IFIP Advances in Information and Communication Technology 506

IFIP – The International Federation for Information Processing

IFIP was founded in 1960 under the auspices of UNESCO, following the first World Computer Congress held in Paris the previous year. A federation for societies working in information processing, IFIP's aim is two-fold: to support information processing in the countries of its members and to encourage technology transfer to developing nations. As its mission statement clearly states:

IFIP is the global non-profit federation of societies of ICT professionals that aims at achieving a worldwide professional and socially responsible development and application of information and communication technologies.

IFIP is a non-profit-making organization, run almost solely by 2500 volunteers. It operates through a number of technical committees and working groups, which organize events and publications. IFIP's events range from large international open conferences to working conferences and local seminars.

The flagship event is the IFIP World Computer Congress, at which both invited and contributed papers are presented. Contributed papers are rigorously refereed and the rejection rate is high.

As with the Congress, participation in the open conferences is open to all and papers may be invited or submitted. Again, submitted papers are stringently refereed.

The working conferences are structured differently. They are usually run by a working group and attendance is generally smaller and occasionally by invitation only. Their purpose is to create an atmosphere conducive to innovation and development. Refereeing is also rigorous and papers are subjected to extensive group discussion.

Publications arising from IFIP events vary. The papers presented at the IFIP World Computer Congress and at open conferences are published as conference proceedings, while the results of the working conferences are often published as collections of selected and edited papers.

IFIP distinguishes three types of institutional membership: Country Representative Members, Members at Large, and Associate Members. The type of organization that can apply for membership is a wide variety and includes national or international societies of individual computer scientists/ICT professionals, associations or federations of such societies, government institutions/government related organizations, national or international research institutes or consortia, universities, academies of sciences, companies, national or international associations or federations of companies.

More information about this series at http://www.springer.com/series/6102

Luis M. Camarinha-Matos · Hamideh Afsarmanesh
Rosanna Fornasiero (Eds.)

Collaboration in a Data-Rich World

18th IFIP WG 5.5 Working Conference on Virtual Enterprises, PRO-VE 2017
Vicenza, Italy, September 18–20, 2017
Proceedings

Springer

Editors
Luis M. Camarinha-Matos
Universidade Nova de Lisboa
Monte Caparica
Portugal

Rosanna Fornasiero
ITIA-CNR
Milan
Italy

Hamideh Afsarmanesh
University of Amsterdam
Amsterdam
The Netherlands

ISSN 1868-4238 ISSN 1868-422X (electronic)
IFIP Advances in Information and Communication Technology
ISBN 978-3-319-65150-7 ISBN 978-3-319-65151-4 (eBook)
DOI 10.1007/978-3-319-65151-4

Library of Congress Control Number: 2017948187

Printed on acid-free paper

This Springer imprint is published by Springer Nature
The registered company is Springer International Publishing AG
The registered company address is: Gewerbestrasse 11, 6330 Cham, Switzerland

Preface

Increasing availability of sensors and smart devices connected to the Internet, and powered by the pervasiveness of Cyber-Physical Systems and Internet of Things, create an exponential growth of available data. We observe the hyper-connectivity of organizations, people, and machines taking us to data-rich environments and often facing big data challenges. All activities in the world, and everyday life of people, leave trails that can be accumulated on cloud-supported storage, while developments in open data movement contribute to the wide availability of such data.

This emerging reality challenges the way collaborative networks and systems are designed and operate. Earlier approaches to collaborative networking however were constrained by scarcity of data, and thus previous solutions in terms of the organizational structures, applied algorithms and mechanisms, and governance principles and models, need to be revisited and redesigned to comply with the speed of evolving scenarios. Furthermore, new solutions need to consider a convergence of technologies, including CPS, IoT, Linked Data, Data Privacy, Federated Identity, Big Data, Data Mining, Sensing Technologies, etc., and the impact of the variables, such as time, location, and population, which suggest a stronger focus on system dynamics. The new abundance of data also raises challenges regarding data validity and quality, with the increasing need for data cleaning and avoiding the cascade of errors. Cyber-security and the impact of non-human data manipulators (bots) become particularly critical, as there is an increasing dependency on data from the society, which may lead to malicious data access and citizen safety and liberty concerns. On the other hand, there is a need to better understand the potential for value creation through collaborative approaches in this context.

PRO-VE 2017 is therefore addressing the timely topic of data-rich world. It will provide a forum for sharing experiences, discussing trends, identifying challenges, and introducing innovative solutions aimed at fulfilling the vision of collaboration in a data-rich world. Understanding, modeling and proposing solution approaches in this area require contributions from multiple and diverse areas, including computer science, industrial engineering, social sciences, organization science, and technologies, among others, which are well tuned to the interdisciplinary spirit of the PRO-VE Working Conferences.

PRO-VE 2017, held in Vicenza, Italy, was the 18th event in this series of successful conferences, including:

PRO-VE 1999 (Porto, Portugal), PRO-VE 2000 (Florianopolis, Brazil), PRO-VE 2002 (Sesimbra, Portugal), PRO-VE 2003 (Lugano, Switzerland), PRO-VE 2004 (Toulouse, France), PRO-VE 2005 (Valencia, Spain), PRO-VE 2006 (Helsinki, Finland), PRO-VE 2007 (Guimarães, Portugal), PRO-VE 2008 (Poznań, Poland), PRO-VE 2009 (Thessaloniki, Greece), PRO-VE 2010 (St. Étienne, France), PRO-VE 2011 (São Paulo, Brazil), PRO-VE 2012 (Bournemouth, UK), PRO-VE 2013

(Dresden, Germany), PRO-VE 2014 (Amsterdam, The Netherlands), PRO-VE 2015 (Albi, France), and PRO-VE 2016 (Porto, Portugal).

This proceedings book includes selected papers from the PRO-VE 2017 Conference. It provides a comprehensive overview of major challenges that are being addressed, and recent advances in various domains related to the collaborative networks and their applications. There is therefore a strong focus on the following areas related to the selected main theme for 2017 conference:

- Collaborative models, platforms and systems for data-rich worlds
- Manufacturing ecosystem and collaboration in Industry 4.0
- Big data analytics and intelligence
- Risk, performance, and uncertainly in collaborative data-rich systems
- Semantic data/service discovery, retrieval, and composition, in a collaborative data-rich world
- Trust and sustainability analysis in collaborative networks
- Value creation and social impact of collaboration in data-rich worlds
- Technology development platforms supporting collaborative systems
- Collective intelligence and collaboration in advanced/emerging applications:
  - Collaborative manufacturing and factories of the future, e-health and care, food and agribusiness, and crisis/disaster management.

We are thankful to all the authors, from academia, research, and industry, for their contributions. We hope this collection of papers represents a valuable tool for those interested in research advances and emerging applications in collaborative networks, as well as identifying future open challenges for research & development in this area. We very much appreciate the dedication, and time and effort spent by the members of the PRO-VE International Program Committee who supported the selection of articles for this conference, and provided valuable and constructive comments to help authors with improving the quality of their papers.

July 2017

Luis M. Camarinha-Matos
Hamideh Afsarmanesh
Rosanna Fornasiero

Organization

PRO-VE 2017 – 18th IFIP Working Conference on Virtual Enterprises

Vicenza, Italy, 18–20 September 2017

Conference Organization Chair

Rosanna Fornasiero, Italy

Program Committee Chairs

Luis M. Camarinha-Matos, Portugal
Hamideh Afsarmanesh, The Netherlands

Program Committee Members

Antonio Abreu, Portugal
Hamideh Afsarmanesh, The Netherlands
Cesar Analide, Portugal
Samuil Angelov, The Netherlands
Dario Antonelli, Italy
Bernard Archimede, France
Américo Azevedo, Portugal
Panagiotis Bamidis, Greece
José Barata, Portugal
Frédérick Bénaben, France
Peter Bertok, Australia
Xavier Boucher, France
Jean-Pierre Bourey, France
Jeremy Bryans, UK
Luis M. Camarinha-Matos, Portugal
Wojciech Cellary, Poland
Vincent Chapurlat, France
Naoufel Cheikhrouhou, Switzerland
Nicolas Daclin, France
Andrea Delgado, Uruguay
Yves Ducq, France
Jens Eschenbaecher, Germany
Elsa Estevez, Argentina
John Fitzgerald, UK
Franck Fontanili, France
Rosanna Fornasiero, Italy
Cesar Garita, Costa Rica
Jose Gonzalez, Norway
Ted Goranson, USA
Paul Grefen, The Netherlands
Jorge E. Hernandez, UK
Dmitri Ivanov, Germany
Javad Jassbi, Portugal
Toshiya Kaihara, Japan
Eleni Kaldoudi, Greece
Dimitris Karagiannis, Austria
Iris Karvonen, Finland
Kurt Kosanke, Germany
Adamantios Koumpis, Ireland
John Krogstie, Norway
Elyes Lamine, France
Fenareti Lampathaki, Greece
Matthieu Lauras, France
Leandro Loss, Brazil

Special Session Organizers

Special Session on Design Science Research in CNs

Special Session on Collaboration in Food and Agribusiness

Special Session on Knowledge Sharing for Production CPS

Special Session on Sustainability Improvements Through CNs

Special Session on Big Data and CNs in Health

Special Session on Manufacturing Ecosystem Collaboration

Pericles Loucopoulos, UK
Yiannis Mourtos, Greece
Rosanna Fornasiero, Italy

Special Session on Risk and Uncertainty in Agriculture

Jorge Hernandez, UK
Janusz Kacprzyk, Poland
Hervé Panetto, France
Alejandro Fernandez, Argentina
Marco De Angelis, UK

Technical Sponsors

ifip

IFIP WG 5.5 COVE
Co-Operation infrastructure for Virtual Enterprises and electronic business

SoCol net

Society of Collaborative Networks

Organizational Co-sponsors

Istituto di Tecnologie Industriali e Automazione
Consiglio Nazionale delle Ricerche

dtg

Università degli Studi di Padova

Department of Management and Engineering

Nova University of Lisbon

UNINOVA

Universiteit van Amsterdam

Contents

Manufacturing Ecosystem Collaboration

Knowledge Sharing for Production CPS

Data-Rich Networked Organizations

Big Data and CNs in Health

Service-Oriented Collaborative Networks

Service Specification and Composition

Collaboration in Industry 4.0

Collaborative Networks as a Core Enabler of Industry 4.0

Luis M. Camarinha-Matos[1(✉)], Rosanna Fornasiero[2], and Hamideh Afsarmanesh[3]

[1] Faculty of Sciences and Technology and Uninova – CTS, Nova University of Lisbon, Campus de Caparica, Monte Caparica, Portugal
cam@uninova.pt

[2] ITIA-CNR, Vicenza, Italy
rosanna.fornasiero@itia.cnr.it

[3] Informatics Institute, University of Asmterdam, Amsterdam, Netherlands
h.afsarmanesh@uva.nl

Abstract. The notion of Industry 4.0 is having a catalyzing effect for the integration of diverse new technologies towards a new generation of more efficient, agile, and sustainable industrial systems. From our analysis, collaboration issues are at the heart of most challenges of this movement. Therefore, an analysis of collaboration needs to be made at all dimensions of Industry 4.0 vision, complemented with a mapping of these needs to the existing results from the collaborative networks area. In addition to such mapping, some new research challenges for the collaborative networks community, as induced by Industry 4.0, are also identified.

Keywords: Industry 4.0 · Collaborative networks · Smart manufacturing

1 Introduction

The idea of a 4th industrial revolution, represented by terms such as Industry 4.0 and Smart Manufacturing, has attracted considerable attention namely as a result of a proposal by the German government and other initiatives from USA, Korea, and other countries [1, 2]. The initial notion primarily pointed to a merging of the physical and virtual worlds – cyber-physical system (CPS) – thus leading to a CPS-based industry. Soon the idea evolved to a symbiosis of CPS with Internet of Things and Internet of Services, justifying the view that it represents an evolution towards digitalization. This idea was then combined with the notion of "smartness" (intelligence dimension) reflected in terms such as smart factory, smart sensors, smart machines, smart products, smart environments, etc. [3]. This move therefore represents a symbiosis among the informatics, and particularly artificial intelligence, engineering, and manufacturing.

More recently, Industry 4.0 has turned into a buzzword [4] and became a catalyzer or "integration factor" for various new technologies and manufacturing concepts – following the "me too" effect. As a result, its scope has increased – a kind of "everything fits" – making this concept even more difficult to grasp, while every technology-related company also tries to give this concept its own description.

L.M. Camarinha-Matos et al. (Eds.): PRO-VE 2017, IFIP AICT 506, pp. 3–17, 2017.
DOI: 10.1007/978-3-319-65151-4_1

Nevertheless, this trend has brought a number of benefits, namely by creating a momentum to drive industrial transformation and upgrading, catalyzing multi-disciplinary contributions, and promoting discussions and identification of new directions and possibilities, as clearly shown by the recent boom of business and academic publications related to Industry 4.0. Furthermore it has also created opportunities for attracting new political and financial support. In fact many countries have been launching local programs on Industry 4.0.

But there is also some risk associated with this new emergence. As usual, the hype creates excessive expectations, and overlooking several hard problems. Many newcomers look at it from a narrow perspective – the perspective of their own field of interest – with a potential loss of the vision and focus. Some publications and talks in conferences resemble the past discussions around the CIM (Computer Integrated Manufacturing) concept of the 1980s, just revamped with some new technologies.

From our perspective, in order to properly understand the vision of Industry 4.0 one needs to look at it from the lens of collaborative networks (CN). It might of course be argued that this is "yet another partial view". Nevertheless, since the collaborative networks area is by nature multi-disciplinary and interdisciplinary, it can enhance getting a more holistic understanding of the issues at stake here. We therefore claim that "collaboration" is at the heart of most challenges in Industry 4.0, and thus the area of Collaborative Networks shall be considered as a major enabler – although certainly not the only one – for this industrial transformation. In fact, some important keywords for Industry 4.0 include "networking", "value chains", "vertical and horizontal integration", and "co-engineering/through engineering", which very well match the issues addressed for the CNs [1, 5]. A recent survey [8] also shows that "interconnection" and "collaboration" are two of the main clusters of terms found in related literature. As such, this work proposes an analysis of the relevant dimensions of Industry 4.0, while identifying their collaboration-related aspects and mapping them into the potential contributions from the CN area. Complementarily, a number of open issues are identified as research challenges with a more "collaborative" flavor of those concept, towards what we could term Collaborative Industry 4.0.

2 Trends and Concepts

2.1 Industry 4.0 Concept Overview

Industry 4.0 is mainly characterized by an increasing digitalization and interconnection of manufacturing systems, products, value chains, and business models. The interconnection between the physical and the virtual/cyber worlds – Cyber-Physical Systems and Internet of Things – is a central feature.

In the literature, this concept is often described in terms of its four main dimensions or characteristics, namely: (1) vertical integration/networking, (2) horizontal integration/networking, (3) through-engineering, and (4) acceleration of manufacturing [1, 6]. Some authors also highlight two additional aspects: (5) digitalization of products and services, and (6) new business models and customer access or involvement [7]. Table 1 summarizes these dimensions.

Table 1. Summary of characteristics of Industry 4.0

	Characteristic	Notion	Some relevant topics	
1	Vertical integration or networking of smart production systems	Focuses on integrating processes vertically across the entire organization, via networking of smart production systems, smart products and smart logistics. [1, 6, 8].	• Extensive CPS • Interoperability • Decentralization • Virtualization • Real-time availability of data • Service orientation	• Modularization • Enterprise wide data analytics & Augmented reality support • Needs-oriented & Individualized • Optimization
2	Horizontal integration through global value chain networks	Involves networking along the whole value chain, from suppliers and business partners to customers [8, 1], "in order to achieve seamless cooperation between enterprises" [5, 9].	• Collaboration • Transparency • Interoperability • Decentralization • Data sharing • Business ecosystem/business community • Track and tracing	• Safety & security • Global optimization • Global flexibility • Suppliers orchestration • Resilience • Regulatory framework
3	Through-engineering across the entire value chain	Integrates all engineering activities considering the complete life-cycle of the product, from design/production to retirement/recycling [1, 6].	• Product life-cycle • Co-engineering • End-to-end integration • Circular economy • Connecting & integrating customers	• Availability of data at all stages • Tracking & tracing • Service-enhance products • Creating new product-service offerings
4	Acceleration of manufacturing	Strive to optimize the whole value chain through the so-called "exponential technologies" (i.e. exponentially growing technologies), accelerating and making industrial processes more flexible [1, 6].	• IoT, CPS • Mobile computing • Robotics and drones • Artificial Intelligence • Additive manufacturing • Industrial biology	• Neuro-technologies • Nanotechnologies • Sensing technologies • Cloud, big data & analytics • Collaborative machines
5	Digitalization of products and services	Moves to smart products, by adding sensors, computing and communication capabilities to products, providing availability of product data along its life-cycle, introducing new digital products, and associating business services to products [7].	• Self-identification • History record and tracing • Augmented reality • Data availability	• Service-enhanced products • Assistance • Self-diagnosis, self-configuration
6	New business models and customer access	Focuses on new business models that take advantage on digitalization and networking in data-rich contexts, along the value chain. Such models will deepen digital relationships with more empowered customers, and accelerate globalization but with distinct local/regional flavors [7].	• Customer experience • Customer intimacy • Co-design/co-creation • Value chain • Link to smart infrastructures	• Product-service ecosystem • Sustainability • Social responsibility • Glocal enterprise

This industrial transformation momentum towards industry 4.0 is driven by two major forces – the new technological possibilities, and the fast changing market demands (Fig. 1).

From a technological perspective, Industry 4.0 is in fact characterized by the combination of large variety of enabling technologies [10, 11]. Furthermore, the role of data – available in fast growing amounts – is becoming central not only challenging the re-design of past systems and solutions, but also motivating new services and products.

Fig. 1. Driving forces

2.2 Collaborative Networks Overview

The area of CNs is nowadays represented by a large literature basis [12, 13] and a great variety of implementations, corresponding to multiple classes of collaborative networks. To support this variety of collaboration forms, a large number of models, infrastructures, mechanisms and tools have been developed, as summarized in Fig. 2.

Many of these developments have been directed to manufacturing and other industrial applications, which make the area a natural contributor to Industry 4.0.

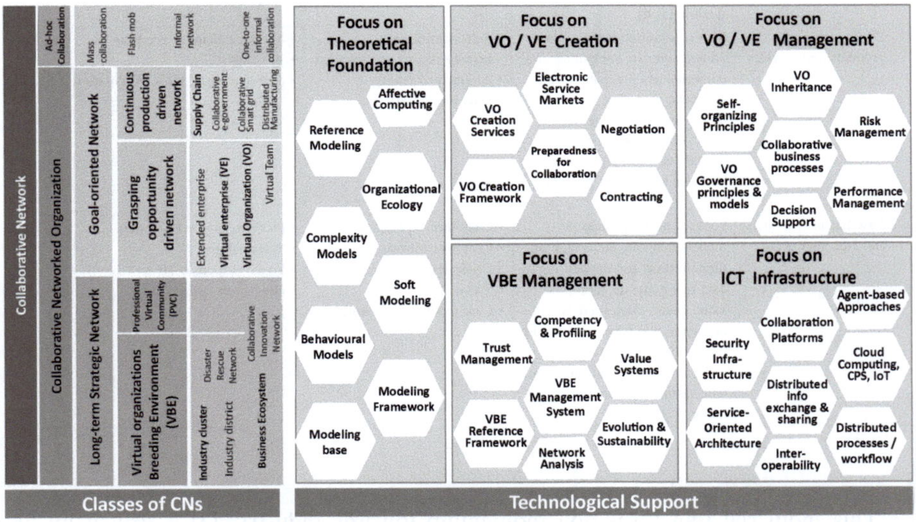

Fig. 2. Collaborative Networks and some of their supporting technologies

3 Collaboration Issues in Industry 4.0

Numerous collaboration issues emerge from the characteristics of Industry 4.0, as summarized in the following Tables 2, 3, 4, 5, 6 and 7. As illustrated in Fig. 3, a good number of contributions to solve these issues can be found in the research on CNs.

Table 2. Collaboration issues in vertical integration of smart production systems

Examples of collaboration-related issues	What CN can contribute
• With the increase of intelligence and autonomy of enterprise systems, vertical integration more and more corresponds to networking of smart systems, which need to collaborate in order to support agile processes. For instance, at shop floor this leads to a move from "control structures" to "collaborative structures" (from CPS and embedded systems to collaborative CPS). • Collaboration between humans and robots is an emerging field, often limited to one-to-one model, but that can be enlarged to a network level. • Future enterprises can be seen as multi-layer networks, involving the interplay of smart production systems, smart products, smart logistics, organizational units, and people. Support for real-time monitoring and agility requires fluid interplay among these multiple layers (up and downstream). • Real-time availability of data and enterprise wide analytics and augmented reality supported data visualization can be better supported by a collaborative model among the various enterprise units.	• Although most CN research has focused on networks of organizations or networks of people, some earlier suggestions to apply the same concepts to networks of machines [14] and CPS [15] are available. • Some works addressed the interplay among CNs [16]. • From the area of multi-agent systems and distributed artificial intelligence, models and protocols for collaboration among agents have been extensively discussed and applied to manufacturing [17]. • The concept of sensing, smart, and sustainable enterprise offers a comprehensive view of integration [18].

Table 3. Collaboration issues in horizontal integration through global value chain networks

Examples of collaboration-related issues	What CN can contribute
• Collaboration among all stakeholders along the value chain, including business partners and customers. • Materialization of business ecosystems, which are strategic cooperative alliances. • Sharing of resources and information along the value chain, one of the facets of collaboration. • Global optimization, which requires a network-oriented perspective and not an enterprise-centric view. • Global flexibility requires dynamic formation of goal-oriented networks to adapt to changes.	• This is the area more extensively covered by CN research [12, 13], [q]. Extensive results are available on: - Organizational models, including strategic alliances (e.g. VBEs, business ecosystems) and goal-oriented networks [19, 20]. - Collaboration platforms, tools and information management supporting needs of the various phases of the CN life-cycle [19, 21, 22]. - Governance and behavioural models [20, 23, 24]. - Trust management [25]. - Reference models [26, 27, 28]. - Resilience and CNs [29]

(continued)

Table 3. (*continued*)

Examples of collaboration-related issues	What CN can contribute
• Resilience, thus the capability to absorb shocks and disruptions, requires collaboration with high level of sharing. • Tracking and tracing functionalities require high level of transparency and sharing among the value chain. • Some authors also explore the integration of smart manufacturing with smart cities [30].	

Table 4. Collaboration issues in through-engineering across the entire value chain

Examples of collaboration-related issues	What CN can contribute
• Involvement of customers in product design (co-design) as well as close interaction among engineers of different nodes along the value chain (co-engineering) require effective collaboration between manufacturers and customers, possibly involving intermediary stakeholders. • Consideration of full-life cycle of product and circular economy requires collaboration among multiple stakeholders. • Service-enhanced products or association of business services to products usually requires well-coordinated networks, involving manufacturers and service providers, namely for delivering integrated service packages. This is particularly critical when there is a need for differentiation according to geographical area.	• Co-design, co-innovation and customer communities are topics addressed in various CN works, e.g. [31, 32]. • The interactions between the product life-cycle and the CNs life-cycle were studied in GloNet [23]. • The role of CNs in supporting service-enhanced products/product-service systems has been a major research topic in recent years [24, 33–35, 52].

These examples, although not a complete list, clearly show the relevance of CNs for the materialization of this industrial revolution. On the other hand, further research areas can also be identified, as presented in Sect. 4.

The above tables are focused on the four main characteristics of Industry 4.0. The two other characteristics mentioned in Fig. 1, although partially overlapping the cases mentioned above, also require a strong collaborative networks component, as shown in Tables 6 and 7.

Table 5. Collaboration issues in acceleration of manufacturing

Examples of collaboration-related issues	What CN can contribute
• Fast introduction of new technologies requires dynamic involvement of new players along the value chain, and thus agile collaborative structures. • Some of the "exponential technologies" strongly based on AI more and more suggest collaboration among machines (M2 M). This trend naturally involves issues such as sharing, interoperability, negotiation and contracting, and trust management, etc. • Mobile technologies challenge the closed ecosystem models and require collaborative models that cope with nomadic systems. • Technologies such as 3D printing allow for distributed and localized manufacturing, involving collaboration among actors located in different geographical locations. • The increasing role of virtual and augmented reality as a tool to collaborate during training activities, to interact in an innovative way and for simulation and management of a certain situation can affect collaboration.	• Combining results from the multi-agent systems area [18] and from CN [36] regarding consortia formation can provide good support to agility. • Till now 3D printing has been studied mostly from a technological point of view and only recently as a new enabler of new collaboration models [37]. • Virtual and augmented reality have been studied as a tool for training and for management of processes, but only recent developments of mobile and connectivity concepts can change the way CNs are conceptualized (virtual and real participants) [http://vf-os.eu/]

Table 6. Collaboration issues in digitalization of products and services

Examples of collaboration-related issues	What CN can contribute
• Leveraging the notion of smart product can only be done through effective collaboration among nodes of the value chain, which use the smart product to mediate their collaboration (ako stigmergy); otherwise the full potential of the concept cannot be achieved. • It is through collaboration that effective history records and tracing can be kept updated and associated to the product. • Data availability next to the product depends on the technological infrastructure but also on the collaboration among all stakeholders involved in the "product history". • Inclusion of assistance and other value-added services typically requires	• Some examples of stigmergic collaboration can be found in mass collaboration in which "agents communicate with one another indirectly through traces left in the shared environment" [38]. A typical example is Wikipedia. • Collaboration of multiple stakeholders in integrated business services provision has been addressed [33, 39, 40], including aspects such as value-added/integrated service composition, service discovery in collaborative environments, etc. • Role of CNs in transition to product-service systems [35, 41]. • Role of CNs in innovation ecosystems and open innovation [42, 43].

(continued)

Table 6. *(continued)*

Examples of collaboration-related issues	What CN can contribute
contributions from various stakeholders, which implies at least some minimal levels of collaboration – being the "smartness of the product" their common goal. • Smart products will inspire/motivate the creation of new services to enhance the value of products, which opens the opportunity for new players, thus creating collaboration communities associated to the product (product-related digital ecosystems.	

Table 7. Collaboration issues in new business models and customer access

Examples of collaboration-related issues	What CN can contribute
• This dimension further extends the "horizontal integration", seeking tight collaboration along the value chain. • Collaboration with customers (co-design/co-creation of products and services), not necessarily under the one-to-one model, but rather under a community perspective (increasing "customer intimacy"). Improving customer experience, namely in global markets, also requires close collaboration among value chain stakeholders. • Addressing global markets taking into account local specificities (notion of global enterprise) requires collaboration between global producers and local providers and other entities close to the customer. • The move towards "servitization" more and more requires tight collaboration between manufacturers and a growing variety of service providers. • Current concerns regarding sustainability and social responsibility require stronger collaboration links between industry and other societal actors. • Hybrid value chains, combining for-profit and non-for-profit organizations.	• Numerous forms of goal-oriented networks have been implemented in diverse industry sectors [44]. • The involvement of customer in co-creation networks has been studied in various sectors, e.g. solar energy [31], consumer goods sector [45, 21], etc. • Materialization of the *glocal* enterprise concept through CNs [40]. • New models for collaboration in Non-hierarchical value chains [22]. • The role of CNs in product-service systems/servitization [35, 41]. • The role of CNs in sustainability has been discussed in various works, e.g. [46, 18] and even been the main theme of the 2010 PRO-VE edition [47]. • Notions of green virtual enterprise and green enterprise breeding environment have been introduced [48].

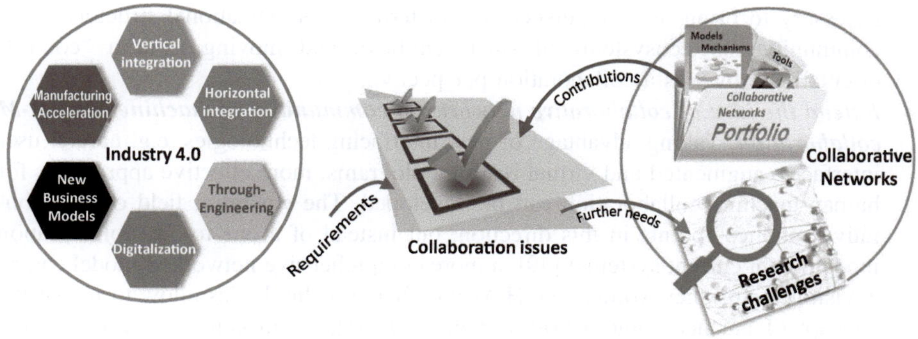

Fig. 3. Mapping Industry 4.0 into Collaborative Networks

4 New Research Challenges

Last decades of research in CNs resulted in a large base of theoretical and empirical knowledge, which provides a strong support to the collaboration requirements of Industry 4.0, as summarized in Sect. 3. Furthermore, the catalyzing "movement" originated with the Industry 4.0 concept is raising new challenges and pointing to areas requiring further research in CNs. Some of these areas include:

- ***Combination and interplay of multiple dynamic networks***. The aimed vertical and horizontal integration dimensions and the need to support the various stages of the product life-cycle lead to the co-existence of multiple networks, formal and informal, involving organizations, people, systems, and machines. These networks have different durations and thus different life-cycles. Understanding the nature and supporting the interactions/interdependences among these networks is crucial for the effectiveness, agility, and resilience of future manufacturing systems. Although some inputs towards this aim can be found in [16], this issue remains an important research challenge.
- ***Coping with and benefiting from data-rich environments***. The increasing availability and use of sensors and smart devices, integrated as cyber-physical systems, combined with the hyper-connection of organizations, people, and systems, generate fast increasing amounts of data. These emerging data-rich environments challenge CNs and associated decision-making systems. Previous design assumptions, based on scarcity of data, need to be revisited, probably leading to new architectures and mechanisms. Furthermore, new collaborative business services that leverage the value of big data are likely to emerge. On the other hand, data-richness also raises issues regarding data validity and quality, data protection, access, and ownership.
- ***Extend the use of a CNs perspective to complex CPS***. Earlier CPS/IoT efforts were focused on the base technological aspects, such as interconnectivity, safe communications, control, and coping with limited energy and computing resources. As the level of intelligence, and thus the autonomy, of devices, machines and systems increases, and the number of interconnected entities grows exponentially, it is

necessary to bring in new perspectives in terms of organizational structures (e.g. communities or ecosystems of smart entities), and moving from a "control-orientation" towards a collaboration perspective.

- ***Extend the idea of collaborative networks to communities of machines and H-M collaboration***. Taking advantage of new interfacing technologies, e.g. natural user interfaces, augmented and virtual reality, holograms, more effective approaches for human-machine collaboration can be developed. The emerging field of "collaborative robotics" points in this direction, but instead of a one-to-one collaboration model (as in current systems) [49], a more comprehensive networked model can be envisioned. In other words, new H-M interfacing technologies allow to revisit the concept of balanced automation systems [50, 51], re-enforcing the collaboration perspective (human-enhancement and human-machine symbiosis).
- ***Networks involving hybrid value systems***. The need to properly consider the societal dimension and systems sustainability require an increasing collaboration of manufacturing industries with other societal stakeholders. Thus a collaboration among public, NGOs, and private entities, guided by different value systems, which calls for a better understanding of the interactions and alignment of value systems in CNs. Furthermore smart cities, smart communities need to include and to consider the role of manufacturing companies for the wealth of the country.
- ***Further develop the sensing, smartness, and sustainability dimensions***. New products, processes, enterprises, communities, and infrastructures need to be envisioned as sensing, smart and sustainable (S3), extending the concept of "S3 enterprise" [18], in order to transcend individual interests and better satisfy collective aspirations. Human capability and machine intelligence need to be integrated within production systems so to achieve maximum efficiency as well as worker satisfaction. Research efforts should tackle social sustainability challenges at all levels of manufacturing industries (from shop-floor to production systems to networks). This implies moving from an enterprise-centric perspective to a business ecosystem-oriented perspective. CNs is a key enabler for the materialization of this idea, which requires the integration and interaction of multiple entities that are heterogeneous, distributed and autonomous, but that must collaborate in order to achieve their collective goals.
- ***Seek inspiration in nature, towards optimized solutions***. Nature is full of examples of successful collaboration processes, shown in a wide variety of forms, and which seem to be highly optimized. On the other hand, seeking optimized, agile and sustainable solutions is a core goal of Smart Manufacturing. Therefore, a study of research results from Nature-related disciplines regarding collaboration can provide good inspiration to better understand and replicate sustainable collaboration mechanisms and organizational structures.
- ***Deployment of open linked data and interlinking of open ontologies*** to enhance collaboration among autonomous and heterogeneous connected agents in collaborative environments. This is crucial to support both vertical and horizontal integration.
- ***Better service specification mechanism***, enhancing service discovery, composition and evolution in collaborative environments, coping with mobility and evolution of manufacturing equipment.

- ***Further develop monitoring and supervision of agents collaboration*** in *coopetitive* environments. This requires further development of behavioral models, and other advanced aspects such as collective emotions, resilience mechanisms and anti-fragility in order to cope with disruptive events, etc.
- ***New business models for new CNs:*** upon the changes enabled by Industry 4.0 the structure, the actors, the interaction mechanisms, the value creation mechanisms of CNs will change. Organizations (both public and private) will be asked to revise their processes, rules of collaboration, as well as regulatory systems. In the specific case of manufacturing companies, service orientation, inclusion of sustainability issues, availability of big data, etc., are strategies that need to be accompanied by new organizational models.
- ***Re-enforce interdisciplinary work***. The increasing levels of integration envisioned by Industry 4.0 clearly require the contribution from multiple disciplines. The CNs area, the result of an interdisciplinary effort in itself, can facilitate the needed dialog among all stakeholders in Industry 4.0, but also needs to be continuously re-enforced, seeking synergies among multiple knowledge areas.
- ***Further education and dissemination of CN concepts in industry***. Performing this industrial revolution is not only a matter of technology. It requires a different mind-set, new ways of working, a new culture. For this to happen, and considering the enabling role of collaborative networks, it is necessary to invest further on education and dissemination of CN concepts in the industrial communities.

5 Conclusions

The vision behind Industry 4.0 and alternative terms such as Smart Manufacturing is having a strong catalyzing effect, reflected in the convergence of various new technologies and mobilization of efforts towards reorganization of industry. To some authors this effect is triggering a new industrial revolution.

An effective materialization of this vision strongly relies, in our opinion, on collaborative organizational structures, processes, and mechanisms. This position is confirmed through an analysis of the Industry 4.0 requirements along its six dimensions – vertical integration, horizontal integration, through-engineering, acceleration of manufacturing, digitalization, and new business models – which allowed us to identify a large number of collaboration-related issues.

From an analysis of literature on collaborative networks, a great number of research results and empirical knowledge gathered along the last two decades which constitute a rich contribution to the identified needs, positioning CNs as a major enabler of Industry 4.0.

Complementarily, this analysis shows that this revolution also raises new research challenges or re-enforces ongoing focus topics in the CN community. A preliminary list of examples of such challenges was elaborated, although further refinement is needed.

Acknowledgments. This work was partially funded by the FCT- Strategic program UID/EEA/00066/2013 (Impactor project) and Socolnet (ARCON-ACM project).

References

1. Gilchrist, A.: Industry 4.0 – The Industrial Internet of Things. Apress, Bangken, Nonthaburi, Thailand (2016). doi:10.1007/978-1-4842-2047-4
2. Bartodziej, C.J.: The Concept Industry 4.0 – An Empirical Analysis of Technologies and Applications in Production Logistics. Springer Gabler, Wiesbaden, Germany (2017). doi:10.1007/978-3-658-16502-4
3. Kang, H.S., Lee, J.Y., Choi, S., Kim, H., Park, J.H., Son, J.Y., Kim, B.H., Noh, S.D.: Smart manufacturing: past research, present findings, and future directions. Int. J. Precis. Eng. Manuf.-Green Tech. **3**(1), 111–128 (2016)
4. Drath, R., Horch, A.: Industrie 4.0: hit or hype? [industry forum]. IEEE Ind. Electron. Mag. **8**(2), 56–58 (2014). doi:10.1109/MIE.2014.2312079
5. Sniderman, B., Mahto, M., Cotteleer, M.J.: Industry 4.0 and manufacturing ecosystems - exploring the world of connected enterprises. Deloitte University Press (2016), https://dupress.deloitte.com/content/dam/dup-us-en/articles/manufacturing-ecosystems-exploring-world-connected-enterprises/DUP_2898_Industry4.0ManufacturingEcosystems.pdf. Accessed 9 Mar 2017
6. Schlaepfer, R.C., Koch, M., Merkofer, P.: Industry 4.0 – challenges and solutions for the digital transformations and use of exponential technologies. Deloitte, Zurich (2015), http://www.industrie2025.ch/fileadmin/user_upload/ch-en-delloite-ndustry-4-0-24102014.pdf. Accessed 9 Mar 2017
7. Geissbauer, R., Vedso, J., Schrauf, S.: Industry 4.0: building the digital enterprise. PwC (2016), https://www.pwc.com/gx/en/industries/industries-4.0/landing-page/industry-4.0-building-your-digital-enterprise-april-2016.pdf. Accessed 9 Mar 2017
8. Hermann, M., Pentek, T., Otto, B.: Design principles for industrie 4.0 scenarios. In: 2016 49th Hawaii International Conference on System Sciences (HICSS), pp. 3928–3937. IEEE Xplore, Koloa (2016). doi:10.1109/HICSS.2016.488
9. Zhou, K., Liu, T., Zhou, L.: Industry 4.0: towards future industrial - opportunities and challenges. In: 2015 12th International Conference on Fuzzy Systems and Knowledge Discovery (FSKD), Zhangjiajie, pp. 2147–2152 (2015). doi:10.1109/FSKD.2015.7382284
10. MTC: From Industry 4.0 to Digitising Manufacturing – An End User Perspective. Conference Report, Manufacturing Technology Center, Coventry (2016), http://www.the-mtc.org/pdf/Industry-4-Report-2016-e.pdf, accessed 9 Mar 2017
11. Wan, J., Cai, H., Zhou, K.: Industrie 4.0: enabling technologies. In: 2015 International Conference on Intelligent Computing and Internet of Things (IC1T), Harbin, China, pp. 135–140. IEEE Xplore (2015). doi:10.1109/ICAIOT.2015.7111555
12. Durugbo, C.: Collaborative networks: a systematic review and multi-level framework. Int. J. Prod. Res. **54**(12), 3749–3776 (2016)
13. Appio, F.P., Martini, A., Massa, S., Testa, S.: Collaborative network of firms: antecedents and state-of-the-art properties. Int. J. Prod. Res. (in press, 2017). doi:10.1080/00207543.2016.1262083
14. Barata, J., Camarinha-Matos, L.M.: Coalitions of manufacturing components for shopfloor agility. Int. J. Netw. Virtual Organ. **2**(1), 50–77 (2003)

15. Nazarenko, A., Camarinha-Matos, L.M.: Towards collaborative cyber-physical systems. In: Proceedings of YEF-ECE 2017–Young Engineers Forum on Electrical and Computer Engineering, Costa de Caparica, Portugal, 5 May 2017, pp. 12–17. IEEE Xplore (2017)
16. Camarinha-Matos, Luis M., Ferrada, F., Oliveira, A.I.: Interplay of collaborative networks in product servicing. In: Camarinha-Matos, Luis M., Scherer, Raimar J. (eds.) PRO-VE 2013. IAICT, vol. 408, pp. 51–60. Springer, Heidelberg (2013). doi:10.1007/978-3-642-40543-3_6
17. Shen, W., Norrie, D.H., Barthès, J.-P.: Multi-Agent Systems for Concurrent Intelligent Design and Manufacturing. Taylor & Francis, London, New York (2003)
18. Weichhart, G., Molina, A., Chen, D., Whitman, L.E., Vernadat, F.: Challenges and current developments for sensing, smart and sustainable enterprise systems. Comput. Ind. **79**, 34–46 (2016)
19. Camarinha-Matos, L.M., Afsarmanesh, H., Galeano, N., Molina, A.: Collaborative networked organizations–Concepts and practice in manufacturing enterprises. Comput. Ind. Eng. **57**(1), 46–60 (2009)
20. Shadi, M., Afsarmanesh, H.: Behavioral norms in virtual organizations. In: Camarinha-Matos, Luis M., Afsarmanesh, H. (eds.) PRO-VE 2014. IAICT, vol. 434, pp. 48–59. Springer, Heidelberg (2014). doi:10.1007/978-3-662-44745-1_5
21. Shamsuzzoha, A., Kankaanpaa, T., Carneiro, L.M., Almeida, R., Chiodi, A., Fornasiero, R.: Dynamic and collaborative business networks in the fashion industry. Int. J. Comput. Integr. Manuf. **26**(1–2), 125–139 (2013)
22. Almeida, R., Carneiro, L.M., Sà, A., Ferreira, P.S., Fornasiero R.: Business Communities Management. In: Intelligent Non-hierarchical Manufacturing Networks. Wiley (2012). ISBN 978184821481
23. Camarinha-Matos, L.M., Oliveira, A.I., Ferrada, F., Sobotka, P., Vataščinová, A., Thamburaj, V.: Collaborative enterprise networks for solar energy. In: 2015 International Conference on Computing and Communications Technologies (ICCCT), Chennai, pp. 93–98 (2015). doi:10.1109/ICCCT2.2015.7292726
24. Camarinha-Matos, L.M., Ferrada, F., Oliveira, A.I., Afsarmanesh, H.: Supporting product-servicing networks. In: Proceedings of 2013 International Conference on Industrial Engineering and Systems Management (IESM), Rabat, pp. 1–7 (2013)
25. Msanjila, S., Afsarmanesh, H.: Trust analysis and assessment in virtual organization breeding environments. Int. J. Prod. Res. **46**, 1253–1295 (2008)
26. Camarinha-Matos, L.M., Afsarmanesh, H.: On reference models for collaborative networked organizations. Int. J. Prod. Res. **46**(9), 2453–2469 (2008)
27. Carneiro, L., Shamsuzzoha, A.H.M., Almeida, R., Azevedo, A., Fornasiero, R., Ferreira, P. S.: Reference model for collaborative manufacturing of customised products: applications in the fashion industry. Prod. Plann. Control **25**(13–14), 1135–1155 (2014)
28. Fornasiero, R., Zangiacomi, A., Franchini, V., Bastos, J., Azevedo, A., Vinelli, A.: Implementation of customisation strategies in collaborative networks through an innovative Reference Framework. Prod. Plann. Control **14**, 1158–1170 (2016)
29. Camarinha-Matos, Luis M.: Collaborative networks: a mechanism for enterprise agility and resilience. In: Mertins, K., Bénaben, F., Poler, R., Bourrières, J.-P. (eds.) Enterprise Interoperability VI. PIC, vol. 7, pp. 3–11. Springer, Cham (2014). doi:10.1007/978-3-319-04948-9_1
30. Lom, M., Pribyl, O., Svitek, M.: Industry 4.0 as a part of smart cities. In: 2016 Smart Cities Symposium Prague (SCSP), pp. 1–6. IEEE Xplore, Prague (2016). doi:10.1109/SCSP.2016.7501015

31. Oliveira, A.I., Camarinha-Matos, Luis M.: Negotiation support for co-design of business services. In: Camarinha-Matos, Luis M., Afsarmanesh, H. (eds.) PRO-VE 2014. IAICT, vol. 434, pp. 98–106. Springer, Heidelberg (2014). doi:10.1007/978-3-662-44745-1_9
32. Romero, D., Molina, A.: Collaborative networked organisations and customer communities: value co-creation and co-innovation in the networking era. Prod. Plann. Control **22**(5–6), 447–472 (2011)
33. Afsarmanesh, H., Shafahi, M., Sargolzaei, M.: On service-enhanced product recommendation guiding users through complex product specification. In: International Conference on Computing and Communications Technologies (ICCCT), Chennai, pp. 43–48 (2015). doi:10.1109/ICCCT2.2015.7292717
34. Bertoni, A., Bertoni, M., Panarotto, M., Johansson, C., Larsson, T.C.: Value-driven product service systems development: Methods and industrial applications. CIRP J. Manufact. Sci. Technol. **15**, 42–55 (2016)
35. Boucher, X.: Economic and organizational transition towards product/service systems: the case of French SMEs. In: Camarinha-Matos, Luis M., Xu, L., Afsarmanesh, H. (eds.) PRO-VE 2012. IAICT, vol. 380, pp. 26–34. Springer, Heidelberg (2012). doi:10.1007/978-3-642-32775-9_3
36. Oliveira, A.I., Camarinha-Matos, L.M., Pouly, M.: Agreement negotiation support in VO creation – an illustrative case. J. Prod. Plann. Control **21**(2), 160–180 (2010)
37. Janssen, R., Blankers, I., Moolenburgh, E., Posthumus, B.: The Impact of 3-D Printing on Supply Chain Management White paper by TNO (2014), http://publications.tno.nl/publication/34610218/0zCfLz/janssen-2014-impact.pdf. Accessed 3 Apr 2017
38. Elliott, M.: Stigmergic Collaboration: a framework for understanding and designing mass collaboration. In: Cress, U., Moskaliuk, J., Jeong, H. (eds.) Mass Collaboration and Education. CCLS, vol. 16, pp. 65–84. Springer, Cham (2016). doi:10.1007/978-3-319-13536-6_4
39. Camarinha-Matos, Luis M., Afsarmanesh, H., Oliveira, A.I., Ferrada, F.: Cloud-based collaborative business services provision. In: Hammoudi, S., Cordeiro, J., Maciaszek, Leszek A., Filipe, J. (eds.) ICEIS 2013. LNBIP, vol. 190, pp. 366–384. Springer, Cham (2014). doi:10.1007/978-3-319-09492-2_22
40. Camarinha-Matos, Luis M., Afsarmanesh, H., Koelmel, B.: Collaborative networks in support of service-enhanced products. In: Camarinha-Matos, Luis M., Pereira-Klen, A., Afsarmanesh, H. (eds.) PRO-VE 2011. IAICT, vol. 362, pp. 95–104. Springer, Heidelberg (2011). doi:10.1007/978-3-642-23330-2_11
41. Fitzgerald, J., Bryans, J., Payne, R.: A formal model-based approach to engineering systems-of-systems. In: Camarinha-Matos, Luis M., Xu, L., Afsarmanesh, H. (eds.) PRO-VE 2012. IAICT, vol. 380, pp. 53–62. Springer, Heidelberg (2012). doi:10.1007/978-3-642-32775-9_6
42. Durugbo, C., Lyons, A.: Collaboration for innovation networks: towards a reference model. In: Camarinha-Matos, Luis M., Bénaben, F., Picard, W. (eds.) PRO-VE 2015. IAICT, vol. 463, pp. 311–322. Springer, Cham (2015). doi:10.1007/978-3-319-24141-8_28
43. Rabelo, Ricardo J., Bernus, P., Romero, D.: Innovation ecosystems: a collaborative networks perspective. In: Camarinha-Matos, Luis M., Bénaben, F., Picard, W. (eds.) PRO-VE 2015. IAICT, vol. 463, pp. 323–336. Springer, Cham (2015). doi:10.1007/978-3-319-24141-8_29
44. Romero, D., Rabelo, R.J., Molina, A.: Collaborative networks as modern industrial organisations: real case studies. Int. J. Comput. Integr. Manuf. **26**(1–2), 1–2 (2013)
45. Fornasiero, R., Zangiacomi, A.: A structured approach for customised production in SME collaborative networks. Int. J. Prod. Res. **51**(7), 2110–2122 (2013)

46. Camarinha-Matos, Luis M., Afsarmanesh, H., Boucher, X.: The role of collaborative networks in sustainability. In: Camarinha-Matos, Luis M., Boucher, X., Afsarmanesh, H. (eds.) PRO-VE 2010. IAICT, vol. 336, pp. 1–16. Springer, Heidelberg (2010). doi:10.1007/978-3-642-15961-9_1
47. Camarinha-Matos, Luis M., Boucher, X., Afsarmanesh, H. (eds.): PRO-VE 2010. IAICT, vol. 336. Springer, Heidelberg (2010). doi:10.1007/978-3-642-15961-9
48. Romero, D., Noran, O., Afsarmanesh, H.: Green virtual enterprise breeding environments bag of assets management: a contribution to the sharing economy. In: Camarinha-Matos, Luis M., Bénaben, F., Picard, W. (eds.) PRO-VE 2015. IAICT, vol. 463, pp. 439–447. Springer, Cham (2015). doi:10.1007/978-3-319-24141-8_40
49. Moniz, A.B., Krings, B.-J.: Robots working with humans or humans working with robots? searching for social dimensions in new human-robot interaction in industry. Societies **6**(3), 23 (2016)
50. Camarinha-Matos, L.M., Rabelo, R., Osório, A.L.: Balanced automation. In: Tzafestas, S.G. (eds.) Computer Assisted Management and Control of Manufacturing Systems. Advanced Manufacturing, pp. 376–414. Springer, London (1997). doi:10.1007/978-1-4471-0959-4_14
51. Romero, D., Noran, O., Stahre, J., Bernus, P., Fast-Berglund, Å.: Towards a human-centred reference architecture for next generation balanced automation systems: human-automation symbiosis. In: Umeda, S., Nakano, M., Mizuyama, H., Hibino, H., Kiritsis, D., Cieminski, G. (eds.) APMS 2015. IAICT, vol. 460, pp. 556–566. Springer, Cham (2015). doi:10.1007/978-3-319-22759-7_64
52. Afsarmanesh, H., Sargolzaei, M., Shadi, M.: Semi-automated software service integration in virtual organisations. Enterp. Inf. Syst. **9**(5–6), 528–555 (2015)

Digital Marketplaces for Industry 4.0: A Survey and Gap Analysis

Sonia Cisneros-Cabrera(✉), Asia Ramzan, Pedro Sampaio, and Nikolay Mehandjiev

The University of Manchester, Manchester, UK
{sonia.cisneroscabrera, asia.ramzan, P.Sampaio, n.mehandjiev}@manchester.ac.uk

Abstract. Industry 4.0 is the called 4th technological revolution, where digital and physical marketplaces and manufacturing technologies converge to enable smart manufacturing and factories of the future. This paper presents an overview of a representative set of marketplace platforms available to support supply chain processes underpinning Industry 4.0. We develop a gap analysis of existing marketplaces assessing their ability to support Industry 4.0 requirements. Finally, we position our survey and gap analysis in the context of the European Union's Horizon 2020 programme, in particular on the Digital Automation call topic addressing the theme of collaborative manufacturing and logistics.

Keywords: Industry 4.0 · Supply chain · Digital marketplace · Collaborative technologies · Gap analysis

1 Introduction

Corporations are steadily moving to a mode of competition and collaboration coined "Industry 4.0", which uses Internet technologies, sensors and big data to develop industry solutions. The shift in computing towards the cloud, the wide availability of information services that can be remotely accessed, and the new business models enabled by the software as a service paradigm, are the catalysts for the vision of Industry 4.0 to become operational. For the full accomplishment of this vision, it will be essential that digital marketplace mechanisms are created to support the service ecosystems arising from the multitude of market players and service portfolios.

In this paper, we present a survey of digital marketplace platforms with a potential towards supporting Industry 4.0 initiatives. In particular, this survey aims to provide an assessment of service marketplace design and configuration platforms that will enable the dynamic evaluation and composition of hundreds of thousands of potential candidate services towards developing Industry 4.0 solutions. We develop our gap analysis taking into account the context of the European Union's Digital Automation call topic aimed at developing technologies towards enabling Industry 4.0 collaborative networks within European organisations [14]. The survey and analysis conducted in this paper have the following research questions, which outline the future directions for developing an Industry 4.0 solution:

L.M. Camarinha-Matos et al. (Eds.): PRO-VE 2017, IFIP AICT 506, pp. 18–27, 2017.
DOI: 10.1007/978-3-319-65151-4_2

1. What concepts, techniques and services of Industry 4.0 are available in current marketplace environments for collaborative supply chain systems?
2. How can a digital marketplace platform address capability gaps in traditional approaches to collaborative supply chains?
3. How can digital marketplace tools impact the business, organisational and Information Technology (IT) architectural approaches within collaborative supply chains?

This document is organised as follows: Sect. 2 discusses background and related work, Sect. 3 presents the research method and our gap analysis. Section 4 includes the discussion on the research questions' answers, and finally, Sect. 5 concludes the paper and presents key findings.

2 Background and Related Work

Industry 4.0 moves towards efficient manufacturing systems, augmenting the automation of the processes and actors involved in Industry, and aiming at a highly efficient response to internal and external events, seeking for resilience and adaptive systems [2, 4]. The EU's Digital Automation call topic, supported by the Horizon 2020 programme, presents a vision towards innovations on collaborative networks across manufacturing value chains within Industry 4.0 [14]. Particularly, the vision presented requires development to support Small and Medium Enterprises (SME) participation and collaboration with large Original Equipment Manufacturer (OEM) companies in the supply chain comprising management, control, manufacturing, and logistics capabilities [14]. The main objectives of the call involve the development of technological means for a resilient, flexible and event-responsive procurement process, capable of coping with a dynamic environment providing automated reconfiguration within the supply chain processes [14]. The research involved in the EU's Digital Automation call topic includes addressing the development of solutions able to optimise and facilitate collaboration among different stakeholders involved, including supply clusters, companies, factory machines and objects [14].

Within EU's Digital Automation call topic, a marketplace refers to the tool that will support the entire supply chain life cycle processes, which will be used by both demand side (requestors) and suppliers when participating in the bidding process, and will enable suppliers to form temporary coalitions, towards fulfilling complex call bids where multiple suppliers might be needed, with a strong focus on enabling SMEs to participate in the marketplace.

3 The Supply Chain Digital Marketplace

Ten platforms were selected and analysed as the representative platforms of today's marketplace. The selection criteria include the relevance of the platform, where the platform should be utilised by at least 1000 members, however, most of the platforms surveyed have millions of users [7–10, 12, 15–17, 19, 21]; a second selection criterion involves the platform's support for business-to-business (B2B) transactions, where companies on both sides of the digital marketplace (requestors and suppliers) participate, rather than only individual users; a third aspect considered was the identification of the platform as an eProcurement one; finally, the marketplace selected should be of high relevance and impact within its domain area, measured by their geographical span (regional or worldwide, but not local). These criteria were defined to eliminate the risk of selecting platforms that might be tackling different objectives to those relevant to Industry 4.0, in such a way that each of the platforms is indeed a tool that supports the supply chain management cycle in a virtual environment.

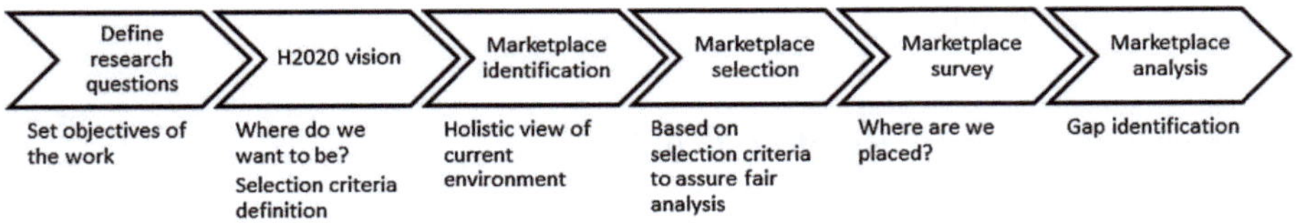

Fig. 1. Gap analysis method applied

Figure 1 outlines the method we utilised to carry out the work presented and define the criteria summarised above. The first step comprised defining the research questions to set the objectives of the analysis. Secondly, we explored the European Union's Horizon 2020 program's vision (H2020), in particular, the Digital Automation call topic towards Industry 4.0; this exploration provided the context of the study and enabled the recognition of the most relevant elements that are needed to develop a working Industry 4.0 solution. Based on the exploration conducted, we were able to define a selection criteria for the platforms to be surveyed accordingly. The third phase gathered information on available marketplaces, where more than 20 trading platforms available to the European market were identified; however, a fourth phase was dedicated to selecting only those platforms that met the criteria defined in the second phase. This was done to avoid creating an unfair comparison and analysis, where there was the risk of including marketplaces out of the scope of the research objectives. Examples of platforms that were left aside include those with little visibility within its domain area, with less than 1000 members, or very low impact and functionalities, and no intention to connect businesses but instead support a peer-to-peer (P2P) approach, as these platforms would provide an exaggerated and not necessarily representative gap. Finally, we proceeded to analyse the selected platforms in terms of the vision identified, thus, we were able to gather insights on the situation of the current representative digital marketplaces and identify the existing gaps.

Table 1 presents an analysis of the platforms surveyed. The analysis considers the platform's capabilities with regards to collaboration in supply chains and production networks, and their functionalities to support a working marketplace. This gap analysis intends to identify the limitations of the current supply chain marketplace solutions towards accomplishing the EU's Digital Automation call's vision.

The first column in Table 1 shows the area in which each platform works; the relevance of pointing out the industry area in which each platform works resides in the

Table 1. Surveyed marketplaces overview. Marketplace platform labels: (UG) UK Government Digital Marketplace (https://www.digitalmarketplace.service.gov.uk/), (AL) Alibaba (https://www.alibaba.com/), (CB) CloudBuy (https://www.cloudbuy.com/), (IM) IndiaMart (https://www.indiamart.com/), (OW) OFweek (http://en.ofweek.com/), (HA) Haizol (https://www.haizol.com/en), (IZ) Izberg (http://www.izberg-marketplace.com/), (AB) Amazon Business (https://www.amazon.com/b2b/info/amazon-business?layout=landing), (MI) Mirakl (https://www.mirakl.com/mirakl-marketplace-platform/), and (TH) Thomas net (http://www.thomasnet.com/).

Marketplace/Category		UG	AL	CB	IM	OW	HA	IZ	AB	MI	TH
Area	IT services	✓		✓							
	Retail/wholesaler		✓	✓	✓			✓	✓	✓	✓
	Industrial			✓		✓	✓				✓
	Services			✓					✓		✓
SME participation	Supported	✓	✓	✓	✓						
	Not supported					✓	✓	✓	✓	✓	✓
Type	Sellers listing			✓					✓		✓
	Sellers & buyers listing	✓	✓		✓	✓	✓				
	Online shop to third party suppliers							✓		✓	
Evaluation	Internal		✓		✓			✓			
	External	✓					✓		✓		
	None			✓		✓				✓	✓
Security	Existent			✓							
	None explicitly	✓	✓		✓	✓	✓	✓	✓	✓	✓
Connection to external systems	Supported							✓		✓	
	Not supported	✓	✓	✓	✓	✓	✓		✓		✓

discovery of the existing degree of coverage, especially for the industrial and services areas, therefore the area in which more development is needed can be identified. The majority of the platforms work with retail and wholesalers, with no specific domain set; second place is taken by those platforms that are focused on a particular vertical domain. Only one of the platforms surveyed is dedicated exclusively to a specific domain area, which is the case of the UK Government Digital Marketplace, dedicated to IT services such as cloud computing offerings. Finally, it can be identified that not all of the platforms support a service marketplace, where business or individuals can offer or request services and parts. The analysis reveals a capability coverage gap in digital marketplaces available specifically for the aerospace and automotive domains.

The EU's Digital Automation call topic has SMEs as one of the main beneficiaries, this is why it is important to analyse the platforms surveyed in terms of SME participation support. The participation of SMEs seems to be a growing area in the marketplace; however, it is not yet fully supported by the majority of the digital marketplaces, as Table 1 shows. This symbolises an opportunity to cover the gaps to provide wide support for SMEs within an important domain besides general trading.

Among the platforms surveyed, three types were identified; the first type is formed by those platforms where the functionality supports products or services listing only for suppliers; the second type of platform identified enables either buyers or contractors to list their requirements as well as suppliers to list their capabilities and interact with each other in a two-way communication, and the third type found is composed of those platforms that provide technological means to create a digital marketplace managed by one of the users, which then will coordinate and be responsible for an internal marketplace available to third party suppliers, called “the sellers”. This is the only form in which a kind of Virtual Enterprise (VE) is supported; however, it is not clearly treated as one. There is also no support in any of the platforms for the management of constructs resulting from the assembly of VEs or cooperation to fulfil the same bid. The type classification is of relevance because this category allows us to identify the most utilised model within digital marketplaces, hence, it could be known where is the major gap to cover, and identify where are the emerging developments going as a perspective.

One important issue to solve when talking about VE formation is to consider how the suppliers will be evaluated to form a viable VE. Within the platforms analysed, not all of them have procedures to evaluate if a supplier is reliable or not; this is presented in Table 1. Normally, the evaluation is done by the same platform (internal evaluation) or the users awarding rates to identify ranges among the available suppliers (external evaluation).

When dealing with bids, sensitive information will be required, such as details of the bid, which might include strategic information, designs not yet ready to be published, contact information from contractors and suppliers, etc., which makes information security and governance information a major concern in the digital marketplace. Among the platforms reviewed only one prioritises security, where Payment Card Industry Data Security Standard (PCI-DSS Level 1) is claimed to be used, and the “buyers” that use the platform are governed by rules selected to limit information access. The last category evaluated is the platform’s functionality to connect to external devices, platforms or things, which can be translated in Internet of Things (IoT) capabilities, which is a core functionality towards Industry 4.0. In this category, only two of the platforms surveyed are able to connect to the major e-Commerce solutions, and none considers a connection to physical devices. IoT seems to be an open area for development within marketplaces solutions.

3.1 Marketplace Gap Analysis Towards Industry 4.0 Aims

Six main processes of the supply chain aligned to the EU’s Digital Automation call topic could be identifiable: Procurement, Engineering, Manufacturing, Delivery, Risk Evaluation, and Monitoring [6]. The marketplace analysis presented in Sect. 3.1 reveals there are some processes not currently available to use from the marketplaces surveyed, and for those processes supported, there is no coverage within the same marketplace platform.

The Procurement process supports the registering of a company to the platform, either to be a contractor or a supplier, this process also supports the functionality to publish a tender or offer a bid, where both sub-processes mentioned are basic functionalities supported by the majority of the platforms. One process not yet available is VE identification and formation [6]. The contract management process, part of the

Procurement process, is supported by some of the platforms analysed, however, most of the time it is offered in a rudimentary form, with no support for custom/personalised legal features.

Another identified process is called Engineering; this provides guidance and availability for the first statement of the requirements towards initialising the Manufacturing process. As part of the Engineering process, a capacity planning sub-process is contemplated, where data models describing the production plans are required to assess and allocate the capacity of individual participants within a VE to fulfil a bid. The capacity planning is not supported by marketplaces yet, this reflects another example of a VE management process not supported.

The Manufacturing process is currently left to be managed by each supplier on their own, without support from any platform. A production planning process and a scheduling process is required [6], in such a way the suppliers and contractors could monitor each and every phase of the manufacturing process, accompanied by risk management tasks on each phase. This is a helpful functionality towards optimising collaboration and resources.

The Delivery process is covered by the majority of the marketplaces nowadays, but it was found to be very limited. The main functionality towards delivery is to let the involved entities know the date of delivery, and then some marketplaces implement a satisfaction or evaluation (ratings) survey once the delivery is completed. The logistics planning is not supported for VE management, and to a lesser degree, it is supported for multi-vendor situations.

Finally, some major Industry 4.0 processes within the manufacturing value chain are novel, such as the automated risk evaluation and monitoring, where this last one if existent, is supported only by manual updates in the majority of the marketplaces. An overview of the findings towards those Industry 4.0 processes and the platforms

Table 2. Designed Industry 4.0 Value Chain processes covered by available marketplaces

Industry 4.0 value chain process	Sub-process	Covered by marketplaces available
Procurement	Registering company	Yes
	Publishing tender	Yes
	Offering bids	Yes
	Forming consortium	No
	Contract management	Yes
Engineering	Capacity planning	No
Manufacturing	Production planning	No
	Scheduling	No
Delivery	Delivery forecasting	Yes
	Logistics planning	No
	Satisfaction evaluation	Yes
Risk evaluation		No
Monitoring		Partially

Table 3. Summary of the marketplaces gap analysis

Category	Expectations	Gaps
VE management support	Support for VE creation, recommendation for VE formation, evaluation for potential suppliers to form a VE, management as if participants were a single company	There is no model to support VE in digital platforms
Logistics management	Availability of capacity planners, contract support, production planners, operational and delivery tools, with resilient, scalable, automated solutions	Logistics management, including delivery details, are approached separately, out of the digital platforms, or even without IT interaction
Monitoring	The main expectation is to monitor in real time with connection to physical items, such as sensors, PLCs, etc.	Monitoring is carried out mainly by manual updates. No IoT for supply chain monitoring is available integrated within a collaboration platform
Risk evaluation	Risk evaluation will be an inherent functionality of the supply chain management, automated and efficient	Risk evaluation if any, are most of the times done outside digital platforms with separated and isolated technological tools

surveyed mentioned above are represented in Table 2 and summarised in Table 3. The gaps presented offer an overview of the areas in which opportunities and challenges to address exist. IoT appears as the major gap to address, with special attention required on protocols and models designed to cover this gap.

4 Discussion and Future Directions

The main goal of the current study was to identify existing gaps within digital marketplaces towards enabling future initiatives for industry, especially those focusing on supply chain management. Although there are research outcomes available to support Industry 4.0 characteristics [1, 11, 18, 20], we evaluate the extent to which existing digital marketplaces are already involved with those developments, and identify those areas that require focus towards enabling a working Industry 4.0 solution to support the whole supply chain management processes.

The first question in this study sought to determine what Industry 4.0 concepts, techniques and services are available in current marketplace tools to support Industry 4.0 collaborative supply chain systems. Industry 4.0 represents a new approach in the value chain, integrating an organisation and control merged with technologies and digitalisation [3]. This paper has found that generally, Industry 4.0 requirements are not fully supported in existing platforms. IoT is not implemented in the majority of the value chain stages of the surveyed platforms, cyber-physical-systems (CPS) are not present, and digitalisation is limited only to the online identification of products or services facing the customer, but not for communication between any of the factories' elements. We also identified that actions are triggered based on manual updates, rather than automated information sharing.

With respect to the second research question, it was found that digital marketplace platforms can address the gaps of traditional approaches in collaborative supply chain by developing protocols and models to cover the gap in the integration of IoT with Industry processes, and developing unified technologies that might support the complete digitalisation of the physical factory and machinery, for which CPS communication and IoT are important parts. We believe industries will need to begin the path to digitalisation underpinned by cloud services, machine-to-machine (M2M) communication standards, embedded systems, and the introduction of new business models. In a separate layer, governance and security issues will arise linked with the new architectures, including challenges in handling Big Data.

The third question driving this research was how digital marketplace tools can impact the business, organisational, architectural and technology approaches within collaborative supply chains. Industry 4.0 will support the development of new business models and new methods of creating value chains, and will widen the marketplace for SMEs by adopting a model in which small-scale batches of products and custom products and services will be competitive against larger enterprises [3]. These benefits will be enabled because of the increased levels of control, micro-work specification and customisation from Industry 4.0 approaches [5].

An example of how digital marketplaces can impact business models is when the information details obtained from a product distribution is at a new deeper micro-work specification level compared to the information that could be obtained before marketplaces from Industry 4.0; this information could provide value when shared among the organisational structures and roles of the companies or collaborators, generating a change in the processes carried out. Organisational aspects will change due to the increased dynamism of the industry, both within and across companies, and new information could be obtained in real time. Together, these developments provide important insights into the steps ahead for Industry 4.0. Making use of the most innovative and recent technologies might not be enough without assuring the business and organisational models reflect the most effective way of doing business.

The industry of the future will reduce the burden involved in traditional supply chain processes, and will also create new opportunities to provide a highly dynamic environment with substantial benefits for businesses. The Industry 4.0 for the supply value chain required platform will support IoT, CPS, and smart technologies (i.e. Semantic Web Standards) that can enable M2M communications within supply chain systems and provide Industry 4.0 solutions. Future research will concentrate on the investigation of Industry 4.0 use cases, with a particular interest in the challenges, benefits and drawbacks.

Future direction also includes the development of several tools and technologies in the context of the Decentralised Agile Coordination Across Supply Chains (DIGICOR) EU project, coined as a platform that will consist of open tools and services for European companies requiring working within collaborative networks supporting Industry 4.0 activities [13].

5 Conclusion

This paper presented an overview of a representative set of marketplace platforms available to support supply chain processes underpinning Industry 4.0, and a gap analysis of existing marketplaces assessing their ability to support Industry 4.0 requirements, positioned in the context of the EU's Digital Automation call topic addressing the theme of collaborative manufacturing and logistics. Results of this paper revealed digital marketplace platforms have not yet moved completely from supporting simple collaboration approaches, where, for example, B2B models are formed by only one company on each side, and although there is research covering different aspects of more elaborated collaborations, such as VE formations and SMEs clusters, we believe there is still significant work to be done in relation to digital marketplaces to incorporate more advanced virtual organisation capabilities such as dynamic search, assessment, selection, and formation of coalitions. The limitations in existing digital marketplaces arise primarily due to a considerable gap between VE research adoption and its dissemination into commercial practice.

Acknowledgements. The work presented has received funding from the European Commission under the European Union's Horizon 2020 research and innovation programme (grant agreement n° 723336). Financial support has been provided by the National Council of Science and Technology (abbreviated CONACYT) to the first author (agreement n° 461338).

References

1. Helo, P., Szekely, B.: Logistics information systems: an analysis of software solutions for supply chain co-ordination. Ind. Manage. Data Syst. **105**(1), 5–18 (2005)
2. Lasi, H., Fettke, P., Feld, T., Hoffmann, M.: Industry 4.0. Bus. Inf. Syst. Eng. **6**(4), 239–242 (2014)
3. Gilchrist, A.: Introducing Industry 4.0. In: Industry 4.0, pp. 195–215. Apress, Springer (2016)
4. Obitko, M., Jirkovsky, V.: Big Data Semantics in Industry 4.0. In: Marik, V., Schirrmann, A., Trentesaux, D., Vrba, P. (eds.) Industrial Applications of Holonic and Multi-Agent Systems. HoloMAS 2015. LNCS, vol. 9266, pp. 217–229. Springer, Cham (2015)
5. Koch, V., Kuge, S., Geissbauer, R., Schrauf, S.: Industry 4.0: Opportunities and Challenges of the Industrial Internet. PWC Stategy (2014)
6. Jiru, F., Harcuba, O.: Main processes and their requirements in the DigiCor platform (2017). (Unpublished)
7. Laissus, L: Mirakl Announces Record Growth, Continued International Expansion (2017). https://www.mirakl.com/mirakl-announces-record-growth-continued-international-expansion/
8. Smith, C.: By the numbers: 90+ Amazing Alibaba Statistics (2017). http://expandedramblings.com/index.php/alibaba-statistics/
9. Su, T.: HAIZOL Announces Operation Expansion (2016). http://www.prweb.com/releases/2016/10/prweb13753925.htm
10. Amazon Inc.: Amazon Business features. https://www.amazon.com/b2b/info/features?layout=landing

11. CONOISE-G: Virtual Organisations and the Grid. http://www.iam.ecs.soton.ac.uk/projects/CONOISEG.html
12. CloudBuy: Company Formations. https://www.cloudbuy.com/solutions/company-formations.html
13. DIGICOR Project. http://www.digicor-project.eu/
14. Digital Automation. http://ec.europa.eu/research/participants/portal/desktop/en/opportunities/h2020/topics/fof-11-2016.html
15. Government Digital Service Cabinet Office: G-Cloud 8 supplier statistics. https://digitalmarketplace.blog.gov.uk/2016/08/04/g-cloud-8-supplier-statistics/
16. IndiaMART InterMESH Ltd.: India-MART. Indian Manufacturers Suppliers: Exporters Directory, India Exporter Manufacturer. https://www.indiamart.com/
17. IZBERG SAS: The Most Advanced Marketplace Platform. http://www.izberg-marketplace.com/
18. ManuCloud project. http://www.manucloud-project.eu
19. OFweek: About OFweek. http://www.ofweek.com/abouten/company.html
20. SMEs undertaking design of dynamic Ecosystem Networks project (SUDDEN). http://cordis.europa.eu/project/rcn/79353_en.html
21. Thomas Publishing Company: Thomas-Net. Product Sourcing and Supplier Discovery Platform. http://www.thomasnet.com/

Relevant Capabilities for Information Management to Achieve Industrie 4.0 Maturity

Volker Stich, Sebastian Schmitz(✉), and Violett Zeller

FIR at RWTH Aachen, Institute for Industrial Management,
Campus-Boulevard 55, 52074 Aachen, Germany
{Volker.Stich,Sebastian.Schmitz,
Violett.Zeller}@fir.rwth-aachen.de

Abstract. Industrie 4.0 is changing the industrial landscape in an unanticipated way. The vision for manufacturing industries is to transform to an agile company, in order to react on occurring events in real-time and make data based decisions. The realization requires also new capabilities for the information management. To achieve this goal agile companies require taking measured data, analyzing it, deriving knowledge out of this and support with the knowledge their employees. This is crucial for a successful Industrie 4.0 implementation, but many manufacturing companies struggling with these requirements. This paper identifies the required capabilities for the information management to achieve a successful Industrie 4.0 implementation.

Keywords: Industrie 4.0 · Agile company · Information management · Manufacturing companies

1 Introduction

The term "Industrie 4.0" - or labelled with different terms as "Industrial Internet of Things" in USA - describes the widespread integration of information and communication technology in industrial manufacturing [1]. Industrie 4.0 can be defined scientifically as real-time, multilateral communication and data transmission between cyber-physical devices with high data volumes rates [2]. The main benefit in realizing Industrie 4.0 concepts is the transformation of companies to an agile and learning company in order to be competitive in a growing dynamic business market. Many studies have shown that manufacturing companies are highly interested in capturing the named benefit within a targeted timeline of five years [3, 4]. However, the actual implementation speed is too slow to achieve this goal. Use cases are dominant, but an end-to-end implementation is necessary to realize the presented potentials. A systematic implementation in companies has not been conducted and companies need a precise development path for a holistic implementation of Industrie 4.0.

Due to the Industrie 4.0 definition, one action field is information management. An efficient information management is the key for successful companies to ensuring that available data and information can be used to make decisions. The relevant task in the

L.M. Camarinha-Matos et al. (Eds.): PRO-VE 2017, IFIP AICT 506, pp. 28–38, 2017.
DOI: 10.1007/978-3-319-65151-4_3

information management and its influence on production processes are not transparent for manufacturing companies [4, 5].

2 Vision of Industrie 4.0 for Manufacturing Companies

The overall objective for producing companies is continuous, long-term enhancement of liquidation and stakeholder value. Quality and time objectives replace traditional objectives like a substantial margin especially in high-wage countries [6]. Flexibility is the key for manufacturing companies to produce and deliver products in high quality and adapt to customer requirements fast. New market entrants, ever-shorter product lifecycles and customized solutions increase the required agility of companies. Industrie 4.0 enables flexibility and agility as two success factors for producing companies [7].

With a better availability of data and information, companies can learn how things are related to each other and can make faster decisions. A faster reaction to events achieve agility, as one key capability required by companies in Industrie 4.0 [2]. Derived from this vision, four corresponding Industrie 4.0 levels describe the business value of Industrie 4.0 for manufacturing companies. The Fig. 1 shows Industrie 4.0 levels defined by the acatech– the national academy of science and engineering [2]. The definition of these levels represent following Industrie 4.0 maturity levels [2]: The starting point is the digital **visibility** of events in the company. This means that all processes and events leave a digital trace. In order to achieve this goal, all kinds of processes, such as management, business or supporting processes have to be captured digitally and be available in real-time. All data are processed and displayed in an appropriate level of detail for the given use-case. Having achieved visibility, decisions are information-based rather than assumption-based.

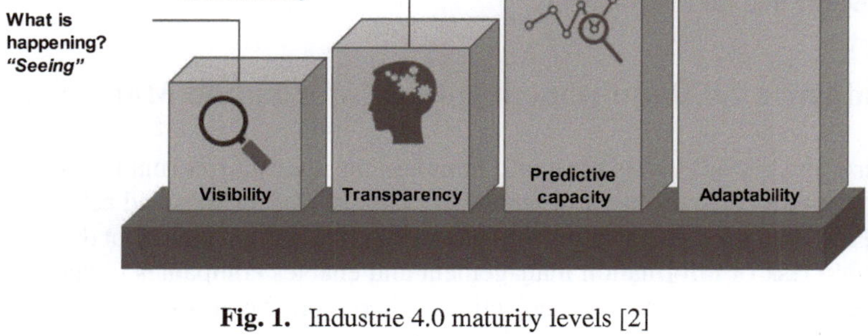

Fig. 1. Industrie 4.0 maturity levels [2]

Given the real-time availability of all relevant data, companies can reach the next maturity level of **transparency** resulting from understanding cause-and-effect relationships in the obtained data. Created process knowledge derived from context specific data combination and aggregation granted decision support. Big Data applications are used in environments where traditional methods of data analysis fail due to size and scope of obtained data. With the help of stochastic methods, these applications reveal unknown cause-and-effect relationships in producing companies. Big data applications fed systems, like enterprise resource planning (ERP) and manufacturing execution systems (MES), with the aggregated data. The configuration of these applications allows that data are transmitted to the right software automatically.

The next target level **predictability** bases on identified cause-and-effect relationships. The conducted measures grant a comprehensive and reliable input in order to make better forecasts and predictions. Probabilistic methods forecast events in the future and developed strategies face them in advance. Hence, best possible reactions can be determined more reliably and initiated faster. With these new capabilities in predicting the company's market environment, the number of unexpected events decreases. Thus, production planning achieves a new level of reliability. The quality of the prognoses is highly dependent to the preliminary work done in the described former stages. Information quality is resulting from a comprehensive digital signature and defined cause-and-effect relationships. Quantifying information quality is crucial in order to make valid prognoses yet remains a challenge. Both practical and expert knowledge are key factors in order to generate sound prognoses.

Companies can accomplish the final level **self-optimization** by continuously adapting insights given by transparency and visibility. In manufacturing, self-optimization controls automatically controlling the manufacturing process. All factors essential to the company's success are included in such a system (e.g. production planning, production control). In order to decide which steps to automate, companies have to determine and evaluate costs and benefits for all manufacturing steps. Repeating manufacturing steps should always be considered when examining the capability to run autonomously. When communicating with suppliers and customers, approval and confirmation notifications have to be supervised critically. Companies reach the target of self-optimization when they able to use the digital signature in a way that the system is able to make decisions quickly and put their measures into practice fast with the best possible outcome for the company.

3 Industrie 4.0 Requirements to the Information Management

All four Industrie 4.0 levels have in common, that relevant information in right time, place and quality are required to enable these databased decisions and achieve business value. Providing time-critical information in the right quality to the right decision maker is the main task of information management and enables companies to achieve targets like flexibility, quality and time objectives. Therefore, this business function handles processes and information systems in order to provide, process, save, generate and transfer data and information to all business processes. This includes data processing to generate knowledge out of data [8]. Information systems are socio-technical systems in which information is provided based on economic criteria by both people and information and communication technology [9].

In order to provide decision-relevant information, access and confidentiality of all required data has to be ensured and a detailed digital picture of the production system has to be enabled. Only providing is not enough. Information have to be filtered, clustered and showing relationships, so that data analysis is a required capability for manufacturing companies. Data processing and interpretation transform raw data into valuable information and knowledge [10]. Data preparation and visualizations reduces for users the complexity of relations. Furthermore, the communication between users and systems has to be bidirectional to enable the user to feed information back.

Providing data and information for decisions, companies' data have to be available throughout different IT systems like Enterprise resource planning (ERP). To do this, it is necessary to create an information system architecture for agile companies with a central platform. This requires horizontal and vertical integration, standardized exchange formats and interfaces as well as appropriate data quality.

4 Methodical Approach of This Paper

The overall target of the research activity is to identify relevant Industrie 4.0 capabilities of the information management and integrate these capabilities in an Industrie 4.0 maturity model –e.g. the acatech Industrie 4.0 maturity index. To achieve that overall target the research activity is split into three models, see Fig. 2. Content of this paper will be the development of the first model. This model derives the required capabilities from literature analysis. The literature analysis bases on relevant Industrie 4.0 studies and fundamental work of information management. The identified capabilities are discussed and validated with expert, who are involved in the acatech project "Industrie 4.0 maturity index" [2]

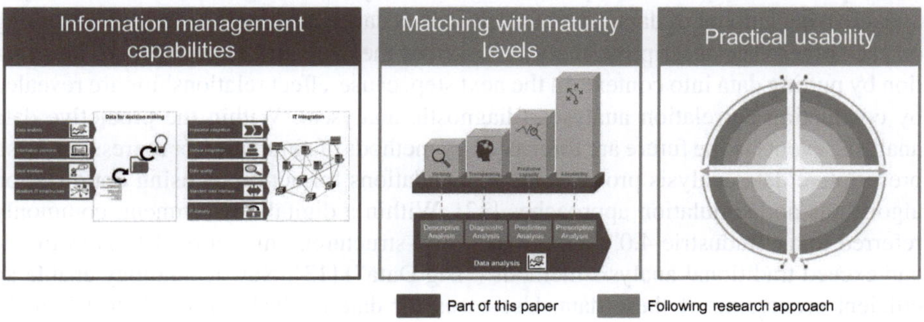

Fig. 2. Methodical approach of this paper

5 Industrie 4.0 Capabilities to the Information Management

Derived from the requirement, this chapter describes the Industrie 4.0 capabilities to the information management. For a successful Industrie 4.0 implementation, two principles are relevant. First, available data should be prepared and processed in a manner that supports decision-making. In order for the data to be usable, the organization must meet technical requirements for real-time access and possess an infrastructure that enables the necessary data processing and seamless information delivery. Second, manufacturing companies require an IT integration in order to enhance data use and increase agility [2]. To realize both principles, producing companies have to possess a level of capabilities. It is the task for the information management to ensure that capabilities and develop a roadmap to realize these capabilities. Figure 3 shows an overview of the required capabilities. An explanation of these capabilities are followed in detail.

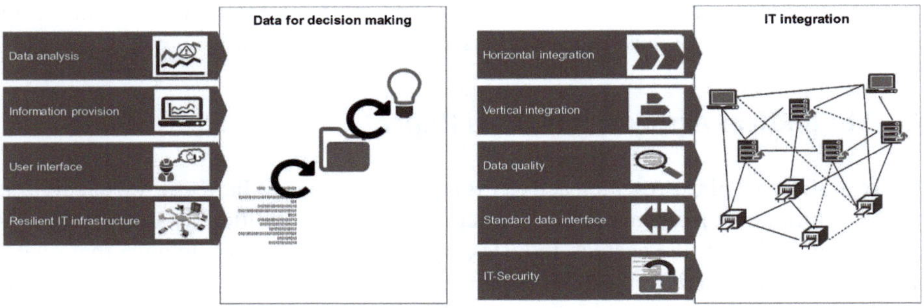

Fig. 3. Required Industrie 4.0 capabilities for a successful implementation

Data analysis Data analysis defines the transformation process from data into information to use the information for valuable decisions [11]. The degree of digitization and interdependence of production plants is continuously increasing. This results directly in an increasing amount of data. Literature describes data analysis along four levels basing on each other: The descriptive analysis describes the evolvement from data to information by putting data into context. In the next step, cause-effect relationships are revealed by conducting correlation analyses (diagnostic analyses). Within the predictive data analysis, events in the future are forecasted by methods of simulation or regression. Last, prescriptive data analysis provides recommendations for action by using optimization algorithms and simulation approaches [12]. Within a digital environment, commonly referred to as "Industrie 4.0", a large and poly-structured amount of data is available and exceed traditional analysis methods ("Big Data") [13]. New technology enable an efficient processing of these data. Use-cases for data analysis in an "Industrie 4.0"-environment are forecasting machine failures and an optimized production planning process.

Information provision Information provision includes the suitable provision of information [14]. Due to increasing amount of information, companies focusing on an efficient information provision [15]. Delivering contextualized information to employees allows that they use the results of the data analysis to support their decision-makings. Companies have to make sure, that the provided information are the right information in that situation. Methods like information modelling or information logistic concepts identify the right information [16].

Instead of searching for the information across several different IT systems and processes, sorting or interpreting it themselves, the IT system delivered the right information in accordance of the specific context of the actual task and the right content. The term system-of-engagement describes an efficient information provision. Systems of engagement focus on the employees instead of daily processes, like systems of enrichment. These system of engagement works similar to apps and collect all required information from available IT-Systems and show these in the right relation to the employees task [17].

Furthermore, companies have to ensure, that employees use the provided information and information system for their tasks and decisions. Not used information or systems leads to redundant data and missing feedback to former processes [18].

User interface User interfaces describe the interface and interaction modus between IT systems and users [19]. IT systems can deliver information in form of tables, animations, Augmented Reality or voice. The better the information are displayed and corresponding to the actual process, companies reach potentials like increasing productivity or quality. Easily understandable visualisation (e.g. 3D-animations) reduces the decision complexity. Its content and presentation should be adapted to the task being performed and the employee's skill level. The used technology must be mobile, highly versatile and easily usable [20]. Users need intuitive possibilities to react on events and communicate with the IT systems. Depending on the actual task though, gesture or voice control are used [21].

Resilient IT infrastructure Resilience defines how an IT system reacts under changes circumstances. Resilient IT systems are stable within foreseeable circumstances [22]. Data analysis and delivery require a resilient IT infrastructure that fulfils the relevant technical data capture, transfer, storage and processing requirements and guarantees the IT system's functionality. A common problem for manufacturing companies is the actual IT infrastructure, which is not designed for the big amount of data [23].

Backups or specialised software prevent threats to people and material assets and guarantee the system's long-term usability. Situation-based data storage ensures that applications can access the data within an appropriate timeframe. In-memory databases allow frequent accessing of the data, so that it can be used to provide rapid and stable decision-making support [24].

Horizontal IT system integration The horizontal integration describes the integration of different process steps within a company. The integration contains operational, executional and administrational processes and IT systems. The horizontal integration abolish different version status over the value stream and enable a single source of truth [25]. A complete horizontal integration along the value stream and without media disruption enables companies to link the order information to product, work and process instructions [2, 26]. Companies can react flexible and data based due to an interconnection between engineering, planning and production data [27]. This interconnection include also an information feedback, e.g. the feedback of production parameter back to the production planning to adapt the planned production time. To implement a horizontal integration of the IT-systems local data storages have to opened and interfaces between IT-systems be connected. Common data storage is the basis for a companywide single source of truth. All users access the same set of information [2].

Vertical IT-system integration A big amount of data is available throughout the value chain. To analyse these data and identify interdependencies between them, a vertical integration of IT systems is required. The vertical integration is one of the Industrie 4.0 key aspects [25]. IT systems and the machines on the field level exchange information continuously between them. It is necessary to create an information system architecture for agile companies with a central platform that connects existing IT systems to each other and provides contextualized information. The vertical IT integration focus on the integration of IT systems on different levels and the dissolution of the automation pyramid [25, 26, 28]. This means the dissolution of the IT systems structures and hierarchies.

Standardize data interfaces Data interfaces describe the transition between two IT systems. Standardized data interfaces is the required communication basis in Industrie 4.0 [29–31]. A continuous information flow between the IT systems and the access for all users on the same set of information requires standardized data interfaces. Data interfaces facilitate the exchange of data and information from individual IT systems. Nowadays many interfaces are proprietary, which means that the interface works only in that individual use case [31]. To react agilely on changing IT-systems and information flows a flexible IT-landscape is required. Neutral or standard interfaces and data exchange formats across all the relevant systems are necessary for this flexible IT-landscape [17].

Data quality Data quality means the degree of data usability for the individual purpose [32]. IT systems integration relies on sufficiently high data quality. Poor data quality in the IT systems results in incorrect aggregated data and inaccurate feedback, ultimately undermining confidence in both the IT systems and their contents [17]. This makes it impossible to achieve the goal of databased decision-making. Data governance policies provide organisations with guidance for the processing, storage, management and presentation of high-quality data within the company. Even a perfect data quality is impossible to reach, goal within the Industrie 4.0 vision is a "fit for use" [33]. Technical capabilities for improving data quality include automated data cleansing (identification, standardisation, duplicate removal, consolidation and enhancement of data) and master data management systems.

Upgrade IT security The increasing integration of information systems as well as human factors and other contributors bear the risk of criminal attacks. The potential damage that these attacks can cause increases in proportion to the degree of integration. IT security encompasses different strategies for identifying and implementing security measures. Compliance with standards such as IEC 62443 can help to contain the risks.

Such standards include proactive measures to maintain IT security and adapt it in response to changing circumstances [34].

6 Conclusion and Outlook

This paper describes possible capabilities for the information management in order to achieve the four maturity levels of Industrie 4.0 successfully. Companies have to master these capabilities to reach the overall goals of Industrie 4.0, like flexibility, quality and time objectives. All capabilities base on a literature research analysis. This paper defines the capabilities and presents the requirement for an Industrie 4.0 implementation.

The following research activities match these capabilities to the described Industrie 4.0 maturity levels. The maturity levels will be described by the configuration of each capability.

Figure 4 shows exemplarily the matching for the capability of data analysis. Literature separates data analysis into descriptive, diagnostic, predictive and prescriptive analysis. Target of the first maturity level is that data are processed and displayed in an appropriate level of detail for the given use-case. To reach this goal, data have to transfer to information by putting data into context. These requirements are given by descriptive analysis. The maturity level "transparency" is described by cause-and-effect relationships in the obtained data. Diagnostic analysis include correlations and identifies these cause-and-effect relationships. Predictive data analysis forecasts events in the future by methods of simulation or regression. This forecast is the central issue in the third maturity level predictability. Prescriptive data analysis provides recommendations for action and optimization algorithms. The fourth maturity level adaptability requires recommendations for action and optimization algorithms to react autonomously.

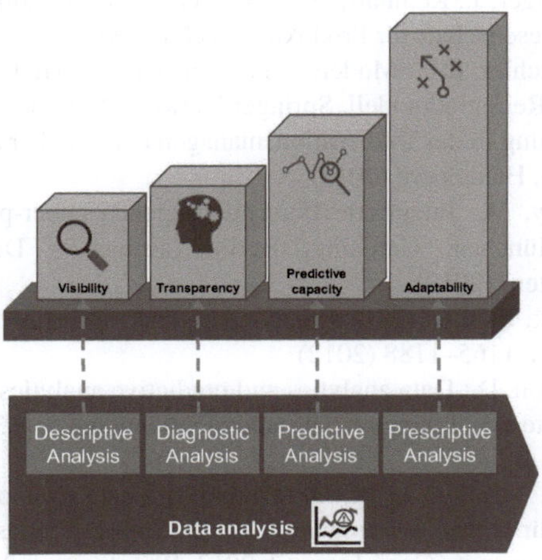

Fig. 4. Example for matching of capabilities to maturity levels

Following research activities will split and match all identified to the maturity levels. The allocation is used for a maturity model that assess the maturity degree of the information management. Furthermore, the validation of the presented approach will include interviews and assessments in producing companies in order to prove that the identified information management capabilities support the achievement of each Industrie 4.0 level.

References

1. Gudergan, G., Stich, V., Schmitz, S., Buschmeyer, A.: The global evolution of the industrial internet of things. a cross country comparison based on an international study on industrie 4.0 for asset efficiency management. In: Dimitrov, D., Oosthuizen, T. (Hg.): Proceedings of International Conference on Competitive Manufacturing. COMA 2016, Stellenbosch, South Africa, 29. January 2016, pp. 489–494. Department of Indutrial Engineering Stellenbosch University, Stellenbosch (2016)
2. Schuh, G., Anderl, R., Gausemeier, J., ten Hompel, M., Wahlster, W.: Industrie 4.0 Maturity Index. Managing the digital transformation. Hg. v. acatech. acatech, Munich (2017)
3. Infosys: Industry 4.0. The State of the Nations. 1. Aufl. Hg. v. Infosys Ltd. Bangalore, India (2015)
4. von Dominik Wee, U.M., Kelly, R., Cattel, J., Breunig, M.: McKinsey: Industry 4.0. How to navigate digitalization of the manufacturing sector. Hg. v. McKinsey (2015)
5. Zühlke, D.: Die Cloud ist Voraussetzung für Industrie 4.0. Präsentation. VDI. VDI-Pressegespräch anlässlich des Kongresses. In: AUTOMATION 2013, Baden-Baden, 25 June (2013)
6. Schuh, G., Kampker, A., Stich, V., Kuhlmann, K.: Prozessmanagement. In: Schuh, G., Kampker, A. (Hg.): Strategie und Management produziernder Unternehmen. Handbuch Produktion und Management, vol. 1, 327–382. Springer, Heidelberg (VDI-Buch) (2011)
7. Bauernhansl, T., Krüger, J., Reinhart, G., Schuh, G.: WGP-Standpunkt Industrie 4.0. Hg. v. Wissenschaftliche Gesellschaft für Produktionstechnik Wgp e. V
8. Mangiapane, M., Büchler, R.P.: Modernes IT-management. Methodische Kombination von IT-Strategie und IT-Reifegradmodell. Springer Vieweg, Wiesbaden (2015)
9. Krcmar, H.: Einführung in das Informationsmanagement. 2., überarb. Aufl. Springer Gabler (Springer-Lehrbuch), Heidelberg (2015)
10. Geisberger, E., Broy, M.: Integrierte Forschungsagenda cyber-physical systems. acatech Studie. Hg. v. München, Garching, Berlin (acatech - Deutsche Akademtie der Technikwissenschaften) (2012)
11. Chen, H., Chiang, R., Storey, V.: Business intelligence and analytics. from big data to big impact. MIS Q. **36**(4), 1165–1188 (2012)
12. Shi-Nash, A., Hardoon, D.: Data analytics and predictive analytics in the era of big data. In: Geng, H. (ed.) The internet of things et data analytics handbook, pp. 329–345. Wiley, Hoboken (2017)
13. Krumpe, J., Knoth, A., Golla, B.: XaaS und big-data-technologien. cloudoptimiertes Datenmanagement für Open-Government-Data. In: Strobl, J., Blaschke, T., Griesebner, G., Zagel, B. (Hg.): Angewandte Geoinformatik 2013. Beiträge zum 25. AGIT-Symposium, pp. 566–575. Wichmann, Salzburg. Berlin, Offenbach (2013)

14. Hermann, M., Pentek, T., Otto, B.: Design Principles for industrie 4.0 scenarios. In: Bui, T.X., Sprague, R.H. (Hg.): Proceedings of the 49th Annual Hawaii International Conference on System Sciences, HICSS 2016, Kauai, Hawaii, 5–8 January 2016, pp. 3928–3937. IEEE, Piscataway (2016)
15. Fiebig, S., Lehmann, M., Wonneberger, K-U., Münnich, M.: Informationen auf dem Shopfloor. In: Rudow, B., Heidecke, H.-C. (Hg.): Betriebliche Informationssysteme in der Automobilproduktion. Soziotechnisches System - Nutzerpersönlichkeit - Nutzungserleben - Rollout und Betrieb - Fabriksteuerung - Informationen auf Shopfloor. IT-Nutzen, pp. 231–259. Oldenburg Wissenschaftsverlag GmbH, München (2014)
16. Krcmar, H.: Informationsmanagement. 6, überarb. Aufl. Berlin, Gabler. SpringerLink, Bücher (2015)
17. Schuh, G., Potente, T., Thomas, C., Hauptvogel, A.: Steigerung der Kollaborationsproduktivität durch cyber-physische Systeme. In: Bauernhansl, T., ten Hompel, M., Vogel-Heuser, B. (Hg.): Industrie 4.0 in Produktion, Automatisierung und Logistik. Springer Fachmedien Wiesbaden, Wiesbaden, pp. 277–296 (2014)
18. Aier, S., Schönherr, M.: Flexibilisierung von Organisations- und IT-Architekturen durch EAI. Technische Universität Berlin, Berlin. Competence Center EAI (2007)
19. Calvary, G., Coutaz, J., Thevenin, D., Limbourg, Q., Bouillon, L., Vanderdonckt, J.: A unifying reference framework for multi-target user interfaces. Interact. Comput. **15**(3), 289–308 (2003). doi:10.1016/S0953-5438(03)00010-9
20. Fallenbeck, N., Eckert, C.: IT-Sicherheit und Cloud Computing. In: Bauernhansl, T., ten Hompel, M., Vogel-Heuser, B. (Hg.): Industrie 4.0 in Produktion, Automatisierung und Logistik, pp. 397–431. Springer Fachmedien Wiesbaden, Wiesbaden (2014)
21. Vogel-Heuser, B.: Herausforderungen und Anforderungen aus Sicht der IT und der Automatisierungstechnik. In: Bauernhansl, T., ten Hompel, M., Vogel-Heuser, B. (Hg.): Industrie 4.0 in Produktion, Automatisierung und Logistik, pp. 37–48. Springer Fachmedien Wiesbaden, Wiesbaden (2014)
22. Laprie, J.-C. (Hg.): From dependability to resilience. In: 38th IEEE/IFIP International Conference on Dependable Systems and Networks, Anchorage (2008)
23. Bartel, J., Pfitzinger, B., et al.: Big Data im Praxiseinsatz. Szenarien, Beispiele, Effekte. Hg. v. BITKOM e.V. Berlin (2012)
24. Porter, M.E., Heppelmann, J.: How smart, connected products are transforming companies. Harvard Bus. Rev. **93**(10), 97–114 (2015)
25. Kaufmann, T., Forstner, L.: Die horinzontale Integration der Wertschöpfungskette in der Halbleiterindustrie. Chancen und Herausforderungen. In: Bauernhansl, T., ten Hompel, M., Vogel-Heuser, B. (Hg.): Industrie 4.0 in Produktion, Automatisierung und Logistik, pp. 359–367. Springer Fachmedien Wiesbaden, Wiesbaden (2014)
26. Schlick, J., Stephan, P., Loskyll, M., Lappe, D.: Industrie in der praktischen Anwendung. In: Thomas Bauernhansl, Michael ten Hompel und Birgit Vogel-Heuser (Hg.): Industrie 4.0 in Produktion, Automatisierung und Logistik, pp. 57–82, Springer Fachmedien Wiesbaden, Wiesbaden (2014)
27. Bloching, B., Leutiger, P., Oltmanns, T., Rossbach, C., Schlick, T., Rename, G., et al.: Die digitale Transformation der Industrie. Hg. v. Roland Berger. München (2015)
28. Müller, R., Vette, M., Hörauf, L., Speicher, C., Jatti, K.: Concept and implementation of an agent-based control architecture for a cyber-physical assembly system. In: Platter, P., Meixing, G., Suhag, S. (Hg.): 3rd International Conference on Control, Mechatronics and Automation. MATEC Web of Conferences. MATEC Web of Conferences. Barcelona, Spanien, 21–22 December, pp. 167–170. Curran Associates, Red Hook (2015)

29. Hoppe, S.: Standardisierte horizontale und vertikale Kommunikation: Status und Ausblick. In: Bauernhansl, T., ten Hompel, M., Vogel-Heuser, B. (Hg.): Industrie 4.0 in Produktion, Automatisierung und Logistik, pp. 325–341. Springer Fachmedien Wiesbaden, Wiesbaden, (2014)
30. European Commission, Enterprise & Industry Directorate General: e-business w@tch. e-Business Interoperability and Standards. A Cross-Sector Perspective and Outlook. e-business watch, Brüssel (2005)
31. Sindermann, S.: Schnittstellen und Datenaustauschformate. In: Eigner, M., Roubanov, D., Zafirov, R. (eds.) Modellbasierte virtuelle produktentwicklung, pp. 327–347. Springer Vieweg, Berlin (2014)
32. Heinrich, L.J., Riedl, R., Stelzer, D.: Informationsmanagement. Grundlagen, Aufgaben, Methoden. 11., vollst. überarb. Aufl. 2014. Oldenbourg Wissenschaftsverlag, München (2014)
33. Strong, D.M., Lee, Y.W., Wang, R.Y.: Data quality in context. Commun. ACM **40**(5), 103–110 (1997). doi:10.1145/253769.253804
34. IEC 62443: Network and system security

Production Information Systems

A Holistic Algorithm for Materials Requirement Planning in Collaborative Networks

Beatriz Andres(✉), Raul Poler, and Raquel Sanchis

Research Centre on Production Management and Engineering (CIGIP),
Universitat Politècnica de València (UPV), Calle Alarcón, 03801 Alcoy, Spain
{bandres,rpoler,rsanchis}@cigip.upv.es

Abstract. Collaboration has increasingly been considered a key topic within the small and medium-sized enterprises, allowing dealing with the intense competitiveness of today's globalised markets. The European H2020 Cloud Collaborative Manufacturing Networks Project proposes mechanisms to encourage collaboration among enterprises, through the computation of collaborative plans. Particularly, this paper focuses on the proposal of a holistic algorithm to deal with the automated and collaborative calculation of the Materials Requirement Plan. The proposed algorithm is validated in a collaborative network belonging to the automotive industry.

Keywords: Materials requirement plan · Collaboration · Cloud computing · Data exchange · Automotive sector · Collaborative planning · Cloud collaborative manufacturing networks · H2020 project

1 Introduction

Collaboration has increasingly been considered a key topic within the small and medium-sized (SME) enterprises (SMEs), allowing dealing with the intense competitiveness of today's globalised markets. The SMEs participation in collaborative networks increases their competitive advantages over large multinational corporations that produce on a large scale, and mass customised products. This situation has involved the design of novel models, algorithms, mechanisms and tools to support companies on establishing collaborative relationships with the network partners. Nevertheless, SMEs are characterised by the scarce of resources to access such collaborative tools. In addition a cultural change is necessary within the SMEs, in the context of exchanging information and calculating their plans collaboratively, with the main aim of obtaining more realistic plans that are beneficial to all partners in the network.

The European Cloud Collaborative Manufacturing Networks project (C2NET), one of the projects funded under the programme H2020 Technologies for Factories of the Future [1, 2], aims to build a novel Cloud Architecture to provide SMEs affordable tools (in term of cost and usability) to help them to overcome the barriers appearing when they are willing to participate in a collaborative network (CN). C2NET Project generates a Cloud Architecture composed by [3] (see Fig. 1): (i) The Data Collection Framework

L.M. Camarinha-Matos et al. (Eds.): PRO-VE 2017, IFIP AICT 506, pp. 41–50, 2017.
DOI: 10.1007/978-3-319-65151-4_4

(C2NET DCF) for IoT-based continuous data collection from supply network resources; (ii) The Optimiser (C2NET OPT) to support manufacturing networks in the optimisation of manufacturing and logistics assets by the collaborative computation of production, replenishment and delivery plans, to achieve shorter delivery times, higher speed and consistency of schedules; (iii) The Collaboration Tools (C2NET COT) for providing a set of tools in charge of managing the agility of the collaborative processes; and (iv) The Cloud Platform (C2NET CPL) to integrate the data module, the optimisers and the collaborative tools in the cloud and allow the access to process optimisation resources to all the participants in the value chain to support their decisions and process enhancement.

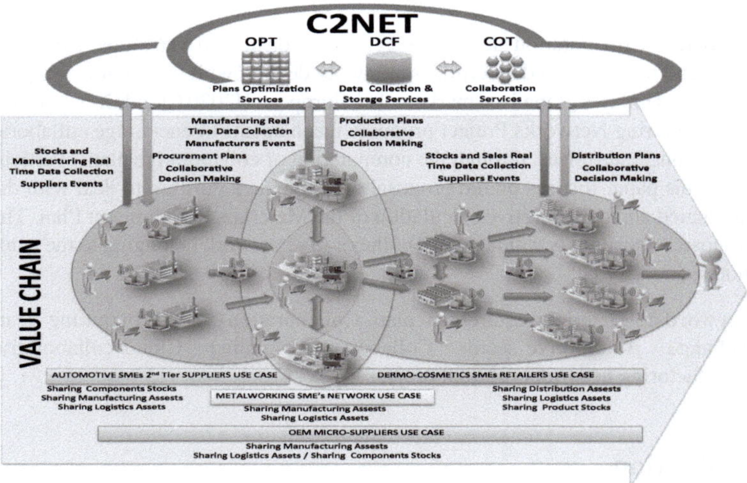

Fig. 1. C2NET project results [4]

This paper presents part of the results obtained in the C2NET OPT and C2NET COT used to compute optimised collaborative plans in an automotive network. Particularly, this paper focuses on the proposal of an approach to deal with the automated and collaborative calculation of the Materials Requirement Plan (MRP) of a CN. The complete approach consists of (i) MRP algorithms embedded in the algorithms repository of C2NET OPT, (ii) collaborative mechanisms defined through workflows in the C2NET COT Orchestration Planning Process (OPP) module, and (iii) cloud-supported tool to exchange the data between the collaborative enterprises. In the light of this, the paper is organised as follows: Sect. 2, in which the problem is identified; in Sect. 3, the complete approach to develop the present contribution is described; in Sect. 4, the results of the related experiments are presented; and finally, in Sect. 5 a discussion of potential generalisation and reuse of the presented results is provided.

2 Problem Description

Current planning processes are characterised by uncertainties derived from the continuously and rapidly changing market conditions and increasingly shorter time-to-market requirements. The significance of establishing collaborative processes to enhance the SMEs competitiveness and increase their agility and adaptability to deal with rapid evolutions of existing and future markets, is cross-examined and widely studied in [5, 6].

When starting to collaborate, the enterprises find that the replenishment, manufacturing and delivery plans are treated and computed short-sighted, within the enterprise, and no planning results are exchanged with upstream and downstream network partners. In this regard, the enterprises are dependent on complex information exchanges and material flows, requiring new approaches inside and outside the enterprise to support them on the establishment of collaborative planning process.

The problem treated in this paper focuses on the collaborative MRP from the automotive industry, applied in a network in which first and second tiers participate. In the current planning process the first tier receives the demand plan from the Original Equipment Manufacturer (OEM) and manually computes its MRP. Then the MRP is exploded into the demand plans for each of its suppliers. The second tier receives the demand plan from the first tier and manually computes its MRP. The only exchange of information is the demand plan that the first tier sends to the second tier. Moreover, there is no collaboration in case the second tier cannot supply the required demand plan to the first tier. Therefore, the second tier has to incur in extra costs, such as inventory costs, urgent purchase costs, delay costs, etc., to meet the demand of components/materials of the first tier. MRPs are manually computed by the company planners, incurring in resources and capacity expenses due to the difficultness and time-consuming associated. The lack of affordable collaborative tools does not motivate enterprises to evolve from traditional to collaborative planning approaches, which involve the application of negotiation and communication mechanisms. The complexity of the collaborative planning process increases, due to the appearance of more restrictions defined by other partners, which sometimes could be conflicting and contradictory.

C2NET leverages the potential of Cloud technologies providing a manufacturing infrastructure for a real-time knowledge of different supply chain components such as manufacturing assets status, inventory levels or current demand at consumption points. By providing specific tools for optimisation and collaboration in the cloud, companies involved in a CN will be able to increase their enterprise resilience to respond quickly, flexibly and efficiently to changes in demand and unexpected events that have place during the planning process [7].

3 Automated and Collaborative Calculation of the Materials Requirement Plan

The three main modules of C2NET Architecture (C2NET DCF, C2NET OPT and C2NET COT OPP) are integrated in the C2NET Cloud Platform (C2NET CPL), in order to allow the industrial enterprises to automatically and collaboratively compute the MRP. A brief description of the components, embedded in the Cloud Architecture, involved in the automated and collaborative calculation process of the MRP is presented next:

Legacy Systems Hub: It virtualises legacy systems hub in order to upload to C2NET the data from the enterprise.

C2NET UCP: It is a web-based application that provides user interfaces for companies users, for each C2NET solution.

C2NET DCF: It is a cloud-supported storage, in which the developments in open data contribute to the wide availability of such data. It also includes the mapping rules that allow transforming the companies' data into C2NET standardised and homogenised data.

C2NET OPT: To support the optimisation of manufacturing and logistics assets by the collaborative computation of production, replenishment and delivery plans. In C2NET OPT, the plan is characterised [8] according to the objectives, restrictions and the solving time. C2NET OPT contains a repository of algorithms that solve different set of individual or collaborative plans related to replenishment, production and delivery (including optimisation mathematical models, heuristic, metaheuristic and matheuristic algorithms). C2NET OPT is developed with the capability of selecting the most appropriate algorithm/s to automatically compute the defined plan taking into account its objectives, restrictions and solving time, considering the minimum GAP. The C2NET heuristics valid for the collaboration and automatically calculation of the MRP are [9]: (i) Lot-by-Lot, exactly provides what is needed, minimising the inventory costs. Both the periods interval between orders and the size of the batch are variable; (ii) Minimum Unit Cost, calculates the unit cost of requesting the net requirements of the 1st period, calculating the $1^{st} + 2^{nd}$ period, and so on until a relative minimum is reached; Indicator: unit cost = (order cost + inventory cost)/units; (iii) Minimum Total Cost: Similar to the previous one but considering the total costs; and (iv) Silver-Meal, selects the batch that results in a minimum total cost (order cost + inventory cost) per period, for the interval covered by the replenishment; Indicator: cost per period = (order cost + inventory cost)/ n° periods covered; (v) Minimum Period Cost (MPC): Similar to the previous one but considering the order and inventory cost per period = (order cost + inventory cost + extra purchase cost + urgent order cost of products)/n° periods covered.

C2NET COT OPP: provides a set of components for value-chain handling of collaborative manufacturing issues in each defined plan. It includes the following modules: (i) OPP Negotiation, defines the interaction between COT and the UCP modules during a workflow execution; (ii) OPP Notification, defines the interface used to notify events and actions related to the process of optimising plans affecting several companies in a network.

In order to compute the MRP the First Tier planner and the Second Tier planner register in the C2NET DCF all the sources of data from its legacy systems, (e.g. products, bill of materials, periods, demand plan, etc.). Some of the data can change along the time, for example the demand plan of the OEM, which can be updated every period and change from the previous demand plan. The data is stored in the C2NET DCF through using the interoperable rules and an ontology created in C2NET. Once all the data needed for calculating the MRP is stored, the automated collaborative replenishment (MRP) planning process starts with the release of the demand plan of OEM (DP^{OEM}), which is also stored in C2NET DCF. In this regard, the First and Second Tier planner define, through the C2NET UCP, the plans to be solved, in this particular case the plan type and subtype refers to Source_MRP (see [8]). Moreover, the objectives, restrictions and the solving time required to automatically compute the Source_MRP are also determined. The defined plans are stored in C2NET DCF.

C2NET OPT contains a repository of algorithms, and it is in charge of selecting the most appropriate algorithm to solve the defined plans, Source_MPR, according to the features assigned. The components assembled by the First Tier, are planned in the same period in which are served, synchronously with the OEM. While, components purchased by the First Tier, to the Second Tier, are computed by applying the MPC algorithm. MPC algorithm, allows the First Tier to accumulate orders for the purchased components, so that the global cost is minimised, balancing the order, purchase and inventory costs. The First Tier extracts from its MRP the Demand Plan of the Second Tier, which has a more discretized (grouped) demand. In this regard, the Second Tier could have problems on supplying the demand of some components in some periods. This is why the Second Tier calculates its MRP, using the MPC algorithm, and checks if it can really satisfy the discrete demand sent by the First Tier. In case the Second Tier cannot cope with the required demand, the Second Tier sends the First Tier the maximum amount of components that can supply. The First Tier computes again the MRP considering the restrictions sent by the Second Tier, with regards to the maximum amount of components that can supply, the First Tier computes again the MRP using the MPC algorithm. A negotiation loop is generated until the components demanded by the First Tier can be satisfied by the Second Tier. The MPC algorithm ensures not having a negative inventory, also allows to use, first the security stock, and when the security stock finishes, is when the MPC algorithm decides to buy the components incurring in a urgent purchase and extra order cost. The Holistic Algorithm for Source_MRP is described next:

Holistic Algorithm for Source_MRP

```
minTotalCost=M
bestFound = false
while bestFound = false
    calculate MRP First Tier
    obtain MRP cost First Tier (Cost_1stT)
    send demand plan to Second Tier
    calculate MRP Second Tier
    obtain MRP cost Second Tier (Cost_2ndT)
    send maximum requirement amounts to First Tier
    if (Cost_1stT + Cost_2ndT) = minTotalCost
      bestFound=True
    elseif (Cost_1stT + Cost_2ndT) < minTotalCost
      minTotalCost = Cost_1stT + Cost_2ndT
    end
```

4 Industrial Application in the Automotive Sector

Cloud-supported storage collaboration and optimisation contributes to the wide availability of data, and afford enterprises to establish collaborative relationships and compute collaborative plans. In order to perform a collaborative MRP the C2NET DCF, C2NET OPT and C2NET COT are considered; allowing the First and Second Tier exchange new input data from the restrictions defined by the partners participating in the negotiation; this negotiation is draft in the workflow presented in Fig. 2.

The data required to compute the collaborative MRP is stored in C2NET DCF. A database, with standardised structure, has been developed in C2NET project. C2NET database consists of Standardised Tables (STables) that contain all the information required to compute the MPC algorithm. The STables used are: (i) *Part*, contains information of the enterprise products; (ii) *Period*, contains information about the periods in which the MRP is computed, (iii) *Part_Part*, contains information of the BOM, (iv) *Part_Period*, contains information of the demand plans; and (v) *Customer_Part*, links the products of the First and Second Tier. For the developed example the First Tier works with 289 products, and the Second Tier works with 237 products. The MRP planning horizon is divided in 53 periods. Each network Tier has its own database and STables.

The holistic algorithm proposed, to automatically and collaboratively compute the Source_MRP plan, is validated through its application in a real scenario in the automotive sector; two network suppliers are considered, the First and Second Tiers. The collaboration negotiation loop initialises $minTotalCost^1$ = M. The First Tier receives the DP^{OEM} and computes its own MRP, which has an associated cost (Cost_1stT). The demand plan of the Second Supplier is extracted from the First Tier MRP. The Second Tier computes its own MRP, according to the First Tier demand plan. If the Second Tier cannot completely satisfy the components demanded by the First Tier, sends the maximum amount of components that is able to supply; the rest of the components will be planned by considering an urgent purchase cost and an extra order cost. The resulting MPR has linked a cost (Cost_2ndT). The $minTotalCost^N$ is computed by the sum of the Cost_1stT and the Cost_2ndT. If this $minTotalCost^N$ is lower than the previous initialised, $minTotalCost^1$, the new $minTotalCost^N$ is stored. The First Tier computes again the MRP by considering the new restrictions defined by the Second Tier, and a new cost is computed ($Cost\_1stT^N$). The First Tier extracts the demand plan of the Second Tier and the negotiation process is repeated until a $minTotalCost^N$ is repeated (see Table 1). In Table 1, the first column is the number of the iteration; second column shows the TotalCost in each iteration; third column stores the minimum of the TotalCost obtained so far; fourth column is True when the TotalCost = minTotalCost, False otherwise; fifth column is True if the minTotalCost has been computed in a previous iteration, False otherwise. The stopping rule of the negotiation process is defined when the minTotalCost is repeated. In the example, the 12th iteration has the same minTotalCost as 6th iteration and the stopping rule is accomplished, obtaining the result of the Fisrt and Second Tier Source_MRP. Looking at Table 1, the TotalCost oscilate between two solutions (e.g. see Iterations 4, 6, 8, 10, and 12; and Iterations3, 5, 7, 9, and 11), but it is not until the 12th iteration when the minTotalCost is repeated, and the negotiation process stopped.

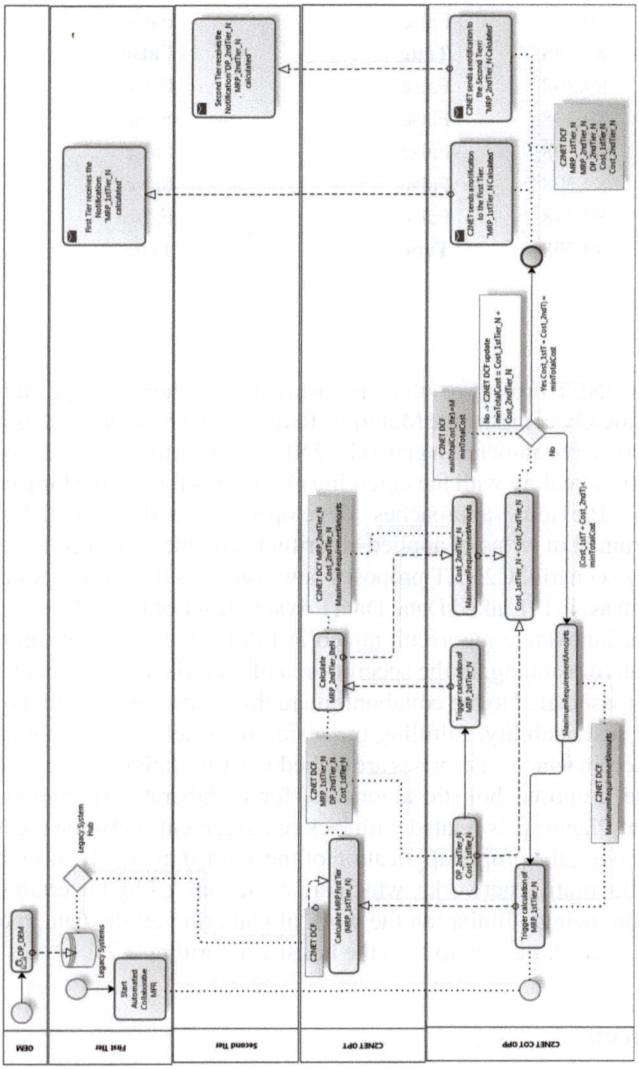

Fig. 2. C2NET COT OPP workflow designed for the collaborative automated MRP

Table 1. Iteration Results of the collaborative Source_MRP

Iteration	TotalCost	minTotalCost	TotalCost = minTotalCost	minTotalCost repeated
1	100,000	100,000	True	False
2	91,260	91,260	True	False
3	106,633	91,260	False	False
4	89,527	89,527	True	False
5	105,243	89,527	False	False
6	**89,398**	**89,398**	**True**	**False**
7	105,319	89,398	False	False
8	89,402	89,398	False	False
9	105,249	89,398	False	False
10	89,527	89,398	False	False
11	105,243	89,398	False	False
12	**89,398**	**89,398**	**True**	**True**

5 Conclusions

This paper is part of C2NET project results, proposing a novel holistic algorithm and data sharing to automatically compute the Materials Requirement Plan in a collaborative network, using the cloud environment. In general C2NET, and particularly the proposed holistic algorithm, allows dealing with the emerging challenges for establishing collaborative relationships. Previous approaches developed to address collaborative networking are constrained in terms of applied algorithms and mechanisms, to comply with this fast evolving scenario. C2NET proposes new solutions that consider convergent technologies, such as, IoT, Linked Data, Data Privacy, Big Data, etc. The proposed solution introduces an innovative algorithm aimed at fulfilling the lack of affordable tools for the collaborative planning, in the specific area of materials requirement plans. The reduction of costs associated to the collaboration highly improves the collaborative network stability and sustainability, fulfilling the vision of beneficial collaboration in current dynamic markets in which enterprises are embedded. Limitations associated with the application of the proposed holistic algorithm, for collaboratively compute the Materials Requirement Planning, is related with lack of agreements between the MRPs obtained results. Moreover, the proper application of the algorithm is influenced by the main drawback of collaborative networks, which are characterized by uncertainty and incomplete information, being a limitation the work of gathering all the data, required by the enterprises, in an accurate way to feed the holistic algorithm.

6 Future Research

The contribution has been verified and validated with two network partners of the automotive industry sector. Future work leads to design generic workflows considering different network typologies. C2NET project will start with a tree supply chain, typically observed in the automotive industry (see Fig. 3). The negotiation workflow and proposed will be designed in order to be extensible in an automated way. The holistic algorithm used to compute the Source_MRP will take into consideration the restrictions given by all the network partners when negotiating. Moreover, negotiation rules will be specifically defined in each pair of nodes. The algorithms used, MPC, allows minimizing the normal and urgent order costs, the normal and extra purchase costs, and the inventory costs. In order compute the costs to the global network; new holistic algorithm will include procedures to redistribute and share costs in an equitable way, so that costs are assigned in a higher extent to the nodes that contribute to have extra purchases and urgent orders in the MRP.

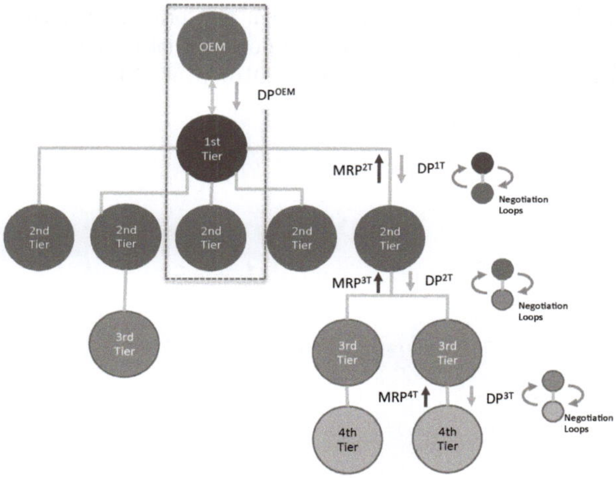

Fig. 3. Diagram for automated and collaborative calculation of the MRP in a tree collaborative network topology

Acknowledgments. The research leading to these results is in the frame of the "Cloud Collaborative Manufacturing Networks" (C2NET) project, which has received funding from the European Union's Horizon 2020 research and innovation programme under grant agreement No. 636909.

References

1. CORDIS Europa: Factories of the Future. H2020-EU.2.1.5.1. - Technologies for Factories of the Future (2014)
2. H2020 Project C2NET (2015). http://cordis.europa.eu/project/rcn/193440_en.html
3. Andres, B., Sanchis, R., Poler, R.: A cloud platform to support collaboration in supply networks. Int. J. Prod. Manag. Eng. **4**(1), 5–13 (2016)
4. Andres, B., Sanchis, R., Lamothe, J., Saari, L., Hauser, F.: Integrated production-distribution planning optimization models: a review in collaborative networks context. Int. J. Prod. Manag. Eng. **5**(1), 31–38 (2017)
5. Camarinha-Matos, L.M., Afsarmanesh, H.: Collaborative networks: a new scientific discipline. J. Intell. Manuf. **16**(4–5), 439–452 (2005)

6. Andres, B., Poler, R.: Models, guidelines and tools for the integration of collaborative processes in non-hierarchical manufacturing networks: a review. Int. J. Comput. Integr. Manuf. **2**(29), 166–201 (2016)
7. Sanchis, R., Poler, R., Lario, F.C.: Identification and analysis of Disruptions: the first step to understand and measure Enterprise Resilience. In: International Conference on Industrial Engineering and Engineering Management, pp. 424–431 (2012)
8. Andres, B., Saari, L., Lauras, M., Eizaguirre, F.: Optimization algorithms for collaborative manufacturing and logistics processes. In: Zelm, M., Doumeingts, G., Mendonça, J.P. (eds.) Enterprise Interoperability in the Digitized and Netwroked Factory of the Future, iSTE 2016, pp. 167–173 (2016)
9. Orbegozo, A., Andres, B., Mula, J., Lauras, M., Monteiro, C., Malheiro, M.: An overview of optimization models for integrated replenishment and production planning decisions. In: Building Bridges Between Researchers and Practitioners. Book of Abstracts of the International Joint Conference CIO-ICIEOM-IISE-AIM (IJC 2016), p. 68 (2016)

BIM Based Value for Money Assessment in Public-Private Partnership

Guoqian Ren[1,2] and Haijiang Li[1,2(✉)]

[1] Cardiff School of Engineering, Cardiff University, The Parade, Cardiff, Wales CF24 3AA, UK
{RenG, lih}@cardiff.ac.uk
[2] BRE Centre for Sustainable Construction, Cardiff University, Cardiff, Wales, UK

Abstract. New urbanization approaches aligned with public- private partnership (PPP) which arose in the early 1990s, have become acceptable and even better solutions to outstanding urban municipal constructions. However, PPPs are still problematic regarding value for money (VFM) process which is the main driving force to deliver public services. The current VFM structure requires an integrated platform to manage multi-performance and collaborative relationship in project life-cycles. Building information modelling (BIM), a popular approach to the procurement in AEC sectors, provides the potential to ensure VFM while also working in tandem with the semantic approach to holistically measure the life cycle performance. This paper suggests that BIM applied to the PPP life cycle could support decision-making regarding VFM and thus meet service targets.

Keywords: Public-private partnership · Value for money · Building information modelling · Collaborative networks

1 Introduction

PPPs (Public – Private Partnerships) have been developed to offer public services designed to relieve the pressures of local debt. The aim of PPP management is to identify clear goals, shared by both the public and private sectors, so that substantial capital gains can be achieved. However, despite the growing status of PPPs, there still exist a number of concerns with reference to infrastructure investment in developing regions regardless of financial uncertainties or poor quality performance [1]. It stress the importance of Value for money (VFM) processes as VFM does not yet receive sufficient attention within project practice. Most of the financial assessments and decisions made by PPPs are formulated without considering the amount of time needed to implement the necessary engineering works [2]. This can result in gross inaccuracies in collaborative networks, with reference to the life cycle of the project, leading to financial crises.

In most of the cases of PPP project, a subsidiary company called special purpose vehicle (SPV) is established at the early stage of the project to serve as counterparty which isolate the project financial risk meanwhile in charge of life cycle management. This new project management model have shown that they deliver a more sustainable

L.M. Camarinha-Matos et al. (Eds.): PRO-VE 2017, IFIP AICT 506, pp. 51–62, 2017.
DOI: 10.1007/978-3-319-65151-4_5

procurement process in comparison to traditional approaches. That said, a holistic approach to project performance provides better VFM with reference to sustainability, something which is necessary to decide whether or not PPP model is appropriate [3]. The information acquired for VFM, currently collected via multi-resources, is mostly second-hand data, any decisions having already been made [4]. The project data often failed to be integrated into management system. This poor quality data makes it very difficult for the public to assess whether the cost is commensurate with the benefits and risks to the public sector [5].

Regarding procurement workflow, BIM (Building Information Modelling) has the potential to be applied to the entire PPP process as opposed to current mainly ad hoc approaches [6]. However, BIM has not yet been used extensively to deliver measurable estimates on work but it does provide the possibility of "future proofing" on PPPs performance based assets. It is suggested here that BIM could be subsumed into PPP frameworks, ensuring that value for money has been provided and to even go a step further and measure and monitor project sustainability.

2 Value for Money Assessment

The definition of value for money (VFM) given by the UK government and the World Bank group is the optimum combination of whole-of-life costs and quality [7]. "Value" in this context represent the performance of project service to meet the user's requirement. It is not just the choice based on the lowest cost bid yet the public agencies must meet the project target on life cycle costs and service quality. In addition, the "value" emphasize more the overall assessment results rather than costs itself. In different project type and background, the weighting system in evaluation criteria could be relatively different yet in most of the cases, the life cycle cost represents by net present value (NPV) take the great proportion of the assessment outcome. Its criteria include business incentives at the procurement stage which could become the initial reference in terms of a good performance benchmark [8]. Even though VFM is a relatively hypothetical construct at present, it lacks clear substance and user guidance toolkits. Measurement lists are not available to guide PPP users to make comparisons of the actual outcomes to use alternative procurement options. Calculations model of VFM quantitative assessment in many countries uses an indicative present value for both PPP options and PSC (Public Sector Comparator) and make comparison. Specifically, PSC is a comprehensive account of procurement strategies across the life cycle of the project by using traditional procurement model. The UK government took the lead in standardizing the content of PSC as a decision making process to define where, when and how to use privately-financed infrastructure solutions [9]. The National Audit Office (NAO), provides a rolling method to compute both PSC and PPP values keeping costings up to date. The key components indicative of the current values in PSC basically covers the raw PSC value (Basic resources costs), the value of risk transfer, retained risk values and the value of Competitive tax adjustment [10].

As showed in the Fig. 1, VFM is not only focused on the whole life costs of assets at early stage quantitative assessment, but also requires the project to achieve a high level of qualitative performance across every aspect of the project [7]. These two

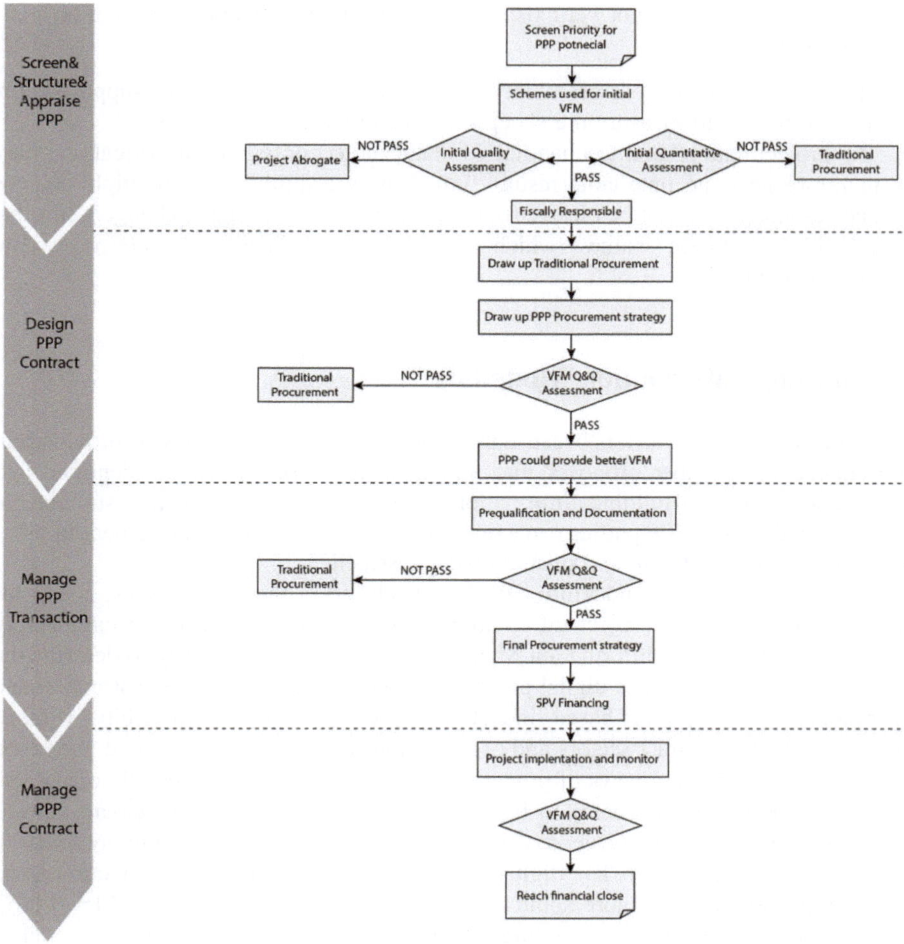

Fig. 1. VFM process through the project life-cycle

assessments work independently of each other providing different but interrelated information. VFM in the project decision phase offers a decision making platform for the use and focus on the discipline of collaborative relationship to achieve common goals between shared parties.

Value for money analysis could be defined as a life cycle assessment for the whole project [11]. Regional variations regarding the use of VFM mean that there is a lack of consistency for both qualitative and quantitative assessments. In China, the only qualitative process required involves completing a very simple form while the quantitative process either does not occur or is postponed due to feasibility issue [12]. The spread of PPPs in infrastructure construction raises issues at various stages including a lack of risk management leading to implementation failure in construction and operations. From the project management point of view, well-organized data management in the initial stages does not yet exist. VFM financial assessment issues can be summarised as follows:

- The current qualitative assessment lacks an information system to support information queries to measure the success and adoption of the projects.
- The project data related to quantitative financial accounting are historical and may therefore generate unreliable results. Information acquired from multiple sources and resources may not be clearly sourced or noted, this raising exchange issues for calculating present values which required more integrated enterprise data management.

3 Building Information Modelling

PPP parties are facing barriers because they cannot guarantee that VFM is provided. In consequence, this paper proposes that indicators of VFM should be identified and communicated using Building Information Modelling. The collaborative structure in BIM could also help PPP parties carry out integrated information management in order to support both qualitative and quantitative assessment.

Building information modelling (BIM), introduced in the early 1990's, is considered the foundation for project information development in construction engineering projects [13]. "Building Information Management" is the accepted way to describe the application of BIM as it is a digital process designed to guide project construction and operations. In the project-based industry, the collaborative relationships (Fig. 2) between different contract sectors and organizations are required to be more integrated to reshape the traditional ways of procurement activities [14]. BIM actually could also offer the opportunity for clients to be involved in procurement management. Nowadays, BIM technologies serve to build low-cost, integrated working systems in infrastructure projects [15]. The digital models have the potentiality to function as an aid to inspection, but are more applicable to management at the municipal level [16].

As showed in the Fig. 2, Building Information Modelling (BIM) has potential to influence the entire process of PPP in the procurement workflow, rather than just part of the project. In the UK, BIM level 2 is generating a comprehensive network, accessible for all parties involved in construction management, it also potentially offers a better quality operational framework for PPPs. The benefits of collaborative network in BIM stress the information delivery and data extraction. Project information attached with digital model could be passed to various project stakeholders in standardized data format. Questions concerned about project quality and objective details could be queried in an easy pattern. Moreover, the semantic extension of BIM makes it even better function on project domain management such as construction risk assessment [17] and low carbon designs [18]. The link data approach functioning between building information modelling and different semantic knowledge bases is becoming increasingly practical in construction industry [19]. The advantages of BIM aligned with semantic approaches in PPP could benefit the procurement decision to achieve better value for money.

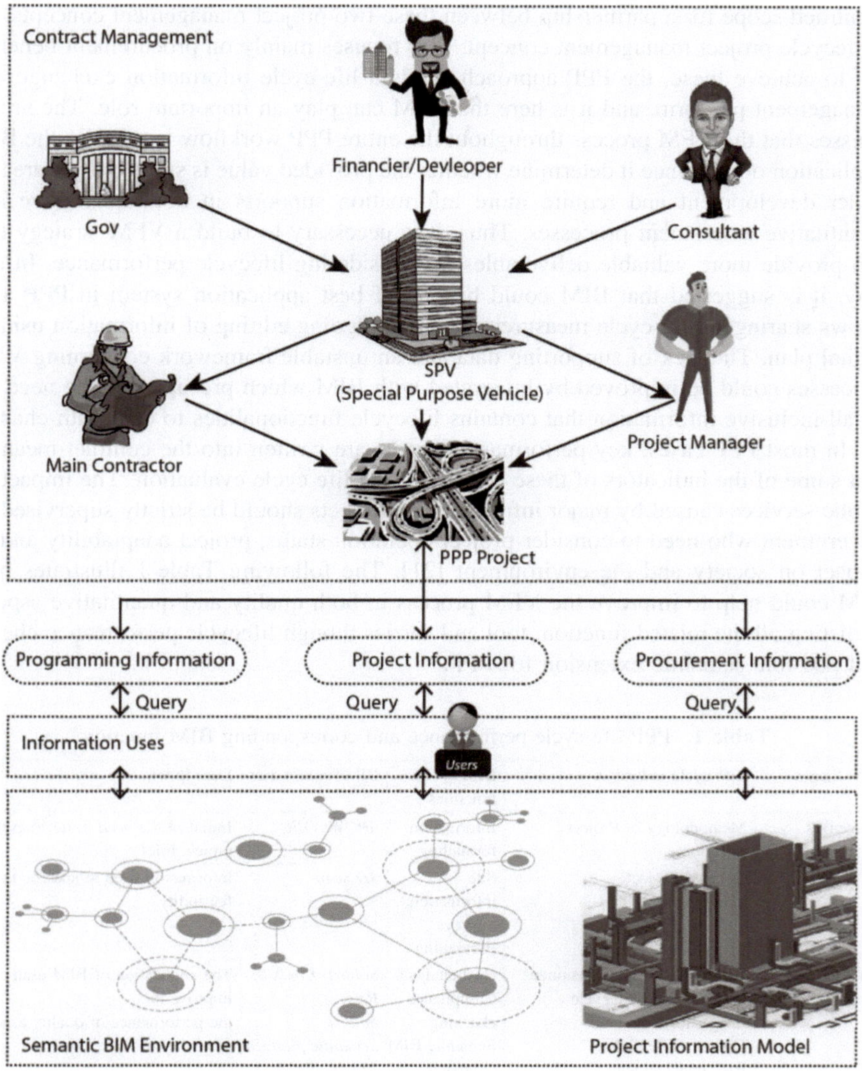

Fig. 2. BIM supported collaborative networks in Public – private partnerships

4 BIM Based VFM in PPP

The development of BIM to date suggests that it has the potential to work with PPP models by challenging electronic procurement [20]. BIM, as seen from an engineering point of view, can be described as providing benefits for management frameworks, tools, standards and assessment methods through the whole project lifecycle in comparison to PPP which is more about standardised and sustainable targets. Through the concept review on both PPP and BIM and their implementation focus, this paper has identified scope for a partnership between these two project management concepts. As a lifecycle project management concept, PPP focuses mainly on procurement benefits; but to achieve these, the PPP approach needs a life-cycle information exchange and management platform, and it is here that BIM can play an important role. The article stresses that the VFM process throughout the entire PPP workflow is actually the BIM application object since it determine whether the provided value is sufficient yet are still under development and require more information supports in both qualitative and quantitative assessment processes. Thus, it is necessary to build a VFM strategy that can provide more valuable deliverables by considering lifecycle performance. In this way, it is suggested that BIM could be one of best application system in PPP as it allows sharing of life cycle measurements and ongoing editing of information using a digital plan. The lack of supporting data and an unstable framework concerning VFM processes could be improved by integrated with BIM which presupposes the need for an all-inclusive information that contains lifecycle functionalities to deal with change.

In most PPP cases, key performance targets are written into the contract meaning that some of the indicators of these could be used life cycle evaluation. The impact on public services caused by major infrastructure projects should be strictly supervised by government who need to consider project operation status, project adaptability and its impact on society and the environment [21]. The following Table 1 illustrates how BIM could help to improve the VFM process in both quality and quantitative aspects by listing all the related function, tool and carries though lifecycle performance checks and possible semantic extension for PPP.

Table 1. PPP life-cycle performance and corresponding BIM function

PPP Stages	Life-cycle indicators	BIM functions	BIMTools/carrier	Description
Screen	Methodology of Project selection	Information formatting	*dPOW; OIR*	Initialize the need to develop the project brief
	Detailed Project plan/programming	Site information; Surveys Formatting	*3D scan*	information used to specific the feasibility
Structure & Appraise	**VFM qualitative assessment** Whole project lifecycle integration Operation flexibility Risk management Contract and assets Duration Incentives and Monitoring Market interest Efficient Procurement	Cost analysis Compliance checking Semantic BIM approach Project management Information exchange Model Simulation; Project management	*Solibri; CostX®;* *Revit* *Solibri* *Semantic platform* *AIR; Cobie* *Navisworks;* *Projectwise* *InfraWorks 360* *BIM 360™;* *Viewpoint*	The application of BIM used to improve the the performance of quality aspects
	VFM Quantitative assessment (PSC) FM costs, Construction costs, Operation costs, Transportation costs, Human resource costs, User fee, Risk costs	Cost analysis; Semantic BIM approach	*Semantic platform;5D BIM related tools*	The Semantic BIM approach help to reasoning the logic of project risk and support the outputs of related indicators of quantitative assessment

(continued)

Table 1. (*continued*)

PPP Stages	Life-cycle indicators	BIM functions	BIMTools/carrier	Description
	Feasibility of task	Cost analysis; Scheduling	*BIM 360™; Viewpoint*	Format the project schedule updated with the project data
Design & Manage	Tender process and competition	Information exchange; Visualization	*EIR; Bentley; Revit*	Deliver the requirement of stakeholders in
	Requirements of stakeholders/Goals	Information formatting; Information exchange	*OIR; EIR;*	Deliver the requirement of stakeholders
	Clear project brief/Contract documents	Information formatting; Information exchange	*OIR; EIR; BIM Execution Plan*	Deliver and translate the objectives of contract digitally
	Transparent procurement process/verify/monitoring	Project management	*BIM 360™; Viewpoint*	Provide progress monitoring and management
	Change in contract/private sector change	Project management	*EIR; BIM 360™; Viewpoint*	Highly efficient deal with progress change
Implementation	Site availability	Surveys Formatting; Space analysis	*IES; Green Building studio*	Information used to input into later design and construction
	Completion/Time Delay	Construction Scheduling	*Navisworks; ProjectWise; Tekla*	Format the scheduling and reduce the costs and delays
	Design deficiency/buildability	Clash detection; Compliance checking	*Navisworks; Solibri; Xsteel*	Improve design quality and benefits construction
	High-quality workmanship	Scheduling; Quantities take off	*3D scan; QTO; Vico*	Improve construction quality
	Site construction safety	Compliance checking; Clash detection	*3D scan; Naviswork; BIM 360™; Solibri*	Improve safety planning by interactive as-build information
	Technical innovation in design to construction	Information exchange	*EIR; AIR; BIM 360™*	Deliver/format the information from design to construction
	Material/Labour/Equipment	Project management	*AIR; BIM 360™; Revit*	Asset Information in Common data environment for F&M
	Construction Cost overrun	Cost analysis; Construction Scheduling	*Solibri; CostX®; Navisworks*	Accurate measurement of cost in construction
	operation cash flow	Maintenance	*ArchiBUS*	Deliver the information from Construction to Operation
	Operation performance	Energy management	*AIR; Energy Plus*	Cost of Energy or electric use in operation stage
	Residual assets	Project management	*AIR; BIM 360™*	Asset Information in Common data environment

This article referenced the PPP process stages based on the World Bank Group and simultaneously referenced construction project flow by using RIBA info exchange [22].

The indicators in PPP life cycle is referenced from different literature sources [23–30]. As discussed below, BIM with its extensive support potential, could theoretically maximize the benefits of VFM process and go step further on project life cycle.

The initial stage of project screening, usually involving investment planning, should be formally approved. Unsolicited proposals and initial projected end results of the project in this phase, could benefit from a digital plan of work (dPOW) related platform such as National Building Specification (NBS), which uses plain language questions (PLQs) to capture the clients' initial needs and gradually generates Organization Information Requirements (OIR). It is also one vital documentation process in previous UK BIM level 2 standard [31]. The information in this phase will then pass to an initial assets management inquiry that considers the clients' need. A Special Purpose Vehicle (SPV), or a related client based organization, could take the responsibility to update information for further asset management and information about prospective employees relevant to project performance. Other factors related to project planning are the physical scale of the project and a review of the constraints of potential sites. Space and site analysis attached to BIM software, has the advantage of providing visual data which is of value in early decision making. Even it is the early stage, VFM assessment has the potential to start building a support information/reference library for PSC projects. Domain and cost related knowledge bases can be structured using the Semantic approach while data could be supported by using BIM related tools.

Second phases which is defined as "structure PPP" and "appraise PPP" in World Bank PPP guidance, involve the collation of core information that helps determine the substance of the project including Risk Identification and Allocation, project feasibility, VFM and viability. Risk management is directly connected with VFM assessment and can be represented using domain-involved indicators to define project risks. A "Semantic BIM" approach is proposed at this stage as interaction of the ontological structure and Industry Foundation Class (IFC) data in the risk management field provide a model which lists the risk events relevant to the PPP. Information can be collated into a semantic environment as "knowledge blocks", represented by a domain-based taxonomy. Because this stage is leading towards the final procurement stage, the quality of data should allow VFM assessment. Figure 2 and Table 1 show how information exchanged within the BIM environment could help to extract the relevant data which could be used in initial design or existing models for Net Present Value (NPV) measurement. 5D representation, regardless of the presence of a digital model, should contain a certain level of detailed information regarding assets during this stage. The use of costing tools aligned with BIM could provide a good measure to structure the cost measurement in general. At this point, quantitative assessment will not depend on non-transparent historical data as the information contained in BIM has its real-time properties [6].

"Manage PPP" refers to the final procurement strategy and business agreement. VFM findings, specifically quantitative output, should be incorporated by the final contract award. Employment information requirements (EIR), includes reference to when contractors need to handover to different sectors. Project goals and assets information could be delivered by using Construction Operations Building Information Exchange (Cobie). The Cobie-UK-2012 is a good application with reference to non-graphical information exchange as it initializes key project information in a standardised format. Information delivery and sharing are often seen in a common data environment (CDE), defined as a single source of information and as the extranet source of information used to import, manage and disseminate all material [22]. The BIM and its CDE are commonly used in most of the cases in DB or BOT procurement model yet only in separated stages. Now it could be used in VFM process as it stress the importance of life cycle costs measurement and performance monitor.

The PPP project implementation stage (Construction and Operation) is likely to be the point at which the benefits of BIM functions at previous points become fully evident. The costs of construction currently account for a large proportion of the NPV of quantitative results in VFM. Theoretically, the cost results should meet the previous value in quantitative assessment, while BIM now has potential to deal with change in real time. There are plenty of resources amenable to BIM application in project design and construction. In most cases, contractors should take the responsibility for integrating processes from "as-built", while BIM could maximise the profits of this. An application in the earlier design stage could be regarded as 3D parametric design, which differs from traditional design approaches; it offers software tools allowing the design team to visualise the architecture, structure, MEP and supported facilities plan. Similarly, 4D and 5D BIM used at the pre-construction stage could eventually output a federated model for construction specifications. Any insufficiency occurring at earlier design stages could be visualised within the bounds of known parameters, in software, to minimise any need for later reworking. The other vital process in the "PPP operation stage" is asset management. Before BIM appears in Facility management, The Radio Frequency Identification (RFID) that discriminates the Quick response (QR) Code on devices, or structural component to track the information needed by operators, can now connect to the assets information model (AIM) which is the result of CDE. More detailed information about operational attributes could also be provided. The tracking system in the BIM environment makes the "future proofing" of VFM easier by enhancing assets maintenance efficiency. The summary of BIM functionality for PPP construction and operation covers the following aspects:

Model Checking: automatic checking comprises two aspects: object-oriented checking and rule-based regulation checking. Software functions e.g. clash detection, could help the project team to solve conflicts before construction starts. This is important specifically for large scale projects or complicated structures as traditional 2D or 3D approaches cannot minimize design fault to a suitable level at pre-construction stages. Performance during the construction stage also needs to satisfy industry standards or sustainability benchmark systems. These automatic checks should be carried out before creation of the combined model. Information extracted, IFC data, could take the form of plain language information in authoritative standards such as LEED and BREEAM, using a rule engine attached to the digital model. The results also could confirm if part of the digital model could help to carry out VFM quality assessment as well.

Model analysis: the availability and diversity of automatic BIM analyses are becoming more adaptable and practical. Current data focus mainly on cost and workload. The cost appraisal during the Planning and construction stage is a vital component of the WLCC as it frequently deals with multiple changes and directly influences the management of assets in the operation stage. Real-time data imported into the analysis system, is used to create CDE output. Theoretically, costings should meet the previous value designated in VFM assessment while CDE now has the potential to deal with change.

Model comparison: the used of point cloud 3D scanning technologies within construction is still limited, but complex quality assessment tasks in VFM like the structural renovation of existing infrastructures which are regarded as "stock assets" in PPP projects, could benefit from these. The process of generating a model from pointed clouds to mesh geometries is also available within the BIM environment, meaning that the 3D scan has access to a combination of data for further assets management [32].

Model Simulation: simulation, a basic software function, provides the potential visualize the build. At the pre-construction stage, BIM modelling and emergency-based software can create an appropriate emergency plan designed to cope with a range of emergencies [33]. Since the majority of PPP projects are urban infrastructures, and VFM in this filed required more comprehensive assessment. The simulation attached with VFM outputs in BIM based project construction is more meaningful to compare with different strategies.

The advantages of the application of BIM based VFM in PPP are as follows:

- The information extracted from BIM is a vital part of the information initialization providing high-quality data, guaranteeing accuracy and high levels of synchronization in VFM qualitative assessment.
- Benefits are created as BIM encompasses the PPP lifecycle project flow and information extraction in VFM quantitative assessment.

5 Conclusion

BIM's comprehensive ability to manage information could facilitate the VFM process by supporting both qualitative and quantitative assessment. Through a literature review on both PPP application and BIM, this paper has identified a potential partnership between these two project management concepts. PPP, as a life-cycle project management concept, mainly focusses on procurement benefits. However, to achieve this, it requires a life-cycle information exchange and collaborative network hence the need for BIM. Regarding PPP as a whole, it can be concluded that VFM processes could determine whether the value provided is effective by using the PPP procurement model as it is a long-term assessment designed to guarantee profits at program, project and procurement level. However, VFM practice is still under development and requires application at a general level and to the whole procurement process to achieve both qualitative and quantitative assessment. Based on this, this paper proposes to create a BIM-based decision-making framework which benefits VFM assessment alone PPP project life cycle. Future work should cover the comprehensive semantic development of this knowledge base, along with automatic means of VFM measurement.

References

1. Zhang, X., Chen, S.: A systematic framework for infrastructure development through public private partnerships. IATSS Res. **36**(2), 88–97 (2013)
2. ACCA, Taking Stock of PPP and PFI around the World (2012)
3. Du, L., Tang, W., Liu, C., Wang, S., Wang, T., Shen, W., Huang, M., Zhou, Y.: Enhancing engineer-procure-construct project performance by partnering in international markets: perspective from Chinese construction companies. Int. J. Proj. Manag. **34**(1), 30–43 (2016)
4. Farquharson, E., Encinas, J., Yescombe, E.R., Torres de Mästle, C.: How to Engage with the Private Sector in Public-Private Partnerships in Emerging Markets (2011)
5. Shaoul, J.: Financial black holes: accounting for privately financed Roads in the UK 20(1) (2011)
6. Love, P.E.D., Liu, J., Matthews, J., Sing, C.P., Smith, J.: Future proofing PPPs: life-cycle performance measurement and building information modelling. Autom. Constr. **56**, 26–35 (2015)
7. HM Treasury, Value for Money Assessment Guidance, p. 49 (2006)
8. Cowper, J., Samuels, M.: Performance benchmarking in the public sector: the United Kingdom experience. Benchmarking, Evaluation and Strategic Management in the Public Sector, pp. 11–32 (1997)
9. Bain, R.: Public sector comparators for UK PFI roads: inside the black box. Transp. (Amst) **37**(3), 447–471 (2010)
10. National Audit Office, Review of the VFM assessment process for PFI, October 2013
11. Office of Transportation Public Private Partnerships, PPTA Value for Money Guidance, pp. 1–60, April 2011
12. M. of F. of the P. R. of China, "政府和社会资本合作项目物有所值评价指引（试行）, pp. 1–8 (2014)
13. van Nederveen, G.A., Tolman, F.P.: Modelling multiple views on buildings. Autom. Constr. **1**(3), 215–224 (1992)
14. Cao, D., Li, H., Wang, G., Luo, X., Yang, X., Tan, D.: Dynamics of Project-Based Collaborative Networks for BIM Implementation: Analysis Based on Stochastic Actor-Oriented Models, pp. 1–12 (2015)
15. Bradley, A., Li, H., Lark, R., Dunn, S.: BIM for infrastructure: an overall review and constructor perspective. Autom. Constr. **71**, 139–152 (2016)
16. Hartmann, T., Van Meerveld, H., Vossebeld, N., Adriaanse, A.: Aligning building information model tools and construction management methods. Autom. Constr. **22**, 605–613 (2012)
17. Ding, L.Y., Zhong, B.T., Wu, S., Luo, H.B.: Cost ontolgoy. Saf. Sci. **87**, 202–213 (2016)
18. Hou, S., Li, H., Rezgui, Y.: Ontology-based approach for structural design considering low embodied energy and carbon. Energy Build. **102**(2015), 75–90 (2015)
19. Abanda, F.H., Tah, J.H.M., Keivani, R.: Trends in built environment semantic web applications: where are we today? Expert Syst. Appl. **40**(14), 5563–5577 (2013)
20. Grilo, A., Jardim-Goncalves, R.: Challenging electronic procurement in the AEC sector: a BIM-based integrated perspective. Autom. Constr. **20**(2), 107–114 (2011)
21. Guo, F., Chang-Richards, Y., Wilkinson, S., Li, T.C.: Effects of project governance structures on the management of risks in major infrastructure projects: a comparative analysis. Int. J. Proj. Manag. **32**(5), 815–826 (2014)
22. RIBA, Guide Information Exchanges (2015)

23. Chou, J., Pramudawardhani, D.: Cross-country comparisons of key drivers, critical success factors and risk allocation for public-private partnership projects. Int. J. Proj. Manag. **33**(5), 1136–1150 (2015)
24. Hwang, B., Zhao, X., Gay, M.J.S.: Public private partnership projects in Singapore: factors, critical risks and preferred risk allocation from the perspective of contractors. Int. J. Proj. Manag. **31**(3), 424–433 (2013)
25. Liu, T., Wang, Y., Wilkinson, S.: Identifying critical factors affecting the effectiveness and efficiency of tendering processes in Public-Private Partnerships (PPPs): a comparative analysis of Australia and China. Int. J. Proj. Manag. **34**(4), 701–716 (2016)
26. Thomas Ng, S., Tang, Z., Palaneeswaran, E.: Factors contributing to the success of equipment-intensive subcontractors in construction. Int. J. Proj. Manag. **27**(7), 736–744 (2009)
27. Tang, L., Shen, Q.: Factors affecting effectiveness and efficiency of analyzing stakeholders' needs at the briefing stage of public private partnership projects. Int. J. Proj. Manag. **31**(4), 513–521 (2013)
28. Toor, S., Ogunlana, S.O.: Critical COMs of success in large-scale construction projects: evidence from Thailand construction industry. Int. J. Proj. Manag. **26**, 420–430 (2008)
29. Wibowo, A., Mohamed, S.: Risk criticality and allocation in privatised water supply projects in Indonesia. Int. J. Proj. Manag. **28**(5), 504–513 (2010)
30. Xu, Y., Chan, A.P.C., Yeung, J.F.Y.: Developing a fuzzy risk allocation model for PPP projects in China. J. Constr. Eng. Manag. **136**(8), 894–903 (2010)
31. British Standard Institution (BSI), PAS 1192-3:2014 - Specification for information management for the operational phase of assets using building information modelling. Br. Stand. Inst. (1), 1–44 (2014)
32. Bosché, F., Ahmed, M., Turkan, Y., Haas, C.T., Haas, R.: The value of integrating Scan-to-BIM and Scan-vs-BIM techniques for construction monitoring using laser scanning and BIM: the case of cylindrical MEP components. Autom. Constr. **49**, 201–213 (2015)
33. Wang, B., Li, H., Rezgui, Y., Bradley, A., Ong, H.N.: BIM based virtual environment for fire emergency evacuation. Sci. World J. **2014**, October 2014

A Collaborative Unified Computing Platform for Building Information Modelling (BIM)

Steven Arthur(✉), Haijiang Li, and Robert Lark

School of Engineering, Cardiff University, Queen's Buildings, 14-17 the Parade, Cardiff, CF24 3AA, UK
{arthurs,lih,lark}@cardiff.ac.uk

Abstract. The current dominant computing mode in the AEC (Architecture, Engineering and Construction) domain is standalone based, causing fragmentation and fundamental interoperability problems. This makes the collaboration required to deal with the interconnected and complex tasks associated with a sustainable and resilient built environment extremely difficult.

This article aims to discuss how the latest computing technologies can be leveraged for the AEC domain and Building Information Modelling (BIM) in particular. These technologies include Cloud Computing, the Internet of Things and Big Data Analytics.

The data rich BIM domain will be analysed to identify relevant characteristics, opportunities and the likely challenges. A clear case will be established detailing why BIM needs these technologies and how they can be brought together to bring about a paradigm shift in the industry.

Having identified the potential application of new technologies, a future platform will be proposed. It will carry out large scale, real-time processing of data from all stakeholders. The platform will facilitate the collaborative interpretation, manipulation and analysis of data for the whole lifecycle of building projects. It will be flexible, intelligent and able to autonomously execute analysis and choose the relevant tools. This will form a base for a step-change for computing tools in the AEC domain.

Keywords: Big Data · Collaboration · Cloud computing · Building Information Modelling · IoT · BIM

1 Introduction

The AEC industry has been slow to adapt to technological change, resulting in stagnation or even decline over the last 40 years [1]. Fragmentation, competition, a deeply embedded conservative approach [2] and other factors have slowed the adoption of new technology but the situation is slowly beginning to change. The most significant development has been the adoption of BIM, a digital representation of the physical and functional characteristics of buildings or infrastructure. The full potential of BIM is far from being fully exploited. This article proposes a BIM Platform to bring together data from

L.M. Camarinha-Matos et al. (Eds.): PRO-VE 2017, IFIP AICT 506, pp. 63–73, 2017.
DOI: 10.1007/978-3-319-65151-4_6

multiple sources and contemporary technologies to achieve BIM's potential through collaboration and the full use of all data.

The current situation results in untapped insights from rich data sources and unrealised collaboration opportunities. Stakeholders work individually on their part of the project with little or no collaboration with other parties. Data is either not collected from potential sources or the expertise is not available to make use of it.

New technologies can unlock the potential of BIM. The Internet of Things provides a rich source of new data which can be analysed using Big Data Analytics. Cloud Computing enables real-time collaboration, high availability and access to scalable resources. This article proposes a BIM Platform which unifies these technologies and brings myriad benefits to stakeholders operating as a truly collaborative network.

This article is organised as follows: Sect. 2 reviews the factors leading to the need for a Collaborative Unified Computing Platform for BIM. Section 3 describes the methods for bringing about a computing paradigm shift for BIM. Section 4 explains the components, architecture, methodology and implementation of the BIM platform. Section 5 discusses specific uses of the BIM Platform. The article ends with a conclusion in Sect. 6.

2 The Need for a Collaborative Unified Computing Platform for BIM

Many industries have been changed, created or have even disappeared because of disruptive technology. Travel, journalism, television, music, advertising and many more have been fundamentally changed. The history and status quo of the AEC domain is very different.

2.1 Technological Inertia in the AEC Domain

There are many reasons for technological inertia in the AEC domain. There is a great amount of fragmentation and a large job could involve dozens of subcontractors, architectural and engineering firms, managers, etc. Furthermore, the parties involved vary from project to project which makes it difficult to synchronise activities or develop collaborative systems which persist. Competition in the industry creates a disincentive to invest in new technology when working on any one project despite long-term advantages. Other factors include concerns about the benefits being too small to justify the initial costs and a conservative approach from senior leadership [3].

The industry has begun to change with more and more projects making use of new software, mobile devices, the internet and sensors. The first steps came in the 1970s with Computer-Aided Design (CAD). In 2002, Autodesk released a paper entitled "Building Information Modelling" [4] and BIM has been central to technological change in the industry since.

2.2 BIM: A Step Toward Change

At its core, BIM is a standardised digital representation of a built asset (such as a building or bridge). This contains data and information linking to spatial relationships, geographic information and properties of building components (e.g. the materials used). More importantly, BIM is a process of standardisation, sharing structured data and managing all the data associated with a building from conception to demolition. With the model at the centre, the aim is for all parties to collaborate on the same rich pool of data but this has not yet been fully achieved.

The adoption of BIM can result in a significant reduction in costs over the lifecycle of a project by detecting issues (such as clashes) early on. Combined with reduced completion times, improved buildings and better safety, the case for adopting BIM is overwhelming. BIM is gaining traction across the world and has been mandatory for all public-sector projects in the UK since April 2016 [5]. Currently, the preconstruction stages widely adopt BIM but it is used progressively less in the later stages of the lifecycle [6]. Fulfilling the potential of BIM for collaboration and data exploitation will require the leveraging of new technology.

3 A Computing Paradigm Shift for BIM

BIM has opened the AEC domain to the possibilities of technological change but the scale of the data, required integration of autonomously orchestrated processes, need for seamless collaborative networking and required data intelligence demand new solutions. Contemporary technologies which complement each other and work together can help bring about the required fundamental step-change in the AEC industry. Those that embrace technological change can reap the benefits and become more competitive, as has happened in many other industries.

3.1 Big Data and Big Data Analytics (BDA)

Big data can be defined as *"High volume, high velocity, and/or high variety information that requires new forms of processing to enable enhanced decision making, insight discovery and process optimization."* [7]. Increasing the volume, velocity or variety (the so-called 3Vs of Big Data) increases the data complexity. The 3Vs are relevant to BIM as follows:

- **Volume** – the size of BIM models and the data associated with them (including sensor data) is gradually increasing. In addition, there is an increasing need to look at multiple buildings, the associated infrastructure and their effect on each other.
- **Variety** – the many formats used in BIM applications include RVT (Revit), IFC, MS formats, sensor data, video, images etc. [6]. The data can be structured, semi-structured or unstructured.
- **Velocity** – data can be streamed continuously from sensors, building management systems (BMS), etc.

BDA includes techniques from interrelated fields including data mining, machine learning, and artificial intelligence [6]. It is used to discover patterns, relationships and dependencies in the data. These are used to get insights and make predictions. Working with Big Data requires a change of mindset [8]. Vast amounts of data (ideally all of it) are analysed – a large amount of messy data is considered better than a small amount of exact data and the analysis is more probabilistic than precise. The questions we want to ask sometimes only emerge when we collect and work with all the data. The value of disparate data can exceed its primary purpose when it is combined. Correlations surface from the data instead of requiring a hunch or hypothesis in advance and their existence is more important than their cause. Bilal et al. presented many opportunities for Big Data in the construction industry [6] but its use is still in its infancy.

3.2 The Internet of Things (IoT)

The IoT consists of sensors and other devices which send and receive live data via the Internet or other networks. Connecting any asset, machine, system or site to the Internet has an almost limitless range of BIM uses throughout the lifecycle. These include measuring and enhancing facility performance, automation and control, improving safety, energy management, optimising inventories and security [1]. The IoT could save $1 trillion dollars a year in maintenance, services and consumables by 2022 [9]. Each IoT solution can require hundreds or thousands of sensors creating a continuous stream of varied data. The IoT and Big Data complement each other with the former providing a rich source of data to be analysed by the latter.

3.3 Cloud Computing

Cloud computing is the delivery of computing services over the Internet (i.e. "the cloud"). Most people are familiar with the delivery of cloud storage but servers, databases, networking, analytics, high performance computing and more can also be delivered. This approach frees people from traditional ways of thinking about computing. It brings benefits including real-time collaboration, lower cost, elasticity, speed and global scale. Productivity, performance and reliability can all be enhanced [10]. Cloud computing is already starting to be used for BIM. Examples include energy management, stakeholder coordination, structural analysis and the integration of management data [6]. Chuang et al. are utilising Cloud Computing to develop a system for BIM visualisation and manipulation through the web [11].

4 A Collaborative Unified Computing Platform for BIM

The proposed platform will combine software, BIM model data and IoT data. The data will be stored in SQL and NoSQL databases, forming a Knowledge Base to be used by the software. BDA can be used to provide insights from the vast amounts of available data, including the real-time analytics of streamed data. A relationship can be maintained between the BIM models and associated IoT devices throughout the lifecycle.

The cloud-based platform will be scalable to multiple built assets all the way up to entire smart cities. A greater amount of data will result in greater potential for BDA to find insights to be exploited in real-time or whenever required. Each project can be stored in the system and analysed. This will provide insights and improvements for future projects and so on.

4.1 BIM Platform Components and Architecture

The main components of the BIM Platform are the IFC Engine, Knowledge Base, IoT Hub and Big Data Analytics Engine. Data enters the BIM Platform from BIM Models and IoT Devices. The BIM Platform will allow collaboration between all parties in the BIM process.

The Industry Foundation Classes (IFC) specification is an open and neutral data format used widely throughout BIM applications. IFC files facilitate the sharing process for a better qualification and validation of data [12]. IFC data enters the IFC Engine from BIM Models. A major problem to be overcome by the BIM Platform is that each discipline (architecture, structural engineering, contractors, suppliers etc.) has a separate distinct model. The IFC Engine assembles the distinct models into a federated model which can be stored in the Knowledge Base.

IoT Devices can be connected, managed and monitored by means of an IoT Hub. Data that comes from BIM Models (such as spatial and component data) can provide a framework for the organisation and analysis of IoT data in a way that is useful for the operation of the building [13]. Information coming from apparently unrelated systems can provide valuable, unique and actionable insights using BDA. Stream Analytics will be used to provide useful insights from live IoT data in real-time.

Federation combined with IoT data results in a data-rich but extremely complex model. This demands a high performance and smart computing framework. This framework must be able to process data and integrate analysis processes to provide proactive and holistic decision making to benefit all stakeholders. The federated models and IoT data can be analysed using a Big Data Analytics Engine to find insights and new uses for the data. Big Data (federated models, traffic congestion, energy consumption, pressure readings from a bridge etc.) can be collected and subjected to advanced analytics to optimise decision-making and boost operational efficiency. Collaboration between stakeholders and between projects increases the data available and the potential for even deeper insights.

All interactions between the components of the BIM Platform are bi-directional. Therefore, for example, data from the IoT Hub can be stored in the Knowledge Base, analysed by the Big Data Analytics Engine and the results fed back to the IoT Hub (and ultimately the IoT Devices themselves) via the Knowledge Base. Data can flow throughout with great flexibility and the results of analysis can be used for diverse applications. The autonomous and self-managing tools work together dynamically. The BIM Platform will be intelligent and implement tools depending on requirements.

Figure 1 illustrates the conceptual architecture of the BIM Platform. The key features are as follows:

- The external inputs (below the BIM Platform) come from IoT Devices and BIM Models.
- The IoT Hub and IFC Engine can exchange data with IoT Devices and BIM Models respectively.
- IoT data captured by the IoT Hub can be analysed in real-time using Stream Analytics or stored in the Knowledge Base for later analysis by the Big Data Analytics Engine.
- The components of the BIM Platform itself are in the cloud.
- The App elements represent compatible third-party applications and applications developed specifically for the BIM Platform. These connect to the IoT Hub, IFC Engine or Big Data Analytics Engine depending on their purpose.
- Data from all elements is stored in databases (SQL or NoSQL) which together constitute the BIM Platform's Knowledge Base.

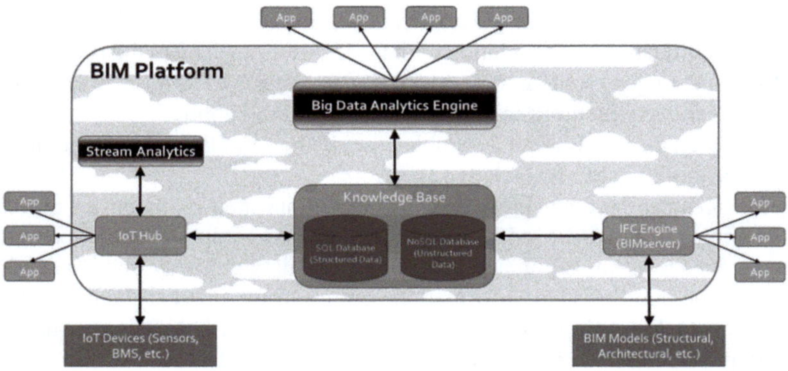

Fig. 1. Architecture of the BIM platform.

The platform will not have a rigid one-size-fits-all architecture. Each part will have several possible outcomes depending on what is required. The system intelligently determines the best approach based on the advantages and disadvantages of each possibility. Some problems will not require analysing streamed data for example. Each problem will only use a subset of the functionality available. The use of the platform can be expanded as further insights are required.

4.2 Methodology and Implementation

The BIM Platform will be hosted using a combination of on-site hardware and Microsoft Azure. The advantages of using on-site hardware include privacy, control and no usage charges. The on-site hardware used includes 8 Intel i7 computers each with 4 cores, 64 GB RAM and 4TB of storage. Microsoft Azure is a cloud computing service that can be used for deploying and managing applications, services and additional virtual machines if required. Azure is highly scalable and charges apply for how many resources are used although this project has been awarded an Azure For Research grant to cover the costs. Azure has been used for its power, convenience and flexibility but open-source alternatives to the services used will also be developed in future. The IFC Engine of the platform is based on BIMserver which runs on an on-site virtual machine. BIMserver adheres to open BIM standards and is an open framework that provides a strong base to build specific BIM applications on top of. BIMserver has an open interface and can be used with any of the various vendors' BIM models. It also has an open API, allowing any applications outside the BIM Platform (e.g. IFC Viewer, BIMserver GUI and IFC Parser) to interact with the models.

The IoT Hub component of the BIM Platform uses Azure IoT Hub for its scalability, multiple communication options, extensive device libraries and seamless integration with Azure Stream Analytics to enable powerful real-time analytics. For the purpose of this research, thousands of IoT devices will be emulated using SQL Server and Enzo Unified [14] (both running on on-site virtual machines). Enzo Unified abstracts the underlying cloud APIs, allowing native SQL commands to be executed against the Azure IoT Hub. Apps to connect to outside of the BIM Platform include Device Monitoring, Configuration Management and Content Distribution.

The Knowledge Base uses both SQL and NoSQL databases to store data on-site. BIM model servers generally map IFC entities into their internal structure one-to-one. Because of the inherently complex structure of the IFC schema, this means many tables, one for each IFC entity. In IFC4 the numbers grew to 766 entities and 327 types [15]. This imposes a heavy burden on the relational (SQL) model when the amount of data becomes "big". However, IFC should still be the first choice since it is the main standard supported by major BIM tools. New approaches will be needed to allow fast and efficient queries and analysis. A tweaked schema can flatten the IFC hierarchy into less tables and reduce the number of steps required to access information.

It is beneficial to integrate multiple data sources to facilitate deeper BDA on a combined data set. The structured IFC data of the BIM models themselves will be stored and analysed using SQL databases. There is also an increasing amount of unstructured data [16] associated with the BIM models such as photos, videos, audio, websites, documents (PowerPoint, PDF), scanned documents etc. The use of NoSQL databases is suitable for a Big Data platform such as this. NoSQL is highly scalable and capable of storing, processing, and managing huge amounts of unstructured data. Combining this with a continuous stream of IoT data results in a large amount of data to be analysed using BDA. The results of these analyses can be used by applications immediately or combined with the original data.

The Big Data Analytics Engine component of the BIM Platform uses Azure HDInsight. HDInsight is a service that deploys and provisions fully managed Apache Hadoop clusters. It provides a software framework for BDA with the analysis and reports being stored in the Knowledge Base. Apps outside of the BIM Platform that can be connected to the Big Data Analytics Engine include Dashboard Tools and Visualisation Tools.

Validation of the BIM Platform will include testing the data from real IoT devices instead of just emulated ones and testing that the integrity of federated BIM Models is maintained upon retrieval from the Knowledge Base after manipulation. Traditional techniques are not viable when validating Big Data and the results of BDA [17]. Autonomous, self-learning Big Data integrity validation and reconciliation tools (e.g. DataBuck) will be used. The accuracy and completeness of the data when moving throughout the BIM Platform will be rigorously validated and checked by an expert. Real life case studies will be published in the near future to present how the BIM Platform works in practice.

5 BIM Platform Uses

Given the flexible nature of the BIM Platform and the diverse range of tools available, the possible uses are extensive. Some examples include:

- **Increased Model Scope** - The gradual increase in the size and variety of the contents of BIM models will restrict the capabilities of traditional BIM based storage and processing systems. Up until recently, BIM was envisaged to contain data from the construction industry only. However, the emergence of other linked building data has changed this perception [6]. There is also a far greater need for collaboration. The BIM Platform supports the increase in scope by being scalable in terms of processing power, memory and storage.
- **Streamed Data Analysis** - The huge amount of data that will increasingly be generated by buildings and infrastructure means they are not just products but providers of services [18]. Rather than the data being archived or just used for its immediate purpose, the BIM Platform enables the analysis of all accumulated data using BDA and also real-time analytics of the data stream using Stream Analytics. For example, sensor data could be analysed to check for the deterioration of a bridge, allowing predictive maintenance [1] and the detection of problems in advance. This not only offers obvious safety benefits but can also help to reduce costs. Parts can be replaced when required instead of at set intervals based on a worst-case scenario.
- **Real-Time BIM Model Collaboration** - The stakeholders involved in a project can collaborate throughout the BIM process to reduce costs, increase efficiency and address problems early on. Architectural, Structural and MEP (Mechanical Engineering & Plumbing) models are currently worked on separately and clashes and other issues are only detected at a late stage causing delays or even problems during construction. Using the BIM Platform, they can be worked on simultaneously. IoT data collected during the operation stage of a building can be analysed using BDA and fed back to the stakeholders to make any required changes or to develop improvements in future buildings. The BIM Platform also facilitates collaboration between stakeholders by allowing them to access the same data and share files. This pooled data can be harnessed by BDA to find hidden patterns and deeper insights for the greater good.
- **Smart Cities** - The BIM platform allows multiple building and infrastructure projects to be considered simultaneously. Data (including Geographic Information System (or GIS) and IoT data) from whole districts or even entire Smart Cities can be analysed together for insights into urban planning, weather, traffic, fire, etc. BDA and powerful hardware are essential for the consideration of an entire city [19].
- **Generative Design** - Many building designs can be generated automatically from specified design objectives including functional requirements, material types, energy use and financial goals [6]. Real-time Generative Design is facilitated by parallelised

algorithms, BDA and the collaborative aspects of the BIM Platform. Figure 2 illustrates some examples of designs generated by Generative Design [20].

Fig. 2. Examples of designs generated using generative design.

6 Conclusion

The data traditionally associated with the construction industry will increasingly pale into insignificance compared with the huge amounts of data from multiple sources now beginning to be seen. This data increases exponentially as we move from considering individual buildings to associated infrastructure, districts and even entire smart cities.

Architects, Engineers, operators and owners of built assets will all want to harness this information to generate insight that they can use to become more efficient, save money and make peoples' lives better. This article has explored unifying Cloud Computing, BDA, the IoT and BIM to bring this about. These technologies will play an important role in the future of the AEC industry.

This article has described a BIM Platform which is Big Data enabled, has an IFC compliant BIM engine and an IoT Hub for handling IoT data. The platform is hosted in the cloud to enable collaboration and the linking of BIM models with other sources. There is a wide range of uses for the BIM Platform including Increased Model Scope, Streamed Data Analysis, BIM Model Collaboration, Smart Cities and Generative Design.

There will be ongoing hurdles to overcome including security, privacy and changing well established processes. There will be compatibility issues between the disparate technologies used in the BIM Platform and by stakeholders so new software will need to be developed. However, these issues have been common in other fields and have been overcome as change was embraced. In the AEC domain, there is still a lingering resistance to change and an understandable suspicion of sharing data amongst stakeholders. With determination, this can be overcome as the long-term advantages become irresistible.

There is a great deal of scope for future work. The BIM Platform forms a foundation for other apps to be connected to. The Apps referred to in this article are a subset of what is possible and Apps will be developed on an ongoing basis. The BIM Platform will connect to compatible third party Apps or new Apps will be developed as required. In future the functionality of the BIM Platform will be expanded to integrate additional data sources into the Knowledge Base. For example, the integration of social media data could lead to insights into what people want from buildings, deciding where new buildings should be located and learning about attitudes to buildings that already exist.

The potential benefits of the BIM Platform include increased efficiency, greater collaboration, new insights from data and reduced costs. But, more generally, it is hoped that it will move forward and accelerate the changes that the industry has started to make. From CAD to BIM and now to a Collaborative Unified Computing Platform for BIM. Unifying BIM with Cloud Computing, BDA and the IoT can help bring about the step-change the AEC domain needs.

References

1. World Economic Forum: What's the future of the construction industry? (2016). https://www.weforum.org/agenda/2016/04/building-in-the-fourth-industrial-revolution/. Accessed Mar 2017
2. Weippert, A., Kajewski, S.L.: AEC industry culture: A need for change. In: CIB World Building Congress 2004, Building for the Future, pp. 1–10 (2004)
3. Migilinskas, D., Popov, V., Juocevicius, V., Ustinovichius, L.: The benefits, obstacles and problems of practical BIM implementation. Procedia Eng. **57**, 767–774 (2013)
4. Autodesk Revit: Building Information Modelling For Sustainable Design (2005). http://images.autodesk.com/latin_am_main/files/bim_for_sustainable_design_oct08.pdf. Accessed Mar 2017
5. Designing Buildings Wiki: Federated building information model (2016). https://www.designingbuildings.co.uk/wiki/Federated_building_information_model. Accessed Mar 2017
6. Bilal, M., et al.: Big Data in the construction industry: a review of present status, opportunities, and future trends. Adv. Eng. Inf. **30**, 500–521 (2016)
7. Gartner: Big Data (2017). http://www.gartner.com/it-glossary/big-data. Accessed Mar 2017
8. Mayer-Schönberger, V.: Big data: a revolution that will transform how we live, work and think (2013)
9. Information Management: Top 10 Predictions for IT in 2017 and Beyond (2016). http://www.information-management.com/gallery/oct-top-reader-pick-top-10-predictions-for-it-in-2017-and-beyond-10030035-1.html. Accessed Mar 2017
10. Microsoft Azure: What is cloud computing? (2017). https://azure.microsoft.com/en-gb/overview/what-is-cloud-computing/. Accessed Mar 2017
11. Chuang, T.-H., Lee, B.-C., Wu, I.-C.: Applying Cloud Computing Technology To BIM Visualization And Manipulation (2011)
12. Vanlande, R., Nicolle, C., Cruz, C.: IFC and building lifecycle management. Autom. Constr. **18**(1), 70–78 (2008)
13. FM Systems: Does BIM have a role in the Internet of Things? (2016). https://fmsystems.com/blog/does-bim-have-a-role-in-the-internet-of-things. Accessed Mar. 2017
14. Enzo Unified: Edge Computing Platform (2017). http://www.enzounified.com/. Accessed Mar. 2017
15. Solihin, W., Eastman, C.: A Simplified BIM Model Server on a Big Data Platform (2016)
16. Conject: Are asset owners and the construction industry really ready for 'Big Data'? (2017). http://www.conjectblog.com/are-asset-owners-and-the-construction-industry-really-ready-for-big-data/. Accessed Mar 2017
17. FirstEigen: Big Data Quality, Integrity Validation, Reconciliation Tool (2017). http://firsteigen.com/databuck/. Accessed Mar 2017

18. Pasini, D., Mastrolembo Ventura, S., Rinaldi, S., Bellagente, P., Flammini, A., Ciribini, A.L C.: Exploiting internet of things and building information modeling framework for management of cognitive buildings. In: 2016 IEEE International Smart Cities Conference, vol. 40545387, pp. 1–6 (2016)
19. Correa, F.R.: Is BIM Big Enough to Take Advantage of Big Data Analytics? (2015)
20. Autodesk: BIM and the Net-Zero Building (2015). http://sustainability.autodesk.com/blog/bim-net-zero-building/. Accessed Mar 2017

Production Networks

A Proposal of Standardised Data Model for Cloud Manufacturing Collaborative Networks

Beatriz Andres[1(✉)], Raquel Sanchis[1], Raul Poler[1], and Leila Saari[2]

[1] Research Centre on Production Management and Engineering (CIGIP), Universitat Politècnica de València (UPV), Calle Alarcón, 03801 Alcoy, Spain
{bandres, rsanchis, rpoler}@cigip.upv.es

[2] Data-Driven Solutions, Technological Research Centre of Finland Ltd. (VTT), Kaitoväylä 1, 90570 Oulu, Finland
leila.saari@vtt.fi

Abstract. The growing amount of data to be handled by collaborative networks raises the need of introducing innovative solutions to fulfil the lack of affordable tools, especially for Small and Medium-Sized Enterprises, to manage and exchange data. The European H2020 Project Cloud Collaborative Manufacturing Networks develops and offers a structured data model, called Standardised Tables, as an organised framework to jointly work with existing databases to manage big data collected from different industries belonging to the CNs. The information of the Standardised Tables will be mainly used with optimisation and collaboration purposes. The paper describes an application of the Standardised Tables in one of the pilots of the aforementioned project, the automotive industry pilot, for solving the collaborative problem of a Materials Requirement Plan.

Keywords: Standardised data model · Management information systems · Manufacturing · Data handling · Modelling · Cloud · Collaborative Networks

1 Introduction

Collaborative approaches have been spreading over the last years due to the advantages associated with the enterprises that take part in collaborative networks (CN). Different areas of research have been studied, such as collaborative planning, performance measurement, strategies alignment, partners' selection, interoperability, data sharing [1]. Current globalised market environments involve open data movement contributing to the wide availability of such data. Nevertheless, earlier approaches to collaborative networking are constrained by the scarcity of data and technologies to deal with the fast evolving scenarios, in terms of data (data exchange/change, and data management). Big data focuses on processing and analysing large data repositories that with the conventional tools of analytical databases will be very difficult to treat. Large data repositories are fed by Radio Frequency IDentification, (RFID) sensors and other Internet of Things (IoT) devices that generate data, faster than people do. To this regard, big data requires smart technologies to efficiently process large quantities of data within a tolerable

L.M. Camarinha-Matos et al. (Eds.): PRO-VE 2017, IFIP AICT 506, pp. 77–85, 2017.
DOI: 10.1007/978-3-319-65151-4_7

amount of time. Technologies being applied to big data include, amongst others, manufacturing execution system (MES), business intelligent systems (BI) or cloud computing platforms, allowing to process big data or repositories based on distributed, cloud and open source systems [2]. In terms of MES, some authors fulfilled a fundamental need of designing data model for MES [3, 4], which are based on entities relationship models [5–7]. These data models are considered to compose the standardised data model for cloud manufacturing collaborative networks.

The main drawback of acquiring technologies for handling big data in CNs, formed by small and medium enterprises (SMEs), is the lack of affordable tools. To achieve the advantages offered from cloud computing capabilities (complex event processing, collaboration technologies, big data management and knowledge processing) enterprises need to start the process of ICT transformation to fulfil the requirements for business innovation and turn technology into competitive advantage. Adopting technologies to deal with collaborative relationships within networked enterprises and adopting future Internet technologies such as cloud computing and data analytics are core competences researchers must deal with in order to support the enterprises technology change.

In this regard, the European H2020 Project Cloud Collaborative Manufacturing Networks (C2NET) develops methods and tools to collect data from real-world and virtualise resources, to collaborate in this data rich world. Addressing data acquisition from different sources interconnected to the C2NET platform and its cloud. Taking into account the diversity and heterogeneity of data resources in CN a proposal of Standardised Data Model is presented to jointly work with existing databases to manage big data collected from different industries belonging to the CN.

In this regard, this paper is structured as follows: Sect. 2 presents a brief overview of the C2NET project in which the paper is contextualised; in Sect. 3 the methodology followed in C2NET project to create the standardised data model is presented; in Sect. 4 the skeleton of the standardised data model is presented with the Standardised Tables (STables) created; Sect. 5 presents the application of the STables in one of the pilots in the C2NET project, the automotive industry pilot; finally, in Sect. 6 the conclusions and future research lines are addressed.

2 C2NET Overview

Cloud Collaborative Manufacturing Networks project (C2NET) [8, 9], will build a Cloud Architecture to support SMEs with affordable tools to help them to overcome the barriers appearing when they are willing to participate in a CN. C2NET Project generates a Cloud Architecture composed by [10]: (i) The Data Collection Framework (C2NET DCF) to provide continuous data collection from supply network resources; (ii) The Optimiser (C2NET OPT) to support SMEs belonging to the CN in the optimisation of collaborative manufacturing and logistics assets. C2NET OPT contains a repository of algorithms that compute and optimise different set of individual or collaborative plans related to replenishment, production and delivery; (iii) The Collaboration Tools (C2NET COT), a set of tools in charge of managing the agility of the collaborative processes; and (iv) The Cloud Platform (C2NET CPL) to integrate the data collection module, the optimisers and the collaborative tools in the cloud and allow the access to process collaboration and optimisation resources to all CN partners.

This paper presents part of the results obtained in C2NET project and provides the standardised data model of the C2NET database for gathering structured information in the C2NET DCF. The stored data will be used by: (i) the C2NET OPT as input of the optimisation algorithms designed in the scope of automatically solving replenishment, production, and delivery plans; (ii) the C2NET COT as an input for collaboration workflows, and monitoring of the optimised plans.

The validation of C2NET project is performed through the implementation of the results in four pilots representing the automotive industry, dermo-cosmetics, metal-working SMEs and OEM equipment manufacturer.

3 Data Base Requirement Analysis

The design of C2NET database raises from the need to define standardised terminologies to manage information in multiple locations and with multiple conceptual areas. A common and structured terminology is created in form of Standardised Tables (STables) to have a shared understanding of all the different needs in terms of collaboration and optimisation, for supporting the definition and calculation of replenishment, manufacturing and delivery plans. Namely, C2NET software developers can develop all kinds of functions for collaboration and optimisation planning, on the basis of the database system. In order to build the C2NET database and STables, two approaches have been considered:

The generic approach: A set of generic problems have been identified from the literature, which were classified using the Supply Chain Operations Reference (SCOR) [11] in Source (S), Make (M) and Deliver (D) plans, and combinations SM, MD and SMD. Each plan type classifies the plan subtypes (see Fig. 1). Around half thousand potential plans were identified in the literature, among which 101 were thoroughly analysed. A detailed analysis has been performed for each of the Literature Plans, regarding the modelling approach, the solution approach, the planning horizon and period, the collaboration level, the algorithm proposed, and the input data, objectives, and output data associated to the algorithm.

The Pilots approach: Some of the generic problems identified in the literature can solve the Pilot problems, while others not. For that reason, the Pilots approach has allowed to identify the Pilot Plans. The input received from the Pilots has allowed identifying problems that include new restrictions to solve the problems that in the generic algorithms have not been considered. Moreover, from the Pilot Plans, a set of input data, objectives and output data have been identified; considering a widespread number of scenarios for building the C2NET database. In this approach, the data that the pilots can provide has been checked, due to sometimes the enterprises do not have available the data required by the algorithms. In this regard, the algorithms must be adapted to the input data that enterprises can provide.

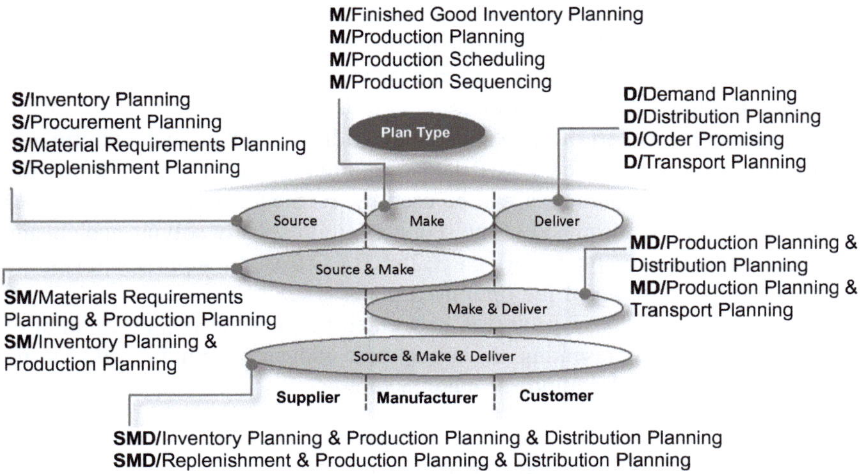

Fig. 1. Plan types and plan subtypes [12–14]

The STables have been built based on the homogenised categories, created to develop a common terminology in C2NET.

4 Data Model: Standardised Tables

The input data, objectives and output data derived from the algorithms reviewed (generic problems) and from the Pilots problems have allowed the completion and refinement of the STables data, according to the needs of the domain modules C2NET DCF, C2NET OPT and C2NET COT. In this regard, STables are built to provide in a structured and standardised way the C2NET data needed.

The STables meta-structure is currently composed by 67 STables (a brief description of each STable is shown in Table 1). The STables are classified into two types: (i) One-dimensional STables which are the master data representing the main entities of C2NET, e.g. the STable *Machine*. This means that the table of Machine will only contain data related to Machine; and (ii) Combined Stables, contains the relations of one or several one dimensional STables; e.g. the STable *Machine_Tool* contains data related to a unique set of machine and tool. This STable contains the field *Setuptime* that is the time needed to setup a specific tool in a specific machine. Each STable contains four fields: (i) fieldname, designation of the field (data) with which the data is identified and/or known; (ii) fieldType, category of the data (string, integer, real, floating-point real number, date, boolean etc.); (iii) fieldUnit, magnitude of the data (length in meters, mass in kilograms, time in hours, etc.); and (iv) fieldDescription, characterisation of the data representing its meaning.

Table 1. The stables of C2NET

STable	Definition
Container	Containers hold Parts for delivery, supply, storage or transport
Customer	Customers buy Parts to the Company
Customer_Order	Associates an Order with a Customer
Customer_Part	Associates a Part with a Customer (parts purchased by the customer to the company)
Customer_Site	Associates a Customer with a Site
Customer_TimeFrame	Associates a TimeFrame with a Customer (available timeslots for supplying parts to the customer)
Labour	Type of Labour of the company
Labour_Period	Associates a Period with a Labour (the number of labours can vary along periods)
Machine	Machines of the company
Machine_Container	Associates a Container with a Machine (the machine needs a number of empty containers to work)
Machine_Labour	Associates a Labour (type of) with a Machine (the machine needs the labour to work)
Machine_Period	Associates a Period with a Machine (the machine can be available or not in such period, or other status)
Machine_Site	Indicates the Site in which the Machine is
Machine_Tool	Associates a Tool with a Machine (the machine needs the tool to work)
Machine_Tool_Labour	Associates a Tool and a Labour (type of) with a Machine (machine needs the tool to work, the tool needs the labour to be setup
Machine_Tool_Period	Associates a Tool with a Machine in each period (the machine and tool can be available or not in such period)
Machine_Tool_Tool	Associates two Tools with a Machine (indicates some characteristics when a tool is setup in the machine having another tool)
Operation	An Operation is a generic phase for changing a thing from one state to another state
Operation_Labour	Associates a Labour (type of) with an Operation (the operation needs the labour to be performed)
Operation_Machine	Associates an Operation with a Machine (the operation needs the machine to be performed)
Operation_Operation	Relate 2 Operations (for establishing sequences)
Operation_Part	Associates a Part with an Operation (the operation needs the part to be performed or generates the part)
Operation_Tool	Associates an Operation with a Tool (the operation needs the tool to be performed)
Order	Generic Order (from a Customer to the Company, or from the Company to a Supplier)
Order_Part	Associates an Order with a Part (the part should be delivered in such order)
Order_Part_Site	Associates an Order of the part with a Site (the part of the order should be delivered in such site)
Order_Period	Associates a Order with a Period
Order_Site	Associates an Order with a Site (the order should be delivered in such site)
Part	Generic Part (raw material, component, final product; purchased or sold by the Company)
Part_Container	Associates a Part with a container (the part needs the container to be stored o transported)
Part_Container_Customer	Associates a Part with a container of a customer (the part of a customer needs the container to be stored o transported)
Part_Container_Machine	Associates a Part with a Container and a Machine. Modelling the picking activity whom load and cost depend on the container (unit, pack, factory box, distribution box, pallet) and the machine used to make the picking activity of the part in the container
Part_Container_Supplier	Associates a Part with a container of a supplier (the part of a customer needs the container to be stored o transported)
Part_Container_Period	Associates a Part with a Customer in a Period (information on such part in the customer in that period)
Part_Machine	Associates a Part with a Machine (the machine produces the part) [a more detailed modelling can be defined using Operation]
Part_Part	Bill of Materials (amount of a part for obtaining one unit of another part)
Part_PartGroup	Associates a Part with a PartGroup (group to which the part belongs)
Part_Period	Associates a Period with a Part (information of the part in such period)
Part_Site	Associates a Part with a Site (the site in which the part is)
Part_Supplier_Period	Associates a Part with a Supplier in a Period (information on such part in the supplier in that period)
Part_Tool	Associates a Part with a Tool (the part needs the tool to be produced)
Part_Vehicle	Associates a Part with a Vehicle (the part needs the vehicle to be transported)
Part_Warehouse	Associates a Part with a Warehouse (the part needs the warehouse to be stored)
PartGroup	Group of Parts
Period	Specifies periods of time (hours, days, week, months, ...)
Person	An individual employee
Person_Labour	Associates a Person with a Labour (a worker able to perform certain type of labour)
Person_Period	Associates a Person with a Period (availability of the worker in such a period)
Route	Generic route
Route_Site_Site	Associates a pair of Sites with a Route (for creating a complete route from the initial site to the end site)
Route_Vehicle	Associates a Vehicle with a Route
Site	Specifies a Site (a location, for a factory, distribution centre, customer, supplier, etc.)
Site_Site	Associates a Site with another Site (information between both Sites)
Site_Site_Vehicle	Associates a Site with another Site and a Vehicle (information between both Sites using the Vehicle)
Supplier	Suppliers deliver Parts to the Company
Supplier_Order	Associates an Order with a Supplier
Supplier_Part	Associates a Part with a Supplier (parts purchased by the company to the supplier)
Supplier_Site	Associates a Supplier with a Site
Supplier_TimeFrame	Associates a TimeFrame with a Supplier (available timeslots for receiving part from the supplier)
TimeFrame	Generic timeframe
Tool	Tools of the company
Tool_Labour	Associates a Labour (type of) with a Tool (the tool needs the labour to setup)
Tool_Period	Associates a Period with a Tool (the tool can be available or not in such period, or other status)
Vehicle	Vehicles of the company
Vehicle_Period	Associates a Vehicle with the period (the vehicle can be available or not in such period, or other status)
Warehouse	Warehouses of the company
Warehouse_Site	Associates a Warehouse with a Site

5 Application Example of C2NET Standardised Data Model

The application is performed in the automotive pilot of C2NET that is specifically for solving the collaborative problem of a Materials Requirement Plan (MRP) between the First Tier and the Second Tier suppliers of an automotive enterprise. The structure of the STables and Fields required for solving the collaborative MRP are presented in Fig. 2.

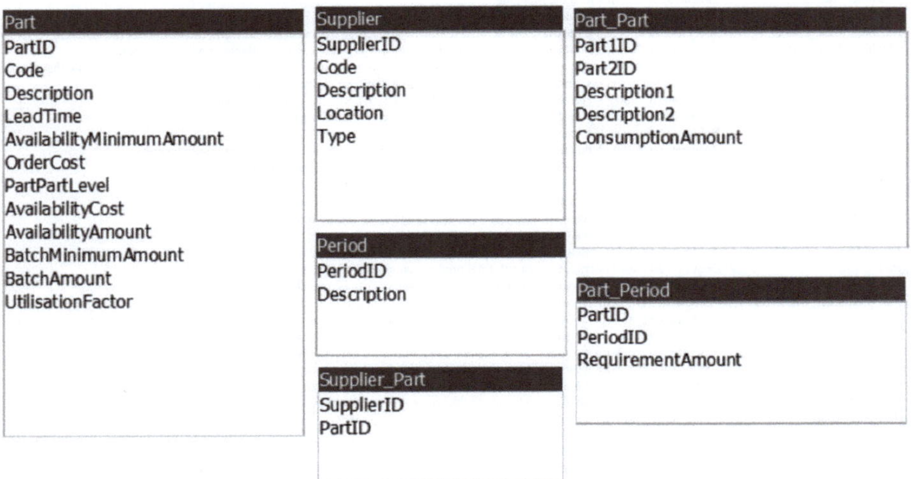

Fig. 2. Data structure required to solve the collaborative MRP.

Table 2. Description of each of the fields

STable.Field	Description
Part.PartID	C2NET unique identifier (autonumeric) for a part (product, raw material, component…)
Part.Code	Company unique identifier for a part
Part.Description	Company description of a part
Part.LeadTime	Supply time of the raw material/component from the supplier to the manufacturer or delivery time of the product from the manufacturer to its customer
Part. AvailabilityMinimumAmount	Minimum inventory of parts, e.g. safety stock
Part.OrderCost	Cost of order release
Part.PartPartLevel	0: product; 1: subassembly; 2: semi-finished; 3: standard; 4: raw material
Part.AvailabilityCost	Inventory cost per unit of the part

(*continued*)

Table 2. (*continued*)

STable.Field	Description
Part.AvailabilityAmount	Current amount of parts available in the inventory
Part.BatchMinimumAmount	Minimum lotsize of parts
Part.BatchAmount	Lotsize of parts taken
Part.UtilisationFactor	Percentage of parts with the required quality (e.g. 85% of the produced parts are within the quality boundaries, the other 15% remaining parts are scrap). The value is given in base 1.
Period.PeriodID	C2NET unique identifier (autonumeric) for a period (hour, day, week, month…)
Period.Description	Company description for the period
Supplier. SupplierID	C2NET unique identifier (autonumeric) for a supplier
Supplier.Code	Company unique identifier for a supplier
Supplier.Description	Company description of a supplier
Supplier.Location	Location of a supplier (e.g. address)
Supplier.Type	Types of suppliers e.g. potential suppliers, current suppliers…
Part_Part.Part1ID	C2NET unique identifier (autonumeric) for a Part1 that is the parent item of Part2
Part_Part.Part2ID	C2NET unique identifier (autonumeric) for Part2 that is the child itemof Part1
Part_Part. ConsumptionAmount	Amount of a Part2ID consumed to create one unit of Part1ID
Part_Period.Part	C2NET unique identifier (autonumeric) for a part
Part_Period.Period	C2NET unique identifier (autonumeric) for a period
Part_Period. RequirementAmount	Demand of a part in a period
Supplier_Part.Supplier	C2NET unique identifier (autonumeric) for a supplier
Supplier_Part.Part	C2NET unique identifier (autonumeric) for a part

Table 2 shows the description of each of the fields required for solving the collaborative MRP as an illustrative example of the input data sets needed and how they are structured.

6 Conclusions and Future Work

The growing amount of data to be handled by CNs, raises the need of introducing innovative solutions to fulfil the lack of affordable tools, especially for SMEs, to manage and exchange data. Considering that there is a need to better understand the potential for value creation through collaborative approaches, this paper presents a standardised data model for manufacturing CN, where organisational data exchange can be highly improved, from the proposed generic and adaptable standardised data model, playing an important role when data sharing and management is carried out in manufacturing CNs.

The STables were defined with the aim of creating a common terminology of C2NET data from the input data, objectives and output data extracted from the generic problems (literature algorithms) and the Pilot problems (developed algorithms).

The process of defining STables is not considered as completely finished, on the contrary, it is under continuous development. The generation of STables depends on (i) the results obtained in the work developed in C2NET project (ii) the new requirements appearing in the implementation and validation of C2NET project, and (iii) further needs that could emerge a posteriori in the exploitation phase, when C2NET project finishes, and when C2NET is implemented in other industrial sectors and contexts.

Acknowledgments. The research leading to these results is in the frame of the "Cloud Collaborative Manufacturing Networks" (C2NET) project, which has received funding from the European Union's Horizon 2020 research and innovation programme under grant agreement No. 636909.

References

1. Andres, B., Poler, R.: Models, guidelines and tools for the integration of collaborative processes in non-hierarchical manufacturing networks: a review. Int. J. Comput. Integr. Manuf. **2**(29), 166–201 (2016)
2. Zikopoulos, P., Eaton, C.: Understanding Big Data: Analytics for Enterprise Class Hadoop and Streaming Data. McGraw-Hill Osborne Media, New York (2011)
3. Zhou, B., Wang, S., Xi, L.: Data model design for manufacturing execution system. J. Manuf. Technol. Manag. **16**(8), 909–935 (2005)
4. Steven, W.: Getting the MES model – methods for system analysis. ISA Trans. **35**(2), 95–103 (1996)
5. Reda, A.: Extracting the extended entity-relationship model from a legacy relational database. Inf. Syst. **28**(6), 597–618 (2003)
6. Teorey, T.J., Yang, D., Fry, J.P.: A logical design methodology for relational database using the extended entity-relationship model. ACM Comput. Surv. **18**(2), 197–222 (1986)
7. Victor, M., Arie, S.: Representing extended entity-relationship structures in relational databases: a modular approach. ACM Trans. Database Syst. **17**(3), 423–464 (1992)
8. CORDIS Europa, Factories of the Future, H2020-EU.2.1.5.1. - Technologies for Factories of the Future (2014)
9. H2020 Project C2NET (2015). http://cordis.europa.eu/project/rcn/193440_en.html
10. Andres, B., Sanchis, R., Poler, R.: A cloud platform to support collaboration in supply networks. Int. J. Prod. Manag. Eng. **4**(1), 5–13 (2016)
11. APICS, "SCOR Framework," Supply Chain Operations Reference model (SCOR) (2017)
12. Orbegozo, A., Andres, B., Mula, J., Lauras, M., Monteiro, C., Malheiro, M.: An overview of optimization models for integrated replenishment and producction planning decisions. In: Building Bridges Between Researchers and Practitioners. Book of Abstracts of the International Joint Conference CIO-ICIEOM-IISE-AIM (IJC2016), p. 68 (2016)

13. Andres, B., Poler, R., Saari, L., Arana, J., Benaches, J.V., Salazar, J.: Optimization models to support decision-making in collaborative networks: a review. In: Building Bridges Between Researchers and Practitioners. Book of Abstracts of the International Joint Conference CIO-ICIEOM-IISE-AIM (IJC2016), p. 70 (2016)
14. Andres, B., Sanchis, R., Lamothe, J., Saari, L., Hauser, F.: Combined models for production and distribution planning in a supply chain. In: Building Bridges Between Researchers and Practitioners. Book of Abstracts of the International Joint Conference CIO-ICIEOM-IISE-AIM (IJC2016), p. 71 (2016)

The Implementation of Traceability in Fashion Networks

Laura Macchion[1(✉)], Andrea Furlan[2], and Andrea Vinelli[1]

[1] Department of Management and Engineering, University of Padova, Vicenza, Italy
{laura.macchion,andrea.vinelli}@unipd.it

[2] Department of Economics and Management, University of Padova, Padua, Italy
andrea.furlan@unipd.it

Abstract. A complete network traceability to identify suppliers and customers' activities and share information along the entire network is not an easy objective to achieve. It requires the involvement of all the network stages: manufacturing, purchasing and distribution processes. This research aims to study traceability for collaborative network within the fashion industry. We conducted an in-depth case study using an interview protocol specifically designed for this research investigating drivers as well as practices for network traceability.

Keywords: Fashion · Traceability · Collaborative networks · Supply network configuration · Supply chain

1 Traceability and the Collaborative Network Context

Traceability is the ability to trace the history, use and location of a particular entity through the implementation of identification systems (ISO 8402:1994). The ISO 9001:2000 extends this definition to networks' traceability, referring to the ability to trace the history, the use and the location of products and processes along the entire network. This way traceability is related to the origin of raw materials and the history of all processes interesting final products within the network [1]. It involves all purchasing, production and distribution stages, in which processes and product units are appropriately identified by a collaborative exchange of information along the network [2, 3]. Two distinct aspects compose traceability: tracing (i.e. the ability to determine the origin and characteristics of a particular product within the network) and tracking (i.e. the ability to follow the path of a product along the network from suppliers to consumers) [1, 2]. Moreover, two different levels of traceability can be identified. The first is related to company's internal traceability, which is the ability to track and trace the products' batch within firm's boundaries [2]. The second is linked to a broader traceability concept that involves the entire network: network traceability represents the ability to track and trace products' batches along sourcing, production and distribution activities, starting from the raw material till final sale [1].

In literature studies mainly focus on agri-food network traceability systems [1, 4–6], with a particular attention on perishable goods chains such as meat [7], grain [8], fish, fruit [10] and vegetables [3]. However, nowadays, other important sectors such as

L.M. Camarinha-Matos et al. (Eds.): PRO-VE 2017, IFIP AICT 506, pp. 86–96, 2017.
DOI: 10.1007/978-3-319-65151-4_8

pharmaceutics are interested in network traceability. Because of the internationalization phenomena that make global networks very difficult to be controlled, also in the fashion industry there is a growing attention to traceability systems to better identify network partners and, in some cases, to protect country of origin strategies. The fashion industry plays a relevant role in the European economy: in 2015 EU fashion industry sales equalled approximately €169 billion, with 174,000 companies [11] and in particular the Italian fashion industry reached €52.4 billion with exports representing about the 56% of the revenue [12].

In recent years some fashion groups have approached the network traceability issue, by focusing specially on the procurement of raw materials. For instance, Patagonia, a manufacture of outdoor clothing, has launched a specific initiative, which allows customers to verify the origin of raw materials used for their products. Despite the growing importance of the network traceability issue for fashion companies, there are no legislations, mandatory requirements or standards identifying the proper method to design a traceability system for collaborative networks. Therefore, companies that decide to implement traceability, face the challenge of creating ad hoc practices. Even the academic literature on fashion traceability appears to be fragmented and limited to some parts of the network. The few contributions available in literature mainly focus on the internal traceability of companies, instead of adopting a network perspective [13] and the alignment with the entire networks, in which many and heterogeneous actors operate, is still a missing point [14].

The achievement of network traceability within the fashion industry needs to be supported by appropriate studies, encompassing the entire network activities to provide relevant value for both companies operating in the collaborative network and customers. This research aims to offer a first contribution in this perspective analysis both drivers and practices in the field of network traceability.

2 Drivers for Network Traceability

Achieving network traceability seems to be a current issue for many industries. For instance, because of the scandals occurred in the '90 s such as the BSE contamination (Bovine Spongiform Encephalopathy), in the agri-food industry strict network traceability legislation has been introduced to reduce risks for consumer health and minimize costs related to the withdrawal from the market of contaminated batches. Therefore for this industry the traceability of the network is already a legal obligation within the European Union, as well as in other countries such as the United States and Japan, attracting considerable attention of both researchers and practitioners to store real time information along the chain. Such studies have led to the identification of proper techniques to trace final products, and their raw materials, ascertain contamination problems and prevent them [2]. Full compliance with existing legislation is therefore the most important driver for agri-food companies to implement network traceability [15].

Nevertheless, other motivations for network traceability exist besides legal and public safety. First, in the fashion industry the development of global networks has increased the attention for sustainability aspects that could be well guaranteed through the implementation of traceability systems [1, 9, 29].

On one hand, production processes that employ chemical components and scarce natural resources, resulting in heavy environmental impacts, characterize the fashion sector. On the other hand, fashion networks are truly planetary, characterized by companies producing and distributing at world-level with different working conditions and Country legislations [19]. Therefore, these aspects encourage the implementation of network traceability to ensure customers the sustainability (both environmental and social) of their network. Second, the network traceability represents a way to provide customers further information about products and processes. Transparency of information becomes a source of competitive advantage that allows companies to differentiate themselves from competitors and build a responsible and reliable brand reputation.

In the fashion world, especially in the luxury segment, country of origin information becomes a guarantee of quality (not only in terms of product quality. but also of social and environmental production conditions). In this way traceability systems represent long-term strategic investment to create consumer confidence, strengthen the company image, and gain a competitive advantage in the market [1, 2]. Third, traceability can also be used to fight fraud in the market [16]. Because of the globalization and the increased use of e-commerce, there has been a strong increase in counterfeit products. Network traceability can be useful in ensuring product authenticity and protecting companies from unfair competition. Counterfeiting can take place at different levels of the chain, from sourcing to customer delivery and different methods (such as holograms, colour-shifting films or inks, sequential product numbering) or tracing technologies (such as RDIF, electronic product codes, barcodes, etc.) have been studied individually by fashion companies to ensure the authenticity of the product [16]. However, a multi-level and dynamic solution that can involve all actors in the network and integrate even different traceability systems is necessary to create an effective anti-counterfeiting mechanism. Fourth, traceability can also be implemented to improve control and communication within complex networks.

A better control of the network could be translated into a reduction in logistics costs (thanks to the reduction of defective products and inventories) and, strengthening cooperation between network partners [17, 1]. Fifth, network traceability allows a better product optimization both in terms of efficiency and quality assurance, by improving the control of network processes. For instance a network traceability system allows to recall only products really affected by quality issues, thus improving process efficiency as well [2, 1]. Sixth, traceability can be a useful tool also to introduce product innovations being a way to facilitate the sharing of improvement proposals among supply chain partners [18].

Finally, companies might choose to implement traceability even in the distribution to geolocalize customers and segment their shopping behaviours [1]. In this way, traceability becomes a way to achieve a strong differentiation in the market.

3 Traceability Practices

The development of traceability for the network still remains an open challenge in the fashion sector. A network traceability system should define the tools and mechanisms to transmit information, the data to be shared, the identification of each product as well as the country of origin of raw materials [4]. The perspective that a network traceability should consider is therefore not only functional, focused on what the system should do, but also organizational, paying attention to the functions and processes composing the system structure [3]. Hence, one of the most critical aspects is the development of a complete inter-organizational traceability that could align different actors and ensure the data exchange in a standardized way.

Two key practices are required for the development of network traceability. First of all, the single Traceability Resource Unit (TRU) (i.e. the individual item or batch to be traced) should be identified [2]. This unit of analysis varies depending on the type of company: for process companies, such as chemical firms, the object to be traced will be the batch; instead product companies, such as the fashion firms, the TRU will be the single product. The TRU evolves along the network as a result of production processes and such transformation must always be documented to guarantee the identification of each step within the network. Therefore the second point interesting the development of traceability practices is represented by the identification of the TRU supported by proper tags, for instance labels, barcodes, microchips or RFID, applied directly to each product or batch or indirectly by fixing the tag on pallets. To each TRU is assigned a code, mainly alphanumeric, with a unique and shared meaning for all actors in the network.

The sharing of product coding with all the actors in the supply chain is therefore a focal point, requiring chain partners to be responsible for the reliability of data provided [2]. Production, movements and storage activities for each TRU will be thus mapped and monitored by all supply partners sharing traceability data [3]. In any case the traceability practices to be implement in the network are strongly subject to specific constraints. In fact the most appropriate traceability system should be identified in accordance to technological and cost constraints, data accuracy possibilities, and reliability of network actors, thus requiring a study of the possibilities of the specific network.

4 Research Objectives

Previous studies mainly analysed traceability based on a single company or have analyzed the traceability issue applied to the entire network in sectors where the network traceability is set by regulations, for instance in the food networks [1]. However, other contexts in which actors decide to implement network traceability based on a voluntary decision require further insights. This research investigates this issue, considering the design and the implementation of a voluntary network traceability within the fashion industry, from raw materials till the end customers and across different supply partners. In particular, fashion industry-specific drivers that led companies to adopt network traceability systems and best practices for network traceability are investigated. The following research questions are investigated:

RQ1: Considering that traceability in the fashion industry is still and mainly a voluntary application, what are the drivers that can encourage the implementation of traceability systems within fashion collaborative networks?
RQ2: What traceability practices are developed in fashion collaborative networks?

5 Methodology

Considering the explorative nature of the research questions the case study method is adopted [20], since it allows achieving a high level of understanding with observations and in-depth case study is particularly encouraged for the study of contemporary events within their real-life context since it increases the external validity of results [21, 20].

The case study methodology is appropriate when the research is exploratory and the phenomenon under investigation is still poorly studied, as it offers the opportunity to achieve in-depth results through direct experience [20]. In setting the eligibility criteria for the case study, the selection included a company that: (i) operate in the fashion industry; (ii) are headquartered in Italy; (iii) have international production and distribution networks (to include a company that have to address different environmental and social international regulations within their SCM); (iv) is brand owners (thus they have the control of their whole SCM).

The organization involved in this research is one of the leading and most representative companies (in terms of turnover and number of employees) of the fashion system producing leather goods, footwear, clothing and accessories. We selected this company for theoretical reasons [22, 23]: the selected case is recognized as exemplar [21] in the fashion industry and it is undertaking an important voluntary project of network traceability for its leather products, involving from third-tier suppliers till final consumers. We interviewed multiple key informants of the company and its suppliers. In particular, we organized with multiple interviewers many meetings with each network partner to cover the entire network traceability issues, achieve a higher level of reliability [20] and enhance the construct validity [23].

To ensure the validity of the collected data senior managers were involved in the research. We interviewed Chief of Sustainability Officer and specialists of the ICT function of the focal company; CEO and COO of slaughterhouse-3rd tier supplier; CEO and COO of hide collector-2nd tier; CEO, CSO, Quality Manager and Import-Export manager of the tannery-1st tier; entrepreneurs, CEOs and specialists of selected façonniers. For triangulation requirements, internal documents provided of network partners were also analysed. Moreover, we had the possibility to visit and have direct observations of all network partners' plants to verify how traceability systems were implemented. Data collection phase took place from February 2013 to December 2013, and was supported by multiple investigators to reduce bias and enhance reliability [23]. A semi-structured interview protocol was specifically designed for this research [20], including questions concerning the traceability practices and drivers. All the interviews were recorded and then transcribed [21]. For every network actors, we stopped the number of interviews when we reached data saturation [22, 20]. Finally, a case summary report were then prepared and reviewed by the research team to improve validity [21].

6 Findings

For what concerns main drivers (RQ1) leading to undertake a network traceability project, the research highlights that several traceability drivers already recognized in other sectors are confirmed also in fashion networks. In particular, the journey towards a traced network was moved by the desire of responding to sustainability pressures from the final markets and from NGOs (i.e. Greenpeace), which are raising always-higher attention towards the provenience of the raw materials and the Countries in which the different activities processes are executed [31]. Gaining comprehensive knowledge on all the partners involved in the supply activities and identifying the different Countries in which every supplier works are company's needs to be able to comply with local laws and have high assurance that processes and workers' conditions are environmental- (i.e. the use of dangerous chemicals during tannery and production stages) and social- (i.e. labour conditions) friendly [24]. Moreover, in the long term the studied company wants to develop a green brand reputation and this goal starts from being unassailable on all network stages through a complete transparency over its processes and suppliers. This network transparency is considered a potential source of competitive advantage, by ensuring the improvement of the perceived quality of the made in effect.

Another strong motivation encouraging fashion companies to invest efforts on traceability project is related to the enhancement of network control and communication to improve the quality of products and components. In fact, the ability to identify the partners taking part in the development of a finished bag, and the related possibility of quickly identifying which partners are affected by quality problems once that a batch is recognized as damaged or not meeting quality standards, was one of the pillars of the network traceability project. However, the achievement of an enhanced control over the raw materials starts from the assumption that a higher level of network communication and integration is requested [17] by stipulating agreements with network partners and developing trust-based relationships for the exchange of data among all the involved actors.

Indeed, one of the drivers of this traceability project was the need to expand the already-existing transactional relations with suppliers to more collaborative ones. Company managers also wished to develop a traceability system useful to control the possible counterfeiting of raw materials and final products: as the products pertaining to the luxury fashion segment, positioned on a high price range, it is strongly critical to ensure the customer about the authenticity of the product and its components.

Moreover, the decision to start a network traceability project was driven by the necessity to refine marketing strategies and in particular to improve the customer geolocation. The application of a RFID tag on every finished product was the final solution implemented to realize this need. Differently from the literature in other industries, the system was not moved by legislation requests: in fact, there are no regulations that impose the adoption of a traceability procedure in the fashion sector, but anyway the analysed firm recognized the need to develop this system to proactively align itself to emerging new market needs.

As for the traceability practices within the fashion network (RQ2), food traceability practice were studied, and subsequently those practices were properly applied to the fashion network composed of many actors (i.e. farmers, slaughterhouses, hide collectors, tanneries, focal company, façonniers, logistic providers and retailers) and of many transformation points in which the raw materials can be joined, transferred, separated or assembled together. These transformation points can lead to relevant problems for traceability purposes [15]. In fact, in the case of foodstuffs, raw materials are often processed directly within one plant without any movements that could damage their healthiness. Below will be analyzed in detail the results to implement traceability with each fashion network partner.

Fourth-tier: Farmer Traceability of livestock at the farms is already adopted: to trace every domestic animal the European food regulations require very strict traceability procedures composed by two ear-tags (with a tracking number), an electronic subcutaneous microchip, a passport containing animal tracking number and the development of an online database with all the information about animals life (for instance vaccinations, etc.) that are also registered within the passports.

Third-tier supplier: Slaughterhouse Thanks to the collaboration with the food sector for which traceability of meat is required by legislation for healthy reason, until the skinning process the traceability of hides is guaranteed. But after it a critical traceability point emerges: by regulation only the meat is labelled and traced through all the downstream steps, where on the contrary hides traceability is not mandatory. To ensure traceability after this point, each hide has been identified by a plastic barcode label. This way all information related to the animal can be maintained. Hides can be then processed through a code scanner and sent to the hide collector with a shipping batch code linked to all the coded hides. Thanks to this traceability code, the hides can be separated based on the hides' country of origin since quality problems in the leather of final products comes from animals' country of origin.

Second-tier supplier: Hide collector Since every hide is marked with a plastic label, traceability within processes of the hide collector (i.e. the actor within the network responsible for the quality leather selection) is preserved. Then, the shipping batch for the tannery is prepared: a new code, the shipping batch code, is generated by the hide collector and is linked to the previous plastic barcode. In this way it is always preserved the network information. As in the previous point, it is fundamental to prepare shipping batches based on the country of origin, for quality reasons.

First-tier supplier: Tannery From this stage in the network the plastic code applied on every hide must be removed, since tannery processes are extremely aggressive and might delete the same code. Moreover, at this point the unit traced becomes the batch composed by many hides that are processed by the tanneries at the same time: all hides coming from the same farmer are processed in the same batch. Even if this means the loss of information on the single hide, this solution is suitable to reach the network traceability objectives, because it is always possible to obtain in every step of tannery process relevant data for network traceability (such as information related to the farmer from which animals come from). For what concerns traceability procedures within the tannery, information could be always traced using a code system that connects shipping batches and production processes. Once again, the information related to the country of origin of batches are guaranteed.

The focal firm and its façonniers Thanks to the implementation of a web ICT solution to share real time information with façonniers, the focal company is able to trace the hides' information during manufacturing processes. The batches shipped by the tannery are codified and registered in the web ICT system. When the focal company sends the batches to façonniers for the production processes, it assigns a proper code of production, which identifies the tannery information and the specific façonnier where the leather will be processed. This code is traced during all the production processes. After the manufacturing activities, every finished product is then associated with a RFID tag, which contains a serial number associated to all network information (such as production code, tannery's shipping code, etc.).

From the focal firm to the retail store Thanks to the RFID tag, traceability at single bag level can be guaranteed beyond this point till the end customer, since the tag can hold also distribution data, such as the store where the bag is shipped.

All in all, given the different network actors involved in the traceability project and their different internal traceability procedures, it was necessary to standardize data coding procedure to allow data to flow downstream, without interrupting the production workflow [25]. All critical points among network partners were connected using proper code numbers that could provide and ensure all data concerning the farmer, the hide collector, the tannery, the focal company, the façonniers and retail stores. As suggested by literature, every single traceability resource unit (TRU) was identified, coded and physically separated from others to guarantee proper identification [2, 3].

7 Conclusions

The study revealed that the drivers that moved the analysed fashion company toward the development of a traceability system were sustainability, product optimization, chain control and communication, counterfeit and competitive advantage reasons. All in all, if in the agri-food chain the protection of consumers' health is the main driver for traceability, in the fashion industry traceability is still seen as a source of an innovative market advantage, able to distinguish a network from competitors. Indeed, in the fashion industry the implementation of network traceability is considered a formidable strategy to better control partners [17]. Moreover, the ability to demonstrate the origin of raw materials and products responds to the need for transparency of environmental aspects, such as the use of dangerous chemicals during production stages, and social aspects, such as labour conditions [1].

Although drivers can be different [30], this research shows that practices used for the implementation of a network traceability in the agri-food sector can be applied to the fashion industry. However, strong collaboration is required for their application to share sensitive data. Accordingly to the literature [2–5, 15] the case study highlights that to achieve network traceability some important aspects should be considered: 1. The identification of which products are involved in traceability practices; 2. The data to be collected, shared along the entire network and then transmitted to customers; 3. The ICTs required within the network for traceability.

This study shows how traceability is strongly related to the network coordination and integration. An effective network traceability is based on the exchange of relevant information between actors. Along this vein, proper network coordination and integration mechanisms should be developed to implement a traceability project and achieve the elimination of inter-organizational barriers. Information regarding finished products are not stored only at the single firm level, but are collected by every actor of the network and then shared to the downstream partners, requiring a high level of alignment and collaboration among all network partners. In this way products and information can be traced from raw materials till final consumers [26].

Moreover, the development of network traceability involves very high costs that only through collaboration between all actors of the network can be supported. According to a sustainability point of view, network traceability allows the implementation of both environmental and social policies, through the effective control of the entire network, in particular of raw materials' suppliers and façonniers [27]. In fact, customers are sensitive about Countries of origin of products and raw materials: some Countries do not have any laws to avoid cruel practices during slaughter processes, and thanks to many NGOs this critical situation and the related sustainability issues are reaching more and more interest by media. Achieving a complete network traceability within all production steps enhance the sustainability profile and ensure the transparency of production and sourcing processes that, starting from an animal, leads to the production and distribution of finished leather products. Unexpectedly, the case study also shows that after the implementation of the traceability project, the company noticed an effective improvement in quality and innovation of products too, thanks to the better alignment with suppliers [28]. Through the development of a network traceability, the company is able to protect very distinctive and particular "made in" competencies [17] that could improve and increase the perceived product quality, based on the Country of origin effect. Moreover, customers are guaranteed about the authenticity of the product they are buying: the improved control along the entire network disincentive not authorised parallel markets, contributing to fight against counterfeiting [16].

From an academic point of view this research contributes to the OM debate on network traceability by adapting food-industry traceability practices to the fashion industry. First we identified the main drivers that lead a fashion company – which is not forced by regulation – to develop a traceability system. Second, we identified the practices that should be adopted to meet network traceability. Despite network traceability have been designed for other industries (e.g. for agri-food contexts), the main best practices can be efficaciously applied also within the fashion industry.

Our research has also implication for practitioners. We detailed the development of a project for network traceability that could be applied by other actors within the fashion leather industry. In particular we developed a system to connect traceability data across network partners, overcoming the problem of loss of traceability data on the single hide from the tanneries. The main limitation of our research is to rely on a single case study, even if in-depth. The analysis could be extended to a broader number of cases in the fashion industry. Besides, the selected case is a very large company, which has high commercial power on its supplier. The results may be different in the case of an SME as a focal company that wants to implement a traceability system within its network. Further studies may also consider the consumer's voice to verify how much traced products are appreciated and then understand if this feature will become a strong order-winner within the fashion system.

Finally, to enhance the debate in the network traceability field future work could deepen the differences between different industries (such as the food and the fashion sector) by considering the drivers and practices implemented.

References

1. Karlsen, K.M., Dreyer, B., Olsen, P., Elvevoll, E.O.: Literature review: does a common theoretical framework to implement food traceability exist? Food Control **32**, 409–417 (2013)
2. Bechini, A., Cimino, M., Marcelloni, F., Tomasi, A.: Patterns and technologies for enabling supply chain traceability through collaborative e-business. Inf. Softw. Technol. **50**, 342–359 (2008)
3. Hu, J., Zhang, X., Moga, L., Neculita, M.: Modeling and implementation of the vegetable supply chain traceability system. Food Control **30**, 341–353 (2013)
4. Regattieri, A., Gamberi, M., Manzini, R.: Traceability of food products: general frame work and experimental evidence. J. Food Eng. **81**, 347–356 (2007)
5. Bendaoud, M., Lecomte, C., Yannou, B.: A methodological framework to design and assess food traceability systems. Int. Food Agribusiness Manag. Rev. **15**(1), 103–125 (2012)
6. Bosona, T., Gebresenbet, G.: Food traceability as an integral part of logistics management in food and agricultural supply chain. Food Control **33**, 32–48 (2013)
7. Smith, G., Pendell, D., Tatum, J., Belk, K., Sofos, J.: Post-slaughter traceability. Meat Sci. **80**, 66–74 (2008)
8. Thakur, M., Hurburgh, C.: Framework for implementing traceability system in the bulk grain supply chain. J. Food Eng. **95**, 617–626 (2009)
9. Da Giau, A., Macchion, L., Caniato, F., Caridi, M., Danese, P., Rinaldi, R., Vinelli, A.: Sustainability practices and web-based communication: an analysis of the Italian fashion industry. J. Fashion Market. Manag. **20**(1), 72–88 (2016)
10. Canavari, M., Centonze, R., Hingley, M., Spadoni, R.: Traceability as part of competitive strategy in the fruit supply chain. Br. Food J. **112**(2), 171–186 (2010)
11. Euratex (2017), http://euratex.eu/press/key-data/, Accessed March 2017
12. Sistema Moda Italia, http://www.sistemamodaitalia.com/it/press/note-economiche/item/9875-consuntivo-2015-e-outlook-2016, Accessed March 2017
13. Bottani, E., Rizzi, A.: Economical assessment of the impact of RFID technology and EPC system on the fast-moving consumer goods supply chain. Int. J. Prod. Econ. **112**(2), 548–569 (2008)
14. Macchion, L., Danese, P., Vinelli, A.: Redefining supply network strategies to face changing environments. A study from the fashion and luxury industry. Oper. Manag. Res. **8**(1–2), 15–31 (2015)

15. Donnelly, K., Karlsen, K., Olsen, P.: The importance of transformations for traceability. - A case study of lamb and lamb products. Meat Sci. **83**, 68–73 (2009)
16. Li, L.: Technology designed to combat fakes in the global supply chain. Bus. Horiz. **56**, 167–177 (2013)
17. Guercini, S., Runfola, A.: The integration between marketing and purchasing in the traceability process. Ind. Mark. Manag. **38**, 883–891 (2009)
18. Macchion, L., Moretto, A., Caniato, F., Caridi, M., Danese, P., Spina, G., Vinelli, A.: Improving innovation performance through environmental practices in the fashion industry: the moderating effect of internationalisation and the influence of collaboration. Prod. Plan. Control **28**(3), 190–201 (2017)
19. Macchion, L., Fornasiero, R., Vinelli, A.: Supply chain configurations: a model to evaluate performance in customised productions. Int. J. Prod. Res. **55**(5), 1386–1399 (2017)
20. Voss, C., Tsikriktsis, N., Frohlich, M.: Case research in operations management. Int. J. Oper. Prod. Manag. **22**(2), 195–219 (2002)
21. Yin, R.K.: Case Study Research: Design and Methods, 2nd edn. Sage, Thousand Oaks (1994)
22. Eisenhardt, K.M.: Building theories from case study research. Acad. Manag. Rev. **14**(4), 532–550 (1989)
23. Eisenhardt, K.M.: Graebner, M.E: Theory building from cases: opportunities and challenges. Acad. Manag. J. **50**(1), 25–32 (2007)
24. New, S.: The transparent supply chain. Harvard Bus. Rev. **88**, 1–5 (2010)
25. Bevilacqua, M., Ciarapica, F.E., Giacchetta, G.: Business process reengineering of a supply chain and a traceability system: A case study. J. Food Eng. **93**, 13–22 (2009)
26. Engelseth, P.: Food product traceability and supply network integration. J. Bus. Ind. Market. **24**(5/6), 421–430 (2009)
27. Zhu, Q., Sarkis, J., Geng, Y.: Green supply chain management in China: pressures, practices and performance. Int. J. Oper. Prod. Manag. **25**(5), 449–468 (2005)
28. Papetti, P., Costa, C., Antonucci, F., Figorilli, S., Solaini, S., Menesatti, P.: A RFID web-based infotracing system for the artisanal Italian cheese quality traceability. Food Control **27**(1), 234–241 (2012)
29. Fornasiero, R., Brondi, C., Collatina, D.: Proposing an integrated LCA-SCM model to evaluate the sustainability of customisation strategies (2017)
30. Fiorentin, E., Contiero, E.: Analysing the features of modules and interfaces across the small consulting firms. In 5th World Conference on P & OM, Havana (2016)
31. Lion, A., Macchion, L., Danese, P., Vinelli, A.: Sustainability approaches within the fashion industry: the supplier perspective. Supply Chain Forum: An Int. J. **17**(2), 95–108 (2016). Taylor & Francis

Digitization in the Oil and Gas Industry: Challenges and Opportunities for Supply Chain Partners

Arda Gezdur(✉) and Jyotirmoyee Bhattacharjya

Institute of Transportation and Logistics Studies, The University of Sydney, Sydney, NSW 2006, Australia
{arda.gezdur,jyotirmoyee.bhattacharjya}@sydney.edu.au

Abstract. Declining oil prices have made it necessary for oil and gas companies to scrutinize their operations and associated costs. The increase in data richness from the digitization of supply chain processes could help these companies manage risks, and increase collaboration and profitability. This paper explores the challenges and opportunities for oil and gas industry in this context.

Keywords: Supply chain digitization · Supply visibility · Supply chain integration · Oil and gas

1 Introduction

Oil and gas are key sources of energy that provide a foundation for global economic growth. Firms in the oil and gas industry require complex machinery and a large amount of capital investment. Thus, there are huge barriers for other companies wishing to enter the industry. Over the years, the industry has experienced high profitability so digitization has largely been a "nice-to-have". However, the recent fall in oil prices due to increasing supply alternatives and slower growth in demand provides motivation for companies to focus on leaner operations and cost reduction.

Oil and gas supply chains are composed of segmented and discrete data hubs. There is little transparency across entities in the supply chain. Even within companies, data is stored and managed separately by different divisions and there is discontinuity in process flows [15]. Decisions are taken based on disparate spreadsheets without consideration of the full picture. Appropriate digitization strategies could help with supply chain integration and information sharing between suppliers, transporters, storage facilities and customers.

2 Supply Chain Digitization in the Oil and Gas Industry

The need for supply chain digitization and the potential benefits have received growing attention in the literature ([12, 14, 17–19]). Current trends in the digitization of supply chains include 3D printing, Uberization, internet of technologies, cloud computing, advanced robotics and drones [7]. The oil and gas industry can be regarded as a

L.M. Camarinha-Matos et al. (Eds.): PRO-VE 2017, IFIP AICT 506, pp. 97–103, 2017.
DOI: 10.1007/978-3-319-65151-4_9

'latecomer industry' [1] in this context. The literature on digitization and supply chain visibility for the oil and gas sector is scarce and diverse. A clear pathway is needed for evolution towards a highly efficient digital ecosystem in the oil and gas industry. Studies on the digitization of supply chains focus on integrating operational technology systems with information technology systems using big data [5]. Use of big data and integration of operational and information technologies are crucial for digitization of supply chains [6].

Digital transformation projects can take considerable effort and time. For instance, a supervisory control and data acquisition (SCADA) project undertaken by Encana in the United States was undertaken over a 12-year period [1]. As an upstream company, Encana senior managers had sought different alternatives for responding to price volatility and reducing production costs by seeking unconventional sources of natural gas. This project helped Encana improve supply chain visibility by embedding digital technologies to integrate its data and establish new information systems policies.

Although the upstream oil companies are not new to big data analytics, most of them are in preliminary stages of implementing relevant technologies [8]. Companies are benefitting from the sensors embedded in their drilling operations and are working on integrating this data with their supply chain information systems. Oil and gas companies need to carry out a gap analysis before investing on digitization. Furthermore, these companies need to create new strategies to utilize the big data for their decision making processes.

The extent of digitization within individual companies influences the digitization within the overall supply chain. Furthermore, supply chain collaboration between the companies also influences and improves companies' performances [21]. Supply chain collaboration is also directly linked with interorganizational dependencies, as past collaboration activities can be used as a basis for defining the dependencies. Among the different types of interorganizational dependencies, sequential and reciprocal dependencies matter for oil and gas companies. If companies in a supplier-customer relation agree to use a specific resource and if the product of one is a raw material for the other company, the arrangement is described as sequential dependency. In such a dependency, the technologies of the supplier and customer companies need to be linked. In reciprocal dependency, the resources are shared in no particular sequential order and in a many-to-many type of dependency to increase collaborative advantage [16]. Oil and gas companies can share onshore and offshore facilities and logistics infrastructure. The extent of dependency can vary across different countries and practices are not consistent throughout the globe. Furthermore, these companies are familiar with linked and complex technologies for information sharing. Thus the interorganizational dependency of the oil and gas companies is sequential or reciprocal varying across different continents throughout the world. When discussing the levels of digitization in companies in the oil and gas industry as a whole, we need to consider upstream and downstream operations separately. Due to narrower profit margins and direct relation with end customers, downstream oil and gas companies have started using digitization strategies earlier than the upstream companies. The past, present and potential future of digitization in oil and gas are summarized in Table 1.

Table 1. Developments in digitization for upstream and downstream companies (Based on [2])

	Upstream	Downstream
Past	Information technology has traditionally not been seen as an essential element of operations	Sensors available but information stored in discrete units
Present	Developing powerful new capabilities to benefit from smarter exploration, easier capture, safer operations and much better utilized labor	Embedded smart sensors in vessels, tanks, compressors, and turbines send real-time data to control rooms in which a handful of experts can monitor processes and provide diagnostics
Future	Dealing with fluid conditions. Tracking the operations to increase operator safety	Connecting biometric data to improve operator safety and in enabling intelligent materials movement within facilities

3 Supply Chain Visibility in the Oil and Gas Industry

The aim of digitization projects is ultimately to improve supply chain visibility. Oil and gas companies need to set the goal as virtualization of a supply chain with the following attributes [15]:

- Complete horizontal integration in which data from feedstock to product trading are integrated
- Achieving strategic fit through convergence in strategy, planning and scheduling
- Modularity to enable flexibility in implementation stage
- Scalability so that the applications are suitable for the most simple or complex supply chains
- Interactivity for collecting effective customer feedback
- Real time optimization speed with direct links to online plant optimization.

Supply chain visibility increases if the company has more control on its supply chain. Fully integrated companies have better control over their supply chains and access to customer feedback [11]. This feedback in turn can influence the quality of their upstream processes. The major Norwegian oil company, Statoil, considered outsourcing five processes: routing of supply vessels, daily coordination of the flow of supplies, performance evaluation of suppliers and logistics providers, problem solving and conflict negotiation and influencing and improving the supply chain [4]. They used transactional cost analysis to understand the effects of outsourcing each of these processes and found that only outsourcing the routing of supply vessels generate a substantial advantage. Although by outsourcing the company can concentrate on its core competencies, it stood to lose visibility into transaction-specific data as well as control over its supply chain.

Supply chain visibility is closely linked with the agility and competitiveness of companies. Lean processes create agility and companies need to reduce waste in their operations to be lean [3]. Agile companies outperform others and thus gain competitive advantage.

Companies in the oil and gas industry employ various software systems for managing their supply chains. However, most solution providers focus only on supply chain management (SCM) or enterprise resource planning (ERP) solutions. Thus, substantial effort may be needed to integrate disparate SCM and ERP solutions. Furthermore, only a few of the SCM software packages incorporate real-time vehicle routing and scheduling (VRS) capabilities. To develop a real-time end-to-end, digital ecosystem, oil and gas companies need to be able to achieve better integration between their software platforms. The current capabilities of the major software packages in the ERP, SCM and VRS space are shown in Fig. 1 (based on [22–24]).

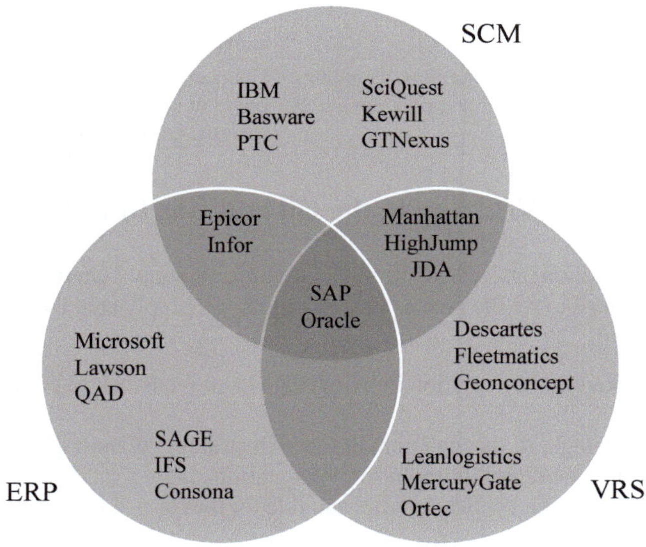

Fig. 1. Capabilities of major software companies in terms of SCM, ERP and VRS (Based on [22–24])

SAP and Oracle are the only two major software vendors which provide all three types of solutions. The choice of solution would depend on different cost and performance considerations for oil and gas companies. When companies choose to use more than one software system, the efficiency of data transfer between the systems becomes vitally important. This necessitates the design of an efficient data integration architecture. Companies need to be able to address problems caused by interruptions in data transfer between the software solutions as well as potential corruptions in the data. The planning and execution processes for a company using multiple software solutions are depicted in Fig. 2. The SCM software requires relevant master and transactional data to generate a plan. This data is stored in ERP system and transferred to SCM system. The SCM software generates a plan after forecasting and optimizing the supply chain drivers. The execution plan generated by the SCM software is then transferred to the ERP system as an order generation, followed by real-time execution and reconciliation. While these processes are running new data is obtained from other data sources like digital data sources and manual entries. The new data is transferred in a batch process to the SCM software to generate the next execution plan. Since the SCM software works discretely and ERP works continuously there is always a gap between the plan and the real-time execution and thus moving the company away from the goal of achieving a fully integrated digital ecosystem. Thus, although it may seem to be cheaper to use multiple software packages at first sight, companies also need to consider the efficiencies that could be gained in a fully integrated digital ecosystem.

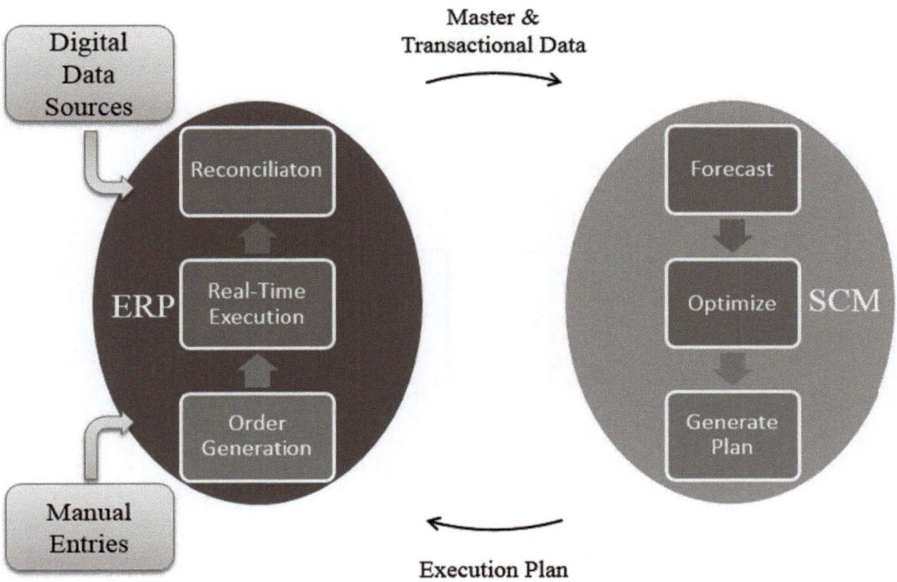

Fig. 2. Planning and execution processes for companies using multiple software solutions

4 Discussions

Digitization forms the backbone for supply chain visibility improvement efforts. As a company invests more in digitization, it starts to get greater insight from its operations. When the company extends its visibility through all operations and removes wasteful information, it starts to become more agile and thus it gains greater ability to respond to the variations in its operations. Supply chain agility and responsiveness are affected by the achievable extent of visibility. In latecomer industries such as oil and gas these changes have been gradual. However, the evolution towards digital ecosystems requires greater intensiveness in digitization efforts among all key players in the supply chain. Figure 3 summarizes these stages in digital evolution. Stage 1 involves digitization efforts and resultant visibility. Stage 2 involves the achievement of agility and responsiveness. Stage 1 and Stage 2 do not represent single instances in time as digitization efforts continue over the period of years and have changing influence on Stage 2. Stage 3 involves a final stage of evolution into a digital ecosystem through the contributions and collaboration of all relevant players in the supply chain.

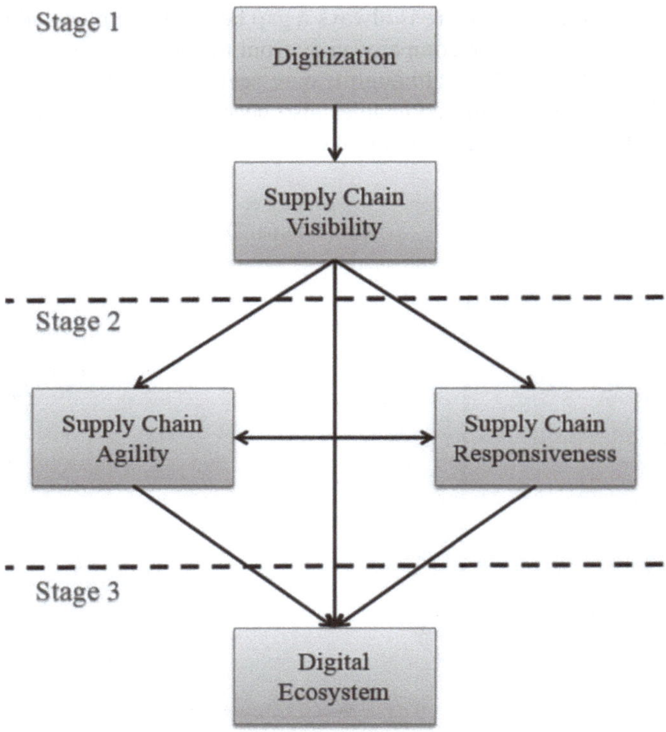

Fig. 3. Supply chain evolution toward digital ecosystem for oil and gas industry

The first author's industry experience and the previous business and academic literature suggest that the oil and gas industry has begun major digitization initiatives. These efforts are far more advanced in the downstream context.

5 Conclusions

Oil and gas companies have understood the importance of digitization and are improving their supply chains by employing digital strategies, using smart manufacturing, designing digital business models and using data analytics as core competencies. A majority of these companies are only at the first stage of the evolution toward a digital ecosystem and are working on their visibility improvement efforts. These companies need to augment their efficiency in exchanging information, increase transparency and remove the friction in their information flow. The development of flexible digital ecosystems involves companies which employ virtualized processes, virtualized customer interfaces, and collaborate with other firms in the industry. However, there is no one-size-fits-all solution for oil and gas supply chains across the world with the increasing speed of digitization and the nature of technologies adopted. Academic researchers have a role to play here in observing and analyzing current efforts, participating in the development of innovative solutions and informing industry of successes, failures and contextual drivers.

References

1. Kohli, R., Johnson, S.: Digital transformation in latecomer industries: CIO and CEO leadership lessons from encana oil & Gas (USA) Inc. MIS Q. Exec. **10**, 141–157 (2011)
2. Strategy. http://www.strategyand.pwc.com/reports/industry4.0
3. Yusuf, Y.Y., Gunasekaran, A., Musa, A., Dauda, M., El-Berishy, N.M., Cang, S.: A relational study of supply chain agility, competitiveness and business performance in the oil and gas industry. Int. J. Prod. Econ. **147**, 531–543 (2014)
4. Aas, B., Buvik, A., Cakic, D.: Outsourcing of logistics activities in a complex supply chain: a case study from the norwegian oil and gas industry. Int. J. Procure. Manage. **1**, 280–296 (2008)
5. Tapping the Power of Big Data for the Oil and Gas Industry, IBM Company (2013)
6. Hamzeh, H.: Application of Big Data in Petroleum Industry (2016)
7. Forbes Logistics and Transportation. https://www.forbes.com/sites/kevinomarah/2016/11/17/digitization-in-supply-chain-five-key-trends/
8. Baaziz, A., Quoniam, L.: How to use big data technologies to optimize operations in upstream petroleum industry. Int. J. Innov. **1**, 19–25 (2013)
9. Henriette, E., Feki, M., Boughzala I.: The shape of digital transformation: a systematic literature review. In: MCIS 2015 Proceedings, vol. 10, pp. 1—13 (2015)
10. Trkman, P., Stemberger, M., Jakli, J., Groznik, A., Indihar, M., Temberger, S.: Process approach to supply chain integration. Supply Chain Manage. Int. J. **12**, 116–128 (2007)
11. Chima, C., Hills, D.: Supply-chain management issues in the oil and gas industry. J. Bus. Econ. Res. (JBER) **5**, 27–36 (2011)
12. Katz, R., Koutroumpis, P., Callorda, F.M.: Using a digitization index to measure the economic and social impact of digital agendas. Info **16**, 32–44 (2014)
13. Xue, L., Zhang, C., Ling, H., Zhao, X.: Risk mitigation in supply chain digitization: system modularity and information technology governance. J. Manage. Inf. Syst. **30**(1), 325–352 (2013)
14. Francis, V.: Supply chain visibility: lost in translation? Supply Chain Manage. Int. J. **13**, 180–184 (2008)
15. Lasschuit, W., Thijssen, N.: Supporting supply chain planning and scheduling decisions in the oil and chemical industry. Comput. Chem. Eng. **28**, 863–870 (2004)
16. Kumar, K., Van Dissel, H.G.: Sustainable collaboration: managing conflict and cooperation in interorganizational systems. MIS Q. **20**, 279–300 (1996)
17. Prater, E., Biehl, M., Smith, M.A.: International supply chain agility — tradeoffs between flexibility and uncertainty. Int. J. Oper. Prod. Manage. **21**, 823–839 (2001)
18. Gunasekaran, A., Lai, K.H., Cheng, T.C.E: Responsive supply chain: a competitive strategy in a networked economy. Omega **36**, 549–564 (2008)
19. ATKearney. http://www.atkearney.com.au/documents/10192/6500433/Digital+Supply+Chains.pdf/
20. Gartner. http://www.gartner.com/technology/topics/digital-ecosystems.jsp
21. Cao, M., Zhang, Q.: Supply chain collaboration: impact on collaborative advantage and firm performance. J. Oper. Manage. **29**, 163–180 (2011)
22. Modern Materials Handling. http://www.mmh.com/article/top_20_software_suppliers
23. Enterprise Innovation. https://www.enterpriseinnovation.net/files/whitepapers/top_10_erp_vendors.pdf
24. Gartner. https://www.gartner.com/doc/3452617/market-guide-vehicle-routing-scheduling

Manufacturing Ecosystem Collaboration

The AUTOWARE Framework and Requirements for the Cognitive Digital Automation

Elias Molina[1(✉)], Oscar Lazaro[1], Miguel Sepulcre[2], Javier Gozalvez[2], Andrea Passarella[3], Theofanis P. Raptis[3], Aleš Ude[4], Bojan Nemec[4], Martijn Rooker[5], Franziska Kirstein[6], and Eelke Mooij[7]

[1] Innovalia Association, Bilbao, Spain
{emolina,olazaro}@innovalia.org

[2] Universidad Miguel Hernández de Elche, Avda. Universidad s/n, 03202 Elche, Spain
{msepulcre,j.gozalvez}@umh.es

[3] Institute of Informatics and Telematics, National Research Council, 56124 Pisa, Italy
{andrea.passarella,theofanis.raptis}@iit.cnr.it

[4] Department of Automatics, Biocybernetics, and Robotics, Jožef Stefan Institute, Jamova 39, 1000 Ljubljana, Slovenia
{ales.ude,bojan.nemec}@ijs.si

[5] TTTech Computertechnik, 1040 Vienna, Austria
martijn.rooker@tttech.com

[6] Blue Ocean Robotics, Odense, Denmark
fk@blue-ocean-robotics.com

[7] PWR Pack, Maxwellstraat 41, 6716 BX Ede, Netherlands
Mooij@pwr-pack.nl

Abstract. The successful introduction of flexible, reconfigurable and self-adaptive manufacturing processes relies upon evolving traditional automation ISA-95 automation solutions to adopt innovative automation pyramids. These new approaches target the integration of data-intensive cloud and fog-based edge computing and communication digital manufacturing processes from the shop-floor to the factory to the cloud. The integration and operation of the required ICT, automation and robotic technologies and platforms is particularly challenging for manufacturing SMEs, which account for more than 80% of manufacturing companies in Europe. This paper presents an insight into the business and operational processes, which motivate the development of a digital cognitive automation framework for collaborative robotics and modular manufacturing systems particularly tailored to SME operations and needs; i.e. the AUTOWARE Operative System. To meet the requirements of both large and small firms this paper elaborates on the smart integration of well-established SME friendly digital frameworks such as the ROS supported robotic Reconcell framework, the FIWARE-enabled BEinCPPS Cyber Physical Production framework and the OpenFog compliant TAPPS hardware framework.

Keywords: Collaborative robotics · Cyber-Physical systems · Modular manufacturing systems · Requirements engineering · Smart factory

L.M. Camarinha-Matos et al. (Eds.): PRO-VE 2017, IFIP AICT 506, pp. 107–117, 2017.
DOI: 10.1007/978-3-319-65151-4_10

1 Introduction and Background

Manufacturing is the second most important sector in terms of small and medium-sized enterprises' (SMEs) employment and value added in Europe [1]. Over 80% of the total number of manufacturing companies is constituted by SMEs, which represent 59% of total employment in this sector. In a global competition arena, companies need to respond quickly and economically feasible to the market requirements. In terms of market trends, a growing product variety and mass customization are leading to demand-driven approaches. It is, therefore, important that production plants can handle small lot sizes and are able to quickly apply changes in product design. In this regard, optimization of manufacturing operations is a major objective for industry. Yet, it still seems difficult for SMEs to understand the driving forces behind digitalization and how they can make use of the vast variety of individualized products and solutions to digitize their manufacturing process, making them cognitive and smart. Moreover, as SMEs intend to adopt data-intensive collaborative robotics and modular manufacturing systems, making their advanced manufacturing processes more competitive, they face the problem to seamlessly connect their physical automation processes with their digital counter parts, leading to difficult and costly digital platform adoption.

This paper is organized as follows. Section 2 reviews the state of the art of the main building blocks behind cognitive digital automation processes. Next, the requirements towards cognitive digital automation are discussed in Sect. 3; along with the details about the AUTOWARE framework. Finally, Sect. 4 concludes the paper.

2 State of the Art

The aim of this Section is to revise the state of the art in terms of both industry 4.0 reference architectures and the five pillars that support the development of cognitive digital manufacturing systems: (1) reconfigurable collaborative robotised capabilities, (2) resilient time sensitive (wireless) communications and data distribution, (3) extension of automation equipment for app-ized operation (open trusted platforms), (4) open service development for added value cognitive industrial services and (5) cross-layer security and certification.

2.1 Industry 4.0 Reference Architectures

With regards to the interoperability of automation systems, the ANSI/ISA-95 and, later, the IEC 62264 standards define a hierarchical model that has been largely used as a reference for manufacturing systems, as well as for specifying interfaces to connect enterprise systems and control operations. Several standards are upon the ANSI/ISA-95, such as the ISO 15746, which is focused on the integration of advanced process control and optimization capabilities for manufacturing systems. However, instead of hierarchical architectures, the industry is moving toward flexible structures, where functions are distributed throughout multiple IT networks and interact across different control levels, as promoted by PathFinder and ScorpiuS projects. As a representative example, the

Reference Architecture Model Industrie 4.0 (RAMI 4.0) is a metamodel that integrates the production system life cycle with a functional control hierarchy, by combining different standards, such as the IEC 62264 or the IEC TS 62832 standard "for the Digital Factory", which defines a framework to specify a factory using digital representation of assets. RAMI 4.0 is especially focused on the process and manufacturing industries, unlike other reference architectures, such as the Industrial Internet Consortium Reference Architecture (IIRA) or the IoT driven SmartM2 M (ETSI), in which manufacturing is just one of the applicable sector (a vertical domain). A thorough review of current manufacturing standards is given in [2], which states that "existing manufacturing standards are far from being sufficient for the service-oriented smart manufacturing ecosystem". Emerging technologies upon which future smart manufacturing systems will rely is described below.

2.2 Cognitive Digital Automation Enabling Platforms

By definition of the U.S. Department of Energy's Advanced Manufacturing Office, "Smart Manufacturing is a network data-driven process that combines innovative automation and advanced sensing and control. Cognitive manufacturing integrates manufacturing intelligence in real-time across an entire production operation while minimizing energy, material use, and costs" [3]. In contrast to traditional automation, in which work cells are generally isolated from each other and based on a static production schedule, advanced manufacturing aims to optimize the production processes and schedules by adopting flexible configurations. With that goal in mind, new monitoring, coordination and communication functions are being increasingly integrated into modern production control systems. "Cognitive Factory" term appeared for the first time in 2009 [4], where the authors identified complex adaptive systems to react autonomously and flexibly to changes. Thus, a Cognitive Factory performs adaptive responses by continuously extracting information and properties from physical objects (e.g., machines, work pieces, etc.) and production processes. Furthermore, besides implementing machine learning and predictive management capabilities, smart factories must rely on reliable networks both at the shop-floor and the enterprise-wide level, and on robots that autonomously adapt to dynamic environmental changes.

2.2.1 Reconfigurable Work Cells

Flexibility of individual work cells has been a research topic for some years [5]. Moreover, the ability of fast reconfiguration of the work cell [6] turns to be even more important. Even more attractive is the possibility of partial or total automatic reconfiguration of the work cells. In such case, robots do not only play the role of universal manufacturing tools, but they are able of automatically reconfiguring the entire work cell layout, including their own base position. This challenge is addressed, for example, in the ReconCell project (http://www.reconcell.eu/), which aims to propose low cost, flexible integrated software and hardware production platform, which will enable quick setup and automatic reconfiguration (see Fig. 1). It incorporates state of the art technologies, such as programming-by-demonstration, adaptive force control, accurate 3D vision sensors, reconfigurable passive elements, intuitive visual programming supported by simulation, use of interchangeable agents based on plug-and-produce approach and optimal gripper design supported by 3D printing technology.

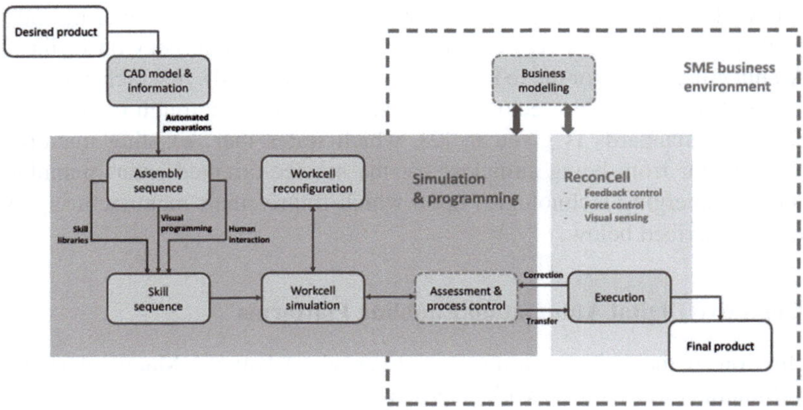

Fig. 1. Block diagram sketches ReconCell workflow for new product preparation.

2.2.2 Resilient Industrial Wired and Wireless Communication Networks

Until now, no real-time communication has been supported in IEEE standardized Ethernet, which caused the emergence of proprietary modifications for industrial automation. To overcome **interoperability** problems, the IEEE Time-Sensitive Networking (TSN) task group is standardizing real-time functionality in Ethernet. Moreover, OPC UA (Open Platform Communication Unified Architecture) has been identified as the reference standard for Industry 4.0. Besides, the Publish/Subscribe enhancement for OPC UA allows for multicast transmission between sensors, machines and the cloud, which combined with IEEE TSN makes the vision of open, real-time machine to machine communication a reality for multi-vendor applications.

In addition, industrial wireless networks play a key role in the **cost and time** reduction for deployment of **plug-and-produce** systems, enabling the connectivity of mobile systems and robots. However, mission-critical applications, demand **reliable and low-latency communications**. **WirelessHART and ISA100.11a** are the most common wireless standards for automation and control systems. They are based on the IEEE 802.15.4 physical and Medium Access Layers, use Time Division Multiple Access (TDMA) combined with Frequency Hopping, and both implement a centralized management architecture. **WirelessHART** reliability, latency or efficiency improvements include multipath routing protocols, link scheduling schemes or relaying and packet aggregation [7]. Furthermore, the interest of IEEE **802.11** in industrial environments started with 802.11e, which allowed prioritization by using the Enhanced Distributed Channel Access (EDCA). 802.11 network reliability enhancements propose the tuning of novel rate adaptation algorithms, and the deactivation of carrier sensing and backoff procedures. More recently, wireless seamless redundancy has been proposed in [8], relying on the IEC 62439-3 Parallel Redundancy Protocol (PRP).

Finally, **4G cellular networks** (based on LTE, Long Term Evolution), initially intended for mobile broadband applications, were not suitable for strict and deterministic industrial QoS requirements. However, factory automation is now a key objective for beyond LTE and 5G networks (3GPP Release 13 onwards); e.g., over-provisioning through instant uplink access (IUA) [9]. Proposals to improve the reliability of cellular transmissions generally focus on the use of spatial and frequency diversity; with novel multi-hop routing diversity being proposed.

2.2.3 Data Management and Elaboration in Large-Scale Industrial Networks

Data-centric operations and decentralization are two fundamental cornerstones of modern industrial automation technologies and form the basis for decision making and control operations [10]. In this context, cloud computing technologies can be used to implement different types of data-centric automation services at reduced costs [11]. However, deploying control-related services in clouds poses significant challenges. For example, jitters become more problematic, as well as a possible loss of control over the data by the legitimate owners. Therefore, it is widely recognized that centralized solutions to collect data in industrial environments are not adequate. The fact that automation control may span multiple physical locations and include heterogeneous data sources, and the upcoming Internet of Things (IoT) make decentralized data management inevitable. This is one of the aspects where Fog Computing, placed between the cloud and the actual machines or plant, can come into play. This will enable more efficient processing, analysis and storing of the data, thereby reducing the delay in communication between the cloud and the machines and providing opportunities for latency-sensitive applications. Components that realize the fog computing architecture are called fog nodes and are characterized by their non-functional properties like e.g., real-time behavior, reliability, availability, safety and security.

2.2.4 Open Cognitive Industrial Service Development Platforms

The Future Internet (FI) PPP has designed a FI core ICT platform, FIWARE, which is released to the general public as an open source project through the FIWARE Foundation. FIWARE enables software engineers and service providers to develop innovative digital products and infrastructures in a vendor-neutral and cost-effective way. It delivers not only a very rich set of open APIs (i.e., Generic Enablers targeted at a wide range of applications), but a catalogue of open source reference implementations. In fact, many of the current digital manufacturing platforms being developed in Europe [12]; e.g., BEinCPPS, PSYMBIOSYS, NIMBLE, vf-OS, among other projects, are adopting F enablers. As a representative example, the BEinCPPS project applied this paradigm to the manufacturing industry, and it provides a smart manufacturing service development framework that support data exploitation from the shop-floor to the factory to the cloud connecting the 3 domains of the Factory 4.0; i.e. the Smart Factories (Internet-of-Things, IoT), the Digital Factories (Internet-of-Services, IoS) and the Virtual Factories (Internet-of-People, IoP). BEinCPPS provides a RAMI 4.0 compliant blueprint as an integrated bundle of FIWARE Generic Enablers (GE) and Industry 4.0 Specific Enablers (SE) developed in projects such as CREMA, C2NET and FITMAN. FIWARE technologies and open source enablers and implementations provide basic support for typical usage scenarios in their target domain, and can be further customized to fit additional needs.

2.2.5 Cross-Layer Security and Certification

With the convergence of Operational Technology (OT) and Information Technology (IT) systems, manufacturers raise concerns about security and confidentiality risks because data is now exchanged between multiple networks. In this regard, ISO/IEC 2700X standards provide a set of guidelines to perform IT protection, including different techniques to prevent, detect and manage cyber-attacks. For example, cryptography modules, firewalls and access control lists, intrusion prevention/detection systems, anti-virus, or Security Information and Event Management (SIEM) software. A sector-specific perspective can be found in the ISA/IEC 62443 standard, which defines procedures to implement secure automation and control systems. Needless to say, to protect manufacturing lines, it is important to secure machine-to-machine (M2 M) communications by using secure protocols or tunneling schemes, and to enforce integrity and authenticity of sensor data. From the counterpart's perspective, the cryptographic services shall not significantly degrade the performance or availability of industrial control services designed to operate without cryptographic protection.

Regarding certification-related aspects, they are a priority in manufacturing scenarios. Certifying safety and security is simplified by the use of standard-based procedures. ISO 10218-X series are the most relevant safety standards for applications of industrial robots. This series are supplemented by the ISO/TS 15066, which specifies safety requirements for collaborative industrial robot systems and the work environment. From a software point of view, for example, the ISO/IEC 15408 standard is commonly used in software certifications; and the ISO/IEC 25010 is focused on the software quality, dealing with aspects of preserving access to data and their modification.

3 AUTOWARE: A Cognitive Digital Operating System

As discussed above, the number of technologies to be integrated to realize a cognitive automation system is large. AUTOWARE (www.autoware-eu.org) proposes an architecture (Fig. 2) based on intensive piloting and solid technological foundations for development of cognitive manufacturing in autonomous and collaborative robotics as extension of ROS/Reconcell frameworks, and for modular manufacturing solutions based on RAMI 4.0. AUTOWARE acts as an Open Digital Automation Operating System (OS) providing full support for digital automation from shop-floor to the cloud.

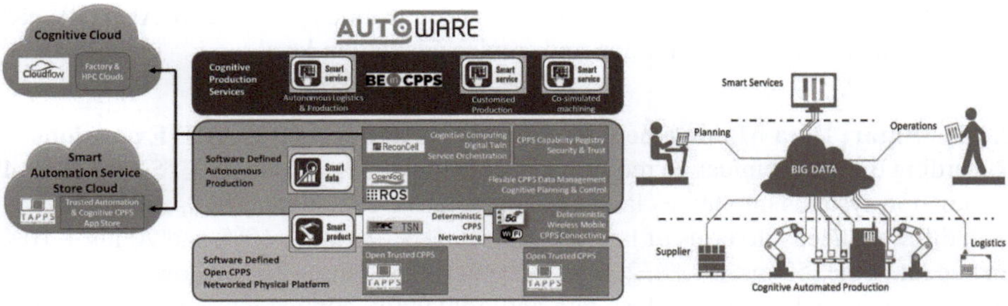

Fig. 2. AUTOWARE reference architecture for cognitive manufacturing.

3.1 AUTOWARE Cognitive Automation Reference Architecture

To facilitate a shift from product-centric to user-centric business models, the layered architecture proposed by the Smart Service Welt initiative defines [13] "smart spaces" where Internet-enabled machines connect to each other, and "smart products" that also encompasses their virtual representations (CPS digital twins). These products know their own manufacturing and usage history and are able to act autonomously. In this architecture, data generated on the networked physical objects are consolidated and processed (smart data) on software-defined platforms, and providers connect to each other via these service platforms to form digital ecosystems. AUTOWARE extends those elements that are critical for the implementation of the autonomy and cognitive features. Specifically, AUTOWARE leverages enablers for deterministic wireless CPPS connectivity (TSN-OPC UA and Fog-enabled analytics) at the **smart product level**. At the **smart data level**, the approach is to develop cognitive planning and control capabilities supported by cloud services and dedicated data management systems, which will contribute to meet the real-time visibility and timing constrains of the planning and control algorithms for autonomous production services. At the **smart service level**, AUTOWARE helps to model and secure trusted CPPS, and their self-configuration policies. In this latter aspect, the incorporation of the TAPPS CPS framework coupled with the provision of a smart automation service store, will pave the way towards an open service market for digital automation solutions *cognitive by-design*. AUTOWARE cognitive OS makes use of a combination of reliable M2 M communications, human-robotics-interaction, modelling & simulation, and cloud-fog based analytics schemes. In addition, considering the mission-critical requirements, this combination is deployed in a secure and safe environment. All this should enable a reconfigurable manufacturing system that enhances business productivity.

3.2 Cognitive Automation Manufacturing Process Requirements and Extensions

The implementation of advanced cognitive manufacturing processes poses challenges in terms of how data should be communicated (latency, reliability) and distributed (availability), and how to react to the working environment (reconfigurability). The following presents two use cases (cognitive-packaging, human-robot collaboration) and associated requirements that motivate the advanced features provided by AUTOWARE at communication, data distribution and service adaptation level.

3.2.1 Smart Data Management Requirements and AUTOWARE Extensions

Regarding the communication requirements of industrial automation. ETSI divides [14] automation systems into three classes (manufacturing cell, factory hall, and plant level) with different needs in terms of latency (5 ms ± 10%, 20 ms ± 10%, and 20 ms ± 10%) and update time (50 ms ± 10%, 200 ms ± 10%, and 500 ms ± 10%). However, all three classes require a 10-9 packet loss rate and a 99.999% application availability. These requirements are confirmed by PWR Pack AUTOWARE use case; a company that develops robotic systems for loading individual products into packaging machines or finished packs into shipping containers. PWR Pack is working on reducing the machine recipe change-over times, and enhance the cognitive and reconfigurability of a packaging line so that it can handle different packaging formats and products with adaptive and auto learning calibration. To this aim, PWR Pack relies on sensor fusion, flexible real-time data processing with programmable hardware and model based analysis and control. Figure 3 illustrates PWR Pack's industrial validation use case that contains four main nodes. The MS (Machine System) handles the product distribution. The HMI (Human Machine Interface) is used by the operators for a day-to-day control using 3D visualization. The PLC (Programmable Logic Controller) controls the servomotors at

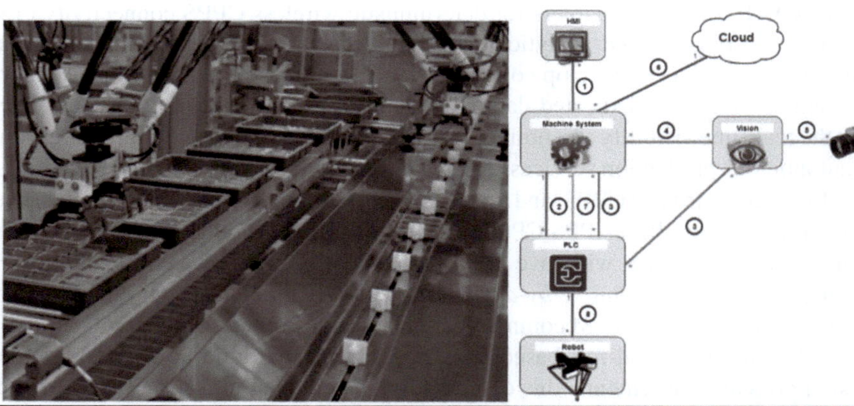

ID	Nodes involved	Data	Max. latency	Data size
1	MS and HMI	Event based data	20 ms	< 20 kb/s
2	MS and PLC	Event based data	10 ms	< 10 kb/s
3	PLC and Vision	Position data	5 ms	< 1 kb/s
4	Vision and MS	Product data (position, orientation…)	10 ms	< 2 kb/s
5	Vision and camera	Image data	5 ms	1-100 Mb per image
6	MS and cloud	Statistical data	100 ms	< 10 kb/s
7	PLC and MS	Recipe and persistent data	20 ms	< 10 kb/s
8	PLC and Robot	Commands	1 ms	< 100 kb/s

Fig. 3. Requirements of the industrial cognitive validation use case by PWR Pack.

robots, conveyors and others, and performs motion tasks and path planning for the robots based on commands received from the MS.

AUTOWARE extensions focus on the management of large amounts of data through smart distribution policies. These policies are based on decentralized cognitive heuristic techniques that replicate data to locations from where they can be accessed when needed within appropriate deadlines. AUTOWARE also provides a data management process that interacts with the routing communication layer (smart product cross-layer approach) to provide efficient data access and end-to-end delay guarantees.

Furthermore, AUTOWARE software-defined autonomous production layer selectively moves data to different network areas and will devise methods on how the data requests will be served, given an underlying routing protocol. The data management module will replicate/store/move data between (i) **(mobile) nodes** in the factory environment (e.g., mobile nodes of operators, nodes installed in work cells, nodes attached to mobile robots, etc.) (ii) **edge nodes** providing storage services, and (iii) **remote cloud storage** services. All the three layers will be used in a synergic way, based on the properties of the data and the requirements of the users requesting it.

3.2.2 AUTOWARE Smart Product Autonomous Adaptation Service Extensions

A truly flexible and reconfigurable work cell should not rely on the specific hardware solution. Moreover, it has to enable quick and transparent change of the specific hardware without applying new programming tools. Thus, the work cell as a basic entity of the flexible production should be unified around the common software architecture. A suitable framework for such an architecture is offered by the Robot Operating System (ROS), which provides tools to create platform independent applications. ROS nodes (i.e., software modules that typically controls a robot, handles vision system, runs simulation system or heavy computing of motion planning, etc.) can communicate directly to each other by passing messages and creating services. AUTOWARE provides an

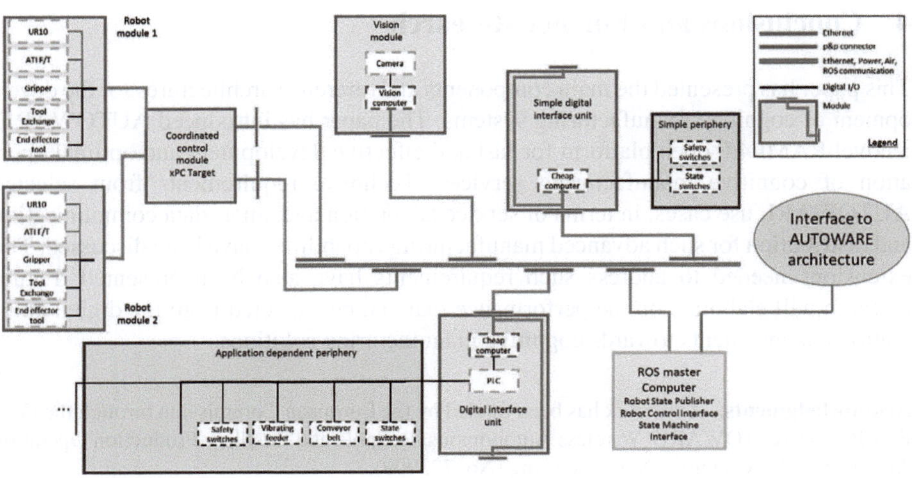

Fig. 4. AUTOWARE ROS-based cognitive reference architecture.

extension (Fig. 4) to the ReconCell software architecture in the form of abstraction to support different robots. The aim is to apply a number of trajectory and feedback control strategies independently of the selected robot, and enable the programming of new strategies via a suitable control interface. For this reason, a real-time server accepts higher-level ROS commands and applies the control strategies to execute the desired robot motion.

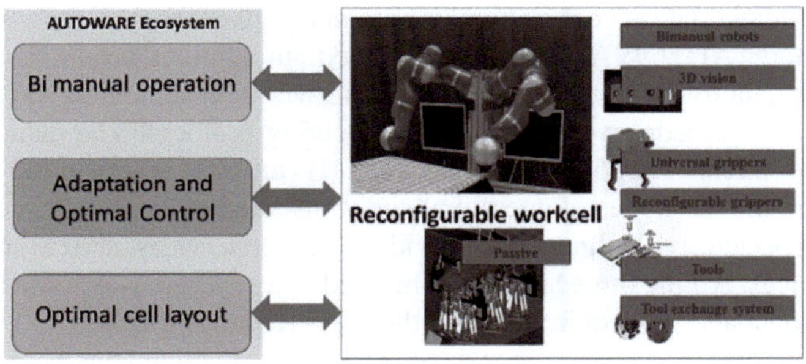

Fig. 5. Enhancement of the existing reconfigurable work cell.

Taking into account the described infrastructure, several enhancements (Fig. 5) are provided by AUTOWARE: autonomous **adaptation of robot trajectories** (improve reinforcement learning and adaptation of the robot skills and policies by more focused search using previous knowledge), **bimanual robot task execution** (provide programming tools to facilitate learning by demonstration), **self-organization and optimal configuration** of the work cell layouts for the given task (simultaneously optimizing both optimal layout design via simulation and search algorithms; while control policies will apply iterative linear quadratic regulator techniques).

4 Conclusions and Further Research

This paper has presented the main components and reference architectures for the development of cognitive manufacturing systems. The paper has introduced AUTOWARE, a novel RAMI 4.0 open platform for fast and effective development and optimal operation of cognitive manufacturing services. Technical requirements from selected AUTOWARE use cases, in terms of service adaptation and smart data communication and distribution for such advanced manufacturing capabilities have been discussed. The extensions needed to address such requirements have also been presented. Future research will elaborate on the performance that can be expected from the digital automation enhancements towards cognitive manufacturing solutions.

Acknowledgments. This work has been funded by the European Commission through the FoF-RIA Project AUTOWARE: Wireless Autonomous, Reliable and Resilient Production Operation Architecture for Cognitive Manufacturing (No. 723909).

References

1. Muller, P., Devnani, S., Julius, J., Gagliardi, D., Marzocchi, C.: Annual Report on European SMEs 2015/2016. European Union (2016)
2. Lu, Y., Morris, K.C., Frechette, S.: Current standards landscape for smart manufacturing systems. National Institute of Standards and Technology, NISTIR (2016)
3. Advanced Manufacturing Office (AMO), U.S. Department of Energy. https://energy.gov/eere/amo/next-generation-manufacturing-processes
4. Zaeh, M.F., Beetz, M., Shea, K., Reinhart, G., Bender, K., Lau, C., Ostgathe, M., Vogl, W., Wiesbeck, M., Engelhard, M., Ertelt, C., Rühr, T., Friedrich, M.: "The Cognitive Factory", in Changeable and Reconfigurable Manufacturing Systems, pp. 355–371. Springer, London (2009)
5. Hedelind, M.: On reconfigurable robotic working cells — a case study. In: Mitsuishi, M., Ueda, K., Kimura, F. (eds.) Manufacturing Systems and Technologies for the New Frontier, pp. 323–328. Springer, London (2008). doi:10.1007/978-1-84800-267-8_66
6. Chen, I.M.: Rapid response manufacturing through a rapidly reconfigurable robotic workcell. Robot. Comput. Integr. Manufact. **17**(3), 199–213 (2001)
7. Sepulcre, M., Gozalvez, J., Coll-Perales, B.: Multipath QoS-driven routing protocol for industrial wireless networks. J. Netw. Comput. Appl. **74**, 121–132 (2016)
8. Cena, G., Scanzio, S., Valenzano, A.: Seamless link-level redundancy to improve reliability of industrial WiFi networks. IEEE Trans. Industr. Inf. **12**(2), 608–620 (2016)
9. Holfeld, B., Wieruch, D., Wirth, T., Thiele, L., Ashraf, S.A., Huschke, J., Aktas, I., Ansari, J.: Wireless communication for factory automation: an opportunity for LTE and 5G systems. IEEE Commun. Mag. **54**(6), 36–43 (2016)
10. Yin, S., Ding, S.X., Xie, X.: A review on basic data-driven approaches for industrial process monitoring. IEEE Trans. Industr. Electron. **61**(11), 6414–6428 (2014)
11. Hegazy, T., Hefeeda, M.: Industrial automation as a cloud service. IEEE Trans. Parallel Distrib. Syst. **26**(10), 2750–2763 (2015)
12. European Factories of the Future Research Association (EFFRA), Platforms for Connected Factories of the Future, Brussels, Belgium (2015)
13. Kagermann, H., Riemensperger, F., Hoke, D., Helbig, J., Stocksmeier, D., Wahlster, W., Schweer, D.: Smart Service Welt: Recommendations for the Strategic Initiative Web-based Services for Businesses. Acatech, Berlin (2014)
14. ETSI TR 102 889-2 V1.1.1, Electromagnetic compatibility and Radio spectrum Matters; System Reference Document; Short Range Devices; Part 2: Technical characteristics for SRD equipment for wireless industrial applications using technologies different from Ultra-Wide Ban (2011)

An Approach for Cloud-Based Situational Analysis for Factories Providing Real-Time Reconfiguration Services

Sebastian Scholze[1(✉)], Kevin Nagorny[1], Rebecca Siafaka[1], and Karl Krone[2]

[1] Institut für angewandte Systemtechnik Bremen GmbH, Wiener Straße 1, 28359 Bremen, Germany
{scholze,nagorny,siafaka}@atb-bremen.de

[2] OAS AG, Caroline-Herschel-Straße 1, 28359 Bremen, Germany
kkrone@oas.de

Abstract. The advances in Information Technology (IT) which allowed the transformation of products into cyber-physical systems (CPS), brought new challenges and opportunities for development in manufacturing. Connected product networks (CPN) which bare more advanced features opposing to regular products, require special resource management and more flexible processes during the whole lifecycle of a product, from conceptualization to development and use. Cloud computing and data analytics enhance the opportunities for reconfiguration and optimization of machines and products, leading to reduced costs for the factories. Situational awareness driven by ontologies, together with Big Data analytics exhibit significant potential for competitive manufacturing that is able to follow the fast-evolving market, nevertheless, with respect to the user and the environment. The current paper suggests an approach for the exploitation of manufacturing context, using sensors and data management techniques in industrial business cases, to achieve reuse of information, resulting to reduced manufacturing waste.

Keywords: Cyber-physical systems · Connected products networks · Cloud computing · Situational awareness · Big data analytics

1 Introduction

Manufacturing of products, nowadays, due to the advances in Information Technologies (IT) that turn products into "smart" devices, and the evolution in device connectivity, becomes increasingly complex. Connected product networks (CPN) and cyber-physical systems (CPS) are bringing new challenges to manufacturing companies. A huge amount of data is produced and new technologies for storage and processing is necessary to cope with this changing condition. Together with this, the increasing diversity of product use and product portfolios, the customer's demand for more customized products and the shorter time-to-market requirements, necessitates flexible manufacturing that can be responsive to the respective context environment. Traditional models of manufacturing,

L.M. Camarinha-Matos et al. (Eds.): PRO-VE 2017, IFIP AICT 506, pp. 118–127, 2017.
DOI: 10.1007/978-3-319-65151-4_11

however, do not exhibit such flexibility, since information flows from product design, over production processes to the manufactured product, unidirectional, leading to "blind" execution of tasks without allowing for adjustment or reconfigurability. Products as well, do not give the opportunity for reconfiguration based on the desired use pattern, failing, in a way, to follow the tendency of the market.

To face these challenges, there is a high need for exploring information from factories and products. Data analyzed from products and machines, will allow for earlier error detection and process optimization. At the same time, the analyzed data can be used already in the design phase of the product lifecycle, leading to reduced manufacturing costs and more robust products.

As shown in Fig. 1, sensor data from the factory and the products will be processed together with situational data and analytics disclosing optimization and reconfiguration opportunities, which will be fed back to the factory and/or product.

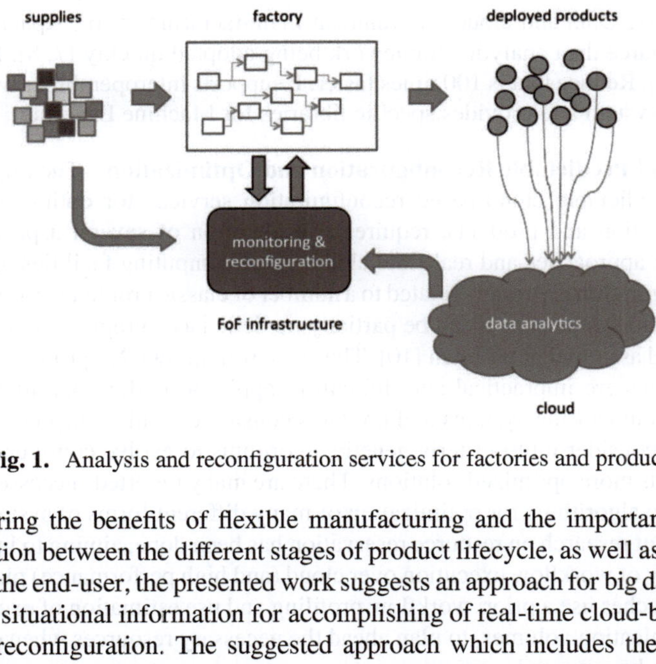

Fig. 1. Analysis and reconfiguration services for factories and products

Considering the benefits of flexible manufacturing and the importance for more communication between the different stages of product lifecycle, as well as between the factory and the end-user, the presented work suggests an approach for big data analytics, considering situational information for accomplishing of real-time cloud-based optimization and reconfiguration. The suggested approach which includes the concepts of predictive analytics, situational awareness, dynamic and predictable reconfiguration/ optimization, cloud computing, and aspects of security, privacy and trust, as well as the benefits from its application in industrial business cases, is described in the following.

2 Overview on State of the Art

Predictive Analytics: Data Management and Analytics, production and operational data come from various data sources. Variety of data types in all forms, from all sources, flow through factory [1, 2]. Big Data Frameworks enable organizations to store, manage and manipulate these vast amounts of disparate data. The Apache Hadoop system is the Big Data standard framework that allows massive data storage in its native form (over HDFS file system), to speed analysis and insight. Hadoop implements its own approach to programming/distributed computing, called Map Reduce [3, 4]. There are many pure Hadoop providers such as Hortonworks, MapR, Pivotal or TeraData. Other Hadoop providers' complete solutions that incorporate their own framework for stream data-processing include AWS Elastic Map Reduce (EMR) with Amazon Kinesis, or Cloudera with Impala. Predictive analytics use data mining analytics, as well as predictive modelling, to anticipate what will likely happen in the future based, on insights gained through descriptive and diagnostic analytics. The ability to predict what is likely to happen next, is essential for improving the overall performance of manufacturing systems, especially operations over products, like maintenance and utilization. Machine Learning is about using patterns found in historical operational data and real-time data to signal what is ahead. Lee et al. describe recent advances and trends in predictive manufacturing systems in Big Data and cloud environment manufacturing [5, 6]. Apache Spark is a new open source data analytics framework being adopted quickly [7, 8]. It is an alternative to Map Reduce that is 100 times faster. It supports interoperability with the wider Hadoop ecosystem and provides specific libraries for Machine Learning.

Dynamic and Predictable Reconfiguration and Optimization: The implementation of timing predictable cloud-based reconfiguration services for optimizing manufacturing production and products, requires consideration of several aspects, including optimization approaches and real-time cloud-based computing facilities. Optimization of any configuration is strongly related to a number of classic problems in multiprocessor and distributed systems, as it can be partially modelled as a graph isomorphism [9], or a generalized assignment problem [10]. Those are well known NP problems. Therefore, exact solutions are impractical and difficult to apply on finding optimizations of the complex manufacturing systems and products considered within the current approach. Instead, we consider multi-criteria genetic algorithms to evolve configurations and to move towards more optimized solutions. There are many reported successes in terms of using genetic algorithms for optimization of many different forms of systems [11].

Significant research on resource reservation has been done, aiming to increase time-predictability of workflow execution over cloud (and high performance) platforms [12]. Many approaches use a priori workflow profiling and use estimation of execution times and communication volumes, to plan ahead the necessary resources when optimization tasks need to be executed.

Situational Awareness is a concept propagated in the domains of Ambient Intelligence and Ubiquitous Computing. It is the idea that computers can be both sensitive and reactive, based on their environment. As situational analysis integrates different knowledge sources and binds knowledge to the user (either human or a system) to guarantee that the understanding is consistent, situation modelling is extensively investigated within Knowledge Management research. Existing research on situational analysis can be classified in two categories: situation-based proactive delivery of knowledge, and capture & utilization of situational knowledge [13].

Current developments in situational-aware systems are mainly directed to the needs of wireless networks and mobile computing [14]. For instance, the middleware solution of Bellavista et al. [15] is ontology-based, concerned with the semantic representation of situations, and personalized service search and retrieval techniques. The need to go beyond situation representation to situation reasoning, classification and dependency is also recognized by Gu et al. [16] and others [17]. Most common approaches to situational modelling are the key-value models, such as the ontology-based models [18]. These provide a rich vocabulary that can be utilized for the representation of situation models. A comparison of different situational modelling techniques is reported by some researchers [19].

Ontologies allow situational modelling at a semantic level, establishing a common understanding of terms, and enabling situational sharing, logic inference, reasoning and reuse in a distributed environment. Shareable ontologies are a fundamental precondition for knowledge reuse, serving as means for integrating problem-solving domain-representation and knowledge-acquisition modules [20], and fit well with the shared situational analysis challenges that will increasingly be encountered in smart factories [21].

Security, Privacy, and Trust: Today, the emerging of Connected Product Networks (CPN) commands increased measures that ensure security in the ICT systems. Those systems, due to their complexity, increasing connectivity, heterogeneity and dynamism, fetch new features that are important to be protected against hostile activities. Traditional security mechanisms, such as firewalls, host and network intrusion detection systems, address-space layout randomization, virtual private networks and encryption of messages, files and disk volumes, which are used for this reason, are inadequate to address the needs that those systems demonstrate.

To provide security in the complex CPN systems, it is necessary to define a *security policy*, namely the allowed and not allowed actions, and develop *security mechanisms* and *assurance activities* that enforce the policy and ensure that this is accordingly implemented and cannot be bypassed or broken. Towards this direction, the concept of *Policy Machine*, work of Ferraiolo et al. [22], is perhaps the frontier in the state-of-the-art. This access control concept, in contrast to the traditional mechanisms, is a flexible approach to enforce a wide variety of policies over distributed systems. Although a recent reference implementation has been made publicly available, it is not yet widely used, proving the lack in applied solutions for security in CPN systems.

3 Proposed Concept

The work presented in this paper is a part of a wider research in which objective is to provide a methodology and a comprehensive ICT solution for cloud-based situational analysis for factories, providing real-time reconfiguration services, allowing for effective extensions of products and existing factory operating systems, for enabling optimization and reconfiguration of products and factories.

The overall proposed reference architecture, which follows the service-oriented architecture (SOA) principles, is illustrated in Fig. 2.

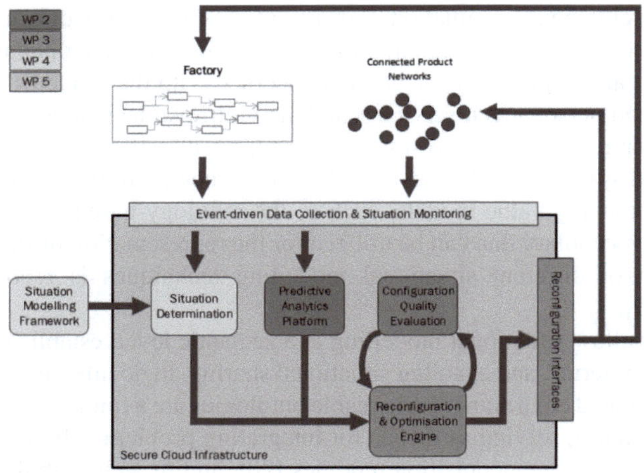

Fig. 2. Technical concept

The components of the proposed system include:

- **Situation Monitoring & Determination:** Services to identify the current situation under which a product/machine is being used or operates. To provide a more sophisticated solution, within the presented approach several mechanisms for checking reliability of the monitored and extracted situation data (applying statistical and reasoning approaches) will be developed. These services will observe activities within the solution.
- **Predictive Analytics Platform:** A new real-time big data framework for manufacturing, a novel architecture based on Kappa architecture approach is proposed instead of the popular Lambda architecture. In the Kappa approach, the main idea is to have an immutable set of records over a stream of processing jobs. It suggests re-calculation of data from an immutable dataset, when the logical process changes, decreasing substantially the processing load and latency. The focus is to avoid the batch, in favor of near-real-time batch processing approach.
- **Reconfiguration and Optimization Engine:** The cloud-based optimization and reconfiguration engine encompasses both reactive optimization (reacting to changes in the system to provide a new configuration) and predictive optimization (planning and predicting likely potential changes in the system functionality), based on past performance and analysis of current configurations, to suggest a range of new configurations before they are required.
  By performing reconfiguration on the optimization engine in the cloud, continuous optimization of a system can be performed, enabling, by far, better reconfiguration control and accuracy, than if performed in either a pre-planned or online manner.
- **Security, Privacy & Trust:** A security, privacy and trust (SPT) framework will be provided to ensure protection of both product and customer data, by implementing a flexible policy-enforcing scheme, suitable for a wide range of factories-of-the-future and product needs. The SPT framework consists of an infrastructure built upon

state-of-the-art existing technologies and tools, extended and integrated seamlessly within the framework of the presented approach. The SPT framework will also provide standard security features, such as monitoring and audit logging.

It is foreseen to package the above described components in portable software-containers – using the de-facto standard Docker – which is supported by most of the established cloud providers. This will allow distributing different components – complete with the necessary runtime infrastructure – to deploy and run them on different cloud infrastructures, without having to reconfigure the component itself.

This approach enables the proposed solution to allow for different deployment modes for the complete solution, leveraging existing cloud infrastructure technologies, such as public clouds, private clouds and mixed clouds.

This will allow users to flexibly adjust deployment scenarios to their needs, especially taking into account the requirements for ensuring the privacy and security of potentially sensitive product and customer data, which can be stored and processed entirely on private clouds.

4 Potential Application and Expected Results

In order to demonstrate the applicability of the proposed approach in the real industrial environment, three different industrial business-case scenarios where developed. The main characteristics of the scenarios follow in the Table 1.

Table 1. Use-case scenarios overview

Domain	Case study	Objectives/technical issues addressed
Control and production systems	Improved Overall Equipment Efficiency (OEE)	Optimize production processes and preventive maintenance activities through reconfiguration, based on big-data analysis in the cloud and thereby improve Overall Equipment Efficiency
Machine tools and control systems	Adaptive machining	Combine process measuring (probing) with high level scripting programming in the CNC, in order to let the process engineer predefine conditional rules for managing and compensating deviation in the electrode wear
Home appliances	Personalization and adaptive control of home appliances	Improved personalization from cloud-based data collection across their connected products Adaptive operation: Re-configuration of home appliances based on environmental variables and/or consumers' behavior

Although, the scenarios focus on different industrial sectors, they all address manufacturing and machine vendors' views, therefore, one business-case scenario applied on a specific industry, is explained in more detail in the following.

In the respective use-case, the company currently provides state-of-the-art services (e.g. continuous improvement, embedded diagnostics, remote diagnostics support and preventive maintenance) with regard to weighing technology, and aims to extend their business in geographically dislocated subsidiaries, suppliers and customer's departments in an innovative organizational form. The focus is to enable improved design/ delivery of the solutions, remote (online) equipment control and disturbance-free, optimal, process operation, increasing the overall equipment efficiency (OEE) of machines/production lines and creating possibilities for new business models (e.g. overtaking full responsibility for process execution).

The company provides diagnostics and maintenance services to the manufacturing process of their customers, using remote access to the control system. The control systems of the company, already include remote monitoring of the processes, so the data from the real processes are used e.g. for diagnostics in dynamically changing production conditions. The company intends, to equip their systems with a number of additional sensors and different ICT solutions enabling remote monitoring of the status of processes and components controlled, and of the system performance, to promptly react to any disturbances, to optimize the maintenance activities, as well as to optimize the production process itself, thereby assuring maximum OEE. The challenging problem to online reconfiguration of a production process, of a highly-customized installation, is to apply services to support both customer staff and (mobile) maintenance staff, enabling effective data mining and integration of data from embedded systems both in the company's control system and other parts of the manufacturing processes (different plants) at the customer. Due to high diversity of customized control and weighing system, the company needs to provide a wide spectrum of services, and these services have often to be adapted to continuously changing customer requirements.

This business case scenario aims to increase OEE of machines/production lines. The scenario will demonstrate the use of the proposed solution to optimize production processes and preventive maintenance activities through reconfiguration based on big-data analysis in the cloud. The aim is to demonstrate the applicability of the approach in the process improvements during run time, and in the control system of the involved company. The control system, which is a high-performance process visualization system for SCADA, is at the same time a control system for the process and production control level (MES). It is optimized for the control and administration of batch-oriented processes, and is particularly suitable for tasks with regard to the weighing technology.

4.1 Validation

In order to ensure reliable validation of the proposed approach, metrics were defined to enable a quantitative assessment of the results achieved. These quantitative metrics include:

- Business metrics (specifically related to improvements in analytics and reconfiguration, business benefits for industrial end users, etc.),

- Technical metrics (requirements upon the software tools and engineering environment) where key measurement will be achievement of the planned Technology Readiness Level (TRL),
- Metrics related to expected results (such as expectations on flexibility of the environment, completeness of the proposed ontology, effectiveness of knowledge/experience provision etc.).

To provide appropriate procedures for the assessment of the proposed solution, an incremental test and assessment strategy if foreseen: laboratory prototype (TRL4), early prototype (TRL5) and full prototype (TRL6).

4.2 Expected Results

The suggested approach is expected to propagate the use of situational information from the factory environment, and along with the exploitation of modern IT solutions in big data analytics, to improve and accelerate manufacturing processes. Situational awareness will allow for more efficient monitoring of resources in material and energy, giving an insight on opportunities where alternative solutions (e.g. different task sequence or the use of different material for specific product lines), based on optimisation metrics, could boost the production keeping the costs at a minimum level. Furthermore, it is expected that the use of cloud infrastructure should impose possible limitations in computational resources from the factory side, supporting parallel processing of vast amount of data, in real time. As a result, complications that might delay the nominal operation of the systems or products, would be revealed in less time, and solutions tailored to the respective working conditions could be proposed, or directly applied when necessary. This should further reduce the costs for maintenance and allow for process adjustability to the changings needs of production. Reuse of manufacturing data from products and machines, as well as from the user's/operator's environment, which is the key characteristic of the suggested approach, should pave the way to a more sustainable user and environmental-friendlier manufacturing, able to conform the challenges (or particularities) of different application-environments.

5 Conclusions

In the fast technologically-evolving era of nowadays, "smart" devices in the form of connected product networks and cyber-physical systems, stress the need for more flexibility in manufacturing of products and machines. The data that such advanced systems produce and use, require more advanced solutions to be able to cope with the amount of (big) data. The application of solutions following the presented approach could pave the way for better information usage, resulting to an optimized production, a more environmental-friendly production, a higher customer satisfaction and cost reduction. Analytics of data can be seen as an enabler for optimization processes that are enabling earlier error detection, optimized maintenance activities, and supporting factories in providing more individualized products and machines.

This paper presented an approach for applying big data analytics combined with situational awareness to provide real-time optimization and reconfiguration opportunities, supporting decision making in all stages of product lifecycle. The applicability of the approach to industry is being demonstrated in three case studies (see Table 1), which cover both the machine and product manufacturing sector.

Although the presented solution is currently under development, the information from the business analysis, concept definition and first laboratory prototypes, revealed important benefits for several actors. Those include optimized machines and products, improvement and cost reduction in the customer support and product maintenance, support in decision making for factories, individualized products for the customers, and more durable products and machines, for both manufacturers and end-users. Therefore, it seems promising that this approach increases the flexibility in manufacturing, and introduces a new concept for exploiting of advanced IT in manufacturing domain.

Acknowledgement. This work is partly supported by the SAFIRE (Cloud based Situational Analysis for Factories providing real-time Reconfiguration Services) project of European Union's Horizon 2020 Framework Program, under the grant agreement no. H2020-FOF-2016.723634. This document does not represent the opinion of the European Community, and the Community is not responsible for any use that might be made of its content.

References

1. Demirkan, H., Delen, D.: Leveraging the capabilities of service-oriented decision support systems: putting analytics and big data in cloud. Decis. Support Syst. **55**(1), 412–421 (2013)
2. Wang, H., Xu, Z., Fujita, H., Liu, S.: Towards felicitous decision making: an overview on challenges and trends of big data. Inf. Sci. **367**, 747–765 (2016)
3. Dean, J., Ghemawat, S.: MapReduce: simplified data processing on large clusters. Commun. ACM **51**(1), 107–113 (2008)
4. Zaharia, M., Xin, R.S., Wendell, P., Das, T., Armbrust, M., Dave, A., Ghodsi, A., et al.: Apache spark: a unified engine for big data processing. Commun. ACM **59**(11), 56–65 (2016)
5. Lee, J., Lapira, E., Bagheri, B., Kao, H.A.: Recent advances and trends in predictive manufacturing systems in big data environment. Manuf. Lett. **1**(1), 38–41 (2013)
6. Lee, J., Bagheri, B., Jin, C.: Introduction to cyber manufacturing. Manuf. Lett. **8**, 11–15 (2016)
7. Zaharia, M., Chowdhury, M., Franklin, M.J., Shenker, S., Stoica, I.: Spark: cluster computing with working sets. HotCloud **10**(10–10), 95 (2010)
8. Barba-Gonzaléz, C., García-Nieto, J., Nebro, A.J., Aldana-Montes, J.F.: Multi-objective big data optimization with jMetal and spark. In: Trautmann, H., Rudolph, G., Klamroth, K., Schütze, O., Wiecek, M., Jin, Y., Grimme, C. (eds.) EMO 2017. LNCS, vol. 10173, pp. 16–30. Springer, Cham (2017). doi:10.1007/978-3-319-54157-0_2
9. Bokhari, S.H.: On the mapping problem. IEEE Trans. Comput. **30**(3), 207–214 (1981)
10. Hölzenspies, P.K., Hurink, J.L., Kuper, J., Smit, G.J.: Run-time spatial mapping of streaming applications to a heterogeneous multi-processor system-on-chip (MPSoC). In: Proceedings of the Conference on Design, Automation and Test in Europe, pp. 212–217. ACM, March 2008
11. Moscato, P.: Memetic algorithms: a short introduction. In: Corne, D., Dorigo, M., Glover, F. (eds.) New Ideas in Optimisation. McGraw-Hill, London (1999)

12. Lecomte, S., Lengellé, R., Richard, C., Capman, F., Ravera, B.: Abnormal events detection using unsupervised one-class SVM-application to audio surveillance and evaluation. In: 2011 8th IEEE International Conference on Advanced Video and Signal-Based Surveillance (AVSS), pp. 124–129. IEEE, August 2011
13. Mazharsolook, E., Scholze, S., Neves-Silva, R., Ning, K.: Enhancing networked enterprise management of knowledge and social interactions. J. Comput. Syst. Eng. **10**(4), 176–184 (2009)
14. Shinde, B.B., Gupta, R.: Use of synchronized context broker cache in cloud. Imperial J. Interdisc. Res. **2**(6), 355–361 (2016)
15. Bellavista, P., Corradi, A., Montanari, R., Stefanelli, C.: A mobile computing middleware for location-and context-aware internet data services. ACM Trans. Internet Technol. (TOIT) **6**(4), 356–380 (2006)
16. Gu, T., Pung, H.K., Zhang, D.Q.: A middleware for building context-aware mobile services. In: 2004 IEEE 59th Vehicular Technology Conference, VTC 2004-Spring, vol. 5, pp. 2656–2660. IEEE, May 2004
17. Yürür, Ö., Liu, C.H., Sheng, Z., Leung, V.C., Moreno, W., Leung, K.K.: Context-awareness for mobile sensing: a survey and future directions. IEEE Commun. Surv. Tutorials **18**(1), 68–93 (2016)
18. Moore, P., Hu, B., Wan, J.: Smart-context: a context ontology for pervasive mobile computing. Comput. J. **53**(2), 191–207 (2010)
19. Bettini, C., Brdiczka, O., Henricksen, K., Indulska, J., Nicklas, D., Ranganathan, A., Riboni, D.: A survey of context modelling and reasoning techniques. Pervasive Mob. Comput. **6**(2), 161–180 (2010)
20. Ziplies, S., Scholze, S., Stokic, D., Krone, K.: Service-based knowledge monitoring of collaborative environments for user-context sensitive enhancement. In: 2009 IEEE International Technology Management Conference (ICE), pp. 1–8. IEEE, June 2009
21. Scholze, S., Barata, J., Stokic, D.: Holistic context-sensitivity for run-time optimization of flexible manufacturing systems. Sensors **17**(3), 455 (2017)
22. Ferraiolo, D., Gavrila, S., Jansen, W.: Policy machine: features, architecture, and specification. NISTIR 7987, National Institute of Standards and Technology, Gaithersburg, Maryland, 109 (2014)

A Proposal of Decentralised Architecture for Optimised Operations in Manufacturing Ecosystem Collaboration

Pavlos Eirinakis[1], Jorge Buenabad-Chavez[2], Rosanna Fornasiero[3(✉)], Haluk Gokmen[4], Julien-Etienne Mascolo[5], Ioannis Mourtos[1], Sven Spieckermann[6], Vasilis Tountopoulos[7], Frank Werner[8], and Robert Woitsch[9]

[1] Athens University of Economics and Business, Athens, Greece
Peir@Aueb.Gr
[2] University of Manchester, Manchester, UK
jorge@Manchester.Ac.Uk
[3] ITIA-CNR, Milan, Italy
rosanna.fornasiero@Itia.Cnr.It
[4] Arcelik A.S., Istanbul, Turkey
Haluk.Gokmen@Arcelik.Com
[5] Centro Ricerche Fiat Scpa, Turin, Italy
Julienetienne.Mascolo@Crf.It
[6] Simplan AG, Maintal, Germany
Sven.Spieckermann@Simplan.De
[7] Athens Technology Center S.A., Chalandri, Greece
V.Tountopoulos@Atc.Gr
[8] Software AG, Saarbrücken, Germany
Frank.Werner@Softwareag.Com
[9] BOC Asset Management Gmbh, Vienna, Austria
Robert.Woitsch@boc-eu.com

Abstract. This paper describes an innovative approach to adopt the next-generation manufacturing paradigm based on flexible production units and eco-systems that can be quickly reprogrammed to provide fast time-to-market responses to global consumer demand, address mass-customisation needs and bring life to innovative products. The approach utilises the capabilities offered by digitalisation to facilitate (i) in-depth (self-) monitoring of machines and processes, (ii) decision support and decentralised (self-) adjustment of production, (iii) effective collaboration of the different IoT-connected machines with tools, services and actors (iv) seamless communication of information and decisions from and to the plant floor and (v) efficient interaction with value chain partners. The paper presents the conceptual architecture under development to support those functionalities for two specific domains in manufacturing.

Keywords: Decentralized platforms · Process optimization · Simulation · Multi-layer platform

L.M. Camarinha-Matos et al. (Eds.): PRO-VE 2017, IFIP AICT 506, pp. 128–137, 2017.
DOI: 10.1007/978-3-319-65151-4_12

1 Introduction

Industry 4.0 or the fourth industrial revolution [1] is the next developmental stage in the organisation and management of industrial processes and the entire manufacturing value chain. By blending the real and the virtual production world through digitalisation, companies will be able to connect all parts of the production process: machines, products, systems, and people. ICT-based systems and service platforms are already playing a major role in this transformation, enabling some forms of monitoring, analysis, simulation, optimization and control of production entities and processes. This is possible through the creation of a virtual copy of the physical world that facilitates decentralised structures of Cyber-Physical Systems (CPS)/Smart Objects (SO). Over the Internet-of-Things (IoT), CPSs communicate and cooperate with each other and humans in real-time. Via the Internet-of-Services (IoS), both internal and cross-organisational services are offered and utilised by participants of the value chain [2].

Such technologies have extensively been presented in the literature and have been the subject of various projects in application domains such as healthcare, energy grids and manufacturing. There are already related cloud offerings by Bosch for the smart office [3], and similar offerings by IBM [4], and Microsoft [5] among others.

The main contribution of the DISRUPT framework is a comprehensive solution to automation of vertical and horizontal operations and decision making for specific use cases in two project partner companies in the automotive and white goods sectors. We have already collected the requirements from these large companies and have developed the target use cases documentation. This paper presents the conceptual architecture to support these use cases. The architecture unifies previously separate production environments into a collaborative virtual ecosystem that seamlessly integrates cyber-physical operations, data analytics and decision support, while also incorporating the structural characteristics of the entire value chain. The architecture is currently being designed considering various reference architectures. We present its main modules in Sect. 3. Main design goals include: be a multi-sided, cloud-based platform that will enable those companies to reduce time, costs or resource consumption and to respond to unexpected events, fluctuations in consumer demand, massively customised products and global competition. It will facilitate the adoption of ICT-enabled innovation in manufacturing by vertically unifying the automation hierarchy of production systems, from IoT and sensors to ERP, MES and SCADA and from advanced analytics tools to production schedulers and capacity planners, all under a seamless data-intensive modelling approach. This will be implemented through modular, decentralised production topologies, empowering Smart Objects with analytics, simulation and optimisation tools and integrating them within a unified monitoring, control and decision support system, thus enabling them to act as intelligent autonomous agents inherent to the plant's virtual production model.

2 Vision and Requirements

In the traditional rigid factory, mass-production is the goal and cost-effectiveness is the drive; this has led many manufacturers to relocate to lower cost regions, and others to totally outsource their production. The new era of manufacturing asks for optimised plants and manufacturing chain networks, transforming them into profitable innovation centers. It requires flexible factories that can be quickly "reprogrammed" to provide faster time-to-market responding to global consumer demand, effectively addressing mass-customisation needs and bringing life to innovative new products. It needs transparent production processes that are responsive to changes or unexpected events originating throughout the value chain. It combines information, technology and human intellect, fundamentally changing how products are invented, manufactured, shipped and sold, materialising an interconnected, efficient manufacturing ecosystem. In that regard, the traditional automation pyramid with its layered, compartmentalised structure of automation systems seems unable to accommodate this transformation.

The proposed decentralized platform aims at disrupting the traditional automation pyramid (Fig. 1) by utilising the capabilities offered by modern ICT to facilitate (i) in-depth (self-) monitoring of machines and processes, (ii) decision support and decentralised (self-) adjustment of production, (iii) effective collaboration of the different IoT-connected machines and devices with tools, services and actors (iv) seamless communication of information, knowledge, and decisions from and to the plant floor and (v) efficient interaction with value chain partners [2].

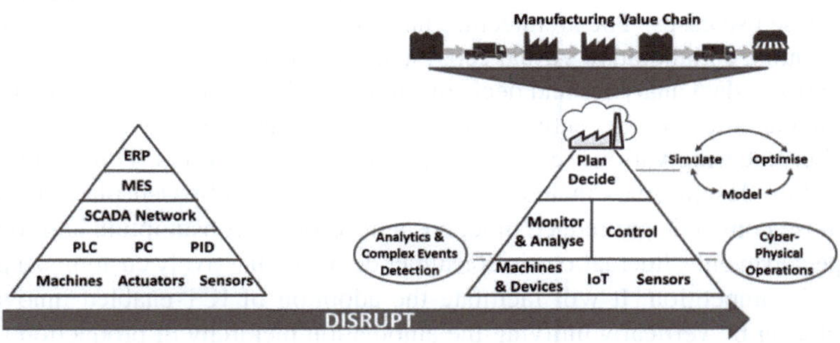

Fig. 1. The DISRUPT concept: disrupting the traditional automation pyramid

More specifically, within DISRUPT, each physical element of production (machine, device, sensor, etc.) is monitored and controlled via the IoT by its virtual counterpart. The vast amount of data collected is processed, refined into information and analysed to detect complex events that, in turn, trigger actions fed back to the physical production units or presented to decision makers along with the appropriate tools to handle them. To that end, DISRUPT proposes a set of decision support tools based on three core interrelated and interacting modules: modelling, simulation and optimisation. These tools should not only incorporate a detailed representation of the production process and the plant floor but also correlate the manufacturing process with information derived from the whole value chain in real-time, refined and analyzed by streaming and predictive analytics as well as complex event processing tools. The platform is cloud-based to accommodate the anticipated high data volume and the computational needs that this volume implies, thus enabling scalability.

The DISRUPT approach is generic to cover different manufacturing settings and scenarios. Nevertheless, it is driven by three concrete business cases that derive from the automotive and the white goods sector, namely:

Market-driven production reconfiguration, scaling and optimisation: Rapid product lifecycles and mass customisation imply an increasing number of phases in product deployment and the involvement of actors along the value chain. Hence, it becomes even more important to consistently reconfigure production processes, to achieve reduced costs and time-to-market, smaller lot sizes and production volumes. Indicatively, this business case is highly applicable to the white goods sector.

Ecosystem-aware, event-enabled production planning and control: This stems from the need to ensure business continuity in the ever-changing contemporary manufacturing environment, where production goals are often derailed by late-cycle changes, the use of unqualified and nonstandard parts, unexpected plant floor events, low supplier involvement and the lack of proper decision support tools to handle the above. Indicatively, this case applies to the automotive sector.

Automated plant floor event handling and self-adjustment: The notion of CPS lies at the very core of Industry 4.0. The incorporation of IoT as a core component of CPSs and their inherent large-scale nature raise a number of specific challenges ranging from system-level management and control to data analytics. On the same time, the evolution of CPSs bundled with analytics and decision support tools leads to manufacturing components that incorporate self-adjustment capabilities.

3 Conceptual Architecture and Modules

The under development reference platform is designed to allow the incorporation of a variety of different tools and services and facilitates a wide range of manufacturing activities from day-to-day and responsive operations to strategic planning, combining an in-depth approach to the actual manufacturing process and the plant floor with a macroscopic value chain perspective. The platform is based on a distributed Service-Oriented-Architecture (SOA) that interconnects the various modules in a seamless manner and provides a “plug-n-play” feel for services and tools to be incorporated in a fast, easy and straightforward manner. Semantic interoperability is utilised to allow the harmonious collaboration of its different modules, enabling them to interact exchanging data with unambiguous, shared meaning. In that regard, the model of the actual manufacturing unit and its value chain relations needs to be conceptually represented via appropriate ontologies of materials, resources, actors, products, machines and processes.

Figure 2 provides a schematic representation of the proposed architecture. The system enables interaction with the actual plant floor (via CPSs and the IoT interrelating machines, sensors, systems and devices), with the manufacturing organisation's Enterprise Information Systems and its Ecosystem (i.e., its value chain partners as well as software developers).

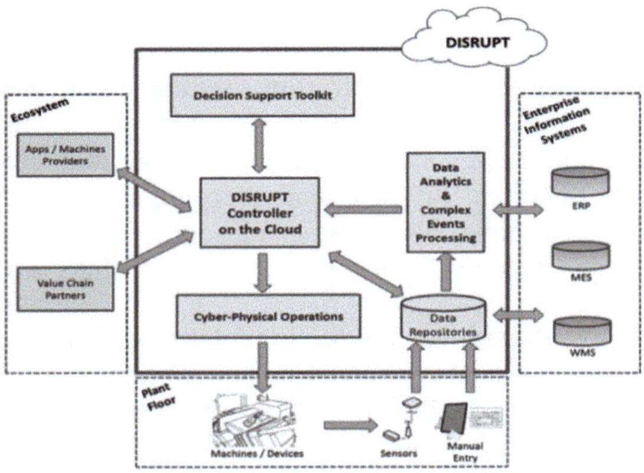

Fig. 2. The DISRUPT system architecture

The DISRUPT system architecture is structured in four interrelated modules.

Module 1: Data Analytics and Complex Event Processing. This module collects, analyses and handles data from diverse sources like specialized sensors or metering devices located at the plant floor along the production process interconnected via IoT, systems embedded in production machinery, on-site or asynchronous manual data entry and Enterprise Information Systems (e.g., ERP, MES, WMS). Depending on their source and form, the appropriate data are retrieved and filtered to avoid transmitting duplicate or non-useful data and processed (if needed) to attain their desirable form. Moreover, this module analyses the vast amount of data pouring in, turning them into meaningful real-time metrics. It detects and analyses patterns, thus producing valuable production, efficiency and business knowledge, addressing "what happened" (querying & reporting), "why it happened" (analysis) and "what will happen" (predictive & streaming analytics).

By utilizing Complex Event Processing (CEP), it allows manufacturing organizations to immediately respond with timely and relevant actions related to operational activities by correlating and analysing events across multiple data streams in real-time. Furthermore, it enables intelligent automated action on fast-moving big data, triggering low-latency actions automatically without human input. To that end, this module will filter, aggregate, enrich and analyse a high throughput of data from multiple disparate live data sources in any data format to identify simple and complex patterns, detect urgent situations and automate immediate response. The integration of sophisticated analytics with native support for temporal arguments and offer flexible event replay for testing new event scenarios and analysing existing ones.

The architectural approach for this module (Fig. 3) is event-driven, collecting information from different sources in vertical and horizontal networks, supporting a plethora of scenarios and simultaneous processing of discrete and streaming events. This architecture guarantees load-balancing and scalability and supports IoT clients with a single messaging platform. To handle the available vast amount of data, it will be empowered by cache static data for fast, in-memory access.

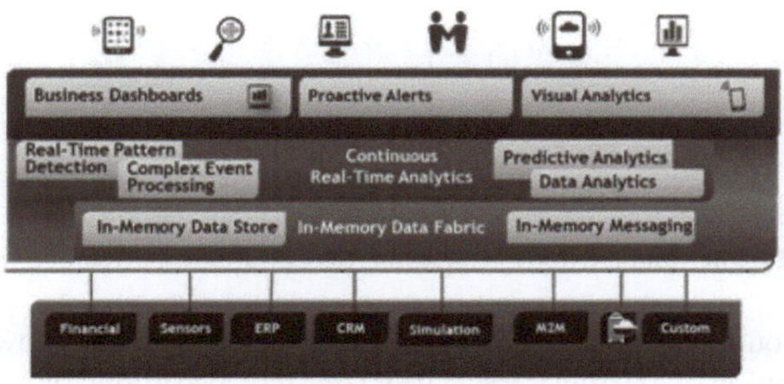

Fig. 3. The DISRUPT streaming analytics architectural approach

Module 2: Cyber-Physical Operations. This module handles the interaction with the production level via the organization's manufacturing systems and enables self-adjustment and self-configuration via a network of modular, decentralized Smart Objects, offering synchronization between the physical plant floor and its virtual representation. More specifically, it accommodates the control of factory operations at machine level by integrating the dynamics of the physical processes with those of software and networking, providing abstractions and tools for each component separately as well as for the integrated whole. To that end, the new platform will adopt a modular, flexible CPS structural architecture that empowers production schemes by facilitating both robustness and concurrent development, offering seamless integration of the organization's CPSs and the simple evolution and incorporation of other existing systems. Modularity does not only serve the purpose of providing a framework for easily integrating CPSs. It also accommodates and empowers the actual operations of such systems. More specifically, the platform will include a virtual counterpart (Smart Object-SO) for each physical entity that not only represents the entity in the virtual factory but also provides computing and networking capabilities to the actual machine. These SOs will be bundled in networks according to the model of the corresponding process step, which will be subsequently interrelated with other process steps to form the processes that comprise the production scheme. Hence, the entire production will be virtualised as a structure of decentralized systems of cooperating, autonomous Smart Objects (Fig. 4) based on the 5C level architecture for CPS [6, 7].

The adopted 5C level architecture will enable DISRUPT CPSs to process and analyse information and handle events at the appropriate level, having the visibility that is required to address the corresponding issue, spanning from local to cross-process or global. Note that with respect to the DISRUPT project this architecture cannot be supported via only local deployment. A cloud-based approach must be followed to deal

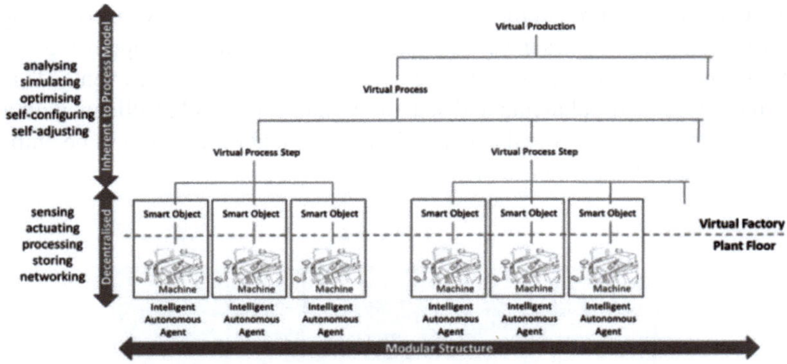

Fig. 4. The DISRUPT modular, decentralised CPS structure

with the vast amount of data and the associated processing power. However, in order to facilitate the adoption of existing CPSs, DISRUPT will also allow for hybrid deployment configurations, including SOs that perform part of the processing activities locally (e.g., perform conversion level analytics locally, at individual sensor nodes, while performing cyber-level methods on the cloud).

Module 3: the decision support toolkit. This module consists of 3 interrelated sub-modules, i.e., Modeling, Simulation and Optimisation, that interact to offer a wide range of decision support tools that cover multiple aspects of the production process or the entire manufacturing chain. Some indicative tools provided by this module are as follows.

Modelling and Design tool: Enterprise Modelling is a particular field in Conceptual Modelling that describes an enterprise in a holistic way in order to enable model processing. In Enterprise Modelling, the business (domain specific aspects) and ICT (technical aspects) are aligned with the organisational goals. Considering a manufacturing chain as a virtual chain that involves multiple independent enterprises, institutions and people which come together to achieve a certain goal [8, 9], the approach of enterprise modelling can be adapted in the context of Industry 4.0 in order to holistically describe the manufacturing processes as well as the technical production level of the whole manufacturing chain. The domain-specific business aspects are the embedded production processes, whereas the technical aspects are the production lines with analogies to enterprise workflows that distinguish between manual, semi-automatic and automatic processes. Moreover, Production Case Management is utilized to enable introducing the flexibility of production processes in a holistic modelling approach independently from the usage of IDEF0, BPMN, or any other modelling method.

Co-Simulator environment: Co-simulation allows coupling simulation environments at runtime in order to link different model descriptions, different parts/components of the overall systems, and possibly different computational algorithms [10]. The communication, the data exchange and the data synchronization is coordinated via a middleware assuming in most cases fixed lengths of communication intervals and a common modelling approach (also denoted as a co-model [11]). The main tasks that should be fulfilled for the development of a decentralised, self-organising co-simulation framework is the communication setup, the control of the co-simulation procedure, the synchronisation of the data exchange and the extrapolation strategies. Moreover, the co-simulation framework must allow its integration with optimisation and predictive analytics to allow not only effective automation in individual plant floors but also for the intensive collaboration of manufacturing sites.

Production Optimisation: This module will be based on algorithms to solve complex scheduling problems with various side constraints, such as utility (renewable resources) and machine maintenance constraints, to offer the capability of treating multiple scheduling objectives in a hierarchical fashion, including combined temporal and energy-aware objectives [12, 13]. In particular, the platform will develop scheduling algorithms in several ways that go beyond the current state-of-the-art, adding significantly to the provided level of accuracy and enhancing their planning capability as follows: (i) Multiple machine configurations will be incorporated into the existing models as decision variables. The available configurations control the operating conditions (such as the speed and the temperature), and they affect not only the completion time but also the energy consumption and the operating cost; (ii) The level of work-in-progress (WIP) inventory that is kept in front of machines (or among the process steps) as well as lot-sizing variables will be considered; (iii) Multiple execution modes will be added, including among others alternative routings and combinations of resource requirements for each production order or operation. For this purpose, in addition to the utility constraints based on renewable resources, non-renewable and doubly constrained resources will be considered. Non-renewable resources are limited for all periods and the entire scheduling horizon, while doubly constrained resources are limited both period by period and for the entire scheduling horizon [14].

Module 4. Controller on the Cloud. This module integrates all tools and modules, enabling their effective collaboration and the seamless communication of information, knowledge, and decisions to the plant floor and across the value chain. The Controller is based upon an integrated meta-model of the major factory modules. In order to realize its full potential, three aspects will be implemented within DISRUPT [15]: horizontal integration across the manufacturing organization, vertical integration of different production modules and SOs, and cross-boundary integration to cover the products' full lifespan.

Events detected by CEP will trigger the system towards possible changes in the Decision Support Toolkit (e.g., involving changes in model design, testing their effects through simulation, utilizing the appropriate optimisation tools) and possibly in the Cyber–Physical Operations module, communicating the appropriate system response to the plant-floor. Such response may be human-controlled or automatic, an example being a machine predicting failures and triggering maintenance processes autonomously. Similarly, changes in production because of exogenous reasons (e.g., involving actors in the value chain) will be communicated by the Controller to the Decision Support

Toolkit, hence allowing for real-time production re-scheduling that will be subsequently fed into production.

The Controller also offers an Ecosystem Gateway. The role of this gateway is twofold. Firstly, it offers a reliable and secure interface for the collaboration of the manufacturing unit with value chain partners, through which all related actors and modules are able to communicate changes in real-time thus virtualizing the actual setting under which the factory's production is implemented. This may include changes in orders by the customers, daily directives from centralized management, the introduction of new partners or unexpected events. Secondly, it allows cooperation with software developers, technology and machine providers, offering a standardized framework for them to interact with DISRUPT. It provides them with the necessary tools for adopting and utilizing the production and value chain semantics scheme, recalibrate their products and offer ready-to-deploy solutions, thus enabling them to showcase the business value of their tools/services/machine utilizing a channel where they can be properly pre-tested and evaluated.

4 Conclusions

The decentralised architecture presented is part of the DISRUPT project [15]. Its purpose is to fully automate vertical and horizontal operations and decision making in project partner companies in the automotive and white goods sectors. We have presented its conceptual architecture and described the functionality of its main modules.

We are currently designing the software architecture details based on already gathered requirements and modelling of specific use cases for each of those sectors; we are also considering the reference architectures by the Industrial Internet Consortium (IIC) [16], the German initiative Industrie 4.0 [17], the EU project IoT-A Internet of Things Architecture [18], and the work-in-progress ISO/IEC Internet of Things Reference Architecture [19]. These reference architectures provide guidelines for the design and development of IoT systems based on standards in order to ensure interoperability.

Many of the advances proposed for the DISRUPT architecture are already used in manufacturing and have been the subject of the literature extensively and similar projects around the world. The ambition of the DISRUPT approach is to radically transform manufacturing in those specific sectors and use cases, through the harmonious integration of those advances into a holistic manufacturing system: isolated, optimised cells that come together as a fully integrated, automated, and optimised production flow, leading to greater efficiencies and changing traditional production relationships among suppliers, producers and customers, as well as between humans and machines.

Our aim is for the DISRUPT platform to be a proof-of-concept in, and a reference implementation for, the automotive and white goods sectors. As a comprehensive solution, it should also be of use in other application domains.

Acknowledgments. The work on this paper is funded mainly by the European Commission through the DISRUPT project (H2020 FOF-11-2016, RIA project no. 723541, 2016–2018). The authors would also like to thank the contributions of the different partners of the DISRUPT project.

References

1. Kagermann, H., Wahlster, W., Helbig, J. (eds.): Recommendations for implementing the strategic initiative Industrie 4.0: Final report of the Industrie 4.0 Working Group (2013)
2. Hermann, M., Pentek, T., Otto, B.: Design Principles for Industrie 4.0 Scenarios. Working Paper No. 01 (2015)
3. Bosch IoT Platform: https://www.bosch-si.com/iot-platform/bosch-iot-suite/homepage-bosch-iot-suite.html
4. IBM Watson Internet of Things: https://www.ibm.com/internet-of-things/
5. Microsoft Internet of Things: https://www.microsoft.com/en-gb/internet-of-things/
6. Lee, J., Bagheri, B., Kao, H.-A.: A cyber-physical systems architecture for industry 4.0-based manufacturing systems. Manufact. Lett. **3**, 18–23 (2015)
7. Bagheri, B., Lee, J.: Big future for cyber-physical manufacturing systems. Design World, 23 September 2015. http://www.designworldonline.com/big-future-for-cyber-physical-manufacturing-systems/
8. Arnold, D., Faisst, W., Haertling, M., Sieber, P.: Virtuelle Unternehmenals Unternehmenstyp der Zukunft? HMD Theorie und Praxis der Wirtschaftsinformatik **32**(185) (1995)
9. Kanet, J.J., Faisst, W., Mertens, P.: Application of information technology to a virtual enterprise broker: the case of Bill Epstein. Int. J. Prod. Econ. **62**, 23–32 (1999)
10. Bleicher, F., Duer, F., Leobner, I., Kovacic, I., Heinzl, B., Kastner, W.: Co-simulation environment for optimising energy efficiency inproduction systems. CIRP Ann. Manufact. Technol. **63**, 441–444 (2014)
11. Fitzgerald, J., et al. (eds.): Collaborative Design for Embedded Systems. Springer, Heidelberg (2014)
12. Plitsos, S., Repoussis, P.P., Mourtos, I., Tarantilis, C.D.: Energy-aware decision support for production scheduling. Decision Support Systems (under review) (2015)
13. Repoussis, P.P., Paraskevopoulos, D.C., Tarantilis, C.D.: Iterated local search algorithm for flexible job shop scheduling problems with resource constraints. In: POMS 2015 Annual Conference, 8–11 May, Washington, USA (2015)
14. Alcaraz, J., Maroto, C., Ruiz, R.: Solving the multi-mode resource-constraint project scheduling problem with genetic algorithms. J. Oper. Res. Soc. **54**, 614–626 (2003)
15. http://www.disrupt-project.eu/
16. Industrial Internet Consortium Reference Archtitecture. https://www.iiconsortium.org/IIRA-1-7-ajs.pdf
17. Reference Architecture Model Industrie 4.0. https://webstore.iec.ch/preview/info_iecpas63088%7Bed1.0%7Den.pdf
18. IoT-A Internet of Things Architecture Project Final Report. http://cordis.europa.eu/docs/projects/cnect/1/257521/080/reports/001-257521IoTAPFRrenditionDownload.pdf
19. ISO/IEC CD 30141:20160910(E). Internet of Things Reference Architecture (IoT-RA). https://www.w3.org/WoT/IG/wiki/images/9/9a/10N0536_CD_text_of_ISO_IEC_30141.pdf

Supporting Product-Service Development Through Customer Feedback

Tapani Ryynänen(✉), Iris Karvonen, Heidi Korhonen, and Kim Jansson

VTT Technical Research Centre of Finland Ltd., PL1000, 02004 VTT, Espoo, Finland
{Tapani.Ryynanen, Iris.Karvonen, Heidi.Korhonen}@vtt.fi

Abstract. When developing product-services (P-S) it is important to take a collaborative and user-centric perspective to ensure that the P-S fits to customer needs. There are different approaches for the user involvement from intensive co-creation to the collection of customer feedback about the P-S design or P-S behavior. The feedback again can be collected using different methods and tools.

The paper discusses different methods for collecting customer feedback for product-service innovation and design. The context of the study is the Manutelligence project in which a P-S collaboration platform is developed, also to support interaction with customer. In the paper four Manutelligence use cases from different industrial fields are analysed to identify the different customer types, lifecycle stages of the feedback, feedback forms and how the platform can support the feedback collection and use. The benefits of the feedback collection in different cases are also described.

Keywords: Platform for collaboration · Co-creation · Product-Service engineering · Customer feedback · Manufacturing intelligence · Use cases

1 Introduction

Manufacturing companies are interested to better engage their customers and to deliver more benefits through offering product-services (P-S) or services related to their products. In this way they can also obtain additional business, which is often not as dependent on economic cycles as pure manufacturing. There are several definitions for a product-service (P-S). For example, it is defined as "a mix of tangible products and intangible service designed and combined so that they are jointly capable of integrated, final customer needs" [1]. Another definition of a service in general (not only P-S) reveals the special nature of services–the intangibility and the importance of interaction with the customer: "A service is an activity or series of activities of more or less intangible nature that normally, but not necessarily, take place in interactions between the customer and service employees and/or physical resources or goods and/or systems of the service provider, which are provided as solutions to customer problems." [2].

Collaboration with the customer is a vital part of any business network and moving into the P-S offering changes co-creation roles and requires different data. Relational coping strategies, including role clarification, role redefinition and role adaption,

L.M. Camarinha-Matos et al. (Eds.): PRO-VE 2017, IFIP AICT 506, pp. 138–145, 2017.
DOI: 10.1007/978-3-319-65151-4_13

may be especially important during the co-creation process [3]. The data collected from the relationship for different roles has wide impact in the whole network. Therefore the quality and management of this data has a domino effect throughout the collaborative network.

The special characteristics address that developing P-Ss needs close collaboration with the customer. This has been discussed for example by the GloNet project which developed support platforms for effective operation of collaborative networks for service-enhanced products [4]. In principle the feedback from customers may come from different customer/user levels and the P-S providers would be interested to get the feedback as early as possible in the lifecycle. However, typically it is not as easy to get feedback from the user level (if not the first customer) in the lifecycle phase when the P-S is still in the design or manufacturing/implementation phase. On the other hand, in the usage phase it is often more simple to get the feedback from the user.

This paper is focused on a specific subtype of co-creation: customer feedback. The paper context is the development of a P-S engineering platform in project Manutelligence ("Product Service Design and Manufacturing Intelligence Engineering Platform", H2020 636951). The objective of Manutelligence platform is to manage manufacturing intelligence; all data, information and knowledge related to the P-S and its lifecycle. In the project, product information is divided into definition data and feedback data [5]. The feedback information can be created in different life cycle stages, like P-S design and P-S operation/use and using different methods. The idea is that the Manutelligence platform supports the collection of customer feedback, for example by visualizing the designed P-S and offering the channels for customer feedback. The platform is based on the integration of existing tools and platforms.

It is clear that extracting customer feedback can make the P-S more attractive to the customers but that it is always not easy to get the feedback. Thus the objective of this paper is to analyze the approaches for customer feedback based on the Manutelligence industrial cases: four industrial pilots from different industrial fields (automotive, ship, smart house, fablab/3D-printing). From the point of the customer two of the pilot products are highly complex (automotive, ship), one is medium complex (fablab) and one is low in complexity (smart house). Respectively the data-richness of the feedback follows the complexity.

The following research questions are discussed:

- What kind of methods can be used to collect customer feedback of Product-Services?
- How can a digital Product-Service engineering platform support the feedback collection and utilization?

2 Approaches for P-S Feedback

Product-service customer feedback is typically linked to the specific, offered, often also customized Product-Service and its behavior. This may happen in the P-S design or manufacturing phase in which case the feedback may be used to modify the P-S according to customer comments. The importance of customer feedback is emphasized due to the co-created nature of value of P-S. Co-creation refers to the customer participating in value creation and value being jointly created by the company, the customer, and often other [6, 7].

It is also possible to collect the feedback once the product is produced, i.e. once a product instance exists. From that moment on, the product instance is affected by loads caused by lifecycle processes (e.g. production, transportation and usage) [3]. These loads affect the degradation and the operation behavior of a product. Feedback information from the use/operation phase allows the producers to learn more about the users, the usage of products and the product behavior [8]. In principle, information about services can also be collected, but the channels may vary and the instantiation of a service is different compared to products. In Manutelligence, a service is instantiated once information is created about it (e.g. a contract or service request) [3]. This is different from the commonly mentioned characteristic that a service is produced and consumed at the same time–technically, the service is instantiated in computer systems before it is consumed.

Often both users and sensors create data about the system. A possibility to manage and compare all data creates new possibilities to understand and verify the system behavior. Zolkiewski et al. [9] say that "In support of this focus on outcomes-based measures, we contend that other data, beyond user's perceptual data, should be employed to enhance customer experience measurement and management." and they mention sources like Big Data, IoT, Cloud and smart assets.

3 Methodology

The platform development is based on existing platforms and their adaptation according to the needs of four use case pilots (automotive, ship, smart house, fablab). The needs were collected and analysed in a requirement engineering process including phases: elicitation, structuration, analysis and validation. In the elicitation phase each of the pilots specified the use scenarios, that is: descriptions of processes or process parts which could be supported by a P-S engineering platform. The description included the objectives, challenges, lifecycle stage and the use cases included. Each scenario could have more than one use case. Each use case again was described with a common format including for example actors, precondition, postcondition, systems involved, diagram and the main steps. The number of scenarios and use cases defined in the first phase was the following:

- Automotive pilot: 3 scenarios and altogether 6 use cases
- Ship pilot: 3 scenarios and 6 use cases
- Smart house pilot: 3 scenarios and 5 use cases
- Fablab pilot: 5 scenarios and 17 use cases.

Thus altogether 14 scenarios and 34 use cases were defined in the first phase of the project. At this time point the companies had not yet decided which use cases will be implemented during the Manutelligence project but the focus was on the identification of future opportunities. Also during the project some new use cases emerged.

The scenario descriptions were used in the elicitation of requirements for the Manutelligence platform.

Currently the project is in its final phase. Most of the use cases have developed into pilot demonstrations. Some of the defined use cases have been left out of the current project and some new use cases have emerged. Validation of the pilots against requirements will take place during the last six months of the project.

This paper describes the analysis of the use case scenarios from the viewpoint of customer feedback. The analysis included the following steps:

1. Identification of the use scenarios and use cases in which customer is involved as an active or passive source of feedback. As a whole in 7 of the 14 scenarios and 9 of the 17 use cases some kind of feedback was included.
2. Analysis of the identified scenarios and use cases using a common approach and template. The main points of the template are presented in Table 1 and as a whole in [10]. It was not possible to find all the information for all the cases in the basic source documents. In some cases prototype presentations and discussions with the use case representatives were needed.
3. Consolidation of the analysis results. This was performed for the items considered most important, like the customer/user type, objectives and benefits, lifecycle stage, feedback type and channels or tools, how the feedback is used and what could be the role of the Manutelligence platform.
4. Identification of similarities and differences; developing a mapping framework and conclusions.

Table 1. Use case analysis framework

Use case name, Scenario, Date, completed by
Product-Service (P-S) delivered
When is the feedback collected? In what P-S lifecycle phase? How often is the feedback collected?
Who is customer or use of the P-S?
Objectives. Why is the feedback from customers needed?
Type of customer interaction? (E.g. B2B, B2C, C2C/P2P, P-S production)
Dimensions of feedback. What does the feedback concern?
What does the feedback include? What is the feedback content? E.g. textual, visual, audio, data, proposition/requirement, free/specified or other format
How is the feedback given? What are current (and future Manutelligence) cannels for delivering feedback? E.g. Listening and asking customers, build with customers, in a meeting/e-mail/platform/IoT
What happens after the feedback is given?
What is the Manutelligence Platform role in customer feedback? How it could help and support in enhancing the use of customer feedback?

4 Results–Feedback Case Analysis

Even if the Manutelligence cases significantly differ from each other in size and complexity, they all express, in different ways, one common objective for the collection of the customer feedback. It is the improvement of the P-S, either of the P-S instant (a specific P-S) or the future P-Ss. The improved P-S is expected to influence the customer satisfaction and thus to improve the competitiveness of the company. Additionally it is expected that the interaction including the feedback and the potential to influence the P-S design strengthens the customer relationship and enables better understanding about the future needs.

The availability of life cycle analysis (LCA) and life cycle cost analysis (LCC) on the platform allows the user to give feedback if the P-S performance is sufficient. The end user can make the decision based on sustainability assessment and long term costs. For example, the customer can predict future energy consumption and adapt.

In addition to high quality P-S, one benefit expected is to speed up the design, P-S specification and implementation processes, and to decrease the costs. Efficient feedback tools enabled by the platform allow faster fixing of the design decisions, but also avoiding errors in the design. Thus there is decreased need to waste time for the correction of errors and the subsequent manufacturing/implementation phases may be more efficient.

In one specific case, fablab, the community of customers (users) is seen important for the manufacturing activity as a whole. The feedback supports the optimization of the use of production machinery for additive manufacturing, sharing knowledge amongst users, design improvement and design reuse.

The feedback or data coming from the P-S use phase also supports the failure management and reduction of repair time as well as activities through predictive maintenance. All this can contribute to the keeping the products in a good shape and thus achieving a longer life for the products.

When analysing the customer feedback, two main distinctive features could be identified:

- The P-S lifecycle phase in which the feedback is collected and analysed. Main phases identified are P-S design/implementation and P-S operation/use phases. The end-of-life phase was not visible in the scenarios.
- The type and method of feedback: type meaning the information type (unstructured information, structured information, data) and method how the feedback is given (customer manual input, customer selection from predefined options, automatic (for example) sensor data). It seems clear that in most cases these are not independent but interlinked: The unstructured information requires some customer activity while the bigger amounts of data are coming automatically from sensors, for example via IoT. The structured feedback (for example selection between options) can be derived either from the customer or from automatic devices.

Thus the main dimensions against which the use cases can be compared and analyzed are: P-S lifecycle phase and the source of feedback: customer activity/automatic retrieval. The customer activity may mean feedback given through platform, email or

Table 2. Use case feedback analysis

	Life cycle phase				
	Sales	Design	Manufacturing	Use/Operation	End of life
Action-based	Ship1 Ship2 Smart-house1	Ship1 Ship2 Smart-house1	Ship2	Automotive1 Automotive2	
Automatic		Automotive2	Fablab1	Automotive1 Automotive2 Fablab2 Fablab3 Smart-house2	

discussions in a meeting etc. In Manutelligence the focus is on feedback which could be supported by the platform; this may be automatic or action-based. In Table 2 the Manutelligence use cases including feedback in some form were analyzed in relation to these dimensions.

The table shows that the different use cases had a different focus in their scenarios and collaboration with customers. The main focus of the ship case was feedback from the ship owner in the design phase, based on virtual models, gamification and augmented reality. As this kind of feedback cannot be automated, the idea was to utilize the virtual models for the easy issue of the observations and again use these as the basis for a managed change management. The smart house scenario included some configuration ideas for the design phase but the main objective was to collect automatically data from sensors to monitor the product behavior and to develop new services. In the automotive case the main point was automatic data collection from testing even if also customer opinions were collected. The fablab case was a specific case where all the lab users (manufacturers) are customers.

Thus, analysis of the Manutelligence case scenarios brings out that there is a need for retrieving customer feedback in all lifecycle phases even if no end of life scenarios were available in the current project. It is clear that an IT platform utilizing IoT (Internet of Things) is needed to collect and manage the large amounts of data given by automatic sensors. The data can be used for use phase services and for further design. Often there is also a need to compare the real data against designed performance (for example energy consumption models).

To receive feedback from the customer through customer actions the P-S provider needs to make the feedback action attractive for the customer. This means that it should be easy and interesting for the customer, for example to understand the current P-S version in the design phase, and also easy to give the feedback. In the use cases this was implemented through visualization, even experimenting through gamification, supported by the platform. The feedback could be directly appointed to the visual models or given by more traditional means, like in meetings. Thus also here the platform is needed both to present the P-S for which feedback is needed but also to save and analyse the collected, often heterogeneous information.

In the fablab case there is a user community which is interested to interact and give feedback to the P-S provider but also to share experiences. Thus the platform needs to offer tools also for this communication and collaboration.

As an important function of the platform in relation to customer feedback is to take care that the customer feedback is handled and used for the current P-S instant or for future P-Ss. Thus systematic change management process, supported by the platform, is needed. The change process also takes care about informing the customer about the results of the feedback process: what changes were made.

Based on the findings in the project a P-S platform may have different roles in the customer feedback process:

- The platform should manage the rich P-S data and information throughout the lifecycle.
- The platform should offer the P-S information to the customer in an understandable interface.
- The platform should offer the customer a possibility to give different types of comments.
- The platform should integrate to IoT to collect data from different types of sensors.
- It should be possible to analyse the feedback data and information using the platform, for example to compare real and designed data.
- The platform should support the change management process.
- The platform should allow communication between different users or different actors.
- The platform should support organizational change management by enabling dynamic changes required by changes in roles and tasks.

5 Summary

This paper is focused on supporting P-S design through customer feedback. The paper is based on Manutelligence pilots (H2020 no. 636951) and their needs and experimentation of the Manutelligence platform. The aim of Manutelligence platform is to manage manufacturing intelligence; all data, information and knowledge related to the P-S and its lifecycle. Even if the main requirements elicited in the beginning of the project were focused on other needs, the customer feedback and collaboration with the customer were visible in 7 out of 21 aggregated requirements [11]. Customer feedback is expected to improve the P-S, customer satisfaction, process efficiency and overall company competitiveness. New methods and channels for customer feedback require that the platform is able to integrate and manage the rich feedback data.

Acknowledgements. This work has been partly funded by the European Union's Horizon 2020 research and innovation program under grant agreement no. 636951 (Manutelligence).

References

1. Tukker, A., Tischner, U. (eds.): New business for Old Europe. Product-Service Development as a Means to Enhance Competitiveness and Eco-efficiency. Final report of SUSPRONET. (2004). http://www.suspronet.org/fs_reports.htm (Accessed 12 May 2011)
2. Grönroos, C.: Service Management and Marketing. Lexington Books, San Fransisco (1990)
3. Sjödin, D.R., Prida, V., Wincent, J.: Value co-creation process of integrated product-services: effect of role ambiguities and relational coping strategies. Ind. Mark. Manage. **56**, 108–119 (2016)
4. Camarinha-Matos, Luis M., Afsarmanesh, H., Koelmel, B.: Collaborative networks in support of service-enhanced products. In: Camarinha-Matos, Luis M., Pereira-Klen, A., Afsarmanesh, H. (eds.) PRO-VE 2011. IAICT, vol. 362, pp. 95–104. Springer, Heidelberg (2011). doi:10.1007/978-3-642-23330-2_11
5. Manutelligence deliverable: D3.1. Semantic facilitator for bridging Product and Service lifecycle phases. H2020 project no 636951 (2017), http://www.manutelligence.eu/
6. Vargo, S.L., Lusch, R.F.: Evolving to a new dominant logic for marketing. J. Market. **68**(1), 1–17 (2004), ISSN 0022-2429
7. Prahalad, C.K., Ramaswamy, V.: The Future of Competition. Harvard Business School Press, Boston (2004)
8. Wellsandt, S., Thoben, K.-D.: Approach to describe knowledge sharing between producer and user. In: Presented at the 26th CIRP Design Conference, Stockholm, Sweden (2016)
9. Zolkiewski, J., Story, V., Burton, J., Chan, P., Gomes, A., Hunter-Jones, P., O'Malley, L., Peters, L.D., Raddats, C., Robinson, W.: Strategic B2B customer experience management: the importance of outcomes-based measures. J. Serv. Market. **31**(2) (2017). doi:10.1108/JSM-10-2016-0350
10. Manutelligence deliverable: D3.3. Methodologies and tools to involve customers in the P-S multi-disciplinary feedback, H2020 project no 636951 (to be published 2017), http://www.manutelligence.eu/
11. Jansson, K., Karvonen, I., Ryynänen, T., Korhonen, H., Corti, D., Cerri, D., Cocco, M.: Processing requirements for a product-service engineering platform - a multiple use case approach. In: Proceedings of International Conference on Engineering, Technology and Innovation/IEEE International Technology Management Conference ICE/ITMC 2016, 13–15 June 2016. IEEE, Trondheim (2016)

Knowledge Sharing for Production CPS

New Requirement Analysis Approach for Cyber-Physical Systems in an Intralogistics Use Case

Günther Schuh, Anne Bernardy(✉), Violett Zeller, and Volker Stich

FIR Institute for Industrial Management, RWTH Aachen University,
Campus-Boulevard 55, 52074 Aachen, Germany
{Gunther.Schuh,Anne.Bernardy,Violett.Zeller,
Volker.Stich}@fir.rwth-aachen.de

Abstract. Nowadays, cyber physical systems support the improvement of efficiency in intralogistics by controlling and manipulating the production and logistic environment autonomously. Due to the complexity of the individual production processes, designing suitable cyber-physical systems based on their existing production environment is a challenge for companies. This paper presents a new methodology on how to design cyber-physical systems conceptually to suit an individual production environment. Compared to existing design approaches, this methodology matches immediately the required functions to existing information and communication technology's components insisting on the neutral assimilation of requirements. Therefore, the requirement specification asks for needed functions in relating to offered functions of information and communication technology (ICT) components. The paper focusses the use case of implementing a cutting-edge mobile network technology into an existing tracking and tracing process.

Keywords: CPS · Matching · Collaboration · Requirements

1 Introduction

Nowadays, companies pursue the implementation of intelligent systems in their production to keep up with the changing demands towards the flexible production of tomorrow. Through a dedicated use of information technologies like monitoring systems to supervise the production status of orders and material flows, the production status can be communicated and visualized in real-time, and an optimized production line can be analysed per order [1]. These potentials are essential factors for small and medium-sized enterprises (SMEs) to maintain their competitiveness.

However, most companies are limited in time and financial resources to integrate CPS into the intralogistics of their production. One major challenge is the conceptual design and the use of information technologies due to the constantly growing market of CPS. Furthermore, the benefit and deployment depend on many factors as individual required functionalities so that SMEs need to rely on external expertise for integration [1, 2].

L.M. Camarinha-Matos et al. (Eds.): PRO-VE 2017, IFIP AICT 506, pp. 149–156, 2017.
DOI: 10.1007/978-3-319-65151-4_14

This complexity is caused by the unclear definition how to design CPS [3, 4]. Historically CPS are an evolution of embedded systems, so that existing design methods are based on system engineering methodologies. Using existing modelling approaches requires the configuration of process models [3–5] but do not support the choice of suitable information and communication technologies (ICT). In addition, the design of complex CPSs requires a comprehensive knowledge of these production processes beneath the knowledge of system engineering, which is usually only known by the user company itself. Since the market for information and communication technologies grows exponentially, a specialized knowledge of these technologies is needed to ensure the best possible solutions for a CPS concept and realization. The process of integrating individual CPSs in manufacturing companies is accompanied by the challenge of knowing and taking into account all relevant interfaces in advance [6].

Hence, this paper proposes a new method to introduce CPS. Since one common use case for CPS is to connect a tracking and tracing system, this use case serves as an example to illustrate the provided approach explaining how to choose systematically information and communicating systems in the intralogistics to transform it to a CPS.

2 State of the Art

These days, the tracking and tracing of products in the intralogistics is essential for different reasons. On the one hand, products in the reclamation allow the interference to the reasons of quality lack. On the other hand, tracking and tracing orders and material helps to point out difficulties of the production and logistic processes. The global logistics use standard identification systems, that can register their status autonomously and which are standardized like the EPCIS, for about 20 years [7]. In contrast, tracking and tracing systems for the intralogistics are mostly insulated applications referring to the individual company [8]. Due to the changing requirements toward the productions effectivity caused by the digitalization, tracking and tracing systems need to get

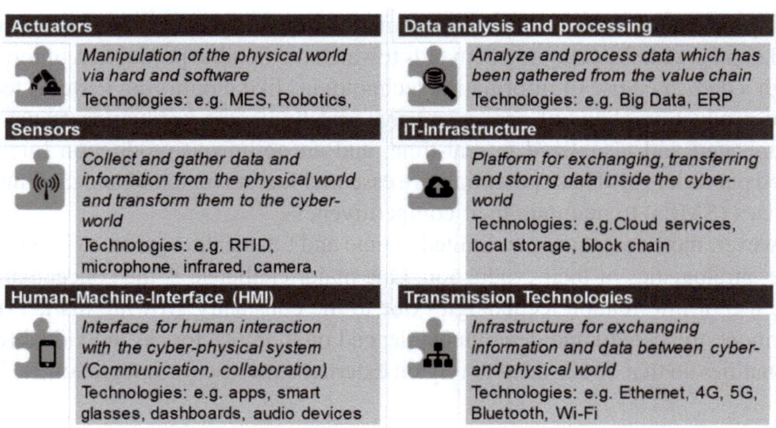

Fig. 1. The six technology clusters and their tasks

connected to the industrial internet as well as the material and orders of the company. Therefore, the tracking and tracing system needs to be transformed into a cyber-physical system.

The conception of a CPS however requires a common definition for all stakeholders, but no commonly acknowledged definition has been established so far [9]. To develop the approach to match applicant's requirements and technology functions, the FIR INSTITUTE FOR INDUSTRIAL MANAGEMENT invented a functional definition based on the definitions of [10–12], which presents six main functions in a CPS [13].

Currently, the only designing and modelling methods for CPS refer to configurations of the chosen components in a simulation environment, e.g. in Modelica, Matlab or Simulink [3, 4, 14]. Since these tools require user skills to simulate the interdependencies between already selected components, they neither support the selection of technologies nor are they suitable for the use by untrained system designers. In addition, they don't involve the applicant into the designing process and do not support requirement engineering approaches to ensure an entire, solution-neutral requirement recording. The selection of the technologies needs to factor new, upcoming ICT because the implementation process of a cyber-physical system takes up to two years in average [15–17]. Screening the ICT market is moreover incessant to ensure the selection of a sustainable and effective technology portfolio.

For a proper decision-making, the alignment between applicant's requirements and technology provided functions needs to be supported by a cost-value-analysis of given matching results between problems and solutions. The following section will describe the foundation of the matching methodology.

3 Scientific Approach - The Matching Method Applied to Tracking and Tracing

As mentioned before, a CPS contains technologies from the cyber and the physical world. Implemented to tracking and tracing systems, they enable more flexibility and environment independence when networking transmission technologies are used to globally connect the tracking and tracing system. Concerning the example use case in this paper of the connected material tracking in a production, the desired cyber-physical system needs sensors to identify the location of the material. Suitable technologies are e.g. Auto-ID technologies such as RFID or barcode systems. Furthermore, the identification has to be connected to the central local or global controlling system.

Hence, transmission technologies have to be used like Bluetooth or mobile connectivity. To fulfil the aim of the tracking and tracing, the data needs to be firstly transformed by tools like e.g. diagrams and then displayed e.g. on a smart device or a terminal. Finally, the cyber-physical system contains an actuator like e.g. a robot which can interact due to implemented logics. If there is no autonomic, technical system to interact, there is at least a human to react to the events during the production process. Finally, the CPS needs a stable IT infrastructure as a backbone. This example illustrates the different functions a CPS has to fulfil. Based on case research, the FIR Institute for Industrial Management at the Aachen University formed six technology clusters to categorize information- and communication systems [13]. Figure 1 gives an overview of the definitions and example technologies for the six technology clusters developed at FIR in Aachen. They were conceived to increase accuracy in describing CPS technologies, allowing for a more systematic approach towards categorizing CPSs. As shown in Fig. 1 the technology clusters are:

- Actuators: Actuators represent the means of a CPS to interact and manipulate the physical world via hard- and software applications. On the one hand, this can be a hardware like a robot or a motor control. On the other hand, software like a MES (manufacturing execution system) can control production systems and change its setup.
- Sensors: Sensors build the antagonist to the actuators cluster. The aim of sensor technologies is the generation of data. Concerning tracking and tracing use cases, sensors especially assimilate localization and identification data. Auto-ID sensors e.g. like RFID-chips support the detection of the location of an item or identification the product being handled, as well as camera systems that automatically recognize the positioning of the work piece and which are monitoring the piece's quality are examples for sensors in the industrial context.
- Human-Machine-Interface (HMI): Human-Machine-Interfaces support the decision support. The visualization of aggregated data is a central aim of the technologies referring to this cluster. Corresponding to the tracking and tracing systems, HMI can appear in the form of a dashboard giving a real-time overview of material and order flows, and can uncover material, information or orders stacks. Theses dashboards can be displayed e.g. on smart devices (smartphone, table) or on BDE-terminals. Other interaction possibilities are realized via speech (e.g. pick-by-voice).
- Data Analysis and processing: The raw data needs to be analysed referring to an individual task. Referring to the tracking and tracing system, methods like deep learning build the basic to reduce order or material stockings automatically. Artificial intelligences (AIs) can predict shifts in machine occupancy and change the job distribution inside the production system to re-establish an equilibrium on their own.
- IT infrastructure: Essentially, all the data assimilation, processing and transfer refers to a stable IT infrastructure. The aim of the technologies of this cluster is to ensure the data, information and knowledge in defined storages like central servers or in the decentral cloud to keep it retrievable at any time. Corresponding to the connected tracking and tracing systems, the data needs to be stored and available for different stakeholders like the production manager to interact if any flow is stacked or the customer supports to calculate the delivery time. E.g. cloud technologies offer the new flexibility to scale the IT infrastructure according to current requirements. However, cloud services decrease the control over the processed data.
- Transmission Technologies: Finally, the transmission of data between admission localization and users need to be realized. Transmission technologies such as mobile communication, Wireless LAN, Ethernet or bus-systems like ProfiNet© provide the technical infrastructure to exchange data and information within the different agents inside the cyber-physical system. In respect to tracking and tracing systems, the requirement towards more flexible ways of data transmission increases so that wireless communication technologies such as 4G, 5G, and

Wireless LAN gain in importance. Depending on the environment, their reliability and their security function lack the requirement so that Ethernet or Fieldbus are the preferable options.

To match the right technologies to individual requirements, a systematical alignment approach is obligatory. Since available technologies of the market can contain several functions of different technology clusters, the matching needs to consider functional overlapping to avoid redundant technology suggestions. Therefore, for all clusters morphologies are designed with categories, attributes and characteristics.

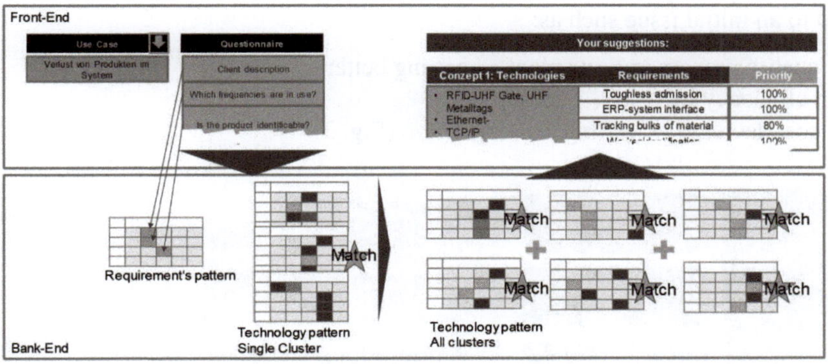

Fig. 2. Example of the matchmaker

The morphologies serve as a pattern to categorize technologies. If a technology is sorted into a technology cluster, it creates an own pattern which later on can be compared to the requirement pattern (see Fig. 2). Every technology assigns for at least one of the clusters. New developments regarding e.g. RFID systems are covering multiple technology cluster aims. They are sorted into several clusters and the matching algorithm proves the redundancy of the functionalities. In relation to the tracking and tracing use case, typical technologies like identification and localization systems are defined by the physical measurement task, the data transmission quality, the existing clients to run IT systems in general and the desired interaction like visualization via a touchable display of the humans.

Theses morphologies form the structure for the systematic requirement assimilation presented in Sect. 3 in this paper and shape the framework of the matchmaking algorithm. Based on the typologies for both the requirements and the technologies, the matching algorithm can then identify the best matches for requirements and solutions. This means that the requirements need to be assimilated into the same kind of pattern like the technologies are clustered. The applicant has to fulfil a questionnaire matching the categories, attributes and characteristics with requirements and to prioritize these requirements by a paired comparison. The ranking decides the alignment process in which or Hence, every question of that requirement guidance is a translation from an available function to a customer need. Mostly, one question asks for one attribute. Since the six clusters contain more than 15 characteristics per cluster with at least two attributes, the applicant needs to answer more than 200 questions. To minimize the effort for the applicant, the questionnaire fades out questions corresponding to answered ones. The fulfilled questionnaire forms than the requirement pattern. The process in the configurator to extract the requirement pattern efficiently is explained in the next section.

4 Requirement Extraction

For the requirement extraction, three overhead-use-case-types are given by the magic triangle of logistic problems [18]. The triangle shows that logistic problems can transferred to an initial issue such as:

- A quality process improvement → getting better
- An efficiency increase → getting faster
- A cost decrease → getting less expensive (Fig. 3).

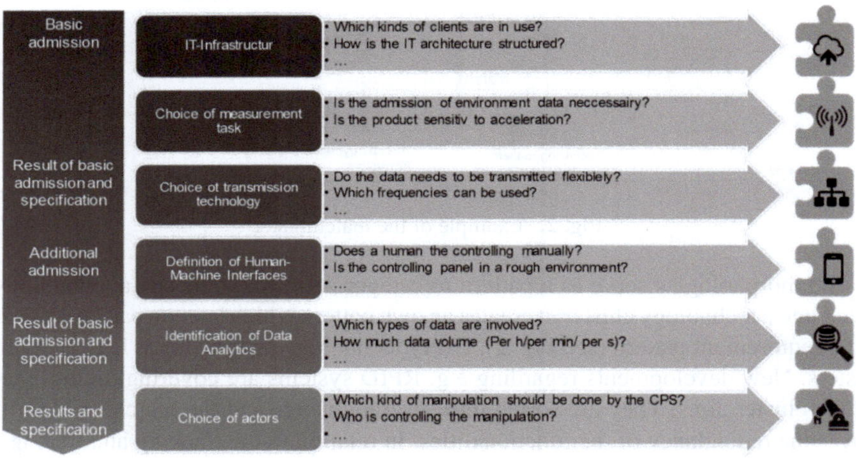

Fig. 3. The questionnaire process

The three types of use-cases require different pre-sets of combinations of attributes of the technology clusters and therefore different pre-sets of characteristics. Nevertheless, two of the technology clusters are essential for every use-case-type because of the definition of a cyber-physical system: the *transmission technologies* to transfer the data of the data sources to a central or decentral data store, which is part of the *IT infrastructure*.

The first use-case-type *Quality* requires e.g. all kinds of proving and checking processes as well as measurement processes. Problems of quality management in the intralogistics are e.g. producing lots of waste or certify critical products. Stage-Gate processes are known in the quality management to decide the status of a product. The second use-case-type *Time* requires support systems and automation systems. The preset questions focus on Human-Machine-Interfaces and the possibilities to assist the worker with wearables.

Talking about industrie 4.0, this use-case-type includes questions about flexibility and an efficient one-piece production [19]. The third use-case-type *costs* brings into focus the problems like too high costs. Compared to the use-case-type *time* material flows are analyzed and have to be improved. The recorded IT infrastructure is essential to detect redundant or unused systems. The data analysis need to be specified by the individual applicant's problem so that the questionnaire is just reduced to typical visualization tasks like the overview of e.g. correlations between environment data (e.g. temperature, humidity) and failures of the products.

5 Summary and Outlook

The matchmaking supports the networking of technology suppliers and applicants and is realized by an online platform; via whose Web front the requirements are recorded. For an efficient determination of requirements, the user selects a problem description from a list of reference application cases, which corresponds to his individual problem situation (see Fig. 2). The pre-selection limits the following questionnaire to a selection of relevant questions. The structure of the questionnaire provides a continuous containment of the questions so that the effort of the filling is reduced to a minimum for the applicant.

Six functional technology clusters built the framework for both, the requirement assimilation and the technology sorting. Hence, the requirement recording is structured and implemented in a way that gradually limits the number of possible technologies to the compatible and application-specific components from the existing framework conditions and the specification of the optimization target.

The questionnaire asserts a solution-neutral requirement assessment to ensure that users are offered the most efficient and effective solution. The CPS matchmaker compares the requirements profile with its broad portfolio of technologies. The solution-neutral formulation prevents companies from using well-known technologies without knowing all the technologies that functionally fulfill the required task.

Currently, the CPS matchmaker is in the process of recording and validating application cases as well as technologies and their providers. According to the project sponsored by the Leitmarkt.IKT agency and the EFRE, the CPS matchmaker will be completed as an online platform by the end of 2018 and will be continually validated by summer 2019. In addition to the application-oriented reference application cases of the application partners, further applications for test purposes may be included in the case of interest. Current information can be viewed at: cyberKMU.de

Acknowledgement. This work has been funded by the Leitmarkt.NRW program of the European Federation R E cooperating with the federation of North-Rhine-Westphalia (NRW) while the project "cyberKMU^2". The authors wish to acknowledge the EFRE and NRW for their support.

References

1. Frey, C., Heinzmann, M., Niggemann, O., et al.: IKT in der Fabrik der Zukunft. ATP Edn. **04**(56), 42–53 (2014)
2. Matt, D., Rauch, E. (eds.): Chancen zur Bewältigung des Fachkraeftemangels in KMU (2014)
3. Akkaya, I., Derler, P., Emoto, S., Lee, E.A.: Systems engineering for industrial cyber-physical systems using aspects. Proc. IEEE **104**(5), 997–1012 (2016)
4. Derler, P., Lee, E.A., Vincentelli, A.S.: Modeling cyber-physical systems. Proc. IEEE **100**(1), 13–28 (2012)
5. Sendler, U.: Industrie 4.0– Beherrschung der industriellen Komplexität mit SysLM (systems lifecycle management). In: Sendler, U. (ed.) Industrie 4.0. Xpert.press. Springer, Heidelberg, pp. 1–19 (2013).doi:10.1007/978-3-642-36917-9_1
6. Acatech, (ed.): Cyber-Physical Systems: Innovationsmotor für Mobilität, Gesundheit, Energie und Produktion. Springer, Heidelberg (2011)
7. Kropp, S.: Entwicklung eines generischen Ereignismodells als Grundlage der Produktionsregelung. Aachen (2015)
8. Bauernhansl, T.: Industrie 4.0 in Produktion, Automatisierung und Logistik: Anwendung, Technologien und Migration. Springer, Wiesbaden (2014)
9. Bettenhausen, K.D., Kowalewski, S.: Cyber-Physical Systems: Chancen und Nutzen aus Sicht der Automation (2013)
10. Lee, E.A.: Cyber physical systems: design challenges. In: Computer Society, pp. 363–369 (2008)
11. National Science Foundation: Cyber-Physical Systems (CPS) (2010)
12. National Science Foundation: Cyber-Physical Systems (CPS) (2016)
13. Jordan, F., Bernardy, A., Stich, V. (eds.): Requirements-Based Matching Approach to Configurate Cyber-Physical Systems for SMEs (2017)
14. Lee, J., Bagheri, B., Kao, H.-A.: A cyber-physical systems architecture for industry 4.0-based manufacturing systems. Manufact. Lett. **3**, 18–23 (2014)
15. Stich, V., Deindl, M., Jordan, F., Maecker, L., Weber, F.: Studie - Cyber physial Systems in der Produktionspraxis. Wuppertal (2015)
16. Lee, E.A.: The past, present and future of CPS: a focus on models. Sensors **15**(3), 4837–4869 (2015)
17. Stich, V., Jordan, F., Birkmeier, M., Oflazgil, K., Reschke, J., Diews, A.: Big data technology for resilient failure management in production systems. In: Umeda, S., Nakano, M., Mizuyama, H., Hibino, H., Kiritsis, D., Cieminski, G. (eds.) APMS 2015. IAICT, vol. 459, pp. 447–454. Springer, Cham (2015). doi:10.1007/978-3-319-22756-6_55
18. Pfeifer, T., Schmitt, R.: Qualitätsmanagement: Strategien - Methoden – Techniken, 4th edn. Hanser, München (2010)
19. Kagermann, H., Gausemeier, J., Anderl, R., Schuh, G., Wahlster, W. (eds.): Industrie 4.0 im globalen Kontext: Strategien derZusammenarbeit mit internationalen Partnern. Herbert Utz Verlag, München (2016)

Self-similar Computing Structures for CPSs: A Case Study on POTS Service Process

Dorota Stadnicka[1], Massimiliano Pirani[2(✉)], Andrea Bonci[2], R.M. Chandima Ratnayake[3], and Sauro Longhi[2]

[1] Faculty of Mechanical Engineering and Aeronautics, Rzeszow University of Technology, Al. Powstancow Warszawy 12, 35-959 Rzeszow, Poland
dorota.stadnicka@prz.edu.pl

[2] Department of Information Engineering DII, Università Politecnica delle Marche, Ancona, Italy
massimiliano.pirani@gmail.com, {a.bonci,sauro.longhi}@univpm.it

[3] Faculty of Science and Technology, Department of Mechanical and Structural Engineering and Materials Science, University of Stavanger, Stavanger, Norway
chandima.ratnayake@uis.no

Abstract. This paper proposes a novel method for the structuring of the knowledge of a service process in order to be processed by lightweight declarative computing infrastructures. Through the identification of self-similarities in the process, the flow of the structured information and the sequence of activities performed in the process are easily implemented by means of cyber-physical systems technologies, in order to timely meet the customer/stakeholder's requirements. The study was performed in a telecommunication service providing organization. Service teams create a collaborative network. With the use of the CPS proposed in this work they can communicate problems and disseminate solutions. This methodology uses the information of a set of performance indicators of the service organization to achieve a better control of the effectiveness and the bottlenecks in the supply network. The methodology is borrowed from the mechatronics field and it is prone to a natural extension and reuse for the similar information structures in manufacturing processes.

Keywords: Cyber-physical system · Service process · Business process management systems · Protocols and information communication · Internet of services and service science

1 Introduction

In this work, the authors propose a multidisciplinary link between two research activities. Both are connected with the concept of Industry 4.0. The first one supports horizontal integration presenting a value flow in manufacturing and service processes by Value Stream Mapping (VSM). The other one is a new computing approach for highly dispersed networks of intelligent automation entities that support human tasks and decisions. The new computing trend refers mainly to the so-called Cyber-Physical Systems

L.M. Camarinha-Matos et al. (Eds.): PRO-VE 2017, IFIP AICT 506, pp. 157–166, 2017.
DOI: 10.1007/978-3-319-65151-4_15

(CPSs). The main research question of this work is whether and how the CPS can be implemented to enhance a collaborative network of service teams.

The methodology proposed here puts process experts in contact, using the VSM methodology, with the programming of the process control system through a computing infrastructure based on declarative paradigms – near to natural language. There are two reasons why the authors decided to use VSM. First was that the VSM was already used in the process analysis and wastes identification of the POTS process. Therefore, this tool was already known in the organization. The second reason was that more sophisticated tools such as, for example, BPMN (Business Process Model and Notation) were too difficult to be understood and adopted by people from the analysed service organization, since they are not IT engineers. Therefore, the Value Stream Map (VSMap) became the base of the development of the knowledge representation method and coupled with the database-centric techniques [1, 2], which are extended to cover the multidisciplinary aspects of tiny agents imitating the knowledge of production or services process experts. This multidisciplinary method will follow the state-of-the-art approaches [3, 4] that capture human experts' decisions, data and actions into the structured knowledge in order to render human and machines collaborative agents in the process design and problem solving. The used case will be conducted on an already well-tested and established procedure for plain old telephone services (POTS) [5]. The key of the methodology is in producing a knowledge representation that develops a VSMap into a relational form. That form allows to answer, with a declarative approach, the fundamental questions ('Who', 'Why', 'Where', 'How' and 'What') that capture the human experts' knowledge into a computing infrastructure. The data and knowledge input into the infrastructure determines the evolution of the process and controls its performance, bottlenecks as well as appearing problems. This a novelty in relation to previously published works.

In Sect. 2, some technological background is provided. Section 3 presents the methodology and the main concepts. In Sect. 4, a case study on POTS service is used to materialize the concepts and explain implementation techniques as means for their validation on the experimental set-up. Section 5 provides the conclusion.

2 Background

A rational agent is defined as an actor that should select an action which maximizes its performance measure for each possible percept sequence and evidence provided by agent's built-in knowledge [6]. An artificial agent is composed by an architecture and a program that transform percepts (inputs) into actions (outputs). The control, based on a logical-reactive (condition-action rules) knowledge model, has the advantage of the naturalness of the "if-then" rules and the possibility of representation of declarative and procedural knowledge [7]. The database-centric architecture [2] is a suitable choice in this sense. The development of technical systems and technological processes opens new opportunities both at the level of embedded control systems of a different scale, and at the level of a group interaction of decentralized multi-agent systems [7–9]. Agent-based automation systems, which realize the vision of CPSs, include increasingly intelligent solutions for managing the information that flows between different layers of products manufacturing or services for the understanding and control of the processes. The information is consumed and generated from the process actors in both human and machine-readable form [10]. The CPS vision implies that the information and the devices will possibly tend to disappear in a dust of collaborating distributed computing elements [11]. This way, the concept of performance measure of the process can be scaled down even to the lowest levels, while all the process elements still remain holistically connected by sharing the same self-similar semantics [1]. The database-centric technology should be based on the capabilities of the full relational model (RM) [12], in a form of a database language and algebra that is expressive enough to encompass both the artificial intelligence aspects and the automated procedures generation. Unfortunately, RM is still not available in lightweight implementation for embedded devices. Nevertheless, the already available database language of SQLite can be applied in dynamical performance optimization problems and smart bottlenecks detection on the highly distributed agent-based systems [1] validated on devices currently priced less than 5$. In this work, the problem of the control of a service process through a typical reflex agent is analyzed.

3 Methodology: Agent-Based Problem Representation and VSM

The methodology suggested in this paper is based on VSM, where the activities can be represented in a descriptive form [13]. In order to be able to use in CPSs, the analysed VSMap [5] is extended in this paper to illustrate additional information (see Fig. 2). The extended version of the VSMap contains the answers for the following questions concerning each step of the process: 'Who', What', 'How', 'Why', and 'Where', as well as the possible challenges/problems that shall be encountered together with countermeasures (see Fig. 2).

The problems in the selected case study process are taken into consideration based on the pre-defined set of rules (i.e. based on experts' knowledge) arranged in a hierarchical pattern. The knowledge gathered from the extended VSMap is used to construct the rule set that controls the evolution and the sequence of the tasks of the selected case study process. Additional information is collected from the analysis of the challenges/problems, which were discovered in the selected case study process. Therefore, it is possible to present the overall business process in terms of business *STEPS*, which correspond to the tasks to be performed. Hence, in different *STEPS*, it is possible to represent the relevant questions as well as the challenges/problems that are highlighted by experts (i.e. an extension of the VSM approach presented in [5]).

It is possible to find a convenient way to express a business process in the form of a tree structure of self-similar tasks [1]. Hence, the decisions made can change the sequence and the structure of the tasks in order to tackle problems dynamically. The division of systems into sub-systems creates a descent on a tree structure. This enables the adoption of the recursive computing structure [1] where the leaf elements will be atomic tasks of the process. Hence, the semantic used for a productive cell is mapped to an atomic activity at the lowest level of the process activity hierarchy. The *STEPS* will be considered as particular systems in the overall systems-of-systems control structure. A step is composed of sub-steps until the lowest level is reached (end of recursion), and hence, it collapses to a cell at the lowest level. With the mapping, an immediate application of the performance metrics can be obtained [1, 14]. That can be used to measure at run-time the drift of the current sequence of the tasks from the initial plan (desired state). For each step, a certain amount of time is dedicated. The desirability of a state is captured by the overall throughput effectiveness (OTE) that evaluates any sequence of the states. The OTE is recursively computed from OEE (overall equipment efficiency), and it can be determined by the value of OEE for the lower atomic tasks. This value depends relationally on which meaning (semantics) is assigned to the lower level tasks in the process. The OEE, and then OTE, capture the rate of time, speed and quality in the execution of the tasks [14]. As the current study concerns a 'service process', the overall performance efficiency (OPE) is used instead of the overall equipment efficiency (i.e. the term 'performance' is selected instead of the term 'equipment'). The use of OEE/OTE is not new and widespread, along with its measurement techniques in continuous and discrete processes (see for example [15, 16]). The novelty in the present work is the leveraging of its well-known and simple computing structure to render treatable the complex control of processes where information is heterogeneous and shared collaboratively between human and machines.

By following the original OEE expression in [14] but with extended meaning, we can define:

$$OPE = Aeff \times Peff \times Qeff \tag{1}$$

Note that the meaning of the three factors can assume different semantics depending on the interpretation (in formal logic sense [6]) adopted for them. The only requirement is to be a dimensionless quantity in the interval [0,1]. Typically: *Aeff* - "availability efficiency", captures the deleterious effects due to breakdowns, time delays, setups and adjustments of a process; *Peff* – "performance efficiency", captures a performance loss due to reduced speed, idling and minor stoppages in performing a task; *Qeff* – "quality efficiency", captures the loss due to mistakes or reworks in a task.

The lead time plays a significant role as it is inversely proportional to the OPE. For a deterministic task without problems, like END, we simply put OPE(END) = 1, as the lead time does not suffer any delays. Reversely, if OPE(Tx) = 0, it means that the task Tx never reaches completion, and it is a critical bottleneck where the correction intervention is highly needed. However, the OTE of some task series (sequence) is affected negatively from the passing of time as well as of delays.

The 'service process' is seen as a task environment for the agents, that is described by Performance, Environment, Actuators and Sensors (PEAS) [6] (Fig. 1).

In order to gather the knowledge concerning the selected service process, the following information is considered according to the proposed methodology: What are the steps of the process? Who should realize a particular step? What exactly should be done? How to do it? Why should these actions be undertaken? Where should the work be done? What documents will be used (If any)? What documents will be created (If any)? Which data bases should be available for the employees performing the step of the process? What problems can appear in the step? What should be done in case of problems appearance? The questions gather the expert's knowledge and they are

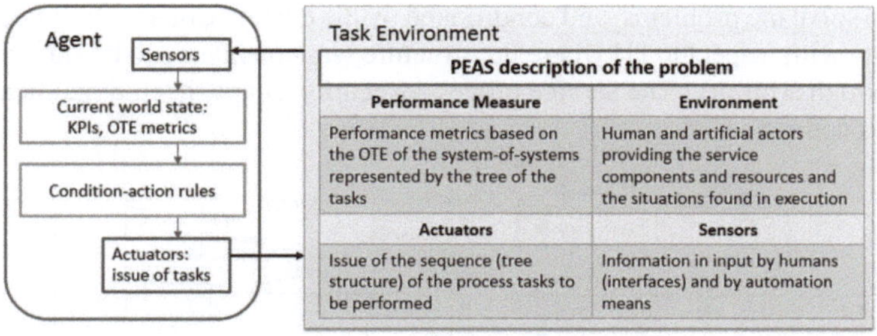

Fig. 1. Representation of the control of the service process through reflex agent scheme.

attributes of the systems and sub-systems (and so steps) with a hierarchical self-repeated structure (a pattern inside of a pattern for the fractal paradigm). The first statement is as follows: The agents participating in the process (machine or human) have a (quick) access to a distributed knowledge base (KB) containing data, documents, semantics, ontologies (if needed), rules and procedures. The information is expressed and modelled in a relational form, following the relational model. The other statement is: The agents can exchange the information with a suitable networking technology and the machine-to-machine or peer-to-peer connections are granted in this infrastructure.

4 A Case Study – POTS Service Process

The case study POTS service process [5] was analyzed using the proposed methodology. The POTS installation process concerns installation of plain old telephone services. Shortly the process can be described as follow. The first step of the process is transmission of an installation order by Polish Telecommunications to a firm providing telecommunication services with all data necessary to perform the installation process. Then a Technical Teams (TT) manager transmits the order to a corresponding team. The installers, who obtained the order check the materials availability on the vehicle and if it is necessary drive to a warehouse for the materials. When the materials are loaded on the vehicle the team go to an installation place. If the client is present they perform the installation and prepare all necessary documentation. In other case they inform TT manager and wait for a decision.

The extended VSMap of the process was developed to illustrate the case study service process together with the experts' knowledge based rules. A fragment of the process representation is shown in Fig. 2. In STEP 1, the question "What if a team is not available?" is going to be posed and verified in relation to the 'Who' attribute. In STEP 2, "What if not all materials are available?" is related to the 'What' attribute: "Checking the status of materials on the car". Typically, a possible problem occurring during the execution of the step may be associated with each of the step attributes (i.e. one of the 5 questions related to the knowledge representation). The answer to the problem creates a specific instance of the possible conditional alternative systems-of-systems structures. It affects the sequence of the subsequent steps. In other words, the instant structure is an instance of all the possible available tree-structures foreseen by the process experts in order to solve the problems, and conditioned by the evidence of a problem status. This is a novelty with respect to [1] where the structure was considered to be statically determined, though arbitrary. The service process execution adapts itself dynamically to the problems occurrence.

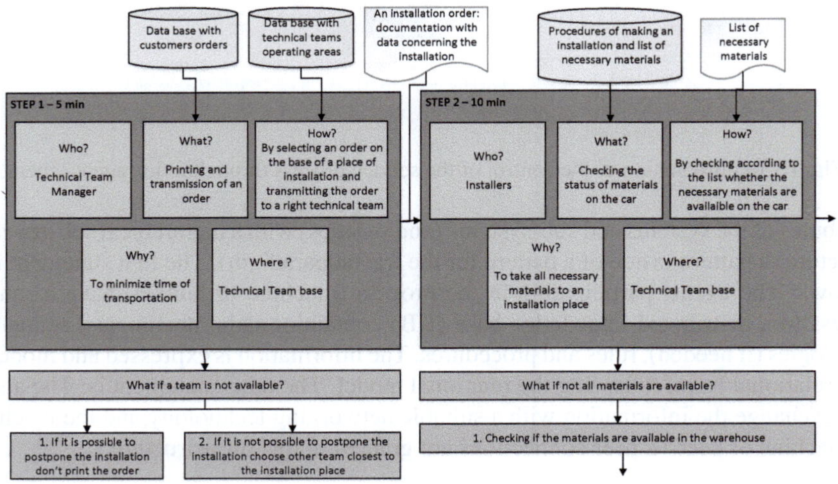

Fig. 2. Graphical representation of the POTS service process – a fragment.

It opens great new possibilities for the presented tool that can be also used in autonomous, evolving and self-organizing systems. The occurring problem appears as a percept to an agent. The agent queries the 5 questions to the knowledge base (or input database) relative to the associated sub-system under control, when the OTE of this subsystem is under the expected quality threshold or is diminished of a certain target rate. Thus, the result is relationally equivalent to the percept information. Depending on the percept, the sub-structure of the current step is changed accordingly.

The whole procedure can be put in a relational form and ready for implementation through the database tables (relations, in general) expressed in Fig. 3. In particular, the core table for the structure instance is the *Condition-action* relation in Fig. 3. This is the plug for artificial intelligence and learning. It can be expressed in other forms as well in order to admit different learning approaches. In the present case, the experience relation is the implementation of a typical decision-tree that captures some of the problem solving skills of human experts. The *Condition-action* table is quite compact as when a NULL (no value) in the cell is present, it means that the perception value can be whatever (undefined). The first column in the *Condition-action* is the identifier of the systems *Sx,x,x*. The comma- separated numbers in this notation indicate the path along the systems structure tree, one index for each of the level descent, in depth dimension, and ordered in breadth along the same level. For example, the S1, S2 are two systems at the top level containing STEP 1 and STEP 2 respectively. S1,1 and S1,2 are at the second level and they appear only when the percept of the problem p1 gives a true output (T). In another case (F), no problems occurred and the structure instantiation process (decision tree descent) stops on S1, and the task of step1 is executed. The action to be done and the descent in the tree are governed by the Sub_system relation attribute of the *Condition-action* relation (Fig. 3). There are commands to descent to the next level and possibly to establish a structure of descendants, as in the "Next_Level (series)" in the third row.

Conditions

Percept	Value	System with OTE under threshold	Semantic
p1	T	S1	Team not available
p2	T	S1,1/S1,2	It is possible to postpone
p3	T	S1,2,1/S1,2,2	Another team available and near to the site
p4	F	S2	All the required materials available in the car
p5	F	S2,1	All the required materials available in the warehouse
...	....	....	....

Condition-action (rules or productions)

System	Question	p1	p2	p3	...	Sub_system
S1	Who	T				Next_Level
S1	Who	F				Task(print order)
S1,1	What		T			Next_Level (series)
S1,2	What		F			Next_Level (series)
S1,1,1						Task(postpone)
S1,1,2						S1
S1,2,1	What			T		Next_Level (series)
S1,2,1	What			F		Task (END)
S1,2,1,1						Task(choose other team)
S1,2,1,2						S1

Fig. 3. Relations that implement the actions through the issuing of questions on the problems detected by the lowering of OTE values.

Other commands tell to simply start executing and controlling the tasks, as when "Task (print order)" or "Task(END)" appears. Otherwise, the substitution of a system with another one, as in the 6th row where S1,1,2 is transformed in S1, can also appear. This creates loops when needed. Given the *Condition-action* relation (here given as a single table for compactness of the paper, but such relation can be in a more structured form across more tables), the agent assigned to a certain step can query about the status of the problem in order to determine the instant system structure as well as the tasks sequence to be performed (actions) in the next business structure instance. For example, the agent produces the following (in SQL pseudocode):

```
SELECT Sub_system FROM experience WHERE
   Question==Who AND p1==(SELECT Value FROM percepts
           WHERE Percept==p1) WHERE System==S1;
```

The result of *SELECT* will command the agent to descend to the next level, and thus, to query again for the systems descendants in the three, i.e. *S1,1* and S1,2, and continue with the queries until it results in a task execution. This recursive procedure can be managed with a single query if the SQL dialect has recursive capabilities, or in the relational model. The result is the compilation of a *systree* table, which enables the computing of the OTE [1]. However, the computing details were not presented here. As an example, the systems generated for STEP 1 are presented in Fig. 4.

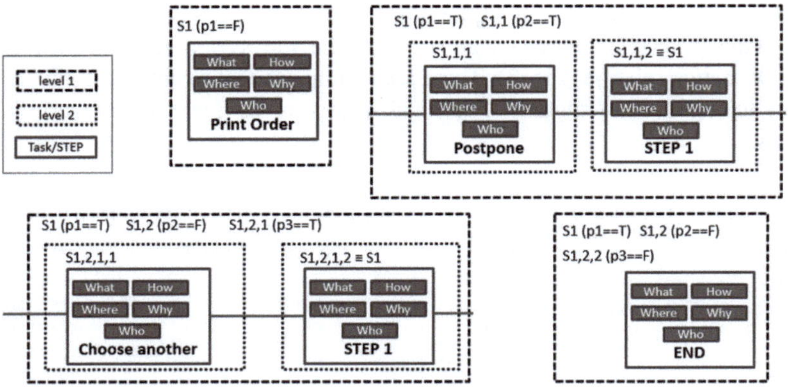

Fig. 4. Graphical representation of the POTS service based on experience table conditions.

The representation shows the structure instantiation obtained with the problem perception from the agents. After an agent obtains the information structure from the *Condition-action* relation, it sees the actual structure and executes it while measuring its OTE. In Fig. 4, all the conditional cases provided in the *Conditions* relation of Fig. 4 are depicted. Each of the four systems in Fig. 4 are obtained through a decision tree. Each of the four systems are alternative structure instances of the process STEP 1, depending on an agent decisions and triggered by the percepts (problems' status) sampled at the beginning of the step. It should be noted that in the presented example the subsystems were considered to have a series structure, but it is not always the case in general [1, 14].

5 Conclusions

This multidisciplinary research work aims at establishing a methodology that links approaches of the process control to the CPSs. From the computer science side, it relies on an extension of a well-known recursive performance metrics method for industrial processes and manufacturing. The tree structure of this computing involves also all the topologies that can be put in a direct acyclic graph form through the four fundamental structures (series, parallel, expansion and assembly) that are proven for completeness in manufacturing layouts [14]. If applied to self-similar structures the computing results greatly simplified and can scale well on tiny devices, also for tree structures of relevant depth. The property of self-similarity is a common feature in manufacturing and other processes, which mostly depends on the appropriate semantics chosen for the indicators. The presented methodology can be straightforwardly applied to the class of problems encompassed from the fractal factory paradigm [1]. The knowledge of experts is conveyed in a declarative (natural-like) language near to humans and readable from machines, in order to program a computing infrastructure for the real-time process control and bottleneck detection. The presented methodology adds value to the well-known VSM method. It was expressed and challenged through a relevant case of POTS services. The performed analysis allows to conclude that the presented methodology enables its executors to understand the realized process and the problems that may appear better. However, it should be underlined that the process has to be well analysed and structured by humans. They should create the knowledge based on a process analysis as well as people's experience to create a graphical representation of the process and the rules being applied in the process realization. Additionally, possible problems should be discussed in order to find solutions that then will be proposed by the created CPS following the process. The analysed POTS process is ready for the future experimental sessions. In the future works, the proposed performance indicators such as OPE and OTE will be calculated on the basis of the data derived from the POTS service process realization.

References

1. Pirani, M., Bonci, A., Longhi, S.: A scalable production efficiency tool for the robotic cloud in the fractal factory. In: IECON 2016-42nd Annual Conference of the IEEE, pp. 6847–6852 (2016)
2. Bonci, A., Pirani, M., Longhi, S.: A database-centric approach for the modeling, simulation and control of cyber-physical systems in the factory of the future. In: 8th IFAC Conference on Manufacturing Modelling, MIM 2016, pp. 249–254. IFAC-PapersOnLine (2016)
3. Qin, H., Hongwei, W., Johnson, A.L.: A RFBSE model for capturing engineers' useful knowledge and experience during the design process. Robot. Comput. Integr. Manufact. **44**, 30–43 (2017)
4. Bruno, G., Taurino, T., Villa, A.: An approach to support SMEs in manufacturing knowledge organization. J. Intell. Manufact. **23**, 1–14 (2016)
5. Stadnicka, D., Ratnayake, R.M.C.: Minimization of service disturbance: VSM based case study in telecommunication industry. In: 8th IFAC Conference on Manufacturing Modelling, Management and Control MIM 2016, pp. 255–260. IFAC-PapersOnLine (2016)
6. Russell, S.J., Norvig, P.: Artificial Intelligence: A Modern Approach. Prentice Hall, Egnlewood Cliffs (2009)
7. Vassilyev, S.N., Kelina, A.Y., Kudinov, Y.I., Pashchenko, F.F.: Intelligent control systems. Procedia Comput. Sci. **103**, 623–628 (2017)
8. Leitão, P., Karnouskos, S., Ribeiro, L., Lee, J., Strasser, T., Colombo, A.W.: Smart agents in industrial cyber-physical systems. Proc. IEEE **104**(5), 1086–1101 (2016)
9. Zhenqiang, B., Weiye, W., Peng, W., Pan, Q.: Research on production scheduling system with bottleneck based on multi-agent. Phys. Procedia **24**, 1903–1909 (2012)
10. Frank, J.A., Kapila, V.: Integrating smart mobile devices for immersive interaction and control of physical systems: a cyber-physical approach. In: Zhang, D., Wei, B. (eds.) Advanced Mechatronics and MEMS Devices II. MN, pp. 73–93. Springer, Cham (2017). doi: 10.1007/978-3-319-32180-6_5
11. Chiang, M., Zhang, T.: Fog and IoT: an overview of research opportunities. IEEE Int. Things J. **3**(6), 854–864 (2016)
12. Date, C., Darwen, H., Lorentzos, N.: Time and Relational Theory, Second Edition: Temporal Databases in the Relational Model and SQL. Morgan Kaufmann, San Francisco (2014)
13. Stadnicka, D., Ratnayake, R.M.C.: Simple approach for Value Stream Mapping for business process analysis. In: Proceedings of the 2015 IEEE IEEM - IEEE International Conference on Industrial Engineering and Engineering Management (IEEM), pp. 88–94 (2015)

14. Muthiah, K.M.N., Huang, S.H.: Overall throughput effectiveness (OTE) metric for factory-level performance monitoring and bottleneck detection. Int. J. Prod. Res. **45**(20), 4753–4769 (2007)
15. Nayak, D.M., Vijaya Kumar, M.N., Naidu, G.S., Shankar, V.: Evaluation of OEE in a continuous process industry on an insulation line in a cable manufacturing unit. Int. J. Innovative Res. Sci. Eng. Technol. **2**(5), 1629–1634 (2013)
16. Muthiah, K.M., Huang, S.H.: A review of literature on manufacturing systems productivity measurement and improvement. Int. J. Ind. Syst. Eng. **1**(4), 461–484 (2006)

Ontology-Based Framework to Design a Collaborative Human-Robotic Workcell

Dario Antonelli and Giulia Bruno(✉)

Department of Management and Production Engineering, Politecnico di Torino, Corso Duca degli Abruzzi 24, 10129 Torino, Italy
{dario.antonelli,giulia.bruno}@polito.it

Abstract. Exploiting the collaboration between human and robots is a fundamental target for industrial Cyber-Physical Systems. Several studies have already addressed the evaluation of collaborative robotic cells, especially in automotive industry. Feasible tasks assignment to workers and robots were proposed in a few use-cases. However, previous studies start from an existing configuration of the collaborative assembly cell. Due to the moderate diffusion of collaborative robotic applications in the industry, it would be better to define a method orienting the design of a new instances of collaborative cells, by taking into account the different classifications of collaboration deriving by the new ISO 15066 standard. The classification depends on the kind of information that must be made available within the cell, and the possible methods of acquisition and communication of such information. This knowledge base will be represented in the form of ontology, as an extension of the CORA (Core Ontologies for Robotics and Automation) ontology, by IEEE Robotics and Automation Society. By adopting this ontology, it will be possible to support the design of new collaborative cell. An industrial case-study will prove the efficacy of the proposed method.

Keywords: Collaborative robots · Cyber physical systems · Ontology

1 Introduction

The design of collaborative environments where robots can work side by side with human operators for the execution of complex industrial tasks is having an increasing interest from both academics and robot manufacturers. In a survey on innovative flexible approaches to automotive assembly technologies, considerable importance is given to cooperation among humans and robots [1]. For example, some complex assembly procedures require both precise handling and other assembly operations, such as inserting fasteners and connecting wire harnesses. Some of these tasks require the precision and speed of automation, while others benefit from the dexterity and intelligence of human operators.

Human-Robot Collaboration (HRC) brings benefits to industrial applications in terms of speed, efficiency, better quality of the production and better quality of the workplace (ergonomic) [2]. However, as far as now, robotic automation was rarely

L.M. Camarinha-Matos et al. (Eds.): PRO-VE 2017, IFIP AICT 506, pp. 167–174, 2017.
DOI: 10.1007/978-3-319-65151-4_16

applied in small batch productions, due to the variety of products and of variable production schedules [3]. The workplace organization leans towards flexibility where manual systems are advantaged. Now, several robot manufacturers are designing special robot architectures, named collaborative robots, allowing the human workers to execute their tasks in the same workplace as the robots, e.g., KUKA LBR [4] and ABB YuMi [5]. However, these robots have limitations in terms of payload, velocity, and strength that prevent their use in several industrial contexts. Some of these limits are related to the necessity of respecting the Technical Specifications ISO 15066 in order to assure human worker safety.

Differently from such architectures, present study focuses on the subset of HRC that exploits standard industrial robots and allows for a safe interaction with the robot, paying a reasonable fee in reduced flexibility. The field of study is the industrial manual and automatic assembly by welding. Small factories usually already have robotic welding cells next to their manual workstations. The aim of this work is to show that it is possible to redesign existing industrial robotic cells for executing a number of collaborative actions, respecting safety requirements.

The rest of the paper is organized as follows. Section 2 revises the state of the art in literature. Section 3 describes the two ontologies necessary in this study, used to classify the kind of information that must be made available within the cell, and the possible methods of acquisition and communication of such information. In Sect. 4, the design and setup of a HRC working cell is described, specifically for an industrial use case. Finally Sect. 5 draws conclusions and states future works.

2 Related Works

The collaborative execution of manufacturing tasks between humans and robots aims to improve the efficiency of industrial processes, for an high adaptability and robustness of the cell Several works are present in literature that address the evaluation of robotic cells, especially in automotive industry [6, 7].

Some efforts have been devoted to investigate the safety of human-robot collaboration [8, 9], and also the problem of define the optimal assignment of tasks between workers and robots was studied in some use-cases [10, 11]. Other problems investigated in literature address the psychological acceptation of the robot as a reliable team member [12, 13].

Some studies are related to the reduction of programming time of robots by exploiting Programming by Demonstration or Learning by Demonstration techniques [14–16]. Even if several human capabilities cannot be fully replaced by robots, it is possible to achieve a solution by combining the capabilities of both. Moving the collaborative robot from laboratory demonstrations to current production cells arises new orders of issues that have not been adequately considered in the past.

What's missing is a solid methodology to configure a HRC cell, based on the manufacturing process under consideration and the kind of collaboration to implement.

3 HRC Ontologies

Ontologies plays a fundamental role in knowledge management because they formally specifies the key concepts, properties, relationships, and axioms of a given domain [17]. Two ontologies are necessary in this study. The first one, named CCORA, is an extension of a standard ontology for robotics and automation (CORA) by adding concepts related to collaborative cells. The second one, named MPRO, is a manufacturing process ontology, which contains concepts related to manufacturing processes and related machines, tools and parameters.

The relationships between CCORA and MPRO with the other existing ontologies in the domain is represented in Fig. 1. The Ontologies for Robotics and Automation Working Group (ORA WG) defined a core ontology for robotics and automation (CORA), which specifies the general concepts in this context [18]. CORA extends SUMO, the Suggested Upper Merged Ontology, which is an open source upper ontology, widely used in several domains [19]. Between CORA and SUMO, there is the CORAX ontology, which represents concepts and relations commonly found in subdomains but that are too general to be included in CORA [20]. We further extended the CORA ontology in the Collaborative CORA (CCORA) by inserting the concepts related to human-robot collaboration. CCORA inherits from both CORA and SUMO, because some CCORA entities are specifications of more general SUMO concepts. The MPRO ontology cover the knowledge related to manufacturing operations, thus is inherits directly from the SUMO concepts.

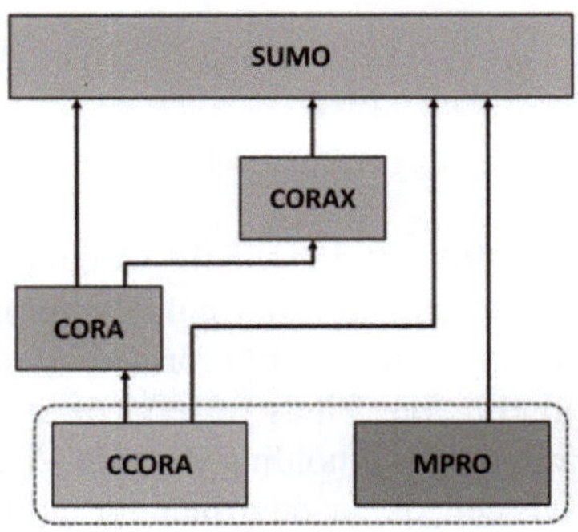

Fig. 1. Relationships between the two defined ontologies (CCORA and MPRO) with respect to previous ontologies SUMO, CORA and CORAX.

3.1 Collaborative CORA (CCORA) Ontology

The most general SUMO category is Entity, given as a disjoint partition of Physical and Abstract entities. The first one represents entities with spatio-temporal extension, while the second one is for entities that do not need have spatio-temporal extension. Both entities are further specialized: Physical into Object and Process, while Abstract into Quantity, Attribute, SetOrClass, Relation and Proposition. SUMO has a total of more than 500 entities, covering a broad spectrum of concepts.

The CORAX ontology defines concepts that are too general to be in CORA, which cover aspects of reality that are necessary for modelling, but are not explicitly or completely covered by SUMO. Examples of CORAX entities are physical environment, interaction, artificial system, processing device, robot motion, human robot communication, robot communication.

CORA focuses on defining a robot, along with the specification of other related entities. The entities defined in the CORA ontology are Robot part, Robot interface, Robot group, Robotic system (further divided into Single Robotic System and Collective Robotic System) and Robotic environment. The relationships among concepts of SUMO, CORAX and CORA are represented in Fig. 2.

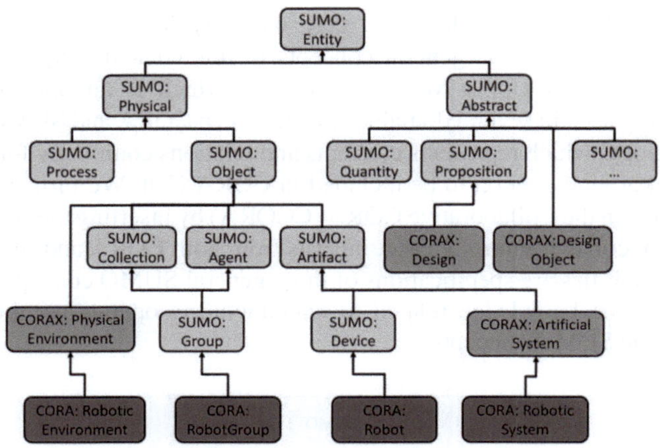

Fig. 2. Relationships among concepts of SUMO, CORAX and CORA.

We further extended the CORA ontology in the Collaborative CORA (CCORA) by inserting the concepts related to human-robot collaboration, as shown in Fig. 3. We defined a collaborative robotic system an entity formed by robots, human workers, and a series of devices. Particularly, four kinds of devices are need: observing devices, pointing devices, gripping devices and holding devices. A collaborative robotic environment, i.e., a collaborative cell, is an environment equipped with a collaborative robotic system.

Three types of collaborative environments exist, the spatial collaboration environment, the temporal collaboration environment, and the spatiotemporal coloration environment. Depending on the kind of collaborative environment, different devices are needed. For example, in the case of a spatial collaboration, where humans and robots work in the same space but in different times, observing devices are mandatory (e.g., laser scanner) to reveal the human presence, to grant that the human worker is not in the cell while the robot is working.

CCORA also extends the SUMO Process with the transport processes, which are not covered by the MPRO ontology.

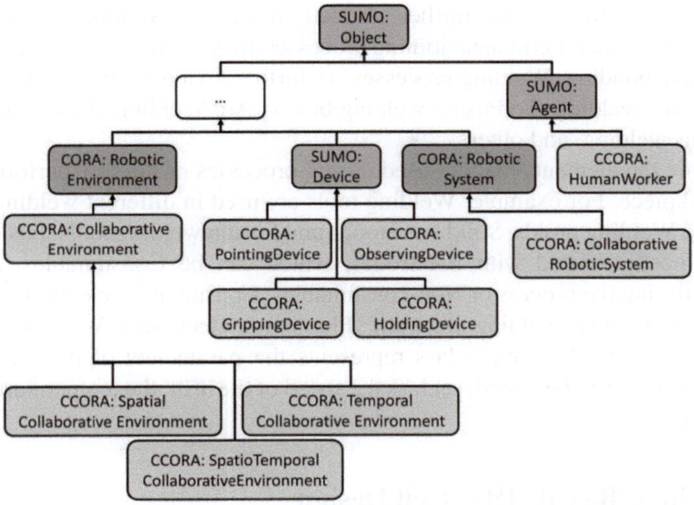

Fig. 3. Relationships among concepts of CCORA, SUMO and CORA.

3.2 Manufacturing Process (MPRO) Ontology

The MPRO ontology cover the knowledge related to manufacturing operations. The main classes of the MPRO ontology are Manufacturing process, Machine, Tool and Parameter [21]. A portion of the MPRO ontology related to the SUMO ontology is shown in Fig. 4.

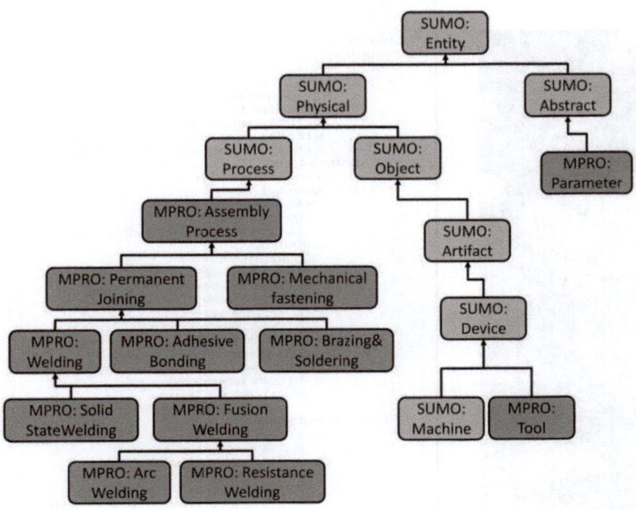

Fig. 4. Relationships between MPRO and SUMO concepts.

Assembly operations are further divided in Permanent joining processes and Mechanical fastening. Permanent joining processes are Welding, Brazing and soldering, and Adhesive bonding. Welding processes are further divided between Fusion welding and Solid state welding. To Fusion welding belong Arc Welding, Resistance Welding, Oxyfuel gas welding, and others.

Tools are the elements that are used during processes or directly perform the work on the workpiece. For example, Welding tools are used in different welding processes and include Welding molds, Solid state tools, and Fusion welding tools. Fusion welding tools are mostly related with Electrodes, which can be Consumables, if they are consumed during the process or Non-consumables. Consumables electrodes are Coated electrodes, Electrogas welding electrode, Flux cored electrodes, Wire electrodes, and GMAW guns. The Parameter class represents the parameters of the manufacturing processes that have to be stored, such as the speed of the drill, the temperature, the water pressure, etc.

4 Ontology-Based HRC Cell Design

The considered industrial process is the assembly of a two-stage cutter (shown in Fig. 5 left), which is used to shred snow and send it to the rear turbine, which throws it out from the roadway. This process was originally executed manually by two operators, but the company wanted to evaluate the introduction of a robot to perform a subset of tasks. By mapping the industrial process on the MPRO ontology, we were able to define

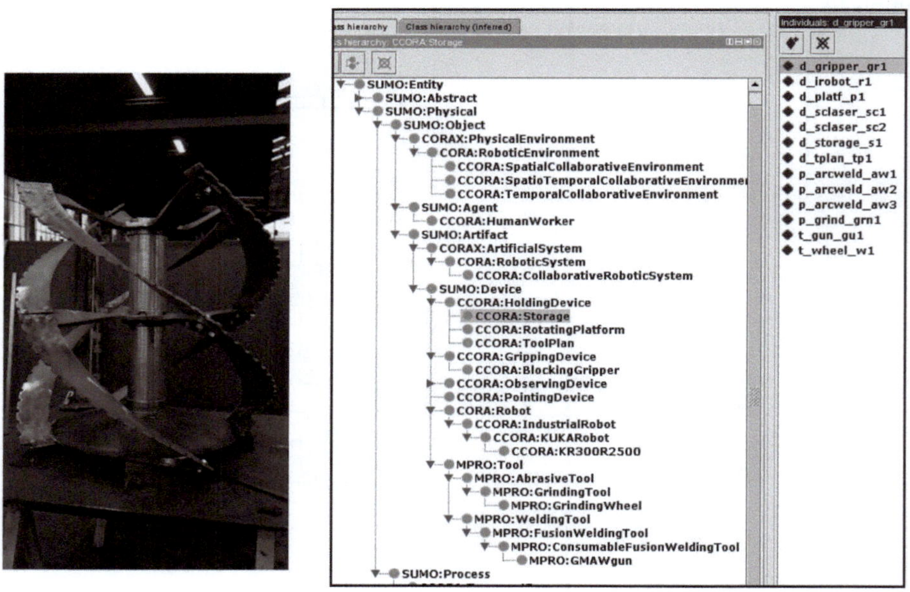

Fig. 5. Image of the cutter considered as use case (left) and the developed ontology with instances (right) shown in the Protégé (http://protege.stanford.edu)

the processes and the corresponding tools that are needed in the cell, i.e., a welding torch for the arc welding and a grinder for the grinding process. These elements were inserted as instances of the corresponding entities in the ontology.

Assuming a task assignment was done (the assignment method is out of the scope of this work), by analysing the tasks assigned to the robot, and knowing that the kind of collaboration of interest in this case is a spatial collaboration, it was possible to exploit the CCORA ontology to select among the vast amount of possible kinds of robots, devices, etc., the set of elements needed in the cell. The following entities were considered: Industrial Robot, Observing device, Gripping device, and Holding device. Among the available industrial robots, the selection was for a KUKA robot KR 300 R2500 ultra C, due to the load and distance capacity. The holding devices are a tool plan to allow the robot executing the operations, a rotating platform so that the robot can easily reach all the positions required for the operations, and a component storage, where the final components are arranged according to a precise order in such a way that the robot can identify and pick them. The gripping device is a blocking gripper, so that the robot can move disks and spiders. The Observing devices are two laser scanners, one for verifying the correct positioning of tools and items, and another one to identify the human worker position. The resulting ontology corresponding to the HRC of such process is shown in Fig. 5 (right).

5 Conclusion

The paper proposed a method to support the design of a human- robotic cell based on the industrial process of interest and the kind of HRC needed. Both the knowledge related to the machines and tools needed for the manufacturing process and the relationships between each kind of collaborative environment and the devices needed in the corresponding cell are stored in the ontology. From this knowledge base it is possible to select the elements needed for the full configuration of the cell.

References

1. Michalos, G., Makris, S., Papakostas, N., Mourtzis, D., Chryssolouris, G.: Automotive assembly technologies review: challenges and outlook for a flexible and adaptive approach. CIRP J. Manuf. Sci. Technol. **2**(2), 81–91 (2010)
2. Helms, E., Schraft, R.D., Hagele, M.: rob@ work: robot assistant in industrial environments. In: Proceedings of the Robot and Human Interactive Communication, pp. 399–404. IEEE (2002)
3. Antonelli, D., Astanin, S., Bruno, G.: Applicability of human-robot collaboration to small batch production. In: Afsarmanesh, H., Camarinha-Matos, L.M., Lucas Soares, A. (eds.) PRO-VE 2016. IFIP AICT, vol. 480, pp. 24–32. Springer, Cham (2016). doi: 10.1007/978-3-319-45390-3_3
4. Bischoff, R., et al.: The KUKA-DLR lightweight robot arm-a new reference platform for robotics research and manufacturing. In: 2010 41st International Symposium on Robotics (ISR). VDE (2010)

5. Kirschner, D., Velik, R., Yahyanejad, S., Brandstötter, M., Hofbaur, M.: YuMi, come and play with Me! A collaborative robot for piecing together a tangram puzzle. In: Ronzhin, A., Rigoll, G., Meshcheryakov, R. (eds.) ICR 2016. LNCS, vol. 9812, pp. 243–251. Springer, Cham (2016). doi:10.1007/978-3-319-43955-6_29
6. Papakostas, N., Michalos, G., Makris, S., Zouzias, D., Chryssolouris, G.: Industrial applications with cooperating robots for the flexible assembly. Int. J. Comput. Integr. Manuf. **24**(7), 650–660 (2011)
7. Pedrocchi, N., Vicentini, F., Malosio, M., Tosatti, L.M.: Safe human–robot cooperation in an industrial environment. Int. J. Adv. Robot. Syst. IJARS **10**(27), 27 (2012)
8. Harper, C., Virk, G.: Towards the development of international safety standards for human robot interaction. Int. J. Soc. Robot. **2**(3), 229–234 (2010)
9. Matthias, B., et al.: Safety of collaborative industrial robots: Certification possibilities for a collaborative assembly robot concept. In: IEEE ISAM (2011)
10. Ding, H., Schipper, M., Bjoern, M.: Optimized task distribution for industrial assembly in mixed human–robot environments – case study on IO module assembly. In: IEEE International Conference on Automation Science and Engineering (2014)
11. Tan, J.T.C., Duan, F., Zhang, Y., Arai, T.: Extending task analysis in HTA to model man-machine collaboration in cell production. In: IEEE International Conference on Robotics and Biomimetics, ROBIO 2008, pp. 542–547 (2009)
12. Hinds, P.J., Roberts, T.L., Jones, H.: Whose job is it anyway? A study of human-robot interaction in a collaborative task. Hum. Comput. Interact. **19**(1), 151–181 (2004)
13. Freedy, A., DeVisser, E., Weltman, G., Coeyman, N.: Measurement of trust in human-robot collaboration. In: International Symposium on Collaborative Technologies and Systems, CTS 2007, pp. 106–114. IEEE (2007)
14. Argall, B.D., Chernova, S., Veloso, M., Browning, B.: A survey of robot learning from demonstration. Robot. Auton. Syst. **57**(5), 469–483 (2009)
15. Antonelli, D., Astanin, S.: Qualification of a collaborative human-robot welding cell. Procedia CIRP **41**, 352–357 (2016)
16. Antonelli, D., Astanin, S., Caporaletti, G., Donati, F.: FREE: flexible and safe interactive human-robot environment for small batch exacting applications. In: Röhrbein, F., Veiga, G., Natale, C. (eds.) Gearing Up and Accelerating Cross-fertilization between Academic and Industrial Robotics Research in Europe. STAR, vol. 94, pp. 47–62. Springer, Cham (2014). doi:10.1007/978-3-319-03838-4_3
17. Bruno, G., Antonelli, D., Korf, R., Lentes, J., Zimmermann, N.: Exploitation of a semantic platform to store and reuse PLM knowledge. In: Grabot, B., Vallespir, B., Gomes, S., Bouras, A., Kiritsis, D. (eds.) APMS 2014, Part I. IFIP AICT, vol. 438, pp. 59–66. Springer, Heidelberg (2014). doi:10.1007/978-3-662-44739-0_8
18. Prestes, E., et al.: Towards a core ontology for robotics and automation. Robot. Auton. Syst. **61**(2013), 1193–1204 (2013)
19. Niles, I., Pease, A.: Toward a standard upper ontology. In: Proceedings of the 2nd International Conference on Formal Ontology in Information Systems (2001)
20. Fiorini, S.R., et al.: Extensions to the core ontology for robotics and automation. Robot. Comput. Integr. Manuf. **33**, 3–11 (2015)
21. Bruno, G.: Semantic organization of product lifecycle information through a modular ontology. Int. J. Circ. Syst. Sig. Process. **9**, 16–26 (2015)

Multi-agent Systems for Production Management in Collaborative Manufacturing

Teresa Taurino(✉) and Agostino Villa

Department of Management and Production Engineering,
Politecnico di Torino, Corso Duca degli Abruzzi 24, 10129 Turin, Italy
{teresa.taurino,agostino.villa}@polito.it

Abstract. The paper aims to analyze multi-agent management structures in Small-Mid Enterprises (SME), such to investigate how collaborations among agents could be improved. A SME manager has generally to face with three issues: data management, organization of the production phases, interactions with mid-level management (denoted by "agents"). Data management is necessary in order to have a clear representation of the many types of data about products, orders and resources of the company. The organization of production phases consists on the management of the production process phases from design up to recycling. Based on a clear representation of the product life cycle, the manager will be able to organize the interactions between these agents (each one dedicated to handle a process phase) so as to facilitate the collaboration, and to make effective each mid-level management as far as it is concerned with controlling the operations to be carried out in each process phase. A model of the mid-layer multi-agent management negotiation, according to the "game theory" viewpoint, is proposed, and its main characters are analyzed, in view of its application.

Keywords: Collaborative manufacturing · Multi-agent systems · Game theory

1 Introduction

In today global markets, factory managers are under pressure to optimize technological processes and to reduce production costs. Adequate tools and sufficiently robust procedures do not support Small and Medium Enterprises (SME) in the organization of work and in the management of the product life-cycle phases. On the other hand, a number of formal approaches have been developed for solving individual processing/managing problems in manufacturing, but their utilization in SMEs find obstacles in the insufficient knowledge of managers and enterprise owners [1, 2].

A SME manager generally face with three issues: how to have a clear representation of data concerning products, orders and resources; how to organize the various phases of the production process, from design up to recycling; how to interact with employees to whom management and control duties have been assigned.

These problems have a common point: use a clear representation of the product life cycle, highlighting the sequence of process steps [3]. Using this representation, the manager will be able to reform/re-engineer the management structure of his/her company based on the following logic:

L.M. Camarinha-Matos et al. (Eds.): PRO-VE 2017, IFIP AICT 506, pp. 175–182, 2017.
DOI: 10.1007/978-3-319-65151-4_17

(a) To organize the stages of the product's life cycle, divide them into management duties, and assign each stage, as management duty, to a mid-level manager of the company with precise responsibilities and authority;
(b) To organize the interactions between these mid-level managers (one dedicated to handle a phase) so as to facilitate the collaboration between the mid-level managers themselves and therefore make them more profitable for the company; this organization aims to optimize the "enterprise integration", i.e. cooperation within the enterprise;
(c) To make effective the management of each mid-level manager as far as it is concerned with controlling the operations to be carried out at each stage; this corresponds - with reference to the "production" phase, for example - at shop-floor management, that is, the collaboration between manufacturing resources within a shop-floor.

The two points (b) and (c) generally represent the greatest difficulty for a top manager/owner. Instead, the organization of the product life cycle phases and the operations to implement them is a simpler task for top management of SMEs since, often, the top manager is also the founder of the enterprise and the "initial designer" of the first product that the company manufactures.

This work is therefore devoted to the analysis of an organizational structure designed to support the manager in solving the problems mentioned in (b) and (c).

2 Some Hints on the Multi-agent Structure of a Manufacturing SME

The multi-agent modeling approach of a manufacturing mid enterprise is here discussed with reference to the main results of the EU project ame-PLM - Advanced Platform for Manufacturing Engineering and Product Lifecycle Management [3].

As above mentioned, product and production engineering in mid industrial companies are typically fragmented across different functional units, dedicated to the complementary phases of a product life cycle. A typical scheme of these phases is in Fig. 1, with reference to a generic product and to its main life cycle phases.

With reference to Fig. 1, conceptual design and preliminary design activities are typical of the SME manager/owner, while other activities involve several mid-level managers, as illustrated in the following figures referred to the "detailed design" phase (Fig. 2), the "production" phase (Fig. 3), and the "utilization" phase (Fig. 4).

The group of mid-level managers that can be recognized in Figs. 2, 3 and 4 are embedded into a network of interactions, each one corresponding to a negotiation. In fact, every mid-level manager has the duty of achieving two goals: (i) to optimize the efficiency of the plant/service/shop-floor managed by himself; (ii) to give the maximum possible contribution to the enterprise profit.

The first goal could be individually obtained by any mid-level manager (for brevity denoted in the following "**agent**"), irrespective of any interaction with the others, but the second goal is of prevailing importance. That generates a two-layer approach in order to manage the enterprise activities: (1) a higher-layer interactions among agents, i.e.

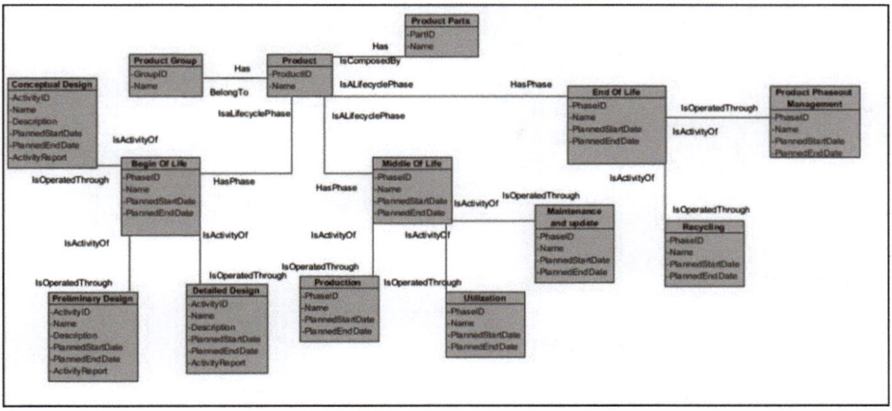

Fig. 1. Main phases of the product life cycle and their macro-activities.

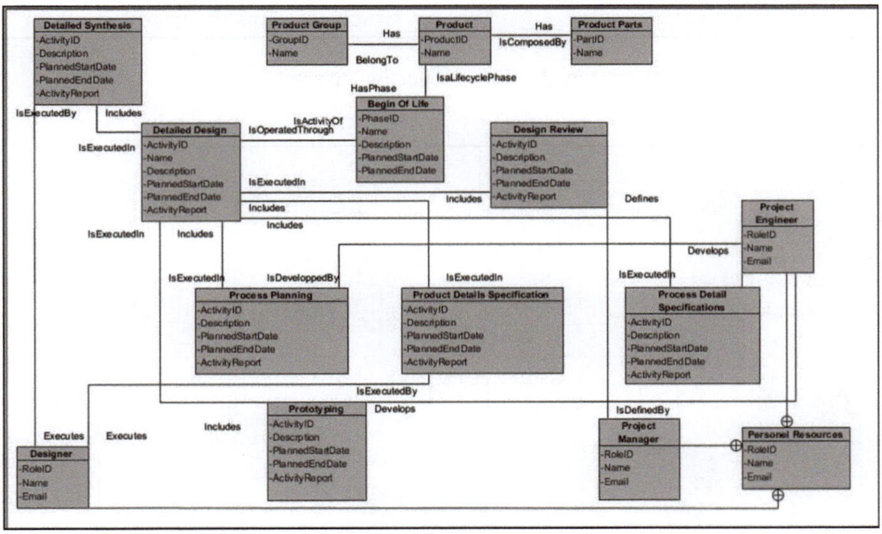

Fig. 2. The detailed design phase.

negotiations with the aim of obtaining the strongest possible coordination of tasks and efforts; (2) a lower-layer individual optimization of the operations required at each phase.

With reference to the higher-layer negotiation, this has to be based on the network of interactions linking agents, as well as on the presence of a "moderator/broker", who will be the owner/top manager. The presence of the "moderator" ensures that negotiation is a converging process towards a common goal [4]. The kind of agents' network can favor the negotiation process, busting conflicts between agents wanting to maximize their own goals, as in case of the managers in a SME network [5–7].

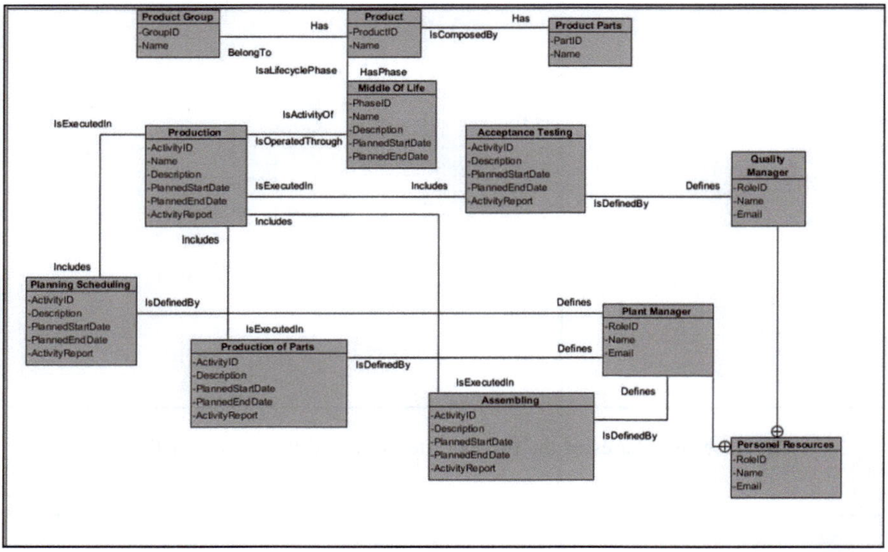

Fig. 3. The “production” phase.

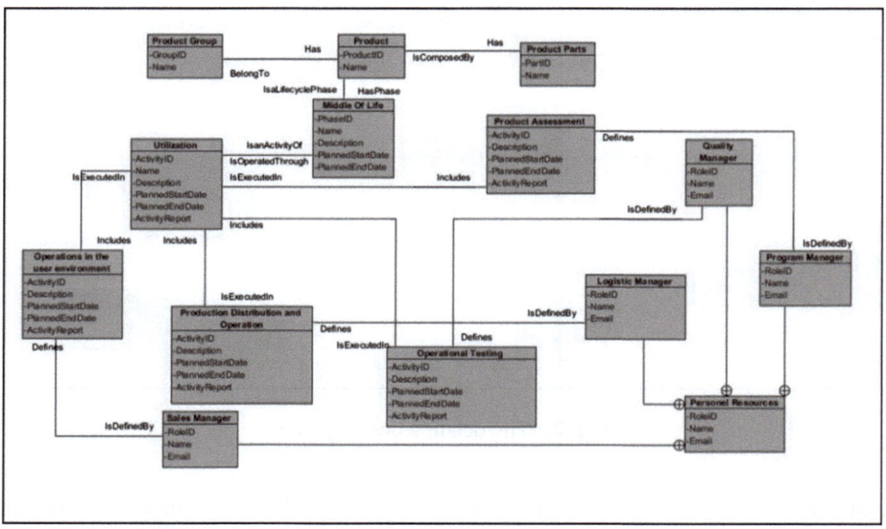

Fig. 4. The product “utilization” phase.

An example of agents' network, that can be derived from Figs. 2, 3 and 4, is illustrated in the following Fig. 5:

- two partial negotiations, one between the "plant manager" in Fig. 3 and the "project manager" in Fig. 2, and the other between the "plant manager" and the "program manager" in Fig. 4;
- one loop transferring requests for improvements from the "program manager" towards the "project manager".

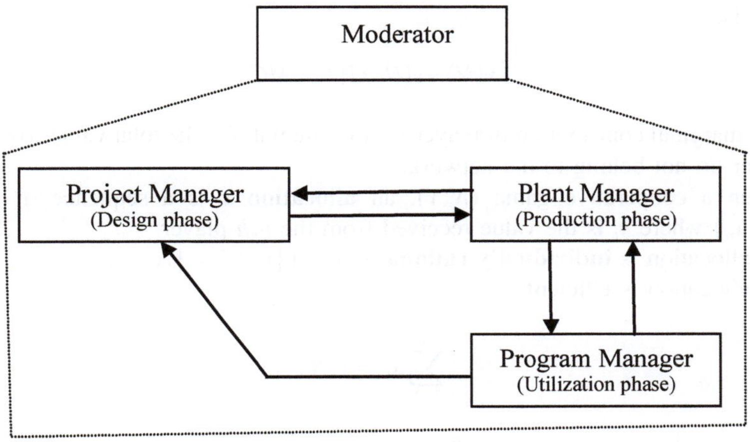

Fig. 5. Simple negotiation scheme among the three agents, with the "Moderator" busting conflicts between agents

Therefore, it is now necessary to discuss a formal model of the multi-agents negotiations, oriented towards the evaluation about when an active collaboration among agents could be activated.

3 Multi-agent Collaboration Model Based on Game Theory

Based on the above considerations, now the agents network of negotiations is modeled by the game theory [4], according to the idea that any agent (in practice, a mid-layer manager) wants to be competitive but must assure his/her best contribution to the enterprise profit.

Then, the requirement from any agent of the network is to understand the payoff of the part of production system managed by himself. In order to evaluate this payoff, it is necessary to adopt a network model based on "cooperative game theory" that shows the different way of "players" (here, the agents) to interact together and cooperate.

A cooperative game (N, v) is constituted by two elements:

- the finite set of players $N = \{1, 2, \ldots, n\}$, i.e. the enterprises that compose the network;
- the characteristic function v, that associates to each subset $S \subset N$ a number $v(S)$ that represents the value created by each subset of players.

$v(N)$ is the total value created, i.e. the value created when all the players in N cooperate together.

Given the set N and a specific player $i \in N$, the **marginal contribution** MC_i of player i is:

$$v(N) - v(N \backslash \{i\}) = MC_i \tag{1}$$

The marginal contribution of player *i* is the amount that the total value would lost if the payer do not belong to the network.

Given a cooperative game (N, v), an **allocation** $\boldsymbol{x}$ is a sequence of numbers $(x_1, \ldots, x_n)$ where x_i is the value received from the *i-th* player.

An allocation is **individually rational** if $x_i \geq v\{i\}\ \forall i = 1, \ldots, n.$

An allocation is **efficient** if

$$\sum_{i=1}^{n} x_i = v(N) \tag{2}$$

An allocation $(x_1, \ldots, x_n)$ satisfies the principle of the **marginal contribution** if

$$x_i \leq MC_i \forall i \tag{3}$$

An allocation is in the Kernel of the game if it is efficient and so that

$$\forall S \in N : x(S) \geq v(S) \tag{4}$$

An efficient allocation is in the Kernel if and only if

$$x(S) \leq MC_S \tag{5}$$

From these definitions and considerations, we can demonstrate the following theorem.

Theorem. The global value generated from the cooperation of all players in set *N* is greater or equal than the sum of the values generated from subsets of *N*:

$$v(N) \geq v(S) + v(N \backslash S) \tag{6}$$

Dim. Let us consider $x(S)$ an allocation of subset S that is in the Kernel and it is individually rational:

$$v(S) \le x(S) \le MC_S \Rightarrow v(S) \le MC_S \tag{7}$$

This means that the marginal contribution that a player or a subset of players in N gives to the network is greater than the value that all the players would generate playing by alone without cooperation.

The definition of marginal contribution is $MC_S = v(N) - v(N \backslash S)$, so by replacing this expression in the previous equation we obtain:

$$\begin{aligned} v(s) \le MC_s = v(N) - v(N \backslash S) \Rightarrow v(s) \le v(N) - v(N \backslash S) \Rightarrow v(N) \\ \ge v(s) + v(N \backslash S) \end{aligned} \tag{8}$$

Thus, the value generated by the cooperation of all the players is greater than the sum of the values generated by any subdivision of players into groups.

This condition will assure the convenience for the system of players (i.e., the multi-agent system) to collaborate.

4 Some Concluding Remarks

From the point of view of practical application in a multi-agent structure, the above approach to organizing the network of agents by maximizing the gain (7) could reflect in supporting agents with higher efficiency.

This theoretical solution, indeed, implies some practical defect, among which that of generating an unbalanced network, with some agents, well organized and with greater impact on the system performance, mainly supported, against some others, not so equipped and assessed.

This consideration suggests that the above "game-theory-based" formal model should be used for clarifying the concept of multi-agent network design, but it must be followed by a validation of the resulting negotiations and of the effectiveness of the collaborations of agents together, as discussed in some EU-funded projects [8, 9].

This further step, even if it could be done by applying a simulation tool, needs a deeper analysis of the completely multi-agent system, as well as of the interactions between the two layers, with a more accurate definition of the lower-layer individual optimizations.

References

1. European Commission, SME Performance Review, Annual Report, November 2016
2. Villa, A., Antonelli, D. (eds.): A Road Map to the Development of European SME Networks – Towards Collaborative Innovation. Springer, London (2009). ISBN/ISSN: 9781848003422
3. amePLM - Advanced Platform for Manufacturing Engineering and Product Lifecycle Management, Project ID: 285171, cordis.europa.eu/project/rcn/100702_it.html

4. Dresher, M.: The Mathematics of Games of Strategy - Theory and Applications. Dover Publications, New York (1981)
5. Villa, A.: Managing Cooperation in Supply Network Structures and Small or Medium-Sized Enterprises: Main Criteria and Tools for Managers. Springer, London (2011). ISBN/ISSN: 9780857292421
6. Villa, A., Taurino, T., Ukovich, W.: Supporting collaboration in European Industrial Districts – the CODESNET approach. J. Intell. Manufact. **23**, 1–10 (2011). doi:10.1007/s10845-011-0516-6
7. Michaelides, R., Morton, S.C., Michaelides, Z., Lyons, A.C., Liu, W.: Collaboration networks and collaboration tools: a match for SMEs? Int. J. Prod. Res. **51**(7), 2034–2048 (2013)
8. GRACE - Integration of process and quality control using multi-agent technology, Project FP7-NMPP2-SA-2009–246203. www.grace.org
9. ARUM – Adaptive Production Management, Project ID: 314056, FP7-2012, NMP-ICT-FoF-314056. http://cordis.europa.eu/project/rcn/104761_en.html

Data-Rich Networked Organizations

Organizational Design and Collaborative Networked Organizations in a Data-Rich World: A Cybernetics Perspective

Paul Jackson[1(✉)] and Andrea Cardoni[2]

[1] Department of Accounting, Finance and Economics Wheatley Campus, Oxford Brookes University, Oxford OX33 1HX, UK
pjackson@brookes.ac.uk

[2] Dipartimento di Economia, Università degli Studi di Perugia, via Pascoli, 20, 06123 Perugia, Italy
andrea.cardoni@unipg.it

Abstract. This paper will examine the importance of big data tools and digital technology for organizational design. Drawing on principles of cybernetics, particularly Ashby's law of requisite variety and Beer's Viable System Model (VSM), it will examine the potential implications of big data and digital developments for whether organizations need to be more centralized, decentralized or adopt networked arrangements with different level of stability and flexibility. The premise of the paper is that, for systems (such as organizations or collaborative networks) to remain viable, their internal complexity needs to reflect that of the environments in which they are based. Examples are provided from the case of the network agreement framework in Italy, which are analyzed using VSM as a theoretical framework.

Keywords: Organizational design · Cybernetics · Collaborative networked organizations · Stability · Flexibility · Centralization · Decentralization

1 Introduction

This paper examines the importance of big data tools and digital technology for contemporary organizational design. It sets out to understand whether, in today's data-rich world, organizations need to be more centralized, decentralized or adopt networked arrangements [1]. While accepting the importance of reference models for analyzing and developing 'Collaborative Networks' [2], the paper provides fresh theoretical insights by drawing on principles of cybernetics, particularly Ashby's law of requisite variety and Beer's Viable System Model (VSM). As Kandjiani and Bernus [3–5] have noted, given the trans-disciplinary nature of the cybernetics field, such ideas provide a potential way of unifying disparate theoretic approaches to the literature on networks. In aiming to contribute to the valuable stream of research Kandjiani and Bernus define as 'Cybernetics of Collaborative Networks', this paper focuses on 'complexity management' in network design and the need for organizational structures to exhibit the

L.M. Camarinha-Matos et al. (Eds.): PRO-VE 2017, IFIP AICT 506, pp. 185–193, 2017.
DOI: 10.1007/978-3-319-65151-4_18

'requisite variety' presented by their environments. Indeed, for many organizations, it is suggested, it is only by forming network arrangements that they can maintain their viability in an increasingly complex, (digital) data-driven world. To maintain viability and deal with this complexity, such networks need to exhibit a range of design features, as described by VSM. The paper seeks to validate these ideas by reference to case examples using the Italian 'Network Agreement Framework', which deal with a series of factors concerning the design of collaborations.

The paper is organized as follows. Section 2 discusses the rise of network structures in recent years and explains why these are closely linked to developments in digital technology and the evolution of big data. Section 3 then sets out the main theoretical framework for the paper, drawing in particular on work in cybernetics by Ross Ashby and Stafford Beer. Section 4 then describes and analyses a number of case examples of formal network agreements (in Italy), before providing a summary and conclusions in Sect. 5.

2 Organizations and Collaborative Networked Structures in the Digital, Data-Rich World

In one way, the modern world is a massive machine for generating, sharing and consuming data, made possible by the growth of digital technologies. The implications stretch beyond the information world itself. For Brynjolfsson and McAffee [6], we are now living through a *Second Machine Age*, in which technology is focused on the creation and manipulation of data. In contrast to the first machine age, where steam-powered machines augmented or replaced human muscle, today's technology augments or replaces human *brains*. This also reflects what Mayer-Schönberger and Cukier [7] call 'datafication' – the transformation of facts about the world into a quantified format so they can be tabulated and analyzed.

Taken together, these developments have provided the impetus behind 'big data' techniques and technologies. What differentiates these from other forms of data manipulation is captured by Laney's [8] notion of 'volume, variety and velocity'. First, we can capture, store, communicate and manipulate data at a *volume* that was not possible in days gone by. Secondly, the *variety* of data – from sensors, databases, websites, etc. – has also expanded. Thirdly, because there is simply more digital technology out there to capture and share data at ever-faster transfer rates, the *velocity* of data creation and communication has also increased.

A further factor about these developments is the *repurposing* of data collected for other reasons (i.e., not readymade datasets). As Mayer-Schönberger and Cukier posit [7], big data reflects 'the ability to harness information in novel ways to produce insights or goods of significant value' (p. 2). As Marr [9] notes, because our actions increasingly leave a digital trace, we can use that data 'to become smarter' (p. 9).

We now turn to the *organizational* implications of the above and their importance to the collaboration agenda. As Yoo [10], observes, among their many facets, digital artefacts are also 'associable' – that is, they can be linked with other actors, artefacts and places. According to Yoo *et al.* [11], digitized products thus engender a new set of 'organizing logics' – arrangements that enterprises need to adopt given a firm's position in its environment and relative to customers and other players. This, Yoo *et al.* [11] say, reflects the 'layered modular architecture' of digital products. There are four layers involved here: (1) the *physical machinery* of devices themselves, (2) the *network capability* that supports the transmission of data to and from them, (3) the *services* available on them (such as the ability to create, access and manipulate content) and (4) the *content* itself (texts, images, videos, and other data).

Whereas for traditional products, whose dominant production logic was the vertically integrated hierarchy, a modular architecture leads instead to *vertical disintegration.* IT plays an additional role here, helping address the communication and coordination requirements of the inter-firm relationships that result [12]. With digital products and services, a diverse range of actors and organizations may be brought into design and production [13]. This is the case in the automotive industry, where digitization has turned automobiles into computing platforms on which outside firms can develop and supply new devices, services and content [14]. The net result is an erosion of industry boundaries and further impetus towards networked organizations. For Castells [15, 16], such examples are emblematic of the contemporary 'network society', in which a range of social, technological and economic transformations come together to produce a new, global structure.

3 The Design of Organizational Structures in a Cybernetics Perspective: Requisite Level of Decentralization and Flexibility

The explosion of IT power bound up with big data is a seeming source of complexity in the world. Quite simply, there are more facts – and insights derived from them – with which to contend. There are also new (value-adding) services, organizations and even industries based upon these. While technology disrupts, however, it can also be used to help cope with (or 'attenuate') complexity. Networked IT, as Castells shows, enables forms of collaborative networked organisation that offer the sort of agility and flexibility hierarchically integrated businesses struggle to achieve [17]. It can also be used to capture and analyse intelligence about the environment (markets, customers, competitors) to support better decision-making about strategy and tactics. To understand this at a deeper level we can turn to ideas from the cybernetics literature.

For cyberneticists such as Ashby [18], complexity can be understood in terms of the 'variety' exhibited by a system. Variety here is the number of distinguishable states an entity (such as an organisation) can assume. Where a system can match the disturbances to its environment's states, it is said to have 'requisite variety'; that is, it can change its own internal states to respond to the world beyond [19].

The notion that 'only variety absorbs variety' is at the heart of work by Beer [20, 21] in his development of the Viable System Model (VSM). The VSM identifies the functional requirements of an organization if it is to have the capacity for self-regulation. Five component subsystems are critical to this (see Fig. 1): System 1 – the *operations* that produce the organization's key outputs (its products or services); System 2 – *coordination,* which enables operational units to work together without clashes or oscillations;

System 3 *delivery management* (including 3*, monitoring), which distributes resources between operations and supports overall cohesion; System 4 – *development management* (such as marketing, training and R&D), which prepares the organization for the future); and System 5 – policy and governance that sets overall direction and ensures a balance between operations and development.

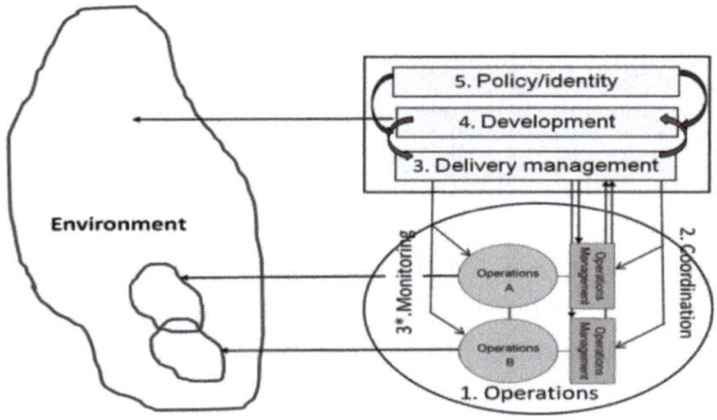

Fig. 1. - Beer's Viable System Model

The fractal nature of these functions (that they should all exist at each level of recursion and exhibit requisite variety in so doing) is crucial to the viability of the whole system. The five subsystems described also need the support of suitable communications channels (with the capacity to deal with the volume, variety and velocity of information flowing through them). Taken together, this provides each level with the capacity to self-regulate its actions and thus match the complexity of the environment [22, 23]. It is through the principles described by VSM that collaborative networks are able to balance stability and change despite being in a state of seeming 'anarchy' – that is, there is no overall leader 'calling the shots'. This stands in contrast to hierarchical structures, which, in directing operations 'from the top', frequently rob lower levels of the variety they need to respond to events and disturbances. The challenge for organizations thereby becomes one of designing enterprises and inter-firm networks that confirm to these principles and, in so doing, balance the need for centralization and decentralization. Returning to Castells [15], we can see that, where modern digital technology supports such viable system designs, the resultant organizations and networks can take on more complex and dynamic forms, thus matching the variety of the wider environment. Such technologies not only help to support the articulation of new business forms; they also allow for better intelligence gathering about the environment, down to the details of customer habits and buying behavior.

We will now turn to the case of network framework agreements in Italy.

4 The Case of the Network Agreement Framework in Italy

At the beginning of the current decade, the Italian government established an innovative legal framework to formalize strategic alliances among business entities. This framework has been recognized by the European Commission as one of the best practices in this area and was included in the 'Innovation and Competence' chapter of the revised version of the Small Business Act in 2011 [24]. The contract allows two or more firms to develop and formalize collaborative strategies without the bureaucratic rigidity of alternative forms of aggregation (i.e. consortia or merger), which are then registered in the Italian Public Register of Business Entities [25]. After seven years of implementation, as at 3 March 2017, 3.479 contracts have been formalized, involving 17.664 business entities.

According to the legal framework defined, the contract [26] must explicitly indicate some mandatory collaborative arrangements regarding (law n. 122/2010): (i) network strategic objectives; (ii) network action plan; (iii) network performance measurement criteria (to assess the progress toward strategic goals achievement); and (iv) network governance model (to manage collaborative activities). Framing this regulatory discipline using the cybernetic perspective above, these conditions reflect the fundamental features of organizational network design. Consequently, the Italian network contract framework offers important opportunities for analyzing the issue of organizational network design to meet the challenges of digital transformation.

Each of the contractual elements listed above can thus be related to VSM components. First, the strategic goal-setting creates a connection between the system in focus (i.e. the networked organizations) and the external environment, in terms of the business entities involved and the objectives they (collectively) seek to achieve. In VSM terms, this reflects the 'policy/identity' (sub-system 5) of the network (the reason for the collaboration) and its 'development' activities (the sub-system 4 function that supports planning). The network action plan provides the organizational steps for the articulation of collaborative tasks and can be framed under 'delivery management' (sub-system 3), where the network performance measures become the fundamental 'monitoring' tools (supported also by sub-system 3* audits). The governance model, finally, defines the characteristics of leadership and responsibility to guide the actors' operational integration. These activities can be attributable to the 'coordination' function (sub-system 2). The operations carried out by the individual partners (sub-system 1) will then performed as part of the network structure, supported by the previous mentioned sub-systems, with the specific design defining the level of centralization/decentralization. Taken together, the approach taken overall will determine the stability/flexibility of the networked system.

To validate these assumptions, the authors explored the official records of the Network Register and selected network contracts whose strategic objectives included some 'digital' issues, such as web technologies, big data, digital transformation and industry 4.0. We found eight agreements, with partners varying from 3 to 10, and located in most Italian macro-regions (North, Centre North and Centre-South). Based on partner specializations and strategic objectives, we classified these into four possible strategic arrangements, identifying an increasing level of complexity based on the concept of the 'business model'[1] [27]. The complexity, here, depends on whether the digital services/

[1] Business model is considered as the organizational and financial architecture based on processes directed to define three main components: 1. Value proposition; 2. Value creation; 3. Value capture (Richardson J.: The business model: an integrative framework for strategy execution. Strategic Change, vol. 17, n. 5-6, 2008, pp. 133-144).

technologies mentioned are intended to integrate: i) the value proposition of partners as service suppliers for marketing processes; ii) the value proposition of partners as service suppliers for production processes; iii) the marketing process of the partners' business model as goods producers; and iv) the production and supply-chain processes of the partners' business model as goods producers.

At the same time the network action plan, performance measurement and governance model were analysed according to different classification criteria, identifying four arrangements of VSM sub-systems design, characterised by an increasing level of network centralization and stability. At the first level it is possible to find network structures whose collaboration is designed for information exchange and sharing, with no specific performance measures and managed by a representative board of directors with low/undefined frequency of meeting. At the opposite level we found a case of a networked structure committed to performing a joint plan of tangible/intangible investments, with specifically defined performance measures and appointing specialized board/experts in charge of the network governance – thus presenting a higher level of centralization and stability.

Table 1 synthesizes the links between formal requirements and VSM components, and indicates the criteria adopted for analysing the network contracts. Applying these criteria to the selected contracts and differentiating them into two groups characterised by different levels of digital complexity (Group 1: value proposition digital integration, and Group 2: business model digital integration), the figure below (Fig. 2) graphically reports the scores related to the VSM components and the average level reached by the two groups on each sub-system.

Table 1. Analysis criteria according to VSM sub-systems

Network contract requirements	Network strategic objectives	Network action plan	Network performance measurement	Network governance model
VSM components	Policy and development (sub-system4&5)	Delivery management (sub-system 3)	Monitoring (sub-system 3*)	Coordination (sub-system 2)
Increasing level of digital complexity (sub-system 4&5) and network centralization stability (sub-systems 3, 3* and 2)	1. Supplying of digital services for marketing processes 2. Supplying of digital services for production processes 3. Integration of digital technologies in marketing processes 4. Integration of digital technology in production processes	1. Information exchange and sharing 2. Process integration and synergies development 3. Joint research on specific projects 4. Tangible and intangible joint investments	1. Not specified 2. Generic measures 3. Macro-process specific measures 4. Projects specific measures	1. Representative with undefined/low frequency 2. Representative with high frequency 3. Specialized/expert with undefined/low frequency 4. Specialized/expert with high frequency

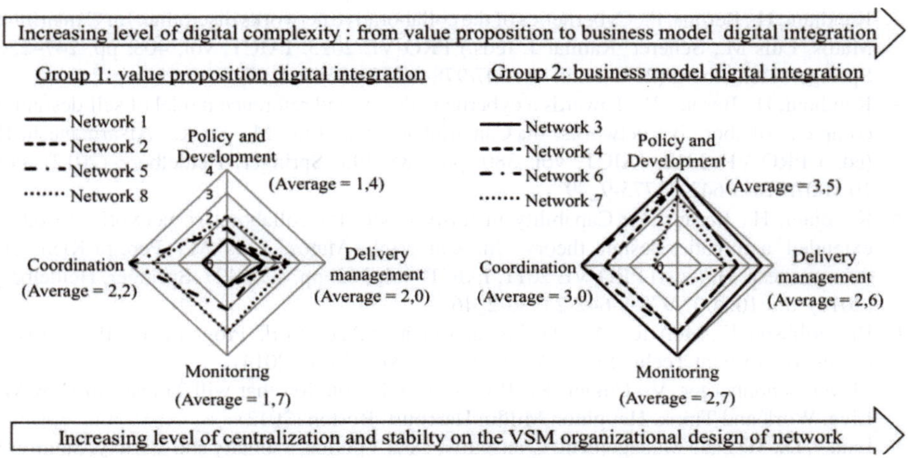

Fig. 2. Features of organizational design for collaborative networked structures

Conversely, the second group includes a contract (Network 7) with a more loosely structured design in terms of management, monitoring and govenance, despite having an ambitious goal in terms of digital integration of the business model. Because this could be related to the limited number of partners (n. 3 partners), it would be important to assess the impact of this less thought-out design on the effective implementation of collaborative operations.

5 Summary and Conclusions

This paper has argued that, in a data-rich world enabled by digital technology, the emergence of networked organizations is a natural consequence of the need to manage the complexity presented by the environment. In doing this, enterprises face a range of design choices, particularly in terms of centralization and decentralization. Getting this right demands a deeper theoretical understanding of how organizations and networks can be designed and managed to handle that complexity (or 'variety'). The paper has argued, using case examples from Italian Network Agreements, that cybernetics theories, particularly the Viable System Model, provides powerful insights in doing this and offers value both to researchers and practitioners.

References

1. Alemany, M.M.E., Alarcón, F., Lario, F.C., Boj, J.J.: An application to support the temporal and spatial distributed decision-making process in supply chain collaborative planning. Comput. Ind. **62**(5), 519–540 (2011)
2. Camarinha-Matos, L.M., Afsarmanesh, H.: On reference models for collaborative networked organizations. Int. J. Prod. Res. **46**(9), 2453–2469 (2008)

3. Kandjani, H., Bernus, P.: Cybernetics of the collaborative networks discipline. In: Camarinha-Matos, Luis M., Scherer, Raimar J. (eds.) PRO-VE 2013. IAICT, vol. 408, pp. 247–256. Springer, Heidelberg (2013). doi:10.1007/978-3-642-40543-3_27
4. Kandjani, H., Bernus, P.: Towards a cybernetic theory and reference model of self designing complex collaborative networks. In: Camarinha-Matos, Luis M., Xu, L., Afsarmanesh, H. (eds.) PRO-VE 2012. IAICT, vol. 380, pp. 485–493. Springer, Heidelberg (2012). doi: 10.1007/978-3-642-32775-9_49
5. Kandjani, H., Bernus, P.: Capability maturity model for collaborative networks based on extended axiomatic design theory. In: Camarinha-Matos, Luis M., Pereira-Klen, A., Afsarmanesh, H. (eds.) PRO-VE 2011. IAICT, vol. 362, pp. 421–427. Springer, Heidelberg (2011). doi:10.1007/978-3-642-23330-2_46
6. Brynjolfsson, E., McAffee, A.: The Second Machine Age. Work, Progress, and Prosperity in a Time of Brilliant Technologies. W.W. Norton, New York (2014)
7. Mayer-Schönberger, V., Cukier, K.: Big Data. A Revolution that will Transform How We Live, Work and Think. Houghton Mifflin Harcourt, Boston (2013)
8. Laney, D.: 3D Data Management: Controlling Data Volume, Velocity and Variety, Stamford. Meta Group, CT (2001)
9. Marr, B.: Big Data: Using Smart Big Data and Metrics to Make Decisions and Improve Performance. Wiley, Chichester (2015)
10. Yoo, Y.: Computing in everyday life. A call for research on experiential computing. MIS Q. **34**, 213–231 (2010)
11. Yoo, Y., Boland, R.J., Lyytinen, K., Majchrzak, A.: Organizing for innovation in the digitized world. Organ. Sci. **23**, 1398–1408 (2012)
12. Sambamurthy, V., Zmud, R.W.: The organizing logic for an enterprise's IT activities in the digital era. a prognosis of practice and a call for research. Inf. Syst. Res. **11**, 105–114 (2000)
13. Yoo, Y., Henfridsson, O., Lyytinen, K.: The new organizing logic of digital innovation. an agenda for information systems research. Info. Syst. Res. **21**, 724–735 (2010)
14. Henfridsson, O., Lindgren, R.: User involvement in developing mobile and temporarily interconnected systems. Inf. Syst. Res. **20**, 119–135 (2010)
15. Castells, M. (ed.): The Network Society. A Cross-Cultural Perspective. Edward Elgar, Cheltenham (2004)
16. Castells, M.: The Rise of the Network Society, 2nd edn. Wiley-Blackwell, Chichester (2010)
17. Andres, B., Poler, R.: Models, guidelines and tools for the integration of collaborative processes in non-hierarchical manufacturing networks: a review. Int. J. Comput. Integr. Manuf. **29**(2), 166–201 (2015)
18. Ashby, W.R.: An Introduction to Cybernetics. Chapman & Hall, London (1960)
19. Ashby, W.R., Goldsteim, J.: Variety, constraint, and the law of requisite variety. E:CO **13**(1–2), 190–207 (2011)
20. Beer, S.: The Heart of Enterprise. John Wiley, Chichester (1979)
21. Beer, S.: Diagnosing the System for Organizations. John Wiley, Chichester (1985)
22. Hoverstadt, P.: The Fractal Organization. Wiley, Chichester (2008)
23. Espejo, R., Reyes, A.: Organizational Systems. Managing Complexity with the Viable System Model. Springer, Heidelberg (2011)
24. European Commission: Review of the "Small Business Act" for Europe (2011). http://eur-lex.europa.eu/
25. Cardoni, A., Tiacci, L.: The "Enterprises' network agreement": the italian way to stimulate reindustrialization for entrepreneurial and economic development of SMEs. In: Camarinha-Matos, Luis M., Scherer, Raimar J. (eds.) PRO-VE 2013. IAICT, vol. 408, pp. 471–480. Springer, Heidelberg (2013). doi:10.1007/978-3-642-40543-3_50

26. Ricciardi, A., Cardoni, A., Tiacci, L.: Strategic context, organizational features and network performances: a survey on collaborative networked organizations of Italian SMEs. In: Camarinha-Matos, Luis M., Afsarmanesh, H. (eds.) PRO-VE 2014. IAICT, vol. 434, pp. 534–545. Springer, Heidelberg (2014). doi:10.1007/978-3-662-44745-1_53
27. Arana, J., Castellano, E.: The role of collaborative networks in business model innovation. In: Camarinha-Matos, Luis M., Boucher, X., Afsarmanesh, H. (eds.) PRO-VE 2010. IAICT, vol. 336, pp. 103–109. Springer, Heidelberg (2010). doi:10.1007/978-3-642-15961-9_11

The Opportunities of Big Data Analytics in Supply Market Intelligence

Salla Paajanen[1(✉)], Katri Valkokari[2], and Anna Aminoff[1]

[1] VTT Technical Research Centre of Finland, Vuorimiehentie 3, P. O. Box 1000, 02044 Espoo, Finland
{Salla.Paajanen,Anna.Aminoff}@vtt.fi

[2] VTT Technical Research Centre of Finland, Tekniikankatu 1, P. O. Box 1300, 33101 Tampere, Finland
Katri.Valkokari@vtt.fi

Abstract. Firms need comprehensive knowledge and understanding of the opportunities available in the market by creating supply market intelligence (SMI). SMI can facilitate in finding the best partners and combination of capabilities within collaborative networks (CN). However, despite of its evident managerial relevance, SMI is still little researched topic. Simultaneously, big data analytics (BDA) has developed rapidly, becoming vital for businesses across industries. The objective of this paper is recognizing the importance of SMI and opportunities of BDA through qualitative research. The data derives from two focus group discussions of 75 purchasing professionals and six qualitative interviews of BDA experts. This research contributes to our understanding of the opportunities of BDA in creating systematic SMI to reinforce strategic collaboration, and to the understanding of knowledge as a strategic resource for forming strategic CN. Collaborative big data intelligence creates value through, for instance, creating transparency in business processes and discovering market changes.

Keywords: Supply market intelligence · Big data analytics · Strategic collaboration · Data-rich systems · Collaborative big data intelligence

1 Introduction

Many firms have developed both horizontal and vertical collaboration networks to respond to the increasing global competition. Particularly in technology based industries, firms' competitiveness depends much on the complementary services and on the entire business ecosystem they are embedded in. Fast developing technology and often very short business opportunity windows create need for fast adaptation to changes in dynamic networked markets, and thus, there is a need for continuous exploration of information about the advancement of technologies and changes in the business environment. Companies need comprehensive knowledge and understanding of the opportunities available in the market to find the best partners and combination of resources to the collaborative networks (CN) [1].

L.M. Camarinha-Matos et al. (Eds.): PRO-VE 2017, IFIP AICT 506, pp. 194–205, 2017.
DOI: 10.1007/978-3-319-65151-4_19

Dynamic sourcing strategies require intelligent actions through collaborative activities, thus supply management has a vital role in understanding the supply environment [2]. In purchasing and supply management (PSM) literature, the concept of supply market intelligence (SMI) has been introduced to answer this call. SMI is defined as "the ability to develop deep insights into key supplier market characteristics, including emerging technologies, price and cost trends, mergers and acquisitions (M&A), capacity requirements, quality and delivery performance, and other key supplier capabilities that form the basis for sound strategic sourcing" [3]. SMI facilitates in selecting partners, making good contracts and developing collaborative business models [4]. Data about potential partners and supply markets are available in many forms and sources, but the challenge is to identify, extract, analyze, present and use the data in processes [5]. Collaborative approach is needed for utilizing the opportunities of big data analytics (BDA) in SMI.

Recently, development of data management technologies and analytics enables leveraging big data in innovative ways [6]. Big data refers to the capability to process and utilize data that has features of volume, variety, velocity (3Vs) and other granular and complex properties that distinguish big data from data in relational databases [7]. BDA consists of processes for identifying new insights that have potential to provide economic value. Fast development of BDA has left little time for maturing discourse and research. Conversely, previous approaches to CN were embarrassed by scarcity of data, and thus they need to be revisited. Therefore, in order to harness the potential of BDA in SMI, the main research question is: What are the opportunities of BDA in creating systematic SMI to reinforce strategic collaboration? Questions that help in answering the main research question are: What is the importance of SMI in creating competitive advantage across collaboration networks?, and How can BDA be utilized for SMI? This paper represents empirical results of two focus group discussions with totally 75 company managers and interviews of six big data experts. The focus group discussions provide broad viewpoints from purchasing professionals, whereas the big data experts bring valuable knowledge of the opportunities of BDA.

This paper is organized as follows. In the second section, we shortly discuss on literature of CN and then review the current literature base on SMI and BDA, in order to understand the current academic and managerial knowledge. In the third section, we describe the research methods of focus groups and qualitative interviews as our empirical research approach. The fifth section describes results from the conducted qualitative research. Discussion and conclusions recapitulate this paper.

2 Literature Review of SMI and BDA

2.1 Collaborative Networks

A digital, hyperconnected economy creates a specific and unique form of value creation wherein the firm and its partners generate value for various users in the networked market [8]. Therefore, organizations frequently form various types of partnerships, such as CN and virtual organization (VO), in order to share knowledge, skills and resources to seize market opportunities, create innovative products, and provide value-added services together with partners. [9] For effective collaboration, new models are required in the era of data-rich world and for instance the concept of collaborative business ecosystem (CBE) has been highlighted [10]. Depending on the type of required support and objectives, these CN with different configurations and purposes are often divided to [11]: (1) Long Term-Strategic Network (i.e. Virtual breeding environments) and (2) Goal-Oriented Network (i.e. VO). In this paper, we focus on supply networks and markets as long-term strategic networks (supply base). Thus, we aim to complement the view by deepening understanding on development of new strategic collaboration networks (supply markets). The full potential of data-rich world can be captured in collaboration with external actors, i.e. CN, as access to and integration of third-party big data sources is required to explore changes in networked business environment.

2.2 SMI in Present Research

SMI includes recognizing and understanding supply market competition, dependencies and dynamics in global supplier corporate hierarchies, networks and linkages. SMI as a concept is often mentioned in PSM research. It is suggested to be an enabler for developing sourcing strategies [12], interpreting supplier behavior and making supply management decisions [13], as well as selecting and committing to suppliers [14]. SMI has an important role in securing availability from risky supply markets, in developing (new) strategic collaboration networks and in supply management and category strategy development as well as other strategic business decisions [15]. Interestingly, 'breakthrough scanning' of the environment for innovations results in higher technical proficiency of the customer company and in increased knowledge sharing with suppliers [16]. SMI is linked with higher levels of internal integration, as the resulting 'valuable information increases the inclusion and integration of supply management in the organization's activities' [2].

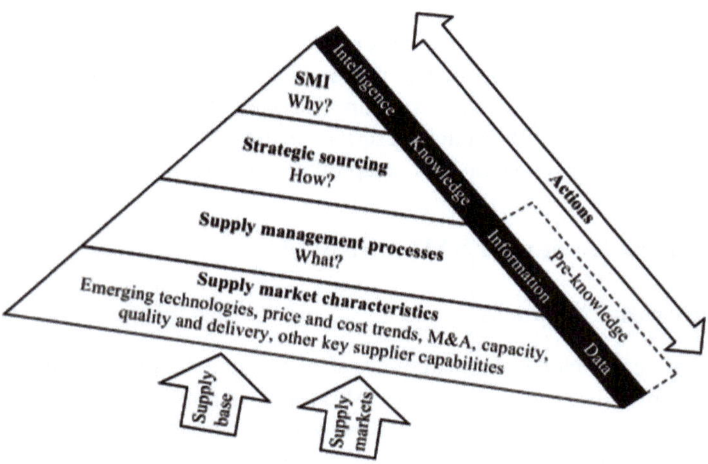

Fig. 1. Data, information, knowledge and intelligence in SMI (Source: [3, 17])

Although the importance of SMI is generally accepted in the literature [15], the research is scattered, and our understanding of capturing the potential of SMI in creating strategic networks and competitive edge is still limited. Data are worthless without context and understanding, thus an intelligence hierarchy is applied (Fig. 1).

Intelligence as the highest level refers to the capacity to acquire knowledge to facilitate actions [18]. Data and information can be called pre-knowledge that are needed for knowledge creation [19]. Intelligence from the supply base and supply markets is generated when pre-knowledge is collected and analyzed to form actionable conclusions that affect a company's ability to strategically locate, secure, and manage sources of supply [20]. Active collaboration is needed during the process of transforming data into intelligence on a timely and precise manner [21].

2.3 SMI and BDA

Data exist in every sector, economy, organization and user of digital technology [22], and the amount of generated data continues to grow rapidly. As per existing literature, data can be categorized based on the form, and ownership or access to the data (as per Fig. 2). The formation of unstructured data to structured data is a continuum, including semi-structured data that does not follow a conventional database system [23]. Structured data are stored in fixed fields, such as relational databases and data spreadsheets, whereas unstructured data resides in various sources and formats, such as free-form text, image, video or untagged audio. [22] Notably, the line between structured and unstructured, relative to internal and external data is indistinct since external data can also be structured or semi-structured.

Business data are often proprietary containing non-disclosure agreements, but firms are realizing the strategic importance of investing in insight based decision-making and value co-creation [24]. As data can be a competitive asset, companies need to understand data, which they hold or have access to by inventorying proprietary data and cataloging external data [22]. Internal data should be organized before acquiring external data [25].

Big data definitions have evolved rapidly, resulting to fragmented classifications [6]. Using the 3Vs characteristics big data is commonly defined as: "high-volume, high-velocity and/or high-variety information assets that demand cost-effective, innovative forms of information processing that enable enhanced insight, decision-making, and process automation" [7]. Besides, concepts like veracity, variability and visibility [26], value and virtual [27] are used subject to sector, size and location of the company [6].

Generating insights from the marketplace to support intelligent decisions requires new analytical tools. Often two categories of analytics are identified as descriptive and predictive. Predictive analytics is a significant aspect of BDA, creating radical new insights and opportunities with third parties via automated algorithms and real-time data analysis [25]. The key in creating value via BDA is collaboration between analytics professionals mining and preparing data, conducting statistical operations, building models and programming business applications, and the businesspeople capable to utilize analyses in processes [28].

BDA applications are increasingly important in strategic sourcing and collaboration. The ability to capture, store, aggregate and analyze data for extracting intelligence is vital for strategic decisions. [25] Big data applications in SMI consist of the areas, which provide insights into key supply market characteristics, consisting of emerging technologies, price and cost trends, M&A, capacity requirements and quality and delivery performance. Patents are an important knowledge resource in identifying technology development trends and opportunities, specifically emerging technologies [29]. Through descriptive statistics, such as the frequency table, retrieved patent documents can be summarized, using representative variables in order to discover novel data for technology forecasting and analysis [30]. Interest and exchange rates analysis is an important part of price and cost trends prediction and financial risk management in the global and unstable economic environment. Exchange rate movements can be forecasted, for instance, from time series of social media channels, such as Tweet counts [31]. M&A actions are influenced by competition policies, which can be analyzed and reveal insights from the retail sites as well as the social side via social media analytics solutions [32]. Furthermore, user demographics can be utilized to find patterns and create insights into usage clusters in order to create multidimensional segmentations and evaluate capacity requirements [33]. Finally, geographic information systems facilitate delivery performance monitoring and optimizing by integrating spatial data into regressions or simulations [22].

Reaching the full potential of BDA in SMI requires accessing third-party data sources that may be public, through collaboration or purchased, and involve several data types [22]. Access to external market and internal enterprise data supports supply management by integrating software between enterprises and supply chain partners.

Research Framework

In studying the research questions, the importance of integrating external data to the company's context and internal data is recognized. Therefore, a data categorization/integration -based research framework is applied (Fig. 2), as a baseline for the research and a tool for analysis of the empirical data.

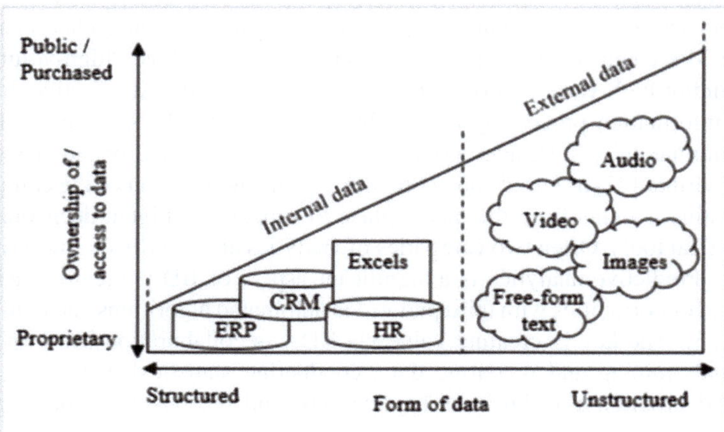

Fig. 2. Data categorization/integration -based research framework (Source: Modified from [22–24])

3 Research Methods

Data collection methods in this paper consist of two focus group discussions with purchasing professionals and six qualitative interviews of big data experts (Table 1). Qualitative research is particularly relevant when there are minor previous insights about a phenomenon under study, which indicates that qualitative research is exploratory and flexible due to unstructured questions [34]. The choice of method was based on the types of research questions [35]. The practical orientation of big data enabled SMI coupled with a lack of academic research proposes a research approach that includes a strong collaboration between academics and practitioners. We consider focus groups an appropriate method for collecting empirical data, as we can benefit from the participants' practical experience related to SMI and need for SMI. In addition, the approach was chosen because focus groups allow idea generation and strong interaction between members of focus groups, which generates new perspectives and in-depth answers [36]. Focus groups can be defined as 'a research methodology in which a small group of participants gathers to discuss a specified issue under the guidance of a moderator' [37]. Focus group participants produce qualitative data during a focused discussion to explore particular areas of interest.

The focus groups allowed us to gather empirically relevant data from large number of purchasing professionals. However, as the application of big data was still limited, we added interviews of big data expert to get an understanding of the potential of technology. The selected BDA experts have expertise from a wide range of data engineering and analytics solutions, thus enabling to receive insights into the opportunities of BDA in creating SMI.

Table 1. Overview of the data collection

Method	Objective	Number of informants	Role of informants
Focus group discussion 1	To get an understanding of the need for SMI in companies and how companies are performing today	35	Purchasing professionals
Focus group discussion 2	To examine what are the fundamentals, pre-knowledge, methods and use cases of systematic SMI by utilizing BDA	40	Purchasing professionals and BDA experts
Semi-structured interviews	To answer how can big data be categorized and what are the most suitable BDA methods, and what opportunities there are in creating SMI and providing value	6	BDA experts

Two focus group sessions were organized, in which 35 participants were invited to the first, and 40 to the second one. The participants were purchasing professionals from different companies, representing various industries and positions in the value chain, providing views of both customers and suppliers. Their shared professional background and identity thus enabled discussion in a shared language and facilitated knowledge sharing [36]. In the first focus groups the participants were divided into three groups which discussed three questions in three rounds lasting 25 min each: (1) Why and when

SMI is important? (2) How SMI is conducted in your company? By whom? Please tell examples from practice. (3) How SMI capabilities should be developed?

In the second focus group, the participants were mostly purchasing professionals, in addition to a few BDA experts. The participants were divided into six groups, in which 1–2 mediators guided the discussions and made notes of the participants' answers. All of the groups discussed two questions lasting 20 min each: (1) Describe an ideal situation of what data from the supply market would you need to reinforce supply management in your company? (2) Which changes in the supply market are most relevant in supply management? How can intelligence be used to prepare for changes in the supply market? Furthermore, two of the groups discussed third question for 10 min: (3) Who creates SMI in your company? Who should do it?, and finally one group discussed last question for 10 min: (4) Which supply management processes can benefit from descriptive analytics? Which processes require and can benefit from predictive analytics?

In addition, we conducted BDA expert interviews to receive valuable insights to creating SMI using BDA. The discussions concentrated mainly on the potential and benefits BDA can create for business through supply management, enabling strategic collaboration with particular partners. Qualitative interviews enable tailoring for the purposes of the research objectives and questions of the study. Three of the interviewees represent BDA solution providers to study analytics solutions and customers' needs for SMI. Furthermore, three interviewees of BDA experts were selected from the academic field to study the current research and knowledge regarding the subject. The interviews were recorded and transcribed for further analysis.

Data coding and analysis was conducted through coding, using a qualitative data analysis software NVivo. The first focus group discussions were analysed by use of coding; identifying the needs and methods for SMI. The analyses of second focus group discussion strongly utilized the framework derived from related literature (Fig. 2). The BDA experts' interviews were analysed in order to discover opportunities for creating SMI using BDA, and analysis use cases to reinforce strategic collaboration.

Data triangulation was ensured through different data collection methods as well as analysis from different perspectives. Data was analysed by two researchers from the perspective of strategic sourcing and one of the researchers brought the point of view of knowledge management into the analysis.

4 Findings

Based on the empirical research, it was discovered that collaboration should be threefold in order to harness the opportunities of BDA in SMI. According to focus group discussions SMI enables (long-term) strategic collaboration with suppliers and other external partners for joint development opportunities and innovative solutions. Secondly, internal collaboration between business units is required for information sharing and strategic alignment. Thirdly, the interviews of BDA experts revealed that collaboration between supply management professionals and big data analysts is a prerequisite for harnessing the full potential of big data solutions to support informed decision-making in networked business environment. This requires analytical mindset and receptive attitude from the supply management professionals and business understanding from the big data analysts. Supply management professionals perceived strategic alignment between business units and suppliers, as well as actions such as joint development opportunities with suppliers as fundamentals for innovation and strategic collaboration.

The company representatives in the focus groups considered SMI to be critical in predicting and identifying changes in the supply base and supply markets among existing and new partners. SMI can be used to find and select new suppliers, and evaluate current suppliers as well as make choices such as when to change partners. SMI is important for reacting to changes in the supplier base, and for anticipating risks, for example connected to raw material availability. Supply risk management, comprising of for example country and image risks, was considered important in all of the second focus groups. Ecosystems may change much faster than the focal company, thus frequently producing new valuable business opportunities by finding new partners. In specific, the ability to scan new supply/partner markets was considered important in new business development, requiring becoming familiar with new supplier bases connected to for instance new geographical areas. Furthermore, SMI allows rapid identification of new opportunities. Up-to-date knowledge about new technologies and capabilities may be important in contributing to innovation and business development.

Moreover, the BDA experts emphasized the importance of going further than just monitoring changes in the markets. One of the interviewees stated: "It is not enough that the system gives an alert, but it needs to justify why it was distributed and what should be done." The system should recommend further actions, or in some cases even automatically solve the issue. Value from BDA derives from applying the analyzed information to decision-making and actions. In supply management, the value from BDA can be divided into backward and forward oriented as well as reactive and proactive processes. Due to the dynamic and complex business environment and supply markets, management of change and staying ahead of market fluctuations is crucial. Forecasting the future and being aware of current market conditions and potential risks via SMI enables proactive actions and fast reactions to unprecedented events. However, as per one of the BDA experts: "In a very critical part is that the one who is using the information understands what it is, and that is the biggest challenge." If the extracted insights are not converted into intelligence across business units, value from the analysis will be unexploited. Hence, collaboration between business people and analysts is important, in collaboration with external partners and across business units for acquiring knowledge and identifying development opportunities.

As today, SMI in the sample companies was still immature and not systematic. The use of BDA was very limited and minor. Internal data in relational databases was mostly not sufficiently organized, and knowledge sharing between business units was infrequent. Segregation of "traditional data" in relational databases and big data was indistinct, even though as per the BDA experts, one of the most important aspects is integrating data from diverse legacy systems and external market data. The research framework (Fig. 2) is utilized to analyze the BDA expert interviewees to present a more precise framework for pre-knowledge categorization in the context of SMI (Fig. 3).

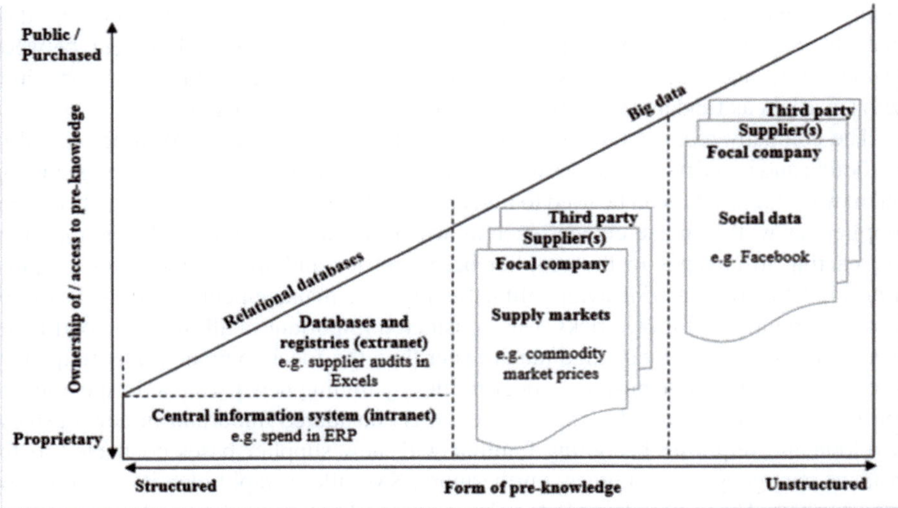

Fig. 3. Pre-knowledge categorization in the context of SMI

Pre-knowledge for creating SMI consist of data and information before refining them into knowledge. Below in Table 2, some examples of pre-knowledge according to the supply management professionals and BDA experts are presented.

Table 2. Examples of pre-knowledge in different categories based on empirical research

Intranet	Extranet	Supply markets	Social data
Supplier spend (per category, supplier) Contracts (purchase prices, terms of payment) Working capital/savings	Total cost of ownership Fast-moving consumer goods Proprietary indices Suppliers' impact on business Suppliers' value proposal and compliance Financial performance	Global price levels Commodity MI Quality and delivery performance Future market (mega)trends Product and service availability/capacity Innovations and technological development Business environment drivers/key players Existing suppliers' abilities and new suppliers and solutions Suppliers' alignment/ accountability Suppliers' personnel turnover Demand and supply M&A and personnel turnover Rules and regulations	Attractiveness of the company/importance of other customers Suppliers' reputation/ experiences perceived by others Corporate hierarchies/ networks and linkages My Data Social media

According to the research findings, the supply markets consist of a wide range of data and information, so before acquiring the data it is important to define what data are needed, why they are needed and how they are utilized to support supply management processes. Hence, as per the big data experts "Asking the right questions is vitally important". One of the most appeared pre-knowledge was recognizing future market trends and megatrends, but also their influence on suppliers' strategy and value proposal. Access to this type of data and information requires collaboration across networks.

5 Discussion and Conclusions

As per recognized in the literature ([4, 15, 20]) and verified by the purchasing professionals, SMI is an important capability for the firm, as firms need comprehensive knowledge and understanding of the opportunities available in the market to find the best partners and combination of capabilities within the CN. However, despite of its evident managerial relevance, SMI is still little researched topic. This research contributes to our understanding of the opportunities of BDA in creating systematic SMI to reinforce strategic collaboration, and to the understanding of knowledge as a strategic resource for the forming of strategic CN. Therefore, the term collaborative big data intelligence is utilized in order to highlight the need for involvement of multiple parties. The radical new source of value and competitive advantage in supply management originates in the intersection of different sources of data, for instance, comparing negotiated prices to market prices and the causal connections of price fluctuations to a company's profitability. With the expertise of a BDA solution provider, and businesses capability to absorb analyses, it is possible to reach more mature BDA and receive comprehensive results.

The results of this paper suggest that decision-making support is one of the most critical benefits that can be achieved through collaborative big data intelligence. Threefold collaboration is needed for reaching the full potential of BDA in SMI for acquiring knowledge and recognizing collaboration opportunities with suppliers. Collaboration between analysts and business people is supported by literature [28], but this research contributes to recognizing collaboration opportunities with external partners. Once an opportunity is recognized, SMI can be used to indicate the win-win situations to external partners. By utilizing big data technologies, multidimensional segmentations based on defined criteria enable, for instance, evaluating capacity requirements, user demographics, and supplier suitability for a particular company.

According to the big data experts, some of the biggest advantages of BDA are advanced algorithms that can automate routine tasks, leaving more time for strategic decisions that require human input. In addition, collaborative big data intelligence provides visibility and openness to processes, allowing perceiving defects and initiating improvements. Also previous literature has proved that there is great potential to benefit from BDA by collecting and analyzing the data, and utilizing them to detect risks [31]. Correspondingly, supply risk management, linked to recognizing needs and opportunities, was perceived as one of the most important aspects according to the purchasing management professionals. Implemented by analysts, BDA makes it possible to receive automatic alerts of threats and changes, or correspondingly opportunities that require actions.

However, simply alerts are not enough, but reasons and understanding of the alerts is required for intelligent actions. BDA can provide suggestions for action plans, but at present human intervention is still required for most critical decisions and processes. BDA can be used to analyze the past via historical data, describe the present in real time and forecast the future. Instead of focusing only on the figures of spend and savings, more forward oriented approach of supply pipeline management should be applied. Utilizing BDA enables to detect risks and opportunities, and proactively develop the pipeline and networks. Ability to accomplish backward focused cost-follow up is needed for moving to forward oriented forecasting.

As in any empirical research, the results of the present study cannot be interpreted without taking into account its limitations. Thus, this study provides many interesting avenues for further research. It may, for instance, take place in the form of multiple case studies of leading firms and their CN in order to more fully understand the potential of SMI.

References

1. Weele, A.J.V., Raaij, E.M.V.: The future of purchasing and supply management research: about relevance and rigor. J. Supply Chain Manag. **50**, 56–72 (2014)
2. Zsidisin, G.A., Hartley, J.L., Bernardes, E.S., Saunders, L.W.: Examining supply market scanning and internal communication climate as facilitators of supply chain integration. Supply Chain Manag. Int. J. **20**, 549–560 (2015)
3. Handfield, R., Petersen, K., Cousins, P., Lawson, B.: An organizational entrepreneurship model of supply management integration and performance outcomes. Int. J. Oper. Prod. Manag. **29**, 100–126 (2009)
4. Iloranta, K.K.: Hankintojen johtaminen: ostamisesta toimittajamarkkinoiden hallintaan. Tietosanoma (2015)
5. Lorentz, H.: Situation awareness as a building block of purchasing and supply management capability. In: Proceedings of 20th Annual Cambridge International Manufacturing Symposium, Cambridge, UK (2016)
6. Gandomi, A., Haider, M.: Beyond the hype: Big data concepts, methods, and analytics. Int. J. Inf. Manage. **35**, 137–144 (2015)
7. Chen, P.C.L., Zhang, C.Y.: Data-intensive applications, challenges, techniques and technologies: a survey on Big Data. Inf. Sci. (NY) **275**, 314–347 (2014)
8. Zott, C., Amit, R.: Business model design: an activity system perspective. Long Range Plann. **43**, 216–226 (2010)
9. Afsarmanesh, H., Camarinha-Matos, L.M.: Collaborative Networks and Their Breeding Environments. Springer, Boston (2005)
10. Graça, P., Camarinha-Matos, L.M.: The need of performance indicators for collaborative business ecosystems. In: Camarinha-Matos, L.M., Baldissera, T.A., Di Orio, G., Marques, F. (eds.) DoCEIS 2015. IAICT, vol. 450, pp. 22–30. Springer, Cham (2015). doi: 10.1007/978-3-319-16766-4_3
11. Oliveira, A.I., Shafahi, M., Afsarmanesh, H., Ferrada, F., Camarinha-Matos, L.M.: Competence matching in collaborative consortia for service-enhanced products. In: Afsarmanesh, H., Camarinha-Matos, L.M., Lucas Soares, A. (eds.) PRO-VE 2016. IAICT, vol. 480, pp. 350–360. Springer, Cham (2016). doi:10.1007/978-3-319-45390-3_30
12. Handley, S.M., Benton, W.C.: Mediated power and outsourcing relationships. J. Oper. Manag. **30**, 253–267 (2012)

13. Kaufmann, L., Michel, A., Carter, C.R.: Debiasing strategies in supply management decision-making. J. Bus. Logist. **30**, 85–106 (2009)
14. Swink, M., Zsidisin, G.: On the benefits and risks of focused commitment to suppliers. Int. J. Prod. Res. **44**, 4223–4240 (2006)
15. Handfield, R.: Organizational structure and application of supply market intelligence. In: ACM International Conference Proceeding Series, p. 36 (2014)
16. Cousins, P.D., Lawson, B., Petersen, K.J., Handfield, R.B.: Breakthrough scanning, supplier knowledge exchange and new product development performance. J. Prod. Innov. Manag. **28**, 930–942 (2011)
17. Rowley, J.: The wisdom hierarchy: representations of the DIKW hierarchy. J. Inf. Sci. **33**, 163–180 (2007)
18. Goertzel, B., Pennachin, C. (eds.): Artificial General Intelligence. Springer, Heidelberg (2007)
19. Erickson, G.S., Rothberg, H.N.: Intelligence in Action. Palgrave Macmillan, London (2012)
20. Jones, J., Barner, K.: Supply Market Intelligence for Procurement Professionals: Research, Process, and Resources (2015)
21. Aydın, B., Ozleblebici, Z.: Should we rely on intelligence cycle? J. Mil. Inf. Sci. **3**, 93–99 (2015)
22. Manyika, J., Chui, M., Brown, B., Bughin, J., Dobbs, R., Roxburg, C., Hung Byers, A.: Big Data: The Next Frontier for Innovation, Competition, and Productivity. McKinsey Glob. Inst, New York (2011)
23. Hashem, I.A.T., Yaqoob, I., Anuar, N.B., Mokhtar, S., Gani, A., Ullah Khan, S.: The rise of "big data" on cloud computing: Review and open research issues. Inf. Syst. **47**, 98–115 (2015)
24. Chang, R.M., Kauffman, R.J., Kwon, Y.: Understanding the paradigm shift to computational social science in the presence of big data. Decis. Support Syst. **63**, 67–80 (2014)
25. Sanders, N.R.: Big Data Driven Supply Chain Management: A Framework for Implementing Analytics and Turning Information into Intelligence. Pearson Education, London (2014)
26. Buyya, R., Calheiros, R.N., Dastjerdi, A.V.: Big Data: Principles and Paradigms. Elsevier, Cambridge (2016)
27. Assunção, M.D., Calheiros, R.N., Bianchi, S., Netto, M.A.S., Buyya, R.: Big data computing and clouds: Trends and future directions. J. Parallel Distrib. Comput. **79–80**, 3–15 (2015)
28. SAS: From Data to Action. Harvard Bus. Rev. Insight Cent. 1–49 (2014)
29. Ma, J., Porter, A.L.: Analyzing patent topical information to identify technology pathways and potential opportunities. Scientometrics **102**, 811–827 (2014)
30. Jun, S., Park, S., Jang, D.: A technology valuation model using quantitative patent analysis: a case study of technology transfer in big data marketing. Emerg. Mark. Financ. Trade. **51**, 963–974 (2015)
31. Fan, Y., Heilig, L., Voß, S.: Design, User Experience, and Usability (2015)
32. Kaye, K.: Data Innovations Help Brands and Retailers Monitor the Competition. Crain Communications (2015)
33. Varela, I.R., Tjahjono, B.: Big data analytics in supply chain management: trends and related research. In: 6th International Conference on Operations and Supply Chain Management, vol. 1, pp. 2013–2014 (2014)
34. Eriksson, P., Kovalainen, A.: Qualitative methods in business research. SAGE Publications, London (2008)
35. Yin, R.K.: Case Study Research: Design and Methods. SAGE, Thousand Oaks (2014)
36. Byers, P.Y., Wilcox, J.R.: Focus groups: a qualitative opportunity for researchers. J. Bus. Commun. **28**, 63–78 (1991)
37. Wibeck, V., Dahlgren, M.A., Oberg, G.: Learning in focus groups: an analytical dimension for enhancing focus group research. Qual. Res. **7**, 249–267 (2007)

Data Rich – But Information Poor

Peter Bernus(✉) and Ovidiu Noran

IIIS Centre for Enterprise Architecture Research and Management,
Griffith University, Brisbane, Australia
{P.Bernus,O.Noran}@griffith.edu.au

Abstract. The article describes the missing link between the information type and quality required by the process of decision making and the knowledge provided using the recent developments of 'big data' technologies, with emphasis on management and control in systems of systems and collaborative networks. Using known theories of decision making, the article exposes a gap in present technology arising from the disparity between the large amount of patterns that can be identified in available data using data analytics, and the lack of technology that is able to provide a narrative that is necessary for timely and effective decision making. The conclusion is that a second level of situated logic is necessary for the efficient use of data analytics, so as to effectively support the dynamic configuration and reconfiguration of systems of systems for resilience, efficiency and other desired systemic properties.

Keywords: Situation awareness · Big data · Decision model · Situated reasoning

1 Introduction

The ability to gather very large amounts of data has preoccupied the research community and industry for quite some time, starting within Defence in the 1990s and gradually evolving in popularity so as to become a buzzword in the 2010s. 'Big data', the 'sensing enterprise', and similar concepts signal a new era in which one hopes to provide 'all necessary' decision-making information for management in the quality and 'freshness' required. Whoever succeeds in building such facility and use the data to derive decision making information efficiently and effectively, or produce new knowledge that was not attainable before, will 'win'. The hope is well founded, if one considers an analogy with the early successes of evidence-based medicine (Evidence Based Medicine Working Group 1992, Pope 2003) that transformed the way the medical profession decided what treatments to use. At the same time, it is necessary to define realistic expectations in order to avoid expensive mistakes; for example, even evidence-based medicine that relies on large scale data gathering through clinical trials and careful statistical analysis is showing signs of trouble (Greenhalgh et al. 2014) with the usefulness of the evidence gathered when it is applied in complex individual cases increasingly being questioned. Generally, it is becoming obvious that finding new ways to correctly interpret complex data in context is necessary – a claim supported by many authors (HBR 2014).

L.M. Camarinha-Matos et al. (Eds.): PRO-VE 2017, IFIP AICT 506, pp. 206–214, 2017.
DOI: 10.1007/978-3-319-65151-4_20

An obvious viewpoint is that when intending to use large amounts of gathered data to create useful decision making information, one must carefully consider the information needs of management and especially how the interpretation of data is influenced by context. The goal of this paper is to investigate and analyse, from a theoretical perspective, what missing links exist in order to put 'big data' to use apart from the obvious 'low hanging fruit' applications.

2 Current Issues in Big Data and Data Warehousing

The role of Management and Control (or Command and Control) is to make decisions on multiple levels, i.e.: Real time, Operational, Tactical and Strategic, often guided by various types of models. Along these lines, two notable systematic models of decision making (which is the essence of management and control) are the GRAI Grid (Doumeingts et al. 1998) and the Viable Systems Model or VSM (Beer 1972). These models are very similar and differ mainly in the details emphasised (Fig. 1). Fundamentally, these generic models identify management, command and control tasks and the information flow between them.

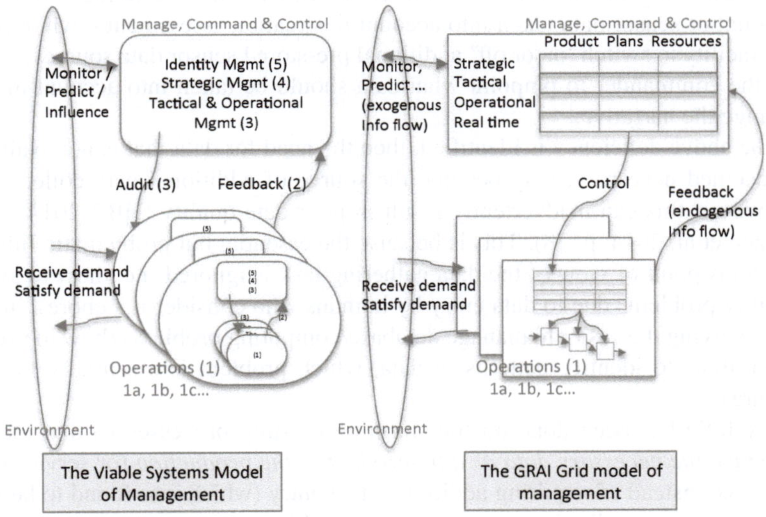

Fig. 1. A simplified view of two equivalent decision making models: Viable Systems Model (Beer 1972) and GRAI Grid (Doumeingts et al. 1998)

To make successful decisions, it is necessary to satisfy the information needs of the management functions as depicted in Fig. 1. The big data movement (discussed in Sect. 1) has a 'little brother': data warehousing (with its associated techniques), which made similar initial claims of creating meaningful insight for management. Even though there exist many success stories, there were some notable failures of data warehousing to deliver on its promises, owing to similar causes (see below).

In data warehousing, the methodology suggested by its proponents was to take copies (snapshots) of operational databases (and other data repositories) and build an interface, based on which the data could be 'mined' (analysed) to find management-relevant information. To build such a facility fast and in an affordable manner, the methodology suggested by Inmon (1992) and Kimball (1996) and others was to create the data warehouse out of existing databases and possibly transaction logs so as to gain management insight. In other words the aim was to create a *narrative* that is characterising the present or predicted future situation, which is essential for strategic decision making. Big data is no different, using traditional data analysis and machine learning techniques the protagonists derive useful interpretations, just on a larger scale than data warehouses can do, as data sources are larger and include multiple sources. However, both the big data and data warehousing movements (even though their scales are different) have in fact similar shortcomings, such as:

- The associated methodologies give not enough weight to first understanding the fundamental information needs of the decision maker;
- Very little is done to *correlate* internal- and external data sources to create useful information for decision making (i.e., relating the endogeneous and the exogeneous);
- Insufficient effort was put into realising what data *would be* needed but was unavailable (for being able to draw useful inferences); Even the recent method to limit the amount of sensor data taken into account in situation assessment – while providing the facility to switch 'on or off' additional pre-stored sensor data sources – is relying on the commander to pinpoint what data should be taken into account to possibly change the narrative;
- If the above deficiency is identified, then the need for data that is not available, but is deemed necessary, may become the source of additional data collection tasks. However, this can inadvertently result in poor data quality (HBR 2014, p. 47 and Hazen et al. 2014, p. 78). This is because the essential but problematic Information Systems point of view of the data gathering task is ignored (i.e., how to avoid data quality problems due to data entry by humans who consider it a chore), in favor of only solving the easier to manage database/computing problems (how to use various algorithms to identify patterns in data, which problem is essentially technical in nature);
- Very little has been done on transforming existing processes so that they would *produce the necessary data as a by-product of the production* (or service delivery) *process*, instead of requiring additional data entry (which was found to be the main source of data quality issues) (Hazen et al. 2014);
- There has been a propensity to disregard the *context* of the collected data, and thus creating the danger of situation mis-identification without even being aware of having committed this mistake (Santanilla et al. 2014).

The data warehouse movement largely concentrated on collecting and making available for analysis the *internal* data of the enterprise, while the big data movement, with its roots in the 1990s (e.g. the 'Dominant Battlefield Knowledge' movement (Szafranski 1995)), concentrates on the ability (initially, of the military) to access an unprecedented amount of *external* data so as to gain advantage over adversaries - and indeed, specialised systems have been built and deployed in order to achieve this goal.

Two issues become apparent when analysing the history of creating useful decision-making information, whether through data warehousing or big data analytics and the associated business intelligence processes:

1. On each decision-making level, we must correlate internal *and* external data;
2. With the opportunity to collect and access very large amounts of data, it becomes difficult to identify patterns that are useful for decision making (there are too many patterns that algorithms can identify) – unless one uses heuristics (i.e., the result of prior learning) to discern what is relevant and what is not. Importantly, the measure of relevance changes with time and with the current interpretation of data.

3 Making Effective Decisions

Tasks that appear in each type and level of decision-making and the feedback that can be used to inform the filters used to selectively observe reality may be studied using a finer model that explains how successful decisions are made. This filter is part of the well-known Observe, Orient, Decide and Act (OODA) Loop devised by John Boyd (Osinga 2006) (see explanation below). It must be noted that on closer inspection, it turns out that OODA is *not* a strict loop because it is precisely the feedbacks inside the high level 'loop-like' structure that are responsible for learning and for decisions about the kind of filters necessary. Note that this 'loop' is often misunderstood to be a strict sequence of tasks (e.g. *cf.* Benson and Rotkoff's 'Goodbye OODA Loop' (2011)) when in fact it is actually an *activity network* featuring rich information flow among the OODA activities and the environment.

A brief review of Boyd's OODA 'loop' can be used to point to potential development directions for a 'big data methodology' for decision support. Accordingly, decisions can be made by the management/command & control system of an entity, in any domain of action and on any level or horizon of management (i.e., strategic, tactical, operational and real-time, performing four interrelated tasks:

- Observe (*selectively perceive data [i.e., filter]* – measurement, sensors, repositories, real-time data streams, using *existing* sensors);
- Orient (*recognise* and become *aware of the situation*);
- Decide (*retrieve existing-*, or *design/plan new* patterns of behaviour);
- Act (execute behaviour, of which the outcome can then be observed, etc.).

According to Boyd and subsequent literature analysing Boyd's results (Osinga 2006), to make the actions effective, decision makers must repeat their decision making loops faster than the opponents, so as to disrupt the opponent's loop. Note that the first caveat: one can only 'observe' using *existing* sensors. Since there is no chance to observe absolutely everything, how does one know that what is observed is relevant and contains (after analysis) all the necessary data, which then can be turned into useful situation awareness (Lenders et al. 2015)? The likely answer is that one does *not* know *a priori*; it is through learning using past positive and negative experiences that a decision system approaches a capability level that is timely and effective in establishing situation awareness. This learning will (or has the potential to) result in decisions, which are able to identify capability gaps (and initiate capability improvement efforts). This is the task of *self-reflective management*, comparing the behaviour of the external world and its demands on the system (the future predicted action space) with the action space of the current system (including the current system's ability to sense, orient, decide and act). In this context, the 'action space' is the set of possible outcomes reachable using the system's current technical-, human-, information- and financial resources.

This learning loop depends on self-reflection and *it is in itself an OODA loop* analogous to the one discussed above, although the ingredients are different and closely associated with strategic management. The questions are: (a) what to observe, (b) how to orient to become situation aware and (c) what is guiding the decision about what to do (within constraints and decision variables and the affordances of action) so as to finally be able to perform some move. The action space of this strategic loop consists of transformational actions (company re-missioning, change of identity, business model change, capability development, complete metamorphosis, etc.).

Essentially, such strategic self-reflection compares the current capabilities of the system to desired future capabilities, allowing management to decide whether to change the system's capabilities (including decision making capabilities), or to change the system's identity (re-missioning), or both. Note that management may also decide that part of the system will need to be decommissioned due to its inability to fully perform the system's mission. Such transformation is usually implemented using a separate programme or project within a so-called Plan-Do-Check-Act (PDCA) loop (Lawson 2006, p. 102) (not discussed further as it is outside the scope of this paper).

The above analysis can be put to use in the following way: to achieve situation awareness, which is a condition of successful action, 'big data' (the collective technologies and methods of data analysis and predictive analytics) has the *potential* to deliver a wealth of domain-level facts and patterns that are relevant for decision-making, which were not available before. However, this data needs to be interpreted, which calls for a *theory of situations* ultimately resulting in a *narrative* of what is being identified or predicted; without such narrative, there is no true situation awareness, which can significantly limit the chances of successful action.

It is therefore argued that having the ability to gather, store and analyse large amounts of data using only algorithms is not a guarantee that the patterns thus found in data can be turned into *useful* information that forms the basis of effective decision-making, followed by appropriate action leading to measurable success.

The process works the other way around as well: when interpreting available data (however large the current data set may be), there can be multiple fitting *narratives* and unfortunately it is impossible to decide which one is correct. Appropriate means of reasoning with incomplete information could in this case identify a need for new data (or new *types* of data) that can resolve the ambiguity. Thus, supporting decision-making using 'big data' requires the collection of a *second level* of data, which is not about particular facts, but about the creation of a 'repertoire' of situation types, including facts that *must* be true, facts that *must be not* true, as well as constraints and rules of *causes and effects* matching these situation types. Such situation types can also be considered as models (or model 'archetypes') of the domain, which then can be matched against findings on the observed data level. Given the inherently perpetual changing nature of the world, these situation types are expected to evolve themselves; therefore, one should *not* imagine or aim to construct a facility that relies on a completely predefined ontology of situation types. Rather, there is a need for a facility that can continuously improve and extend this type of knowledge, including the development and learning of new types that are not a specialisation of some previously known type (to ensure that the 'world of situations' remains open, as described by Goranson and Cardier (2013)).

4 Using Big Data in Decision-Making for System of Systems

The Dominant Battlefield Knowledge movement (Szafranski 1995) pointed out quite early that in spite of the ability to deploy a large number of sensors, in order to achieve situation awareness data needs to get filtered based on 'relevance'. The word 'relevant' is in inverted commas, because it is precisely the possible situations of interest that dictate what data are or would be relevant – however, one does not know *a priory* (and/or unambiguously) what situation one is actually in! Therefore, the *continual narrative* of the situation changes the data needs (Madden 2012), as well as what needs to be filtered out and should be kept.

In the real world of cooperative action (whether business, government or military), such as in collaborative networks (Camarinha-Matos et al. 2011) or virtual organisations created by them (both being socio-technical kinds of systems of systems (SoS)), decisions are not taken in a completely centralised way. The participants of a system are systems themselves, in control of their own resources; moreover, usually each participating system has its own *system identity* as well as multiple commitments at any given time (with one of these commitments being to belong to the SoS in question). The types of strategies that need to be used in such scenarios have recently been reviewed in the extensive state of the art report by the Committee on Integrating Humans, Machines and Networks (CIHMN 2014), which calls for an interdisciplinary approach, similar e.g. to the collaborative networks research area (instead of relying on a purely computational viewpoint as a background discipline).

A SoS must be robust to cope with the situation when a participating system is not performing (e.g. becomes faulty, is destroyed, or otherwise unavailable, or due to communication channels being compromised, etc.). Successful SoS level decision-making must be framed as a *cooperative conversation* of information exchange and commitments, however with the added complexity that important systemic properties (e.g., availability) of the SoS need to be maintained, without being able to completely rely on the same property (i.e., availability) of individual participating systems.

To overcome this difficulty, the architecture of a successful SoS must be dynamically reconfigurable, so that the functional integrity of the SoS is preserved, including its mission fulfilment and its management and control. The robustness of the decision system is only achievable, if (i) the decision function is built to cope with incomplete information (at least for a limited time), (ii) the decision function can pro-actively provide guidance regarding its information needs to the contributing systems that 'observe', so as to resolve ambiguity or to replace information sources that became unavailable, (iii) the allocation of the OODA loop functions to resources is dynamic – similar to how cloud computing can achieve required capacity, availability, scalability, and other desirable systemic properties (the 'ilities') (Lehrig et al. 2015).

This self-awareness requirement for a SoS is in addition to the self-reflection requirement discussed (Sect. 3), as it requires operational (and real-time) reconfiguration, based on the need for timely and always available reliable narrative.

Although it is not possible to go into the technical details within the limits of this article, the theory that allows the two levels – situation theory and domain level theory(ies) to coexist is *channel logic* (Barwise and Seligman 2008). Mathematically, given the category of situations (that represent situation types) there exist a mapping between situation types that regulates the way complete lines of reasoning can be 'transplanted' from one situation type to another. This transplanting works as follows: when there exist a logic in a known situation type A, and the facts suggest that the situation is of a related type B, many but not all facts and inferences should also be valid in type B. As a result, if we have a known situation (of type A) with facts supporting this claim, and we only have scarce data about another situation of interest (of type B), channel logic allows us to deduce the need for data that can be used to 'fill in the details' about this second situation.

The mapping from one category to another is a morphism between categories, and can be implemented using functional programming techniques. The practical consequence is that the decision maker can use this (strictly formal) analogical reasoning to come to valid conclusions in an otherwise inaccessible domain (or if this is not possible, narrow down the need for specific data that can support a valid conclusion). This is a rudimentary explanation of the ability of the situation theoretic logic to infer that for decision making there is a need for specific unavailable data that can disambiguate the interpretation of data available at the time.

5 Conclusions and Further Work

The conceptual analytical work presented in this paper can be extended and used as the concept of a solution creating an ongoing *situation awareness* capability. All application domains (e.g. business, government, military, etc.) have typical situations and thus maintain a specific 'repertoires' of actions known to work. The knowledge of these situations can be acquired partially through education and partially through practical experience. The efficient use of these patterns depends on them being utilised fast, without too much explicit thought; in other words, efficient behaviour is typically based on the use of *tacit* skills and knowledge (irrespective of the fact that some of this knowledge would also be available in an explicit, formal form).

As pointed out, the effectiveness of the OODA loop is also dependent on its efficiency – hence, *whoever does it better and faster will win*. If, for example, one is not able to process the gathered information in a timely manner, the resulting action/s may become irrelevant, because one's adversary may have already acted and thus, changed the situation. Given the complexity of situations and the amount of data available, using data analytics *in conjunction with situation recognition* could dramatically speed up the loop, hence increasing the chance of success.

The technology for data analytics and predictive analytics is currently subject to substantial ongoing effort in research and in industry. The authors are observing the technical side of this movement, while concentrating their effort on the promising, however difficult to implement and mathematically challenging technology that is developed on the basis of situation theory (Goranson and Cardier 2013). The main aim is to demonstrate the use of such technology to construct resilient Systems of Systems through dynamic management, command and control of a large number of cooperating participating agents.

Acknowledgements. The authors would like to acknowledge the research grant (Strategic Advancement of Methodologies and Models for Enterprise Architecture) provided by Architecture Services Pty Ltd (ASPL Australia) in supporting this work.

References

Barwise, J., Seligman, J.: Information Flow: The Logic of Distributed Systems. Cambridge Tracts in Theoretical Computer Science. Cambridge University Press, Cambridge (2008)

Beer, S.: Brain of the Firm. Allan Lane Penguin Press, London (1972)

Benson, K., Rotkoff, S.: Goodbye, OODA loop: a complex world demands a different kind of decision-making. Armed Forces J. **149**(3), 26–28 (2011)

Camarinha-Matos, L.M., Pereira-Klen, A., Afsarmanesh, H. (eds.): PRO-VE 2011. IAICT, vol. 362. Springer, Heidelberg (2011). doi:10.1007/978-3-642-23330-2

CIHMN (Committee on Integrating Humans, Machines and Networks): A global review of data-to-decision technologies. Complex operational decision making in networked systems of humans and machines a multidisciplinary approach. National Academy of Sciences. National Academy Press, Washington (2014)

Doumeingts, G., Vallespir, B., Chen, D.: GRAI grid decisional modelling. In: Bernus, P., Nemes, L., Schmidt, G. (eds.) Handbook on Architectures of Information Systems, pp. 313–337. Springer, Heidelberg (1998). doi:10.1007/978-3-662-03526-9_14

Evidence Based Medicine Working Group: Evidence based medicine. A new approach to teaching the practice of medicine. JAMA **268**, 2420–2425 (1992)

Goranson, H.T., Cardier, B.: A two-sorted logic for structurally modeling systems. Progress Biophys. Mol. Biol. **113**(2013), 141–178 (2013)

Greenhalgh, T., Howick, J., Maskrey, N.: Evidence based medicine: a movement in crisis. BMJ 2014 **348**, g3725 (2014)

Hazen, B.T., Boone, C.A., Ezell, J.D., Jones-Farme, A.: Data quality for datascience, predictive analytics, and big data in supply chain management: an introduction to the problem and suggestions for research and applications. Int. J. Prod. Econ. **154**, 72–80 (2014)

HBR: From data to action (a Harvard Business Review Insight Center report). Harvard Business Review (2014)

Inmon, B.: Building the Data Warehouse. Wiley, New York (1992)

Kimball, R.: The Data Warehouse Toolkit. Wiley (1996). ISBN 978-0-471-15337-5

Lawson, H.: A Journey Through the Systems Landscape. College Publications, London (2006)

Lehrig, S., Eikerling, H., Becker, S.: Scalability, elasticity, and efficiency in cloud computing: a systematic literature review of definitions and metrics. In: Proceedings of the 11th International ACM SIGSOFT QoSA, pp. 83–92. ACM, New York (2015)

Lenders, V., Tanner, A., Blarer, A.: Gaining an edge in cyberspace with advanced situational awareness. IEEE Secur. Priv. **13**(2), 65–74 (2015)

Madden, S.: From databases to big data. IEEE Internet Comput. **16**(3), 4–6 (2012)

Osinga, F.P.B.: Science, Strategy and War: The Strategic Theory of John Boyd. Routledge, London (UK) (2006)

Pope, C.: Resisting evidence: the study of evidence-based medicine as a contemporary social movement. Health **7**, 267–282 (2003)

Santanilla, M., Zhang, D.W., Althouse, B.M., Ayers, J.W.: What can digital disease detection learn from (an external revision to) Google Flu trends? Am. J. Prev. Med. **47**(3), 341–347 (2014)

Szafranski, R.: A Theory of Information Warfare. Airpower J., **9**(1), 1–11 (1995)

Big Data Analytics

From Periphery to Core: A Temporal Analysis of GitHub Contributors' Collaboration Network

Ikram El Asri(✉), Noureddine Kerzazi, Lamia Benhiba, and Mohammed Janati

National Higher School for Computer Science and System Analysis (ENSIAS), Rabat, Morocco
{ikram.Asri,n.Kerzazi,lamia.Benhiba, a.Janati}@um5s.net.ma

Abstract. Open-source projects in GitHub exhibit rich temporal dynamics, and diverse contributors' social interactions further intensify this process. In this paper, we analyze temporal patterns associated with Open Source Software (OSS) projects and how the contributor's notoriety grows and fades over time in a core-periphery structure. In order to explore the temporal dynamics of GitHub communities we formulate a time series clustering model using both Social Network Analysis (SNA) and technical metrics. By applying an adaptive time frame incremental approach to clustering, we locate contributors in different temporal networks. We demonstrate our approach on five long-lived OSS projects involving more than 700 contributors and found that there are three main temporal shapes of attention when contributors shift from periphery to core. Our analyses provide insights into common temporal patterns of the growing OSS communities on GitHub and broaden the understanding of the dynamics and motivation of open source contributors.

Keywords: Collaboration · Core-periphery · Socio-technical relationships · SNA

1 Introduction

Open source communities grow and fade over time. Understanding how to maintain, sustain, and grow a community of contributors is crucial for the survival and success of any open source project [1]. That said, more than 12,000 individuals have contributed to Linux since 2005, from which more than 4,000 contributed in just the last 15 months (50% are first-time contributors); 3000 for Rails; and 1403 for AngularJs. Scaling from one to thousands highly distributed developers in an interesting challenge of collaboration [2]. However, there is very little evidence as to how those virtual communities grow? And more interestingly, how newcomers can navigate from the periphery of a given project (i.e., first-time contribution) to the core contributors of the project (i.e., constantly committing, commenting, and participating in important decision-making)?

Recent studies have shown that only small portion of contributors leads an OSS project making a large proportion of technical contributions [3–8]. For instance,

L.M. Camarinha-Matos et al. (Eds.): PRO-VE 2017, IFIP AICT 506, pp. 217–229, 2017.
DOI: 10.1007/978-3-319-65151-4_21

Mockus et al. [8] studied two open source projects: Apache and Mozilla and revealed that only 10 to 15 developers collaborate to carried out 80% of the contributions. Similarly, Dinh-Trong and Bieman [6] stated that only 28 to 42 contributors performed 80% of the development activity. Koch and Shneider [3] showed that 17% (51 out of 301 developers) provides core functionalities to the GNOME project. However, again these previous works do not help to understand how these small portions of contributors shift from the periphery, or even stick, to the core.

The picture that emerged from this evidence- contribution of developers in OSS projects- has been taken to shape OSS organization structures. OSS communities can be seen such as a Core-Peripheral structure [5]. At the core, there are those contributors who have been involved with the project for a relatively long time, are leading the project, and making significant contributions (80%) to the evolution of OSS projects. In the other side, at the periphery there are newcomers or people interested in the project and making few contributions with much less notoriety.

The key idea in our work is to analyze temporal patterns by which newcomers to OSS project shift from the periphery to the core teams. This shift remains largely uncovered even in organizational theories. Understanding this phenomenon within open source project can help gain insights on how to maintain virtual communities and how to attract new world wild contributors in order to accelerate software development projects in both OSS and traditional commercial organizations [9].

In this paper, we have undertaken a socio-technical analysis of five OSS collaborative communities aiming at uncovering the dynamics of growing and fading of those communities over time. Particular attention has been paid to the migration of newcomers from the periphery to core team.

Paper organization. The remainder of the paper is organized as follows. Section 2 presents related work. Section 3 provides our reasoning about core-periphery structure for the open source context. Section 4 describes our methodology including description of studied systems and data collection, for which the results are presented in Sect. 5. Section 6 discusses our finding and highlights some limitations. Finally, Sect. 7 draws conclusions and enlightens future work.

2 Related Work

Open source software is built by teams of volunteers. A series of efforts in recent years have focused on the OSS development organization [1]. Newcomers are explorers who must orient themselves within an unfamiliar landscape. As they gain experience, they eventually settle in and create their own places within the landscape [10].

Understanding Motivation. Members of OSS communities are volunteers whose motivation to participate and contribute is a necessary condition to the success of open source projects. Ye and Kishida [11] argued that learning is one of the major driving forces that motivate people to get involved in OSS communities. Hars and Ou [12] categorized open source participants' motivations into two broad categories: internal factors meaning that open source programmers are not motivated by monetary rewards but by their own hobbies and preferences. External rewards, when contributors are interested in receiving indirect rewards by increasing their marketability and skills or demonstrating their capabilities in programming. Whatever the motivation behind the contribution the most interesting is a contributor level of activity and engagement within a project. In this paper, we are interested in that engagement in the project and how contributors gain notoriety and fade over time from core-periphery structure throw investigating technical and social collaboration activities of developers.

Detecting the Core-Periphery Structure. A series of efforts in recent years have focused on detecting the core-periphery structure in OSS projects. For example, from Social Perspective- Dabbish et al. [13] performed a series of in-depth interviews with central as well as peripheral GitHub users. Authors found that people make a rich set of social inferences from the networked activity information within GitHub and then combine these inferences into effective strategies for coordinating their work, advancing technical skills and managing their reputation. More concretely, Bosu and Carver [14] proposed a K-means classifier based on SNA metrics. for detecting core-periphery structure. We build upon these previous works to develop a further social perspective of collaboration. Our approach is based on k-means classifier using three classes (core, gray area, and peripheral) instead of two. We use three classes to include transitional states where nodes are neither core nor peripheral, which gives us a higher accuracy (80%) in identifying and dealing with peripheral vs core contributors.

Amrit and van Hillegersberg [15] examined core-periphery movement in open source projects and concluded that a steady movement toward the core is beneficial to a project, while a shift away from the core is not. Toral and et al. [16] found that a few core members post the majority of messages and act as middlemen or brokers among other peripheral members.

Our study, by contrast is a field study of the migration of contributors from the periphery to core team. We, therefore, aim to analyze and understand interactions and contributors' evolvement per month. Specifically, we would like to address a practical question: can the activities of newcomers reveal who would be part of the core team leading the project?

Predicting Who Will Stay. Zhou et al. [17] attempted to predict who will stay in OSS communities. The authors proposed nine measures of involvement and environment based on events recorded in the issue tracking system. One of their funding stipulates that newcomers who are able to get at least one issue reported in the first month to be fixed are doubling their odds of becoming a long-term contributor. Gamalielsson et al. [18] studied the sustainability of Open Source software communities beyond a fork. Forking an OSS means that a sub set of contributors take another direction of the project because they are not in line with decisions made by notorious contributors.

3 Core-Peripheral Contributors

The existing literature provides a number of theories and approaches that may help identifying core-peripheral structures in OSS projects [5]. We could classify the OSS structure, as most of these previous works, in two classes core/peripheral. However,

Table 1. K-means classifier precision

	Number of sub-graphs	Precision for 2 classes (%)	Size (#Nodes by cluster)	Precision for 3 classes (%)	Size (#Nodes by cluster)
AngularJs	79	67.0	(50, 1379)	80.1	(39, 169, 1221)
Docker	50	64.3	(92, 1540)	84.1	(24, 146, 1462)
Rails	62	67.1	(110, 3164)	85.0	(78, 519, 2677)
Symfony	86	68.7	(133, 1296)	81.7	(26, 172, 1231)
TensorFlow	16	74.2	(43, 622)	87.6	(24, 56, 585)

found that classification into three groups provides a more accurate model as reported in Table 1.

More specifically, we start from discovering and retrieving SNA metrics for co-edition files networks. Then we run a k-means classifier to identify three classes (core, gray area, and peripheral). Finally, we evaluate our classification using O(m) Algorithm for Cores Decomposition of Networks [19].

Step 1: The first step in this analysis was to compute the social networks (SNA) metrics for each project. We use an SNA package implemented in python, named Networkx[1], to compute automatically SNA metrics for each graph. As described in Sect. 4, historical collaboration data have been processed to create one Network per month. Table 1 shows, in column 1, the number of generated sub-graphs for each project.

Step 2: The second step was to identify core/periphery contributors. To identify the core/peripheral structure in our OSS projects, we use K_means classifiers (k = 3). The underlying idea is to classify contributors in three groups according to their SNA metrics and see whether they belong to Core – Peripheral – Gray area groups. Table 1, presents the size of each cluster (k = 2 and k = 3).

Step 3: We cross validate the resulting k-means clusters for core-periphery using two methods. First, we compare k-means classification against the result of O(m) Algorithm for Cores Decomposition of Networks [19]. The algorithm takes as input a graph and provides partitions as an output. For randomly selected networks, we computed the k_core function provided by Networkx implementing the O(m) algorithm. The matching between the two algorithms was 100% agreement for small network. For large networks, we obtained a 68% agreement matching for core nodes (for example 24 node of 35 identified as core were in the partition with max k_core score).This can be due to the evolution of the collaboration network structure into an onion shape [20] with multiple layers of peripheral nodes and thus the increasing fuzziness of the gray-area-periphery border as the network grows in size.

[1] https://networkx.github.io/.

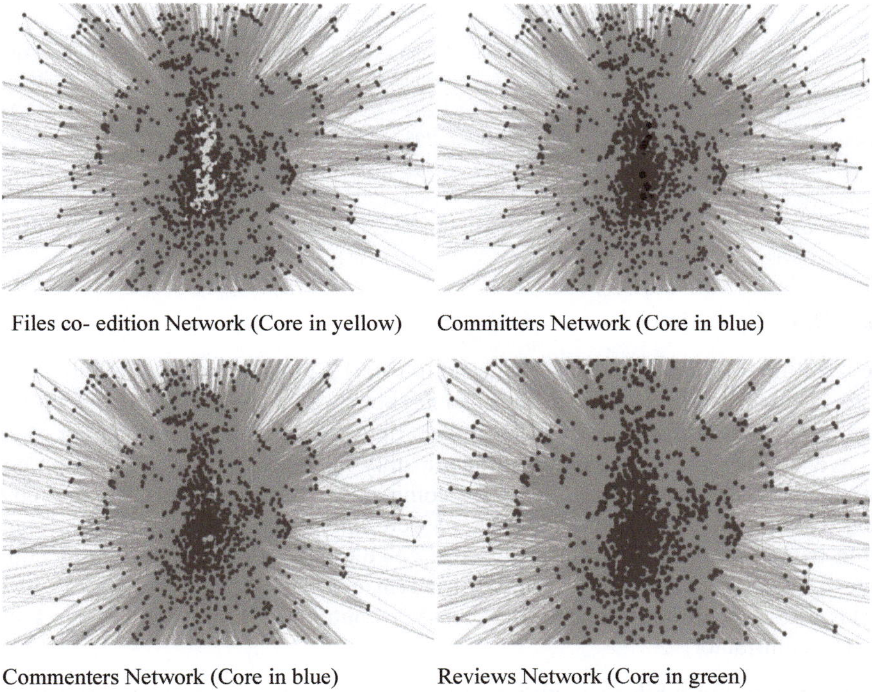

Fig. 1. Illustrative examples of networks visualization. (Color figure online)

We then manually inspect the visualization of a random sample of graphs using Cytoscape. We validated that identified core contributors effectively belong to a dense and cohesive bloc showing core members physically centered in the network, as depicted in Fig. 1.

4 Methodology

4.1 Study Subjects

In order to understand how a newcomer makes a shift from the periphery to being part of the core team within OSS projects, we studied socio-technical interactions for five long-lived and highly stared projects from GitHub. Hence, we have carefully chosen projects with approximately a thousand of contributors, with different lifespan, programming languages, and different domain in order to have diverse histories. Table 2 shows general information about the chosen OSS projects. In total, we have analyzed 850 stories of contributors spanning five different projects.

Table 2. Overview of the studied systems

	Language	Contributors	Commits	Commits comments	Reviews	Reviews comments	Line of code
AngularJs	JavaScript	1,430	8,403	1,292	497	3,013	543,246
Docker	Go	1,633	31,291	298	4,754	23,153	1,039,309
Rails	Ruby	3,273	61,782	9,986	302	5,028	413,393
Symfony	PHP	1,424	30,106	2,309	3,226	17,014	744,619
TensorFlow	C++	700	15,221	147	111	872	1,349,495

4.2 Data Collection

We used the REST (Representational state transfer) API[2] provided by Github in order to get access to all the available information about hosted projects. The API provides access to a lot of information in JSON (JavaScript Object Notation) format. For each of the five studied projects we retrieved data history including: (1) information on commits [author, date, code churn, count of comments on commits, reviews, and edited files]; (2) and then for each edited file we were interested to investigate the collaboration between contributors with respect to co-edition files (Two contributors collaborate if they modify the same file). It is worth noting that the collaboration in our context is asynchronous (timeless) because a contributor can edit files years after another contributor.

Collaboration Over Files Co-edition. OSS projects such as GitHub are collaborative repositories hosting services including social features brought a new transparency to the development project [21]. Collaboration among GitHub users can be seen in different ways and forms several kinds of social networks. The most intuitive one is the network of collaboration between developers over projects. On the other hand, collaboration within the repository is of great importance and gained interests in OSS collaboration analysis [13]. In our case, coediting the same file is the dependent variable indicating whether or not the collaboration between two developers happened. We leverage on information of co-edition files to construct our collaborative networks.

4.3 Data Processing: Building Networks

The data sets have been processed and sliced by month to provide time frames (TF) for dynamic data analysis. For each time frame (for instance, 86 TF for Angular), we constructed three undirected, weighted cumulative networks: The first network is related to **Files co-edition Network** (FCN) where nodes represent contributors and edge weights represent the quantity of interactions between those contributors based on the amount of files they both edited. The second is **Committed Comments Network** (CCN) where nodes are commenters and edge weights are the amount of commits they interacted together. Finally, the **Review's comments Network** (RCN) based on comments interactions on reviews. Figure 1 illustrates the three examples of generated graphs.

[2] https://developer.github.com/v3/.

We performed a dynamic network analysis on monthly sequences of collaboration networks based on files co-edition. By progressively adding one month activity after another, we obtained a sequence of cumulative collaboration networks that allows us to study the evolvement of social structures of each community as well as its contributor's evolution according to the core-periphery perspective.

5 Results

RQ1. *Are some activities more prevalent than others for a newcomer to become a core contributor?*

Motivation. Few newcomers in OSS end up being into the core of the project suggesting that somehow, they are gaining notoriety due to their participation in some collaborative activities such as changing source code, reviewing contributions from others, and commenting on commits and reviews. We aim at discovering what kind of contribution or collaboration are more relevant. We are interested in detecting existing correlations between social position and technical participation. Our primary goal is to equip the community of OSS with a better understanding of collaborative activities and potential guidelines for newcomers to play an efficient role.

Approach. We first identify the ascension of the top 10 core contributors for each. Next, we trace back the history of contributions aiming at quantifying collaboration activities. Then we considered contributors' activities under three types of contributions (#commits, #comments on commits, #comments on reviews, #editedFiles, and #changed Line of Code. We use a k-mean clustering approach to identify core contributors (see Sect. 3) in monthly networks. This task requires us to identify different stages through which sequences of activities progress and then segment individual sequences according to the discovered stages. Finally, we measured the most correlated collaborative activity with respect to the contributors' social network metrics.

Results. Figure 2 shows the monthly evolution of core contributors for each studied project. It also illustrates how attractive is the project in terms of its capacity to build a large community of contributors. We were also interested to quantify the amount of contributors' transition from a status to another. Figure 3 illustrates a dynamic movement from periphery to the core and vice versa. For instance, we can track only the evolvement of core developer over time (CC) as well as the contributors that quit the core for a gray area (CG).

Our monthly analysis of OSS structure networks reveals a relatively stable evolution of the core teams. An average of 19.1 contributors per month for Docker, 11.6 for Angular, 16.46 for Symfony, and 16.2 for Tenserflow. We observed, for all projects, a monthly evolution of core contributors ranging between [.4 and 10.4].

In terms of featured activities, we found that newcomers spend significant portions of their time committing, editing source code files obviously adding and deleting lines of code more than commenting on commits and reviews.

Table 3 shows the correlation between SNA centrality metric and the measure of each activity feature. One can notice that activities related to source code changes are

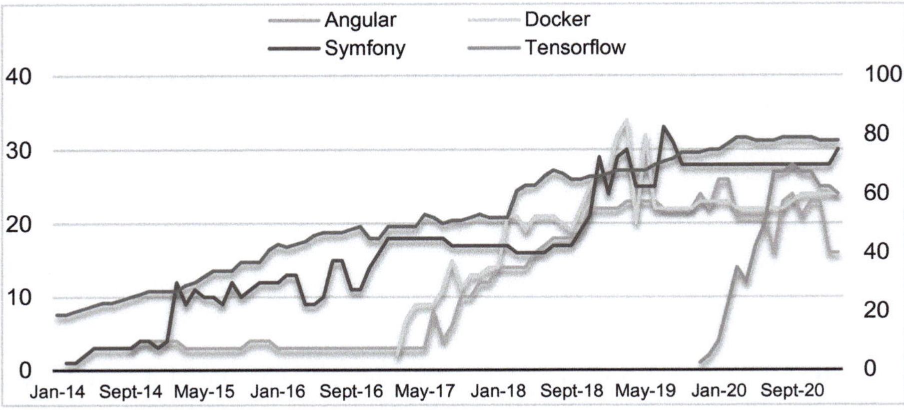

Fig. 2. Monthly evolution of core contributors.

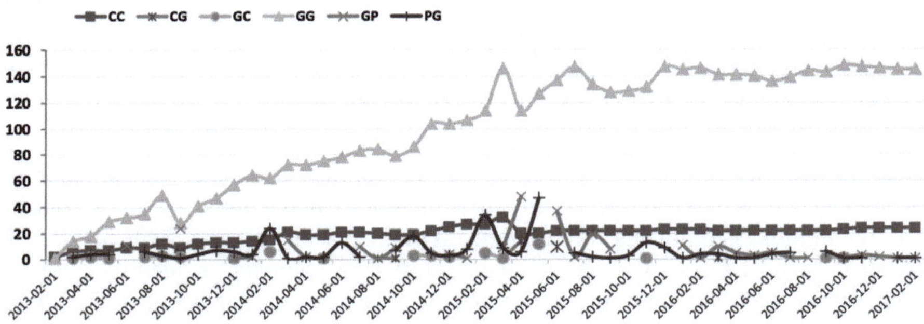

Fig. 3. Monthly evolution of contributors' status shifting for Docker

more correlated to the position of contributors within the structure core/periphery. For instance, we found for AngularJs project a correlation factor of .76 between staying in the core team and the number of contributor's commits.

RQ2. *What collaboration activities can influence how long it takes for a contributor to be a core team member?*

Motivation. We aim at identifying those collaborative activities that are more supporting newcomers gaining notoriety and being part of the core team.

Approach. Knowing the most correlated metric from RQ1, we calculated the number of commits for core contributors of each project as well as the amount of Line of code add to the project.

Results. Figure 4 shows the medians for four projects, (52, 5465) for AngularJS, (109, 21787) for Docker, (154, 7975) for Rails, (145, 6421) for Symfony, and (80, 36155) for Tenserflow. The results show that the number of commits and the amount of line of code add are both a statistically significant characteristics of core contributors.

Table 3. Average correlation between centrality metric and activity features

	Source code changes				Commenting	
	Commits	Edited files	Lines additions	Lines deletions	Commits comments	Reviews comments
AngularJs	0.76	0.77	0.70	0.72	0.28	0.60
Docker	0.73	0.81	0.75	0.72	0.43	0.06
Rails	0.68	0.74	0.62	0.60	0.71	0.31
Symfony	0.77	0.83	0.85	0.84	0.54	0.39
TensorFlow	0.69	0.72	0.73	0.79	0.68	0.27

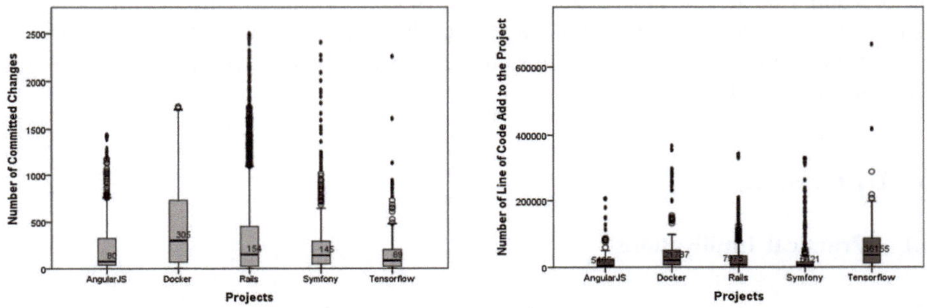

Fig. 4. Number of commits (left) and LOC add from core contributors

RQ3. Does the extent of involvement and environment predict whether a core contributor will churn from the project?

Motivation. Enormous effort over the past decades was spent in attempts to understand factors that affect involvement and sustainability of OSS communities. We contribute to that body of knowledge through our predicting model.

Approach. To answer *RQ3* and predict who will leave the project, given the collaborative metrics, we applied the *J48* decision tree algorithm on the data clustered previously using k-means for all projects in WEKA[3]. To the purpose of this analysis, we filtered out only contributors that shift from the core to the gray area (CG) before the final transition to the periphery (GP), meaning leaving the project.

Results. Table 4 reports the results of our supervised machine learning approach regarding the four projects. For instance, we have 27 contributors within Angular project shift from the core to the gray area (CG). With a decision tree approach, we are able de predict 74.07% (.93 recall) the shift from C to G with only 7 out of 27 misclassified case. Interestingly, we found the root node of the decision tree to be the "EditedFiles" <= 871.39. This means that the amount of edited file is the most closely related metric to contributors' churn. The tree showed that if the number of edited files

[3] http://www.cs.waikato.ac.nz/ml/weka/downloading.html.

Table 4. Machine learning: decision tree results (J48)

	Correctly classified	Incorrectly classified	Precision	Recall	Root activity
AngularJs	20	7	74.07	.93	# Edited Files
Docker	43	0	100	1	# Commits
Rails	39	14	73.58	.84	CommentsOnReview
Symfony	19	13	59.37	.94	CommentsOnReview
TensorFlow	23	3	88.46	.70	# Commits

keep dropping then the contributor is likely to leave the core. However, the root activity of decision tree is not always the same for each project. We hypothesis that this difference is due to the progression stage of each project. For instance, it's easier to be part of the core team of Tenserflow, a relatively new project on Github, by just committing new changes.

6 Discussion

6.1 Practical Implications

Understanding the involvement of contributors and their gain of notoriety can help the OSS communities to attract more valuable and highly motivated individuals. Moreover, analyzing the history of contributors 'activity may help to build a sustainable community of contributors around OSS.

Providing guidelines for whom want to lead future decisions of an OSS. We found the ascension of a newcomer becoming a core contributor to be associated mainly with technical contribution, especially the amount of code changes and interactions with existing source code. Most importantly, the number of commits and the amount of Line of code added rather than other activities such as commenting and reviewing others work. This may reflect some inherent differences between OSS projects and industrial ones in which we have other collaborative contributions such as requirement analysis, testing, etc.

Predicting who will churn along and who will stay is important. Allows project owners to find potential long-term contributors earlier and helps newcomers to improve their behaviors. Figure 5 illustrates tracking one contributor from Docker project. This contributor has belonged to the core team and then churned from the project at the end of 2013. If we could predict contributors 'turnover according to some aspects of behavior that we are able to model and quantify then we have the ingredients to build a sustainable long-lived community of contributors.

In summary, understanding the shift from peripheral to core contributors and then sustainable core team in OSS projects requires an understanding of "Hidden" collaborative activities as well as the motivation behind observable developers' commitment. Therefore, while our results may be statistically valid, more care must be taken in

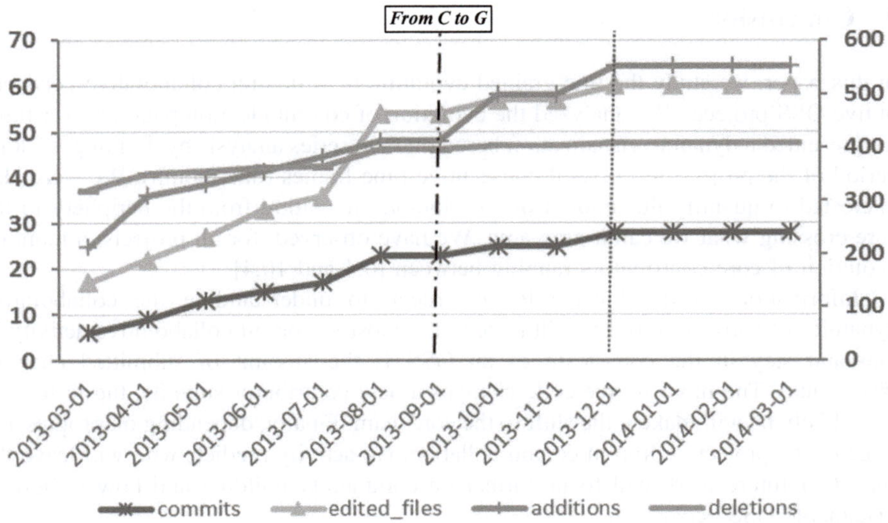

Fig. 5. Contributor turnover

interpreting their meaning to draw, for instance, a recipe to guide newcomer's behavior within OSS projects. Much work remains to be done in studying sustainable collaboration in open source projects.

6.2 Threats to Validity

We recognize few threats to our reported results. First, we did not check the bug database to assess the quality of contributions; instead we rely on crowd comments and code reviews that OSS communities use to enhance the software quality. Our choice was deliberate since we assume that core teams have gained their notoriety by performing in the quality also. However, such choice possesses threats of over estimation the quality of contributions. To mitigate the threat, we evaluate our classification against manual annotation. Second, we make certain assumption based on how we slice and build our co-edition, comments, and reviews graphs. For instance, we consider cumulative data for the co-edition network per month, and thus, building networks from the beginning of the projects up to the studied month. We consider source code collaboration as a sustainable activity in the sense that contributors leverage on the previous work of each other.

Finally, our study is the subject of statistical conclusion validity which refers to the ability to make an accurate assessment of the strength of the relationship between our independent and dependent variables. For instance, in Sect. 3, we used k-means to cluster and segregate contributors in three categories (core, peripheral, and gray area) according to a series of metrics. To gain more confidence on our classification approach, we triangulate our results using different methods such as SNA metrics, O(m) Algorithm, GitHub information, and visual inspection of collaborative networks.

7 Conclusion

In this paper, we study the fine-grained evolution of structural collaborative networks of five OSS projects. We analyzed the evolution of communication patterns over time, we presented a dynamic visualization based on time series analysis by dividing the long period of the project into several consecutive time frames (one month). We were also interested to quantify the amount of contributors' transition from the periphery to the core crossing what we call a gray area. We have observed, for all projects, a monthly evolution of core contributors ranging between [0.4 and 10.4].

Information on developer roles is crucial to understanding the collaborative dynamics of software projects. Ultimately, the most important collaborative activity to join and stay in the core team of an OSS is the amount of submitted changes (#commits). The more source code changes a new contributor submits, the faster and more likely he will make it the shift to the core team. Finally, depending on progression stage of the project, a drop in certain collaborative activity predicts who will leave the core. Our future work will focus further on community building and how to build a sustainable OSS ecosystem.

References

1. Zhou, M., Mockus, A.: What make long term contributors: willingness and opportunity in OSS community. In: Proceedings of the 34th International Conference on Software Engineering (ICSE 2012), Zurich, Switzerland, pp. 518–528 (2012)
2. Hinds, P., McGrath, C.: Structures that work: social structure, work structure and coordination ease in geographically distributed teams. In: Proceedings of the 20th International Conference on Computer Supported Cooperative Work, Banff, Alberta, Canada, pp. 343–352 (2006)
3. Koch, S., Schneider, G.: Effort, cooperation and coordination in an open source software project: Gnome. Inf. Syst. J. **12**(1), 27–42 (2002)
4. Goeminne, M., Mens, T.: Evidence for the pareto principle in open source software activity. In: The 1st International Workshop on Model Driven Software Maintenance and 5th International Workshop on Software Quality and Maintainability, pp. 74–82 (2011)
5. Geldenhuys, J.: Finding the core developers. In: 36th Euromicro Conference on Software Engineering and Advanced Applications, Lille, France, pp. 447–450 (2010)
6. Dinh-Trong, T.T., Bieman, J.M.: The FreeBSD project: a replication case study of open source development. IEEE Trans. Softw. Eng. **31**(6), 481–494 (2005)
7. Robles, G., Koch, S., Gonzalez-Barahona, J.M., et al.: Remote analysis and measurement of libre software systems by means of the cvsanaly tool. In: Proceedings of the 2nd ICSE Workshop on Remote Analysis and Measurement of Software Systems, pp. 51–55 (2004)
8. Mockus, A., Fielding, R.T., Herbsleb, J.D.: Two case studies of open source software development: Apache and Mozilla. ACM Trans. Softw. Eng. Methodol. **11**(3), 309–346 (2002)
9. Lussier, S.: New tricks: how open source changed the way my team works. IEEE Softw. **21**(1), 68–72 (2004)
10. Dagenais, B., Ossher, H., Bellamy, R.K.E., et al.: Moving into a new software project landscape. In: Proceedings of the 32 International Conference on Software Engineering (ICSE 2012), Cape Town, South Africa, pp. 275–284 (2010)

11. Ye, Y., Kishida, K.: Toward an understanding of the motivation open source software developers. In: Proceedings of the International Conference on Software Engineering (ICSE 2003), pp. 419–429 (2003)
12. Hars, A., Shaosong, O.: Working for free? Motivations of participating in open source projects. Int. J. Electron. Commer. **6**, 25–39 (2001)
13. Dabbish, L., Stuart, C., Tsay, J., et al.: Social coding in GitHub: transparency and collaboration in an open software repository. In: Conference on Computer Supported Cooperative Work, Seattle, WA, USA, pp. 1277–1286 (2012)
14. Bosu, A., Carver, J.C.: Impact of developer reputation on code review outcomes in OSS projects: an empirical investigation. In: Proceedings of the 8th International Symposium on Empirical Software Engineering and Measurement, Torino, Italy, pp. 1–10 (2014)
15. Amrit, C., van Hillegersberg, J.: Exploring the impact of socio-technical core-periphery structures in open source software development. J. Inf. Technol. **25**(2), 216–229 (2010)
16. Toral, S.L., Martínez-Torres, M.R., Barrero, F.: Analysis of virtual communities supporting OSS projects using social network analysis. Inf. Softw. Technol. **52**(3), 296–303 (2010)
17. Zhou, M., Mockus, A.: Who will stay in the FLOSS community? Modeling participant's initial behavior. IEEE Trans. Soft. Eng. **41**(1), 82–99 (2015)
18. Gamalielsson, J., Lundell, B.: Sustainability of open source software communities beyond a fork: how and why has the LibreOffice project evolved? J. Syst. Softw. **89**, 128–145 (2014)
19. Batagelj, V., Zaversnik, M.: An O(m) algorithm for cores decomposition of networks. Adv. Data Anal. Classif. **5**(2), 129–145 (2003)
20. Louzada, V.H.P., Daolio, F., Herrmann, H.J., et al.: Smart rewiring for network robustness. J. Complex Netw. **1**(2), 150–159 (2013)
21. McDonald, N., Blincoe, K., Petakovic, E.V.A.: Modeling distributed collaboration on Github. Adv. Complex Syst. **7**(8), 1450024 (2014)

Big Valuable Data in Supply Chain: Deep Analysis of Current Trends and Coming Potential

Samia Chehbi-Gamoura(✉) and Ridha Derrouiche

EM Strasbourg Business School, Université de Strasbourg, HuManiS EA 7308, 67000 Strasbourg, France
samia.gamoura@gmail.com

Abstract. Today, Big Data Analytics (BDA) are definitely the key basis of competitiveness for enterprises in their Supply Chains. The outburst of data captured, accumulated and analyzed is impacting the value-added-chain at all levels from manufacturers to customers. In this paper, we develop a structured methodology to provide a deep analysis of Big Data Analytics methods across the Supply-Chain Operations Reference (SCOR) model processes. An exhaustive literature review is illustrated to afford a comprehensive Mind-Map cartography with a BDA-SCOR matching matrix. The proposed approach points to a number of research concerns that need to be addressed by research community. Outcomes of this study may highlight relevant guidelines for upcoming works of both academics and industrials. It highlights the need for collaborative Big Data to manage SCM more intelligently. Our objective is to provide an effective analysis to understand how Big Data Analytics become even more valuable for better Supply Chain Management.

Keywords: Big valuable data · Analytics · Supply Chain Management · SCOR model · Mind-Map cartography

1 Introduction

There is no doubt; Big Data Analytics (BDA) is progressively becoming inevitable practice to extract more and more business values [1]. The main motive of Supply Chain (SC) managers is certainly to possess meaningful insights that allow them to better forecast, predict, reveal hidden patterns, and then to gain wider edge of competitiveness [2]. Henceforth, academics and industrials are aware that conventional databases are not capable to process such Big Data [3]. Analytics are reforming the way Supply Chain Management (SCM) handle acquired data internally; such as transactional information systems, and externally such as social networks, mobile devices, and IoT (Internet of Things) sensors [4].

Beyond considerate what Big Data earns, companies now are focusing on how analytics might be used to obtain business meaningful insights [5]. Given the variety and complexity of very large unstructured and high-dynamic datasets, this task is not trivial and may be very challenging [6].

L.M. Camarinha-Matos et al. (Eds.): PRO-VE 2017, IFIP AICT 506, pp. 230–241, 2017.
DOI: 10.1007/978-3-319-65151-4_22

Accordingly, we propose this paper with multifold purposes: (a) Foremost, it carried out a profound literature review across past and present patterns in academic publications. The bibliographical analysis is conducted by observing contributions, synthetizing knowledge, drawing tendencies, and making causality relationships by classifying intakes and highlighting further research opportunities. (b) Secondly, it provides a Mind-Map cartography of using BDA methods in Supply-Chain Operations Reference (SCOR) model as a clear synopsis of current research trends. (c) Lastly, this study draws future research trajectories and sheds light on the gaps that need to be overcome. Scholars can leverage this paper as a reference for future research opportunities, and SC specialists can use it as a methodology to benchmark BDA methods and measure impact in valuable information for SC.

This paper is structured as follows. We begin by introducing BDA methods and SCOR model reminder. We then develop the proposed methodology of bibliography analysis. Finally, we conclude by underlining the current trends of SCM-BDA researches, the untaken breaks, and the expected potential in the near future.

2 Related Works and Research Gaps

Analytics are ranged into several collections of methods, sub-methods and techniques that diverge in their objectives, prerequisites and applicability [7]. Hence, prior to hastily study applicability of these methods in SCM, there is a prerequisite to first understand their settings and features. The next sub-section offers a brief overview.

2.1 Big Data Analytics Methods and Techniques

The word 'value' in the context of BD denotes extraction of worthy information by investigating the accumulated data through transformation and processing. Aligned with [8], BDA are emerging as the 'next big thing' and is defined as a collection of technologies that handle, incorporate, and report massive data by transforming it into new insights not attainable with traditional technologies.

In one hand, academics are aware that decision makers progressively view in BDA an imperative driver of modernization and a substantial source of value creation for competitive benefit [9]. In fact, since 2014, there is an increasing emerging of research works: case studies ([10–12], etc.), original works ([13–15], etc.), surveys ([16, 17], etc.), and a variety of literature papers ([18–20], etc.). Likewise, industrials are attentive to the potential of analytics in management of SC. Indeed, the worldwide leader in research and advisory Gartner's® has mentioned in [21] that BDA appear among the Top 25 SC research topics for 2016. Forbes®, also, argued in [22] that no single research topic in the last decade has as much effect on incumbent investments for industrials.

Approaches of BDA are numerous and may be alienated into several methods and sub-methods; to be employed solely or combined jointly [17]. Each method/sub-method uses one or a mixture of statistical or mathematical techniques, up on the expected business value. According our literature review, the main root methods that concerned by SC are: Exploratory Data Analysis (EDA) [8], Confirmatory Data Analysis (CDA) [11], Qualitative Data Analysis (QDA) [23], and Real-Time Analysis (RTA) [24]. Based on the underlying methods, sub-methods and techniques can also be categorized into several groups, but given the breadth of these techniques, an exhaustive list exceeds the extent of a single paper. Though, a relevant sub-list which has already been used in the field of SC covers mainly: regression [25], optimization [26], induction [27], fuzzy logic [28], classification [10], aggregation [12], and so on.

2.2 Supply Chain Operations Reference (SCOR) Model

In order to expand in competiveness of companies, SCOR model was developed by Supply Chain Council (SCC) for designing and enhancing SCs. It offers standard frame for deciding, organizing and fulfilling SC processes [29]. Nevertheless, it is traditionally used in benchmarking studies [30]. SCOR model governs five processes; they are consecutively named and briefly described in Table 1.

Table 1. Brief definition of processes in SCOR Model (SCOR model V.9.0 [29])

Plan	Process that includes planning activities
Source	Process that includes procurement activities
Make	Process that includes transformation of contents or services
Deliver	Process that includes fulfilment of customer orders
Return	Process that includes reverse movements of goods from customers

Based on pre-defined processes, SCOR can detect where action is required. It can also help to arrange more accurate projections. Accordingly, we base our study through SCOR processes. The next section describes step-by-step our methodology.

3 Proposed Methodology

3.1 Data Collection

By using Harzing's Publish or Purish V.5® [31], we queried out the more relevant and recent publications in the topic of BDA and SCM (from 2014 to 2017). Parameters of Harzing's search request are itemized in Table 2.

Once the information were sorted, we then cleansed and filtered the academic database by deleting unwanted columns (ranking, types, ISSN) and rows (programs, books, technical reports, white papers, patents, literature reviews, unrelated researches, etc.). We kept only used columns (cites, authors, title, year, source, publisher, URL, countries) and rows (journals).

Table 2. Search request in Harzing's Publish or Purish V.5® [31]

Query date	2017-03-22
Maximum papers number	100
Any of the words	{Big Data Analytics, Supply Chain, Management, Value}
Publication type	Journal
Since year	2014
Publisher	All
Search engine	Google Scholar Engine
Location	Title, abstract, key words

3.2 Analysis and Findings

By using the sorted list of last step, we reviewed each contribution and recorded a matrix that matched information with respect to BDA methods and SCOR processes. Discussion of our relevant findings and empirical results are in following sections.

Finding1: SCOR-BDA matching matrix. For each row (reference), we analyzed BDA methods, sub-methods and techniques (Sect. 2.1), and then recorded matching cells with regard to SCOR processes according to Table 1. Table 3 below illustrates the SCOR-BDA matrix as applied to the collected bibliographical dataset.

Finding 2: Mind-Map Cartography of SCOR-BDA. We constructed cartography by using Mind-Mapping technique [32] with Coggle® tool [33]. The branching out in (Appendix, Fig. 3) illustrates that all defined methods are employed in all SCOR processes but not with the same techniques. For instance, the FUzzy Logic technique (FUL) is used in Data Statistical-inference Methods (DSM) in 'Make' process but not in 'Source' process. Another ascertainment; the process 'Deliver' is the most prolific branch regard to methods and techniques already addressed in literature.

Finding 3: Overview of SCOR-BDA evolution. Bars diagrams in Fig. 1; summarize the total number of publications for each process in SCOR, in the current three years (2014–2017).

As seen in Fig. 1, there is an exponential increase in the number of contributions for all SCOR processes with an overall exponential variation of +0.064 (R^2 = ~0,90). A few publications was issued in early 2014 (equal and less than 11%), and at the end of 2015 (~11%–~23%). However, in just two consecutive years later (2016 and 2017), publication rates have almost doubled for each year and each process (for instance; in plan process, the rate jumped from 11% to 26%, and then to 53%). This demonstrates that BDA tools have emerged as one of the fastest growing fields in SCM in recent years. On the other hand, as we observe an unequal growing interest for processes, we then broke down the total numbers by processes.

Finding 4: Detailed view of SCOR-BDA evolution. Figure 2 sorts the number of contributions for each process in the matrix BDA-SCOR of the selected dataset.

Table 3. SCOR-BDA matching matrix according to the bibliographical dataset.

References	Method-Data Discovery and Visualization	Method-Predictive Data Analysis	Method-Data Reduction Methods	Method-Data Deduction Methods	Method-Data Statistical-inference Methods	Method-Data Quantification Methods	Method-Data Event-oriented Methods	Technique-Optimization	Technique-Regression	Technique-Classification	Technique-Association rules learning	Technique-Dimensional reduction	Technique-Aggregation	Technique-Operations Research	Technique-Fuzzy logic	Technique-Real-Time reporting score	Technique-Sequential Analysis	Technique-Rules Induction	Streamlining and modeling	SCOR-Plan Process	SCOR-Source Process	SCOR-Make Process	SCOR-Deliver Process	SCOR-Return Process
[8]	X							X													X			X
[25]					X				X														X	
[12]				X									X		X					X	X			
[1]		X							X											X				
[11]					X				X													X		
[6]				X										X						X				
[34]				X										X						X				X
[2]	X								X											X			X	
[24]	X						X		X							X				X			X	
[15]				X													X			X		X		
[14]	X								X														X	
[35]				X										X									X	
[27]		X	X															X	X			X		
[36]			X														X			X	X	X	X	
[37]				X													X			X				
[26]	X			X	X			X												X				
[38]				X				X														X	X	
[16]				X														X		X				
[39]	X			X														X		X				
[40]		X		X				X	X														X	
[10]		X								X											X		X	
[23]				X		X					X		X							X				X
[5]	X																	X					X	
[41]			X				X		X							X				X		X		X
[42]							X									X				X	X		X	
[43]				X								X										X		
[44]											X												X	X
[45]	X										X												X	X
[46]	X		X				X							X		X	X						X	
[47]		X										X	X							X				
[28]	X			X					X	X					X					X				
[48]	X					X												X		X			X	
[49]				X								X										X		
[50]				X			X									X			X	X				
[51]							X									X			X			X		
[9]				X													X		X	X				
[13]				X			X	X								X						X		
[3]				X							X											X		
[52]		X		X					X													X		
[53]				X		X					X								X		X			X
[7]		X							X	X										X				
[54]				X				X												X				
[55]		X						X												X				
[56]		X									X									X				
[57]	X																		X			X		
[58]				X							X								X	X				
[59]				X															X	X				
[60]	X				X			X			X									X				
[61]		X		X							X		X						X	X				
[62]	X																	X		X				
[63]	X	X							X								X	X		X				
[64]			X				X				X		X						X				X	
[65]				X			X									X			X	X				
[66]				X							X									X			X	
[4]								X											X				X	

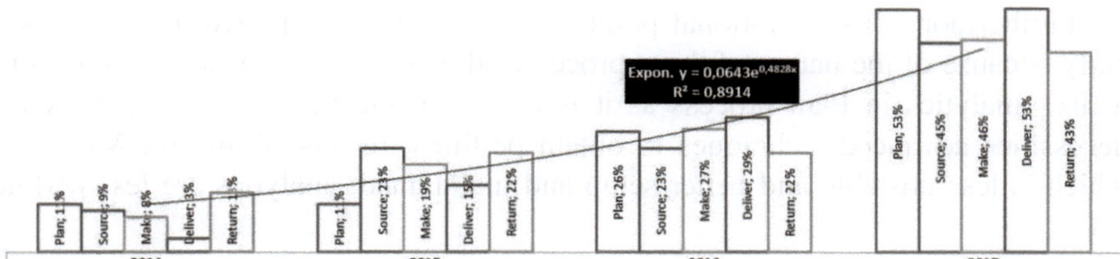

	2014	2015	2016	2017
□ Plan	11%	11%	26%	53%
□ Source	9%	23%	23%	45%
□ Make	8%	19%	27%	46%
□ Deliver	3%	15%	29%	53%
□ Return	13%	22%	22%	43%

Fig. 1. Normalized total numbers of publications in BDA-SCOR matrix according to the bibliographical dataset (2014–2017)

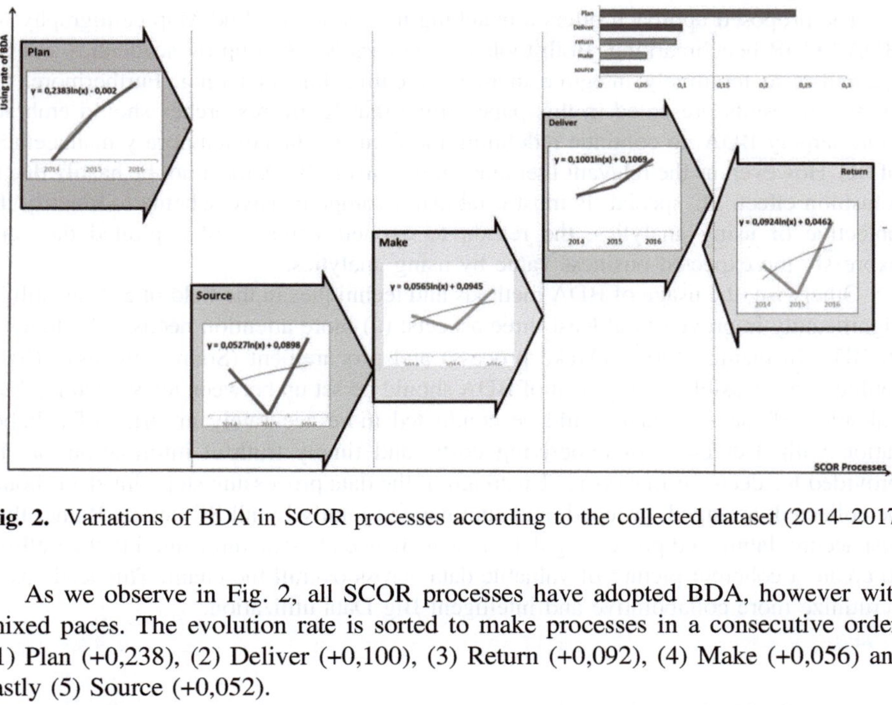

Fig. 2. Variations of BDA in SCOR processes according to the collected dataset (2014–2017)

As we observe in Fig. 2, all SCOR processes have adopted BDA, however with mixed paces. The evolution rate is sorted to make processes in a consecutive order: (1) Plan (+0,238), (2) Deliver (+0,100), (3) Return (+0,092), (4) Make (+0,056) and lastly (5) Source (+0,052).

Subsequently, we assume that: the more operations are oriented inside the company (manufacturer), the less analytics are exploited. In other words, researchers need valuation of the data that are positioned at company's connectivity with the outside (mainly Deliver, Return and Plan). This indicates a lack of collaboration between companies in the process of valuing their data. We can explain this by the fact that these companies compete to extract as much value from data, but unfortunately each company acts separately. This point is very significant as it raises the need for collaborative Big Data to exploit it intelligently in SCM.

Furthermore, from a rational point of view, BDA are applied to processes differently because of the nature of these processes themselves. In instance, it seems normal to use analytics in Plan process as it is the most uncertain activity and then which necessities advanced techniques to obtain pertinent results. While for Make process, which is less unstable and better setup and maintained, analytics are less pertinent.

4 Conclusion: Discussion and Future Trends

It is true that the proposed approach may have some limits such as restriction in dataset collection. Indeed, we have collected data by the way of Harzing's Publish or Purish® tool which is itself limited in search queries and cannot combine searching engines. Despite this, the study allowed us to have a deep overview of the BDAs and their positioning in the SC processes.

The proposed approach offers a matching matrix and a Mind-Map cartography for BDA-SCOR benchmarking. Both tools can be largely taken up by academics and SC specialists to intuitively integrate them in orienting understanding. Furthermore, the empirical results presented in this paper argue that future researches should embrace more largely BDA, to continue redefining the focus of the contemporary management of SC. However, as the relevant literature shows, using BDA must not be hastily due to a fashion effect. SC specialists must establish a comprehensive schema to identify the objective of using analytics, the reason to expand volumes of exploited data and expressly the expected business value by using analytics.

Otherwise, the usage of BDA methods and techniques in the field of SC can still be significantly improved in at least three aspects: (a) more attention needs to be focused to BDA in manufacturing (Make process) and procurement (Source process). (b) A faultless and feasible deployment of BDA should be set up between all SC actors, thus, valuation of massive data would be conducted more accurately in terms of collaboration with decreasing of underlying costs, and timely truthful information can be provided for decision-makers (c) Upstream of the data processing step, this data should be collected, arranged, grouped, and summarized jointly by all SC actors. Rather than just accumulating and processing data, managers need to structure, and link their efforts to create a coherent picture of valuable data across overall the chain. This leads us to scrutinize more collaborative and intelligent Big Data utilization.

Appendix

Figure 3 bellow illustrates the Mind-Map cartography according the collected dataset.

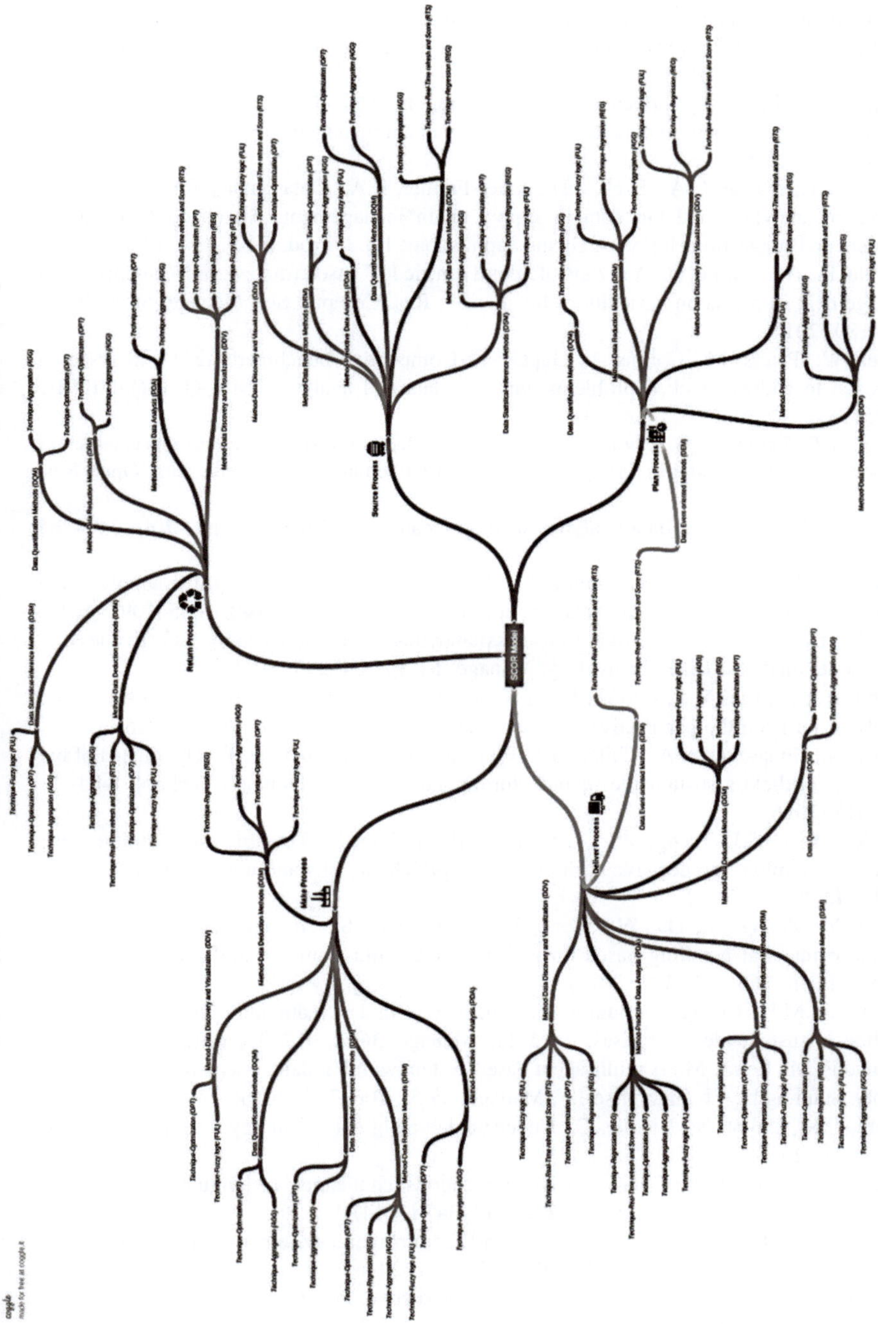

Fig. 3. MindMap of BDA- SCOR according to the bibliographical dataset (available under public access on [67])

References

1. Gunasekaran, A., Papadopoulos, T., Dubey, R., Wamba, S.F., Childe, S.J., Hazen, B., Akter, S.: Big data and predictive analytics for supply chain and organizational performance. J. Bus. Res. **70**, 308–317 (2017)
2. Bendoly, E.: Fit, bias, and enacted sensemaking in data visualization: frameworks for continuous development in operations and supply chain management analytics. J. Bus. Log. **37**(1), 6–17 (2016)
3. Hazen, B.T., Boone, C.A., Ezell, J.D., Jones-Farmer, L.A.: Data quality for data science, predictive analytics, and big data in supply chain management: An introduction to the problem and suggestions for research and applications. Int. J. Prod. Econ. **154**, 72–80 (2014)
4. Satpute, P., Tembhurne, O.: A review of: cloud centric IoT based framework for supply chain management in precision agriculture. Int. J. Adv. Res. Comput. Sci. Manage. Stud. **2**(11), 175–180 (2014)
5. Ketter, W., Peters, M., Collins, J., Gupta, A.: Competitive benchmarking: an IS research approach to address wicked problems with big data and analytics. MIS Q. ERS-2015-01 (2015)
6. Hazen, B.T., Skipper, J.B., Boone, C.A., Hill, R.R.: Back in business: Operations research in support of big data analytics for operations and supply chain management. Ann. Oper. Res. 1–11 (2016)
7. Bi, Z., Cochran, D.: Big data analytics with applications. J. Manage. Anal. **1**(4), 249–265 (2014)
8. Zhao, R., Liu, Y., Zhang, N., Huang, T.: An optimization model for green supply chain management by using a big data analytic approach. J. Clean. Prod. **142**, 1085–1097 (2017)
9. Cao, G., Duan, Y., Li, G.: Linking business analytics to decision making effectiveness: A path model analysis. IEEE Trans. Eng. Manage. **62**(3), 384–395 (2015)
10. Chong, A.Y.L., Liu, M.J., Luo, J., Keng-Boon, O.: Predicting RFID adoption in healthcare supply chain from the perspectives of users. Int. J. Prod. Econ. **159**, 66–75 (2015)
11. Dubey, R., Gunasekaran, A., Childe, S.J., Wamba, S.F., Papadopoulos, T.: The impact of big data on world-class sustainable manufacturing. Int. J. Adv. Manufact. Technol. **84**(1–4), 631–645 (2016)
12. Wu, K.J., Liao, C.J., Tseng, M.L., Lim, M.K., Hu, J., Tan, K.: Toward sustainability: using big data to explore the decisive attributes of supply chain risks and uncertainties. J. Clean. Prod. **142**, 663–676 (2017)
13. Zhang, Y., Zhang, G., Du, W., Wang, J., Ali, E., Sun, S.: An optimization method for shopfloor material handling based on real-time and multi-source manufacturing data. Int. J. Prod. Econ. **165**, 282–292 (2015)
14. Rehman, U.M.H., Chang, V., Batool, A., Wah, T.Y.: Big data reduction framework for value creation in sustainable enterprises. Int. J. Inf. Manage. **36**(6), 917–928 (2016)
15. Giannakis, M., Louis, M.: A multi-agent based system with big data processing for enhanced supply chain agility. J. Enterprise Inf. Manage. **29**(5), 706–727 (2016)
16. Emani, C.K., Cullot, N., Nicolle, C.: Understandable big data: a survey. Comput. Sci. Rev. **17**, 70–81 (2015)
17. Chen, C.P., Zhang, C.Y.: Data-intensive applications, challenges, techniques and technologies: a survey on Big Data. Inf. Sci. **275**, 314–347 (2014)
18. Akter, S., Wamba, S.F.: Big data analytics in E-commerce: a systematic review and agenda for future research. Electron. Mark. **26**(2), 173–194 (2016)
19. Schoenherr, T., Speier-Pero, C.: Data science, predictive analytics, and big data in supply chain management: Current state and future potential. J. Bus. Log. **36**(1), 120–132 (2015)

20. Duan, L., Xiong, Y.: Big data analytics and business analytics. J. Manage. Anal. **2**(1), 1–21 (2015)
21. Gartner: Survey Analysis: What Does Increased Adoption of Big Data Mean to Supply Chain Strategists? Research Analysis, Gartner, Inc., California (2016)
22. Forbes: 51% of Enterprises Intend to Invest More in Big Data. Research Press Report, Forbes Inc., California (2016)
23. Luthra, S., Garg, D., Haleem, A.: Critical success factors of green supply chain management for achieving sustainability in Indian automobile industry. Prod. Plann. Control **26**(5), 339–362 (2015)
24. Vera-Baquero, A., Colomo-Palacios, R., Molloy, O.: Real-time business activity monitoring and analysis of process performance on big-data domains. Telematics Inform. **33**(3), 793–807 (2016)
25. Papadopoulos, T., Gunasekaran, A., Dubey, R., Altay, N., Childe, S.J., Fosso-Wamba, S.: The role of Big Data in explaining disaster resilience in supply chains for sustainability. J. Clean. Prod. **142**, 1108–1118 (2017)
26. Dutta, D., Bose, I.: Managing a big data project: the case of ramco cements limited. Int. J. Prod. Econ. **165**, 293–306 (2015)
27. Tan, K.H., Zhan, Y., Ji, G., Ye, F., Chang, C.: Harvesting big data to enhance supply chain innovation capabilities: An analytic infrastructure based on deduction graph. Int. J. Prod. Econ. **165**, 223–233 (2015)
28. Chang, H.-T., Mishra, N., Lin, C.C.: IoT big-data centred knowledge granule analytic and cluster framework for BI applications: a case base analysis. PLoS ONE **10**(11), e0141980 (2015)
29. Supply Chain Council (SCC): Supply Chain Operations Reference Model: Release 11.0. Supply Chain Council (SCC), New York (2012)
30. Jamehshooran, G.B., Shaharoun, M., Haron, N.H.: Assessing supply chain performance through applying the SCOR model. Int. J. Supply Chain Manage. **4**(1) (2015)
31. Harzing. Harzing's Publish Or Perish, 19 February 2017. http://www.harzing.com/. Accessed 22 Mar 2017
32. mindmapping.com. Mind Mapping. 31 December 2016. http://www.mindmapping.com/fr/. accès le 25 Mar 2017
33. Coggle.it. Coggle Mind-Map, 31 December 2016. https://coggle.it. accès le 25 Mar 2017
34. Song, M.L., Fisher, R., Wang, J.L., Cui, L.B.: Environmental performance evaluation with big data: theories and methods. Ann. Oper. Res. 1–14 (2016)
35. Wedel, M., Kannan, P.K.: Marketing analytics for data-rich environments. J. Mark. **80**(6), 97–121 (2016)
36. Li, J., Tao, F., Cheng, Y., Zhao, L.: Big data in product lifecycle management. Int. J. Adv. Manufact. Technol. **81**(1–4), 667–684 (2015)
37. Miklos, A., Vasarhelyi, A.K., Tuttle, B.M.: Big Data in accounting: an overview. Account. Horiz. **29**(2), 381–396 (2015)
38. Xu, J., Huang, E., Chen, C.H., Lee, L.H.: Simulation optimization: a review and exploration in the new era of cloud computing and big data. Asia-Pacific J. Oper. Res. **32**(03), 34 (2015)
39. Alles, M.G.: Drivers of the use and facilitators and obstacles of the evolution of big data by the audit profession. Account. Horiz. **29**(2), 439–449 (2015)
40. Phillips-Wren, G., Hoskisson, A.: An analytical journey towards big data. J. Decis. Syst. **24**(1), 87–102 (2015)
41. Lee, J., Ardakani, H.D., Yang, S., Bagheri, B.: Industrial big data analytics and cyber-physical systems for future maintenance & service innovation. Procedia CIRP **38**, 3–7 (2015)

42. Vera-Baquero, A., Colomo-Palacios, R., Molloy, O.: Measuring and querying process performance in supply chains: an approach for mining big-data cloud storages. Procedia Comput. Sci. **64**, 1026–1034 (2015)
43. Zhong, R.Y., Xu, C., Chen, C., Huang, G.Q.: Big data analytics for physical internet-based intelligent manufacturing shop floors. Int. J. Prod. Res. 1–12 (2015)
44. Xu, M., Cai, H., Liang, S.: Big data and industrial ecology. J. Ind. Ecol. **19**(2), 205–210 (2015)
45. Chae, B.K.: Big data and IT-enabled services: ecosystem and coevolution. IT Prof. **17**(2), 20–25 (2015)
46. Hsu, C.Y., Yang, C.S., Yu, L.C., Lin, C.F., Yao, H.H., Chen, D.Y., Robert, L.K., Chang, P. C.: Development of a cloud-based service framework for energy conservation in a sustainable intelligent transportation system. Int. J. Prod. Econ. **164**, 454–461 (2015)
47. Zakir, J., Seymour, T., Berg, K.: Big data analytics. Issues Inf. Syst. **16**(2), 81–90 (2015)
48. Donnelly, C., Simmons, G., Armstrong, G., Fearne, A.: Digital loyalty card 'big data' and small business marketing: Formal versus informal or complementary? Int. Small Bus. J. **33**(4), 422–442 (2015)
49. Gölzer, P., Simon, L., Cato, P., Amberg, M.: Designing global manufacturing networks using Big Data. Procedia CIRP **33**, 191–196 (2015)
50. Vera-Baquero, A., Colomo-Palacios, R., Molloy, O., Elbattah, M.: Business process improvement by means of big data based decision support systems: a case study on call centers. Int. J. Inf. Syst. Project Manage. 2182–7788 (2015)
51. O'Donovan, P., Leahy, K., Bruton, K., O'Sullivan, D.T.J.: An industrial big data pipeline for data-driven analytics maintenance applications in large-scale smart manufacturing facilities. J. Big Data **2**(1), 25 (2015)
52. Lee, J., Kao, H.A., Yang, S.: Service innovation and smart analytics for industry 4.0 and big data environment. Procedia CIRP **16**, 3–8 (2014)
53. Govindan, K., Kaliyan, M., Kannan, D., Haq, A.N.: Barriers analysis for green supply chain management implementation in Indian industries using analytic hierarchy process. Int. J. Prod. Econ. **147**, 555–568 (2014)
54. Milliken, A.L.: Transforming big data into supply chain analytics. J. Bus. Forecast. **33**(4), 23 (2014)
55. Schlegel, G.L.: Utilizing big data and predictive analytics to manage supply chain risk. J. Bus. Forecast. **33**(4), 11 (2014)
56. Chae, B., Olson, D., Sheu, C.: The impact of supply chain analytics on operational performance: a resource-based view. Int. J. Prod. Res. **52**(16), 4695–4710 (2014)
57. Lasi, H., Fettke, P., Kemper, H., Feld, T., Hoffmann, M.: Industry 4.0. Bus. Inf. Syst. Eng. **6** (4), 239–242 (2014)
58. Baars, H., Felden, C., Gluchowski, P., Hilbert, A., Kemper, H.G., Olbrich, S.: Shaping the next incarnation of business intelligence. Bus. Inf. Syst. Eng. **6**(1), 11–16 (2014)
59. Vera-Baquero, A., Colomo-Palacios, R., Molloy, O.: Towards a process to guide Big data based decision support systems for business processes. Procedia Technol. **16**, 11–21 (2014)
60. Chae, B.K., Yang, C., Olson, D., Sheu, C.: The impact of advanced analytics and data accuracy on operational performance: a contingent resource based theory (RBT) perspective. Decis. Support Syst. **59**, 119–126 (2014)
61. Stefanovic, N.: Proactive supply chain performance management with predictive analytics. Sci. World J. **17** (2014)
62. Bhimani, A., Willcocks, L.: Digitisation, 'Big Data' and the transformation of accounting information. Account. Bus. Res. **44**(4), 469–490 (2014)
63. Chae, B.K.A.: Complexity theory approach to IT-enabled services (IESs) and service innovation: Business analytics as an illustration of IES. Decis. Support Syst. **57**, 1–10 (2014)

64. Yesudas, M., Menon, G., Ramamurthy, V.: Intelligent operational dashboards for smarter commerce using big data. IBM J. Res. Dev. **58**(5/6), 13 (2014)
65. Bärenfänger, R., Otto, B., Österle, H.: Business value of in-memory technology–multiple-case study insights. Ind. Manage. Data Syst. **114**(9), 1396–1414 (2014)
66. Zhu, J., Huang, Z.: Banks' micro enterprises loan credit risk decision-making model innovation in the era of big data and internet finance. J. Manage. Strateg. **5**(2), 63 (2014)
67. samiagamoura.com. SCOR-BDA Mind-Map. Vers. 1.0, 20 February 2017. http://www.samiagamoura.com/mes-outils-my-coggle-mind-maps.html. Accessed 22 Mar 2017

Simplifying Big Data Analytics Systems with a Reference Architecture

Go Muan Sang(✉), Lai Xu, and Paul de Vrieze

Faculty of Science and Technology, Bournemouth University, Poole, Dorset BH12 5BB, UK
{gsang, lxu, pdvrieze}@bournemouth.ac.uk

Abstract. The internet and pervasive technology like the Internet of Things (i.e. sensors and smart devices) have exponentially increased the scale of data collection and availability. This big data not only challenges the structure of existing enterprise analytics systems but also offer new opportunities to create new knowledge and competitive advantage. Businesses have been exploiting these opportunities by implementing and operating big data analytics capabilities. Social network companies such as Facebook, LinkedIn, Twitter and Video streaming company like Netflix have implemented big data analytics and subsequently published related literatures. However, these use cases did not provide a simplified and coherent big data analytics reference architecture as well as currently, there still remains limited reference architecture of big data analytics. This paper aims to simplify big data analytics by providing a reference architecture based on existing four use cases and subsequently verified the reference architecture with Amazon and Google analytics services.

Keywords: Big data · Analytics · Reference architecture

1 Introduction

Cloud computing and the evolution of Internet of things technology with their applications (digital data collection devices such as mobile, sensors, etc.) have exponentially increased the scale of data collection and data availability [1, 2]. Digital technology (social network applications, etc.) facilitates people interact with data and more data is shared ever before [1]. Across every industry, businesses focus on putting data at the core of business transformation to better understand their customers, create product and service differentiation as well as to simply lower their costs and to increase efficiency [1–3]. As a result, data becomes one of the primary assets for organizations [2].

The need of enterprise agile analytics is growing rapidly to satisfy the demands driven by big data, and increasingly complex business analysis and analytics [1]. Thus, data-driven analytics become a mainstream process for businesses [2]. [4] defined analytics as "techniques used to analyse and acquire intelligence from big data". We refer analytics as "the collection, processing, analysis (machine learned models, statistics, etc.,) and visualization of big data to produce insight".

Contemporary data analytics systems cannot sufficiently handle big data as well as current systems handling big data consist of inflexible and complex platforms, tools

L.M. Camarinha-Matos et al. (Eds.): PRO-VE 2017, IFIP AICT 506, pp. 242–249, 2017.
DOI: 10.1007/978-3-319-65151-4_23

and information. This needs to be restructured into much more centralized but flexible analytical infrastructure [1]. The problem of how to do this presents a challenge to businesses and the research community. Reference architecture can help in the creation of concrete architectures [19], however there still remains a lack of reference architectures as well as a coherent architecture of big data analytics.

The aim of this paper is to explore the realization of simplifying big data analytics systems, and subsequently proposes a new high level abstract reference architecture. Key aspects and considerations such as architecture design of the system, utilization of underlying processes, technologies and services are important for the realization of a big data analytics system [5]. The contributions of this work are: a) to provide high level independent reference architecture for design a big data analytics platform based on existing publications b) to verify the proposed reference architecture using existing different big data analytics.

The structure of the paper is as follows: Related work and literature study are presented in Sect. 2. Production of the reference architecture with big data use cases as well as LinkedIn big data use case and its mapping the reference architecture are presented in Sect. 3. Due to page limitation, we do not present all other use cases. Finally, a short conclusion is provided in Sect. 4.

2 Related Work

In this section, we reviewed existing big data analytics use cases and related reference architectures based on past publications.

2.1 Big Data Analytics System

Over the last few years, several large-scale data driven analytics have been published from Social network domain such as Facebook, Twitter and LinkedIn to Entertainment Video-streaming such as Netflix. Also, other industry like the health industry has recognized and demonstrated their huge interest and opportunity of big data analytics. Data including streaming are collected by Facebook, LinkedIn and Twitter from their users [6, 9–12]. Facebook and LinkedIn often deals with both traditional data such as web logs and streaming whereas Twitter mostly deals with streaming data [6–8, 10–12]. The collected data are then managed on a batch or streaming processing with own custom functionalities. Several data analysis and aggregations such as Deep Analytics, trained models and specified jobs, algorithm service with Hadoop HDFS are largely implemented in clustering and distributed computations. Furthermore, Netflix collects users' events, which are then processed in Online, Nearline and Offline computations [13, 14]. Recommendations processed via the Online data analysis are available to users.

2.2 Reference Architecture of Big Data Analytics System

Service-oriented architecture and its principles facilitate software design, architecture and implementation in the enterprise software domain [16, 17]. In addition, several reference architectures have been published. Galster and Avgeriou [18] proposed software reference architecture based on a step-wise process. It includes six steps; deciding a type for reference architecture, selection of design strategy, empirical acquisition of data, construction of reference architecture, enabling of variability, and evaluation. Angelov, Grefen and Greefhorst [19] presented software reference architectures and subsequently claimed that it facilitate better architecture design, and hence will lead to better success. Their framework is for design and analysis of software reference architectures which forms of a multi-dimensional classification space, and five types of reference architectures.

For the context of big data, limited architectures have been suggested. Paakkonen and Pakkala [5] presented reference architecture and classification of technologies, products and services based on published big data use cases and associated commercial products. A high level description of big data lifecycle and infrastructure for a big data architecture framework was presented by [20]. A service and deployment model for implementing big data pipeline in the cloud domain was suggested by Schmidt and Möhring [21]. Reference architectures for the integration of SQL and NewSQL databases was proposed for supporting different growth patterns in enterprise data traffic [22]. In addition, big data architecture for in-memory storage system and distributed task execution analysis was suggested and validated [23]. Another tiered architecture (SOLID) for separating big data management from data generation and semantic consumption was also proposed [24]. For predictive and real-time analytics, a generalized software architecture was suggested. This was intended for structured historical and temporal data [25].

Literature review shows that there are limited reference architectures in the big data analytics context as well as lack of concrete or coherent reference architecture. This establishes a need for further research in reference architecture for big data analytics.

3 Reference Architecture for Big Data Analytics

Reference architecture can help in the creation of concrete architectures as well as the understanding of the overall architecture with typical related functionality and data flows in a big data analytics system [19]. A reference architecture is also useful for analysing existing big data systems, providing the base of classification of data analysis processes and technologies. Categorizing the processes, technologies and services into groups (components) further facilitate decision making regarding the realization of system processes and functionalities.

In the comparison of big data analytics use cases as shown in Table 1, we have divided the key elements of big data uses into five components: Data source; Data

Integration; Data Analysis and Aggregation; Interface and Visualization; and Job and Model Specification.

a. *Data Source*: it refers to the original source of data to be collected. Data can be stored as traditional database such as relational data or NoSQL. Data can be structured, unstructured, semi-structured or streaming.

Table 1. Big data analytics user case comparison

Big Data Analytics Use Case	Data Source	Data Integration	Data Analysis, Aggregation	Model, Job	Interface, Visualization
Facebook	MySQL, Web Servers Logs	Dump database copy, Scribe, Hadoop raw data, Replication.	Cube, Deep analytics, Hive jobs	Jobs stored Database	Microstrategy Visualization and User Applications
LinkedIn	Oracle, Users Activity Data	Oracle (Snapshot), Kafka, Hadoop Data cleaning, De-duplication, Replication.	Deep Analytics, Hive, Pig, MR, Voldemort, Avatara.	Azkaban Framework	Visualization applications (enterprise), LinkedIn users
Twitter	Firehose (tweets), Updater, Queries	Tokenization, Stats Queries, Filter and Personalization of Firehose, Ranking	Hadoop HDFS (Ranking algorithm, analysis), Cache database	Ranking algorithm	Twitter users
Netflix	Stream data (Users and online service)	Chukwa, Stream signals, Manhattan Framework	Deep Analytics: Off/Online Nearline. Algorithm	Machine Learning, Pig .	Netflix Users, Visualization applications (enterprise)

b. *Data Integration*: it involves the Collection, Processing and Loading of data. The collection deals with getting data from sources (multiple) for storage or analysis. There are several techniques for this such as Snapshot. Data Processing covers the executions required for processing the source data before moving into the Loading stage. Data Processing represents functionalities such as data cleaning, replication, filtering, algorithm service, etc. Data Loading can then be executed, meaning the collected and processed data are now loaded into a data storage such as Hadoop HDFS.
   We group three items (Data Collection, Processing and Loading) in one component because each item closely links to each other. For example, data collection requires data processing for cleaning or formatting as well as loading the data into a storage. At high level architecture, we believe that this improves logical linkage and flow between items closely related, and hence provides clearer and effective overall architecture.
c. *Data Analysis and Aggregation*: Data analysis refers to the related data analysis tasks and processes whereas the Aggregation refers to the data storage (including multi-dimensional) which stores the results of the analysis.
d. *Interface and Visualization*: they represent the end users (i.e. ad hoc analysis, queries, etc.) as well as visualization based applications such as dashboards.
e. *Model and Job Specification*: This covers machine learning, models trained, specifications and scheduling of jobs with their storages.

Furthermore, we have introduced our own mapping notations (based on data flow, integration, processing, analysis and interface) for modelling the big data uses. Our primary intention was of simplifying a big data system and effective understanding of its overall architecture. Additionally, our study of literatures and use cases of big data analytics prompted a gap for improvements in mapping notations. Thus, we created our mapping notations which are presented in Table 2 and subsequently produced a reference architecture which is presented in Fig. 1.

Table 2. Big data analytics reference architecture notations

No	Notation	Description
1		The notation of a data store or database which can represent structured, unstructured or semi-structured data. We often indicate a short text or description of the notation.
2	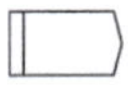	This represents the Extraction Process of data from a source to a destination. We often indicate a short text or description of the notation.
3	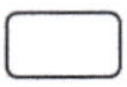	This notation represents Data Processing and Computation. We often indicate a short text or description of the notation.
4		This specifically indicates Visualization based applications. We include a short text.
5		This specifically indicates Ad Hoc or End Users based applications. We include a short text.
6	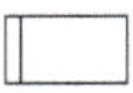	This represents the Job Schedule for batch processing. A short text is included.
7	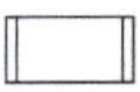	This represents the Job Specification for batch processing. A short text is included.
8		This indicates the flow between two notations. The left arrow of the line indicates the flow of the connection occurs from left to right notation.
9		This line indicates the flow between two notations. The line does not have any arrow so we can say that the flow can occur both ways.

Notations 1, 2 and 3 present in 'data source', 'data integration', 'data analysis and aggregation, 'job model specification'. Notation 4 and 5 are used in 'interface and visualization'. Notations 6 and 7 are used in 'job and model specification'. And Notations 8 and 9 are links between elements of Notation 1-7.

3.1 Mapping LinkedIn

At LinkedIn, users' activity data is collected and transferred via database snapshots. The activity data refer to the usage of LinkedIn' services which are treated as streaming events. Kafka, a distributed, publish/subscribe messaging system, is used for the collection of the streaming events [7].

With Kafka, producers report events to a broker, and consumers read data at their own space [7]. The event data of Kafka are moved to Hadoop ETL cluster for further processing tasks such as combining, de-duplication. Data from the Hadoop ETL cluster is copied into production and development clusters.

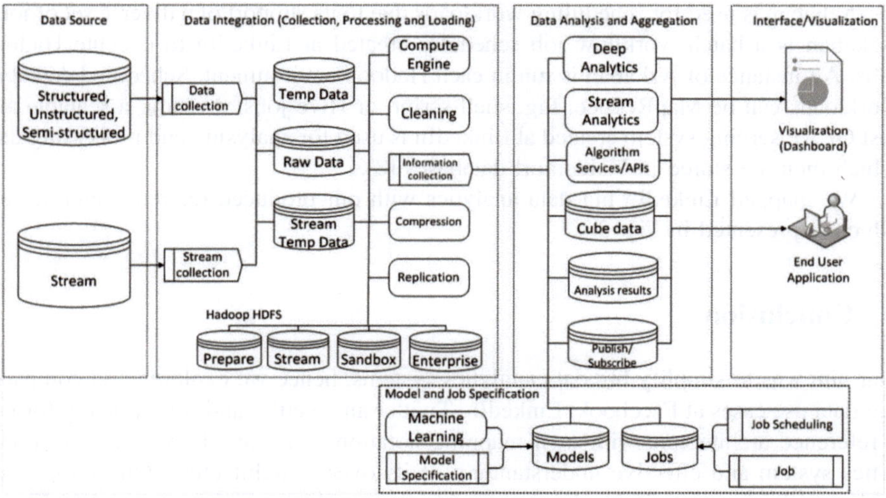

Fig. 1. Big data analytics reference architecture

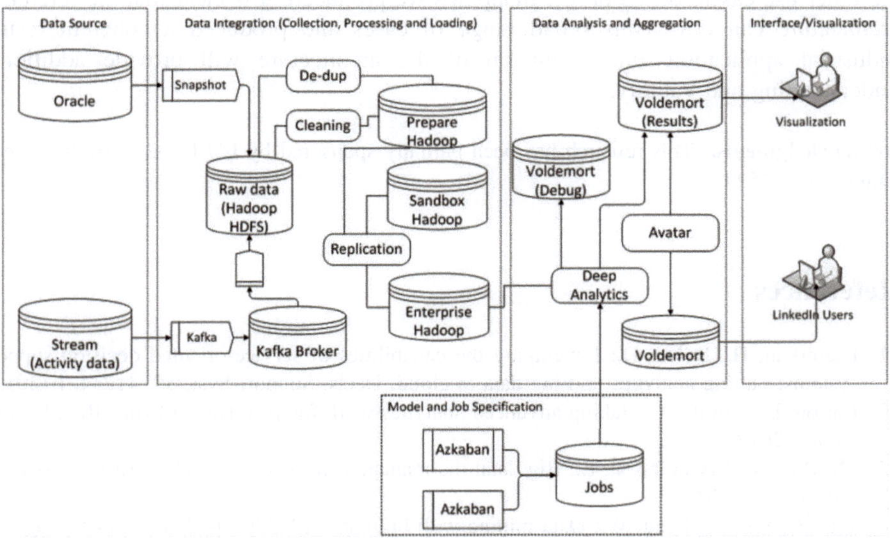

Fig. 2. Mapping LinkedIn big data analytics reference architecture

Workloads are typically performed in this way; initial experiments are carried out in the Development cluster, and then are transferred to the production cluster upon successful review and testing. Analysis results from the production cluster are stored in both offline (debugging) and online database. Moreover, these results may also be used again in the Kafka cluster [7].

Azkaban is used for scheduling workloads due to its support of a diverse set of jobs. Azkaban is a batch workflow job scheduler created at LinkedIn to execute Hadoop jobs. An instance of Azkaban is run in each Hadoop environment. Scheduled Azkaban workloads can be MapReduce, Pig, shell script, or Hive jobs. Avatara, a scalable and fast OLAP serving system created at LinkedIn is used for analysing and processing data which then are stored in Voldemort databases [8].

We mapped LinkedIn big data analytics with our produced reference architecture which is presented in Fig. 2.

4 Conclusion

Our aim was to simplify big data analytics systems, hence we explored and compared big data use cases at Facebook, LinkedIn, Twitter and Netflix and subsequently formed a reference architecture with own mapping notations for simplifying a big data analytics system and effective understanding of its overall architecture. Our comparison table can be found at Table 1 and our reference architecture is presented in Fig. 1. Furthermore, we mapped and produced LinkedIn Use Case Reference Architecture which is presented in Fig. 2. Due to the page limitation, we did not present our work of the other use cases. Based on the mappings we produced, it is clear that the reference architecture can cover this broad range of cases and produced a coherent result. Industrial application and evaluation of the architecture will provide additional understanding and validity.

Acknowledgments. This research has been partially sponsored by EU H2020 FIRST project, Grant No. 734599.

References

1. Demirkan, H., Delen, D.: Leveraging the capabilities of service-oriented decision support systems: putting analytics and big data in cloud. Decis. Support Syst. **55**, 412–421 (2013)
2. Barton, D., Court, D.: Making advanced analytics work for you. Harvard Bus. Rev. **90**(10), 79–83 (2012)
3. McAfee, A., Brynjolfsson, E.: Big data: the management revolution. Harvard Bus. Rev. **90** (10), 60–68 (2012)
4. Wu, X., Wu, G., Ding, W.: Data mining with big data. IEEE Trans. Knowl. Data Eng. **28**, 97–106 (2014)
5. Paakkonen, P., Pakkaka, D.: Reference architecture and classification of technologies, products and services for big data systems. Big Data Res. **2**, 166–186 (2015)
6. Thusoo, A., Shao, Z., Anthony, S., Borthakur, D., Jain, N., Sarma, J.S., Murthy, R., Liu, H.: Data warehousing and analytics infrastructure at Facebook. In: 2010 ACM SIGMOD International Conference on Management of Data, Indianapolis, Indiana, USA, 6–11 June (2010)
7. Kreps, J., Narkhede, N., Rao, J.: Kafka: a distributed messaging system for log processing. In: The 6th International Workshop on Networking Meets Databases, Athens, Greece, 12 June (2011)

8. Wu, L., Sumbaly, R., Riccomini, C., Koo, G., Kim, H.J., Kreps, J., Shah, S.: Avatara: OLAP for web-scale analytics products. In: 38th International Conference on Very Large Databases, Istanbul, Turkey, 27–31 August (2012)
9. Mishne, G.: Fast data in the era of big data: Twitter's real-time related query suggestion architecture. In: The 2013 ACM SIGMOD International Conference on Management of Data, New York, USA, 22–27 June (2013)
10. Lin, J., Ryaboy, D.: Scaling big data mining infrastructure: the Twitter experience. ACM SIGKDD Explor. Newsl. **14**, 6–19 (2013)
11. Lee, G.L., Lin, J., Liu, C., Lorek, A., Ryaboy, D.: The unified logging infrastructure for data analytics at Twitter. In: The 38th International Conference on Very Large Databases, Istanbul, Turkey, 27–31 August (2012)
12. Busch, M., Gade, K., Larson, B., Lok, P., Luckenbill, S., Lin, J.: EarlyBird: real-time search at Twitter. In: 2012 IEEE 28th International Conference on Data Engineering, Washington, DC, USA, 1–5 April (2012)
13. Amatriain, X.: Big & personal: data and models behind Netflix recommendations. In: The 2nd International Workshop on Big Data, Streams and Heterogeneous Source Mining: Algorithms, Systems, Programming Models and Applications, Chicago, Illinois, USA, 11 August (2013)
14. Amatriain, X., Basilico, J.: System architectures for personalized recommendations, http://techblog.netflix.com/2013/03/system-architectures-for.html, Accessed 05 Aug 2016
15. Boulon, J., Konwinski, A., Qi, R.: Chukwa: a large-scale monitoring system. In: Cloud Computing and its Applications, Chicago, Illinois, USA, 22–23 October (2008)
16. Zimmermann, A., Sandkuhl, K., Pretz, M., Falkenthal, M., Jugel, D., Wissotzki, M.: Towards and integrated service-oriented reference enterprise architecture. In: International Workshop on Ecosystem Architectures, Saint Petersburg, Russia, 19 August (2013)
17. Zachman, J.A.: A framework for information systems architecture. IBM Syst. J. **26**(3) (1987)
18. Galster, M., Avgeriou, P.: Empirically-grounded reference architectures: a proposal. In: Joint ACM SIGSOFT Conference on Quality of Software Architectures and ACM SIGSOFT Conference on Quality of Software Architectures and ACM SIGSOFT Symposium on Architecting Critical Systems, Boulder, Colorado, USA, June 20–24 (2011)
19. Angelov, A., Grefen, P., Greefhorst, D.: A framework for analysis and design of software reference architectures. Inf. Softw. Technol. **54**, 417–431 (2012)
20. Demchenko, Y., Ngo, C., Membrey, P.: Architecture framework and components for the Big Data Ecosystem, SNE Technical Report, University of Amsterdam, 12 September (2013)
21. Schmidt, R., Möhring, M.: Strategic alignment of cloud-based architectures for big data. In: 17th IEEE International Enterprise Distributed Object Computing Conference Workshops, Vancouver, Canada, 9–13 September (2013)
22. Doshi, K.A., Zhong, T., Lu, Z., Tang, X., Lou, T., Deng, G.: Blending SQL and NewSQL approaches reference architectures for enterprise big data challenges. In: The International Conference on Cyber-Enabled Distributed Computing and Knowledge Discovery, Beijing, China, 10–12 October (2013)
23. Zhong, T., Doshi, K.A., Tang, X., Lou, T., Lu, Z., Li, H.: On mixing high-speed updates and in-memory queries a big-data architecture for real-time analytics. In: IEEE International Conference on Big Data, Santa Clara, California, USA, 6–9 October (2013)
24. Cuesta, Carlos E., Martínez-Prieto, Miguel A., Fernández, Javier D.: Towards an architecture for managing big semantic data in real-time. In: Drira, K. (ed.) ECSA 2013. LNCS, vol. 7957, pp. 45–53. Springer, Heidelberg (2013). doi:10.1007/978-3-642-39031-9_5
25. Westerlund, M., Hedlund, U., Pulkkis, G., Bjork, K.: A generalized scalable software architecture for analyzing temporally structured big data in the cloud. New Perspect. Inform. Syst. Technol. **1**, 559–569 (2014)

Data Mining and Data Services

Mining Governmental Collaboration Through Semantic Profiling of Open Data Catalogues and Publishers

Mohamed Adel Rezk(✉), Adegboyega Ojo, and Islam A. Hassan

Insight Centre for Data Analytics, National University of Ireland Galway, Galway, Ireland
{mohamed.adel,adegboyega.ojo,islam.hassan}@insight-centre.org

Abstract. Due to the increasing adoption of open data among governments worldwide especially in the European Union area, a deeper analysis of the newly published data is becoming a mandate. Apart from analyzing the published dataset itself we aimed on analyzing published dataset catalogues. A dataset catalogue or a dataset metadata contains features that describe what the data is about in a textual representation. So, we first acquire data from open data portals, choose descriptive dataset catalogue features, and then construct an aggregated textual representation of the datasets. Afterwards we enrich those textual representations using Natural Language Processing (NLP) methods to create a new comparable data feature "Named Entities". By mining the new data feature we are able to produce datasets and publishers relatedness network. Those networks are used to point similarities between the published data across multiple open data portals. Pointing all possible collaborations for integrating and standardizing data features and types would increase the value of da1ta and ease its analysis process.

Keywords: Unstructured data analysis · Data mining · Collaborative network · Open data · E-government

1 Introduction

Despite the availability of data loaded into open data portals worldwide[1] [1, 2], methods to maximize stakeholders' engagement and ease data integration still not complete [3–5]. We believe that a proper mining of collaboration channels within a single data portal internally as well as between multiple open data portals are not introduced yet. Our work is aiming to develop an open data portals collaboration channels mining framework as shown in Fig. 1. To achieve this, we start with data acquisition by harvesting metadata of datasets published on the portal then restructure and store them in MongoDB[2]. Afterwards we construct textual representation from the dataset metadata's unstructured features, apply DBpedia [6] Named Entity Recognition pipeline called DBpedia Spotlight [7] to extract information that represent those dataset and their publishers as well. After that we end up with a semantically enriched dataset upon which we can apply our

[1] http://opendatabarometer.org/.
[2] https://www.mongodb.com.

L.M. Camarinha-Matos et al. (Eds.): PRO-VE 2017, IFIP AICT 506, pp. 253–264, 2017.
DOI: 10.1007/978-3-319-65151-4_24

profiling [5] and collaboration opportunities analysis. To illustrate our work, we organized the paper as follows: Sect. 2 presents a background on Open Government Data, NLP and Collaboration Mining. Section 3 discusses our approach to tackle the research question. Section 4. Discussing our research findings, conclusions and future plan.

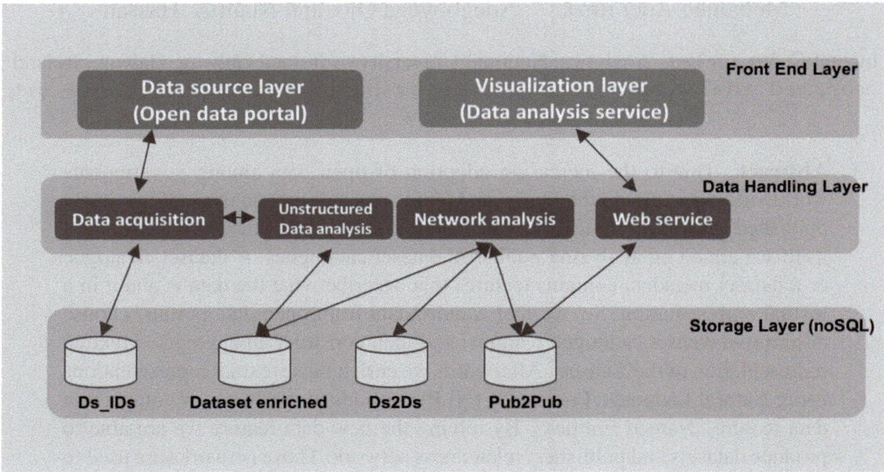

Fig. 1. Open data catalogues and publishers' semantic profiling conceptual framework.

2 Background and Related Work

Following concepts definitions and a literature review of correlated research areas Open Government Data, NLP and Collaboration Mining:

2.1 Open Government Data

Open Government Data referred to the datasets generated and published by governmental departments "without any restrictions on its usage or distribution" and it doesn't contain any personal or undisclosed data [8]. OGD vary by multiple aspects for example: (a) OGD publishing department or agency domain e.g. Agriculture Data, Transport Data, Environmental Data, Financial Data and Telecommunication Data. (b) Data format e.g. Excel, Text, PDF, CSV, Theoretically, Government Open Data is operational or administrative governmental data available to use, redistribute, and analyze "in any form without any copyright restrictions" [9]. Regarding the open government working group draft in 2007[3] they generated initial open data principles: data must be complete, primary, timely, accessible, machine-processable, nondiscriminatory, nonproprietary, and license-free. Then they generated further open data principles, data must be online and free, permanent, trusted, assumed to be open, documented, safe to open, and

[3] http://public.resource.org/8_principles.html.

designed with public input. Figure 2 shows the Irish government's open data portal which we used for our experiments[4].

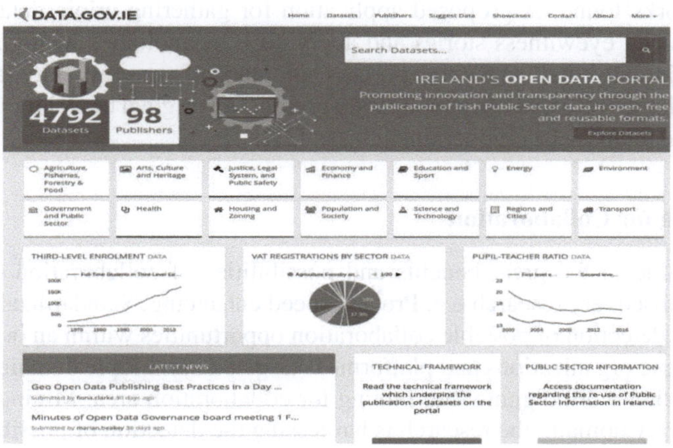

Fig. 2. Irish government's open data portal.

2.2 Natural Language Processing

Following we discuss the correlated features of Natural Language Processing to our research. Specifically, Named Entity Recognition applications:

2.2.1 Named Entity Recognition

Named Entity Recognition is the process of discovering Named Entities (NE) laying within a given text, a common definition of NE is as follows [10], "an information unit described by the name of a person or an organization, a location, a brand, a product, a numeric expression including time, date, money and percent found in a sentence." [11]. NER applications are implemented using multiple methodologies:

The Supervised Learning techniques use a big manually categorized dataset. Then this dataset is used for training the recognition algorithm. Supervised Learning techniques apply Conditional Random Fields [12], Hidden Markov Models [13], Decision Trees [14], Support Vector Machines [15] and Maximum Entropy Models [16] The objective of these methods is to identify and categorize related key-words. The unavailability of manually categorized datasets and the high cost of generating them, represent a challenging obstacle against Supervised Learning Techniques.

The Semi-Supervised Learning and Unsupervised Learning techniques use either a small categorized dataset for training the algorithm [17], or a clustering based algorithm. Further Unsupervised Learning techniques depend on lingual resources e.g. WordNet, and statistics to solve the NER task as a prediction problem [18].

---

[4] http://data.gov.ie.

2.3 Natural Language Processing in E-Government

There are few implementations of NLP technologies in the e-government area. Examples from the works found: A proposed application for gathering crime data from police departments and eyewitness stories and apply NLP technologies with GATE [19]. A system that imitate email answering process automatically or semi-automatically using NLP technologies [20]. Another application presents an original model for incorporating multimedia data to assist e-government tasks [21].

2.4 Mining for Collaboration

In general, due to the great benefits and possibilities of collaboration opportunities mining and discovery research e.g. Process speed enhancing, Standardization and Integration. The detection of possible collaboration opportunities within an organization or across multiple organizations and platforms is targeted in multiple domains. Following the few existing work digging into mining for collaboration area: Mining for collaboration in library domain, the research is harnessing the detection of possible collaboration opportunities with academic professional based on their publications to increase the benefits of students [22]. Collaboration mining between governmental levels and departments based on their objectives, resources and services to increase the government efficiency regarding public policy development and implementation, crisis management, etc. [23]. Collaboration mining tool using agent technology to analyze the collaboration between information on the web to help the tool users to get their desired materials more accurately and faster [24]. Collaboration mining of team members using summaries of successful past projects to increase moderator efficiency to promote project partner's awareness of best way to formulate a proposal for a European research project [25].

3 Semantic Profiling for Collaboration Mining

As shown in Fig. 1 and zoomed in Fig. 3 we have designed a solution pipeline that incorporates Data Acquisition, Data Modeling, Data Analysis, and Data visualization technologies to enable the existence of a collaboration mining tool. We start with inputting the targeted open data portal(s) in which we seek mining for collaborations then we start acquiring metadata (catalogue) of the datasets. Then we restructure the catalogue to fit into the predesigned storage model (semantic profile), within this model we enhance, filter and exclude less important catalogue features – regarding our use case - and we add new features that are corresponding to our collaboration mining requirements e.g. we add "textual representation" feature by merging original textual features of the data catalogue, we add "Entities" feature to the new catalogue storage model by applying NER over the new "textual representation" feature of the catalogue, we filter features like "author" and "creator" to end up with only "publisher ID" feature, and we exclude "groups" and "tracking summary" features. After constructing and storing the new data model (semantic profile) we start the unstructured data analysis (text mining) pipeline by applying NER algorithm. At the end of that process we generate a comparable feature "Entities" and add it to the new data model to be used for collaboration mining. After that we construct dataset's publisher data model (semantic profiles) which contains aggregated features' values from their published datasets. Finally, we compute relation strengths between dataset publishers based on *comparing* their semantic profiles that we built using the aggregation of unique entities they publish datasets about and store it as shown in Fig. 4 for later visualization and web service usages as shown in Figs. 10 and 11.

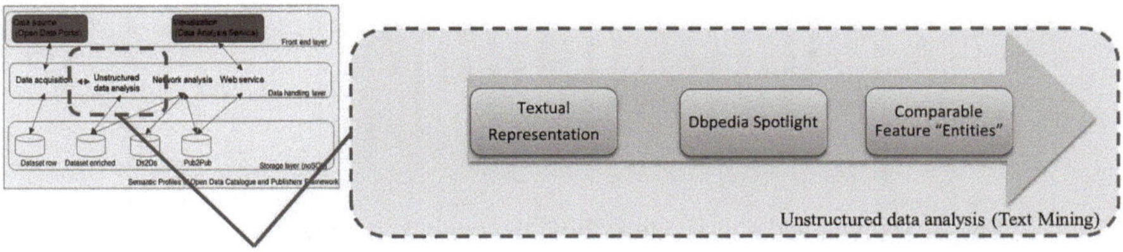

Fig. 3. Unstructured data analysis (Text Mining).

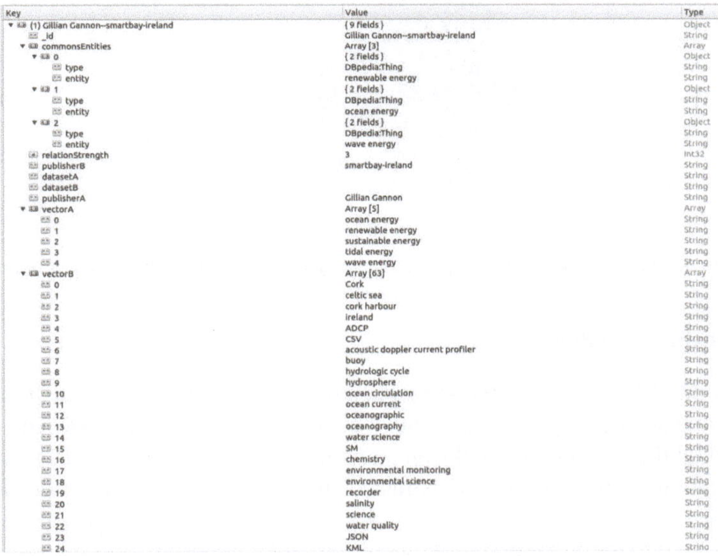

Fig. 4. Publisher collaboration network.

Following we discuss and represent the results of our Semantic Profiling for Collaboration Mining approach.

3.1 Profiling the Catalogues

By querying the stored enriched metadata of open data portal we are able to generate charts that are profiling the underlying open data catalogue. As an example of those queries we are able to retrieve the named entities detected from mining unstructured textual representations of data catalogues generated by our tool. Those named entities which are originally derivate from dataset metadata are - same as their origin – able to demonstrate a description of the contents of the data portals see Figs. 5 and 6.

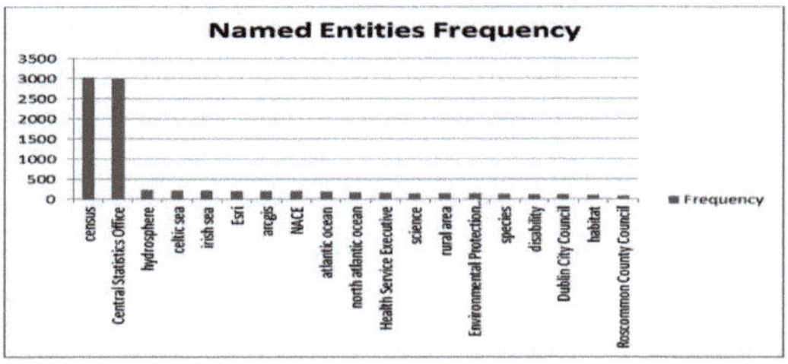

Fig. 5. Top named entities describing the open data portal “data.gov.ie”.

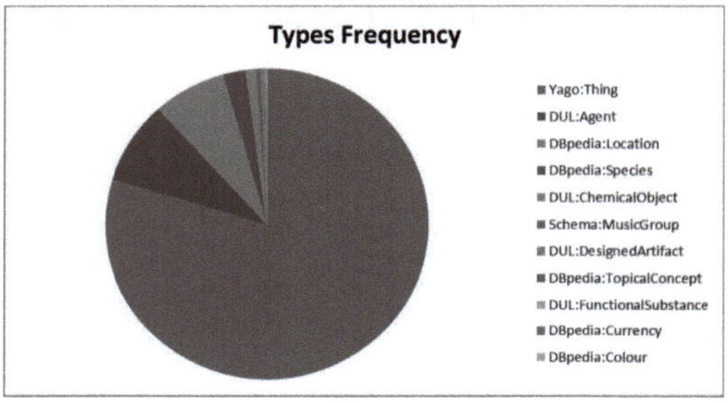

Fig. 6. Top named entities types describing the open data portal “data.gov.ie”.

3.2 Publishers Profiles

Open data publishers are an interesting open data analysis feature; publishers could be governmental departments, councils, etc. which make their profiles a key component of governmental data integration and standardization. An open data publisher’s profile is the aggregation of the information extracted from its published dataset metadata. One

Open Data Publisher	Named Entities;Frequency
central-statistics-office	Central Statistics Office;2985, census;2863, county;269, NACE;194, Irish;142, rural area;140, disability;97, Irish Travellers;68
department-of-housing-planning-community-and-local-government	department;209, Helena;96, Constitution;38, referendum;35, local authority;35, census;21, county;18, mortgage;15, gener
health-service-executive	Health Service Executive;140, achi;73, icd 10;73, Discharge;62, DRG;62, AM;62, AR;60, Irish;59, ACS;56, birthweight;54, gest
environmental-protection-agency	Environmental Protection Agency;139, REST;102, WMS;74, Water Framework Directive;73, Informatics;59, WFD;43, irish se
marine-institute	hydrosphere;119, atlantic ocean;91, north atlantic ocean;87, celtic sea;85, irish sea;85, CSV;61, biology;56, life science;54,
dublin-city-council	Dublin City Council;105, Dublin City;60, .csv;49, Irish;20, ID;18, Dublin;16, DCC;14, MAP;10, DAT;10, urban planning;9, recyc
roscommon-county-council	KML;85, CSV;85, Roscommon County Council;85, Shapefile;81, Esri;80, Rest API;80, arcgis;80, Roscommon;65, roscommon;
geological-survey-of-ireland	geological survey;58, earth science;55, GSI;53, science;49, lithosphere;43, ireland;38, Irish;32, WMS;29, JSON;28, bedrock;
c2f170ca-63d0-4498-9e81-759827708e97	Ordnance Survey;57, Shapefile;56, CSV;56, KML;56, Rest API;56, Esri;56, arcgis;55, OSI;55, level crossing;3, watercourse;2,
national-transport-authority	statute;56, Dublin Transport Authority;56, Oireachtas;56, National Transport Authority;56, public transport;55, Peter;54, D
all-island-research-observatory	demography;55, CSV;43, REST;30, JSON;30, SA;22, CSO;19, Service economy;14, population density;13, ED;12, Northern Cro
fingal-county-council	Fingal County Council;53, county;52, .csv;35, Fingal;24, WGS84;20, .zip;5, ID;4, datasheet;3, water quality;2, recycling;2, Du
department-of-education-and-skills	department;50, census;40, county;11, Leaving Certificate;3, .csv;3, ireland;2, national school;2, Junior Certificate;2, xls;2, I
revenue-commissioners	Revenue Commissioners;47, income tax;8, Wicklow;7, Kerry;7, Cavan;7, Monaghan;7, Longford;7, Meath;7, Scheme;7, Kilk
health-research-board	census;42, ICD 10;12, Health Service Executive;9, group sex;3, database;2, disability;2, fibrosis;1, scooters;1, lumbar;1, imr
galway-county-council	Shapefile;42, CSV;42, Galway County Council;42, KML;41, Rest API;36, Esri;36, arcgis;36, county;35, Galway County;19, Galw
national-biodiversity-data-centre	wildlife protection;40, wildlife sanctuary;40, species;40, data centre;40, synecology;40, wildlife conservation;40, wildlife;
sustainable-energy-authority-of-ireland	ireland;38, renewable energies;26, renewable energy;26, Atlas;23, WMS;19, JSON;18, celtic sea;18, irish sea;18, north atla
dun-laoghaire-rathdown-county-council	DLR;18, .csv;7, sbn;6, shp;6, dbf;6, Cycling;5, st;3, ards;3, xls;3, Cherrywood;3, Sandyford;2, WW1;2, A2;2, Dev;2, A1;2, INFO
department-of-communications-climate-action-and-environment	department;36, hydrosphere;35, KML;32, CSV;31, WMS;30, WFS;29, north atlantic ocean;26, atlantic ocean;26, celtic sea;2

Fig. 7. Top named entities describing data posted by top publishers to the open data portal “data.gov.ie”.

of the usages of a publisher's profile is to understand more about the domain of the publisher see Fig. 7 for an example.

3.3 Interlinking Publishers

The resulted publisher profiles are used to mine possible collaboration channels between data publishers at data portal level and among portals level by using the added comparable feature "Entities" see Figs. 8, 9 and 10.

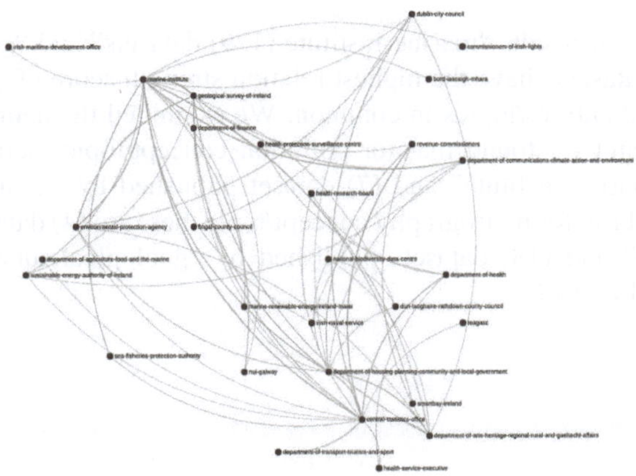

Fig. 8. Publishers collaboration network of open data portal "data.gov.ie" with relation strength >20.

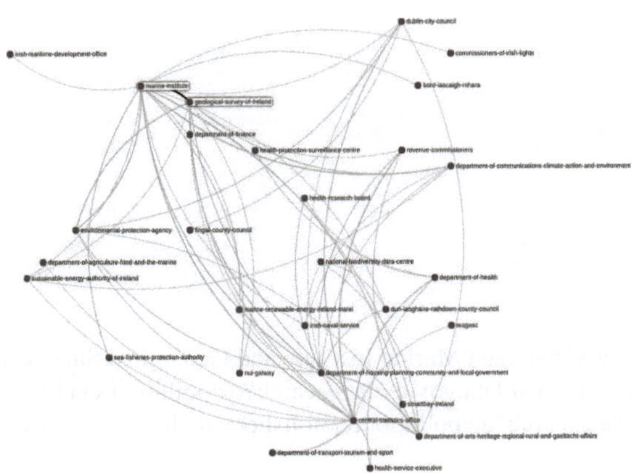

Fig. 9. Publishers collaboration network of open data portal "data.gov.ie" – Showing highest relation strength score between "marine-institute" and "geological-survey-of-ireland".

publisherA	publisherB	stregnt	commons
marine-institute	geological-survey-of-ireland	82	[('DBpedia:Thing', 'pollution'), ('DBpedia:Thing', 'hydrography'), ('DBpedia:Thing', 'habitat'), ('DBpedia:
department-of-communications-climate-action-and-environment	marine-institute	66	[('DBpedia:Location', 'United Nations'), ('DBpedia:Thing', 'hydrography'), ('DBpedia:Thing', 'North Atlar
central-statistics-office	marine-institute	62	[('DBpedia:Thing', 'hake'), ('DBpedia:Species', 'whiting'), ('DBpedia:Thing', 'probability'), ('DBpedia:Loc
central-statistics-office	revenue-commissioners	62	[('DBpedia:Thing', 'Stamp Duty'), ('DBpedia:Thing', 'Exchequer'), ('DBpedia:Thing', 'communication'), ('
marine-institute	environmental-protection-agency	58	[('DBpedia:Thing', 'aquatic'), ('DBpedia:Thing', 'hydrography'), ('DBpedia:Thing', 'estuary'), ('DBpedia:T
environmental-protection-agency	geological-survey-of-ireland	55	[('DBpedia:Thing', 'topography'), ('DBpedia:Thing', 'hydrography'), ('DBpedia:Thing', 'habitat'), ('DBped
department-of-housing-planning-community-and-local-government	marine-institute	53	[('DBpedia:Thing', 'habitat'), ('DBpedia:Thing', 'Density'), ('DBpedia:Thing', 'Shapefile'), ('DBpedia:Thin
central-statistics-office	department-of-health	51	[('Wikidata:Q12136', 'brucellosis'), ('Wikidata:Q12136', 'influenza'), ('DBpedia:Thing', 'birthweight'), ('W
department-of-housing-planning-community-and-local-government	geological-survey-of-ireland	50	[('DBpedia:Thing', 'habitat'), ('DBpedia:Location', 'Fingal'), ('DBpedia:Thing', 'Shapefile'), ('DBpedia:Thi
department-of-housing-planning-community-and-local-government	central-statistics-office	48	[('Wikidata:Q386724', 'Excel'), ('DBpedia:Location', 'Tipperary'), ('DBpedia:Thing', 'county'), ('DBpedia:T
department-of-housing-planning-community-and-local-government	department-of-arts-heritage-regional-rural-and-gaeltacht-affairs	48	[('DBpedia:Thing', 'wildlife protection'), ('DBpedia:Thing', 'habitat'), ('DBpedia:Thing', 'wildlife conserv
central-statistics-office	department-of-transport-tourism-and-sport	47	[('DUL:Agent', 'iveco'), ('DBpedia:Thing', 'skoda'), ('DBpedia:Thing', 'vauxhall'), ('DUL:Agent', 'piaggio'),
central-statistics-office	dublin-city-council	43	[('DBpedia:Thing', 'tonne'), ('DBpedia:Thing', 'road safety'), ('DBpedia:Thing', 'force'), ('DBpedia:Thing',
central-statistics-office	geological-survey-of-ireland	42	[('DBpedia:Thing', 'copper'), ('DBpedia:Thing', 'aluminium'), ('DBpedia:Thing', 'force'), ('DBpedia:Thing'
department-of-communications-climate-action-and-environment	geological-survey-of-ireland	42	[('DBpedia:Thing', 'geophysical'), ('DBpedia:Thing', 'hydrography'), ('DBpedia:Thing', 'Shapefile'), ('DBp
sea-fisheries-protection-authority	marine-institute	42	[('DBpedia:Thing', 'hake'), ('DBpedia:Species', 'whiting'), ('DBpedia:Thing', 'fish'), ('DBpedia:Location', '
department-of-arts-heritage-regional-rural-and-gaeltacht-affairs	geological-survey-of-ireland	41	[('DBpedia:Thing', 'limestone'), ('DBpedia:Thing', 'Sligo'), ('DBpedia:Thing', 'habitat'), ('DBpedia:Locatio

Fig. 10. Publishers mined relations of open data portal "data.gov.ie".

According to our results "marine-institute (129) datasets" and "geological-survey-of-ireland (67) datasets" have the highest relation strength score of (82) which means that they share 82 entities/topics in common. We examined the datasets published by both publishers and we found that for pollution concept/topic there are (7) datasets published by "marine-institute" and (7) dataset published by "geological-survey-of-ireland" and similarly for hydrography concept/topic there are (4) datasets published by "marine-institute" and (18) datasets published by "geological-survey-of-ireland" as shown in Figs. 11 and 12.

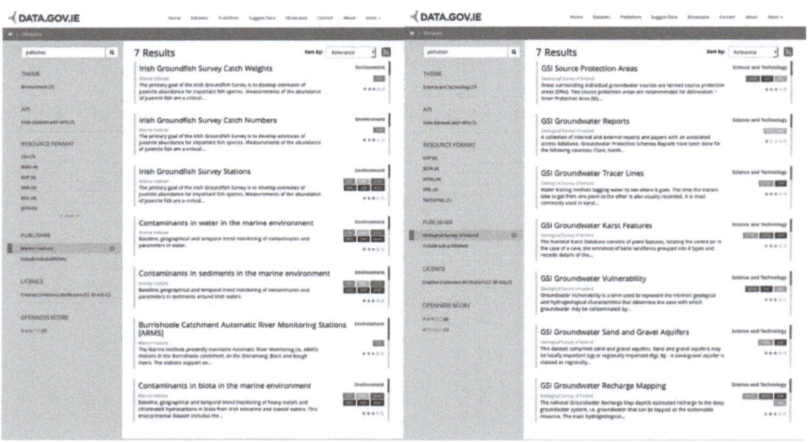

Fig. 11. Datasets shared between Marine Institute and Geological Survey of Ireland around the concept pollution (https://data.gov.ie/data/search?q=pollution&publisher=marine-institute) (https://data.gov.ie/data/search?q=pollution&publisher=geological-survey-of-ireland)

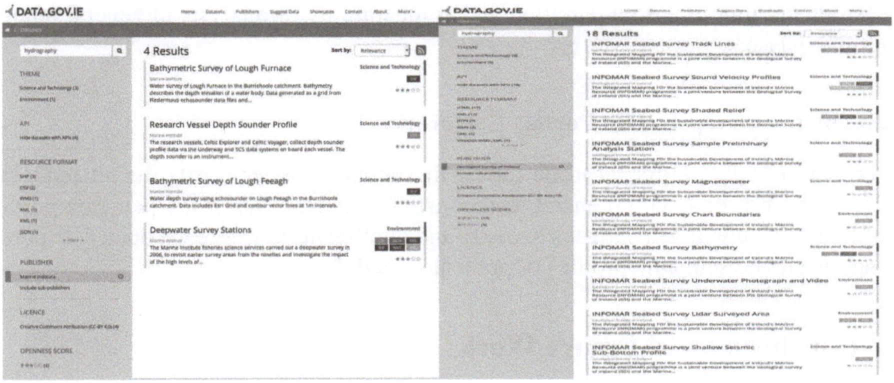

Fig. 12. Datasets shared between Marine Institute and Geological Survey of Ireland around the concept hydrography. (https://data.gov.ie/data/search?q=hydrography&publisher=marine-institute) (https://data.gov.ie/data/search?q=hydrography&publisher=geological-survey-of-ireland)

3.4 Limitations

Named Entity Recognition area of the work is tightly coupled with the training and the quality of the Named Entity Recognition algorithm. Through this research we have experimented Natural Language Tool Kit (NLTK), Stanford NER and Stanford NER with nGram of (3) enhancement, then we ended up using DBpedia Spotlight as the NE source as through our manual examination of the text analysis phase results DBpedia out performed the other methods in its NE detection quality. DBpedia spotlihght still have its limitations though and we reported one of the issues we faced to their github repository[5].

4 Applications

4.1 Standardization and Collaboration Analysis

Despite most of governments already publishing their data via their open data portals, when a government decides to integrate their data sources over its variant departments and councils, this heterogeneous domain dependent data will consume huge analysis resources and a considerably extended period of time to be fitted into an integrated data repository. Our profiling service will lead the way for data analysts to define integration channels, and necessary concepts standardizations between governmental departments and councils, using the available data published on open data portals. Same example would fit a multinational enterprise as well.

For example "marine-institute" and "geological-survey-of-ireland" share the named entity (pollution), this concept shall be standardized regarding its code and its

[5] https://github.com/dbpedia-spotlight/dbpedia-spotlight/issues/407.

measurement unit to ease integration and comparability or analysis in general among multiple datasets.

4.2 Intelligent Open Data Portals Exploration

Open data portals are meant to be facing the public in other words the citizens, but citizens can't directly comprehend, and consume this row data [4]. Open data portals profiling service will help citizens to easily and intelligently explore the open data portal using visualized semantic profiles of publishers and datasets.

5 Conclusion and Future Work

Regarding our approach results we believe that we are on the right track to tackle the collaboration mining problem in open governmental data domain, as we are getting interested collaboration recommendations out of our pipeline in a visualized way that is easy to comprehend by general public users of open governmental data.

Our future plan is to overcome the NE limitation by developing a new text analysis pipeline that integrates statistical text analysis, babel.net[6], and DBpedia[7] as our NE source. Also we are planning to replace the string comparison module with semantic relatedness comparison module as the way of calculating relation strength between open governmental data publishers.

Acknowledgments. This paper is partially supported by European Union's Horizon 2020 research and innovation programme under grant agreement No. 645860, project ROUTE-TO-PA (Raising Open and User-friendly Transparency-Enabling Technologies for Public Administrations).

References

1. Shadbolt, N., O'Hara, K., Berners-Lee, T., Gibbins, N., Glaser, H., Hall, W., Schraefel, M.C.: Linked open government data: lessons from data.gov.uk. IEEE Intell. Syst. **27**, 16–24 (2012)
2. Breitman, K., Salas, P., Casanova, M.A., Saraiva, D.: Open government data in Brazil. Intell. Syst. IEEE. **27**, 45–49 (2012)
3. Mutuku, L.N., Colaco, J.: Increasing Kenyan open data consumption. In: Proceedings of 6th International Conference on Theory and Practice of Electronic Governance, ICEGOV 2012, p. 18 (2012)
4. Artigas, F., Chun, S.A.: Visual analytics for open government data. In: 14th Annual International Conference on Digital Government Research, From E-Government to Smart Gov.dg.o 2013, pp. 298–299 (2013)
5. Ribeiro, D.C., Freire, J., Vo, H.T., Silva, C.T.: An urban data profiler. In: WWW Workshop Data Science Smart Cities, pp. 1389–1394 (2015)

[6] http://babelnet.org/.
[7] http://wiki.dbpedia.org/.

6. Auer, S., Bizer, C., Kobilarov, G., Lehmann, J., Cyganiak, R., Ives, Z.: DBpedia: a nucleus for a web of open data. In: Aberer, K., Choi, K.-S., Noy, N., Allemang, D., Lee, K.-I., Nixon, L., Golbeck, J., Mika, P., Maynard, D., Mizoguchi, R., Schreiber, G., Cudré-Mauroux, P. (eds.) ASWC/ISWC -2007. LNCS, vol. 4825, pp. 722–735. Springer, Heidelberg (2007). doi: 10.1007/978-3-540-76298-0_52
7. Mendes, P.N., Jakob, M., García-Silva, A., Bizer, C.: DBpedia spotlight: shedding light on the web of documents. In: Proceedings of the 7th International Conference on Semantic Systems, pp. 1–8 (2011)
8. Janssen, M., Charalabidis, Y., Zuiderwijk, A.: Benefits, adoption barriers and myths of open data and open government. Inf. Syst. Manag. **29**, 258–268 (2012)
9. Kassen, M.: A promising phenomenon of open data: a case study of the Chicago open data project. Gov. Inf. Q. **30**, 508–513 (2013)
10. Nadeau, D.: A survey of named entity recognition and classification. Linguist. Investig. **30**, 3–26 (2007)
11. Grishman, R.: Message Understanding Conference-6: A Brief History. In: Proceedings of COLING 1996 (1996)
12. McCallum, A., Li, W.: Early results for named entity recognition with conditional random fields, feature induction and web-enhanced lexicons. In: Proceedings of the Seventh Conference on Natural Language Learning at HLT-NAACL 2003, pp. 188–191. Association for Computational Linguistics, Morristown (2003)
13. Bikel, D.M., Miller, S., Schwartz, R., Weischedel, R.: Nymble. In: Proceedings of the Fifth Conference on Applied natural language processing, pp. 194–201. Association for Computational Linguistics, Morristown (1997)
14. Borthwick, A., Sterling, J.: NYU: description of the MENE named entity system as used in MUC-7. In: Conference on MUC-7 (1998)
15. Asahara, M., Matsumoto, Y.: Japanese Named Entity extraction with redundant morphological analysis. In: Proceedings of the 2003 Conference of the North American Chapter of the Association for Computational Linguistics on Human Language Technology, NAACL 2003, pp. 8–15. Association for Computational Linguistics, Morristown (2003)
16. Hoffart, J., Yosef, M.A., Bordino, I., Fürstenau, H., Pinkal, M., Spaniol, M., Taneva, B., Thater, S., Weikum, G.: Robust disambiguation of named entities in text, pp. 782–792 (2011)
17. Ji, H., Grishman, R.: Data selection in semi-supervised learning for name tagging, pp. 48–55 (2006)
18. Alfonseca, E., Manandhar, S.: An unsupervised method for general named entity recognition and automated concept discovery. In: Conference on General WordNet (2002)
19. Ku, C.H., Iriberri, A., Leroy, G.: Natural Language Processing and e-Government: Crime Information Extraction from Heterogeneous Data Sources. In: The Proceedings of the 9th Annual International Digital Government Research Conference. ACM International Conference Proceedings Series, pp. 162–170. ACM Press (2006)
20. Dalianis, H., Rosell, M., Sneiders, E.: Clustering e-mails for the Swedish social insurance agency – what part of the e-mail thread gives the best quality? In: Loftsson, H., Rögnvaldsson, E., Helgadóttir, S. (eds.) NLP 2010. LNCS, vol. 6233, pp. 115–120. Springer, Heidelberg (2010). doi:10.1007/978-3-642-14770-8_14
21. Amato, F., Mazzeo, A., Moscato, V., Picariello, A.: Semantic management of multimedia documents for e-government activity. In: 2009 International Conference on Complex, Intelligent and Software Intensive Systems, pp. 1193–1198 (2009)
22. Williams, L.M., Cody, S.A., Parnell, J.: Prospecting for new collaborations: mining syllabi for library service opportunities. J. Acad. Librariansh. **30**, 270–275 (2004)

23. Basanya, R., Ojo, A., Janowski, T., Turini, F.: Mining collaboration opportunities to support joined-up government. In: Camarinha-Matos, Luis M., Pereira-Klen, A., Afsarmanesh, H. (eds.) PRO-VE 2011. IAICT, vol. 362, pp. 359–366. Springer, Heidelberg (2011). doi: 10.1007/978-3-642-23330-2_40
24. Wan, L., Chen, J., Gu, D.: An information mining model of intelligent collaboration based on agent technology. In: International Conference on Applied Sciences, Engineering and Technology, ICASET 2014. Scientific.net (2014)
25. Palmer, C., Harding, J.A., Swarnkar, R., Das, B.P., Young, R.I.M.: Generating rules from data mining for collaboration moderator services. J. Intell. Manuf. **24**, 313–330 (2013)

A Model-Based Environment for Data Services: Energy-Aware Behavioral Triggering Using ADOxx

Wilfrid Utz(✉) and Robert Woitsch

BOC Asset Management GmbH, Operngasse 20b, 1040 Vienna, Austria
{wilfrid.utz,robert.woitsch}@boc-eu.com

Abstract. This paper demonstrates an application case for the concept of Data Service design and composition techniques established by the Big-Data Data Service (BD-DS) modelling method realized using the ADOxx meta-modelling platform. In the domain of energy-efficiency assessments of buildings and their operations, the collection of energy related data does not pose a problem anymore as the necessary infrastructure is available in a non-intrusive way, at low installation and operation costs. An issue identified relates to the realization of value-adding services based on these continuous data streams in such distributed, heterogeneous environments. In the context of the ORBEET project, a dynamic, close-to-real-time data access/composition design and exploration framework has been realized. This framework builds upon the concept of Energy Data as a Service combining different sources for a dynamic and enhanced operational rating deployed in 4 different pilot sites in Europe.

Keywords: Data as a service · IoT · Sensor network · Big data · Service composition · Energy rating and certificates · Modelling · Meta-modelling

1 Introduction

The design of data access and processing mechanism has gained importance in the past years as a result of the technological evolution on device and infrastructure level. This evolution allows to install and use sensors in various situations and settings, to access, to store and to process larger amount of diversely structured data from the environment surrounding us. A technological challenge that has been identified in [1] relates to the continuous evolution and update of schema information. Since any connected device, application or service deployed online is potentially a data source that could be used to as input to implement value-adding capabilities as an identified trend in [2], (e.g. enable understanding and decision support) a novel approach is required to handle this variability in access and composition. Data is not hand-crafted anymore, but continuously generated by computers, devices, sensors, search results [3]; The related schema is evolving over time along the development of new devices and sensors. When realizing functionality that builds on these dynamically changing and/or attached sources, a flexible approach is needed to continuously adapt access and processing mechanisms accordingly. The "Big-Data Data Service" (BD-DS) modelling method as described in

L.M. Camarinha-Matos et al. (Eds.): PRO-VE 2017, IFIP AICT 506, pp. 265–275, 2017.
DOI: 10.1007/978-3-319-65151-4_25

[1] established an approach and tool support for the concept of Data Services. Using diagrammatic, conceptual models as put forward in [4], following a well-structured modelling procedure, it is possible to design access to data sources of any type, classify composition techniques and provide standardized interfaces for integration, having the format, syntactical and semantical characteristics of the sources and intended target schema as a guiding frame; at the same time the design is readable by the user, externalizing the calculation techniques and methods. The stakeholders involved along the line of realization of novel functionalities (visualization, analysis) are involved and work collaboratively on the design.

This paper demonstrates the application of the above method in an application case from the energy efficiency assessment domain. BD-DS acts as a mitigation layer between energy sensors, visualization/prediction techniques and the end-user in a close to real-time setting. Based on the requirements of the project, the modelling method has been extended and adapted to the specifics of the domain.

The remainder of paper is structured as follows: Sect. 2 provides background information on the OrbEEt project and related work to set the results presented in context of its objectives. Section 3 introduces the challenges and requirements from a conceptual perspective, observed and mapped to the BD-DS approach. Section 4 describes the prototypical implementation and preliminary results of evaluation in the pilot settings. The paper concludes by outlining future work in the context of the project and beyond.

2 Energy Data as a Service: The OrbEEt Case

The contribution presented in this paper is based on the work performed in the OrbEEt project (http://www.orbeet.eu/), a research and innovation action funded by the European Commission's Horizon 2020 Energy Efficiency programme. The objective of the project is to introduce an innovative ICT solution to facilitate public and social engagement to action for energy efficiency by providing real-time assessments of the energy impact and energy-related organisational behaviour [5]. As such it combines and integrates building and operations/business process information with energy data on high granularity level. In current energy assessment techniques three major deficiencies have been identified:

(a) Assessment Approach: as put forward in the legal framework [6] by the European Commission, the objective is to reduce energy use by 20%. Current assessments are performed by expert teams in a static way. Static means that it is done periodically (e.g. yearly) by expert consultants, information of results achieved are not set in context of the changing organisation and occupants' behaviour. Therefore the impact of the results is limited;
(b) Correlation capabilities are limited and do not allow for a combination of the information with operational behavioural aspects. The solution presented in this paper aims to propose a solution to this challenge.
(c) Collaboration techniques and analysis of the environment in a virtualized setting: energy-efficiency initiatives need to be run in a balanced way, therefore

collaboration is required between involved stakeholders in the business ecosystem [7]. Such balancing must consider behaviour of the stakeholders, strategy considerations of the organisation, operation and business process adaptation and impact of the supply-chain and distribution network, resulting in a multi-dimensional collaborative composition and aggregation of information as discussed in [8].

Figure 1 shows the overall concept of the project. In this paper we focus on the Systemic Enterprise Operational Rating (SEOR) Engine that acts as a mitigation layer between data sources (energy, operation, building characteristics and location, baselining) and the representation/interaction layer (enhanced Display Energy Certificate, behavioral triggering, gamification). Further details on the project's objective are available in [5].

The SEOR Engine accesses data from different sources, granularity and variability: Energy data is provided in 10 min intervals by sensors, business process/operation information is less variable but space and people aspects needs to be considered and annotated. As output from the engine, harmonized data streams, are required that feed into visualization and behavior triggering frameworks, updating and changing the energy behavior of occupants and operations.

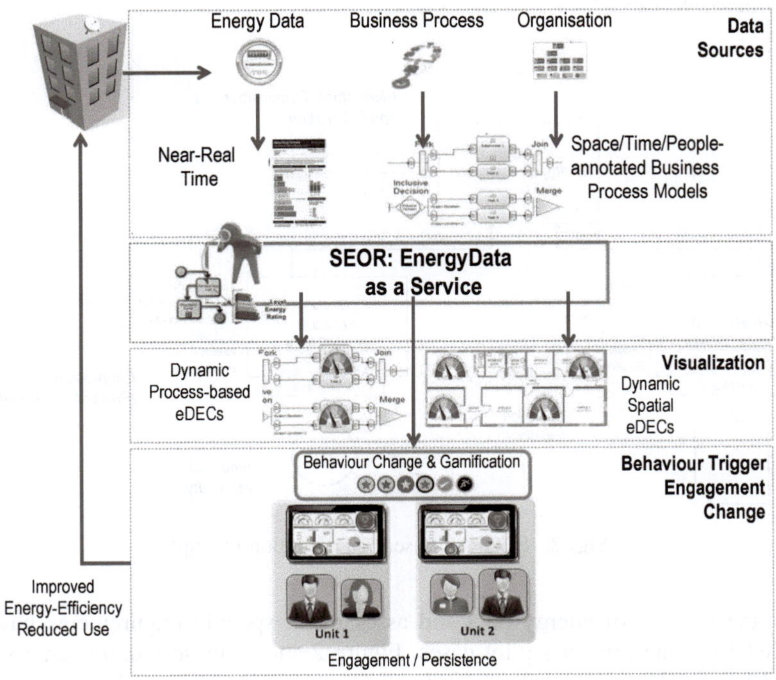

Fig. 1. OrbEEt overall concept [9]: positioning the SEOR layer

As a collaborative project, the consortium is composed of nine partners from six European countries with different competences and experiences. A strong aspect in the consortium relates to the involvement of pilots. These pilot building are located in 4 different countries (Spain, Austria, Germany, and Bulgaria) with different operational usages and construction characteristics. The project started on March 1, 2015 and will run for a period of 36 month with a budget of 1.7 MEUR.

3 Concept: Extending BD-DS for Energy Data as a Service

As a starting point for conceptualizing the of the SEOR mitigation layer, the BD-DS modelling method has been selected. Based on the generic modelling method framework developed by Karagiannis and Kühn in [10], the modelling method comprises of the modelling procedure realized as a domain-independent guideline, supported by a corresponding model structure and model processing mechanisms/algorithms.

Further details on the modelling method components are available in [1], complemented by a proof-of-concept implementation (modelling toolkit and operation/deployment mechanisms for data services) available online via the Open Models Initiative Laboratory (www.omilab.org) at [11]. Following the Agile Modelling Method Engineering approach [12], BD-DS is iteratively extended to include domain-specific aspects.

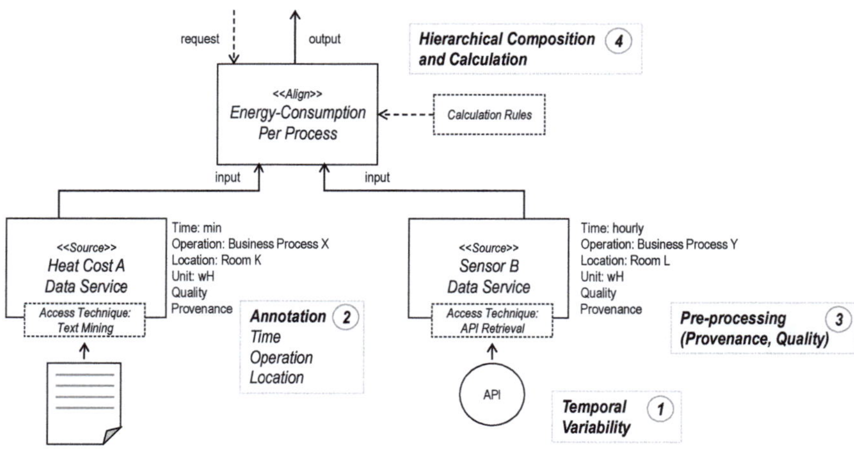

Fig. 2. SEOR data service definition example

For the domain of energy data and assessment, specific requirements have been identified from the project's pilot cases. Figure 2 shows these requirements visually, detailed below. The core challenge relates to support decision making and behavior triggering in a distributed, heterogeneous environment, whereas distribution is understood from a technical observation but also organizational (e.g. skills, competences, involved stakeholders). The user of the system should have the possibility to understand the meaning of data and its impact on the behavioral triggers that are put in place in a transparent way. Graphical models act here as the knowledge-bearing entity: they can be interpreted by the end-user, providing means to reason and derive action from the provided results and are also machine executable by a real-time access and composition engine. The requirements for the extension are:

1. *Temporal Variability:* as data sources with varying temporal dimensions are input to the composition, harmonization techniques need to be applied to create combinable data series. An example for this challenge relates to the different update intervals of energy sensors: electricity sensors provide their input in 10 min intervals, whereas heating data is captured on a bi-monthly to monthly basis. Operation information is captured manually by analyzing the business processes with a lower variability and the building structure is described as the Building Information Model (BIM) using the gbXML standard [13].
2. *Semantic Annotation:* during the design of data service compositions, modelling support mechanisms are required. Through semantic annotation of data sources, initial compositions and filters become feasible using the temporal, spatial and operational context annotations as input.
3. *Data Quality, Provenance:* due to the technical distribution of providing sources and integration via a loosely-coupled architecture as detailed in [14] and [15], quality and provenance information needs to be captured dynamically and composed along the calculation logic.
4. *Hierarchical Composition:* the calculation of complex data services is designed in a hierarchical manner. Calculation techniques are made available as plugins to provide flexible extension and modification mechanisms. The processing engine interprets the hierarchy, binds the calculation plugins dynamically and performs the composition as well as orchestration.

The extensions to BD-DS on a conceptual level based on the above requirements are discussed in the following.

3.1 Modelling Language Extension: Metadata Annotation

The BD-DS modelling language as presented in [5, Fig. 4] is extended to provide means for annotation of data-services with energy related metadata and contextual information. The objective of this extension is to keep the core meta-model stable and provide dynamic means to extend the semantic expressiveness of artefacts created. The Semantic Lifting approach from [16] is re-purposed for BD-DS, extending the available "Metadata" view. The characteristic of the extension is twofold: (a) it establishes on tool-level a dynamic and adaptive mechanisms to cope with changing domain-specific semantics and their evolution, and (b) enriches the semantic expressiveness of the artefacts created to realize model-value functionality in the form of domain-specific analysis features, graph-rewriting techniques and composition layouts. Model-value capabilities aim to elevate the model quality from a user interaction and interpretation point of view with the graphical conceptual models used to specify the data service logic.

This repository for annotation is made available as an ontological representation using RDF syntax [17] on vocabulary and instance level: the energy domain semantics of OrbEEt are captured in a custom, high-level vocabulary that can be imported into the system, updated and modified. Related instances are derived from the domain context of the observed building, device sensor and operation. Instance information is considered to reside in an external environment. The combination of both vocabulary and instance information represents the annotation and tagging base as shown in Fig. 3.

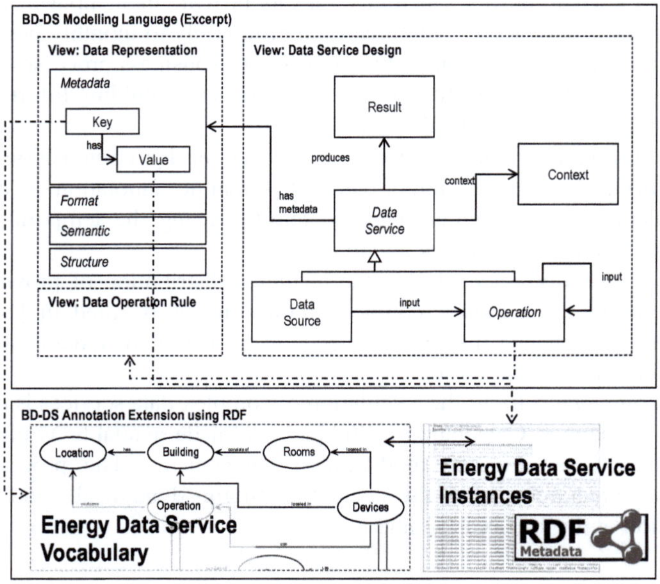

Fig. 3. Extended BD-DS meta-model with RDF annotations

3.2 Mechanisms and Algorithms: Annotation-Based Modelling Support

The annotation technique of above is used as input to dynamically derive data service compositions. Based on the context made available in the model, composite services are dynamically created and added to the model. The algorithmic solution is available as pseudo code below. The algorithm uses defined data source services from a common information layer (an abstraction from actual sensor information) and their annotations as input.

Pseudo-code: Annotation-based Composite Data Services

```
# retrieve all source services
set sources to GET_BASE_DATA_SOURCES
set annotations to map (a_key, a_value_list)
for i=0 to source.size
  set a_src to GET_DATA_SOURCE_ANNOTATIONS (source(i))
  set annotations to union(annotations, a_src)
endfor
# create aggregate service
set r_list to annotations.get(r_key).values
for k=0 to r_list.size
  CREATE_AGGREGATE_DATA_SERVICE (l, r)
  set rel_src to GET_SERVICE_BY_ANNOTATION (r_key,
room(k))
  CREATE_INPUT_RElATlON (new_aggrate_ds, rel_src)
endfor
RADIAL_WEDGE_LAYOUT (model)
```

The algorithm is available for the end-user to create complex design, validate the composition logic and visualize results interactively.

Through these extensions on meta-model and mechanism/algorithm level, the requirements of the energy domain in data service design can be satisfied. Evaluation was performed by realizing a prototypical implementation of the extension and validating its operation with the OrbEEt framework.

4 Evaluation: SEOR Data Service Designer and Engine

The proof-of-concept implementation has been performed as the SEOR Data Services Designer, supporting the modeling of energy data as a service, and Engine supporting the operationalization of these services in the cloud.

4.1 SEOR Data Service Designer

The realization of the prototype builds upon the available implementation of BD-DS on ADOxx [18] resulting in the SEOR Data Service Designer. The extensions have been implemented using metamodeling concepts and techniques, adapting the meta-model with required constructs for annotation and temporal update definitions for dynamic data series.

Figure 4 shows the results of the implementation in the SEOR Data Service Designer:

1. Data sources are retrieved from the abstract sensor information layer. The step is performed through automated import mechanisms (detection) and manual interaction of the energy expert.

2. The domain expert annotates the data source services with semantic constructs, imported in RDF Turtle syntax. Annotation is performed for location, operational and temporal attributes as well as energy type, based using RDF subjects and objects (see Fig. 4a);
3. The tool derives additional properties are using ADOxx Expressions (composition serial, temporal cron expressions).
4. The system automatically creates the composed data services based on the annotation (see Fig. 4b) and performs a radial layout algorithm on the model for better readability.

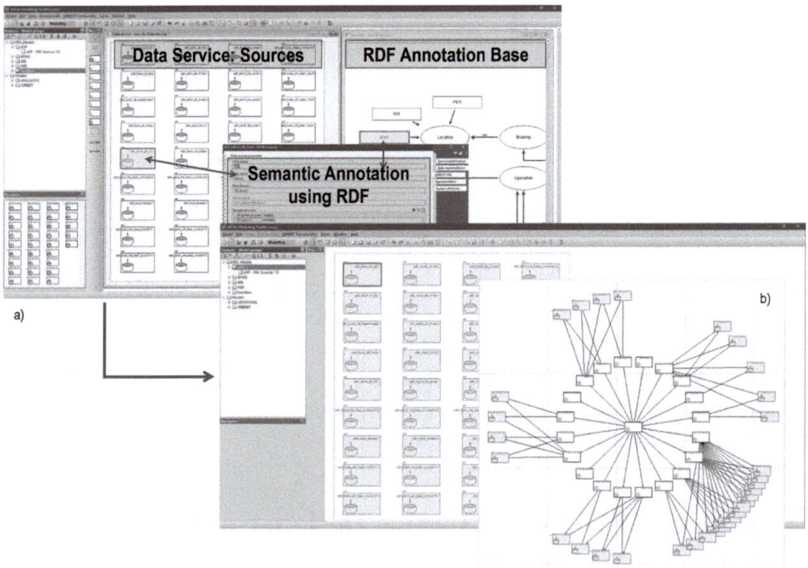

Fig. 4. SEOR data service designer: (a) Annotation and (b) Composite Service Generation

The SEOR Data Service Designer enables additional interaction capabilities, provided by the meta-modelling platform ADOxx such as visualization options, analysis and query techniques, reporting and open interfaces.

4.2 SEOR Data Service Engine

The SEOR Data Service Engine has been implemented as a web-application using Java 8.0 on the server side and JavaScript/HTML5/CSS for the user interface. The applications logic is dynamic upon the design artifacts and operationalizes them using web-service technologies. As an interaction layer with the engine, all data services (source- and composed service) are accessible through standard service protocols (SOAP and ReST) to reduce integration effort. A validation UI is provided to assess the operational status of each service, values and historical information.

The characteristics of this implementation are summarized below:

- *Interpretation of conceptual model:* the engine interprets the diagrammatic representation in the designer and executes them. This approach provides flexibility to the designer as artifacts created can be verified and validated in operation without further implementation/coding
- *Plugin-based Composition Logic:* Composition and aggregation logic in the engine is supported by a plugin-based approach, meaning that arbitrary composition techniques for data services can be realized as individual plugins in the engine, dynamically made available in the designer following [19].
- *Time-series handling:* to support the requirement of temporal variability and data quality, the engine builds on locally cached, streamed data. According to the derived temporal variability, the engine runs update threads for each service in the background and enables close to real-time processing. Additional aggregation techniques are supported to condense/expand a time-series. In the evaluation environment for the project, growing time-series data of 531 data services (atomic and composed) consisting of 9700 entries per series (as of writing this publication) are handled in a performant and efficient way. A re-design of the composition logic is by the designer is supported at any point in time.
- *Dynamic filtering and visualization techniques*: review results of the SEOR engine execution for specific time-frames and visualize results as charts.

Figure 5 shows the SEOR Data Service Engine's user interface. The Data Explorer provides functionality to access data services in a hierarchical manner, visualize the change history and drill-down/up to related services.

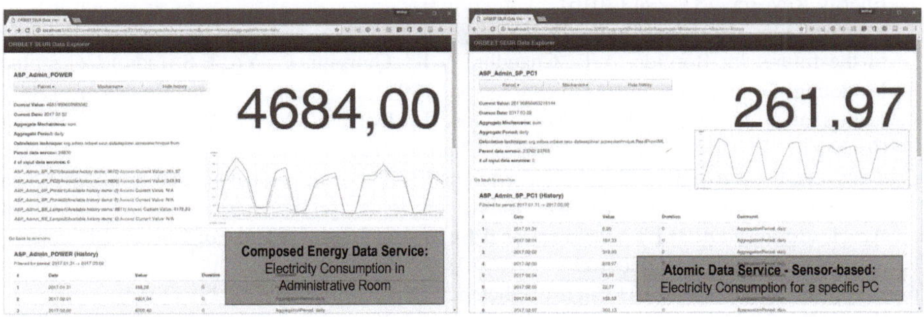

Fig. 5. SEOR data service engine: data explorer (atomic and composed)

5 Conclusion and Outlook

The work presented in this paper provides insights into results achieved within the energy data modelling and composition task of the OrbEEt project, applying the BD-DS Data Service concept in a practical setting. An initial technical and user evaluation of the results took place, resulting in the finding that due to the flexible approach, an efficient design and deployment process as well as agile adaptation in the system could be performed. A challenge identified during the work relates to the observed knowledge gap between business views captured in the operation and data processing experts. Interpretation of finding and therefore optimization techniques on both ends are currently only of limited value due to this gap. Different levels of visual and conceptual techniques are going to be developed in the coming period, summarized under the keyword "Conceptual Analytics", to foster the creation of value-adding, innovative service offerings in the domain and their application in networked organisational settings. This work contributes to elevate (big) data related work to a conceptual and decision making level, involving stakeholders from different background, expertise and create organisational value, not only through data analytics but also in conceptually understanding data assets in the company.

Acknowledgments. The OrbEEt project has received funding from the European Community Horizon 2020 Program for European Research and Technological Development (2014-2020) within the funding line H2020-EU.3.3.1. - Reducing energy consumption and carbon footpint by smart and sustainable use. Contract no. 649753-OrbEEt-H2020-EE-2014-2015/H2020-EE-2014-2-RIA.

References

1. Roussopoulos, N., Utz, W.: Design semantics on accessibility in unstructured data environments. In: Karagiannis, D., Mayr, H., Mylopoulos, J. (eds.) Domain-Specific Conceptual Modeling, pp. 79–101. Springer, Cham (2016). doi:10.1007/978-3-319-39417-6_4
2. Camarinha-Matos, L.M.: Collaborative smart grids – a survey on trends. Renew. Sustain. Energy Rev. **65**, 283–294 (2016)
3. Roussopoulos, N., Karagiannis, D.: Conceptual modeling: past, present and the continuum of the future. In: Borgida, A.T., Chaudhri, V.K., Giorgini, P., Yu, E.S. (eds.) Conceptual Modeling: Foundations and Applications, pp. 139–152. Springer, Berlin Heidelberg (2009)
4. Karagiannis, D., Mayr, H.C., Mylopoulos, J.: Domain-Specific Conceptual Modeling: Concepts, Methods and Tools. Springer, Cham (2016)
5. Tsatsakis, K., Hatzoplaki, E., Martínez, J.: ORBEET: organizational behaviour improvement for energy efficient administrative public offices. http://www.gridinnovation-on-line.eu/Articles/Library/ORBEET-Organizational-Behaviour-Improvement-For-Energy-Efficient-Administrative-Public-Offices.kl
6. European Commission: EU Energy Efficiency Directive (32012L0027) (2012)
7. Graça, P., Camarinha-Matos, Luís M.: A proposal of performance indicators for collaborative business ecosystems. In: Afsarmanesh, H., Camarinha-Matos, L.M., Lucas Soares, A. (eds.) PRO-VE 2016. IAICT, vol. 480, pp. 253–264. Springer, Cham (2016). doi:10.1007/978-3-319-45390-3_22
8. Matei, O., Orio, G., Jassbi, J., Barata, J., Cenedese, C.: Collaborative data mining for intelligent home appliances. In: Afsarmanesh, H., Camarinha-Matos, L.M., Lucas Soares, A. (eds.) PRO-VE 2016. IAICT, vol. 480, pp. 313–323. Springer, Cham (2016). doi:10.1007/978-3-319-45390-3_27
9. OrbEEt: OrbEEt Project Website. http://orbeet.eu/

10. Kühn, H., Bayer, F., Junginger, S., Karagiannis, D.: Enterprise model integration. In: Bauknecht, K., Tjoa, A.M., Quirchmayr, G. (eds.) EC-Web 2003. LNCS, vol. 2738, pp. 379–392. Springer, Heidelberg (2003). doi:10.1007/978-3-540-45229-4_37
11. OMiLab.org: Project BD-DS. http://austria.omilab.org/psm/content/bdds/info
12. Karagiannis, D.: Agile modeling method engineering. In: Proceedings of the 19th Panhellenic Conference on Informatics, pp. 5–10. ACM (2015)
13. gbXML - An industry supported standard for storing and sharing building properties between 3D Architectural and Engineering Analysis Software. http://www.gbxml.org/
14. Utz, W., Woitsch, R., Karagiannis, D.: Conceptualisation of hybrid service models: an open models approach. In: 2011 IEEE 35th Annual Computer Software and Applications Conference Workshops (COMPSACW), pp. 494–499. IEEE (2011)
15. Woitsch, R., Karagiannis, D.: Process oriented knowledge management: a service based approach. J UCS. **11**, 565–588 (2005)
16. Woitsch, R., Utz, W.: Business process as a service (BPaaS). In: Janssen, M., Mäntymäki, M., Hidders, J., Klievink, B., Lamersdorf, W., Loenen, B., Zuiderwijk, A. (eds.) I3E 2015. LNCS, vol. 9373, pp. 435–440. Springer, Cham (2015). doi:10.1007/978-3-319-25013-7_35
17. W3C Consortium: RDF 1.1 concepts and abstract syntax (2014)
18. ADOxx.org: ADOxx Metamodelling Platform. https://www.adoxx.org/live/home
19. Utz, W., Kühn, H.: A model-driven data marshalling approach for capturing learning activities in heterogeneous environments. In: 2014 Conference of the eChallenges e-2014, pp. 1–9. IEEE (2014)

The Network Structure of Visited Locations According to Geotagged Social Media Photos

Christian Junker[1(✉)], Zaenal Akbar[2], and Martí Cuquet[2]

[1] Fanlens.io, Baumkirchen, Austria
christian@fanlens.io
[2] Universität Innsbruck, Technikerstraße 21a, 6020 Innsbruck, Austria
{zaenal.akbar,marti.cuquet}@sti2.at

Abstract. Businesses, tourism attractions, public transportation hubs and other points of interest are not isolated but part of a collaborative system. Making such collaborative network surface is not always an easy task. The existence of data-rich environments can assist in the reconstruction of collaborative networks. They shed light into how their members operate and reveal a potential for value creation via collaborative approaches. Social media data are an example of a means to accomplish this task. In this paper, we reconstruct a network of tourist locations using fine-grained data from Flickr, an online community for photo sharing. We have used a publicly available set of Flickr data provided by Yahoo! Labs. To analyse the complex structure of tourism systems, we have reconstructed a network of visited locations in Europe, resulting in around 180,000 vertices and over 32 million edges. An analysis of the resulting network properties reveals its complex structure.

Keywords: Complex networks · Social media · Collaborative tourism · YFCC100M dataset · Travelling patterns · Social networks

1 Introduction

The current ubiquity of digital and hyperconnected activities generates an ever-growing amount of available data. Coupled with the increasing ability to process, link, analyse and exploit them, it is producing a radical impact in our society and how individuals and organisations function and interact.

This new reality of data-rich environments is posing novel challenges and opportunities emerge that are not only technical [1], but also expand into the economic, social, ethical, legal and political fields. Some examples are an increased efficiency and innovation speed, the appearance of new business models, raising concerns on data quality, reliability and trust as well as privacy, protection and accountability issues, among others [2–4].

As a result, businesses and economic sectors are adapting to this new reality. Research is also quickly embracing the potential of using and analysing this expanding number of data sources. The study of complex and collaborative systems can also substantially benefit from these large amounts of evolving data. Indeed, the use of big data, which share the large scale (volume), complexity (variety) and dynamics

L.M. Camarinha-Matos et al. (Eds.): PRO-VE 2017, IFIP AICT 506, pp. 276–283, 2017.
DOI: 10.1007/978-3-319-65151-4_26

(velocity) properties of complex systems [5], enhanced by the innovative potential of open data [6], and machine learning, data mining and natural language processing tools, among others, set an ideal framework for a data-driven approach to the study of collaborative networks of autonomous entities cooperating to achieve a common or compatible goal. Characterising how these networks are organised will shed new light into what are the relations between the main actors in a network, how they collaborate and what are the building blocks for a successful ecosystem.

In some applications, this approach is proving very productive, e.g. in air traffic management [7], face-to-face behavioural networks in human gatherings [8], and movements of farmed animal populations [9]. Data-centric fields, of which these are examples, provide an empirical framework where advances in network science, and particularly in collaborative networks, can be tested. The complex structure of actors and their relations is particularly relevant in socioeconomic systems. This has triggered a long history of interdisciplinary collaboration between network science and fields such as computational sociology [10], transportation systems [7, 11], economy [12], and also that of collaborative networks, which is increasingly benefiting from data-driven approaches [13, 14].

A field with a particularly big potential to benefit from intensive data-driven network research but that has still been hardly explored is the tourism sector. Some early studies include a characterisation of the worldwide network of tourist arrivals at the country level [15] and of touristic destinations [16–19]. The tremendous increase in the abundance of data sources in the tourism sector is boosting a new data intensive approach [20]. Examples of sources are online bookings, the process of tourists informing themselves before the travel, and the sharing of their experiences during and after it via social media. Some examples are the use of geotagged data of tourists to show the destination preference and the hotspots in a city [21], analyse sentiment by neighbourhoods [22], describe city and global mobility patterns [23, 24] and predict taxi trip duration [25]. Social media data may be used as a source to reveal business and points of interest relationships and thus open the ground for collaborative value-creation.

In this paper, we reconstruct a European network of locations visited by tourists using fine-grained data from Flickr, an online community for photo sharing. We have used a publicly available set of Flickr data provided by Yahoo! Labs [26]. The network design relies on the use of collaboratively contributed data by users: The locations where photos were taken make the nodes of the network, and are connected if at least two different Flickr users took a photo in both locations. The objective of the present work is to perform a characterisation of this network and its basic properties, to lay the ground for future research on tourism segmentation based on locations visited, detection of communities of businesses and points of interest to enable collaboration among them, and identification of motifs and business functions within the network to correct and enhance the tourism ecosystem in cities.

Social media networks in particular contain salient data that highlights real-world behaviour patterns of their users. Due to these properties, these networks can act as the catalyst for the reconstruction of complex, possibly multilayered connections in seemingly unrelated networks. This study shows the feasibility and potential of using social media data in the collaborative networks field, and reconstructs the relationships between relevant places for tourists with the aim to contribute to a better understanding of what constitutes the central and most relevant points of interest. Further, results of the study could make a significant contribution in assisting the design of collaborative networks of city entities in the face of tourism, be they businesses, landmarks, attractions, public transport authorities or others. Finally, it lays the ground for future research to reconstruct multiplex location networks, where each of the layers corresponds to different segmentation of users, such as locals and tourists or by country of origin.

This paper is organised as follows. In Sect. 2 we present the network of locations in Europe visited by Flickr users. First, the YFCC100M dataset is briefly presented and discussed. We then outline the methodology used to prepare the network from this dataset, and finally proceed to the network analysis. Section 3 discusses the results and we conclude with some remarks in Sect. 4.

2 Network Reconstruction and Analysis

2.1 Flickr Dataset

The Yahoo Flickr Creative Commons 100 Milion Dataset (YFCC100M) [26], released in 2014, is a public dataset of 100 million media objects uploaded to Flickr, a social image and video hosting website. Almost all of its contents cover the period between 2000 and 2014. The dataset is very rich in metadata, enabling a large variety of applications. Since its release, it has been used in a variety of contexts, such as photo clustering [27], multimodal learning [28], situation recognition [29], trajectory recommendation [30], and tag recommendation.

The metadata contained in the dataset, aside from Flickr-related data such as a photo identifier and the user that created it, include tags used by users to annotate it (68 million objects have been annotated), camera used, time when the photo was taken and when it was uploaded, location and license. For this paper, only the metadata related to the geolocalisation has been used, although future work would largely benefit from consideration of at least tags and timing, to enable e.g. a dynamic analysis of the network. In total, 48 million objects are annotated with the geolocalisation of the object, and the most prominent cities represented in the dataset are London, Paris, Tokyo, New York, San Francisco and Hong Kong [26]. Figure 1 shows the locations of all those photos, linked as described below in Sect. 2.2.

2.2 Collaborative Network Reconstruction

To analyse the complex structure of tourism systems, we have used Apache Spark for the pre-processing of the YFCC100M dataset and converted it into a GraphX graph to construct a network of locations visited by users of Flickr. In this undirected weighted network, a vertex corresponds to the geolocation of a media object in the YFCC100M dataset as specified by the latitude and longitude fields. We used a precision of 10^{-3} degrees both in latitude and longitude, which at 45° of latitude roughly corresponds to 111 m of latitude and 79 m of longitude. In practice, this means that media objects show up as the same vertex if they are on the same street or neighbourhood.

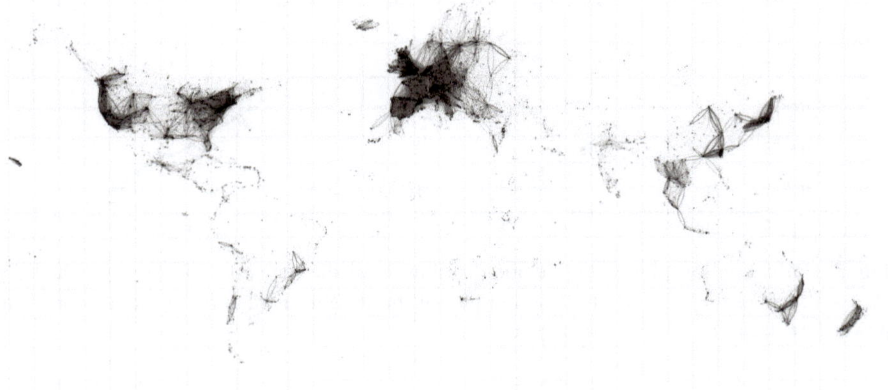

Fig. 1. Global overview of the geolocalised photos of the YFCC100M dataset [26]. Locations where photos were taken have been linked following the method described in Sect. 2.2. For clarity, only links connecting locations separated by less than 10° are displayed.

The network is represented by a graph $G = \{V, E\}$, where V is the set of vertices and E is the set of edges. Two vertices u and v are connected by an undirected edge (u, v) if at least two different users have a media object in the two locations corresponding to such vertices (i.e., both visited the two locations). Reconstructing the network without this constraint leads to tremendous noise, i.e. spurious connections between singular points of interest. The weight w_{uv} of an edge (u, v) is the number of users that visited locations u and v. The resulting network for Europe has N = 178,661 vertices and M = 32,753,756 edges.

2.3 Network Analysis

The network of visited locations in Europe consists of one giant connected component of 174,699 nodes, accounting for 97.8% of the total, and 1,575 other small components of sizes ranging from 2 (most of them) to 29.

The degree k_u of vertex u is the number of edges attached to the vertex. In the present network, it is the number of locations that were visited by the same users that visited a given location, and thus indicates what are the hotspots in the city or region. One of the most important characteristics of real-world networks is their degree distribution p_k [31]: the probability that a randomly chosen vertex has degree k. In the binomial random graph model, each of the $\binom{N}{2}$ pairs of vertices holds an edge with a certain probability $p = \langle k \rangle/(N-1)$, with $\langle k \rangle$ the average degree. For large graphs with $N \to \infty$, its probability distribution tends to a Poisson distribution, $p_k = \langle k \rangle^k e^{-\langle k \rangle} \big/ k!$. Real-world networks, on the other hand, typically have a larger number of nodes of high degree, and follow a distribution that decays as a power law,

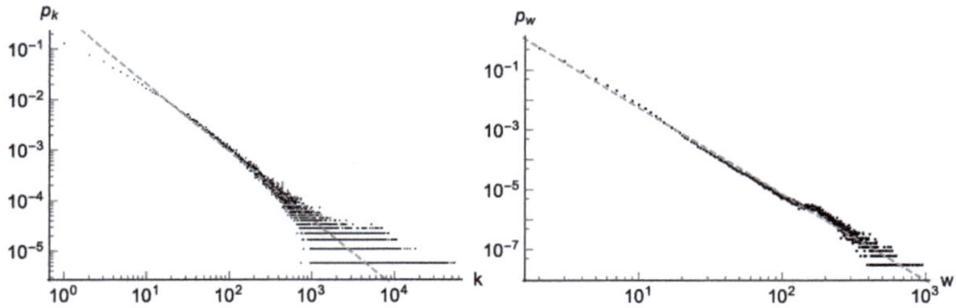

Fig. 2. Left: Log-log plot of the degree distribution of the network, with a power law decay $P_k \sim k^{-\theta}$, where $\theta = 1.34$. Right: Log-log plot of the weight distribution of the network, with a power law decay $P_w \sim w^{-\gamma}$, where $\gamma = 2.89$.

$P_k \sim k^{-\theta}$, rather than exponentially [31]. In our case of the European network of locations, it decays as a power law with exponent $\theta = 1.34$, as shown in Fig. 2.

In a weighted network, the degree alone is not enough to characterise the relation between a node and the rest of the network. Indeed, each edge (u, v) in our network is weighted according to the number of users that visited both endpoints, u and v, of the edge, with each user adding 1 to the weight w_{uv}. The range of weights goes from 2 to 944 users with an average of 303.78. The probability distribution of weights, shown in Fig. 2, follows again a power law $p_w \sim w^{\gamma}$ with exponent $\gamma = 2.89$.

We also analyse if there is a correlation on how locations are linked to each other in terms of the location degree. Typically, social networks tend to show assortative mixing, i.e. nodes tend to be connected to other nodes of similar degree. On the contrary, economic, technological and biological networks tend to show disassortative mixing, where nodes of high degree tend to connect to nodes of low degree [32]. To examine the assortativity of our network, we consider the average degree of the neighbours of a node with degree k,

$$\langle k_{nn} \rangle = \sum\nolimits_{k'} k' p'(k'|k), \tag{1}$$

where $p'(k'|k)$ is the conditional probability that an edge leaving a node of degree k leads to a node of degree k'. This probability is proportional to $k' p_{k'}$ if it is independent of k. Figure 3 shows the $\langle k_{nn} \rangle$ distribution for our network and indicates a rather weak degree-degree correlation. We thus computed the Pearson correlation coefficient of the degrees at the ends of an edge,

$$r = \frac{1}{\sigma_q^2} \sum\nolimits_{j,k} jk\left(e_{jk} - q_j q_k\right), \tag{2}$$

which is in the range $-1 \leq \mathrm{r} \leq 1$. Here q_k is the remaining degree distribution,

$$q_k = \frac{(k+1)p_{k+1}}{\sum_j jpj}, \tag{3}$$

e_{jk} is the joint probability distribution of the remaining degree for the two vertices of a same edge, and σ_q^2 is the variance of q_k [32]. In our network, $r = -2.36 \times 10^{-6}$, showing no assortative mixing and confirming the results in Fig. 3.

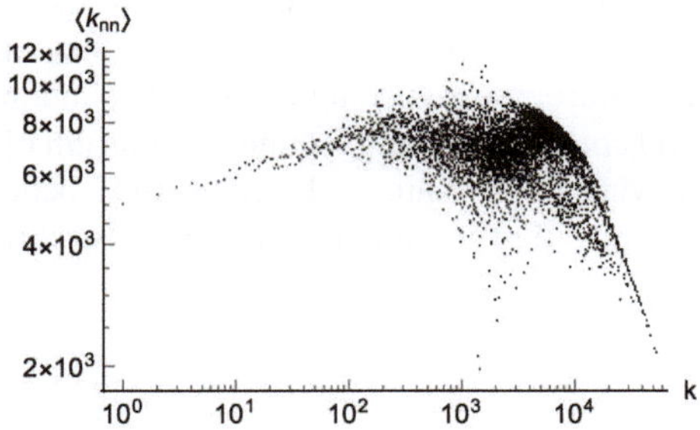

Fig. 3. Log-log plot of the average neighbour degree with respect to the node degree. It indicates no assortative mixing, confirmed by a correlation coefficient of $r = -2.36 \times 10^{-6}$.

3 Discussion

The work presented in this paper shows how to use the YFCC100M dataset to reconstruct a network of locations visited by Flickr users. The resulting network of around 180,000 vertices and over 32 million edges, comprising all locations in Europe with a granularity at the street/neighbourhood level, displays a complex structure with a scale-free degree and weight distribution, in line with other social, economic and technological networks [33]. An analysis of degree-degree correlations, however, shows no assortative mixing, as opposed to different results in other real-world networks [32], and thus further analysis is recommended that take into account the edge weights and node strengths, as well as exploring the clustering properties.

The increasing data richness of activities associated with tourism activities, especially from the social media domain, exemplified by the present study, make it a highly promising testbed for the study of collaborative networks in the tourism sector. After linking coordinates of the dataset to points of interest (e.g. local business, landmarks, transportation hubs), communities of actors and motifs with specific functions in the tourism ecosystem may be identified, to assist in the characterisation and potentiate innovation in collaborative tourism. As an example, the role that transportation hubs play in a city could assist in the restructuration of the transportation network. Additionally, smaller networks with a higher detail resolution can be readily obtained with our methodology, enabling the comparison between different cities and possibly revealing different ecosystem patterns.

4 Concluding Remarks

This study shows the feasibility and potential of using social media data in the collaborative networks field, to link local business, landmarks and other points of interest based on social media users visiting them. It lays the ground for further data-driven studies that make use of the richness of the metadata of similar sources, aside from the geotagging, that allow for future research on multilayered collaborative networks. In that case, different layers could correspond to e.g. countries of origin of the users and assist in the segmentation of users via e.g. community detection, and a better understanding of the role of different user segments ties in the collaborative possibilities of tourism.

References

1. Jagadish, H.V., Gehrke, J., Labrinidis, A., Papakonstantinou, Y., Patel, J.M., Ramakrishnan, R., Shahabi, C.: Big data and its technical challenges. Commun. ACM **57**(7), 86–94 (2014)
2. Manovich, L.: Trending: the promises and the challenges of big social data. In: Gold, M.K. (ed.) Debates in the Digital Humanities, pp. 460–475. University of Minnesota Press (2012)
3. Metcalf, J., Keller, E.F., Boyd, D.: Perspectives on Big Data, Ethics, and Society, The Council for Big Data, Ethics and Society (2016)
4. Cuquet, M., Vega-Gorgojo, G., Lammerant, H., Finn, R., Ul Hassan, U.: Societal impacts of big data: challenges and opportunities in Europe (2017). arXiv preprint: arXiv:1704.03361
5. Diebold, F.X.: 'Big Data' dynamic factor models for macroeconomic measurement and forecasting. In: Advances in Economics and Econometrics, Eighth World Congress of the Econometric Society, vol. 32(1), pp. 115–122 (2003)
6. Ojo, A., Porwol, L., Waqar, M., Stasiewicz, A., Osagie, E., Hogan, M., Harney, O., Zeleti, F. A.: Realizing the innovation potentials from open data: stakeholders' perspectives on the desired affordances of open data environment. In: Afsarmanesh, H., Camarinha-Matos, L. M., Lucas Soares, A. (eds.) PRO-VE 2016. IFIP AICT, vol. 480, pp. 48–59. Springer, Cham (2016). doi:10.1007/978-3-319-45390-3_5
7. Cook, A., Blom, H.A.P., Lillo, F., Mantegna, R.N., Miccichè, S., Rivas, D., Vázquez, R., Zanin, M.: Applying complexity science to air traffic management. J. Air Transp. Manag. **42**, 149–158 (2015)
8. Isella, L., Stehlé, J., Barrat, A., Cattuto, C., Pinton, J.-F., Van den Broeck, W.: What's in a crowd? Analysis of face-to-face behavioral networks. J. Theor. Biol. **271**(1), 166–180 (2011)
9. Bajardi, P., Barrat, A., Natale, F., Savini, L., Colizza, V.: Dynamical patterns of cattle trade movements. PLoS ONE **6**(5), e19869 (2011)
10. Lazer, D., Pentland, A., Adamic, L., Aral, S., Barabasi, A.-L., Brewer, D., Christakis, N., Contractor, N., Fowler, J., Gutmann, M., Jebara, T., King, G., Macy, M., Roy, D., Van Alstyne, M.: Social science. computational social science. Science **323**(5915), 721–723 (2009)
11. Kaluza, P., Kolzsch, A., Gastner, M.T., Blasius, B.: The complex network of global cargo ship movements. J. R. Soc. Interface **7**(48), 1093–1103 (2010)
12. Schweitzer, F., Fagiolo, G., Sornette, D., Vega-Redondo, F., Vespignani, A., White, D.R.: Economic networks: the new challenges. Science **325**(5939), 422–425 (2009)
13. Harb, A., Hajlaoui, K., Boucher, X.: Competence mining for collaborative virtual enterprise. In: Camarinha-Matos, L.M., Pereira-Klen, A., Afsarmanesh, H. (eds.) PRO-VE 2011. IFIP AICT, vol. 362, pp. 351–358. Springer, Heidelberg (2011). doi:10.1007/978-3-642-23330-2_39

14. Benaben, F., Montarnal, A., Fertier, A., Truptil, S.: Big-Data and the Question of Horizontal and Vertical Intelligence: A Discussion on Disaster Management, pp. 156–162. Springer, Cham (2016)
15. Miguéns, J.I.L., Mendes, J.F.F.: Travel and tourism: into a complex network. Phys. A Stat. Mech. Appl. **387**(12), 2963–2971 (2008)
16. Shih, H.-Y.: Network characteristics of drive tourism destinations: an application of network analysis in tourism. Tour. Manag. **27**(5), 1029–1039 (2006)
17. Baggio, R., Scott, N., Cooper, C.: Network science. Ann. Tour. Res. **37**(3), 802–827 (2010)
18. Scott, N., Cooper, C., Baggio, R.: Destination networks. Ann. Tour. Res. **35**(1), 169–188 (2008)
19. González-Díaz, B., Gómez, M., Molina, A.: Configuration of the hotel and non-hotel accommodations: an empirical approach using network analysis. Int. J. Hosp. Manag. **48**, 39–51 (2015)
20. Crampton, J.W., Graham, M., Poorthuis, A., Shelton, T., Stephens, M., Wilson, M.W., Zook, M.: Beyond the geotag: situating 'big data' and leveraging the potential of the geoweb. Cartogr. Geogr. Inf. Sci. **40**(2), 130–139 (2013)
21. Paldino, S., Bojic, I., Sobolevsky, S., Ratti, C., González, M.C.: Urban magnetism through the lens of geo-tagged photography. EPJ Data Sci. **4**(1), 5 (2015)
22. Alshamsi, A., Awad, E., Almehrezi, M., Babushkin, V., Chang, P.-J., Shoroye, Z., Tóth, A.-P., Rahwan, I.: Misery loves company: happiness and communication in the city. EPJ Data Sci. **4**(1), 7 (2015)
23. Hawelka, B., Sitko, I., Beinat, E., Sobolevsky, S., Kazakopoulos, P., Ratti, C.: Geo-located twitter as proxy for global mobility patterns. Cartogr. Geogr. Inf. Sci. **41**(3), 260–271 (2014)
24. Liu, Y., Sui, Z., Kang, C., Gao, Y.: Uncovering patterns of inter-urban trip and spatial interaction from social media check-in data. PLoS ONE **9**(1), e86026 (2014)
25. Zarmehri, M.N., Soares, C.: Collaborative data analysis in hyperconnected transportation systems. In: Afsarmanesh, H., Camarinha-Matos, L.M., Lucas Soares, A. (eds.) PRO-VE 2016. IFIP AICT, vol. 480, pp. 13–23. Springer, Cham (2016). doi:10.1007/978-3-319-45390-3_2
26. Thomee, B., Shamma, D.A., Friedland, G., Elizalde, B., Ni, K., Poland, D., Borth, D., Li, L.-J.: YFCC100M: the new data in multimedia research. Commun. ACM **59**(2), 64–73 (2016)
27. Tang, M., Nie, F., Jain, R.: Capped Lp-norm graph embedding for photo clustering. In: Proceedings of the 2016 ACM on Multimedia Conference - MM 2016, pp. 431–435 (2016)
28. Zahálka, J., Rudinac, S., Jónsson, B.Þ., Koelma, D.C., Worring, M.: Interactive multimodal learning on 100 million images. In: Proceedings of the 2016 ACM on International Conference on Multimedia Retrieval - ICMR 2016, pp. 333–337 (2016)
29. Pongpaichet, S., Tang, M., Jalali, L., Jain, R.: Using photos as micro-reports of events. In: Proceedings of the 2016 ACM on International Conference on Multimedia Retrieval - ICMR 2016, pp. 87–94 (2016)
30. Chen, D., Ong, C.S., Xie, L.: Learning points and routes to recommend trajectories. In: Proceedings of the 25th ACM International on Conference on Information and Knowledge Management - CIKM 2016, pp. 2227–2232 (2016)
31. Barabási, A.-L.: Emergence of scaling in random networks. Science **286**(5439), 509–512 (1999)
32. Newman, M.E.J.: Assortative mixing in networks. Phys. Rev. Lett. **89**(20), 208701 (2002)
33. Albert, R., Barabási, A.-L.: Statistical mechanics of complex networks. Rev. Mod. Phys. **74** (1), 47–97 (2002)

Data Acquisition and Analysis

Customer Experience: A Design Approach and Supporting Platform

Maura Mengoni[1(✉)], Emanuele Frontoni[2], Luca Giraldi[1], Silvia Ceccacci[1], Roberto Pierdicca[2], and Marina Paolanti[2]

[1] Department of Industrial Engineering and Mathematical Sciences, Università Politecnica delle Marche, Via Brecce Bianche, 12, 60131 Ancona, Italy
{m.mengoni,l.giraldi,s.ceccacci}@univpm.it

[2] Department of Information Engineering, Università Politecnica delle Marche, Via Brecce Bianche, 12, 60131 Ancona, Italy
{e.frontoni,r.pierdicca,m.paolanti}@univpm.it

Abstract. The purpose of the research is to develop an intelligent system able to support the design and management of a Customer Experience (CX) strategy based on the emotions tracked in real time at the different touchpoints in a store. The system aim is to make the shopping experience responsive to the customers' emotional state and behaviour and to suggest successful product/service design guidelines and customer experience (CX) management strategies whose implementation may affect current and future purchases. In this particular, the present paper focuses on the description of the integrate approach developed to design the overall CX and on the emotional recognition tools to elaborate the rich-data captured by a network of optical and audio sensors distributed within the shop.

Keywords: Customer experience · Collaborative CX design approach · Emotional recognition · Big Data

1 Introduction

Retailers have begun to pay more and more attention to the design of experiential services to stimulate customer emotions and create unique experiences at shops [1]. This has determined a focus shift from the service design to the customer experience design [2] and led the retail to be considered not only as a market in which products are exhibited for sale but mainly as a space where events happen [3].

However, providing entertainment and organizing funny and creative events are not enough to ensure satisfactory Customer Experience (CX). Companies must manage all the clues they are sending to costumers according to a well-conceived and comprehensive CX strategy [4]. In general, the clues that may affect the customer experience are everywhere inside a shop (e.g., from the colors of walls to the lights, the odors and sounds of the store; the style of exhibitors; the uniform of shop assistants, etc.).

Current distributed networks of sensors and the availability of internet connections within shops, provide an interesting opportunity for retailers and for all CX stakeholders

L.M. Camarinha-Matos et al. (Eds.): PRO-VE 2017, IFIP AICT 506, pp. 287–298, 2017.
DOI: 10.1007/978-3-319-65151-4_27

to observe what customers do, how they interact in the space and with the object populating it and with others and to understand what they feel, how they perceive the clues, which is their emotional state and why it changes if an incidental event occurs [5]. Such rich data represents a base:

1. To develop successful clues within the shops able to focus the customer attention and enjoy him/her;
2. To implement CX management strategies able to influence customer purchase probability [6], customer satisfaction [7] and customer loyalty [8];
3. To design improved visual merchandise and shop layout and finally,
4. To provide some drivers for the design of the offered product/service.

The emerging technologies for tracking customer behavior and emotion and the attention to CX challenge the way to design both product and services for retail [9] and highlight the needs for new tools able to collect raw data, arrange and represent such information based on the stakeholder work purpose and propose proper actions to make the shopping experience more engaging, the product more appealing, the services more responsive to the individual needs.

However, based on our knowledge, no study exploited intelligent system based on emotion recognition tools to monitor in real time the customer's experience along his/her journey and make the shopping experience responsive to the customers' emotional state and behaviour. Consequently, the introduction of systems based on affective computing is innovative in the CX research filed.

Starting from these general considerations, a long-term project, called EMOJ, has been launched in 2015 with the aim to answer to this challenging reality by reaching two main objectives as follows:

- Research and Modeling of a holistic approach to define the requirements for the development of every clue (i.e., product/service) which characterizes the store in a comprehensively way. The approach must embrace the holistic nature of CX, consider the unconscious needs of customers and of all process stakeholders and support the drawing of the customer journey and every touchpoint;
- Study and development of implement an intelligent system to support the definition, design and management of the CX strategy to make the shopping experience responsive in the various touchpoints based on the recognized customer's behavior and emotional state.

A significant step to reach the above-mentioned objectives is the definition of what CX is and how this definition impacts on traditional User-Centered design methodologies. The type and density of data necessary for customer analysis represent the starting point for the development of the supporting platform.

2 Customer Experience and Big Data Analytics: Main Challenges

2.1 The Design of Customer Experience

Customer Experience can be defined as the person's response (internal and subjective) to all interactions (direct or indirect) with a company [10]. Such response is holistic in nature and is determined by customers' cognitive, affective emotional and social responses to the stimuli perceived during the interaction. In particular, CX is affected by all the product and services or clues with which customer get in contat along his/her journey [4]. If a company is able to correctly identify the touchpoints that most affect shopping experience and understand which stimulus they have to provide for ensure the best CX, depending on the nature of touchpoint in which the interaction takes place, it will be actually able to influence the customer in choose/repurchase the products in a more profitable way.

However, despite many authors seem to agree on this perspective, no studies provide a holistic approach able to support the development of product and services in an integrated way, according to a determined CX strategy [11]. To support CX design, the well-known User-Centered Design (UCD) approach [12] seems to be suitable for the multi-disciplinary disciplines it requires and for the methods and tools it proposes to ensure that products meet users' expectation. However, UCD focuses only on specific touch-point (i.e., the product use), so that it lacks in consider all the interaction between the customer and the company. Moreover, it mainly focus on needs of particular customers (i.e., the users, the persons who effectively will use the product), so that it lacks in consider all stakeholders needs that the product must meet to ensure customer satisfaction in every stage of CX.

Finally, most of the reported studies in CX pointed out the importance to contract the emotional curve along the customer journey to measure the customer response and define each touchpoint design requirements [13, 14].

Today several methods and technologies allow the recognition of human emotions, which differ in level of intrusiveness. Obviously, the use of invasive instruments (e.g., ECG or EEG, biometric sensors) can affect the subjects' behavior and in particular it may adulterate his/her spontaneity and consequently the emotions experienced by them. The majority of such techniques, methods and tools refer to three research areas: facial emotion analysis [15], speech recognition [16] and biofeedback emotion analysis [17]. All techniques elaborate the data captured by a network of sensors embedded either in wearable systems or distributed in space and collected by data management systems as described in the following section.

2.2 Data-Rich Shop: An Opportunity for CX

Increasing availability of sensors and smart devices connected to the Internet, and powered by the pervasiveness of Cyber-Physical Systems and Internet of Things, create an exponential growth of available data. These advances are transforming traditional network application to be more human-centric [18]. We observe the hyper-connectivity of organizations, people, and machines taking us to data-rich environments and often facing big data challenges. All activities in the world, and everyday life of people, leave trails that can be accumulated on cloud-supported storage, while developments in open data movement contribute to the wide availability of such data. The key will be the introduction of sophisticated tagging algorithms that can analyze images either in real time when pictures are taken or uploaded from RGB-D sensors. To enable such evidence-based decision making, retailers need efficient processes to turn high volumes of fast-moving and diverse data into meaningful insights. The overall process of extracting insights from big data can be broken down into five stages formed by two main sub-processes: data management and analytics. Data management involves processes and supporting technologies to acquire and store data and to prepare and retrieve it for analysis. Analytics, on the other hand, refers to techniques used to analyze and acquire intelligence from big data. Thus, big data analytics can be viewed as a sub-process in the overall process of 'insight extraction' from big data. The data generated by RGB-D cameras in retail can be extracted for business intelligence. Currently, Big Data analytics is being applied at every stage of the retail process, working out what the popular products will be by predicting trends, forecasting where the demand will be for those products, optimizing pricing for a competitive edge, identifying the customers' attraction and working out the best way to approach them, for an optimization of CX strategy. For instance, retailers can collect demographic information about customers, such as age, gender, and ethnicity. Likewise, they can count the number of customers, measure the time they spend in the store, detect their movement patterns, measure their passing time in different areas, and monitor queues in real time. Valuable insights can be obtained by correlating this information with customer demographics to drive decisions for product placement, price, assortment optimization, promotion design, cross-selling, layout optimization, and staffing [19]. Another potential application of big data collection in retail lies in the study of buying behavior of groups. Among family members who shop together, only one interacts with the store at the cash register, causing the traditional systems to miss data on buying patterns of other members. Data from RGB-D sensors can help retailers address this missed opportunity by providing information about the size of the group, the group's demographics, and the individual members' buying behavior.

The customer-specific data can drive dynamic and personalized CX. By capturing important moments in the customer journey, and analyzing this customer-specific activity, retailers can help navigate customers through the ideal interaction points to reach desired outcomes. In this way, they can predict the products a customer will most likely be interested in and offer personalized options in real time across any number of channels.

3 CX Design Approach

The proposed approach to support Shopping Experience Design is characterized by a customer-centered iterative procedure consisting of the following five main activities:

5. Analysis of customers in the store: it implies the observation of behaviours of customer and the understanding of their emotional state during the interactions with

products and staff. The results of the analysis can be represented through the construction of the customer journey map, which represents the main touchpoints in the store, and the creation of the emotional curve to graphically show the level of customers' satisfaction and to recognize which touchpoints need to be redesigned or adapted.

6. Planning of strategies to improve the shopping experience: definition of all changes to be applied to product and services and all strategical short-term and long-term actions that the company must implement in every touchpoint to maximize shopping experience.
7. Development of all intended products, services and clues for every critical touchpoint: the implementation of a CX strategy may imply the design of new products and/or services as so as the re-design of every product and service affecting each touchpoint.
8. Implementation of the prototypal CX strategy: introduction of prototypes of all products, services and clues along the customer journey to test the achieved CX performance.
9. Testing and evaluation of resulted shopping experience: experimentation of the prototyped solution in real stores and measurement of customers' satisfaction to define possible improvements. Results of this activities include the elaboration of data collected through the construction of the emotional curve and guidelines to improve CX.

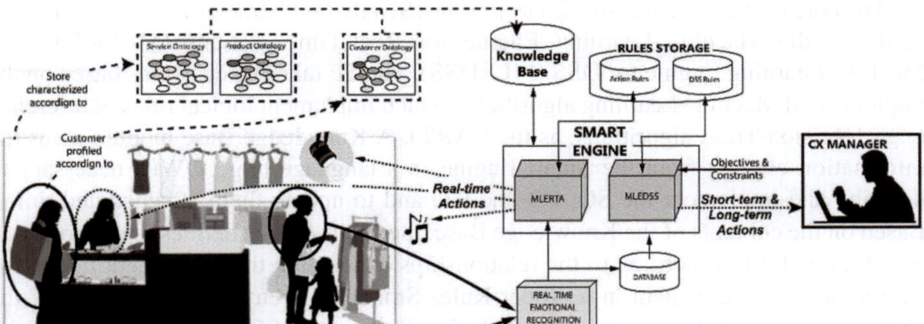

Fig. 1. The overall architecture of the KB platform

It is worth to notice how much strategic the analysis of the customer emotions, their mapping with his/her behaviour and the definition of related real time, short and long term actions are. For this purpose, a Knowledge-based System, which implements Machine Learning algorithms and Ontologies is defined and showed in Fig. 1. The system can:

- Monitor the emotional state of customers along all the touchpoints that characterize the Customer Journey Map;
- Manage real-time actions to improve shopping experience;

- Support decision-making to define what are the most appropriate short and long term solutions to be adopted to improve the shopping experience.

4 A KB Platform to Support CX Management

The proposed knowledge-based system adopts two different strategies. On one hand, it acts directly on the shopping environment, surrounding the customer, to improve his/her buying experience in a reactive way. On the other hand, it provides a Decision Support System (DSS) able to help CX management in defining the optimal CX strategy and planning short and long-term actions. It requires the presence of a real time emotional recognition module to trace the customer emotional state in store.

The system exploits artificial intelligence algorithms (Machine Learning) based on inductive inference and makes decisions on the basis of logical rules derived from a knowledge framework composed by three main modules: the Service Ontology (SO), the Product Ontology (PO) and the Customer Ontology (CO).

SO and PO allow the retailer's knowledge related to product/service to be mapped, structured and managed to design the service and product semantic model. UO provides semantic data structure related to the user characteristics and behavior. In this way, the knowledge necessary to manage the system reaction per emotions is defined through the relations among the entities of such ontologies, according to the results of psychological and marketing studies.

The core of the system is the Smart Engine (SE) that is characterized by two distinct modules: the Machine Learning Engine for Real-Time Actions (MLERTA) and Machine Learning Engine for DSS (MLEDSS). The SE takes its decisions based on the implemented Machine Learning algorithms, which implement logical rules of inference (e.g., Decision Trees algorithms, as the CART). A Knowledge Base module maps the information coming from the Smart Engine in a language (e.g., OWL) necessary to describe and implement the SO, PO and CO and to update them at scheduled times. Based on the contents of the Knowledge Base, the smart engine defines logical rules, in an "if-then" form, according to the relationships connecting the various entities of the Ontologies, and save them in a proper Rules Storage. Given the dual purpose of the platform, two kind of rules are defined: Action Rules and DSS rules. Action Rules aim to manage the system reactive behavior, through the changing of characteristics of service (e.g., number of opened counters) and products (e.g., the color of lighting) into the shop, according to the level of satisfaction experienced by the customers. In general, DSS rules allow the management of the behavior of the business strategy according to proper objectives and constraints. To define DSS rules the Ontology-Driven Business Rules technique can be used, to generate the enterprise model from the ontology domain [20]. To define Action Rules homogeneous or hybrid approaches can be used. Hybrid approaches are usually used to solve knowledge representation problems: they are based on models implemented through Answer Set Programming languages (e.g., AnsProlog) [21]. Homogeneous approaches, implemented by using SWRL language, allow to define logical rules just inside the Knowledge Base, using directly the OWL concepts [21].

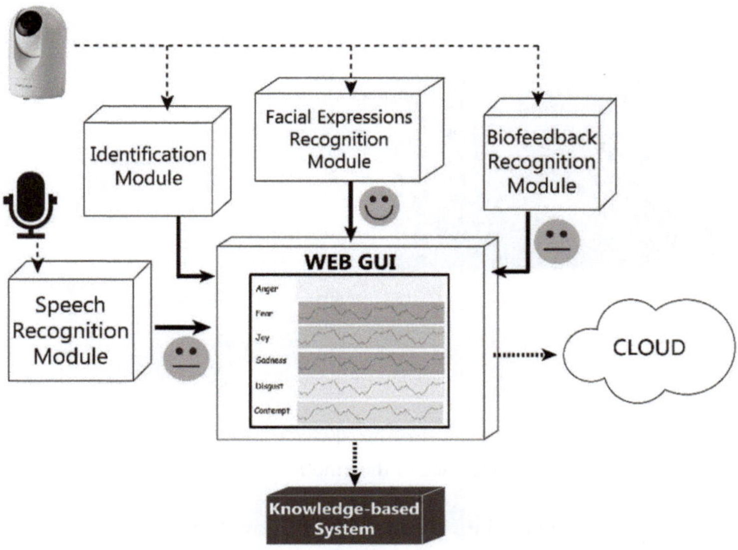

Fig. 2. The Architecture of the proposed Real Time Emotional recognition platform

Every time the Smart Engine receives data in input, coming from the emotional recognition platform (e.g., a specific emotional curve in a specific touchpoint), it takes a decision based on the corresponding Action Rule and activates the proper service and product reactions (e.g., providing personalized offers for a specific customer, changing the music genre in the shop, etc.).

At the same time, all input data are stored in a Database in order to enable statistics elaborations. Based on the resulting statistical data, the DSS tool, provide to the CX manager some suggestions on possible actions to improve planning of a CX Strategy, according to pre-defined objectives and constraints.

4.1 The Emotional Recognition and Analytics Module

The proposed tool is composed by four modules (Fig. 2). The first module provides person identification whenever he/she is detected in the proximity of a Touchpoint. The other three modules allow to acquire and analyze emotional information. Each of them is design to work as a standalone tool, so that the functionality of system is not compromised when the others are missing. They are as follows: Facial expression recognition, Speech recognition and the Biofeedback analysis modules.

The facial expression recognition module makes use of IP Wi-Fi full-HD cameras equipped with PTZ technology with autofocus. Each camera is installed in correspondence of every Touchpoint and continuously sends the video streams to the central server, which processes every video frame and returns the measure of the customer's emotions. This module embeds the Affectiva opensource engine Affdex [22], that provides in output a percentage value associated to the intensity of the main Ekman's emotions (i.e., Joy, Sadness, Anger, Fear, Contempt, Disgust and Surprise). Moreover, it provides

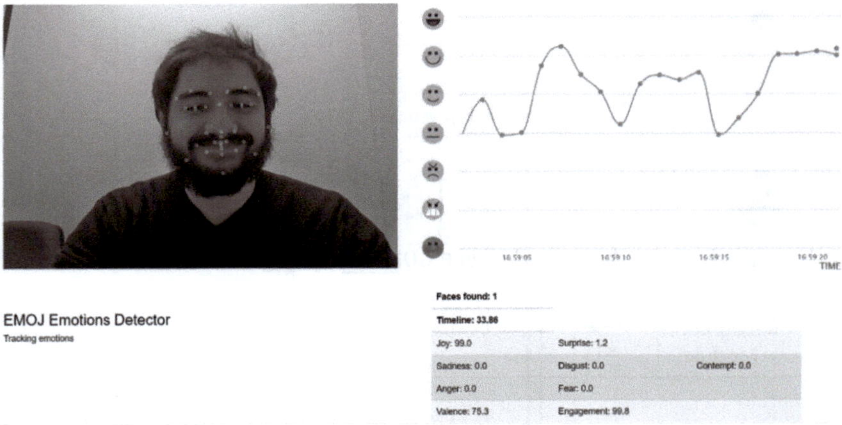

Fig. 3. The user interface of the emotional recognition module

measures for the Engagement (i.e., the measure of how the subject is "engaged") and the Valence, which gives a measure of positivity and negativity of the experience. The Speech recognition module refers to speech samples collected during organized surveys, or recorded from microphones installed in every Touchpoint. Also in this case, our software will be integrated with an already existing emotion recognition engine. At the time the research is focused on the evaluation of the most reliable algorithms to process voice parameters.

Several tools can be used depending on the speech analysis approach we want to adopt. For example, it is possible to use Google APIto convert the human voice in written text, and the IBM Watson software, for the text emotional analysis. Otherwise, we can adopt the AudioProfiling tool to directly extract emotions from the voice features (i.e., Loudness, Articulation, Time, Rhythm, Melody and Timbre). The third module allows the biometric data analysis through the acquisition of heartbeat and/or breath rate. Such bio-information are usually monitored by using intrusive sensors (e.g., ECG). However, VPGLIB (ex QPULSECAPTURE) is used to monitor such parameters in a non-intrusive way. The application is an OpenCV extension library that uses digital image processing to extract the blood pulse rate and provides an estimation of breath frequency from the video of the human face. In this way it is possible to acquire the breath rate and heartbeat of the person through the same camera used for facial recognition, with an absolute error in most cases less than 5 bpm. The next step is to trace these measurements to the emotional percentage values (Joy, Anger etc.). In fact, it has been demonstrated that exists a correlation between these measurements and the emotional state [17]. To this purpose, the APIs available by SensauraTech is adopted (Fig. 3).

To ensure the customer identification in each touchpoint, the Identification Module implements a face recognition engine that uses a database of previously stored images (e.g., such images can be collected during the customer registration required for loyalty card).

In this way, the customer is identified every time that he/she passes in from of a camera. Face Recognition APIs, from Lambda Lab allow to obtain this purpose.

A web GUI displays the data provided in output by emotional recognition platform. Such interface provides a representation of the customers emotional curve as a function of the Time and of the Valence values, measured on a scale that goes from -100 to 100. Moreover, it displays the percentages related to the primary emotions. Real time data related to each touchpoint can be plotted for one or more customers. In this last case, average values are provided.

The analytics module is based on the information provided by the previously described system and is a cloud based infrastructure previously designed for intelligent retail environments [22, 23] and used also in this project. The tool aims to analyze big data coming from massive customer emotions mining along with the customer journey in a pervasive computing scenario. The analytics module architecture describes the policy used, from the beginning of the project. The system main aspects are the data and the cloud.:

The Data are sent, in real time, to server by string or JSON form. Strings are sent in a queue URL using HTTPSv protocol. HTTPS (also called HTTP over TLS, HTTP over SSL, and HTTP Secure) is a protocol for secure communication over a computer network which is widely used on the Internet. HTTPS consists of communication over Hypertext Transfer Protocol (HTTP) within a connection encrypted by Transport Layer Security or its predecessor, Secure Sockets Layer. The main motivation for HTTPS is authentication of the visited website and protection of the privacy and integrity of the exchanged data.

In its popular deployment on the internet, HTTPS provides authentication of the website and associated web server with which one is communicating, which protects against man-in-the-middle attacks. Additionally, it provides bidirectional encryption of communications between a client and server, which protects against eavesdropping and tampering with and/or forging the contents of the communication. HTTPS is especially important to avoid anyone on the same local network can packet sniff and discover sensitive information.

In the project Amazon Web Services (AWS) cloud service is used. AWS, is a collection of cloud computing services that make up the on-demand computing platform offered by Amazon.com. Cloud computing exhibits the following key characteristics:

- Agility. It improves with users' ability to re-provision technological infrastructure resources.
- Cost reductions claimed by cloud providers. A public-cloud delivery model converts capital expenditure to operational expenditure. This purportedly lowers barriers to entry, as infrastructure is typically provided by a third party and need not be purchased for one-time or infrequent intensive computing tasks. Pricing on a utility computing basis is fine-grained, with usage-based options and fewer IT skills are required for implementation (in-house).
- Device and location independence that enable users to access systems using a web browser regardless of their location or what device they use (e.g., PC, mobile phone). As infrastructure is off-site (typically provided by a third-party) and accessed via the Internet, users can connect from anywhere.
- Maintenance of cloud computing applications that is easier, because it does not need to be installed on each user's computer and can be accessed from different places.

- Multitenancy that enables sharing of resources and costs across a large pool of users, increases of peak-load capacity (users do need not to be engineers), utilization and efficiency improvements.
- Productivity that may be increased when multiple users can work on the same data simultaneously, rather than waiting for it to be saved and emailed. Time may be saved as information does not need to be re-entered when fields are matched, nor do users need to install application software upgrades to their computer.
- Reliability improving with the use of multiple redundant sites, which makes well-designed cloud computing suitable for business continuity and disaster recovery.
- Scalability and elasticity via dynamic ("on-demand") provisioning of resources on a fine-grained, self-service basis in near real-time (Note, the VM startup time varies by VM type, location, OS and cloud providers), without users having to engineer for peak loads. This gives the ability to scale up when the usage need increases or down if resources are not being used.
- Security that is improved due to centralization of data and resources, etc., but sometimes there can be a loss of control over certain sensitive data, and the lack of security for stored kernels. However, the complexity of security is greatly increased when data is distributed over a wider area or over a greater number of devices, as well as in multi-tenant systems shared by unrelated users. In addition, user access to security audit logs may be difficult or impossible.

5 Conclusion

The present paper introduced an approach, based on a customer-centered process to support the achievement of a completely satisfying customer experience in a retail context. Such approach aims to support the definition of requirements and drive the development of every clue (i.e., product/service) which characterizes the store in a comprehensively way. A prototypal Knowledge-based system to analyze the emotions experienced by every customer in every touchpoint is here described. It implements Machine Learning algorithms and Ontologies.

In the context of retail, such system introduces several innovations:

- Monitoring of real customer experience in an automatic way along all the touchpoints: the system implements an innovate Real-time Emotional Recognition Platform able to monitor customers in a non-intrusive way. Consequently, the system will be able to provide to the company an enormous amount of data about consumers (including spontaneous emotions) that so far has never been possible to collect with traditional ethnographic techniques. In particular, the use of this technology will allows to have a more elaborate customer profile than that obtainable from simple personal data or from surveys, and will make possible to propose customizable offers.
- Automatic management of the shop environment based on machine learning: for the first time an automation system, responsive to customer emotions, is introduces in a retail context.
- Decision Support System based on customers' emotions: traditional DSS lack to consider the impact of management decisions on customer's emotions.

The proposed Real-time Emotional Recognition and Analytics Platform, compared to the most common tools and methods applied for emotional recognition and analysis, presents the following advantages:

- Not invasive solution that integrate several technologies: the presented tool will allow monitoring the emotive status of customers without being aware of it (although, for privacy issues, they should be informed that they are monitoring). Moreover, it exploits several tools and method of emotional recognition; it will be able to provide data that are more reliable that any other existing system.
- Totally modular architecture: each technology used for emotional recognition constitute an independent module. In this way, each module can work as a standalone tool, so that the functionality of system is not compromised when the others are missing.
- Web-based user-interface: easily and remotely accessible (protected by security protocols). In this way, the user can access data in a cloud-based environment.
- Emotion recognition technology inserted in a Customer Experience context, a totally innovative element

The introduction of this system in retail environments can result in important benefits. However, its implementation in practical context will require a lot of other research. The platform for the recognition of emotions still requires testing to verify its effectiveness in the various possible operating conditions (e.g., changing light conditions, noise, various number of customers present in the store). It will also be necessary to define a model for the analysis of data from the various tools and test it through appropriate training set. Finally, several future studies will be needed to define the KB implemented by the proposed knowledge-based system and define the solutions that must be adopted for the implementation of the Smart Engine.

References

1. Zomerdijk, L.G., Voss, C.A.: Service design for experience centric services. J. Serv. Res. **13**(1), 67–82 (2010)
2. Chen-Yu, H.J., Kincade, D.H.: Effects of product image at three stages of the consumer decision process for apparel products: Alternative evaluation, purchase and post-purchase. J. Fashion Mark. Manag. Int. J. **5**(1), 29–43 (2001)
3. Giraldi, L., Mengoni, M., Bevilacqua, M.: How to enhance customer experience in retail: investigations through a case study. In: Transdisciplinary Engineering: Crossing Boundaries: Proceedings of the 23rd ISPE Inc. International Conference on Transdisciplinary Engineering 3–7 October, vol. 4 (2016)
4. Berry, L.L., Carbone, L.P., Haeckel, S.H.: Managing the total customer experience. MIT Sloan Manag. Rev. **43**(3), 85–90 (2002)
5. Liciotti, D., Contigiani, M., Frontoni, E., Mancini, A., Zingaretti, P., Placidi, V.: Shopper analytics: a customer activity recognition system using a distributed RGB-D camera network. In: Distante, C., Battiato, S., Cavallaro, A. (eds.) VAAM 2014. LNCS, vol. 8811, pp. 146–157. Springer, Cham (2014). doi:10.1007/978-3-319-12811-5_11
6. Grewal, D., Levy, M., Kumar, V.: Customer experience management in retailing: an organizing framework. J. Retail. **85**(1), 1–14 (2009)

7. Ofir, C., Simonson, I.: The effect of stating expectations on customer satisfaction and shopping experience. J. Mark. Res. **44**(1), 164–174 (2007)
8. Wallace, D.W., Giese, J.L., Johnson, J.L.: Customer retailer loyalty in the context of multiple channel strategies. J. Retail. **80**(4), 249–263 (2004)
9. Sturari, M., Liciotti, D., Pierdicca, R., Frontoni, E., Mancini, A., Contigiani, M., Zingaretti, P.: Robust and affordable retail customer profiling by vision and radio beacon sensor fusion. Pattern Recogn. Lett. **81**, 30–40 (2016)
10. Meyer, C., Schwager, A.: Understanding customer experience. Harvard Bus. Rev. **85**(2), 117–126 (2007)
11. Teixeira, J., Patrício, L., Nunes, N.J., Nóbrega, L., Fisk, R.P., Constantine, L.: Customer experience modeling: from customer experience to service design. J. Serv. Manag. **23**(3), 362–376 (2012)
12. Maguire, M.: Methods to support human-centred design. Int. J. Hum Comput Stud. **55**(4), 587–634 (2001)
13. Frow, P., Payne, A.: Towards the 'perfect' customer experience. J. Brand Manag. **15**(2), 89–101 (2007)
14. Verhoef, P.C., Lemon, K.N., Parasuraman, A., Roggeveen, A., Tsiros, M., Schlesinger, L.A.: Customer experience creation: determinants, dynamics and management strategies. J. Retail. **85**(1), 31–41 (2009)
15. Bailenson, N.J., Pontikakis E.D., Mauss, I.B., Gross, J.J., Jabon, E., Hutcherson, C.a.C., Nass, C., John, O.: Real-time classification of evoked emotions using facial feature tracking and physiological responses. Int. J. Hum. Comput. Stud. **66**(5), 303–317 (2008)
16. Ververidis, D., Kotropoulos, C.: Emotional speech recognition: resources, features, and methods. Speech Commun. **48**(9), 1162–1181 (2006)
17. Quintana, D.S., Guastella, A.J., Outhred, T., Hickie, I.B., Kemp, A.H.: Heart rate variability is associated with emotion recognition: direct evidence for a relationship between the autonomic nervous system and social cognition. Int. J. Psychophysiol. **86**(2), 168–172 (2012)
18. Chen, M., Zhang, Y., Li, Y.: EMC: emotion-aware mobile cloud computing. IEEE Network **29**(2), 32–38 (2015)
19. Gandomi, A., Murtaza, H.: Beyond the hype: Big Data concepts, methods, and analytics. Int. J. Inf. Manage. **35**(2), 137–144 (2015)
20. Gailly, F., Geerts, G.L.: Ontology-driven business rule specification. J. Inform. Syst. **27**(1), 79–104 (2013)
21. Eiter, T., Ianni, G., Polleres, A., Schindlauer, R., Tompits, H.: Reasoning with rules and ontologies. In: Barahona, P., Bry, F., Franconi, E., Henze, N., Sattler, U. (eds.) Reasoning Web 2006. LNCS, vol. 4126, pp. 93–127. Springer, Heidelberg (2006). doi: 10.1007/11837787_4
22. Frontoni, E., Raspa, P., Mancini, A., Zingaretti, P., Placidi, V.: Customers' activity recognition in intelligent retail environments. In: Petrosino, A., Maddalena, L., Pala, P. (eds.) ICIAP 2013. LNCS, vol. 8158, pp. 509–516. Springer, Heidelberg (2013). doi: 10.1007/978-3-642-41190-8_55
23. Frontoni, E., Mancini, A., Zingaretti, P., Placidi, V.: Information management for intelligent retail environment: the shelf detector system. Information **5**(2), 255–271 (2014)

Self-learning Production Control Using Algorithms of Artificial Intelligence

Ben Luetkehoff(✉), Matthias Blum, and Moritz Schroeter

Production Management, FIR at RWTH Aachen University,
Campus-Boulevard 55, 52074 Aachen, Germany
{lh,bl,sch}@fir.rwth-aachen.de

Abstract. Manufacturing companies are facing an increasingly turbulent market – a market defined by products growing in complexity and shrinking product life cycles. This leads to a boost in planning complexity accompanied by higher error sensitivity. In practice, IT systems and sensors integrated into the shop floor in the context of Industry 4.0 are used to deal with these challenges. However, while existing research provides solutions in the field of pattern recognition or recommended actions, a combination of the two approaches is neglected. This leads to an overwhelming amount of data without contributing to an improvement of processes. To address this problem, this study presents a new platform-based concept to collect and analyze the high-resolution data with the use of self-learning algorithms. Herby, patterns can be identified and reproduced, allowing an exact prediction of the future system behavior. Artificial intelligence maximizes the automation of the reduction and compensation of disruptive factors.

Keywords: Production control · Self-learning algorithms · Data analytics

1 Introduction

Driven by the Internet of Things and countless initiatives in the context of Industry 4.0, the shop floor level is steeped by IT. This poses the question as to which extent these approaches can be used to reduce and control the increasing production complexity. The collection of real-time data and its interpretation with data analytics are supposed to enable improved planning decisions. The research project "Intelligent Production Control" (iProd) takes exactly this point into account: technologically and theoretically the progress towards completion, machine condition and the current flow of material can be captured by installing sensor systems and identification technology. The difficulty lies in, on the one hand, the connection of heterogeneous data to form an overall picture to generate recommended actions [1, 2]. On the other hand, the reaction speed of implemented planning and control solutions is limited by the detection and evaluation of deviations by the employee [3]. Moreover, current algorithms are based on inflexible heuristic optimizations and static analyses. Even though, simulation can be based on this kind of information, the reality is still far away from a self-learning production control that, to a certain degree, compensates deviations and disturbances independently [4, 5].

L.M. Camarinha-Matos et al. (Eds.): PRO-VE 2017, IFIP AICT 506, pp. 299–306, 2017.
DOI: 10.1007/978-3-319-65151-4_28

Therefore, the goal of this project is the application of existing technologies, architectures and algorithms from the field of artificial intelligence to the problems of production, so that the open loop production control is expanded to an advanced closed loop production control.

Before the project is described in detail, the motivation of this paper is outlined and a short outline of the necessary basics and state of the art is given. Additionally, the requirements for an intelligent closed loop production control are presented. Afterwards, the concept itself is introduced and discussed before a conclusion is given and necessary further research is outline.

2 Motivation

Data analytics is a scientific process of mathematical-logical transformation of data to improve decision making [6]. Four stages of the decision-making process exist: descriptive, diagnostic, predictive and prescriptive analytics. The decision making process assisted by data analytics can be described as a four-stage model. The first stage is called descriptive analytics and deals with the question "What happened?". This stage aims at analyzing large amounts of data in order to find out what happened in the past. The next stage, called diagnostic analytics, deals with the question "Why did it happen?" by analyzing interactions in the first stage. The third and fourth stage also allow proactive optimization. Predictive analytics focusses on the question "What will happen?" and predicts future behavior by applying methods of pattern recognition as well as the use of statistics. Prescriptive analytics focusses on the question "What should I do?". The assistance of data analytics either serves as a support mechanism for the decision process or implements decisions autonomously. [7]

3 State of the Art

In this chapter, the basic principles deviation management, information modelling, Artificial Intelligence, machine learning and their application in production planning and control are discussed.

A multitude of software solutions has been developed in the past in order to manage the dynamics of production planning and control with the use of IT. In context of production control, especially Enterprise Resource Planning and Manufacturing Execution Systems have been used for detailed production planning and control [8]. Approaches that focus on closed loop production, i.e. an additional feedback loop to regular open loop control, can be found in several dissertations [4, 9, 10]. However, these are not based on artificially intelligent methods but instead on procedures of discrete-event simulation. These require exact models of influencing variables, which come along with manual effort. Even the automatic generation of models has only been theoretically discussed within this field [11].

Intelligent, self-learning systems are aware of their current performance. They are therefore able to evaluate it in comparison to the ideal performance, enabling them to develop strategies to improve the solution. Machine learning (ML) methods enable intelligent systems to complete tasks in unexpected situations [12]. Learning the behavior strategies of a technical system with the use of ML has already been used for many purely virtual scenarios and for a few scenarios in robotics. The best-known examples for this come from the technology company Google, e.g. the latest application example for learning gripping operations [13]. Recently, data-driven ML has become progressively more important in the context of Industry 4.0. However, significant research results have not yet been presented.

Research for the application of Artificial Intelligence in the context of Production Planning and Control is nothing new. In the 90ies, the application of artificial neuronal networks in business has already been researched by Schneider, who identified different adequate network types and parameters [14]. Huang analyzed the suitability and weaknesses of existing approaches for the application of neuronal networks in production systems [15]. In the following years, approaches to build groups for flexible manufacturing systems were developed [16] for capacity planning and sequencing. Reddy et al. used artificial neuronal networks for pattern recognition on the production process level [17]. Scholz-Reiter et al. introduced a system with cascaded control loops for a neuronal closed loop production control. Implicit knowledge is integrated into the network with the help of case based reasoning. The training and selection of the suitable artificial neuronal network remains a task for experts [18]. Hamann developed a control concept for production systems that is based on "Computational Intelligence". Neuronal networks control the stock of work systems by determining the optimal target stock heuristically. Next, the quality of the model is shown with theoretical observations and practical examples. The quality can be increased continuously by training the neuronal networks with new examples [4]. This approach is suited mainly for bottlenecks due to the high implementation complexity and does not represent a universal concept for the entire production control. Di Orio et al. discuss a paradigm called Self-Learning Production System (SLPS) to ensure the evolvability of industrial systems over time. This is achieved with context-awareness and data mining techniques in order to ensure the adaption of a system to changing processes. The discussed approach focusses on the systemization of technical and theoretical developments to provide a baseline for the SLPS solution [19].

The State of the Art shows that existing approaches for the rapid elimination of disturbances and deviations often focus solely on reproducing interdependencies in simulation models or do not offer the feedback of real-time data. The implementation and adaption of these models is despite extensive research effort in the context of automated model generation linked to manual input [11, 20]. In the framework of simulation models, forecasts can be calculated for different scenarios, the exact reproduction of real interdependencies in the form of these scenarios is linked to high manual effort. Methods of pattern recognition allow the formalization of knowledge. Because of increasing computing capacities, promising approaches can be found in the field of artificial intelligence – especially in ML. The high requirements for reliable and robust processes as well as an efficient use of resources complicate the application of complex trial and error methods parallel to the ongoing production. Extended data driven solutions are needed that can be applied purposefully and allow efficient learning of new tasks. Here, a combination of ML and model driven approaches seems imaginable in order to achieve a broad field of application [21].

4 Requirements

The research project has five requirements in order to achieve an intelligent closed loop production control: (1) a real-time capability, (2) a pattern recognition, (3) an analysis of deviations, (4) a derivation of response strategies and (5) a feedback.

Real-time representation of data is required and the essential element for handling with deviations. Decisions are based on data and therefore the provision is one of the main challenges. The earlier data are available and presented in a useful way the better the response time of the system. Furthermore, the real-time representation serves to a better overview of the production processes. With the help of data, the production is presented in a transparent manner, which leads to a better process understanding and can help to stabilize the production processes.

Another condition is the pattern recognition. Machine learning methods evaluate a database to detect anomalies. A basic prerequisite for machine learning methods is the reliability and real time availability of data. Through this, machine-learning methods are able to discover patterns early and just in time. Pattern recognition support the analysis of error causes and error sequences. This draws on specifically designed algorithms. If there is a deviation in the production process, the deviation needs to be captured completely.

Afterwards the deviation has to be analyzed, which is the next main requirement of the system. It is very important to understand the causes and effects of the deviation. The analysis is the fundament of the classification process, in which deviations allocated to clusters.

The next step is to create a link between a type of deviation and a response strategy. For this allocation, different response strategies have to be defined. According to this, response strategies are another requirement for a working system. A distinction is made between automated, semi-automated and manual response strategies. One aspect of a response strategy is the development of a morphology with characteristic attributes and properties captured by sensors and IT. In order to prioritize the reaction strategies, the aspect of time needs to be regarded as well.

5 iProd – A Concept for Data Driven Closed-Loop Production Control

The research project iProd intends to develop a robust and intelligent closed loop production control that continuously reacts to deviations within the production system by target-performance comparison. It configures the parameters of the production order accordingly, based on model-based forecast scenarios. With a basis of real-time, high-resolution data from the direct production environment, the optimization model applies algorithms of artificial intelligence in order to deduce effective recommended actions. These recommendations are supposed to contain (partly) autonomous decisions, made by a pattern recognition system. The system analyses the observations, assesses them with reaction strategies and links them to a course of action. A feedback into the control loop rates the result of the measures. The research project reproduces the application of a closed loop production control very precisely and describes one of the relevant problems of manufacturing companies – the simple control and laying-up of the production with regard to a turbulent environment. All of the addressed processes are collected on a data platform. The concept is visualized in the following Fig. 1.

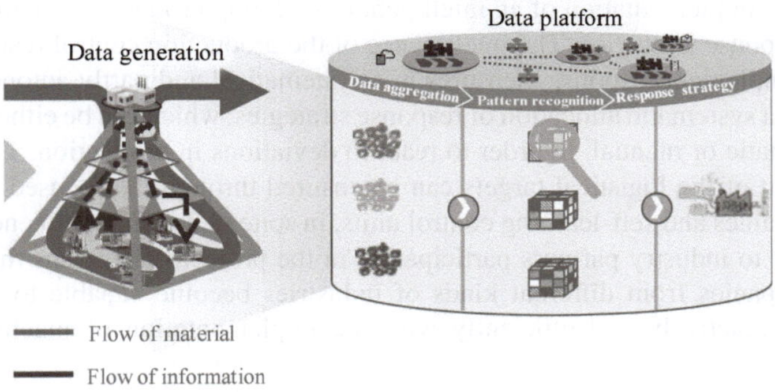

Fig. 1. The concept of the research project

The result is an increased capacity of the personnel that allows the search, analysis and removal of causes. This leads to a sustainable stabilization of the entire production and relieves employees by reducing the amount of short time, highly critical decisions. A positive impact on cycle times and work in progress affect delivery dates positively. The degree of capacity utilization – for employees and machines – is harmonized and sudden surge in workload can be averted. Thus, the capacity can be planned better without risking the flexibility of the company.

The proposed concept is based on four elements: (A) the collection and aggregation of real-time data, (B) the ability to recognize patterns with self-learning algorithms, (C) the deduction of response strategies and (D) the implementation of a data platform for production control.

(A) Real-time feedback data: The basis for the concept is the identification and virtual representation of real-time data along the material flow. The analysis and evaluation of structured and unstructured real-time data enables an optimization of complex production systems. The digital shadow of the production is the basis for a databased predictability of future situations within a real system and for the realization of potentials for innovation and optimization [22].

The overarching goal of iProd covers the development and validation of an Industry 4.0 suitable solution concept, which exploits technical possibilities in digitalization. Therefore, the digital image of a production forms the basis for a holistic analysis an evaluation of the automatized captured data.

(B) Pattern recognition: The collected data in form of a digital shadow allows recognizing patterns that would otherwise stay hidden. This is achieved by descriptive, predictive or prescriptive analysis of the data. Different methods can be applied for data analytics. For example, there classical data mining and machine learning tools that can be used on structured data and other tools that can be used for unstructured data [23]. In this case, there is only structured data from the production environment. Classical tools for the analysis of structured data are, for example, Online Analytical Processing (OLAP), querying and reporting [24] and will mainly be used in this project. Based on patterns from the production system, the project enables the accurate forecast of the future system behavior in consideration of influencing disruptive factors. This is the basis for the implementation of an intelligent closed loop production control.

(C) Response strategies: The intelligence of the production control results from the ability to implement response measures in a systematical and partly autonomous way. The goal is a systematic allocation of response strategies, which can be either automatic, semi-automatic or manual, in order to react to deviations in production. This way, the achievement of the logistical targets can be ensured through the focused feedback of measured values and self-learning control units, in spite of dynamic influencing factors. Transferred to industry partners participating in the project, this means that manufacturing companies from different kinds of industries become capable to design their production reactively and efficiently with the implementation of machine learning methods.

(D) Data platform: The production control is the fundamental condition for capturing and comparing the relevant control variables with the planning guidelines (reference variables) continuously and in real-time. For the approximation of the control variable, the action alternatives are rated in the data platform of iProd. For the determination of the regulating variables, for example work- and machine usage plans, the optimal configuration can be defined. This way, adequate measures for the parameterization of the order-generation, the order-authorization, the sequencing and the capacity-coordination of the production can be derived.

In summary, iProd intends the substitution of classical control logic, in which for example set-up times, process times and transition times are based on average values or even on subjective evaluation. Instead of this, iProd allows the forecast of future disruptive factors and resulting deviations besides the identification of current deviations, to fix the control difference in a proactive way by an optimized parameter configuration.

6 Conclusion and Further Research

Manufacturing companies are facing an increasingly turbulent market defined by products growing in complexity and shrinking product life cycles. This leads to an increase in planning complexity and higher error sensitivity. In practice, IT systems and sensors integrated into the shop floor in the context of Industry 4.0 are used to deal with such challenges. However, while existing research provides solutions in the field of pattern recognition or recommended actions, a combination of the two approaches is neglected. This leads to an overwhelming amount of data without contributing to an improvement of processes. Therefore, this paper presents a new platform-based concept that enables an increased logistical capability. This is achieved by collecting and analyzing high-resolution data with the use of self-learning algorithms. Thereby, patterns can be identified and reproduced, allowing an exact prediction of the future system behavior influenced by interfering factors. The use of artificial intelligence maximizes the automation of the reduction and compensation of the identified disruptive factors.

However, the presented paper also has a few shortcomings. First, further research is needed to enable and improve the proposed concept. It is necessary to elaborate the discussed approach to solve the discussed problem of production control. Moreover, the concept still only focusses on the manufacturing industry while other industries are neglected. Furthermore, use cases need to be found for a possible application and validation of the proposed concept. In addition, it is important to improve the man-machine interaction, e.g. visualization, to enable a broad dissemination of the concept.

References

1. Kropp, S.K.: Entwicklung eines Ereignismodells als Grundlage der Produktionsregelung, 1st edn. Schriftenreihe Rationalisierung, vol. 137. Apprimus, Aachen (2016)
2. Schuh, G., Blum, M.: Design of a data structure for the order processing as a basis for data analytics methods. In: Portland International Conference on Management of Engineering and Technology (PICMET), pp. 2164–2169, Honolulu (2016)
3. Meier, C.: Echtzeitfähige Produktionsplanung und -regelung in der Auftragsabwicklung des Maschinen- und Anlagenbaus, 1st edn. Edition Wissenschaft, vol. 117. Apprimus, Aachen (2013)
4. Hamann, T.: Lernfähige intelligente Produktionsregelung. Informationstechnische Systeme und Organisation von Produktion und Logistik, vol. 7. GITO, Heidelberg (2008)
5. Hauptvogel, A.: Bewertung und Gestaltung von cyber-physischer Feinplanung, 1st edn. Produktionssystematik, vol. 6. Apprimus Verlag, Aachen (2015)
6. Knabke, T., Olbrich, S., Lehner, W., Piller, G. (eds.): Towards agile BI: applying in-memory technology to data warehouse architectures (2011)
7. Stich, V., Hering, N.: Daten und Software als entscheidender Wettbewerbsfaktor. Industrie 4.0 Magazin: Zeitschrift für integrierte Produktionsprozesse, pp. 8–13 (2015)
8. Kletti, J., Schumacher, J.: Die perfekte Produktion. Manufacturing Excellence durch Short Interval Technology (SIT), 2nd edn. Springer, Heidelberg (2014)
9. Simon, D.: Fertigungsregelung durch zielgrößenorientierte Planung und logistisches Störungsmanagement. iwb Forschungsberichte, vol. 85. Springer, Heidelberg (1995)
10. Zetlmayer, H.: Verfahren zur simulationsgestützten Produktionsregelung in der Einzel- und Kleinserienproduktion. iwb Forschungsberichte, Bd. vol. 74. Springer, Berlin, New York (1994)
11. Selke, C.: Entwicklung von Methoden zur automatischen Simulationsmodellgenerierung, vol. 193. Utz, München (2005)
12. Giese, H., Burmester, S., Klein, F., Schilling, D., Tichy, M.: Multi-agent system design for safety-critical self-optimizing mechatronic systems with UML. In: Crocker, R. (ed.) Proceedings of the 18th Annual ACM SIGPLAN Conference on Object-oriented Programing, Systems, Languages, and Applications, pp. 21–23. n.n. (2003)
13. Levine, S., Pastor, P., Krizhevsky, A., Quillen, D.: Learning Hand-Eye Coordination for Robotic Grasping with Deep Learning and Large-Scale Data Collection (2016), http://arxiv.org/pdf/1603.02199

14. Schneider, B.: Neuronale Netze für betriebliche Anwendungen: Anwendungspotentiale und existierende Systeme. Universität Münster (1993)
15. Huang, S.H., Hong-Chao Zhang: artificial neural networks in manufacturing. Concepts, applications, and perspectives. IEEE Trans. Compon. Packag. Manuf. Technol. Part A, 212–228 (1994)
16. Kulkarni, U.R., Kiang, M.Y.: Dynamic grouping of parts in flexible manufacturing systems — a self-organizing neural networks approach. Eur. J. Oper. Res., 192–212 (1995)
17. Reddy, D.C., Ghosh, K., Vardhan, V.A.: Identification and interpretation of manufacturing process patterns through neural networks. Math. Comput. Model., 15–36 (1998)
18. Scholz-Reiter, B., Hamann, T., Gronau, N., Bogen, J.: Fallbasierte neuronale Produktionsregelung: Nutzung des Case-Based Reasoning zur Produktionsregelung mit neuronalen Netzen. wt - Werkstattstechnik Online, pp. 293–298 (2005)
19. Di Orio, G., Cândido, G., Barata, J.: Self-Learning production systems: a new production paradigm. In: Sustainable Design and Manufacturing, Part 2, pp. 887–898 (2014)
20. Bergmann, S., Straßburger, S., Schulze, T.: Automatische Generierung adaptiver Modelle zur Simulation von Produktionssystemen. TU Ilmenau Universitätsbibliothek, Ilmenau (2014)
21. Schaal, S., Peters, J., Nakanishi, J., Ijspeert, A.: Learning movement primitives. In: Dario, P., Chatila, R. (eds.) Robotics Research. The Eleventh International Symposium. STAR, vol. 15, pp. 561–572. Springer, Heidelberg (2005). doi:10.1007/11008941_60
22. Schuh, G., Blum, M., Reschke, J., Birkmeier, M.: Der Digitale Schatten in der Auftragsabwicklung. ZWF, 48–51 (2016)
23. Gröger, C., Kassner, L., Hoos, E., Königsberger, J., Kiefer, C., Silcher, S., Mitschang, B.: The Data-driven Factory. In: ICEIS 2016, pp. 40–54 (2016)
24. Kassner, L., Gröger, C., Mitschang, B., Westkämper, E.: Product life cycle analytics – next generation data analytics on structured and unstructured data. In: Procedia CIRP, pp. 35–40 (2015)

Business Modelling for Smart Continual Commissioning in ESCO Set-Ups

Karsten Menzel(✉) and Andriy Hryshchenko

School of Engineering, University College Cork, Western Gateway Building, Western Road, Cork T12 XF62, Ireland
k.menzel@ucc.ie

Abstract. The availability of sensors, smart meters, and so called 'intelligent devices' (IoT) enables owners and tenants to better understand and flexibly adjust the status of buildings and their systems according to their needs. However, it also requires a more intense and detailed knowledge about how to exploit, analyse and manage 'big data' compiled from these devices. Building operators, facility managers and energy suppliers are expected to collaborate and to share this data aiming to deliver more holistic, comprehensive services to clients (i.e. owners and tenants of buildings). This paper discusses how so called ESCO-business models (energy service companies) and CC-business models (continuous commissioning) can be integrated through sharing of big data and collaboration of major stakeholders involved in building operation, energy supply and engineering consultancy. It explains how building owners will benefit from the availability of such comprehensive, collaborative services.

Keywords: Big data · Collaboration · Continual commissioning · Energy service company · Facility management

1 Introduction

ESCOs emerged in the United States in the 1970s, after the oil crisis. The concept then gradually spread to Europe and Japan where the ESCO industry has successfully developed. Today, the ESCO concept has spread with varying success to most industrialised and developing countries worldwide. [1] There are a variety of descriptions of what an ESCO is. The EU Energy Service Directive defines an ESCO as "*a natural or legal person that delivers energy services and/or other energy efficiency improvement measures in a user's facility or premises, and accepts some degree of financial risk in doing so. The payment for the services delivered is based (either wholly or in part) on the achievement of energy efficiency improvements and on the meeting of the other agreed upon performance criteria*" [2].

The terms ESCO and Energy Performance Contracting (EPC) [3] were not widespread in Ireland, but instead an ESCO-type work is often referred to as Contract Energy Management (CEM). As of 2009, there were only 15 companies identified as energy service providers [4]. More recent reports [5] indicate that the potential market size for ESCOs in Ireland could be as high as €110 million per year by 2020.

L.M. Camarinha-Matos et al. (Eds.): PRO-VE 2017, IFIP AICT 506, pp. 307–319, 2017.
DOI: 10.1007/978-3-319-65151-4_29

The ESCO market in Ireland is mainly focussed on co-generation and supply-side projects in the service sector (e.g. hotels and leisure centres). A smaller section of the industry targets district heating and renewable energies. [6] Build Own Operate Transfer (BOOT) arrangements are the most commonly used contract type, these having no performance guarantees [4].

Continuous Commissioning (CC) is - according to a definition developed by the Energy Systems Laboratory (ESL) – "*… an ongoing process to resolve operating problems, improve comfort, and optimize energy use*". CC® is trademarked by ESL. CC® can be broken down in two phases, consisting of a total of seven steps (Table 1).

Table 1. Phases and steps of CC®

Phase 1	Phase 2
Visit the site to identify and quantify potential measures and savings	Implement Continuous Commissioning measures
Develop performance baselines for energy and comfort	Identify changes in operating procedures for the building staff. Document energy savings and comfort improvements in accordance with the International Performance Measurement and Verification Protocol (IPMVP)
Examine the building in detail to identify: * operating and comfort problems * component failures or * degradation, and causes of system inefficiency	Train the building staff Track/verify energy and comfort performance for at least one year in accordance with the IPMVP

Figure 1 overleaf summarises the 'integration challenge'. The traditional business model of FM-operators is presented on the top; i.e. specialist contractors operate single building services systems using their detailed expertise. Secondly, energy providers sell one or multiple forms of energy to owners and FM-providers (central part of figure).

Currently, the thermal comfort monitoring is either not or only in a very limited format executed (centre right).

The lower part of Fig. 1 represents the extended scope (and thus the extended risk) for ESCO providers or building owners, since energy transformation (e.g. from renewable co-generators) and energy distribution (e.g. across groups of buildings and CHP, storages, etc.) are pre-requisites for holistic energy provision and management.

The right part of Fig. 1 depicts the different 'real time' data sources and the stakeholders. 'Real-time' data sources can be better described as "time-series data" and may include: (i) information about the status of systems and components (log-files, e.g. valve on/off etc.), (ii) meter data (e.g. from smart meters), (iii) sensor data (e.g. room temperature), (iv) process documentation (e.g. from maintenance tickets).

These 'time-series data streams' are also called dynamic data or fact data. This data delivers "big data" to the FM and constructions sectors in the range of hundreds of million data sets per building. [7]

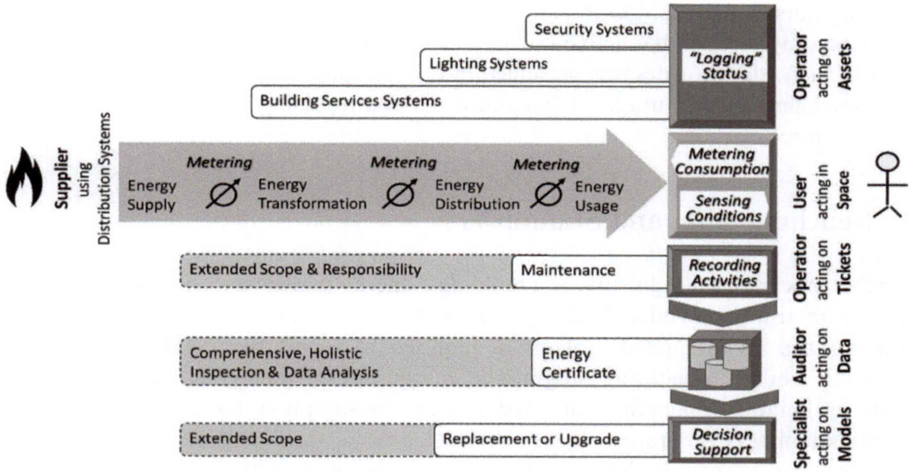

Fig. 1. The ESCO & CC® integration challenge

For data analysis purposes dynamic data can be combined with so called 'static data' (also called dimensional data) which can be compiled from (i) EMS (energy management systems), (ii) BAC (building automation and control systems), (iii) Documentations or computer models (e.g. BIM), and (iv) MMS (maintenance management systems) (see Fig. 2).

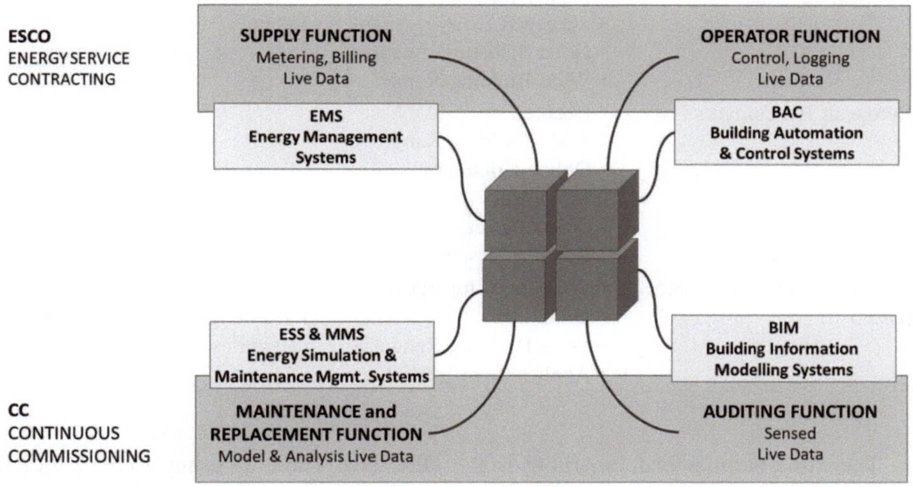

Fig. 2. Integration of dynamic, big data with static data

The extension of ESCO-models with up-to-date CC® business models can be achieved only through the active collaboration of all involved stakeholders. An overview of these stakeholders was presented in Fig. 1(right). Collaboration can be heavily supported through the usage of integrated, shared reporting and analysis tools (see Fig. 2 centre).

2 Benchmarking and Standards

Benchmarks are used to identify if a buildings' energy performance is poor, average or good with respect to other buildings of its type. An accurate energy model of the building and its integrated systems is required to assess the building energy use potential, while a monitoring programme is required for the systematic collection of plant or building operating data and energy consumption through the Continual Commissioning (CC) processes.

There are several building performance assessment methods which have been deployed to assess building environmental performance. Table 2 presents a comparison of selected international energy benchmarks in relation to their applicability in Ireland.

Table 2. International Benchmarks comparison.

Benchmarks	Pros	Cons
UK Benchmarks	• Detailed Information • Wide Building Range • Applicable to Ireland	• Not normalized for Ireland
USA Energy Star	• Highly Detailed • Surveyed Every 4 Years • Good Statistical Accuracy • Wide Building Range	• Not easy to normalize for Ireland
European Benchmarks	• Detailed • Wide Building Range • Online Continuous Monitoring • Public Access • Ranking System	
Display Energy Certificates (DEC)	• Normalized for Ireland by SEAI • Wide Building Range • Applicable to Ireland	• Information not as detailed • Buildings are grouped into categories

The most popular benchmarking is the DEC (see Table 2) using a conventional Energy Performance Indicator (EPI) expressing the energy usage per usable floor area [unit kWh/m^2]. [8] This is a robust and simple instrument for peer group benchmark. However, there are many variables which can skew the comparison, e.g. Climate (Degree Day Variation), Occupancy, Sample Size, Jurisdiction, Building Standards, Hours of Operation etc.

These issues must be factored into any comparison. Allowances can be made for those variables through different normalisation processes.

Furthermore, more comprehensive methods for performance benchmarking are required, which support the holistic evaluation of (i) energy use, (ii) user comfort, (iii) the integrated operation of building services systems, and (iv) the efficient usage of building spaces. An example for such a methodology has been developed in the EU-FP7 project CAMPUS 21 by researchers from industry and numerous academic partners [9].

3 Business Models

A Business Model (BM) describes the rationale of how an organization creates, delivers and captures value. [10] Business models have changed and adapted over time to suit market conditions. There have been various creators of business model frameworks, but one particularly stands out. Developed by A. Osterwalder, Yves Pigneur, Alan Smith, and 470 practitioners from 45 countries, this is one of the most used BM-frameworks [11, 12].

Osterwalder et al. [10] believes that a BM can best be described through nine basic building blocks showing the logic of how a company intends to make money. These nine blocks cover the four main areas of a business, such as: customer interface, product, infrastructure, and financial aspects. Each of these building blocks are related to other building blocks. The interdependency of these blocks is key to the success of the model. Figure 3 shows how the blocks are linked to each other.

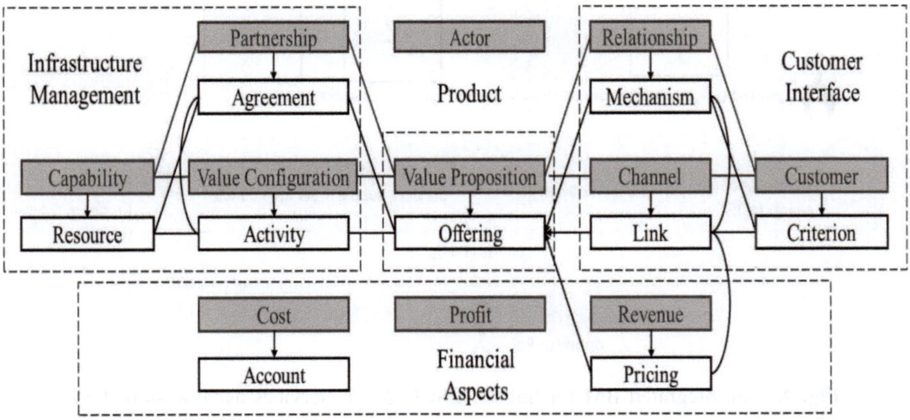

Fig. 3. Interdependency of 9 BM blocks (as per [10])

This business model canvas can be taken as a strategic management template for developing new or documenting existing business models for those providers offering Continual Commissioning services. It will also work as a visual representation describing ESCO's value proposition, infrastructure, customers, and finances for the selected case study to be discussed in subsequent sections.

4 BM Solutions for Integrated ESCO & CC®-Services Models

To profit from innovation, those companies offering CC service within an ESCO framework need to count not only on product innovation but also on business model design, understanding business design options as well as customer needs and technological trajectories. [13] In this chapter business models for ESCOs providing Continual Commissioning services will be examined against the above Key Elements.

Figure 4 clearly illustrates that integrated ESCO & CC-BM still benefit from the strong 1:1 customer relationship of FM-providers with users on a "location" (building) basis. However, it benefits from the availability of an additional "auditing and benchmarking" function (lower right). Big data and holistic data analysis are the "enablers" for this advanced services offer. The integration of big data (dynamic data) with the building expertise from specialist services (top right) allows the exploitation of the benefits from semantically enriched data, i.e. BIM models.

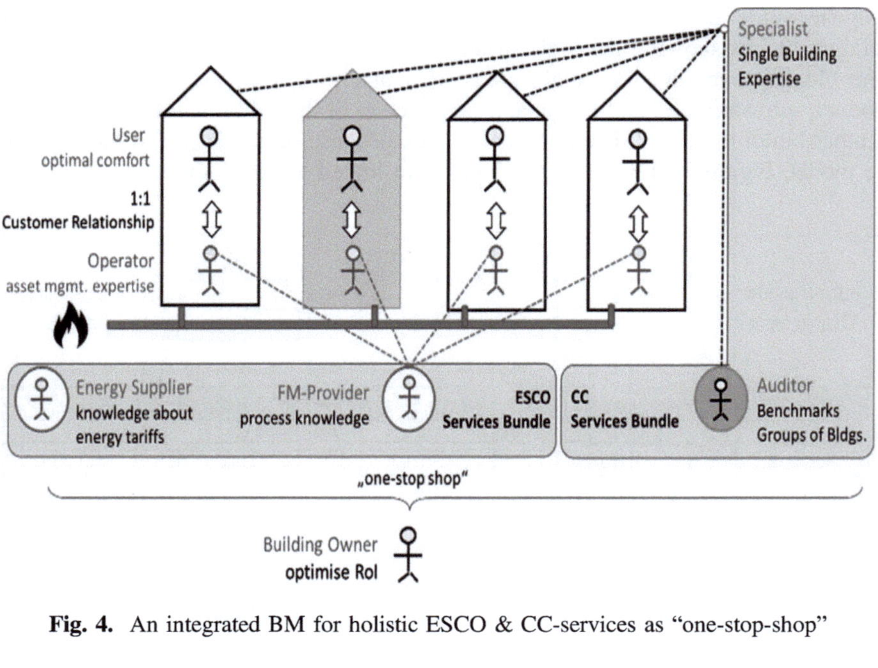

Fig. 4. An integrated BM for holistic ESCO & CC-services as "one-stop-shop"

In summary, CC-business services provide a substantial 'evaluation and risk management' element which complements existing ESCO business models. The implementation of such an 'ESCO & CC' business model is based on the intensive collaboration of four well known stakeholders, such as: energy suppliers, FM-providers, energy auditors, and engineering specialists. Building owners clearly benefit from such a collaborative approach, since they are provided with access to 'integrated services' through a single interface.

4.1 Analysis of BMs Available for an ESCO Offering CC® Service

The purpose of this section is to examine several BM suitable for ESCO offering CC® service, based on Osterwalder's BM-canvas. Each model will have its advantages and disadvantages for both the client and the ESCO. The information on Key Partners, Key Activities, Key Resources, Customer Relationship, and Channels & Customer Segments generally remain the same, no matter what type of financing arrangement is decided upon. Thus, for the potential BM the authors will concentrate on Value Proposition, Cost Structure & Revenue Streams factors as shown in Table 3 overleaf.

Table 3. Comparison of BM - contracting types for ESCO offering CC.

Type of financing	EPC	Value proposition	Cost structure	Revenue streams
Integrated Energy Contract	n/a	Supply of Heat and Power managed by ESCO plus Energy Efficiency Upgrades using an EPC	Cost structure varies and depends on individual contracts	ESCO sells heat and power to Customer. This is combined with one of the EPC models below
Shared Savings	Yes	Reduction in CO_2 emissions and associated energy costs Reduction in maintenance & operation costs	Cost and savings are split for a pre-determined length of time in accordance with a pre-arranged percentage	ESCO & Customer incentivised to outperform targets as energy savings are shared Revenue recovered through reduced energy consumption, operation and maintenance costs
Guaranteed Savings	Yes		Customer: No upfront cost, invites capital ESCO: guarantees a certain level of energy savings Advantage: interest rates of loan usually much lower	Only the Customer is incentivised to reach energy targets. Revenue recovered through reduced energy consumption, operation and maintenance costs

(*continued*)

Table 3. (*continued*)

Type of financing	EPC	Value proposition	Cost structure	Revenue streams
Chauffage Model	Yes		Supply by demand long-time (20–30 years) contract Less complex with lower transaction costs and without need of costly measurements and verifications	Heated/Conditioned space at a specified price per energy unit
BOOT (Build-Own-Operate-Transfer)	No	Reduction in CO_2 emissions to be agreed between ESCO and Customer. Complete outsourced model	Usually no upfront cost for Customer. ESCO invites capital	The ESCO operates under an agreement with the Customer and receives BOOT payments dependant on the ESCO's performance
Energy Performance Related Payments (EPRP)	Yes	Reduction in CO_2 emissions and associated energy costs	Low capital costs. Improvements done by ESCO paid by the Customer	ESCO is incentivized to improve energy efficiency with performance-related payments

5 Case Study

The purpose of this section is to present an initial case study based on the building of the Environmental Research Institute (ERI) located on the campus of University College Cork, Ireland. The case study illustrates how energy monitoring analysis (as it would be executed by an ESCO) could be extended with additional CC®-services enabled by holistic sensor data analysis. It explains how CC®-services can be used in a collaborative way, to identify potential sources for slow system's degradation.

5.1 Energy Use

The usage of supplies (i.e. electricity, natural gas and mains water) for the ERI building is monitored daily and available to authorised stakeholders through a web interface. For the initial pre-commissioning analysis, it was decided to analyse the information available for the last five years, i.e. from 2012 to 2016. All necessary data is obtained

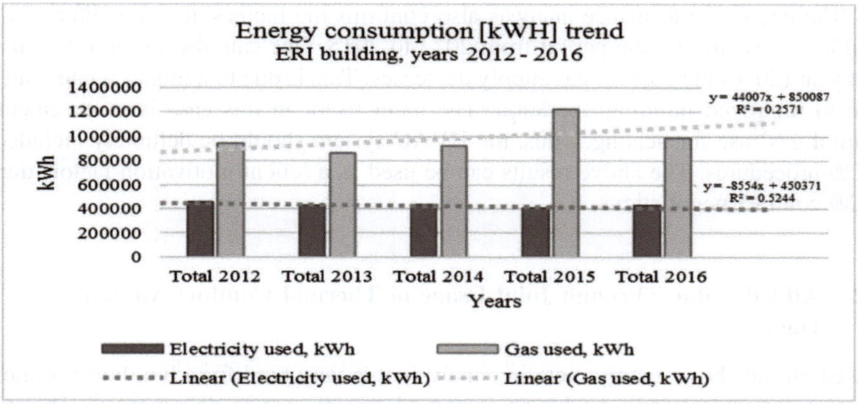

Fig. 5. The ERI energy consumption trend for the last five years.

and compiled with additional calculations, so the trend of the building's energy performance became clearly visible. The following Fig. 5 aggregates these data.

At this point it is possible to suggest while electricity use in the building remains stable, the natural gas consumption (which is mostly used for heating and for preparation of the domestic hot water) constantly increases. This indicates that there might be an urgent need to arrange for the execution of continuous commissioning services aiming to identify the reason(s) of such an increase. Furthermore, these commissioning procedures, if repeated continually, would prevent such an increase in the future.

The following Fig. 6 is representing the financial aspect of the building's ownership, i.e. the combined costs of consumed energy-resources and water in the building for the same last five years' period.

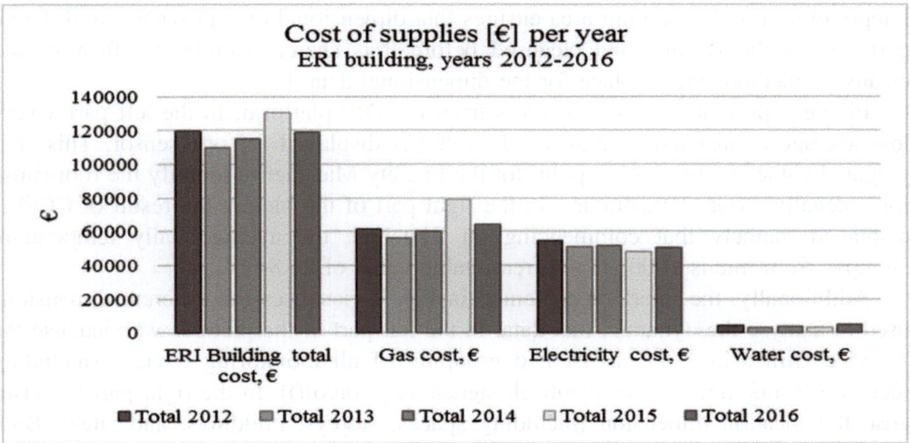

Fig. 6. Cost of supplies for the building, 2012–2016.

The energy performance analysis also confirms the increasing expenditure for the building's use during the period from 2013 to 2015. One can also observe that in the last year (2016) the cost for gas supply decreases. This is due to a milder winter and not due to improved building operation. The main factor in this case is incensement of natural gas' use for heating. Thus, the HVAC-system should be definitely included in CC®-procedures. The above results can be used as a 'client-motivation factor' during CC® contract negotiations.

5.2 Added Value Through Joint Usage of Thermal Comfort Analysis Data

Based on the above energy metering analysis it is very hard for a building operator to develop an understanding why an increased energy use is documented. The usual approach would be to work on a boiler inspection and maintenance.

However, with increasing "building intelligence" malfunctioning monitoring and control components can also contribute to a degradation of building services systems. In case of our example building, the heating system starts to operate in the event that in three rooms the temperature falls below a set threshold (e.g. 18 °C). Thus, the commissioning of (temperature) sensors becomes equally important to e.g. the CC® of boilers and pumps.

One should notice that the example building is equipped with approximately 300 data points. Assuming 15 min reading intervals ca. 30000 values need to be analysed by the local facility manager daily. One should further notice that the selected building has a total floor area of approx. 2.500 m^2 distributed across three floors (only), i.e. the building is a relatively small commercial building.

It becomes easily clear that modern, innovative data analysis techniques are required.

In our show case an Oracle Data Warehouse Platform is used to integrate dynamic data from different systems with dimensional data from BAC and BIM. The data integration through a staging area ensures that dimensional data provided by different partners can be verified and cleansed before it is shared. Similar verification and cleansing methods are in place for the dimensional data. [7]

Figure 7 presents two screen shots from the DW-platform. In the left part a very low average annual temperature (−11.64 °C) is displayed for one sensor. This "aggregated value" is the starting point for the Facility Manager to identify the root-cause for a negative room temperature. In the right part of the picture the result of CC® is displayed, namely that commencing on 21st-June the average daily temperature "jumps" from minus 1000 °C to a reasonable value of 23.84 °C.

Additionally, the interface presented in Fig. 7 visualises the different dimensions used to analyse the dynamic, fact data. In the left part of the pictures we visualise the "Device Dimension", i.e. a list and grouping of all monitoring devices (including meters, sensors, and control feedback signals (e.g. on/off)). In the right part we visualise the location dimension (including spaces, storeys, buildings, and sites). Both views also include a time dimension, with three hierarchy levels, such as year, month, and day.

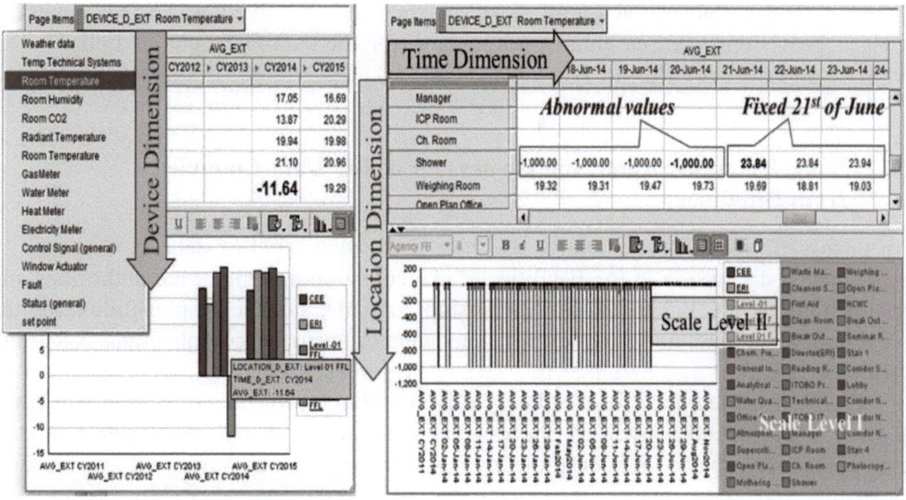

Fig. 7. Identification of malfunctioning sensor through comfort analysis.

The above visualisation demonstrates that different stakeholders joint forces, since the data analysis platform benefits from (i) the topological and electrical engineering knowledge defining how automation components are interconnected (device dimension), (ii) the topological and architectural knowledge defining what spaces exist, of what type these spaces are and how these spaces are grouped e.g. on storeys (location dimension), and (iii) the mechanical engineering knowledge defining what components are installed in what rooms and what additional sensors and meters exist to monitor building services systems (e.g. supply and return temperature).

6 Summary and Conclusions

In general, the market for Energy Services Companies (ESCO) in Ireland has been underdeveloped. A holistic view towards Continual Commissioning as part of ESCO-BM should be developed with involvement of all relevant stakeholders working collaboratively together. A radical paradigm shift is required to achieve this goal.

Business model innovation allows for the creation of new services when fully exploiting the potential of advanced infrastructure features (e.g. the availability and accessibility of big data). Additionally, companies must understand their competitive advantages. For example FM-providers will benefit from their 'in-depth' 1:1 customer relationship and their detailed understanding of various building services and automation systems and thus can deliver 'local services' in an efficient way. In comparison stakeholders must also be capable to identify challenges and disadvantages. In our case study none of the so called 'traditional' stakeholders had access to all available monitoring data. This 'limited' access to dynamic (big) data and the absence of static or 'dimensional' data restricts the capabilities of all stakeholders to execute deep data analysis. The collaboration of all stakeholders being involved in ESCO and CC® service provision is an essential pre-requisite for the establishment of holistic data analysis and the provision of performance audits.

6.1 Some Thoughts About the Ownership of Big Data Compiled from Buildings

An unsolved problem in the above use case is the ownership of data. Furthermore, it also needs a discussion in the Facilities Management community what authorities and responsibilities are linked to the 'ownership' of data, i.e. the responsibility for the compilation, storage, and long-term maintenance of accurate, complete and consistent data sets.

The "lessons learned" from industry-driven research projects [14, 15] in which the authors were recently involved shows, that required 'up-front' investments in data consistency pay back in later project phases through much lower efforts for data cleansing and data quality management. Thus, providers of CC®, ESCO, and FM-services shall aim to convince their clients to enter 'mid-term' or 'long-term' contractual agreements. Those contractual agreements exist, e.g. in the form of public-private-partnerships.

The government, as the creators of policy and legalisation, need to drive the ESCO agenda. Policy needs to reward businesses for tackling CO_2 emissions. They also need to create an environment whereby the buildings' owners and managers be more comfortable when dealing with ESCOs. In Ireland the National Energy Services Framework [16] will convey regulation to the ESCO market to bring clarity to both the ESCO industry and potential clients. The BM extension approach proposed in this paper could also support the development of an Irish Continual Commissioning market, especially by those stakeholders currently utilising "reactive maintenance" BM.

Acknowledgements. Parts of this work were supported by the European Commission, projects CAMPUS 21 and BaaS.

References

1. Fang, W.-S., Miller, S.M.: The effect of ESCOs on carbon dioxide emissions. Appl. Econ. **45**, 4796–4804 (2013)
2. Parliament, E.U.: Energy end-use efficiency and energy services (Directive 2006/32/EC). European Parliament, Brussels (2006)
3. SEAI: Energy Performance Contracting Handbook, 25 October 2012. http://www.seai.ie/Your_Business/Energy-Contracting/Support-and-Guidance/
4. IFC: Energy Service Company Market Analysis. International Finance Corporation, Washington, DC 20433 USA (2011)
5. Codema: Codema Publications. Codema, 16 October 2015. http://www.codema.ie/publications. Accessed 1 Nov 2016
6. SERVE Consortium: Deliverable D6.10. EC, Brussels (2012)

7. Menzel, K., Hryshchenko, A., Mo, K.: Why and how to assess the quality of building performance data. In: eWork ad eBusiness in AEC - Proceedings ECPPM, Vienna (2014)
8. CIBSE: Guide F – Energy Efficiency in Buildings. Chartered Institution of Building Services Engineers, London (2008)
9. Browne, D., Menzel, K., Deng, S.: Performance indicators to evaluate buildings' systems' performance. In: eWork and eBusiness in AEC - Proceedings of ECPPM, London (2014)
10. Osterwalder, A., Pigneur, Y.: Business Model Generation, Self Publ. (2009)
11. OMICS: Business model (2014). http://research.omicsgroup.org/index.php/Business_model
12. Burkhart, T., et.al.: Analyzing the business model concept - a comprehensive classification of literature. In: ICIS 2011, Saarbrücken, Germany (2011)
13. Teece, D.: Business Models, Business Strategy and Innovation (2009)
14. Katsigarakis, K., Kontes, K.D., Rojicek, J., Valmaseda, C., Hernandez, J., Rovas, D.: An ICT platform for building analytics. In: eWork and eBusiness in AEC - Proceedings of ECPPM, London (2014)
15. Mahdavi, A., Schuss, M., Menzel, K., Browne, D.: Realization of ICT potential in improving the energy efficiency of buildings. CAMPUS 21. In: eWork and eBusiness in AEC - Proceddings ECPPM, London (2011)
16. SEAI: National Energy Services Framework Overview. Sustainable Energy Authority of Ireland, Dublin (2013)

Big Data and CNs in Health

How MyData is Transforming the Business Models for Health Insurance Companies

Marika Iivari(✉), Minna Pikkarainen, and Timo Koivumäki

Oulu Business School, University of Oulu, P.O. Box 4600 90014 Oulu, Finland
{Marika.Iivari,Minna.Pikkarainen,Timo.Koivumaki}@oulu.fi

Abstract. This paper discusses the potential impacts of MyData in healthcare business, more precisely occupational health insurance companies, and how the coming of MyData will transform the business models and the whole logic of value creation and capture of health insurance businesses. These companies have traditionally acted alone and relied on organization-centric business models. Through an empirical study, we demonstrate how these organizations are now heading towards acting as active members of collaborative health service ecosystems.

Keywords: Business model · MyData · Personal data · Occupational health · Insurance business

1 Introduction

Within the past years, the use of data in the healthcare sector has become increasingly important. People are embracing a future healthcare system that allows them to control and share their personal health information for receiving improved personalized care. The adoption of cloud technologies and mobile devices, for instance, enable novel ways to generate, access, and manage personal health data. People voluntarily agree vast amounts of personal data to be stored and utilized by companies in exchange of services. For the use of personal health data, the MyData paradigm has therefore emerged to address to strengthen digital human rights while simultaneously opening new opportunities for businesses to develop personal data-driven services. MyData refers to an approach that seeks to transform the current organization-centric system to a human centric-system to use personal data as a resource that individuals themselves can access, control and share based on mutual trust. MyData both enables and requires active collaboration among healthcare businesses for fulfilling the human-centric service perspective through technological solutions. A shared MyData infrastructure enables decentralized management of personal data, improves interoperability, eases to comply with tightening data protection regulations, and allows individuals to change service providers without proprietary data lock-ins [1].

The continuing growth in personal data is thus paving way for data-driven business solutions. Sharing individual's data between actors is crucial especially in preventive healthcare services. This kind of collaboration is seen as a way to differentiate from

L.M. Camarinha-Matos et al. (Eds.): PRO-VE 2017, IFIP AICT 506, pp. 323–332, 2017.
DOI: 10.1007/978-3-319-65151-4_30

competition, requiring new kinds of collaborative business models. Because MyData is only becoming for business use through technological and regulatory developments, there is a clear research gap in studying how MyData-based collaboration is projected in business models. The aim of this study is to increase knowledge on the business potential of MyData in the field of occupational healthcare, in the case of health insurance companies. Sharing and use of data between health professionals – including insurance companies – could contribute to increased health and wellbeing through preventive healthcare, and result in e.g. lowered insurance costs, bringing added value to the individual client. How MyData eventually impacts the insurance business, is thus a very topical and relevant question. Building on business model literature, the research question of this study calls, *how MyData is transforming health insurance companies' business models?*

The paper first discusses the theoretical foundations on business models in data-driven business. It then dives deeper into MyData as a human-centric approach to healthcare. Research methodology and the empirical case are described next. The study ends with discussing research results, findings and conclusions.

2 Toward Data-Driven Business Models

One of the buzzwords of contemporary business is the concept of business model [2, 3]. Previous literature has described and defined business models in various ways, such as a structure, an architecture or a business frame; a representation of a firm's relevant interactions and activities [4]. Although scholars are debating on a unanimous definition for the concept, the common view nevertheless is that business models act as pathways to fulfill unmet needs, profitability and the promise of service ([4] that will lead to competitive advantage [2, 5]. Thus, business models are to "create and capture value in an inimitable way and through rare and valuable resources that are utilized efficiently" [6]. This means that a business model is a system of specific activities conducted to satisfy the perceived needs of the market, as well as specifying who does what (whether it is the firm or its partners), and how do these activities link to each other. From collaborative perspective, a business model also acts as a system of interconnected activities that determine the way the company does business with its customers, partners and vendors [7].

Business models are often imposed by technological innovation that creates the need to bring discoveries to market, and the opportunity to respond to unmet customer needs [5]. Stemming from this background, the concept of data-driven business model has emerged to address connectivity issues, the Internet of Things, and Big Data [8]. [9] define data-driven business models as business models that rely on data as a key resource. According to [9], the source for this data can be either internal or external, the offering can consist of data itself, information or non-data product or service. Revenues can consist of, e.g. sale, licensing or subscriptions, but their definition does not consider data sharing and re-use [8], as implied in MyData paradigm. According to research conducted by [8], in current data-driven business, data sharing is still uncommon, to which this research contributes to contribute to from business model perspective.

Still, using data has become as a necessity for many organizations in order to remain competitive or survive in their field [10]. In healthcare, the most successful services should place the sensing and supporting technologies around the needs of individuals in a manner that is highly personalized and makes the person as a driver of his own health and wellbeing. The key challenges of integrating personal data are both data availability from different silos, and consumer protection laws that currently hinder data usage especially in the health sector. Recently, open source solutions around modern web interfaces or database solutions have started to break the data silos from different sectors. This has resulted in "API Economy" [11], which means that companies separately create revenues through application programming interfaces (APIs) - either licensing, use-for-fee or other monetization models - very much on personal data sets. An aggregator model on the other hand emphasizes the controlling role of a central organization. In open business environment, a shared MyData infrastructure enables decentralized management of personal data, makes it easier for companies to comply with tightening data protection regulations, and allows individuals to change service providers without proprietary data lock-ins [1]. MyData model means that organizations are moving from traditional, technology and aggregator models towards a human-centric data management approach (Fig. 1).

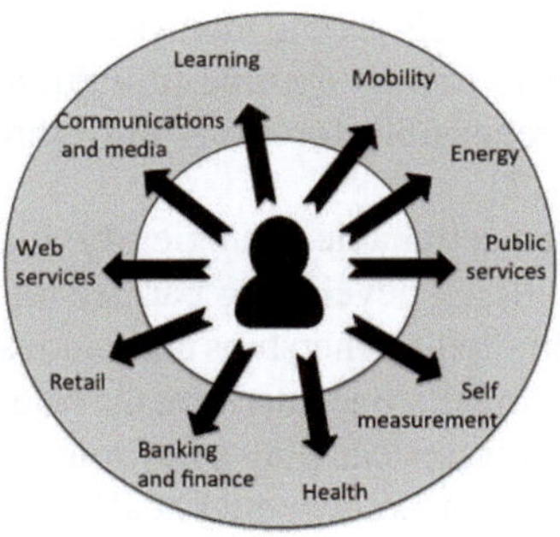

Fig. 1. MyData model (adapted from [1]).

In the traditional "structureless" API economy, there is no clear infrastructure or platform in place for controlling and organizing the use of data in a logical manner. Organizations do not systematically collaborate, and the ecosystem is governed by closed business models. Aggregating data control would make life easier for organizations and individuals, but different aggregators do not have a built-in incentive to develop interoperability between them. In this model, there is an ecosystem in place, however, it is a closed system, dominated by large corporations. Compared to the aggregation model, MyData is a resilient model because it is not dependent on a single organization, but works as a shared open infrastructure [1], thus relying on open innovation approach. MyData can been seen as a way to convert data from closed silos into an important, reusable resource. It can be used to create new services that help individuals to manage their lives. The providers of human-centric services can therefore create new data sharing based business ecosystems and new business models, leading to economic growth to the society as whole [1].

Thus, business models can be seen as the focal firm's boundary-spanning transactions with external parties [2]. Indeed, collaboration of the focal firm with its network can be considered as one of the main functions of the business model. This approach is well captured in the MyData paradigm, yet it brings a lot of challenges for organizations to realign their current strategies and business models. As [12] state, the transformation of an existing business brings special challenges on business models. Business model transformation is about transforming an existing organization through repositioning the core business and adapting the current business model into the altered market place [6, 12]. With the emergence of data sharing and the control of individuals over their health data will transform healthcare business. This means shifting away from the transactional fee-for-service model towards a strategic value-based care [13]. It provides an opportunity to "better understand their true customer, the patient-consumer; tailor products to meet their needs; and to capture a high share of distinct customer subsets who will pay for and be loyal to their brand" [14].

However, transforming an organization requires a lot of commitment from the management, as the old ways of doing things may become a challenge [15]. The activities and logic related to the new business model may be incompatible with the status quo [16]. Therefore, business models should always be evaluated and calibrated against the business context in order to find an optimal fit with the environment [5]. Business models become fully comprehensible for firms only through action in the business context where they emerge [12].

According to [14], the main actionable strategies driving the transformation of health insurance companies start with (1) developing partnerships with right parties, moving away from volume towards limited partnerships and innovative treatment pathways. (2) Predictive care paths, when correctly executed, are the true offerings for future hospitals and physicians. Insurance businesses can play a key role in building such collaborations that have the power to achieve measurably better health outcomes at lower overall costs. In the (3) systematic transformation, payers will have a significant role to play in bridging the divide that is between providers and patients [14]. Thus, it is important to be aware that business model creation in start-ups is a different process from business model transformation within established firms [12].

It is also important to acknowledge that a firm does not have to bind itself to a single business model, but should, in fact, experiment with several simultaneously [17]. During the transformation process, it is not clear what the new business model will be like, but by experimenting the data needed to justify the transformation can be gained. The search for a new business model thus often requires a period of co-existence for the current and the new model(s) [16]. However, although the business model as an actionable concept includes an underlying assumption of a process, academic research has not widely addressed the issues related to business model transformation [12].

3 Methodology, Data Collection and Analysis

As this study seeks to gain an in-depth understanding of the mechanisms of change in an organizational setting, an action-based research methodology was applied for data collection [18]. [19] suggest that action research is a valuable method to study dynamic and turbulent environments. As MyData paradigm shift is still to come, the method enables researchers to get close to the business reality as of now, and thus foster the development of deep and rich insights of the complexities within (data-driven) decision-making [20] in the context of MyData.

The data utilized in this study is part of a wider research project on healthcare service ecosystem, Digital Health Revolution DHR2. The primary data was collected from ten in-depth interviews with insurance company representatives and stakeholders related to the insurance business during 2016 (Table 1). We intentionally selected both insurance players and their stakeholders in order to understand the business of insurance players from different perspectives. In addition, early 2017, the data collected from the interviews was further elaborated during a joint 3 h workshop with insurance companies and their stakeholder ecosystem to validate the identified impact of MyData on business models. All the interviews and workshop material was recorded and transcripted.

Table 1. Data collection of the study.

Company	Key business area	Interviewee	Duration
SME	Technology provider	CEO	106 min
Health provider	Healthcare	Development Director	45 min
Insurance player	Banking, finance, healthcare	Chief actuary	60 min
SME	Wellness training	CEO and Director of Intl. Growth	75 min
SME	Wellness training	Two personal trainers	45 min
Insurance player	Insurance	Business developer	35 min
Insurance player	Insurance	Manager	45 min
Large company	Mobile network operator	Innovation Manager	45 min
Large company	Technology provider	Head of Ecosystems Research	73 min
SME	Technology provider	CEO	56 min

In the data analysis, statements were identified, sorted and structured to identify impacts of MyData to healthcare insurance companies. The business model wheel [6] was used as a tool to analyze the data derived in order to thematically identify the potential impact and use of MyData on healthcare insurance business, as this tool helps to identify the points of action and collaboration in a simplistic manner. The template addresses the following elements: (1) what, comprising offering, value proposition, customer segments, and differentiation, (2) how, covering key operations, basis of advantage, mode of delivery, and selling and marketing, (3) why, describing base of pricing, way of charging, cost elements, and cost drivers, and (4) where are all these items located, internally or externally to the firm, as each part of the business model can be executed through collaborating with outside partners [6]. This template is depicted in Fig. 2.

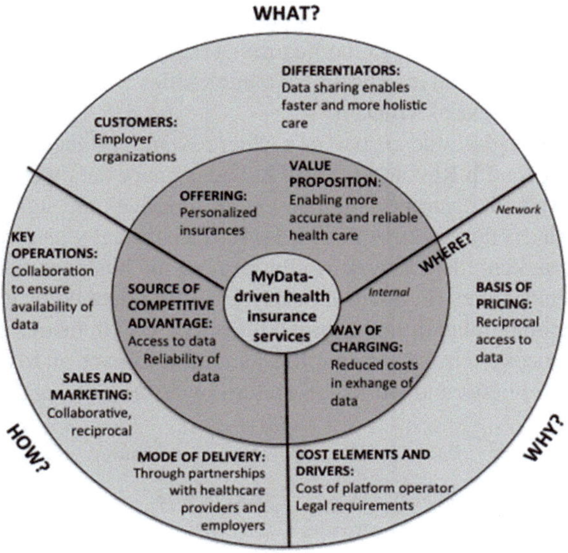

Fig. 2. MyData-driven health insurance business model.

4 Findings

In exploring how MyData will potentially impact the business models of health insurance companies, we thematically categorized our interview findings and mapped them together with the themes discussed during the joint workshop. The results are summarized in Fig. 2, and discussed in more detail below through business model elements, where collaboration is addressed in all components.

4.1 Business Opportunities of MyData

New type of access to human-centric data provides a novel possibility for insurance companies to take a bigger role in preventive healthcare field. The aim for insurance companies is to help their end customers to live more healthy and safe life, which will also support insurance business to decrease the compensation costs related to chronic disease and accidents. In this new field, insurance companies see that *"Our role is not anymore just to buy compensation, it is more to help to make sure that everything is fine with individual"*. At a concrete level, insurance companies consider that *"Mydata approach will offer us new opportunities to give better and updated information for example about the value of their property or risks for future accidents and the like."*

But, MyData is seen to enable also a more general approach to wellbeing, as *"As soon as end users buy from us we can start to offer the services that helps them to improve their health and life style"*. This is based on some initial work insurance companies have conducted in the field, such as "*We have noticed in our research that it is important to offer bonus or some price for people when they are changing their life style"... "smoking is a good example, if you get 3000 if you stop it perhaps people will do it"*. This indicates that in the future system the insurance companies can be characterized more as a service providers than as a player that buys compensations of general risks or issues that already have occurred.

4.2 Value and Competitive Advantage of MyData for Insurance Business

What. MyData was seen to enable extended and novel offerings based on collaborative use of data: "*the data sharing would make it possible that both insurance company and doctor sees the same information and we could serve the individuals better*". Also new players will emerge to collect and analyze data. First, insurance companies aim to use data to achieve close to real-time customer insights to better align themselves with customers for better services. Value could be captured especially in situations when a person has been using one service provider for 10 years and then decides to change. "*that could be the case in which the end user could do some effort to be able to transfer information easily*". Secondly, insurance companies could base the costs of insurance on real, not estimated, situations. This means that people with high-risk profile will have bigger costs whereas those who are living healthy life could get some compensation. Costs would be based on a person's lifestyle and activity level, which is not currently possible due to legal regulations. Thirdly, with MyData, insurance companies could offer a feeling of safety, such as using data from sensors and devices to detect likelyhood for potential accidents. Early risk detection services can be an opportunity for the insurance business. "*... if we could use the sensor and personal data with the permission of end user to check that there is something wrong with the car tire and it is better to fix it before a long journey*".

Insurance services can also be customized based on the data. For example, in many cases the insurance companies are supporting groups in employee organizations. "*The use of Mydata approach will especially change the role of employer organizations in the occupational health business sector during the next 10 years of time*". Indeed, employer organizations were seen as a core player who would benefit from the transformation to MyData enabled healthcare most: "*In the new Mydata based model, the employee organizations should be able to better take into account the coping, energy level, wellbeing and health of their own employee*s" Other important players in this new business model could be banks, food stores, aviation industry, utilities and housing companies.

How. Utilizing collaborative networks were identified as the key strategic approach in MyData, as it is not possible to build open access to data open business or innovation models." "*We have opened the interfaces and helped developers to build interfaces and open data sources.*" "*we have organized hackathons that targeted to give* *developers a possibility to use their data as a basis for new application development.*" However, insurance companies mentioned that there is a key player, an operator, missing in this field who could take the responsibility of data sharing and offer the needed collaboration interfaces. Supporting customers to decide which data to share is important in Mydata transformation. Without an operator in place, it might be difficult for insurance companies to get access to the personal data without legal problems. Insurance companies have interest to lead this but their challenge is that it could be seen scary from citizen perspective.

Insurance companies aim to develop rapid data usage as source of competitive advantage: "*the faster we can use the data either as a service or information or to do better pricing the better we can manage in the business compared to our competitors*". Combining personal data with environmental data like cars or housing, insurance players could maximize the probability of customers finding products that they want to buy. It was also mentioned in the interviews that data usage is not only a competitive advantage but must-to-have for insurance players in the future if they want to survive: "*The basic model in which we just send bills and compensations does not work anymore in the current digital world. If we cannot use the data we will stay behind in the insurance marke*t".

Why. From revenue perspective, the individual was highlighted as the most important player in the future MyData-driven business: In the new insurance business model, individuals can get discounts of their insurance if they are improving their lifestyle. At the same time the assumption was that the insurance companies should pay less compensations on chronic diseases and accidents. However, insurance companies do not yet have evidence that the costs actually decrease if data is better used. One approach could be reciprocal data sharing among within the collaborative network that includes also the end customer: "*I think some players are ready also to buy the data from individuals*". Equally, "*You need to buy if you want to get the valuable services based on your data*". Help is needed from other players such as individuals, developer organizations and data operators. Who owns the data and has the right to use or sell the data within MyData – based collaborative networks is a key issue.

5 Discussion and Conclusions

It seems that data-driven business models will be mandatory in future insurance business. It will open new opportunities for new services and therefore help insurance players to stay as a significant player in the preventive healthcare business. It was evaluated that the key players who will buy new MyData based services are individuals and employee organizations who will clearly financially benefit from new data-driven services. The way to achieve MyData transformation is to open the interfaces and organize hackathons to help developers to build solutions. This means that in order to attract and retain customers, insurance companies can offer lowered prices for those who voluntarily share their health data. This results in lowered income in the form of insurance payments (the higher the risk indicators, the more one has to pay), but equally lowers the amounts of compensations paid to individuals. Thus in general both losses and profits will decrease.

The results of the study thus indicate that the use of personal data, and the coming of MyData will dramatically transform the business models of health insurance companies from transaction-based to service based business. This has also important policy implications for data regulations and legislation, as consent and control on the use of personal data is a central aspect of MyData, in terms of how for-profit companies can utilize it for business gain.

Through addressing an emergent phenomenon, this study contributes to business model literature, and especially on data sharing within data-driven business models. Thus, this study also contributes to data based aspects of sharing economy discussion as well. The main limitations relate to empirical validity. As MyData yet is a still a paradigm, the results of this study still address the potential use and implications, and cannot be validated through large scale empirical studies. Similarly, as the project took place among occupational healthcare sector, the implications on revenue models and competitive advantages for organizations involving also public institutions and healthcare provides. Hence, larger scale future scenario work would be useful to validate the business potential of MyData, especially from regulations and legislation points of view. We are yet to see, if the findings of this study will become the reality of health insurance business soon enough. In the meanwhile, further research on the design and orchestration on networks around MyData would be extremely valuable, especially from the point of view of MyData operator business. Moreover, the voice of the individual consumers from user driven innovation perspective could contribute to human-centric data management.

Acknowledgments. The authors would like to acknowledge DHR2 – Digital Health Revolution – project consortium.

References

1. Poikola, A., Kuikkaniemi, K., Honko, H.: MyData - A Nordic Model for Human-Centered Personal Data Management and Processing. Ministry of Transport and Communication, Open Knowledge Finland (2014)
2. Zott, C., Amit, R., Massa, L.: The business model: recent developments and future research. J. Manag. **37**(4), 1019–1042 (2011)
3. Onetti, A., Zucchella, A., Jones, M.V., McDougall-Covin, P.P.: Internationalization, innovation and entrepreneurship: business models for new technology-based firms. J. Manage. Governance **16**, 337–368 (2010)
4. Wirtz, B., Pistoia, A., Ullrich, S., Göttel, V.: Business models: origin, development and future research perspectives. Long Range Plan. **49**(1), 36–54 (2016)
5. Teece, D.: Business models, business strategy and innovation. Long Range Plan. **43**, 172–194 (2010)
6. Ahokangas, P., Juntunen, J., Myllykoski, J.: Cloud computing and transformation of international e-business models. Res. Competence-Based Manag. **7**, 3–28 (2014)
7. Zott, C., Amit, R.: Business model design: an activity system perspective. Long Range Plan. **43**(2–3), 216–226 (2010)

8. Pujol, l., Osimo, D., Wareham, J., Porcu, F.: Data-driven business models in the digital age: the impact of data on traditional businesses. Paper presented at the 3rd World Open Innovation Conference, Barcelona, 14-15 December 2016
9. Hartmann, P.M., Zaki, M., Feldmann, N., Neely, A.: Big Data for Big Business? University of Cambridge Service Alliance, working paper, pp. 1–29 (2014)
10. Brownlow, J., Zaki, M., Neely, A., Urmetzer, F. Data and Analytics – Data-Driven Business Models: A Blueprint for Innovation. University of Cambridge Service Alliance, working paper, pp. 1–15 (2015)
11. Anuff, E.: Almost everyone is doing the API economy wrong, TechCrunch, 21 March 2016. https://techcrunch.com/2016/03/21/almost-everyone-is-doing-the-api-economy-wrong/
12. Ahokangas, P., Myllykoski, J.: The practice of creating and transforming a business model. J. Bus. Models **2**(1), 6–18 (2014)
13. Kaiser, L.S., Lee, T.H.: Harvard Business Review Turning Value-Based Health Care into a Real Business Model, 08 October 2015. https://hbr.org/2015/10/turning-value-based-health-care-into-a-real-business-model
14. Numerof, R.: 3 strategies for changing the health insurance business model. FierceHealthcare, 26 October 2015. http://www.fiercehealthcare.com/payer/3-strategies-for-changing-health-insurance-business-model
15. Giannopoulou, E., Yström, A., Ollila, S.: Turning open innovation into practice: open innovation research through the lens of managers. Int. J. Innov. Manag. **15**(3), 505–524 (2011)
16. Chesbrough, H.: Business model innovation: opportunities and barriers. Long Range Plan. **43**(2–3), 354–363 (2010)
17. Trimi, S., Berbegal-Mirabent, J.: Business model innovation in entrepreneurship. Int. Entrepreneurship Manag. J. **8**, 449–465 (2012)
18. Ballantyne, D.: Action research reviewed: a market-oriented approach. Eur. J. Mark. **38**(3–4), 321–337 (2004)
19. Daniel, W., Wilson, H.: The role of dynamic capabilities in e-business transformation. Euro. J. Inf. Syst. **12**(4), 282–296 (2003)
20. Carson, D., Gilmore, A., Perry, C., Gronhaug, K.: Action Research and Action Learning. Qualitative Marketing Research. Sage, London (2001)

Managing Business Process Variability Through Process Mining and Semantic Reasoning: An Application in Healthcare

Silvana Pereira Detro[1,2(✉)], Eduardo Alves Portela Santos[1], Hervé Panetto[2], Eduardo de Freitas Rocha Loures[1], and Mario Lezoche[2]

[1] Graduate Program in Production Engineering and Systems (PPGEPS), Pontifícia Universidade Católica do Paraná (PUCPR), Curitiba, Paraná, Brazil
silvana.detro@pucpr.edu.br,
{eduardo.portela, eduardo.loures}@pucpr.br

[2] Research Centre for Automatic Control (CRAN UMR 7039), Université de Lorraine, CNRS, Boulevard des Aiguillettes, B.P. 70239, 54506 Vandoueuvre-lès-Nancy, France
{herve.panetto, mario.lezoche}@univ-lorraine.fr

Abstract. Managing process variability enable the process model adaptability according changes in the application environment. In the healthcare area, flexibility is essential to provide a quality treatment because, even patients with the same diagnostic, may follow different paths and suffer different proceedings. Besides, there are many aspects to be considered for the selection of a path, as patient's symptoms, and clinical guidelines, among others. In this context, this research presents a framework for the management of the process variants through semantic reasoning. The enrichment of the business process with semantics enables the automation of the configuration, thus promoting more flexible and adaptive solutions. The proposed framework helps selecting the appropriate process variant according the patient's symptoms by reasoning on ontologies based known expertise. In our specific use case, we will use the expertise of the Brazilian guideline for acute ischemic stroke.

Keywords: Process variability · Process mining · Semantic reasoning

1 Introduction

Healthcare processes occur in constantly changing environments, making the management of this kind of process a challenge, due the flexibility and the amount of processes involved [1]. During the patient treatment, there are several paths that can be followed or activities that can be executed according different aspects, such as the patient's symptoms, the response to the treatment, the expert knowledge, the clinical guidelines, among others. Thus, any process must be able to evolve to provide a quality treatment to the patient.

In this way, the business process variability plays a major role since it is related with the ability of a process to change according the different contexts and its

L.M. Camarinha-Matos et al. (Eds.): PRO-VE 2017, IFIP AICT 506, pp. 333–340, 2017.
DOI: 10.1007/978-3-319-65151-4_31

requirements. However, managing process variability is a non-trivial task because it requires specific standards, methods and technologies [2, 3].

Besides, due the syntactic and semantic constraints of the configuration of the process variants, this is a complex task involving many parameters not always formally defined. Design the reference process model, which represent the commonalities from the process family is a challenge, as well the adjustments necessary to configure a specific process variant from the reference process model. Ensuring the evolution is also a challenge faced by the configurable process model [2, 4, 5].

To overcome some of these challenges, this research proposes a framework to manage the process variants through semantic annotations and reasoning. The framework proposes to select the appropriate process variant according the patient's symptoms, by reasoning on ontologies based known expertise. In our specific use case, we will use the expertise of the Brazilian guideline for acute ischemic stroke [6], both as an accepted expert knowledge for discovering different aspects about the selection of a patient's path. These aspects are essential, since they define all the conditions for the selection of any process variant in the case of acute ischemic stroke.

The benefits provided by the semantic enrichment of the business process includes the improvement of its representation and understanding; the automation of tasks related to the modelling, configuration and evolution; and the adaptability of the business process according the changes in the requirements [7]. Besides, it makes possible to validate the configurable process model in a semantic way, which is not yet done in the literature. Indeed, all existing approaches are validating the processes through a syntactic control [8].

Our framework also proposes to obtain a configurable process model based in the analysis of an event log related to the treatment of patients diagnosed with acute ischemic stroke. The event log analysis provides knowledge about how the process is performed, thus helping on making appropriate decisions to improve it. However, despite the benefits that the event log analysis can provide, many enterprises do not use such data appropriately.

Obtaining the configurable process model by means of the event log enables us to improve the process variants by correcting deviations, if they exist, anticipating problems, discovering if the requirements have been followed, etc. [9]. Besides, the implicit knowledge can be captured and made explicit, thus enabling to enrich the process variants.

The contribution of the framework presented in this paper is about variability management, which captures the semantics of the processes for improving the efficiency and quality of the treatment, the process model validation and a decision-making support grounded on the patient conditions and existing standards. The paper is structured as follows: Sect. 2 provides the required background knowledge. The Sect. 3 introduces the proposed framework for discovering the process variants. In Sect. 4, the conclusions and the future work are discussed.

2 Literature Review

This Section addresses the configurable process model approach, the process mining technique, followed by an introduction about ontology and semantic reasoning. The process mining techniques enable to analyse the event log, and thus, to extract the process variants. The knowledge for the selection of a process variant is formalized in ontologies. Thus, by reasoning on the ontologies, the process variant can be selected.

2.1 Configurable Process Model

The configurable process model (CPM) [10] emerged with the objective of integrating different process variants into one model. Thus, the configurable process model enables extracting a process variant, which is a process model different from the original one, but that fits better in the application environment. This approach enable to represent the commonalities of the process variants only once thus eliminating the model redundancies. By sharing the particularities among multiple variants, this approach also promotes the model reuse [4].

Several aspects related to the business process variability have been discussed, such as: management and (re)design [11], modelling [10], configuration [12], among others. Furthermore, most of the proposed approaches present a low level of automation. Besides, after the configuration of the process variant it is necessary to verify if the resulting process model respect the requirements, in a syntactical and semantical level [13].

Besides, when dealing with process variants, most of them do not consider that what happens during the process execution may be not planned to happen. The process mining technique enables extracting information from an event log, showing what is happened [9]. Thus, by analysing the process model generated from an event log, some aspects that can improve the process variant may be discovered as well problems may be corrected.

2.2 Process Mining

The Process mining technique aims to analyse the event log, promoting the understanding of process behaviour, to check the process model conformance and to enable it enhancement [14]. In this way, this technique facilitates to control and improve the process behaviour. In the healthcare environment, process-mining techniques are applied to the analysis and discovery of process behaviour [15], the discovery and the analysis of the pathways [16], etc.

Despite being a quite mature technique, process mining suffers from a lack of automation between business and IT, requiring a huge human effort in the translation between both domains. Besides, the analyses provided by process mining technology are purely syntactic, i.e. based in the string of the labels. To overcome these issues, emerged the Semantic Business Process Mining (SBPM), which the basic idea is to annotate the log with the concept derived by one or more ontologies. By annotating the event log with ontologies new knowledge can be discovered [17]. Different issues were addressed by using the concept of SBPM, but few authors applied this approach to solve problems related to the configurable process models. Besides, these papers do not use the knowledge embedded in the ontology to manage the business process variability.

2.3 Ontologies and Semantic Reasoning

The ontology enable to capture, represent, re(use), share and exchange common understanding in a domain [18]. The ontology is composed by commonly agreed terms, thus describing the domain of interest. However, knowledge sharing and reuse among applications and agents is possible only through the semantic annotation.

Semantic annotation enable to reasoning over the ontology, thus ensuring the quality of the ontology and enabling to derive new knowledge [19–21].

The semantic enrichment of the business process was proposed to increase the level of BPM lifecycle [22], to compliance checking [23], among others. Regarding to the configurable process model, semantic technologies have been applied for semantic enrichment [8] and for the semantic validation [15]. However, these papers do not use the knowledge embedded in the ontology to manage the business process variability.

3 Framework for Managing Business Process Variability

The selection of activities to be performed during the treatment relies in several aspects such as the patient conditions and the patient's health record, the clinical guidelines, some expert knowledge, etc. Thus, the criteria for the selection of the treatment provided to the patient are based on knowledge that is, generally implicit and not yet computed, making necessary the use of semantics.

Thus, the framework presented in this research, proposes the selection of the appropriate process variant through semantic reasoning. For appropriate process variant, we mean the process variant that meets the patient needs and respects the clinical guidelines. The Fig. 1 shows the first part of the proposed framework, which is related to the discovery of the process variants.

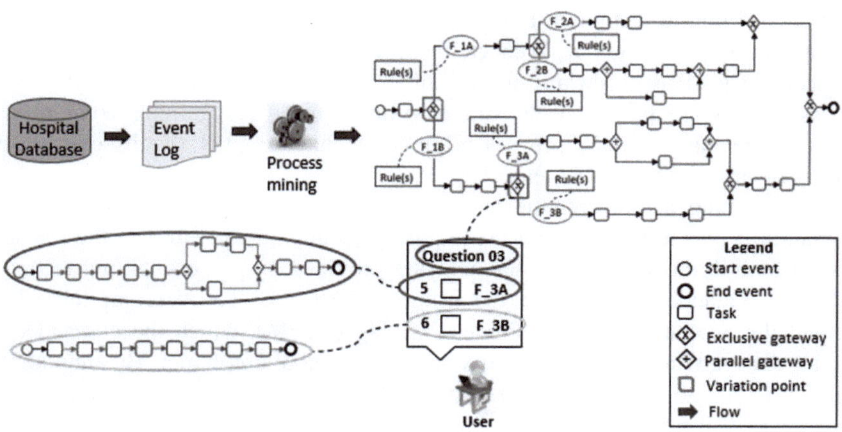

Fig. 1. Discovering the process variants

By analysing the event log through the process mining techniques, all instances of all paths are obtained. Then, the properties of those instances are identified to build a generic model from which all instances may have come from.

For obtaining a configurable process model, three aspects must be identified in the process model: the variation points, which are the parts of the model that are subjects to variation, the alternatives available for the variation points and the rules to select a path instead of another [4].

To discover these aspects is applied the decision point analysis, a process mining technique, which enable to identify the variation points, the alternatives and the rules to choose one path instead another [24]. By identifying these aspects, we obtain a configurable process model, thus the process variants can be extracted.

By analysing the rules for choosing a path, we can note that the user should provide some information once that they are related to the patient's symptoms. Therefore, the questionnaire-model approach [13], is applied to guide the configuration process. In this approach, each variation point has associated a question, whose alternatives determine the path selection. Thus, by selecting an alternative related to a question, the user configures a process variant. In the proposed framework, the questionnaire is developed using the analysis provided by the decision point analysis.

By discovering the process variants, the ontologies are applied to manage them. We propose to formalise the knowledge about the variation points, the available alternatives and the rules related to the acute ischemic treatment from a hospital in an ontology. Another ontology will formalise the knowledge about the Brazilian clinical guideline for the acute ischemic stroke. This last ontology is also complemented with some expert knowledge. Then, the semantic mapping between both ontologies is established. The next step refers to link the configurable process model with the ontologies through semantic annotation as presented in the Fig. 2.

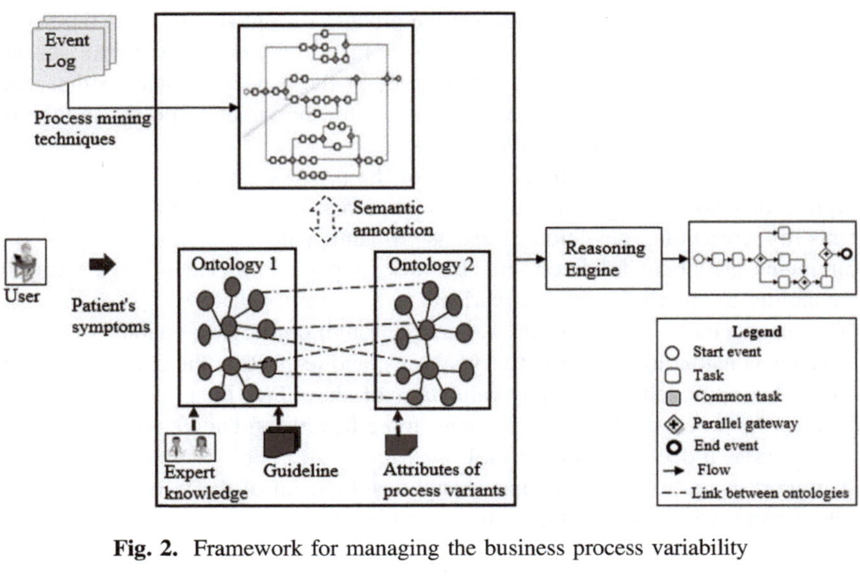

Fig. 2. Framework for managing the business process variability

In this way, when the user provides an information related to the patient's symptoms, by reasoning on the first ontology we obtain an activity to be performed according the information provided, and the second ontology ensures that the activity selected respects the guidelines. For example, when the patient arrives to the hospital, usually the first action is the evaluation of the vital functions. Thus, some exams must be performed, such as, blood pressure, glucose level, etc. The symptoms presented by the patient determine the treatment. Therefore, the result of these exams must be provided for the process variants configuration.

The process variant configuration through ontologies have been proposed by some authors, such as Huang et al. in [25]. However, the framework proposed in this research enable to identify the process variants and its characteristics from an event log. In this way, the process model can be correctly individualized by meeting the requirements of the context application. Besides, as the process variants are extracted from the event log, they reflect what is happening during the patient treatment, enabling to act in a more effective way to correct or improve the process variants. Another advantage of the proposed framework is the possibility to configure the process variants as the user answer the posed questions.

4 Conclusion and Future Work

In the healthcare environment, the management of the process variants is not an easy task, since many aspects must to be considered for the treatment. As result, this environment is characterized by the existence of several paths that may be followed by the patients. Thus, to provide a quality treatment, the business process needs to be able to change according the different requirements.

In this way, this research aims to present a framework for the management of the process variants through semantic reasoning enabling the configuration of the process model. The framework proposes to select the process variant according to the patient's symptoms by reasoning on ontologies based in the Brazilian guideline for acute ischemic stroke, in the expert knowledge and, in the aspects related to the process variants, i.e., the variation points, the alternatives for the variation points and the rules for the selection of the available alternatives.

The framework proposes the discovery of the process variants from the event log through a process mining technique. This approach enable to improve the process variants by correcting deviation if exists, to anticipate problems, discover if the requirements are being followed, etc. Besides, implicit knowledge can be captured, thus enabling to enrich the process variants.

The management of the process variants, through ontologies, enables to configure the variants considering the patient's symptoms, and respecting the clinical guidelines. Besides, this approach enable the validation of the CPM in a semantic level, the analysis of the process behaviour, promotes more flexible and adaptive solutions and it may be used as a decision support tool.

The work is on-going by the operational development of the framework presented in this research within a prototype and its validation.

Acknowledgments. This work is partially supported by Science Without Borders, CAPES, Brazil.

References

1. Rebuge, A., Ferreira, D.R.: Business process analysis in healthcare environments: a methodology based on process mining. Inf. Syst. **37**(2), 99–116 (2012)
2. Reichert, M., Weber, B.: Enabling Flexibility in Process-Aware Information Systems: Challenges, Methods, Technologies. Springer, Heidelberg (2012)
3. Valença, G., Alves, C., Alves, V., Niu, N.: A systematic mapping study on business process variability. Int. J. Comput. Sci. Inf. Technol. **5**(1), 1–21 (2013)
4. Ayora, C., Torres, V., Reichert, M., Weber, B., Pelechano, V.: Towards run-time flexibility for process families: open issues and research challenges. In: Rosa, M., Soffer, P. (eds.) BPM 2012. LNBIP, vol. 132, pp. 477–488. Springer, Heidelberg (2013). doi:10.1007/978-3-642-36285-9_49
5. Sbai, H., Fredj, M., Kjiri, L.: To trace and guide evolution in configurable process models. In: 2013 ACS International Conference on Computer Systems and Applications (AICCSA), pp. 1–4. IEEE (2013)
6. Oliveira-Filho, J., Martins, S.C.O., Pontes-Neto, O.M., Longo, A., Evaristo, E.F., Carvalho, J.J.F.D., Fernandes, J.G., Zétola, V.F., Gagliardi, R.J., Vedolin, L., Freitas, G.R.D.: Guidelines for acute ischemic stroke treatment: Part I. Arq. Neuropsiquiatr. **70**(8), 621–629 (2012)
7. El Faquih, L., Sbaï, H., Fredj, M.: Towards a semantic enrichment of configurable process models. In: 2014 Third IEEE International Colloquium in Information Science and Technology (CIST), pp. 1–6. IEEE (2014)
8. El Faquih, L., Sbai, H., Fredj, M.: Semantic variability modelling in business processes: a comparative study. In: 2014 9th International Conference for Internet Technology and Secured Transactions (ICITST), pp. 131–136. IEEE (2014)
9. Van der Aalst, W.M.P., et al.: Process mining manifesto. In: Daniel, F., Barkaoui, K., Dustdar, S. (eds.) BPM 2011, Part I. LNBIP, vol. 99, pp. 169–194. Springer, Heidelberg (2012). doi:10.1007/978-3-642-28108-2_19
10. Gottschalk, F., van der Aalst, W.M., Jansen-Vullers, M.H.: Configurable Process Models - A Foundational Approach. Reference Modeling, pp. 59–77. Physica-Verlag HD (2007)
11. Kumar, A., Yao, W.: Design and management of flexible process variants using templates and rules. Comput. Ind. **63**(2), 112–130 (2012)
12. La Rosa, M., van der Aalst, W.M., Dumas, M., Ter Hofstede, A.H.: Questionnaire-based variability modeling for system configuration. Softw. Syst. Model. **8**(2), 251–274 (2009)
13. El Faquih, L., Sba, H., Fredj, M.: Configurable process models: a semantic validation. In: 10th International Conference on Intelligent Systems: Theories and Applications (SITA), pp. 1–6. IEEE (2015)
14. van Der Aalst, W.M.P.: Process Mining: Discovery, Conformance and Enhancement of Business Processes. Springer, Heidelberg (2011)
15. Fei, H., Meskens, N.: Discovering patient care process models from event logs. In: 8th International 530 Conference of Modelling and Simulation, MOSIM, pp. 10–12 (2008)
16. Caron, F., Vanthienen, J., Vanhaecht, K., Van Limbergen, E., Deweerdt, J., Baesens, B.: A process mining-based investigation of adverse events in care processes. Health Inf. Manag. J. **43**(1), 16–25 (2014)

17. De Medeiros, A.K.A., Pedrinaci, C., van der Aalst, W.M.P., Domingue, J., Song, M., Rozinat, A., Norton, B., Cabral, L.: An outlook on semantic business process mining and monitoring. In: Meersman, R., Tari, Z., Herrero, P. (eds.) OTM 2007, Part II. LNCS, vol. 4806, pp. 1244–1255. Springer, Heidelberg (2007). doi:10.1007/978-3-540-76890-6_52
18. Musen, M.A.: Dimensions of knowledge sharing and reuse. Comput. Biomed. Res. **25**, 435–467 (1992)
19. Liao, Y., Lezoche, M., Panetto, H., Boudjlida, N., Loures, E.R.: Semantic annotation for knowledge explicitation in a product lifecycle management context: a survey. Comput. Ind. **71**, 24–34 (2015)
20. Obitko, M.: Translations between ontologies in multi-agent systems. Ph.D. dissertation, Czech Technical University, Faculty of Electrical Engineering (2007)
21. Staab, S., Studer, R.: Handbook on Ontologies. Springer, Heidelberg (2013)
22. Hepp, M., Roman, D.: An ontology framework for semantic business process management. In: Wirtschaftinformatik Proceedings (2007)
23. Szabó, I., Varga, K.: Knowledge-based compliance checking of business processes. In: Meersman, R., et al. (eds.) OTM 2014. LNCS, vol. 8841, pp. 597–611. Springer, Heidelberg (2014). doi:10.1007/978-3-662-45563-0_36
24. Decision Miner. http://www.processmining.org/prom/decisionmining?s[]=decision&s[]=mining
25. Huang, Y., Feng, Z., He, K., Huang, Y.: Ontology-based configuration for service-based business process model. In: 2013 IEEE International Conference on Services Computing (SCC), pp. 296–303. IEEE (2013)

Ontology-Based Decision Support Systems for Health Data Management to Support Collaboration in Ambient Assisted Living and Work Reintegration

Daniele Spoladore(✉)

Institute of Industrial Technologies and Automation,
Italian National Council of Research, Milan, Italy
daniele.spoladore@itia.cnr.it

Abstract. The modern evolution of healthcare systems towards even more complex networks has highlighted the emerging need of a standardized and interoperable model for the management of health data. Several studies in the past years have underlined how the adoption of Semantic Web technologies can provide a valuable solution for both of the aforementioned needs. Semantic modelling of health-data can indeed provide a sound and sharable conceptualization of a patient's health condition and can leverage automatic generation of new knowledge related to the clinical contexts. In fact, thanks to reasoning processes these technologies can be used as part of decision-support systems in a variety of domains. In this paper two examples of ontologies are presented. Both models rely on a worldwide-known classification and are the basis for two decision-support tools related to the Ambient Assisted Living and Work Reintegration domains, which enable cooperation among different clinical and non-clinical stakeholders.

Keywords: Ontology · Semantic web · Decision Support System · Data integration · Health

1 Introduction

The evolution of healthcare systems towards more complex networks has highlighted the need of a standardized model for health-data management. Clinical personnel, rehabilitators, care-providers and non-clinical professionals need to access and interpret many heterogeneous sets of data related to the health condition of patients to provide them with optimal and customized solutions. In details, specialized personnel can exploit these data at two different levels. The first one consists in the so-called primary use of health information: in this case, data are used to deliver direct healthcare services, which are care, therapy and drug administration. The latter is the secondary use, which involves the usage of heterogeneous data for applications placed outside the process of direct healthcare delivery as, for instance, clinical research, public health surveillance and quality measurement. It consists in the analysis of aggregated data to study a variety of issues related to the health. In this second scenario, it is even more difficult for

L.M. Camarinha-Matos et al. (Eds.): PRO-VE 2017, IFIP AICT 506, pp. 341–352, 2017.
DOI: 10.1007/978-3-319-65151-4_32

researchers and non-clinical personnel retrieving patients' data, since they are often inconsistent in formats and models. One of the most promising answers to this issue is the adoption of solutions based on Semantic Web (SW), which allows the integration of different types of data collected from different kind of patients and provides a standard set of languages to model knowledge – namely Resource Description Framework (RDF) [1] and Ontology Web Language (OWL) [2]. Domain knowledge is modeled into ontologies, explicit, shared and Description Logic-based conceptualizations of the knowledge and the relationships of the concepts composing a domain [3]. In addition, with the use of ontologies it is possible to derive new facts – which are not explicitly expressed – through reasoning, thus discovering new chunks of knowledge and adding value to several knowledge-based businesses and fields [4]. This feature is particularly interesting and enriches the scenario of the secondary uses of health data with the possibility to infer new information related to a patient's health condition in several domains.

This paper describes two ontologies that can be framed among the secondary uses of health data, since they deal with two health-related domains, the Ambient Assisted Living (AAL) and the Work Reintegration (WR) and involve both clinical and non-clinical professionals. The presented ontologies model the health condition of patients through the World Health Organization's International Classification of Functioning, Disability and Health (ICF) [5], an international standard acting as common language that allows diverse clinical and non-clinical professionals to exchange and use the patient's health data. In fact, the use of ontologies permits to support the collection and use of a vast amount of patients' data by making them interoperable, thus enhancing the collaboration among different stakeholders (e.g. rehabilitators, physicians, lab technicians, therapists, caregivers).

In the AAL scenario, the ontology is used to model the patient's health condition, from which it is possible to infer the most suitable sets of appliances to help him/her to cope with his/her impairments in everyday-life. The model serves as a Decision Support System (DSS) for the smart home designers, to support them in the design of a living environment for impaired users. In the WR scenario, the ontology is used to identify possible alternative jobs for novice wheelchair users who need to be reintegrated in the workplace after a trauma, providing a list of suitable jobs tailored on specific users. This ontology acts therefore as a DSS for vocational and rehabilitation therapists and employers, enabling them to choose the most suitable options for the to-be-reintegrated wheelchair user.

This paper is organized as follow: Sect. 2 presents the existing works in the fields of semantic health-data modelling for secondary uses and DSSs. Section 3 introduces the ICF as a common background for the two ontologies developed. Section 4 focuses on the description of the AAL ontology and the use of its derived knowledge in a design application. Section 5 describes the ontological model for WR and the possible inferences to support a DSS. Finally, Sect. 6 summarizes the main outcomes.

2 Related Works

The topic of modeling the health-data is one of the main issues when tackling the interoperability among various data sources. Data integration is not an easy task: the possibility to link different health-data is complicated by the heterogeneity of data formats and different naming conventions [6]. The importance of this topic gave birth to the Semantic Web for Health Care and Life Sciences Interest Group [7], whose mission is to advocate, support and develop the adoption of SW technologies across clinical research, healthcare and life sciences. These matters have been addressed in [8], where the authors used semantic archetypes based on ontologies to provide a formal representation of knowledge deriving from health domains and integrating this model with clinical data. A similar solution is explained in [9], where the interoperability of electronic health records (EHR) is approached by turning the attention to SW technologies, providing a representation of the health-data using OWL. The issue of EHR reusability is also addressed in the European project EHR4CR [10], where the authors overcame the interoperability issues adopting a platform able to provide semantic interoperability services based on standard terminologies. In [11], the need to provide services oriented to the patients encompassing an holistic vision brought to the adoption of a SW-based approach.

The benefits deriving from the adoption of semantic-based technologies in healthcare also concern the possibility to discover new knowledge through reasoning processes. In [12], these features are used to develop a knowledge-mediated personalized care planning. The authors highlighted how the application of the SW technologies can lead to the identification of a planning system that automatically generates ad adaptive care plan, tailored on the patient's profile. In [13], the authors presented a semantic - and SWRL [14] - based DSS for clinical decision making. Doucette et al. [15] adopted a similar approach in their work, which develops a semantic framework for AI-based clinical DSS, which also supports data interoperability. Subirats et al. [16] developed an SWRL-based DSS providing a personalization of therapies in a rehabilitation scenario, using ICF as a framework.

However, the DSSs presented in these works, although leveraging on the SW interoperable capabilities, are all focused on clinical aspects and are not suitable to enhance and support the cooperation between clinical and non-clinical professionals.

3 ICF: A Sharable and Standard Language for Disability

The International Classification of Functioning, Disability and Health (ICF) [4] is a framework aimed at providing a standard tool for the description of health and its related states. It conceptualizes the functioning of an individual as a "dynamic interaction between a person's health condition, environmental factors and personal factors" [17]. ICF acts as a tool able to ease the communication among the health-stakeholders (therapists, clinicians) providing a standard and worldwide comparable description of the functional experiences of the individuals. Due to its vocabulary, which is easily interpretable also by non-clinical personnel, ICF can also be used in health-related domains, such as AAL and WR, as a common means to support and facilitate the collaboration of different actors. The classification is organized in two main parts: the first, "*Functioning and Disability*", provides a description of the components *Body functions*, *Body structures* and *Activities and participation*; and the second, "*Contextual Factors*", provides the means to describe the impact of the components *Environmental factors* and *Personal factors*. Each component is further deepened into Chapters, which identify the addressed domain. The functioning of a person is then described through the interaction between his/her health condition and the context where he/she acts. Each component is identified by a letter (*b* for Body functions, *s* for Body structures, *e* for Environmental factors, *d* for Activities and participation) and can be deepened by adding digits (Fig. 1). According to the number of digits following the letter, it is possible to get a code, whose length indicates the level of granularity – up to five digits.

B2 *«Sensory functions and pain»*	Component and chapter – first level item
B210 *«Seeing functions»*	Second level item
B2102 *«Quality of vision»*	Third level item
B21020 *«Light sensitivity»*	Fourth level item

Fig. 1. An example of ICF code.

The functioning or disability of an individual can be assessed selecting the suitable category and its corresponding code and then adding a qualifier (from 0-no impairment to 4-complete impairment). ICF has also been represented into an ontological model in RDF/OWL [18], which can be used as reference in the modelling of more complex ontologies. However, it has to be underlined that this model inherits some shortcomings belonging to the whole classification, such as problems regarding incongruent classification of some concepts, a lack of clarity between activities and their qualities, incorrect parent-child relationships and overemphasis on subsumption [19–21].

4 DSS for Collaborative Configuration of Living Environments

The AAL-DSS is developed within Design For All, an Italian research project aimed at providing elderly or impaired people with a set of tools able to cope their physiological status. AAL should assure them the ability to perform several daily life activities during their domestic lives that would otherwise be precluded or strenuous. In this context, the semantic-based DSS is composed of five sets of domain ontologies.

The ontologies were developed following the NeOn methodology [22], a methodology requiring several domain experts to collaborate. An Ontology Requirements Specification Document [23] has been drafted and then completed with a set of Competency Questions [24] – a list of the questions that an ontology should be able to answer. The related answers provided the terminology for a pre-glossary of terms, which were later formally represented into the set of ontologies using the Protégé ontology editor [25].

The first set is the User Model, which gathers a dweller's registry records (full name, date of birth, birthplace, full address, telephone number, Tax Identification Number) and describes a person's physiological status using a partially re-engineered version of the ICF ontology [18]. In this particular module, the specific ICF codes originally modelled as individuals are converted into datatype properties, in order to enable to model several health conditions using the same ICF codes. The result of this process consists of a simplified TBox, containing the datatype properties describing the four main components of the classification (Body functions, Activities and participation, Body structures and Environmental factors). For each of the components, the Chapters are also specified, providing a grade of detail with sub-datatype properties for the second and third level categories (Fig. 2). These datatype properties, linked to a Health Condition individual, allow to specify the generic qualifier (with a range of acceptable `int` value restricted to 0, 1, 2, 3 or 4) to be associated to a specific category. Following this modelling expedients, it is possible to keep the inferences strictly related to the Health Conditions and to build general SWRL rules regarding specific codes and impairments.

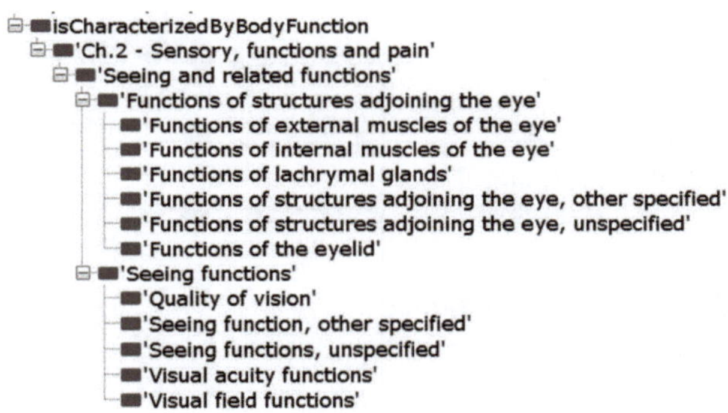

Fig. 2. An excerpt of the ICF TBox, illustrating the second Chapter of the "Body functions" component and the degree of specification with the use of datatype properties.

Every person living in the house is associated with his/her Health Conditions – modelled in a separate module –, according to an already tested Ontology Design Pattern (ODP) [26]. For each dweller, several Health Conditions can be assessed in different moments in time by clinicians. Health Conditions described by means of the ICF module can then be classified through reasoning process. In fact, the reasoning performed on the Health Condition module allows to understand if a person is characterized by a mild, moderate, severe or complete impairment and the quality of the impairment (visual, hearing, motor or cognitive).

The second set of ontologies is the Smart Object Model, which formally describes the appliances and sensors that can be potentially placed in the house and their related functionalities. This set allows to classify each appliance according to its typology (dishwasher, refrigerator, oven, etc.) and to the benefits it provides to specific categories of impaired dwellers. The description of the Smart Objects takes advantage of the HicMO [27] "grammar", a set of XML properties able to describe the features of any appliance. The description of a Smart Object is integrated with a module describing the list of programs available for each appliance. Reasoning process on this module allows to determine the most suitable appliance for each of the dwellers modelled in the User Module.

The third set of ontologies deals with the Measurements Description and allows to model the measurements performed by a Smart Object. Each measurement is classified according to its typology (environmental, physiological or machinery if they refer respectively to rooms, people or Smart Objects) and described with a set of objects and datatype properties (Fig. 3). This model serves as a completion for the description of the appliances and provide a formal way to describe the domestic comfort metrics. Another relevant advantage offered by this module, is the possibility to get semantic interoperability among the various measurements performed by the different Smart Objects, thanks to their formal description and the use of reference ontology for the description of the physiological measurements – Vital Sign Ontology (VSO) [28] – and comfort-related measurements – Units Ontology [29].

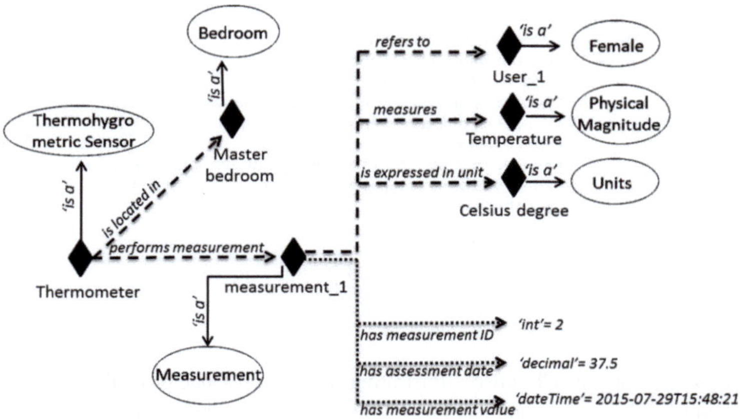

Fig. 3. An example of modelling of a Smart Object performing a measurement; dashed lines represent object properties, while dotted lines represent datatype properties.

The fourth set of domain ontologies is the Domestic Environment Model, whose goal is to provide a description of the dwellers' house and its structures, together with the comfort metrics that must be effective in providing a comfortable and safe permanence inside the house. The description of a person's house is performed with a simple taxonomy, which is composed of a set of classes categorizing the different rooms of a domestic environment (living room, kitchen, bathroom, etc.). Comfort dimensions are expressed as environmental measurements and allow to describe air quality (in terms of CO_2 concentration in a room), amount of illuminance and internal temperature during winter and summer. According to the typology and grade of impairment it is possible to set specific comfort dimensions for a particular dweller; for instance, a visual-impaired user characterized by hyposensitivity to light may need a customized (higher) level of illuminance to perform daily life activities.

Finally, the fifth set of ontology provides a description of the customization work provided by the designers. In this model, a description of the projects for the configuration of a living environment is provided; thanks to the entailments performed on the User Model and on the Smart Object Model, this ontology allows to formalize the choices performed by a designer (Fig. 4).

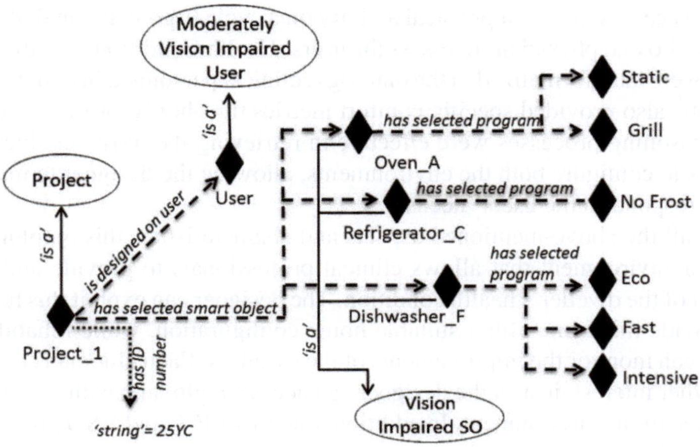

Fig. 4. An example of modelling of a Project for a moderately visual-impaired user; the designer has chosen the appliances and their programs (dashed lines represent object properties, dotted lines represent datatype properties).

The aggregated data regarding the user's health condition, the list of suitable Smart Objects, the user's house and the entailments performed by the AAL-DSS are retrieved via SPARQL queries [30] and fed to a Virtual Reality-based application that enables designers to reproduce a virtual model of the user's domestic environments (Fig. 5).

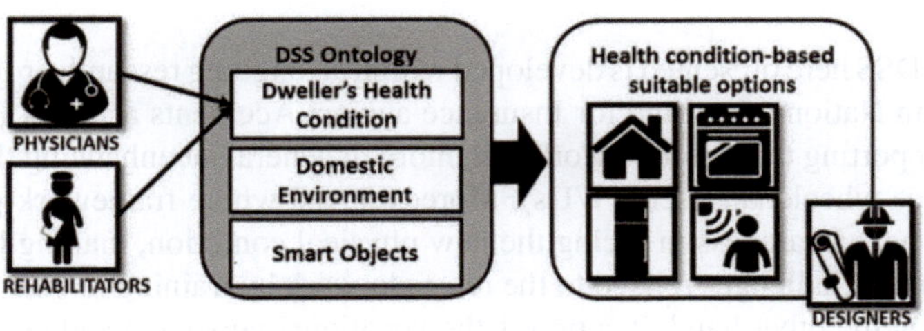

Fig. 5. An example of support to collaboration among different professionals provided by the application of ontology.

Inside this virtual environment, the designer can place the Smart Objects by choosing from the list of most suitable options provided by the reasoning process on the Smart Object Model. As already described, the entailments are performed taking into account the user's current Health Condition: in this way, it is possible to update the list of suitable

Smart Objects whenever an enhancement or deterioration of the health condition is modelled in the User Model.

To validate the ontology-based DSS implemented within the Design For All project, two specific use cases were developed. The first one foresees the configuration of a kitchen for a 68-year-old moderately visual-impaired male user, while the second foresees the configuration of a bedroom for a 70-year-old female user characterized by frailty, who needs to perform physical activity on a cycle-ergometer on daily basis. The framework allowed physicians to assess the users' Health Condition with the use of ICF: these data were later formalized in the ontology; clinical personnel, in collaboration with ergonomists, also provided specific comfort metrics thresholds for illuminance and air quality. Reasoning processes were effective in retrieving the most suitable appliances and sensors to configure both the environments, allowing the designer to make the best choices to respond to the users' needs.

Due to all the above-mentioned aspects and characteristics, this ontology acts as a cooperation environment that allows clinical professionals to provide and ICF-based assessment of the dweller's health condition. The designer can exploit this health condition to provide the users with a suitable home configuration, while rehabilitators and caregivers can monitor the improvements of the dwellers. Each clinician can deepen the data of his/her interest, just as the designer can access to global health condition data to configure the living environment. In addition, the use of ICF and VSO provides clinical personnel with descriptions and measurements able to ease the communication among physicians, domestic caregivers, rehabilitation therapists and dwellers. As a result, this semantic DSS enhances the collaboration between clinical and non-clinical professionals through the exchange of health-related data in an interoperable way, providing non-clinical personnel with aggregated and holistic data and clinical personnel with in-depth health data.

5 Collaborative DSS for Novice Wheelchair Users' Rehabilitation and Work Reintegration

The second DSS here presented is developed within an ongoing research project financed by the Italian National Institute for Insurance against Accidents at Work (INAIL) and aimed at supporting the return to work and, more in general, at enhancing the quality of life of novice wheelchair users (WUs). Moreover, the whole framework provides the WU with a new awareness in facing the new physical condition, making him/her able to deal with the challenges related to the return to work by training in safe virtual environments. On the other hand, it supports the vocational personnel and employers with technological means able to discriminate the still suitable jobs for that specific user. In this framework, the role of Semantic Web technologies is in fact to assess, with the help of clinicians, the WU's health conditions and, basing on this assessment, (1) to provide a list of eligible jobs for the WU's new health condition and (2) to set the difficulty of the training exercises in the virtual environments (Fig. 6).

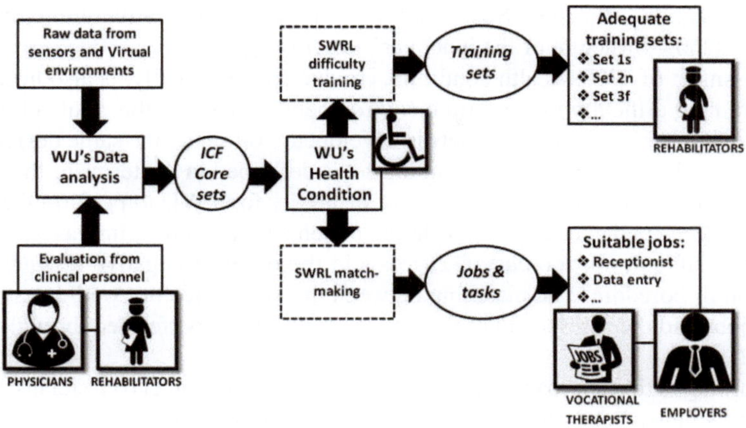

Fig. 6. A representation of how the health data flow among the three ontologies eases the cooperation among different stakeholders.

To this purpose, a set of three domain ontologies is developed. Also for this DSS, the NeOn methodology for ontology development has been chosen, since it provides a framework able to assess the purpose of the semantic models through the Ontology Specification Requirements Document and the list of Competency questions.

The first set of ontologies foresees the modelling of four ICF Core Sets [31] – corresponding to the main causes that force a person on a wheelchair: Spinal Cord Injury, Traumatic Brain Injury, Stroke; Vocational Rehabilitation Core Set is added as a fourth set to better address work reintegration. Together with this module, following the same ODP characterizing the AAL-DSS, the set describes the WU's registry record and Health Condition. Therefore, this model allows to provide a holistic view on the WU's health condition and to assess his/her residual functional capability. Since the focus of the project is very specific, it was preferred to develop the ICF Core Sets ontologies from scratch, instead of reusing the already existing ontology – which would have been too wide for the WU's Health Conditions description. Since some of the categories belonging to different ICF Core Sets are the same, a meta-model is implemented. In this meta-model it is possible to state the equivalency between the same categories and to classify them according to the four ICF components. For instance, the category "b126 – Temperament and personality functions" is used in all the four considered Core Sets. It is modelled as datatype property inside all the respective Core Sets models and then, in the meta-model, it is set as equivalent among the different tokens of this same category; in this way, it is possible to model exhaustively the ICF Core Sets domains while avoiding redundancy of the information.

The second set of ontologies provides an ICF-based description of the jobs and the tasks composing them. Its goal is to assess the impairment typology and the maximum grade of disability that is acceptable to perform a certain job. Each job is thus analyzed assigning it ICF-based employment factors, with the aim of identifying the acceptable conditions that a worker must fulfill to perform that job. For instance, a specific job like Receptionist can be suitable for WUs with a grade of impairment in the codes "b2300

– Sound detection", "b2304 – Speech discrimination", "s250 – Structure of the middle ear" and "s260 – Structure of the inner ear" lower or equal to 1.

Assessment of WU's health condition, conducted periodically, is also necessary to set the training difficulty in the virtual environment: to achieve this goal, a third set of ontologies describing the training sets is developed. Following the same design pattern used for the jobs' modelling, each training set is described in the terms of the typology of impairment and the maximum grades of disability for a WU to perform the training set. It is indeed fundamental to provide the patients with challenging tasks, which are neither too difficult nor too easy [32] to avoid the onset of negative feelings such as frustration or boredom. The matching between the WU's Health Condition, the list of eligible jobs and the assessment of the training difficulty is performed through two sets of SWRLs.

According to this approach, the DSS allows clinical personnel (physicians and rehabilitation therapists) and different health care structures (different hospital wards, rehabilitation structures) to periodically assess the WU's progresses and provides vocational therapists and rehabilitators with an up-to-date tool to evaluate (work-related) residual capabilities. The model then provides employers with reasoned suggestions regarding WU's suitable jobs and with a set of environmental modifications that can be implemented to ease the WU's reintegration in the working place. The DSS is therefore able to enhance the cooperation between clinicians, rehabilitators and non-clinical stakeholders. This DSS is part of a framework which will be validated and later integrated into the return to work process adopted by INAIL as a further development of this work.

6 Conclusions

This work addresses the secondary use of health-related data with SW technologies, describing two DSSs. Both of them are based on a worldwide-known standard (International Classification of Functioning, Disability and Health) and allow to model into ontologies the patient's health condition. Thanks to reasoning processes, it is possible from these formalized models to infer several new information regarding different health-related domains – such as Ambient Assisted Living and work reintegration. This information can be enriched and used by a variety of clinical and non-clinical professionals who may intervene to improve several aspects of impaired patients' lives. Relying on ICF and its structured vocabulary provides a common language for clinicians, rehabilitators, vocational personnel and non-clinical personnel (designers and employers), offering a standard for the description of a patient's functioning, thus enhancing cooperation among different actors both from health and not health related fields. In addition, ICF's structure represents a suitable means to allow the development of ontologies with Semantic Web standard technologies. The developed ontologies can also be aligned with the upper-level ontologies [33], thus providing a common semantic framework for data interoperability and granting horizontal scalability.

References

1. Pan, J.Z.: Resource description framework. In: Liu, L., Özsu, M.T. (eds.) Handbook on Ontologies, pp. 71–90. Springer, Heidelberg (2009)
2. Heflin, J., et al.: An introduction to the OWL web ontology language. Lehigh University. National Science Foundation (NSF) (2007)
3. Gruber, T.R., et al.: A translation approach to portable ontology specifications. Knowl. Acquisit. **5**(2), 199–220 (1993)
4. Aiello, C., Catarci, T., Ceravolo, P., Damiani, E., Scannapieco, M., Viviani, M.: Emergent semantics in distributed knowledge management. In: Evolution of the Web in Artificial Intelligence Environments, pp. 201–220. Springer, Heidelberg (2008)
5. World Health Organization: International Classification of Functioning, Disability and Health: ICF. World Health Organization (2001)
6. Cheung, K.-H., Prud'hommeaux, E., Wang, Y., Stephens, S.: Semantic web for health care and life sciences: a review of the state of the art (2009)
7. Semantic Web for Health Care and Life Sciences Interest Group. https://www.w3.org/2011/09/HCLSIGCharter
8. Moner, D., Maldonado, J.A., Bosca, D., Fernández, J.T., Angulo, C., Crespo, P., Vivancos, P.J., Robles, M.: Archetype-based semantic integration and standardization of clinical data. In: 28th Annual International Conference of the IEEE Engineering in Medicine and Biology Society, EMBS 2006, pp. 5141–5144. IEEE (2006)
9. Tao, C., Jiang, G., Oniki, T.A., Freimuth, R.R., Zhu, Q., Sharma, D., Pathak, J., Huff, S.M., Chute, C.G.: A semantic-web oriented representation of the clinical element model for secondary use of electronic health records data. J. Am. Med. Inf. Assoc. **20**(3), 554–562 (2013)
10. Hussain, S., Ouagne, D., Sadou, E., Dart, T., Jaulent, M.-C., De Vloed, B., Colaert, D., Daniel, C.: EHR4CR: a semantic web based interoperability approach for reusing electronic healthcare records in protocol feasibility studies. In: SWAT4LS (2012)
11. Kashyap, V., Prud'hommeau, E., Chen, H., Stenzhorn, H., Pathak, J., Fostel, J., Oniki, T., Anderssen, B., Forsberg, K., Marshall, M.S., et al.: Clinical observations interoperability: a semantic web approach. In: 2009 AMIA Spring Congress (2009)
12. Abidi, S.S., Chen, H.: Adaptable personalized care planning via a semantic web framework. In: 20th International Congress of the European Federation for Medical Informatics (MIE 2006), Maastricht. Citeseer (2006)
13. Artikis, A., Bamidis, P.D., Billis, A., Bratsas, C., Frantzidis, C., Karkaletsis, V., Klados, M., Konstantinidis, E., Konstantopoulos, S., Kosmopoulos, D., et al.: Supporting tele-health and AI-based clinical decision making with sensor data fusion and semantic interpretation: The USEFIL case study. In: International Workshop on Artificial Intelligence and NetMedicine, p. 21 (2012)
14. Horrocks, I., Patel-Schneider, P.F., Boley, H., Tabet, S., Grosof, B., Dean, M., et al.: SWRL: a semantic web rule language combining OWL and RuleML. W3C Member submission 21, 79 (2004)
15. Doucette, J.A., Khan, A., Cohen, R., Lizotte, D., Moghaddam, H.M.: A framework for AI-Based clinical decision support that is patient-centric and evidence-based. In: International Workshop on Artificial Intelligence and NetMedicine, p. 26 (2012)
16. Subirats, L., Ceccaroni, L., Gómez-Pérez, C., Caballero, R., Lopez-Blazquez, R., Miralles, F.: On semantic, rule-based reasoning in the management of functional rehabilitation processes. In: Management Intelligent Systems, pp. 51–58. Springer, Heidelberg (2013)

17. World Health Organization, others: How to use the ICF: a practical manual for using the international classification of functioning, disability and health (ICF). Exposure draft for comment (2013)
18. International Classification of Functioning, Disability and Health NCBIO BioPortal. https://bioportal.bioontology.org/ontologies/ICF
19. Della Mea, V., Simoncello, A.: An ontology-based exploration of the concepts and relationships in the activities and participation component of the international classification of functioning, disability and health. J. Biomed. Semant. **3**(1), 1 (2012)
20. Kumar, A., Smith, B.: The ontology of processes and functions: a study of the international classification of functioning, disability and health. In: Proceedings of the AIME 2005 Workshop on Biomedical Ontology Engineering, Aberdeen, Scotland (2005)
21. Andronache, A.S., Simoncello, A., Della Mea, V., Daffara, C., Francescutti, C.: Semantic aspects of the international classification of functioning, disability and health: towards sharing knowledge and unifying information. Am. J. Phys. Med. Rehabil. **91**(13), S124–S128 (2012)
22. Suárez-Figueroa, M.C., Gómez-Pérez, A., Fernández-López, M.: The NeOn methodology for ontology engineering. In: Suárez-Figueroa, M.C., Gómez-Pérez, A., Motta, E., Gangemi, A. (eds.) Ontology Engineering in a Networked World, pp. 9–34. Springer, Heidelberg (2012)
23. Suárez-Figueroa, M., Gómez-Pérez, A., Villazón-Terrazas, B.: How to write and use the ontology requirements specification document. In: On the Move to Meaningful Internet Systems, OTM 2009, pp. 966–982 (2009)
24. Grüninger, M., Fox, M.S.: The role of competency questions in enterprise engineering. In: Rolstadås, A. (ed.) Benchmarking — Theory and Practice. IAICT. Springer, Boston, MA (1995). doi:10.1007/978-0-387-34847-6
25. Gennari, J.H., Musen, M.A., Fergerson, R.W., Grosso, W.E., Crubézy, M., Eriksson, H., Noy, N.F., Tu, S.W.: The evolution of Protégé: an environment for knowledge-based systems development. Int. J. Hum Comput Stud. **58**(1), 89–123 (2003)
26. Sojic, A., Terkaj, W., Contini, G., Sacco, M.: Modularising ontology and designing inference patterns to personalise health condition assessment: the case of obesity. J. Biomed. Semant. **7**(1), 12 (2016)
27. Peruzzini, M., Germani, M.: A service-oriented architecture for ambient-assisted living. In: ISPE CE, pp. 523–532 (2015)
28. Goldfain, A., Smith, B., Arabandi, S., Brochhausen, M., Hogan, W.R.: Vital sign ontology. In: Bio-Ontologies 2011 (2011)
29. Gkoutos, G.V., Schofield, P.N., Hoehndorf, R.: The Units Ontology: a tool for integrating units of measurement in science. Database (2012). bas033
30. SPARQL Query Language for RDF. https://www.w3.org/TR/rdf-sparql-query/
31. Bickenbach, J., Cieza, A., Rauch, A., Stucki, G.: ICF core sets: manual for clinical practice for the ICF research branch. In: Cooperation with the WHO Collaborating Centre for the Family of International Classifications in Germany (DIMDI). Hogrefe Publishing (2012)
32. Maclean, N., Pound, P.: A critical review of the concept of patient motivation in the literature on physical rehabilitation. Soc. Sci. Med. **50**(4), 495–506 (2000)
33. Hoehndorf, R.: What is an upper level ontology? Ontogenesis (2010)

Service-Oriented Collaborative Networks

A Comparative Assessment of Collaborative Business Process Verification Approaches

John Paul Kasse[(✉)], Lai Xu, and Paul de Vrieze

Computing and Informatics, Bournemouth University,
Poole BH12 5BB, Bournemouth, UK
{jkasse, lxu, pdvrieze}@bournemouth.ac.uk

Abstract. Industry 4.0 is a key strategic trend of the economy. Virtual factories are key building blocks for Industry 4.0 where product design processes, manufacturing processes and general collaborative business processes across factories and enterprises are integrated. In the context of EU H2020 FIRST (vF Interoperation suppoRting buSiness innovaTion) project, end users of vFs are not experts in business process modelling to guarantee correct collaborative business processes for realizing execution. To enable automatic execution of business processes, verification is an important step at the business process design stage to avoid errors at runtime. Research in business process model verification has yielded a plethora of approaches in form of languages and tools that are based on Petri nets family and temporal logic. However, no report specifically targets and presents a comparative assessment of these approaches based on criteria as one we propose. In this paper we present an assessment of the most common verification approaches based on their expressibility, flexibility, suitability and complexity. We also look at how big data impacts the business process verification approach in a data-rich world.

Keywords: Petri nets · Temporal logic · Collaborative business process · Big data · Virtual factory

1 Introduction

Virtual factories (vF) arise out of the amalgamation of distributed manufacturing, virtual enterprises, and business management. A vF describes a distributed and integrated computer-based model simulating total manufacturing environment. It incorporates all the tasks and resources necessary to accomplish the operation of designing, producing and delivering a product [1, 2]. From the manufacturing practice, the machines, processes, related products and services are directly made compatible to support automated design and verification of collaborative business processes (cBP). Individual enterprise business processes integrate into a cBP jointly designed and implemented. The pool of skills, resources and technology is exploited to support the analysis of different design alternatives, performance evaluation and reduced time-to-production.

cBPs are complex; they are dynamic, cross organizational boundaries and rely on data from partners for their design and execution. They differ from single organization business processes (sBP) in nature and structural design [3, 4] more so in virtual

L.M. Camarinha-Matos et al. (Eds.): PRO-VE 2017, IFIP AICT 506, pp. 355–367, 2017.
DOI: 10.1007/978-3-319-65151-4_33

environments where execution is automated. It is resonant therefore to verify cBPs before their implementation to avoid errors at execution. We posit that verification should be supported with canonical approaches. Literature is scanty concerning approaches and tools applicable to verify cBP models especially for vF yet sBP verification has been well addressed with various approaches [3, 5–9, 10, 11]. However, these approaches present realizable knowledge gaps; they concentrate on control flow aspects [3, 4, 9–12, 14, 15] and abstract from other perspectives like data which is a major input for smart devices and machines in a vF. Besides, best practice linking verification approaches to vF cBPs is missing. The EU H2020 FIRST project aims to develop a method to support non expert end users to model and verify vF cBPs.

This paper presents the state of art in business process verification approaches and makes a comparative assessment of their fitness to verify vF cBPs. The vF cBPs being data intensive, we describe their requirements and how to support their verification in a vF environment. The rest of the paper is structured as follows; Sect. 2 presents the requirements for cBP verification by describing their characteristics in a vF setting, Sect. 3 presents the state-of-art in process verification. In Sect. 4 we present a framework of cBP verification while Sect. 5 discusses the related work. We make conclusions and outlook for future work in Sect. 6.

2 Requirements of CBP Model Verification

For us to support cBP verification, it is objective to understand their nature and requirements. We postulate that cBPs should conform to a set of requirements described below:

Span different organisations: Collaboration involves different partners working together for a common goal. In terms of business process management the partners jointly define business and technical solutions. The business solution describes partner behavior in the cBP while the technical solution defines the specifications and implementation of the supporting system [16]. The approach to verify such processes should consider the diversity of users, their roles and the distributed nature of the cBP.

Communication/Interaction Protocol: Typical of the cBP are the forms of communications and interactions expressed as message exchanges among partners who engage in discussions before reaching a decision. cBPs require dedicated interaction protocols through which partners can communicate. Various interaction protocols are proposed [4, 17] but they do not pass the criteria to support cBP verification.

Dynamism, Flexibility and Complexity: CBPs may be composed from services offered by partners using Service oriented architecture. The partners timelessly and continuously push in changes that impact on the process outcome. Such volatility should be taken care or at design time through verification to prevent execution flaws and support change integration, propagation and continuous verification.

Data requirements: cBP data requirements relate to several issues to support operations and analytics for decision making. Workflow systems embraced 2 kinds of data i.e.

control data (for routing purposes) and production data (information objects like documents, forms, and tables) [8]. For the smart factory data is exploited by the cyber physical systems, internet of things and cloud computing to support operations by autonomously exchanging information, triggering actions and controlling operations. Factory automation relies on intelligent data gathering and exchange between the systems. Verification should cater for data requirements and data patterns to support analytics for decision making and driving operations at the factory floor. A verification tool should be able to support verification of such requirements.

The following section presents the state of art in business process verification by discussing how existing approaches and tools compare in regard to supporting cBP model verification given the suggested requirements.

3 State of the Art in Business Process Verification

3.1 Business Process Verification Approaches

Business process verification as a concept of model checking (MC) has various applications; i.e. Variability - checking to ascertain how business processes vary in behavior over a set of conditions [12, 18]. Compliance - model conformance with requirements, laws or standards [13–15, 19–21]. Compatibility - aligning partner processes to the choreography i.e. the interaction architecture through which the cBP is executed [18, 22]. Verification – checking models to correct errors. During business process design, more time is spent on verification than actual design. Formal verification leads to seminal advantages as described in [19, 23].

Various verification approaches exist along with supporting tools. This section presents a description of some of the most commonly applied verification approaches and tools in literature. The tools are broadly categorized according to the technique or language on which they are semantically based .i.e. *Petri nets and Temporal Logic*. Petri nets describe a bipartite directed graph with two nodes i.e. Places (circles) and Transitions (rectangles) [24] connected by directed arcs. Petri nets are applied in workflows to create Workflow Nets. A workflow net must meet a syntactical requirement of having each place or transition on a direct path from start to end. Such requirement satisfies the workflow property of soundness [3, 11, 25, 26]. For details on petri nets and workflow verification the reader is referred to [6]. Classical petri nets become very large, inaccessible and difficult to interpret [3]. The color petri nets solve the limitations. A discussion of some of the most common petri net based tools follows;

Colored Petri Nets (CPN Tools); support modelling of data, objects and structures using color [27] and support verification [28, 29]. Color expresses each instance as unique in a case, time captures time related information to track capacity of a process, and hierarchy supports hierarchical design of process models and sub models. CPN tools integrate with other tools to support verification of models, for instance Protos and E-C-A [29].

Yet Another Workflow Language (YAWL); it is both a workflow modelling and verification tool based on the Petri nets [25] and workflow patterns [30]. It provides a graphical editor enhanced with built-in verification functionality supporting early time detection of model errors. It provides support for verification based on Reset nets and transition invariants (WofYAWL editor plug-in) [31]

Protos: Protos supports process model definition and analysis based on different perspectives of data and control flow. It supports simulation of models before their enactment and execution. Protos2CPN tool is an integration of Protos with CPN tools to support process model verification [29].

FlowMake: The tool supports design time identification of errors in models before implementation in WFMS [32]. Graph reduction algorithm [33] is employed to verify workflows for syntactic correctness by identifying and eliminating structural conflicts like deadlocks and lack of synchronization. Correct structures are removed until the WF graph remains empty through a conflict reserving reduction process.

Application Development based on Encapsulated pre-modelled Process Templates (ADEPT)/AristaFlow; a family of tools used to support modelling and verification of flexible and dynamic business processes [34–37]. Based on clinical business scenarios, ADEPT enables process implementers, application developers and end users to model and verify models through its features like; extended graphical interfaces, on-the-fly correctness checks [37], process templates and structural transformation of processes. It supports for ad-hoc changes and their propagation.

The tools described from this point are based on Temporal Logic formalism. Temporal Logic supports ways to specify systems and check models for correctness against a set of properties expressed in form of event orderings in time [20, 38]. It is widely applied to verify concurrent systems, distributed systems, context aware and collaborative systems. For details on temporal logic and its various branches and application the reader is referred [39].

Declarative Service Flow Language (DecSerFlow): DecSerFlow supports specification, enactment, and monitoring of service flows in a declarative nature. Verification of service workflow conformance is achieved by subjecting models to temporal logic constraints enforced by the engine and guarded against their violations. The engine monitors the violations as well [11, 14].

HYbrid TECHnology (HyTech); supports automatic verification of system models against properties specifications expressed in real time temporal logic through symbolic computation [7]. Models are verified for reachability, liveness, time boundedness and duration properties [40]. HyTECH is recommended for verification of mission critical systems. However, the tool is limited to verification of small systems [41] and linear hybrid systems [42]. Some of the limitations have been overcome by HyTECH+ tool [42] which is an extension to the classical HyTECH.

Symbolic Model Verifier (SMV); operates like HyTECH to exhaustively verify models and provide counter examples. It is limited by state explosion. NuSMV is a modified version to verify synchronous finite-state and infinite-state systems [43, 44].

SPIN; supports verification of asynchronous systems by verifying for correctness. The properties are expressed as standard temporal logic while model specifications as a Buchi automaton. The Buchi automaton is a product from computation of the claims and the automaton representing the global state space. The product is then checked, if empty then the claims are not satisfied for a given system, otherwise it contains the behavior that satisfies the original temporal formula. To limit state explosion, partial order reduction method is employed [25, 45–47]. However state explosion remain a challenge limiting applicability to verify cBP model.

KRONOS; applies timed automata and timed temporal logic to verify models for reachability properties [48, 49] like; safety (system never enter unsafe states), non zenoness (the state of the system does not prevent time to diverge) and bounded response (ability to respond to requests issued in specified time)

UPPAAL; supports on-the-fly verification of real time systems modelled as timed automata with extended data. It checks models for reachability and invariability properties with support for diagnostic trace [5, 50, 51]. State explosion remains a challenge limiting its application to cBP model verification. Table 1 presents a summary of the tools and the related properties that they verify in business process models.

Table 1. Showing summary of tools and properties

Language\Technique	Tool	Properties
Petri Nets	Woflan	Soundness (deadlocks, reachability and liveness)
	YAWL	Soundness and liveness
	FlowMake	Synchronization, Deadlocks, consistency, boundedness, liveness
	CPN Tools	Performance analysis, coverability and occurrence
	Protos2CPN	Soundness and liveness
Temporal logic	SPIN	Correctness and logical consistency
	UPPAAL	Bounded liveness and deadlocks
	KRONOS	Reachability (safety and bounded response)
	SMV \NuSMV	Correctness, safety, and liveliness
	HyTECH	Reachability, safety, liveness, time-bounded, duration
	ADEPT	Semantic correctness, deadlock and Safety
Petri Nets & Temporal logic	DecSerFlow	Constraints and their variations

3.2 Limitations of the Verification Approaches to Verify cBP Models

Based on the assessment in Table 1, we find verification approaches lacking in terms of the support they accord to users to verify cBPs. We expound on these limitations; *Support sBP verification*; existing approaches were developed to support modelling and simulation of single organization business processes, not cBPs. Simulation is not an exhaustive way to verify models since it is based on assumptions that may deviate from actual. Some tools integrate with other tools to support verification (e.g Protos and E-C-A integrate with CPN tools) [29] while others like YAWL verify models modelled in the same language. Woflan was created as an independent verification tool to verify models developed in Staffware, COSA and MQ [52]. These tools remain limited for vF cBP verification.

The semantical and architectural structure: The tools do not support the semantical structure and architectural requirements for cBP verification i.e. the lack of interfaces or open structures to permit integration with other systems manifests their inability to support collaborative environments. YAWL avails web based plugins for integration with other systems but support for simultaneous model and sub models verification is limited. Additionally the semantical structure of other tools is ambiguous and a source of semantical errors and conflicts when models are merged for verification [53].

Support for data and data analytics: Most approaches target verification based on control flow perspective and abstract from other perspectives like data, resources, tasks and applications [6, 8, 9, 16, 52]. The justification advanced for abstraction never anticipated future data requirements that vF processes currently present. The smart factory heavily relies on data routed between interconnected smart devices to drive the automated machines at the factory floor. Moreover, data is used to support analytics for other seminal benefits like decision making, projections and future planning. Therefore during verification data and data analytics should be supported at both design time and runtime.

4 Framework for Assessing CBP Model Verification Approaches

4.1 Assessment Criteria

Language comparisons are based on different factors that may be objective or subjective [53]. A set of parameters to compose our criteria intended to assess the inherent traction and precision of the verification approaches and their appropriateness to verify vF cBP models. The following section briefly describes these parameters;

Expressibility; assesses the degree to which an approach can represent any number of models in different application domains [54, 55]. In [33], the expressive power of a modelling technique was gauged in terms of its capability to represent specific process requirements. In our case, we consider expressiveness of a model verification tool in terms of the degree to which it supports one to verify different properties of cBP models given their specifications.

Flexibility; describes the ability to support exception handling, possibility to make changes at design time or runtime, and support for scalability especially as the cBPs evolve and grow.

Suitability; describes the appropriateness of a tool to a particular application domain [5, 54]. In our case we assess suitability in terms of the degree to which a tool is applicable to verify vF cBP models given their structure and architecture for instance; verify semantical correctness of main models and sub models simultaneously.

Complexity and Limitations; assesse the level of difficulty an approach presents to work with [33] or its features that make it easy to work with while being used to verify process models. The limitations refer to the different forms of inadequacies of a tool that render it inappropriate and inapplicable to verify vF collaborative business process models.

4.2 Application of the Assessment Framework

This section presents the application of the assessment framework criteria to assess the existing verifications approaches and tools. A summary of this assessment is presented in Table 2 after which we discuss the assessment results in the section that follows after;

Table 2. Showing a Comparative assessment of the verification tools

Tool	Expressibility	Flexibility	Suitability	Complexity \Limitation
Woflan	Control flow specific Non domain specific Imports models from other tools	No adhoc changes Verifies complete models.	Non-collaborative Single model verification	Graphical interface Hard to trace Errors
YAWL	Control flow specific Non domain specific Integrates data	Exception handling at Design time	Non-collaborative Single model verification	Extensible with web plugins Graphical interface
FlowMake	Control flow specific Integrates data Non-domain specific	Supports exception handling Non scalable	Non-collaborative Single model verification	Graphical interface Hard to trace Errors
CPN Tools	Non domain specific Concurrent systems Integrates data	Exception handling supported	Non-collaborative Integrates with other tools	Graphical interface
Protos2CPN	Control flow specific Integrates data	Static analysis Exception handling supported	Non-collaborative Integrates with CPN tools	Known application and user support Graphical interface

(*continued*)

Table 2. (*continued*)

Tool	Expressibility	Flexibility	Suitability	Complexity \Limitation
SPIN \XSPIN	Non domain specific Viable for vF cBP Wide application	Exception handling supported	State explosion - smaller systems Non-collaborative	Complex syntax and semantics. Graphical interface Counter examples
UPPAAL	Non scalable Error traceability	Supports on-the-fly verification.	No support for data Non-collaborative	Graphical interface with supported tools
KRONOS	Unknown application to vF domain No support for data	Exception handling supported	Non-collaborative Single model verification Verifies smaller models	Graphical interface Counter examples
SMV\ NuSMV	Non- domain specific	Exception handling Supported	Non-collaborative Single model verification State explosion	Graphical interface Counter examples
HyTECH	No support for data integration	Exception handling not supported. Non scalable	Verifies smaller models State explosion Non-collaborative	Complex syntax and semantics Counter examples
ADEPT	On-the-fly verification Integrates data	Exception handling supported	Lack of known application Single model verification	Process templates for easy creation of processes
DeScerFlow	Non-domain specific Control flow specific	Adhoc changes supported Plug & play style	Single model verification	Graphical interfaces Process templates for process creation

Assessment based on the proposed criteria as summarized in Table 2 and in reference to Table 1 reveals various properties being checked by the existing tools. However, these properties are expressed in relation to single organization business processes. The interpretation and connotation of these properties may not be the same for cBPs: for instance having sound models for a single organization business process does not guarantee their soundness in a collaborative environment. Furthermore verifying for reachability, safeness, liveness and boundedness in a single organization process is not as complex as verifying the same properties for cBPs where the requirements differ. Moreover, there is no silver bullet solution; no single approach verifies all necessary properties for all situations. For example Petri net based tools like YAWL, Woflan, and CPN are lacking in terms of time based requirements for models. Temporal logic based tools like SPIN, KRONOS and HyTECH suffer from state explosion problem that limits the number and size of models that can be checked. Besides, the counter examples they provide on discovery of errors remain difficulty to understand for the ordinary users. Above of all, the inability and inconsideration for data perspective leaves them inappropriate to verify cBPs that are highly data intensive. In summary, using the parameters in the proposed criteria we note the following in view of cBPs;

Expressiveness - most approaches are not specific to a particular application domain but incapable of representing as many models for interacting enterprises as may be required. To that effect such approaches would not verify the structure, data and execution requirements of cBPs.

Flexibility - besides HyTECH, UPPAAL and Woflan, all other tools reviewed have the capability for exception handling, permitting ad hoc changes and scalability. Such attributes meet the requirements of cBPs that are highly variable and dynamic due to the diversity of process owners and environment in which they apply. However the tools verify already completely designed models. This renders them rigid and inflexible for application to cBPs [17].

Suitability - the techniques are inappropriate and not suitable for verification of vF cBP models. The tools support single model verification at a time which makes it difficult for cBPs that are composed of many sub models that are merged for verification. Lack of standardized semantics introduces semantical errors when models to be verified are developed from different tools. This further limits the application of these tools to vF cBP verification.

Complexity\ Limitations - most tools present graphical user interfaces making them easy for the non-expert users to apply. Moreover, temporal logic based tools provide counter examples where model errors exist. However, the provided counter examples are not a guarantee for correctness of the model. Besides, temporal logic expressions remain complex for non-expert users in the collaborative environments [40].

5 Related Work

This section presents work related to our study but we are keen to highlight how our work differs.

In [33] a survey of comparative business process modelling approaches is presented based on graph based vs rule based approaches. The comparison criteria included parameters like expressibility, flexibility, adaptability, dynamism and complexity, and an analysis of how the approaches score was presented. The work is presented under the umbrella of process modelling while ours is based on supporting cBP model verification in a vF environment. In [23], a survey of formal verification approaches for business process diagrams is presented and compared with respect to motivation behind their development i.e. the aim of verification, method of formalization and logics. This survey was based on verification of single organization business process models where our work concentrates on assessment of approaches that support cBP verification. Moreover they do not assess the tools based on their application or competency but rather on what motivated their developers. In our study the assessment is based on how well the approaches can support verification in a collaborative environment.

Further work by [56] presents an analysis of verification tools based on the forms and application of verification by categorizing it into variability, compliance and compatibility. The approaches are then discussed and compared under the same breadth. Our work differs in a way that we propose and present an assessment framework to analyze verification tools based on their traction, precision and competency to verify cBP in vF environment.

6 Conclusion and Future Work

Verification is a way to ensure error free business process models at execution time. The existing research reveals various efforts towards business process modelling and verification in form of theories, approaches, tools and methodologies but realizable knowledge gaps exist. Verification of single organization business processes is well addressed in literature but work remains at large concerning techniques and tools specific for verification of cBP models more so for vF environments. The nature of cBPs in vF relies on data to enable real-time actionable intelligence. Supporting data analytics presents the potential to increase productivity, undertake preventive maintenance through projected breakdowns and generate cost savings. Recommendation for a verification method specific to cBP models in a vF environment is appropriate to meet the expressiveness, flexibility, suitability and complexity required in such environment given its requirements as discussed above.

Acknowledgements. This research has been partially sponsored by EU H2020 FIRST project, Grant No. 734599, FIRST: vF Interoperation suppoRting buSiness innovaTion.

References

1. Jain, S., Choong, N.F., Aye, K.M., Luo, M.: Virtual factory: an integrated approach to manufacturing systems modeling. Int. J. Oper. Prod. Manage. **21**(5/6), 594–608 (2001)
2. Wenbin, Z., Xiumin, F., Juanqi, Y., Zhu, P.: An integrated simulation method to support virtual factory engineering. Int. J. **2**(1), 39–44 (2002)
3. van der Aalst, W., van Hee, K.: Workflow Management (2004)
4. van der Aalst, W.: Loosely coupled interorganizational workflows: modeling and analyzing workflows crossing organizational boundaries. Inf. Manage. **37**(2), 67–75 (2000), http://www.sciencedirect.com/science/article/B6VD0-3YJ9Y2V-2/2/d9c28a0dfa2816dcd7f419de6a56d7cf\, http://www.sciencedirect.com/science/article/pii/S0378720699000385
5. Larsen, K.G., Pettersson, P., Yi, W.: UPPAAL in a Nutshell, pp. 134–152 (1997)
6. Van Der Aalst, W.M.P.: Verification of Workflow Nets (1997)
7. Alur, R., Henzinger, T.A., Ho, P.: Automatic Sybolic Verification of Embedded Systems. IEEE Trans. Softw. Eng. **22**(3), 2–11 (1996)

8. Aalst, W.M.P.: Workflow verification: finding control-flow errors using petri-net-based techniques. In: Aalst, W., Desel, J., Oberweis, A. (eds.) Business Process Management. LNCS, vol. 1806, pp. 161–183. Springer, Heidelberg (2000). doi:10.1007/3-540-45594-9_11
9. van der Aalst, W.M.P., Ter Hofstede, A.: Verification of workflow task structures: a petri-net-based approach. Inf. Syst., pp. 43–69 (2000)
10. Anderson, B.B., Hansen, J.V, Lowry, P.B., Summers, S.L.: Model checking for e-business control and assurance **35**(3), 445–450 (2005)
11. Pesic, M., van der Aalst, W.M.P.: A declarative approach for flexible business processes management. In: Business Process Management Workshops, pp. 169–180 (2006)
12. Varea, M.: Mixed Control/data-flow representation for modelling and verification of embedded systems (2002)
13. Adamides, E.D., Karacapilidis, N.: A knowledge centred framework for collaborative business process modelling. Bus. Process Manage. J. **12**(5), 557–575 (2006)
14. Aalst, W.M.P., Pesic, M.: DecSerFlow: towards a truly declarative service flow language. In: Bravetti, M., Núñez, M., Zavattaro, G. (eds.) WS-FM 2006. LNCS, vol. 4184, pp. 1–23. Springer, Heidelberg (2006). doi:10.1007/11841197_1
15. Norta, A., Grefen, P., Narendra, N.C.: A reference architecture for managing dynamic inter-organizational business processes. Data Knowl. Eng. **91**, 52–89 (2014), http://dx.doi.org/10.1016/j.datak.2014.04.001
16. Roa, J., Villarreal, P., Chiotti, O.: A methodology for the design, verification, and validation of business processes in B2B collaborations. In: International Conference on Business Process Management, pp. 293–305. Springer, Heidelberg (2011)
17. Villarreal, P.D., Lazarte, I., Roa, J., Chiotti, O.: A modeling approach for collaborative business processes based on the UP-ColBPIP language. In: Rinderle-Ma, S., Sadiq, S., Leymann, F. (eds.) BPM 2009. LNBIP, vol. 43, pp. 318–329. Springer, Heidelberg (2010). doi:10.1007/978-3-642-12186-9_30
18. Aiello, M., Bulanov, P., Groefsema, H.: Requirements and tools for variability management. In: Proceedings of International Computer Software and Applications Conference, pp. 245–250, July 2010
19. Knuplesch, D., Reichert, M., Fdhila, W., Rinderle-Ma, S.: On enabling compliance of cross-organizational business processes. In: Daniel, F., Wang, J., Weber, B. (eds.) BPM 2013. LNCS, vol. 8094, pp. 146–154. Springer, Heidelberg (2013). doi:10.1007/978-3-642-40176-3_12
20. Kochanowski, M., Fehling, C., Koetter, F., Leymann, F., Weisbecker, A.: Compliance in BPM today–an insight into experts' views and industry challenges. In: Informatik 2014, Big Data - Komplexität meistern, pp. 769–780 (2014)
21. Fdhila, W., Rinderle-Ma, S., Knuplesch, D., Reichert, M.: Change and compliance in collaborative processes. In: Proceedings of 2015 IEEE International Conference on Services Computing, SCC 2015, pp. 162–169 (2015)
22. De Backer, M., Snoeck, M., Monsieur, G., Lemahieu, W., Dedene, G.: A scenario-based verification technique to assess the compatibility of collaborative business processes. Data Knowl. Eng. **68**(6), 531–551 (2009)
23. Morimoto, S.: A survey of formal verification for business process modeling. In: Bubak, M., Albada, G.D., Dongarra, J., Sloot, Peter M.A. (eds.) ICCS 2008. LNCS, vol. 5102, pp. 514–522. Springer, Heidelberg (2008). doi:10.1007/978-3-540-69387-1_58
24. Kim, S., Smari, W.W.: A Petri Net-based Workflow Modeling for a Human-centric Collaborative Commerce System **5**(Cd), 28–31 (2006)
25. Petri, C.A.: General net theory. In: Computing System Design: Proceedings of the Joint IBM-University of Newcastle upon Tyne Seminar, September 1976 (1977), papers3://publication/uuid/80FAA443-1FAC-47FD-9828-B7D271194C80

26. Aalst, Wil M.P.: Business process management demystified: a tutorial on models, systems and standards for workflow management. In: Desel, J., Reisig, W., Rozenberg, G. (eds.) ACPN 2003. LNCS, vol. 3098, pp. 1–65. Springer, Heidelberg (2004). doi:10.1007/978-3-540-27755-2_1
27. Fahland, D., Luebke, D., Mendling, J., Reijers, H., Weber, B., Weidlich, M., Zugal, S.: Declarative versus imperative process modeling languages: the issue of understandability. In: Halpin, T., et al. (eds.) Enterprise, Business-Process and Information Systems Modeling. LNBIP, vol. 29, pp. 353–366. Springer, Heidelberg (2009). doi:10.1007/978-3-642-01862-6_29
28. Jensen, K., Kristensen, L.M., Wells, L.: Coloured Petri Nets and CPN Tools for modelling and validation of concurrent systems. Int. J. Softw. Tools Technol. Transf. **9**(3–4), 213–254 (2007)
29. Gottschalk, F., van der Aalst, W.M.P., Jansen-Vullers, M.H., Verbeek, H.M.W.: Protos2CPN: using colored petri nets for configuring and testing business processes. Int. J. Softw. Tools Technol. Transf. **10**(1), 95–110 (2008)
30. van der Aalst, W.M.P., Kiepuszewski, B., Hofstede, A.: Workflow patterns. distributed and parallel databases **14**(1), 5–51 (2003), http://link.springer.com/article/10.1023/A:1022883727209
31. Foundation, T.Y.: YAWL - User Manual (2016)
32. Sadiq, W., Orlowska, Maria E.: Applying graph reduction techniques for identifying structural conflicts in process models. In: Jarke, M., Oberweis, A. (eds.) CAiSE 1999. LNCS, vol. 1626, pp. 195–209. Springer, Heidelberg (1999). doi:10.1007/3-540-48738-7_15
33. Lu, R., Sadiq, S.: A survey of comparative business process modeling approaches. In: Abramowicz, W. (ed.) BIS 2007. LNCS, vol. 4439, pp. 82–94. Springer, Heidelberg (2007). doi:10.1007/978-3-540-72035-5_7
34. Reichert, M., Dadam, P.: ADEPTflex - supporting dynamic changes of workflows without losing control. J. Intell. Inf. Syst. **10**(2), 93–129 (1998)
35. Weber, B., Reichert, M., Rinderle-Ma, S.: Change patterns and change support features - Enhancing flexibility in process-aware information systems. Data Knowl. Eng. **66**(3), 438–466 (2008)
36. Weber, B., Reichert, M., Rinderle-Ma, S., Wild, W.: Providing integrated life cycle support in process-aware information systems. Int. J. Coop. Inf. Syst. **18**(1), 115–165 (2009)
37. Dadam, P., Reichert, M.: The ADEPT project: A decade of research and development for robust and flexible process support: Cllenges and Achievements. Comput. Sci. Res. Dev. **23**(2), 81–97 (2009)
38. Lowe, G.: Specification of communicating processes: temporal logic versus refusals-based refinement. Formal Aspects Comput. **20**(3), 277–294 (2008)
39. Baier, C., Katoen, J.-P.: Principles of Model Checking. MIT Press (2008). http://mitpress.mit.edu/books/principles-model-checking
40. Henzinger, T.A., Wong-toi, H.: HyTech: a model checker for hybrid systems 1 introduction. Int. J. Softw. Tools Technol. Transf. (STTT) **1**(1997), 110–122 (1997)
41. Bérard, B., Bidoit, M., François, A.F., Antoine Petit, L., Petrucci, L., Schnoebelen, P., Pierre, M.: HYTECH — Linear Hybrid Systems.pdf (2001)
42. Henzinger, T.A., Horowitz, B., Majumdar, R.: Beyond HyTech, pp. 89–95 (1999)

43. Cimatti, A., Clarke, E., Giunchiglia, E., Giunchiglia, F., Pistore, M., Roveri, M., Sebastiani, R., Tacchella, A.: NuSMV 2: an opensource tool for symbolic model checking. In: Brinksma, E., Larsen, K.G. (eds.) CAV 2002. LNCS, vol. 2404, pp. 359–364. Springer, Heidelberg (2002). doi:10.1007/3-540-45657-0_29
44. Kadono, M., Tsuchiya, T., Kikuno, T.: Using the NuSMV model checker for test generation from statecharts. In: 2009 15th IEEE Pacific Rim International Symposium on Dependable Computing, PRDC 2009, pp. 37–42 (2009)
45. Holzmann, G.J.: The model checker SPIN. IEEE Trans. Software Eng. **23**(5), 279–295 (1997)
46. Holzmann, G.: The Design and Validation of the CLASS.pdf, March 2017
47. Holzmann, G.J., Godefroid, P., Pirottin, D.: Coverage preserving reduction strategies for reachability analysis, vol. 6, pp. 349–363 (2013). https://books.google.com/books?hl=en&lr=&id=Q1EvBQAAQBAJ&oi=fnd&pg=PA349&dq='establish the correctness of systems of interacting concurrent processes by an Sections 3 and 4 discuss the foundation for a partial order semantics' "the actions aff
48. Daws, C., Olivero, A., Tripakis, S., Yovine, S.: The tool Kronos. In: Alur, R., Henzinger, Thomas A., Sontag, Eduardo D. (eds.) HS 1995. LNCS, vol. 1066, pp. 208–219. Springer, Heidelberg (1996). doi:10.1007/BFb0020947
49. Yovine, S.: Kronos: A verification tool for real-time systems. Int. J. Softw. Tools Technol. Transf. **1**(1–2), 123–133 (1997)
50. Larsen, K.G., Pettersson, P., Yi, W.Y.W.: Compositional and symbolic model-checking of real-time systems. In: Proceedings 16th IEEE Real-Time Systems Symposium, pp. 76–87 (1995)
51. Bengtsson, J., Rs, B., Larsen, K.G., Yi, W.: In 1995, December 1996
52. Verbeek, H.M.W., Basten, T., Van Der Aalst, W.M.P.: Diagnosing workflow processes using Woflan. Comput. J. **44**(4), 246–279 (2001)
53. Koliadis, G.: Verifying semantic business process models in verifying semantic business process models in inter-operation (2007)
54. Falkenberg, E., Hesse, W., Lindgreen, P.: A framework of information systems concepts. Ifip Wg (1998), http://citeseerx.ist.psu.edu/viewdoc/download?doi=10.1.1.89.1492&rep=rep1&type=pdf
55. Hommes, B.J.: The Evaluation of Business Process Modeling Techniques (2004)
56. Groefsema, H., Bucur, D.: A survey of formal business process verification: from soundness to variability. In: Proceedings of the Third International Symposium on Business Modeling and Software Design, pp. 198–203 (2013)

The User Perspective on Service Ecosystems: Key Concepts and Models

Garyfallos Fragidis(✉)

Faculty of Business and Economics, Technological Education Institution of Central Macedonia, Terma Magnisias, Serres, Greece
gary.fragidis@teicm.gr

Abstract. The concept of service ecosystems emerged recently in service research as an important notion that underlines the complexity of structures in service interactions and the need for comprehensive approaches for the study of service systems. In this paper we focus on the role of the user as the 'keystone entity' of service ecosystems – especially for the creation of value. The research objective is to understand better the requirements and the implications of a user-centric perspective on service ecosystems and provide some basic modelling abstractions for the analysis of the structure and the objectives of the service ecosystem. The paper develops the concept of the user-centric service ecosystem at the beginning and then provides a conceptual model of its structure and a goal model for the intentions of the actors. The paper can contribute to the better understanding of service ecosystems, the explanation of the role of the user and the fulfilment of the initial phases of requirements analysis for service ecosystems.

Keywords: Service ecosystem · Service value · Requirements analysis · Conceptual model · Goal model

1 Introduction

We live in a service world, which is characterized by the great variety and multiplicity of the services people use in their daily life practices. The complexity of the modern life practices is reflected on the service processes and relationships for the development, the provision and the use of services. Moreover, service processes are considered 'co-creational' as they commonly receive contribution and require the collaboration of various service actors and stakeholders.

The concept of service ecosystems emerged recently in service research as an important notion for the better understanding of the complexity of service processes and relationships and the development of service systems that address the requirements of the service world of today. The ecosystemic nature of services is obvious in the definition of a service system as "a dynamic value co-creation configuration of resources that are connected internally and externally to other service systems by value propositions" [13]. In this regard, service ecosystems are systems of actors who interact with their environment through mutual service flows [23].

L.M. Camarinha-Matos et al. (Eds.): PRO-VE 2017, IFIP AICT 506, pp. 368–380, 2017.
DOI: 10.1007/978-3-319-65151-4_34

In this paper we emphasize on the role of the user (or else the end-customer) as the 'keystone entity' [10] of service ecosystems. The user, first of all, may participate as co-producer in service processes and interactions. More importantly, taking into account the basic definition of service as "the application of resources for the benefit of another entity" [22], we gather the purpose of the processes of service providers (i.e. the application of resources) is reflected on the use of service and the benefit/value that is created for/by the user. Hence, the user, with his intentions, skills and additional resources, has the most critical role in service usage and in value creation, as he determines the actualization of service value as 'value-in-use' [22]. For this, we consider the analysis of service ecosystems from the user's perspective is important and meaningful and, additionally, it can inspire alternative approaches for the design of service systems that go beyond the operations and the concerns of the service providers to support service innovations, business model innovations and improved service value.

The paper proposes a user-centric perspective on service ecosystems and focuses on the initial phases of requirements analysis ('requirements elicitation') for service ecosystems. Taking into account the importance of requirements analysis for the design and development of successful information systems [6, 20], the paper can contribute to the better understanding of the role of the user in service ecosystems, the analysis of the context and the objectives of service ecosystems and the design of user-centric service processes.

The modeling procedures in requirements elicitation include domain descriptions that express the viewpoint of the analysis, conceptual models that describe the structure and relationships of the key concepts and goal models that describe the intentions of the actors [21, 28]. Following this approach as a rule of action, the rest of the paper is structured as such: after a short review of the concept of service ecosystems in the recent literature (Sect. 2), we propose a user-centric perspective on service ecosystems (Sect. 3). Next we provide an analysis of the conceptual structure of the user-centric perspective on service ecosystems in the form of a class diagram (Sect. 4) and the intentions of the actors of service ecosystems in the form of a goal model (Sect. 5). The paper concludes with a discussion of the importance of the research outcomes and the future research directions.

2 Basic Concepts of Service Ecosystems

The notion of ecosystems was introduced in the business literature firstly by Moore [16], who examined the analogy of the business operations to the relationships and the operations of biological entities in the natural environment. Iansity and Levien [10] developed further the strategic aspects of business ecosystems and Peltoniemi and Vuori [17] described their key attributes (complexity, self-organization, emergence, adaptation and co-evolution).

In ICT the notion of ecosystems was termed usually as 'digital ecosystems' or 'digital business ecosystems' [7], 'software ecosystems' [11] and 'collaborative networks' [5]. Digital ecosystems pay attention to the complexity and the distributed nature of the computing environment, the development of open, self-organized and adaptive socio-technical systems, the importance of the role of the user/customer and the interdisciplinary nature of research [7]. The applications of digital ecosystems refer typically to collaborative software development processes [1], SOA environments [2], cloud computing [3], and smart system environments [18]. Software ecosystems emphasize on the relationships among the actors of the software industry for the development and use of software and services [11]. The software industry becomes more and more an ecosystem under the influence of platforms like Google Android and Apple iOS [14]. Manikas [15] characterizes the field multidisciplinary, proposes the characteristics of software ecosystems and highlights the predominant areas of research. The interdisciplinary structure of technological ecosystems is obvious also in the research in collaborative networks, which emphasize on the collaboration and the interrelationships of business and technological actors for the development of products and services [5]. In sum, service ecosystems have a mixed nature that combines both business and technological concerns.

The concept of ecosystems has greatly influenced the research of service systems in general. Service science defines service systems as "dynamic value co-creation configurations of resources, including people, organizations, shared information (language, laws, measures, methods), and technology, all connected internally and externally to other service systems by value propositions" [13]. Using a less technical language, Spohrer, Demikan and Krishna [19] describe service systems as complex business and societal systems that include other technological and human-made systems and create benefits for customers, providers and other stakeholders. Camarinha-Matos et al. [4] regard service ecosystems as architectures that can address both the business/economic aspects of services on the physical world and the technological aspects of services, as computing mechanisms for the implementation of the business service.

In the service management literature, Vargo and Lusch [24] defined a service ecosystem as "a spontaneously sensing and responding spatial and temporal structure of largely loosely coupled, value-proposing social and economic actors interacting through institutions, technology, and language to co-produce service offerings, engage in mutual service provision and co-create value". Hence, the Service Dominant (SD) logic emphasizes on interactions that co-create value in nested and overlapping service ecosystems [23]. The focal role of the customer in service ecosystems was introduced in Voima et al. [25]. The customer ecosystem, clearly influenced by the ideas of the Customer Dominant (CD) logic [9], is a system of actors (e.g. providers, other customers and other actors) related to the customer that are relevant to a specific service [25]. The customer ecosystem augments a service ecosystem with the dimensions of the idiosyncratic character of the customer and the social context. The interest is placed on what the customer is doing with services and how he involves the service offerings of the providers in his daily life practices.

3 The User-Centric Service Ecosystem

Service ecosystems, as complex and multidimensional structures, can be approached from different points of reference. For instance, in business ecosystems the focus is on the business organization and the strategic relationships with its environment; in digital and software ecosystems the attention is on the digital technologies that can be employed and their operations; in collaborative business ecosystems the interest lies on the production and delivery of products/services through the collaboration of the participating business entities.

In this paper we approach the analysis of service ecosystems from the point of view of the service user. The user has a key role in service processes in general, but especially in the phase service usage, as his intentions, skills and resources, together with the contextual parameters, can determine the service value. Our analytical scope is focused on the use of services in the daily life practices of the user for the creation of value. The business processes for the development and delivery of the service offering are supportive to service usage and concern also the service ecosystems.

A user-centric service ecosystem is defined as a system of actors, with the user as the keystone entity with the focal role, and other elements related to the service. The actors include also service providers, technology providers, other users/customers, other social actors, such as communities and social groups, and institutional actors, such as regulatory bodies. The actors can play various roles in the service processes and in the value creation process. The other elements of the service ecosystem include resources and other inputs that are used in the service processes, physical and virtual structures related to the service, social norms and structures and institutional arrangements.

The proposed definition provides a comprehensive and extended view on service ecosystems that combines elements from previous relevant works in business ecosystems (e.g. the complexity and the symbiotic nature of service relationships), software ecosystems (the importance of ICT in service provision), collaborative networks (collaboration between a variety of business entities for the development and delivery of service), service science (the ecosystemic approach on services as socio-technical systems), CD logic (the customer logic for the creation of service value in the daily life practices of the user) and SD logic (the importance of the social context and the intuitions in service processes).

The proposed conceptualization of service ecosystems is comprised of five sub-domains: (a) the user sub-domain that refers to the use of service, (b) the business sub-domain that refers to the service development and provision, (c) the technological sub-domain that refers to the use of ICT for the development, the provision and the use of service, (d) the social sub-domain that describes the social context of the service provision and usage, and (e) the institutional sub-domain that includes the various institutions, rules, ethics, and beliefs that regulate and affect service provision and use. All the sub-domains are related to each other and affect the service processes.

The proposed conceptualization of the user-centric service ecosystem is depicted on Fig. 1. The user sub-domain is the epicenter of the analysis and the various service processes are approached from the point of view of the user who uses services in the daily life practices.

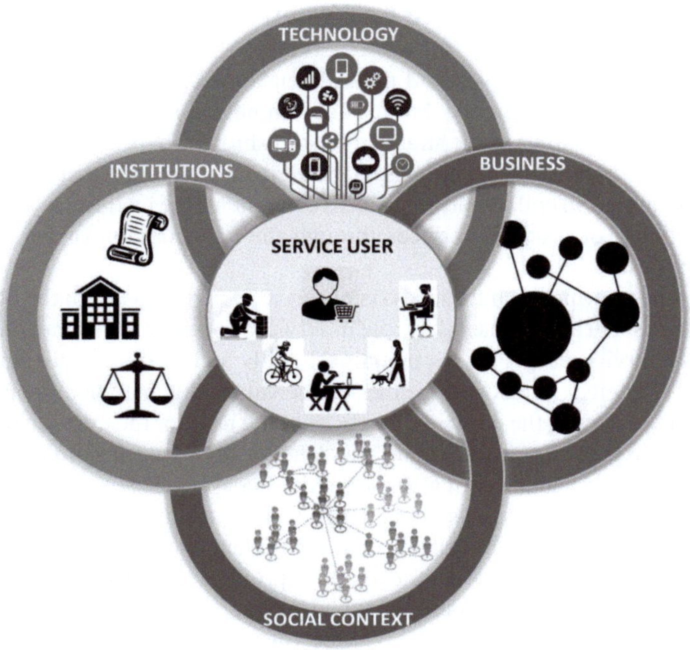

Fig. 1. The user-centric service ecosystem

The user sub-domain. The core entity of the service ecosystem is the service user (or else the customer as the end user of service), who resides in the user sub-domain. The attention here is on what the user is doing with services in his daily activities to accomplish his own personal goals. The user sub-domain is based on the 'customer logic' [8, 9] as an idiosyncratic life pattern and a set of actions, practices, preferences and decisions about how the user uses services as a part of his life. The main goal is the creation of service value, which emerges as value-in-use, that is when the service is used in the life practices. The service value derives fundamentally from the functional and non-functional aspects of the service and is affected by the experiences and expectations of the user.

The business sub-domain. The business sub-domain refers to the business processes performed by the service providers –and their collaborators– for the development and delivery of service. It corresponds to the concept of the business ecosystem as a network of interacting business entities that produces services. The service offering conveys a value proposition to the user based on the functional and non-functional characteristics of the service; the value proposition can be actualized and converted into real value when the service is used, according to the skills and preferences of the user. Key characteristics of the business ecosystem are the symbiotic relationships between various business entities, including suppliers, producers, competitors, customers and other stakeholders, and their mutual fate for the growth and the advancement of the ecosystem [10].

The technological sub-domain. It refers to the various computing resources and software, hardware and network technologies that are used by the service providers for the development, management and dissemination of services and by the users for the acquisition and use of services. The technological sub-domain corresponds to the notion of the digital or software ecosystems from the literature.

The social sub-domain. The daily activities of the people that require the use of services take place in a particular social context, which is shaped by social structures, common experiences, cultural elements, as well as the physical environment. For instance, in SD logic value creation is approached as a 'value-in-social-context' phenomenon and *all economic entities* are 'social actors' that integrate resources to create value [23]. The social sub-domain is relevant to the notion of the 'network society', as today social structures and activities tend to be organized around online networks. The social structures (e.g. friends or peers in groups and communities) can support or enhance the use of services provided by business providers or provide alternative services, which may complement or compete the business services.

The institutional sub-domain. The role of institutions in service ecosystems is emphasized in SD logic [23]. Institutions are humanly devised rules, norms, ethics and beliefs that enable and constrain action and make social life practical and meaningful. Hence, institutions and the institutionalization process are keys to understanding the structure and functioning of service ecosystems.

Figure 1 shows the interrelated nature of the different sub-domains as service processes require input from several or all of these sub-domains. The multilateral interaction between the different sub-domains increases the complexity of service ecosystems. For instance, technologies are used for the development and provision of service in the business sub-domain, the use of service by the user, the operation of the social structures (especially the online ones), while institutions govern the use of technologies in all these domains and social attitudes affect the development and use of technologies in business processes, in social processes and in life practices. Likewise, business processes and models are enabled by technologies, shaped by the preferences of the customers and adapted to the social impact and the institutional requirements. In general, the inter-relationship between the elements of the different sub-domains can be supportive or restrictive. For instance, institutions and technologies affect service development in the business domain supportively or restrictively; or social structures can support, impede or even compete the business organizations in the development and provision of services.

It is important to notice the customer-centric service ecosystem is an abstract conceptual structure for the analysis of service relationships and service value from the user's point of view. If we wished to analyze a particular occasion of service usage by a particular user, then the analysis would refer to the particular parameters of service provision and usage at a particular context (e.g. usage circumstances, technologies used by the user and the provider, accompanied or support services, social interactions, institutional arrangements, etc.). Similarly, if we wished to analyze a particular business service model from the user's point of view, then the analysis would refer to the particular usage patterns and the particular impact of the technological, social and institutional parameters.

4 A Conceptual Model of the User-Centric Service Ecosystem

Following the working definition of the user-centric service ecosystem presented in the previous section, we gather the user perspective on service ecosystems contains several concepts, which can be grouped in six categories: (a) service actors, (b) service processes, (c) inputs and resources, (d) service (offering), (e) service value, and (f) rules and social standards.

The *service actors* are the entities that participate in the service processes. We distinguish four basic types of service actors: service users, service providers, social actors and technology providers. The service users are the individuals who use services in their life practices in order to achieve personal goals. We prefer the term 'user' –rather than 'customer'– to emphasize on the actor who uses services for personal benefit. The service providers are business entities that develop and provide services to the service users in order to support them in their life practices and in their effort to achieve personal goals. The social actors are other non-business entities that can have a role in the effort of the service users to achieve their personal goals. The technology providers possess technological resources that are used to enable or support the service processes of the other service actors. Hence, technology providers are different from service providers, as they do not develop and provide directly service offerings, but support the service providers in their processes.

The *service processes* refer to activities that are performed by the service actors. We distinguish three main types of such service processes: service development, service provision and service usage. Service development refers to the production of service; service provision refers to the offering and delivery of service; service usage refers to the use of service in the daily life practices of the individual. Service development and provision are the typical activities of service providers that are performed with the support of technology providers. Social actors and service users can also participate in service development and provision, when they are co-producing, supporting or enhancing these processes. Service usage is the typical activity of service users, who can be supported in addition by technology providers for the acquisition and use of the service and social actors (e.g. peers). The idea that the service value is co-created and manifested as value-in-use [22, 23] is based on this collaboration of the service actors during service usage.

Service inputs and resources include any kind of physical (e.g. equipment), digital (e.g. software) or mental (e.g. knowledge and skills) input of the service actors to the service processes. As an example, service usage requires the user has some basic knowledge and skills about how to choose a service and how to use it properly. In addition, it may require some particular technological resources for the acquisition and use of the service (e.g. for location-aware services, it is required a GPS equipment, software, online connection, etc.) and contribution from social groups, such as advices and guidelines.

The *service,* or *service offering,* is the output of the service development and provision processes and the input to the service usage process. The service is described by its functional and non-functional characteristics. According to these, the service offering has some value potential and conveys a value proposition to the user.

The *service value* is the outcome of the service usage process, or in other words it is the value that is created when the service is used by the user. The service value is based on the value proposition of the service offering (and hence on the functional and non-functional characteristics of the service), but it can vary from it, because it is shaped from the way the service is used by the user and depends on the knowledge and skills of the user, the contribution of other service actors, contextual parameters of the life practices of the user, etc. The service value can be of different types, such as functional, social, emotional, aesthetic value, etc.

The *rules and social standards* include a variety of norms that influence or regulate the service processes. They include elements of the social context and the institutional context, such as rules, norms, common experiences, cultural elements, ethics and beliefs.

In Fig. 2 we provide a conceptual model that describes the structure of the main concepts and relationships of the user-centric service ecosystem as a UML class diagram. The model aims at the better understanding of the relationships and the characteristics of the service ecosystem. Therefore, the model classifies the major actors, resources and service processes in service ecosystems and portrays the concept of service value and how it derives. In addition, the model can serve as a metamodel that guides the analysis and design of service systems.

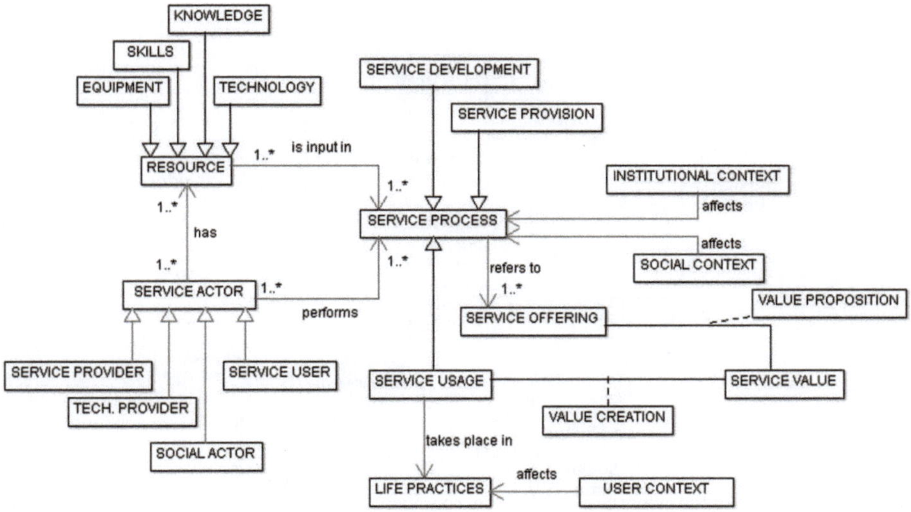

Fig. 2. A class diagram of the user-centric service ecosystem

5 A Goal Model of the User-Centric Service Ecosystem

The concept of ecosystems underscores the symbiotic relationship and the interdependency of the actors in achieving their particular purposes. The analysis of the intentions of the actors with the development of goal models is important for the better understanding of the system requirements and the design of successful systems [26]. A goal model is a high level abstraction that describes the intentions of the actors ('why'), even without specifying their exact actions ('how'). Especially for the analysis of service ecosystems, we consider goal modeling as particularly important because it can explain the complex structure of the service ecosystem and the multifarious influences by individual behaviors, business practices, institutional arrangements and social structures. In Fig. 3 we provide a strategic dependency model of the goals of the main types of actors of the service ecosystem. We use the i* modeling framework, which has been used for the modeling of software ecosystems [27] and for social modeling in information systems [12, 28].

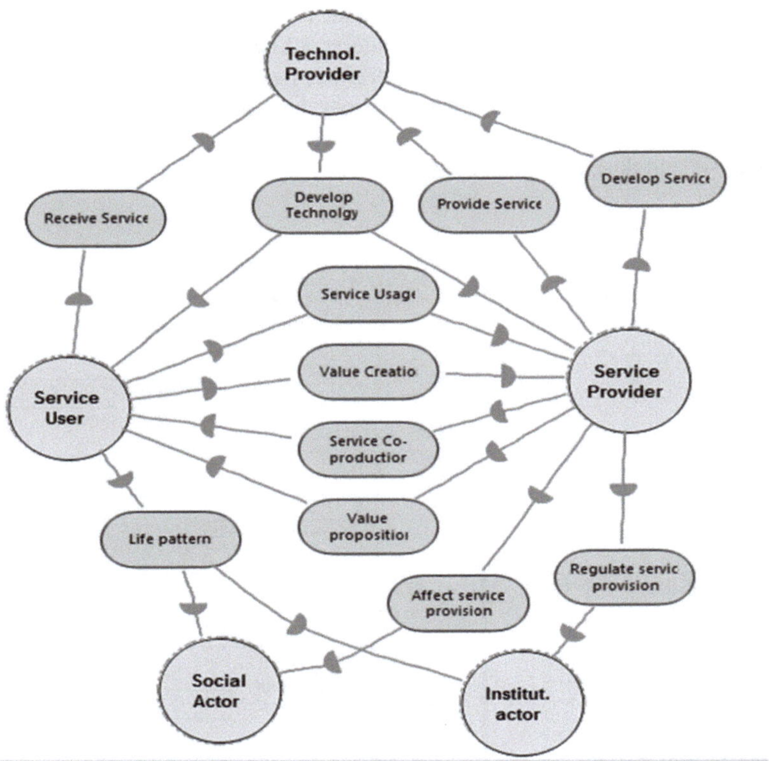

Fig. 3. A goal model of the user-centric service ecosystem (Color figure online)

The model provides a high level view of the major goals of the actors and their interdependencies. The actors are depicted with round shapes (in blue color) and their goals with oval shapes (in green color). According to the proposed user-centric service ecosystem, next to the service user and the service provider, who have the principal role, we have technology providers, social actors (e.g. social structures) and institutional actors (e.g. regulatory bodies).

The service user has several goals. The major ones are the usage of service and the creation of service value (in fact these goals are interrelated, as service usage takes place in order to create service value. This means-ends relationship can be further analyzed in a 'strategic rational' model in the i* framework. By the same token, value creation is not a stand-alone goal, but a means for the satisfaction of personal needs in the realm of the daily life practices). The model shows the user 'depends' for the achievement of these goals on service providers (i.e. curved arrows showing at the direction of the service providers). Another goal of the user is to receive service, which depends on technology providers. The user's life practices are affected by the life patterns (social norms, institutions, etc.) that are formulated by social actors and institutional actors.

Service providers perform service processes with two major goals: to develop service and to provide service. The achievement of these goals depends largely on the resources provided by the technology providers. In addition, service providers have the business goal to make a value proposition to the users, the acceptance of which depends on the users. Service providers may wish to involve users in co-production service processes, the outcome of which depends on the willingness, the effort and the skills of the users. Lastly, service providers depend on the goals of the social and the institutional actors to affect and regulate respectively the service processes.

Understanding the interdependencies of the actors of the service ecosystem is important for the better understanding of certain key service concepts. For instance, in the goal model we can see clearly the interdependency between service users and providers. First of all, service production can be a collaborative process ('service co-production') between the user and the service provider. However, reflecting some recent approaches of the literature [9, 23], the provider does not create value, but only makes a value proposition to the user, which is based on the service offering. If the user accepts the value proposition and uses the service offering, then value is created by the user – based on the provider's service input and contribution. As a general term, the user depends on the provider for the use of services in his life practices.

The structure of goals can be more detailed and further analyzed with 'strategic rational' models in the i* modeling framework. In any particular model, the structure of goals should contain the particular idiosyncratic variables for each user/actor and the contextual parameters of each situation.

6 Conclusions

In this paper we presented a multi-disciplinary approach for the study of service ecosystems that combines business aspects for the provision and use of service and the creation of service value with technological aspects for the requirements analysis and design of service systems. The study of service ecosystems was approached from the user's point of view that emphasizes on what users are doing with services in their life practices, rather than how providers develop and market services in their business practices. The paper aims at the better understanding and the modeling of service ecosystems – from the user perspective. We explained the rationale and the key ideas of the user perspective in service ecosystems and developed a conceptual model and a goal model that help visualize, analyze and understand the structure of the concepts, the intentions and the interdependencies of the actors in the service ecosystem. These models can support for the design of service systems. The user perspective in the analysis and design of service ecosystems suggests the need for a comprehensive analytical framework that incorporates the technological, the business and the user concerns and takes into account the social and the institutional context. The concurrent analysis of all these concerns will provide insights for their relationships and interdependencies. The emphasis on service usage can reveal the real value of services for the users – that can be different from the designed value that derives from the functional and non-functional service attributes. Such knowledge can help the providers to understand better their customers and their service offerings and develop alternative services or alternative technological and business models.

As service ecosystems are complex structures that accommodate various actors with different goals and concerns, it is extremely important for future research to develop methodologies that incorporate all these concerns in the same analytical framework. This paper presented some ideas and an initial approach for this. Future research can seek the further development of the modeling approach for service ecosystems both at methodological, conceptual and practical level. Methodologically, the development of a multi-view modeling procedure that explicates the use of the underlying conceptual knowledge for the development of structural and intentional models and analyzes their interrelationship and transitions between them can be important for the requirements analysis of service ecosystems. Equally important is the development of approaches for the exploitation of the knowledge of requirements analysis for the exploration of alternatives in the design of service systems. At the conceptual level, particular views of the proposed conceptual and intentional models (e.g. conceptual models that emphasize on certain services processes; intentional models that emphasize on specific goals and on their strategic rational) can provide in-depth knowledge and support the better understanding of service ecosystems. Moreover, particular models that derive from case studies can improve the modeling process by relating the abstract modeling knowledge to the real world requirements of the life practices of the users and the business processes. At practical level, particular models that derive from particular service practices and instantiated models that take into account the particular requirements of system implementations can support the development of technological solutions for service ecosystems.

References

1. Boley, H., Chang, E.: Digital ecosystems: principles and semantics. In: Digital EcoSystems and Technologies Conference, pp. 398–403 (2007)
2. Briscoe, G., De Wilde, P.: Digital ecosystems: evolving service-orientated architectures. In: Proceedings of the 1st International Conference on Bio-inspired Models of Network, Information and Computing Systems, paper no. 17 (2006)
3. Briscoe, G., Marinos, A.: Digital ecosystems in the clouds: towards community cloud computing. Digital Ecosyst. Technol. **2009**, 103–108 (2009)
4. Camarinha-Matos, L.M., Rosas, J., Oliveira, A.I., Ferrada, F.: Care services ecosystem for ambient assisted living. Enterp. Inf. Syst. **9**(5–6), 607–633 (2015)
5. Cardoso, T., Camarinha-Matos, L.M.: Pro-active service ecosystem framework. Int. J. Comput. Integr. Manufact. **26**(11), 1021–1041 (2013)
6. Cheng, B.H., Atlee, J.M.: Research directions in requirements engineering. In: Proceedings of 2007 Future of Software Engineering, pp. 285–303 (2007)
7. Dini, P., Darking, M., Rathbone, N., Vidal, M., Hernandez, P., Ferronato, P., Briscoe, G., Hendryx, S.: The Digital Ecosystems Research Vision: 2010 and Beyond. European Commisssion, Position Paper, Bruxelles (2005)
8. Heinonen, K., Strandvik, T., Voima, P.: Customer dominant value formation in service. Eur. Bus. Rev. **25**(2), 104–123 (2013)
9. Heinonen, K., Strandvik, T.: Customer-dominant logic: foundations and implications. J. Serv. Mark. **29**(6/7), 472–484 (2015)
10. Iansiti, M., Levien, R.: The Keystone Advantage: What the New Dynamics of Business Ecosystems Mean for Strategy. Harvard Business Press, Boston (2004)
11. Jansen, S., Finkelstein, A., Brinkkemper, S.: A sense of community: a research agenda for software ecosystems. In Proceedings of 31st IEEE International Conference on Software Engineering, pp. 187–190 (2009)
12. Liu, L., Yu, E.: Designing information systems in social context: a goal and scenario modelling approach. Inf. Syst. **29**(2), 187–203 (2004)
13. Maglio, P.P., Vargo, S.L., Caswell, N., Spohrer, J.: The service system is the basic abstraction of service science. IseB **7**(4), 395–406 (2009)
14. Manikas, K., Hansen, K.M.: Software ecosystems: a systematic literature review. J. Syst. Softw. **86**(5), 1294–1306 (2013)
15. Manikas, K.: Revisiting software ecosystems research: a longitudinal literature study. J. Syst. Softw. **117**, 84–103 (2016)
16. Moore, J.F.: Predators and Prey: a new ecology of competition. Harvard Bus. Rev. **71**(3), 75–83 (1993)
17. Peltoniemi, M., Vuori, E.: Business ecosystem as the new approach to complex adaptive business environments. Proc. eBusiness Research Forum **18**, 267–281 (2004)
18. Reinisch, C., Kofler, M.J., Kastner, W.: ThinkHome: a smart home as digital ecosystem. In: Digital Ecosystems and Technologies, pp. 256–261 (2010)
19. Spohrer, J.C., Demirkan, H., Krishna, V.: Service and science. In: Demirkan, H., Spohrer, J., Krishna, V. (eds.) The Science of Service Systems. Service Science: Research and Innovations in the Service Economy, pp. 325-358. Springer, Boston (2011). doi:10.1007/978-1-4419-8270-4_18
20. Van Lamsweerde, A.: Requirements engineering: from craft to discipline. In: Proceedings of 16th ACM SIGSOFT International Symposium on Foundations of Software Engineering, pp. 238–249 (2008)

21. Van Lamsweerde, A.: Goal-oriented requirements engineering: a guided tour. In: Proceedings of 5th IEEE International Symposium on Requirements Engineering, pp. 249–262 (2001)
22. Vargo, S.L., Lusch, R.F.: Service-dominant logic: continuing the evolution. J. Acad. Mark. Sci. **36**(1), 1–10 (2008)
23. Vargo, S.L., Lusch, R.F.: Institutions and axioms: an extension and update of service-dominant logic. J. Acad. Mark. Sci. **44**(1), 5–23 (2016)
24. Vargo, S.L., Lusch, R.F.: It's all B2B… and beyond: toward a systems perspective of the market. Ind. Mark. Manage. **40**(2), 181–187 (2011)
25. Voima, P., Heinonen, K., Strandvik, T., Mickelsson, K.J., Arantola-Hattab, J.: A customer ecosystem perspective on service. In: Advances in Service Quality, Innovation and Excellence, QUIS 2012, pp. 1015–1024 (2011)
26. Yu, E., Mylopoulos, J.: Why goal-oriented requirements engineering. In: Proceedings of 4th International Workshop on Requirements Engineering, vol. 15, pp. 15–22 (1998)
27. Yu, E., Deng, S.: Understanding software ecosystems: a strategic modeling approach. In: Proceedings of 3rd International Workshop on Software Ecosystems, pp. 65–76 (2011)
28. Yu, E.S.: Social modeling and *i**. In: Borgida, A.T., Chaudhri, V.K., Giorgini, P., Yu, E.S. (eds.) Conceptual Modeling: Foundations and Applications. LNCS, vol. 5600, pp. 99–121. Springer, Heidelberg (2009). doi:10.1007/978-3-642-02463-4_7

Service Oriented Collaborative Network Architecture

Mahdi Sargolzaei(✉) and Hamideh Afsarmanesh(✉)

Springer-Verlag, Computer Science Editorial, Tiergartenstr. 17, 69121 Heidelberg, Germany
{M.sargolzaei1,H.afsarmanesh}@uva.nl

Abstract. A service-oriented collaborative network (SOCN) supports collaboration among a network of organizations through their shared business services. SOCN in comparison with traditional collaborative networks, promotes and simplifies reusability and interconnection of shared software services, in a distributed manner. Our work contributes to comprehensive support of software service oriented collaboration among networked organizations enabling semi-automated service discovery, selection, and composition in collaborative environments. With the help of an organizational monitoring tool, we improve the accuracy of claimed characteristics based on non-functional criteria of services. The reference framework and implementation architecture are defined in this paper to support implementing SOCN.

Keywords: Service oriented architecture (SOA) · Business services · Service composition · Virtual organization

1 Introduction

In today's economy, cooperations between organizations tend to change from traditional static supply chains to/dynamic organization networks [24]. In general, making relationships with business partners for the organizations brings forth lower cost, higher quality service/product, larger service/product portfolio, faster delivery, and more agility. The pace by which these changes need to occur results in high demands on supporting collaboration in a network of organizations, i.e. on establishing collaborative networks (CNs). On the other hands, organizations constantly search for innovative ways to improve their business processes and to enrich the collaborations of their distributed workers [10]. Therefore in this paper, the promising paradigm of Service Oriented Architecture (SOA) is investigated and applied to the enhancement of collaborative networks. Besides proposing the use of SOA in the construction of CNs, we extend the generic model of SOA as a reference framework to better support them. An implementation architecture is then needed to be elaborated based on the findings identified from the reference framework.

This paper specifically aims to introduce this new framework supporting collaboration among a network of organizations through their shared business services (BSs). Applying this framework results facilitates SOCN, which in comparison with traditional collaborative networks, promotes and simplifies reusability and interconnection of

L.M. Camarinha-Matos et al. (Eds.): PRO-VE 2017, IFIP AICT 506, pp. 381–394, 2017.
DOI: 10.1007/978-3-319-65151-4_35

shared software services, in a distributed manner. Furthermore, a set of sub-systems are designed and interconnected within an implementation architecture, to support all SOCN's needed functionality.

Service oriented architecture (SOA) is gaining more and more attention in business and industry since it offers new, agile and flexible ways of supporting the activities inter- and intra-organizations. These kinds of organizations propounds the idea of service orientated collaborative networks (SOCNs). However, the current implementations of the SOA approaches often do not deliver the expected advantages [24]. Several major problems in this area can be identified. First, a complete and clear understanding of the notion of SOCN is missing. As a consequence, it is unclear what functionality should be implemented to realize such system [2]. Second, an appropriate framework for specifying business services is needed to supplement insufficient information for the business services concerning various aspects of the respective services [24] and [6]. Third, an enhanced service discovery mechanism is needful in order to give more flexibility and efficiency to search for services in more impressive ways rather than only through general keyword-based delineation of required services [1] and [6]. Finally, to fully leverage the opportunities provided by the service oriented architecture within organizations, integration of existing services must be simplified [9, 23] and [2]. As a consequence, approaches for automated service composition, as well as the execution of the integrated services are needed. The above problems present the motivation of this paper.

The paper starts with a brief description of some related works in Sect. 2. In Sect. 3, a short introduction of the Service Oriented Architecture is represented. In Sect. 4 the role of SOA in today's organizations is discussed. An extended model of SOA paradigm is addressed in Sect. 5 to identify the basic requirements to support SOCN. Here a reference framework and architecture to facilitate assisting the implementation of our proposed model is presented thereafter, identifying and brie y describing its main components. We conclude the paper in Sect. 6.

2 Related Work

Multiple approaches are developed by research community in the area of service oriented computing (SOC). However, only a few address the comprehensive design of a framework that can encompass all aspects required to efficiently support semi-automated service discovery and composition within SOA-based virtual organizations.

Specification of services is the first base step of SOC that can improve discovery and composition of services. Nowadays, research on web services constitutes the base in Service-Oriented Architecture research [1], and has been widely accepted by service industry. One key point for the success of web service technology is the employment of XML-based standards, such as SOAP and WSDL for communicating and self-describing it [4]. These standards enable web services to become independent of the programming language, operating system, and hardware [9]. It therefore supports communication in heterogeneous environments, and is ideally suited to provide dynamic information and functionalities over the CNs. However, applying WSDL as the most adopted base standard for web Service description is limited to self-describing of the structure of the messages and operations, and not supporting the conceptual description or the capability of the service. This limitation, which is known as lack of semantics and behavior in describing web services [2], consequently required human intervention to ensure valid and befitting use of the services. Currently, the most promising research works in the area of software service specification are semantic service description frameworks, such as OWL-S, WSMF, and WSDL-S that provide machine understandable semantic description of services in order to enable automatic service discovery and composition. Behavior of the services represents the configuration of stateful web services. In fact, the behavior specification of a service indicates the valid sequence of the operations' invocations in that service, which is also absent in WSDL. Thus, lack of semantics and behavior representation is a major drawback of WSDL, and consequently become a barrier in achieving automatic or semi-automatic service discovery, composition and execution [2].

A handful of researchers have investigated the problem of business process discovery and reuse based on process similarity, and discovery of processes based on search through repositories. However, as a consequence of insufficient information in the current service specifications, precise matchmaking required to locate a demanded service is also not supported [21]. For instance, WSXplorer [25] presents a method to retrieve desired web service operations of a given textual description. The method uses the concept of tree edit distance to match similar operations. Meanwhile, a few other algorithms are proposed for measuring and grouping similar operations. The proposed algorithms suggested for measuring and grouping similar operations catche not only the structures, but also their semantic information. Although, they still ignore behavioral and non-functional properties of services. VU+ [13] is another approach that supports semantic discovery of web services. It also performs a QoS enabled ranking of web services based on their quality compliance. The framework could be used either as a centralized discovery component or as a decentralized repository system. However, VU + is also suffers from the lack of supporting behavioral matching of services.

Service composition also has received much interest for supporting collaboration among enterprise applications [26]. Many research projects have studied this issue as the most promising choice to implement service oriented architecture and its strategic objectives. Some earlier approaches, such as the SWORD project [19] give a simple mechanism for finding and combining web services, without considering the existing complexities such as coordination among the component services. SWORD uses an expert system to check whether or not a desired composite service can be realized using existing services. If so, it designs a plan for that service composition. SWORD does not benefit from service-description standards (e.g. WSDL, SOAP, RDF and etc.), instead it uses the Entity-Relationship (ER) model to specify Web services. SWORD focuses more on the data integration and no coordination has been addressed. Some other research works on service composition rely more on QoS concerns rather than service interoperability and coordination, in order to optimize the quality of service composition. The eFlow project, WSQoSX, and UPWSR are some instances of this kind of research efforts. BPEL4WS (Business Process Execution Language for Web Services) [12], or BPEL in short, is an XML-based language for web service composition through orchestration that also supports specification of processes that involve operations provided by one or several web services. Furthermore, BPEL4WS draws upon concepts developed in the area of workflow management. When compared to languages supported by existing workflow systems and to related standards (e.g. WSCI), BPEL4WS is relatively more expressive. BPEL however does not provide a full graphical notation, and thus needs to be combined with the BPMN to fully support service interactions [12]. Moreover, according to the principal of "separation of concerns" as a main concern in software engineering, employing the BPMN and BPEL simultaneously is not recommended. Doedt et al. [5] argue that while a business expert is aware of the BPs in an organization, he/she does not often know how to implement a service. Similarly, while the programmer knows how to implement a described service, he/she is not properly aware of the nature of processes running at the organization. It is therefore advised to deal with these two perspectives separately through different notations and standards for business process modeling and coordination. With this strategy, we have used Reo [11] as a graphical coordination language, only to implement the coordination aspects of web services.

3 Service Oriented Architecture

Recently, Service Oriented Architecture (SOA) has become a well-known and somewhat imprecise term. For example, an organizational methodology to design systems, an IT infrastructure in business, and a structure for increasing the efficiency of IT are definitions of SOA from three different points of view.

As a preliminary definition, SOA is a loosely-coupled architecture designed to meet the business requirements of the organization. It means that the dependency among services is minimized, while they only require to be aware of each other. Being open, extensible, federated, and composable are the characteristics of SOA, formally defined by Erl in [7], promoting service-orientation in enterprises. In his point of view, services in SOA are autonomous, QoS-capable, vendor diverse, interoperable, discoverable, and potentially reusable, which are implemented as Web services.

Organization for the Advancement of Structured Information Standards (OA-SIS) also represents a holistic definition of SOA as below:

"Paradigm for organizing and utilizing distributed capabilities that may be under the control of different ownership domains. It provides a uniform means to offer, discover, interact with and use capabilities to produce desired effects consistent with measurable preconditions and expectations" [15].

Indeed, Service Oriented Architecture is a programming paradigm that uses "services" as the constructs of distributed business applications to support reusability and agility. Services in this architecture are autonomous and platform-independent computational entities that can represent the steps of a business process and communicate with each other [17]. These services can be described, published, discovered, and dynamically integrated in order to developing massively distributed, interoperable, and evolvable applications. Each service can perform some functions that are able to execute either simple requests or complex business processes through peer-to-peer relationships between service clients and providers.

For a long time, increasing the level of abstraction in programing has been a main motivating goal in software engineering. Therefore, we have witnessed evolutions in programming approaches from sequential programming, respectively to procedural programming, object-oriented programming, component-based programming, and finally service oriented programming. Figure 1 shows the time-line of increasing abstraction level in programming paradigm from procedural methodology to SOA. Service oriented programming holds the promise of moving beyond the simple exchange of information and remotely invocation of methods on objects, to the concept of encapsulating data and application to services and passing messages between them. An important economic bene t of this shift in programing paradigm is that it improves the effectiveness of software development activities and enables enterprises to bring their new applications to the market more rapidly and cost-effectively than ever before, by developing composite services from the existing component applications [16] and [17].

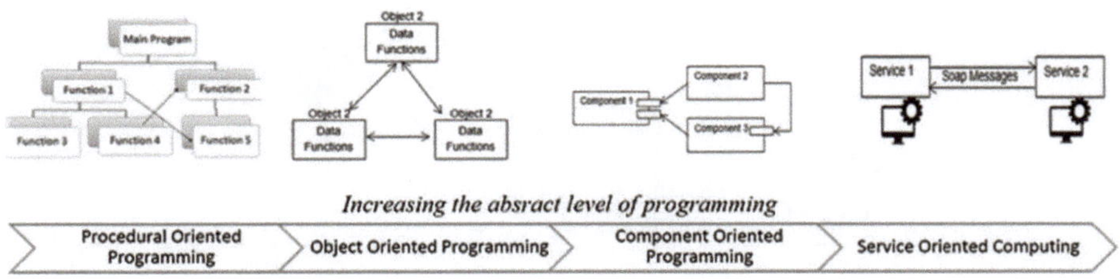

Fig. 1. The history line of SOA

Currently, web services are the most promising technology that implements the concept of SOA, and provides the basis for the development and execution of business processes that are distributed over the Internet. A web service is defined as a self-contained, modular, loosely coupled, reusable software application that can be described, published, discovered, and invoked over the World Wide Web [18, 20] and [3].

4 SOA-Based Organizations

Nowadays, SOA is a very promising methodology for supporting the business processes of organizations. Applying the service oriented architecture paradigm and technologies in organizations leads to reduced complexity and costs, reusing business functionality and operations, and finally increasing flexibility and efficiency [17]. These advantages allow organizations to adapt more readily to needed changes; therefore, it is expected that the SOA paradigm improves the e efficiency of organizations more than previous approaches and technologies.

SOA offers new and flexible ways to develop tools for supporting the activities inter- and intra-organizations. Thus, two types of usages, Intra-Organizational and Inter-Organizational platforms, can utilize service oriented computing (SOC) tools. In a large enterprise/organization, single departments can share their services stored in a repository, and offer them to other departments to be accessed and applied to their own activities, and even to use them for purposes different than what the business service was originally built. So, this usage of SOC tool could be seen as Intra-Organizational application of SOA. The other type of using SOA in organizations is in Inter-Organizational platform, which can be established among a variety of organizations and SMEs as stakeholders that form a VO. Each VO partner should announce their services in a collaboration space, i.e. a directory of shared services, to be identifiable and accessible for other VO partners. Figure 2 shows these two kinds of usages of SOA-based organizations.

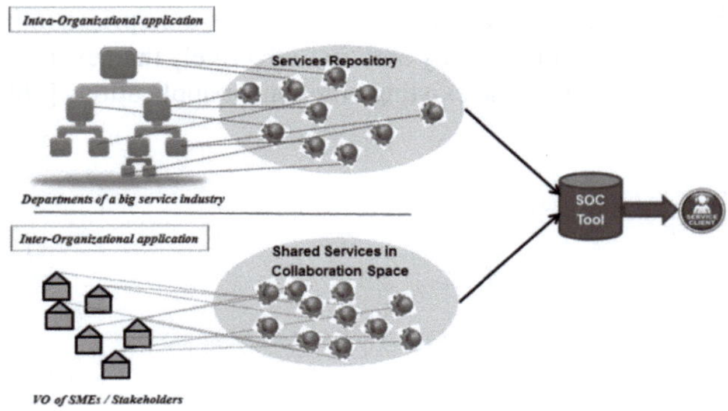

Fig. 2. Two kinds of SOA-based organizational applications

5 Towards Service Oriented Collaborative Networks

We believe that applying SOA paradigm to collaborative networks ensures a high level of abstraction for data and operations in the form of business services. Thanks to the higher abstraction level, the ease of integration with functional capabilities (i.e. services) has gradually gained power.

Business services (BSs) constitute the base construction element in service oriented virtual organizations (VOs). Each BS shared at the VO is represented as a set of Business Processes (BPs), while each BP involves the invocation of one granular software service. Therefore, designed BSs may be specified either as atomic services or composite services, whereas each composite service in turn is composed of several other atomic services as its constituent. In VOs, there are usually two kinds of business services, including the manual services and the software services. In our proposed framework, we only address software services, which correspond to their defined BPs. For manual services, if desired, we can define a simple software service to include two basic operations: Start and Stop. Only through this specification, manual tasks cab also be specified as software services in the framework, otherwise they are outside the scope of this paper.

To support the challenging task of business service composition in VOs, such software services need to be both discoverable and integrable, as it is considered in the designed framework. We need to study the life cycle of BSs in VOs to explore the needs and challenges of establishing a service oriented collaborative network.

Business services are naturally dynamic; therefore, the supporting tools for their development and deployment are needed to be used at different stages of the Service Life Cycle (SLC). At the macroscopic level, the life cycle of business services consists of four phases, i.e. Design, Construction, Operation, and Innovation, as illustrated in Fig. 3. The need for each phase of the SLC is brie y described below.

- **1st SLC phase- Design:** This stage deal with strategic planning and rough design specification of business services. In this stage, we need to identify the required services (manual task or software services), their goals and functionalities.
- **2nd SLC phase- Construction:** This stage deals with the logistics, construction, and procurement of business services. Therefore, a number of functionalities (operations of a service) need to be implemented in this stage to support the configuration and establishment of the needed business services, for the purpose of service implementation. Moreover, this stage encompasses a fully detailed specification of business services, such as the interface of services (WSDL documents).
- **3rd SLC phase- Operation:** It is considered as the long operation phase of existing business services. Therefore, it encompasses a large number of functionalities related to the operation, management, deployment, announcement and delivery of the services. The utilization of offered services, such as service registry, discovery and execution continue heavily in this stage. Moreover, in this stage of SLC, the quality of services is measured in order to make service level agreements (SLAs).
- **4th SLC phase- innovation:** Finally, the innovation or design of new business services would be necessary for solving some emerged problems, or service enhancement/adaptation. In this stage of SLC, service designers can design new value added services through adaptation of the service interfaces, or composing some existing services. Moreover, it is possible to identify exactly the same services (functionality) and replace them with the optimized alternative service (non-functionality).

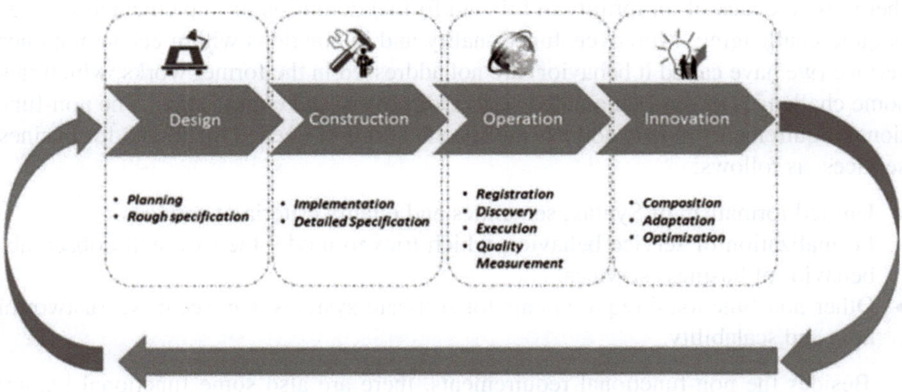

Fig. 3. Service life cycle's phases

Figure 4 shows the UML sequence diagram for the main operations involved with business services in SLC. At first, a Service Developer must add its provided services to the Service Registry. Then, a Service Client can ask Service Discovery for his/her desired business services, and consequently receive a WSDL URI as the response. The Service Discovery should send a query and receive corresponding results from the Service Registry to provide response for the Service Client. Moreover, for the purpose of providing composed business services, a Service Integrator can retrieve two or more business services from the Service Registry as the "Constituent Services", and then integrate them as a composite or composed business service, and finally publish it in the Service Registry.

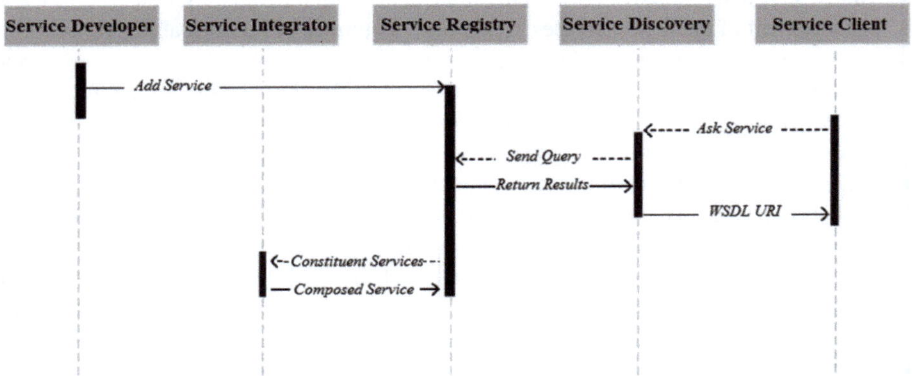

Fig. 4. The UML sequence diagram for SLC

Considering the discussion above, we have identified a set of functional and non-functional requirements to establish a framework for business service inter-operation in CNs. Note that SMEs (VO members) in the VBE are fully independent and autonomous; therefore, the lack of uniformity in full and formal definition of implemented software is quite challenging. Moreover, functionality and interactions within each component service (we have called it behavior) are not addressed in the former works, which raise some challenges in semi-automated service discovery and composition. The non-functional requirements mostly address the specifications of needed meta-data for business services, as follows:

- Unified formalism of Syntax, semantics and quality criteria of services.
- Formalization of service behavior, which tries to model the externally observable behavior of business services.
- Other non-functional requirements for software systems, e.g. security, trustworthiness and scalability.

Besides the non-functional requirements, there are also some functional requirements for business services as described below, which need to be supported:

- Service specification/registration tool to store and index the specified meta-data for services.

- Effective service discovery to search among registered services, based on their specifications.
- Support of Bundled/composite services to make a bundle of atomic business services as an integrated composed business service.

We address these functional and non-functional requirements in design of our proposed reference framework for service oriented collaborative networks (see next section), except some non-functional requirements, such as security and authorization that are out of the scope of this paper.

5.1 Reference Framework

Figure 5 shows the traditional view of service oriented architecture, which consists of three major tasks: Service Consumption, Service Provision and Service Registry. In order to customize the traditional view of the SOA for our purpose, at first we should add a sub-task, namely "Service Design & Implementation" besides the "Service Provision". Figure 6 shows this variation of the SOA paradigm. In fact, we have extended the traditional view of SOA by separating design/implementation from the provision task, which involves providing common VO business service meta-data and selection criteria. The meta-data specifies capability of a business services. Moreover, VBE that facilitates collaborative environment for business services, monitor and adjust the non-functional values claimed for such services.

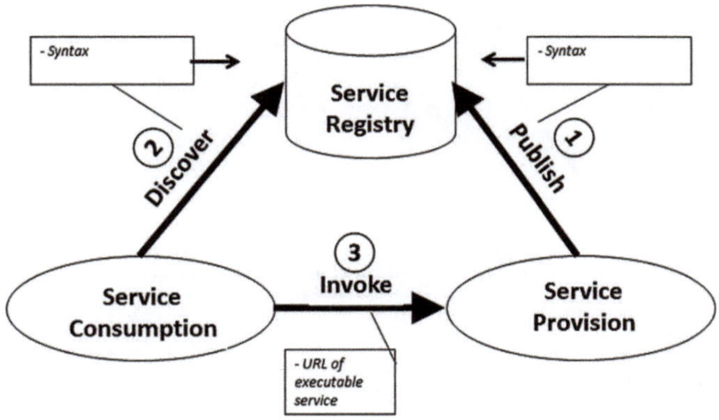

Fig. 5. Traditional view of Service oriented architecture

Figure 7 shows the second variation of the SOA that addresses service composition for SOCN precisely. Similar to the atomic services (see Fig. 6), composite service provision is also separated from the composite service design and implementation. To design composite services, at first "Service Integrator" should discover (from registry) the constituent services that form the composite service. After that, one proxy should be automatically generated for each selected constituent service to assist end users in execution of the services. In fact, the generated

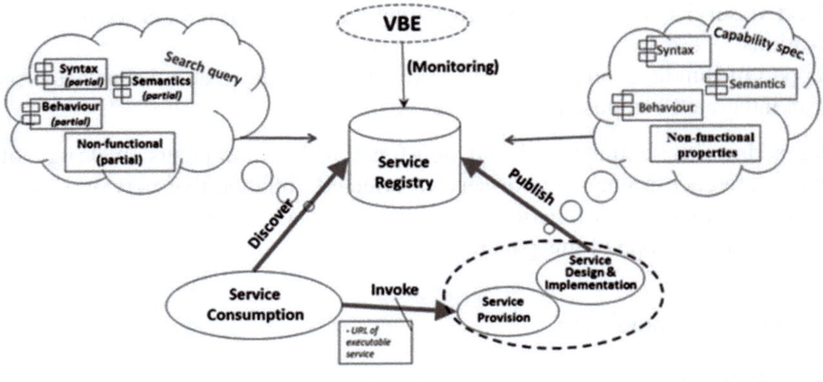

Fig. 6. The first variation of SOA needed for SOCN

proxies are required to support automated invocation and data exchanging among services. Moreover, an integrated service designer/implementer is needed to interconnect (coordinate) the selected services, and then de ne a full specification of the integrated services as a new (composite) business service. Finally, the provided composite services should be published in the "Service Registry". Thus, such services can be discovered in the SOA triangle like atomic services.

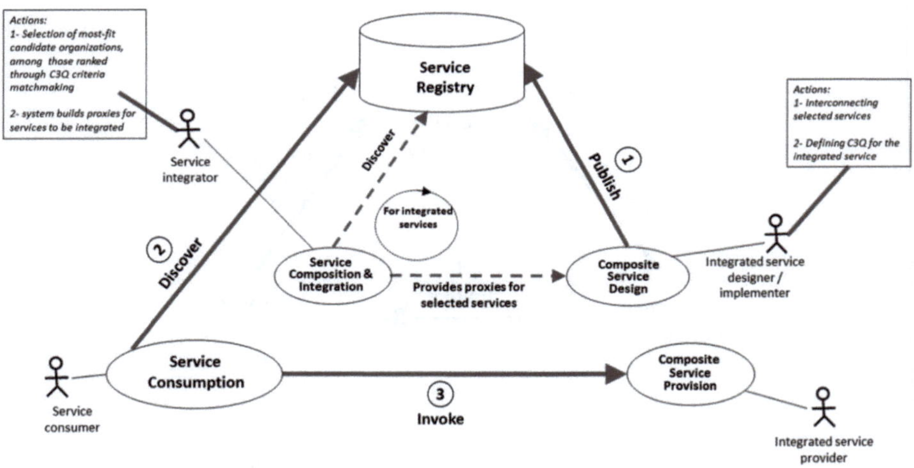

Fig. 7. The second variation of the SOA addressing service composition in SOCN.

5.2 Implementation Architecture

Figure 8 illustrates an implementation architecture capturing the needed elements for establishing service oriented computing in VOs. This architecture is designed in order to identify significant entities and relationships between them, for the development of the extended SOA model (represented in Fig. 7). Note that the proposed architecture is not directly tied to any standards, tools or other concrete implementation technologies. This architecture conceptually is composed of three software modules, including Specification Module, Discovery Module, and Composition Module, as further explained below.

- **Specification Module** is involved with software services that are offered by different members/stakeholders of the VO in the role of service providers. The shared services are published in a service registry or directory, such as the UDDI [3], according to specific Operational Level Agreement (OLA) [6]. An OLA is agreed among the VO stakeholders, to describe the responsibilities of each VO member/stakeholder toward the specified composite services. OLAs are also supported by Service Level Agreements (SLAs) among web services [9]. At the service binding time, SLA defines the agreement between the client and the service provider to represent the expected quality and performance of the web service. Our approach to service quality assessment is rooted in [15], which identifies the level of VO partners' trustworthiness through monitoring their behaviors. Based on this approach, all agreements in OLA and SLA are considered as promises exchanged among the VO members. Using VO Supervisory Assisting Tool (VOSAT) [15], at any point in time, the trust level of a VO member would be reflected on its claims about different QoS properties of its provided services, as well as on its feedbacks related to its consumed services.
  The function that is labeled as "Agreement Management" manages all tasks related to the service agreements, and keep the results in the Service Registry. The other function of this module named "Software Service Specification", which presents the triple meta-data content as the means of accurate formalization for every atomic software service. Every composite service, is then specified by a set of meta-data, as the concrete formalization of its associated atomic services. To support machine-to-machine service interoperation in a VO, our proposed meta-data reflects the three aspects of each service, namely its syntax, semantics, and behavior, where they facilitate discovery and composition of services. Moreover, these specifications are deployed to execute the services in an automated way. All of the specifications will be registered in the "Service Registry".
  We have introduced XWSDL, as our extension to WSDL that can support all information aspects needed for our semi-outdated service discovery and composition. We have also implemented a GUI for the behavioral specification of web services. As Fig. 9 shows, the GUI accepts one WSDL file as its input and then depict its behavior in the form of constraint automata. Figure 9 shows a snapshot of this GUI.
- **Discovery Module** of the proposed architecture represents the needed tasks for service discovery and selection of the existing web services in the VO. Automated and successful application of search services at this module needs to the functional meta-data (i.e. syntax, semantics, and behavior of services) provided in the Specification Module. The Search function returns a list of alternative services from the Service Registry that can be matched with the service query (based on the functional properties of services). After that, the Service Selection function chooses one of the service alternatives that optimize non-functional properties of services.
  We have implemented a tool for the proposed discovery module of the architecture. It is able to rank the shared service descriptions in VBE, according to the matched

similarity score for each service description against the service desired by a user. More details about this tool has represented in [21].

- **Composition Module** of the implementation architecture involves the functions needed for service composition, to allow service integrators bundle several shared services in the VO, and offer a new composite service. An efficient service composition in this module requires not only the rich meta-data captured in the Service Registry, but also the coordination model that reflects the demanded interactions among the constituent services that form a composed service. The information of the constituent services as well as the orchestration model should be kept in the Service Registry.
  We also implemented ProxCG as a proxy generator to realize the composition module of the architecture. The proposed approach is based on Reo, which is a graphical and domain specific language for coordination of services. The details of ProXCG can be found in [11]. Figure 10 shows a screenshot of the ProxCG, which is implemented within a tool that works with Reo, so-called ETC [11].

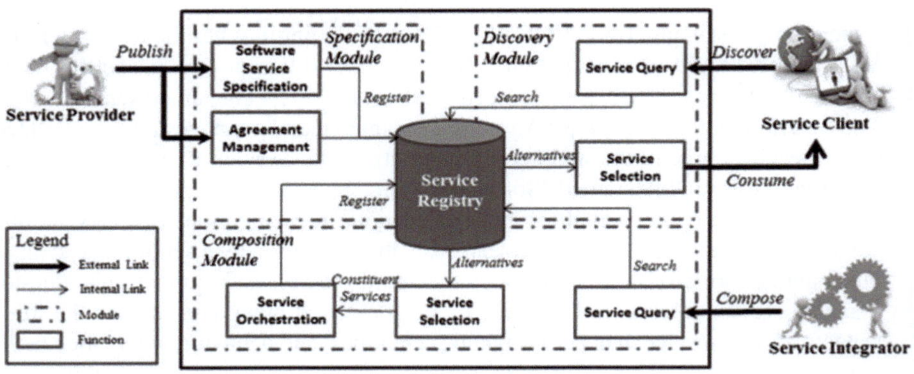

Fig. 8. Implementation Architecture of SOCN.

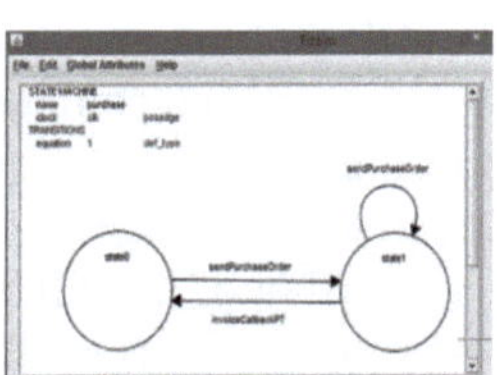

Fig. 9. A snapshot of the GUI

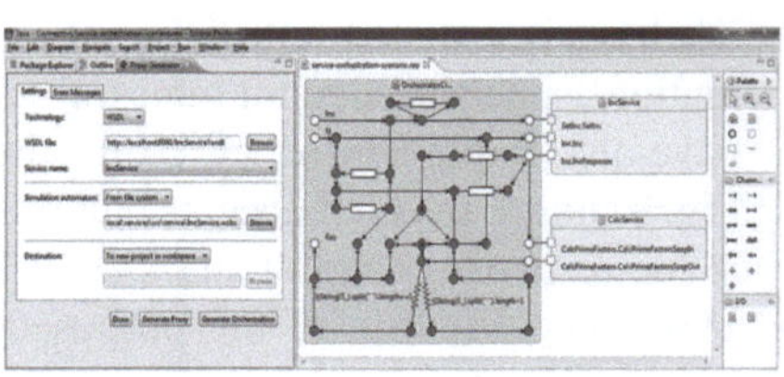

Fig. 10. A snapshot of the ProxCG.

6 Conclusion

Emerging developments under the umbrella of "Future Internet" and particularly on web services, highlight SOA-based paradigms and approaches to support service oriented collaborative networks. Software services, e.g. the web services, and SOA paradigm provide rapid, cost-effective and standard-based means to improve service interoperability and collaboration in CNs. Although the research area of collaborative networks is active, the higher-level abstraction of the activities that simplify the collaboration among members using SOA is still lacking. The goal of this paper is to address a comprehensive framework in order to support a semi-automated service discovery and compositions in VOs. With this in mind, we propose a reference framework and an implementation architecture that allows us to efficiently support service-oriented collaborative networks. The implementation of the proposed framework consists of three software modules that realize functional and non-functional requirements of SOCN addressed in this paper.

References

1. Afsarmanesh, H., Sargolzaei, M., Shadi, M.: A framework for automated service composition in collaborative networks. In: Camarinha-Matos, Luis M., Xu, L., Afsarmanesh, H. (eds.) PRO-VE 2012. IAICT, vol. 380, pp. 63–73. Springer, Heidelberg (2012). doi: 10.1007/978-3-642-32775-9_7
2. Afsarmanesh, H., Sargolzaei, M., Shadi, M.: Semi-automated software service integration in virtual organisations. Enterp. Inf. Syst. **9**(5–6), 528–555 (2015)
3. Curbera, F., Duftler, M., Khalaf, R., Nagy, W., Mukhi, N., Weerawarana, S.: Un-raveling the web services web: an introduction to SOAP, WSDL, and UDDI. IEEE Int. Comput. **6**(2), 86–93 (2002)
4. Dhara, K., Dharmala, M., Sharma, C.: A Survey Paper on Service Oriented Architecture Approach and Modern Web Services (2015). http://opus.govst.edu/capstones/157
5. Doedt, M., Stefien, B.: An evaluation of service integration approaches of business process management systems. In: 2012 35th Annual IEEE Software Engineering Workshop (SEW), pp. 158–167. IEEE (2012)
6. Du, X.: Semantic service description framework for efficient service discovery and composition. Ph.D. thesis, Durham University (2009)
7. Erl, T.: Service-Oriented Architecture: Concepts, Technology, and Design. Pearson Education, Mumbai (2005)
8. Guidara, I., Chaari, T., Fakhfakh, K., Jmaiel, M.: A comprehensive survey on intra and inter organizational agreements. In: 2012 IEEE 21st International Workshop on Enabling Technologies: Infrastructure for Collaborative Enterprises (WETICE), pp. 411–416. IEEE (2012)
9. Huma, Z., Gerth, C., Engels, G., Juwig, O.: Automated service discovery and composition for on-the-fly SOAs. Technical report, TR-RI-13-333, University of Paderborn, Germany (2013). http://is.uni-paderborn.de/uploads/txsibibtex/tr-ri-13-333.pdf
10. Jerstad, I., Dustdar, S., Thanh, D.V.: A service oriented architecture framework for collaborative services. In: 2005 14th IEEE International Workshops on Enabling Technologies: Infrastructure for Collaborative Enterprise, pp. 121–125. IEEE (2005)
11. Jongmans, S.S.T., Santini, F., Sargolzaei, M., Arbab, F., Afsarmanesh, H.: Orchestrating web services using Reo: from circuits and behaviors to automatically generated code. SOCA **8**(4), 277–297 (2014)
12. Kopp, O., Leymann, F., Wagner, S.: Modeling choreographies: BPMN 2.0 versus BPEL-based approaches. In: EMISA, pp. 225–230 (2011)
13. Le-Hung, V., et al.: A search engine for QoS-enabled discovery of semantic web services. Int. J. Bus. Process Integr. Manag. **1**(4), 244–255 (2006)

14. Ludwig, H., Keller, A., Dan, A., King, R.P., Franck, R.: Web service level agreement (WSLA) language specification. IBM Corporation, pp. 815–824 (2003)
15. MacKenzie, C.M., Laskey, K., McCabe, F., Brown, P.F., Metz, R., Hamilton, B.A.: Reference model for service oriented architecture 1.0. OASIS standard 12, p. 18 (2006)
16. Mallayya, D., Ramachandran, B., Viswanathan, S.: An automatic web service composition framework using QoS-based web service ranking algorithm. Sci. World J. **2015** (2015)
17. Papazoglou, M.P., Traverso, P., Dustdar, S., Leymann, F.: Service-oriented computing: a research roadmap. Int. J. Coop. Inf. Syst. **17**(02), 223–255 (2008)
18. Petritsch, H.: Service-Oriented Architecture (SOA) vs. Component Based Architecture. Vienna University of Technology, Vienna (2006)
19. Ponnekanti, S., Fox, A.: SWORD: a developer toolkit for web service composition. In: Proceedings of the Eleventh International World Wide Web Conference, Honolulu, HI, vol. 45 2002
20. Prakash, C.J., Rohini, P.M., Ganesh, R.B., Maheswari, V.: Hybrid reliability model to enhance the efficiency of composite web services. In: 2013 International Conference on Emerging Trends in Computing, Communication and Nanotechnology (ICE-CCN), pp. 79–83. IEEE (2013)
21. Sargolzaei, M., Santini, F., Arbab, F., Afsarmanesh, H.: A tool for behaviour-based discovery of approximately matching web services. In: Hierons, R.M., Merayo, M.G., Bravetti, M. (eds.) SEFM 2013. LNCS, vol. 8137, pp. 152–166. Springer, Heidelberg (2013). doi:10.1007/978-3-642-40561-7_11
22. Shadi, M., Afsarmanesh, H., Dastani, M.: Agent behaviour monitoring in virtual organizations. In: 2013 IEEE 22nd International Workshop on Enabling Technologies: Infrastructure for Collaborative Enterprises (WETICE), pp. 9–14. IEEE (2013)
23. Tabatabaei, S.G.H., Kadir, W.M.N.W., Ibrahim, S., Dastjerdi, A.V., et al.: Integrating discovery and composition of semantic web services based on description logic. J. Comput. Sci. Inform. Electr. Eng. **3**(1) (2009)
24. Terlouw, L.I., Albani, A.: An enterprise ontology-based approach to service specification. IEEE Trans. Serv. Comput. **6**(1), 89–101 (2013)
25. Hao, Y., Zhang, Y., Cao, J.: WSXplorer: searching for desired web services. In: Krogstie, J., Opdahl, A., Sindre, G. (eds.) CAiSE 2007. LNCS, vol. 4495, pp. 173–187. Springer, Heidelberg (2007). doi:10.1007/978-3-540-72988-4_13
26. Yu, T., Lin, K.-J.: Service selection algorithms for composing complex services with multiple QoS constraints. In: Benatallah, B., Casati, F., Traverso, P. (eds.) ICSOC 2005. LNCS, vol. 3826, pp. 130–143. Springer, Heidelberg (2005). doi:10.1007/11596141_11

Service Selection and Ranking: A Framework Proposal and Prototype Implementation

Firmino Oliveira da Silva(✉), Claudia-Melania Chituc(✉), and Paul Grefen(✉)

School of Industrial Engineering, Eindhoven University of Technology, 5612 AZ Eindhoven, The Netherlands
{F.Oliveira.da.Silva,C.M.Chituc,P.W.P.J.Grefen}@tue.nl

Abstract. Organizations that are part of collaborative service networks need to handle increasing amounts of data in their information systems to construct complex customer-oriented solutions from dynamically selected service elements. This brings numerous challenges in today's highly competitive markets, where companies need to provide customers with services that have a high level of quality, in a time and cost effective manner. Having prior knowledge of the performance associated with specific choreographies of services allows companies to provide customers with services tailored to their specific requests, while maintaining a high quality of the services. This paper presents an approach for service selection and ranking considering customers' requirements, knowledge of the historic behavior of services, business process constraints and the characteristics of the execution environment. Following the specifications of the proposed framework, a prototype has been implemented targeting the automotive sector. Tests of this prototype illustrate the usability and validity of the proposed approach.

Keywords: Collaborative network · Service selection · Service ranking · Prototype

1 Introduction

The increasing digitization of the business world creates new opportunities for companies [1]. More and more devices are connected and new services are available, generating a huge traffic and volume of data, creating challenges for enterprises that have to constantly adapt to new demands. Customers' demands for high quality services tailored to their specific needs are increasingly high, and companies need to rethink their business strategy and focus on their core activities. Offering tools to customers that allow to configure the requested services (that may be provided by different partners that are part of a collaborative network), and enabling an accurate estimate of the results based on their expectations (e.g., estimates of service cost, duration, and quality level) is nowadays of great importance to face competition. In today's dynamic business environment, organizations increasingly form partnerships in order to improve their performance, increase their competitive advantage to share knowledge, skills and resources to seize

L.M. Camarinha-Matos et al. (Eds.): PRO-VE 2017, IFIP AICT 506, pp. 395–403, 2017.
DOI: 10.1007/978-3-319-65151-4_36

market opportunities and reduce operating costs [2]. Assessment and monitoring of cross-organizational business processes plays an important role in this dynamic environment to evaluate the performance of the services of the involved partners [3]. The development of methods of service selection and ranking that most appropriately apply to complex customer's requests is thus a relevant matter of concern.

The aim of this paper is to present an approach for service selection and ranking, considering customers' requirements, knowledge of the behavior of services, business process constraints and the characteristics of the execution environment. Following the specifications of the proposed framework advanced in [4, 5], a prototype has been implemented targeting the automotive sector. We illustrate in this paper how the prototype can be used to obtain the most appropriate services considering customers' requirements. Tests of this prototype illustrate the usability and validity of the proposed approach.

The rest of this paper is organized as follows. The proposed framework for service selection and ranking is briefly presented next. The implementation of the prototype and results of its tests are discussed in Sect. 3. Related work is analyzed in Sect. 4. The article concludes with a section addressing future research work.

2 Framework for Service Selection and Ranking

The framework developed for service selection and ranking using service choreography advanced in [4, 5] follows an adaptive control system approach, as described in [6, 7], and integrates the basis of the hierarchical model of [8]. The hierarchical control model was built to allow a self-adaptation of the system by obtaining information from the monitoring and assessment mechanism for a learning process in order to ensure its evolution and adjust deviations.

Figure 1 illustrates the dynamic cycles of the proposed framework. Following specifications of a complex adaptive system (as in [9]) and adaptive control system [10], the proposed framework allows to achieve and maintain a desired level of control when variables dynamically change in time (e.g., product cost, availability). The framework is built upon four main modules that interact with two levels of repositories [4, 5]: the *Basic Application Setup module* contains elements that depend on the customer criteria and preferences, allowing them to enter the data required to fulfill the characteristics of the service; *Core module* elements support the definition of the business and scoring rules for the provider, the identification of the services that will build up the specific business, the pools where all the services with similar functions will compete, and the definition of metrics to evaluate the performance of services; *Choreography Engine Setup module* contains elements that assemble and instantiate the choreography; *Monitoring and Assessment System module* whose elements support the instantiation of the monitoring and assessment mechanism; *Central Operational Repository* which stores operational information; and *Knowledge repository* which stores historical information from metrics assessments and choreography execution results.

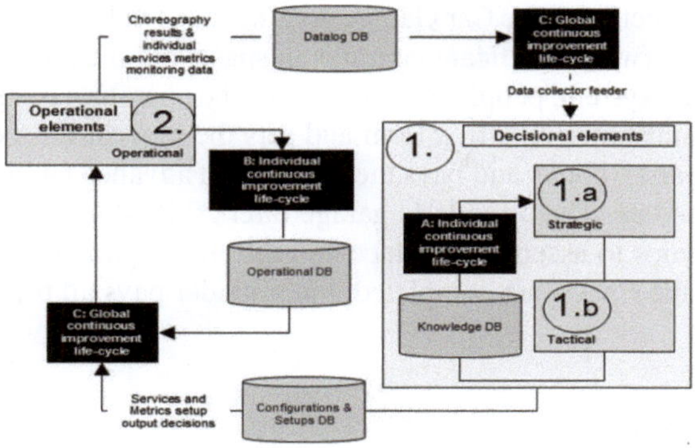

Fig. 1. Framework dynamic improvement cycles (following the specifications in [4, 5])

The modules of the framework are organized in hierarchical levels so that each role can be applied in each center of competences. The first functional group (*Decisional: 1*) integrates elements for setting strategic and tactical approaches, i.e., the provider business rules, types of metrics definition to assess service behaviors. The second group of elements (*Operational: 2*) is responsible for the instantiation of elements that fulfill requirements of a specific instance requested by the customer and retrieve data from the assessment mechanism.

Following these specifications, the prototype that supports the service selection and ranking method is described next.

3 Prototype Implementation and Discussion of Results

The prototype implemented follows the specifications of the framework for service selection and ranking using service choreography advanced in [4, 5] and its dynamic cycles illustrated in Fig. 1. This prototype targets the automotive business sector, in particular, the aftermarket automotive environment, that is: a manufacturer independent Car Garage that develops Car Maintenance Operations (CMOs).

3.1 Introduction

A high percentage of CMO interventions are basically summarized to a standard set of operations that depend on vehicle mileage or a contract formalized between the customer and the brand. These standard interventions are likely to predict which car parts are targeted by a CMO intervention, reflected in the services that will use the respective car parts. The customer (who is the car owner) can change or decline a suggested car part indicated by the car manufacturer and select another one if it is compliant. A customer may also request to replace other car parts not listed in the CMO mapping of the car manufacturer. Each brand, model, and year of manufacturing car series maps all the operations according to the characteristics of the vehicle, and this allows the Car Garage to perform CMOs based on an advanced knowledge of the operations required to meet the maintenance objectives. The Car Garage does not need to have a conventional warehouse to stock parts (with significant earnings in space, building, electricity, air conditioning, information system, people) which reduces the operating costs. The main activities as follows: a customer fills in a form and sets the request for the CMOs (e.g., by choosing the car parts), books and pays the car parts in advance taking into account the CMO intervention date. The provider's garage offers skilled labor in mechanics, electricity and electronics to assemble, replace and install car parts to perform the agreed CMOs. When all the CMOs are completed, the provider pays all the partners involved in the CMO.

3.2 Customer Front-End

For the client side, the front-end interface has been designed to allow a wide variety of service choices in order to proceed with the CMO, such as: different alternatives for the car parts to be include in the CMO, the quantity and the part brand availability; the criteria of the brand price (i.e., highest price/best price/normal), the quality criteria (highest/medium/normal), the intervention date and the prioritization of the criteria (where the default mode is: 1st - Quality and Brand Availability; 2nd - Price; 3rd - Quality). The weights assigned to each metric by the customer (and controlled by the provider through scoring and metrics tables) are automatically calculated based on the choices selected from this *Front-end* form. Each time a new request is submitted, different alternatives (considering the customer weights) are calculated by the Service Selection Services and Services Ranking Matrix elements into the matrix of calculus, as explained in [5]. The matrix is associated to a pool that stores in the database all the customer requests. After a service is selected, the values of the metrics associated with the respective service are updated.

3.3 Simulation Builder

After a customer submits its requirements and preferences for the CMO, the *Generator of the Pools of Services* (Fig. 2) builds a number of service pools that the provider may test, and the services to compete in each pool. It also produces, at the provider's request, a number of metrics by service pool, needed to monitor and assess each service. In the example illustrated in Fig. 2, ten service pools and ten metrics for each pool were chosen for the simulation. The number of services by each pool is randomly generated in a range of [300..500] in order to simulate a market service database. Each metric varies in predefined ranges and all the data types are Numeric and Boolean. The provider configures tables with scoring rules that implement a more aggressive strategy, or gives the customer more decision power to influence this behavior. For each customer request a matrix to perform the service selection and ranking is generated (as explained in [4, 5]). The definition of metrics[1] for the monitoring system is identified at each layer (e.g.,

[1] An example of a metric considered in this selection is the *Global Service Cost* referring to all the costs of all the operations and parts, including the required labor effort and a fee that is applied in order to support the operational business cost.

service's composition layer), considering a specific dimension (e.g., technical infrastructure), data types, range of values, and impact on other metrics. Assigning the customer's weight to metrics is automatic, according to the tables managed by the provider.

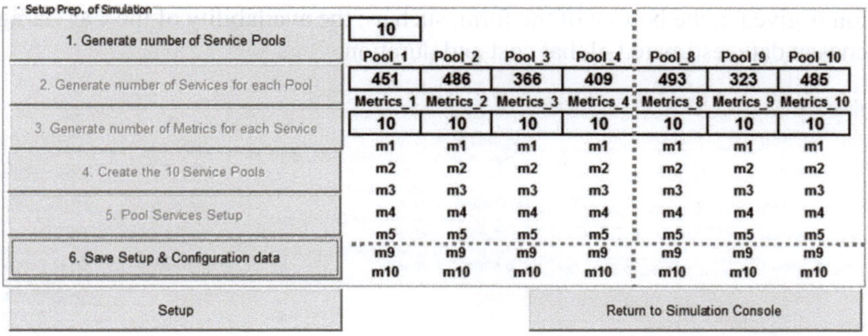

Fig. 2. Generator of pools of services.

3.4 Service Proposal and Service Request Results

The customer needs to submit a service request in order to get the estimated cost of the CMO. After the customer requests a "New Proposal", the method for selecting and ranking the services is executed. The algorithm consists of (1) selecting the services whose priority is defined in terms of "Prioritize Criteria", and (2) obtaining as a result the first sub-set of services whose pool of performance range values are in accordance with what the customer selected as the first criterion. In the next iteration, the first subset of services is used to evaluate the second priority and the resulting subset matches the performance range values for the second criterion. Another iteration is run (for the third criterion) until a reduced set of services is achieved, responding with an estimate to the request submitted. On this latter subset, an algorithm for ranking is run that allows obtaining the best service positions in the pool. This classification depends on:

- the criteria and preferences of the customer and the weight assigned to each metric that analyzes the performance of each service;
- the business rules that the provider imposes which allow to control the performance of the system;
- the number of entries in the best rated choreographies of services;
- the evaluation of the service performance resulting from the comparison between the estimated value and the actual value (with direct attribution of a penalty or a bonus);
- and the ratio between the number of participations in the best choreographies and in the lower rated ones.

From this processing we obtain the identification of the services that will participate in the choreography. The expected values for the performance of the services are recorded taking into account the existing knowledge in the pools.

The results obtained are displayed to the client, as illustrated in Fig. 3. Different colors may be used to differentiate between the results (e.g., green for the best choreography). Considering the result of "Pool 4", for example, the service identified as the best service has the ID = 327 (with a score of 3,906) cannot assure the Best price for the brand, given the percentage obtained (at yellow signage: 50%). Additional information is given at the bottom of the form, such as: the availability of the Car Garage on the chosen date, estimated global cost and duration.

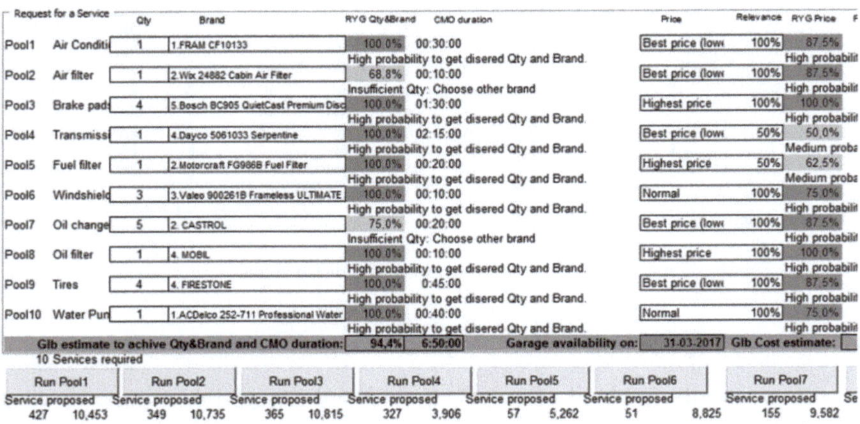

Fig. 3. Service proposal partial layout. (Color figure online)

Taking the example of Pool 3 (Fig. 4), the part of the matrix responsible for calculating the scoring rules is visible in *a)* and reflects the ranking of the top three services in that pool. The application of "wAct" described in [5] makes the service ID = 365 pass from the 8th to the 4th (in rank2 column of *(a)*), precisely because it obtains superior performances for all the metrics having weights in *(b)*. SC1 [5] determines that the service ID = 65 moves from 3rd to 1st position since it has benefited in the last participation in a choreography with *(b)* 0,5. SC3 [5] allows the service with the ID = 365, which has the highest number of entries in the most valued choreographies, to move from the 2nd to the 1st position and to remain in this position since the ratio between the number of participations in best choreographies and in the normal rated ones SC4 [5] is higher (0.729) than the other services (0,403: Service ID = 65) and (0,063: service ID = 85) respectively. In case the client does not accept some of these values, he/she can re-submit a request for another proposal by changing the service parameter that is below expectations or by filling in other values (i.e., choose other "Brand" in the "Front-end" form), and repeat the execution for specific service pools. If the customer accepts the proposal presented, the next step is to obtain the order of the global service and proceed with the payment.

a)

perf coefficient	rank1	wAct	rank2	r2-r1	scoring algorithms: SC1 - oriented perf coeff : factor : ranked value	rank3	r3-r2	SC2 - service utility (nSI <=> factor) : ranked value	rank4	r4-r3	SC3 - part. in best chor (factor) : ranked value	rank5	r5-r4	SC4 - nBPC / nSC (factor) : ranked value	pool ranking	rf-r5	services
66,8%	8°	2,943	4°	-4	4,12	2°	-2	5,15	2°	0	7,21	1°	-1	10,815	1°	0	365
84,5%	2°	2,977	3°	1	4,466	1°	-2	5,583	1°	0	6,979	2°	1	9,771	2°	0	65
63,1%	12°	2,432	11°	-1	3,405	3°	-8	4,767	3°	0	6,674	3°	0	8,343	3°	0	85

b)

		Weights	16,7%	16,7%	0,0%	0,0%	16,7%	0,0%	0,0%	16,7%	16,7%	16,7%	
in best chor (nBPC)	penalty/benefit	iteractions (nSI)	m1	m2	m3	m4	m5	m6	m7	m8	m9	m10	services
200	0,4	274	92,0%	90,2%	19,0%	27,0%	100,0%	27,8%	25,0%	100,0%	91,1%	95,6%	365
71	0,5	176	72,0%	93,4%	97,0%	88,3%	100,0%	77,8%	48,5%	100,0%	82,7%	84,9%	65
195	0,4	3091	14,0%	94,8%	75,0%	55,3%	100,0%	29,8%	21,0%	100,0%	54,4%	87,0%	85

Fig. 4. Pool 3: partial view of *(a)* ranked services and *(b)* the metrics services behavior

The last step of this process is to receive the feedback information from the monitoring and assessment system to update the performance values of the services of the different pools from the submitted request. For various market circumstances, some of the performance values may differ. This aspect is managed by the method implemented by the parameter "penalty/benefit" explained in [5] which is related to the comparison between the expected performance of each service and its actual performance. Differences resulting from this comparison allow to classify the degree of (in)success of the choreography, compared to its expected performance.

4 Related Work

Several works are concerned with decoupling the data flow from the control flow [11, 15]. Monitoring and assessing service compositions are fundamental to allow the provisioning of a valid business process. Several approaches for service monitoring exist. Some approaches are concerned with identifying erroneous situations after they occur and early detection of faults [12, 13]. Different from these works, this approach takes into account the performance results of services executed and its benefits or penalties according to the estimated values of the performance metrics. Other approaches are concerned with discovering the main factors of influence of process performance [3]. In this research work the control of the performance of the framework is determined by the provider strategy through business scoring rules. The present work relates to the monitoring of choreographies in a cross-organizational setting, similar to [3]. The added value of the approach presented in this article lies in the strong responsiveness addressing the customer's request, in which the service that is selected as the most suitable is the one that is executed. It does not focus on the analysis during the execution process related to predicting failures, adaptations and corrections of service violations [12–14]. The analysis of the most appropriate service is carried out before being submitted to the market, based on previous behavior recorded in pools of historical data. The framework learns and enhances results iteratively, iterating each time a customer submits a request.

5 Conclusions and Future Work

This work presents a prototype implemented following the framework specifications presented in [4, 5], supporting the service selection and ranking. The analysis of data shows that the weights that the customer assigns to the selection criteria, and which are automatically channeled to the respective metrics, provide clients with service proposals according to their expectations. This approach also allows the supplier to adjust the parameters of the scoring rules such that the framework behaves as expected. The results of the tests performed showed that the framework evolves and self adjusts with the execution of customer requests, and improved services are offered at each new customer iteration. The novelty of the proposed approach is related to the fact that it allows the selection of the services that best fit the customer requests as a result of a refined processing of several variables (i.e., the criteria defined by the customer). This approach can be easily applied to other business sectors that involve the composition of several services to fulfill the customers' requests. Future work will focus on the implementation of the instantiation modules of the services choreography.

References

1. Weill, P., et al.: Thriving in an increasingly digital ecosystem. MIT Sloan Manag. Rev. **56**(4), 27–34 (2015)
2. Afsarmanesh, H., Camarinha-Matos, L.M.: A framework for management of virtual organization breeding environments. In: Camarinha-Matos, L.M., Afsarmanesh, H., Ortiz, A. (eds.) PRO-VE 2005. IFIP, vol. 186, pp. 35–48. Springer, Heidelberg (2005). doi: 10.1007/0-387-29360-4_4
3. Wetzstein, B., et al.: Cross-organizational process monitoring based on service choreographies. In: Proceedings 2010 ACM Symposium on Applied Computing (2010)
4. Silva, F., Chituc, C.-M.: Towards the definition of a framework supporting high level reliability of services. In: Ghose, A., Zhu, H., Yu, Q., Delis, A., Sheng, Q.Z., Perrin, O., Wang, J., Wang, Y. (eds.) ICSOC 2012. LNCS, vol. 7759, pp. 143–154. Springer, Heidelberg (2013). doi:10.1007/978-3-642-37804-1_16
5. Silva, F., Chituc, C.-M., Grefen, P.: An approach for automated service selection and ranking using services choreography. In: Proceedings WEBIST 2015, pp. 259–266 (2015). ISBN: 978-989-758-106-9
6. Landau, I.D., et al.: Adaptive Control – Algorithms, Analysis and Applications. Communications and Control Engineering. Springer, London (2011). ISBN: 978-0-85729-664-1
7. Hellerstein, J.L., Diao, Y., Parekh, S., Tilbury, D.M.:Feedback Control of Computing Systems. Wiley Interscience, IEEE Press (2004)
8. Kaplan, R.S., Norton, D.P.: Mastering the Management System. Harvard Bus. Rev. **86**, 62–77 (2008)
9. Holland, J.H.: Complex Adaptive Systems. Daedalus, A New Era in Computation, vol. 121, pp. 17–30. The MIT Press (1992)
10. Feng, G., Lozano, R.: Adaptive Control Systems. Newnes, Oxford (1999)
11. Hahn, M., Karastoyanova, D., Leymann, F.: Data-aware service choreographies through transparent data exchange. In: Bozzon, A., Cudre-Maroux, P., Pautasso, C. (eds.) ICWE 2016. LNCS, vol. 9671, pp. 357–364. Springer, Cham (2016). doi:10.1007/978-3-319-38791-8_20
12. Wetzstein, B., et al.: Preventing KPI violations in business processes based on decision tree learning and proactive runtime adaptation. J. Syst. Integr. **3**(1), 3–18 (2012)

13. Leitner, P., et al.: Monitoring, prediction and prevention of SLA violations in composite services. In: Proceedings of the IEEE ICWS 2010, pp. 369–376. IEEE Computer Society (2010)
14. Rajaram, K., et al.: Monitoring flow of web services in dynamic composition using event calculus rules. In: IEEE International Conference on Computer Communication and Control (IC4) (2015)
15. Hahn, M., et al.: A management life cycle for data-aware service choreographies. In: Proceedings of the 23rd IEEE ICWS 2016, pp. 364–371 (2016)

Service Specification and Composition

Agnostic Informatics System of Systems: The Open ISoS Services Framework

A. Luis Osório[1(✉)], Adam Belloum[2], Hamideh Afsarmanesh[2], and Luis M. Camarinha-Matos[3]

[1] ISEL - Instituto Superior de Engenharia de Lisboa, Instituto Politécnico de Lisboa, and POLITEC&ID, Lisbon, Portugal
lo@isel.ipl.pt

[2] University of Amsterdam (UvA), Amsterdam, The Netherlands
{a.belloum,h.afsarmanesh}@uva.nl

[3] Faculty of Sciences and Technology and Uninova-CTS, NOVA University of Lisbon, Monte Caparica, Portugal
cam@uninova.pt

Abstract. The upward integration endeavor is making informatics systems (I-systems) increasingly complex. The modeling techniques, methodologies, development strategies, deployment and execution environment, maintenance and evolution, and governance, to mention just a few aspects are making the resulted (un)integrated informatics technology system a vendor lock-in landscape. The relation between informatics science and engineering and the organization's business or control processes automation, or services provisioning and adaptation, has demonstrated to be difficult to converge to a common understanding of clear computational responsibility borders. Existing approaches and standards fail to be complete with respect to establishing a landscape of informatics technology under vendor agnostic model (lock-in free). In this context, this paper extends previous research by proposing an organization´s level modularity framework aiming at formally identifying an agnostic, and open informatics system of systems (ISoS). A definition of its components is provided, and a validation case study is discussed.

Keywords: Complex informatics system · Open modularity framework · Collaborative networks · Integrated I-system of systems

1 Introduction

The role and value of informatics science and engineering can be significantly improved if the gap between the technology landscape and the business processes domain is reduced [24]. Current informatics solutions are often difficult to be substituted, paving the way for vendor lock-in cases, which weakens their value [27]. This problem has been studied in the context of multi-sectorial standards, network effects, and the impact of lock-in patterns in informatics systems industry, often leading to the conclusion that "*lock-ins are not in general avoidable*" [8]. It is thus necessary to develop strategies to

L.M. Camarinha-Matos et al. (Eds.): PRO-VE 2017, IFIP AICT 506, pp. 407–420, 2017.
DOI: 10.1007/978-3-319-65151-4_37

reduce such dependencies. The challenge cannot, however, be addressed exclusively from an informatics point of view. It requires a common strategy including the business and administration areas in order to reach a common understanding of the complexity of integrating informatics systems in the enterprise/organization and the need to induce competition among solution providers. One approach is the moderation of innovation strategies based on consensus agreements, associated with the consolidation of open specifications leading to a wider, coordinated, and complete suite of standards. A proposal of an open infrastructure as a facilitator to integrate legacy systems, and developed under an open community goes into this direction [29]. Nevertheless, the complexity of the challenge is demonstrated by the crescent recognition that a holistic model for systems integration is lacking.

The software engineering discipline, while key for the development of informatics systems (I-systems) has pursued various alternative development strategies. For instance, the agile methodologies are an evolution of the waterfall model, later converging to hybrid approaches, and more recently to the formalization of the OMG's Kernel and Language for Software Engineering Methods (Essence) specification [21]. Research work on software engineering feasibility discusses the management driven decision by adopting an agile or plan-driven (waterfall) approach, guided by value creation management decision [18]. However, even if a systematic approach is considered, the focus is on software development and not how to integrate different I-systems and its components, and to cope with the substitutability principle [24]. A first attempt to solve the lock-in problem was proposed with the Collaborative Enterprise Development Environment (CEDE) platform as a way to structure the software development landscape [24].

This paper presents and discusses an approach to reduce the above-mentioned vendor dependency risks and the gap between processes and the I-systems technology environment. The proposed approach is a step further on our previous research aiming at contributing towards an open informatics systems modularity and framework for organizations. By the end of 2002, in the early days of service-oriented paradigm (SOA), we formulated an autonomous system abstract implementing services, which was then applied to the Intelligent Transport Systems Interoperability Bus (ITSIBus) [25]. Later in 2011, we enhanced the modularity of the design based on the experience acquired with other projects (Horus and SINCRO) targeted to develop open architectures for nation-wide informatics systems, leading to the concept of Cooperation Enable System (CES) [22]. This paper proposes the formalization of the Informatics System of Systems (ISoS) framework as a conceptualization based on the CES modularity abstraction. The proposed I-system notion ranges from simple to complex entities made of CES elements, and able to answer one or more requirements sets. As an application example, the enterprise collaboration network (ECoNet) [26] infrastructure and platform, operationalized by the enterprise collaboration manager (ECoM) I-system is discussed as a validation of the ISoS adaptive integration framework.

2 Problem Domain and the State of Research

Achieving an effective organization's agnostic ISoS technology landscape is an open problem without a known and well-founded approach. This problem is commonly addressed from two main research streams: (i) system's development and operation cycles, and (ii) organization's informatics systems architecture, in conjunction with processes and services models [9]. A convergence of approaches is, however, needed. Establishing the foundations for integrated I-systems at the level of organizations (enterprises and other) requires, in fact, multidisciplinary research contributions. As such, state of the art is at the level of "islands of automation", where different I-systems, developed under different specific industry cultures, are difficult to manage, integrate and extend [15]. More recently, the collaborative dimension needed to support interactions between organizations added further structuration requirements for the involved computational responsibilities. Besides interoperability requirements, the challenge is to reach an adaptive and cooperative system of systems whose components are provided by multi-suppliers. The need to cope with the evolution of systems requires the capability of smoothly replacing I-systems by other (new generation) I-systems, which represents an even more complex challenge.

A number of recent and ongoing initiatives have tried to contribute to partial solutions to some of these challenges. For instance, the ISO/IEC/IEEE 42010:2011 systems and software engineering standardization proposal, an evolution of the IEEE 1471:2000 architectural description of software-intensive systems, embeds a systemic approach. The efforts to map existing enterprise architecture frameworks (e.g. Zachman Framework, TOGAF, RM-ODP, GERA, and ArchiMate) demonstrate a general concern on how to formalize enterprise informatics systems modeling [10]. From another direction, the Engineering Service Bus suggests an approach addressing the integration of heterogeneous engineering and modeling tools, contributing to resolving some technical and semantic gaps [3]. Another academic contribution is represented by the collaborative enterprise development environment (CEDE) platform [24], focuses on the reduction of vendor dependencies regarding services development. The enterprise service bus (ESB) concept was introduced as an adaptation layer for the integration of monolithic enterprise systems. The model-driven data independence, efficiency and functional flexibility using feature-oriented software engineering (DIEFOS) is an example of the trend towards an efficient model-driven adapter framework [15]. In a more recent initiative, and in line with the idea of microservices [13], a model for a mini enterprise application description (EA-Mini-Descriptions) was proposed. This is an interesting modeling strategy based on the OMG's MOF[1] [20], establishing a layered meta-data modeling framework, and based on M0 (Run-Time Data), M1 (Architectural Model, Meta-Data), M2 (Integration Rules, Architectural Ontology, Architectural Meta-Model), and M3 (ArchiMate, OWL) [4]. Further developments of the microservice model, such as in the Microservices Inner and Outer Architecture as defined in [19] and its relation to the Enterprise Services Architecture Reference Cube, seem promising although requiring further clarification.

[1] MOF - OMG's Meta Object Facility.

Modularity has been a research topic for a long time. E.g. [11] applies modular systems theory to the SOA paradigm. Based on an empirical study the same authors conclude that "*Implementing new, dedicated decision-making bodies for SOA hampers organizations in achieving higher degrees of IT flexibility and reuse*", pointing to the need for new decision-making and governance approaches regarding technological strategies in the organizations. However, most existing research work does not include any discussion about the multi-supplier issue and its impact in the organizations' I-systems. As an exception, in [16, 17] a mathematical model for the dynamics and modularity degree analysis of an elevator system is proposed and discussed. A similar research discusses the fact that Airbus abandoned a proprietary modular cabinet from Honeywell, replacing it by the ARINC 600 open Integrated Modular Avionic (IMA), an open modularity specification that was applied in the design of the A380 airplane [5]. It is quite interesting that the main motivations for this move were to guarantee alternative suppliers for the same components and as a side effect (also important aspect) cost reduction. Also interesting is the fact that IMA was founded by Honeywell, the supplier that used to be unique to offer the mentioned proprietary component.

Nevertheless, in spite of these efforts from the research and practice communities, a well-founded strategy to deal with the growing complexity of I-systems is lacking.

The Collaborative Network Dimension. Beyond the intra-organization dimension (vertical integration), the integration of I-systems has to answer the growing number of interactions between informatics systems of business partners (horizontal integration along the value chain). Existing technological approaches to support Collaborative Networks (CNs) do not seem to address the needs of inter-systems collaboration properly.

Seen from the informatics science and engineering point of view a CN [1] establishes a directed graph of nodes and edges, where nodes correspond to organizations with their own process and specific technological culture. In practice, these graphs can involve a complex mesh of dedicated connections, based on different transport and payload message formats. In order to cope with this complexity the grid community has suggested the grid infrastructure to support Virtual Organizations (VO) which require "*unique authentication, authorization, resource, access, resource discovery, and other challenges*" answered by the grid technology [7]. A more recent work on cloud computing extends the idea, proposing an application driven network (ADN) to establish the quality of service links between business applications (our I-systems) under the quality of service (QoS) constraints [28]. Nevertheless, the CN abstraction requires more than using distributed workstations to share and interchange resources [6]. Another initiative, the KeyVOMS server as a VO Management System (VOMS), suggests that application services share a common infrastructure to manage virtual organizations [12]. But one key problem is that no unified approach is able to cope with all requirements, making potential frameworks only partially successful; "*there will always be tools, which are unique for specific use cases*" [3]. In spite of the many efforts to establish a robust network infrastructure to support CNs, a major problem is a cost associated with instantiating and maintaining the services [6].

Therefore, an open framework is needed to induce a move from current proprietary approaches in enterprise systems (e.g. SAP, Oracle, IBM, and Microsoft) towards establishing a collaborative-oriented informatics system landscape with substitutable components. The proposed ISoS framework presented in the next section goes in this direction.

3 ISoS Model and Framework

In this paper, we formalize the open I-system of systems (ISoS), extending previous research on Cooperation Enabled System (CES) [22]. The proposed framework is based on two main entities: (i) the **I-system**, as an organization's level autonomous computational responsibility under some business model, and (ii) the **Cooperation Enabled System** (CES), as an atomic component integrating an I-system.

For a CES to be used in an organization's informatics landscape, it has to be integrated into an I-system. Therefore we can say that the informatics environment of an organization is made of I-systems which in turn are composites of CES. The CES model establishes an atomic modularity abstraction able to support substitutability. A CES_x has a substitutable CES_y from a competing supplier if the services implemented by CES_x are structurally and semantically equivalent to the services implemented by CES_y. Moreover, the substituted and substitute need to implement migration mechanisms able to recover current and historic state data. This requires that a CES implements specialized migration services to be called by the substitute when assuming the roles of the substituted CES. The substitution process might be complex enough to require human intervention. Nevertheless, the model assumes the development of standard mechanisms for each class of CES, making competing products substitutable. Therefore, a CES abstraction is defined as:

Definition 1. CES: A Cooperation Enabled System (CES) is an autonomous computational entity with an independent deployment and operation lifecycle, and defined as a tuple: CES = (I_0, SA, CS), where:

- I_0 is the system Interface, a standard entry point used by peers to access metadata and CES services;
- SA is the embedded self-awareness meta-data making CES aware to peers; the SA capabilities are accessed through I_0;
- CS is the set of implemented services, formalized through the interfaces CS = {I_0, I_1, …, I_N}, where $N \geq 1$, being each interface a point of interaction or a cooperation point.

This model maintains the essence of the concept introduced in [22] considering that security, monitoring, events and resources management are part of the CS interfaces.

Definition 2. I-system: An I-system is defined as a tuple: I-system = (I_0, SA, MC), where:

i. I_0 is the entry point service for the self-awareness mechanism responsible for adaptability;
ii. SA is the Self-Awareness element, following the CES definition;

iii. MC is a modular composite that can be based on CES (CESc) or other equivalent structure. If a CES composite, CESc = {CES_0, CES_1, …, CES_N} where $N \geq 0$; and the CES_0 is the system CES, responsible for managing the composite and its I_0 the entry-point (self-awareness); to deal with legacy assets the model does not impose a strict CES implementation. However, the SA(I_0) entry point needs to conform the service I_0 of the CES model specification.

This framework is adaptive considering that implementation is free to adopt any existing competence, components and technology assets. Only the availability of an equivalent I_0 (awareness entry point) is mandatory for ISoS structural compliance. The openness of an I-system can range from fully open to close, crossing possible hybrid situations, depending on the substitutability of its atoms (a CES or any other modularity framework) since the I-system complies with the ISoS mandatory specifications. The general structure of an I-system and its relation to the CES atom are depicted in the Fig. 1.

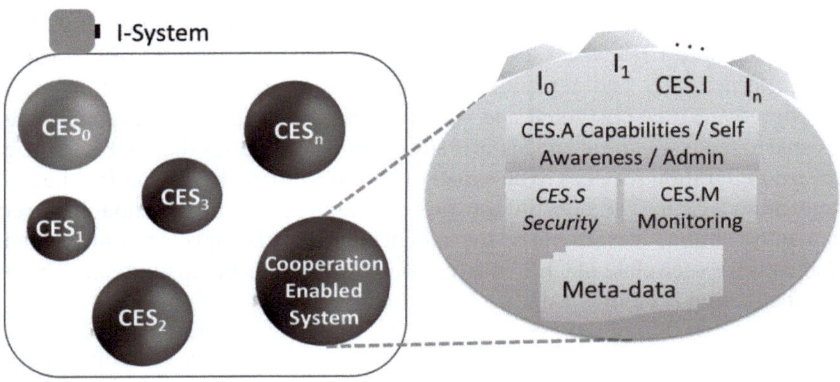

Fig. 1. Model of an Informatics system (I-system)

The proposed I-system model is transparent regarding the adopted implementation technologies. An adaptive virtual execution environment, supported by the respective CES_0, manages heterogeneity and execution location (cloud or on-premises). Furthermore, the model aims to simplify the integration of legacy I-systems by considering the respective CES_0 as a wrapper. The integration of I-systems such as (i) federated data sharing, and data management (data lifecycle management; backups/recovery, historical data); (ii) unified authentication and role-based access control; (iii) unified administration of deployed I-systems; (iv) unification of the user interface considering the participation of each I-system in user interactions; (v) unified security strategy for data privacy, data integrity and (programmatic) access to computational services; is aimed.

Definition 3. ISoS: An I-system of systems (ISoS) is defined as a tuple: ISoS = (I_0, SA, ISC), where:

i. The I_0 is the entry point service, supporting the self-awareness mechanism, following the I_0 service of a CES and I-system;

ii. The Self-Awareness (SA) follows the I-system and CES definitions;
iii. The I-system composite (ISC) is defined as a set ISC = {I-system$_0$, I-system$_1$, …, I-system$_M$}, where $M \geq 0$; for simplicity the ISC is also represented by **S** = ISC.

Following the strategy adopted for an I-system, the minimal requirement for an organization to be considered conforming to the ISoS framework is to implement an equivalent I-system$_0$ and the respective I_0.

The I-system$_0$ plays an enterprise integration, coordination, operationalization, and mediation role. Through the I-system$_0$ the proposed ISoS framework establishes an open adaptive coupling infrastructure (OACI) as a generic logical bus connecting the enterprise I-systems, as illustrated in Fig. 2. Comparing with the practiced enterprise service bus (ESB) where one or more informatics systems mediate the required interconnections, the OACI is based on the simple I-system$_0$, CES$_0$, and I_0 mechanisms to establish peer-to-peer adaptive interconnections among I-systems. The integration mediators (integration hubs) that establish additional dependencies are not requited in the proposed ISoS framework. Every shared informatics capability has to be formalized under the I-system concept.

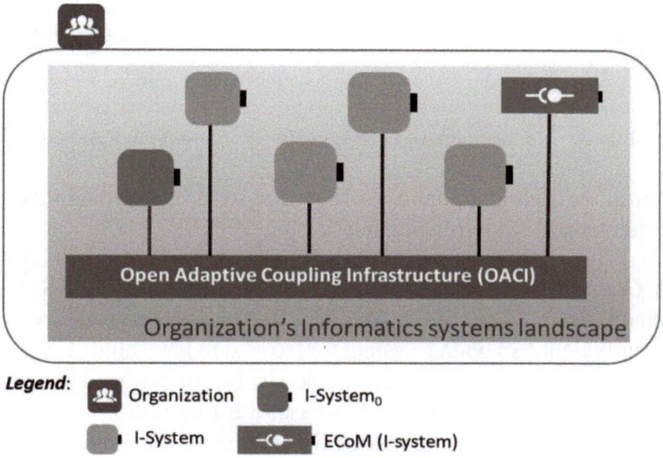

Fig. 2. The organization's I-system of systems (ISoS)

As an example, one of the I-systems can be the ECoM if the ECoNet [26] collaborative platform is adopted, as depicted in Fig. 2. The other I-systems can look-up for and obtain access credentials to the ECoM services from the organization's I-system$_0$, CES$_0$, service I_0. The ISoS framework makes possible for the organization's informatics landscape to evolve for a coordinated composite of I-systems potentially substitutable if developed under open specifications.

Therefore, the I-system$_0$ is a kind of meta-system responsible for coordinating the remaining deployed I-systems. It is the responsibility of I-system$_0$ to implement common governance functions, e.g. a unified security, services discovery mechanisms, and user authentication and authoring. The I-system model is flexible enough to support component's I-systems distributed across on-premises or cloud computational resources. Such flexibility is possible because the CES_0 component is responsible for the management of the I-system composite as a consistent, unity entity, and the computational responsibility (Fig. 3).

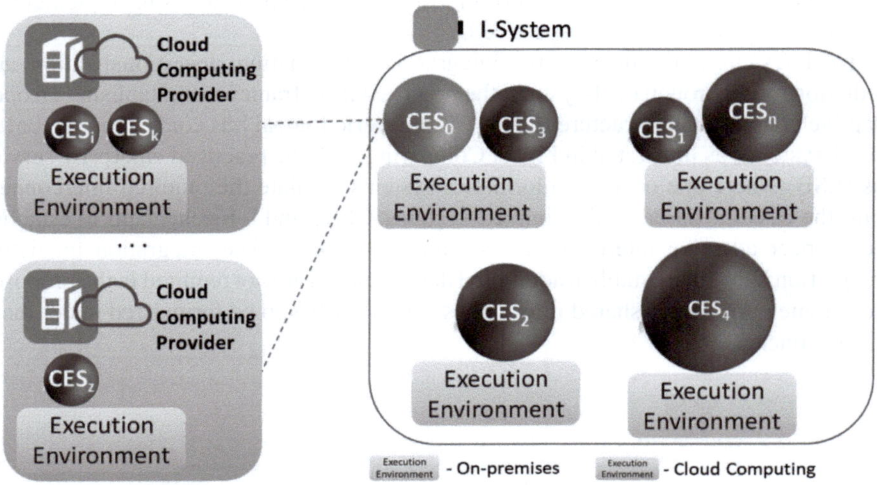

Fig. 3. Management of heterogeneous execution environments

Furthermore, we define openness of an I-system, substitutability, equivalence between I-systems and I-system's openness:

Definition 4. Openness: An ***I-system is open*** $\forall$x (CES_x) if $\exists$y: $CES_y \Leftrightarrow CES_x$. Two CES components are equivalents if $CS_x \subseteq CS_y$ and the services are structural and semantically equivalent. An open I-system is also said to have all its CES under external modularity [24]. If not all CES are substitutable, the I-system is said to be partially open. It is closed if none is substitutable. In this case, the I-system is said to be developed under an internal modularity strategy. A CES under an external modularity is said to be open.

Definition 5. Substitutability: An I-system is ***substitutable*** $\forall$x (I-system$_x \in$ S) if $\exists y$: I-system$_y \Leftrightarrow$ I-system$_x$. is the capability of a CES or an I-system that makes possible to replace them by an equivalent through a migration process. Substitutability can happen at two different levels: (i) I-system level (substitutable CES), and (ii) ISoS level (substitutable I-systems).

Definition 5.1. Equivalence: Two I-systems are ***equivalent***, or I-system$_x \Leftrightarrow$ I-system$_y$, if $MC_x \subseteq MC_y$ and the services are structural and semantically equivalent (where MC is a modular composite as formalized by definition 2).

Definition.5.2. Openness: An ISoS is open (ISoS $\in$ O), if $\forall x$, $\exists y$: I-system$_y$ $\Leftrightarrow$ I-system$_x$. If $\exists x$: I-system$_x$ $\notin$ S then the ISoS is said to be ***partially open*** (ISoS $\in$ O^P). If $\forall x$: I-system$_x$ $\notin$ S then the ISoS is said to be ***closed*** (ISoS $\in$ C).

A validation of the proposed model in the context of the EU European MIELE project to the ports administration ecosystems was applied to develop the logistics single window vision. This case is briefly described below.

The Logistics Single Window Collaborative Network. The Logistics Single Window (LSW) [2] and Port Community System (PCS) [14] research granted by the European MIELE project aimed at establishing a European-wide collaborative framework for door-to-door freight and logistics management [23, 26]. The number of connected stakeholders, the involved heterogeneity (processes and technology) and the complexity of business data and services exchanges, establishes a web of I-systems difficult to develop and maintain. The LSW services provided by business organizations interact through the ECoNet infrastructure (as depicted in Fig. 4) [26].

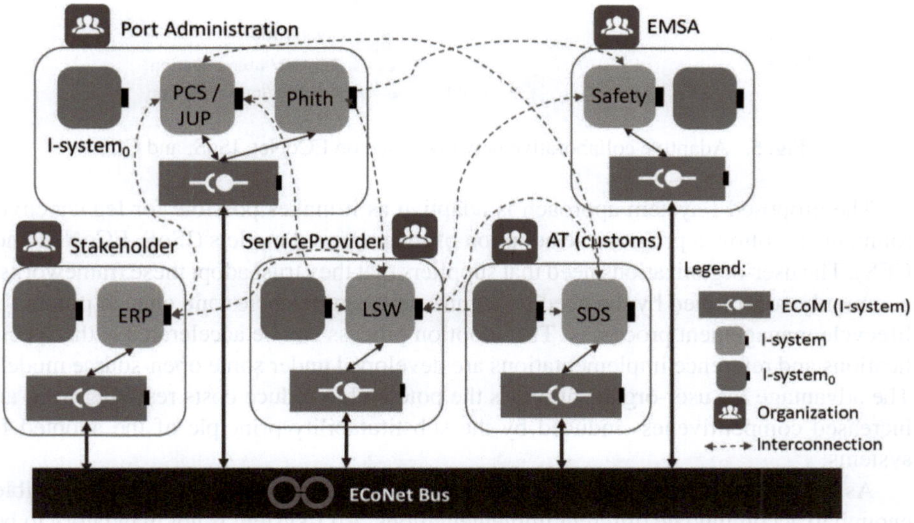

Fig. 4. The collaborative network established by the LSW services

The LSW I-system offers transport and logistics services or composites of services involving a number of stakeholders participating in the door-to-door freight offerings. The I-system approach formalizes the current point-to-point model based on adapters for the data interchanges, using a common and open infrastructure where adapters are formalized as collaboration contexts (CoC) [23]. However, for organizations that have not yet adopted ECoNet neither the ISoS framework, they can continue to use adapters, providing that their peers make the necessary changes to cope with legacy practices, see Fig. 5.

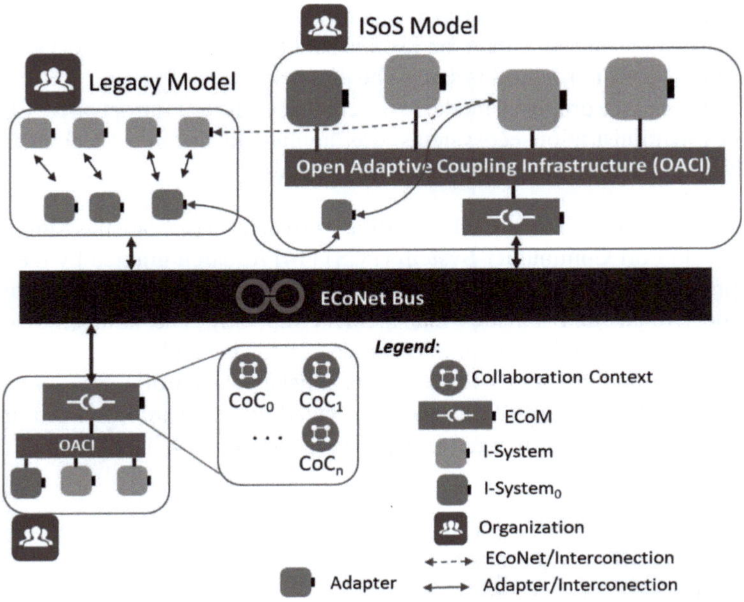

Fig. 5. Adaptive collaborative network based on ECoNet, ISoS, and CES

The proposed I-system approach is adaptive as it makes possible for legacy environments to follow a progressive adoption of the proposed models (ISoS, ECoNet, and CES). The user-organizations need that suppliers that they trust adopt these frameworks, commonly constrained by the need to acquire new competencies and change product's lifecycle management processes. The adoption process can be accelerated if the specifications and reference implementations are developed under some open-source model. The advantage for user-organizations is the potential to reduce costs resulting from an increased competitiveness induced by the substitutability principle of the adopted I-systems.

As far as a structural dimension is concerned, the proposed models are flexible enough to accommodate different implementations. An I-system is not mandatory to be implemented based on a composite of CES. In fact, an I-system is a black-box with a single well-known entry point, the (or equivalent) I_0 service of the CES_0 component. What is important is that any peer can introspect implemented functionalities and technology constraints for a dynamic coupling between I-systems. For simplicity, the sharing of functionalities implemented by different computational responsibilities (different suppliers) are restricted to I-systems. This means that if a CES component has value beyond a single I-system, its services can be available through a new I-system. The example of a CES implementing a wide organization's persistence service configures a specialized I-system with that specific responsibility.

For a user-organization to evolve to an agnostic (or dependence free) informatics landscape, a semantics consolidation is necessary. We propose to develop reference models for I-systems targeted to specific application domains. Considering the need to promote substitutability of LSW provider, the challenge is to develop a reference implementation - LSWreference - establishing common interfaces for all derived implementations (market LSW I-system products offerings). Furthermore, considering that different logistics stakeholders might adopt different LSW providers, the proposed model makes possible for them to join a virtual collaboration context [26].

4 Impact on Existing Practices

The proposed ISoS challenges current practices considering it introduces an application level modularity framework requiring a novel structuration of existing approaches. It promotes the adoption of open models and technical specifications whose products are verified through a conformance certification process. This means that existing market competition based on unique product features or development services for specific I-systems is expected to move towards standardized computational responsibilities capable of being substituted. This can, however, happen under a smooth changing process without disturbance of complex operating legacy I-system. In fact, the proposed framework makes possible a partial migration of existing I-systems considering that no constraint exist to incorporate existing technologies. The ISoS framework considers an adaptive coupling among I-systems making possible the convergence for patterned computational responsibilities. Such standard computational responsibilities as I-systems can even wrap legacy systems in order to cope with the recognized difficulty from industry to change their development processes and technologies.

Furthermore, a novel collaborative governance model is required considering there is a need for an integrated monitoring and maintenance management strategy. As I-systems tend to be more interdependent/cooperative, malfunction detection and diagnostic needs to be performed by a unified I-system. Such I-system shall be responsible for the first monitoring line and dispatch the maintenance responsibility for each I-system according to the identified problems.

5 Conclusions and Further Research

The informatics system of systems (ISoS) framework in conjunction with the cooperation enabled system (CES) establish an adaptive strategy for evolving organizations to dependency-free technology landscapes. The CES abstraction makes possible for an informatics system (I-system) to adopt different implementations of an equivalent suit of computational capabilities, promoting in this way substitutability at the component level. The I-system as a composite of CES or any agglomeration of computational capabilities is the organization's modularity level able to make the technology landscape to converge for cooperative and substitutable informatics systems. The proposed ISoS framework establishes a unique I-system, the I-system$_0$ as the unique responsibility to coordinate and manage the other I-systems.

A validation scenario considering the development of the logistics single window (LSW) concept was developed to make possible user organizations and other stakeholders collaborate even if they subscribe LSW services from different providers. This is made possible by adopting the ECoNet collaborative platform, and its ECoM I-system targeted to manage data exchanges under specific contexts and virtual collaboration groups (while multi-tenant collaboration domains). However, in spite of the demonstrated value, I-systems as products requires further investments to gear the market towards the adoption of the ISoS framework.

At the semantic level, the approach for future work is to develop an I-systems ontology establishing a sufficient set of reference I-systems and the respective reference implementations to support conformity certification processes. The strategy is in line with the EA-Mini-Descriptions [4]. It is also aligned with the Generic Enabler implementations as developed and maintained by the Future Internet Lab (FIWARE Lab) [30]. One main problem to get such a sufficient set of I-systems reference definitions is how to convince I-systems developer companies to frame their products under the ISoS framework. Our approach is to invite public and private user-organizations to invest on reference implementations on the proved certainty that in subsequent acquisitions the induced costs reduction pay off the investments in research and development.

Acknowledgements. This work has been partially supported by Administration of the Port of Lisbon and Leixões through the MIELE project, A-to-B (former Brisa Innovation and Technology), through a yearly research grant, Galpgest and BP through the Horus project and ANSR (National Road Security Authority) through the SINCRO project. Partial support also from FCT - Fundação para a Ciência e a Tecnologia within the research unit CTS – Center of Technology and Systems (project UID/EEA/00066/2013).

References

1. Afsarmanesh, H., Camarinha-Matos, L.M.: A framework for management of virtual organization breeding environments. In: Camarinha-Matos, L.M., Afsarmanesh, H., Ortiz, A. (eds.) PRO-VE 2005. IFIPAICT, vol. 186, pp. 35–48. Springer, Boston, MA (2005). doi: 10.1007/0-387-29360-4_4
2. Ahn, K.: The study of single window model for maritime logistics. In: 2010 6th International Conference on Advanced Information Management and Service (IMS), pp. 106–111 (2010)
3. Biffl, S., Schatten, A.: A platform for service-oriented integration of software engineering environments. In: Proceeding of the 2009 Conference on New Trends in Software Methodologies, Tools and Techniques: SoMeT 2009, pp. 75–92. IOS Press, Amsterdam, The Netherlands (2009)
4. Bogner, J., Zimmermann, A.: Towards integrating microservices with adaptable enterprise architecture. In: 2016 IEEE 20th International Enterprise Distributed Object Computing Workshop (EDOCW), pp. 1–6 (2016)
5. Butz, H.: Open integrated modular avionic (IMA): State of the art and future development road map at airbus deutschland. Department of Avionic Systems at Airbus Deutschland GmbH (2004). www.aviation-conferences.com
6. Foster, I., Kesselman, C.: The history of the grid. **20**(21), 22 (2010). http://www.ianfoster.org/wordpress/wp-content/uploads/2014/01/History-of-the-Grid-numbered.pdf
7. Foster, I., Kesselman, C., Tuecke, S.: The anatomy of the grid: enabling scalable virtual organizations. Int. J. High Perform. Comput. Appl. **15**(3), 200–222 (2001)
8. Heinrich, T.: Standard wars, tied standards, and network externality induced path dependence in the ICT sector. Technol. Forecast. Soc. Change **81**, 309–320 (2014)

9. Huxtable, J., Schaefer, D.: On servitization of the manufacturing industry in the UK. In: Procedia CIRP, The Sixth International Conference on Changeable, Agile, Reconfigurable and Virtual Production (CARV2016), vol. 52, pp. 46–51 (2016)
10. ISO_IEC_IEEE_42010: Systems and software engineering–architecture description; survey of architecture frameworks, January 2017
11. Joachim, N., Beimborn, D., Weitzel, T.: The influence of SOA governance mechanisms on IT flexibility and service reuse. J. Strateg. Inf. Syst. **22**(1), 86–101 (2013)
12. Lee, C.A., Desai, N., Brethorst, A.: A keystone-based virtual organization management system. In: 2014 IEEE 6th International Conference on Cloud Computing Technology and Science, pp. 727–730 (2014)
13. Lewis, J., Fowler, M.: Microservices a definition of this new architectural term, March 2014. https://www.martinfowler.com/articles/microservices.html
14. Long, A.: Port community systems. World Customs J. **3**(1), 63–67 (2009)
15. Habich, D., Lehner, W., Bohm, M., Bittner, J., Wloka, U.: Model-driven generation of dynamic adapters for integration platforms. In: Proceedings of the First International Workshop on Model Driven Interoperability for Sustainable Information Systems (MDISIS 2008), CEUR Workshop Proceedings, vol. 340, pp. 105–119, June 2008. CEUR-WS.org
16. Mikkola, J.H.: Modularity and interface management of product architectures. In: Portland International Conference on Management of Engineering and Technology, PICMET 2001, vol. 2(Supplement), pp. 599–609 (2001)
17. Mikkola, J.H.: Modularity and interface management: the case of Schindler elevators. In: IVS/CBS Working Papers 2001-6, Department of Industrial Economics and Strategy, Copenhagen Business School (2001)
18. Myburgh, A.: Situational software engineering complex adaptive responses of software development teams. In: 2014 Federated Conference on Computer Science and Information Systems (FedCSIS), pp. 841–850, September 2014
19. Olliffe, G.: Microservices: building services with the guts on the outside, January 2015. http://blogs.gartner.com/gary-olliffe/2015/01/30/microservices-guts-on-the-outside/
20. OMG-MOF. Meta object facility (MOF), November 2016
21. OMG-SEMAT. Omg_semat-essence-kernel and language for software engineering methods-v1.1. Web, December 2015
22. Osório, A.L., Camarinha-Matos, L.M., Afsarmanesh, H.: Cooperation enabled systems for collaborative networks. In: Camarinha-Matos, L.M., Pereira-Klen, A., Afsarmanesh, H. (eds.) PRO-VE 2011. IFIPAICT, vol. 362, pp. 400–409. Springer, Heidelberg (2011). doi: 10.1007/978-3-642-23330-2_44
23. Osório, A.L., Camarinha-Matos, L.M., Afsarmanesh, H.: Enterprise collaboration network for transport and logistics services. In: Camarinha-Matos, L.M., Scherer, R.J. (eds.) PRO-VE 2013. IFIPAICT, vol. 408, pp. 267–278. Springer, Heidelberg (2013). doi: 10.1007/978-3-642-40543-3_29
24. Osório, A.L.: Towards vendor-agnostic IT-system of IT-systems with the CEDE platform. In: Afsarmanesh, H., Camarinha-Matos, L.M., Lucas Soares, A. (eds.) PRO-VE 2016. IFIPAICT, vol. 480, pp. 494–505. Springer, Cham (2016). doi:10.1007/978-3-319-45390-3_42
25. Osório, A.L., Abrantes, A.J., Gonçalves, J.C., Araújo, P., Machado, J.M., Jacquet, G.C., Gomes, J.S.: Flexible and plugged peer systems integration to ITS-IBUS: the case of EFC and LPR systems. In: Camarinha-Matos, L.M., Afsarmanesh, H. (eds.) PRO-VE 2003. ITIFIP, vol. 134, pp. 231–240. Springer, Boston, MA (2004). doi:10.1007/978-0-387-35704-1_24

26. Osório, L.A., Camarinha-Matos, L.M., Afsarmanesh, H.: ECoNet platform for collaborative logistics and transport. In: Camarinha-Matos, L.M., Bénaben, F., Picard, W. (eds.) PRO-VE 2015. IFIPAICT, vol. 463, pp. 265–276. Springer, Cham (2015). doi: 10.1007/978-3-319-24141-8_24
27. Sydow, J., Windeler, A., Müller-Seitz, G., Lange, K.: Path constitution analysis: a methodology for understanding path dependence and path creation. Bus. Res. **5**(2), 155–176 (2012)
28. Tegueu, F.S., Abdellatif, S., Villemur, T., Berthou, P., Plesse, T.: Towards application driven networking. In: 2016 IEEE International Symposium on Local and Metropolitan Area Networks (LANMAN), pp. 1–6 (2016)
29. West, J.: Seeking open infrastructure: Contrasting open standards, open source and open innovation. First Monday **12**(6) (2007)
30. Zahariadis, T., Papadakis, A., Alvarez, F., Gonzalez, J., Lopez, F., Facca, F., Al-Hazmi, Y.: FIWARE Lab: managing resources and services in a cloud federation supporting future internet applications. In: Proceedings of the 2014 IEEE/ACM 7th International Conference on Utility and Cloud Computing, UCC 2014, pp. 792–799. IEEE Computer Society, Washington, DC, USA (2014)

Enhancing Network Collaboration in SOA Services Composition via Standard Business Processes Catalogues

Roque O. Bezerra[1(✉)], Maiara H. Cancian[2], and Ricardo J. Rabelo[1]

[1] Department of Automation and Systems Engineering, Federal University of Santa Catarina, Florianopolis, (SC), Brazil
{roque.bezera, ricardo.rabelo}@ufsc.br

[2] Estácio Florianopolis, Rodovia SC401 Km 01, Florianopolis, (SC), Brazil
maiara.cancian@estacio.br

Abstract. Resources sharing between members are a key issue in Collaborative Networked Organizations (CNO). In the software services sector most of companies develops their services by their own and stores them at their local silos without sharing them with other partners. However, the development of services-based applications can be very complex and costly, which is a difficult issue to overcome as most of IT companies are SMEs. In this line this paper proposes a digital catalogue environment to leverage services sharing and larger reuse between CNO members. It is strongly grounded on standard business processes models that would be adopted by all the involved members. The catalogue acts as a collaborative environment that logically embraces all the public services made available by the CNO members, enabling software services developers to compose new services-based applications more agilely. A prototype has been implemented and its results are presented and discussed.

Keywords: Business process · Catalogue · Repository · SOA · UBL

1 Introduction

Likewise in other sectors, SMEs (Small and Medium Sized Enterprises) from the software sector have been increasingly pushed to adopt advanced IT and more sustainable business models to stay competitive in the market [1, 2]. However, they use to be very limited in their capacity to engage the required assets for that. Collaborative Networked Organizations (CNO) has emerged as a powerful strategy for SMEs to overcome such limitations [3].

In this sector, *SOA* (Service Oriented Architecture) and services-based principles have been gradually adopted by software companies to more agilely create new solutions that are better aligned to their business strategy as well as to foster more advanced business models. Recent advances on IT have grounded the emergence of new models, e.g. the ones based on the vision of larger scale provision and offering of software services by pervasive providers from digital ecosystems, that are distributed over the Internet and that can be accessed on demand, from everywhere, anytime [4].

L.M. Camarinha-Matos et al. (Eds.): PRO-VE 2017, IFIP AICT 506, pp. 421–431, 2017.
DOI: 10.1007/978-3-319-65151-4_38

Working in a CNO can leverage many competitive advantages. For example, the sharing of resources [5], including software active assets [4]. Such collaboration dimension can help software services providers to save development costs, share losses and offer more value to customers [6]. Empirical observations show that, however, such providers use to keep their (*web-services*-like software) deployed exclusively at their local silos to both support their own Business Processes (BP) and to attend their customers' process/systems needs [7]. Operationally, this prevents providers from increasing the potential of services' reuse and ROI (*Return of Investment*) as services are not shared among companies. Strategically, this prevents them from the benefits of getting involved in larger value chains [4]. This limitation gets even bigger as providers and customers use to adopt their own and proprietary BP models [7], which ends up requiring made-to-fit and hence more expensive IT solutions. This, in turn, use to create vendors dependency and technology lock-in [7].

An approach to face this issue is via BP catalogues and repositories. Yan et al. [8] have highlighted the importance of having catalogues to organize, manage and handling BPs repositories and their life cycle in an organization. Nurmilaakso [9] has pointed out the potential of a larger adoption of standard BPs by organizations in terms of processes interoperability and reuse. Actually, a number of BP models have been proposed since decades (e.g. *ISO 19440, ISA-95, EDIFACT, ebXML, Rosettanet* and *UBL*), although with an emphasis on interoperability and BP modeling [7]. Many works also have been addressing BP management and BP:SOA layers integration to enhance business agility and IT alignment (e.g. [10]).

This paper investigates the hypothesis that such issues could be mitigated if CNO members adopt catalogues and repositories based on open and standard BP reference models to boost their collaboration so as to increase their competitiveness.

Applying the Design Science methodology [11], a standard-based BP digital catalogue environment was built to experimentally and mostly qualitatively verify the general feasibility of its use as an open and "unified" collaborative platform to create SOA/services-based applications. This artifact was used to create a scenario where reference BP models would be largely adopted by both software providers (when they develop their software services) and by their customers (when they specify their internal business processes). This would create a global logical view over all the software services (repositories) developed by the providers (and even by some customers) members of a CNO so that new SOA/services-based applications would be composed in a more agile and BP-coherent ways.

Although the model is flexible to deal with other BP models, UBL (*Universal Business Language*) [12], from OASIS, has been chosen for this proof of concepts regarding it is open, free and comprehensive.

This paper is organized as follows. Section 1 has introduced the problem and paper's goal. Section 2 summarizes the review of related works and identifies the scientific contribution of this research. These two sections represent the expression of awareness of the problem and the initial basis for the intended artifacts' design in the Design Science methodology. Section 3 describes the developed catalogue's rationale, its prototype and experimental results, representing the requirements, the artifact itself and the performance measurement steps in Design Science. Finally, Sect. 4 presents some conclusions, representing the achieved results step.

2 Literature Review

As the result of a literature review it was identified that a number of authors have made important contributions on some of the issues pointed out in Sect. 1. They have inspired this paper's authors in the design of the envisaged catalogue environment. For example, Cancian *et al.* [4] have identified the list of BPs that software service providers have to support in the collaboration life cycle (including services provision and support) considering aspects like partners' and services' certifications, governance and trustworthiness. Perin et al. [10] have developed a dynamic services discovery environment that works over disparate UDDI-based services repositories considering BPs' context and QoS to better support BPM-SOA integration. Using different IT supporting approaches, Camarinha-Matos et al. [13] and Obidallah [14] have developed platforms to identify and to better link BPs' needs to partners' competences and software services within a CNO. Rabelo et al. [15] have developed an open and plug & play SOA/services-based ICT platform to support dynamic offering of software services by CNO members and their link to collaborative BPs, including the organization of services within a so-called federation. Pinheiro et al. [16] have used a grid computing platform to support the sharing of computing resources (memory and storage) between CNO members.

Related to BP catalogues, it was observed that the existing ones are essentially repository management systems of proprietary BPs' models, including BP mining in some tools [8]. Eighteen catalogues & repositories were found out in the search, but only six were considered as relevant and compared with the one being proposed in this work regarding the tackled scenario (Table 1). This comparison, however, does not aim at stating which one is the "best", or that the one developed is a full-fledged environment. Instead, it aims at highlighting the main differences and commonalities with the proposed BP catalogue when supporting that scenario.

Table 1. Basic comparison among BP catalogues

Requirements	Process Handbook	SBPR	IBM BPEL	RepoX	Oryx	APRO-MORE	Proposed Model
Reusable BPs	Yes	Yes	Yes	Yes	Yes	Yes	Yes
BP Language Independence	Yes	No	No	No	Yes	Yes	Yes
Flexibility for BPs extensions	No	Yes	Yes	Yes	No	No	Yes
Semantics support	No	Yes	No	No	No	No	Yes
Non-proprietary BP model	No	No	No	No	No	No	Yes
Non-proprietary modeling language	Yes	Yes	Yes	Yes	Yes	Yes	Yes
SOA integration	No	No	Yes	No	No	Yes	Yes
BPM editor integration	No	No	Yes	Yes	Yes	No	Yes
Open source	No	No	No	No	No	No	Yes
CNO support	No	No	No	No	No	No	Yes

The evaluated catalogues were: *MIT Process Handbook* [17], *Semantic Business Process Repository (SBPR)* [18], *IBM BPEL Repository* [19], *RepoX* [20], *Oryx* [21] and *APROMORE* [22]. The requirements' subset used in Table 1 came from the surveys [7, 8], and the 'CNO support' aspect was added by the authors as it was not covered by these two surveys. The classification *yes* does not mean the full support for the elicited requirements, but rather at least some basic support.

Regarding this paper's goals and as a summary of this general comparison, it was realized that none of those works or other similar found out in the literature have proposed a BP catalog as a "common platform" to be used at CNO level enabling members to compose SOA/services-based software applications by means of massive reuse from a large-scale pool of shared services adopting open reference BP models.

About UBL, the *Universal Business Language*, it is a royalty-free library of standard XML business documents supporting commercial and logistical BPs for supply chains, such as procurement, purchasing, transport, logistics and intermodal freight management. UBL can act as a *lingua-franca* supporting disparate business applications and trading communities to exchange information using common format and terminology. It is modeled as XML schemas, which are modular, reusable and extensible, allowing its evolution and application to other domains [12].

3 Business Process Catalogue's Model and Prototype

3.1 The Catalogue's Rationale

The BP catalog has been conceived taking the requirements highlighted in the previous section into account, also considering the envisaged CNO scenario and current trends in BPM (Business Process Management): SOA integration [7, 8, 23]. This includes the use of open standards in all parts of the entire environment in order to mitigate interoperability problems.

The catalog is basically represented by an environment through which right actors from a CNO of software services providers can more agilely generate new software applications that are compliant to the respective BPs' UBL specifications when attending their customers. Customers would also adopt UBL. The applications themselves would be composed of a set of distributed software services.

Different services implementation models can co-exist. Equivalent services (from the functional point of view) can have different QoS levels, support different technologies- (e.g. web services, SOAP, etc.), billing- and access- models, multi-tenancy, etc., depending on each provider's strategy and its internal development skills and practices. However, such equivalent services should adopt a common service's interface (i.e. the same parameters for the service's *WSDL*, in this case). Once published, they will act as the services' references for further discovery, binding and invocation. There can be multiple equivalent services being provided by a sort of different providers for the same BP.

Providers are autonomous to decide which services will be shared within the federation also respecting contracted businesses and SLAs. The general management of such providers, their services' governance, reputation, revenues distribution, CNO's conventions, etc., as covered in [4], are subjects out of the scope of this work.

The to-be generated SOA/services-based application can be very complex in terms of e.g. interoperation, security and resilience capabilities. Besides that, services can be of different types, such as related to business, shop-floor, utilities, infrastructure, etc. A composed application via the catalog environment will rarely be ready to be deployed and executed. Actually a number of technical adjustments of many natures usually have to be made in real cases, besides the fact the, depending on the planned deployment and access models, non-software services can be required (e.g. manual integrations at the customers' site, configuration of the eventual ESB in use, adjustments in the generated BPEL file due to BPMN limitations, helpdesk, etc.) [24].

A given SOA/services-based application can vary from customer to customer for the same BP depending on the required non-functional requirements, both at global level (e.g. end-to-end QoS) and at individual services level (e.g. when a given system's functionality should respect specific performance metrics). For example, an application to cope with the UBL *Invoicing* BP for some customer can be composed of a different number of services (and their versions and respective providers) than one for the same BP to attend other costumer's requirements.

3.2 The Catalogue's Architecture and Prototype

The catalogue's architecture can be seen as a partial instantiation of the BPM reference architecture proposed in [7]. It provides some support to design processes, handle applications' repository and manage related services enactment [7].

The catalogue itself is a SOA application, being its modules implemented as services too. It is integrated to a BP editor (at the BPM level) and to a dynamic service discovery environment (at the SOA level), besides interacting with other modules. This global environment helps managers to design, reuse or modify existing services-based applications (developed following UBL), to discover and bind services from the CNO federation, to store the composed application, and to execute it when necessary. Figure 1 provides a general view of the catalogue environment's architecture.

In general, the IT architect and/or the Process analyst from a given CNO starts interacting with the BPM editor looking for the (UBL) BP for which they want: to create a new (services-based) software application; to modify a previous one (to reuse it) already developed for e.g. an older BP's version; or to bind another services to the application regarding new QoS requirements. The catalog provides the usual functionalities for this, as *edit, search, delete, merge, compose, monitor, save*, among others. Users also specify the QoS for the application (out of 11 parameters, such as *performance* and *response time*), being further transformed into a SLA.

Figure 2 shows a case where the *Ordering* UBL process would be accessed from the BP catalogue aiming at generating a respective application. An auxiliary graphical interface allows assigning the required QoS. In the case this application had been already generated in the past (it would be stored in the catalogue BPEL's repository) and it can be recovered for further refinements.

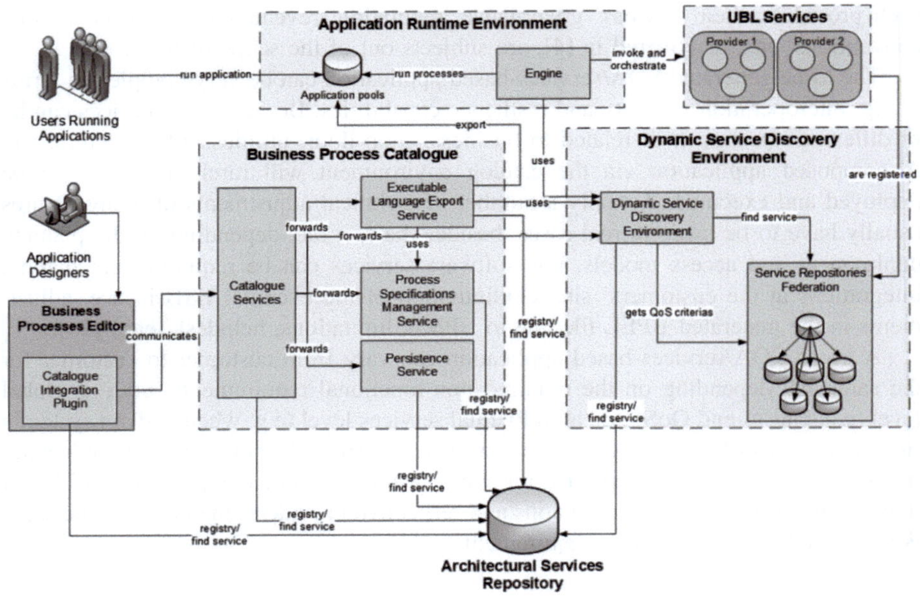

Fig. 1. Catalogue environment's general architecture.

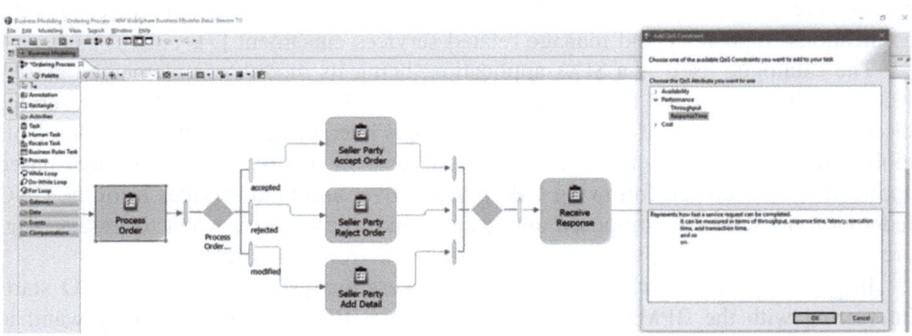

Fig. 2. Loading a given UBL process and QoS constraints.

Processes are modeled in BPMN and are further converted into BPEL files. Figure 3 shows an excerpt of the generated BPEL file.

The UBL repository can work over a single CNO member's services repository or the so-called CNO federation, which creates a "cloud-like" view over the distributed providers' repositories. The catalogue is a web-based application and uses an Internet browser as its front-end. The catalogue environment acts as a 'unified' platform through which the collaboration among consumers and providers is leveraged and supported. Depending on the agreed deployment model, each member can have access to the federation and catalogues via such front-end.

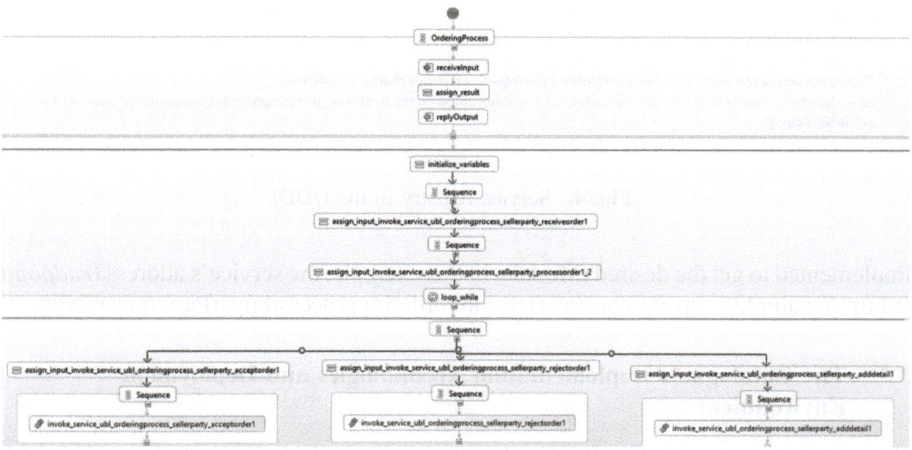

Fig. 3. Generated BPEL file.

One of the key elements of the catalogue environment is the discovery service [10], developed in the scope of this work. It supports the search, analysis, selection and final binding of the services (from the services federation) that fit best the set of functional and non-functional requirements of the application(s) under construction. The discovery service permanently checks in background the services' properties and availabilities, and maintains a ranking of up to five services for each BP's sub processes so as to always have a service ready to be invoked. This means that services binding are done dynamically instead of statically.

In the case none service can be discovered to match a given BP's requirement then the IT architect and/or Process analyst can or should relax some QoS constraint. In the worst case, if the situation persists then a new service should be developed.

As the BPEL execution is not triggered as soon as services are discovered, the involved actors can check the suggested (five) services for each BP's sub process and manually modify the ranking. This ranking is based on the QoS fitness range. Once everything is set up for the given BP then the respective BPEL file is stored into the BPEL catalogue repository for further execution.

Although the management of the federation is a subject out of the scope of this work, new services and repositories can be added or deleted from the environment. This dynamics is automatically handled by the discovery service as it always checks the registered services and available repositories.

Services and their interfaces should be previously and properly registered (following the SOA principles and the UBL specifications). Figure 4 shows a fragment of the code used to register a service related to the *OrderingProcess* UBL process, which has an activity called *placeOrder* that is performed by the *BuyerParty* actor. This is modeled in a UDDI information structure (metadata) devoted for that, called *tModel:uddi:ubl:services:ordering_orderingprocess_buyerparty_placeorder*. Every information (e.g., QoS attributes in this case) related to a given service has a tModel, and the UDDI supporting software has 'services' to access them. A generic *getServiceQoS()* method was

```
publishService(
  "UBLOrderingProcessBuyerPartyPlaceOrder",
  "UBL Payment -> Ordering Process -> Buyer Party -> Place Order",
  "http://examplecompany.com/services/ubl/orderingprocess/buyerParty/placeOrder",
  new TModelInstanceInfo[] {getTModelInstanceInfo("uddi:ubl:services:ordering_orderingprocess_buyerparty_placeorder")},
  getServiceQoS()
);
```

Fig. 4. Service registry in the UDDI

implemented to get the desired tModels. In this example, the service's address (*endpoint*) is http://examplecompany.com/services/ubl/orderingprocess/buyerParty/placeOrder.

3.3 The Catalogue's Implementation Technologies and Deployment Environment

The catalogue was fully implemented in Java, using the *Eclipse* platform. The BPM editor has used the *IBM Websphere Business Modeler* tool and a plug-in was developed as a connector to support the implementation of the *UBL* specification. Process models are generated in *BPMN*. The whole SOA environment has adopted the *SCA* architecture (*Service Component Architecture*) and was executed in the *Apache Tuscany* environment. The execution environment was supported by the *Intalio BPMS*, a suite that generates and uses *BPEL* (version 2.0 compliant), using the *Apache ODE*. *Hibernate/HSQLDB* was the database used to store the UBL BP models. Services are registered and stored using *jUDDI*, compliant with *UDDI 3.0*. The services used to test the catalogue were implemented using the *Apache CXF* framework. Only *web services, WSDL* and *SOAP* were supported.

Five servers were used to simulate the scenario of largely distributed repositories and CNO members. A set of 50 services was implemented in a very thin way, emulating the different activities of the several UBL processes. One hundred instances of these services were automatically generated, only and randomly varying the 11 possible QoS attributes so as to simulate the natural different services' "quality" of the CNO's providers. This total of 5000 services was equally deployed in 5 servers and also randomly registered in 5 repositories, deployed in a local network.

BPs that had some human intervention in their execution were implemented in way to provide a simple graphical interface for users to type what was required. This was inspired in the BPEL4People standard [12].

3.4 Catalogue Evaluation

A set of formal unit and integration tests were performed to verify the correctness of the catalogue against its requirements, especially the ones listed in Table 1.

After a sort of experiments based on many samples of UBL-based BPs modeled in the BPM environment, the systems run smoothly, supporting all the planned functionalities. In more particular, it allowed the generation and execution of new SOA/services-based applications (or changes in previously stored ones) as a result of compositions of (reused) services coming from the diverse CNO members. The intense use of open standards at all the involved levels has strongly mitigated interoperability problems and hence has facilitated the whole implementation. In other words, it was technically feasible to support compositions via the sharing of assets from the CNO members.

Considering that the developed prototype is a proof of concepts instrument handling a relatively advanced scenario, it was not feasible to test the catalogue close to a real CNO of services providers. Therefore, a more qualitative analysis had also to be done, using the *expert panel* technique [25] for that.

Nine experts on BPM and SOA were carefully selected via their curricula and previous experience on these areas for a general evaluation of the catalogue. Six experts were from the academia and the other three from IT companies, being two private and one public ones. After explaining and presenting the catalogue, they answered a questionnaire with seven questions, adopting the *Likert* scale (from *totally agree* to *totally disagree*). Some questions had a number of sub questions.

In summary, all of them agreed that: a catalogue like this can mitigate business and IT alignment problems; the catalogue is reasonably easy and intuitive to use in all of its main actions, which is suitable for SME managers; the catalogue isolates many technical details from the users when composing and generating applications; the catalogue can help companies to generate new applications in a faster and lower cost way thanks to the intense reuse. On the other hand, the interviewees expressed some concerns. In general, they were mostly related to the organizational and cultural obstacles to adopt a solution like that, both at SMEs and CNO levels. Actually, in essence, most of the identified obstacles are essentially the same than the ones pointed out in the deployment and operation of a general CNO, as depicted in [26].

4 Conclusions

This paper has presented a digital business process and software services catalogue environment as a contribution and approach to boost collaboration between CNO members of IT providers when the development of SOA/services-based applications.

Based on the research and experiments that have been carried out it was concluded that: (i) an open digital catalogue environment has the potential to work as a "unified" collaborative platform for creating services-based applications within a CNO; and (ii) it is technologically feasible to be built using open standards. It was also realized that the ultimate goal of a composition via the catalogue is not necessarily the development of an application for a very final concrete customer. The catalogue can also be used as a basis for: (i) idealizing future applications or even acting as a supporting platform for collaborative innovation in software services, as in [27]; and (ii) identifying gaps inside the CNO, which in turn can demand new services developments and can trigger other collaborations and joint results' exploitations.

The scenario created by the catalogue environment ends up representing a win-win underlying business model that tries to take advantage of the increasing pervasiveness of providers and services. For clients, this allows to flexibly find alternative services (instead of developing them) and to bind them to their BPs considering the needed functional and non-functional requirements. For providers, their software services can be more easily discovered and more intensively used, maximizing their sustainability.

Although the model was evaluated using the UBL process model, the catalogue's architecture is open to cope with other process models. In the same line, providers can offer new or equivalent services for different process models – even simultaneously via e.g. multi-tenant services architecture – and hence for other customers.

A number of assumptions were made to evaluate this work. The main one is that CNO partners have to adopt a common business process reference model when modeling their BPs and develop related software services. On the other hand, the adoption of conventions and models for BPs and software's interfaces by companies and their partners is a common practice since decades. IT systems have been more and more developed using open standards to reduce interoperability problems and development costs as well as to maximize software reuse and ROI. Regarding this, it is believed that providers will be increasingly interested to develop their services following reference process models.

Next main steps of this research refer to implement an ontology for helping providers to map their services' interfaces regarding UBL's semantics, and to develop a resilience module to support the proper execution of the generated applications.

References

1. Ukita (2017), http://www.ukita.co.uk/what-is-ukita/, Accessed March 2017
2. Kramer, W., Jenkins, B.: The role of the information and communications technology sector. In: Expanding Economic Opportunity Series. Report No. 22. Harvard Press (2007)
3. Camarinha-Matos, L.M., Afsarmanesh, H.: A comprehensive modeling framework for collaborative networked organizations. J. Intell. Manuf. **18**(5), 529–542 (2007)
4. Cancian, M.H., Rabelo, R.J., Wangenheim, C.G.: Collaborative business processes for enhancing partnerships among software services providers. Enterp. Inf. Syst. **9**(5–6), 634-659 (2015). Taylor & Francis
5. Afsarmanesh, H., Camarinha-Matos, L.M., Msanjila, S.S.: Models, Methodologies, and Tools Supporting Establishment and Management of Second-Generation VBEs. IEEE Trans. Syst. Man Cybern. **41**(5), 692–710 (2011)
6. Adner, R.: A Sad Lesson in Collaborative Innovation. Harvard Business Review, May 2012
7. Van der Aalst, W.: Business Process Management: A Comprehensive Survey. In: ISRN Software Engineering (2013)
8. Yan, Z., Dijkman, R., Grefen, P.: Business Process Model Repositories - Framework and Survey. J. Inf. Technol. **54**(4), 380–395 (2012)
9. Nurmilaakso, J.M.: EDI, XML and e-business frameworks: a survey. Comput. Ind. **59**(4), 370–379 (2008)
10. Perin-Souza, A., Rabelo, R.J.: A dynamic services discovery model for better leveraging BPM and SOA integration. Int. J. Inf. Syst. Service Sector **7**(1), 1–21 (2015)
11. Järvinen, P.: Action Research is Similar to Design Science. Qual. Quant. **41**(1), 37–54 (2007). Springer
12. OASIS (2017), https://www.oasis-open.org/committees/_abbrev=ubl
13. Camarinha-Matos, Luis M., Afsarmanesh, H., Koelmel, B.: Collaborative networks in support of service-enhanced products. In: Camarinha-Matos, Luis M., Pereira-Klen, A., Afsarmanesh, H. (eds.) PRO-VE 2011. IAICT, vol. 362, pp. 95–104. Springer, Heidelberg (2011). doi:10.1007/978-3-642-23330-2_11

14. Obidallah, W.J., Raahemi, B., Kamali, S.: Service oriented virtual organizations: a service change management perspective. In: Proceedings 26th Annual IEEE Canadian Conference on Electrical and Computer Engineering, pp. 1–6 (2013)
15. Rabelo, Ricardo J., Gusmeroli, S.: The ecolead collaborative business infrastructure for networked organizations. In: Camarinha-Matos, Luis M., Picard, W. (eds.) PRO-VE 2008. ITIFIP, vol. 283, pp. 451–462. Springer, Boston, MA (2008). doi:10.1007/978-0-387-84837-2_47
16. Pinheiro, F.R., Rabelo, R.J.: Experiments on Grid Computing for VE-Related Applications. In: Camarinha-Matos, Luis M., Afsarmanesh, H., Ortiz, A. (eds.) PRO-VE 2005. ITIFIP, vol. 186, pp. 483–492. Springer, Boston, MA (2005). doi:10.1007/0-387-29360-4_51
17. The MIT Process Handbook Project (2003), http://ccs.mit.edu/phbook.htm
18. Ma, Z., Wetzstein, B., Anicic, D., Heymans, S.: Semantic business process repository. In: Proceedings on Semantic Business Process and Product Lifecycle Management, pp. 92–100 (2007)
19. Vanhatalo, J. IBM BPEL Repository (2005), http://domino.research.ibm.com/library/cyberdig.nsf/papers/A4037428EF9DD28D85256FA5004FF88A/$File/rz3582.pdf
20. Song, M., Miller, J.A., Arpinar, I.B.: REPOX: an XML repository for workflow designs and specification (2001), https://pdfs.semanticscholar.org/c247/13c44e48d3536130b5394415fb02274bfd83.pdf
21. The Oryx Project (2017), http://bpt.hpi.uni-potsdam.de/Oryx
22. La Rosa, M., Reijers, H.A., Van der Aalst, W.: APROMORE: an advanced process model repository. Exp. Syst. Appl. **38**, 7029–7040 (2011)
23. Fiammante, M. Dynamic SOA and BPM: Best Practices for Business Process Management and SOA Agility. IBM Press (2010)
24. Rabelo, R.J., Noran, O., Bernus, P.: Towards the next generation service oriented enterprise architecture. In: Proceedings IEEE 19th EDOC, pp. 91–100 (2015)
25. Zelkowitz, M.V., Wallace, D.R.: Experimental models for validating technology. Computer **31**(5), 23–31 (2002)
26. Romero, D., Rabelo, R.J., Molina, A. (Orgs): Collaborative networks as modern industrial organizations: real case studies. Int. J. Comput. Integr. Manuf. **26**(1–2), 182 pages (2013)
27. Santanna-Filho, João F., Rabelo, Ricardo J., Pereira-Klen, Alexandra A.: A flexible collaborative innovation model for soa services providers. In: Camarinha-Matos, Luis M., Bénaben, F., Picard, W. (eds.) PRO-VE 2015. IAICT, vol. 463, pp. 366–376. Springer, Cham (2015). doi:10.1007/978-3-319-24141-8_33

C3Q: A Specification Model for Web Services Within Virtual Organizations

Mahdi Sargolzaei(✉) and Hamideh Afsarmanesh

Computer Science Editorial, Springer-Verlag, Tiergartenstr. 17, 69121 Heidelberg, Germany
{M.sargolzaei1,H.afsarmanesh}@uva.nl

Abstract. Generic representation of web services is targeted, in order to generate machine readable specification of business processes that run at each partner organization within the virtual organization (VO). A holistic and formal service specification model is defined that can then be used unambiguously for discovery of business services, i.e. for finding a suitable service available at the VO to perform a given task. Especially, the proposed model, called C3Q, augments the description of service by its behavioral specification. A light extension of the WSDL documents is represented to specify all aspects of C3Q. Finally, a GUI is implemented to assist users with the behavioral description of the VO services.

Keywords: Service oriented architecture (SOA) · Web services · Service specification

1 Introduction

Fast pace in development of services prompts exploration of the role of Service Oriented Architecture (SOA) in assisting organizations to deal with service interoperability and flexibility demands. Using SOA and its available standards enable organizations to better connect their operations. In VOs, as a first step, the services should be specified concisely, such that they are recognizable, discoverable, comparable and integrable. Currently, web services are the most promising technology that implements the concept of SOA, and provides the basis for the development and execution of business processes that are distributed over the Internet. A web service is defined as a self-contained, modular, loosely coupled, reusable software application that can be described, published, discovered, and invoked over the World Wide Web [1]. In the last decades, the Web Service Definition Language (WSDL) has emerged as the most prominent standard for the specification of business services (BSs). This standard however does not provide the specification basis for a service client to get a full understanding of "What of the service does exactly" and "How the service performs". This lack of information about services results in the mismatch of provider's objective with consumer's demands, considering the functionality of the corresponding service. In spite of several proposed additional standards, a comprehensive view on which aspects of a service is required to be concisely specified is still missing [27]. In fact, in order to share effectively the BSs and facilitate their reusability and integration in VOs, it is needed to define and register

L.M. Camarinha-Matos et al. (Eds.): PRO-VE 2017, IFIP AICT 506, pp. 432–443, 2017.
DOI: 10.1007/978-3-319-65151-4_39

the BSs in a common VO directory. Despite the simple appearance of the above requirements, several complexities and challenges rise that need to be addressed, as mentioned below:

- No uniformity in service definitions, since VO partner organizations are and remain independent and autonomous.
- Lack of common ontology for defined services.
- No defined specification as needed for formal and concise representation of services.
- No address of service functionality, as required for developing and deploying software services.
- Lack of unambiguous machine interpretable (e.g. an XML-based standard) representation of services.

This research work aims to define a model to address and resolve these obstacles and challenges, and to provide a basis for discovery and composition of services in VOs discussed in [1, 13, 23].

The paper is organized as follows. Section 2 briefly outlines some theoretical and technical aspects from the related works in order to serve as the base for our service specification. In Sect. 3, we sketch out our model of VO services, called C3Q. Moreover, a GUI is implemented to assist users with the behavioral description of the services, as demonstrated in this section. Section 4 represents how we extend the WSDL documents in order to describe all aspects of C3Q. Finally, we conclude the paper in the last section.

2 Related Work

Nowadays, web services have turned into a main area of research in the field of Service-Oriented Architecture [12], and has been widely accepted by service industries. One key point for the success of web services technology is the employment of XML-based standards, such as SOAP and WSDL for communicating and self-describing [8]. The Web Services Description Language (WSDL) as the most adopted standard for web Service description is limited to self-describing of the structure of the messages and operations, not the concept and the capability of the service. This limitation which is known as "lack of semantics" [9] in describing service capability, consequently required human intervention to interpret the semantics of the message content and the capability of the web service in order to ensure a valid and befitting use of the service. Apart from lack of semantics, another limitation of WSDL is that it does not address the configuration of stateful web services, so-called the behavior of the services. The behavior plays a vital role in service composition and improve service discovery as discussed in the [23]. Thus, lack of semantics and behavior is a major drawback of WSDL, and consequently become a barrier in achieving automatic or semi-automatic service discovery, composition and execution.

A numerous standards and languages have been proposed to describe semantics of web Services, such as OWL-S [22], WSMF [10], WSMO [16]. Due to the lack of semantics definition in WSDL documents, many research efforts are being put into the extension of WSDL by semantics annotations, such as WSDL-S [2] and SAWSDL [15].

WSDL-S can annotate the information provided in WSDL using different semantic languages, such as RDF and OWL. SAWSDL is also defined as an extension of WSDL to describe the semantics of its elements through providing the mechanisms to bind ontology concepts to semantic annotations of WSDL.

Although several researchers have tackled "the lack of semantic" problem and some tools (e.g., [21]) have achieved good results by specification of syntactic and semantic properties of web services, they hardly consider the behavioral signature of a service, which describes the sequence of operations, which the user is actually interested in. This is partly due to the unavoidable limitations of today's standard specifications, e.g. WSDL, which do not encompass such aspect. Despite this, the behavior of stateful services representation is a very important issue to be considered during discovery and composition of services, to provide users with an additional means to refine the search and automate the composition in such a diverse environment. A few formalisms have been proposed that are able to model the behavior of a service. For example, session types as a formalism for structuring interactions and reasoning over communicating processes, can be applied as a model to describe the behavior of services. Session types, which can be assigned to end-point processes, describe the user view of an interaction. In [7], the authors have specified component behavior as session types showing that session types can also describe the behavioral signature of services.

Besides the functional description of services, it is essential to capture non- functional properties of BSs or quality of services (QoS) in order to meet the performance requirements of clients (such as availability) and even providers' requests (e.g. cost). Several research works in this area are instead in favor of extending the WSDL capabilities rather than introducing additional languages on top of it. The works done in [6, 20] are two instances that capture the QoS specifications with WSDL file. A lightweight WSDL extension called Q-WSDL (QoS-enabled WSDL) is introduced in [6], to specify the QoS characteristics of web services.

3 C3Q Model of VO Services

For the sake of developing an architecture to support service oriented VOs, we first define a holistic service model, on top of which this architecture can be founded. Here, a new meta-data based on this mode is introduced to formalize the description of business processes. This model aims at addressing all characteristics of BSs, through an unambiguous formal description. From the service analysis point of view, all BSs intended to be shared and reused within the VO need to be unambiguously specified according to C3Q specified by their service providers.

We propose a concise representation of BSs as web services, C3Q model, namely addressing the Capability, Costs, Conspicuity, and Quality criteria of services. As such, VO web services can be uniformly defined and published in order to support their sharing and reusing. The Capability is the most important part of the C3Q, which represents the functional properties of the BSs including syntax, semantics, and behavior. The other elements of C3Q model, including cost, conspicuity and quality criteria of services, contain the other important required description of non-functional properties of BSs.

These three are also defined in the next subsections. Since different BSs may offer similar functionality with distinct non-functional characteristics, it is necessary to consider both functional and non-functional properties as the BS competency, in order to fully satisfy the demands of a service client, especially during the service selection phase [17, 18].

We can apply a number of different notational options for representing each C3Q's aspect. We have however adopted one specific notation and specification way for formalizing each of these aspects, as it is later addressed in this section.

3.1 Syntax

The description of the syntactic properties of a service are usually represented by XML-based standards and languages, such as Web Service Description Language (WSDL), Universal Description, Discovery, and Integration (UDDI) and Simple Object Access Protocol (SOAP) [5]. A WSDL description is an XML document that contains the following information about a specific web service:

- **What** the service does, which is described in terms of the service's operations, as well as the input and output parameters that define the operation's messages.
- **How** the service is acceded, that describes data structures, binding implementation and protocols needed for sending messages through the web to reach the service location.
- **Where** the service is located, i.e. the hosting address that executes the service implementation.

3.2 Semantics

We refer to the conceptual description of web services as their semantics, which are typically defined with an ontology, i.e. an explicit specification of a conceptualization of knowledge related to services. The definition of service ontology in the VO context encompasses a group of vocabularies that specify semantic attributes of services (e.g. context) which together provide a meaningful concept about the service [3]. In fact, the semantic description of BSs would enrich the information about services to the level that cannot be specified by their mere syntactic description. Purpose-classification of the BS (e.g. goals and context) are good examples of the semantic aspects of the BS specification, aims to categorize services in order to improve service discovery and matchmaking.

The proposed service semantics within our C3Q-based service description consists of a set of semantic attributes. These semantic attributes provide a rich description of the Conceptual information needed for representing semantics related to services. For example, goal as a semantic attribute can describe the business logic of the service (e.g. Monitoring). It is possible to also define a semantic attribute for the existing elements of the WSDL document, e.g. the operation's category.

In order to obtain semantic information about items used in the semantic attributes for the sake of semantic discovery, we must link to a particular reference domain ontology for that item. Such ontologies encompass a set of well-founded structured data that provide significant concepts with their semantic relationships, which can be used to improve the matchmaking of the services. In this research, we do not deal with the problems of ontology construction and matching. Rather, we assume the existence of a pre-defined domain-specific ontology or simply a taxonomy for a specific domain, which is related to a semantic attribute. Therefore, we capture the elements described below to specify a semantic attribute.

- **name**, which represents the title of attribute, e.g. goal or context.
- **taxonomyUri** that refers to the link of a related domain ontology or taxonomy for the attribute.
- **value** that represents the value of the attribute for this service.

An example of semantic specification in our model is represented in Fig. 1.

```
<xwsdl:semantics>
    <attribute>
        <name> context </name>
        <taxonomyUri>
        http://example.org/onto\#context
        </taxonomyUri>
        <value> Purchase </value>
    </attribute>
    <attribute>
        <name> goal </name>
        <taxonomyUri>
        http://example.org/onto\#goal
        </taxonomyUri>
        <value> Monitoring </value>
    </attribute>
</xwsdl:semantics>
```

Fig. 1. Example of the WSDL extension by the semantic description.

3.3 Behavior

Beyond the semantic description of the operations that a service can provide, and the syntax of how they are to be invoked, a specification of the proper order in which those operations can be invoked is a prerequisite for correct implementation and use of a service. Behavioral specification of a service, refers to the specification of all admissible invocation orders of the operations of that service. The discovery of suitable services matching a query must consider the behavioral specification of candidate matches. What operations can be performed at a given point in time by a client of a service may depend on the history of the previous operations that have already been performed (usually, by the same client) on that service. Therefore, specification of the behavior of a service is, in general, “stateful”. However, these states are not always maintained within the service itself.

Consider a hotel booking example, as in Fig. 2 illustrated, rooted in [14]. However, this service cannot be used properly unless, for instance, *getHotelDetails* operation is invoked only after a search operation. Any proper use of this service requires remembering whether or not a search has indeed been performed yet, and perhaps the results of such a search, etc. The REST architecture requires such information to be kept outside of the service implementation itself, on the client/user side (perhaps as cookies), and passed back and forth between the client and the service. From the perspective of a client, however, the stateless service in Fig. 2 cannot be used without considering the specification of its stateful behavior depicted in [23].

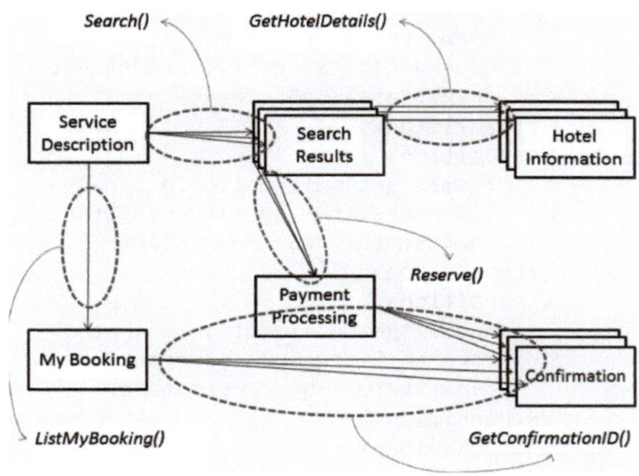

Fig. 2. Operations of the example: the Hotel booking service rooted in [14]

As a consequence, we extend the WSDL document to incorporate behavioral information of services. Our approach retains the original structure of the WSDL documents but enhances them by adding new tags. Figure 3 shows an example of the WSDL extension with the behavior description.

Since modelling the behavior of services in term of constraint automata (CA) seems rather difficult for the users, a GUI is developed to ease the behavioral specification of services and to allow its visualization. For this implementation, we have extended an open source java library, so-called Fizzim, which enables graphical modeling and designing of finite state machine (FSM). The GUI accepts a WSDL document as its input, then provides its behavioral description as a stateless web service. In fact, the preliminary behavioral-specification of the web service as a stateless web service consists of a single state automaton for each operation of the web service. For the stateful services, the states might be connected to each other to indicate the desired sequence of the operations' invocations during the service execution. Thus, a service integrator as a user of the GUI, should be able to add or remove transitions between the states of constraint automata. Fizzim supports our required extensions. It also exports the revised CA in the form of WSDL document, which is extended by the needed tags to model the behavioral specification of the service, according to the XWSDL.

```
<xwsdl:behaviour>
    <transition>
        <name> Search </name>
        <currentState> q0 </currentState>
        <nextState>  q1 </nextState>
    </transition>
    <transition>
        <name> getHotelDetails </name>
        <currentState> q1 </currentState>
        <nextState>  q2 </nextState>
    </transition>
    <transition>
        <name> reserve </name>
        <currentState> q1 </currentState>
        <nextState>  q3 </nextState>
    </transition>
    <transition>
        <name> getConfirmationId </name>
        <currentState> q0 </currentState>
        <nextState>  q5 </nextState>
    </transition>
    <transition>
        <name> getConfirmationId </name>
        <currentState> q3 </currentState>
        <nextState>  q4 </nextState>
    </transition>
</xwsdl:behaviour>
```

Fig. 3. Example of the WSDL extension by the behavior description.

3.4 Quality Criteria of Services

Quality criteria of service consists of a numbers of properties, in which every property has its own effect on overall quality of service (QoS). A wealth of research work has been done to support QoS for BSs. Although so many QoS solutions are proposed, service developers and clients still are not able to handle QoS-related concerns easily. The reason lies in the fact that a universal QoS specification standard is still absent.

We may consider that a QoS specification should contain the elements described below, in order to assure an expressive formal description of quality of services.

- **Criterion** which represents a quantifiable aspect of a service like availability.
- **Unit** Unit that is used as a standard for counting or measuring the corresponding quality criterion, e.g. hours per day, hours per week, decimal, etc. for the availability.
- **Range (Min and Max)** which depicts the highest and lowest possible values of the quality criteria. The range is needed when we want to compare the same quality criteria with different units.
- **Value** that represents the amount of the corresponding quality criterion.

An example of QoS specification in XWSDL is represented in Fig. 4. The <Quality-Criteria> tag is a container tag, which contains at least one <Criterion> tag.

```
<xwsdl:QualityCriteria>
    <Criterion>
        <Name> availability </Name>
        <Unit> hours </Unit>
        <Value min="0", max="24"> 24 </Value>
    </Criterion>
    <Criterion>
        <Name> reliability </Name>
        <Unit> Percentage </Unit>
        <Value min="0", max="100"> 90 </Value>
    </Criterion>
</xwsdl:QualityCriteria>
```

Fig. 4. Example of the WSDL extension by the quality criteria of services.

The <Criterion> tag is also a container tag indicating the required attributes of the corresponding criterion including "Name" "Unit" and "Value". The <Value> tag also provides the minimum and maximum values of the criterion, i.e. the "min" and "max" attributes.

3.5 Cost

Cost is a key economic attribute that affects the selection and usage of BSs. Thus, we introduce cost as an additional QoS parameter for specification of BSs. The cost specification consists of three parts:

- **Initial price** which represent the value of the cost, e.g. 5 or 10.
- **Unit** that defines the unit of the cost, e.g. Dollar or Euro.
- **Price plan** which is used to model the method of cost estimating, e.g. per invocation, per transmitted byte charges, etc.

In Fig. 5, an example of cost description in our proposed specification, i.e. XWSDL is represented.

```
<xwsdl:Cost>
    <InitialPrice> 10   </InitialPrice>
    <Unit> Dollar </Unit>
    <PricePlan> Per invocation  </PricePlan>
</xwsdl:Cost>
```

Fig. 5. Example of the WSDL extension by the cost.

3.6 Conspicuity

Conspicuity for a BS is the quality or state of being well-known and marked by a noticeable violation of good taste from the service client prospective. It represents means for identifying the validity of information related to a service, as claimed by its provider. A web service's conspicuity can either be measured through studying the behavior of the corresponding service provider or by capturing the past service consumers' feedbacks.

We have used the VO Supervisory Assessment Tool (VOSAT) [25] to assess the conspicuity. The approach adopted for VOSAT borrows ideas from [26], that monitors the behavior of VO members for identifying their level of trustworthiness. In this approach, all agreements in Operational Level Agreement (OLA) and Service Level Agreement (SLA) are considered as promises among the involved partners in the VO. The trustworthiness of each VO partner is reflected in this framework, as calculated by the VO Supervision Tool during the VO operation phase, related to the claims made by each partner, as explained in [19, 26]. In [24], different introduced states for promises include: conditional, unconditional, kept, not kept, withdrawn, released, and invalidated, which address different stages within the entire life-cycle of every promise. The life-cycle of every promise is then formalized and monitored, and the trust level of VO partners are assessed through a set of pre-defined causal-relationships among different promise states and the trustworthiness of VO members. Therefore, at any point in time, the trust level of the VO member would be reflected on its claims about different characteristics of its provided services, as well as on its feedback about others' services. The trust level of each partner is calculated in reference to its own performance in the VO by VOSAT during the VO operation phase. This information, i.e. the trust level is used as the conspicuity specification in the C3Q service competency model defined in this research. An example of conspicuity specification in the proposed XWSDL is shown below. Please note that the value of trust level would be between 0 and 1. An example of conspicuity description in our proposed specification is represented in Fig. 6.

```
<xwsdl:Conspicuity>
    <Trustlevel> 0.6   </Trustlevel>
</xwsdl:Conspicuity>
```

Fig. 6. Example of the WSDL extension by the conspicuity.

The technical details of measuring the organizations' trustworthiness is reported in [25].

4 XWSDL

We extend WSDL description of web services in order to support the C3Q. The XWSDL extension follows the rules for extending WSDL [4] to guarantee that any service consumer unaware of the extensions can still parse, validate and use the extended version of WSDL files, i.e., XWSDL documents. A new namespace "XWSDL" should be used to identify the tags part of the extension.

Our approach retains the original structure of the WSDL documents and enhances it by new tags to the XML-based files. In order to extend WSDL, we need to define a schema of the elements of XWSDL as its name space. We used XML-Liquid 2.0 to design the schema and then translate it to an XML documents, which consist of XSD tags in order to define the elements of the schema. This XML document is used later as the namespace for defining XWSDL documents.

The Object Management Group (OMG) has proposed "Model Driven Architecture" to support existing and future OMG standards and object models, so they would become assets instead of expenses during the transforming technologies. Model Driven Architecture focuses on providing meta-model, which is simply a model of a modeling language. These kind of meta-models are defined by use of the Meta Object Facility (MOF1), which is the OMG's standard to specify meta-models aimed at describing other model. Nowadays, employing MDA in web service standards has received significant attention to assist the automated generation and extension of web service models [6, 11]. Therefore, we apply MDA to our definition of XWSDL, in order to appropriately enrich web service descriptions based on the C3Q.

Representing an XML-based language in terms of a meta-model allows to enhance its comprehensibility and facilitate its extension [6]. Figure 7 introduces the XWSDL meta-model, as an extension of WSDL meta-model, from which the XWSDL XML Schema is derived. The basic WSDL meta-model is represented in the portion of Fig. 7 bounded by a dashed line shape. Note that some classes related to specific documenting and extensibility features of XML are removed from this basic WSDL meta-model in favor of brevity and readability. The other classes and associations outside the dashed line shape in Fig. 7 indicate our extension of the WSDL meta-model to include the description7 of C3Q for a web service. In other word, the whole classes and association in represented Fig. 7, i.e. both inside and outside the dashed line shape, forms the XWSDL meta-model. Obviously, multiplicities 0..1 or 0..* indicate optional associations, while associations with multiplicities 1 or 1..* reveal needed associations. This means, for example, that the transition is obligated for the Behavior class, while the Attribute is optional for the semantics (see Fig. 7). Note that the introduced meta-model of XWSDL can assist service providers in order to transform their WSDL documents to the proposed XWSDL descriptions.

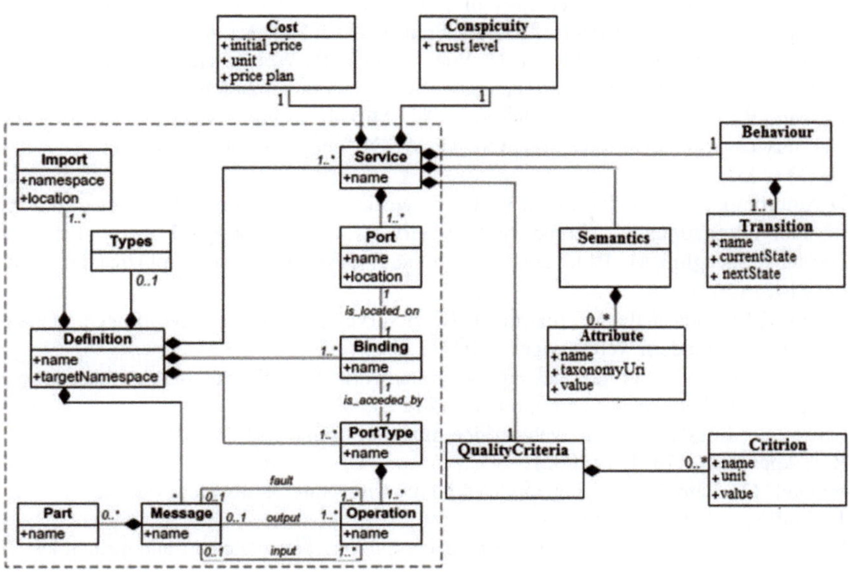

Fig. 7. The XSD tags of the schema

5 Conclusion

In this paper, we presented an extension and improvement to the current web service description approaches and standards, in order to support more efficient service discovery and composition in VOs. First, we depict a data model namely C3Q to represent the various information needed for description of the BSs as web services. The C3Q is considered as the service's competency model within the VOs. Then, we introduce a light extension of WSDL that we have called XWSDL, to specify web services according to the C3Q model. XWSDL is the first model that provides a comprehensive description of capabilities over web services and highlights the important role of service behavior in the realization of the semi-automated service oriented computing. Since XWSDL is a lightweight extension of standard WSDL, the existing WSDL documents can easily be enriched without altering their original content. The meta-model of XWSDL is also presented here to assist transforming WSDL documents to the proposed XWSDL descriptions. In XWSDL, the power and flexibility of the C3Q model has been combined with the simplicity and convenience of standard WSDL, thus reaching the right balance between flexibility and expressivity for VO services.

References

1. Afsarmanesh, H., Sargolzaei, M., Shadi, M.: Semi-automated software service integration in virtual organisations. Enterp. Inf. Syst. **9**(5–6), 528–555 (2015)
2. Akkiraju, R., Farrell, J., Miller, J.A., Nagarajan, M., Sheth, A.P., Verma, K.: Web service semantics- WSDL-S (2005)
3. Camarinha-Matos, L.M., Afsarmanesh, H., Oliveira, A.I., Ferrada, F.: Collaborative business services provision. In: Proceedings of ICEIS 2013 – 15th International Conference on Enterprise Information Systems, Angers, France, 4–7 Jul 2013, vol. 2, pp 382–392 (2013)
4. Chinnici, R., Moreau, J.J., Ryman, A., Weerawarana, S.: Web services description language (WSDL) version 2.0 part 1: Core language. W3C Recommendation 26, 19 (2007)
5. Curbera, F., Duftler, M., Khalaf, R., Nagy, W., Mukhi, N., Weerawarana, S.: Unraveling the web services web: an introduction to SOAP, WSDL, and UDDI. IEEE Internet Comput. **6**(2), 86–93 (2002)
6. D'Ambrogio, A.: A model-driven WSDL extension for describing the QoS of web services. In: 2006 International Conference on Web Services, ICWS 2006, pp. 789–796. IEEE (2006)
7. Dezani-Ciancaglini, M., Padovani, L., Pantovic, J.: Session type isomorphisms. In: PLACES, pp. 61–71 (2014)
8. Dhara, K.M., Dharmala, M., Sharma, C.K.: A survey paper on service oriented architecture approach and modern web services (2015)
9. Du, X.: Semantic service description framework for efficient service discovery and composition. Ph.D. thesis, Durham University (2009)
10. Fensel, D., Bussler, C.: The web service modeling framework WSMF. Electron. Commer. Res. Appl. **1**(2), 113–137 (2002)
11. Frankel, D., Parodi, J.: Using model-driven architecture to develop web services. IONA Technologies White Paper (2002)
12. Huhns, M., Singh, M.: Service-oriented computing: key concepts and principles. IEEE Internet Comput. **9**(1), 75–81 (2005)

13. Jongmans, S.S.T., Santini, F., Sargolzaei, M., Arbab, F., Afsarmanesh, H.: Orchestrating web services using reo: from circuits and behaviors to automatically generated code. SOCA **8**(4), 277–297 (2014)
14. Kopecky, J., Gomadam, K., Vitvar, T.: hRESTS: an HTML microformat for describing RESTful web services. In: 2008 IEEE/WIC/ACM International Conference on Web Intelligence and Intelligent Agent Technology, WI-IAT 2008, vol. 1, pp. 619–625. IEEE (2008)
15. Kopecky, J., Vitvar, T., Bournez, C., Farrell, J.: SAWSDL: semantic annotations for WSDL and XML schema. IEEE Internet Comput. **11**(6), 60–67 (2007)
16. Lara, R., Roman, D., Polleres, A., Fensel, D.: A conceptual comparison of WSMO and OWL-S. In: Zhang, L.-J., Jeckle, M. (eds.) ECOWS 2004. LNCS, vol. 3250, pp. 254–269. Springer, Heidelberg (2004). doi:10.1007/978-3-540-30209-4_19
17. Ludwig, H.: Web services QoS: external SLAs and internal policies or: how do we deliver what we promise? In: Proceedings of 2003 Fourth International Conference on Web Information Systems Engineering Workshops, pp. 115–120. IEEE (2003)
18. Menasce, D.: QoS issues in web services. IEEE Internet Comput. **6**(6), 72–75 (2002)
19. Msanjila, S., Afsarmanesh, H.: Trust analysis and assessment in virtual organization breeding environments. Int. J. Prod. Res. **46**(5), 1253–1295 (2008)
20. Pei, S., Chen, D.: Research on dynamic web services composition framework based on quality of service. Inf. Technol. J. **10**(8), 1645–1649 (2011)
21. Plebani, P., Pernici, B.: Urbe: web service retrieval based on similarity evaluation. IEEE Trans. Knowl. Data Eng. **21**(11), 1629–1642 (2009). http://dx.doi.org/10.1109/TKDE.2009.35
22. Rohallah, B., Ramdane, M., Zaidi, S.: Agents and OWL-S based semantic web service discovery with user preference support. arXiv preprint arXiv:1306.1478 (2013)
23. Sargolzaei, M., Santini, F., Arbab, F., Afsarmanesh, H.: A tool for behaviour-based discovery of approximately matching web services. In: Hierons, R.M., Merayo, M.G., Bravetti, M. (eds.) SEFM 2013. LNCS, vol. 8137, pp. 152–166. Springer, Heidelberg (2013). doi:10.1007/978-3-642-40561-7_11
24. Shadi, M., Afsarmanesh, H.: Behavior modeling in virtual organizations. In: 2013 27th International Conference on Advanced Information Networking and Applications Workshops (WAINA), pp. 50–55. IEEE (2013)
25. Shadi, M., Afsarmanesh, H.: Behavioral norms in virtual organizations. In: Camarinha-Matos, L.M., Afsarmanesh, H. (eds.) PRO-VE 2014. IAICT, vol. 434, pp. 48–59. Springer, Heidelberg (2014). doi:10.1007/978-3-662-44745-1_5
26. Shadi, M., Afsarmanesh, H., Dastani, M.: Agent behavior monitoring in virtual organizations. In: 2013 IEEE 22nd International Workshop on Enabling Technologies: Infrastructure for Collaborative Enterprises (WETICE), pp. 9–14. IEEE (2013)
27. Terlouw, L.I., Albani, A.: An enterprise ontology-based approach to service specification. IEEE Trans. Serv. Comput. **6**(1), 89–101 (2013)

E-Service Culturalization: New Trend in E-Service Design

Rasha Tolba[1(✉)], Kyrill Meyer[2], and Christian Zinke[2]

[1] Department of Computer Science, University of Leipzig, Leipzig, Germany
rasha@informatik.uni-leipzig.de

[2] Institute for Applied Informatics, University of Leipzig, Leipzig, Germany
{meyer,zinke}@informatik.uni-leipzig.de

Abstract. In this paper, we draw attention to the importance of incorporating aspects of localization into design of e-Services in order to address the differences among e-Services consumers such as linguistic differences, and cultural diversity. In the past, many companies have realized that the idea of promoting an e-Service through a single version of a portal/website is not suitable for all of the potential users or customers. This has led companies to consider new and creative design principles for e-Services, especially those who are in direct interaction with the consumer and act as service provider in a Business-to-Customer (B2C) setting. In this regard, this paper initially reviews the different aspects of service design that highlight the need to include cultural usability aspects in the service design process and successively determines the different cultural dimensions that have a substantial influence in determining the level of e-service localization.

Keywords: E-Service design · E-Service culturalization · Human-Service interaction (HSI) · User interface design (UID)

1 Introduction

As part of the development of different service promotion channels, business services are increasingly delivered through the Internet, which is commonly referred to as e-Business or e-Services [1]. One general category, which clarifies the nature of the relationship between service provider and service consumer using different electronic means (e.g. website, portal, mobile applications), focused on the end user of a service is called Business-to-Customer/Consumer (B2C).

Service Engineering [2] and Service Science [3] are concerned with studying all the methodologies and technologies that could help to improve the performance of these services directed to customers. As part of these efforts, Human-Service Interaction (HSI) has been proposed as a means of bringing together the structured development of e-services with the more general concept of Human-Computer Interaction (HCI) [4]. So far, there has been a limited research on the role of human/sociality in e-service design. Understanding the requirements of both, e-Service provider and e-Service consumer, is a persistent need for various changes (e.g. market changes, customer's interests, e-Service demand, effects of web and social media, online shopping norms). Up to now, the perspective of the customer (customer–centered design) seems to be neglected, with the result of poorly

L.M. Camarinha-Matos et al. (Eds.): PRO-VE 2017, IFIP AICT 506, pp. 444–451, 2017.
DOI: 10.1007/978-3-319-65151-4_40

designed and customized e-services. The resulting amplification of social/cultural gaps between what users expect and what developers anticipated should be addressed to minimize the effects.

The purpose of this paper is to advance the understanding of the importance of including the culture usability aspect in the service design process. In doing so, we review the relevant aspects of service design and Human-Service Interaction particularly focusing on e-Services (Sect. 2). Subsequently, we explore the different cultural dimensions who have a substantial influence on the level of e-service localization (Sect. 3).

2 Research Background

2.1 Human Service Interaction

Human Service Interaction (HSI) is the field of research that emerged and has expanded rapidly after the development of the service innovation field in the 1990s [6]. With respect to the definition of the Human Computer Interaction (HCI) it is concerned with the designing and implementation process of interactive services for the human use (see [7]), in order to let the users interact with the service system in a usable manner. It includes the perspective of a systematic development of service systems (Service Engineering), which is understood as a "technical discipline concerned with the systematic development and design of services using suitable procedures, methods, and tools" [2], including IT-enabled services [8]. The main goal of the service engineering is to develop modular and configurable systems for services [6, 9, 10]. It requires a comprehensive understanding of a service system, ideally based on a formal system model. The system provides a common basis for the description of a Human-Service Interaction for IT-enabled services.

The system model, which is an important development object of the service engineering, can also be used within the human-computer interaction. Differently from HCI the focus of HSI is not only the design of an adequate interaction within single process tasks of an employee, it is about the whole communication that takes place in a service system [8, 9]. The service systems view helps to clarify customer (human) requirements that need to be fulfilled for e-services [9]. Understanding and addressing these requirements will lead to better usability and an adequate customer interface. It will however in most case influence the services itself (e.g. the shipping options or payment methods offered) and address intangible factors such as customer loyalty and perceived service quality.

2.2 E-Service Definition

In literature many different overlapping definitions of e-Services exists. They are focusing on different criteria, such as (1) the delivery infrastructure of the e-Services, (2) the definition and essence of the term itself, (3) the benefits expected by the customer from using the e-Service [11], or (4) the difference between service production and service outcomes [12, 13]. E-Services have previously been defined as:

- "Those services that can be delivered electronically" [14].
- "Provision of services over electronic networks" [15–17].
- "Interactive services that are delivered on the Internet using advanced telecommunications, information, and multimedia technologies" [18].
- "Internet-based applications that involve a series of parallel executed transactions performed by e-service providers as they locate, negotiate, and handle requests from each other" [19].
- "An actor performance offered by one party to another an economic activity that creates value and provides benefits for customers" [12, 13].
- "An act or performance that creates value and provides benefits for customers through a process that is stored as an algorithm and typically implemented by networked software" [11].

According to [5, 19], e-Services can be categorized into three different groups. The differentiation factor is the question what kind of offering is provided through the e-Service:

- Physical: The consumer will receive a physical good. The e-service will provide additional value for the customer regarding the "assembly, design, aggregation, and delivery" of the physical good (e.g. parcel tracking services) [19].
- Digital: The consumer will in the end receive a digital good of binary coded information that "primarily exists in electronic form" [21] (e.g. digital music or book download services).
- Pure Service: The consumer is not receiving a physical or digital product. The offered service interaction brings the value for the customer by itself. Therefore, characteristics of digital and physical services may be included (e.g. an instant messaging solution) [19].

Generally, e-Services are the provision of services over an electronic network such as the Internet [24]. The scope of the e-Services should be described in the context of the type of channels and organization uses. Here, an e-Service provider interacts with customers through downstream channels and with suppliers through the upstream channels [15–17]. The type of the interaction can be (1) information-based interaction, (2) negotiations interaction, (3) promotion flow, (4) title exchange, (5) and product/service flow. Largely, e-Services include both channels and all interactions except for the transfer of physical products [16]: The downstream channels may encompass concepts such as extra-organizational interactions (e.g. Customer/Citizen Relationship Management (CRM), Relationship Marketing, Customer Care), and the upstream channels will be in relations to concepts of intra-organizational interactions (e.g. E-procurement, Supply Chain Management, Inventory Management).

Further, e-Services delivery have many forms: (1) as a service embedded in a website [26] or in portal [27], (2) as a web application backend [26] or e-Commerce application [17], (3) as a "packaged solution comprising multiple outsourced e-Services." [26], (4) as a "portfolio of related services delivered on a metered basis" [26], or (5) as a service offered in an e-government scenario G2C [27] (e.g. making an appointment with to license plates for your car).

Different domains of e-Service have been discussed in [16]. Focuses are (1) information services and web services as done in the IT sector, (2) connectivity and related services in the Telecommunications sector (3) marketing themes to move the focus from products to services in the commercial sector (4), and a Government agency's view of governmental accountability to citizens.

2.3 E-Services Design

E-Service Design is "a new holistic, multi-disciplinary, field. It concerns to either innovate or improve e-Services to make them more useful, usable, desirable for customers, as well as more efficient and effective for organizations" ([33], see also [5]). E-Service design activities are part of the service development process [13, 33, 34], and contributes to a set of modeling techniques for service experiences. That includes service-scape, customer journeys, service interface, etc. [33–35]. E-Service design as a new trend lacks in design standards. It becomes evident that (1) there aren't any specific criteria belonging to the context of e-Services [36], (2) approaches are limited and have not enough details [36], (3) approaches are not sufficient [37, 38], (4) they are derived from a specific theory or perspective [39, 40], (5) often only usability in user interface design is considered, (6) evaluation of the usability is often not related to the web or online services, (7) some of the approaches do not support a human-computer interaction perspective [41], and mainly not focus on the support of the design of IT-mediated communication between humans [42]. The first contribution to develop design criteria for e-Service was proposed in [43] as part of the social action theory Others researches focus on the business action, and use a social action perspective on IT-systems to discuss the communication as one type of action [36, 39, 44].

3 E-Service Culturalization

The e-Service culturalization concept is not entirely new. It can be understood as a customization of an e-Service through a special design for a group audience of customers according to specific customer's requirements. What is important to note, as the scope of the customization, is, that it takes into consideration the need of understanding the different customer's cultural norms. The differences and similarities in any culture are joint directly with the geographical location of customers, or to which countries customers belong to, which give attention to another term "Localization".

According to (LISA)[1], "Localization is the process of modifying products or services to account for differences in distinct markets" [45], in order to transform them into more understandable, usable, and culturally suitable services for target customers. The localization process is divided into three main levels [5]:

---

[1] Localization Industry Standards Association: is the trade body concerning the translation of computer software (and associated materials) into multiple natural languages, which existed between 1990 to February 2011 in Switzerland..

1. Linguistic level: includes the linguistic aspects (e.g. language translation, software source code, database content), rather than the adaption of the "e-Service to technical aspects such as dates, time, currency formats, addresses, measurements, weights, punctuation, and so on" [46] – suitable for the initial stages of the localization process.
2. Cultural level: includes the adaption of design components to a specific culture (e.g. graphics, visual elements, images, terminologies, metaphors, colors) and all cultural aspects of certain audience groups.
3. Technical level: includes the e-Service redesign, by means of changing components in order to make them more culturally usable.

The localization of products and e-Services is an important issue, which helps to increase: (1) customers trust if the e-Services matches their cultural needs and preferences [47] (2) customers satisfaction (3) customers loyalty (they will be more loyal to localized services that is compatible with their cultural needs and preferences) [47] and reduce "training costs, limited user risk, and enhanced performance" [48].

E-Service culturalization, includes all the procedures for cultural adaptation of e-Services including the consideration of the cultural characteristics of customers and their culture diversity as part of the e-Service design. The most comprehensive and influential model aiming to understand the culture diversity around the world is the Hofstede model [48], which has been used to understand the culture diversity in many fields.

Hofstede [48] derived his model through a survey conducted with (IBM) employees in 40 different countries. His resulting model consist of six specific dimensions:

1. Power Distance: the degree of expectation and acceptance of unequal power distribution within a culture.
2. Individualism vs. Collectivism: the role and function of the individual and group and their relation in a society.
3. Masculinity vs. Femininity: Gender roles, not restricted to physical appearance such as assertiveness or tenderness.
4. Uncertainty Avoidance: how people deal with risks and degrees of uncertainty
5. Time Orientation: related to the choice of focus for people's efforts and planning in the future or their effort in present and past.
6. Indulgence vs. Restraint: society permissions, which includes relatively free fulfilment of human desires (good life and happiness).

E-Services, which are embedded on a website or portal, should not be designed in separation of designing the web interface or website design. Five user interface design components have been suggested by [46], which include information visualization and web-based services. They have been mapped into Hofstede's cultural dimensions as a matrix to find out the relationship between interface design and culture norms. User interface design components contain (1) Metaphors: capture the essential concepts in words, images, icons and sounds with the intention to provide a understanding of the service provided; (2) Mental Model: the organization of the data so that it relates to the perception und predictive behavior of someone – the person relates to the e-Service in their consciousness; (3) Navigation: the predicted movement through the e-Service in relation to the mental model; (4) Interaction: the grade of the user interaction within the service system; and (5) Appearance: the perceptual characteristics of the presentation including audio, style, colors and themes as well as other visuals.

4 Conclusion

In this initial research paper, we tried to bring attention to e-Service culturalization as a new orientation in e-Service design. The approach outlined will require further effort in order to provide a broad and dynamic understanding of culture, and how such an understanding can be employed by e-Service designers/developers.

It is necessary for service designers to realize that services are designed for interaction with people with different cultures and social backgrounds, which means that they differ in interaction patterns. Thus being not only linguistics differences, but variations in respect to personal beliefs, values and attitudes. Service Design will have to make sure those aspects are adequately accounted for as part of the service design process. This will help to provide e-Services that match the different cultural groups in order to provide customers with services which are more usable, relevant, homecoming, and familiar. In that sense, service design can provide a holistic view regarding the activates about human centered design and the human understanding, where a service is tailored to satisfy the real requirements of both customers and service providers.

References

1. Riedl, C., Leimeister, J.M., Krcmar, H.: Why e-Service development is different. a literature review. e-Serv. J (2011). doi:10.2979/eservicej.8.1.2
2. Bullinger, H.-J., Fähnrich, K.-P., Meiren, T.: Service engineering—methodical development of new service products. Int. J. Prod. Econ. **85**(3), 275–287 (2003)
3. Maglio, P.P., Spohrer, J.: Fundamentals of service science. J. Acad. Mark. Sci. **36**(1), 18–20 (2008)
4. Meyer, K., Fähnrich, K.-P.: Ein Plädoyer für eine human-service-interaction. In: Schroeder, U. (ed.) Interaktive Kulturen - Workshop Band, pp. 118–123. Logos, Berlin (2010)
5. Alhendawi, R., Meyer, K.: The importance of cultural adaptation of B2C e-services design in Germany. World Acad. Sci., Eng. Technol. Int. Sci. Index 105 **9**(9), 544–549 (2015)
6. Miles, I.: Introduction to service innovation. In: Macaulay, L.A., Miles, I., Wilby, J., Tan, Y.L., Zhao, L., Theodoulidis, B. (eds.) Case Studies in Service Innovation. SSRISE, pp. 1–15. Springer, New York (2012). doi:10.1007/978-1-4614-1972-3_1
7. Hewett, T., Baecker, R., Card, S., Carey, T., Gasen, J., Mantei, M., Perlman, G., Strong, G., Verplank, W.: ACM SIGCHI Curricula for Human-Computer Interaction (1996). http://sigchi.org/cdg/cdg2.html#2_1. Accessed 21 June 2017
8. Meyer, K.: Software-Service-Co-Design – Eine Methodik für die Entwicklung komponentenorientierter IT-basierter Dienstleistungen., Leipzig (2010)
9. Meyer, K., Fähnrich, K.-P. (eds.): Why We Need a Human-Service-Interaction. Business Information Systems - Universität Leipzig, Leipzig, Germany (2010)
10. Edvardsson, B., et al.: New service development and innovation in the new economy. Studenlitteratur (2000)

11. Hahn, J., Kauffman, R.J.: Information foraging in internet-based selling: a system design value assessment framework. In: E-business management integration of Web technologies with business models (2002)
12. Lovelock, C.H., Wirtz, J.: Services Marketing. People, Technology, Strategy. Pearson/Prentice Hall, Upper Saddle River (2004)
13. Lovelock, C., Gummesson, E.: Whither services marketing? In search of a new paradigm and fresh perspectives. J. Serv. Res. **7**(1), 20–41 (2004)
14. Javalgi, R.G., Martin, C.L., Todd, P.R.: The export of e- services in the age of technology transformation challenges and implications for international service providers. J. Serv. Mark. **18**(7), 560–573 (2004)
15. Rust, R.T., Kannan, P.K.: E-Service: a new paradigm for business in the electronic environment. Commun. ACM **46**(6), 37–42 (2003)
16. Rust, R.T., Kannan, P.K.: E-service. New Directions in Theory and Practice. ME Sharpe (2002)
17. Meier, A., Stormer, H.: eBusiness & eCommerce. Managing the Digital Value Chain. Springer Science & Business Media, Heidelberg (2009)
18. Boyer, K.K., Hallowell, R., Roth, A.V.: E-services: operating strategy - a case study and a method for analyzing operational benefits. J. Oper. Manage. **20**(2), 175–188 (2002)
19. Tiwana, A., Balasubramaniam, R. (eds.): e-Services: Problems, Opportunities, and Digital Platforms. IEEE Computer Society (2001)
20. Mecella, M., Pernici, B.: Designing wrapper components for e-services in integrating heterogeneous systems. VLDB J.—Int. J. Very Large Data Bases **10**, 2–15 (2001)
21. Fielding, R.T., et al.: Web-based development of complex information products. Commun. ACM **41**, 84–92 (1998)
22. Sheth, J.N., Sharma, A.: E-Services: a framework for growth. J. Value Chain Manage. **1**(1/2), 8–12 (2007)
23. Prahalad, C.K., Ramaswamy, V.: Co-creating unique value with customers. Strategy Leadersh. **32**, 4–9 (2004)
24. Hogan, J.E., Lemon, K.N., Rust, R.T.: Customer equity management. Charting new directions for the future of marketing. J, Serv. Res. **5**, 4–12 (2002)
25. Bridges, E., Goldsmith, R.E., Hofacker, C.F.: Attracting and retaining online buyers. Comparing B2B and B2C customers: advances in electronic marketing. In: IGI Global, pp. 1–27 (2005)
26. Seybold, P.B.: Preparing for the e-services revolution: designing your next-generation e-business. Patricia Seybold Group (1999)
27. Phifer, G. (ed.): Enterprise Portals (1999)
28. Usunier, J.-C.: International Marketing. Prentice-Hall, New York, NY. Harcourt Brace Jovanovich College Publ, Fort Worth (1993)
29. Hofacker, C., et al.: E-services: a synthesis and research agenda. J. Value Chain Manag. **1**(1/2) (2007)
30. Bitner, M.J.: Servicescapes: the impact of physical surroundings on customers and employees. J. Mark. 57–71 (1992)
31. Bernd Stauss, P.M.: "Culture shocks" in inter-cultural service encounters? J. Serv. Mark. **13**, 329–346 (1999)
32. Barber, W., Badre, A. (eds.): Culturability: The Merging of Culture and Usability, Atlanta, GA, USA (1998)
33. Moritz, S.: Service Design: Practical Access to an Evolving Field. Masters of Science thesis, KISD (2005)
34. Evenson, S. (ed.): Designing for Service (2005)

35. Shostack, L.: Designing Services That Deliver (1984)
36. Röstlinger, A., Cronholm, S. (eds.): Design criteria for public e-services (2009)
37. Cronholm, S., Goldkuhl, G.: Actable Information Systems-Quality Ideals Put into Practice, Information Systems (ISD). Riga, Latvia (2002)
38. Cronholm, S., Goldkuhl, G.: Actability at a Glance. VITS/IEI Linkoping University (2005)
39. Nielsen, J.: The Usability Engineering Lifecycle: Usability Engineering Usability Engineering Usability Engineering, pp. 71–114. Elsevier (1993)
40. Nielsen, J.: Enhancing the explanatory power of usability heuristics. In: Proceedings of the SIGCHI Conference on Human Factors in Computing Systems, pp. 152–158. ACM, New York (1994)
41. Gould, J.D., Lewis, C.: Designing for usability: key principles and what designers think. Commun. ACM **28**, 300–311 (1985)
42. Liu, K., et al. (eds.): Coordination and Communication Using Signs. Studies in Organizational Semiotics. Springer, Boston (2002)
43. Weber, M.: Economy and society. Can. J. Linguist. (1978)
44. Searle, J.R.: Speech Acts – an Essay in the Philosophy of Language. A Philosophical Study. Cambridge University Press, Cambridge (1969)
45. Lommel, A., Ray, R.: The Globalization Industry Primer. The Localization Industry Standards Association, Switzerland (2007)
46. Sun, H.: Building a culturally-competent corporate web site: an exploratory study of cultural markers in multilingual web design. In: Sun, H. (ed.) Building a Culturally-Competent Corporate Web Site: An Exploratory Study of Cultural Markers in Multilingual Web Design, pp. 95–102. ACM, New York, (2001)
47. Marcus, A., Gould, E.W.: Crosscurrents: cultural dimensions and globalweb user-interface design. Interactions **7**, 32–46 (2000)
48. Hofstede, G.: Cultural dimensions in management and planning. Asia Pacific J. Manage **1**, 81–99 (1984)

Digital Platforms

Toward CNO Characteristics to Support Business/IT-Alignment

Ronald van den Heuvel(✉), Jos Trienekens, Rogier van de Wetering, and Rik Bos

Faculty of Management, Science and Technology, Open University of the Netherlands, Heerlen, The Netherlands
{ronald.vandenheuvel,jos.trienekens, rogier.vandewetering,rik.bos}@ou.nl

Abstract. Increasing market dynamics rapidly change the business landscape. Collaboration amongst organizations is a common way to cope with these dynamics. Achieving a state of Business/IT-alignment (BITA) within Collaborative Networked Organizations (CNOs) appears to be a valuable endeavor. Therefore, this paper investigates CNO characteristics, as a basis, to incrementally design BITA artifacts that facilitate CNO-dynamism. Via a structured literature review and an expert session, we synthesized a list of 6 main and 22 sub-characteristics for CNOs. This list provides more detailed characteristics than we found in the literature. We also discuss the importance of the characteristic "Dynamic and self-regulating network" and the need for new BITA models that can cope with the dynamics.

Keywords: Business/IT-alignment · Collaborative networked organization · Characteristics · Dynamism

1 Introduction

Collaborative networks have become a common organizational form in current dynamic markets. A CNO consists of multiple participants that collaborate to achieve common goals [1]. This field of CNOs is not new (1990s). However, studies used inconsistent conceptualizations of the term and a broadly accepted ontology currently is missing [2, 3]. CNOs emerge from the pressing need to innovate, change and collaborate and efficaciously deal with environmental dynamics. This need becomes even more pressing since the speed in which market and environment evolve is increasing [4, 5]. This increase of dynamism in the environment could increase dynamism within the CNO leading to creation, reconfiguration/(re)partnering and decommission. This requires intense collaboration within the CNO, something that is only possible through the extensive use of IT.

Achieving a state of alignment within these CNOs appears to be a valuable endeavor that could provide benefits on agility and performance [6]. However, extant literature on BITA predominantly focusses on uniminded organizations (opposed to networked organizations) and does not consider the network dynamics 'lens' [6–10].

L.M. Camarinha-Matos et al. (Eds.): PRO-VE 2017, IFIP AICT 506, pp. 455–465, 2017.
DOI: 10.1007/978-3-319-65151-4_41

Recently, both management and Information Systems (IS) research increased attention towards the adaptive and co-evolutionary nature of BITA [11, 12] and dynamic, multi-faceted processes to align IT and the business in constantly-changing business environments [8, 13, 14].

This research paper investigates CNO characteristics to develop a basis for our research project to create new BITA models that facilitate CNO-dynamism. The paper is organized as follow. Section 2 provides some background on the concept CNO and BITA. Section 3 describes the research methodology that was used. Section 4 describes the results and contains the list of characteristics. This paper ends with a discussion (Sect. 5) and conclusion (Sect. 6).

2 Background

2.1 Collaborative Networked Organizations (CNO)

Organizations operate in dynamic environments where stakeholders and their wishes quickly change and they continuously need to innovate, change and collaborate to cope with these dynamics [7, 15]. Under these conditions, collaborative networks are emerging. This is a transformation from a uniminded system, which has the form of a single autonomous legal entity, to a multiminded social model, that has the form of joint ventures or collaborative relationships [16, 17]. Collaborative networks manifest in a large variety of forms [1, 15]. Camarinha-Matos and Afsarmanesh [1] argue that a CNO is "constituted by a variety of entities (e.g., organizations and people) that are largely autonomous, geographically distributed, and heterogeneous in terms of their operating environment, culture, social capital, and goals". Literature describes different characteristics related to CNOs like: exploit fast-changing market opportunities; flexible, rapid, dynamic and reactive network; partnership among independent companies and the high dependence on IT [3]. These characteristics reflect the network, environmental aspects and the goal-oriented focus of a CNO. These characteristics could operate on different levels, which can be classified as: (1) Participants level, (2) Context level and (3) the Marketplaces level [18]. The current body-of-knowledge provides various examples of CNOs. However, despite valuable research effort, the vast majority of studies does not provide clear characteristics for these organizations.

2.2 Business/IT-Alignment (BITA)

In a CNO, IT is directly used to manage the information exchange and communication between participants [1, 15, 19]. To manage the whole IT landscape, BITA is commonly used. BITA refers to applying IT in an appropriate and timely way, in harmony with business strategies, goals and needs and leads to an increase in agility and performance [6]. Henderson and Venkatraman [20] argue that organizations should embrace continuous adaptation and change to achieve alignment and business goals. As such, they argue that 'no single IT application – however sophisticated and state of the art it may be – could deliver a sustained competitive advantage' [20]. Recent studies support this view [6, 8, 12, 21]. However, how alignment is achieved within complex networks remains largely unaddressed [6–8], and mainstream concepts for BITA are developed for uniminded organizations [7, 22]. BITA models that recognize and can cope with CNO-dynamism do not exist yet.

3 Research Methodology

Three steps can be recognized, respectively structured literature review, expert session and confrontation. The structured literature review is executed based on methods of Levy and Ellis [23], Armitage and Keeble-Allen [24]. The literature is processed by title & abstract selection, reading, comprehending, evaluating the literature until only relevant literature was left. Forward and backward searching is applied to the results to get additional literature. The quality parameters for this review were: (1) peer reviewed; (2) not older than ten years (not applicable to seminal papers); (3) written in the English language. No limitations to geographical locations were applied. We used EBSCO Host (Academic Search Elite, Business Source Premier and E-Journals) to acquire the literature. Some special interest journals were selected based on the "MIS Journal Rankings" list [25]. We built queries based on the three main research components (Table 1) and the above mentioned quality parameters. The following combinations were used: CS + CNO + BITA; CNO + BITA; CS + CNO; CS + BITA. Depending on the number (<100) of results, additional parameters (Year and Special Interest Journals) were added. Experts involved with this research project provided additional, recent, literature ([8, 26, 27]).

Table 1. Search queries on research components

Complexity science (CS)	CNO	BITA
("co-evolution" OR coevolution OR "evolutionary theory*" OR "self organization" OR evolution OR tension OR adoption OR emergence)	("networked organization" OR "collaborative networked organization" OR "collaborative networks" OR "network organization" OR multiminded OR "business network" OR "virtual organization" OR "virtual organization breeding environment" OR uniminded OR multiminded)	("IT/business alignment" OR "IT/business strategy" OR "business strategy" OR "IT strategy" OR "IT governance" OR "enterprise architecture")

The team did an expert session using the Metaplan® method [28] and consists of three scientific researchers on the senior level and one Ph.D. researcher. All in IT, complexity sciences and/or BITA/CNOs field. All participants were given literature to prepare for the session, [2–6, 19, 22, 26, 27, 29–32]. The duration of the session was 2 h.

The session was divided into the following phases: (1) Describe goal; (2) Individual brainstorm about characteristics of CNO; (3) Explanation of characteristics; (4) Group characteristics; (5) Review groups; (6) Map expert session characteristics groups on groups from literature review; (7) Recap & finish-up. The characteristics from the literature review were not provided as preparation material. The team activity started with phase 3. As the first team step, participants had to describe their insights and ideas to the other participants. In phase 4, these characteristics were categorized, grouped and duplicates were removed from an overall CNO characteristics list. In phase 5, the characteristics and groups were incrementally reviewed and reformulated. During phase 6 the characteristics and groups from phase 5 were mapped on the characteristics from the literature review. This resulted in a set of relationships between the characteristics from the expert session and the characteristics from the literature review. Finally, phase 7 recapped the session and the results. The facilitator processed and distributed the results for validation to all participants.

In the confrontation, the characteristics from literature and the expert session were critically reviewed and compared. The identified relationships from the expert session served as a foundation for the confrontation. As the synthesis subsequently developed, studies and outcomes were read and reread to check all the relevant topics and interpretations. The final list of CNO characteristics was created by categorizing, combining, splitting, rewriting and restructuring the characteristics. This step within the confrontation process resulted in an ordered schema of main and sub characteristics. Characteristics could operate on different levels, being: Participants; Context; ECO-Systems [18]. We categorized the characteristics on these specific levels to synthesize our list. Traceability of these actions was logged during the process.

4 CNO Characteristics

The literature review resulted in a large amount of results (Table 2). Criteria were added to limit the results and focus on higher quality literature. This was done for the combination CNO + CS and BITA + CS. The search queries resulted in 108 articles that could be reviewed and used for forward and backward searching on the references. The highest results came from the combination BITA + CS. BITA is a broad researched area and by adding criteria, the results were limited to 52. Switching criteria did not have relevant effects on the articles included in the review.

Table 2. Results from literature review and additional quality criteria

Input	Results	Added year	Added journals
BITA + CNO + CS	5		
CNO + CS	162	120	4
BITA + CS	2.000+	1.543	52
BITA + CNO	47		

In most cases literature used the term "characteristics", but "attributes" and "viewpoint" were also used. We did not exclude articles based on the usage of a different term. Table 3 shows the synthesized common characteristics derived from this review, coded as L1–L12.

Table 3. CNO Characteristics from literature review

#	Characteristic	References
L1	Decentralized decision-making unit/non-Hierarchical	[2–5, 22, 30–32]
L2	Lack of a consistent strategy across participants	[2, 4, 5, 22]
L3	Dynamic and self-regulating network	[2–5, 22, 26, 27, 30, 31]
L4	Highly rely on IT	[1–5, 15, 19, 22, 26, 27, 32]
L5	Equality between the participants	[2, 3, 31, 32]
L6	Shared knowledge, capabilities, risk. High amount of trust	[2, 3, 26, 27, 30–32]
L7	Evolution and continuous interaction with the environment	[2, 22, 26, 27, 30]
L8	Autonomous participants	[1–5, 15, 26, 27, 30–32]
L9	Geographically distributed	[1, 15]
L10	Heterogeneous operations (culture, social capital and goals)	[1, 3, 15, 31]
L11	Common goals between participants in a fast-changing market	[1, 3, 15, 30–32]
L12	Co-creation of customer solutions	[26, 27, 31]

Esposito and Evangelista [3] describe several shared characteristics: Exploit fast-changing market opportunities (L11); Share costs/risk, skills and core competencies (L6); Flexible, rapid, dynamic and reactive network (L3); Partnership among independent companies (L8); Temporary relationships (L3); Collaborative/Cooperative relationships (L5, L11); Extensive use of ICT and computer networks (L4). Esposito and Evangelista [3] mention a clash within the literature in the field of management. One part of the literature focusses on hierarchical structures and others on so-called holarchical structures. They state that "In the holarchical VE, partners act as a single business entity and the self-organisation approach is the main coordination mechanism". In this quote, VE can be interpreted as CNO. This clash is visible in the model of Camarinha-Matos, Afsarmanesh [15] where hierarchical structures could map to long-term strategic partnerships and holarchical structures to goal oriented networks.

Dekkers [22] pays attention to CNOs from a manufacturing perspective and states that an important difference between monolithic companies and CNOs is the absence of a central decision-making unit (L1), the lack of a consistent strategy across all the agents (L2) and the capability to reconfigure the network (L3). Concha, Espadas [19] address the need for specific ICT solutions (L4) to make sure participants can communicate with each other within the dynamics of a collaborative network.

Walters and Buchanan [2] state that: CNOs are not hierarchical but participants are equal within the network (L5); The network is dynamic and self-regulating (L3); There is knowledge sharing within the network (L6); The network is evolving and constantly interacting with its environment (L7); It's a learning organization (L6).

Camarinha-Matos, Afsarmanesh [15] mention the following common characteristics for CNOs: Networks composed of a variety of entities which are largely autonomous (L8), geographically distributed (L9) and heterogeneous in terms of their operating environment, culture, social capital and goals (L10); Participants collaborate to (better) achieve common or compatible goals (L11); the interaction among participants are supported by computer networks (L4).

Weber [30] researched the supply chain agility of CNOs. In her study, she synthesized the following characteristics for CNOs: Loosely related group of companies formed to enable collaboration towards mutually agreed on goals (L1, L8, L11); Focus on adaptability, flexibility and the ability to react quickly to changes in the market (L3, L8, L7); Substantial cost reductions, higher productivity and greater satisfaction of both employees and customers because they provide the means to create greater focus and integration (L6).

Van Alstyne [31] synthesized the following characteristics from literature: A network organization maintains permeable boundaries either internally, among business units or externally with other firms (L3, L5, L8); Management is less hierarchical (L1); deriving its authority more from expertise than from rank (L1, L6); Higher degree of intangible, local, or specialized know-how (L6, L10); Communication is direct and point-to-point rather than “through channels” (L1); knowledge of emerging problems and opportunities may arrive via multiple loose associations or weak ties (L3); Resources are specialized and customizable within a given product or service scope (L11); less vertically integrated than their hierarchical counterparts (L1); Purposeful agents may establish ties to other agents and organizations (L1, L3); Tasks are more project and less functionally driven (L11); Differentiated products (L11, L12); integrated staff conception and line executing (L1); local concerns are more locally addressed and thus owned (L1); High degree of trust and commitment between parties; sharing risk (L5).

Rahman and Bhattachryya [32] also mentioned characteristics for organizations: They have a shared vision and goal and/or common protocol of cooperation (L8, L11); They cluster activities around their core competencies (L6); They work jointly in teams of core competence groups, to implement their activities in a holistic approach throughout the value chain (L1); They process and distribute information in real time throughout the entire network, which allows them to make decisions and coordinate actions quickly (L4); They tend to delegate from the bottom up whenever economies of scale can be achieved, new conditions arise, or a specific competence is required for serving the needs of the whole group (L1) Also Rahman and Bhattachryya [32] mention the characteristics: Autonomous participants that collaborate in VO (L8). Shorter lived organizations focused on a common goal shared among participants (L11); Sharing risk, knowledge and capabilities (L6).

There are different views in the literature on these collaborative networks like a business process management point of view [26, 27], social view [16], manufacturing view [22]. The characteristics used within these different viewpoints overlap.

In the expert session, the participants provided in total 37 characteristics (Table 4) coded as M1-M37. In most cases, the characteristics could be related to the literature review. At the end of the session, consensus was achieved on the characteristics, groups and relationships to characteristics from the literature review. M1; M2; M3; M7; M18; M19 are new characteristics. M1, M29, M35, M37 were mentioned multiple times by the experts. Also, relationships between characteristics from the experts were established. We agreed that there was a relationship between M2 and M3, M2 and M4, M4

Table 4. Characteristics from expert session

#	Characteristic	#	Characteristic
M1	Long-term/short-term	M20	IT is an integral part of collaboration
M2	Level of collaboration (business, information, tech)	M21	Infrastructure
		M22	Essential capabilities (IT, strategy, communication)
M3	Maturity (integrated/connected)		
M4	Modular (loosely coupled)	M23	Trust basis
M5	Many-to-many relations epistatic relations	M24	Distributed capabilities
		M25	Complementary partnerships
M6	Interaction patterns (int./external)	M26	Sharing of resources
M7	Size CNO (# orgs, #employees, #revenue)	M27	Panarchy life-cycle (adaptive cycle)
		M28	Möbius-strip organization
M8	Control function	M29	(in)Dependence from partners
M9	No mandatory central org. struct.	M30	Location/time zone
M10	Control of the network (central, decentralized, hybrid)	M31	Culture
		M32	Diversity
M11	Collaboration fixed/dynamic	M33	Common goals within the networked organization
M12	Dynamic partnering (join/leave)		
M13	Change/adaptation	M34	Goal(s)
M14	Complex landscape of organization	M35	Product vs. service-orientation (product/process)
M15	Networks can change in volatility	M36	Individual org. cannot achieve the shared goals
M16	Environmental turbulence		
M17	Non-linear	M37	Developments/manufacturing vs co-creation (customer)
M18	Emergent		
M19	Multi-level effects		

and M5, M5 and M6. These relationships fit within the topics of modularity, interaction levels and the level on which modularity is described. M18 is related to M17 and M19, which are related to adaptation and evolution of the CNO. Lastly, the experts concluded that M27 has a relationship with M28 (Panarchy life-cycle follows a Möbius-strip movement).

In phase 6, most of the characteristics from the expert session were related to L3 (9x), L1-L6-L7-L8-L11 (5x). Characteristics L2 and L5 did not have any characteristics attached from the expert session. This could be related to a different interaction maturity level as described by Camarinha-Matos, Afsarmanesh [15], Camarinha-Matos and Afsarmanesh [29]. In their articles, they describe a lower interaction level called "cooperation" or "coordinated network" where organizations do not have these characteristics.

The confrontation resulted in 6 main characteristics (Table 5) coded as N1-N6. In this process, characteristics were rewritten, combined, and split up into multiple characteristics. For instance, N1 was created from the characteristics L11, M33, M34, M36, L12, M37, all these characteristics are related to common goals between participants. L6 was split up into N2.1, N2.2, N2.3, N2.4. N2.4 was combined from L6 and M23.

Table 5. CNO Characteristics

#	Characteristic	#	Characteristic
N1	Common goals between participants within a fast-changing market (co-creation)	N4	Autonomous participants
		N4.1	Non-hierarchical determined control function for the network (centralized, decentralized, hybrid)
N2	Complementary partnerships, shared & distributed capabilities	N4.2	Modular (loosely coupled)
N2.1	Shared knowledge	N4.3	Lack of a consistent strategy across participants
N2.2	Shared capabilities		
N2.3	Shared risk	N4.4	Equality between the participants
N2.4	High amount of trust	N4.5	No geographical limitations on distribution of the organizations
N2.5	IT is an essential capability		
N2.6	Level of collaboration (business, information, technology)	N4.6	Diverse/heterogeneous operations in culture, social capital and goals
N3	Evolution (change/adaptation) and continuous interaction with the environment	N5	Dynamic and self-regulating network
		N5.1	Dynamic partnering (join/leave, fixed/dynamic, short/long)
N3.1	Adaptive cycle (Panarchy cycle)	N5.2	Complex landscape of organization
N3.2	Environmental turbulence	N5.3	Many-to-many relations epistatic relations
N3.3	Emergent behavior		
N3.4	Multi-level effects	N5.4	Interaction patterns (int./external)
N3.5	Non-linear effects	N5.5	Maturity (integrated/connected)
		N6	Size CNO (#organizations, #employees, #revenue)

Both are related to trust within the network. Another example is N2.5 that was combined from M20, M21, M22, L4 because all these characteristics were related to the fact that "IT is an essential capability". The groups, being: (1) Participants; (2) Context; (3) Marketplaces [18], provided some guidance in the process.

We noticed that the characteristics from the literature review were in most cases on a higher abstract level than characteristics from the expert session. We also noticed that the characteristics from the literature review were not directly linked to each other, but by combining the results from the expert session, relations manifested. A relationship is visible between the cluster around IT (L4) and the cluster related to capabilities, risk and trust (L6) via M22. This relationship shows that IT can be seen as an expertise of a participant, and resulted in the combination of the two characteristics in N2. A relationship is also visible between the cluster around dynamics within the network (L3, N3) and continuous interaction with the environment (L7, N5). Where the first is categorized in (2) Context and the latter in (3) Marketplaces. This shows the relationship between the internal dynamics within the network and the external dynamics within the environment that both influence the CNO. The relationship between the clusters around dynamics within the network (L3, N3), CNO hierarchy (L1, N1) and participant autonomy (L8, N4), show the independent and autonomous nature of the participants. This is in line with the definition of CNO provided in Camarinha-Matos and Afsarmanesh [1].

5 Discussion and Future Research

Ever increasing market dynamics and turbulence rapidly changes the business landscape and ecosystem of organizations. CNOs are a common organizational form to cope with environmental dynamics [1, 4, 5]. Participating organizations need to efficaciously adapt and co-evolve with the dynamics within the network and the environment. The synthesized characteristics (Table 5) try to capture these dynamics.

From literature we understand that CNOs highly rely on IT to collaborate within their network of participants [1–5, 15, 19, 22, 26, 27, 32] and that IT systems are a core element of high-performance configurations [33]. According to El Sawy, Malhotra [33] a complex configuration of multiple elements could lead to higher performance and thus strategic sustainable advantages. Current BITA models do not specifically address this CNO-dynamism and are predominantly focused on uniminded organizations opposed to CNOs [6–9]. Also, IT is an important enabler within CNOs, and IT systems are a core element of high-performance configurations. We therefore argue that CNOs could benefit from BITA models that could increase agility and performance [6]. Therefore, we continue our research to synthesize and design BITA models. We argue, based on the outcomes of this study, that these types of models should fit the dynamic nature of CNOs, the environment they operate in and acknowledge that IT systems facilitate rapid creation, reorganization or decommissioning of CNOs in these turbulent and dynamic times. This dynamics "lens" fits the characteristic group "N5 Dynamics and self-regulating networks". By combining results from the SLR and expert session to one set of characteristics, we try to assist researchers to examine CNOs and CNO-dynamism. In our future research, we will specifically use the characteristic group "N5 Dynamics and self-regulating networks" to design BITA models to facilitate CNO-dynamism.

Obviously, this study has several limitations. First, by executing a SLR, with clear constructed queries, qualitative journals and multiple indexes, we tried to achieve a broad view on the research topic. Nevertheless, literature could be missed due to these particular parameters and the addition of parameters could limit the results. Second, bias, i.e. the inclination to hold a particular perspective, among experts could be an issue since the authors of this article took part in the expert session. We think this effect is limited due to the fact that we used a systematic expert review and validated the characteristics against the characteristics found in the literature review. Finally, no additional validation currently has been performed on the outcomes of this research, i.e. the list of characteristics. This will be part of our future research. We do think that the constructs, like CNOs and their characteristics, are sufficiently valid by using high-quality literature, an expert session and the structured confrontation of the two results.

6 Conclusion

Outcomes of this paper contribute to IT and CNO literature through three key findings which raise several theoretical and managerial implications. First, extant (IT) literature does not adequately address and explain how CNO-dynamism is facilitated through the use of IT-resources and capabilities. Hence, we argue that the design of adequate BITA models is an important step in order to explain how CNO-dynamism can be supported. Moreover, these insights could be beneficial for executives and business managers in practice in order to drive organizational and collective CNO efforts that would increase agility, performance and ultimately competitive advantage.

Second, the complex multi-faceted interrelations and interactions among the many stakeholders and (IT) resources can only be investigated through a methodological 'lens' that explains non-linear dynamics among the many interacting agents and components [34].

Third, the current study synthesized a list of 6 main characteristics (Table 5) that can assist researchers to examine CNOs. Via the creation of characteristics for CNOs, we observed that there could be a relationship between complexity science and CNO-characteristics. Future research can investigate and identify specific configurational and contingency alignment patterns within the CNO-context.

References

1. Camarinha-Matos, L.M., Afsarmanesh, H.: Collaborative networks: a new scientific discipline. J. Intell. Manuf. **16**(4), 439–452 (2004)
2. Walters, D., Buchanan, J.: The new economy, new opportunities and new structures. Manag. Decis. **39**(10), 818–834 (2001)
3. Esposito, E., Evangelista, P.: Investigating virtual enterprise models: literature review and empirical findings. Int. J. Prod. Econ. **148**, 145–157 (2014)
4. Grefen, P., et al.: Dynamic business network process management in instant virtual enterprises. Comput. Ind. **60**(2), 86–103 (2009)
5. Grefen, P.: Networked business process management. Int. J. IT/Bus. Align. Gov. (IJITBAG) **4**(2), 54–82 (2013)
6. Coltman, T., et al.: Strategic IT alignment: twenty-five years on. J. Inf. Technol. **30**(2), 91–100 (2015)
7. Bernus, P., Noran, O., Molina, A.: Enterprise architecture: twenty years of the GERAM framework. Annu. Rev. Control **39**, 83–93 (2015)
8. Wetering, R., Bos, R.: A meta-framework for efficacious adaptive enterprise architectures. In: Abramowicz, W., Alt, R., Franczyk, B. (eds.) BIS 2016. LNBIP, vol. 263, pp. 273–288. Springer, Cham (2017). doi:10.1007/978-3-319-52464-1_25
9. Heuvel, R., et al.: Business/IT-alignment adaptation in dynamic networked environments. In: PRO-VE 2016 Porto, Portugal (2016)
10. Cuenca, L., et al.: Business-IT alignment and service oriented architecture - a proposal of a service-oriented strategic alignment model. In: Proceedings of the 16th International Conference on Enterprise Information Systems, ICEIS 2014, vol. 3, pp. 490–496 (2014);
11. Benbya, H., McKelvey, B.: Toward a complexity theory of information systems development. Inf. Technol. People **19**(1), 12–34 (2006)
12. Benbya, H., McKelvey, B.: Using coevolutionary and complexity theories to improve IS alignment: a multi-level approach. J. Inf. Technol. **21**(4), 284–298 (2006)
13. Vessey, I., Ward, K.: The dynamics of sustainable IS alignment: the case for IS adaptivity. J. Assoc. Inf. Syst. **14**(6), 283 (2013)
14. Wetering, R.: Modeling alignment as a higher order nomological framework. In: Abramowicz, W., Alt, R., Franczyk, B. (eds.) BIS 2016. LNBIP, vol. 263, pp. 111–122. Springer, Cham (2017). doi:10.1007/978-3-319-52464-1_11

15. Camarinha-Matos, L.M., Afsarmanesh, H., Galeano, N., Molina, A.: Collaborative networked organizations – Concepts and practice in manufacturing enterprises. Comput. Ind. Eng. **57**(1), 46–60 (2009)
16. Gharajedaghi, J.: Systems Thinking: Managing Chaos and Complexity: A Platform for Designing Business Architecture. Elsevier, Burlington (2011)
17. Binder, M., Clegg, B.T.: A conceptual framework for enterprise management. Int. J. Prod. Res. **44**(18/19), 3813–3829 (2006)
18. Dyer, L., Ericksen, J.: Complexity-based agile enterprises: putting self-organizing emergence to work. In: Wilkinson, A., Bacon, N., Redman, T. (eds.) The SAGE Handbook of Human Resource Management. SAGE Publications Ltd, London (2010)
19. Concha, D., et al.: The e-HUB evolution: from a custom software architecture to a software-as-a-service implementation. Comput. Ind. **61**(2), 145–151 (2010)
20. Henderson, J.C., Venkatraman, N.: Strategic alignment: leveraging information technology for transforming organizations. IBM Syst. J. **32**(1), 4–16 (1993)
21. Peppard, J., Campbell, B.: The co-evolution of business/information systems strategic alignment: an exploratory study. Manuscript for Journal of Information Technology Special Issue Strategic IT Alignment: Twenty Five Years On (2014)
22. Dekkers, R.: Distributed manufacturing as co-evolutionary system. Int. J. Prod. Res. **47**(8), 2031–2054 (2009)
23. Levy, Y., Ellis, T.J.: A systems approach to conduct an effective literature review in support of information systems research. Inform. Sci.: Int. J. Emerg. Transdiscipl. **9**(1), 181–212 (2006)
24. Armitage, A., Keeble-Allen, D.: Undertaking a structured literature review or structuring a literature review: tales from the field. In: 7th European Conference on Research Methodology for Business and Management Studies, Ecrm 2008. Academic Conferences Limited (2008)
25. Association for Information Systems. MIS J. Rank. (2016). https://aisnet.org/?JournalRankings. Cited 21 May 2016
26. Rasouli, M.R., Eshuis, R., Trienekens, J.J.M., Kusters, R.J., Grefen, P.W.P.J.: Information quality in dynamic networked business process management. In: Debruyne, C. et al. (eds.) On the Move to Meaningful Internet Systems: OTM 2015 Conferences. LNCS, vol 9415, pp. 202–218. Springer, Cham (2015). doi:10.1007/978-3-319-26148-5_12
27. Rasouli, M.R., et al.: Information governance requirements in dynamic business networking. Ind. Manage. Data Syst. **116**(7), 1356–1379 (2016)
28. Metaplan: Metaplan basic techniques. Moderating group discussions using the Metaplan approach (2009)
29. Camarinha-Matos, L.M., Afsarmanesh, H.: Collaborative Networks: Reference Modeling. Springer, New York (2008)
30. Weber, M.M.: Measuring supply chain agility in the virtual organization. Int. J. Phys. Distrib. Logist. Manage. **32**(7), 577–590 (2002)
31. Van Alstyne, M.: The state of network organization: a survey in three frameworks. J. Organ. Comput. Electron. Commer. **7**(2–3), 83–151 (1997)
32. Rahman, Z., Bhattachryya, S.K.: Virtual organisation: a stratagem. Singap. Manage. Rev. **24**(2), 29 (2002)
33. El Sawy, O.A., et al.: Research commentary—seeking the configurations of digital ecodynamics: it takes three to tango. Inf. Syst. Res. **21**(4), 835–848 (2010)
34. Merali, Y., Papadopoulos, T., Nadkarni, T.: Information systems strategy: Past, present, future? J. Strateg. Inf. Syst. **21**(2), 125–153 (2012)

Standardising Public Policy Documentation to Foster Collaboration Across Government Agencies

Mohamed Adel Rezk(✉), Mahmoud H. Aliyu, Hatem Bensta, and Adegboyega Ojo

Insight Centre for Data Analytics, National University of Ireland Galway, Galway, Ireland
{mohamed.adel,mahmoud.aliyu,hatem.bensta, adegboyega.ojo}@insight-centre.org

Abstract. Public policies documents convey strategic directions and framework of actions of government in a particular sector. For most societal challenges, there is a need for government entities at the same and different levels to coordinate their policies and collaborate on the implementations of policies. However, this coordination and collaboration efforts are seriously hampered by the lack of a central repository for public policy documents from which policy makers and researchers can access related policies on a particular topic, industry or group of stakeholders. To address this challenge, this paper describes the development of Vocabulary to underpin the implementation of a shared public policy repository in Europe. The Core Public Policy Vocabulary (CPPV) is developed as a semantic interoperability resource for government organizations for consistent description and documentation of public policies to enable efficient discovery, cross-referencing and analysis of policy documents. We describe our approach, conceptual model, elements of the vocabulary, its implementation and concrete scenarios for the use of the vocabulary.

Keywords: Core Public Policy Vocabulary (CPPV) · Inter-agency collaboration · Standardisation · Open policy · Policy repository · e-Government

1 Introduction

Service Delivery and Policy Networks are one of the most common Governance Networks in the public sector in which entities within government and outside government work together to tackle complex societal challenges [1]. Collaboration in public policy making is pivotal to coherence of government programs in general. Policy coherence entails systematic promotion of mutually reinforcing policy actions across government departments and agencies creating synergies towards achieving the agreed objectives [2]. In the context of Sustainable Development, integrated policy making and coherence aims to foster synergies across economic, social and environmental policy areas; identifying trade-offs and reconcile domestic and international

L.M. Camarinha-Matos et al. (Eds.): PRO-VE 2017, IFIP AICT 506, pp. 466–477, 2017.
DOI: 10.1007/978-3-319-65151-4_42

objectives; and addressing the spill-overs of domestic policies on other countries and on future generations (*ibid*).

There are three main approaches towards assessing the coherence of public policies. These include: (1) Analytical approaches: Modelling of cause-and-effect relations; (2) Participatory approaches: Involving stakeholders; and (3) Knowledge management: collection and processing of data[1]. The knowledge management dimension requires some form of standardization in collecting the relevant data on policies to be stored in the knowledge base. Standardisation here entails specifying some minimum agreed information to be provided by different parties (i.e. government agencies) responsible for producing and publishing public policies. For instance, the European Commission's Interoperability Solutions for Public Administrations (ISA) provides a number of similar standards - Core vocabularies about organizations, person, public services, locations, public organizations etc.; to facilitate semantic interoperability among public administrations across the European Union [3]. These vocabularies are data models which capture the fundamental characteristic of an entity in a context-neutral fashion thus enabling public administration to use these models as basis for information exchange, data integration and publishing of open data or information[2].

The development of the vocabulary – Core Public Policy Vocabulary (CPPV) presented in this article was motivated by the lack of a public repository or knowledge base of open public policies and the unavailability of existing standards in the form of ontologies, schema or data models that could be adapted to underpin the development of such repository. To address this problem, we have developed a conceptual model and a vocabulary to implement the model as a basis for a public policy repository or knowledge base.

This rest of the paper is structured as follows: Sects. 2 describes some of the basic concepts underpinning CPPV vocabulary. The methodology employed for the development of the vocabulary is presented in Sect. 3 while the details of the vocabulary are provided in Sect. 4. Section 5 discusses the application scenario of the vocabulary followed by some final discussions in Sect. 6.

2 Concepts

This section briefly explains some core concepts underpinning the CPPV vocabulary. It describes the concept of public policies in Sect. 2.1 and the notion of vocabularies and ontologies in Sect. 2.2.

2.1 Public Policies

A *Public Policy* is a commitment made by a government (or inter-governmental) entity to accomplish a single or set of objectives. It could also be described as "*a principled guide to action taken by the administrative executive branches of the state with regard*

[1] http://www.liaise-kit.eu/ia-method/methods-analyse-coherence-policies.

[2] https://ec.europa.eu/isa2/solutions/core-vocabularies_en.

to a class of issues in a manner consistent with law and institutional customs"[3]. A policy might be detailed using laws or other formal documents to discuss the institutional settings e.g. executing organization, and rewards/fines system [4]. A Public policy is could also as the aggregation of actions, legal acts, governing measures, duties, sequences of operations and resource allocation precedence that are completed, in the 'public's' name [5].

Examples of policies include regulatory policies, redistributive policies, fiscal policies and monetary policies [6]. Regulatory policies allow the government to exert control over the conduct of certain activities. The most obvious examples of regulation techniques include civil and criminal penalties for certain behaviors. Redistributive policies are used for managing the economy as a whole. The techniques of control involve fiscal (tax) and monetary (supply of money policies. Fiscal techniques employ tax rates and government spending to affect total or aggregate demand. Each particular approach to taxing or spending can have a different impact on the overall economy, so political entrepreneurs often propose or initiate policies with the goal of achieving specific impacts. Monetary policies attempt to regulate the economy by changing the rate of growth of the money supply or manipulating interest rates.

Public policies documents are usually published on government agencies websites responsible for their development and implementation. In exceptional cases (e.g. the UK government[4]), policy documents are accessible through one central point. Even when this is the case, cross-analysis and linking of these policies is not possible.

2.2 Vocabularies and Public Policies

Vocabularies are represents the definitions of concepts and their relationships in a certain domain of interest. Practically, vocabularies represent the base component for the semantic web inferencing framework [7]. Vocabularies also enable semantic integration and interoperation and understanding of the domain [8]. Ontologies are more complex form of vocabularies which are described formal explicit specification of a shared conceptualization [9].

Ontologies are employed to perform following: organizing and structuring information, reasoning and problem solving, semantic indexing and search, semantic integration and interoperation and understanding of the domain [8]. Ontologies like vocabularies do not only describe the data model, it also supports the specification of concrete exemplars (also called individuals) of such models.

There have been past efforts in describing public policies using other methods of formalism associated with the subject of policy modelling. For instance in the OCOPOMO (Open Collaboration Policy Modelling) project, the goal was to engage stakeholders in policy making [10]. Public policies such as renewable energy policy of the Kosice region in Slovakia, housing policy of the city of London or the distribution of structural funds in the Campania region in Italy were analysed and modelled. OCOPOMO provided so-called Consistent Conceptual Description for these policy cases.

---

[3] https://www.jstor.org/topic/public-policy/.

[4] https://www.gov.uk/government/policies.

The OCOPOMO framework also supported semi-automatic transformation of conceptual policy descriptions in the CCD into formal policy models. In a second example the Open Preservation Data project [11], designed a policy vocabulary to control the digital preservation process and as enabling preservation systems to collaborate more effectively. Thirdly, some standardization efforts in the United States on publishing strategy related documents and performance plans of government agencies have produced the Strategy Markup Language (StratML) [12]. StratML was designed to enable the publishing of these documents in open and machine readable format.

However, so far, none of these efforts have resulted in a scalable public policy standard that could be adopted to underpin (pan European) Public Policy repository.

3 Methodology

This section describes our overall approach in the development of the Core Public Policy Vocabulary. There are popular alternatives to developing vocabularies. The first is to adopt a lightweight version of ontology development approaches. The second approach is to adopt the more general conceptual modelling process. We adopted the latter approach due to the importance we gave the underpinning conceptual model for the vocabulary.

Conceptual modelling (CM) is the elicitation and the representation of the general knowledge that an information system operating in a specific domain needs to know [13, 14]. In particular, conceptual modelling aims at representing static (e.g., objects, entities) and dynamic phenomena (e.g., events and processes) in a particular domain [15]. Conceptual modelling encompasses four elements [15]:

CM grammar [16] (or CM notation [17]) that provides a set of constructs and rules showing how to combine the constructs in order to model the real world domain [15]. The IS literature includes a vast variety of conceptual modelling grammars including data oriented, process oriented and object-oriented ones, [13, 15, 17–20].

CM method (or modelling technique [17, 21] that prescribes how to map the real phenomena of the domain into a model of the domain [15]. A rather limited number of CM methods exist in the literature [15, 18].

CM script (or conceptual schema [13, 14, 17, 18, 22] or conceptual model [17, 18] is the output of the CM method and is constructed using a CM grammar [15]. It is usually one (or more) diagrams [18] depicting the domain's concepts. A great variety of conceptual scripts have been proposed in the literature [13, 15, 18, 21, 23].

CM context, which is the setting in which conceptual modelling occurs and scripts are used.

Guide by the above Conceptual modelling framework, we started by developing concrete scenarios and general use cases for the vocabulary. Following this we analysed over 20 well documented public policy documents across different sectors and from different public administration cultures in Europe. These documents serve as primary sources of requirements for what could constitute core elements in describing the public policies (as shown in Fig. 1).

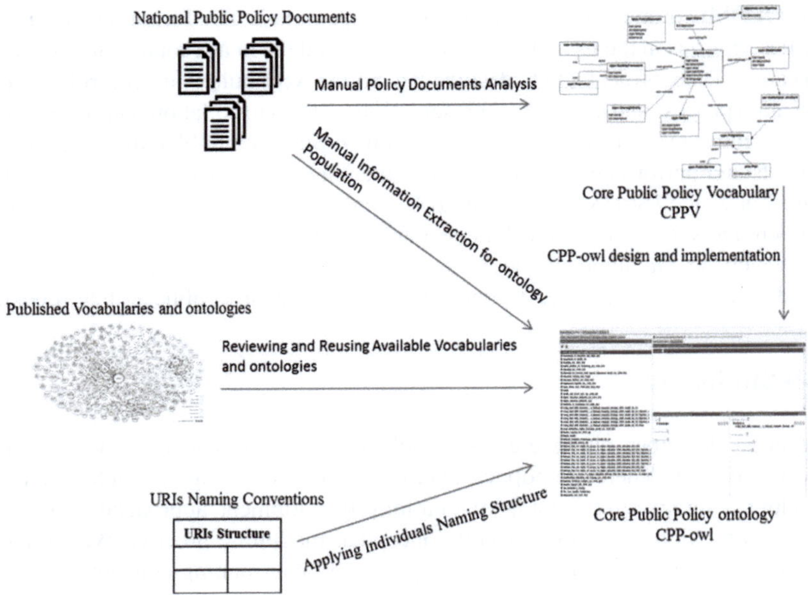

Fig. 1. The Core Public Policy Vocabulary modeling methodology

A minimalist orientation was adopted in identifying these core elements in line with the guiding principles for the European Commission's Core Vocabulary[5] as agreements are easier when the standards are simple enough to enable exchange and concomitantly allow for possible extensions by individual collaborating government entities using the standards.

4 Core Public Policy Vocabulary

This section provides some details about the elements of the CPPV vocabulary. Section 4.1 describes the conceptual model while

4.1 Conceptual Model

The Core Public Policy Vocabulary (CPPV) contains the following classes and properties to model elements public policies resulting from the process described above. Elements were included in the vocabulary after detailed analysis of their necessity in being part of the core or minimal set. Subsequently, the Core Public Policy Ontology was manually populated (CPP-owl)[6] by extracting and mapping information from

---

[5] https://joinup.ec.europa.eu/site/core_vocabularies/Core_Vocabularies_user_handbook/ISA%20Hanbook%20for%20using%20Core%20Vocabularies.pdf.

[6] http://vmogi01.deri.ie/egovcppv/.

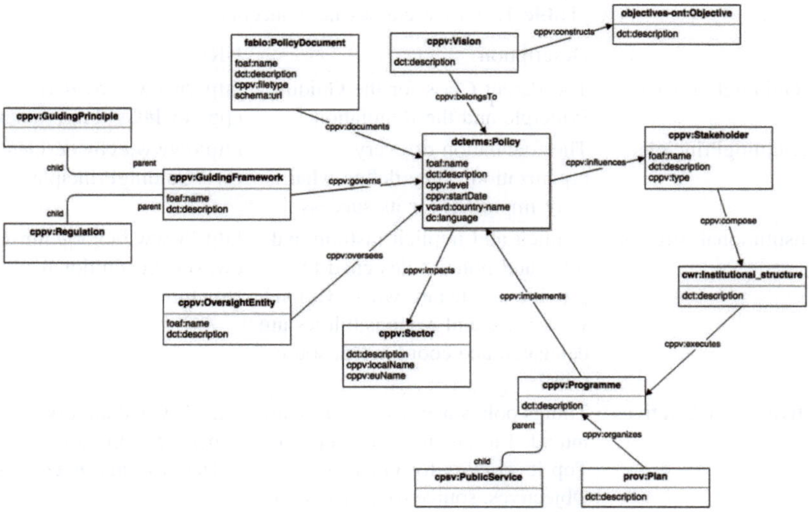

Fig. 2. Core Public Policy Vocabulary (CPPV) conceptual model

sample public policies as shown in Fig. 2. A detailed description of the CPPV elements is listed in Tables 1 (the main classes) and 2 (properties). The definitions of these elements are provided in respective tables.

Policy coordination and coherence can be analysed and effected through a number of relationships such as impacts which specified which sectors are impacted by a policy, implements which indicates which programmes are linked to specific policies or governs which specifies a legislation or higher level framework that binds a set of policies. All these properties with a supporting Uniform Resource Identifier (URI) strategy provide strong mechanism for linking in a policy ecosystem (Table 2).

4.2 Vocabulary Implementation

The above vocabulary was implemented in number of ways. First, we created an ontology based on this vocabulary in Protégé (one of the most popular open source ontology editor and management tool) so that basic analysis and reasoning could be performed on exemplar policies. By capturing the policies in Protégé, a linked data of public policy could be generated and published as open data on the government open data portals. Figure 3 below the screen shot of the implementation,

In our second implementation, the vocabulary was on the employed for publishing our sample policies as open policies on the popular Comprehensive Knowledge Archive Network (CKAN)[7] platform developed by the Open Foundation. CKAN is the most popular open data platform available. CKAN in our instance represents an open policy repository providing one central point of access to the public and policy makers.

---

[7] https://ckan.org/this.

Table 1. CPPV classes i.e. concepts

Class	Description	URI
cppv:GuidingFramework	The Parent Class for the Guiding Principle and the Regulation	http://www.egov.deri.ie/cppv.owl#GuidingFramework
cppv:GuidingPrinciple	The foundation of every organization. They define what is truly important for its success	http://www.egov.deri.ie/cppv.owl#GuidingPrinciple
cwr:institutional_structure	Explicit and implicit institutional rules and policies designed to provide a structure where various work roles and responsibilities are delegated and coordinated. source:(cwr)	http://www.fao.org/aims/aos/cwr.owl#institutional_structure
objectives-ont:Objectives	Things policy actions set out or are intended to attain or accomplish. Top level class for Goals and Objectives. source:(objectives-ont)	http://www.daml.org/experiment/ontology/objectives-ont#Objectives
cppv:OversightEntity	A distinct or independent body charged with supervision and observation of policy implementation	http://www.egov.deri.ie/cppv.owl#OversightEntity
terms2:PeriodOfTime	An interval of time that is named or defined by its start and end dates. source:(dublin core)	http://dublincore.org/documents/2012/06/14/dcmi-terms/?v=terms#PeriodOfTime
prov:Plan	A detailed proposal for doing or achieving something. A plan is an entity that represents a set of actions or steps intended by one or more agents to achieve some goals. source:(prov)	http://www.w3.org/ns/prov#Plan
cppv:Poilcy	A combination of law, rules and guidelines that determine or control results, management and information usage – that designs the role of information in a community	http://www.egov.deri.ie/cppv.owl#Policy
fabio:PolicyDocument	A document embodying a policy that descibes and defines how something should be done. source:(fabio)	http://purl.org/spar/fabio/PolicyDocument
cppv:Programme	A planned series of future events or performances. Structures for implementing and executing policies	http://www.egov.deri.ie/cppv.owl#Programme

(*continued*)

Table 1. (*continued*)

Class	Description	URI
cpsv:PublicService	This class represents the service itself. A public service is the capacity to carry out a procedure and exists whether it is used or not. It is a set of deeds and acts performed by or on behalf of a public agency for the benefit of a citizen, a business or another public agency. source:(cpsv)	http://purl.org/vocab/cpsv#PublicService
cppv:Regulation	The system of rules which a particular country or community recognizes as regulating the actions of its members and which it may enforce by the imposition of penalties	http://www.egov.deri.ie/cppv.owl#Regulation
cppv:Sector	A distinct part, especially of society or of a nation's economy that is impacts or impacted by the public policy	http://www.egov.deri.ie/cppv.owl#Sector
cppv:Stakeholder	All key parties influenced or affected by the implementation of a policy	http://www.egov.deri.ie/cppv.owl#Stakeholder
cppv:Vision	An organisation's road map, indicating both what it wants to become and guiding transformational initiatives by setting a defined direction for growth or achievement	http://www.egov.deri.ie/cppv.owl#Vision

Table 2. CPPV object properties i.e. relations

Object property	Domain	Range	Is inverse of
belongsTo	Vision	Policy	hasVision
compose	Stakeholder	institutional_structure	composedOf
constructs	Vision	Objective	constructedBy
documents	PolicyDocument	Policy	documentedby
executes	institutional_structure	Programme	executedBy
governs	GuidingFramework	Policy	governedBy
impacts	Policy	Sector	isImpactedBy
implements	Programme	Policy	implementedBy
influences	Policy	Stakeholder	influencedBy
organizes	Plan	Programme	organizedBy
oversees	OversightEntity	Policy	overseenBy
relatedTo	Thing	Thing	relatedTo

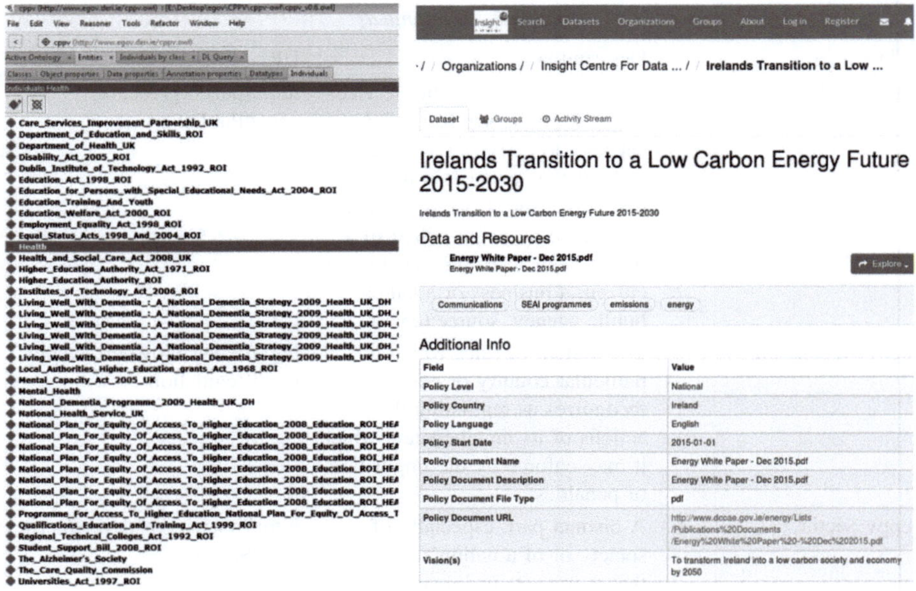

Fig. 3. Core Public Policy Vocabulary implementations in Protégé and CKAN

In addition to the vocabulary, the use of standard code lists and entity identifiers are required to fully link up the published policies.

5 Applications

This section describes in more details how the vocabulary could be exploited to enable collaboration among government entities in the implementation of public policies. Following this, we present a few other application scenarios of the CPPV vocabulary and discuss how it could be formally adopted.

5.1 The Collaboration Scenario

Let's assume the availability of the above CKAN based Open Policy Repository in a Public Administration jurisdiction. In addition, we could assume that all public authorities are mandated to publish the policies on the Open Policy Platform. Supposing the Environment department would like to design a policy to address the increasing level of air pollution in a city produced by cars. One of the policy makers in the Environment searches for "air pollution" on the policy repository to identifier other policies that may be addressing issues related to air pollution. He discovers that the Trade and Transport ministries are two other departments interested on the issue. The reference from the Trade department referred to levels of emissions permitted from imported cars and the Transport department reference was linked to the road worthiness assessment.

The policy officer from the environment investigates the programmes associated with respective policies and sets up meetings to better understand how the new policy to be design could leverage the existing programs. The officer also wishes to know how the environment department could participate in pollution related programs of these other departments.

5.2 Other Application Scenarios

Here we highlight two other application scenarios for the CPPV vocabulary.

Scenario 2: Semantic Policy Search Engine: Researchers and Business users of a CPPV ontology based search engine to browse the public policies or run complex queries, to discover opportunities in a market. Example: Firm X is specialized in the energy sector; they would like to extend their business to Country Y. To get a better understanding of the market they need to review Country Y's energy policies and related policies using a search engine such as the semantic policy search engine.

Scenario 3: "Policy learning" - During the policy making or policy update processes, governments may review policies from the Open Public Policy platform to find best practices or certain policy aspects to adopt. Example: Government Y is developing a new Health policy and would want to review different Health polices implemented in the European Union, query for certain aspects of the Health policies to improve their policy decisions.

5.3 Formal Adoption of the Core Public Policy Vocabulary

Finally, we briefly highlight the vision for the adoption of the vocabulary. Currently, the vocabulary is being reviewed by experts involved in public sector information modelling practices in Ireland, Scotland and UK, semantic interoperability and standards in Europe for staged adoption. After the adoption by a these governments, the follow-up steps entails submitting the vocabulary to the European Commission's ISA programme as a candidate Core Vocabulary.

6 Conclusion

Our work was motivated the lack of the of central repository for government policies in Europe and the underpinning semantic data model or vocabulary to facilitate the inter-linking and exchange of public policies in the European Public Administration Ecosystem. The unavailability of such infrastructure makes the collaboration among public agencies and development of coherent public policies difficult. In addressing this challenge, we have developed a public policy ontology guided by the principles driving the ISA's Core Vocabulary initiatives. Our Core Public Policy Vocabulary complements existing core vocabularies and reuses elements of these vocabularies.

We are currently in the second stage of the third-party country expert review process of the vocabulary. We intend to develop many uses cases to demonstrate policy collaboration opportunities afforded by the CPPV. In addition, we plan to provide reference implementation using other technologies such as Semantic Media Wiki or Wiki Data[8]. In the near future, we intend to propose the CPPV vocab as a candidate ISA Core Vocabulary.

References

1. Ojo, A., Mellouli, S.: Deploying governance networks for societal challenges. Gov. Inf. Q. (2016)
2. OECD: Policy coherence for development (2010)
3. ISA: Core Vocabularies Specification (2012)
4. CDM – Executive Board: Definitions of policy and programme of activities (2001)
5. Siobhan, L.: Community Development (2006)
6. Cochran, C.L., Malone, E.F.: Public Policy: Perspectives and Choices (2005)
7. W3: Ontologies - W3C. https://www.w3.org/standards/semanticweb/ontology
8. Valente, Andre: Types and roles of legal ontologies. In: Benjamins, V.Richard, Casanovas, Pompeu, Breuker, Joost, Gangemi, Aldo (eds.) Law and the Semantic Web. LNCS, vol. 3369, pp. 65–76. Springer, Heidelberg (2005). doi:10.1007/978-3-540-32253-5_5
9. Gruber, T.R.: A translation approach to portable ontology specifications. Knowl. Acquis. **5**, 199–220 (1993)
10. Wimmer, M.A., Furdik, K., Bicking, M., Mach, M., Sabol, T., Butka, P.: Open Collaboration in Policy Development: Concept and Architecture to integrate scenario development and formal policy modelling. In: Charalabidis, Y., Koussouris, S. (eds.) Empowering Open and Collaborative Governance, pp. 199–219. Springer, Heidelberg (2012)
11. Kulovits, H., Kraxner, M., Plangg, M., Becker, C., Bechhofer, S.: Open Preservation Data: Controlled vocabularies and ontologies for preservation ecosystems. In: Proceedings of the 10th International Conference on Preservation of Digital Objects (IPRES 2013) (2013)
12. Strategy Markup Language Committee: stratml. http://stratml.us
13. Olivé, A., Cabot, J.: A research agenda for conceptual schema-centric development. In: Krogstie, J., Opdahl, A.L., Brinkkemper, S. (eds.) Conceptual Modelling in Information Systems Engineering, pp. 319–334. Springer, Heidelberg (2007)
14. Rolland, C.: Capturing system intentionality with maps. In: Krogstie, J., Opdahl, A.L., Brinkkemper, S. (eds.) Conceptual Modelling in Information Systems Engineering, pp. 141–158. Springer, Heidelberg (2007)
15. Wand, Y., Weber, R.: Research commentary: information systems and conceptual modeling a research agenda. Inf. Syst. Res. **13**, 363–376 (2002)
16. Wand, Y., Monarchi, D.E., Parsons, J., Woo, C.C.: Theoretical foundations for conceptual modelling in information systems development. Decis. Support Syst. **15**, 285–304 (1995)
17. Mylopoulos, J., Chung, L., Yu, E.: From object-oriented to goal-oriented requirements analysis. Commun. ACM **42**, 31–37 (1999)
18. Rolland, C.: Information Systems and Web Information Systems: A Methodological Perspective. In: Information Technology and Communication at the Dawn of the New Millennium, p. 1 (2000)
19. Olle, T.W., Sol, H.G., MacDonald, I.G.: Information Systems Methodologies; A Framework for Understanding. Addison-Wesley Longman Publishing Co., Inc. (1991)

[8] https://www.wikidata.org/wiki/Wikidata:Main_Page.

20. Rolland, C., Prakash, N.: From conceptual modelling to requirements engineering. Ann. Softw. Eng. **10**, 151–176 (2000)
21. Davies, I., Green, P., Rosemann, M., Indulska, M., Gallo, S.: How do practitioners use conceptual modeling in practice? Data Knowl. Eng. **58**, 358–380 (2006)
22. Bubenko Jr., J.A.: From information algebra to enterprise modelling and ontologies – A historical perspective on modelling for information systems. In: Krogstie, J., Opdahl, A.L., Brinkkemper, S. (eds.) Conceptual Modelling in Information Systems Engineering, pp. 1–18. Springer, Heidelberg (2007)
23. Frisse, M.E., Johnson, K.B., Nian, H., Davison, C.L., Gadd, C.S., Unertl, K.M., Turri, P.A., Chen, Q.: The financial impact of health information exchange on emergency department care. J. Am. Med. Informatics Assoc. **19**, 328–333 (2012)

From Data Sources to Information Sharing in SME Collaborative Networks Supporting Internationalization: A Socio-Semantic Approach

Eric Costa[1,2(✉)], António Lucas Soares[1,2], and Jorge Pinho de Sousa[1,2]

[1] INESC TEC – INESC Technology and Science, Campus da FEUP, Rua Dr. Roberto Frias 378, 4200-465 Porto, Portugal
{eric.m.costa, jsousa}@inesctec.pt, als@fe.up.pt
[2] FEUP – Faculty of Engineering, University of Porto, Rua Dr. Roberto Frias S/N, 4200-465 Porto, Portugal

Abstract. Information is a crucial asset to successful internationalization, as it allows to reduce risks and uncertainty and to facilitate international expansion. Information about foreign markets and activities can be obtained by companies from internal or external sources, and in formal or informal ways. Industrial business associations (IBAs) are one of the external information sources. Due to their resource constraints, small and medium enterprises (SMEs) tend to highly depend on the services and information of IBAs to expand their business overseas. However, to improve their role in supporting SME internationalization, one important development is for IBAs to evolve towards more collaborative networks, by sharing more organized and valued information with their associates, but also by fostering information flows and more collaborations between them. This paper contributes to this view by synthetizing current data and information sources to support SME internationalization, based on a literature review, on interviews with Portuguese IBAs, and on expert opinion. An innovative aspect is to present a first instantiation of a socio-semantic model, opening paths for further developments in this area, and contributing to the community of Collaborative Networks.

Keywords: Data and information sources · Internationalization of SMEs · International business · Business associations · Collaborative networks · Socio-semantic approach

1 Introduction

Today, in a Big Data era and information overload, the ability of companies to extract vital information from the vast amount of available data sources represents one of the main key success factors for achieving competitive advantage [1]. Thus, in this data-rich world, having access to valued information is also a crucial asset for companies to remain successful in international markets [2]. Internationalization requires high quality information extracted from a variety of different data sources but the

L.M. Camarinha-Matos et al. (Eds.): PRO-VE 2017, IFIP AICT 506, pp. 478–490, 2017.
DOI: 10.1007/978-3-319-65151-4_43

problem is that many small and medium enterprises (SMEs) still face major challenges to have access and to manage internationalization-related information and knowledge, to reach more effective international endeavors [3]. Therefore, having more support from external entities and having access to credible information sources is a fundamental aspect for SMEs to improve their international operations.

Although existing different opinions about the utility of their services, industrial business associations (IBAs) are institutional actors that provide some support to SME internationalization, who are also identified in previous studies as one source of information about international trade activities [4, 5]. Nevertheless, previous research also points that the IBAs' role as information providers and as external support to internationalization may be improved by progressing to a collaborative network, by sharing more organized and valued information, and by promoting flows of information and knowledge, and more collaborations among their associate companies [6–8].

Therefore, this paper presents one important step for contributing to this view, by identifying, characterizing, and synthetizing current data and information sources to support SME internationalization. These findings allow to make a contribution for improving the first stage of the information management life-cycle of IBAs, which is the information acquisition stage [9]. Other stages of the information management life-cycle (information organization, storing, distribution, and use) will be explored in future developments of this study.

2 Research Methodology

The research methodology of this study was composed by four parts: (i) an exploratory literature review; (ii) interviews with IBAs; (iii) the use of expert opinion; (iv) the adoption of a socio-semantic approach.

A literature review was first performed to synthetize the data and information sources indicated in previous studies that are used by companies in their internationalization processes (Sect. 3.1). After that, one of the information sources was explored in more detail, i.e. the IBAs (Sect. 3.2.).

To increase the knowledge about this specific context of IBAs, an empirical study was performed by collecting data through interviews with 20 IBAs in Portugal (Sect. 4). This part of the study helped to reinforce the practical relevance of the research, as well as to identify specific information sources that IBAs use to support the international activities of their associate SMEs.

In addition to that, expert opinion was also used, by contacting people with knowledge on existing information sources for internationalization, allowing to discover additional sources (Sect. 5).

Finally, the socio-semantic approach of Pereira et al. [10, 11] was adopted in this paper to present the first instantiation of a socio-semantic model of a collaborative network for internationalization (Sect. 6). This approach was adopted as it allows to obtain a more socio-cognitive perspective to create more effective tools that can better represent the complexity of information and knowledge sharing in collaborative networks of organizations [10]. Therefore, in this approach, organizational networks are modelled as socio-semantic networks. A socio-semantic network is then a network of relationships between the organizational actors (individuals and groups of the organizations that form the collaborative network) and the concept structures (concepts and conceptual structures organized in business domains) [11]. At the end, it is possible to obtain a socio-semantic network model composed by three networks: (i) the social network (links between individuals); (ii) the semantic network (links between concepts); and (iii) the socio-semantic network (links individuals to concepts). As stated by Pereira et al. [10, 11], this integrated view can help researchers that are studying collaborative networks to better understand the interplay between knowledge structures and social structures.

3 Literature Review Findings

3.1 Information Sources for International Business

A systematic search and acquisition of information about foreign markets and foreign partners has been considered, in the International Business (IB) literature, as one of the most critical factors for achieving the internationalization success [12]. Theodosiou and Katsikea [13] consider that the export/internationalization information system comprises four key dimensions: information sources, information acquisition, information dissemination, and information utilization. In this paper, we are specifically concerned about the information sources.

Quality and relevant information is required to compensate the lack of prior knowledge and experience in foreign markets, and as a way to reduce internationalization uncertainties [14]. Therefore, companies tend to rely on multiple sources of information to satisfy their internationalization needs [3, 13]. These information sources can be classified in different ways [4, 15]:

- Primary and secondary sources;
- Formal and informal sources;
- Internal and external sources.

Information can be collected from primary sources, based on specific actions developed by the own company, such as market studies, or can come from secondary sources that has been already collected by other entities, such as statistics from governments. Information can be derived from formal sources, where data is acquired through formal actions, such as meetings and focus group discussions, or from more informal sources, when the information is obtained by personal and casual interactions with partners. Information can also be acquired from internal company sources, based on previous experiences in international markets and by using internally stored information, such as financial accounts. Finally, companies can also rely on information from sources external to the organization, by using the experience of others and externally available information.

There are many ways for a firm to acquire information and knowledge about foreign markets [12]. Xie and Amine [14] found that decision-makers typically choose their information sources as a function of their perceived utility. Nonetheless, it has been shown in previous studies that different information sources are not equally useful for the internationalization process [13]. The use of information sources depends on many factors, among which the size of a company, and the advancement and level of experience regarding its international activity, are some of the most important to have in consideration [16]. For example, previous studies agree that SMEs tend to use less expensive, easily accessible, and more informal sources when compared to large companies [17, 18]. From other side, large companies rely more on primary sources, by conducting their own studies and market analyzes [16].

Due to the existence of a large variety of classifications of information sources in the literature, we summarize the information by cross-casing the analyzed literature and create our own classification (Table 1).

Table 1. Data and information sources for internationalization from the literature, according to location

Information sources	References
Internal sources	
Personal contacts (e.g. export customers, own agents and distributors)	[2, 4, 5, 13, 17, 19–22]
Company's own knowledge and experience	[5, 16, 22]
Company's sales people and offices, and export agents	[4, 13, 16–21]
Foreign market visits	[4, 12, 13, 17, 19, 20, 22]
Company's studies and market research	[2, 4, 16, 17, 19, 21]
Company's records (e.g. reports from sales people, statistical reports, trade contracts and invoices)	[4, 16–19, 22, 23]
External sources	
Business networks	
Suppliers	[4, 5, 17, 19, 22, 23]
Competitors	[16, 17, 22]
Customers	[4, 5, 16–19, 22, 23]
Strategic partners and other organizations in the industry	[4, 20, 22]
Overseas agents, distributors and representatives	[4, 5, 16–19, 23]
Commercial brokers and freight forwarders	[4, 17, 19, 20, 22]
Social networks	
Friends	[5, 14]
Family	[5, 14]
Institutional networks	
Government offices/ministries	[2, 4, 13, 17, 19–21]
Embassies	[4, 13, 16–20]
Chambers of commerce	[4, 13, 16, 17, 19, 21, 22]
Business, trade and industry associations	[2, 4, 5, 13, 17–21]
Export agencies	[2, 4, 5, 12, 13, 16, 17, 19, 22]
Consulting and research agencies and institutes	[2, 4, 12, 13, 16–18, 20–22]
Universities and polytechnics	[2, 17]

(*continued*)

Table 1. (*continued*)

Information sources	References
Banks	[4, 16, 17, 19–22]
Physical documents and publications	
Trade catalogues, journals, magazines, and books	[4, 13, 16–19, 21, 22]
Local and international periodicals, journals and newspapers	[4, 13, 17–22]
Internet (e.g. trade lists, statistics, ratings and rankings, on-line market studies and surveys, on-line journals and newspapers, clients and customers' webpages)	[2, 12, 13, 16, 22, 23]
Databases, directories and repositories	[4, 16–18]
Public and commercial libraries	[2, 4, 17, 19]
Trade missions, trade fairs/exhibitions and other export/promotion programs	[4, 12, 13, 16, 17, 19, 22]

3.2 Business Associations as Information Sharers

Looking at the diversity of entities and organizations that act as information sources to support internationalization processes of companies (Table 1), chambers of commerce and IBAs are many times referred as one of those institutional entities of support. These entities represent different firms of a specific industrial sector or act as intermediaries within a multi-sectoral network of companies [7]. Therefore, they are characterized by their collective and member-based nature, where members share a common interest and membership is most of the times voluntary [24, 25]. In addition to that, they are intermediaries between business sectors and government action, and they provide services for their members [25, 26].

Many empirical studies have been made to study the information source behavior of exporting SMEs and large companies, in order to understand the most used information sources in internationalization processes. Regarding the usefulness of the information provided by IBAs, there are mixed opinions about that. By performing an integrative review of the literature, Leonidou and Theodosiou [4] conclude that although the experience of chambers of commerce and trade associations offer first-hand information about foreign markets, this information was not extensively used nor regarded as useful by companies. Looking at other specific empirical studies, Benito et al. [18] report the results of a survey with 221 Norwegian exporting companies, revealing that large companies, in contrast to smaller ones, generally give higher priority to the information of industry associations rather that the information that is provided by the export council. In a more qualitative fashion, Walters [20, 21] performs a first study with 33 companies from the USA and a second one, with the same sample size, but focusing in Norway. In both studies, industry associations are considered by companies as a useful information source to have access to more general, cheap and easy to acquire information about markets and exports (e.g. exports/imports, trade barriers), and to obtain contacts in foreign markets. However, companies also consider that more expensive information sources, with more detailed and market related experience, can be more helpful for their international expansion. The counterpart of using this kind of sources is the intrinsic costs that will limit their use.

By analyzing the information source behavior of 80 export firms in Cyprus, Leonidou and Katsikea [17] demonstrate that companies tend to rely more on personal contacts rather than impersonal sources, such as chambers of commerce and industry associations, when gathering information for internationalization. In fact, the analyzed companies, from one side, recognize the existence of information services from those institutional entities but, from the other side, they often consider to be information of low value. In contrast, Riddle and Gillespie [5] measure the company owners' awareness of the role of two business associations that act as information sources for SMEs in the Turkish clothing export industry. Results show that these business associations are perceived as very important information sources for companies' exports, mainly to have access to information about the export laws, foreign markets and the export process. More recent studies show that business associations and chambers of commerce are perceived to be the most important institutional information sources for Polish exporters [16, 22]. Gashi et al. [27] and Patel-Campillo and DeLessio-Parson [28] suggest a positive influence of membership in business associations to the propensity of SMEs to export. Finally, findings of Costa et al. [7] show that, although recognized by some Portuguese companies as a useful source of information, their information management role can be improved to better meet their internationalization needs.

In summary, previous literature shows that business associations and chambers of commerce have the potential to be important information sources to support internationalization processes, mainly for SMEs. However, as stated by Costa et al. [6, 7], these institutional actors might have a more active role as information managers and in fostering collaboration between associates. The next section starts to contribute to these aspects by identifying and characterizing current internal and external information sources that are used by IBAs to support SME internationalization.

4 Insights from Industrial Business Associations

Results from the interviews show that Portuguese IBAs use different data and information sources to provide information to support the internationalization of their members. Compared to the information sources found in the literature (Table 1), the ones used by IBAs are, in general, similar. Nonetheless, some other specific internal and external information sources are identified in this section, as well as some particular websites and cooperative entities. The findings allow to add new elements to the list of available information sources useful for internationalization.

According to the interviewees, the use of information sources for internationalization processes is very flexible and different from case to case. The information can be acquired for obtaining more macro-economic views of industrial sectors and countries, or can be more detailed, by using information sources to share specific information about promotional actions or internationalization opportunities. Most of the IBAs also have a large diversity of members and sub-sectors in the same industrial sector, making it difficult to obtain information to satisfy the specific needs of each company. Naturally, this situation complicates the process of synthetizing all the information sources used by IBAs, but an attempt to achieve this is presented in Table 2.

The IBAs' network of contacts is referred as one of the most important information source. Most of them have many established and trusted contacts that comes from decades of experience, acquired in previous studies and internationalization projects. So the own experience and know-how is a vital information source for the IBAs. A particular case to highlight here is the specific IBAs' members that often serve as a

Table 2. Data and information sources used by IBAs to support SME internationalization

Type of source	Category	Information source
Internal sources	Own experience and know-how	Previous market studies and industrial sector studies
		Previous internationalization projects
		Previous promotional activities
		Previous international experiences and visits to foreign countries
	Contacts	Network of contacts with different entities
		Associates (members)
	Human resources	Export agents
		People from commercial and international trade areas
	Promotional activities	Trade fairs and exhibitions
		Trade missions
		Events, meetings and collaborative workspaces
		Other promotional actions
External sources	Entities and organizations	National institutional entities (government, embassies, federations, chambers of commerce, and other business associations)
		Foreign institutional entities (governments, embassies, federations, chambers of commerce, and other business associations)
		Consulting agencies
		Other companies (not members of the IBA)
		The press (e.g. press TV, journalists, news media)
		Overseas agents and distributors
		Universities and research institutes
		Banks
	Internet	International market studies and surveys
		Statistics
		Websites
		Search engines
		Databases, directories and repositories
		On-line journals and newspapers

relevant information source. The associates express not only their needs to the IBAs but also indicate some specific countries that can be of interest for the exportations of the sector, or even some specific internationalization projects and opportunities. What they expect in return is for the IBA to use its contacts, services and knowledge base, and to act as intermediary between them and entities of interest. The use of databases are also mentioned by the interviewees, but only some of them are actually using this data source because it has high costs of acquisition. Some particular entities and organizations are also mentioned by the interviewees as being important sources of information about international trade and activities:

- International sources:
  - European Commission; Horizon 2020; OECD (Organization for Economic Co-operation and Development); WTO (World Trade Organization); BusinessEurope (confederation of European business), nTrade (statistics).
- National sources:
  - CIP (business confederation of Portugal), AICEP (external trade and investment agency of Portugal), INE (national institute of statistics), Republic Diary and Assembly of the Republic (for more legal information), IAPMEI (public agency for competitiveness and innovation), Bank of Portugal, and Portugal 2020 (a partnership agreement between Portugal and the European Commission that provides funding opportunities for the Portuguese business).

5 Expert Opinion and Additional Information Sources

Findings from the expert opinion allowed to identify additional international portals, databases, directories and repositories from specific entities and websites. These data and information sources can be accessed and used by IBAs to support SME internationalization. Table 3 presents only the ones that represent new information sources, not identified in the previous sections.

Table 3. Additional data and information sources identified with expert opinion

Type of source	Information source
External sources	FITA (Federation of International Trade Associations) Global Trade Portal
	World Bank
	WAIPA (World Association of Investment Promotion Agencies)
	United Nations
	IMF (International Monetary Fund)
	ITC (International Trade Center)
	Enterprise Europe Network
	Trade Map (International Trade Center)

(*continued*)

Table 3. (*continued*)

Type of source	Information source
Statistics of international trade	Comtrade (United Nations Commodity Trade Statistics Database)
	United Nations Data Retrieval System
	Eurostat (European Commission)
	OECD.Stat
Tariff and non-tariff barriers	Market Access Map (International Trade Center)
	WTO - Tariffs
	The Market Access Database (European Commission)
	I-TIP Goods (WTO)
Business directories	Bureau Van Dijk
	FITA Global Trade Portal
	GlobalTrade.net
	Kompass
	Thomasnet
Countries' reports, ratings and indicators	Doing Business (World Bank)
	World Competitiveness Center (IMD business school for management and leadership courses)
	World Economic Forum
	IPS (Institute for Industrial Policy Studies)
	The Global Innovation Index
	Economist Intelligence Unit (The Economist Group)
	External Markets (AICEP)
	Country Profiles and Resources (FITA)
	Multilateral Investment Guarantee Agency (World Bank)
Sectorial reports	Oxford Economics
	Industry analysis (Economist Intelligence Unit)
	Frost & Sullivan
	D&B Hoovers
	Plimsoll World
	BMI Research
	Datamonitor Healthcare (Pharma intelligence)
	Euromonitor International
Portals	SME internationalization portal (European Commission)
	European Small Business Portal (European Commission)

6 A Socio-Semantic Model of a Collaborative Network Mediated by a Digital Platform

Previous research show that IBAs can have a more active role in supporting SME internationalization, by fostering more collaborations between associates [6]. This support can also be enhanced by improving their information management role to better meet companies' informational needs [8]. Therefore, one important development for the positive impact of IBAs on the internationalization process can be the evolution towards a more collaborative network, fostering flows of information between associates [7]. Consequently, by having in consideration these previous findings, and with the new findings described in this paper, it is a natural conclusion that an effective collaborative network, where one of the main goals is to share information and knowledge about internationalization processes, can be achieved by means of a digital platform which can mediates social relations, levered in data and information management.

Therefore, based on a socio-semantic perspective [10, 11], we present the conceptual skeleton of the IBA-SME digital platform (Fig. 1) modelling the users (SMEs) structural links through descriptive profiles (implementation of a social network), the basic information structure to organize information gathered from the internationalization information sources (semantic network), and the linkage between users and information (socio-semantic network).

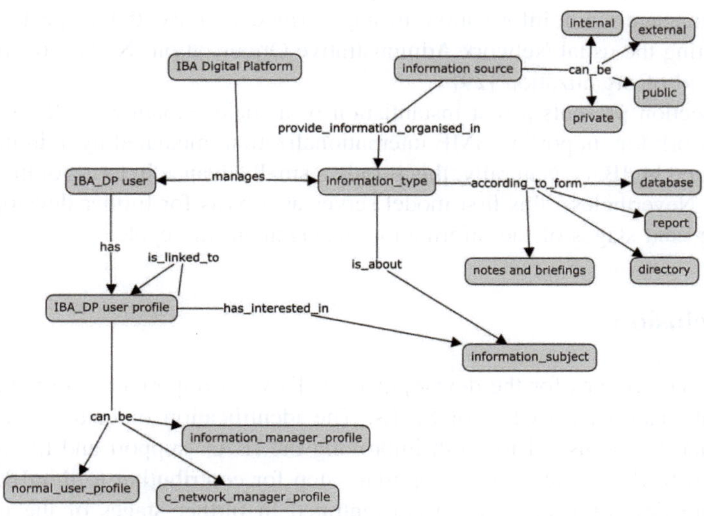

Fig. 1. Conceptual model of an IBA-SME digital platform

Figure 2 shows an instantiation of the conceptual model where the socio-semantic network becomes clear. A set of round shaped nodes representing the users (or, institutionally, the SMEs) are linked through `is_linked_to` named edges. This implements the usual social network connections.

The set of rectangle shaped nodes representing the information subjects are linked through `is_a` or `is_type_of`, `is_part_of`, or a general binary relationship. On its turn, this implements a semantic network. The dotted edges, labelled as `has_interest_in`, connect users with information subjects. From these links, a second social network can be derived connecting users through their common

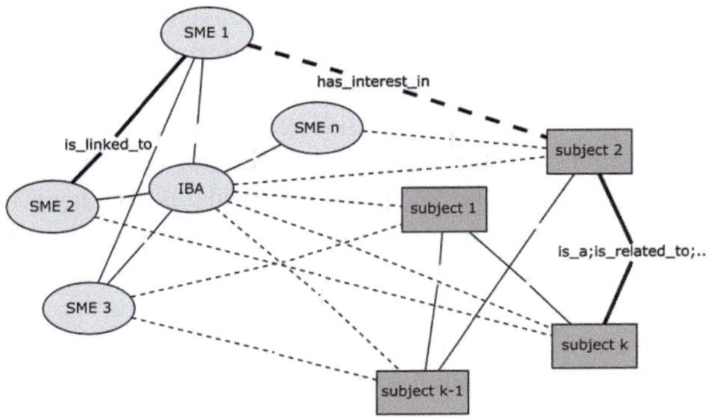

Fig. 2. Socio-semantic network model of a collaborative network mediated by the IBA-SME digital platform

information subject interests. The management of the IBA accumulates the roles of network manager and information manager (modelled by the respective profiles) implementing the usual Network Administrative Organization (NAO) governance type for this kind of organization [29].

This section presents a first instantiation of a socio-semantic model of a collaborative network for supporting SME internationalization, mediated by a digital platform and managed by IBAs. Naturally, this is only a small advance in terms of the modelling approach. Nevertheless, this first model serves as a basis for further developments for improving next stages of the information management life-cycle.

7 Conclusion

This study contributes for the development of IBAs as important information sources for the international activities of SMEs. The identification of data and information sources that can be useful for both improving the IBAs' support and the internationalization of SMEs, represents an important step for contributing to this IBAs' evolution. Future developments will be concentrated in further stages of the information lifecycle, by identifying specific information content and categories from the identified sources, by studying ways of organizing and storing this information, and by understanding the means and channels to be used for distributing this information.

In complementarity to this, the socio-semantic network model will progress and will evolve in the following ways: (i) by adding more detail on the relations and links between the social organizations (social network); (ii) by adding new concepts and domains, and their relations in terms of conceptual structures (semantic network); and (iii) by exploring the links between these previous networks (socio-semantic network).

Finally, this paper can also contribute to the broader community of Collaborative Networks, by showing the application of the socio-semantic approach developed by Pereira et al. [10, 11]. Results of this study allow to support the arguments of these authors about using this approach for obtaining a more integrated view between knowledge structures and social structures, when analyzing collaborative networks of organizations. This opens avenues for other researchers to use and explore this approach in their collaborative network projects.

Acknowledgments. This research was funded by the Portuguese funding agency, Fundação para a Ciência e a Tecnologia (FCT), through the Ph.D. Studentship SFRH/BD/110131/2015. It was also supported by the Project "TEC4Growth - Pervasive Intelligence, Enhancers and Proofs of Concept with Industrial Impact/NORTE-01-0145-FEDER-000020" financed by the North Portugal Regional Operational Programme (NORTE 2020), under the PORTUGAL 2020 Partnership Agreement, and through the European Regional Development Fund (ERDF).

References

1. Smallwood, R.F.: Information Governance: Concepts, Strategies and Best Practices. Wiley Online Library, Hoboken (2014)
2. Knight, G., Liesch, P.: Information internalisation in internationalising the firm. J. Bus. Res. **55**, 981–995 (2002)
3. Costa, E., Soares, A.L., Sousa, J.P.: Information, knowledge and collaboration management in the internationalisation of SMEs: a systematic literature review. Int. J. Inf. Manage. **36**, 557–569 (2016)
4. Leonidou, L.C., Theodosiou, M.: The export marketing information system: an integration of the extant knowledge. J. World Bus. **39**, 12–36 (2004)
5. Riddle, L.A., Gillespie, K.: Information sources for new ventures in the Turkish clothing export industry. Small Bus. Econ. **20**, 105–120 (2003)
6. Costa, E., Soares, A.L., Sousa, J.P.: A new insight in the SMEs internationalization process. In: Camarinha-Matos, Luis M., Bénaben, F., Picard, W. (eds.) PRO-VE 2015. IAICT, vol. 463, pp. 398–410. Springer, Cham (2015). doi:10.1007/978-3-319-24141-8_36
7. Costa, E., Soares, A., Sousa, J., Jamil, G.: Information management for network transformation in industrial enterprises associations: the case of the internationalization process. In: Jamil, et al. (eds.) Handbook of Research on Information Management for Effective Logistics and Supply Chains, pp. 415–436. IGI Global, Hershey (2017)
8. Costa, E., Soares, A.L., Sousa, J.P.: Situating case studies within the design science research paradigm: an instantiation for collaborative networks. In: Afsarmanesh, H., Camarinha-Matos, Luis M., Lucas Soares, A. (eds.) PRO-VE 2016. IAICT, vol. 480, pp. 531–544. Springer, Cham (2016). doi:10.1007/978-3-319-45390-3_45
9. Detlor, B.: Information management. Int. J. Inf. Manage. **30**, 103–108 (2010)
10. Pereira, C., Sousa, C., Lucas Soares, A.: A socio-semantic approach to collaborative domain conceptualization. In: Meersman, R., Herrero, P., Dillon, T. (eds.) OTM 2009. LNCS, vol. 5872, pp. 524–533. Springer, Heidelberg (2009). doi:10.1007/978-3-642-05290-3_66
11. Pereira, C., Sousa, C., Soares, A.L.: Supporting conceptualisation processes in collaborative networks: a case study on an R & D project. Int. J. Comput. Integr. Manuf. **26**, 1066–1086 (2013)
12. Nguyen, T., Barrett, N., Fletcher, R.: Information internalisation and internationalisation: evidence from Vietnamese firms. Int. Bus. Rev. **15**, 682–701 (2006)
13. Theodosiou, M., Katsikea, E.: The export information system: an empirical investigation of its antecedents and performance outcomes. J. Int. Mark. **21**, 72–94 (2013)
14. Xie, Y., Amine, L.: Social networks and the internationalization of Chinese entrepreneurs. Glob. Bus. Organ. Excell. **29**, 61–78 (2009)

15. Akerman, N.: An international learning typology: strategies and outcomes for internationalizing firms. Balt. J. Manag. **9**, 382–402 (2014)
16. Bartosik-Purgat, M., Schroeder, J.: Polish exporters' use and perception of various sources of market information. Poznań Univ. Econ. Rev. **14**, 97–117 (2014)
17. Leonidou, L.C., Katsikeas, C.S.: Export information sources: the role of organizational and internationalization influences. J. Strateg. Mark. **5**, 65–87 (1997)
18. Benito, G.R.G., Solberg, C.A., Welch, L.S.: An exploration of the information behaviour of Norwegian exporters. Int. J. Inf. Manage. **13**, 274–286 (1993)
19. Leonidou, L.C.: Types and sources of export information: insights from small business. Int. Small Bus. J. **17**, 30–48 (1999)
20. Walters, P.: International market information infusion: data acquisition behaviour in Norwegian exporters. Int. J. Inf. Manage. **16**, 437–444 (1996)
21. Walters, P.G.P.: Export information sources: A study of their usage and utility. Int. Mark. Rev. **1**, 34–43 (1993)
22. Danik, L.: Information Sources applied in search for a foreign business partner and the perception of barriers in establishing international cooperation. In: Ann. Univ. Mariae Curie-Sklodowska, vol. XLIX, pp. 39–48 (2015)
23. Nguyen, T.D., Barrett, N.J.: The adoption of the internet by export firms in transitional markets. Asia Pacific J. Mark. Logist. **18**, 29–42 (2006)
24. Bennett, R.: Business associations and their potential contribution to the competitiveness of SMEs. Entrep. Reg. Dev. **10**, 243–260 (1998)
25. Traxler, F., Huemer, G.: Handbook of Business Interest Associations, Firm Size and Governance: A Comparative Analytical Approach. Routledge, London (2007)
26. Boléat, M.: Managing Trade Associations. Trade Association Forum, London (2003)
27. Gashi, P., Hashi, I., Pugh, G.: Export behaviour of SMEs in transition countries. Small Bus. Econ. **42**, 407–435 (2013)
28. Patel-Campillo, A., DeLessio-Parson, A.: Why types of operations, trade associations, and production trends matter in the geographic branding of an emerging industry. J. Wine Res. **27**, 242–256 (2016)
29. Provan, K., Kenis, P.: Modes of network governance: structure, management, and effectiveness. J. Public Adm. Res. Theory **18**, 229–252 (2008)

Risk and Trust Analysis in CNs

Influence of Information Sharing Behavior on Trust in Collaborative Logistics

Morice Daudi[1(✉)], Jannicke Baalsrud Hauge[2,3], and Klaus-Dieter Thoben[1,2]

[1] International Graduate School for Dynamics in Logistics (IGS), University of Bremen, Bremen, Germany
mdaudi@uni-bremen.de, tho@biba.uni-bremen.de

[2] Bremer Institut für Produktion und Logistik, University of Bremen, Bremen, Germany
baa@biba.uni-bremen.de

[3] School of Engineering, Technology and Health, KTH, Royal Institute of Technology, Stockholm, Sweden

Abstract. Collaborations are based on mutual trust to strengthen confidence in the sharing of various resources such as information. Particularly in logistics, collaborations benefit emerged rich-data environments to successfully manage demand fluctuation and visibility of in-store logistics; as well as the sharing of physical assets. Shared information is gathered from various sources and manipulated by specific partner to match or maximize individual payoff. Such information may become vulnerable to information sharing behavior of the partner to henceforth affect trust. This paper investigates the influence of the information sharing behavior on trust. It focuses on a dimension of information accuracy to answer a research question: how do information sharing behaviors of partner affect trust in logistics collaboration? A framework of information behavior is established, and subsequently a trust model specified. Afterwards, simulation experiments are conducted to observe resulting impacts. Results unveil that both, the positively and negatively manipulated information influence trust in similar magnitudes. It is further argued that partner's deceitful behavior underlying information sharing can be reduced although it might be difficult to eliminate.

Keywords: Trust · Logistics collaboration · Rich-data environments · Information behavior · Information uncertainty · Veracity information

1 Introduction

Logistics collaboration advocates an efficient use of shareable resources to mitigate underlying and encountered inefficiencies. Through collaboration, partners can reduce logistics costs, improve the quality of service, gain market position, and reduce harms to the environment [1]; as well as increase the utilization of physical and non-physical assets. Although beneficial, logistics collaboration is challenged by a lack of trust amongst collaborating partners. One key area contributing to this challenge are uncertainties which stem from the information sharing behavior of partners. The sharing of information enables the implementation of planning and control of chain operations [2].

L.M. Camarinha-Matos et al. (Eds.): PRO-VE 2017, IFIP AICT 506, pp. 493–506, 2017.
DOI: 10.1007/978-3-319-65151-4_44

Information sharing is one of the key determinants of trust in logistics collaboration, on the one hand. On the other hand, it is a construct from which both the certain and uncertain behavioral elements of an enforcing partner emerge. Uncertain information lacks quality, and may negatively affect chain operations and trust. For example, the sharing of untimely, irrelevant, inaccurate and incomplete information may escalate uncertainties due to unreliable variations in an actual belief of the world. Notwithstanding with this, sharing of quality data may be impeded with the perceived (or existing) opportunism; fear of exposing private business models to competitors, and; misuse of proprietary information. This problem may even be large in the present era where supply chain and logistics operate in data-rich environments where veracity information is largely featured.

Information behavior in logistics and supply chain is normally conceptualized in qualitative and/or quantitative forms. The literature [3–5] conceive the qualitative form using constructs such as "*no information sharing*", "*limited information sharing*", and "*full information sharing*". Such constructs have been used in [3, 6, 7]. The no information sharing, according to [8] means sharing only actual orders and excluding tiers of width and distance of sharing. The full information sharing construct implies that all information is visible to the entire chain without any barrier. This implication is however contradicted because collaboration occurs in a world which is neither totally invisible nor completely visible. In addition, the full information sharing is even exaggerated because the world cannot be made risky-free. The no information sharing construct denies prediction and implies that transactions are risky and untrustworthy. To this end, the limited information sharing remains the potential and practical belief that surrounds daily living of humans. It is the world in which humans, organizations, and objects interact and collaborate. Therefore, this paper advances on the limited information sharing that is featured by the information sharing behaviors of collaborating partners. It concentrates on a dimension of information accuracy to investigate how information sharing behavior of partners impact trust. It particularly answers the following Research Question (RQ): *how do information sharing behavior of the partner affect trust in logistics collaboration?* Besides this RQ, the paper contributes also by establishing a trust framework of information behavior that may potentially be applicable in logistics collaboration and related areas.

The remainder of the paper is organized into 7 sections. Section 2 presents discussions of data-rich environments, trust in logistics collaboration, and information behavior. Section 3 describes a methodology this study has employed while Sect. 4 presents a framework of information behavior. Whereas Sect. 5 presents the trust model and hypotheses, Sect. 6 presents the design and setups of the experiments. Section 7 presents results and discussions while Sect. 8 provides conclusion and outlook.

2 Information Sharing: A Trust-Based Perspective

This section presents discussions of data-rich environments in logistics and it highlights the current and future benefits of such environments to collaboration. In addition, it reviews literature which addresses trust in a standpoint of information sharing. A primary goal of such review is to recognize previous contributions and identify a resulting knowledge gap. Final discussion is focused on building a foundation of information and information-seeking behavior. This foundation supports the establishment of a corresponding trust-based framework that guides a trust model.

2.1 Data-Rich Environment in Logistics Collaboration

Emerging information and communication technologies enrich the world with more data. Such data enables efficient distribution goods, services, and as well as mobility of humans. It further facilitates visibility of logistics features such as the size, weight, content, location, condition, and the state of usage of asset. Rich-data has enabled customers to gain more control in the delivery of tangible goods thereby supporting a direct customer interaction especially at pickup and delivery [9]. Other improvements are such as the: prediction of consumer demands; production planning, and; distribution and storage of goods. In the matter of feedbacks the manufacturers and retailers can nowadays obtain consumers' reviews about products and services they offer. Nevertheless, it is now relatively quite easy to figure out an optimum delivery route that leads into saving the cost of fuel.

However, data-rich environments are challenged to deceitful behaviors. The deceitful behaviors emerge from many sources such as actors (partners). Partner may purposely distort Information Quality (InfQ) either for just malicious purpose or individual interests. The accuracy of exchanged data, for example, may intentionally be manipulated to maximize individual payoffs. This challenge may be referred to as veracity data in logistics collaboration. It is the challenge encountered when opportunistic partners generate rich but inaccurate data that in the end offer a high chance to deteriorate trust.

2.2 Trust in the Context of Information Sharing in Logistics

Trust is generally understood as an extent to which an object will behave in an expected manner. It is a critical ingredient of humans' everyday life and plays a profound role in networked collaborations. Although a plethora of definitions exists, in this paper, trust is defined in accordance to [10]. Trust is a level of confidence developed by trustor in trustee based on the expectation that trustee will perform a particular action necessary to the trustor, irrespective of the ability to monitor or control trustee.

Literature has addressed trust in a standpoint of information sharing. In the [11] authors investigate the role of information sharing and quality in the development of trust. In [3] authors explore how trust impacts the level of shared information. Using the supplier and manufacturer as subjects, authors in [6] investigate the role of trust in supply forecast. Moreover, in [7] authors study supply chain coordination with the trust-embedded cost-sharing contract. In the overall, previous studies tend to address the role and impact of information sharing on trust. Such studies lack to take into account sufficient consideration of information sharing behavior exhibited by partners.

In a standpoint of trust in logistics collaboration, information sharing is more than a degree to which information can be exchanged. One crucial step ahead, for example, is to understand how information sharing behaviors of partners lead to the growth or deterioration of trust. This understanding strengthens previous contributions and subsequently updates both the academic and practitioner communities. In essence, collaborating partners exhibit multiple information sharing behaviors which may be valuable or harmful. Valuable behavioral practices entail information exchange that conforms to a purpose of collaboration, while harmful ones lack this conformity. Both behaviors can be described or represented using the InfQ dimensions such as those belonging to data use in the process. A critical analysis of the literature on logistics collaboration characterizes the data use in process to consist of various attributes (see in [12, 13]) such as the information accuracy. Information accuracy means that every set of data represents a real world situation [13]. If partners exchange data that do not represent a factual belief of the world causes low chain visibility as well as trust deterioration.

2.3 Information Behavior in Logistics Collaboration

Information and information-seeking behavior are becoming more imperative in this era of information age. These multidisciplinary constructs are drawn from disciplines of the information science, psychology, and decision-making. The literature [14] define the: information behavior as the totality of human behavior in relation to sources and channels of information, whereas; information-seeking behavior is the purposive seeking for information as a consequence of a need to satisfy some goal.

Partners source (capture) and exchange (share) information amongst them to satisfy goals of collaborating. For this to be possible partners have to possess cognitive ability for sensing [15]: information that reflects the state of their environments (beliefs); state of the environment they prefers (desire), and; state of the environment they try to achieve. Since captured information is not only meant for internal consumption, it has to be shared to peers for a specific purpose. In view of this, author [8] emphasizes that information sharing is typically a: *collaborative/collective behavior* since it does not only involve an individual behavior, but a collective and collaborative effort occurring in a sharing community; *mutual-benefit behavior* because partners expect to respectively gain values out of it, and; *relationship-based behavior* because it is supported and facilitated by relationships that connect partners. In spite of a fact that partners work to attain common goals they may still differ in decision-making. This difference is largely brought about by uncertainties in states of their environments as well as intrinsic and incongruent behaviors of partners. Partners may correspondingly be deceitful and manipulate (distort) captured information before sharing it. Consistent with the principle of sense-making, such shared information may be subjective because its production is internally guided by partners [16].

The information sharing behavior can be described and represented using the Wilson's revised model of information behavior [17] and Dervin's sense-making framework [16]. These model and framework are potentials for establishing the linkage and dependency among the information behavior, sense-making, expectation and trust. Author in [18] builds from [16] to clarify that sense-making is implemented:

- *In situation of time and space* (context in which information problems arise);
- *In a gap* (difference between the contextual and desired situation);
- *An outcome* (consequences of the sense-making process), and;
- *A bridge* (means of closing the gap).

This implementation correlates strongly to human trusting process and the structure of belief-desire-intention. To briefly explain, trust has a meaning in a situation of dependency featured by a fact that trustor cannot accomplish its task without relying on trustee. In this dependency the trustor is uncertain (gap) if a trustee can accomplish a task to be delegated in a manner the trustor expects. In this endeavor, the trustor collects and assesses information about the trustee to close the uncertainty it has in the trustee. Once satisfied, the trustor accepts to be vulnerable to consequences of the trustee and executes an action to trusting.

3 Research Methodology

This study builds up on social behavior of human agents in computer controlled settings. It uses the Multi-Agent Systems (MAS) simulation to observe impact that results from the bottom-up interactions of individual human-representatives. The MAS complements the case study and/or action research due to difficulties of obtaining industrial testbed platform. The remaining part of the methodology is described as follows. Firstly, a framework is built to link the concepts of logistics collaboration, information behavior, and trust. In this framework, key collaborating partners are identified and modeled using the agent-based modeling approach. Secondly, a trust simulation model that draws largely from [19] is formalized and corresponding hypotheses derived. Thirdly, simulation experiment is designed and necessary settings specified to run experiments. The simulation uses the randomly generated data (*model*) and system data (*system*). The system data has been validated in [20]. For model inputs, independence of data is established using linear-congruential generators. Additionally, the chi-square test is carried to ensure data is uniformly distributed.

The internal validity technique is used to ensure that conceptualization as well as assumption, and representation of the information sharing behavior is reasonably accurate and credible. It is worthy to note that the trust mechanism behaves stochastically due to individual agent's actions. For this reason, the internal validity is attained by running several replications to determine the amount of (internal) stochastic variability [21]. Moreover, two aspects are involved to ensure that results are not only reliable but also bear an operational level of accuracy. Firstly, the output behaviors of the component of Interaction Trust (IT) of the FIRE [22] model and trust model (*trust mechanism*) are compared. The second aspect entails comparing outputs behavior of model data to that of the system data. Mixed techniques, namely: statistical tests and graphical displays are employed to provide the subjective and objective decision in judging results of the aforementioned comparison.

4 A Framework of Information Behavior

In this section a trust-based framework of information behavior is proposed. The framework provides loose connectedness among concepts used in this study. The framework is built up by integrating the revised model of information behavior in [17], and the concepts of information sharing, partner behavior, logistics collaboration, and trust (Fig. 1). This framework depicts logistics collaboration as a context by which partners desire to improve information visibility. It is further described as follows. Shippers, carriers, and receivers desire information (world beliefs) to achieve an ideal full information visibility. This desire may be satisfied or not. Struggling to achieve this desire partners activate their information seeking behaviors to obtain needed information. Such information relates to logistics functions such as the capacities, demands, forecasts, inventories, and backorders.

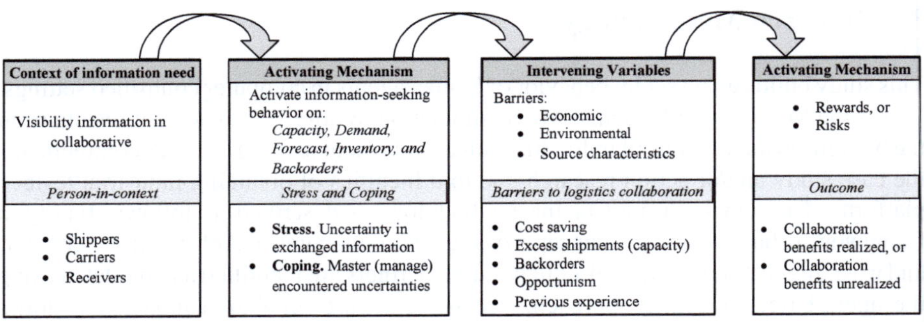

Fig. 1. A framework of information behavior in the context of logistics collaboration

However, during this struggle partners encounter stresses in respect underlying uncertainties in information they are looking for (sensing). To master such stresses partners need to be cognitive. Such kind of ability help partners to reduce or mitigate encountered uncertainties thereby collecting needed information from all sources they are able to sense. While attempting to manage uncertainties, partners face barriers related to the economy, environment, and source characteristics.

To emphasize this, barriers partners face are such as: how much cost they can save by collaborating; costs emerging from excess capacity they provide, and; back orders. Other barrier is a possibility that some partners want to benefit more on the cost of others (opportunism) by providing misleading information. Additionally, previous experience may become a barrier especially when benefits to collaboration were least than it was expected. On the whole, depending on the information sensed (captured) and individual cognitive reasoning, partner chooses how to behave when providing (exchanging) information to its logistics network. In the end, logistics function becomes executed and outcomes (reward or risks) observed. Depending on the states of outcome and prior expectation partners may maintain a trust or distrust in the network they are involved. Moreover, obtained trustworthy forms part of an experience to future engagements where partner may adjust its information sharing behavior to suit the forthcoming context (stress, barriers, and outcome).

5 Trust Model and Hypotheses

This section proposes the trust model that is used to investigate the impact of information sharing behavior on trust. Conception proceeds as follows. A decision partner undertakes is largely influenced by prevailing circumstances (collaborative situations) and is guided by individual ability of the partner to reason. The collaborative situation and individual ability account for a degree of the certainty and uncertainty in information partners can share or exchange. Partners can exchange uncertain (manipulated or distorted) information in an attempt to recover from previous bad outcome or to purposely maximize individual gains (opportunism). The outcome and opportunism constitute the internal and external environments which influence partners' decisions.

Information accuracy, which is the attribute of InfQ, is used to investigate the information sharing behavior of partners. It is modeled using the quantitative stream. Under this stream information accuracy stands on a continuum of information certainty and uncertainty. Concordant to [6], logistics elements such as the production capacity, market demand, and forecasts are modeled to be affected by a specific factor. This means that collaborating partners are enabled to manipulate (modify/distort) or retain the factual beliefs (true/actual information) before they exchange it. A degree to which partners distort the actual information is determined by influential situations that surround them, such as previous trustworthiness. Three kind of factors (or affection) are formalized to affect the degree of information accuracy. Meaning that partners retain or distort accuracy of information in three ways: negative distortion (or negative information accuracy) that is denoted by a symbol "$\boldsymbol{\gamma}$"; no distortion (or neutral information accuracy) that is denoted by the symbol "$\boldsymbol{\alpha}$", and; positive distortion (or positive information accuracy) that is denoted by the symbol "$\boldsymbol{\beta}$". Such factors imply that partners choose to exchange information that is: below the exact value (affection by factor γ); equal to the exact information without distorting (affection by factor α), and; above the exact value (affection by factor β). Each factor has its set whose elements are selected by partner to affect the accuracy.

Partners are guided by the information behavior (*stress, coping, barriers, and likely outcome*) to choose which factor to use when affecting the accuracy of information. This affection is realized by multiplying the chosen factor with a real world situation data. For example, let the real world data be denoted by $\boldsymbol{q_0}$ and the value after affection be denoted by $\boldsymbol{q_n}$. Then the affection is of the form: $q_n = q_0 + q_0 * factor$. To illustrate, if q_0 is 100 units and *factor* is –0.15 then the value after affection is 85 units ($q_n = 100 + 100 * -0.15$). The factor is a coefficient whose value may be negative, zero, and positive. Particularized to this study the sets of information accuracy for each affection are defined as follows:

- *Negative information accuracy*: $\boldsymbol{\gamma} \leftarrow \{-0.45, -0.40, -0.35, -0.30, -0.25, -0.20, -0.15, -0.10\}$. Partner who exhibits this behavior is considered untrustworthy and acts in a manner of maximizing individual payoff. The partner exchange information that is underestimated and is affecting the accuracy negatively.
- *Neutral information accuracy:* $\boldsymbol{\alpha} \leftarrow \{-0.05, 0, 0.05\}$. Partner who affect logistics elements using this factor are considered honest, congruent, and can certainly be relied upon. If a factor chosen is zero then the partner is absolutely honest and reports the true information. Otherwise it is a normal honest partner.
- *Positive information accuracy:* $\boldsymbol{\beta} \leftarrow \{0.10, 0.15, 0.20, 0.25, 0.30, 0.35, 0.40, 0.45\}$. Partner who exhibits this behavior is still considered untrustworthy (similar to the negative information accuracy). He instead exchange overestimated information.

Besides the established affections, further enrichment to the trust model are provided.

If a partner had previously experienced the best (or better) trustworthy it becomes realistic by reporting almost undistorted information, on the one hand. On the other hand, if it had previously experienced the worst (or worse) trustworthy it struggles to recover by reporting distorted information. In each cycle partner develops an expectation that is to be compared with reality thereof. In the matter of this, this paper advances on the trust mechanism proposed already in [19]. This mechanism emphasizes that human trusting process propagates in three stages: intention to trusting; action to trusting, and; transaction to trusting. In a second stage, the trustor develops specific expectation in the trustee with respect to a task (transaction) it desires to delegate. Once transaction is executed the trust level is assessed by comparing resulting score (outcome) against the expectation.

In the present study the predictor and response variables are specified (Fig. 2). The main predictor variable, information accuracy, consists of three sub-variables: *negative information accuracy, neutral accuracy, and positive accuracy.*

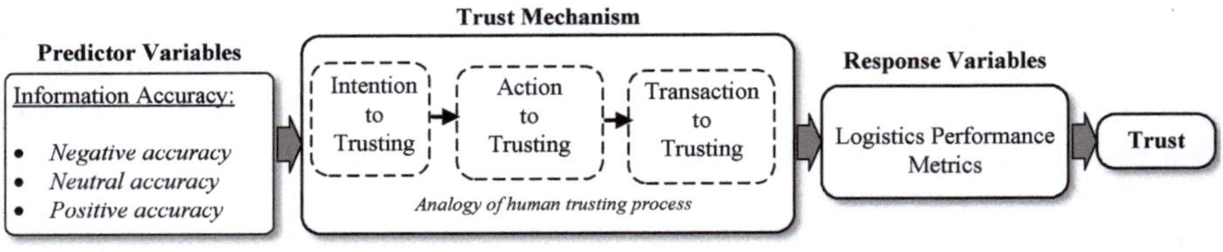

Fig. 2. The trust model used in simulation

Five response variables used to observe and evaluate trust. They are forecast accuracy, cost saving, full truck load, order fill rate, and vehicle fill (refer Sect. 6 for further details).

Moreover, two hypotheses (claims) are derived to help understand how information sharing behavior of the collaborating partners affects trust. Struggling to fulfill goals, partners have options decrease, increase, or even retain actual information about their orders and/or capacities. What is still unestablished is whether distorting information by decreasing or increasing orders and/or capacity marks a distinctive impact on trust level. As well, if the distinction exists what affection may relatively be better? To unveil this, the following claim is set:

Claim 1: *The positive and negative information accuracies generates trust levels which are equivalent.*

It has been conceived that partners who are normally stressed tend to master a situation they encounter by trying to choose options which can maximize their expected gains. Although the factor (α) is assumed to be entirely certain, still the {0} element is the only absolute member of a set by which partners may report exact information compared to the rest: *{−0.05, 0.05}*. In this case, it is gain necessary to understand whether partners prefer to *exactly* be honest or they deviate slightly. The {0} and {−0.05, 0.05} factors are referred to as the *absolutely exact* and *slightly deviated* information accuracy, respectively. To realize this, the second claim is set as follows:

Claim 2: *Under the neutral information accuracy partners prefer to report the slightly deviated than the absolutely exact information accuracy.*

6 Design and Setup of Experiments

The design and setups of experiments proceed as follows. A logistics network applied in this study correlates partly to that in [23]. The network comprises of 7 shippers and 7 receivers (to simplify interactions), and 3 carriers. One shipper serves one and only receiver but with multiple orders. Each carrier owns one vehicle truck that is put in a pool and the carrier cannot choose who customer to serve. Three predictor variables (Fig. 2) are manipulated to affect the trust mechanism. An outcome of such manipulation is observed using five response variables: forecast accuracy, cost saving, full truck load, order fill rate, vehicle fill. Each experiment yields 12 samples, and it is replicated 5 times to yield 60 samples in total. Settings involved are benchmark values for each response variable. These benchmark values are essential for deriving a trust meter. The forecast accuracy in sales is benchmarked to 32.5% [24] using MAPE[1] while cost saving ranges between 10 and 15% of the original transportation charge per pallet [25]. Vehicle fill is derived from benchmark value of the full truck load [26] and are both benchmarked to 95%. Finally, the order fill rate is benchmarked to 95% [24]. Except the cost saving, a width for assessing trust to remaining benchmark values is established by creating an interval of ± 5 units. For example, forecast accuracy (32.5 ± 5) has a Lower value ($\boldsymbol{L_v}$) of 27.5 and Upper value ($\boldsymbol{U_v}$) of 37.5 units. This interval is further divided into Likert scale of size 5 to yield a class width ($\boldsymbol{w}$) of 2 units. For cost saving, $\boldsymbol{L_v}$ and $\boldsymbol{U_v}$ are 10 and 15, respectively, while a width ($\boldsymbol{w}$) is set 1 unit. In the end, trust is measured and assessed based on a trust meter established in Table 1.

[1] Mean Absolute Percentage Error.

Table 1. Trust meter.

Range	Quantitative value	Qualitative value
(L_v <= score < (L_v + w)	1	Least trustworthy[a]
(L_v + w) <= score < (L_v + 2w)	2	Less trustworthy
(L_v + 2w) <= score < (L_v + 3w)	3	Trustworthy
(L_v + 3w) <= score < (L_v + 4w)	4	More trustworthy
(L_v + 4w) <= score < U_v	5	Most trustworthy[b]

[a]If a score is less than L_v the trust level is also assessed as the least trustworthy

[b]If a score is greater than U_v the trust level is still assessed as the most trustworthy

7 Results and Discussions

Obtained results are analyzed and summarized in both graphical and statistical forms. In Fig. 3, a subjective comparison of the FIRE model and trust mechanism based on the graphical display technique is presented. To a large extent, the graphical patterns between the FIRE and trust mechanism correlate although variations are also observed. On the whole the trust mechanism scores higher than its rival, the FIRE.

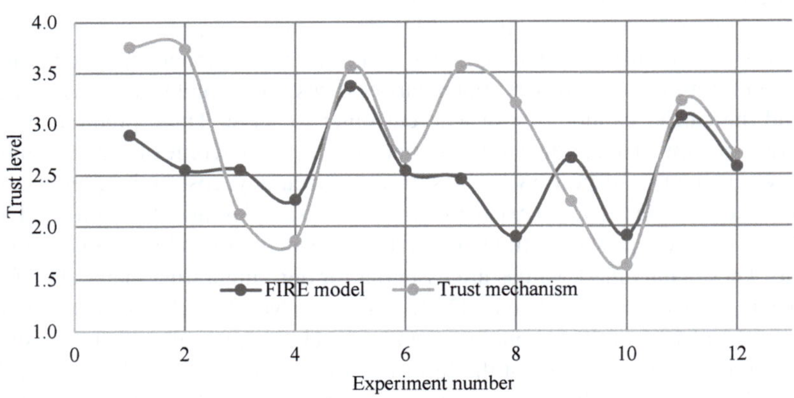

Fig. 3. Comparison of the FIRE and Trust mechanism

To establish a clear difference or correlation, outputs of the FIRE and trust mechanism are compared using the t-test. The t-test compares only the outputs for positive information accuracy. Since the two models evaluates trust differently this comparison employs unpaired observations technique. With a sample size of 60 for each model the mean trust level for the FIRE and Trust mechanism are 2.18 and 3.38, respectively. The standard error of the estimate for both models coincides to 0.20 trust level. The 96% CI for difference ranges in the interval: $\{-1.762, -0.617\}$. With reference to the internal, conceptual, and operational validity what do these results imply?

Firstly, building on the subjective decision, the trust mechanism is credibly accurate since it produces outputs whose pattern match to that of the valid model, the FIRE model. Secondly, the range for CI excludes a null value. If the range excludes the null value it implies that the two models are significantly different, and that one model is better than the other. A decision on which model is better depends comparing mean trust levels of the two. The model with higher trust level is statistically better. It is thus established with 96% confidence the trust mechanism yields better performance than its rival. To this end, theories and assumptions underlying the employed trust mechanism are reasonably accurate and credible. This credibility counts also from the standard error whose magnitude is observed to be small and tolerable.

Furthermore, Figs. 4, 5, and 6 present graphical displays to compare output behavior (trust level) resulting from the model and system data. The output behavior in Figs. 4, 5 produce similar trends (patterns), although slight variation may be observed in Fig. 6.

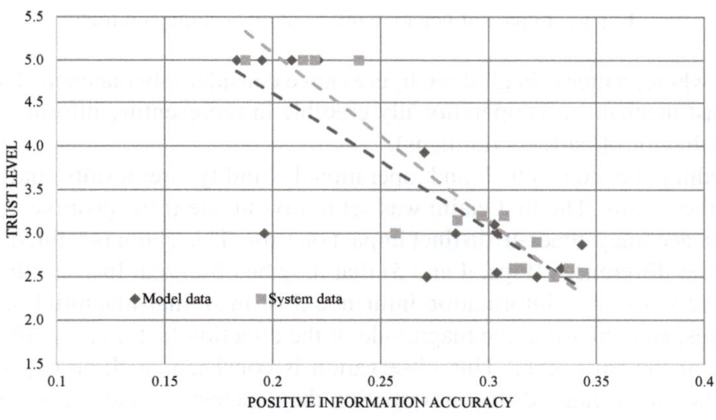

Fig. 4. Impact of positive information accuracy on trust

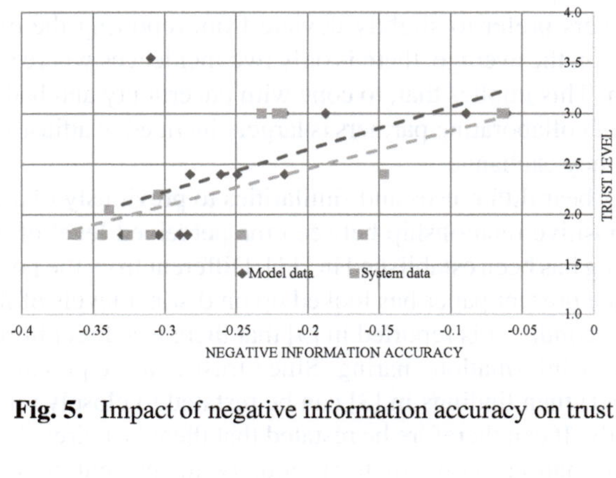

Fig. 5. Impact of negative information accuracy on trust

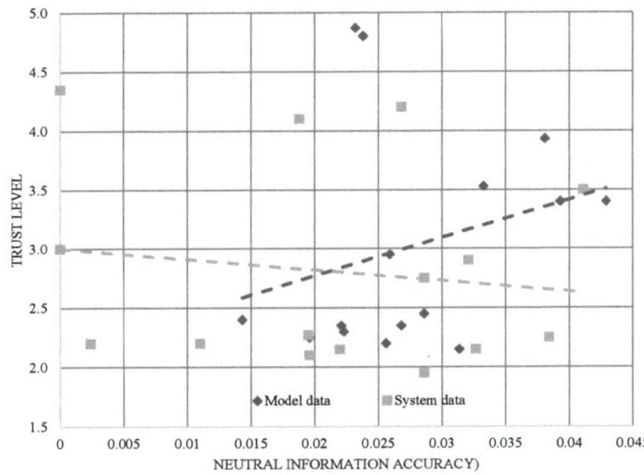

Fig. 6. Impact of negative information accuracy on trust

On the whole, patterns in all three figures have considerably matched. This signifies that the trust mechanism is operationally credible in representing information sharing and trust behavior of partners (humans).

Succeeding the conceptual and operational validity are results and discussion regarding the claims. The first claim was set to investigate if the positive and negative information accuracy generate distinct impact on trust. This claim is refuted as there are no significant differences (Figs. 4 and 5) that may be observed. Instead, the positively and negatively distorted information influence trust in similar magnitudes. Moreover, in both cases, an increase in the magnitude of the affection factor (γ and β) results into a decrease of the trust level. This observation is consistent with an expectation that partners who increasingly distort information they exchange create equivalent distrust in the network.

The second claim was set to investigate if under the neutral information accuracy (α) situation partners prefer to be exactly honest or not. This claim is supported. To a large extent, partners prefer to slightly deviate from reporting the exact information. Looking at Fig. 6, on the average, there is only two incidences where partners report the exact information. This implies that, to cope with uncertainty and bad outcomes, information behavior of collaborating partners is largely inclined to adjusting (distorting) the true information they exchange.

These findings bear differences and similarities to previously related works in literature. Firstly, a positive relationship between the perceived level of InfQ and level of information sharing has been established in [11]. Different from the positive relationship reported in [11] the present paper has looked up on distinct levels of the InfQ and their impact on trust. Secondly, it is reported in [3] that there is a direct impact of trust to the level and quality of information sharing. Since trust is a reciprocal construct (both a cause and an effect) then findings in [3] can be restated to closely relate to the context of the present study. It can therefore be restated that there is a direct impact on the level and quality of information sharing on trust. Equally, the present findings relate to those in [3]. Similar to [11], one key difference is that findings in [3] do not reveal an extent of this impact as it has been addressed in the present paper. Finally, it has been found that supplier tends to deviate from reporting true information [6]. This finding relates to what this study reports especially on the aspect of certain (neutral) information accuracy. One difference is that there are few cases in which partners report true (exact) information (Fig. 6). On the whole, a major difference of this study to related works is that it explore in details about an extent to which the information sharing behavior of partner affect trust.

Referring to the RQ and general implications of this study, the following can be stated. Information behavior of the collaborating partners affects trust in different magnitudes. Less distortion in the accuracy of the shared information remains relatively trustworthy than larger distortions. It also appears that collaborating partners are as not honest as it is ideally desired. Instead when they realize fairness they exchange nearly true information which is not harmful. These findings are helpful to designers of information systems who suggest encapsulating exchanged information to avoid risks of exposing proprietary business models. That the encapsulated information may be distorted slightly to maintain company's privacy, and still achieve chain visibility and sustain the trustworthy.

8 Conclusion and Outlook

Information sharing marks a core heart of collaboration and daily living of humans as it affects way collaborating partners can trust each other. The quality of shared information depends on information sharing behaviors of partners. In a viewpoint of such behavior, collaborating partner may deceitfully manipulate information they exchange to maximize individual gains. Focusing on a dimension of information accuracy, this paper has investigated how the information behavior of partner affects trust. Both, the positively and negatively manipulated information accuracies influence trust in similar magnitude. It is argued that partner's deceitful behavior on information accuracy can be reduced but not eliminated. Future works is unlimited to exploring the impact of the positively, negatively, and neutrally manipulation of information accuracy in combination. As well, replicating this study by expanding the size of collaborative network (such as increasing number of partners) may strengthen the present findings.

References

1. Xu, X.: Collaboration Mechanism in Horizontal Logistics Collaboration. Dissertation, Ecole Nationale Supérieure desMines de Paris (2013)
2. Simatupang, T.M., Sridharan, R.: Supply chain discontent. Bus. Process Manag. J. **11**(4), 349–369 (2005)
3. Ouzrout, Y., Chaze, L., Lavastre, O., Dominguez, C., Akhter, S.H.: Simulation of trust in supply chains. Supply Chain Perform. Collab. Alignment Coord. 267–315 (2013)
4. Zhou, Q., Lee, T.: The interactive effects between internal and external resources constraints on supply information sharing. J. Syst. Manag. Sci. **4**(3), 22–41 (2014)
5. Zhao, X., Xie, J.: Forecasting errors and the value of information sharing in a supply chain. Int. J. Prod. Res. **40**(2), 311–335 (2002)

6. Firouzi, F., Jaber, M.Y., Baglieri, E.: Trust in supply forecast information sharing. Int. J. Prod. Res. **7543**(December), 1–12 (2015)
7. Han, G., Dong, M.: Trust-embedded coordination in supply chain information sharing. Int. J. Prod. Res. **53**(18), 5624–5639 (2015)
8. Bao, X., Bouthillier, F.: Information Sharing: As a Type of Information Behavior, pp. 1–14. McGill Univ, Canada (2007)
9. Jeske, M., Grüner, M,. WeiB, F.: Big Data in Logistics: A DHL perspective on how to move beyond the hype. Report (2013)
10. Mayer, R.C., Davis, J.H., Schoorman, F.D.: An integrative model of organizational trust. Acad. Manag. Rev. **20**(3), 709–734 (1995)
11. Chen, J.V., Yen, D.C., Rajkumar, T.M., Tomochko, N.A.: The antecedent factors on trust and commitment in supply chain relationships. Comput. Stand. Interfaces **33**(3), 262–270 (2011)
12. Daudi, M., Baalsrud Hauge, J., Thoben, K.-D.: Behavioral factors influencing partner trust in logistics collaboration: a review. Logist. Res. **9**(1), 19 (2016)
13. Bobrowski, M., Marré, M., Yankelevich, D.: A homogeneous framework to measure data quality. In: Fourth Conference on Information Quality, pp. 115–124 (1999)
14. Wilson, T.D.: Human information behaviour. Inf. Sci. **3**(2), 49–55 (2000)
15. Huhns, M.N., Singh, M.P.: Cognitive agents. IEEE Internet Comput. **2**(6), 87–89 (1998)
16. Dervin, B.: An overview of sense-making research: concepts, methods and results to date. In: International Communications Association Annual Meeting (1983)
17. Wilson, T.D.: Information behaviour: an interdisciplinary perspective. Inf. Process. Manag. **33**(4), 551–572 (1997)
18. Wilson, T.D.: Models in information behaviour research. J. Doc. **55**(3), 249–270 (1999)
19. Daudi, M., Hauge, J.B., Thoben, K.-D.: Effects of Decision Synchronization on Trust in Collaborative Networks. In: Afsarmanesh, H., Camarinha-Matos, Luis M., Lucas Soares, A. (eds.) PRO-VE 2016. IAICT, vol. 480, pp. 215–227. Springer, Cham (2016). doi: 10.1007/978-3-319-45390-3_19
20. Datta, P.P., Christopher, M.G.: Information sharing and coordination mechanisms for managing uncertainty in supply chains: a simulation study. Int. J. Prod. Res. **49**(3), 765–803 (2010)
21. Sargent, R.G.: Verification and validation of simulation models. J. Simul. **7**(1), 12–24 (2013)
22. Huynh, T.D., Jennings, N.R., Shadbolt, N.R.: An integrated trust and reputation model for open multi-agent systems. Auton. Agent. Multi. Agent. Syst. **13**(2), 119–154 (2006)
23. Zolfagharinia, H., Haughton, M.A.: The benefit of information sharing in a logistics outsourcing context. Int. J. Logist. Syst. Manag. **13**(2), 187 (2012)
24. Supply Chain Consortium: Supply Chain Core Benchmarks: Understanding Key Metrics (2011). Retrieved from http://www.tompkinsinc.com/wp-content/uploads/2012/07/core benchmarksreport.pdf
25. Tseng, M., Yan, J., Cruijssen, F.: Position paper on compensation rules. CO3 Deliverable D2.5 (2013). http://www.co3-project.eu/wo3/wp-content/uploads/2011/12/CO3-D-2-5-Position-Paper-on-Compensation-Rule.pdf
26. VICS: Collaborative Transportation Management: White Paper. Lawrencevill, NJ Volunt. Interindustry Commer. Solut. Assoc., pp. 0–32 (2004)

A Supply Chain Risk Index Estimation Methodological Framework Using Exposure Assessment

Arij Lahmar[1,2(✉)], François Galasso[2], Habib Chabchoub[1], and Jacques Lamothe[2]

[1] Unit of Logistic, Industrial and Quality Management (LOGIQ), Faculty of Economics Sciences and Management, University of Sfax, Sfax, Tunisia
Arij.lahmar@hotmail.fr

[2] Industrial Engineering Center (CGI), University of Toulouse, Mines Albi, Campus Jarlard, 81013 Albi, France
{francois.galasso,jacques.lamothe}@mines-albi.fr

Abstract. The objective of this article is to move a step forward towards the general knowledge about how to manage supply chain risks by developing a theoretical risk index using exposure analysis. Two questions "why logistics systems are exposed to risks? to which type of risk, a supply chain organization is exposed to?" have to be raised and investigated. The answers to these questions will be used as a basis for the risk index methodology, which allows organizations to assess their exposure level and also to identify which type of risk they need to deal with it. The results of previous step will be computed into a supply chain risk index. To achieve our objective, the article is organized as follows: Sect. 2 provides a brief literature review to position the proposed model against other existing theoretical models. Section 3 provides the methodology used to develop our approach. Section 4 presents the conclusion, limitations and future research.

Keywords: Supply chain risk · Exposure supply chain trends · Probability of occurrence · Disruptive events · Hazard

1 Introduction

According to [1], different types of disruptions are threaten supply chain causing several financial losses. Thus protecting supply chains and making them less vulnerable to different types of disruptions have become one of the main priorities for both researchers [5–10] and practitioners (Resilience Report 2012, 2013 and 2015, Generix Group 2015, Accenture 2014, etc.), where there is a common consensus about the need to determine the causing factors of supply chain susceptibility to risks and the their occurrence impacts [1–4]. The attempts to give answers to these basic questions have been the topic of years of research and experiments, resulting in a plethora of tools, methods and practices that deal with different issues related to supply chain risks [3]. The need for an effective approach to manage supply chain risks seems apparent.

L.M. Camarinha-Matos et al. (Eds.): PRO-VE 2017, IFIP AICT 506, pp. 507–514, 2017.
DOI: 10.1007/978-3-319-65151-4_45

[11–14] highlight that the search for a mitigation strategy or solution required first and foremost a clear understanding of what the supply chain risk concept means, which still missing in the literature review [3, 14]. According to the authors, "the real challenge in the field of supply chain risk management is still the quantification and modeling of supply chain risk". For instance, [16, 17] characterize supply chain risk by the combination of three terms: consequence, vulnerability and disruptive events; where consequence is the maximum possible loss, vulnerability is the potential exposure of supply chain to potential disruptive events scenarios and disruptive event is the possibility of occurrence per time frame. Moreover, [18] highlight the important for of disruptions detection for defining effective risk management practices. Following the same line of thinking, [19] emphasize the significance of disruption detection using a manufacturer case study by integrating this dimension, "detection" into occurrence models to calculate the duration of a risk event. The results of this study prove that in large supply chains it may be challenging to detect the occurrence of a risk event. According to this study, it had taken the manufacturer several weeks to discover the source of the disruptions and to estimate their likelihood and their impacts, which resulted in a loss of market share to competitors. As a result, the authors suggest that academics and practitioners need to invest more in discovering and developing more appropriate dimensions to assess supply chain risks and to develop new approaches to manage the critical risks [20]. Although that the domain of supply chain risk management extend to 30 years, the quantification and computation frameworks of supply chain risk are just beginning to emerge and more research progress is expected to be made in the future research [21]. [22–25] believe that supply chain characteristics need to be considered when assessing and measuring supply chain risks to guarantee the accuracy of developed risk measurement methods. [26] underline that risk cannot be measured without taking into account the supply chain exposure level and the safety measures applied. And these latter are changeable and depend on both risk type and supply chain characteristics. [27] suggest that identifying risk factors and most exposed or vulnerable component within supply chain is a crucial sub-problem of a general risk management process. Therefore, there is a need for additional analysis of causing path of supply chain risks to capture the impact of supply chain on risk dimensions.

Informed by the above critical aspects of this issue, this article proposes an comprehensive essay to estimate supply chain risk occurrence based on exposure analysis. We extend the general risk quantification model to propose a broader quantification approach focusing on probability perspective. We assume that supply chain risk is defined with regard to two perspectives, the causal aspect and the consequence one. In this article, we focus on the causality perspective of supply chain risks: How supply chain risk is generated? and we model Risk probability as a function of exposure factors and the occurrence of one or a set of disruptive events.

To reveal the reasons and to describe the method to incorporate exposure factors into the probability quantification of supply chain risk formula, this paper is organized as follows: after the introduction, Sect. 2 presents an overview of the most common frameworks of supply chain risks from the probability perspective. Section 3 discusses a conceptual model to include exposure in the supply chain risk occurrence analysis. Section 4 details the conclusions, limitations, and future directions regarding our conceptual model.

2 Research Background

According to [28–30], a huge variety of works with diversified themes and approaches have been developed to define supply chain risks. And this can be explained by the nature of risk that is inherent from the concept of life. It implicitly reflects the complexity, instability and diversity of managerial interactions. As a result, no universally accepted definition of supply chain risk exists [31, 32]. However, whereas specific definitions of risk might vary, a few characteristics are common to all definitions, which are: the probability of occurrence of a particular disruptive event, hazard or negative outcome and the consequence of the particular disruptive event, hazard or negative outcome if it is occurring. [33] confirm that risk management strategy or method needs to address all three dimensions to effectively manage supply chain risk. This could explain why 67% scientific articles define supply chain risk as a measure of the likelihood (probability) that unexpected disruptive event(s) will cause negatives impacts or losses to supply chain performance [13]. Different terms are often used synonymously to refer to these events, such as risk drivers, risk trigger, hazard, risk sources [38], disturbance or conditions that leads to the occurrence of a risk. To avoid confusion in the terminologies used, "disruptive event" will be used for the rest of this article. These events could be considered as one of the characteristics of the underlying supply chain as well as an external driver from supply chain environment. The likelihood of a disruptive event is specified by the probability of occurrence, which has been considered as the central aspect of risk perception in most research areas and the core of various definitions developed in the context of supply chain risk management [3]. Thus assessing supply chain risks consequences merely requires the definition of the disruptive events occurrence and then, the estimation of their occurrence probability and then their possible effect on supply chain objectives [34, 35]. However, these events have been always considered as distinct from the characteristics of supply chain although that [21, 24] highlight the need to consider these characteristics when modeling and assessing supply chain risk. To summarize, all previous frameworks have often attach slightly different meanings of supply chain risk upon the context in which it is viewed [12, 13]. The notion of explicitly establishing the context in which supply chain risk is evaluated to ensure that appropriate measures and interpretations are made. This context is referred to it as exposure factors. There is a need to understand the causal factors leading to the occurrence of Supply Chain Risk, related to the identification and the estimation of trigging events and the manner in which they lead to different types of risks. In order to address the problematic identified, a general theoretical risk exposure estimation model is developed in Sect. 3.

3 Research Methodology

The results of the previous section emphasis that events are one of the important ingredients to understand the occurrence process. However, the transformation mechanisms of these events to potential supply chain risks is missing in the literature review. Probability of disruptive events (fire, natural disasters, etc.) is a risk metric that only quantifies uncertainty. It does not address the supply chain exposure to these events and its consequences, which depends upon the extent to which a supply chain is susceptible to a specific or unspecific risk events. These hazardous events may be potentially harmful to supply chain process, activities, flows, and organizations but also to the entire network, which are all grouped together under the term Elements-at-risk or assets. According to the survey's results published by [39, 40] the frequency of the disruptive events is increasing. The results have underlined that there is nearly 1500 disruptive events threaten supply chain each year [40, pp. 3–4] and 49.9% of companies have experienced supply chain disruptive events during 2016. These statistics prove that not all supply chain organisations are exposed neither to the same level and nor to the same type of disruptive events. As a result, it is becomes crucial for a company to determine whether it is truly exposed to any of the possible risks or hazards that exist. It becomes important to know whether its perception of exposure is adequate with the risk level (sets of likelihoods multiplied by impacts) that can be anticipated. As organizations are not vulnerable to every possible risk that may exist, it is a real concern to be able to define the level of risk susceptibility or exposure. The ability to deal with (and over time adapt to) various risk factors is an important element for continued existence, placed after their possibility of detection and evaluation. As a result, exposure to risk has been highlighted by several researchers in the field of supply chain risk management. [33] defined it as "the susceptibility to risks". According to [5, 38] each supply chain organization is "exposed" to unforeseen disruptive events caused by unexpected changes in its environment. These changes are referred to them as potential risk factors. e.g. political instability, strikes which have been considered as a potential risk factors. Hence, researchers defined the risk exposure as "the measure of the sensitivity of a firm's to fluctuations in the relevant risk factor that could affect a firms continuity" [36, 37]. The term exposure is used to indicate those elements-at-risk that are subject to potential losses. Then, exposure describes the characteristics of an asset or a supply chain that make it vulnerable to the negative effects of a disruptive events [22]. Following the work of [41], supply chain risk occurrence is a combination of an action (disruptive events) and condition (SC characteristics) that could leads to negative impacts [15]. The authors [15] considers that all type of risk are triggered by a disruptive events (which have been considered as the active component of risk) and a set of conditions (supply chain characteristics). Without these two previous elements or dimensions, risk doesn't exist. Following this logic of thinking, we model Risk probability as a function of exposure factors and the occurrence of disruptive events (see Fig. 1).

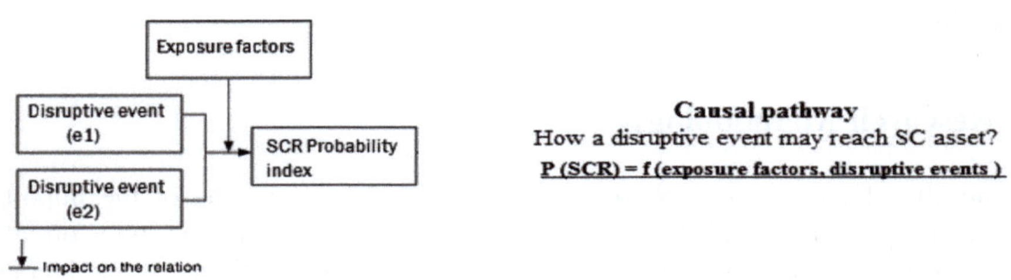

Fig. 1. Proposed model.

Supply chain risk occurrence is not only a conceptual model as it had been described in Fig. 1. It can also be actually calculated. A general risk function is introduced to compute the risk occurrence probability as a function of:

1. The occurrence of disruptive events reflects the number of times a particular type of event happens over a period of time. It can be modeled using a Poisson distribution with the assumption that events are not correlated, as follow:

$$p(k) = P(X = k) = \frac{\lambda^k}{k!} e^{-\lambda} \tag{1}$$

   Where

   λ is the number if occurrence per time period
   K is the disruptive event (under study)

2. The amount of exposure factors that characterize supply chain. [15, 25, 39] highlight that supply chain trends are considered as exposure factors that could leads to potential risks. [31] use Normal Accident Theory to investigate how supply chain trends leads to increase the level of exposure to risks. The results of their study demonstrate that certain supply chain practices comprise certain exposure factors that increase the probability of supply chain risk occurrence. Let us assume that there are (n) trends applied for company (j) where the relative importance weight for (i) managerial trend (tij) is measured by (wij). As the result, the total number of trends applied in company (j) is modeled by the Eq. (1). Each applied trend cause a set of exposure factors. As a result, potential exposure (PE) equation for a specific company (j) could be modelled as follow:

$$\mathrm{T(j)} = \sum\nolimits_{i=0}^{n} \mathrm{w(ij)} * \mathrm{t(ij)} \ \text{ with } \mathbf{n} = \boldsymbol{7} \textbf{ and } \mathbf{0} \leq \mathbf{w} \leq \mathbf{1} \tag{2}$$

$$\mathrm{EF(i)} = \left[\sum\nolimits_{i=0}^{p} \mathrm{ef(ki)} * \mathrm{t(ki)}\right] / \mathrm{p} \ \text{ with } \mathbf{P{=}7} \tag{3}$$

$$\downarrow$$

$$\mathrm{PE(j)} = \sum\nolimits_{i=0}^{n} \mathrm{w(ij)} * \left[\left(\sum\nolimits_{i=0}^{p} \mathrm{ef(ki)} * \mathrm{t(ki)}\right) / 7\right] \tag{4}$$

3. As a result, the first equation need to be adjust it basing on this assumption, to compute the new occurrence probability of supply chain risk and will help understanding its causal pathway. To compute the new index, different scenarios need to be considered. A definition of a risk scenario includes a combination of a set of disruptive events and a selected number of exposure factors to determine the potential causal links between them. These scenarios will be defined basing on experts judgement and historical data and ranged between 0 (no risk) and 1 (risk is occurring) (Fig. 2).

The result of described methodology is "a set of causal matrix and initial hypotheses about the structure of the causal chain of supply chain risks which must then be tested. The matrix can offer two forms of assistance in dealing with multifarious

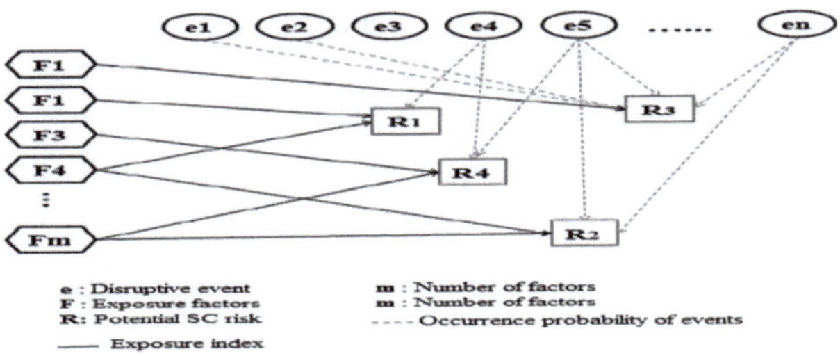

Fig. 2. Scenario development.

supply chain risks. Then the new probability occurrence for each risk could be then calculated as follow

$$P(x = k + PE) = \left(\frac{e^{-(k+PE)}}{k!}\right)(K + PE)^{k}$$

4 Conclusion

Managing supply chain risk is becomes today one of the most important issue for both academics and practitioners. However, to effective deal with risks and mitigate its impacts, a need to understand and to define the potential risks threaten supply chain. Probability approach has been widely used to address this need. Although that several researchers have emphasis the need to develop other alternatives that could taking into account the risk dimensions in side and the supply chain characteristic in other side. Trying to address the need, a new attempt has been developed basing in the exposure analysis. We present a first essay to quantify the probability of occurrence of supply chain risk considering the supply chain characteristics through the exposure analysis. The first step was to understand the measurement and the assessment approach of supply chain risks probability. Then in second step, the identification of the exposure factors was carried out. The results of this step has reveal that managerial trends applied increase the level of exposure to supply chain risks through a set of factors. These latter, combined with the probability of disruptive events are computed to develop a new risk probability index. The Poisson distribution was used in this research to quantify the occurrence probability of potential disruptive events. Then, we integrate an estimated exposure index into the calculated probability to give more accurate index of supply chain risks occurrence.

The developed approach is a work in progress. Future evaluation and experimental analysis are expected.

References

1. Supply Chain Resilience, 6th Annual Survey, Business Continuity Institute (2014). http://knowledge.zurich.com/supply-chain/supply-chain-resilience
2. Hallikas, J., Lintukangas, K.: Purchasing and supply: an investigation of risk management performance. Int. J. Prod. Econ. **171**(Part 4), 487–494 (2016)
3. Ho, W., Zheng, T., Yildiz, H., Talluri, S.: Supply chain risk management: a literature review. Int. J. Prod. Res. **53**, 1–39 (2015)
4. Jury, G., Matteo, K.: Supply risk management and competitive advantage: a misfit model. Int. J. Logist. Manage. **26**(3), 459–478 (2015)
5. Peck, H.: Reconciling Supply Chain Vulnerability, risk and supply chain management. Int. J. Logist. Res. Appl. **9**(2), 127–142 (2006)
6. Svensson, G.: A conceptual framework for the analysis of vulnerability in supply chains. Int. J. Phys. Distrib. Logist. Manage. **30**(9), 731–750 (2000)
7. Tang, C.S.: Robust strategies for mitigating supply chain disruptions. Int. J. Logist. Res. Appl. **9**(1), 33–45 (2006)
8. Wagner, S.M., Bode, C.: An empirical investigation into Supply Chain Vulnerability. J. Purch. Supp. Manage. **12**(6), 301–312 (2006)
9. Wagner, S.M., Neshat, N.: A comparison of supply chain vulnerability indices for different categories of firms. Int. J. Prod. Res. **50**(11), 2877–2891 (2012)
10. Scholten, K., Sharkey, S.P., Fynes, B.: Mitigation processes–antecedents for building supply chain resilience. Supp. Chain Manage. Int. J. **19**(2), 211–228 (2014)
11. Pfohl, H.-C., Gallus, P., Thomas, D.: Interpretive structural modeling of supply chain risks. Int. J. Phys. Distrib. Logist. Manage. **41**(9), 839–859 (2011)
12. Heckmann, I.: Towards Supply Chain Risk Analytics: Fundamentals, Simulation. Optimization. Springer, Heidelberg (2016)
13. Heckmann, I.: Supply chain risk analysis–common flaws, core areas, and main tasks. In: Towards Supply Chain Risk Analytics, pp. 77–129. Springer, Wiesbaden (2016). doi:10.1007/978-3-658-14870-6_4
14. Heckmann, I., Comes, T., Nickel, S.: A critical review on supply chain risk–Definition, measure and modeling. Omega **52**, 119–132 (2015)
15. Paulsson, U., Nilsson, C.H., Wandel, S.: Estimation of disruption risk exposure in supply chains. Int. J. Bus. Contin. Risk Manage. **2**(1), 1–19 (2011)
16. Lahmar, A., Galasso, F., Chabchoub, H., Lamothe, J.: Towards an integrated model of supply chain risks: an alignment between supply chain characteristics and risk dimensions. In: Camarinha-Matos, L.M., Bénaben, F., Picard, W. (eds.) PRO-VE 2015. IAICT, vol. 463, pp. 3–16. Springer, Cham (2015). doi:10.1007/978-3-319-24141-8_1
17. Ayyub, B.M., McGill, W.L., Kaminskiy, M.: Critical asset and portfolio risk analysis: an all-hazards framework. Risk Anal. **27**(4), 789–801 (2007)
18. DuHadway, S., Carnovale, S., Hazen, B.: Understanding risk management for intentional supply chain disruptions: risk detection, risk mitigation, and risk recovery. Ann. Oper. Res. 1–20 (2017)
19. Handfield, R., McCormack, K.P. (eds.): Supply Chain Risk Management: Minimizing Disruptions in Global Sourcing. CRC Press, Boca Raton (2007)
20. Christopher, M., Peck, H.: Building the resilient supply chain. Int. J. Logist. Manage. **15**(2), 1–14 (2004)
21. Wagner, S.M., Neshat, N.: A comparison of Supply Chain Vulnerability indices for different categories of firms. Int. J. Prod. Res. **50**(11), 2877–2891 (2012)

22. Karningsih, P.D., Kayis, B., Kara, S.: Development of SCRIS: a knowledge based system tool for assisting organizations in managing supply chain risks. In: 2010 IEEE 24th International Conference on Advanced Information Networking and Applications Workshops (WAINA), pp. 55–60. IEEE, April 2010
23. Heckmann, I., Nickel, S., Saldanha-da-Gama, F.: The risk-aware multi-period capacitated plant location problem (CPLP-Risk). In: International Conference on Information Systems in Supply Chain (2016)
24. Craighead, C.W., Blackhurst, J., Rungtusanatham, M.J., Handfield, R.B.: The severity of supply chain disruptions: design characteristics and mitigation capabilities. Decis. Sci. **38**(1), 131–156 (2007)
25. Bode, C., Macdonald, J.R.: Stages of Supply Chain Disruption Response: Direct, Constraining, and Mediating Factors for Impact Mitigation. Decision Sciences (2016)
26. Bogataj, D., Bogataj, M.: Measuring the supply chain risk and vulnerability in frequency space. Int. J. Prod. Econ. **108**(1), 291–301 (2007)
27. Kamalahmadi, M., Parast, M.M.: An assessment of supply chain disruption mitigation strategies. Int. J. Prod. Econ. **184**, 210–230 (2017)
28. Gao, Y., Simchi-Levi, D., Teo, C.P., Yan, Z.: Disruption Risk Mitigation in Supply Chains-The Risk Exposure Index Revisited (2016)
29. Levner, E., Ptuskin, A.: An entropy-based approach to identifying vulnerable components in a supply chain. Int. J. Prod. Res. **53**(22), 6888–6902 (2015)
30. Tang, O., Musa, S.N.: Identifying risk issues and research advancements in supply chain risk management. Int. J. Prod. Econ. **133**(1), 25–34 (2011)
31. Snyder, L.V., Atan, Z., Peng, P., Rong, Y., Schmitt, A.J., Sinsoysal, B.: OR/MS models for supply chain disruptions: a review. IIE Trans. **48**(2), 89–109 (2016)
32. Ponis, S.T., Ntalla, A.C.: Supply chain risk management frameworks and models: a review. Int. J. Supp. Chain Manage. **5**(4), 1–11 (2016)
33. Spekman, R.E., Davis, E.W.: Risky business: expanding the discussion on risk and the extended enterprise. Int. J. Phys. Distrib. Logist. Manage. **34**, 414–433 (2004)
34. Chopra, S., Sodhi, M.S.: Reducing the risk of supply chain disruptions. MIT Sloan Manage. Rev. **55**(3), 73 (2014)
35. Zsidisin, G.A.: A grounded definition of supply risk. J. Purchas. Supp. Manage. **9**, 217–224 (2003)
36. Hallikas, J., Karvonen, I., Pulkkinen, U., Virolainen, V.M., Tuominen, M.: Risk management processes in supplier networks. Int. J. Prod. Econ. **90**(1), 47–58 (2004)
37. Svensson, G.: Dyadic vulnerability in companies' inbound and outbound logistics flows. Int. J. Logist. **5**(1), 13–43 (2002)
38. Svensson, G.: Interactive vulnerability in buyer-seller relationships: a dyadic approach. Int. J. Phys. Distrib. Logist. Manage. **34**(8), 662–682 (2004)
39. Jüttner, U., Peck, H., Christopher, M.: Supply chain risk management: outlining an agenda for future research. Int. J. Logist. Res. Appl. **6**(4), 197–210 (2003)
40. Lahmar, A., et al.: Development of supply chain vulnerability drivers interrelationships model using interpretive structural modeling. In: Proceedings of the 28th International Business Information Management Association Conference - Vision 2020: Innovation Management, Development Sustainability, and Competitive Economic Growth, pp. 2675–2689 (2016)
41. World Economic Forum: A Global Risk Network Report 2017. World, Economic Forum, Geneva (2017)
42. Resilinc Company: EventWatch® Supply Chain Disruption Annual Report (2016)
43. Peck, H.: Drivers of supply chain vulnerability: an integrated framework. Int. J. Phys. Distrib. Logist. Manage. **35**(4), 210–232 (2005)

A Classification Taxonomy for Reputation and Trust Systems Applied to Virtual Organizations

Luís Felipe Bilecki(✉) and Adriano Fiorese

Department of Computer Science, Santa Catarina State University, Joinville, Brazil
luis.bilecki@gmail.com, adriano.fiorese@udesc.br

Abstract. Online interactions between unknown parties are increasingly common. This is particularly exemplary in Virtual Organizations (VO). A VO is understood as a permanent or temporary alliance of enterprises that share their resources and skills to achieve specific business goals (collaboration opportunity). In this sense, the lack of trust between partners is seen as an hindrance to the VO's operation. Thus, reputation systems can be applied to trust establishment and management among VO's partners. Therefore, this paper presents a taxonomy to classify and compare trust and reputation systems applied to VO's context. The taxonomy is based on literature studies regarding characteristics observed through a systematic review process. In order to evaluate the proposed taxonomy, it was applied to trust and reputation systems obtained through a systematic review process. Finally, according the presented results, it is possible to note a gap concerning reputation systems applied to the context of VO and Cloud Computing integration.

Keywords: Virtual Organizations · Trust · Reputation · Taxonomy · Systematic review

1 Introduction

Nowadays, the interactions between people, enterprises and unknown services that have not previously interacted, is becoming more common in the online environments [1]. Some examples of online environments include the social networks, peer-to-peer networks, forums, and the collaborative networks, such as, the Virtual Organization [2].

A Virtual Organization (VO) is understood as an alliance of heterogeneous, geographically disperse, and independent entities (enterprises), that share common risks and skills to achieve a business goal [3]. The interactions are supported by the Internet, and the VO's can use the resources provided by the cloud computing to support the business and transactions [4].

In this sense, the interactions in online environments can be supported by the application of trust and reputation concepts. In VOs the entities share, combine, and integrate information in an environment, where the lack of trust and security represents a major issue [4]. Also, one of the obstacles during collaboration opportunity attendance is the establishment, management, and the lack of trust between involved parties [5].

L.M. Camarinha-Matos et al. (Eds.): PRO-VE 2017, IFIP AICT 506, pp. 515–526, 2017.
DOI: 10.1007/978-3-319-65151-4_46

In general, trust is a single measure that is understood as a numerical value composed of indicators, which represents the confidence level about an entity, and others use that value to their decision-making processes [6]. To manage and establish trust, the reputation systems are used. For example, if an entity needs to interact with another one, then it uses the reputation for decision-making and for establishing a trust relationship [7].

The reputation concept are closely related to the trust [8]. However, these concepts present different meanings. According to Resnick et al. [9], reputation is a collective measure defined as a value generated through an aggregation methodology of a feedback collection and/or values related to the historical performance.

Thereby, the reputation assists people when choosing trusted partners in a virtual world (e.g., e-commerce), who are honest in real world. In an environment guided by reputation, people encourage trustworthy behavior, disregarding the participation of immoral or dishonest people [7].

Considering the trust and reputation issue, the main objective of this paper is to present a taxonomy to classify and compare the reputation systems and trust models applied to the VO's context. This taxonomy is based on reviewing studies present in the literature and through the characteristics obtained by a systematic review process. The proposed taxonomy comprises seven characteristics: information type, network or architecture model, value representation, aggregation methodology, information source, VO's phase, and VO's application.

Through the application of the proposed taxonomy in articles obtained by means of systematic review process (related to reputation systems and trust models), it is intended to identify gaps, how the systems are applied in the VO, and whether they are related to business partners, cloud or grid providers. Furthermore, it is possible to compare novel approaches in a qualitative way related to existing ones.

The remainder of this work is organized as follows. Section 2 presents the general background. Section 3 elaborates on the systematic review process. Section 4 addresses the proposed classification taxonomy. Following, Sect. 5 presents and discuss the results of the taxonomy application in the reviewed works obtained through a systematic review process. Section 6 shows related work. Finally, Sect. 7 presents conclusions and future work.

2 General Background

2.1 Virtual Organization

Nowadays the enterprises work in a collaborative way dealing with the competitiveness and the market dynamicity. The enterprises join in a collaborative network to achieve common business goals in order to have a greater flexibility and agility [10].

A Virtual Organization (VO), a collaborative network, is a temporary or permanent cluster of entities (enterprises) that share their skills, resources, and competences to attend a specific business goal (collaboration opportunity) [3]. Their activities are supported by a communication infrastructure, such as, the Internet. In this way, VO is understood as a single entity through the union of the core competences of its members [11].

According to Camarinha-Matos et al. [3], a VO has its life-cycle, composed of four phases, Creation, Operation, Evolution, and Dissolution.

In Creation step the business partners are selected, contracts are signed and the VO is launched. In Operation phase occurs the exchange of information between partners to achieve a common business goal. Evolution step can occur during the VO's operation motivated by small changes in the demand, roles, principles, and affiliations. Finally, in Dissolution, the VO ends its activities, by two ways, motivated for the achievement of the proposed objectives in VO's creation or due to several issues during the VO's operation.

Newest concepts on infrastructure and communication technology, such as, grid and cloud computing, brings a new approach to the VO and its operation. Therefore, the VO can use these concepts, for example, network, processing, storage, and systems made available by cloud computing to achieve a collaboration opportunity with greater quality of service [4].

2.2 Trust and Reputation

Trust is a multidisciplinary concept used in several areas, such as, psychology, sociology, e-commerce, and in computing [6]. According to Gambetta [12], trust is understood as a particular level of probability, where a member evaluates other member or a group of members, who will perform a particular action, before it can monitor such action and in a context in which this affects their own action.

In a computational implementation, trust is understood as a numeric value that indicates the trustworthy level of an entity/agent/resource, that others members can take into account in order to interact or not [6].

Through the concept provided by Gambetta [12], some trust characteristics can be identified, such as: subjective, context-dependent, and dynamic over time, and new observations.

Thus, the reputation concept is closely related to the trust [8]. Therefore, they present different meanings, while reputation is related to a collective measure, that is, several evaluations of diverse members regarding someone, the trust is understood as an individual opinion for someone else [13].

In this sense, the reputation is defined as a value generated through an aggregation methodology of feedback data collection and/or values related to historical performance [1]. This value can be used to assist a trust relationship establishment.

These concepts, trust and reputation, share common characteristics, for example, context sensitive, multi-faceted, and dynamic [14]. Context Sensitive is explained by the scenario where Alice trusts Bob as her medic, but she distrusts Bob as her mechanic to repair her car. Therefore, in the "medic" context Bob is reliable, however in the "mechanic" context Bob is not trustworthy [14]. Multi-Faceted means that the concepts can be composed by different set of indicators. Finally, these concepts are dynamic, that is, their values may increase or decrease with further experiences, and in some cases the recent values have greater importance than old values [6].

Finally, reputation systems are responsible for collecting feedback, aggregating these feedbacks or other data and returning the calculated reputation. Besides this, the reputation value can be used as an indicator to support decision-making process, when a participant trusts or distrusts in someone else [15].

3 Systematic Review Methodology

This Section describes the methodological procedure used to obtain the characteristics of the proposed classification taxonomy and to identify reputation systems and trust models applied to the VO's context. Following this methodological procedure, a systematic review process was realized.

A systematic review is a research type that uses as a source of data the literature on a particular topic. In addition, it provides means to identify, evaluate, and interpret the relevant literature to one or more research questions [16].

Therefore, the systematic review method proposed by Kitchenham and Chartes [16] was applied. Thus, it was searched for articles written in English, full papers (more than four pages – not abstract/proposal paper), published between 2005 and 2016, and using the following academic search engines (ASE): IEEEXplore, ScienceDirect, ACM-DL, and Springer Link. The search process was guided by the following combination of words:

("Reputation" OR "Reputation System" OR "Trust System" OR "Trust") AND ("Virtual Organization" OR "Virtual Organisation")

Using ASE's search engines and with the application of the aforementioned filters, it was resulted in 261 articles to the analysis process. From these works, 63 articles are in *IEEEXplore*, 18 articles are in *ScienceDirect*, 24 articles in *ACM-DL*, and 156 articles are indexed by the *Springer Link*.

Following this, the TOPIC (title, abstract, and keywords) of each one article was analyzed and verified whether it was related to VO's and presented or applied a reputation system, trust model or trust indicator in this context. This process was resulted in 21 articles for the review and identification of classification characteristics, which are presented in Sect. 4.

4 The Proposed Taxonomy

Through the analyzed articles in the systematic review [2, 4, 5, 7, 8, 11, 17–32], and the review articles [1, 6, 13–15, 33] that presented classification characteristics for reputation and trust system in general, a taxonomy was designed to classify and compare the works that are applied in Virtual Organization's context.

The proposed classification taxonomy, depicted in Fig. 1, has seven characteristics: information type, network model or network architecture, trust or reputation value representation, aggregation methodology, information source, VO's phase, and VO's application.

Reputation systems and trust models can use different information types in order to support the decision-making process. According to Tavakolifard and Almeroth [15], these types are defined as: implicit and explicit. The implicit is used in social networks, such as Facebook and LinkedIn, and does not characterize a reputation system because, the reputation or trust level are obtained through a friendship analysis [1]. Conversely, the explicit are reputation systems and trust models particularly developed for those

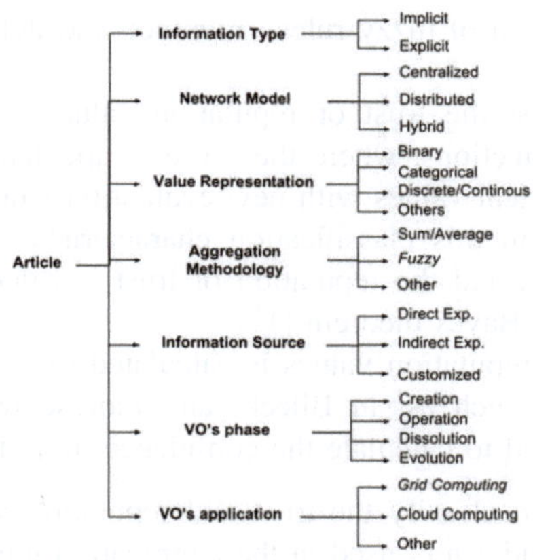

Fig. 1. The proposed taxonomy

environments, in which there is a need to establish trust relationship, access control, among other characteristics [1].

The network model or architecture determines how the values are collected and stored in a reputation/trust system, where the two main types are: centralized and distributed [1]. The centralized model has a centralized element, called Trusted Third Party (TTP) [4], which is responsible to receive the members' feedback and provide the trust or reputation value.

The distributed model is commonly used in Peer-to-Peer (P2P) networks, where each one participant stores the feedback regarding the interaction with others [34]. For example, a participant C wants to interact with A, but they have not interacted previously, then participant C asks her community about A reputation's, so the participant B responds to A the reputation of the participant C.

Other network model is the hybrid one, that combines the characteristics of the two aforementioned models. The hybrid model presents a centralized reputation mechanism for the service provider's reputation and other distributed mechanism that refers to each one member in the community, that owns their data repository and stores information regarding the interactions with others [35].

The trust or reputation value representation is discussed in several ways, such as: categorical, continuous, binary, range or interval, and customized. Categorical is represented by a set of linguistic variables, such as unreliable, reliable, extremely reliable, among others. Continuous is understood as integers or fractions in a scale interval. Binary values assume only two values [7] or accept only positive and negative evaluations [22].

The aggregation methodology refers to the trust or reputation calculation method based on the historical collected data [15]. Some aggregation forms are defined as:

- **Sum or average:** this method performs the sum of the positive and negative transactions amount to calculate the reputation of an entity;
- **Fuzzy Models:** the values are represented by means of fuzzy variables, in which the membership functions describe the trust or reputation level of a participant.

Through the application of fuzzy rules, inference and defuzzification, the value is calculated [36];

- **Probabilistic Models:** the trust or reputation value is calculated by means of probability density functions, where the score is updated and calculated with the combination of historical values with new evaluation values [7, 18, 23];
- **Stochastic Models:** in this classification characteristic, the events are modeled using Markov's chain and the reputation or trust is calculated using a stochastic method, for instance, Bayes theorem [17];
- **Hybrid:** the trust or reputation values is calculated by using one or more models (customized or not), such as, in Bilecki and Fiorese [8] the data envelopment analysis (DEA) is used to calculate the confidence in a cloud provider.

Also, it is possible to classify the trust and reputation systems according to the information sources or indicators used in the aggregation methodology. According to Sabater et al. [6], they can be classified as:

- **Direct Experience:** obtained by means of direct interaction between the participants, for example, a participant A interacts with B and at the end A gives an evaluation about B. The evaluation can be a value in an interval [7] or a set of values [37];
- **Indirect Experience:** obtained through the participant community, because it comes from other participants who interacted with such participant [6]. For example, the PeerTrust [38] uses several information sources to calculate the reputation of a participant: direct experience and indirect experience, for example, context community factor, and the amount of transactions;
- **Customized Indicators:** other set of indicators are used to calculate the trust or reputation. For example, Bilecki and Fiorese [8] used the Quality of Service (QoS) indicators to calculate the amount of trust in cloud providers. In addition, other indicators that represent the performance of an enterprise can be used (e.g., financial, logistical, among others) [17].

The characteristic VO's phase refers to the VO's phase in which the reputation system or trust model is applied. It can be applied only in the VO's creation phase [7, 8] assisting the decision-making process in the search and selection step. Also, it can be applied in the VO's operation and/or dissolution [4] or even in other VO's phases existent in its life-cycle [3], such as, VO's evolution which can be assisted by the reputation value, for example, a change of business partners guided by reputation.

A significant and decisive differential for VO's is the use of resources made available by the information and communication technologies [39]. Therefore, at using these resources, the VO's application characteristic aims to classify the articles that apply the reputation or trust in the context which uses cloud computing [8, 30, 31] or grid computing [4, 23] resources. Finally, in order to apply the proposed taxonomy, the Sect. 5 presents a comparative table using the proposed taxonomy and the obtained results.

5 Results and Discussion

The proposed taxonomy was applied to the result of the systematic review process presented in Sect. 3. Thus, the results of the application are presented in the Table 1, showing the differences between the analyzed works.

The comparative table classified the articles by the publication year and the characteristics present in the taxonomy, such as:

- **Information Type (C1):** explicit (E) and implicit (I);
- **Value Representation (C2):** it is classified as a binary method (B), continuous (C), and in some cases, it is not possible to identify (NI);
- **Network Model (C3):** centralized (CE) or distributed (DI);
- **Aggregation Methodology (C4):** it is classified as probabilistic (PR), stochastic methods (ST), sum and average (S/A), average (A), hybrid (H), fuzzy logic (FZ), probability and average (PR/A), and factors (FA);
- **Information Source (C5):** direct experience (DE), indirect experience (IE), customized indicator (CI), quality of service (QoS), and other (O);
- **VO's phase (C6):** the system/model can be applied in Creation/Formation (FM), Dissolution (D), Evolution (E), and Operation (OP);
- **VO's application** (C7): can be applied in the level of business partners (BP), enterprises (EP), Grid Computing (G), Cloud Computing (CC), and agents (AG).

The information type between analyzed articles was predominantly explicit, because they are reputation systems, trust models, among others, developed directly for the application in environments where the need, for example, is to establish a trust relationship [1].

Comprising the value representation, seventeen articles presented the trust or reputation value in continuous format, that is, included in a predefined range [8, 17], while only two works presented the binary method, and one article was not identified (NI) [2]. The binary format is used in PathTrust [7] to represent feedback, which can be positive or negative, and in Arasteh et al. [24] trust value under binary is used in the access control.

The most used network model is the centralized, showing that the reputation or trust system application in VO has been performed in a centralized way, unlike other environments such as P2P networks. In some cases, such as [5, 8, 11, 23, 30–32], it was not possible to identify the network model, due to some works are classified as trust models.

With regard to the aggregation methodology, the articles presented calculation methods based on the probabilistic, stochastic, average, sum and average, sum of factors, fuzzy logic and hybrid methods. In the sum of factors method, for example, Kaur and Sengupta [27, 28] calculate the reputation considering the sum of transactions, direct experiences, user's satisfaction, credibility and the community and transaction context factor. Also, in Bilecki and Fiorese [8] a hybrid aggregation method is presented based on a non-parametric method, Data Envelopment Analysis (DEA), applied into a set of historical QoS data.

Table 1. Application of the proposed taxonomy

Article	Year	C1	C2	C3	C4	C5	C6	C7
[7]	2006	E	B	CE	PR	DE	FM	BP
[17]	2008	E	C	CE	ST	CI	FM	BP
[19]	2012	E	C	CE	A	DE/IE	FM	G
[20]	2013	E	C	CE	S/A	CI	FM	BP
[21]	2005	E	C	CE	A	DE	FM	BP
[18]	2008	E	C	CE	PR	CI	FM	BP
[22]	2009	E	B	CE	S/A	DE	FM	BP
[4]	2010	E	C	CE	S/A	DE/QoS	FM/D	G
[23]	2010	E	C	NI	PR	DE	FM	G
[8]	2016	E	C	NI	H	QoS	FM	CC
[32]	2011	E	C	NI	FZ	CI	FM	BP
[5]	2011	E	C	NI	S/A	DE	NI	AG
[2]	2011	E	NI	CE	NI	NI	FM/O/D	BP
[11]	2011	E	C	NI	S/A	DE/IE	FM	BP
[24]	2012	E	B	CE	PR/A	DE/IE	FM	BP
[25]	2010	E	C	CE	FZ	DE/IE	FM	EP
[26]	2009	E	C	CE	S/A	QoS	FM	G
[27, 28]	2012	E	C	DI	FA	DE	NI	G
[30]	2012	E	C	NI	FZ	CI	NI	CC
[31]	2014	E	C	NI	FA	DE/QoS	NI	CC
[29]	2008	E	C	CE	FZ	DE/O	NI	G

Table 2. Most relevant values

Most relevant			
C1	E	(21)	100%
C2	C	(17)	80,95%
C3	CE	(13)	61,90%
C4	S/A	(6)	28,57%
C5	DE	(6)	28,57%
C6	FM	(14)	66,67%
C7	BP	(10)	47,62%

In terms of the information source, it is possible to note that many works use direct experience, that is, a participant interacts with other and evaluates him. Also, the in formation source is presented in a customized method, such as, STORE [17] that uses several business performance indicators to compose the trust indicator, and Javaid et al. [20] use several indicators to compose the reputation, such as, collaboration, operational resources, operational costs, feedback, among others.

Comprising the VO's phase characteristic, the most part of the analyzed works address the VO's creation/formation phase, supporting the search and selection process [7]. Also, others articles address the Dissolution phase, collecting new evaluations referring to new transactions. The VO's application characteristic refers to the object the reputation/trust system is applied for. Thus, the most part is related to the VO's business partners and fewer works present the application in a VO that uses the resources provided by grid or cloud computing.

So, the most relevant characteristics were summarized in the Table 2. According to the summarized results it is possible to note that the most of analyzed works present the following characteristics: explicit information type, continuous value representation, centralized network model, sum and average aggregation method, direct experience information source, and VO's formation phase related to business partners.

Through the application of the proposed taxonomy, it is possible to note that the reputation or trust systems and models are mostly applied at the level of business partners, and to calculate/evaluate the trust or reputation, the feedback ratings (direct experience) are mostly used. However, in addition to feedback rating, other indicators can be used together to assess the reputation/trust value of members, for example, STORE [17] uses the business performance indicators.

Also, there is a gap in the reputation systems/trust models applied in a cloud based VO, that is, a VO that uses the resources of a cloud provider to achieve a common business goals. In this sense, three articles are applied into this context. In [30], trust is used for resource scheduling in a cloud based VO, in [31] a trust model is presented and in [8] a confidence indicator coping with cloud providers is presented.

The gap in the cloud based VO's indicates that there is a growing trend and a newest application area. The first work was performed in 2012 [30] identified by the systematic review process. In addition, further studies are necessary in a cloud based VO's addressing the reputation and trust concepts, and its application in this context, just as the adaptation or study in virtual organizations of other reputation/trust systems that are intended for cloud computing and are applied in other contexts, such as, a platform to recommend cloud services based on reputation for clients [37].

All in all, it was not possible to identify a reputation system applied in a cloud based VO, to manage, update and establish the trust from business partners to a cloud provider.

6 Related Work

Wang and Vassileva [14] present a survey about the application of the trust and reputation concepts in the web service search process. This work generated a taxonomy that allowed the classification of these works, by means of three characteristics: centralized or decentralized, person/agent or resource, and global or customized [14].

Tavakolifard and Almeroth [15] present a taxonomy for trust and reputation systems in general with some characteristics, such as information type, value type, among others. In addition, it is presented several challenges as future work, which are related to issues existent in these current systems that are related to feedback generation, distribution and aggregation.

Hendrikx et al. [1] present a survey and a classification taxonomy applied to reputation systems in general. This work address a taxonomy with common characteristics, such as, information source, context, representation, aggregation, network model, among others and also presents a set of uncommon characteristics, such as, node organization (structured and unstructured), interoperability (open and proprietary), control (rules and incentives/penalties), among others.

Dellarocas [40] presents a survey with challenges and future directions in the research and development of the trust and reputation systems. Also, it is presented some issues related to implementation, use, and evaluation of these mechanisms.

Resnick et al. [9] introduce the reputation concept and its application through reputation systems. This work describes some issues in the application of reputation systems, such as, how the feedback is collected and distributed, and the reputation should help to distinguish between trusted and untrusted people/enterprise/partners, among others.

Therefore, through the related works it is possible to note that none has presented a taxonomy and classified the reputation systems or trust models that are applied in

Virtual Organization, considering their life-cycle's phases, which technology is used or where it is applied (business partners, cloud or grid providers), among other factors, such as: customized information source, hybrid network model, and hybrid aggregation method.

7 Conclusions and Future Work

This paper presented a classification taxonomy for reputation systems and trust models that are used in Virtual Organization. The taxonomy was based on some related work available in the specialized literature and other articles obtained through a systematic review process.

The proposed classification taxonomy is based on seven characteristics: information type, network model, value representation, aggregation methodology, information source, VO's phase and VO's application. Through the proposed taxonomy it was possible to classify and compare the works involving trust and reputation systems that are applied in Virtual Organization context.

In order to apply the proposed taxonomy, a systematic review process was carried out, comprising 286 articles that after some filtering processes remained for analysis and classification 22, which were related to reputation systems and trust models applied in VO's.

Through the results of the application of the proposed taxonomy, it is possible to note that the reviewed papers present reputation systems, trust models, trust indicators and the use of trust in access control in a VO's context. Also, it was possible to identify relationships between the characteristics, gaps in the analyzed systems. The mostly reviewed works calculate the reputation/trust value for business partners and are more applied in the VO's formation phase, where it supports the decision-making during the search and selection of these partners guided by reputation/trust value.

Through the reviewed works and the taxonomy's application, it was not possible to identify a reputation system that is applied in a cloud based VO's to manage, update and establish the trust from business partners to a cloud provider.

Besides that, it is possible to identify a growing trend in cloud based VO's indicating that it as a new area (systematic review process identified first work in 2012 [30]), that need further studies in several concepts such as trust, reputation, access control, among others and their applications in this context.

Finally, as future work, it is intended to add new characteristics to this taxonomy, and improve this taxonomy for the application in other scenarios and collaborative networks, such as, Virtual Enterprises.

References

1. Hendrikx, F., Bubendorfer, K., Chard, R.: Reputation systems: a survey and taxonomy. J. Parallel Distrib. Comput. **75**, 184–197 (2015)
2. Squicciarini, A.C., Paci, F., Bertino, E.: Trust establishment in the formation of virtual organizations. Comput. Stand. Interfaces. **33**, 13–23 (2011)

3. Camarinha-Matos, L.M., Afsarmanesh, H., Galeano, N., Molina, A.: Collaborative networked organizations – concepts and practice in manufacturing enterprises. Comput. Ind. Eng. **57**, 46–60 (2009)
4. Arenas, A.E., Aziz, B., Silaghi, G.C.: Reputation management in collaborative computing systems. Secur. Commun. Networks. **3**, 546–564 (2010)
5. Neata, S., Urzica, A., Florea, A.M.: Trust model for virtual organizations. In: Proceedings of the 2011 13th SYNASC, pp. 357–364. IEEE, Washington, DC, USA (2011)
6. Sabater, J., Sierra, C.: Review on computational trust and reputation models. Artif. Intell. Rev. **24**, 33–60 (2005)
7. Kerschbaum, F., Haller, J., Karabulut, Y., Robinson, P.: PathTrust: a trust-based reputation service for virtual organization formation. In: Stølen, K., Winsborough, W.H., Martinelli, F., Massacci, F. (eds.) iTrust 2006. LNCS, vol. 3986, pp. 193–205. Springer, Heidelberg (2006). doi:10.1007/11755593_15
8. Bilecki, L.F., Fiorese, A.: A confidence indicator model for virtual organization creation in cloud computing environment. In: Afsarmanesh, H., Camarinha-Matos, L.M., Lucas Soares, A. (eds.) PRO-VE 2016. IAICT, vol. 480, pp. 200–211. Springer, Cham (2016). doi:10.1007/978-3-319-45390-3_18
9. Resnick, P., Kuwabara, K., Zeckhauser, R., Friedman, E.: Reputation systems. Commun. ACM **43**, 45–48 (2000)
10. Alawamleh, M., Popplewell, K.: Risk in virtual organisation: a case study. Int. J. Netw. Virtual Organ. **11**, 142–155 (2012)
11. Li, M., Yu, Y., Huang, Z.: a group-choose model for partner selection in virtual organization. In: Proceedings of the 2011 IEEE Ninth DASC, pp. 674–681. IEEE, Washington, DC, USA (2011)
12. Gambetta, D.: Can We Trust Trust? In: Trust: Making and Breaking Cooperative Relations, pp. 213–237 (2000)
13. Mousa, H., Ben Mokhtar, S., Hasan, O., Younes, O., Hadhoud, M., Brunie, L.: Trust management and reputation systems in mobile participatory sensing applications: a survey. Comput. Networks. **90**, 49–73 (2015)
14. Wang, Y., Vassileva, J.: Toward trust and reputation based web service selection: a survey. Trans. Syst. Sci. Appl. **3**, 118–132 (2007)
15. Tavakolifard, M., Almeroth, K.C.: A taxonomy to express open challenges in trust and reputation systems. J. Commun. **7**, 538–551 (2012)
16. Kitchenham, B., Charters, S.: Guidelines for performing systematic literature reviews in software engineering version 2.3. Engineering **45**, 1051 (2007)
17. Haller, J.: STORE stochastic reputation service for virtual organisations. In: Karabulut, Y., Mitchell, J., Herrmann, P., Jensen, C.D. (eds.) IFIPTM 2008. ITIFIP, vol. 263, pp. 367–370. Springer, Boston, MA (2008). doi:10.1007/978-0-387-09428-1_25
18. Haller, J.: A Bayesian reputation system for virtual organizations. In: Gimpel, H., Jennings, N.R., Kersten, G.E., Ockenfels, A., Weinhardt, C. (eds.) Negotiation, Auctions, and Market Engineering. LNBIP, vol. 2, pp. 171–178. Springer, Heidelberg (2008). doi:10.1007/978-3-540-77554-6_12
19. Mashayekhy, L., Grosu, D.: A reputation-based mechanism for dynamic virtual organization formation in grids. In: 2012 41st International Conference on Parallel Processing, pp. 108–117 (2012)
20. Javaid, S., Majeed, A., Afzal, H.: A reputation management system for efficient selection of disaster management team. In: Proceedings of ICACT 2013, pp. 829–834 (2013)
21. Avila-Rosas, A., Luck, M.: A direct reputation model for VO formation. In: Pěchouček, M., Petta, P., Varga, L.Z. (eds.) CEEMAS 2005. LNCS, vol. 3690, pp. 460–469. Springer, Heidelberg (2005). doi:10.1007/11559221_46

22. Kerschbaum, F.: A verifiable, centralized, coercion-free reputation system. In: Proceedings of the 8th ACM Workshop on Privacy in the Electronic Society, pp. 61–70 (2009)
23. Papaioannou, T.G., Stamoulis, G.D.: Reputation-based estimation of individual performance in collaborative and competitive grids. Futur. Gener. Comput. Syst. **26**, 1327–1335 (2010)
24. Arasteh, M., Amini, M., Jalili, R.: A trust and reputation-based access control model for virtual organizations. In: ISCISC 2012, pp. 121–127 (2012)
25. Chen, T.-Y., Chen, Y.-M., Lin, C.-J., Chen, P.-Y.: A fuzzy trust evaluation method for knowledge sharing in virtual enterprises. Comput. Ind. Eng. **59**, 853–864 (2010)
26. Dessi, N., Pes, B., Fugini, M.G.: A distributed trust and reputation framework for scientific grids. In: IEEE RCIS Proceedings, pp. 265–274 (2009)
27. Kaur, D., SenGupta, J.: P2P trust and reputation model for securing grid resource management. In: ICAESM Proceedings, pp. 524–529 (2012)
28. Kaur, D., SenGupta, J.: A trust model based on P2P trust models for secure global grids. In: International Conference on Trust, Security and Privacy in Computing and Communications, pp. 1103–1108 (2012)
29. Ni, X., Luo, J.: A clustering analysis based trust model in grid environment supporting virtual organizations. In: Proceedings of the 2008 AINAW, pp. 100–105 (2008)
30. Lu, K., Jiang, H., Li, M., Zhao, S., Ma, J.: Resources collaborative scheduling model based on trust mechanism in cloud. In: Proceedings of 2012 IEEE TrustCom, pp. 863–868 (2012)
31. Qi, L., Dou, W., Ni, J., Xia, X., Ma, C., Liu, J.: A trust evaluation method for cloud service with fluctuant QoS and flexible SLA. In: Proceedings of 2014 ICWS, pp. 345–352. IEEE (2014)
32. Mun, J., Shin, M., Jung, M.: A goal-oriented trust model for virtual organization creation. J. Intell. Manuf. **22**, 345–354 (2011)
33. Petri, I., Rana, O., Rezgui, Y., Silaghi, G.C.: Evaluating trust in peer-to-peer service provider communities. In: 2011 Proceedings of CollaborateCom, pp. 407–414 (2011)
34. Vavilis, S., Petković, M., Zannone, N.: A reference model for reputation systems. Decis. Support Syst. **61**, 147–154 (2014)
35. Silva, V.T., Hermoso, R., Centeno, R.: A hybrid reputation model based on the use of organizations. In: Hübner, J.F., Matson, E., Boissier, O., Dignum, V. (eds.) COIN -2008. LNCS, vol. 5428, pp. 111–125. Springer, Heidelberg (2009). doi:10.1007/978-3-642-00443-8_8
36. Lin, H., Li, Z., Huang, Q.: Multifactor hierarchical fuzzy trust evaluation on peer-to-peer networks. Peer Peer Netw. Appl. **4**, 376–390 (2011)
37. Noor, T.H., Sheng, Q.Z., Yao, L., Dustdar, S., Ngu, A.H.H.: CloudArmor: Supporting Reputation-Based Trust Management for Cloud Services. IEEE Trans. Parallel Distrib. Syst. **27**, 367–380 (2016)
38. Xiong, L., Liu, L.: Peertrust: Supporting reputation-based trust for peer-to-peer electronic communities. IEEE TKDE **16**, 843–857 (2004)
39. Zamanian, M., Mohsenzadeh, M., Nassiri, R.: A novel framework for virtual organization creation on cloud. In: Camarinha-Matos, L.M., Afsarmanesh, H. (eds.) PRO-VE 2014. IAICT, vol. 434, pp. 435–442. Springer, Heidelberg (2014). doi:10.1007/978-3-662-44745-1_43
40. Dellarocas, C.: The digitization of word of mouth: promise and challenges of online feedback mechanisms. Manage. Sci. **49**, 1407–1424 (2003)

Exploratory Study on Risk Management in Open Innovation

João Rosas[1,3(✉)], Paula Urze[1,4], Alexandra Tenera[1,5], António Abreu[2,3], and Luis M. Camarinha-Matos[1,3]

[1] Faculty of Sciences and Technology, NOVA University of Lisbon, 2829-516 Monte de Caparica, Portugal
{jrosas, cam}@uninova.pt, {pcu, abt}@fct.unl.pt
[2] Instituto Politécnico de Lisboa, Rua Conselheiro Emídio Navarro 1, 1959-007 Lisbon, Portugal
ajfa@dem.isel.ipl.pt
[3] Uninova Institute, Centre of Technology and Systems, Lisbon, Portugal
[4] CIUHCT – Interuniversity Center for the History of Science and Technology, Lisbon, Portugal
[5] UNIDEMI/SEM, Systems Engineering and Management, Lisbon, Portugal

Abstract. Open innovation is a strategy with increasing adoption by value-seeking companies using or sharing technology with the outside world. But this strategy is also accompanied by risk. However, risk management seems to have been overlooked by researchers on open innovation networks. This exploratory work clarifies to what extent the issue of risk has been considered in open innovation research. Presented results are based on interviews and analysis of existing literature on open innovation.

Keywords: Open innovation · Risk management · Collaborative Networks · Text mining

1 Introduction

The combination of ideas from Collaborative Networks (CN) and Open Innovation (OI) is creating new synergies through which companies seek collaborative innovation practices outside their boundaries [1]. Although the topic of OI is receiving considerable attention in the last years, and a progressive opening of the boundaries of companies has been taking place, this openness is not immune to risks.

Open innovation is on a growing trend, as suggested by a recent survey [2], which found that 79% of company executives believe that their companies were effectively gaining from open innovation, and more specifically, from using innovations from other industries. Furthermore, 71% of the enquired entrepreneurs hoped to increase their investment in OI-based projects in the following year. Their motivation is to increase commercial success and share risk, as new products and services have always been prone to failures, as illustrated by the 102 paradigmatic examples of product failures reported in [3]. But failure is intrinsic to innovation processes [4]. A recent work curiously titled "*failure is the mother of innovation*" [5] offers the following

L.M. Camarinha-Matos et al. (Eds.): PRO-VE 2017, IFIP AICT 506, pp. 527–540, 2017.
DOI: 10.1007/978-3-319-65151-4_47

quote: "*Many people dream of success. Success can only be achieved through repeated failure and introspection. Success represents the one percent of your work that results from the 99 percent that is called failure*", which constitutes a paramount driver of the open innovation dynamics.

According to [6], the failure rate of new products is defined as the percentage of new products that are introduced in the market and then fail to meet the commercial expectations. Based on this definition, this work mentions several empirical studies which show an average failure rate of 35%. But considering a less strict notion of failure rate, not just commercial but also including concepts, ideas and prototypes that did not go further, the failure rate is much higher, although difficult to assess because these cases are usually not reported. Therefore, and according to the mentioned study, common belief arguably puts the number of failure rate above 80%. Complementarily, Table 1 shows a number of cases collected from online media documents regarding organizations, news products and open innovation, which are in the neighborhood of this value.

Table 1. Failure manifestations.

Case	Value	Ref.
Startups ending in failure	90%	[7]
Business partnership failures	80%	[8]
Introduction of new products	40% to 90%(1)	[9, 10]
Failure rate in Open Innovations	40% to 70%(2)	[11]

(1) Depending of the category of products; (2) in food and beverage products

Unfortunately, beyond the food and beverage example in this table, figures concerning OI failure rates were difficult to find. But the openness and partnership-based characteristics of OI suggest that we can extrapolate from these numbers and consider that OI failures might also be leveled to high values. Furthermore, OI has got its own specific risks. For instance, "*lack of awareness of the benefits of co-operating*", "*limited information on functional capabilities of potential partners*" and "*limited information on trustworthiness*" were identified as OI failure causes in [12].

Therefore, the risk of failure is intrinsic to OI. However, something which causes some surprise is the apparent absence of literature addressing risk in open innovation. For example, a search performed in Publish or Perish [13] for publications between 2013 and 2017 which had "open", "innovation" and "risk", as keywords in titles of the papers, provided just 10 results, 4 of which were published in 2016. On the other hand, a similar search, using the same criteria, for literature with "risk", "supply", and "chain" in papers' titles provided 1090 results, which amounts to 100 times more than the previous search for OI. Although we could search with other keywords, this order of magnitude between the amounts of literature in these two areas may indicate that risk has been overlooked in OI literature. This contrasts with the failure rates manifestations mentioned before.

Therefore, it is important to find out to which extent and which aspects of risk are addressed in open innovation literature. The objective of this work is, therefore, to perform an exploratory analysis of risk in OI in order to contribute to clarify its nature, namely the most important dimensions. This analysis is based on testimonies of participants in open innovation projects and analysis of open innovation literature, using a text mining approach.

The remaining of this paper addresses Open Innovation and Risk Management, which is then followed by the description of the exploratory analysis, the result analysis, and future work.

2 Background

2.1 Open Innovation

Innovation and its impacts on social, economic and political markets are widely acknowledged among policymakers and other stakeholders as an important endeavor. Recently, there has been a dense production of literature on the importance of innovation in contemporary societies [14].

The term innovation has become part of the public and political discourse and indelibly marks the various scientific areas. Various definitions of innovation are available. The one that is usually given states that innovation occurs when the invention reaches the market [15]. The concept of open-innovation (OI) has reassessed the role of innovation in the current context of the global economy [16, 17], contributing to updating innovation networks. OI has both academic and business relevance, bearing in mind that R&D activities are increasingly distributed, collaborative, and global, requiring novel forms of governance. The OI concept introduced by Chesbrough in 2003 [16] broke with the classical linear model associated with the paradigm of closed innovation and introduced new challenges in the process. OI is, by definition, "open" and shows some facet of "public domain". When promoted by the states, governments and international public institutions, it becomes an important driver of the development of innovation in society in general.

But OI is also a "game" between public and private knowledge sources, being crucial to balance these two parts. On one hand, companies want to be unique in terms of the products and processes they offer, an aim that seems to be a paradox in relation to OI itself. On the other hand, they gain essential value to their internal products by making them available in the market. OI is a continuous process balancing knowledge that cannot be made available and must be kept secret by the company and other knowledge that must be disclosed to the market.

If companies want to incorporate the concept of OI and make it part of their market strategy they must be at the cutting edge of technology and at the forefront of innovation itself. If this is not the case, they can lose their expert knowledge to other companies who may utilize this knowledge to develop newer products that might surpass those initially presented by the leading company. As a result, these companies may also take the driving position in the market.

Thus, although an OI approach may create positive outcomes, it also bares some risk. Thus, companies should have a proper strategy to protect innovation within their organizations, to generate boundaries and make achievements measurable. The governance model that various collaborating partners have (large companies, start-ups, S&T community, and others) is also very important [18]. When organizations work in an OI environment they must be aware of the greater risks involved in order to keep their competitive edge.

2.2 Base Concepts in Risk Management

According to the ISO 31000 standard [19], risk can be defined as a concept which expresses the effect of uncertainty on achieving pre-established objectives, in which an effect can be seen as a positive or negative deviation from an expected outcome. Risk is usually characterized by establishing associations between events and consequences, and corresponding likelihoods of events occurrence. Uncertainty represents a state, which arises from deficient (or lacking) information or understanding related to the events, consequences or likelihoods.

Risk Management corresponds to a set of activities that organizations use to control the many risks which may undermine their ability to achieve objectives [19]. Organizations try to manage these risks, which implies, among other aspects, an accurate identification of their sources, modes and effects. Then risks are leveled to allowable "levels", namely, reducing the likelihood of events or minimize their severity. Risk sources may come from different contexts, so there will always be some degree of uncertainty during the development of any project, particularly in the conceptual and design phases, because we are not able to have a complete picture of all factors that may affect projects.

Globalization brings higher opportunities, namely through possible involvement in global value chains, but also higher hazards and unknowns, so different types of risks must be considered since early stages and during all project life. As such, for example, since 2008, Portuguese public tenders have compulsory specifications for risk activities. It is required that contractors have to perform risk management activities process [20], demanding for contractual rules which directly or indirectly concern risk sharing and transferring, benefit sharing, and establishing rules for situations of non-compliance of contracting parties with the work plan of the public contractor [21]. This induces the need to add additional risk activities for risk and uncertainty modeling and scheduling in public tender proposals [22].

Also in 2011 the ISO Technical Committee on Information Security Risk Management updated their corporate or enterprise processes [23] incorporating ISO 31000 standard on "Risk management - principles and guidelines" [19] and identified associated tools [24], which are mostly focused on negative risk management and security practices, while also reinforcing the use of several classical risk tools as Brainstorming, SWOT and scenario analysis, FMEA (Failure-Mode-and-Effects) analysis [25].

More recently, since 2015, the idea of risk-based thinking and knowledge management has been spreading on enterprise management processes, embedding risk management more deeply on current companies' management practices [26]. This trend is aligned with the classical international standard on Project, Programme and

Portfolio Management practices and competencies approaches [27–29], and introduces on the enterprise's processes not only hazard and negative risks but also opportunities or positive risks management.

3 The Exploratory Study

As mentioned previously, this work consists of a study of the risk aspects present in OI literature, while assuming a risk management perspective on OI. A text mining knowledge extraction process based on a risk taxonomy is adopted.

3.1 Methodological Steps

The adopted method for risk-related OI literature analysis includes the following steps:

- Get aware of standards concerning risk from a risk management perspective.
- Propose of a taxonomy of risks, as a result of the previous step.
- Collect further evidence from experts through interviews.
- Collect a corpus composed of open innovation literature which also addresses risks.
- Use of the risk taxonomy as input to a text mining process in order to discover which factors or dimensions of risk are more emphasized in the OI literature.
- Evaluate the obtained results.

3.2 A Risk Management Based Taxonomy

Considering international standards on entrepreneurial management process risk and project management professional practices, namely, ISO 21500, ISO 31000 and PMI global standards PMBOK®Guide, a reference risk management structure can be organized as a taxonomy as illustrated in Fig. 1. This taxonomy identifies main risk management processes and sub-processes and associated risk tools. An aspect on this taxonomy which will be mentioned recurrently consists of the positive and negative aspects of risk.

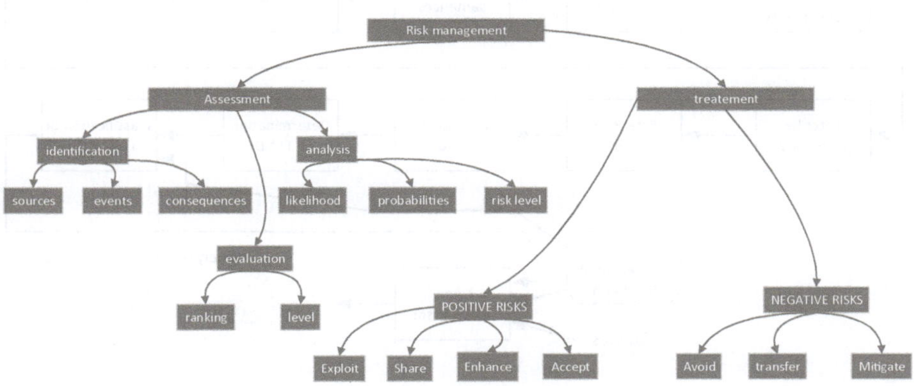

Fig. 1. Conceptual representation of the risk taxonomy.

This taxonomy shows that risk management includes two principal dimensions, namely, assessment and treatment, and that each dimension is also split in more granular aspects. For instance, risk assessment, on the left side of the figure, requires the identification of the source events and consequences. An example of a risk assessment method which addresses these aspects is the Failure Mode and Effects Analysis.

The risk management taxonomy is an input for the next step of our analysis of the literature concerning OI.

3.3 The Text Mining Process

Much of the available information is an unstructured format, like the many documents that are written in natural language. But, this information holds valuable knowledge, which may become reusable if transformed by some process into a more structured format, allowing knowledge extraction. This process is called Text Mining [30].

A Text Mining process (TMP) can in general be used, for example, in the initial stages of a literature review, allowing identifying which documents are associated with topics of interest [31]. It can also be used in the extraction or discovery of knowledge that can be used, for instance, in the construction of ontologies [32]. In the context of our work, TMP is used to examine OI documents for the discovery of the more relevant risk dimensions.

Developing the Text Mining Process. A TMP follows a number of steps in which a specific technique is applied on a set of documents, usually named as corpus. A variety of such techniques are available and well established [30, 31]. Therefore, our TMP starts by preparing a corpus composed of literature related to OI and which also addresses risk. The whole text mining process is shown in Fig. 2.

As shown in the figure, the collected corpus in fed to TMP at the beginning of the process, in which the contents of each document is extracted. Each document is then

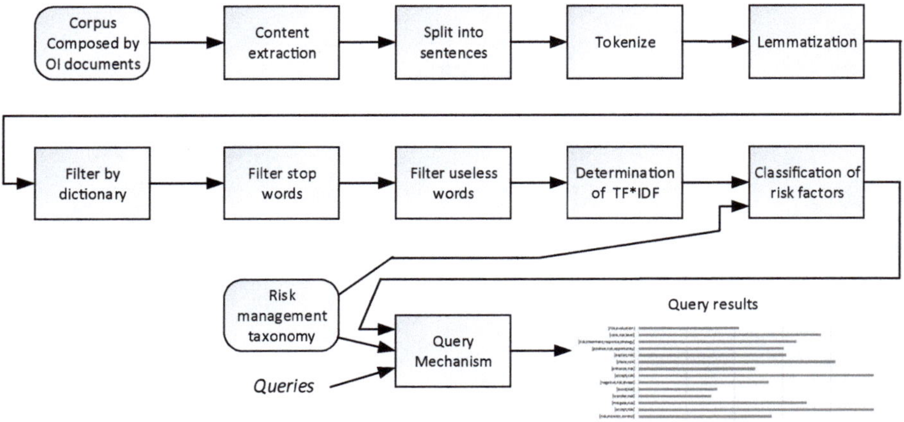

Fig. 2. Representation of the text mining process.

split into individual sentences (those that can be split by '.', '?', '!', and so on). Then each sentence is decomposed into individual words, in a step usually named as tokenization. Each word is then subject to a lemmatization operation. After that, each word that is not in the dictionary is removed from each sentence. The next process is to eliminate words that have no meaning from the point of view of Text Mining, which is usually described as "stop words" [31]. After that, some words that are considered useless from the point of view of risk in OI are eliminated (actually, we did not use this feature, but reserved it for later use).

The next step consists in the statistical analysis of the words from each document and each sentence. This step provides two Term Frequency (TF) tables, one that accounts the frequency of each word in a document and another that accounts the frequency of each word in a sentence.

Our approach to account words frequency within each sentence, instead of within the same document, was inspired in [33], which allows increasing the granularity of the knowledge extraction process. For example, it has more meaning that two terms, e.g. "risk" and "management", appear in the same sentence than in separate sentences of a document. Another approach to account associated terms is to use n-grams [34].

Many text mining methods also perform an adjustment to attenuate the importance level of the most frequent words. That is, if a word appears very frequently across the documents in a corpus, then it is considered a common word, without relevant meaning. Therefore, the relative frequencies TF obtained before are adjusted by a function called Inverse Document Frequency (IDF) [35].

Finally, we proceed to the classification of the risk factors that are present in the risk taxonomy introduced before. The classification process picks each sentence from documents and compares it to keywords present in the taxonomy. Depending on the correspondences between each sentence and the keywords, two vectors u and v are created, one for a sentence and another for the keywords. Each component of the vector is filled with a value which corresponds to $u_i = TF_i * IDF_i$ for vectur u and similarly for vector v. The comparison is made through a similarity function that corresponds to the determination of the cosine between the vectors of sentence u and keywords v using Eq. 1 [31].

$$cosine(\vec{u}, \vec{v}) = \frac{\sum_{i=1}^{n} u_i \times v_i}{\sqrt{\sum_{i=1}^{n} u_i^2} \times \sqrt{\sum_{i=1}^{n} v_i^2}} \quad (1)$$

After these steps, the last block of the TMP, the query mechanism, allows the user to input queries using the Prolog language (in our implementation). The results of a query are written to CSV files, which are then used to create charts allowing a better visualization of the answers provided by the query mechanism, as illustrated in the next section.

The whole process supported by an implementation in the JAVA language. A number of third party components were also used, such as API for reading the contents of PDF documents [36].

4 Exploratory Phase

In this section, we provide the results of the exploratory work concerning risk in OI. The discovery of risk aspects in OI may provide better results if we rely on a comprehensive exploratory approach divided into two complementary parts, and afterwards, synergistically combine them. These two lenses of analysis will allow reaching a deeper comprehensive understanding on the OI logic as well as of its relation with risk.

In the first part, we aim to obtain information regarding perception of risks in OI from participants in OI projects, namely from managers and engineers. This empirical research includes the construction of interviews scripts and *in-locu* observation. The targeted experts have deep experience and understanding on OI, but do not usually disseminate their knowledge, that is, they rarely publish papers. The viable way to obtain empirical knowledge from them consists of targeted interviews.

In a second part, we aim to obtain information regarding risk in OI from researchers who work in the scientific and academic fields. With some exceptions, these researchers do not usually participate directly in OI projects, those of an industrial and commercial nature, but are dedicated to the study of the phenomenon and dynamics of OI. These people achieve more aggregated and theoretical knowledge, which they disseminate mainly through the publication of papers. In this case, given the availability of papers which come from these researchers, a practical method to reach that knowledge consists on the utilization of Text Mining.

4.1 Interviews to OI Practitioners

During an OI network event in 2015 [37], twelve interviews were conducted with participants in open innovation projects and holding different positions to triangulate the gathered qualitative data. The participants included product development managers, project coordinators, system developers and a CEO. The questions aimed at clarifying the subject of risk in IO projects. According to experts' opinion, the risks and the way they are seen in OI are listed in Table 2.

An example of novel capability (benefit "i.a" in Table 2) is the case of the Brisa/Via-Verde project that focused on moving from a closed to an open electronic toll collection (ETC) system. According to the CEO of the Brisa company, this move resulted in a significate reduction of costs, e.g. one-third decrease in the cost of the system used to electronically identify vehicles based onboard radio frequency identifier; a kind of RFID (Dedicated Short Range Communication - DSRC) antenna. This reduction resulted from a change from a single supplier to a multi-supplier model. The former unique supplier experienced a reduction of its market share to a half when having to face a crescent competition, with obvious benefit to the customer.

As far as risks are concerned, a reported example (risk "i.a" in Table 2) was the taking over of a market position by a start-up involved in an innovation project. The problem was not in the start-up itself but in the lack of clear competing rules in a science and engineering area without clear subcontracting procedures. This demonstrates the need for creating contractual rules to be agreed by all partners in order to avoid similar situations.

Table 2. Results of interviews to OI practitioners.

Identified risks and benefits
Open innovation risks: i. For user-organizations a. Potentially fragile competitive advantages considering others may use and adopt shared achievements; b. Core knowledge differentiation might be blurred considering competitors run on concurrency; c. Potential use of shared knowledge and open specifications of offered services increases the risk of malicious attacks. ii. For product/service organizations a. Potentially fragile competitive advantages considering others may use and adopt shared achievements; b. "Opportunity window" related to novel products or services might be difficult to maintain; c. Core knowledge differentiation might be blurred considering competitors run on concurrency; d. Increases the risk of markets being occupied by competitors that worked and got competencies in common OI projects.
Open-innovation potential benefits: i. For user-organizations a. Novel capabilities based on the network effect, considering the potential to develop competing product/service organizations; b. Potential cost reductions of required resources, products or services supporting innovation processes; c. Potential reduction of dependency paths namely those associated with vendor lock-in situations [16]. ii. For product/service organizations a. Provides easier access to competencies; b. Promotes a faster convergence to normalized (generally adopted) processes and technologies; c. Potential decrease of production costs induced by faster generalization and normalization trends; d. Faster network effects for known and novel products and services; e. Reduction of dependency on workers with specific competencies; f. Substitution of developers is easier considering that competencies tend to become normalized and widespread.

4.2 Using the Text Mining Process

The TMP described in the previous section was applied to a set of OI documents, the corpus, mentioned before. The objective is to find out which risk dimensions are most mentioned in these documents. For that, we proceeded as follows:

- Using Google Scholar, search for articles that contain "open" and "innovation" in their title and that also mention the term "risk" in their contents.
  - We collected the first 110 PDF documents.
- Perform the TMP steps in these documents, namely splitting the documents in their corresponding sentences. Furthermore, each sentence was subjected to tokenization and remaining operations described before.
  - We obtained 35 535 sentences with 10103 distinct words.
- The words in the sentences were subjected to frequency determination.

- Document-term frequency (DTF) tables were obtained, one for the documents and one for the sentences.
- Using the DTF table and the risk factors presented before, each sentence was transformed into vectors.
- The keywords from the risk taxonomy were also transformed into vectors.
- Using the cosine similarity indicator, each sentence vector was compared with the keywords vector, using the similarity function (Eq. 1).
- A table was generated comprising each risk factor and the frequency they appear in the documents, according to the similarity result.
- A risk factor frequency was increased whenever cosine provides a value above a 0.9 threshold.

The result of this process is illustrated in Fig. 3, which presents the risk factors that are more frequently mentioned in the OI literature. As illustrated, "risk management" seems to be highlighted in the literature as an important aspect of OI. This confirms our

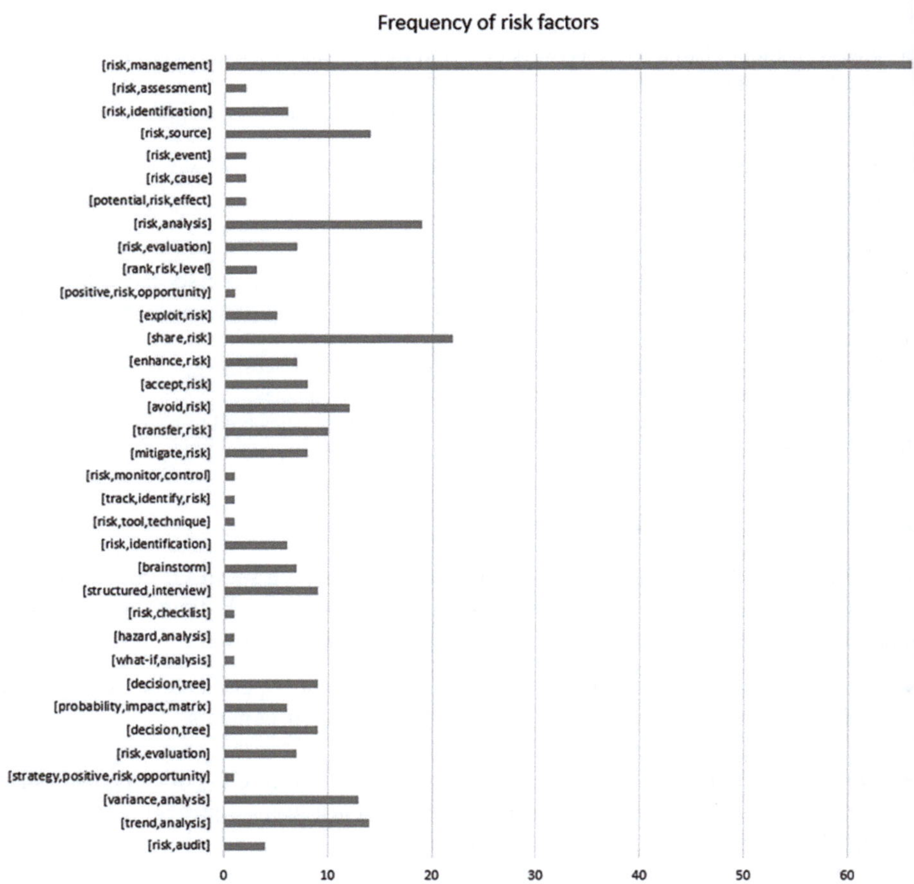

Fig. 3. Risk dimensions accounted in the OI documents.

intuition that if OI projects occur with a high level of failures, as mentioned before, then adequate risk management strategies must be adopted for the sake of sustainability. The sustainability aspect might be partially achieved through risk sharing which, according to the TMP results, is the second most identified factor in the literature. Perhaps entrepreneurs are also adopting OI as a way to share and mitigate these risks. The other aspects also identified refer to the analysis of risks, their effects, and eventual acceptance or avoidance, which point towards some risk assessment approach, such as Failure Mode and Effect Analysis (FMEA) [38]. The utilization of FMEA in OI is illustrated in [18].

4.3 Results Discussion

As mentioned, the exploratory phase was split in two parts, performed using two complementary approaches. One was based on interviews with OI practitioners to obtain their empirical knowledge regarding OI risks. The other approach was based on the extraction of the knowledge using Text Mining on the literature provided by OI researchers.

Regarding interviews, the posterior compilation and interpretation of the various answers allowed a more specific perspective of risk in OI, as shown in Table 2. Although still preliminary, we can consider a classification framework based on risks versus benefits dimensions. Inside each dimension, the underlying factors were grouped in terms of organizational or product (or service) related ones. Furthermore, the consideration of risks versus benefits seems slightly similar to the positive versus negative risks specified in the Risk Management standard.

During the second part, the TMP allowed to highlight the risk dimensions which appeared more frequently in the OI literature. In this part, a risk management taxonomy was given a priory, which contrasts with the previous part, in which a preliminary classification framework was obtained a posteriori. The results collected from the TMP are of statistical nature. Based on the frequency of occurrences, we could infer risk management and risk sharing as important aspects related to failures in OI projects.

After this exploratory phase, a question that remains is whether OI projects can be considered just projects. If yes, then Risk Management standards may be adequate to manage risk in OI. On the other hand, risk management might not be suitable to deal with the specific risks of OI, such as the ones related to collaboration, openness, and know-how sharing aspects. A possible approach which might help clarifying these questions consists on synergistically combining the results from the two parts. For the first part, additional questions that focus on the more frequent dimensions, which surfaced during the TMP part, can be formulated. For the second part, the combination of both results may enable the synthesis of a risk taxonomy more suitable for OI.

5 Conclusions

This work involved an exploratory analysis of risk in open innovation. Initially, we came across that innovation projects are characterized by their high number of failures being thus necessary to rely on risk management techniques for sustainability.

On the other hand, risk literature in OI seems to be scarce, which is an aspect at odds considering a projected failure rate of OI projects. Therefore, to have a concrete perspective of risk in OI, two complementary activities were carried out during our research. The first one comprised interviews with experts in open innovation, which were performed during an OI workshop. The other activity consisted of the application of a Text Mining process aimed at identifying the risk factors which are highlighted in open innovation literature. Risk management and risk sharing were the more highlighted aspects by the Text Mining Process.

As for future work, we intend to perform a deeper analysis of risk factors in OI using complementary approaches like, for instance, Opinion Mining or Sentiment Analysis.

Acknowledgments. This work has been supported by Faculdade de Ciências e Tecnologia da Universidade Nova de Lisboa, by Uninova-CTS research unit, by national funds through FCT - Fundação para a Ciência e a Tecnologia within the research unit CTS - Centro de Tecnologia e Sistemas (project UID/EEA/00066/2013). The authors would like to thank all the institutions, by CIUHCT: Interuniversity Center for the History of Science and Technology, and by DEMI/FCT/UNL.

References

1. Appio, F.P., Martini, A., Massa, S., Testa, S.: Collaborative network of firms: antecedents and state-of-the-art properties. Int. J. Prod. Res. **55**(7), 2121–2134 (2016)
2. NineSigma: Survey Shows Innovation Budgets Increasing in 2015 (2015). http://www.ninesigma.com/news-and-events/press-releases//2014/survey-shows-innovation-budgets-increasing-in-2015. Seen on 2017/02/27
3. Cbinsights: When Corporate Innovation Goes Bad - The 102 Biggest Product Failures of all Time (2016). https://www.cbinsights.com/blog/corporate-innovation-product-fails/. Seen on 2017/02/27
4. Gillin, P.: How to encourage innovative thinking in your organization (2006). http://gillin.com/blog/2006/06/how-to-encourage-innovative-thinking-in-your-organization/. Seen on 2017/03/30
5. Sloane, P.: Failure is the mother of innovation (2012). http://www.innovationmanagement.se/imtool-articles/failure-is-the-mother-of-innovation/. Seen on 2017/03/30
6. Castellion, G., Markham, S.K.: Perspective: new product failure rates: influence of argumentum ad populum and self-interest. J. Prod. Innov. Manag. **30**(5), 976–979 (2013)
7. Patel, N.: 90% of startups fail: here's what you need to know about the 10% (2015), https://www.forbes.com/sites/neilpatel/2015/01/16/90-of-startups-will-fail-heres-what-you-need-to-know-about-the-10/#4993261e6679. Seen on 2017/03/30
8. Simoons, P.: The 80% rule of business partnerships (2013). https://www.petersimoons.com/2013/07/the-80-percent-rule/. Seen on 2017/03/25
9. Gourville, J.T.: Eager Sellers and Stony Buyers: Understanding the Psychology of New-Product Adoption. https://hbr.org/2006/06/eager-sellers-and-stony-buyers-understanding-the-psychology-of-new-product-adoption. Seen on 2017/03/25
10. Fisher, A.: Why most innovations are great big failures (2014). http://fortune.com/2014/10/07/innovation-failure/. Seen on 2017/02/20

11. Martinez, M.G. (ed.): Open Innovation in the Food and Beverage Industry. Elsevier, Cambridge (2013)
12. Hewitt-Dundas, N., Roper, S.: Exploring market failures in open innovation. Int. Small Bus. J. (2017). doi:10.1177/2F0266242617696347
13. Publish or Perish (2017). http://www.harzing.com/resources/publish-or-perish
14. Fagerberg, J., Martin, B.R., Andersen, E.S.: Innovation Studies. Oxford University Press, Oxford (2013)
15. Godinho, M.M.: Inovação em Portugal. Fundação Francisco Manuel dos Santos (2013)
16. Chesbrough, H.: Open Innovation: The New Imperative for Creating and Profiting from Technology. Harvard Business Press (2003)
17. West, J., Salter, A., Vanhaverbeke, W., Chesbrough, H.: Open innovation: The next decade, Research Policy 43, pp. 805–811. Elsevier (2014)
18. Rosas, J., Macedo, P., Tenera, A., Abreu, A., Urze, P.: Risk assessment in open innovation networks. In: Camarinha-Matos, Luis M., Bénaben, F., Picard, W. (eds.) PRO-VE 2015. IFIP AICT, vol. 463, pp. 27–38. Springer, Cham (2015). doi:10.1007/978-3-319-24141-8_3
19. ISO 31000, Technical Committee, ISO/TC 262, Risk management – Principles and guidelines, ISO/IC (2009)
20. DL 18/2008, Ministério das Obras Públicas Transportes e Comunicações, Código dos Contratos Públicos (CCP), 29 Janeiro (2008)
21. Roxo, J.: Análises de Risco em Empreendimentos de Construção Civil: Do conceito à prática. Dificuldades e Limitações contratuais. 4º Encontro Nacional de Riscos, Segurança e Fiabilidade (ENRSF)/ESRA, IST, Lisboa Portugal, pp. 841–854, ISBN: 978-972-689-247-2. (2012)
22. Tenera, A.: A Gestão do Risco de Derrapagem da Duração de Projetos. 4º Encontro Nacional de Riscos, Segurança e Fiabilidade (ENRSF)/ESRA, IST, Lisboa Portugal, pp. 789–809 (2012). ISBN: 978-972-689-247-2
23. ISO/IEC 27005, Technical Committee, ISO/IEC JTC 1/SC 27, Information technology - Security techniques - Information security risk management, ISO/IEC (2011)
24. IEC 31010, Technical Committee, ISO/TC 262, Risk management – Risk assessment techniques, ISO/IC (2009)
25. Jodkowski, L.: Possibilities and Methods of Risk Assessment under ISO 9001: 2015. Int. J. Manag. Stud. Res. (IJMSR) **3**(10), 14–23 (2015)
26. ISO 9001, Technical Committee, ISO/TC 176/SC 2, Quality management systems – Requirements, ISO/TC 176 (2015)
27. PMI: A Guide to the Project Management Body of Knowledge (PMBOK® Guide), Project Management Institute (2013)
28. IPMA: Individual Competence Baseline for Project, Programme & Portfolio Management (ICB), International Project Management Association (2015)
29. ISO 21500, Technical Committee, ISO/TC 258, Guidance on project management, ISO/TC 258 (2015)
30. Weiss, S. M., Indurkhya, N., Zhang, T., & Damerau, F.: Text mining: predictive methods for analyzing unstructured information. Springer Science & Business Media (2010)
31. Aggarwal, C.C., Zhai, C.: A survey of text clustering algorithms. In: Mining Text Data, pp. 77–128. Springer, USA (2012)
32. Bloehdorn, S., Cimiano, P., Hotho, A., Staab, S.: An ontology-based framework for text mining. In: LDV Forum, vol. 20, No. 1, pp. 87–112 (2005)
33. Rajpathak, D.G.: An ontology based text mining system for knowledge discovery from the diagnosis data in the automotive domain. Comput. Ind. **64**(5), 565–580 (2013)
34. Cavnar, W.B., Trenkle, J.M.: N-gram-based text categorization. Ann. Arbor MI **48113**(2), 161–175 (1994)

35. Tokunaga, T., Makoto, I.: Text categorization based on weighted inverse document frequency. In Special Interest Groups and Information Process Society of Japan (SIG-IPSJ) (1994)
36. Apache PDFBox - A Java PDF Library. https://pdfbox.apache.org/
37. BIT - Brisa Group's hub for innovation. http://www.brisa.pt/en/Mobility-and-Innovation/Brisa-Inova%C3%A7%C3%A3o-e-Tecnologia
38. Stamatis, D. H.: Failure mode and effect analysis: FMEA from theory to execution. ASQ Quality Press (2003)

Sustainability Improvements Through CNs

The CPS and LCA Modelling: An Integrated Approach in the Environmental Sustainability Perspective

Andrea Ballarino, Carlo Brondi(✉), Alessandro Brusaferri, and Guido Chizzoli

ITIA-CNR Institute for Industrial Technologies and Automation,
12 Alfonso Corti, 20133 Milan, Italy
{andrea.ballarino,carlo.brondi,alessandro.brusaferri,
guido.chizzoli}@itia.cnr.it

Abstract. The present paper clarifies the methodological framework to implement the integration of Cyber Physical Systems (CPS) in the perspective of environmental sustainability. Firstly, authors identify main methodological, software and hardware pre-requisites enabling the use of CPS systems in accordance with the literature and environmental standards. Then, the paper focuses on the main barriers in the case the information is distributed along a flexible supply chain and identifies a methodology to coordinate environmental information from ubiquitous sources by the use of modularization. This methodology is applied in the field of energy management for the steel sector for different production lines. In particular, it is highlighted as the consumption tracking may be linked to the real-time management of suppliers and processing cycles in order to pursue strategies for environmental impact minimization. Results emphasized as the development of the CPS systems that are designed for sustainability can produce relevant results for the effective restrain of industrial environmental impacts.

Keywords: CPS · LCA · Industrial sustainability · Modular LCA · Industry 4.0

1 Application of CPS for Environmental Sustainability

The Cyber Physical Systems (CPS) are identified by many authors as key technology for the development of manufacturing industry in the next future [1–4]. Such technology in fact introduces a number of significant potential for production systems such as the ability to process a large amount of data in real time, the ability to optimize operations by flexible and automatic solutions, and finally the ability to enhance collaboration between different levels of the factory and suppliers.

In particular, some authors identify the features that are obtained through the CPS systems such as a prodromal condition for the actual sustainability of production systems [3–6]. Some authors emphasize also that the development of the CPS systems could lead further barriers to sustainability by massive production of devices and by causing significant social effects on employment market [3]. Despite such remarks, various beneficial contributions to sustainable manufacturing paradigm can be identified.

L.M. Camarinha-Matos et al. (Eds.): PRO-VE 2017, IFIP AICT 506, pp. 543–552, 2017.
DOI: 10.1007/978-3-319-65151-4_48

In the first place, the support of the CPS systems to Sustainable manufacturing can be performed through new instruments for sustainability policies. The Sustainable Manufacturing in fact requires the implementation of strategic objectives such as zero waste, the benign emissions, the use of renewable resources, the circular economy, the process efficiency, social investment, and the modification of trade criteria goods. Each of these objectives entails increasing complexity, operation intelligence and a growing integration between the operations along the supply chain and the facility [7–9]. The development of the CPS majorly affects these areas by increasing monitoring, collaboration and efficiency across several areas [1, 3] while in other cases the CPS constitutes the bulk of new sustainability-oriented technologies [6].

The second contribution of CPS regards the building of an infrastructure to ease the calculation of Key Performance Indicators (KPIs) for the sustainability of industrial practices. The environmental impact assessment of production operations, in fact, involves interdisciplinary areas and requires a data-intensive process. Such assessment increases in complexity with the concurrent increase of the production constrains. The development of CPS allows to reduce this convolution in calculation by capturing latent properties of ubiquitous systems. Furthermore, the independent behavior of CPS also enables to manage this exponential complexity in relation to response actions and decisional support [4]. Through such support, CPS makes possible to develop integrated environmental management systems that are constantly connected to the analytical values and environmental accounting and create a continuous stream of verifiable environmental information.

From another point of view, the implementation of CPS and industry paradigm 4.0 introduces a series of constraints that are needed to fully implement this potential capability. The main involved issues seem to concern the information role, its transfer, and the complexity management [5] as inevitable problems to be treated. Another important aspect is the reliability of data that are collected through sensor networks as well as their reuse [10–12].

CPS applications for sustainable manufacturing, by literature, include applications for circular economy in the modelling of Industrial Park [13], green computing to increase efficiency in energy consumption [1, 14] and other [6] applications.

2 Requirements for the LCA Integration Within the CPS Framework

The intended purpose of such work is to sequentially clarify pre-requisites, current barriers and potentialities for LCA integration within CPS. The use of CPS in the environmental perspective, may allow a real time quantification of the environmental impact of a set of productive activities that are subject to a certain variability. From one side, this usage enables most reliable Life Cycle Assessment (LCA) calculation in comparison to traditional ex-post LCAs. According to CPS framework, LCA seems a suitable methodology to be integrated within CPS to quantify environmental implication of a certain activity by virtue of certain characteristics: LCA is designed to provide quantitative data; LCA is directly connected to business areas that monitor the business flows and which provide monitoring data for Life Cycle Inventory (LCI) phase; taking a perspective on the entire life cycle, the LCA methodology manage data that are external to company boundaries; finally, the LCA methodology is well supported in standardization by various ISO standards in the international arena, and then the generation and verification of the environmental information tend to be more congruent between different countries.

The expected progression CPS functions is characterized by five hierarchical levels [15], each level corresponds to a stage of CPS functional development. Equally, it is possible to define a progression of functions for real-time analysis of environmental impact that can be linked with the LCA. Each of these layers includes a number of prerequisites regarding the different elements involved, such as the sensors, the data management systems, the simulation methods, and the standardization and optimization criteria (Fig. 1).

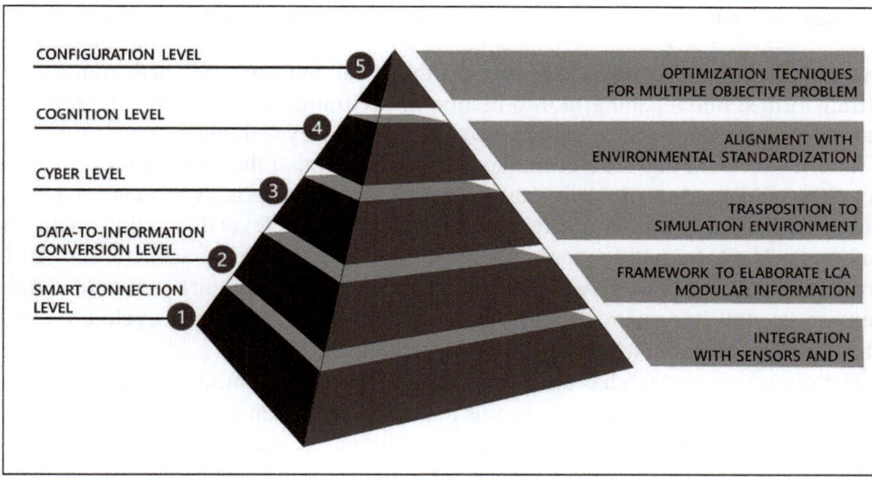

Fig. 1. Requirements for CPS use in the LCA framework

Smart connection level At this level, the challenge to create a reliable LCA from distributed data depends on the chance to record data on the environmental aspects and to bring them to a higher level.

Therefore, it is necessary that CPS glean data from a distributed network of data sources regarding direct tracking trough sensors or indirect tracking through Information Systems (IS). Such data should be attributed to local mass and energy balances for a set of activities. The data collection system should track consumption of materials, energy or items as well as solid, liquid or gaseous emissions. The sequence of data collection assumes different trends depending on the characteristics of the flow to be monitored.

As an example, the tracking of a homogeneous gaseous flow over the time will require an instantaneous flow rate measurement system while in the case the composition changes over time an extra measurement device is needed (e.g. a mass spectrograph) in order to identify the chemical composition. The data used by CPS systems is not necessarily derived from field sensors but can also be obtained through IS such as Enterprise

Resource Planning (ERP) or Supply Chain Management (SCM) tools. CPS should recognize and capture these data from remote systems through the use of complementary information that must travel together to the data on physical features. In this sense, methodologies such as the semantic web could support the identification of standard protocols for data transmission. The data collection system also influences the temporal trend of its tracking (e.g. solid waste can be monitored on a monthly basis while electric power consumption can be monitored on a shorter basis). It would therefore be important to understand through a preventive analysis which are the critical flows and the related measurement policies.

Another key issue concerns the monitoring cost. The calculation of a time-variant mass/energy balance can be expensive for a company. Therefore, the development of "smart inventory" systems allows to produce more information through a single measure or a measures combination. Such indirect measurement can require inference methods and data combination in order to extrapolate the investigated environmental aspects.

Data-to-information connection level At this level, the data collected from the field are transformed into meaningful information in environmental terms. As an example, it becomes possible to trace the carbon dioxide produced by a single task.

In terms of LCA this kind of transposition requires that the local impact is defined through a modification of traditional LCA calculation criteria. The Goal and Scope phases, for example, can become reconfigurable at an upper level depending on the end-user needs. The information storage becomes no longer a remote activity, instead the information is continuously available. Such a transformation requires a modularization of environmental information that no longer refers to the entire life cycle but can be considered as congruent assembly of gate-to-gate modules.

The modular approach has already been applied in the manufacturing environment [16]. A second important aspect concerns the final assessment quality that must be suitable for a major precision in comparison to traditional LCAs.

Data to be processed should be attributable to the same functional units and should be supplied with standard information to support upper level calculation as allocation and quality assessment. As a fundamental requirement, the application of the LCA modularization requires connecting the material and energy flow monitoring, namely the inventory of the environmental aspects, with the environmental profile of individual flows. Therefore data are associated with database that are external to the physical CPS. The databases roles include both data storing for long-term strategies and active capabilities in supporting CPS to govern the production systems operations [5]. These stored data, which are updated by a different rate in comparison to physical flow data, requires also an intermediate step for respective association in order to be referred to the same activity (e.g. an absorbed current should be referred both to a certain operation and to an incoming energy flow from a specific supplier).

Cyber level At this level, it becomes possible to express the aggregate environmental impact and to simulate the LCA-based environmental efficiency of the CPS through the mirroring of the behaviour of a production unit in a virtual environment. The CPS should express a function for instantaneous and predictive impact on the environment for the cumulated activities under its control. Simulation is the essential step to perform such activity. In environmental terms, environmental profile function can be calculated as modular variable environmental profile constituted by the instantaneous value of the different impact categories.

At this level, the CPS also coordinates with other analogous units to exchange information on other activities that have influence on its environmental impact. Also in this case, the communication should be supported by protocols aiming to coordinate and address information. Such aspect concerns the automatization of LCA procedures such as allocation of field measurements and information alignment. The CPS unit should report together with the final data, information on the overall quality of the calculation, complementary information on calculation criteria (allocations, the system boundaries, geography, period sampling etc.). In the absence of these complementary information, the environmental impact function risk to be inferred by incongruent modules leading to a worse result than the traditional LCA. Some examples of protocols for standardization of environmentally-related information has been studied for the UML language for the Manufacturing Execution System (MES) [17] and the Product Life Cycle Management (PLM) [18].

In terms of simulation criteria, different criteria can be linked to LCA. Discrete event simulation [19, 20] has been applied to model the environmental impact for different production scenarios. According to these criteria, modelling of the behaviour of a production unit is separated from its actual field operation, the same impact tends to depend on general purpose database.

The application of a simulation that is connected with the real time operational value can introduce a direct link with industry-driven data within simulation both in term of inventory data and performed assessment. In addition, the introduction of dynamic simulation methods allows to extend the LCA beyond its normal scope of and to create the basis for the application of the optimization criteria.

On the other hand, the creation of a CPS "virtual twin" requires the application of calibration methods. An initial calibration relates to the explicit link between environmental drivers and environmental effects within the simulation model. The LCA methodology is based on "black box" structure while the simulation requires a certain degree of explication for the links between the environmental drivers and their effects according to a logic of "grey box". In this sense, the modularization should be designed in such a way that the information might be cut out in the perspective use for the simulation. A second type of calibration regards the temporal correlation between the field measurements and simulation of an activity. If the sampling of the mass flows and energy are delayed in time with respect to the range of the simulation calculation system may inherit an implicit inaccuracy.

As an example, a certain input value function (e.g. a function for a processing material) may report constant value between two sampling moments while other input values (e.g. compressed air functions) are varying independently from the source behaviour. It appears therefore necessary to partially align the sampling times and simulation times. Finally, the time trend of some driver value that comes from remote sources can be unpredictable. It will be necessary therefore to use regression methods to reduce uncertainty in "time machine" simulation.

Cognition level At this level data from CPS level are further elaborated in order to provide key performance indicators that are compliant with existing environmental standards. At this level, it is also possible to link CPS data with other sustainability accounting systems (e.g. cost accounting or social accounting) or company accounting system (Fig. 2). The existence of misaligned industrial simulation areas can limit the transition from an accounting system to another due to the fact such areas are still not integrated (e.g. product design, process simulation, ergonomics, etc.). Further integration of simulation areas can create a holistic simulation area that affects different decision areas. In such sense, knowledge domain integration performed by ISA 95 and other standards can also foster CPS development.

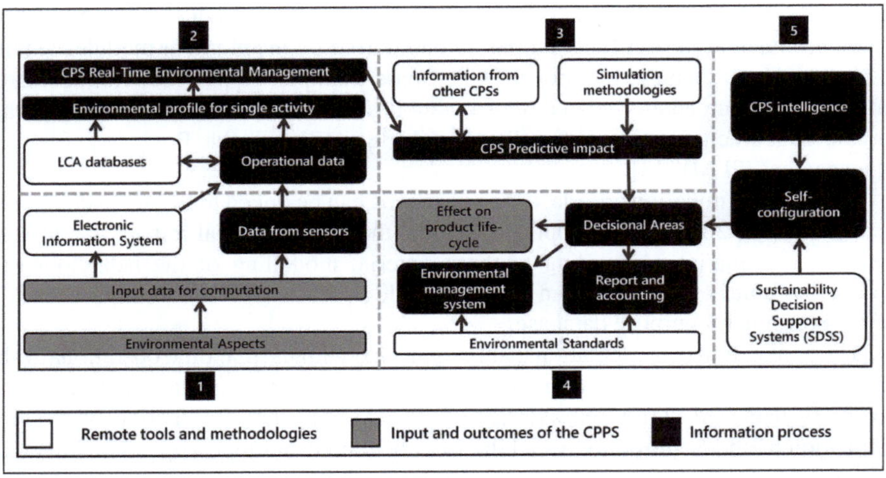

Fig. 2. Data elaboration in the environmental perspective through different CPS levels

In terms of environmental performance CPSs can pave the way to new generation of Environmental Management Systems (EMS) within companies through the creation of a continuous digitized assessment of environmental information. The modular and flexible structure of environmental data from CPSs should allow to quantify the environmental performance of different business areas as well as of different stages of the product life cycle.

Configuration level At this last stage, CPS can self-configure itself based on real time LCA outcomes, system constraints and Objective Functions (OF) related to sustainability targets or other targets. The proper development of this function requires that environmental optimization criteria are clearly addressed. LCA can be already applied for process optimization according to an environmental sustainability perspective. The general problem for optimization has a multi-objective nature cause to the distinctive features of the LCA characterization indicators, the key performance representation according to international standards, and the perspective integration of these indicators with other non-environmental performance indicators. In mathematical terms, the branch of the Sustainability Decision Support System includes a range of analytical support methods that are based on artificial intelligence (Expert System-ES, Genetic Algorithm-GA, Artificial Neural, Network-ANN, Intelligent Agents- IA, Case Based Reasoning-CBR), but also other Geographic Information System-GIS-based methodologies, Internet-based services, and Business Intelligence BI. In the presence of different criteria and priorities, effective automatic self-configuration by the CPSs exist in case multi-objective optimization system is transparently and congruently addressed.

3 Application of CPS to Energy Grids for LCA Based Optimization

The potential application of CPS systems has been explored in the case of an energy supply system for a European process industry company. The application of CPS framework was implemented in a smart grid in order to manage real-time data to optimize energy consumption in the sustainability perspective from the point of view of the final consumer industry. These CPSs can exchange real-time information on energy attributes and real-time demand in a coordinate way (Fig. 3).

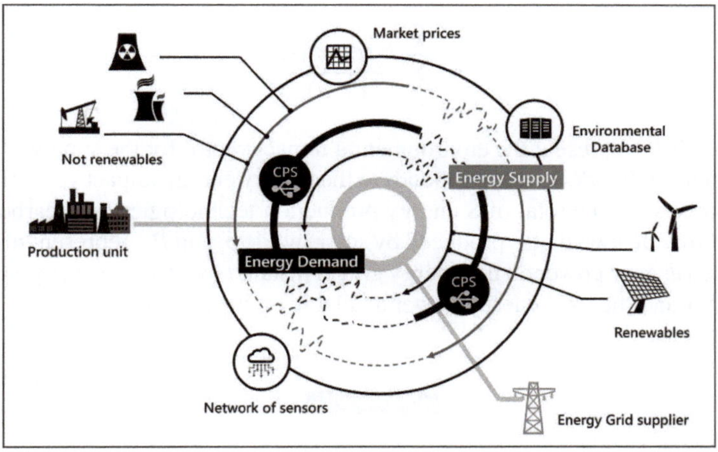

Fig. 3. Application of CPS for Environmental optimization of energy grid

The user company has already implemented a system of sensors that can record energy consumption from electrical grid and the CPS system is able to estimate the energy consumed for each work cycle and, prospectively, the energy required for subsequent scheduling through a Time-machine system. User can gain more insight on the system variation and self-adjust consumption according to prediction of ever-changing attributes of energy production pattern (costs, environmental impacts etc.).

Similarly, the energy supplier is able to transfer a series of real-time information regarding the average hourly energy price and, at the same time, the LCA-based environmental information impact. Both information are based on regression analysis when CPS simulate the future energy supply. Information on price is based on open-source database for energy market while the Environmental impact is based on combined information by the national energy authority on the actual allocation between renewable energy and fossil-based energy production. The system thus incorporates the ideal features for the implementation of CPS systems since the monitoring of environmental aspects (energy consumption) and energy consumptions present performance that are time dependent. In this case, the CPS allows to represent the environmental performance through Eq. 1:

$$\boldsymbol{I}_w(t+1) = A \cdot \int_t^{t+1} \boldsymbol{k}(t) * w(t) \tag{1}$$

In such equation, ***I*** represents the energy performance indicator at a given moment t + 1 for a number of monitored operations, ***k(t)*** represents the vector of unit flow performance, w(t) represents the instantaneous absorbed power by the company at the moment t for the monitored operations while A is a normalization coefficient.

The variable **k**(t) depends on the monitoring of the CPS on energy network conditions and is partly based on the LCA databases support, while *w(t)* depends on the instantaneous monitoring of consumption within the company through sensor system.

$$\boldsymbol{k}_e(t) = \sum_{s=1}^{S} \frac{\boldsymbol{k}_s(t) \cdot p_s(t)}{P_{tot}(t)} \tag{2}$$

In Eq. 2, $\mathbf{k_e}$(t) represent the environmental impact vector for the supply of energy at time t from the network. $\boldsymbol{k}_s$(t) corresponds to the unitary energy impact vector for a given energy source *s* for the total of S energy production technologies (e.g. carbon dioxide equivalent for one kwh that is produced by solar) while p_s and P_{tot} represent respectively the provided energy power on the energy grid at instant *t* by using the energy generation technology *s* and the total energy power available on the grid (Fig. 4).

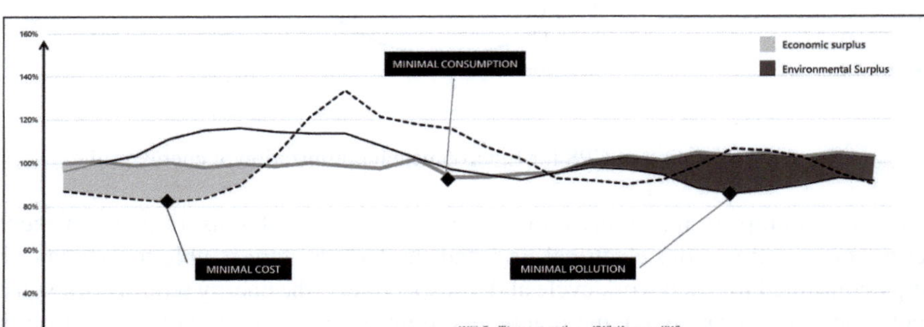

Fig. 4. Daily regression energy analysis according to CPS real-time monitoring system

The objective function to be optimized in this case coincides with a multi-objective function that concurrently minimizes I_w as a set of indicators. Outcome for such applications regards the identification of time spans for focusing production in correspondence of minimal energy cost or minimal environmental impact. Sustainability profile resulting from operations arrangement of the examined factory can be improved simply by introducing time constrains to single operations. Open issues still remain in identifying methodologies for concurrent optimization of cost and environment that are not based on arbitrary weighting of such categories. At the same time, the formalization of production constrains in the optimization model could better emphasize margins for green manufacturing policies.

4 Conclusion and Remarks

The implementation of CPS can have positive and remarkable effect for the implementation of Sustainable Manufacturing policies. In particular, the implementation of LCA tools can introduce a quantitative basis to provide effective environmental improvements in virtue of its intrinsic characteristic. The proper implementation of CPS systems integrating LCA features can concurrently provide real-time management systems integrating factory and supply chain level, efficient EMS and provide effective tools to adapt operational management to high-level sustainability targets. Such progresses introduce the possibility of intelligent production unit that are able to adjust and record their environmental impact. CPS can in fact include the ubiquity of information in the production chain and manage the complexity of the criteria to calculate the environmental impact. However, its implementation poses a number of challenges and constrains to industry automation at semantic, physical, operational and decisional levels. In particular, protocol development for data integration appears as an indispensable key area to foster CPS application for eco-efficiency. Apparently, the use of CPS seems to imply major effects in presence of certain operational characteristics as the congruency between variance of different operational drivers, the cost and availability of field data and margins for company to address such indications within decisional areas. According to the presented case, the application of CPS to smart energy grids seems to meet all these features. Improvements in real-time and foresight LCA assessments introduce measurable improvements on specific sustainability target. Perspective work can be oriented on the further formalization of production constrains as well as to reliability of regression analysis by a comparison of an ex-ante optimization policies and ex-post gate-to-gate analysis of effective environmental impacts. In parallel, further research on multi-criteria optimization can enforce CPS intelligence for such purpose.

References

1. Schuh, G., Reuter, C., Hauptvogel, A.: Increasing collaboration productivity for sustainable production systems. Procedia CIRP **29**, 191–196 (2015)
2. Siemieniuch, C.E., Sinclair, M.A., Henshaw, M.J.: DeC.: global drivers, sustainable manufacturing and system ergonomics. Appl. Ergon. **51**, 104–119 (2015)

3. Waibel, M.W., Steenkamp, L.P., Moloko, N., Oosthuizen, G.A.: Investigating the effects of smart production systems on sustainability elements. In: 14th Global Conference on Sustainable Manufacturing, GCSM 3–5 October 2016, Stellenbosch, South Africa. Procedia Manufacturing, vol. 8, pp. 731–737 (2017)
4. Dumitrache, I., Caramihai, S.I.: The enterprise of future as a cyber-physical system. In: 7th IFAC Conference on Manufacturing Modelling, Management, and Control June 19–21, Saint Petersburg, Russia, pp. 1310–1315 (2013)
5. Bonci, A., Pirani, M., Longhi, S.: A database-centric approach for the modeling, simulation and control of cyber-physiscal system in the factory of the future. In: IFAC-PapersOnLine, pp. 49–12, 249–254 (2016)
6. Estevez, C., Wu, J.: Green cyber-physical systems. In: Cyber-Physical Systems, chap. 15. Elsevier (2017)
7. Esmaeilian, B., Behdad, S., Wang, B.: The evolution and future of manufacturing: A review. J. Manuf. Syst. **39**, 79–100 (2016)
8. Zhang, H., Calvo-Amodio, J., Haapala, K.R.: A conceptual model for assisting sustainable manufacturing through system dynamics. J. Manuf. Syst. **32**(4), 543–549 (2013)
9. Haapala, K.R., Zhao, F., Camelio, J., Sutherland, J.W., Skerlos, S.J., Dornfeld, D.A., et al.: A review of engineering research in sustainable manufacturing. J. Manuf. Sci. Eng. **135**(Jul (4)) (2013)
10. Tang, L., Yu, X., Kim, S., Gu, Q., Hana, J., Leung, A., La Porta, T.: Trustworthiness analysis of sensor data in cyber-physical systems. J. Comput. Syst. Sci. **79**, 383–401 (2013)
11. Wang, D.: Data reliability challenge of cyber-physical systems. In: Cyber-Physical Systems, chap. 6. Elsevier (2017)
12. DeSmit, Z., Elhabashy, A.E., Weels, L.J., Camelio, J.A.: An approach to cyber-physical vulnerability assessment for intelligent manufacturing systems. J. Manuf. Syst. (in press, 2017)
13. Pan, M., Sikorski, J., Kastner, C.A., Akroyd, J., Mosbach, S., Lau, R., Kraft, M.: Applying industry 4.0 to the Jurong Island Eco-industrial Park. Energy Procedia **75**, 1536–1541 (2015)
14. Gupta, S.K.S., Mukherjee, T., Varsamopoulos, G., Banerjee, A.: Research directions in energy-sustainable cyber–physical systems. Sustain. Comput. Inf. Syst. **1**, 57–74 (2011)
15. Kao, H.A., Jin, W., Siegel, D., Lee, J.: A cyber physical interface for automation systems-methodology and examples. Machines **3**, 93–106 (2015)
16. Brondi, C., Carpanzano, E.: A modular framework for the LCA-based simulation of production systems. CIRP J. Manufact. Sci. Technol. **4**, 305–312 (2011)
17. Lee, H., Ryu, K., Son, Y.J., Cho, Y.: Capturing Green Information and Mapping with MES Functions for Increasing Manufacturing Sustainability. Int. J. Precision Eng. Manuf. **15**(8), 1709–1716 (2014)
18. Zhao, W.-B., Park, Y.H., Lee, H.Y., Jun, C.M., Noh, S.: Design and implementation of a PLM system for sustainable manufacturing. In: Rivest, L., Bouras, A., Louhichi, B. (eds.) PLM 2012. IAICT, vol. 388, pp. 202–212. Springer, Heidelberg (2012). doi:10.1007/978-3-642-35758-9_18
19. Logfren, B., Tillman, A.: Relating manufacturing system configuration to life-cycle environmental performance: discrete-event simulation supplemented with LCA. J. Clean. Prod. **19**, 2015–2024 (2011)
20. Sproedt, A., Plehn, J., Schonsleben, P., Hermann, C.: A simulation-based decision support for eco-efficiency improvements in production systems. J. Clean. Prod. **105**, 389–405 (2015)

Collaborative Perspective in Bio-Economy Development: A Mixed Method Approach

Manfredi Vale[1(✉)], Marta Pantalone[2], and Morena Bragagnolo[3]

[1] Aghetera Sas, Venice, Italy
vale@aghetera.eu
[2] Economic Department, Ca' Foscari University of Venice, Venice, Italy
[3] Environmental Science, Informatics and Statistics Department, Ca' Foscari University of Venice, Venice, Italy

Abstract. The hybrid Economic Input Output - Life Cycle Assessment (EIO-LCA) coupled with qualitative methods for consensus creation and participative policy building is a proposed methodology for dealing with complex and data-rich contexts that have to be connected in order to construct a robust regional bioeconomic profile that informs policy makers and other stakeholders about socio-economic and ecological impacts – and suggest at the same time strategies for its validation and implementation. An important result of this work is that the process of data collection and systematisation also provided ample opportunity to be in touch with a wide and diverse range of actors that characterize the different supply chains, ranging from the primary (farming, aquatic resources, forest sector) to manufacturing and services-related companies. These contacts encouraged the establishment of a network exchanging knowledge on crucial aspects for the further development of bioeconomy.

Keywords: Supply chains integration · Economic input-output · Life cycle analysis · Sustainability · Resilience

1 Introduction

The concept of 'bioeconomy' is gathering momentum in European Union (EU) policy circles as a sustainable model of growth to reconcile continued wealth generation and employment with bio-based sustainable resources usage. Bio-based industries and bio-based products can represent a new development opportunity for European areas fighting with a still stagnating economy. The development of a bio-based economy is a long-term process that requires the involvement of many stakeholders on multiple levels and sectors [1] and could have great impacts on local communities. According to the definition of the European Commission, the bioeconomy comprises those parts of the economy that use renewable biological resources from land and sea – such as crops, forests, fish, animals and micro-organisms – to produce food, materials and energy [2]. Standing this wide definition, in order to strengthen its profile, it is necessary to bring into vision the main actors of the bioeconomy, primarily the companies that are taking

L.M. Camarinha-Matos et al. (Eds.): PRO-VE 2017, IFIP AICT 506, pp. 553–563, 2017.
DOI: 10.1007/978-3-319-65151-4_49

action to achieve the objectives set by both the European Union and the United nations [3–5]. The bioeconomy is by and large an assemblage of regional activities that have their own regional character. For this reason, the choice of the most suitable strategy should be based on the involvement of all stakeholders [6], through participatory methods [7], that brings stakeholders together and let them confront each other on specific issues, agree on common meanings, and foreshadow a strategy for action. These participatory processes should empower participants to have an impact on the local/ regional context, making them active in the strategic planning in the areas where they live, supporting the policy-making process in accordance with politicians, technocrats, lobbies and civil society groups. The aim is to find an agreement on development scenarios and a general strategy to pursue common interests, breaking the 'vicious circle of non-participation' [8]. The stakeholders are not always aware of their significant role in the co-creation of policies [9] and they need the support of methodologies that are able to promote their participation, encourage the interaction, and provide an operational synthesis of this process, leading to a strategy which could support the public decision-makers and policy-makers. The innovation beyond the state of the art of this project is to delineate and model the regional Bioeconomy with a hybrid Economic Input Output-Life Cycle Analysis (EIO-LCA) using statistical data of economic flows, conventional pollutants emissions, energy use, waste production of the 37 regional economic sectors (according to NACE[1] classification) and integrate this information with sociological survey data collected during interviews and focus groups sessions.

The paper begins with a critical review of the literature on recent bio-economy impact-focused studies and on participative methods for policy design involving experts and diverse 'publics', thus suggesting that a mixed quantitative-qualitative approach is more appropriate for planning in highly complex contexts. The other sections present a synthetic description of methodologies and tools involved in this research, starting with an analysis of the baseline, as well as the main results on both disciplinary fields invoked, the economic-environmental modelling and the policy building through participative approaches. The concluding discussion recalls the importance of a mixed-method approach in order to better exploit its data richness and, at the same time, the importance of creating collaborative networks of different stakeholders in the field of bio-economy.

2 Literature Review

Bio-based products can include a diverse cross-section of items like enzymes; bio-based end-use products; commodity, fine, and specialty chemicals; intermediates and polymers; feed, food and food additives; fuels; flavours and fragrances; pharmaceuticals; and bio-based energy. These products are woven into the economy in complex ways, making it difficult to compute the impact on the economy. Defining what will and will not be considered part of the core bioeconomy is important and has a great impact on the magnitude of various indicators of impact. For the bioeconomy to grow, many different segments of the economy must effectively interact. The connectedness of the

[1] Statistical Classification of Economic Activities in the European Community.

bioeconomy can most easily be discussed in a supply chain framework. Supply chains are defined as all of the players involved in the movement of a product or service to the end customer. These networks transform natural resources into an end-use product, often via many different companies that add incremental value along the way [10–12].

Input-Output modelling is a linear modelling approach which involves the examination of the economic cycle of production by analysing the relationship between the flow of production inputs and resultant flow/destination of outputs in an economy. Input-output analysis has received attention also as a means for delineating the bioeconomy development in Europe and abroad, with a number of works attempting to gauge the impacts that bioeconomy is producing and will produce in economic, environmental and social terms [13]. There are relatively few studies attempting a quantitative impact analysis of the existing and projected bioeconomy, also dealing with the problem of defining the scope, sectors and supply chains involved. An EU study [14] has attempted an economy-wide quantitative assessment covering the full diversity of the European bioeconomy by employing social accounting matrices (SAMs) for each EU27 member encompassing a highly disaggregated treatment of traditional 'bio-based' agricultural and food activities, as well as additional identifiable bioeconomic activities from the national accounts data. The aim was to profile and assess comparative structural patterns both across bioeconomic sectors and EU Member States. The results indicate six clusters of EU member countries with homogeneous bioeconomy structures. Irish researchers applied an input-output framework to define the scope of the national bioeconomy [15], thus establishing a Bio-Economy Input Output model (*BIO*) which can be used to analyse the linkages between the bio-economy sectors and the wider economy. Two major strategies have been developed in recent years to develop the Agri-Food and Ocean Economy sectors in Ireland: the *Food Wise 2025* and the *Harnessing our Ocean Wealth* strategies. The report contains analytical studies utilising *BIO* to quantify, among other things, the impact of reaching *Food Wise 2025* growth scenarios and *Harnessing our Ocean Wealth* 2020 targets. Another work prepared for the U.S. Department of Agriculture and the Congress [16] seeks to answer questions regarding the contributions of the bio-based products industry in the United States: the quantity of biobased products sold; the value of the biobased products; the quantity of jobs created; the quantity of petroleum displaced; other environmental benefits; and areas in which the use or manufacturing of biobased products could be more effectively used.

The studies mentioned above highlight the data richness available on this matter and the need to capitalize on the wealth of information in order to promote policies effectively supporting the bioeconomy. The challenge to be grasped then becomes to "let the quantitative data speak" bringing it to the attention of those who, from different perspectives, work in the field of – or ar involved in – bioeconomy. The high uncertainty, of economic and regulatory nature, as well as the fact that it still mostly is a series of market niches, makes it necessary for the actors involved to identify a common glossary, a field of shared meanings that allows for the construction of alternative scenarios, in order to identify paths for collective action. Faced with the growing complexities of reality, the co-construction of bottom-up policies has taken hold in many fields [17–20]. If planned and appropriately applied, participation can contribute to the design of policies and practices that are better suited to serving the needs of those concerned, that are perceived to be holistic and fair, accounting for a diversity of values and needs [21]. These processes increase the legitimacy of decisions taken and contribute in saving time in the long path due to lower resistance among stakeholders.

Starting from the above literature analysis and state of the art, this paper aims to answer the following research questions:

- RQ1 Identifying the sectors that make up the regional bio-economic mosaic;
- RQ2 (By using the EIO-LCA model): measuring the extent of the difference - in terms of environmental and socio-economic impacts - between conventional and bio-economic sectors;
- RQ3 (Starting from the living labs experience): building a network of inter-sectoral integration (combining agriculture, manufacturing and services) through a system of contractual guarantees that can be a model for developing the bioeconomy in Veneto region.

3 Methods

An Input-Output Analysis based approach for calculating environmental impacts of the economy that has become relatively widespread across the academic and institutional community around the themes of decision support systems is the Economic Input Output Analysis - Life cycle Assessment approach, based on Wassily Leontief's [22] I-O method for environmental analysis. The approach defines the whole economy as the boundary of analysis and uses transactions between industry sectors, along with environmental emissions data to determine the environmental impacts throughout supply chains within the economy. To answer the research questions we developed a hybrid Economic Input Output table (EIO) of the regional bioeconomy in a life cycle (LCA) perspective to make it available for the environmental and socio-economic *ex-ante* and *ex-post* assessments of (regional) plans and programs. The Veneto economy was taken into consideration as a whole to get a clear view of the bioeconomy; then, in cooperation with Unioncamere del Veneto and Emilia-Romagna (Regional Unions of Chambers of Commerce) and IRPET (Tuscany Regional Institute for Economic Planning) we identified through the Regional Input-Output Table (IOT) the sectors and companies that are momentarily the main bearers of the development of bioeconomy. Given the fact that the bioeconomy is a broad field, we decided to study a representative sample of Veneto companies (2000) with at least one product certified as organic, trying to strengthen a more respectful agriculture and transformation of raw materials. Therefore on a macro-economic scale it makes sense to analyze such economic input/outputs and the corresponding interactions among organic and conventional supply chains by considering at the same time the pressures they exert on the environment and the socioeconomic system as a whole.

The process continued with the construction of a regional version of the NAMEA[2] matrix (*National Accounting Matrix including Environmental Accounts*) for Veneto region (Italy) by disaggregating emissions based on a proxy variable defined as follows: number of employees per sector in Veneto Region compared to the total number of employees in the same sector in Italy. A second Matrix was derived from the regional Inventory of air emissions (INEMAR), 2013 version. This inventory estimates the municipal emissions of the main pollutants for each activity of the *Corinair* classification and type of fuel. Despite these figures can be considered more accurate than those obtained from the NAMEA data processing, they are aggregated according to categories not directly comparable with the classification of economic activities used to estimate the bioeconomy. The data available at INEMAR were processed to obtain results to be included in the NAMEA table. Three drivers of environmental pressures relate to: greenhouse categories (GWP); acidification (AP); ground-level ozone, while the 10 pollutants are: methane (CH_4), carbon monoxide (CO), carbon dioxide (CO_2), nitrous oxide (N_2O), ammonia (NH_3), non-methane volatile organic compounds (NMVOC), nitrogen oxides (NO_x), particulate matter (PM10 and PM2,5) and sulphur oxides (SO_x).

For the socio-economic analysis, we involved stakeholders in focus group and brainstorming sessions, on one hand, and in depth interviews, on the other. Both these moments were crucial for sharing knowledge with experts (entrepreneurs, farmers, NGO's members, researchers), to putting together the distinctive visions from different stakeholders and to drawing possible policy actions. A first source of data comes from 3 case studies of companies (in the fields of bio-plastics, bio-food, bio-materials for the construction industry). The aim of these in-depth interviews was to analyse the characteristics of the 'bio-company', highlighting the economic and cultural context in which it operates. A second source of data comes from a Living Lab (LL) experience. Living Labs are open innovation platforms described as "functional regions where stakeholders have formed a Public-Private-Partnership of firms, public agencies, universities, institutes and people, all collaborating for creation, prototyping, validating and testing of new services, products and systems in real-life contexts" [23, 24]. One precondition of LL activities is that the innovation processes are strongly connected to real-world contexts, including exploration, experimentation, co-creation and evaluation with consumers in real life environments.

In the LL experience we involved all people who, at the local/regional level, felt themselves committed to the improvement of the bio-economy business as a whole. All people were recruited from participants to a European Union's Horizon 2020 coordination and support action (*Bio-STEP*) aimed at engaging citizens and various stakeholders in discussions about the future development of Europe's bioeconomy. The group was then expanded according to a snowball sampling procedures. The role of all these actors is significant not only when describing the problem, but also when pointing out for solutions and conditions to develop shared visions. Sadly, it appeared very difficult to get policy-makers involved. These participants were recruited first by phone, then

[2] The NAMEA consists of the framework of National Accounts with the supply and use of goods and services expressed in monetary units linked with integrated environmental accounts where the input of resources and output of emissions and pollutants are expressed in physical units.

through a one-to-one interview, and when interested, they received an e-mail with a formal invitation to participate in focus group sessions or more in-depth interviews. The aim of this part of the study was to outline a set of policies that can enhance best practices in order to coordinate and improve the effectiveness of bio-economic actions. We collected the voices of different stakeholders and let them dialogue on different topics: the potential of networking with other bio-economic actors, the critical issues to be addressed in the bio business sector, the willingness to cooperate with other conventional and bio actors.

4 Results

In the case of Veneto Region for the year 2012 the IOT is a square matrix of 37 × 37 sectors representing how the various economic sectors are dependent on each other because in the columns and rows there are, respectively, the monetary values of their inputs and outputs. We notice that, despite the sector *Crop and animal production, forestry, hunting and related services* consists of more than half of the companies identified as contributors to the Venetian bioeconomy, it represents one of the sectors with less information available: hardly ever these are capital companies and then budget information is not available on the databases available so far. By coupling the Economic Input Output (EI-O) table with the RAMEA (*Regional Accounting Matrix including Environmental Accounts*) it has been possible to extend the previously existing knowledge about direct and indirect environmental impacts: the ratio of value added for the whole economy compared with that of each of the bioeconomic sectors comprised in our sample of some 2000 companies has been used to estimate the impacts associated with bioeconomy in a life cycle perspective (LCA). Moreover, it is possible to further separate the contribution of final demand by distinguishing e.g. the internal aggregated one from that generated by the exports. By carefully screening the results of this combination of economic and environmental information, it is possible to select out of the 37 "canonical" IO industry categories, those economic sectors that at this stage (data refers to year 2012) (a) are/were referable to bioeconomy and (b) showed significant potential impacts - associated with the emissions to the atmosphere - on one or more standard impact categories. Some overestimation is possible under e.g. the NACE 'Manufacture of food products, beverages etc.' where the relatively high ratio of bioeconomic activities on the total is due to the inclusion in the calculations of conglomerated realities of large-scale distribution retailers with their massive turnovers, despite the transition to organic is rapid but still partial indeed. Other sectors of interest for the regional bioeconomy are obviously 'Crop and animal production' (despite the very low added value, which still is one of the issues of the "average" agricultural supply chain in Italy and Veneto), the 'Manufacture of coke and oil' (similar argument to the one concerning retail chains) - that is partially converting to renewables – 'Rubber and plastic products', 'Wholesale and retail trade', 'Accommodation and food service activities'. The same applies to the export quota of demand. By referring to e.g. the manufacture of food products, the pressure exerted from the export quota in terms of direct and indirect emissions is on average higher for an order of magnitude when compared with emissions produced by the internal regional demand. This is not strange for highly internationalized economies as the Veneto one[3]. When moving from emissions to the associated potential impacts through dedicated LCA software, it is possible to quantitatively measure the proportion of the Venetian bioeconomy as an aggregate of multiple supply chains compared with the regional economy as regards to Global warming, Acidification, Nutrient Enrichment and Photochemical Ozone Formation (see Fig. 1).

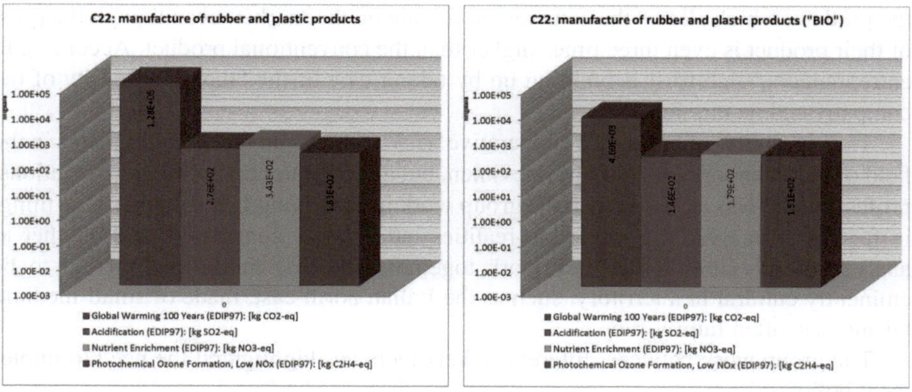

Fig. 1. Main impact categories associated with the emissions of conventional vs bio-based rubber and plastics production (logarithmic scale; ordered: values in thousands).

Definitely our sample of 2000 companies when compared with the total number of companies in Veneto represents 0.4%. The data obtained from this first estimate shows that the bioeconomy in Veneto has an interesting growth potential, representing, in terms of added value, 2.86% of the regional total.

So, what are the policies that, according to stakeholders, can help the increase of Veneto's bio-economic sector?

The in-depth interviews and case studies on bio factories have allowed us to outline the economic and cultural context within which bio activity in Veneto is developing. These markets are "niches", populated by a few or very few actors[4] (at national, European and international level). In these niches, because of the low number of actors and the strong ethical instances of some key players, the competition assumes a peculiar characteristic: it becomes "Coopetition", a hybrid between cooperation and competition that brings to light the positive results of the first concept while not losing the characteristics of the latter. Being very few, these companies may not be subject to the "*mors tua, vita mea*" rule, which regulates the conventional markets, but, while not abandoning the logic of

---

[3] http://venetointernazionale.it/.

[4] From the case study on bio-building factory emerges that in this field the analyzed enterprise is unique in its kind in Italy by the type of product proposed and, at international level, is one of the six existing in the field. Similar numbers are also found in relation to the production of bioplastic materials.

profit, they can adopt ethical behaviors by which all can implement their profits minimizing losses (win-win logic).

The adoption of this logic has enabled companies, once they enter their market niche, to raise its standards. Rigorous controls on raw materials and production processes, with the aim of certifying their product as organic or their processes as sustainable, have introduced virtuous logics between competitors, creating a "standard upgrade process" aimed at giving the consumer more trustworthy products. It is the consumer's trust in the product, which allows the company to remain on the market, even though the price of their product is even three times higher than the conventional product. According to entrepreneurs, such trust is building up by taking care of the "moral" integrity of the company and its mission.

The possibility of building a cooperative network between the different actors in the field of bio-economy (not only businessmen, but also researchers, cultural associations, professionals) was assessed with the group work in the Living Lab sessions. One thing, in fact, is to analyze the single bio-realities individually considered, and another to analyze the possibility that they work together. The first hurdle has proved to be eminently cultural in a territory, such as the Italian north-east, made of small-medium businesses, often family-run.

The group work between different stakeholders has highlighted the need to implement policies:

1. for the creation of a network of bio actors [e.g. (a) Provide a common glossary to match the language with which reference is made to the activities carried out or (b) adopt an ethical code that protects patents and original ideas and prevents opportunistic behaviors];
2. for the consolidation of relationships with other actors [e.g. (a) with the university research, in order to create dialogue between the world of production and the world of scientific research and to optimize and finalize the resources in programs that have then possible productive effects (systems, biomaterials, crops) or (b) for vertical and horizontal integration of the supply chain, with the aim of building certified chains from the producer to the consumer].

It is, in this sense, to create the background for dialogue among niche markets and to ensure that individual actors are no longer "dwarfs" in a giant world (the 'conventional' one), but part of a cooperative network getting more and more resilient. The restructuring of the bio-economic sectors, in fact, moves the "power" on who, normally, does not have it: small producers (farmers, breeders), consumers, the civil society and their networks.

5 Conclusions

This research project has allowed to more reliably gauge the value of bioeconomy – a complex and data-rich aggregation of market niches - beyond its current economic and monetary weight in the Veneto region. The theme of the higher value of bio-products and bio-supply chains has emerged, as well as the ongoing process of rebalancing supply chains and giving more power to historically disadvantaged stakeholders.

From an economic point of view, the adoption of a mixed approach has highlighted the sectors linked to bio-economy as showing higher value of production, higher added value and lower staff turnover, but at the same time they still account for only 0.4% of the total number of companies in the region and in many cases they are converting imported raw materials - from other regions or from the rest of the world - because regional production does not meet their demand.

From an environmental point of view, according to the first outcomes of the EIO-LCA analysis, there is evidence - across some sample bioeconomic supply chains - of reduced environmental impacts; however, further analyses are required to confirm those insights, both at the sectors' and system scale.

From a sociologic point of view, it has emerged that the true drivers of change are relatively small economic actors (both on the demand and supply side) capable of raising standards across the entire industry and promoting at the same time its resilience. Within these market niches, those actors are capable of imposing their "regulatory discipline" to other actors, going beyond their own boundaries and influencing the whole sector. These 'little ones' - being a cultural and knowledge-intensive *avant-garde* - demonstrate the link between culture, ethical instances, *coopetition* capacity, networking potential, increased resilience, win-win logic. Culture has in fact demonstrated to be the hidden engine behind this change of paradigm towards bioeconomy: familiar and entrepreneurial culture often dates back to the last century in Italy, with a very clear distinction between family and business, being still today the main prerequisite towards business managerialisation and development in this geographic area. Another important driver of change are consumers who, with their behaviours in terms of preferences and demand, affect and redirect the market, thus indicating in advance to the regulators the direction of future policies. Conversely, politicians are perhaps those less capable of vision and innovation among the various stakeholders, and tend to hardly chase the progress of others.

All of the above boils down to a very first attempt of defining an operational/managerial model which moves from the academic interaction of sciences and humanities - having realized that none of the two disciplinary fields can be exhaustive by itself - towards a hybrid approach to big (and diversified) data management that allows for the definition of a measurable link between knowledge -based and aware business management, increasing environmental performance - at the product and process scale - and a corresponding improvement of socioeconomic performance.

References

1. Munda, G.: Social multi-criteria evaluation: Methodological foundations and operational consequences. Eur. J. Oper. Res. **158**, 662–677 (2004)
2. European Union: Innovating for Sustainable Growth. A Bioeconomy for Europe. Directorate-General for Research and Innovation (2012)
3. United Nations: Sustainable Development Goals (2016). http://www.un.org/sustainable development/sustainable-development-goals/

4. McCormick, K., Kautto, N.: The bioeconomy in Europe: an overview. Sustainability **5**, 2589–2608 (2013). http://www.mdpi.com/2071-1050/5/6/2589
5. European Commission: Commission proposes strategy for sustainable bioeconomy in Europe (2012). http://europa.eu/rapid/press-release_IP-12–124_en.htm
6. Patel, M., Kok, K., Rothman, D.S.: Participatory scenario construction in land use analysis: an insight into the experiences created by stakeholder involvement in the Northern Mediterranean. Land Use Policy **24**, 546–561 (2007)
7. Lopolito, A., Nardone, G., Prosperi, M., Sisto, R., Stasi, A.: Modeling the bio-refinery industry in rural areas: a participatory approach for policy options comparison. Ecol. Econ. **72**, 18–27 (2011)
8. Sisto, R., van Vliet, M., Prosperi, M.: Puzzling stakeholder views for long-term planning in the bio-economy: a back-casting application. Futures **76**, 42–54 (2016)
9. Odugbemi, S., Jacobsoon, T.: Governance reform under real world conditions. Citizens, stakeholders, and voice. Washington, DC: The International bank for Reconstruction and Development/The World Bank (2008)
10. United States Department of Agriculture: Biobased economy indicators (2011). https://www.usda.gov/oce/reports/energy/USDA%20Bioindicators982011_2.pdf
11. Macchion, L., Moretto, A., Caniato, F., Caridi, M., Danese, P., Spina, G., Vinelli, A.: Improving innovation performance through environmental practices in the fashion industry: the moderating effect of internationalisation and the influence of collaboration. Prod. Plann. Control **28**, 1–12 (2016)
12. Lion, A., Macchion, L., Danese, P., Vinelli, A.: Sustainability approaches within the fashion industry: the supplier perspective. Supp. Chain Forum: Int. J. **17**(2), 95–108 (2016)
13. Vagnani, G., Volpe, L.: Alla ricerca del valore della filiera vitivinicola: verso la formulazione di un modello di analisi. Mercati e Competitività n. **4**, 21–43 (2009)
14. Philippidis, G., Sanjuán, A.I., Ferrari, E., M'barek, R.: Employing social accounting matrix multipliers to profile the bioeconomy in the EU member states: is there a structural pattern? Span. J. Agric. Res. **12**(4), 913–926 (2014)
15. Grealis and O'Donoghue: The bio-economy input-output model: development and uses (2015). www.nuigalway.ie/semru/documents/economic_impact_of_the_irish_bioeconomy_07_10_15.pdf
16. Golden, J.S., Handfield, R.B., Daystar, J., McConnell, T.E.: An economic impact analysis of the u.s. biobased products industry: a report to the congress of the united states of america. A Joint Publication of the Duke Center for Sustainability & Commerce and the Supply Chain Resource Cooperative at North Carolina State University (2015)
17. Claude, S., Ginestet, S., Bonhomme, M., Moulène, N., Escadeillas, G.: The Living Lab methodology for complex environments: Insights from the thermal refurbishment of a historical district in the city of Cahors. Energy Res Soc Sci, France (2017)
18. Lepik, K., Krigul, M., Terk, E.: Introducing living lab's method as knowledge transfer from one socio-institutional context to another: evidence from helsinki-tallinn cross-border region. J. Univ. Comput. Sci. **16**(8), 1089–1101 (2010)
19. Liedtke, C., Welfens, M.J., Rohn, H., Nordmann, J.: LIVING LAB: user-driven innovation for sustainability. Int. J. Sustainab. High. Educ. **13**(2), 106–118 (2012)
20. Canzler, W., Engels, F., Rogge, J., Simon, D., Wentland, A.: From "living lab" to strategic action field: bringing together energy, mobility, and Information Technology in Germany. Energy Res. Soc. Sci. **27**, 25–35 (2017)
21. Gruszka, K.: Framing the collaborative economy —Voices of contestation. Environmental Innovation and Societal Transitions (2016)

22. Leontief, W.: Environmental repercussion and the economic structure: an input output approach. In: The review of Economics and Statistcs, pp. 263–271. The MIT Press (1970)
23. Almirall, E., Wareham, J.: Living labs and open innovation: roles and applicability. Electron. J. Virtual Organ. Netw. (EJov) **10**, 22–46 (2008)
24. Wendin, K., Åström, A., Ståhlbröst, A.: Exploring differences between central located test and home use test in a living lab context. Int. J. Consum. Stud. **39**, 230–238 (2015)

Sustainable Development for Rural Areas: A Survey on the Agritourism Rural Networks

Salvatore Ammirato[1(✉)], Alberto Michele Felicetti[1], Marco Della Gala[2], Nicola Frega[1], and Antonio Palmiro Volpentesta[1]

[1] Department of Mechanical, Energy and Management Engineering, University of Calabria, 87036 Arcavacata di Rende, CS, Italy
{salvatore.ammirato,alberto.felicetti,nicola.frega, antonio.volpentesta}@unical.it

[2] Countryside and Community Research Institute, University of Gloucestershire, Oxstalls Campus, Oxstalls Lane, Gloucester GL2 9HW, UK
mdellagala@glos.ac.uk

Abstract. The topic of sustainable growth is becoming central in the debate over the rural development policies. Rural communities can completely fulfil the new challenges in the area of sustainability only with the implementation of innovative forms of collaborations among their business networks. In this work, we consider a particular form of business collaboration arising within rural communities, namely Agritourism Rural Network (ARN). In an ARN, a farm, providing agritourism activities, represents a touchpoint between a network of business and organizations in a rural area and tourists interested in enjoying the local territory. With the aim to deeper the extend of the agritourism phenomenon in a rural region and the potential of the related ARNs in being means of sustainable development, we report main results of an empirical survey carried out in 2016 on a sample of 105 agritourism farms all belonging to the same region (Calabria, Italy). Results confirm our intuitions about the importance at farm level of setting agritourism activities and their impact for the ARN related to the farm and for the sustainable development of a local community as a whole.

Keywords: Sustainable development · Agritourism · Collaborative network · Agritourism rural network · ICT

1 Introduction

Rural communities have been heavily impacted from a wide range of changes, mainly consisting in the loss of economic importance of agricultural activities, low wages, a dramatic fall in employment rates and a large amount of people that left rural areas for big cities. Such changes exposed rural communities to the risk of inexorable decline, from an economic, social and environmental point of view.

To overcome the present unsustainable development model, rural communities are gaining an increasing awareness on the importance of territorial specific resources (e.g. typical foods, landscape, monuments, history, traditions) as a way to produce a long lasting development for rural area as a whole. Agrifood producers and other

L.M. Camarinha-Matos et al. (Eds.): PRO-VE 2017, IFIP AICT 506, pp. 564–574, 2017.
DOI: 10.1007/978-3-319-65151-4_50

organizations (e.g., suppliers of touristic service, craftsmen, local administrations) operating in rural areas have spontaneously started organizing in rural networks, as a way to answer the rural communities' needs in terms of socio-economic development, improving their revenue streams, developing new market niches and increase their competitiveness against large retail companies. Collaboration in the agrifood sector is characterized by a re-connection among producers and consumers that is known in literature as "re-localisation" whose aims are: "re-vitalisation of territory identity and rural community relations to local food and agriculture, linking with sustainable agriculture, economically viable and socially responsible practices" [1, 2]. Collaboration based organization models which rise under the principle of re-localization are generally named Alternative AgriFood Networks (AAFNs) [3]. In this work we consider a particular form of AAFNs, namely Agritourism Rural Networks (ARNs), where farms, which deploy agritourism activities, represent a touchpoint between a network of rural actors (organizations, companies, public administrations) and tourists interested in enjoying the local territory [4]. This work aims to provide a deeper understanding of the ARN phenomenon evaluating its potentials in fostering socio-economic development of rural areas. Agritourism is able to balance needs of rural tourists with those of rural communities, offering a real opportunity for the economic and social development while mitigating undesirable impacts on environment and other socio-cultural aspects. In particular, we report main results of an empirical survey carried out in 2016 on a sample of 105 farms offering agritourism activities and all located in the same region (Calabria, Italy). After analysing the extent of the agritourism phenomena in the region, the survey was aimed to evaluate the presence of ARNs and their characteristics. A specific section has been devoted to introduce ICT tools useful to support collaboration among the ARN's members and to exploit the collectable big amount of data in order to design new patterns of sustainable development.

2 Theoretical Background

Over the last decades, both at political and scientific level there has been an increasing consensus on the need of a transition to sustainable rural development strategies [5, 6]. Such strategies are aimed to balance economic growth with cultural and natural resource conservation [7], taking into account the three pillars of sustainability which are known as the Triple Bottom Line (TBL) [8]. Several authors have argued that the agricultural sector represent a 'seedbed' for sustainable rural development and has the potential to foster the interrelationships between farms and people, both within rural areas and between rural and urban areas [9, 10]. To foster sustainable development pathways, scholars advocate the necessity to re-construct local agro-food systems [11] leveraging on the concepts of re-territorialization, re-localization [2], diversification [12] and on the adoption of organizational models which allows the re-connection between producer and consumers. Thanks to the renewed interest in local food production, new organizational networks, based on processes of synergic collaboration between farmers, consumers and other rural actors, have emerged in recent years [3]. These collaborative networks (that have been called AAFNs) aim at shortening the physical and social distances between producers and consumers by minimizing the number of intermediaries in the food supply chain [13, 14]. AAFNs have the potential to positively affecting the sustainable development of rural areas along all the three pillars of sustainability in agricultural systems [15, 16].

Strictly related to the sustainable rural development and to the sustainable agriculture, there is the topic of sustainable rural tourism. Rural tourism represents a growing market offering to rural communities growth opportunities that arise from the emerging trends in tourism demand, which tent to pay more attention to the values of culture, food, and to the countryside. It can bring a valuable contribution to the sustainable development of rural areas. Its contribution can be expressed not only in financial terms, but also in terms of jobs, enhancement and revitalization of community pride, encouragement to the adoption of new working practices, and the injection of a new vitality into sometimes weakened economies [17]. In particular, within rural tourism, agritourism offers to small farmers a chance for the economic diversification. In [7] agritourism is defined as "tourism activities exercised by farmers through the exploitation of their own farm according to logic of connection complementarity and non-prevalence" of tourism activities with respect to agricultural based activities. This definition is in line with the Italian Legislative System. In the scientific literature the term "agritourism" is often understood as a synonym for "farm tourism," "farm-based tourism," and "rural tourism" [18]. In our work, while the term "rural tourism" refers simply to tourism services provided in a rural context, we refer to agritourism as "tourism services provided by agricultural entrepreneurs within their own farm, allowing also visitors to take part, directly or indirectly, in agricultural activities". It has been observed that agritourism offers many opportunities to small and medium farms, including increased farm gross income, the generation of cash flow and the creation of job opportunities. Moreover, it has the potential to affect positively the local rural development as a whole because its positive impacts extend beyond the farm gates through the interrelated activities with other local economic sectors [19]. Strictly connected with the concept of agritourism, the concept of Agritourism Rural Network, ARN, has been first introduced in [4]. Within a rural community it is possible to identify particular kinds of *Collaborative Networks,* namely ARNs, whose members are agritourism farms and other rural organizations (craftsmen, artists, local public administration, transportation services, typical agrifood producers, etc.) that collaborate to offer tourists the opportunity to enjoy the local territory. Rural communities, by means of the ARNs, could achieve the common goal of sustainable local development in order to increase their general competitiveness in a larger area.

The aim of this regional study is to analysing the extent of the agritourism phenomena and, in particular, its potentials to trigger and support ARNs as means of sustainable development for rural areas. To pursue the above purpose, we operationalized it in three research questions which can be formulated as follows according to [4, 20].

- RQ1: Do farmers understand the importance of setting agritourism activities within their farm (i.e.: to what extend do farmers engage in agricultural activities)?
- RQ2: Can the agritourism farm be a direct contact point between the rural community offer of products/services and the tourist request for relocalization?
- RQ3: Is it possible to highlight the presence of an agritourism rural network in supporting the activities of the agritourism farm?"

3 The Research Design, Results and Discussion

To answer the research questions, we analysed:

- secondary data from the Italian National Institute of Statistics – ISTAT [21], and Confagricoltura, [22], related to agribusiness sector in Calabria for the year 2015;
- results of a survey carried out among the Calabrian agritourism farms in the period 02 January 2016 to 31 January 2016 concerning activities they performed in 2015.

Moreover, to give a better understanding of the evolution over time of the surveyed phenomenon, results of this study are compared with those obtained from a similar research conducted in 2012 [20]. The period between the two surveys was characterized by a strong economic crisis in the EU agricultural sector, thus putting in contrast results of the two surveys helped us to better understand the role of agritourism and ARNs in giving sustainable answers to the rural development question. At the end of 2015, 521 agribusinesses were authorized to offer agritourism activities, in Calabria [21]. They represent the population of interest, *P*, of this study. In other Italian regions agritourism was much more widespread both in absolute and proportional terms. Tuscany and Trentino Alto Adige were the regions where agritourism was most diffused. In Tuscany, in the 2013 on 66.584 agribusinesses, 4.108 deployed agritourism activities (6,16%) while in Trentino Alto Adige on 34.693 farms, 3.506 of them offered agritourism activities (10.10%). At the national level, on 758.953 Italian agribusiness, only 22,238 (2,93%) offered agritourism activities [22]. In Calabria only 521 to 30.857 agribusinesses offered agritourism activities meaning that the rate (1,69%) was lower than the national one. In 2012 data were more promising in Calabria: on 20474 agribusinesses, 610 were authorized to offer agritourism activities (1,96%). After three years, the already limited percentage of agritourism on the total agribusinesses in Calabria was further decreased (from 1,96% to 1,69%). Moreover, while the overall number of agribusiness showed a growth rate of 8,62%, in the same three years, the number of agritourism farms decreased at a rate of 14,6% [23].

A questionnaire was set up containing 16 questions aimed to answer the research questions. The questionnaire has been delivered to managers of all the farms belonging to *P*. On 521 agritourism farms in *P*, 105 of them (20,1%) returned the filled questionnaires with the requested data. Such farms constituted the sample *S* of our survey; for each farm in *S*, we analysed their responses and statistical results are reported.

When requested to quantify the percentages of farm's yearly turnover and overall costs coming from the agritourism activities, 74% of respondents affirmed that more than 20% of turnover come from agritourism while 90% of respondents reported that agritourism costs represent more than 20% of the overall farm's costs. While data about turnover is essentially in line with the analogous data in [20], surprisingly, percentage of agritourism costs on overall farm's costs is more than double in 4 years (from 44% to 90%). Details can be found in Table 1.

Moreover, when asked to point out trends of evolution of turnover and costs of agritourism activities on the overall farm's turnover and costs in 2015, with respect to the first year of activity of the agritourism, what emerges is:

Table 1. Percentages of farm's yearly turnover and overall costs coming from the agritourism activities

% of respondents	% of Yearly turnover coming from agritourism activities		% of overall farm's costs coming from agritourism activities	
	2012	2015	2012	2015
<20%	33%	27%	56%	10%
Between 20% and 50%	29%	61%	23%	69%
>50%	38%	12%	21%	21%

- 29% of respondents stated that in 2015 agritourism turnover is decreasing respect the first year of activity, 19% reported a stable trend of evolution, 34% reported a growth while 18% did not answer the question.
- 1% of respondents stated that in 2015 agritourism costs are decreasing respect the first year of activity, 27% stated a stable trend of evolution, 48% stated a growth while 24% did not answer the question.

The small number and percentage of agritourism farms present in Calabria in 2015, together with the strong decrease of them in 4 years (−14,6% while the total number of agribusiness in the region remained unchanged in the same period) highlight that we cannot positively answer to RQ1. This result confirms the conclusion in [20]. Data from the survey have a twofold interpretation. On the one side, investments in agritourism activities give farmers a good return in terms of turnover that is durable through time. On the other side, percentage of farm costs imputable to the agritourism costs have been increasing considerably in the last 4 four years and, generally, since the beginning of the agritourism activity.

To answer RQ2, respondents were enquired to indicate which of the activities in Table 2 they offered to tourists as part of the agritourism products portfolio. Activities in Table 2 go in the direction to make the agritourism a contact point between the tourist and the local territory. The aim of these questions is to understand if agritourism farms have potentials to be drivers for the development of ARNs. In Table 2, results of the survey are compared with results in [30].

Data highlights that farmers well understand the importance to enlarge the product portfolio with territory-related activities that let tourists enjoy the cultural/naturalistic heritage of the region (also in the form of participation to farm life) as well as to buy typical agrifood products of the region (both self-produced and purchased from local producers). When put in contrast with data from the 2012, 2015 results become more important considering the growth rate in the offering of activities from surveyed farms. We can give a positive answer to RQ2; agritourism is no more conceived only as a means to sell products/services self-produced as in 2012 but it can be considered a sort of tourist's bridgehead to the rural network. This result is in contrast with result of the 2012 survey when "agritourism is still intended by farmers only as a means to sell products/services self-produced" [20].

Table 2. Activities offered to tourists and percentage of agritourism which offer them

Activity	Agritourism farms offering the activity in **2012**	Agritourism farms offering the activity in **2015**
Meal provision	94,23%	96,19
Selling of self-produced food	71,15%	93,33
Selling of products of other local farms	13,46%	68,5%
Visits to touristic/cultural/naturalistic places close to the agritourism (Excursion)	53,8%	67,7%
Active participation in the life of the farm (e.g. 'pick-your-own' facilities, participation in farm tasks) also in the form of "Educational farm" (e.g. milking cows, sheepdog display, feeding animals)	48,5%	60,9%

To answer RQ3, respondents were asked about the presence of formal cooperation agreements with other local service/product providers to carry out the agritourism activities and the percentage of agrifood products utilized in agritourism activities coming from local producers. Moreover, respondents were asked about the numbers of local workers engaged by the farm exclusively to carry out the agritourism activities. Results are present in Table 3 together with similar data from the 2012 survey [20].

Data highlights that ARNs are present and consolidated in Calabria, thus we can positively answer to RQ3. Local service/product providers definitely benefit from the agritourism presence considering that almost 90% of farms declare some kind of formal cooperation with them. Moreover, local products are purchased from 95% of agritourism farms.

4 ICT and Agritourism

On the basis of a recent literature and empirical exploration we can suggest how ICTs can provide noteworthy opportunities for organizations belonging to an ARN in term of reduction of operational and management costs [24, 25]. ICTs have in fact a considerable impact in improving internal business processes (e.g. reservation management, back-office activities), facilitating business transaction and networking among partners in ARNs. From ARNs perspective, ICTs have not only a considerable impact in process efficiency, thus reducing operational costs, but represent also an effective advertising medium and a fundamental distribution channel in order to increase customers and visitors the (e.g. booking platforms). Moreover, social interactions between organizations in an ARN and tourists enable new learning opportunities, educating tourists about local tangible and intangible assets (monuments, typical foods, traditions, cultural heritage). Hence, the use of ICTs is able to engender trust and cooperation within a community and supports the exchange of local knowledge that can revitalise local/traditional knowledge and encourage sustainable territorial management.

Table 3. Agritourism connections with the local territory

	2012	2015
The farm has some kinds of formal cooperation with other local service/product providers to carry out the agritourism activities	40%	89,5%
How many local workers are engaged by the farm exclusively to carry on the agritourism activities? (mean value among answers)	5	1,53
More than 20% of agrifood products utilized in agritourism activities (direct selling, meal provision, etc.) come from local producers	12%	60%
Less than 20% of agrifood products utilized in agritourism activities (direct selling, meal provision, etc.) come from other local producers	61%	35%
The farm utilized only self-produced agrifood products for its agritourism activities.	27%	5%
Overall farms using products supplied from local producers.	71%	95%

ICT can be deployed in many business activities carried out by the ARN. When evaluating the business opportunities coming from tourism activities, farmers can be helped by the large amount of data available from a variety of sources. A good starting point can be offered by social media platforms which are taking an important role in supporting tourists in decision support both for planning and enjoy a journey experience. Data coming from the social activities of tourists are important to point out new trends in destination choices and preferences in tourism experience. According to [26], a multidimensional analysis of such a data can be deployed to improve marketing strategies. The use of mobile devices, during the journey experience, generate another class of data very useful to depict and track tourist behaviors in different contextualized scenarios. Smartphones can interact with other smart "objects" to generate an "augmented tourism experience" within the local territory [24]. Internet-of-Things technologies let farmers create and manage *cyber-physical systems*, CPS, in tourism activities in order to perform virtual interactions with visitors using sensors already present in their devices [27]. Bluetooth beacons, NFC tags, GPS positioning, e.g., can help user to improve the information quality of the destination, to digital control and manage access to physical resources, to guide and support orienteering [28]. In [29], a service oriented architecture of CPS in tourism infomobility is proposed in order improve the tourism management activities. The concept of CPS, as integration of digital and physical processes, can lead to the achievement of valid smart tourism management to ensure its sustainability and efficiency. All these interactions can be analyzed both at farm and at ARN level to better tune the overall experience and plan an improved bundle of suggested activities within the ARN territory [30].

E-commerce platforms can be the main digital touchpoint through which tourist can buy ARN products and services. In planning phase of the tourism experience, tourists can book events and services to enjoy in situ. In experience phase, tourists can do the same and can buy food or ingredients used during cooking experiences; tourists can buy products previously delighted at farms site and eat them at home. In [31], authors have analyzed and explored some case studies in introducing ICT to increase the value proposition of a touristic organization. ARNs should consider the influence and impact of social media (as part of tourism marketing strategy) for all involved actors in agritourism sector to determine the economic contribution of social media networks [32]. It is crucial, for farmers in ARN, get experienced in using social media tools to meet marketing objectives quickly and improve their competitiveness.

From a supply-chain point of view, ARN member might adopt many ICT solutions to support collaboration and cooperation. B2B e-commerce solution or digital multi-sided platforms (DMSPs) can be a valid support for supply chain management for meal and services provisioning. One goal can be an e-Marketplace framework in which all cooperative actions of ARN members can take place. One of the pre-requirement to deploy such an innovative strategy can be the partial adoption of process automation (for example, using basic ERP solutions) to support farmer organization internal activities [33].

5 Conclusion

Overall, Calabrian farmers do not understand the importance of setting agritourism activities within their farm. In this sense, they look less far-sighted than farmers in other Italian regions, like Tuscany and Trentino Alto Adige. Such result is more serious considering that survey results confirm the potential of agritourism activities in improving the revenue streams of Calabrian farms. Anyway, among the Calabrian farmers there is a leading group (the 521 ones that offer agritourism activities) who exploit the potential of agritourism in giving sustainable development to the farm and in being a contact point between the tourist and the local territory through the presence of consolidated ARNs. The ARNs can be means of sustainable development for local areas also in order to react to the economic crisis. This conclusion is in contrast with [20] who stated that, in 2012, “Local suppliers, through their long-term contracts with the farm, offer agritourists their goods and services having an indirect contact with them (mediated by the farm)”. Survey results demonstrate that, in 2015, local suppliers can have a direct contact with tourists selling them their products and services, even if this is mediated through the agritourism.

A change in the ARNs structure is evident respect to the 2012 survey:

- farms which declare some kinds of formal cooperation with other local service/ product providers to carry out the agritourism activities increase from 40% in 2012 to 89,5% in 2015.
- farms using products supplied from local producers increase from 71% in 2012 to 95% in 2015.
- farms selling products of other local suppliers through the agritourism surprisingly increase from 13,46% to 68,5%.
- Percentage of respondents who declare a yearly turnover coming from agritourism activities more than 20% of the overall farm turnover remains almost the same in

2012 and 2015 among while % of respondents who declared that overall farm's costs coming from agritourism activities are more that 20% of the overall farm costs grow up from 44% to 90%.

- The mean value of the number of local workers engaged by the farm exclusively to carry out the agritourism activities decreased from 5 to 1,53.

It seems that farmers reacted to the economic crisis improving collaboration with local suppliers, so strengthening the connection within the ARN, and reducing the number of direct employers. Unfortunately, in the same period when such forms of outsourcing were set up, an overall increase in the agritourism costs was evident. Whether it was the outsourcing the motivation of the cost increase or vice-versa, the question remains unclear. What is certain is that the increase of operational costs is a problem for agritourism farms. At the same time, it is evident how the growth of tourist number would have a direct impact on improving farm's turnovers and on increasing the number of ARN customers. Lastly, agritourism farm owners should increase service value and their competitiveness exploiting the potential of ICT, both to consolidate the relationships with ARN partners and to meet and anticipate travelers' needs and expectations. Further questions on this topic will be investigated in future research.

Acknowledgments. This work has been partially supported by a Marie Skłodowska-Curie Individual Fellowship of the European Union's Horizon 2020 Programme, 'Situated learning Opportunities Fostered by Ict adoption in AAFN – SOFIA' (G.A. 702884). This paper only reflects the authors' views and funding agencies are not liable for any use that may be made of the information contained herein.

References

1. Marsden, T.: The Condition of Rural Sustainability. Royal Van Gorcum, Assen, The Netherlands (2003)
2. Volpentesta, A., Ammirato, S., Della Gala, M.: Classifying short agrifood supply chains under a knowledge and social learning perspective. Rural Soc. **22**(3), 217–229 (2013)
3. Volpentesta, A.P., Ammirato, S., Della, G.M.: Alternative agrifood networks as learning communities: some issues for a classification model. Commun. Comput. Inf. Sci. **278**, 293–300 (2013)
4. Ammirato, S., Felicetti, A.M.: The potential of agritourism in revitalizing rural communities: some empirical results. In: Camarinha-Matos, L.M., Scherer, R.J. (eds.) PRO-VE 2013. IAICT, vol. 408, pp. 489–497. Springer, Heidelberg (2013). doi:10.1007/978-3-642-40543-3_52
5. Watts, D., Ilbery, B., Maye, D.: Making reconnections in agro-food geography: alternative systems of food provision. Prog. Hum. Geogr. **29**(1), 22–40 (2005)
6. Feagan, R.B., Morris, D.: Consumer quest for embeddedness: a case study of the Brantford Farmers' Market. Int. J. Consum. Stud. **33**, 235–243 (2009)
7. Sonnino, R.: For a 'piece of bread'? Interpreting sustainable development through agritourism in Southern Tuscany. Sociologia Ruralis **44**(3), 285–300 (2004)
8. Elkington, J.: Cannibals With Forks: the Triple Bottom Line of 21st Century Business. Capstone, Oxford (1997)

9. Miller, E., Van Megen, K., Buys, L.: Diversification for sustainable development in rural and regional Australia: how local community leaders conceptualise the impacts and opportunities from agriculture, tourism and mining. Rural Soc. **22**(1), 2–16 (2012)
10. Sonnino, R., Kanemasu, Y., Marsden, T.: Sustainability and rural development. In: Unfolding webs: the dynamics of regional rural developmen, pp. 29–52. Royal Van Gorcum, Assen, Netherlands (2008)
11. Berti, G., Mulligan, C.: Competitiveness of small farms and innovative food supply chains: the role of food hubs in creating sustainable regional and local food systems. Sustainability **8**, 616 (2016)
12. Volpentesta, A.P., Ammirato, S.: A collaborative network model for agrifood transactions on regional base. In: Lytras, M.D., Ordonez de Pablos, P., Ziderman, A., Roulstone, A., Maurer, H., Imber, J.B. (eds.) WSKS 2010. CCIS, vol. 112, pp. 319–325. Springer, Heidelberg (2010). doi:10.1007/978-3-642-16324-1_34
13. Kneafsey, M., Venn, L., Schmutz, U., Balázs, B., Trenchard, L., Eyden-Wood, T., Bos, E., Sutton, M., Blackett, M.: Short food supply chains and local food systems in the EU. A state of play of their socio-economic characteristics. European Commission (2013)
14. Goodman, D.: Editorial the quality "turn" and alternative food practices: reflections and agenda. J. Rural Stud. **19**, 1–7 (2003)
15. Sonnino, R., Moragues Faus, A., Maggio, A.: Sustainable food security: an emerging research and policy agenda. Int. J. Sociol. Agric. Food **21**(1), 173–188 (2014)
16. Forssell, S., Lankoski, L.: The sustainability promise of alternative food networks: an examination through alternative characteristics. Agric. Hum. Values **32**(1), 63–75 (2015)
17. Irshad, H.: Rural Tourism – an overview. Alberta, Canada (2010)
18. Tew, C., Barbieri, C.: The perceived benefits of agritourism: the provider's perspective. Tour. Manag. **33**, 215–224 (2012)
19. Yang, L.: Impacts and challenges in agritourism development in Yunnan. China. Tour. Plann. Dev. **9**(4), 369–381 (2012)
20. Ammirato, S., Felicetti, A.: The Agritourism as a means of sustainable development for rural communities: a research from the field. Int. J. Interdiscipl. Environ. Stud. **8**(1), 17–29 (2014)
21. ISTAT: Report on Agritourism activities in Italy (2016)
22. CONFAGRICOLTURA: imprese agricole nel 2012 (2013)
23. UNIONCAMERE: Rapporto economico sulla Calabria. Collana dell'Ufficio Studi di Unioncamere Calabria (2016)
24. Ammirato, S., Felicetti, A., Della Gala, M.: Rethinking tourism destinations: collaborative network models for the tourist 2.0. Int. J. Knowl. Based Dev. **6**(3), 178–201 (2015)
25. Ammirato, S., Felicetti, A.M.: Tourism breeding environment: forms and levels of collaboration in the tourism sector. In: Camarinha-Matos, L.M., Scherer, R.J. (eds.) PRO-VE 2013. IAICT, vol. 408, pp. 517–524. Springer, Heidelberg (2013). doi:10.1007/978-3-642-40543-3_55
26. Mariani, M.M., Di Felice, M., Mura, M.: Facebook as a destination marketing tool: Evidence from Italian regional destination management organizations. Tour. Manag. **54**, 321–343 (2016)
27. Rho, S., Vasilakos, A., Chen, W.: Cyber physical systems technologies and applications. Future Gener. Comput. Syst. **56**, 436–437 (2016)
28. Nitti, M., Pilloni, V., Giusto, D., Popescu, V.: IoT architecture for a sustainable tourism application in a smart city environment. Mob. Inf. Syst. **2017**, 9 (2017)
29. Smirnov, A., Shilov, N., Kashevnik, A., Ponomarev, A.: Cyber-physical infomobility for tourism application. Int. J. Inf. Technol. Manage. **16**(1), 31 (2017)
30. Li, Y., Hu, C., Huang, C., Duan, L.: The concept of smart tourism in the context of tourism information services. Tour. Manag. **58**, 293–300 (2017)

31. Vassalosa, M., Lim, K.H.: Farmers' Willingness to Pay for Various Features of Electronic Food Marketing Platforms. Int. Food Agribus. Manage. Rev. **19**(2), 131–149 (2016)
32. Zeng, B., Gerritsen, R.: What do we know about social media in tourism? A review. Tour. Manage. Perspect. **10**, 27–36 (2014)
33. Yoo, K.-H., Gretzel, U.: The role of information and communication technologies (ICTs) in marketing tourism experiences. In: The Handbook of Managing and Marketing Tourism Experiences, pp. 409–442 (2016)

Achieving the Sensing, Smart and Sustainable "Everything"

Dante Chavarría-Barrientos[1(✉)], Luis M. Camarinha-Matos[2], and Arturo Molina[1]

[1] Tecnologico de Monterrey, School of Engineering and Science, 14380 Mexico City, Mexico
{dante.chavarria, armolina}@itesm.mx

[2] Faculty of Sciences and Technology and Uninova – CTS, Nova University of Lisbon, 2829-516 Monte Caparica, Portugal
cam@uninova.pt

Abstract. The vast diversity of current sensing devices and mechanisms enable the creation of data-rich environments which gives the opportunity to create smart systems. The smartness of systems must transcend individual interests and fulfill collective aspirations and environmental needs. Therefore, new products, processes, enterprises, communities and any kind of systems must be envisioned as Sensing, Smart and Sustainable (S^3). This paper discusses the trends and challenges for S^3 applied to everything. Furthermore, it suggests that the knowledge produced in the field of collaborative networks might be used to leverage the S^3 capabilities.

Keywords: Collaborative networks · Sensing systems · Smart systems · Sustainability

1 Introduction

The generalized use of technologies such as cloud computing, cyber-physical systems, big data analytics, and sensor systems lead to data-rich environments. In industry, these environments can promote an increase in productivity because they boost the creation of knowledge. Having access to the right information at the right time gives enterprises the ability to better compete and sustain their operations. Consequently, the idea of Sensing, Smart and Sustainable (S^3) Enterprise was recently introduced [1]. The S^3 Enterprise is concerned with the analysis and management of all data sources to feed smart systems that react rapidly and flexibly to environment changes. As a result, enterprises can become sustainable in the economic, social and environmental senses.

This research proposes the adoption of the S^3 concepts not only in enterprises, but in any human-designed system, e.g. products, processes (business and manufacturing), communities and cities. We call this vision as the S^3 of everything. The creation of S^3 systems will promote and rely on collaboration, information access, open innovation, and sustainable development. However, the concept must be well studied to be adopted by practitioners.

L.M. Camarinha-Matos et al. (Eds.): PRO-VE 2017, IFIP AICT 506, pp. 575–588, 2017.
DOI: 10.1007/978-3-319-65151-4_51

As a contribution in this direction, this paper discusses the trends and challenges when developing the S^3 of everything. Section 2 provides a definition of the S^3 concept and a brief literature review of current approaches in developing these systems. Section 3 introduces a list of challenges to make this vision a reality. Finally, Sect. 4 describes the enablers while trying to identify further research opportunities.

2 The S^3 Concept: Sensing, Smart and Sustainable

The sensing enterprise, the smart organization and the sustainable enterprise are the concepts that give birth to the S^3-Enterprise vision where the S^3 concepts were used together for the first time. The sensing enterprise [2] can anticipate future decisions by using multidimensional information that enhances its global context awareness. The smart organization [3] is defined as an enterprise that is internetworked, knowledge driven, and therefore able to adapt rapidly in response to opportunities. Finally, the sustainable enterprise maintains its economic, social and environmental dimensions when it operates [4]. Figure 1 tries to capture the S^3 characteristics of generic systems based on such definitions. The conceptual model proposed details the S^3 system definition, and each of the characteristics are explained next.

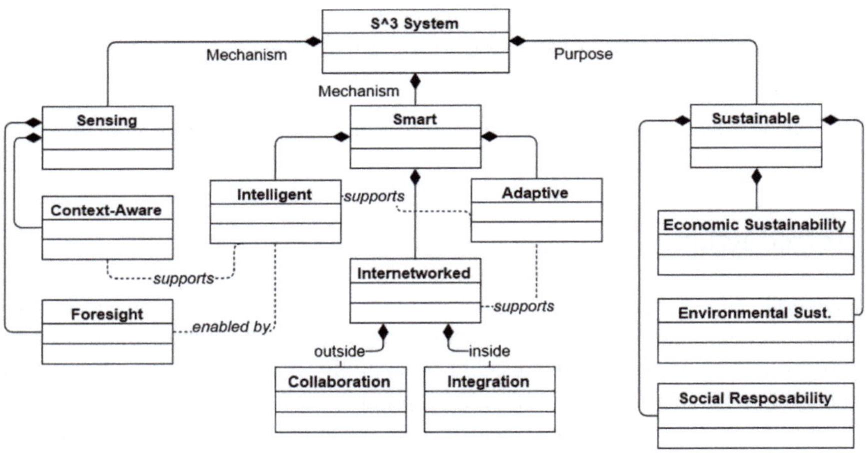

Fig. 1. A conceptual model of a Sensing, Smart and Sustainable system

Context-awareness is a key characteristic of any sensing system which refers to the acquisition of relevant information to make better decisions. The monitoring activities of any sensing system must be directed towards reliability and usability. Reliability guarantees the level of trust needed to make decisions based on information, while usability gives a purpose that helps designers in prioritizing monitoring efforts.

One of the associated goals when acquiring information is the foresight ability which is proposed as a second characteristic of a sensing system. To anticipate its future, the system must have a reasoning mechanism that makes inferences.

Predictions are enhanced when the information is captured in real-time. A smart system is based on intelligent artefacts which imply the use of information to make decisions. An autonomous cognitive reasoning facet is needed to use the information effectively and efficiently. The intelligence is reflected in the way the system decides.

Internetworking is a characteristic of current smart systems that can be approached at two levels. At the external level, it refers to the collaboration with other systems whose interaction provides value to the system tasks. At the internal level, interconnectivity is used to provide integration of the system's parts. Both levels suggest the creation of collaborative networks.

Using the internetworking and knowledge-based capacities, a smart system must be able to adapt to disruptions on its environment. The adaptability of a system can be enhanced by having a wide range of operating conditions or by having reconfigurability to change its type of operations to provide new capabilities. The first approach provides faster response times; however, it increases complexity.

The notion of sustainability is typically divided in three pillars. The economic dimension is maintained when the system produces more than what it costs. Therefore, the goals must be to minimize operational costs while increasing productivity or value generation. In addition, a sustainable system must participate in the co-creation of a world where humans survive and thrive. Being socially responsible is therefore an obligation. Finally, environment sustainability refers to a resource consumption rate that allows the environment to restore itself. Complementarily, the production rate of wastes must be less than the absorption capacity of the ecosystem. Collaborative networks have been discussed as a major pillar of sustainability implementation [5].

As shown in Fig. 2, different application areas can be found for the deployment of the S^3 concept. Products, processes, enterprises, business environments, communities

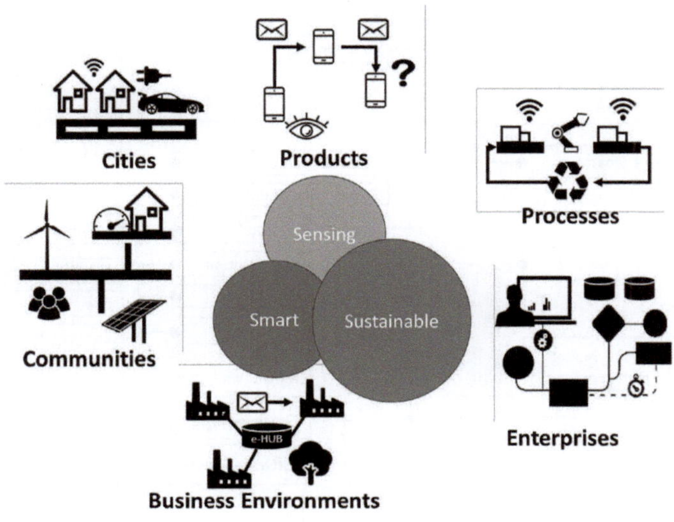

Fig. 2. Some application areas for Sensing, Smart and Sustainable concepts

and cities improve their functionality and behavior when they become Sensing, Smart and Sustainable. Let us now have a closer look at each of them:

S^3 Products. Customers want cheaper, personalized and innovative products with better quality and reliability [6]. The S^3 products idea is an approach to satisfy these requirements. Miranda et al. [7] have proposed the product model (See Fig. 3) for the S^3 products based on different approaches such as smart products where computational technologies are utilized to join physical processes with cyber representations [8]. These products have a mechatronics characteristic since they integrate mechanical, electronic and IT components. But they have more interaction with geographically distributed parts, and even relying on external components or services to provide product's functionality [9]. The sensing characteristic of S^3 products involves all types of sensors which provide additional information to enhance context-awareness and self-description. The smartness characteristic is divided into the physical components, smart components and connectivity. For physical components, new smart materials need to be introduced to provide proactive behavior. The smart components, conformed by processing, storage and user interfaces, must be enhanced towards intelligent control, AI planning, and machine learning, in order to provide the product functionality in different conditions and following customers needs. Finally, the connectivity components are for interaction of the products with other products and different actors during the product lifecycle. The sustainable characteristic is realized by

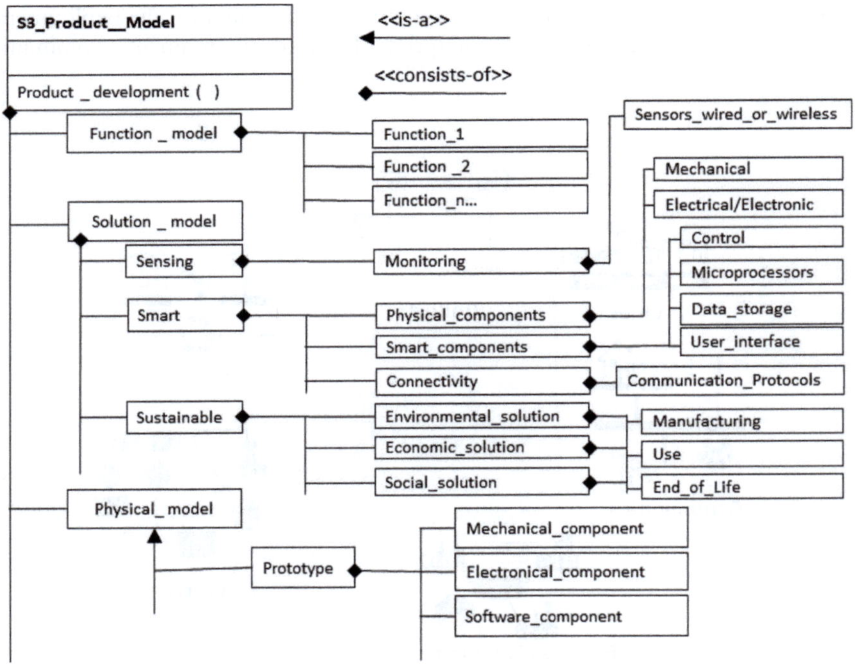

Fig. 3. Sensing, Smart and Sustainable Product Model [7]

adopting sustainable product development which includes traditional product requirements criteria (economic, quality, market, technical feasibility) but adds environmental and social impacts [10]. Thus, the S^3 products must produce benefits such as reduced volume of hazardous material and raw material in general, reduced energy consumption and elimination/reduction of waste. For developing sustainable products, the lifecycle approach is currently used to measure their economic, social and environmental impacts [11]. Adding sustainable considerations to the Smart Product concept is a step towards S^3 products.

S^3 Processes. In todays' world, innovation drives economy, therefore new products are being introduced at a faster and faster pace. The processes (manufacturing and business) need to adapt to this rate. We propose the S^3 processes as solutions for the everchanging environment in the digital economy. Figure 4 shows an S^3 material transformation process using the morphological definition provided in [12] to illustrate what is expected in a S^3 manufacturing processes. The processes should become smart and sensing, which implies that there is a continuous monitoring of operations which gives processes the ability to create the desired products in efficient and flexible ways [13]. The continuous monitoring and processing will be provided by the use the emerging technologies i.e. Internet of Things, Cloud Computing, Big Data, embedded systems. Autonomous cooperative elements will connect in situation dependant ways, conforming Cyber-Physical Production Systems [14]. The production processes used by most industries are not sustainable [15]. In fact, traditional industrial production is linked to environmental disruptions, such as global warming and pollution, and consumption of nonrenewable resources. However, in S^3 processes, the energy and material utilizations should be minimized and the production waste reduced to almost zero seeking sustainable production [16]. Intelligent technologies for sustainable energy management are been developed to this end (energialab.com). These processes are related to the concept of Industry 4.0 where the cooperative interconnectivity will also affect the business processes and the data must be trusted without always knowing their origin. As a consequence, benefits such as scenarios anticipation, increased resources

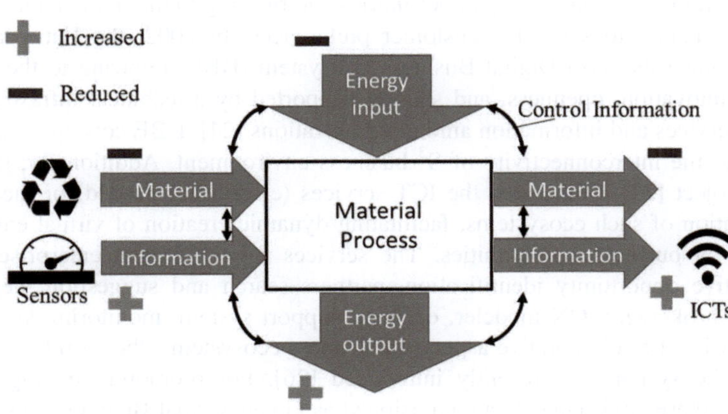

Fig. 4. Sensing, Smart and Sustainable Material Processes

efficiency and reduced risks will be found [17]. Business and engineering processes in Industry 4.0 promote sustainability [18].

S^3 Enterprises. If enterprises want to thrive in the ever-changing business environments, they need to operate efficiently and adaptively. The S^3 Enterprises [1] will achieve this through various mechanisms that promote sustainability. All type of sensors in all hierarchical levels of the Enterprise [19] will give the self-awareness needed to operate efficiently, Additionally, digitalization will be the mechanism that supports the foresight ability and transformation of enterprises by providing modularity and reconfigurability [20]. For becoming intelligent, model-based engineering and operation would guide the enterprise behavior. The concept of service is adopted as a building block that describes the operation of the enterprise providing reconfiguration capability. For heterogeneous supply networks, a core ontology will facilitate the exchange and interoperation of information systems. These systems can rely on intelligent autonomous agents that need executable models. The executable models will enable the creation of Enterprise Operating Systems [21], where enterprise operations are controlled and executed through computers. For sustainability, the indicators will include the fulfilment of survival and purpose needs of the socio-ecological system in which it is emerged [22]. According to the S^3 vision, enterprises must follow the road to sustainable development by minimizing consumption (e.g. energy, goods, and water); maximizing societal and environmental benefit, rather than prioritizing economic growth; emphasizing delivery of functionality and experience, rather than product ownership; and promoting collaboration and sharing, rather than aggressive competition [23]. These goals should be pursued at each hierarchical level of the enterprise. Figure 5 shows the hierarchical levels together with some sensing requirements and decisions to be considered in a S^3 manufacturing enterprise.

S^3 Business Ecosystems. New business ecosystem should create a climate conductive to investments, innovation and entrepreneurship, which is supported by the progress of the ubiquitous and pervasive computing and networking, i.e. S^3 Business Ecosystems. Figure 6 illustrates the combination of concepts that define these ecosystems. For context awareness and foresight, these business environments will be in continuous contact with markets, harvesting opportunities and reacting to them. Social media in an important enabler to sense the customer preferences. In 2002, the European Commission coined the term Digital Business Ecosystem (DBE) referring to the achievement of innovation, openness, and sharing supported by a technical infrastructure to connect services and information among organizations [24]. DBE concept is applied to understand the interconnectivity of S^3 business environment. Additionally, the ECO-LEAD project [25] synthesized the ICT services (e-services) needed for the creation and operation of such ecosystems, facilitating dynamic creation of virtual enterprises, triggered by business opportunities. The services for the virtual enterprise include collaborative opportunity identification, partners search and suggestion, negotiation wizard (e-brokerage), CN modeler, decision support system, monitoring system, etc. To emphasize the collaborative aspects in business ecosystems, the term Collaborative Business Ecosystem was recently introduced [26]. For promoting intelligence and adaptivity, these environments are envisioned as Green Virtual Breeding Environment (GVBE) which is considered as an intelligent network of assets that are shared to create

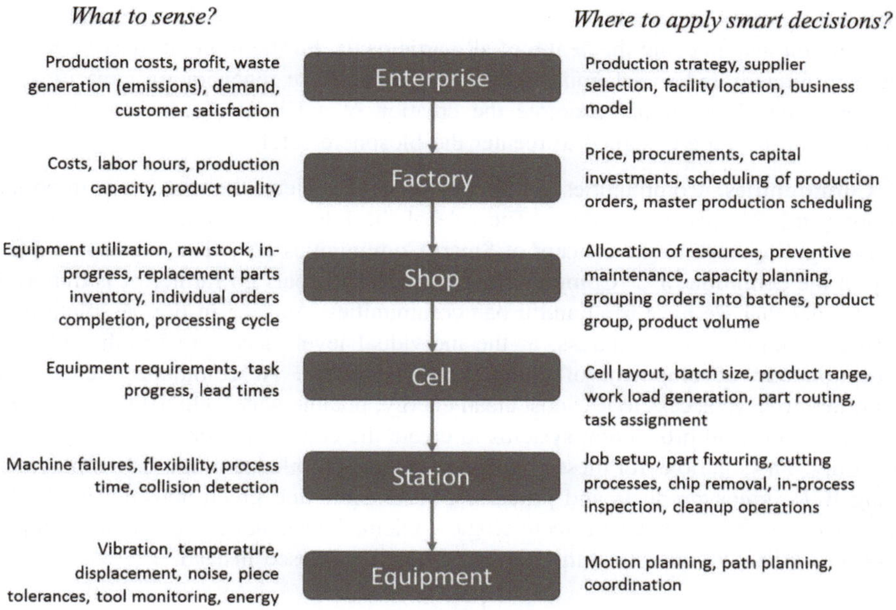

Fig. 5. Examples of what to sense and decide in a S^3 Manufacturing Enterprise

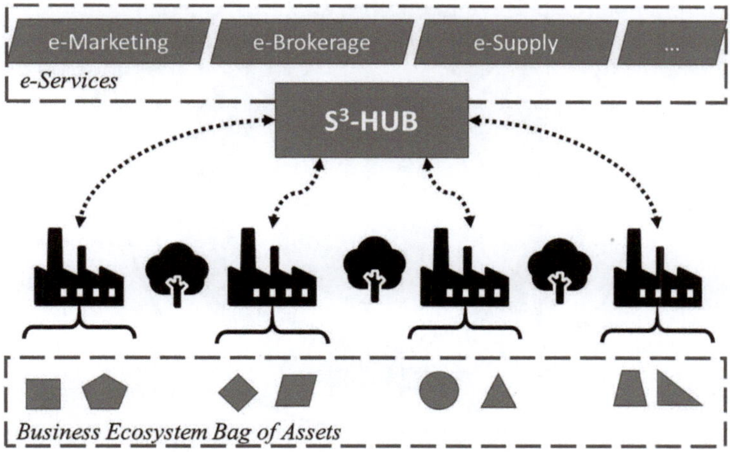

Fig. 6. A view of Sensing, Smart and Sustainable Business Ecosystems.

sustainable value [27]. This view of the GVBE gives the opportunity to consider business ecosystems as a bag of assets that must be assigned, monitored and managed by and in effective ways to save costs, co-create value, efficiently utilize resources and develop trust among Green Enterprises. The S^3 HUB [28] acts as the mediator among enterprise assets and provider of e-services. The S^3 HUB must also govern the sustainable issues of the Business Ecosystem. It should balance the cooperation and competition guaranteeing the health of all participants. Furthermore, it must verify that the environment and social impacts do not overcome the regeneration capacities. To this end, the HUB should promote the creation of a Circular economy, where all elements utilized are designed to reenter the biosphere safely.

S^3 Communities. Communities are the keystone of society; therefore, it is important to apply the S^3 concepts to them. The role of the Internet of Things (IoT) has been revised, giving birth to the concept of Smart Communities [29]. This concept is a first step in the definition of S^3 Communities, however the goals go further. It is important to consider that we have rural and urban communities. As seen in Fig. 7, solutions to rural communities must address, at the individual level, access to health, nutrition, education and development of competencies to work. At community level, it is important to have access to low cost clean energy, potable water, efficient management of waste, and local production systems to create the conditions for a sustainable local economy. The solutions for these challenges include mobile learning, self-employment using ICTs, green products and processes, sustainable and green housing, waste disposal technologies, renewable technologies, telemedicine, nutraceuticals and bioprocess. For urban communities, the term S^3 cities is proposed instead.

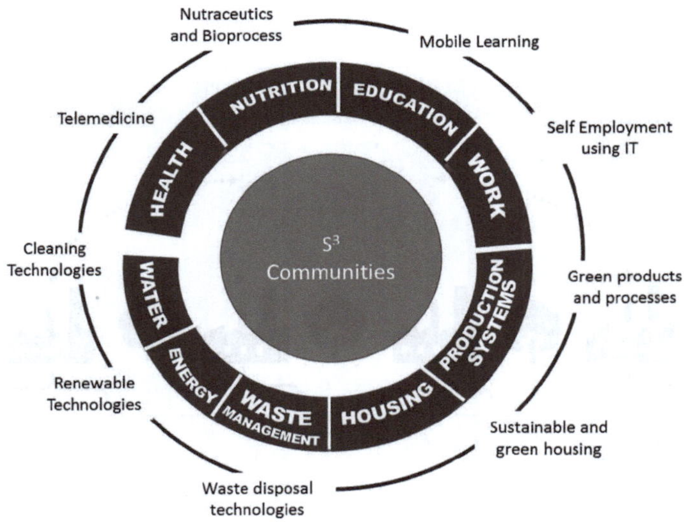

Fig. 7. Challenges and solutions for Sensing, Smart and Sustainable Communities (Rural).

S^3 Cities. These cities are defined based on the Smart city concept, and the ICT-enabled sustainable strategies (See Fig. 8). However, this is not the first time Smart and Sustainable cities have been defined. Hojer and Wangel [30] propose the term Smart Sustainable City as a "*city that meets the needs of its present inhabitants without compromising the ability for other people or future generations to meet their needs, and*

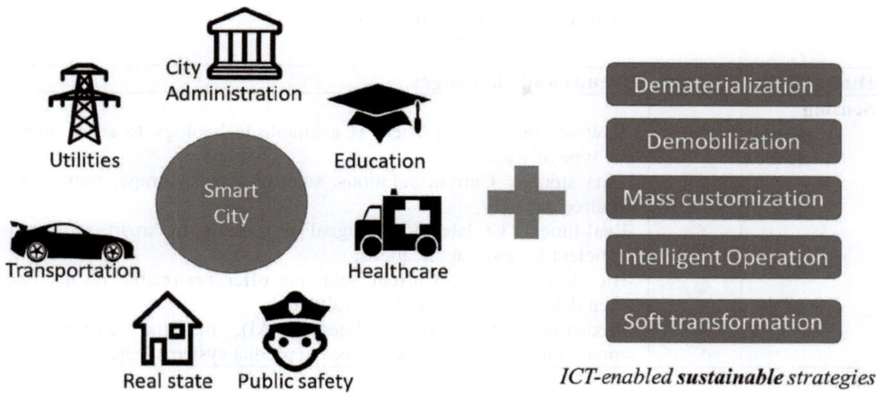

Fig. 8. Towards Sensing, Smart and Sustainable Cities (Urban Communities).

thus, does not exceed local or planetary environmental limitations, and where this is supported by ICT." The goal in S^3 cities is to select the ICT investments that cause the greatest benefit to environment and society. The Internet of Things must be used to provide Sensing as a service which promotes the development of activities such as waste management, smart agriculture and environmental management [31]. In addition, human interaction with technology should be monitored to provide a digital representation of the social phenomena [32]. The digital representation must be analyzed with Big Data technics to provide increasing quality of life. Seven core services have been enlisted as the components of the Smart City where the ICT-enabled intelligence can be applied to improve life quality [33] (i.e. city administration, education, healthcare, security, real state, transportation and utilities). In these cities ICT also improves sustainability by providing dematerialization, demobilization, mass customization, intelligent operation and soft transformation [34]. Effective materialization of these cities requires the involvement and collaboration of multiple public and private stakeholders.

3 Trends and Challenges

Despite the advances in different applications areas, the development of truly S^3 systems is still a challenging and not yet fully understood task. Following the model proposed in Sect. 2, Table 1 shows some challenges and the status related to the deployment of S^3. The status has been determined according to the literature review done in the previous section. The sensing challenges are mostly accomplished since current technologies allow collecting and keeping almost any type of data. This situation varies for the smartness-related challenges because often the "smart" label has been naively assigned to simple use of ICT. However, there is a need for further developments in smart facets, such as cognition and adaptability. Finally, the main challenge regarding sustainability is the ability to measure the impacts on society and environment to avoid partial and therefore incomplete approaches to sustainability. Current methods (e.g. Lifecycle assessment) need to be standardized and sharpened.

Table 1. Trends and challenges in S^3

Dimension	Status	Trends and challenges
Sensing		
Context-aware	●	-Raw sensor systems: There is available technology to sense almost any type of variable.
	●	-Data storage: Current solutions, such as cloud storage, provide the required capacity.
	●	-Real-time: The latency of signal processing in smart sensors is sufficient for most applications.
Foresight	◐	-Big data analytics: Current solutions offer reasonable results only when data is pre-organized and validated.
	◐	-Predictions: Artificial Intelligence (AI), machine learning and simulation provide first approaches to predict systems behavior.
Smart		
Intelligent	◐	-Common understanding: standards are a first approach, but core domain ontologies are needed to allow knowledge sharing.
	●	-Effective AI: current intelligent systems have proved to provide the required precision needed in standard applications.
	○	-Flexible AI: current AI systems are focused on specific tasks; flexible reasoning systems are needed in seek of adaptivity.
Interconnected	●	-Physical Interconnectivity: ICTs allow communication in different scenarios using different resources.
	◐	-Interoperability: hierarchical IT architectures need to be broken to allow a more open communication among system components.
Adaptive	◐	-Modularity: components must provide their functionality as on-demand services that can be accessed by both humans and bots.
	○	-Autonomy: an agile response depends on the ability of the system components to self-organize.
Sustainable		
Economic	●	-Value generation: Because technologies have a cost, the value propositions should overcome traditional proposals.
	●	-Economic assessment: Different KPIs and evaluation techniques are available to measure costs and profit of any system.
Environmental	◐	-Green technologies: Alternative technologies are being developed to substitute harmful resources.
	◐	-Environmental impacts assessment: Standards such as ISO 14000 are the first aproach in getting universal measure for impacts.
Social	◐	-Social developments technologies: ICTs have promoted varying befits to societies providing wide access to services.
	○	-Social assessment. There is a need to define clear and universal measures of social impact.

● - Solved challenges ◐ - Partially solved challenges ○ - Open challenges

4 Enablers to Achieve S^3 Realization

4.1 S^3 Technologies

The main component that is leading to the conceptualization of S^3 "things" is the advancement in ICTs and sensing technologies. These technologies alone (e.g. RFID, sensors, microprocessors and mobile networks) have the potential of supporting the S^3

"things". However, there is an aggregated version of such technologies that allow a straightforward adoption of S^3 concepts, i.e. S^3 Technologies. These technologies are integrated hardware, software, and network technologies that provide real-time awareness, advanced analytics, collaboration capabilities and adaptability to help in intelligent and sustainable decision making. An example is the smart grid because it promotes the use of renewable energy using of real-time information to balance supply and demand [35]. The Advanced Metering Infrastructure (AMI) is a key component that provides reliable, real-time data about each component of the power grid. The concept of Collaborative Smart Grid was recently introduced [36] to reflect a trend towards establishing collaborative networks among all stakeholders in a smart grid environment. Smart grids have enabled the creation of S^3 communities and cities. There is a need for similar developments that impulse the implementation of S^3.

4.2 S^3 Collaborative Networks (CNs)

As mentioned above and already evidenced in current trends, the area of CNs is a key enabler for the realization of the S^3 concept. In fact, all cases mentioned in Sect. 2 involve multiple entities – organizations/enterprises, people, smart machines, smart sensors, smart systems – which are typically heterogeneous, distributed, and with growing levels of autonomy. The "integration" and "interaction" of these entities – which are progressively more interconnected – into a consistent whole require effective collaboration among them in order to ensure proper (and desirably optimal) functioning.

Nevertheless, the full achievement of the S^3 vision raises several challenges for the CN research community, including:

- *Interplay among diverse networks:* various networks, with different life cycles co-exist in the same environment – e.g. networks of machines and networks of organizations or networks of people - and the interplay among these networks needs to be better understood and supported.
- *Hybrid value systems:* in some cases, e.g. smart cities, and smart infrastructures, there are actors (public and private) with very different value systems along the value chain. Finding ways of combining those diverse value systems is necessary in order to ensure healthy global behaviors.
- *Culture/training:* some of the mentioned application domains are often addressed from very partial perspectives, e.g. from a technology-only perspective, requiring the creation of a CN culture and training the involved human actors with the already vast knowledge base of the CN discipline.
- *S^3 KPIs:* a new set of performance indicators oriented to assess the level of S^3-ness in each application domain needs to be developed.

5 Conclusions

The S^3 of everything invites researchers to see the sensing and smart capabilities as a medium to achieve system sustainability. S^3 characteristics as requirements for system design would allow the development of systems that thrive and survive in the ever-changing world. This approach take the advantage of the technologies that are shaping the digital era. Furthermore, the usual design goals are taken further through considerations such as minimizing waste generation, enhancing working conditions, improving social conditions, and promoting green societies.

For adopting the S^3 conceptualization and setting the requirements of such systems, a generic description of each characteristic has been provided. This generic model is an initial step towards the construction of a formal and well-recognized vision of Sensing, Smart, and Sustainable everything. In addition, several challenges and their status have been introduced to guide and leverage research related to S^3 everything. Furthermore, collaborative networks have been identified as a major vehicle for S^3 realization. Nevertheless, the full realization of the vision requires further research. We expect that this preliminary work may encourage researchers to develop the area of S^3 of everything into a recognized and active approach for systems development.

Acknowledgments. This research is a product of the project 266632 "Laboratorio Binacional para la Gestión Inteligente de la Sustentabilidad Energética y la Formación Tecnológica" ["Bi-National Laboratory on Smart Sustainble Management and Technology Training"], funded by the CONACyT SENER Fund for Energy Sustainability (agreement: S0019-2014-01); the project S^3-Microfactory (Sensing, Smart & Sustainable) funded by the Seed Grant from CITRIS, which support the connected communities' initiative; the project S^3-Makerspace funded by the NOVUS program at Tecnologico de Monterrey; and the impactor project funded by the Portuguese FCT-PEST program UID/EEA/00066/2013.

References

1. Weichhart, G., Molina, A., Chen, D., Whitman, L.E., Vernadat, F.: Challenges and current developments for sensing, smart and sustainable enterprise systems. Comput. Ind. **79**, 34–46 (2016)
2. Santucci, G., Martinez, C., Vlad-Câlcic, D.: The sensing enterprise. In: Proceedings of FInES-Aalborg Workshop, European Commission, DG CONNECT 02 (2012)
3. Filos, E.: Smart organizations in the digital age. In: Mezgar, I. (ed.) Integration of ICT in Smart Organizations, pp. 1–38. IGI Global, London (2006)
4. Zollo, M., Cennamo, C., Neumann, K.: Beyond what and why: understanding organizational evolution towards sustainable enterprise models. Organ. Environ. **26**(3), 241–259 (2013)
5. Camarinha-Matos, Luis M., Afsarmanesh, H., Boucher, X.: The role of collaborative networks in sustainability. In: Camarinha-Matos, L.M., Boucher, X., Afsarmanesh, H. (eds.) PRO-VE 2010. IAICT, vol. 336, pp. 1–16. Springer, Heidelberg (2010). doi:10.1007/978-3-642-15961-9_1
6. Penas, O., Plateaux, R., Patalano, S., Hammadi, M.: Multi-scale approach from mechatronic to Cyber-Physical Systems for the design of manufacturing systems. Comput. Ind. **86**, 52–69 (2017)

7. Miranda, J., Pérez-Rodríguez, R., Borja, V., Wright, P.K., Molina, A.: Integrated product, process and manufacturing system development reference model to develop cyber-physical production systems – the sensing, smart and sustainable microfactory case study. In: IFAC 2017 World Congress, Toulouse France (2017)
8. Lee, E.A.: Cyber physical systems: design challenges. In: 11th IEEE International Symposium on Object Oriented Real-Time Distributed Computing (ISORC), pp. 363–369. IEEE (2008)
9. Mühlhäuser, M.: Smart products: an introduction. In: Mühlhäuser, M., Ferscha, A., Aitenbichler, E. (eds.) AmI 2007. CCIS, vol. 11, pp. 158–164. Springer, Heidelberg (2008). doi:10.1007/978-3-540-85379-4_20
10. Maxwell, D., Van der Vorst, R.: Developing sustainable products and services. J. Clean. Prod. **11**(8), 883–895 (2003)
11. Gmelin, H., Seuring, S.: Determinants of a sustainable new product development. J. Clean. Prod. **69**, 1–9 (2014)
12. Todd, R.H., Allen, D.K., Alting, L.: Manufacturing processes reference guide. Industrial Press Inc., New York (1994)
13. Bott, T., Gerlinger, W., Barth, J.: Tailor made products by smart processes. Macromol. React. Eng. **9**(5), 396–400 (2015)
14. Monostori, L.: Cyber-physical production systems: roots, expectations and R&D challenges. Procedia CIRP **17**, 9–13 (2014)
15. Mbow, C., Smith, P., Skole, D., Duguma, L., Bustamante, M.: Achieving mitigation and adaptation to climate change through sustainable agroforestry practices in Africa. Curr. Opin. Environ. Sustainab. **6**, 8–14 (2014)
16. Kong, D., Choi, S., Yasui, Y., Pavanaskar, S., Dornfeld, D., Wright, P.: Software-based tool path evaluation for environmental sustainability. J. Manufact. Syst. **30**(4), 241–247 (2011)
17. Liebert, A.: Industry 4.0–the intended impact of Cyber Physical Systems in a Smart Factory on the daily business processes: a study on BMW (UK) Manufacturing Limited (2016). www.diva-portal.se/smash/get/diva2:944759/FULLTEXT01.pdf. Accessed 27 Mar 2017
18. Wang, S., Wan, J., Li, D., Zhang, C.: Implementing smart factory of industrie 4.0: an outlook. Int. J. Distrib. Sens. Netw. **12**(1), 1–10 (2016)
19. Jones, A.T., McLean, C.R.: A proposed hierarchical control model for automated manufacturing systems. J. Manufact. Syst. **5**(1), 15–25 (1986)
20. Ramesh, R.: Architecting digital transformation. J. Inf. Technol. Manage. **29**, 6–11 (2016)
21. Chen, D., Youssef, J.R., and Zacharewicz, G.: Towards an enterprise operating system-requirements for standardisation. In: Zelm, M. (ed.) Proceedings of the 6th Workshop on Enterprise Interoperability, Nîmes, France, 27 May 2015 (2015). http://ceur-ws.org
22. Parrish, B.D.: Designing the sustainable enterprise. Futures **39**(7), 846–860 (2007)
23. Bocken, N.M.P., Short, S.W., Rana, P., Evans, S.: A literature and practice review to develop sustainable business model archetypes. J. Clean. Prod. **65**, 42–56 (2014)
24. Nachira, F., Dini, P., Nicolai, A.: A Network of Digital Business Ecosystems for Europe: Roots, Processes and Perspectives. European Commission, Brussels (2007)
25. Camarinha-Matos, L.M., Afsarmanesh, H., Galeano, N., Molina, A.: Collaborative networked organizations–concepts and practice in manufacturing enterprises. Comput. Ind. Eng. **57**(1), 46–60 (2009)
26. Graça, P., Camarinha-Matos, L.M.: Performance indicators for collaborative business ecosystems – literature review and trends. Technol. Forecast. Soc. Chang. **116**, 237–255 (2017)

27. Romero, D., Noran, O., Afsarmanesh, H.: Green virtual enterprise breeding environments bag of assets management: a contribution to the sharing economy. In: Camarinha-Matos, L.M., Bénaben, F., Picard, W. (eds.) PRO-VE 2015. IAICT, vol. 463, pp. 439–447. Springer, Cham (2015). doi:10.1007/978-3-319-24141-8_40
28. Molina, A., Mejia, R., Galeano, N., Najera, T., Velandia, M.: The HUB as an enabling IT strategy to achieve smart organizations. In: Integration of ICT in Smart Organizations, pp. 68–100. IGI Global (2006). http://www.digital-ecosystems.org/book/pdf/0.3.pdf
29. Li, X., Lu, R., Liang, X., Shen, X., Chen, J., Lin, X.: Smart community: an internet of things application. IEEE Commun. Magaz. **49**(11), 68–75 (2011)
30. Höjer, M., Wangel, J.: Smart sustainable cities: definition and challenges. In: Hilty, L.M., Aebischer, B. (eds.) ICT Innovations for Sustainability. AISC, vol. 310, pp. 333–349. Springer, Cham (2015). doi:10.1007/978-3-319-09228-7_20
31. Perera, C., Zaslavsky, A., Christen, P., Georgakopoulos, D.: Sensing as a service model for smart cities supported by internet of things. Trans. Emerg. Telecommun. Technol. **25**(1), 81–93 (2014)
32. Sagl, G., Resch, B., Blaschke, T.: Contextual sensing: integrating contextual information with human and technical geo-sensor information for smart cities. Sensors **15**(7), 17013–17035 (2015)
33. Washburn, D., Sindhu, U., Balaouras, S., Dines, R.A., Hayes, N., Nelson, L.E.: Helping CIOs understand "smart city" initiatives. Growth **17**(2), 1–17 (2009)
34. Kramers, A., Höjer, M., Lövehagen, N., Wangel, J.: Smart sustainable cities–Exploring ICT solutions for reduced energy use in cities. Environ. Model Softw. **56**, 52–62 (2014)
35. Yan, Y., Qian, Y., Sharif, H., Tipper, D.: A survey on smart grid communication infrastructures: Motivations, requirements and challenges. IEEE Commun. Surv. Tutor. **15**(1), 5–20 (2013)
36. Camarinha-Matos, L.M.: Collaborative smart grids - a survey on trends. Renew. Sustain. Energy Rev. **65**, 283–294 (2016)

Circular Economy

A PLM Vision for Circular Economy

Sofia Freitas de Oliveira[1(✉)] and António Lucas Soares[1,2]

[1] INESC TEC, Centre for Enterprise Systems Engineering, Rua Dr. Roberto Frias, 4200-465 Porto, Portugal
sofia.f.oliveira@inesctec.pt, als@fe.up.pt

[2] FEUP, Faculdade de Engenharia da Universidade do Porto, Rua Dr. Roberto Frias, 4200-465 Porto, Portugal

Abstract. Due to growing concerns with sustainability issues and the emergence of the Circular Economy (CE) paradigm, combined with recent technological changes and consequent increase in competitiveness, there is a pressing need to redefine the Product Lifecycle Management (PLM) approach. PLM needs to incorporate aspects that would enable the shift to this paradigm, such as enhanced collection and evaluation of information coming from production processes, distribution, retail, consumers, and collaboration in an extended enterprise context, by implementing enabling technologies such as the Internet of Things (IoT) and Big Data. This paper proposes a vision, based on the state of the art, for a CE enabled PLM, having the Portuguese footwear industry scenario as a reference.

Keywords: Product Lifecycle Management · Circular Economy · Collaboration · Information management · Footwear industry · Industry 4.0 · IoT · Big Data

1 Introduction

Today, the concept of Product Lifecycle Management (PLM) is being redefined by the shift from the mass production paradigm to a new personalized, on demand, customer-driven and knowledge-based production paradigm [1], which requires the enhancement of information coming from design, production processes, distribution, retail, consumers, among the whole product lifecycle, from its initial inception to its end of life. The increase in complexity of products has led to enterprise unbundling, with most companies focusing on their core activities and externalizing support activities, leading to a value chain distribution among several organizations. In this decentralized knowledge intensive environment, collaboration between the stakeholders involved in all product lifecycle activities, in an extended enterprise context (network of retailers, consumers, producers, among others) is a challenge that needs to be addressed in PLM, enabled by technologies such as the IoT and Big Data. At the same time, new challenges related to growing concerns with sustainability issues and the increasing significance of Circular Economy (CE) concept are emerging, which require improved products that can be used for longer, with multiple lifecycles. This scenario poses challenges to future

L.M. Camarinha-Matos et al. (Eds.): PRO-VE 2017, IFIP AICT 506, pp. 591–602, 2017.
DOI: 10.1007/978-3-319-65151-4_52

PLM systems, especially those intended for SMEs, which have limited internal resources and strongly rely on collaboration with external partners, suppliers and customers.

This paper proposes a vision for a CE enabled PLM, targeting SMEs needs, having the Portuguese footwear industry as a reference in order to illustrate the current scenario, and is structured as follows. The Portuguese footwear industry, which consists mainly of SMEs, is a success story in the Portuguese industry, being responsible for the greatest positive contribution to the Portuguese trade balance. Leading European footwear players, such as Portugal and Italy, pursue a strategy based on technological innovation, quality-competition, and product differentiation. Differentiation is a crucial factor for the fashion cluster, as a result of accelerated changes in consumer preferences and fashion trends [2]. These changes require a reduction of the footwear development cycle, with repercussions to companies' strategies and PLM approaches.

The volume of business growth in the footwear sector witnessed in recent years, together with product differentiation and a decrease in time to market, translates into an almost exponential increase of references, each one with a reduced production volume. This new reality, while enhancing new opportunities for the most dynamic footwear companies, entails enormous organizational and technical challenges regarding product data management throughout the entire product lifecycle.

Moreover, the increase in complexity of footwear products led to specialization and consequent unbundling. Currently, few footwear companies internalize all their processes, leading to a value chain distribution among several organizations (from the end customer, either an individual store or a distribution chain, through the manufacturer and its partners, often in the form of subcontractors, to raw material suppliers), which greatly increases the need for interaction between agents, with large amounts of data, information and knowledge being constantly exchanged. In this heterogeneous and dispersed environment, the alignment of people, information and processes poses a big challenge. In order to be competitive in the described context, companies must manage their value chains effectively, with the aim of reducing lengthy product development cycles and costs, while improving quality [3].

Traditionally, the management of this dynamic in SMEs is done in a very ad-hoc way, without any specific methodologies, usually by using tools designed for personal productivity (text documents, spreadsheets, e-mail messages). This approach, in addition to requiring a huge consumption of human resources, greatly limits the ability to exploit the value associated with the increase in data exchanged, and its transformations into information and even knowledge. Many SMEs have strong gaps in management and execution of activities with a strong collaborative nature, both horizontally (inter-company relations along the value chain) and vertically (information exchange between business processes within the same organization).

Today's knowledge-intensive product development setting requires a computational framework that allows the acquisition, representation and reuse of product and process knowledge. In a manufacturing environment, all product information should be shared along the value chain and continuously synchronized with updates. During product utilization, product data must be used by the service chain in order to provide support. Sharing and managing product data, information and knowledge is the cornerstone of

PLM [3]. PLM is defined as business strategy for building and sustaining a product-centric knowledge environment, seeking to integrate people, processes, resources and information. A PLM environment allows collaboration between multiple stakeholders of a product along its lifecycle [4]. Over the last two decades, PLM emerged as a strategy to enable end-to-end product development [5]. Ideally, companies manage products from cradle to grave as part of their PLM strategy, according to a linear model in which products are developed, manufactured, used and disposed. However, environmental problems such as biodiversity loss; water, air and soil pollution; resource depletion; excessive land use, among other sustainability issues, are increasingly compromising the earth's life-support systems, pressing the need to transition to more sustainable paradigms [6]. To address these issues, the concept of Circular Economy, while not entirely new, has recently been gaining importance. Based on different contributions [6] define Circular Economy as "a regenerative system in which resource input and waste, emission and energy leakage are minimized by slowing, closing and narrowing material and energy loops. This can be achieved through long-lasting design, maintenance, repair, reuse, remanufacturing, refurbishing and recycling" [6]. Ongoing European Project FUTURING – Futuring European Industry[1] defines an approach for the definition of CE that is structured in Building Blocks, Pillar Actions and impacts on Profit/Planet/People, covering the extent of CE. The Building Blocks represent the different dimensions of CE, defined as Science & Technology, Business & Innovation, Human Being & Society, Policy & Finance, Environmental Sustainability, Education & Training. The Pillar Actions describe some complimentary ways to implement CE – Regenerate, Share, Optimize, Loop, Virtualize, Exchange. A fundamental principle of circular economy is that after the utilization phase, products should be returned to manufacturers instead of being disposed, creating new flows of recyclables with extremely high values. Therefore, circular economy will require new PLM enabling solutions and supporting services [5].

According to a study conducted by McKinsey & Company [7], companies can benefit largely from consumer-focused lifecycle thinking and cross-functional collaboration, as it helps capturing more value from the resources they consume. Some companies are already adopting circular economy practices to create durable products that are easy to reuse or recycle and profitable, by devising a highly collaborative product development process that helps determining sourcing requirements, production methods, marketing, sales and other aspects of how products are created and managed at the end of their lives. However, these aspects are far from being a reality in PLM solutions designed for SMEs, and even in PLM solutions overall [8, 9]. The rest of the paper is organized as follows: Sects. 2, 3 and 4 cover a brief literature review regarding PLM and its main aspects: data and information management and collaboration; Sect. 5 provides a vision for the support of Circular Economy in PLM; the paper concludes with final remarks on the contributions of this study, and interesting fields for further research.

[1] www.futuring-project.eu.

2 PLM and PLM Systems

In the last few years, PLM has become the paramount management approach in engineering in the manufacturing industry [8]. According to Stark [4], PLM is the business activity of managing a company's products all the way along their lifecycles; from the very first idea until products are retired and disposed of, in the most effective way. PLM is an integrated paradigm that includes a consistent set of methods, models and tools for managing product information, engineering processes and applications along the phases of product lifecycle [8]. The core functionalities of PLM systems include information management, process management and application integration, as well as a set of additional PLM methods and tools such as engineering collaboration support, user access management and data analysis, reporting and visualization [8].

As clearly defined by Stark [4], the generic product lifecycle has five phases: Imagine, Define, Realize, Support/Use, Retire/Dispose. During the imagination phase, the product in an idea. In the "Define" phase, ideas are translated into detailed descriptions. By the end of the realization phase, the product is ready be used by the customer. During the use/support phase, the product is being used by the customer. Ultimately, the product reaches a phase in which it is no longer useful, and is retired by the company or disposed by the customer. The specific activities that occur across the lifecycle phases can be different, depending on the particular industry. PLM activities enable a company to grow revenues by improving innovation cycles, reducing time-to-market for new products, and providing support and new services for already existing products [4]. PLM can improve the development of new products and reduce manufacturing costs by controlling products' data throughout their lifecycle [10].

The main weakness of current PLM solutions is poor support of product lifecycle phases and activities besides product development [8]. Another problem of available PLM solutions is their very high complexity and the huge customizing efforts that are necessary. The total costs involved in the installation, usage and maintenance of PLM systems means that the most powerful and popular PLM systems are only affordable to large companies, and a mirage for SMEs [11]. In recent years, light and low cost PLM solutions have started to appear in the market for SMEs [12]. However, according to studies carried out by several authors [9], SMEs continue to consider PLM solutions complex, with high cost and high dependence on software services, which constitutes a barrier to the adoption of this technology. In this context, one of the biggest challenges in PLM is the reduction of costs related to IT technology and infrastructure investment, as well as the development of easy-to-use, intuitive software with features that are very oriented to the real needs of organizations, with the objective of enabling their adoption by SMEs, which represent 99% of the European Union's manufacturers [13].

3 Data and Information Management in PLM

The Industry 4.0 term, which originates from a German government strategy project [14], defines the complete digitization and integration of the industrial value chain. The technical foundation for Industry 4.0 is the combination of information and communication technologies with automation technologies, embodying the Internet-of-Things (IoT) and Internet-of-Services (IoS). The combination of these technologies enables high levels of network communication, encompassing people, equipment, products, services, as well as business-to-business communication. This way, it becomes possible to create intelligent supply chains, covering all phases of the product lifecycle - from the initial idea to the end of its life, through development, production, use and service [14]. The Reference Model for Industry 4.0 - RAMI 4.0, consists in a three-dimensional coordinate model that describes all the important aspects of Industry 4.0, in order to reach a common understanding of required standards and use cases. According to RAMI 4.0, presented in Fig. 1, the complex interrelationships can be decomposed into elementary clusters: "Layers" axis, "Life Cycle & Value Stream" axis and "Hierarchy Levels" axis [15].

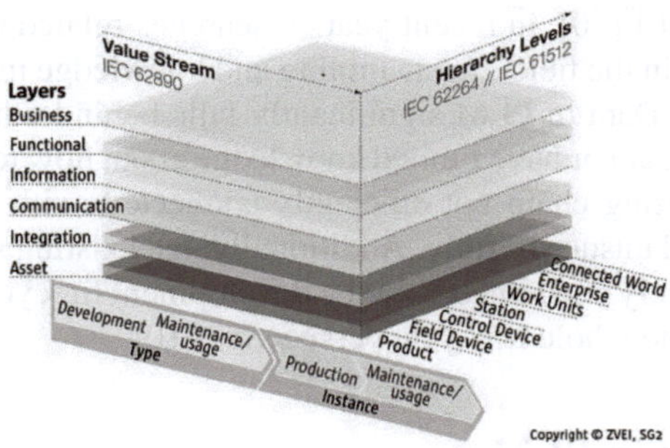

Fig. 1. RAMI 4.0

RAMI 4.0 maps the relationship between the lifecycle of products and value streams, the hierarchical levels of business information systems connected via the Internet, and the IT structure of an Industry 4.0 component. The description of the product lifecycle is done considering that a product has a lifecycle as a virtual "type" (during the design and development phases) and as a physical instance (after the manufacturing phase, through use, service and end of life). During the entire product lifecycle, as a type and an instance, the data generated in the process chains is processed by PLM systems, creating product-service centered collaboration among the connected world [16].

Due to technological advances and the emergence of the Industry 4.0 paradigm, which generate and must deal with extremely high volumes of data, new opportunities for the application of PLM in areas such as SMAC (Social, Mobile, Analytics, Cloud), Internet of Things (IoT), Big Data and Smart Products have recently emerged. PLM has been evolving continuously towards a digital paradigm, under which products are managed throughout their lifecycle using digital information and communication. The reporting of product performance using technologies such as the IoT, GPS and RFID, which allows real-time perception of its performance and customer satisfaction level, is a pressing trend [4].

The aim of the IoT application in PLM is to establish a smart information cycle along the whole product lifecycle. From data sensed and communicated by smart products, manufacturers can understand products' behavior when they are being used by the customer. From the analysis of product data, innovative new products and services can be identified in order to better fit customer's requirements. In the product's end of life, components can be identified and tracked, which can lead to better decisions being taken regarding how to treat products in an environmentally correct way. These aspects can reduce costs and improve compliance with environmental rules and regulations [4].

Top PLM manufacturers are already defining visions for enabling digitalization in their PLM solutions. Siemens Automation is building a "Smart Innovation Portfolio", with the aim of activating digitalization in manufacturing. Siemens AG's "Digital Enterprise Software Suite" extends digitalization from development and operation through production [17]. PTC FlexPLM, a powerful retail oriented PLM, is leveraging PTC's own IoT technology, ThingWorx [18]. However, the integration of these aspects in PLM is at an early stage, and far from becoming commonplace in PLM solutions for SMEs. According to Li [10], in recent years researches related to the increase of data have been conducted in the field of data mining and knowledge management. However, the utilization of Big Data in PLM significantly falls behind other areas. Most manufacturers do not store data or have limited knowledge about how to use these data, which makes the manufacturing chain not efficiently connected, with data being generated, transmitted and stored unsuccessfully. Additionally, the existing studies about Big Data and PLM are exclusively concerned with the development lifecycle phase, and have not been explored from the whole lifecycle perspective [10].

4 Collaboration in PLM

In nowadays global economy, manufacturing companies must be considered in the context of their input to the whole value chain. Extended or virtual enterprises, which consist of connected chains of suppliers, manufacturers, assemblers, distributors and customers, compete to provide customized products and services to competitive markets [19]. Virtual enterprises and manufacturing networks have been largely discussed in the last decade [1]. According to Camarinha-Matos [1], "a Virtual Enterprise represents a temporary alliance of enterprises who join to share skills or core competencies and resources in order to better respond to business opportunities, and whose cooperation is supported by computer networks". An extended enterprise is defined as a particular case of a virtual enterprise, which arises when an organization "extends" its boundaries to all or some of its supply chain stakeholders [1]. Due to the growing complexity of products, their variability and the continuous transformation of customer needs, product lifecycle has become increasingly challenging, requiring collaboration between heterogeneous teams, holding expertise in different fields [20]. Internally, collaboration among associated departments, such as marketing, development and production, is the most crucial factor in the successful on-time delivery of new products to market, which is one of PLM goals [21]. Externally, collaboration among various stakeholders, such as customers, suppliers and other partners, such as service suppliers, is also a contributing factor to improve processes efficiency and customer satisfaction.

Therefore, the modern product lifecycle is characterized by an interdisciplinary interaction between a large number of actors, intra and extra organization, such as departments, customers, suppliers and partners, in an extended enterprise environment. Traditionally, PLM solutions focus on collaboration between various departments of the same company. However, as a business integration platform, PLM systems must take into account the entire network of partners and customers, in order to improve information access and sharing inside the company and outside the company [22]. This way, PLM can provide the capability of collaborative creation as well as management and use of product data, information and knowledge in a virtual enterprise environment, merging people, processes and technology [23].

Siemens PLM software solution for apparel, footwear and accessories provides the supply chain stakeholders (buyers, designers, merchandisers and managers) with a central location to effectively manage the fashion product development process, enabling collaboration across the supply chain [17]. PTC Flex PLM integrates internal and external teams, as well as third-party customers [18]. However, fashion industry PLM solutions aimed at SMEs, such as Infor Fashion PLM, are more focused on devising collaboration within the enterprise, by linking planning, design, development and execution on a common platform [24]. The effective implementation of an extended PLM raises a concerning challenge, which is the need to process information gathered from multiple sources into knowledge for making effective decisions in real-time. This technical challenge addresses the goal to integrate the collaborative network partners' information systems, so that cooperation can occur flawlessly [1]. The interaction between the various agents is marked by the use of IT tools such as CAD, CAE and CAM, among others, which creates a very heterogeneous data scenario [8].

5 Vision for the Support of Circular Economy in PLM

As evidenced in the previous sections, recent work shows that PLM is evolving from a system mainly supporting product development and engineering processes to a platform destined at encompassing the whole product lifecycle. This future PLM platform is about integration, collaboration and connectivity of devices, across disciplines and enterprise borders, supported by enabling technologies such as the IoT and Big Data [25]. Scarcity of materials and energy resources, combined with rapid degradation of the environment, is pressing the reformulation of economic and industrial systems. As briefly mentioned in the opening section, nowadays most manufacturers still follow a linear model of production, in which materials are extracted, turned into products, used and discarded, with their value being lost, according to a "take, make, use and throw away" approach. The Circular Economy approach, which includes reuse, recycling and remanufacturing principles, presents an opportunity for manufacturers, since it enables the creation of flows of valuables capable of generating new business opportunities. However, there are challenges in closing the loop [25], particularly the information gaps along the end-of-life stages of product lifecycle. The development of efficient and robust PLM systems for Circular Economy will require excellence in IT, supporting collaboration among the extended enterprise and management of multiple lifecycles [25]. In this context, a Circular Economy PLM Strategy is defined along these lines [26]:

Mission: To provide products capable of satisfying customer needs, while taking full advantage of the company's sustainable production system and innovation competency, considering all impacts along the lifecycle.
Vision: To generate data, information and knowledge within the supply chain and to manage it from the perspective of sustainable product design and development, manufacturing, distribution, use and service and recycling and recovery.
Objective: To share data, information and knowledge of all the product lifecycle phases among all the stakeholders (internal and external); to encourage collaboration between customers, designers, producers and suppliers; and to enable sustainability through environmentally conscious products and processes.

Figure 2 illustrates the concept of managing the entire product lifecycle from a Circular Economy outlook, supporting and driving the value chain. This concept is focused on the footwear industry scenario.

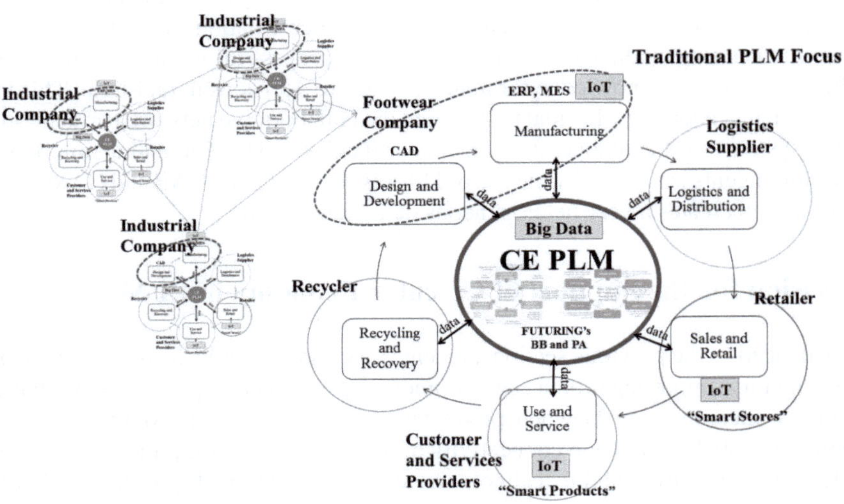

Fig. 2. CE enabled PLM concept

The vision for a CE-enabled PLM proposed in this research encompasses the CE dimensions defined in the scope of the FUTURING approach, represented by Science & Technology, Business & Innovation, Human Being & Society, Policy & Finance, Environmental Sustainability and Education & Training Building Blocks (BB) and the Pilar Actions (PA) needed to implement CE - Regenerate, Share, Optimize, Loop, Virtualize, Exchange. The vision is grouped into four categories: Enabling technologies; Types of products; Product lifecycle phases and stakeholders; Virtual enterprises and industrial symbiosis. Each category is described below.

Enabling Technologies. There is a consentual opinion among various authors [4, 5, 7, 27] that digital technologies are the main drivers to the transition to the Circular Economy paradigm in PLM. The Internet can link together multiple supply chain partners, improving transparency and helping optimize cost, service, agility and resilience [27]. The use of the IoT technology is especially important during the Manufacturing, Sales and Retail and Use and Service product lifecycle phases, as shown in Fig. 2. During the Manufacturing phase, the IoT helps optimizing production efficiency, by using data across the manufacturing value chain. During the Use and Service phase, the IoT enables companies to track their products, offering numerous opportunities to get an improved understanding of products behavior, as well as to manage their related services. At the store level, during the Sales and Retail phase, the IoT enables the collection of valuable data regarding consumers' preferences.

Due to recent technological advances and the evolution of PLM into a digital paradigm, under which products are managed using digital information and communication, the volumes of data generated along the whole lifecycle are increasing at a high rate, which poses an opportunity for the application of Big Data in PLM [4]. There is the need to analyze and extract information from the large volumes of data collected along the product lifecycle, in order to capture knowledge that can lead to improvements in product lifecycle's activities all along the supply chain. Therefore, a CE enabled PLM should support IoT and Big Data technologies integration.

Types of Products. Anext generation PLM should support "smart products", embedding information devices such as RFID or on-board computers, capable of tracking and tracing all the product information over the entire lifecycle in real-time. PLM solutions should also manage intangible products such as software or services, and in a more complex level PSS (Product Service Systems) [8].

Currently, there are concluded and ongoing R&D projects that address product and stores sensorization. Shoe-ID project, concluded successfully, addressed the incorporation on RFID technology in the initial phase of the footwear production cycle, in order to simplify the whole supply chain follow-up, from manufacturing to the final consumer [28]. The ongoing project FASCOM aims at creating a solution that enables the collection of sales related data from the store and its access by product developers, manufacturers and distributers [29]. Data collected from the store regarding the perception of products by customers, as well as reasons for lost sales, can provide valuable information to designers and manufacturers that can lead to improvements in the development of new products. The integration of these technological solutions with PLM solutions is not yet explored and therefore is an area for further research. A CE enabled PLM should support smart products and smart stores, connected by the IoT.

Product Lifecycle Phases and Stakeholders. As previously stated in Sect. 4, currently the focus of SME oriented PLM solutions is within one manufacturing company, which may include various distributed locations [8]. A CE-enabled PLM approach for footwear industry should integrate all supply chain stakeholders along the whole product lifecycle: logistics suppliers, materials suppliers, retailers, manufacturers, customer and recyclers.

Specific models, methods and tools from actual PLM solutions are mainly focused on product design and development, providing little or no support to other lifecycle phases [8]. CE-enabled PLM platforms must provide support in managing other downstream product phases such as manufacturing, distribution and logistics, sales and retail, use and service, recycling and recovery, focusing on value-added activities. A CE enabled PLM system should consider not only the management of a single life cycle but multiple product life cycles in which the products used can be changed or reconfigured in a sustainable way. These aspects are represented in Fig. 2. As previously mentioned, PLM platforms must support smart, connected products and stores enabled by the IoT, improving product design through feedback on in-use performance and durability. This information flow should continue seamlessly through reuse to the end of use, with further feedback to the designer and producer, supporting improved design and material choice. In the design and development phase, components normalization and modularity aspects must be considered, thinking of the products end-of-life from an early stage, which can include reuse, remanufacturing, recycling and disposal. In the CE context, the use and service phase is particularly relevant, since the product and its related services must be managed in order to provide customer support. CE enabled PLM systems should focus on generating product data during utilization and end-of-use phases, which is more complex than generating product data at the development and manufacturing phases. Data, information and knowledge flows break down after the delivery of the product to the customer, preventing the feedback of data, information and knowledge from service and recycling providers back to designers and manufacturers [30]. CE PLM solutions should close this information gap, feeding information about in-use and end-of-use to inform product development, materials selection and support circular business models. The recycling and recovery phase is characterized by various scenarios, such as product reuse with refurbishing, components reuse with disassembly and refurbishing, material reclamation with disassembly and disposal with or without incineration, material reclamation without disassembly, remanufacturing [30]. Therefore, in the recycling and recovery phase PLM systems must be capable of managing activities related to materials recovery, recycling, remanufacturing and disposal.

Virtual Enterprises and Industrial Symbiosis. Industrial symbiosis engages traditionally independent industries in a collaborative approach to competitive advantage by involving tangible exchange of materials, energy, water, and byproducts. The key elements to successfully implement industrial symbiosis are collaboration and the synergistic potential offered by geographic adjacency [31]. Relating this concept to the virtual enterprise concept, there are some opportunities in extending PLM not only to the company's supply chain, but also to other companies with whom they have resources synergies. The aim would be to establish a knowledge base that would involve a network of enterprises, offering the necessary conditions to efficiently promote the sharing information regarding materials, water, energy and infrastructure, with the intention of achieving sustainable development in a collaborative way [32]. This is especially relevant for SMEs, which have limited internal resources, since it reinforces their capacity without the need to make large investments. Figure 2 illustrates the concept of connecting multiple enterprises with symbiotic relationships, incorporating this data in PLM.

6 Conclusions

A CE enabled PLM would be a fundamental tool to improve companies' competitiveness in a collaborative and sustainable way, particularly footwear industry SMEs, which have complex interactions along the supply chain. Due to the growing market demands in this field, translated by product differentiation and a reduction in time to market, as well as increasing environmental awareness, there is a need to implement a new PLM paradigm. This circular PLM paradigm should be focused on generating data, information and knowledge within the organization and its stakeholders and manage it along the product's multiple lifecycles, from the perspective of sustainable product design and development, manufacturing, use and service, recycling and recovery. Technologies such as the IoT and Big Data will have a major role in enabling collaboration throughout the whole lifecycle. Although the design and development phase can be defined as the main phase responsible for driving the sustainability impact [26], future works must be done regarding its connection with other critical lifecycle phases such as use and service and recycling and recovery. Currently, efforts are being made in the development of technological solutions aimed at supply chain integration and smart products and stores. However, the integration of these technologies with PLM is nonexistent and therefore should be explored. The integration of a knowledge database regarding industrial symbiosis in PLM is also an area for further research.

Acknowledgments. The research leading to these results has received funding from the European Union´s Horizon 2020 – The EU Framework Programme for Research and Innovation 2014–2020, under grant agreement No 723633.

References

1. Ferreira, F., Faria, J., Azevedo, J., et al.: Product lifecycle management in knowledge intensive collaborative environments: an application to the automotive industry. Int. J. Inf. Manage. **36**, 1474–1487 (2016)
2. Batista, F., Matos, J.E., Matos, M.C.: Assessing the Competitiveness of the Portuguese Footwear Sector, GEE Papers, No. 66 (2017)
3. Terzi, S., Bouras, A., Dutta, D., Garetti, M., Kiritsis, D.: Product lifecycle management – from its history to its new role. Int. J. Product Lifecycle Manage. **4**(4), 360–389 (2010)
4. Stark, J.: Product Lifecycle Management (Volume 2): The Devil is in the Details. Decision Engineering, 3rd edn. Springer, Cham (2016)
5. Raconteur, Supporting the Circular Economy. https://www.raconteur.net/business/supporting-the-circular-economy
6. Geissdoerfer, M., Savaget, P., Bocken, N.M.P., Hultink, E.J.: The circular economy – a new sustainability paradigm? J. Clean. Prod. **143**, 757–768 (2016)
7. Bouton, S., Hannon, E., Rogers, M.: The circular economy: Moving from theory to practice. McKinsey Center for Business and Environment. Special edition (2016)
8. Abramovici, M., Aidi, Y.: Next generation product lifecycle management (PLM). In: Fathi, M. (ed.) Integration of Practice-Oriented Knowledge Technology: Trends and Prospectives, pp. 143–156. Springer, Heidelberg (2013)

9. Messaadia, M., Baudry, D., Louis, A., Mahdikhah, S., Evans, R., Gao, J., Paquet, T., Sahnoun, M., Mazari, B.: PLM adoption in SMEs context. Comput. Aided Des. Appl. **13**(5), 618–627 (2016)
10. Li, J., Tao, F., Cheng, Y., et al.: Big data in product lifecycle management. Int. J. Adv. Manuf. Technol. **81**, 667–684 (2015)
11. Baptista, A., Lourenço, E., Oliveira, S., et al.: PLM4all – a novel approach for product lifecycle management of mechatronic equipment in SME. FAIM (2015)
12. Stackpole, B.: Vendors try to rightsize PLM for smaller businesses, desktop engineering. http://www.deskeng.com/articles/aabjyf.htm
13. European Commission. Internal market, industry, entrepreneurship and SMEs. http://ec.europa.eu/growth/smes/business-friendly-environment/sme-definition_is
14. Acatech: Recommendations for implementing the strategic initiative Industrie 4.0: Final report of the Industrie 4.0 Working Group. Federal Ministry of Education and Research (2013)
15. Hankel, M., Rexroth, B.: Industrie 4.0: The Reference Architectural Model Industrie 4.0, ZVEI: Die Elektroindustrie (2015)
16. Phoenix Contact, RAMI 4.0: the three-dimensional reference architecture model. goo.gl/4f04J5
17. Siemens PLM. https://www.plm.automation.siemens.com/en_gb/
18. PTC Flex PLM. http://www.ptc.com/retail-plm/flexplm
19. Browne, J., Zhang, J.: Extended and virtual enterprises – similarities and differences. Int. J. Agile Manage. Syst. **1**, 30–36 (1999)
20. Penciuc, D., Durupt, A., Belkadi, F., et al.: Towards a PLM interoperability for a collaborative design support system. Procedia CIRP **25**, 369–376 (2014)
21. Oh, J., Lee, S., Yang, J.: A collaboration model for new product development through the integration of PLM and SCM in the electronics industry. Comput. Ind. **73**, 82–92 (2015)
22. Soto-Acosta, P., Placer-Maruri, E., Perez-Gonzalez, D.: A case analysis of a product lifecycle management framework for SMEs. Int. J. Inf. Manage. **36**, 240–244 (2015)
23. Ming, X., Yan, J., Lu, W., et al.: Mass production of tooling product families via modular feature-based design to manufacturing collaboration in PLM. J. Intell. Manuf. **18**, 185–195 (2007). Springer Science+Business Media, LCC
24. Infor Fashion PLM. http://www.infor.com/product-summary/plm/fashion/
25. ResCoM – Resource Conservative Manufacturing. http://www.rescoms.eu/
26. Vila, C., Abellán-Nebot, J., Albiñana, J., et al.: An approach to sustainable product lifecycle management (Green PLM). Procedia Eng. **132**, 585–592 (2015)
27. Weetman, C.: A Circular Economy Handbook for Business and Supply Chains: Repair, Remake, Redesign, Rethink. Kogan Page Publishers, New York (2016)
28. INESC TEC. https://www.inesctec.pt/cese/projetos/casos-de-sucesso/shoe-id/
29. CTCP. http://www.ctcp.pt/info/email/index.asp?valores=4|1|2016|3515
30. Kiritsis, D.: Closed-loop PLM for intelligent products in the era of the Internet of things. CAD Comput. Aided Des. **43**, 479–501 (2011)
31. Chertow, M.R.: Industrial symbiosis: literature and taxonomy. In: Annual Review of Energy and the Environment, vol. 25, pp. 313–337. Annual Reviews (2000)
32. Romero, D., Molina, A.: Green virtual enterprise breeding environments: a sustainable industrial development model for a circular economy. In: Camarinha-Matos, Luis M., Xu, L., Afsarmanesh, H. (eds.) PRO-VE 2012. IAICT, vol. 380, pp. 427–436. Springer, Heidelberg (2012). doi:10.1007/978-3-642-32775-9_43

Green Virtual Enterprise Breeding Environments Enabling the RESOLVE Framework

David Romero[1,2(✉)], Ovidiu Noran[2], and Peter Bernus[2]

[1] Tecnológico de Monterrey, Monterrey, Mexico
david.romero.diaz@gmail.com
[2] Griffith University, Nathan, Australia
{ovidiu.noran,p.bernus}@griffith.edu.au

Abstract. Shifting towards Circular Economy will have significant implications on how value offerings are created, delivered and their residual value recovered as well as how shared value is created and captured by various actors in a collaborative (business) network where information, materials, water, energy and cash will flow in different cycles and based on various dynamic interactions within a closed-loop value system. In this context, Green Virtual Enterprise Breeding Environments (GVBEs) will act as long-term strategic networks of green enterprises and their related support institutions established with the aim of providing the necessary conditions, including common (circular) operating principles and infrastructure, for increasing their members' preparedness towards rapid configuration of Forward- and Reverse-Green Virtual Enterprises (GVEs) in order to provide a dynamic model for operations management of closed- loop supply networks. This paper focuses on how GVEs and their breeding environments can contribute to enable McKinsey's RESOLVE framework of six core-principles, and corresponding actions, for circularity: REstore/REgenerate, Share, Optimise, Loop, Virtualise and Exchange.

Keywords: Collaborative networked organisations · Green virtual enterprises · Breeding environments · Sharing economy · Circular Economy · Collaborative consumption · Industrial ecology · Sustainability · Shared value

1 Introduction

A strategic transition towards the *Circular Economy (CE)* [1] requires: (a) the use of renewable energy sources and materials that can be recycled, as well as circular product designs, which support these two conditions, (b) the adoption of new circular business models, (c) global closed-loop networks that support circular material flows, and (d) various enabling conditions of the above [2].

Shifting towards the CE will have significant implications on how value offerings are created, delivered and their residual value recovered as well as how shared value is created and captured by the members of a collaborative (business) network where information, materials, water, energy and cash will flow in different cycles based on various dynamic interactions within a closed-loop value system.

L.M. Camarinha-Matos et al. (Eds.): PRO-VE 2017, IFIP AICT 506, pp. 603–613, 2017.
DOI: 10.1007/978-3-319-65151-4_53

In this context, this paper explores how the *Collaborative Networks discipline* can enable, by creating 'Green Virtual Enterprises and their Breeding Environments' [3–7], the circular business practices of McKinsey's RESOLVE framework of six core-principles, and corresponding actions, to achieve 'circularity' in business operations: REstore/REgenerate, Share, Optimise, Loop, Virtualise and Exchange [8].

2 Green Virtual Enterprises and Their Breeding Environments

A *Green Virtual Enterprise Breeding Environment (GVBE)* has been defined as a "long-term strategic alliance of green enterprises and their related support institutions aimed at offering the necessary conditions (viz. human, financial, social, infrastructural and organisational) to support the rapid configuration of GVEs"… towards the creation of dynamic closed (circular) supply networks [3–5], and inter-organisational Circular [1, 8] and Sharing Economies [9]. *Green Virtual Enterprises (GVEs)* are "short-term alliances of green enterprises, known as GVE partners, which have come together to share their green skills or core-competences and resources in order to better respond and exploit green (circular) business opportunities, and that have been dynamically created within a GVBE". Such GVEs, according to [6] and [7] respectively, must be created as "(a) *dynamic forward supply networks (F-GVEs)* for delivering green and circular products and/or services to the market, as well as (b) *dynamic reverse supply networks (R-GVEs)* for recovering such products sold under the GVBE brand (product stewardship) for service provisioning, product recovering or for safe disposal". Both GVE types are created in order to support the collaborative management of sustainable closed (circular) supply networks [4]. Further details on concepts related to GVEs and their breeding environments can be found in the following references: [3–7].

3 Enabling the RESOLVE Framework

The RESOLVE framework has been developed by McKinsey's Centre for Business and the Environment [8] with the aim of emphasizing six strategies to incorporate Circular Economy concepts into a business, as follows: Restore/REgenerate, Share, Optimise, Loop, Virtualise and Exchange strategies (see Table 1).

'RE' for Restore and Regenerate According to Mckinsey [8], *REstorative/REgenerative (RE) systems* aim to "reclaim, retain and restore the health of natural and industrial ecosystems, and return recovered resources to the bio-sphere and techno-sphere to renew feedstocks". GVBEs aim to develop *RE capabilities* in the techno-sphere (i.e. the industrial ecosystem) in order to reduce virgin materials extraction and materials waste flows, and to increase materials productivity and recovery in the Circular Economy. *RE industrial systems* [1, 8] focus on maximising the usage and value of either products themselves or of their components, and eventually their incorporated materials, by the 'power of circling materials longer' through their reuse, remanufacturing or recycling, and by the 'power of their cascaded use' by using materials discarded as by-products

Table 1. McKinsey's RESOLVE Framework [8]

Circularity Actions	Examples
Restore/Regenerate	• Shift to renewable energy and materials • Reclaim, retain, and restore health of ecosystem. • Return recovered biological resources to the biosphere.
Share	• Share assets (e.g. cars, rooms, appliances). • Reuse/Second-hand • Prolong life through maintenance, design for durability, upgradability, etc.
Optimise	• Increase performance/efficiency of product. • Remove waste in production and supply chain. • Leverage big data, automation, remote sensing and steering.
Loop	• Remanufacture products or components. • Recycle materials • Digest anaerobic • Extract biochemical form organic waste.
Virtualise	• Dematerialising directly (e.g. books, music, travel, etc.). • Dematerialising indirectly (e.g. online shopping).
Exchange	• Replace old with advanced non-renewable materials. • Apply new technologies (e.g. 3D printing). • Choose new products/services (e.g. multimodal transport).

from one value chain to replace virgin materials inflow in another (e.g. Industrial Symbiosis [10]). Hence, GVBEs can act in different industrial sectors as *REstorative systems* (e.g. of land) by becoming 'urban miners' (*cf.* urban mining [11, 12], see Fig. 1), which extend their responsibility beyond their own ecological/environmental footprint, and transform landfills into 'mines' to reclaim the scraps of different materials (e.g. plastics, metals, wood, rubber, etc.) from discarded (landfilled) products. Such action allows recovering lost land and reintroduces various materials as reusable ones in their respective cyclic material flows, allowing the GVBEs to also act as *REgenerative systems* for such materials stocks in the techno-sphere of the Circular Economy.

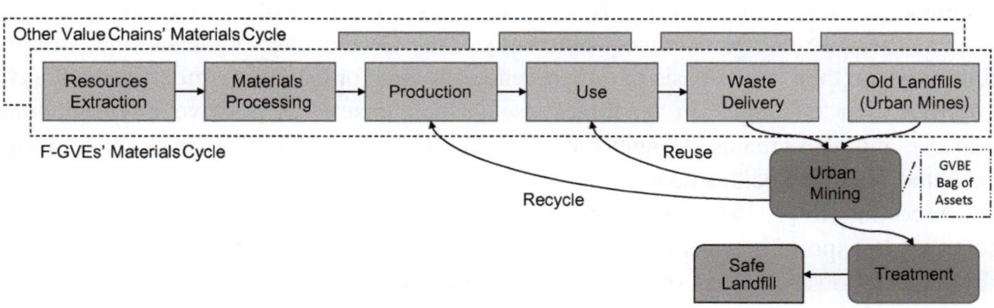

Fig. 1. GVBE Urban Mining based on GVEs Materials Lifecycle (Based on [12])

Other *regenerative* or *conservation actions* performed by GVBEs are the use of renewable sources of energy and sustainable (recyclable and renewable) materials. These actions are enabled by GVBE green practices such as:

(a) Recruiting *GVBE members*/selecting *GVE partners* based on various quantitative and qualitative sustainability metrics [13] (viz. economic, social and environmental (e.g. recyclable materials, eco-design, clean technologies, emissions, waste) performance indicators) to select the most suitable *green enterprises* for GVBE membership and collaboration in F- and R-GVEs, and
(b) The adoption of *green Information Systems (IS)* (software) focus on improving the flow and management of information (e.g. environmental management systems, lifecycle analysis tools), while *green Information Technologies (IT)* focus on the ecological footprints of hardware and other Information and Communication Technology (ICT)-infrastructure, designed and managed under an environmental-care perspective [14].

A good example of such greening effort in IT is the 'GVBE advanced Collaborative Business ICT-Infrastructure' [15], which adopts the *Cloud Computing paradigm* [16], to share hardware and ICT-infrastructures in order to reduce dispersed IT usage, maximise energy efficiency, adopt hardware recycling practices, lower emissions, and minimise water usage in cooling data centres [17].

'S' for Sharing. According to [18], "the *Sharing Economy* is founded on the principle of maximising the utility of assets and other shareable resources by means of renting, lending, swapping, bartering and giving them away in order to avoid their 'idle existence'". The *Sharing Economy* requires the adoption of wider business practices that, while economically sustainable, are able to reduce the environmental footprint of businesses, and also enable socially responsible business behaviours [9]. The concept of a '*GVBE bag of assets*' was introduced in [9] as a virtual repository and/or physical warehouse, including collaborative procurement and shareable assets[1] management strategies and services, with the purpose of facilitating the sharing of tangible and intangible assets and resources among *GVBE members*, so that economies of scale and scope can be achieved and an 'inter-organisational' sharing economy enabled within a GVBE [9] (see Fig. 2). Hence, the *GVBE bag of assets* aims to develop a sharing economy business model that enables GVBE members to share their assets and resources in the sense of the RESOLVE framework, *shareable assets and resources* that would otherwise not be used cost-efficiently. This GVBE inter-organisational sharing economy can then be the basis of new revenue streams for GVBE members as well as to improve their efficiency in resources use (which ensures a positive environmental impact), and also creates stronger connections and trust among GVBE members (with expected positive social impact).

According to [9, 19], some example of *shareable assets* can be: "(a) tangible assets such as transportation vehicles (e.g. collaborative logistics), physical spaces (e.g. shared warehouses, excess space), infrequent-use items (e.g. event equipment), durable goods (e.g. productive assets), etc., and (b) intangible shareable assets like individuals' knowledge, skills and services (both business and software services), data, time and experiences".

[1] A *shareable (tangible) asset* "is characterised by its high acquisition price, low availability and low frequency of use" [9].

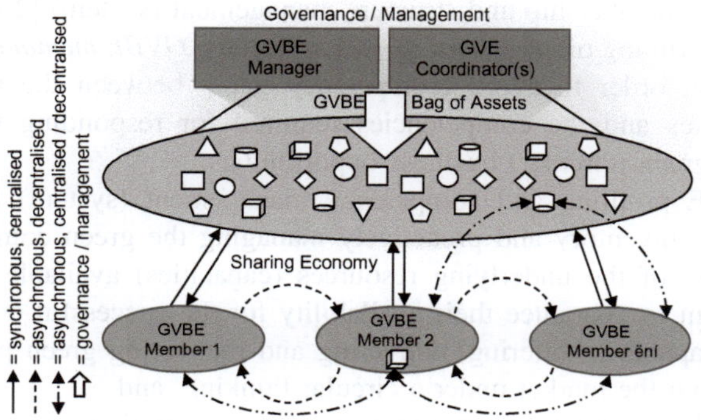

Fig. 2. GVBE Sharing Economy Scenario [9]

Other (quasi) *sharing actions* that GVBEs support are different strategies/services for prolonging life of products or components through their re-use, re-sale, repair, upgrade/refurbishment and/or re-manufacturing, as well as through the recovery of their residual value at their end-of-life via cannibalisation, recycling and/or smart incineration (viz. waste-to-energy) [20], based on the creation of *R-GVEs* [7].

As detailed in [7], *R-GVEs* must be able to sustainably manage 'reverse logistics', despite the sometimes uncertain nature of the reverse material flows in closed-loop (circular) supply networks, and be able to take advantage of new green (circular) business opportunities based on second-hand markets, repair champions, sharing societies, service-life extension programs and resources security initiatives (viz. materials, energy and water), also known as 'Circular Economies'. Moreover, *GVBEs* and *GVEs brokers* [6, 21] will play a fundamental role in marketing, selling and branding GVEs circular products[2] and services (e.g. products as a service, products based on recycled, biodegradable and/or compostable resources, or products/assets in sharing platforms [22]) towards promoting their acceptance in a growing environmental conscious (green) marketplace.

'O' for Optimise. GVEs and their breeding environments aim to integrate and *optimise* complementary, and when needed, redundant green skills or core-competencies and resources (e.g. technologies and practices) of their GVBE members/GVE partners, and through this improve their competitiveness and environmental performance. According to [3], the advantage is to be able to offer green products and/or services that are circular, conserve natural resources, and importantly, are economically viable and socially rewarding for all stakeholders involved. Such *optimisation* is conducted at different scales within the breeding environment and involving different GVBE actors. Some examples of GVBE *optimisation actions* at the *breeding environment level* include:

---

[2] A *circular product* is "a product designed for servitization, lifecycle extension and easy-disassemble for composting and recycling, so their materials can circulate in closed-loops without generating waste" [22].

(a) The GVBE membership and structure management (system) [23] focused on the strategic recruiting of *green enterprises* to become *GVBE members,* and later *GVE partners,* in order to avoid 'competency gaps' between the GVBE available competencies and the competencies required for responding to designed and emerging green (circular) business opportunities,
(b) The GVBE profiling and competency management (system) [23] focused on building an inventory and proactively managing the green competencies (capabilities) and of the underlying resources (capacities) available in the breeding environment to guarantee their availability for the successful creation of F- and R-GVEs capable of offering, delivering and recovering green products and services to/from the market under a circular thinking, and
(c) The GVBE lifecycle management itself (viz. creation, operation, evolution, metamorphosis and dissolution). This includes the GVBE 'evolution lifecycle stage', which refers to a set of feedback (*cf.* optimisation) processes through the GVBE performance management (system) [23], responsible for managing the continuous improvement of the breeding environment's operations, and the GVBE 'metamorphosis lifecycle stage', which refers to various strategic imperatives such as changes in the GVBE mission, strategic adaptation of its business processes, ICT-infrastructure, governance principles and rules, etc. This may be necessary because of new market challenges or observed/predicted trends in the marketplace to remain competitive.

Furthermore, examples of *optimisation actions* at *GVE level* comprise:

(a) The GVE partners' search and selection process (tool) [24] focused on assisting in the selection of the most suitable (optimal) *GVBE members* to become *GVE partners* based on 'multi-criteria' approach (e.g. quality, cost, delivery time, geographical distance, flexibility, green practices, health and safety practices, trust, etc.) to meet customer requirements and sustainability standards and regulations, and
(b) The GVE lifecycle management itself (viz. creation, operation, evolution and dissolution), where the GVE 'evolution lifecycle stage' is supported by simulation and decision support tools [25] for (re-)scheduling activities, optimising the production/service delivery plans, and finding solutions during operation when the original plan cannot be kept. Lastly, *optimisation actions* at *green enterprises level* focus on incentivising GVBE members' sustainability continuum [26, 27] in order to increase their chances for involvement in GVEs as partners.

Generally, GVBEs' goals are to increase and *optimise* the preparedness of their members based on mechanisms for enhancing their readiness for collaboration [28] (e.g. development of common working and sharing principles, governance rules and bylaws, a common ontology (terminology), shared (green) principles of operation, and an ICT-infrastructure that supports interoperability, etc.). This is necessary in order to support the rapid configuration of F- and R-GVEs [4] as closed (circular) supply networks, and to *optimise* GVE partners' collaborative performance[3] [29] based on systems and tools for GVEs creation and management [25].

'L' for Loop As developed in [5], GVBEs aim to *loop* their information, materials, water, energy and infrastructure (services) flows in their closed (circular) supply networks to achieve zero-waste in a three-level holistic sustainable industrial development model for achieving a Circular Economy (see Fig. 3). At a micro-level (small-cycle), *Green Enterprises* (GVBE members) focus on developing an 'industrial ecology' at factory level by linking "material, energy, water and waste (including by-products) flows between their manufacturing operations, supporting facilities and the surroundings buildings in order to increase resources productivity and pursue zero-waste" [30].

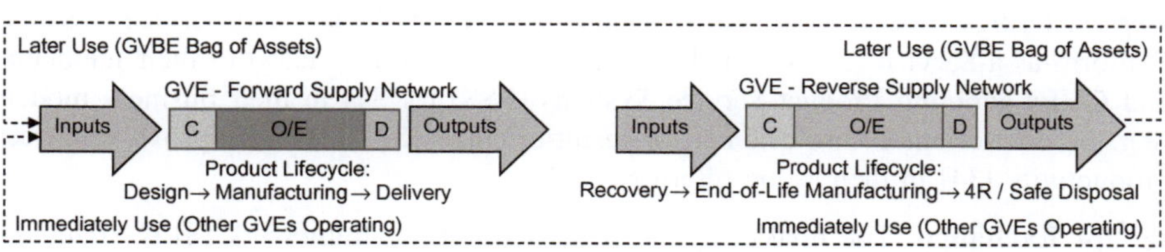

Fig. 3. GVEs Loops based on Industrial Symbiosis Strategies [5]

At meso-level (mid-cycle), *GVEs creation* aims to facilitate the development of dynamic closed-loop (circular) supply networks through the agile operation of *F-* and *R-GVEs* within a breeding environment in order to develop synergies between GVE partners. According to [5], this is performed "so the waste and/or surplus of downstream operations within a GVE lifecycle, through a certain degree of technical processing, return to the upstream operations of other GVEs in order to close various resources loops". Lastly, at macro-level (big-cycle), GVBEs will act as 'intelligent collaborative networks' *optimising* the different core-competencies and resources (viz. capabilities and capacities) of their members. These resources include human and technology as well as financial ones, but also information and knowledge resources whether available in the breeding environment itself or through its GVBE members to become as 'lean' as possible in all its operations. For example, this may involve the removal of some members, activities and/or resources, or continuously improving those [5].

The most natural *loop* for GVBEs is the creation of R-GVEs (dynamic reverse supply networks) [7] for the purpose of recovering the products sold under the GVBE brand (product stewardship), through F-GVEs [6], for service provision (e.g. repair), product recovery (e.g. re-manufacturing), or safe disposal [22], and therefore close-the-loop for closed (circular) supply networks based on GVEs creation [3–5].

---

[3] Collaborative Performance is "the effectiveness and efficiency in creating an environment in which enterprises can merge their processes for performing joint activities in a non-hierarchic way" [29].

'V' for Virtualise As discussed in [3, 21], GVBEs as *virtual* eco-industrial clusters possess certain advantages over traditional eco-industrial clusters (located in one site) based on their nature of being geographically distributed (virtual) and supported by collaborative business ICT infrastructures [15] that allow to the breeding environment to act as a *'glocal networked enterprise'* [21] with low environmental impact (e.g. on land).

Moreover, GVBEs as 'glocal networks' can have a *global* presence with *locally* available GVBE members/GVE partners to serve customers worldwide, creating in this way sustainable economic, environmental and social benefits for all stakeholders.

Other examples of GVBEs' actions towards *virtualisation* are the shifting of physical products, services and/or processes by displacing or replacing those with the delivery of utilities through virtual channels. Such could be the case of a GVBE 'Cloud-based' Collaborative Business ICT-Infrastructures [15, 16] delivering (e-)service offerings based on cloud models like Software-as-a-Service (SaaS), Platform-as-a-Service (PaaS) and Infrastructure-as-a-Service (IaaS) to their members, and GVEs adopting Product-Service Systems (PSS) [6, 31] in their business models (e.g. product-oriented, use-oriented or result-oriented [32, 33]) to improve resources productivity [34] in their value offerings.

'E' for Exchange. The final category of the RESOLVE framework [8] is *exchange,* and this action refers to adopting new green (circular) technologies and systems as well as to upgrading or replacing older ways of working (e.g. green (circular) practices and principles) at the GVBE as it evolves based on a sustainable development maturity model [35].

Such *exchanges* can take place at different scales within the breeding environment and involving different GVBE actors. Some examples of 'greening' (circular) efforts at GVBE members (green enterprises) and GVEs levels may include the adoption of:

(a) Technologies, in the broad sense of the term, focused on sustainable materials (e.g. green chemistry [36]), circular product and service designs (e.g. designed for ease of maintenance and repair, upgradability and adaptability, and dis- and re-assembly [22]), green business processes (e.g. green marketing [37]), circular manufacturing [30, 38], reverse [39] and collaborative logistics [40], green packaging [41], to mention a few,
(b) Systems, information technology based and non-information technology based, supporting Design for the Environment (DFE), Closed-loop Product Lifecycle Management (CPLM), Life Cycle Analysis (LCA), Lean Manufacturing, Total Quality Environmental Management (TQEM), Environmental Management Systems (EMS), Closed-loop Supply Chain Management (CSCM), ISO14000 series' requirements, etc., and
(c) Practices and principles, in addition to the Circular Economy ones, (viz. waste is food, diversity is strength, renewable energy, prices must tell the truth, and systems thinking [1]) like biomimicry (innovation inspired by nature) [42], industrial ecology (closed-loop processes) [43], cradle-to-cradle (regenerative industrial systems) [44] and blue economy (cascading systems) [45].

Furthermore, at GVBEs level 'greening' (circular) efforts will focus on advanced eco-industrial networking strategies [35, 46] in domains such as materials, energy, transportation, marketing, human resources, information and communication systems, environmental, health and safety, production processes, quality of life and community, and waste management.

4 Conclusions

This paper has presented the manner GVEs and their breeding environment/s can act as enablers of McKinsey's RESOLVE framework of six core-principles, and corresponding actions, for circularity, namely REstore/REgenerate, Share, Optimise, Loop, Virtualise and Exchange. Thus, a brief explanation of the RESOLVE framework was followed by a mapping of each of the principles against GVEs and breeding environments' features and capabilities, emphasizing all relevant aspects. This has shown that a) the way Mckinsey's framework can be employed to structure complex Circular Economy artefacts such as Virtual Enterprises and their breeding environments, and b) the GVE and breeding environments are soundly grounded concepts that can be effectively used to model multifaceted Circular Economy scenarios at various levels. This work also contributes towards the further development of a GVBE toolkit for supporting a Circular Economy on the basis of Collaborative Networks discipline.

References

1. Ellen MacArthur Foundation: Towards the Circular Economy: Accelerating the Scale-Up across Global Supply Chains – Report (2014)
2. Lewandowski, M.: Designing the business models for circular economy: towards the conceptual framework. Sustainability **8**(43), 1–28 (2016)
3. Romero, D., Molina, A.: Green virtual enterprises and their breeding environments. In: Camarinha-Matos, Luis M., Boucher, X., Afsarmanesh, H. (eds.) PRO-VE 2010. IAICT, vol. 336, pp. 25–35. Springer, Heidelberg (2010). doi:10.1007/978-3-642-15961-9_3
4. Romero, D., Molina, A.: Green virtual enterprise breeding environment reference framework. In: Camarinha-Matos, Luis M., Pereira-Klen, A., Afsarmanesh, H. (eds.) PRO-VE 2011. IAICT, vol. 362, pp. 545–555. Springer, Heidelberg (2011). doi:10.1007/978-3-642-23330-2_59
5. Romero, D., Molina, A.: Green virtual enterprise breeding environments: a sustainable industrial development model for a circular economy. In: Camarinha-Matos, Luis M., Xu, L., Afsarmanesh, H. (eds.) PRO-VE 2012. IAICT, vol. 380, pp. 427–436. Springer, Heidelberg (2012). doi:10.1007/978-3-642-32775-9_43
6. Romero, D., Molina, A.: Forward - green virtual enterprises and their breeding environments: sustainable manufacturing, logistics and consumption. In: Camarinha-Matos, Luis M., Afsarmanesh, H. (eds.) PRO-VE 2014. IAICT, vol. 434, pp. 336–346. Springer, Heidelberg (2014). doi:10.1007/978-3-662-44745-1_33
7. Romero, D., Molina, A.: Reverse – green virtual enterprises and their breeding environments: closed-loop networks. In: Camarinha-Matos, Luis M., Scherer, Raimar J. (eds.) PRO-VE 2013. IAICT, vol. 408, pp. 589–598. Springer, Heidelberg (2013). doi:10.1007/978-3-642-40543-3_62

8. McKinsey's Center for Business and the Environment, Ellen MacArthur Foundation: Growth Within: A Circular Economy Vision for a Competitive Europe – Report (2015)
9. Romero, D., Noran, O., Afsarmanesh, H.: Green virtual enterprise breeding environments bag of assets management: a contribution to the sharing economy. In: Camarinha-Matos, Luis M., Bénaben, F., Picard, W. (eds.) PRO-VE 2015. IAICT, vol. 463, pp. 439–447. Springer, Cham (2015). doi:10.1007/978-3-319-24141-8_40
10. Chertow, M.R.: Industrial Symbiosis: Literature & Taxonomy. Annu. Rev. Energy Env. **25**, 313–337 (2000)
11. Baccini, P., Brunner, P.H.: Metabolism of the Anthroposphere: Analysis, Evaluation Design. The MIT Press, Cambridge (2012)
12. Cossu, R., Salieri, V., Bisinella, V. (eds.): Urban Mining – A Global Cycle Approach to Resources Recovery from Solid Waste. CISA Publisher (2012)
13. Verdecho, M.J., Alfaro-Saiz, J.J., Rodríguez-Rodríguez, R.: An approach to select suppliers for sustainable collaborative networks. In: Camarinha-Matos, Luis M., Boucher, X., Afsarmanesh, H. (eds.) PRO-VE 2010. IAICT, vol. 336, pp. 304–311. Springer, Heidelberg (2010). doi:10.1007/978-3-642-15961-9_36
14. Sarkis, J., Zhu, H.: Information Technology and Systems in China's Circular Economy: Implications for Sustainability. J. Syst. Info. Technol. **10**(3), 202–217 (2008)
15. Rabelo, R.: Advanced collaborative business ICT infrastructures. In: Camarinha-Matos, L. M., Afsarmanesh, H., Ollus, M. (eds.) Methods and Tools for Collaborative Networked Organizations, pp. 337–369, Springer, Boston (2008)
16. Ruaro, Andre F., Rabelo, Ricardo J.: Do cloud computing tools support the needs of virtual enterprises? In: Afsarmanesh, H., Camarinha-Matos, Luis M., Lucas Soares, A. (eds.) PRO-VE 2016. IAICT, vol. 480, pp. 481–493. Springer, Cham (2016). doi:10.1007/978-3-319-45390-3_41
17. Sarkis, J., Koo, C., Watson, R.T.: Green information systems & technologies – this generation and beyond. Inf. Syst. Front. **15**(5), 695–705 (2013)
18. Botsman, R., Rogers, R.: What's Mine is Yours: How Collaborative Consumption is Changing the Way We Live. HarperBusiness (2010)
19. Latitude and Shareable: The New Sharing Economy: A Study by Latitude in Collaboration with Shareable Magazine (2010)
20. Thierry, M., Salomon, M., Numen, J.V., Van Wassenhove, L.: Strategic issues in product recovery management. Calif. Manag. Rev. **37**(2), 114–135 (1995)
21. Romero, D., Cavalieri, S., Resta, B.: Green virtual enterprise broker: enabling build-to-order supply chains for sustainable customer-driven small series production. In: Grabot, B., Vallespir, B., Gomes, S., Bouras, A., Kiritsis, D. (eds.) APMS 2014. IAICT, vol. 439, pp. 431–441. Springer, Heidelberg (2014). doi:10.1007/978-3-662-44736-9_53
22. Bakker, C.A., den Hollander, M.C., van Hinte, E., Zijlstra, Y.: Product that Last: Product Design for Circular Business Models. TU Delft Library (2014)
23. Afsarmanesh, H., Msanjila, S., Ermilova, E., Wiesner, S., Woelfel, W., Seifert, M.: VBE management system. In: Camarinha-Matos, L.M., Afsarmanesh, H., Ollus, M. (eds.) Methods and Tools for Collaborative Networked Organizations, pp. 119–154. Springer, Boston (2008)
24. Camarinha-Matos, L.M., Oliveira, A.I., Demsar, D., Sesana, M., Molina, A., Baldo, F., Jarimo, T.: VO creation assisting services. In: Camarinha-Matos, L.M., Afsarmanesh, H., Ollus, M. (eds.) Methods and Tools for Collaborative Networked Organizations, pp. 155–190. Springer, Boston (2008)

25. Negretto, U., Hodik, J., Král, L., Mulder, W., Ollus, M., Pondrelli, L., Westphal, I.: VO management solutions: VO management e-Services. In: Camarinha-Matos, L.M., Afsarmanesh, H., Ollus, M. (eds.) Methods and Tools for Collaborative Networked Organizations, pp. 257–274, Springer, Boston (2008)
26. Willard, B.: Next Sustainability Wave: Building Boardroom Buy-In. New Society Publishers, Gabriola Island (2005)
27. Graedel, T.E., Howard-Grenville, J.A.: Greening the Industrial Facility: Perspectives, Approaches, and Tools, Springer, US (2005)
28. Romero, D., Galeno, N., Molina, A.: Mechanisms for assessing and enhancing organisations' readiness for collaboration in collaborative networks. IJPR **47**(17), 4691–4710 (2005)
29. Westphal, I., Mulder, W., Seifert, M.: Supervision of collaborative processes in VOs. In: Methods and Tools for CNOs, pp. 239–256. Springer (2008)
30. Despeisse, M., Ball, P.D., Evans, S., Levers, A.: Industrial ecology at factory level - a conceptual model. J. Cleaner Prod. **31**(1), 30–39 (2012)
31. Romero, D., Rossi, M.: Towards circular lean product-service systems. In: 9th CIRP IPSS Conference: Circular Perspectives on Product/Service-Systems, Procedia CIRP (2017)
32. Bocken, N.M.P., de Pauw, I., Bakker, C., van der Grinten, B.: Product design and business model strategies for a circular economy. J. Ind. Prod. Eng. **33**(5), 308–320 (2016)
33. Tukker, A.: Eight types of product-service system: eight ways to sustainability? experiences from SusProNet. Bus. Strategy Environ. **13**(4), 246–260 (2004)
34. Cook, M.: Understanding the potential opportunities provided by service-orientated concepts to improve resource productivity. In: Design and Manufacture for Sustainable Development, pp. 123–134 (2004)
35. Romero, D., Molina, A.: Towards a Sustainable Development Maturity Model for Green Virtual Enterprise Breeding Environments. IFAC Proc. **47**(3), 4272–4279 (2014)
36. Anastas, P.T., Warner, J.C.: Green Chemistry: Theory and Practice, p. 30. Oxford University Press, New York (1998)
37. Liu, Y., Wang, B.: Research on the construction of green marketing channel of manufacturing enterprise based on circular economy. J. Beijing Inst. Technol. (Soc. Sci. Ed.) (2010)
38. Cerdasa, F., Kurle, D., Andrew, S., Thiede, S., Herrmann, C., Zhiquanc, Y., Jonathan, L.S. C., et al.: Defining circulation factories – a pathway towards factories of the future. In: 22nd CIRP Conference on Life Cycle Engineering, Procedia CIRP, vol. 29, pp. 627–632 (2015)
39. Ellen MacArthur Foundation: Waste not, Want not – Capturing the Value of the Circular Economy through Reverse Logistics: An Introduction to the Reverser Logistics Maturity Model – Report (2016)
40. Langley, J.: 7 Immutable Laws of Collaborative Logistics. NISTEVO Consulting (2000)
41. Ma, C., Zhang, G., Zhiping, W., Dehua, L.: Research on green packaging of circular economy. In: International Conference on Optoelectronics and Image Processing, vol. 2, pp. 229–232 (2010)
42. Benyus, J.: Biomimicry: Innovation Inspired by Nature. William Morrow & Company, NY (1997)
43. Allenby, B.: The Ontologies of Industrial Ecology. Prog. Ind. Ecol. **3**(1/2), 28–40 (2006)
44. McDonough, W., Braungart, M.: Cradle to Cradle: Remaking the Way We Make Things. North Point Press, New York (2002)
45. Pauli, G.: The Blue Economy. Paradigm Publications (2010)
46. Cohen-Rosenthal, E.: Management of Eco-Industrial Parks, Networks and Companies. Eco-Industrial Strategies: Unleashing Synergy between Economic Development and the Environment, Part 3, chap. 11, pp. 163–185 (2003)

How to Make Industrial Symbiosis Profitable

Mohammadtaghi Falsafi[1,2(✉)], Rosanna Fornasiero[1], and Umberto Dellepiane[3]

[1] ITIA-CNR Institute of Industrial Technologies and Automation, Via Corti 12, 20133 Milan, Italy
{mohammadtaghi.falsafi, rosanna.fornasiero}@itia.cnr.it
[2] Department of Mechanical Engineering, Politecnico di Milano, Via la Masa 1, 20157 Milan, Italy
[3] ACT Operations Research, Via Nizza 45, 00198 Rome, Italy
umberto.dellepiane@act-OperationsResearch.com

Abstract. Industrial symbiosis can well represent a new kind of collaborative network which demands resolute attention to the flow management of materials, by-products, and waste through local and regional economies. Industrial symbiosis engages traditionally separate companies in a collaborative approach to competitive advantage involving physical exchange of different kind of products which are usually disregard by traditional market transitions. The identification of innovative models to support decision-making process in this kind of networks is urgent since it is necessary to close the loop assuring profitability at a single node as well as at system level. This paper proposes the application of the bi-level optimization model as a way to handle this two-stage problem organized into two cooperating layers. As a preliminary result, the model is applied to a simplified case where the nodes can sell their output to the market or share them in the industrial symbiosis to increase the global efficiency.

Keywords: Industrial symbiosis · Flow management · Bi-level optimization

1 Introduction

Due to the increase of production costs, organizations are becoming more concerned to find new efficient approaches. Industrial symbiosis not only reduces the supply chain costs through geographical proximity but also suggests innovative ideas to increase the income of an organization thanks to closing the loop between the output (i.e. by-products and waste of a company) to be used as input for another. Industrial symbiosis (IS) is a type of collaborative networks for regional economic relationships providing a richer, more meaningful representation of local industry drivers and regional dynamics than do traditional methods.

In this paper, it is assumed that the Production Unit (PU) is the atomic decision unit within a collaborative network and we will treat each of them as a single decision maker. Thus, we are implicitly assuming that each single PU works with a high level of efficiency, but this does not seem restrictive since if this is not the case, at single PU level, it is possible to optimize the planning and scheduling and increase the efficiency level. Moreover, the decision autonomy of each PU has to be maintained.

L.M. Camarinha-Matos et al. (Eds.): PRO-VE 2017, IFIP AICT 506, pp. 614–625, 2017.
DOI: 10.1007/978-3-319-65151-4_54

Indeed, when the PU makes a decision, it has to consider also what is happening at network level. For this reason, we can introduce the concept of upper-level decisions. They are optimized with respect to network-level KPIs (Key Performance Indicators), which in turn have a twofold purpose: from one side to increase the wealth related to a symbiotic approach at cluster level while on the other maintain the single PU decision autonomy.

In Sect. 2, a literature overview of the recent trends in the applicability of optimization techniques in different perspectives is presented. Section 3 explains the optimization model of the problem in this paper. The application of the model in a case study and the input data and the assumptions is described in Sect. 4. In Sect. 5, the results of applying the model to the numerical example with their analyses are demonstrated. Finally, Sect. 6 gives a brief overview of what has been done in this paper and what is going to be done to expand the model.

2 Theoretical Background

Organizations can benefit from shared resources in an IS while they can still make decisions independently. However, there are some challenging issues that prevent organizations from easily accepting to apply it. Shared resources incur some limitations for a better collaboration among organizations [1]. In addition, according to Chertow [2], the most prominent reason that many organizations are not willing to participate in IS is that they do not see sufficient material flow to make it worth wide. Chertow also emphasizes the importance of the analysis of specific industries based on key materials.

Bi-level optimization is concerned with a class of problems characterized by a particular nested structure. Some decision variables of the inner level problem may act as parameters for the objective function of the second level problem and may also influence its constraints. The nesting of these problems may be deeper and involve more than two levels, and in this case, we refer to Multilevel Programming. More in detail, a problem called lower or inner problem is nested inside the feasible region of another problem, called upper level or outer problem.

Bi-level problems, or more generally multi-level problems, allow modelling the complex situations and decision dynamics. However, their capability of capturing the complex reality results in a problem hard to solve. For this reason, a compromise between consistency with the reality and modelling simplifications is often sought.

Bi-level problems are NP-hard problems. Several approaches to solving this kind of problem have been proposed in the literature. Possible drawbacks to this formulation are:

- The problem can have large dimension, and the proposed approaches may be negatively influenced;
- To assure the convergence of an algorithm, some assumptions have to be made, and they cannot be representative of the reality we intend to model.

Why using a bi-level formulation for modelling the industrial symbiosis problem?

For answering this question, we will use a parallelism with another sector that has drawn great benefit from the development of bi-level programming. Many Transportation

Management problems, in fact have been well represented with bi-level formulations. For more details, readers can refer to Marcotte (1986) or Marcotte and Marquis (1992) [3, 4].

Usually, these formulations try to model, at the inner level, the choices or the behaviors of the network users while at the upper level they represent the decision problem faced by the manager of the transport system, which wants to improve the performance of the system.

Many other applications of bi-level optimization can be found in different application fields. For example, the management and the engineering sectors also obtained advantages from this kind of optimization. In particular, in the work of Neittaanmäki and Stachurski (1992) [5], control problems with unilateral boundary-value are addressed (a typical problem with these characteristics could be represented by Optimal Shape Design problem). The bi-level structure is the result of a finite difference approximation of the original optimal control problem with boundary value. The resulting bi-level problem involves the minimization of a functional (different according to the particular problem) that depends on control variables and state variables. The state variables are the solution of an auxiliary quadratic problem which is characterized by parameters that depend on the control variables. Some features of this problem are the expensiveness of the functional evaluation and the large scale of the inner level problem. It is important to stress that these features are often common in many real two-level problems.

Indeed, an important motivation for the widespread use of bi-level models in the management field is the consistent presence of decentralized decision-making processes. This kind of decisions is particularly common within companies where different choices, which will affect each other, are taken by different parties in some points of the supply chain. Two papers which deal with decentralized decision process in supply chain are [Patriksson and Wynter (1999) [6] and Júdice and Faustino (1988) [7].

Recently bi-level applications have also appeared in financial studies, and examples can be found in the works of Carriòn et al. (2009) [8] and Conn and Vicente (2012) [9].

Another Network Design problem has been faced in Ben-Ayed et al. (1992) [10] where the upper-level decision maker (the manager of the system) would like to allocate some investments to strengthen an existent interregional highway network. Choosing an investment allocation, the manager of the system changes the users' preferences. In consistence with this dynamic, the users are the inner-level decision makers who have the goal of minimizing their travel costs.

Furthermore, to answer the previous question, we need to report also two important assumptions that we cannot relax:

1. each single PU works with a high level of efficiency
2. the decision autonomy of each PU has to be maintained.

Focusing on the last example and considering that the following assumptions cannot be relaxed, we understand the reason of the use of bi-level programming for modelling the symbiosis problem.

First of all, the inner level of the problem is the decisions related to the single Production Units (PUs) within each plant. These are optimized with respect to some proper KPIs. In this study, we will assume that the PUs are the atomic decision units within a collaborative network and we will treat each of them as a single decision maker.

Indeed, it is necessary to consider what happens at the network level. For this reason, we can introduce the concept of the upper-level decisions. These are optimized with respect to network-level KPIs, which in turn have a twofold purpose: from one side to increase the wealth related to a symbiotic approach while on the other maintain the single PU decision autonomy.

In order to make things work, coordination to improve the whole symbiotic network performance is necessary, measured in different ways, for example economic (profit or costs), environment impact (energetic, waste) or social. This coordination is provided by an organization that is a physical organization or more easily a virtual platform which is called the network coordinator. Of course, for maintaining the decision autonomy of each PU, a top-down approach (i.e. a centralized network coordinator) cannot be considered.

We then conceive a multi-layer architecture organized into two cooperating layers. At the company level, each industry performs its Supply Chain Optimization (SCO) to gain a high efficiency operative level optimizing its short-term and long-term decisions. These decisions do not take into account any of the decisions of the other industries in the cluster or in other words, are completely independent. To govern the whole cluster performance, we introduce the cluster-level optimization, whose aim is the increasing of the global cluster efficiency. This two-layer architecture is formulated by a bi-level optimization problem.

3 Methodology

The objective of the model is to integrate the two decision levels: decisions at PU level for managing flows in supply chain and at the network level for managing the industrial symbiosis (IS) among PUs. The aim of the model is to support the optimization of the flow in the cluster (IS) while maximizing the total benefit of each PU and dynamically maximize the benefit for the IS. Accordingly, the upper level of the bi-level model maximizes the total flow inside the IS among PUs, and the inner level maximizes the total benefit of each of the PUs.

Input parameters

i	*Index for PU under consideration where* $i = 1, 2, .., S$
j	*Index for PU other than considered PU where* $j = 1, 2, .., S - 1$ *where* $j \neq i$
k_i	*Index for finished products at each PU i where* $k_i = 1, 2, .., K_i$
b_i	*Index for by − products at each PU i where* $b_i = 1, 2, .., B_i$
w_i	*Index for waste products at each PU i where* $w_i = 1, 2, .., W_i$
l_i	*Index for materials purchased from market by PU i where* $l_i = 1, 2, .., L_i$
mkt	*Index for market*
IS	*Index for industrial symbiosis cluster*
SA	*Index for standalone mode for each PU*
op	*Index for output products*
ip	*Index for inputproducts*

P	*Index for product, regardless if it is output or input of a PU*
s	*Set of PUs for IS where* $s = 1, 2, .., S$
SP^{i}_{op}	*Selling price of output products op sold by PU i*
PC^{i}_{op}	*Production cost of output products op produced at PU i*
C^{i}_{ip}	*Cost of purchasing input products ip by PU i*
$CT^{i}_{w_i}$	*Cost of disposing waste* w_i *at PU i*
d^{mkt}_{p}	*Market demand for product p at PU i*
$PCap^{i}_{op \in k_i}$	*Production capacity of final products at PU i*
$ICap^{i}_{ip}$	*Inventory capacity of input products ip at PU i*
$ICap^{i}_{op}$	*Inventory capacity of output products op at PU i*
H^{i}_{ip}	*Inventory holding cost of input products ip at PU i*
H^{i}_{op}	*Inventory holding cost of output products op at PU i*
$I^{i,0}_{ip}$	*Initial inventory level of input products ip at PU i*
$I^{i,0}_{op}$	*Initial inventory level of output products op at PU i*

The assumption is that finished products and by-products could be sold to both the market and other PUs in the IS with the same price ($i.e. SP^{i}_{op \in k_i}, SP^{i}_{op \in b_i}$). Also, the price and purchasing cost for a specific material is the same for all the PUs. The waste is normally disposed with the cost $CT^{i}_{w_i}$, while it could be exchanged in the IS without any cost ($SP^{i}_{op \in w_i} = 0, C^{i}_{ip \in w_j} = 0$).

The inventory level of each PU is the input inventory for input products and output inventory for output products. For each of them we assume an initial inventory level (i.e. $I^{i,0}_{ip}$ and $I^{i,0}_{op}$).

For each product, there is a specific demand in the market (d^{mkt}_{p}). This is a general demand regardless of the product type (finished product, by-product) of each PU. In other words, if two PUs produce the same product (finished product or by-product), the market demand of that product for both of them is the same.

Decision variables (Positive)

X	*Amount of goods from/to the market*
Y	*Amount of goods from/to the IS*
W	*Amount of waste disposed*
I	*Final inventory level*

W is the proportion of waste which is disposed. The remaining proportion is transacted in the IS with the other PUs.

1. Upper Level Objective Function

$$\mathrm{MaxZ} = Max \sum_{i \in IS} \sum_{j \in \{IS \setminus i\}} Y^{i,j}_{p}$$

The objective function of the upper level maximizes the total flow inside IS.

2. Balance of demand

$$\sum_{i \in IS} X^{i,mkt}_{op \in k_i \cup b_i} \leq d^{mkt}_{p} \quad \forall i \in 1, 2, \ldots, S$$

3. Balance of production capacity

$$\sum_{j\{IS \backslash i\}} Y^{i,j}_{op} + X^{i,mkt}_{op} + I^{i}_{op} - I^{i,0}_{op} \leq PCap^{i}_{op \in k_i} \quad \forall i \in 1, 2, \ldots, S$$

4. Balance of output products

$$\sum_{j\{IS \backslash i\}} Y^{i,j}_{op} + X^{i,mkt}_{op} + I^{i}_{op} - I^{i,0}_{op} = f_i \left(\sum_{j\{IS \backslash i\}} Y^{i,j}_{op \in k_i} + X^{i,mkt}_{op \in k_i} + I^{i}_{op \in k_i} - I^{i,0}_{op \in k_i} \right) \quad \forall i \in 1, 2, \ldots, S$$

5. Balance of input products

$$\sum_{j\{IS \backslash i\}} Y^{i,j}_{ip} + X^{i,mkt}_{ip} + I^{i}_{ip} - I^{i,0}_{ip} = h_i \left(\sum_{j\{IS \backslash i\}} Y^{i,j}_{op \in k_i} + X^{i,mkt}_{op \in k_i} + I^{i}_{op \in k_i} - I^{i,0}_{op \in k_i} \right) \quad \forall i \in 1, 2, \ldots, S$$

6. Balance of input inventory capacity

$$I^{i}_{ip \in l_i} \leq ICap^{i}_{ip \in l_i} \quad \forall i \in 1, 2, \ldots, S$$

7. Balance of output inventory capacity

$$I^{i}_{op} \leq ICap^{i}_{op} \quad \forall i \in 1, 2, \ldots, S$$

8. Inner Level Objective Function - Maximization of the profit of each PU independently from the IS

$$\begin{aligned} MaxZ_i = & \sum_{op \in k_i \cup b_i} \left\{ (SP^{i}_{op} - PC^{i}_{op}) \times \left(X^{i,mkt}_{op \in k_i} + \sum_{j} Y^{i,j}_{op \in k_i} \right) \right\} - \sum_{ip \in l_i} \left\{ C^{i}_{ip} \times \left(X^{mkt,i}_{ip} + \sum_{j} Y^{j,i}_{ip} \right) \right\} \\ & - \sum_{w_i} \left(CT^{i}_{w_i} \times W^{i}_{w_i} \right) - \sum_{ip \in l_i} (H^{i}_{ip} \times I^{i}_{ip}) \\ & - \sum_{op \in k_i \cup b_i} (H^{i}_{op} \times I^{i}_{op}) \forall i \in 1, 2, \ldots, S \end{aligned}$$

(a) Balance of demand

$$\sum_{i \in IS} X^{i,mkt}_{op \in k_i \cup b_i} \leq d^{mkt}_{p \in k_i \cup b_i} \qquad \forall k_i, b_i$$

(b) Balance of production capacity

$$\sum_{j\{IS \setminus i\}} Y^{i,j}_{op} + X^{i,mkt}_{op} + I^{i}_{op} - I^{i,0}_{op} \leq PCap^{i}_{op \in k_i} \qquad \forall k_i$$

(c) Balance of output products

$$\sum_{j\{IS \setminus i\}} Y^{i,j}_{op} + X^{i,mkt}_{op} + I^{i}_{op} - I^{i,0}_{op} = f_i \left(\sum_{j\{IS \setminus i\}} Y^{i,j}_{op \in k_i} + X^{i,mkt}_{op \in k_i} + I^{i}_{op \in k_i} - I^{i,0}_{op \in k_i} \right) \quad \forall b_i, w_i$$

(d) Balance of input products

$$\sum_{j\{IS \setminus i\}} Y^{i,j}_{ip} + X^{i,mkt}_{ip} + I^{i}_{ip} - I^{i,0}_{ip} = h_i \left(\sum_{j\{IS \setminus i\}} Y^{i,j}_{op \in k_i} + X^{i,mkt}_{op \in k_i} + I^{i}_{op \in k_i} - I^{i,0}_{op \in k_i} \right) \quad \forall ip$$

(e) Balance of input inventory capacity

$$I^{i}_{ip \in l_i} \leq ICap^{i}_{ip \in l_i} \qquad \forall ip$$

(f) Balance of output inventory capacity

$$I^{i}_{op \in k_i \cup b_i} \leq ICap^{i}_{op \in k_i \cup b_i} \qquad \forall k_i, b_i$$

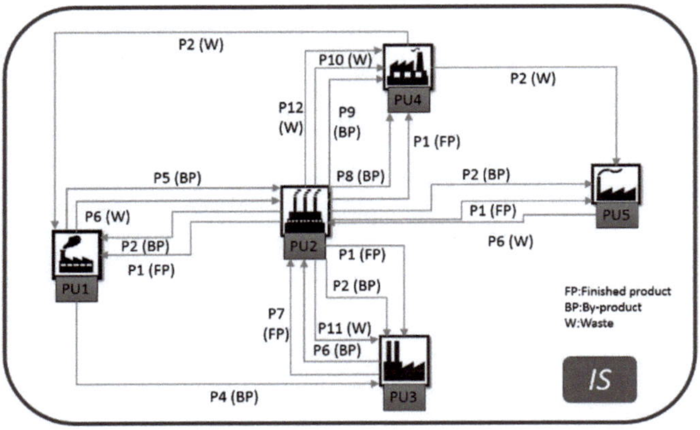

Fig. 1. Schematic view of PUs and potential interconnections

4 Illustrative Example

The above model has been applied to a simplified example of an IS case with five PUs, and it is partially taken from the paper of Gonela and Zhang (2014) [11]. Each PU produces a set of finished products, by-products, and wastes. It is assumed that the waste is either disposed or transacted inside the IS among PUs. Furthermore, for some products, there is the possibility to transact with one or more PUs as well as the market, while some products could solely be purchased/sold to the market. Figure 1 shows the

Table 1. Input data

i	ip	$C^i_{ip\in l_i \cup k_j \cup b_j}$	$C^i_{ip\in w_j}$	H^i_{ip}	$ICap^i_{ip}$	$I^{i,0}_{ip}$
1	P1 (0.5)	5	n.a.	n.a.	n.a.	n.a.
	P2 (2)	3	0	n.a.	n.a.	n.a.
2	P5 (50)	1.5	n.a.	0.55	200	20
	P7 (1)	4	n.a.	1	5	2
	P6 (30)	0.02	0	n.a.	n.a.	n.a.

i	op			$PC^i_{op\in k_i}$	SP^i_{op}	PC^i_{op}	$CT^i_{w_i}$	H^i_{op}	$ICap^i_{op}$	$I^{i,0}_{op}$	d^{mkt}_p
	k_i	b_i	W_i								
1	P3			60	13	10		1	0.5	0	70
		P4 (0.5)			2.5	1		0.02	1	0.2	100
		P5 (30)			1.5	0.5		0.5	15	5	1500
			P6 (30)		0	0	0.002	n.a.	n.a.	n.a.	0
2	P1			99	5	4		n.a.	n.a.	n.a.	110
		P2 (1)			3	1		n.a.	n.a.	n.a.	90
		P8 (30)			1	0.5		n.a.	n.a.	n.a.	4000
		P9 (50)			2.2	0.5		0.2	300	50	10000
			P10 (10)		0	0.5	1	n.a.	n.a.	n.a.	0
			P11 (10)		0	0	0.75	n.a.	n.a.	n.a.	0
			P12 (12)		0	0	0.005	n.a.	n.a.	n.a.	0

schema of the PUs and the potential interconnections among them. For each potential product, it is also specified if it is a finished product (FP), by-product (BP), or waste (W).

Table 1 shows the input data for the first two PUs. For each PU, it is considered a set of inputs (*ip*) that could be supplied from the market or, potentially, from the PUs in the network. The purchasing cost is the same if the product is supplied from the market or it is a finished product or by-product of another PU inside the IS ($C^i_{ip \in l_i \cup k_j \cup b_j}$). Alternatively, if the input product is a waste of another PU inside the IS, it is transacted without any cost ($C^i_{ip \in w_j} = 0; \forall w_j$). For producing each unit of finished product, a specific amount of each input product is consumed and a specific amount of by-product and waste is produced. Hence, it is defined by a coefficient which is specified in parenthesis in the column *ip* and *op*.

The three types of outputs are finished products, by-products, and waste. Finished product is the main output of the PU. For each PU, there are also one or more by-products and wastes. Based on the configuration of the PU, it is capable of producing a certain amount of finished product ($PCap^i_{op \in k_i}$). All the other parameters are the same as is explained in Sect. 3. There are some products for which some dimensions are not applicable (n.a.). For example, in case of P1 (which could represent electricity) it is not possible to keep inventory for it.

5 Results and Discussion

Table 2 shows the first part of the results from applying the bi-level optimization. The decision variables are the flows to/from the market, the wastes that are disposed, and the final inventory level. The numbers in parenthesis represent the flows for each PU. For instance, the product P12 ($X^{mkt,i}_{P12}$) is the input for PU 4 and therefore, it is possible to have a flow greater than zero which is 2412. The results also show that some products do not interact with the market when considering the IS. For example, the output product P2 from PU 2 does not have any interaction with the market. In other words, it is entirely transacted within the IS.

Figure 2 shows the flows between PUs inside IS. For example, 90 units of finished product P1 which is produced by PU 2, goes to the market and 4 and 5 units is sold to PUs 1 and 3 respectively. However, there is no transaction with the other potential PUs (i.e. 4, 5). So, production amount of P1 in PU 2 is 99 units.

Table 3 compares the results when the PUs operate as standalone and independently from the IS (SA) with the results obtained by the bi-level optimization in the IS. In other words, the standalone mode is the result of the inner function when the transaction flows within the cluster is set to zero (Y = 0). In the standalone mode, production units 1, 2, 3, and 5 produce less than their production capacity (i.e. 60,99,150 and 100 respectively) to maximize their profit. Contributing with the cluster, the PUs 1, 2, and 3 produce with the maximum production capacity, and therefore their utilization arrives at 100%. This difference stems from the fact that collaborating in the IS, companies can produce more than the market demand and transact the additional production within the cluster.

Table 2. Optimization results – Flow from/to the market, amount of waste disposed, and Inventory level

Decision variable	PU (i)					Decision variable	PU (i)				
	1	2	3	4	5		1	2	3	4	5
$X_{P8}^{mkt,i}$	0	0	0	(0)	0	$X_{P8}^{i,mkt}$	0	(1100)	0	0	0
$X_{P7}^{mkt,i}$	0	(85)	0	0	0	$X_{P7}^{i,mkt}$	0	0	(90)	0	0
$X_{P4}^{mkt,i}$	0	0	(12.8)	0	0	$X_{P13}^{i,mkt}$	0	0	0	(360)	0
$X_{P1}^{mkt,i}$	(26)	0	0	(144)	(14.3)	$X_{P4}^{i,mkt}$	0	0	0	0	0
$X_{P11}^{mkt,i}$	0	0	0	0	0	$X_{P1}^{i,mkt}$	0	(90)	0	0	0
$X_{P9}^{mkt,i}$	0	0	0	0	0	$X_{P3}^{i,mkt}$	(60)	0	0	0	0
$X_{P5}^{mkt,i}$	0	(2965)	0	0	0	$X_{P9}^{i,mkt}$	0	(3190)	0	0	0
$X_{P2}^{mkt,i}$	(0)	0	(0)	0	(0)	$X_{P5}^{i,mkt}$	(0)	0	0	0	0
$X_{P10}^{mkt,i}$	0	0	0	(720)	0	$X_{P14}^{i,mkt}$	0	0	0	0	(140)
$X_{P12}^{mkt,i}$	0	0	0	(2412)	0	$X_{P2}^{i,mkt}$	0	(0)	0	0	0
$X_{P6}^{mkt,i}$	0	(0)	0	0	0	W_{P11}^{i}	0	(935)	0	0	0
$I_{P8}^{i}\ (ip)$	0	0	0	(0)	0	W_{P2}^{i}	0	0	0	(35.4)	0
$I_{P7}^{i}\ (ip)$	0	(5)	0	0	0	W_{P10}^{i}	0	(0)	0	0	0
$I_{P4}^{i}\ (ip)$	0	0	(10)	0	0	W_{P12}^{i}	0	(0)	0	0	0
$I_{P11}^{i}\ (ip)$	0	0	(0)	0	0	W_{P6}^{i}	(45)	0	(0)	0	(0)
$I_{P4}^{i}\ (ip)$	0	0	0	(0)	0	$I_{P7}^{i}\ (op)$	0	0	(0)	0	0
$I_{P4}^{i}\ (ip)$	0	(200)	0	0	0	$I_{P4}^{i}\ (op)$	(0)	0	0	0	0
$I_{P4}^{i}\ (ip)$	0	0	0	(110)	0	$I_{P3}^{i}\ (op)$	(0)	0	0	0	0
						$I_{P9}^{i}\ (op)$	0	(300)	0	0	0
						$I_{P5}^{i}\ (op)$	(0)	0	0	0	0
						$I_{P14}^{i}\ (op)$	0	0	0	0	(5)

Regarding the economic impact, there is an increase in four PUs. The companies with more collaboration with the IS observe more increase in their profits. As Fig. 2 represents, most of the connections in the cluster are related to PU 2. Consequently, this PU has the highest profit increase with around 42%. The increase of the profit is due to the free transaction of waste inside the IS while it is costly for the PU to dispose them. On the contrary, PU 5 with the lowest symbiotic interaction, its profit decreases slightly to approximately 4%.

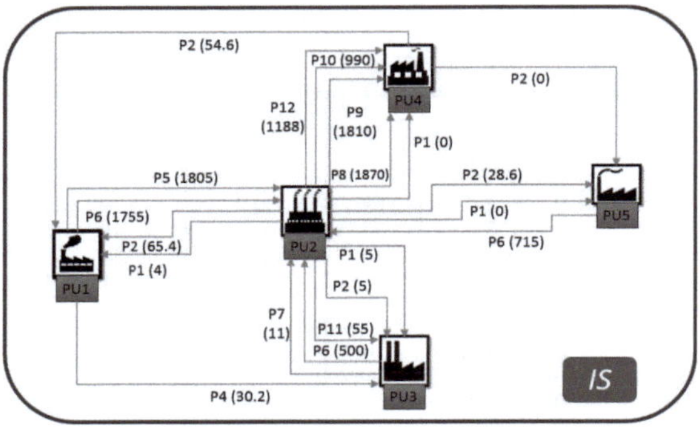

Fig. 2. Optimization results – Flows to the other PUs inside IS

Table 3. Impacts of the model

PU	Production capacity	Production SA	Utilization SA %	Profit SA	Production IS	Utilization IS %	Profit IS	Profit difference %
1	60	49.83	83	1,260.6	60	100	1,684	+ 14.4
2	99	90	91	777.6	99	100	1,926.8	+ 42.5
3	100	89	89	124.2	100	100	155.3	+ 11.1
4	360	360	100	4,665.7	360	100	5,564.7	+ 8.8
5	150	138	92	128.2	143	95	117.7	− 4.3

6 Conclusion

The emergence of environmental and sustainability regulations is asking companies to define new collaboration mechanisms to close the loop of waste and by-product and to put them back into the system as an input for other companies. IS is one of the sustainable strategies that can help to reduce waste production and logistic costs. In IS, traditionally separate plants collocate in order to efficiently utilize resources, reduce waste and increase profits for the entire system as well as each player in the IS. This paper focuses on developing an innovative approach for supporting the definition of the IS configurations based on the total profit and on the profit of each PU.

An innovative decision framework that combines two decision levels is proposed to determine the optimal configuration of IS and to design the optimal network flows of various products in the network. An empirical case has been conducted to study the efficiency and effectiveness of the proposed model, and the results suggest a significant increase in profitability for the single nodes and the rest of the players in the network when IS is applied. In this case, the collaboration is based on the possibility to share resources as a way to gain profit for all the partners in the network. The model is still under development and will be further improved introducing other decision variables (e.g. transportation costs) and enlarging the case study to a larger network.

References

1. van Donk, D.P., van der Vaart, T.: A case of shared resources, uncertainty and supply chain integration in the process industry. Int. J. Prod. Econ. **96**, 97–108 (2005)
2. Chertow, M.R.: Industrial symbiosis: literature and taxonomy. Annu. Rev. Energy Environ. **25**, 313–337 (2000)
3. Marcotte, P.: Network design problem with congestion effects: a case of bilevel programming. Math. Program. **34**, 142–162 (1986)
4. Marcotte, P., Marquis, G.: Efficient implementation of heuristics for the continuous network design problem. Ann. Oper. Res. **34**, 163–176 (1992)
5. Neittaanmäki, P., Stachurski, A.: Solving some optimal control problems using the barrier penalty function method. Appl. Math. Optim. **25**, 127–149 (1992)
6. Patriksson, M., Wynter, L.: Stochastic mathematical programs with equilibrium constraints. Oper Res Lett **25**, 159–167 (1999)
7. Júdice, J.J., Faustino, A.: The solution of the linear bilevel programming problem by using the linear complementarity problem. Investigação Operacional **8**, 77–95 (1988)
8. Carrion, M., Arroyo, J.M., Conejo, A.J.: A bilevel stochastic programming approach for retailer futures market trading. IEEE Trans. Power Syst. **24**, 1446–1456 (2009)
9. Conn, A.R., Vicente, L.N.: Bilevel derivative-free optimization and its application to robust optimization. Optim. Methods Softw. **27**, 561–577 (2012)
10. Ben-Ayed, O., Blair, C.E., Boyce, D.E., LeBlanc, L.J.: Construction of a real-world bilevel linear programming model of the highway network design problem. Ann. Oper. Res. **34**, 219–254 (1992)
11. Gonela, V., Zhang, J.: Design of the optimal industrial symbiosis system to improve bioethanol production. J. Clean. Prod. **64**, 513–534 (2014)

Advanced CN Design and Evolution

Evolution of a Collaborative Business Ecosystem in Response to Performance Indicators

Paula Graça[1,2(✉)] and Luis M. Camarinha-Matos[1]

[1] Faculty of Sciences and Technology and Uninova CTS, NOVA University of Lisbon, Campus de Caparica, 2829-516 Caparica, Portugal
mgraca@deetc.isel.pt, cam@uninova.pt

[2] Instituto Superior de Engenharia de Lisboa, Instituto Politécnico de Lisboa, Rua Conselheiro Emídio Navarro 1, 1959-007 Lisbon, Portugal

Abstract. Business Ecosystems supported by the increasing use and expansion of communication networks represent nowadays a powerful form of collaboration, enabling organizations better responding to more challenging business opportunities. In this context, performance indicators are needed for measuring collaboration benefits of a business ecosystem as a whole and of its individual members, the organizations. But such indicators may also induce a self-adjustment of the organizations' behavior, as there is a natural tendency of individuals and organizations to adapt to the way they are evaluated. As such, an adequate selection of performance indicators can help the sustainability of the ecosystem. The level of reaction to indicators is nevertheless not the same for all members of the ecosystem, i.e. there are different classes of responsiveness. Using system dynamics and multi-agent systems, the focus of this paper is the study of the evolution of the agents of a collaborative business ecosystem, depending on the performance indicators used to assess their performance and considering their class of responsiveness.

Keywords: Collaborative networks · Business ecosystem · Performance indicators

1 Introduction

Nowadays, as the world is getting further interlinked via technological platforms, business ecosystems represent a new era of business environments. The term Business Ecosystem was introduced by Moore [1, 2] as a metaphor inspired by natural ecosystems. Moore also stated that in a business ecosystem *"companies co-evolve capabilities around a new innovation: They work cooperatively and competitively to support new products, satisfy customer needs, and eventually incorporate the next round of innovations*" [1]. On the other hand, the research area of Collaborative Networks (CN) [3], which has a broader scope, identifies a business ecosystem as a form of CN, i.e. a case of Virtual organizations Breeding Environment (VBE), allowing a better understanding of its structure, lifecycles, endogenous characteristics, and exogenous interactions. As such, based on [4] and as defined in [5], a collaborative

L.M. Camarinha-Matos et al. (Eds.): PRO-VE 2017, IFIP AICT 506, pp. 629–640, 2017.
DOI: 10.1007/978-3-319-65151-4_55

business ecosystem (CBE) can be modeled as an environment of agents, representing the organizations, which collaborate creating virtual organizations (VOs) to accomplish business opportunities.

Collaboration is expected to benefit both the participants of a CBE and the CBE as a whole. But the collaborative behavior of agents is likely to be influenced by the performance indicators adopted by the CBE. Thus, selecting a proper set of performance indicators for CBEs is of particular importance. In this work, a simulation model is proposed to study the evolution of a CBE when exposed to evaluation through a given set of indicators.

The remaining sections of this paper are organized as follows: section two presents the proposed performance indicators and metrics to be used for the CBE evaluation, acting as a mechanism of influence in the behavior of the organizations; section three presents the hypothesis proposing a performance assessment and adjustment model to address it; section four presents a simulation scenario using elements of agent-based modeling and system dynamics [6]. The last section discusses the contributions and future work.

2 Performance Indicators and Metrics for CBEs

Performance evaluation is an important issue being used in various fields, particularly in the business area, with the balanced score cards (BSC) [7] being the most well-known mechanism for individual organizations. However, for the present research we are interested on collaboration benefits and metrics, for which only limited contributions can be found in literature. As an example, in [8] an estimation model for business benefits in horizontal collaborative networks is proposed for product development. Another example suggests a set of collaboration benefits identifying cooperation variables and the corresponding target goals [9]. Another contribution for this research, is a conceptual model for value systems in collaborative networks [10], which suggests methods to assess the alignment of value systems of different members of a network [11]. For the case of supply chain collaboration there is a great multiplicity of metrics and methods, as found in [12–14] and [15], some of which can be adopted for collaborative networks in general and for CBEs in particular. Finally, the area of social network analysis provides a well-established set of metrics of structural network analysis, which can also contribute to CBEs assessment, namely as in [16, 17].

The performance indicators described in the next sub-sections, were chosen based on a previous literature analysis [18], and considering their relevance according to the dynamics and trends of current business environments [19]. Business ecosystems enable collaboration among multiple actors, the organizations, which diversity and collective ability leverage new ways to innovate and create value for society. The proposed performance indicators address these concerns by measuring the innovation due to collaboration, the new collaboration opportunities brought in or gained from the CBE, and the distribution of the collaboration among organizations in the CBE. These measures are expected to influence the organizations in self-adjusting their behavior, improving their performance and thus improving the CBE as a whole by promoting its sustainability.

Innovation Indicator. The Innovation Indicator (II_i) of an individual organization member of a CBE, measures the potential of the organization to create new products, services or patents. The result is a ratio between the number of new products and the portfolio of the organization. Metrics and calculations for II_i are described in Table 1.

Table 1. Innovation indicator for an individual organization.

Innovation Indicator (II_i)	
Measures the innovation potential of a member of the CBE	
$O_1,\ldots,O_n$	Organizations in the CBE
METRICS	
#PortPd$_i$	Portfolio of products/services/patents of the member O_i
#NewPd$_i$	Number of new products/services/patents generated by the member O_i
PERFORMANCE INDICATORS	
$II_i = \frac{\#NewPd_i}{\#PortPd_i}$	Is calculated by the ratio between the two metrics #NewPd$_i$ and PortPd$_i$

Note: II_i is a ratio

The Innovation Indicator of the whole CBE (II_{CBE}) sums the innovation potential of all organizations in the CBE. The resulting ratio is then weighted by the correlation (Spearman's or Pearson's) [20] between the number of collaborations (#VOs), and new products, services or patents (#NewPds) created. Metrics and calculations for II_{CBE} are described in Table 2.

Table 2. Innovation Indicator of the whole CBE.

Innovation Indicator (II_{CBE})	
Measures the innovation potential of the CBE as a whole	
CBE	Whole CBE
METRICS	
{#VO$_1$, …, #VO$_n$}	No. of VOs in which the members O_1, …, O_n participated
$\sum_i$ #PortPd$_i$	Total portfolio of products, services, or patents of the CBE
{#NewPd$_1$, …, #NewPd$_n$}	No. of new products, services, or patents generated by the members O_1, …, O_n
$\sum_i$ #NewPd$_i$	Total no. of new products generated in the CBE
PERFORMANCE INDICATORS	
$II_{CBE} = \frac{\sum_i \#NewPd_i}{\sum_i \#PortPd_i} * r(\#VO, \#NewPd)$	The ratio of the totals is weighed by the correlation r between the two metrics #VO and #NewPd

Note: II_{CBE} is a ratio weighted by a correlation

Contribution Indicator. The Contribution Indicator (CI_i) of an individual organization member of a CBE, measures the capacity of the organization to create value, which is brought in or gained from the CBE's new collaboration opportunities. Metrics and calculations for CI_i are described in Table 3.

Table 3. Contribution indicator for an individual organization.

Contribution Indicator (CI_i)	
Measures the contribution for value creation of a member of the CBE	
$O_1,\ldots,O_n$	Organizations in the CBE
METRICS	
#CoOp$_i$ in	No. of collaboration opportunities the member O_i gained from the CBE (indegree)
#CoOp$_i$ out	No. of collaboration opportunities the member O_i brought in the CBE (outdegree)
Act in/out(O_i)	Activity in/out of the member O_i in the CBE Act(O_i) can be measured by the weighted indegree/outdegree centrality (C_D) of the member O_i in the CBE, which stands for the sum of direct connections in/out of the member O_i to the n members O_j with weight #CoOp$_{ij}$ $Act\ in/out(O_i) = C_D\ (O_i)\ in/out = \sum_j O_{ij}\#CoOp_{ij}\ in/out$
PERFORMANCE INDICATORS	
$CI_i = (CI_i\ in, CI_i\ out)$	Is calculated by two indicators
Where, $CI_i\ in = \frac{\sum_j O_{ij}\#CoOp_{ij}\ in}{\max C_D(O_i)\ in}$	$CI_i\ out = \frac{\sum_j O_{ij}\#CoOp_{ij}\ out}{\max C_D(O_i)\ out}$

Note: CI_i in and CI_i out are normalized values

The Contribution Indicator of the whole CBE (CI_{CBE}) is calculated by two indicators, the ratio of the total number of collaboration opportunities created in the CBE by the number of organizations in the CBE, and the degree to which the most active member exceeds the contribution of the others. Metrics and calculations for CI_{CBE} are described in Table 4.

Prestige Indicator. The Prestige Indicator (PI_i) of an individual organization member of a CBE, measures the influence/prominence of a member of the CBE, i.e., the likelihood of the organization be contacted towards potential collaboration opportunities. Metrics and calculations for PI_i are described in Table 5.

The Prestige Indicator of the whole CBE (PI_{CBE}) measures the average difference between the most influent member and that of all members of the CBE. Metrics and calculations for PI_{CBE} are described in Table 6.

Table 4. Contribution indicator of the whole CBE.

Contribution Indicator (CI_{CBE})	
Measures the value creation of the collaboration in the CBE as a whole, and the degree to which the most active member exceeds the contribution of the others	
CBE	Whole CBE
METRICS	
$\sum_i \#O_i$	Number of organizations in the CBE
$\sum_i \#CoOp_i$	Total no. of collaboration opportunities created in the CBE
$\{\#CoOp_1, \ldots, \#CoOp_n\}$	No. of collaboration opportunities in which the members $O_1, \ldots, O_n$ participated
Act(CBE)	Activity of the members of the CBE
	Act(CBE) can be measured by the weighted degree centrality (C_D) of the CBE as a whole, i.e. the sum of the differences between the activity of the most active member (O^*) and that of all members of the CBE $Act(CBE) = C_D(CBE) = \sum_i [C_D(O^*) - C_D(O_i)]$ Where, $C_D(O_i) = \sum_j O_{ij} \#CoOp_{ij}$; $C_D(O^*) = max[C_D(O_i)]$
PERFORMANCE INDICATORS	
$CI_{CBE} = (CI_{CBE}t,\ CI_{CBE}d)$	Is calculated by two indicators
Where, $CI_{CBE}t = \frac{\sum_i \#CoOp_i}{\sum_i \#O_i}$	$CI_{CBE}d = \frac{\sum_i [C_D(O^*) - C_D(O_i)]}{\max C_D(CBE)}$

Note: $CI_{CBE}t$ is a ratio and $CI_{CBE}d$ a normalized value

Table 5. Prestige indicator for an individual organization.

Prestige Indicator (PI_i)	
Measures the influence/prominence of a member of the CBE	
$O_1,\ldots,O_n$	Organizations in the CBE
METRICS	
$\#CoOp_i$	No. of collaboration opportunities of the member O_i participated in the
$\#CoOp_{kj}$	No. of collaboration opportunities of the member O_{kj} participated in the
Inf(O_i)	Influence of the member O_i in the CBE, i.e., the likelihood of O_i to be contacted towards potential collaboration opportunities
	Inf(O_i) can be measured by the weighted betweenness centrality (C_B) of the member O_i in the CBE, assuming that connections between any member O_k and any other O_j have weight of $\#CoOp_{kj}$ $Inf(O_i) = C_B(O_i) = \sum_k \sum_j O_{kj}(O_i)$ $k < j,\ k \neq j \neq i$
PERFORMANCE INDICATORS	
$PI_i = \frac{\sum_k \sum_j O_{kj}(O_i)}{\max C_B(O_i)}$	$k < j,\ k \neq j \neq i$

Note: PI_i is a normalized value

Table 6. Prestige indicator of the whole CBE.

Prestige Indicator (CI_{CBE})	
Measures the average difference between the most influent member and that of all members of the CBE	
CBE	Whole CBE
METRICS	
{$\#CoOp_1$, …, $\#CoOp_n$}	No. of collaboration opportunities in which the members O_1, …, O_n participated
$\sum_i [Inf(O^*) - Inf(O_i)]/(n-1)$	Average of the differences between the influence of the most influent member and that of all members of the CBE
Inf(CBE)	Influence of the members of the CBE Inf(CBE) can be measured by the weighted betweenness centrality (C_B) of the CBE as a whole, assuming that connections between any member O_k and any other O_j have weight of $\#CoOp_{kj}$ $Inf(CBE) = C_B(CBE) = \sum_i [C_B(O^*) - C_B(O_i)]$ Where, $C_B(O_i) = \sum_i [C_B(O^*) - C_B(O_i)]$ $C_B(O^*) = \max[C_B(O_i)]$
PERFORMANCE INDICATORS	
	$PI_{CBE} = \frac{\sum_i [C_B(O^*) - C_B(O_i)]}{\max C_B(CBE)}$

Note: PI_{CBE} is a normalized value

3 Modeling a System for Performance Assessment of a CBE

The purpose of the indicators introduced in the previous section is anchored in the following hypothesis:

Performance indicators are a useful mechanism for assessing a CBE if they can contribute as a factor of influence for organizations to evolve, self-adjusting their behavior, and thereby improving the ecosystem performance and sustainability.

To verify the hypothesis, a CBE can be seen as a closed environment where organizations live, interact and collaborate with each other to realize business opportunities. The organizations are characterized by an endogenous behavior which can be influenced by the adopted performance indicators to evaluate the CBE (assessment engine). Then, according to the purpose of each indicator, organizations react differently depending on the characteristics of their profile which react to a set of factors of influence. As an example, organizations in a highly competitive and innovative CBE are likely to have a higher responsiveness to the innovation indicator. On the other hand, organizations in healthcare service delivery are more likely to respond to indicators of contribution and quality. In addition, organizations with a similar profile may react with different intensity to the same factors of influence, allowing the establishment of classes of responsiveness.

For the present study, considering the assumptions described above, we propose a Performance Assessment and Adjustment Model (PAAM) as depicted in Fig. 1. The

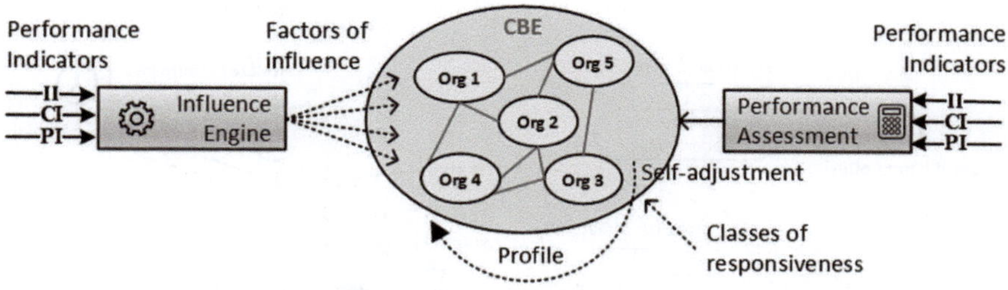

Fig. 1. PAAM (Performance Assessment and Adjustment Model) for a CBE.

purpose of this model is to explore the impact of indicators in the assessment of organizations in a CBE, namely how they can influence an improvement of behavior, thus contributing for a better performance of the CBE.

4 Modeling an Evaluation Scenario

In order to study the above ideas, the proposed PAAM was implemented as a system based on simulation, using agent-based modeling (ABM) and system dynamics (SD). ABM is used for simulating the actions and interactions of the autonomous organizations (the agents) in the CBE (the environment). SD is a mathematical modeling method to enhance learning in complex systems, supporting simulation models which help to understand the dynamics of complexity, allowing designing more effective policies and organizations [21]. Discrete elements (statecharts, events, timers, etc.) can be used to combine the different techniques and models [22], controlling state transitions, delays, or even capture exogenous values.

4.1 Setting-up the Simulation Model

Figure 2 illustrates the designed PAAM simulation system, where the organizations are autonomous agents, operating and collaborating in an environment which represents the business ecosystem. A system dynamics model simulates the evolution of the behavior of the organizations (and the CBE as a whole). This behavior is influenced by a mechanism of evaluation, i.e., when assessed according to the proposed performance indicators (II, CI, and PI).

When a new business opportunity is acquired by an organization (Org_i), it is brought in the CBE as a new collaboration opportunity (CoOp), which triggers the creation of a virtual organization (VO) formed by a set of selected candidate organizations (the partners). The selection is based on the required competencies (matching skills) for that collaboration opportunity, and a ranking of the organizations according to a set of attributes which characterize their profile (attributes such as innovation index, accomplishment index, quality assurance index, and reputation index). These indexes (could be more) were selected for the simulation model, since they are directly related to the adopted performance indicators, i.e., when the CBE is evaluated through the calculation

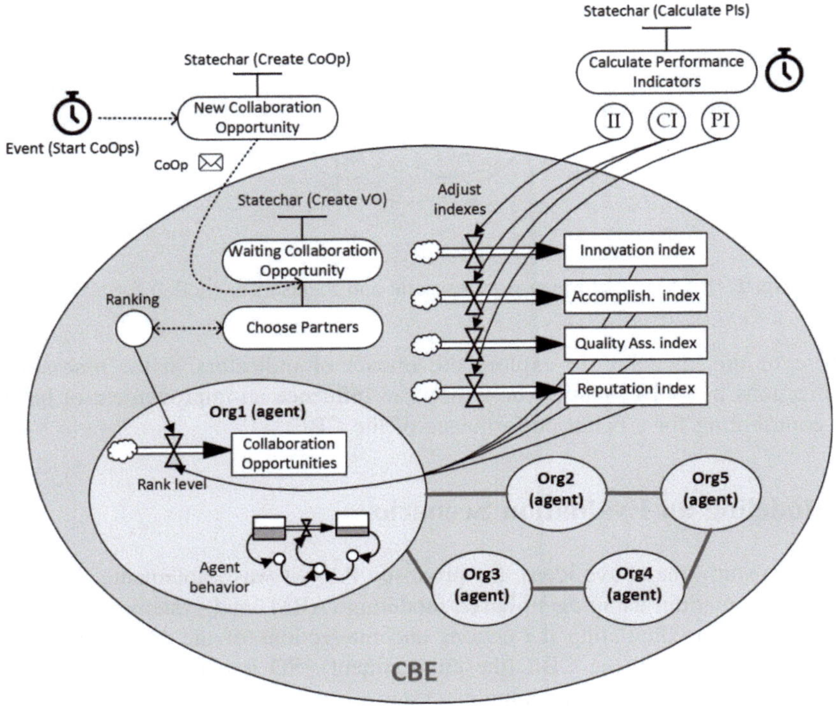

Fig. 2. General schema of the simulation PAAM system.

of the proposed performance indicators, this assessment is expected to induce some self-adjustment of the organizations' profile, as there is a natural tendency of individuals and organizations to adapt to the way they are evaluated. Thus, the performance indicators act as factors of influence, causing different responses according to the profile and class of responsiveness of the organizations. For instance, as suggested in Fig. 2, the II influences de innovation index, the CI is more related to the accomplishment and quality assurance indexes, and the PI influences the reputation index.

4.2 Setting-up the Simulation Scenario

To set-up a complete simulation scenario to study de evolution of a CBE when assessed by the proposed performance indicators, we need to focus on the agent's behavior. The agent's behavior is modeled by system dynamics, and can represent a concern or a problem of the organization, as the generic example based on [21], depicted in Fig. 3.

The example in Fig. 3, comprising a causal loop diagram, aims to explore the causes of late delivery for an organization's design work [21]. The model shows the behavior of a team of engineers trying to conclude the tasks of a project against a deadline. The shorter the time remaining, the more schedule pressure they feel. When the pressure is high, the team has several choices. If they work overtime, the

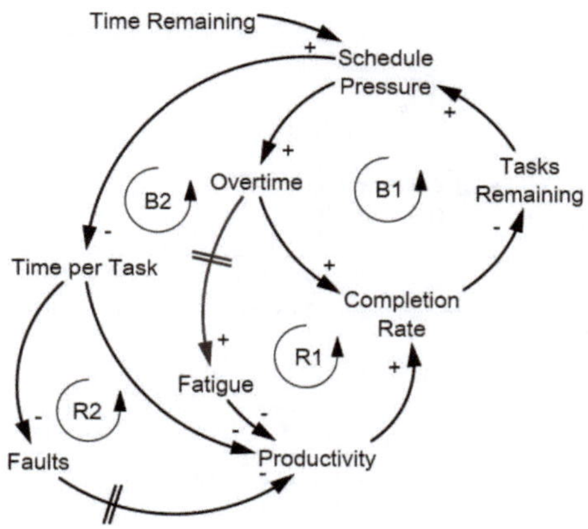

Fig. 3. Behavior of a team trying to complete a project against a (based on [21]).

completion rate increases, thereby decreasing the number of remaining tasks and easing the schedule pressure (balancing loop B1). However, after a certain time, productivity drops due to fatigue, lowering the completion rate and increasing again the schedule pressure (reinforcing loop R1). Another way to meet the deadlines is to devote less time to each task, which increases the productivity as more tasks are done. Consequently, the schedule pressure is relieved (balancing loop B2), but the quality assurance is neglected, causing more faults, lowering productivity and forcing more scheduled pressure (reinforcing loop R2).

To complete the simulation scenario, the behavior of the agents, as the example illustrated in Fig. 3, should be expressed by a stock and flow map coupled to the PAAM system. Figure 4 depicts a zoom in one organization (Org_1) showing the corresponding agent's behavior. The factors of influence and class of responsiveness should be parametrized for each agent.

The ongoing work is focused on completing the development of the PAAM system using AnyLogic Multimethod Simulation Software [22], a tool that supports discrete event, agent based, and system dynamics simulation. The objective is setting-up a simulation scenario as described above, representing a CBE with organizations with different profiles (implying different factors of influence), and classes of responsiveness. By varying these parameters, it is expected that the model will allow understanding the evolution of the behavior of the organizations, namely their self-adjustment as a reaction to the assessment through the proposed performance indicators, and then verifying if that contributes for the improvement of both the organizations and the CBE as a whole.

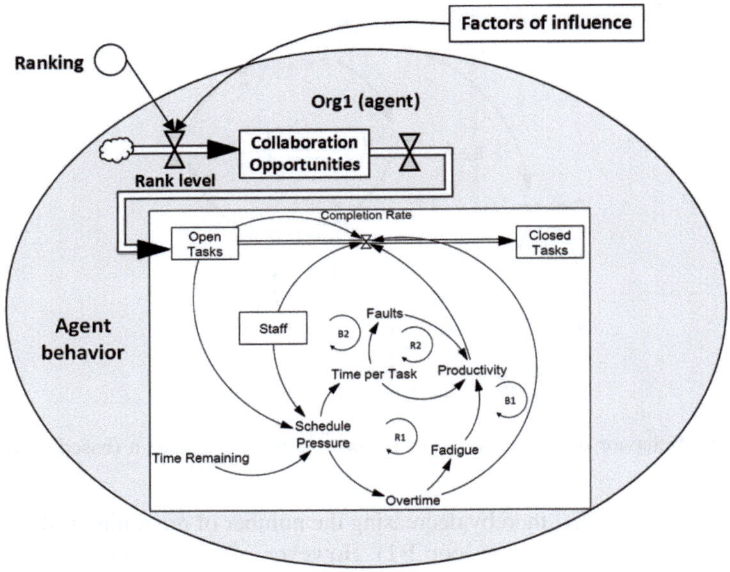

Fig. 4. Zoom in one organization (Org_1), showing the corresponding agent's behavior in a stock and flow map (based on [21]).

5 Conclusions and Further Work

The performance indicators and metrics for CBEs presented in this paper, as well as the proposed PAAM system, contribute as a first approach to verify the hypothesis stated in section three, providing a simulation model to study the evolution of organizations in a CBE influenced by a given set of performance indicators. As such, the model is designed to allow identifying the indicators that lead to an improvement of the behavior of the organizations, thus improving the CBE and its sustainability.

The ongoing work, as mentioned above, comprises finishing the creation of the proposed PAAM system using AnyLogic Multimethod Simulation Software [22], to allow the configuration of multiple simulation scenarios, where the organizations in a CBE are represented by an ABM (agents in an environment), and the autonomous behavior of the organizations, by SD. "*System dynamics seeks endogenous explanation for phenomena*" [21]. The "interactions" between the agents and the variables, factors of influence, and responsiveness, are expected to provide a mechanism to study the effects of different sets of indicators.

The future work is aimed to continue the next steps of the modeling process [21]. i.e., after the problem articulation, dynamic hypothesis, and formulation, covered in the presented approach, comes next the testing phase, and the policy design and evaluation phase. The testing phase will consider concerns such as boundary adequacy, structure and parameter assessment, extreme conditions, behavior reproduction and anomaly, sensitivity analysis, among others. Finally, the policy design and evaluation phase allows designing and evaluating policies for improvement.

Thus, the proposed PAAM system, configured using several scenarios and parametrisation, is expected to reveal important insights, to make us understand the dynamics and evolution of a CBE when assessed by a given set of indicators.

Acknowledgments. This work benefited from the ongoing research within the CoDIS (Collaborative Networks and Distributed Industrial Systems Group) which is part of both the New University of Lisbon (UNL) - Faculty of Sciences and Technology, and the UNINOVA - Institute for the Development of New Technologies. Partial support also comes from Fundação para a Ciência e Tecnologia through the PEST program UID/EEA/00066/2013 (Impactor project).

References

1. Moore, J.F.: Predators and prey: a new ecology of competition. Harvard Bus. Rev. **71**(3), 75–83 (1993)
2. Moore, J.F.: The Death of Competition: Leadership and Strategy in the Age of Business Ecosystems. HarperCollins Publishers, New York (1996)
3. Camarinha-Matos, L.M., Afsarmanesh, H.: Collaborative networks: a new scientific discipline. J. Intell. Manuf. **16**(4–5), 439–452 (2005)
4. Camarinha-Matos, L.M., Afsarmanesh, H.: Collaborative Networks: Reference Modeling. Springer, Heidelberg (2008)
5. Graça, P., Camarinha-Matos, L.M.: The need of performance indicators for collaborative business ecosystems. In: Camarinha-Matos, L.M., Baldissera, T.A., Di Orio, G., Marques, F. (eds.) DoCEIS 2015. IAICT, vol. 450, pp. 22–30. Springer, Cham (2015). doi:10.1007/978-3-319-16766-4_3
6. Forrester, J.W.: Industrial Dynamics. MIT Press, Cambridge (1961)
7. Kaplan, R.S., Norton, D.P.: The Balanced Scorecard: Translating Strategy into Action. Harvard Business Press, Boston (1996)
8. Piot, G., Pouly, M., Cheikhrouhou, N., Glardon, R.: An estimation model for business benefits in horizontal collaborative networks. In: Camarinha-Matos, L.M., Afsarmanesh, H., Novais, P., Analide, C. (eds.) PRO-VE 2007. ITIFIP, vol. 243, pp. 345–352. Springer, Boston (2007). doi:10.1007/978-0-387-73798-0_36
9. Abreu, A., Camarinha-Matos, L.M.: A benefit analysis model for collaborative networks. In: Camarinha-Matos, L.M., Afsarmanesh, H. (eds.) Collaborative Networks: Reference Modeling, pp. 253–276. Springer, Heidelberg (2008). doi:10.1007/978-0-387-79426-6_18
10. Camarinha-Matos, L.M., Macedo, P.: Á conceptual model of value systems in collaborative networks. J. Intell. Manuf. **21**(3), 287–299 (2010)
11. Macedo, P., Camarinha-Matos, L.M.: A qualitative approach to assess the alignment of value systems in collaborative enterprises networks. Comput. Ind. Eng. **64**(1), 412–424 (2013)
12. Vereecke, A., Muylle, S.: Performance improvement through supply chain collaboration in Europe. Int. J. Oper. Prod. Manage. **26**(11), 1176–1198 (2006)
13. Lorentz, H., Shi, Y., Hilmola, O.-P., Srai, J.S., Ramanathan, U., Gunasekaran, A., Subramanian, N.: Supply chain collaboration performance metrics: a conceptual framework. Benchmarking Int. J. **18**(6), 856–872 (2011)
14. Ramanathan, U., Gunasekaran, A.: Supply chain collaboration: impact of success in long-term partnerships. Int. J. Prod. Econ. **147**, 252–259 (2014)
15. Ramanathan, U.: Performance of supply chain collaboration - a simulation study. Expert Syst. Appl. **41**(1), 210–220 (2014)

16. Freeman, L.C.: Centrality in social networks conceptual clarification. Soc. Netw. **1**(3), 215–239 (1978)
17. Jackson, M.O.: Social and Economic Networks, vol. 3. Princeton University Press, Princeton (2008)
18. Graça, P., Camarinha-Matos, L.M.: A proposal of performance indicators for collaborative business ecosystems. In: Afsarmanesh, H., Camarinha-Matos, L.M., Lucas Soares, A. (eds.) PRO-VE 2016. IAICT, vol. 480, pp. 253–264. Springer, Cham (2016). doi:10.1007/978-3-319-45390-3_22
19. Kelly, E.: Introduction: Business Ecosystems Come of Age (2015)
20. Myers, J.L., Well, A., Lorch, R.F.: Research Design and Statistical Analysis. Routledge, New York (2010)
21. Sterman, J.D.: Business Dynamics: Systems Thinking and Modeling for a Complex World. McGraw-Hill Education, Boston (2000). Number HD30. 2 S7835 2000
22. Borshchev, A: The Big Book of Simulation Modeling: Multimethod Modeling with AnyLogic 6. AnyLogic North America (2013)

Establishment of Collaborative Networks – A Model-Driven Engineering Approach Based on Thermodynamics

Frederick Benaben[1(✉)], Vincent Gerbaud[2], Anne-Marie Barthe-Delanoë[2], and Anastasia Roth[2]

[1] IMT Mines Albi-Carmaux, Campus Jarlard – Route de Teillet, 81000 Albi, France
frederick.benaben@mines-albi.fr

[2] Laboratoire de Génie Chimique, Université de Toulouse, CNRS, INPT, UPS, Toulouse, France
{vincent.gerbaud,annemarie.barthe,anastasia.roth}@ensiacet.fr

Abstract. The setup of an efficient collaborative situation between organizations can be considered according to four main complementary dimensions: the *context* (geographical, social, economical environment), the *partners* (the actors, their capabilities, their resources and their relationships), the *objectives* (the collaborative goals of the network, the risks to be avoided, etc.) and finally the *behaviour* (the collaborative processes to be implemented by the *partners* to achieve the *objectives* considering the *context*). Some research works try to infer the *behaviour* based on the three other issues assumed to be known, by using different approaches such as model-driven engineering (MDE), optimization, heuristics, planning, etc. MDE helps studying the opportunity of inferring the *objectives* part from the *context* and *partners* dimensions in order to feed the *behaviour* issue. We use a non-equilibrium thermodynamics analogy where *partners* and *context* attributes and methods are mapped to thermodynamic state variables of an organisation seen as an open system in the frame of dissipative structure thermodynamics. We apply it specifically to enterprises and discuss briefly the analogy of *behaviour* as an irreversible trajectory aiming to maintain the enterprise activity alive.

Keywords: Collaborative network · Thermodynamics · Metamodel · Model-driven engineering · Knowledge management

1 Introduction

The starting point of this article is quite simple: *Would one be able to know some state variables of a set of atoms (about their structure, energy, etc.) and about the environment of these atoms (pressure, temperature, etc.), one can infer the way these atoms will self-organize and self-structure within the next periods of time.* Could we reasonably think about having the same kind of approach for organizations? Is there any chance to characterize organizations, their ecosystems and their kinetics in a way that would allow us to define laws and rules to predict or infer the evolution and structure of networks of organizations? Is that a fantasy to try to find state variables and evolution laws for extended enterprises and collaborative networks?

L.M. Camarinha-Matos et al. (Eds.): PRO-VE 2017, IFIP AICT 506, pp. 641–648, 2017.
DOI: 10.1007/978-3-319-65151-4_56

This article focuses on both these dimensions: state variables and laws. Consequently, this article is structured in two main parts. The first one (Sect. 2) presents a theoretical framework to model collaborative networks of organizations according to four dimensions: the *context* (geographical, social, economical environment), the *partners* (the actors, their capabilities, their resources and their relationships), the *objectives* (the collaborative goals of the network, the risks to be avoided, etc.) and finally the *behaviour* (the collaborative processes to be implemented by the *partners* to achieve the *objectives* considering the *context*). The second one (Sect. 3) describes principles to deal with models and define rules and mechanisms that could exploit those models to support the design of efficient and relevant collaborative networks. Basically, the idea is to use *context* and *partners* models to create *objective* models. These three points of views (*context, partners* and *objective*) could then be used in a model-driven engineering approach to build the fourth one; *behaviour* point of view.

2 Modelling Framework for Collaborative Situations

The characterization of a collaborative situation requires describing several points of view. To describe clearly these points of view, this article directly refers to system modelling (as far as a network of organizations can be considered as a system, or a system of systems) and to enterprise modelling (as far as organizations may be considered as enterprises from a modelling perspective). On the one hand, system modelling is traditionally based on three main dimensions [1]:

- *Requirement/Functional view*[1]: This dimension describes mainly the expectations of the system. It is dedicated to clarify its purposes.
- *Structural view*: This dimension presents on the one hand the components of the system and the relations they have with each other, and on the other hand the environment of the system and the relationships between the system (its components) and that environment.
- *Behavioural view*: This dimension describes the dynamic aspect of the system and the way it performs. It is dedicated to model the processes and the performances of the system.

Enterprise modelling, on the other hand, is often considered according to four points of view [2]:

- Informational view: This point of view describes the embedded data and associated knowledge of the organization.
- Functional view: This point of view presents the whole capability of the organization through its behaviour and its processes.
- Organizational view: This point of view describes the responsibilities, allocations and hierarchical schemes of the structure of the organization.
- Resources view: This point of view presents the means and the individual capabilities of people, software, machines composing the organization.

[1] The name can be different (*e.g.* in SysML formalism or in System Engineering domain).

Considering that the main objective of setting up a collaborative network can be seen as "*the design of an organization, which is a system of organizations*" the previously described points of views (about system modelling and enterprise/organization modelling) should be considered to define the modelling framework of collaborative situations.

Based on the overall idea presented in Fig. 1, the main challenge is to exploit the modelling dimensions inherited from Enterprise/System modelling framework to create the appropriate modelling framework (and its relevant points of view) for collaborative situations.

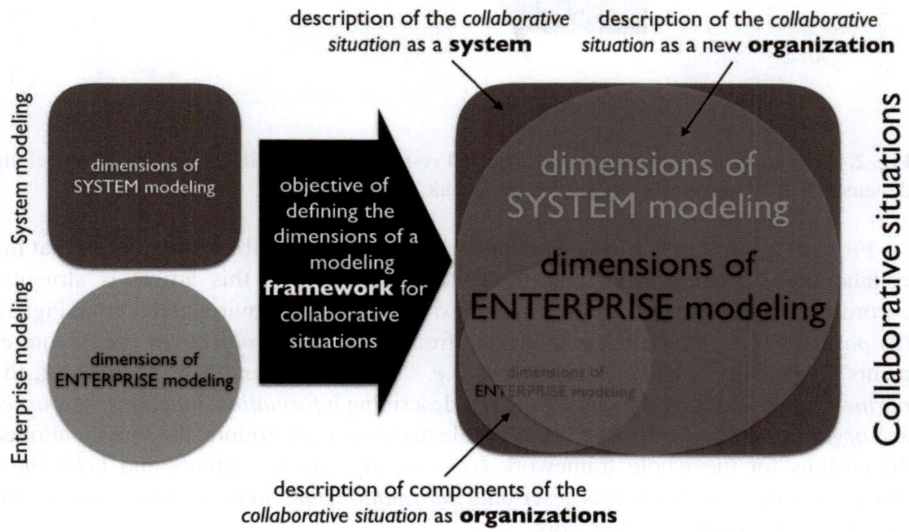

Fig. 1. The use of *enterprise* and *system* modelling dimensions with regards to the objective of defining the modelling dimensions of a *collaborative situation* framework.

The basic principles to reach that objective are the following:

1. The collaborative situation modelling framework should be based on the system modelling dimensions (*because the collaborative situation is a system*).
2. Considering the way the collaborative situation should be integrated in its environment, the structural view of the framework could be split in two parts: components (*i.e.* partners) and environment of the network.
3. A collaborative situation model should embed knowledge about information, functions, resources and organisation of the network as a whole (*because the collaborative situation is an organization*).
4. The dimension (of the collaborative situation modelling framework) specifically describing components (*i.e.* partners) should be based on the enterprise modelling dimensions (*because partners are enterprises*).

Figure 2 presents the consequences of these principles on the basis of the big picture presented on Fig. 1.

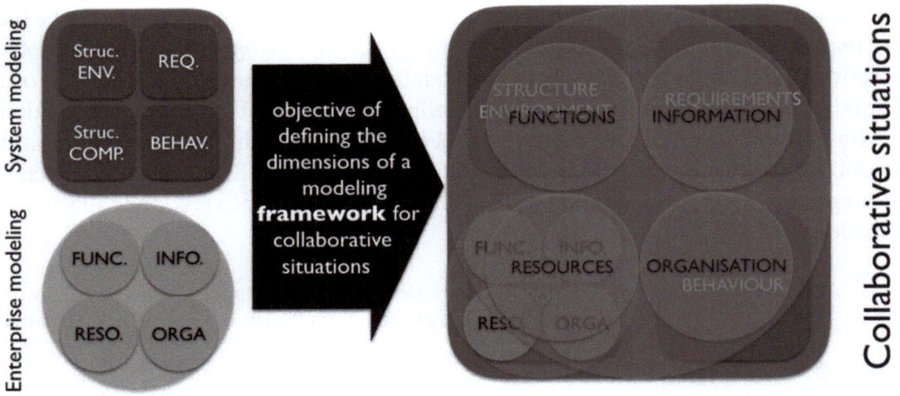

Fig. 2. The mapping principle of *enterprise* and *system* modelling dimensions on the modelling dimensions of a *collaborative situation* framework.

From Fig. 2 and the previously listed principles, it is possible to legitimate that the collaborative situation modelling framework presented in this article is structure according to four main dimensions: (i) *context* (*i.e.* "structure environment" from Fig. 2), (ii) *partners* (*i.e.* "structure components" from Fig. 2), (iii) *objectives* (*i.e.* "requirements" from Fig. 2) and (iv) *behaviour* (*i.e.* "behaviour" from Fig. 2). Besides, the *partner* dimension should include concepts describing *information*, *functions*, *resources* and *organization* of the involved or available partners. Furthermore, the four mentioned dimensions for the whole framework (*context*, *objectives*, *partners* and *behaviour*) should include as well concepts describing *information*, *functions*, *resources* and *organization* of the collaborative network.

Consequently, the framework (Fig. 3) proposed in this article is the following:

- *Context dimension* (light grey) including components and characteristics of the considered environment, and also opportunities or threats specific to these environment characteristics.
- *Partner dimension* (strong grey) expresses the different resources and know-how of the partners. This includes notably capabilities, patterns, instructions, resources (information, material, people, etc.), flows (linking capabilities) and connector/mediator able to orchestrate the different business processes.
- *Objective dimension* (medium grey) containing characteristics of collaborative network (common objective and facts that the collaboration has to manage).
- *Behaviour dimension* (dark grey) that characterized the concrete operations, which are deployed to concretize the collaboration. This includes business processes/activities and their associated events and messages. Besides, this dimension includes as well a *Performance point of view* (white) that assesses the overall performance of the collaboration by comparing, through dedicated Key Performance Indicators (KPIs), the performance objective to the measures on the field.

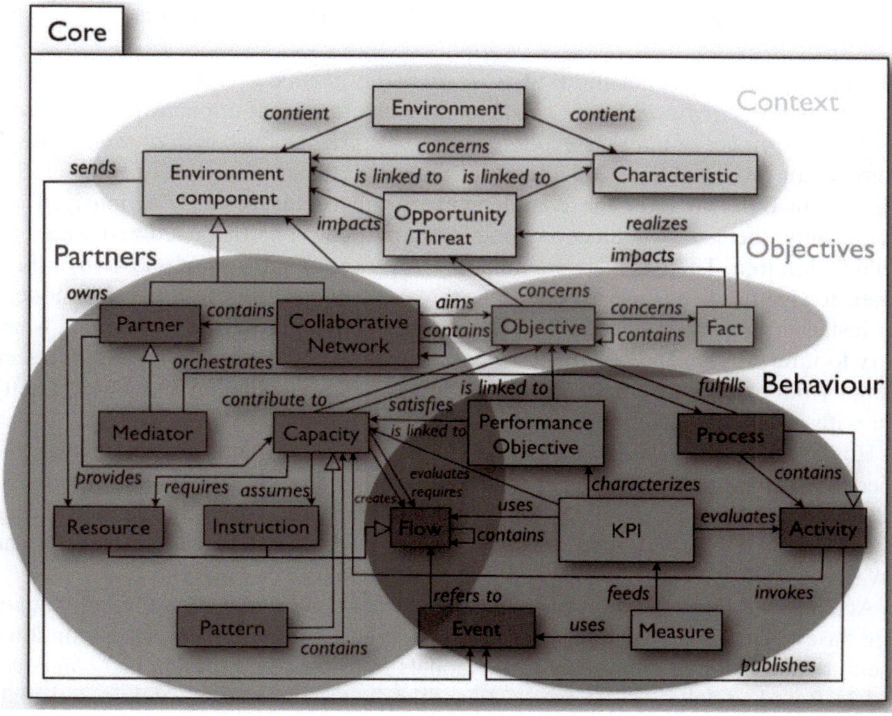

Fig. 3. *Concepts* and *relationships* between concepts embedded in the four-dimension framework of collaborative situation modelling (from [3]).

Figure 3 presents the modelling framework for collaborative situations with the four aforementioned dimensions embedding concepts and relations between concepts to describe a collaborative situation (whatever the concerned business domain).

Based on the previous statements, this article claims that a collaborative situation may be modelled by instantiating *concepts* and *relations* of the previous diagram presented in Fig. 3, which is actually a *collaborative situation metamodel.* The next question at this point is "*how can such a collaborative situation model be used to infer the way a collaborative situation could be established, could evolve and even catch opportunities or re-organize to remain successful?*" and more precisely: "*is it possible to model part of the collaborative situation (e.g. partners and context) and infer the other part?*". This is a direct echo to the question asked in the introduction of this article: considering the characteristics of a set of organizations (partners) and the characteristics of the environment they are involved in (context), is it possible to define what could be done by such a group of organizations in that environment (objectives) and how should this network of partners perform (behaviour).

3 Designing and Implementing Collaborative Situations

The initial question (introduction) was: "*Is there any chance to characterize organizations, their ecosystems and their kinetics in a way that would allow us to define laws and rules to predict or infer the evolution and structure of networks of organizations?*" From the conclusion of Sect. 2, the resulting purpose is to partially model a collaborative situation in order to infer the complementary part of the model. Obviously, from Sect. 2 only, there is no indication about what part could be modelled and what part could be inferred. There is huge combinatory coverage of sub-sets of one, two or three dimension models to be done to deduce the three, two or one missing dimension models. For instance, the objective could be to model *partners* and *objectives* (who and what) to try to infer *context* and *behaviour* (where and how). But there are actually fourteen options (four options with three modelled dimensions, six options with two and finally four with one modelled dimension).

However, from the initial question and the analogy with atoms or molecules, the objective is definitely more precise: from the model of a set of organizations (partners) and of the environment they are involved in (context), the purpose is to define what could be done by such a group of organizations in that environment (objectives) and how should this network of partners perform (behaviour).

Actually, previous research works [4, 5] use model transformation through knowledge bases (ontologies for some application domains and graph data bases for some others) to automatically infer *behaviour* models from *context, partners* and *objectives* models. Based on stakes and characteristics of the *context*, capabilities of *partners*, goals to reach and risks to avoid from *objectives*, model transformation rules automatically build collaborative business process models in BPMN-like format. These contributions are our starting point and show that it is possible to infer *behaviour* from *context, partners* and *objectives*. But we feel reasonable to go a step further by attempting to get the *objectives* model from the *context* and *partners*' dimensions and then thanks to [4, 5], infer the *behaviour* model (Fig. 4).

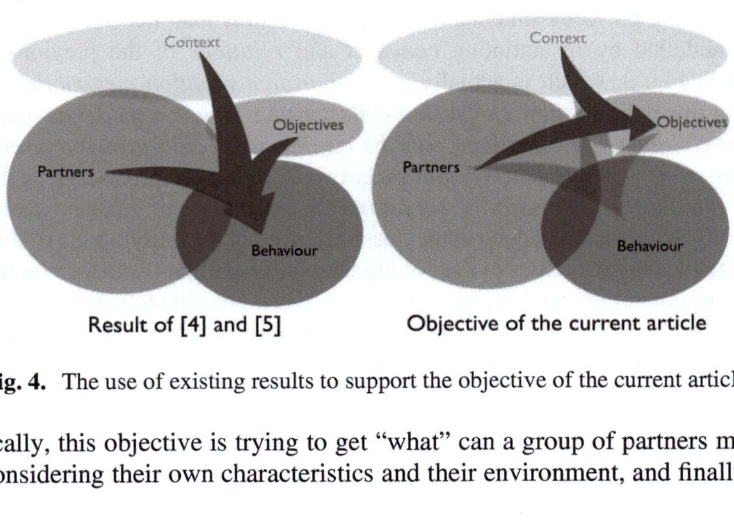

Fig. 4. The use of existing results to support the objective of the current article.

Basically, this objective is trying to get "what" can a group of partners make altogether considering their own characteristics and their environment, and finally, "how" could they reach these objectives. From [6], "a *collaborative network* (CN) is constituted by a variety of entities (e.g., organizations and people) that are largely autonomous, geographically distributed, and heterogeneous in terms of their: operating environment, culture, social capital, and goals". This definition strongly highlights three main features: (i) autonomy of partners, (ii) distribution of partners and (iii) heterogeneity of partners.

We now focus on an enterprise seen as an organisation and carry on with a non-equilibrium thermodynamic (NET) analogy. The second law of Thermodynamic states that closed systems evolve to maximize their entropy, reaching the equilibrium state, often referred as a dead state. Instead, we consider the enterprise as open system, developing in the so-called the *context* (see Sect. 2). We can further define the *context* by three state variables: *opening* (presence of strong competitors/demanding partners and suitable informational/physical connections between them), *easiness* (favourable legal, cultural and financial frame) and *wideness* (expanse of the environment). They can be assigned respectively to the thermodynamic *temperature* T (ability to move), *pressure* P (constraint to a move) and *volume* V (Fig. 5). As is usual, an equation of state can relate P easiness, T opening and V wideness, like the Virial Equation of state: $PV/(n\mathrm{R}T) = 1 + \mathrm{B}(n/V) + \mathrm{C}(n/V)^2\ldots$ R is the ideal gas constant and N is the number of potential partners. 1 is the ideal gas contribution (no partner interaction) whereas B (C) is the second (third) virial coefficient accounting for two (three) partners interactions. Notice that *easiness* and *opening* can be obtained from the metamodel (Fig. 3) respectively as (i) the number and the nature of *environment components*, together with some of the *characteristics* of the environment and (ii) *opportunity* and *threat*, together with some of the *characteristics* of the environment.

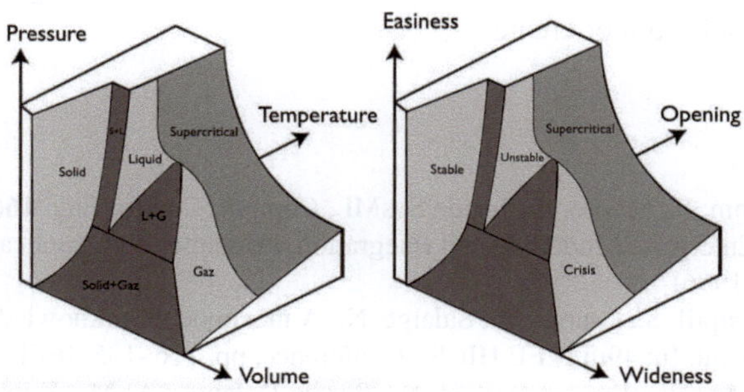

Fig. 5. Thermodynamics analogy for the context of collaborative situation.

According to NET, open systems are subjected to forces that counter gradients: e.g. heat flows from high to low temperature so as to make temperature uniform at the equilibrium state. We postulate that the enterprise lies in a non-equilibrium stationary state as forces and gradient may be balanced over time in the enterprise *context*. Being out of equilibrium, its internal entropy is lower than the equilibrium maximal entropy and that entropy decrease ΔS can be interpreted in two ways: (i) it increases the system free energy $\Delta A = \Delta U - T\Delta S$. A is assimilated to the ability to perform work and U describes the enterprise assets [7], (ii) as a degree of internal organisation. This later meaning could be discussed further by using extremal principles under external constraints, like Bejan's constructal law or thermodynamics' MaxEP [8].

The enterprise *behaviour* translates into a trajectory from its present state to a new one within a modified *context*. Such a trajectory is not reversible, since its duration would be infinite according to thermodynamics fluctuation theorems, which deal with the success probability of a trajectory [7]. Hence, the activity generated through the trajectory is irreversible and in compliance with the 2nd law, it induces a dissipation, comparable to heat, consecutive to the activity's work. We also postulate that the enterprise decision to move to another state is driven by the information gathered by the enterprise, including all the constraints narrowing the path. Then it is processed as *objectives* in order to initiate a *behaviour* that ensures the enterprise's survival.

4 Conclusion

The current article tries to make the link between an approach for modelling collaborative situations based on a metamodel covering the four main dimensions of such a system of organizations and scientific domains such as thermodynamics and chemistry. The ultimate goal of these emerging considerations is about the way to characterize the *context* and the *partners* of a collaborative situation with regards to state variables and characteristics of atoms and molecules. This article is a tentative first step into this field. The expected benefit would be a modelling environment where organizations and their context could be characterized and the obtained models could be constantly updated. Based on the laws and rules inherited from chemistry and thermodynamics, the system could provide the organizations with decision support regarding the collaborative networks they could join or create.

References

1. Hause, M., Thom, F., Moore, A.: Inside SysML. Comput. Control Eng. **16**(4), 10–15 (2005)
2. Vernadat, F.: Enterprise Modelling and Integration, Principles and Applications. Chapman & Hall, London (1996)
3. Benaben, F., Truptil, S., Lauras, M., Salatge, N.: A metamodel for knowledge management in crisis management. In: 49th IEEE HICSS Conference, pp. 126–135. IEEE Press (2016)
4. Benaben, F., Mu, W., Boissel-Dallier, N., Barthe-Delanoë, A.-M., Zribi, S., Pingaud, H.: Supporting interoperability of collaborative networks through engineering of a service-based Mediation Information System (MISE 2.0). Enterp. Inf. Syst. **9**(5–6), 556–582 (2015). Taylor & Francis
5. Benaben, F., Montarnal, A., Truptil, S., Lauras, M., Fertier, A., Salatgé, N., Rebière, S.: A conceptual framework and a suite of tools to support crisis management. In: 50th IEEE HICSS Conference, pp. 237–246. IEEE Press (2017)
6. Camarinha-Matos, L., Afsarmanesh, H.: Collaborative networks: a new scientific discipline. J. Intell. Manuf. **16**(4–5), 439–452 (2005)
7. Demirel, Y.: Nonequilibrium thermodynamics: transport and rate processes in physical, chemical and biological systems, 3rd edn. Elsevier, Amsterdam (2014)
8. Dewar, R.C., et al. (eds.): Beyond the Second Law, Understanding Complex Systems. Springer, Heidelberg (2014)

Dynamic Integration of Mould Industry Analytics and Design Forecasting

João M.F. Calado[1,2(✉)] and A. Luis Osório[1]

[1] IPL – Instituto Politécnico de Lisboa, POLITEC&ID,
ISEL – Instituto Superior de Engenharia de Lisboa, Rua Conselheiro Emídio Navarro,
1959-007 Lisbon, Portugal
jcalado@dem.isel.ipl.pt, lo@isel.ipl.pt

[2] IDMEC/LAETA, Instituto Superior Técnico, Universidade de Lisboa,
Avenida Rovisco Pais, 1049-001 Lisbon, Portugal

Abstract. The aim of this paper is concerned with a conceptual framework to get about the smart factory concept in the mould/tools industry, by retrieving knowledge from historical data and data analysis. Specifically, it will be addressed the requirements to design and develop the next generation of open decision making informatics systems as tools for high variability manufacturing systems as in the tooling industry. The proposed open computational platform as open informatics systems (I-systems) developed under the specifications of the conceptual framework mention above will combine new balancing and simulation algorithms that allow the optimization of the production systems suggesting new and credible collaborative production sequences in a forecasting manner. Coupling smart monitoring with real-time decision support I-systems, the proposed approach will be able to cope with the aim of reducing lead-times and costs on the shop floor. The proposed open system of systems approach aims at contributing to adaptive higher integration levels, contribute for a collaborative factory and, at the same time, reduce the vendor lock-in dependencies risks.

Keywords: Mould/tools industry · Dynamic integration · Co-operation · Collaborative organizations · Smart analytics · Self-learning

1 Introduction

The new industrial reality has brought up an increased complexity to the production structures, requiring new management and organization ways making them more flexible, agile, efficient and effective. This emergent reality implies that companies need to develop products and innovative engineering solutions that put them in a technology leadership [1]. This can be attained through the more efficient use of technologies and resources, practices and methods based on information intelligence [2]. It also depends on a founded strategy to manage complex business partnerships through making them prepared for collaboration in dynamic virtual organizations [11].

The products manufactured by the Engineering and Tooling industry are unique. This is an industry of small series and/or unit production. These companies have a large

L.M. Camarinha-Matos et al. (Eds.): PRO-VE 2017, IFIP AICT 506, pp. 649–657, 2017.
DOI: 10.1007/978-3-319-65151-4_57

amount of data, improperly collected, that alone are just numbers, text and tables, humanly impossible to be analysed to generate knowledge. The collection, structure, compilation, analysis, sharing and monitoring of this data free of any contamination and its processing/interpretation in intelligible information, leading to what is called business intelligence, is of fundamental importance to facilitate decision making within the company [3]. For that purpose, there is a need to use smart monitoring systems on the factory shop floor, including distinctive functionalities for sensing, sensor networks, monitoring hardware and software, connected with manufacturing management and planning forecasting. Such smart systems require high levels of automation and information processing but allow quick reaction to changes on the shop floor. With this come new decision support tools sustained on Open Specification. Such tools should be able to support decision making based on the available data in a predictive or adaptive manner [4]. The approach proposed below combines new balancing and simulation algorithms that allow the optimization of the production system suggesting new and credible production sequences. The combination of smart monitoring and the real-time decision support system will cope with the aim to reduce lead-times and costs on the shop floor by the improvement of the flexibility of the manufacturing processes and by the increasing of the management control supported on new decision support tools based on smart analytics and self-learning [5]. The goal of this paper is to propose a conceptual framework to evolve the Smart Factory by retrieving knowledge from historical data and data analysis. Specifically, to design and develop the next generation Open Source decision making tool for high variability manufacturing systems: Allowing manufacturing decisions based on data reflecting the system past behaviour; Extracting knowledge from past data; Allowing performance measurement based on real-time data and performance evaluation based on manufacturing system status; Allowing risk analysis for more informed decisions and negotiations (with clients, suppliers, sub-contractors and other stakeholders involved); Allowing new Lean manufacturing methodologies responding to special requirements of Mould/Tooling Industry, such as waste reduction of all kinds, namely overproduction, holding time, unnecessary movements, transport, process, stock and defects, which can be translated into increasing productivity. Therefore, a service oriented cooperation enabled systems (CES) [12] is adopted as a modularity abstraction to reduce technology dependencies and empower modelling and intelligence capabilities.

Thus, the paper is organized as follows: Sect. 2 describes the challenges to be addressed to achieve the objectives mentioned above; Sect. 3 describes a conceptual framework for the development of mould/tool plant based on a smart factory concept; in Sect. 4 some conclusions are drawn.

2 Challenges to Be Addressed

Industrial globalisation created a new scenario for the Tooling industry, characterised by intense competition, short windows of opportunity in the market and frequent changes on ramp-up phases. Towards handling the mention challenges, this sector has been investing in technology and in the development of internal skills, both at the level of technological knowledge and in the investment market in terms of trying to identify opportunities and strategies to offer products and services of high technological intensity and with high standards of quality and innovation.

The long-term future impact of high performance computing power and communication speed, smart sensor technologies for generating and exploiting "big data", the convergence of the embedded world and the Internet/Cloud world in cyber-physical systems (CPS), multi-modal visualization and interaction technologies, upon our society as a whole, will be the framework to make a wider variety of products available at reasonable prices combined with high levels of variety, customization, timeliness, newness and quality [6]. Hence, in addition to invest in new technologies, companies will need to develop new strategies for each business area; more flexible organizational structures designed to implement strategies based on timeliness, innovation and product augmentation; sophisticated policies for human resource management; different accounting systems; and financial analysis algorithms [7].

Based on advances in information and communication technologies (ICT) will be new ways for the manufacturing industries to serve society and a new style of competition in the global marketplace. Thus, since the traditional approaches of computer integrated manufacturing (CIM) will make the technology for achieving flexible, low-cost, high-quality production systems available to all competitors, the real competitive advantages will shift from production economies to innovation approaches – where the skills needed are as follows: identify a market niche and its special needs; design a "product/service" that will meet that need better than anyone else can meet it and in a way that is hard to copy; quickly design, produce and distribute the product, to be able to move onto the next product quickly; and to be able to manage the complexity of many different products and many different customers being served from the same facility and at the same time [7]. Firms will also need to change their concepts of strategic thinking - from a focus on products and markets to a focus on competitive advantage in terms of process technology and systems and the institutional learning that allows the companies effectively and efficiently utilized advanced technology [8].

Aiming to achieve competitive advantages the new CIM approaches should be based on advanced analytics and smart decision support systems with self-learning capabilities exploiting the availability of "big data" from smart sensors, historical process files, or human-authored data; and addressing aspects, e.g. interactivity, real-time, data-fusion, imprecise computing, compressed sensing, advanced visualization, security, and privacy [9], ensuring coordination and collaborative activities involving many performers. Coordination and collaboration can be achieved in many ways. Integration is one of them, which means unity, connection, and interrelationships between elements and processes of a given manufacturing structure. In management processes, an especially important role is played by the flow of information between participants of an organization. Information media include technical means and people. The problems consist in the rational division of functions between the people and the machines, as well as a correct way of integration (co-operation and collaboration) of the people and the machines. Technical and social integration create an integrated manufacturing environment.

Between other types of one-of-a-kind product (OKP) manufacturing industries, a typical OKP company can be an injection mould/tool manufacturer. However, in injection mould/tool manufactures, due to a high customization involving uncertainties, resulting in a lot of reworking, the product development cost is normally higher and the development lead time is longer than in product-focused manufacturing companies. Anyway, in a smart factory, the rapid development of an OKP will be a holistic organizational concept that describes the development process by combining and integrating various innovative technologies and tools, such as rapid manufacturing (e.g. 3D printing), computer supported cooperative and collaborative tools and a supportive environment. Furthermore, an injection mould/tool manufacturing company pose some challenges to the factory of the future that could be characterized as follows: high customization; successful product development and production in one go; optimal or rational utilization of technologies and resources; adaptive production planning and control; continuous customer influence throughout the production; distributed control and inter-organizational autonomy. Thus, aiming to cope with the above-mentioned challenges the following section presents a conceptual dynamic integration framework concerned with a smart factory concept to the mould/tools industry.

3 Conceptual Dynamic Integration System

Moulds manufacturing are highly variable systems, often OKP production. These complex and engineering ordered products require dynamic engineering but face low levels of processes standardization. This leads to difficulties in planning and control that might yield high discrepancies between initial planning and execution. Manufacturing data from the past exist but does not talk with the manufacturing system in the sense that no (very little) information is retrieved from history. The conceptual approach proposed here aims to define a framework for the development of a new system fed by real-time data from smart sensors. Thus, it should be considered the integration of knowledge-based systems covering the complete product life-cycle with advanced analytics, smart decision support systems with self-learning capabilities exploiting the availability of "big data" from smart sensors, historical process files, or human-authored data, addressing aspects, such as interactivity, real-time, data-fusion, imprecise computing, compressed sensing, advanced visualization, security, and privacy. Hence, the authors' proposed approach is focused on how to establish a clear evolution from the current tacit culture (predominant) to an informed/founded factory (reasoned factory) where workers have the efficient tools, and, thus, we strategically shift the name for informatics systems (I-systems) an open structuration of computational responsibilities [13], aiming to help them to decide. Such I-systems deeply depend on heterogeneous data sources that require effective and simple interaction views to be accessible by factory workers helping them to decide accurately. This requires the collection of real-time data from a diversity of proveniences (mould components, machines, cells, legacy systems, and tools), integrated and dispatched to specialized decision making computational systems (services) in a complex fusion of data from disparate sources and in a diversity of formats. Furthermore, such web of heterogeneous data needs a transformation to be accessed by factory persons in a simple and clear way, through coordinated decision making tools suite (consistently integrated). The proposed decision-making tools should deal with the failure and with incomplete data by presenting useful and accurate results.

Hence, addressing the challenges mentioned above and aiming to contribute to the concept of a smart factory in the injection mould/tools industry, a conceptual, computational framework is presented. Such an approach is concerned with the development of a supervision and control system based on an open platform, designed to cooperate and collaborate with other systems of an organization through a bus service. The computational platform itself concerned with the mould/tool process supervision and control, should be based on an open service-oriented architecture (SOA) as a network of I-systems, services, and devices with a dynamic interconnection based on a "plug and play" logic and standard interfaces. All elements of overall integrated system are structured as adaptive and discoverable entities abstracted through the CES model independently if they embed simple computational or cyber-physical parts [12]. The challenge starts from the question that considers an open architecture for a supervision and control system, service oriented, as the best strategy for an agile solution, flexible, secure, adaptive and autonomic. Each service corresponds to an autonomous computational entity, which could be an intelligent agent, having an autonomic response to the resolution of exceptions with the guarantee of the service quality level required. Furthermore, the supervisory and control production system interconnects to the organization's service bus providing a set of services to other legacy systems (ERP, CRM, BI). The adoption of a cooperative and collaborative approach to the system development requires the implementation of open interfaces. Considering the complexity of a factory landscape, in special for the cases where it is very challenging to collect accurate real-time data, e.g. the mould production shop-floor, the strategy is to develop complementary approaches for data acquisition. On the one hand, the association of a transponder (as a thing) able to supply real-time data about a piece position and status (and potentially with some local intelligence). On a complementary approach, 3D vision should be used to interpret shop-floor areas and complement (fuses) the data for an accurate decision making.

On the other hand, the high product variability observed in the moulds industry together with the time shortened product-life-cycles require agile and flexible production environments, which can be adapted rapidly to new product demands. This degree of flexibility cannot be achieved by traditional process automation approaches. Instead, modular factory structures composed of smart devices – the so-called CPS – establishing an Internet of Things (IoT), are key elements to overcome the current rigid planning and production processes [10]. Thus, to successful achieve highly modular factory infrastructures it should be based on multi-vendor automation interoperable technology. Thus, the core focus of the conceptual proposed approach is on the Dynamic Integration System (DIS) that combines input from a Data Acquisition Systems (DAS) and available Open Specified I-systems. Both DAS and DIS will include aspects of Big Data, especially data with various origins and formats, such as built-in sensors, manual input, quality control protocols, and customer feedback, etc. Thus, the DIS approach and the corresponding main key features are depicted in Fig. 1. The system here proposed can collect data from smart sensors attached to each part or component giving continuous information about the location, resources, operation time, and setup time, among other. All this information will be used to create new knowledge about the design and manufacturing phases and will be stored on databases and historical data. The smart analytics of the DIS will include machine learning approaches to improve the suggestions for actions and their impact on the process chain.

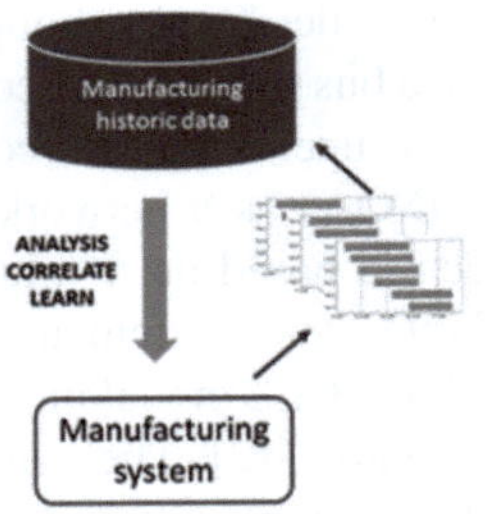

Key Features

- Reference models/tools for data collection;
- Smart sensors for machines and products/parts;
- Data structures for historical data;
- Models for data analysis and process optimization; Human-Machine Interaction for collecting human-authored data and provide instructions;
- Manufacturing Execution System (MES) integration;
- Cloud based infrastructure for (near) real-time monitoring and feedback;
- Methodologies for data collection and data analysis.

Fig. 1. The Dynamic Integration System conceptual framework.

DIS is the formulation of a strategy towards the establishment of a digital collaborative factory as an open community of open informatics systems able to cooperate for intelligent factory services. The approach considers both an intra-factory and an inter-factory integration of the informatics systems. It ranges from cyber-physical systems as specialized bridges between the physical and the computational world [14], to informatics systems managing collaborations. The bridge is made through a special CES component targeted to abstract specific shop floor equipment and sensors interacted based on proprietary protocols or even if standards are adopted as implementations might differ at some interaction level (wire, data payload format, semantic model or coordination), as depicted in Fig. 2.

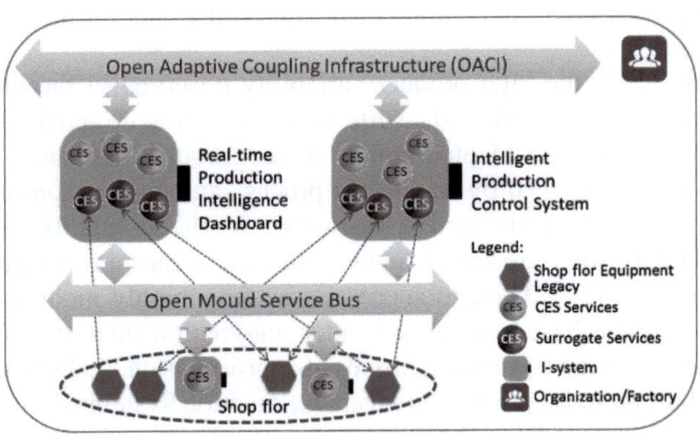

Fig. 2. The two-layered open service bus based on the CES model.

The proposed approach follows the CES adaptive framework model where a computational entity is developed for the cooperation [12]. The CES services components are structured as I-systems as a minimal instantiation (deploy) grouping a set of CES components. The proposed model accommodates the evolution of legacy systems or shops floor cyber-physical systems/equipment. The special surrogate CES components also depicted in Fig. 2, play a bridge role between making this way possible a smooth evolving migration to the new open informatics systems framework. The surrogate abstraction mechanism is a transitory mechanism considering that when all the shop-flor evolve for the adoption of the open CES model, the adaptation role is not anymore necessary. This way, the proposed model makes possible a convergence for the novel, innovative Informatics systems (I-systems) to be developed under independent and possibly multi-supplier dynamics. Furthermore, the new generation of shop floor equipment, if CES enabled, can simplify their internal computational capabilities and complement intelligence with CES running on-premises or in the cloud as cooperative autonomous services. Some of them can inherit from the Intelligent Agents achievements by embedding (business or control) intelligence capabilities.

In addition, for the mould industry to answer the crescent collaborative dimension requiring the exchange of data in different formats and size among partners, the Enterprise Collaborative Network (ECoNet) platform [15] is adopted. The ECoNet platform aims at structure the business to business relations under a common multiple formats data exchange and integrated/coordinated mechanisms. It replaces the current adaptation chaos that contributes for a tight coupling between I-systems from business partners, potentially developed under different processes and technological cultures. The proposed open adaptive coupling infrastructure (OACI) as a loose coupling strategy based on the CES and I-systems concepts, unifies the computational infrastructure of the factory of the future making this way possible to separate (decouple) intelligent processes sharing a common distributed computational infrastructure (security, coordination, fault tolerance, scalability, reliability quality of services, and costs moderation by a multi-supplier model). The possibility to establish hybrid computational execution environments on premises, and on the cloud, in line with the microservices dynamics [16], makes our approach scalable (elasticity) and prone (open) for novel intelligent services and added value composites (integrated business intelligence applications).

4 Conclusions

The continuous competitiveness of the Tooling industry is determined by the ability to understand and respond quickly to the needs of its customers associated with the capacity to reformulate their manufacturing systems to achieve gains in cost, quality and performance and delivery times. This goal involves the adoption of new and better technologies supported by improved management tools allowing higher performances on manufacturing, higher competitiveness, and sustainability of the companies. The Open Source decision-making tools will have the ability to see the preceding and work in process, and to simulate the working charge and resources balance, giving fundamental information that will help to reduce the time from design to manufacturing. Such a computational platform will improve the cooperation with the customer, by the possibility of having a faster answer to customer´s demands and modifications and its implications on shop floor planning. Through this tool, the customer will have access to all information related to the work in process. Furthermore, it will provide important information to improve the balance of the resources and work in process, even with new changes and modifications promoted by the client, because these changes could implicate a new balance and distribution of resources. By implementing this new tool, it is expected to achieve the following benefits for moulding/tooling industry: Real-time data collection during tool production used to optimise and standardise the tool production process; Improve tool maintenance procedures (adaptive preventive maintenance); Improve tool total value and decrease total costs; Improved cost efficiency and accuracy, reliability and speed of simulation techniques for manufacturing processes and/or full complex products.

A concept prove is planned to be implement in a near future, in a mould/tool manufacturer shop floor, based on the conceptual framework described in this paper.

Acknowledgments. This work was partially supported by FCT, through IDMEC, under LAETA, project UID/EMS/50022/2013. It was partially supported by Brisa Innovation and Technology (BIT), Lisbon Ports Administration (APL), MIELE project, BP Portugal research grants.

References

1. O'Keeffe, A., Ozuem, W., Lancaster, G.: Leadership marketing: an exploratory study. J. Strateg. Mark. **24**(5), 418–443 (2016)
2. Yin, S., Li, X., Gao, H., Kaynak, O.: Data-based techniques focused on modern industry: an overview. IEEE Trans. Ind. Electron. **62**(1), 657–667 (2015)
3. Mourtzis, D., Doukas, M., Fragou, K., Efthymion, K., Matzrou, V.: Knowledge-based estimation of manufacturing lead time for complex engineered-to-order products. Procedia CIRP **17**, 499–504 (2014)
4. Monostori, L.: Cyber-physical production systems: roots, expectations and R&D challenges. Procedia CIRP **17**, 9–13 (2014)
5. Wang, S., Wan, J., Zhang, D., Li, D., Zhang, C.: Towards smart factory for industry 4.0: a self-organized multi-agent system with big data based feedback and coordination. Comput. Netw. **101**, 158–168 (2016)
6. Pereira, V.: Perspectives and approaches for the Internet of Things. MSc Thesis, Faculdade de Ciências e Tecnologia, Universidade Nova de Lisboa, Lisbon, Portugal (2014)
7. Goldhar, J.D., Jelinek, M.: Manufacturing as a service business: CIM in the 21st century. Comput. Ind. **14**(1–3), 225–245 (1990)
8. Liu, T., Wang, H., He, Y.: Intelligent knowledge recommending approach for new product development based on workflow context matching. Concurr. Eng. **24**(4), 318–329 (2016)
9. Doumeingts, G., Vallespir, B., Chen, D.: Methodologies for designing CIM systems: a survey. Comput. Ind. **25**(3), 263–280 (1995)
10. Broy, M., Kargermann, H., Achatz, R.: Agenda Cyber Physical Systems: Outlines of a New Research Domain. Acatech, Berlin (2010)

11. Camarinha-Matos, L.M., Afsarmanesh, H., Ollus, M.: Ecolead: a holistic approach to creation and management of dynamic virtual organizations. In: Camarinha-Matos, L.M., Afsarmanesh, H., Ortiz, A. (eds.) PRO-VE 2005. ITIFIP, vol. 186, pp. 3–16. Springer, Boston, MA (2005). doi:10.1007/0-387-29360-4_1
12. Osório, A.L., Camarinha-Matos, L.M., Afsarmanesh, H.: Cooperation enabled systems for collaborative networks. In: Camarinha-Matos, L.M., Pereira-Klen, A., Afsarmanesh, H. (eds.) PRO-VE 2011. IAICT, vol. 362, pp. 400–409. Springer, Heidelberg (2011). doi: 10.1007/978-3-642-23330-2_44
13. Osório, A.L.: Towards vendor-agnostic IT-system of IT-systems with the CEDE Platform. In: Afsarmanesh, H., Camarinha-Matos, L.M., Lucas Soares, A. (eds.) PRO-VE 2016. IAICT, vol. 480, pp. 494–505. Springer, Cham (2016). doi:10.1007/978-3-319-45390-3_42
14. Lee, E.A.: CPS foundations. In: Proceedings of the 47th Design Automation Conference, DAC 2010, pp. 737–742. ACM, New York (2010)
15. Osório, L.A., Camarinha-Matos, L.M., Afsarmanesh, H.: ECoNet platform for collaborative logistics and transport. In: Camarinha-Matos, L.M., Bénaben, F., Picard, W. (eds.) PRO-VE 2015. IAICT, vol. 463, pp. 265–276. Springer, Cham (2015). doi: 10.1007/978-3-319-24141-8_24
16. Fetzer, C.: Building critical applications using microservices. IEEE Secur. Priv. **14**(6), 86–89 (2016)

Automated Emergence of a Crisis Situation Model in Crisis Response Based on Tweets

Aurélie Montarnal[1(✉)], Shane Halse[2], Andrea Tapia[2], Sébastien Truptil[1], and Frederick Benaben[1]

[1] IMT Mines Albi, University of Toulouse, Albi, France
{aurelie.montarnal,sebastien.truptil, frederick.benaben}@mines-albi.fr

[2] Penn State University, State College, USA
{seh297,atapia}@ist.psu.edu

Abstract. During a crisis, being able to understand quickly the situation on-site is crucial for the responders to take relevant decisions together. Social media, in particular Twitter, have proved to be a means for rapidly getting information from the field. However, the deluge of data is heterogeneous in many ways (location, trust, content, vocabulary, etc.), and getting a model of the crisis situation still requires laborious human actions. In addition, depending on which kind of information is mined from them, tweets have to be handle one-by-one (e.g. find victims), or as a whole - amount of tweets - (e.g. occurence of an event). This paper proposes a framework for automatically extracting, interpreting and aggregating streams of tweets to characterize crisis situations. It is based on a specific metamodel that determines the different concepts required to model a crisis situation.

Keywords: Crisis situation modeling · Decision support system · Crisis management · Cross-organizational collaboration

1 Introduction

It is commonly accepted that crisis management can be divided into four phases: prevention, preparation, response and recovery [1]. While the prevention, preparation and recovery phases deal with avoiding or being more ready to crisis situations, the response phase has to deal with adaptation and improvisation in an emergency situation. In particular, the actors involved in the crisis response have to operate in a relevant and timely manner, which requires from decision-makers to make decisions in consequence. Charles et al. [2] emphasizes the challenge of having heterogeneous partners mounting a one-shot suitable Virtual Organization in time of crisis situations.

It has been observed that a limitation in this process is related to the difficulties to manage their coordination and collaboration [3]. About this, Wolbers and Boersma [4] argue that enhancing the responders' situational awareness indeed leverages the coordination of the actors, and this implies to be able to provide them with a common

L.M. Camarinha-Matos et al. (Eds.): PRO-VE 2017, IFIP AICT 506, pp. 658–665, 2017.
DOI: 10.1007/978-3-319-65151-4_58

operational picture that includes the important concepts (i.e. elements on the field) that need to be taken into account.

In parallel, disaster management comes with an ever-increasing amount of generated and potentially accessible data. On any crisis site, heterogeneous and potentially undedicated data sources (sensors, opendata, witnesses and social networks, etc.) generate a deluge of data. As an example, Alexander [5] highlights that only 50 min after the 2012 earthquake in Lombardy, a clear and comprehensive picture of the situation was available mostly established from social media information.

This paper aims at exploring the automated exploitation of social media data (in particular tweets for their easy access thanks to the Twitter API), that have shown an invaluable potential but are so far humanly exploited in most of the cases, to convey a situation model of the crisis that will in turn be used as a basis to support the responders' collaborations.

Two main issues have to be tackled to implement such a system:

- How to aggregate tweets to detect "breaking news" within the massive flow of data?
- How to instantiate those data into instances of the situational model?

In our study, only the tweets gathered on specific geographical area (according to their geotagging metadata) are considered, as they can be assumed as the most informative in real-time.

The first part of the paper brings some visibility to the readers about which are the concepts mined to build a situational model, and then takes an example of flow of tweets during the specific crisis of the Boston Marathon in 2013 to highlight the challenges that need to be tackled. Then, a state of the art shows the already existing methodologies that have emerged these last years and their limitations for our specific use. Finally, a new proposition is explored and discussed.

2 Background of the Research Works

2.1 Which Concepts to Mine to Build a Situational Model?

According to Vieweg [6] situational awareness is defined as "understanding the big picture in time and safety critical situations. According to [7], situation awareness is performed through three levels: *perception*, *comprehension* and *projection*. These three terms are defined by as follows [8]: the *perception* refers to the ability of the system to get the "status, attributes and dynamics of relevant elements" in the environment; *comprehension* to provide a "synthesis" to support decision makers; *projection* to forecast near term future actions. While the first part can be provided by data sources (i.e. social media and in particular Twitter in our case), the second part required to be framed to know which kind of concepts have to be included in the synthesis. The third part will not be explored in this paper. We propose the synthesis to be a crisis situation model, just defined as proposed in the metamodel of Benaben et al. [9]. As a summary, two main packages are required to describe the crisis situation itself: (i) the *context* and (ii) the *objectives* packages. The *context* includes all elements of the environment, at stake, such as *goods*, *people*, *natural sites*, *civilian society*, within a specific *territory*, and also consequently inferred elements such as the corresponding *dangers* and *intrinsic risks*. In particular, in the *objectives* package, the *event* and *emerging risks* are the most interesting concepts to extract from datasets, since it can be used to infer the consequent *facts*.

2.2 Problem Statement Illustrated Through the 2013 Boston Marathon Example

To better clarify the challenge to tackle to automatically define crisis situation models, from social media data, an example is given. A set of 5473 tweets on the 2013 Boston Marathon Bombing, geotagged in Boston area from 2013-04-15 20:49 CET (14:49 local time) to 2013-04-16 01:59 CET (19:59 local time), was manually classified along several classes partly related to the metamodel. Two bombs exploded at the marathon finish line at 14:50 local time; after a short while a fire is declared at the close JFK Library; several minutes later, fake rumors of other devices were spread from several places in the city. A short observation quickly led to several evidences. The diagram in Fig. 1 below shows the evolution of the number of tweets related to specific classes, cumulated on 10 min' windows.

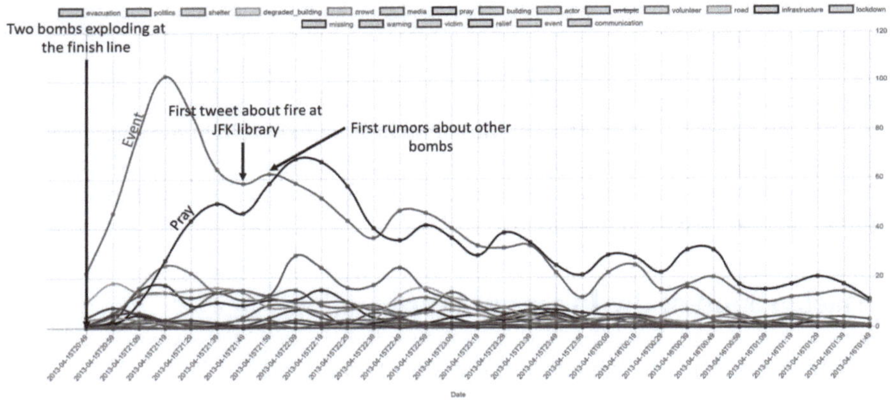

Fig. 1. Number of tweets for each studied class, along the crisis response.

We observed that: (i) such classes as Event, produce expected spikes, but those can occur after the event in question (see frequent increasing slope after 22:00 CET), which can eventually produce a 'noise'; (ii) sometimes isolated tweets (e.g. about victims, or even rumors) conveyed as much information as sets of tweets (e.g. occurrence of an event).

In general, considering the two following statements:

- Depending on the type of concept mined, either isolated tweets or the important amount of similar tweets triggers the instantiation on the model.
- An important amount of tweets related to a class becomes eventually a noise which prevents to detect new information.

The challenge that these works aims to tackle is: *How to aggregate tweets, so that isolated or packs of tweets can be considered equally meaningful, and how to detect in an amount of similar tweets, if the information provided is new, or just an 'echo' throughout the crisis?*

3 State of the Art

When exploring a way to use Big-Data as a means to support the inter-organizational collaborations that articulate the responders' actions and decisions, [10] highlights that this is a challenge on both (i) a social layer with the necessity to support the inter-organizational collaborations (among the crisis' responders) at a macro-level and, in the same time, (ii) a technological layer with the lack of methodology to deal with unknown sources of data that needs to be "understood" to be exploited by decision-makers. Benaben et al. [10] especially summarize that, in disaster management, being able to use and "understand" data is required to support the coordination issues. Hence, focusing on the use of social media data, the following presents a specific study on existing methodologies to exploit and interpret this kind of data in such a context.

Yin et al. [7] have developed a tool to mine and extract data from micro blogs related to the crisis in a near-real-time manner. This tool allows users, both in a crisis decision making or general public role, to visualize information about the incident and the potential impact it may have. The tool is based on burst detection, numerous messages with similar wording or from the same area with an automated data collection. Sakaki et al. use Twitter data flows to detect earthquake in real-time [11]. They built a reporting tool that embeds two parts: the detection of tweets that are about earthquakes and a service dedicated to location detection. [12] provide a four-step approach to take advantage of tweets in crisis situations: (i) burst detection, (ii) text classification to find tweets about infrastructures status, (iii) online clustering and (iv) geotagging of the tweets.

Overall, these solutions are rather about providing decision-makers with visualization tools. As such, even if it is of help for the users, the resulting outputs remain at a data level of abstraction, i.e. *the users still need to put them into a context by themselves if they want to obtain usable information for their decision-making process.*

Many works have based their approach on classification problems, i.e. labelling each tweet with specific class(es), that have been predefined. Among them, [13, 14] propose tweets datasets with many crises cases. In the first case, the tweets have been classified informative or not thanks to a crowdsourcing service. In the second case, as a first step, tweets have been classified between on-topic and off-topic thanks to crowdsourcing, and the authors have use this training dataset to extract specific terms related to crisis (app. 380 terms). In line, [15] built a lexicon EMTerms 1.0 of more than 7200 terms directly related to 23 specific crisis categories. Both lexicons are available online[1]. Using lexicons with keywords occurrence can show some good enough results, providing that the lexicons were built on suitable use cases (i.e. if they are built on hurricane and earthquake cases, there are good chances that the results will be bad in the case of a terror attack),

[1] http://www.crisislex.org.

however, extending lexicons with new cases is time-consuming and results are not always guaranteed, because it is rather hard to detect the terms that could make the lexicons too specific.

In Natural Language Processing (NLP), many methods can be used to classify corpus of documents (in our case a set of tweets, each one belonging to a specific class). Among them, a Convolutional Neural Network model, as presented in [16] allows to adapt an Artificial Neural Network model for analyzing *n-grams*. [17] provide comparative results of tweets classification over several methods: Support Vector Machines, Artificial Neural Networks (ANN), Convolutional Neural Networks (CNN) through unigrams, unigrams + bigrams and unigrams + bigrams + trigrams. As a result, they show that in their two-class (on-topic or off-topic) classification case, CNNs are the most suitable.

Finally, this state of the art shows that, in order to "go up" in abstraction (i.e. instantiate the concepts into the model), *the current systems miss to take into account the interactions among the tweets*, which could be enabled thanks to a deeper semantic analysis.

4 Solution Proposal

4.1 "Concept-Similarity" Graph Emergence

Our proposal is to take advantage both of the classification methods that have shown decent results in the literature, but are too generic to lead to any instantiation, and semantics that allows to get a deeper meaning out of tweet data.
Our framework includes an analysis of the tweets decomposed into three dimensions:

- A time dimension: a sliding time window should be set as a parameter, during which the analysis is executed (e.g. all tweets from t-30 min to t are analyzed). This dimension ensures a memory to the system, and, in the same time, allows it to "forget" information to avoid "echo" or "amalgam" effects resulting from a massive amount of outdated information.
- A class dimension: this dimension includes all concepts (classes of the metamodel) that should be extracted from the tweets. These classes are used as sets that can potentially overlap, and on which the set theory principles can be applied. For each tweet retrieved, it can either belong to none of the classes (i.e. non-informative tweet), or to 1 to several classes.
- A semantic dimension: the goal of this dimension is, considering the time window and the later classification of the tweets, to define semantic similarities between tweets, to aggregate them.

As a result, for a sliding time window, at all time, a "concept-similarity" graph can be established as illustrated in Fig. 2.

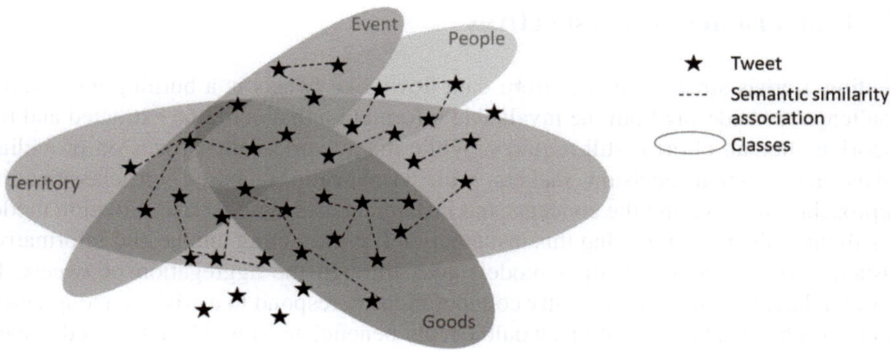

Fig. 2. "Concept-similarity" graph: semantic aggregation of classified tweets.

4.2 Exploitation of the "Concept-Similarity" Graph

Based on this type of graph, rules can be established to determine if a set of similar tweets (1 or more) should trigger a new instantiation on the crisis situation model.

One example of such rule could be (the function Near(Tweet1, Tweet2) relates to a *near* semantic association between Tweet1 and Tweet2):

Let T be the monitored Territory,
Let E be the set of all Events,
Let Tw_1 *be a "new" tweet,*
Let Tw_2 *be a tweet involved in the instantiation of an event* $E_1 \subset E$ *(i.e.* $Tw_2 \in E_1$*)*
If $((Tw_1, Tw_2) \in T \cap E)$ *AND (Near(*Tw_1*,* Tw_2*))**Then,***
Aggregate Tw_1 *and* Tw_2 *together (i.e.* $Tw_1 \in E_1$*, no new instantiation)*

The overall expected architecture to be implemented can be seen in Fig. 3: two services are expected to work in parallel to classify the tweets and, in the same time, establish semantic relationships among them. A rules engine then run predefined rules to trigger or not instantiation into the crisis situation model. The graph obtained by the two first services is updated all along the crisis, according to the time window defined as a parameter.

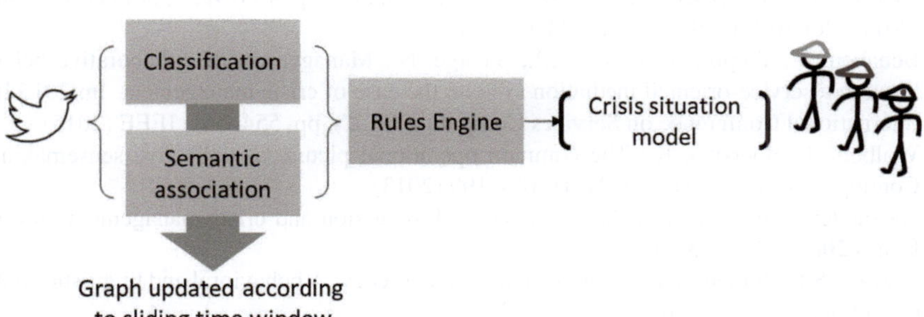

Fig. 3. Functional architecture proposed.

5 Conclusion and Perspectives

Getting a crisis situation model from data flows like tweets is a burning topic and a challenge, considering both the invaluable information that could be extracted and the laborious human effort it still requires. While many works rather focus on providing crisis management decision makers with visualizations, based on classification approaches, discovering the concepts and instantiate them into a crisis situation model is still up to them. Automating this instantiation (i.e. extracting unique and informative instances of the crisis situation model) goes through the aggregation of tweets. In parallel, having to mount on-the-fly collaborations to respond to a crisis is a tough task, hence, such virtual organizations would deeply beneficiate from this automated instantiation of a crisis situation model leveraging both the efficiency and the speed of the collaborative response.

To tackle this challenge, this paper aims to explore a new approach that embeds both the strength of classification methodologies and semantics, to exploit and interpret geotagged tweets on a particular monitored area. A system in three functional parts is proposed as follows: (i) a classification service of tweets along predefined classes used to model the situation, (ii) a service dedicated to the emergence of semantic associations among the tweets to aggregate them and (iii) a rules engine to automatically exploit the graph obtained in (i) and (ii) and trigger the instantiations.

The proposed framework will be used to implement such system and assess it through different real use-cases extracted from past crises. In further step, this system could be improved by adding a correlation service, to compare extraction from social media data and sensors data: this could improve the reliability and the trust of the final crisis situation model.

References

1. Altay, N., Green, W.G.: OR/MS research in disaster operations management. Eur. J. Oper. Res. **175**(1), 475–493 (2006)
2. Charles, A., Lauras, M., Barthe, A. M., Bénaben, F.: Gathering, Structuring and Modeling Business Process Knowledge of the Response to a Nuclear Crisis: Towards a Simulation Platform for Better Coordination. In: Camarinha-Matos, L.M., Pereira-Klen, A., Afsarmanesh, H. (eds.) PRO-VE 2011. IAICT, vol. 362, pp. 486–493. Springer, Heidelberg (2011). doi:10.1007/978-3-642-23330-2_53
3. Benaben, F., Truptil, S., Lauras, M., Salatge, N.: Management of collaborative behavior through a service-oriented mediation system: the case of crisis management. In: 2015 IEEE International Conference on Services Computing (SCC), pp. 554–561. IEEE (2015)
4. Wolbers, J., Boersma, K.: The common operational picture as collective sensemaking. J. Contingencies Crisis Manag. **21**(4), 186–199 (2013)
5. Alexander, D.E.: Social media in disaster risk reduction and crisis management. Sci. Eng. Ethics **20**(3), 717–733 (2014)
6. Vieweg, S.E.: Situational awareness in mass emergency: A behavioral and linguistic analysis of microblogged communications (2012)

7. Yin, J., Karimi, S., Lampert, A., Cameron, M., Robinson, B., Power, R.: Using social media to enhance emergency situation awareness. In: Twenty-Fourth International Joint Conference on Artificial Intelligence. (2015)
8. Endsley, M.R.: Toward a theory of situation awareness in dynamic systems. Hum. Factors: J. Hum. Factors Ergon. Soc. **37**(1), 32–64 (1995)
9. Benaben, F., Montarnal, A., Truptil, S., Lauras, M., Fertier, A., Salatge, N., Rebiere, S.: A conceptual framework and a suite of tools to support crisis management. In: Proceedings of the 50th Hawaii International Conference on System Sciences (2017)
10. Benaben, F., Montarnal, A., Fertier, A., Truptil, S. Big-data and the question of horizontal and vertical intelligence: a discussion on disaster management. In: Afsarmanesh, H., Camarinha-Matos, L., Lucas Soares, A. (eds) PRO-VE 2016. IAICT, vol. 480, pp. 156–162. Springer, Cham (2016). doi:10.1007/978-3-319-45390-3_14
11. Sakaki, T., Okazaki, M., Matsuo, Y.: Earthquake shakes Twitter users: real-time event detection by social sensors. In: Proceedings of the 19th International Conference on World Wide Web, pp. 851–860. ACM (2010)
12. Cameron, M.A., Power, R., Robinson, B., Yin, J.: Emergency situation awareness from twitter for crisis management. In: Proceedings of the 21st International Conference on World Wide Web, pp. 695–698. ACM (2012)
13. Olteanu, A., Vieweg, S., Castillo, C.: What to expect when the unexpected happens: Social media communications across crises. In: Proceedings of the 18th ACM Conference on Computer Supported Cooperative Work & Social Computing, pp. 994–1009. ACM (2015)
14. Olteanu, A., Castillo, C., Diaz, F., Vieweg, S.: CrisisLex: A Lexicon for Collecting and Filtering Microblogged Communications in Crises. In: ICWSM (2014)
15. Temnikova, I., Castillo, C., Vieweg, S.: EMTerms 1.0: a terminological resource for crisis tweets. In: ISCRAM 2015 Proceedings of the 12th International Conference on Information Systems for Crisis Response and Management (2015)
16. Johnson, R., Zhang, T.: Effective use of word order for text categorization with convolutional neural networks. arXiv preprint arXiv:1412.1058 (2014)
17. Caragea, C., Silvescu, A., Tapia, A.H.: Identifying informative messages in disaster events using convolutional neural networks. In: International Conference on Information Systems for Crisis Response and Management (2016)

Design Science Research in CNs

Digital Social Learning – How to Enhance Serious Gaming for Collaborative Networks

Christian Zinke(✉) and Julia Friedrich

Institute for Applied Informatics e.V., Leipzig, Germany
{zinke,friedrich}@infai.org

Abstract. Virtual organizations and enterprises are prominent examples for collaborative networks (CN). Trends like Web 2.0 and Social Media refine the technological base of CN, namely through enterprise social networks (ESN). To strengthen knowledge management and through it the innovation capabilities of CN, further research on supporting knowledge exchange and social learning within ESN is needed. Approaches like serious gaming or digital social learning already tackle this problem. However, there is still a significant lack in integrated approaches, concepts or tools for ESN and digital social learning. In order to address this issue, within the work presented in this paper a design research approach has been chosen to consider the lack of methodological clearness of the iteration process. Thus, the paper will firstly introduce a framework for the iteration process of design research and secondly show first insights on how to integrate ESN and digital social learning.

Keywords: Digital social learning · Enterprise social network · Collaborative network · Design research

1 Introduction

An important driver for collaborative networks (CN) is the digitalization, based amongst others on the rise of computer networks. The forms of CN that can be distinguished are virtual organizations, virtual enterprises or collaborative laboratories [1]. CN in that respect are to be defined as an "alliance constituted by a variety of entities (e.g. organizations and people)" [2]. These entities are spread out over a multitude of domains. In general, they are independent, geographically distributed and vary in their culture and their goals [1, 2]. Further, CN enable a better objective attainment for all stakeholders. One key factor for establishing successful CN is the handling of knowledge, especially its exchange and management [3]. Web 2.0, social media and networks enable a novel technical basis for CN termed enterprise social networks (ESN). Amongst others, important functions of ESN are knowledge sharing, learning as well as training by means of exercises and document sharing [4, 5]. Knowledge management and social learning as an integrated element of human resource development in ESN have already been developed and are field tested in small scale settings [6]. In order to strengthen knowledge management in CN, more research addressing barriers as well as motivation for

L.M. Camarinha-Matos et al. (Eds.): PRO-VE 2017, IFIP AICT 506, pp. 669–677, 2017.
DOI: 10.1007/978-3-319-65151-4_59

knowledge exchange within ESN, considering social as well as personal needs and demands, is required. However, some serious game approaches almost address learning and explicit knowledge exchange within virtual groups and teams. While in the private sector some social networks do already have social games implemented, on enterprise and CN level this is a new ground, especially serious game implementation. Up to now, both worlds – digital social learning (DSL) by means of serious gaming and ESN are side by side when it comes to the lack of integrated considerations or designs combining them. This paper presents research in process with the aim of bridging the gap between DSL and ESN with the special consideration of employee's needs and requirements.

This is not only a thematically, but also a methodological challenge. As there already are approaches for serious gaming and ESN, the chosen design research approach does not start on green fields. So far, an artefact, in our case the serious game Yeepa, has been implemented and elaborated in various fields. The problem is a lack of methodological clarity of the design research process in such cases – starting with elaboration of an artefact to develop requirements for a new one. To sum up, the paper will contribute by developing a methodological design research procedure, focusing on the iteration process. Therefore, a framework to classify evaluation results will be presented. The method will be used exemplarily to develop problem descriptions and detailed requirements for linking DSL and ESN.

2 Methodology

The methodology chosen is use case driven and conducted within the design research approach (especially for Information Systems – IS). Design Science Research (DSR) can be described as a constructive research paradigm [7] focusing on the design and evaluation of artefacts. These artefacts are designed to solve human problems [8]. To do so, Peffers developed four main steps (see [9]), firstly, the problem has to be described and analyzed, secondly the objective has to be set, thirdly, the artefact needs to be designed and developed and fourthly, the impact of the artefact will be evaluated. While some authors differ as to the granularity of the research process [7, 10], they agree in principle to the iterative character of the methodology. Research conducted within design science does often focus on problem descriptions, designing and implementing artefacts, while the evaluation process is often performed poorly [11]. Thus, common models of design research cycle easily link the evaluation results to the problem description (e.g. [12–15]). This approach implies an easy way to match problems, requirements, design objects and impacts of the artefact, but research works with one or more iterations are very rare. The problem is that design research is an explorative approach, where even solved problems may cause novel ones. In order to strengthen the evaluation and iteration of the design research approach, the presented paper will focus methodologically on the evaluation and the transition to an enhanced problem description for an improved design. Figure 1 illustrates the adapted approach of the paper.

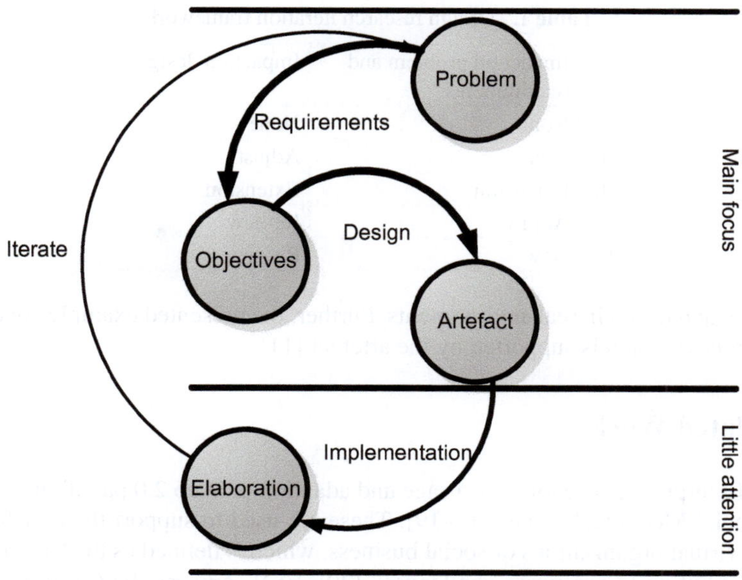

Fig. 1. Design research process

In order to do so, five cases of the iteration process can be described (see also Table 1).

I. Artefact does fulfill the given requirements. (most cases, e.g. [15])

II. Artefact does not fulfill effectively its role, elaboration results show that artefact does not have intended use.
Problem and requirements are the same. The design of the artefact has to be improved.

III. The artefact causes unintended consequences.
The original problem is solved, but novel problems raise up because of the artefact. This leads to extended problem descriptions and requirements.

IV. Elaboration results show goal attainment, but for some reasons the conditions are changing, which lead to an ineffective artefact.
Novel conditions (e.g. technologies or legal boundaries) lead to rethinking and adjust the problems and requirements.

V. Elaboration results show goal attainment and artefact may be suitable for other contexts.
Successful solutions need to be transferred and re-innovated in new context. Development of novel problem description and requirements based on evaluation and cross-cases analysis [16] is needed.

The following work focusses on case V, where a successful solution needs to be evaluated and analyzed in order to transfer it into other contexts. However, Pries-Heje et al. [11] developed a framework to classify the evaluation. According to this classification, the presented use case is ex post and naturalistic, which means that an artefact

Table 1. Design research iteration framework

	Impact on problem and requirements	Impact on design
I	None	None
II	None	Adjust
III	Extension	Extension
IV	Adjust	Re-new
V	New	Re-new

is existing and tested in real environments. Further, the presented example concentrates on the process which is supported by the artefact [11].

3 Related Work

ESN or Enterprise 2.0 denotes the usage and adaption of Web 2.0 paradigms and especially Social Media techniques [17–19]. These are used to support the transformation towards virtual organisations or social business, which is defined as the "application of social computing to enterprise challenges" [20]. ESN supports the CN to accomplish their aims by supporting work-related goals and communication [21, 22]. One of the many functions is the support of knowledge exchange and learning [4]. While a lot of existing work concentrates on traditional Web 2.0 technologies (such as blogs and tags) to realise ESN functions [23–25], examples of explicit knowledge exchange is rarely considered. In addition to ESN, one concept for implementing explicit knowledge transmission and training is serious gaming.

The concept of serious gaming is the conjunction of game mechanics and design with a learning approach [26]. It combines playful elements with serious content, skill improvement through repetition and excitement [27]. Due to the fact that the repetition of content is embedded in a playful and challenging experience, learning is performed automatically while the focus of the user is on the enjoyment and challenge. There is a large variety of possibilities for serious game design. Well-known examples are the flight simulator, learning software or applications for mental fitness. Typically adopted game mechanics are shown in Fig. 2.

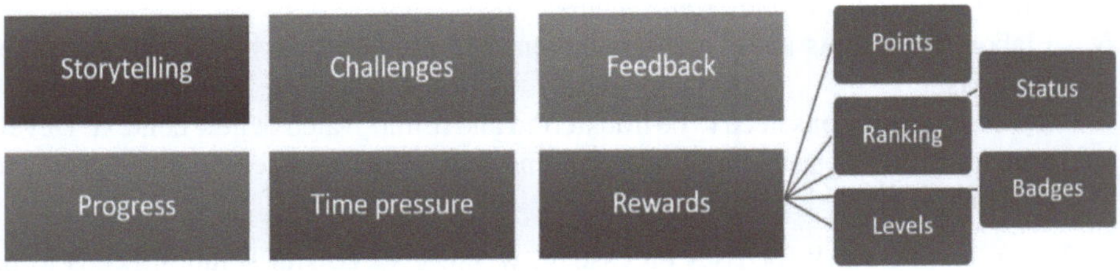

Fig. 2. Serious game mechanism [28]

In the following, with regard to the use case, we will focus on challenges, feedback and progression. Playing a game confronts the player with a certain uncertainty and suspense. The mastering of tasks in increasing levels of difficulty pose a challenge for users. The intrinsic motivation, especially of ambitious players but also of those players with a weak ambition, is affected by cognitive challenges. Feedback, which is bounded to the need for recognition, is another motivating mechanism. Other than challenge, feedback is affecting the extrinsic motivation. It enables the recipient to reflect and contextualize its own work. This way, feedback supports the learning progress and motivates the player at the same time. Progression, too, is supporting the reflection of performance. Progression in serious games can be adapted in different contexts. On the one hand, it may be used in form of a progress bar which shows the achieved but also the forthcoming efforts. On the other hand, it can be applied in form of a curve that illustrates skill improvements and achieved mile stones. This way, gaming mechanisms like feedback and progress impart a feeling of competence and positively affect self-reported learning outcomes [29]. All three components, challenge, progression and feedback, positively affect users motivation and are therefore appropriate mechanics for Serious Game in a corporate context.

4 Use Case

Yeepa is a serious gaming solution designed to create an innovative digital learning approach, which allows for an integration of a group level instead of focusing on the individual player only. The key element of Yeepa is a quiz. The players are answering multiple choice questions individually, however, the analysation is done on a group basis – with direct **feedback** after every game – including supervision to improve players' knowledge. The playful quiz atmosphere promotes motivation by creating fun and **challenge** which may lead to a will to repetition. Every repetition leads to **progression**. In order to evaluate the benefits users derive by playing Yeepa, the solution has been implemented into two settings. In context of the German national IT summit, school kids on the one hand and IT-experts on the other hand were invited to play Yeepa, answering questions about online safety and data security. Within a defined time frame of one week altogether 4000 pupils played a pool of 160 questions taken from ECDL (European Computer Driving License). On the whole, 400.000 questions where played which allowed for a psychometric calibration by using the Rasch model [30]. This way, 43 questions/items with a valid balance of knowledge competence and probability of success could be identified. These questions built the basis for the Yeepa game, played by IT-experts during the IT summit.

The results of all players where analyzed by use of the so-called Yeepa Index. Next to the probability of success, validated on basis of a psychometric analysis, the Yeepa Index calculates with a score that weights the degree of difficulty of every item. The Yeepa Index allows for a comparison of results within and between groups and topics. Additionally, progression analysis with regard to time can be done.

The surprising result that every category was dominated by the pupils, strengthens the argument of knowledge progression through repetition, because the pupils got much more time to improve their knowledge (pupils more than one week, IT experts only one day). Further the result shows the impact of digital social learning. These results do not directly lead to obvious problems in order to start the next loop of design research. Therefore, we analyzed the different settings, including the new one, where Yeepa should be implemented, as a cross case analysis (see Table 2) [16]. Part of the analysis is the comparison of network type of the implementation setting. The topology of network type originate from computer science [31], but can be also be applied for the social game setting. Next we will describe the most important in short. Mesh networks are networks, where every system user is directly connected to another user, so everybody know each other. A star network is a network, where all participants are connected to one central hub (the initiator), and do not know each other. A hierarchical network have multiple groups connected to one hub, these hubs can also be connected to a subordinated hub. All of these network types have implications on knowledge transfer and social embedment. While "hub-based" network needs a coordination of the knowledge through this hub (increased control mechanisms), mesh networks can share and distribute knowledge much more independently (less control possible).

Table 2. Cross-case analysis serious gaming in enterprises

	School	Summit	Enterprise
Network type	Mesh networks	No or Star network	Hierarchical or Mesh networks
Networking origin	Social group	Randomized	Project or Departments
Network focus	Learning	Exploring	Business
Game focus	Instruction	Fun	Instruction
Interaction rate	High	Raw	High
Themes	Static theme	Static theme	Dynamic themes
Guidance	Teacher	Administrator	Supervisor, Cross-domain or Intergenerational expert

The network type is very important, because motivation comes not only from the challenge, it is also about social embedment of the challenge – the networking origin. Further, the interaction rate may support the will for repetition. While in school, social group-based and highly interactive mesh networks created good results, the randomized networks or little star networks on the IT summit with very raw interactions had problems to keep up. Another important difference between the given settings and enterprises are the themes. While in school and on summit, the theme was static given by an administrator, knowledge exchange in enterprises is highly dynamic – given by supervisors, cross-domain and intergenerational experts.

Now we got a clear vision of what the digital social gaming tool Yeepa can handle. Knowledge creation within social group-based networks which concentrate on learning, with a high interaction rate and static themes set by an administrator, seems to be a very fruitful setting. In contrast, a randomized setting, including no networks or small star networks, with raw interactions, where the actors focus on other things, are not very sufficient. Changing the conditions means to change the impact of the artefact. Analysis of the conditions leads to a problem description and first requirements for an artefact of digital social learning as part of the ESN:

1. How to strengthen motivation of hierarchical or star-networks?
2. How to combine network focus and serious gaming in order to enhance motivation for knowledge exchange and training?
3. How to implement dynamic themes within the given context (1&2)?

The motivation and the willingness to repetition of the employee are the key factors for a successful learning. Also, social distance in hierarchical or star-networks which is quite higher than in mesh networks seems to be an important factor of motivation[1]. Further, compatibility of employee's needs, business goals and gaming theme need more consideration in order to apply the solution within ESN. While, Yeepa already supports the user in the generation of new content, so far, the corresponding process is time-consuming and not compatible with daily business. Thus, the main problem, we may focus on is the knowledge creation process in Yeepa within ESN.

5 Summary and Further Work

The paper concludes with two major results. Firstly, (1) we focus on methodological clearness on design research iteration. Thus, we developed a framework, which describes the main cases and their impacts on the research process. The developed framework can be used as a guide for further iterations and the assessment of the impact of the elaboration. Further work is needed to include this framework into common evaluation methods as well as to establish novel methods which support the presented framework. With the help of this foundational description, we implement, secondly, (2) this process in order to develop novel problem descriptions, research questions and goals for adapting serious gaming into ESN as a foundation CN. The main contributions of the paper are the developed problem specifications and requirements for an artefact of digital social learning as part of the ESN. This work is only the starting point for adapting Yeepa to ESN contexts and evaluate its impacts. Therefore, new models and artefacts are needed, which will be developed next – such as a knowledge discovering tools and ESN adapter.

Acknowledgement. The German Federal Ministry of Education and Research have funded the work leading to this publication under grant number 02L15A070 (Project: SB: Digital). Furthermore, the article is based on the results of the joint research project "MACKMA" which was funded by the German Ministry of Education and Research (Grant Number: 01IS15057C) under the supervision of the PT-DLR. The authors thank for the funding.

[1] Here anonymization have contradiction results, in supporting and weaken motivation.

References

1. Camarinha-Matos, L.M., Afsarmanesh, H.: Collaborative networks: a new scientific discipline. J. Intell. Manuf. **16**(4–5), 439–452 (2005). doi:10.1007/s10845-005-1656-3
2. Camarinha-Matos, L.M., Afsarmanesh, H.: On reference models for collaborative networked organizations. Int. J. Prod. Res. **46**(9), 2453–2469 (2008). doi:10.1080/00207540701737666
3. Allee, V.: Reconfiguring the value network. J. Bus. Strategy (2000). doi:10.1108/eb040103
4. Turban, E., Bolloju, N., Liang, T.-P.: Enterprise social networking. opportunities, adoption, and risk mitigation. J. Organ. Comput. Electron. Commer. (2011). doi: 10.1080/10919392.2011.590109
5. Cormican, K., Dooley, L.: Knowledge sharing in a collaborative networked environment. J. Inf. Knowl. Manage. (2007). doi:10.1142/S0219649207001706
6. Fulk, J., Yuan, Y.C.: Location, motivation, and social capitalization via enterprise social networking. J. Comput.-Med. Commun. **19**(1), 20–37 (2013)
7. Baskerville, R., Pries-Heje, J., Venable, J.: Soft design science methodology. In: Vaishanvi, V., Purao, S. (eds.) The 4th International Conference, Philadelphia, Pennsylvania, p. 1 (2009). doi:10.1145/1555619.1555631
8. March, S.T., Smith, G.F.: Design and natural science research on information technology. Decis. Support Syst. (1995). doi:10.1016/0167-9236(94)00041-2
9. Peffers, K., Tuunanen, T., Rothenberger, M.A., Chatterjee, S.: A design science research methodology for information systems research. J. Manage. Inf. Syst. (2007). doi:10.2753/MIS0742-1222240302
10. Holmström, J., Ketokivi, M., Hameri, A.-P.: Bridging practice and theory. A design science approach. Decis. Sci. (2009). doi:10.1111/j.1540-5915.2008.00221.x
11. Pries-Heje, J., Baskerville, R., Venable, J.: Strategies for design science research evaluation. In: Proceedings of ECIS 2008, pp. 1–12 (2008)
12. Gill, A.Q., Chew, E.K., Kricker, D., Bird, G.: Adaptive enterprise resilience management. Adaptive action design research in financial services case study. In: 2016 IEEE 18th Conference on Business Informatics (CBI), Paris, France, 29 August 2016–01 September 2016, pp. 113–122. IEEE (2016). doi:10.1109/CBI.2016.21
13. Oyelere, S.S., Suhonen, J.: Design and implementation of MobileEdu M-learning application for computing education in nigeria. A design research approach. In: 2016 International Conference on Learning and Teaching in Computing and Engineering (LaTICE), Mumbai, India, 31 March 2016–03 April 2016, pp. 27–31. IEEE (2016). doi:10.1109/LaTiCE.2016.3
14. Keijzer-Broers, W., Florez-Atehortua, L., Reuver, M.: Prototyping a health and wellbeing platform. An action design research approach. In: 2016 49th Hawaii International Conference on System Sciences (HICSS), Koloa, HI, USA, 05 January 2016–08 January 2016, pp. 3462–3471. IEEE (2016). doi:10.1109/HICSS.2016.432
15. Crepon, R.: Application of design research methodology to a contex-sensitive study in engineering education. In: Proceedings of 2014 IEEE Frontiers in Education Conference (FIE), Madrid, Spain, 22 October 2014–25 October 2014, pp. 1–4. IEEE (2014). doi:10.1109/FIE.2014.7044254
16. Eisenhardt, K.M.: Building theories from case study research. Acad. Manage. Rev. **14**(4), 532–550 (1989)
17. McAfee, A.: Enterprise 2.0. New Collaborative Tools for Your Organization's Toughest Challenges. Harvard Business Press, Boston (2009)
18. Menzel, C.M.: Web 2.0 as approach for the enterprise information technology, Universität, Fak. III, Wirtschaftsinformatik (2007)

19. Back, A.: Enterprise 2.0 – digitale transformation durch soziale technologien. In: Hoffmann, C.P., Lennerts, S., Schmitz, C., Stölzle, W., Uebernickel, F. (eds.) Business Innovation: Das St. Galler Modell. BIUSG, pp. 123–138. Springer, Wiesbaden (2016). doi: 10.1007/978-3-658-07167-7_9
20. Hinchcliffe, D., Kim, P.: Social business by design. Transformative social media strategies for the connected company. Jossey-Bass, A Wiley Imprint, San Francisco (2012)
21. Ellison, N.B., Gibbs, J.L., Weber, M.S.: The use of enterprise social network sites for knowledge sharing in distributed organizations. The role of organizational affordances. Am. Behav. Sci. (2014). doi:10.1177/0002764214540510
22. Ellison, N.B., Gibbs, J.L., Weber, M.S.: The use of enterprise social network sites for knowledge sharing in distributed organizations: The role of organizational affordances. Am. Behav. Sci. **59**(1), 103–123 (2015)
23. Mausz, N.: Enterprise social network (2012). http://docplayer.org/2217553-Enterprise-social-network.html
24. Büchner, T., Matthes, F., Neubert, C.: A concept and service based analysis of commercial and open source enterprise 2.0 tools. In: KMIS, pp. 37–45 (2009)
25. McKinsey: Business and web 2.0: an interactive feature (2013). http://www.mckinsey.com/business-functions/digital-mckinsey/our-insights/business-and-web-20-an-interactive-feature. Accessed 23 Jan 2017
26. Breuer, J., Bente, G.: Why so serious? On the relation of serious games and learning. J. Comput. Game Cult. **4**, 7–24 (2010)
27. Garris, R., Ahlers, R., Driskell, J.E.: Games, Motivation, and Learning. A Research and Practice Model. Simul. Gaming (2002). doi:10.1177/1046878102238607
28. Darejeh, A., Salim, S.S.: Gamification solutions to enhance software user engagement—a systematic review. Int. J. Hum.-Comput. Inter. (2016). doi:10.1080/10447318.2016.1183330
29. Bakhuys Roozeboom, M., Visschedijk, G., Oprins, E.: The effectiveness of three serious games measuring generic learning features. Br J Educ Technol (2017). doi:10.1111/bjet.12342
30. Rasch, G.: Probabilistic models for some intelligence and attainment tests. Univ. of Chicago Pr, Chicago (1980)
31. Groth, D., Skandier, T.: Network + Study Guide, 4th edn. Sybex, Alameda (2005)

A Semantics-Based Approach for Business Categorization on Social Networking Sites

Atia Bano Memon[1(✉)], Christian Zinke[2], and Kyrill Meyer[2]

[1] Department of Computer Science at the University of Leipzig, Leipzig, Germany
memon@informatik.uni-leipzig.de

[2] Institute of Applied Informatics at the University of Leipzig, Leipzig, Germany
{zinke,meyer}@informatik.uni-leipzig.de

Abstract. As the number and adoption of social networking sites (SNSs) supporting business representation in the form of business pages continues to escalate, more scalable and robust mechanisms for integrating data from different networks in order to serve the special purposes need to be envisaged. An important concern of such SNS data integration is the platform dependencies that different networks impose in collecting, organizing, and presenting the business information hosted on their servers. In this esteem, this paper deals with overcoming the challenge of different business categorization schemes being varyingly used by the existing SNSs. In doing so, we present a content-oriented approach for determining the business category on the basis of a semantic analysis of the textual information available in the business profile. The approach has been operationalized in the CoDiT (Company Discovery Tool) which is a web-based tool to facilitate the integrated business page search over multiple SNSs.

Keywords: Business page integration · SNS integration · Semantics-based category tagging · Business categorization

1 Introduction

Social networking sites (SNSs), a relatively new mechanism of human interaction, has gained a rapid popularity among a broader part of the population, many of whom have integrated these sites into their daily practices [1]. SNSs are the web 2.0 based applications that facilitate an online platform for the people to build social relations with other people and thus offer a new method of communicating, accelerating group formation, and escalating group scope and influence [2]. Today's SNSs originated in 1997 with the launch of SixDegrees.com that allowed the users to create profiles, list their friends, and add friends-of-friends to their own friend lists [1]. Since that time, the trend has gained such a rapid momentum that currently there exist several networks facilitating not only the interpersonal interaction, but also the online representation of all types of business organizations in the form of business pages (aka company pages). Through the business pages, the SNSs offer many opportunities for the businesses that were previously not available or very difficult to acquire for many of them [3].

L.M. Camarinha-Matos et al. (Eds.): PRO-VE 2017, IFIP AICT 506, pp. 678–687, 2017.
DOI: 10.1007/978-3-319-65151-4_60

Increasingly, there exist a number of SNSs that offer the creation and hosting of business pages. Since these sites vary as to their scope as well as functionality [4], they cater a different type of audience. For example, whereas Facebook has a great appeal to the masses, LinkedIn is more focused on professionals [5]. Accordingly, the organizations are variously represented on different platforms in order to reach the audience that they target as Stelzner [6] has reported that the LinkedIn is most preferable platform among Business-to-Business (B2B) marketers while the Facebook is the most popular platform among Business-to-Customer (B2C) marketers. Since all of these platforms work in isolation from each other, useful information remains dispersed and confined to specific platform boundaries which in turn hampers the business discovery and information retrieval without actually getting on a specific platform [7]. Recently, however, the leading SNSs have started exposing their data for third-party applications through their Application Programming Interfaces (APIs). The social networking APIs facilitate the third party developers to fetch, aggregate, and transform SNS user data according to user's specific interests [8]. Accordingly, they enable the integration of business information available on different SNSs in order to serve special purposes and offer a data rich and seamless user experience.

While by leveraging the potential of SNS APIs, the platform boundaries of SNSs can be significantly dissolved, the issue of platform dependencies of the business information becomes more considerable. The existing SNSs support business representation in their own platform dependent ways and thus collect different pieces and types of business related information, impose different structure in information collection and presentation, employ varying search procedures, and offer different search management and page interaction functionalities [7]. A key challenge in this regard comes from the varying business categorization schemes being used by the existing SNSs. Specifically, the application developers have to envisage a mechanism for mapping the platform dependent categorization schemes of SNSs to a uniform scheme in order to support the efficient clustering and filtering of businesses in integrated result sets and thereby offer a seamless data integration. In this esteem, this paper presents a content-oriented approach for determining the business category on the basis of semantic analysis of the textual information available in the business profile. The approach has been operationalized in the CoDiT (Company Discovery Tool) which is a web-based tool for facilitating the integrated business page search over Facebook and LinkedIn platforms (cf. [7] for a detailed description of the tool). The methodology presented herein, besides addressing the issue of differing business categorization schemes of SNSs for the SNS business data integration, can also be applied by the existing SNSs themselves in order to uniformly tag the businesses represented on their servers.

2 Methodological Remarks

The work discussed in this paper is oriented around Design Science Research (DSR) approach which combining the disciplines of engineering and 'the science of the artificial' [9] seeks to solve hitherto unresolved practical and theoretical problems by creating new and innovative artifacts [10]. The creation of DSR artifacts is initiated either to solve an identified problem, achieve an objective, implement a required functionality, or fulfill a client's requirement [11]. For the development of successful artifacts, various DSR methods have been suggested in the academic literature such as 'Build - evaluate - theorize – justify' [12], 'Problem identification - intervention - evaluation – reflection or learning [13] ', 'Construct - develop - analyze - build - observe [14] ', 'Awareness of problem - suggestion - development - evaluation – conclusion [15] ', 'Develop or build – justify or evaluate [10] ', and 'Problem identification and motivation - objectives of a solution - design and development - demonstration - evaluation – communication [11] '. The work described herein is aimed at solving a problem, and is undertaken in four steps drawn upon Takeda et al. [15] and Peffers et al. [11]: investigation and motivation of the problem and related challenges (Sect. 3), designing a suitable solution of the identified problem (Sect. 4), implementation of the proposed solution in a suitable context to demonstrate its usability (Sect. 5), and evaluation of proposed solution to test its validity and performance (Sect. 6).

3 Problem Description

The existing SNSs employ different structure for categorizing the business pages hosted on their servers. An examination of the four leading SNSs that facilitate the business page paradigm - Facebook[1], LinkedIn[2], Google+[3], and Xing[4] – indicates that the existing SNSs are adopting a structured approach for categorizing the business pages, i.e. they offer a predefined list of business categories and users are asked to select any of them to tag in their business profile. The Facebook, LinkedIn, and Google + platforms employ a linear categorization scheme with more than 100 categories each. On the Facebook platform a business can be tagged with a maximum of 3 categories, the LinkedIn platform allows to select only one category (referred to as industry), and the Google+ platform allows to select any number of categories designating one as a primary category and others as additional categories. On the contrary, the Xing platform employs a hierarchical categorization scheme of 23 main categories with additional 121 sub-categories whereby a business can be tagged with a single parent category and one more subcategory relative to the parent category.[5]

Accordingly, while integrating business information from multiple SNSs the developers are faced with the question that 'how the business category information coming from different SNSs can be integrated into a uniform categorization scheme in order to support the efficient clustering and filtering of businesses in the integrated result sets?'. One obvious approach of addressing this is to manually map the respective business categories of different platforms to a uniform category system. However, such an approach tends to be very tedious and time consuming as the developers have to recognize the categorization schemes of all the platforms that are

[1] https://www.facebook.com/.
[2] https://www.linkedin.com/.
[3] https://plus.google.com/.
[4] https://www.xing.com/.
[5] As on March 19, 2017.

intended to be connected and develop a mapping module for each platform individually. Moreover, the manual mapping approach brings the following three challenges:

1. The existing category schemes of SNSs include some very general categories such as 'Company', 'Organization', and 'Local business'. When the categories are mapped abstractly, it becomes impossible to categorize the businesses tagged with such broad categories into more meaningful and relevant categories.
2. When the business pages from different SNSs are integrated in order to address a specific task of a particular business domain, with the manual mapping it becomes challenging to further categorize the high-level (abstract) categories tagged to a business into more specific low-level (concrete) sub-categories in order to facilitate the drilling down to certain sub-domains.
3. When the category mapping is done explicitly, any future changes in the underlying categorization schemes of the integrated platforms are not captured by the application. Thus, the application becomes incapable to aggregate all the available business category information in an efficient and effective manner.

4 Semantics-Based Business Categorization Approach

In this section, we propose a semantics-based approach for uniformly categorizing the business pages retrieved from different SNSs. According to the proposed approach, given a predefined business category list designating the uniform category scheme in which the business category information is to be represented (hereafter referred to as category list), relatedness of a business to the appropriate categories is determined on the basis of the semantic analysis of the concatenated textual information (hereafter referred to as business description) available in various free text fields of business profile such as 'about', 'general information', 'description', 'overview', 'products', 'specialties', and the like. As the category text usually consists of few words with no or minimal interdependence and all the words are equally important in determining category appropriateness, business categorization is considered as a classification task whereby one-to-one similarity decision is made. Accordingly, iterating through the given category list, the appropriateness of a particular category is determined in three steps: (1) preprocessing of category tag, (2) expansion of category tag, and (3) similarity measurement of the expanded category tag and the business description (cf. Figure 1).

1. **Preprocessing of category tag:** During the first step, the category tag is initially normalized by converting it into lower case and removing any discrepancies present therein such as trailing whitespaces, or multiple spaces between the words. Subsequently, the normalized category tag is tokenized into individual words. For example, if a given normalized category tag is 'computer graphics', the tokenization returns an array (say T) of two words such that $T = \{T_1, T_2\}$ = {'computer', 'graphics'}. Finally, the tokenized array of category tag is parsed to discard any stop words present therein, for example 'and', and 'of'.

2. **Expansion of category tag:** During the second step, the token list generated in step 1 is semantically and morphologically expanded. The semantical expansion corresponds to expanding the given token with the words similar to it in meaning (synonyms) in order to overcome the vocabulary mismatch problem. The semantical equivalents of a given word can be generated by different measures referring to either a suitable corpus or a standardized thesaurus. The morphological expansion corresponds to expanding the given token with its different lexical forms (singular/plural of nouns, different tenses of the verbs) in order to address the variances in the structure of sentences available in the business description. Accordingly, taking each token in the category tag, one at a time (say T_i), its semantically similar words (S_1 to S_n) are generated, and subsequently all morphological forms of the token itself (T_iM_1 to T_iM_n) and its semantical equivalents ($T_iS_1M_1$ to $T_iS_nM_n$) are generated. This step results into a bag of words (T) for the token T_i such that $T = \{T_i, T_iM_1, \ldots, T_iM_n, T_iS_1, \ldots., T_iS_n, T_iS_1M_1, \ldots, T_iS_1M_n, \ldots\ldots\ldots., T_iS_nM_1, \ldots, T_iS_nM_n\}$.
3. **Measuring similarity:** During the third step, the inclusion of the T bag of words is determined in the business description through any appropriate text matching algorithm such that the similarity is positive if any of the words in T is present within the business description text. This process is iterated for each token of the category tag generated in step 1. The category is tagged to the business only if each token in any of its semantical or morphological form is present in the business description.

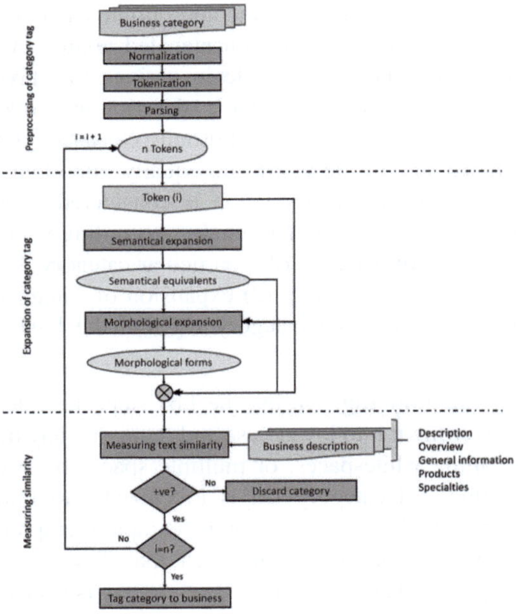

Fig. 1. Semantics-based business categorization approach

5 Implementation

The semantics-based business categorization approach given in Sect. 4 has been implemented in a web-based tool – Company Discovery Tool (CoDiT) - that facilitates an integrated business page search over Facebook and LinkedIn platform together with business specific functionalities in order to support the business partner discovery for open innovation alliances. The key features of the tool include different types of search (keyword search with additional field restriction, advanced search in terms of business category, offered services, and location, and navigational search with respect to business category, offered services, and location), an integrated geographic map, faceted filtering in terms of business-specific attributes, search management functionalities such as bookmarking and networking the business pages, direct page interaction (liking/following, and reading/writing the feed), and uniform representation of the business information retrieved from Facebook and LinkedIn platforms (cf. [7] for more details).

In the CoDiT system, the proposed approach is applied to identify the business category as well as the services offered by a certain business. The business pages retrieved from the Facebook and LinkedIn are mapped to a uniform linear category scheme of 168 categories that includes the general category tags (e.g. company, organization), high-level business domains (e.g. computers, engineering, technology), and low-level specific categories (e.g. computer hardware, computer software, computer graphics). The CoDiT system implements the proposed approach as follows:

1. **Semantical expansion:** For generating the semantically similar words of the given tokens in the category tags, the CoDiT system employs the corpus-based web services available from Leipzig Corpora Collection[6] (LCC) using its REST API[7] (for a description of REST architecture, cf. [16]). LCC is the collection of a large corpus of freely available electronic media consisting of the web, newspapers, and Wikipedia. The resources are collected by employing different data collection methods. The resulting crawled resources are processed, and for each language, a full form dictionary with frequency information for each word is calculated. In addition, the significant co-occurrence statistics (the words that co-occur significantly often with a given word) are precomputed and two kinds of co-occurrence data are stored: words occurring together in sentences, and words found as immediate (left or right) neighbors [17, 18]. The LCC collects corpora for more than 200 languages and for each language different corpora releases are available. For the implementation of the CoDiT system, the English language corpus based on Wikipedia with 1 M sentences (eng_wikipedia_2012_1M) is referenced. The 'similarity-service' of the LCC returns the words related to the given word on the basis of the similarity of their significant sentence and neighbor co-occurrences in the reference corpus.

6 http://corpora.uni-leipzig.de/.

7 http://wortschatzwebservices.informatik.uni-leipzig.de/ws/swagger-ui.html.

2. **Morphological expansion:** For retrieving the different lexical forms of given tokens in the category tags, the CoDiT system leverages the PHP based phpMorphy library[8]. The phpMorphy is a morphological analysis library that provides the dictionary-based morphological services for the English, Russian, German, Ukrainian, and Estonian languages. For every word, phpMorphy provides three types of information: a base form of the word (lemma), all morphological forms of the word, and grammatical information of the word (part of speech, case, etc.).
3. **Similarity measurement:** For computing the similarity between tokens of the category tag and the business description text, the CoDiT system applies the cosine similarity measure which is the most common measure used for determining text similarity [19] and is the baseline for most of the similarity studies [20]. The basic idea behind cosine similarity is to transform each text string into a vector in some high dimensional space such that similar strings are close to each other. The cosine of the angle between two vectors is a measure of how similar they are, which in turn, is a measure of the similarity of given texts. Accordingly, at first, a high dimensional space V is created where each term in text T1 (the token, its similar terms, and morphological forms of the token and its similar terms), and text T2 (the business description) defines an independent dimension, such that $V = (T1_1, \ldots, T1_n) + (T2_1, \ldots, T2_n)$. Then, the texts (T1 and T2) are transformed into their respective binary vectors (V1 and V2) in this high dimensional space. Operating in the positive quadrant of the Euclidean space (i.e. no term is assigned a negative value), vectors represent the presence and absence of a particular term in each text string by a non-negative value (1 or 0) along the dimension corresponding to the term. Finally, the cosine of the angle between V1 and V2 is computed which is identical to their normalized inner product, such that

$$\mathrm{Sim}_{\cos}(\mathrm{T1},\ \mathrm{T2}) = \frac{V1.V2}{\sqrt{V1^2}\sqrt{V2^2}}$$

Since, non-negative values are used in the vectors, the cosine measure returns positive numerical value in the range of 0 (for the orthogonal vectors) and 1 (for the identical vectors).

6 Evaluation

We have tested the validity of proposed approach on a data set of business descriptions of 10 randomly selected businesses represented on Facebook platform. In doing so, at first, we manually analyzed and annotated each business description with relevant categories from the predefined list of 168 categories. Subsequently, we compared the results of proposed approach (as implemented in CoDiT) with this manual standard. As shown in Fig. 2, the proposed approach has an average recall of 0.85 (min. 0.67, max. 1), precision of 0.75 (min. 0.6, max. 1), and F-measure of 0.79 (min. 0.67, max. 0.91).

[8] http://phpmorphy.sourceforge.net/dokuwiki/.

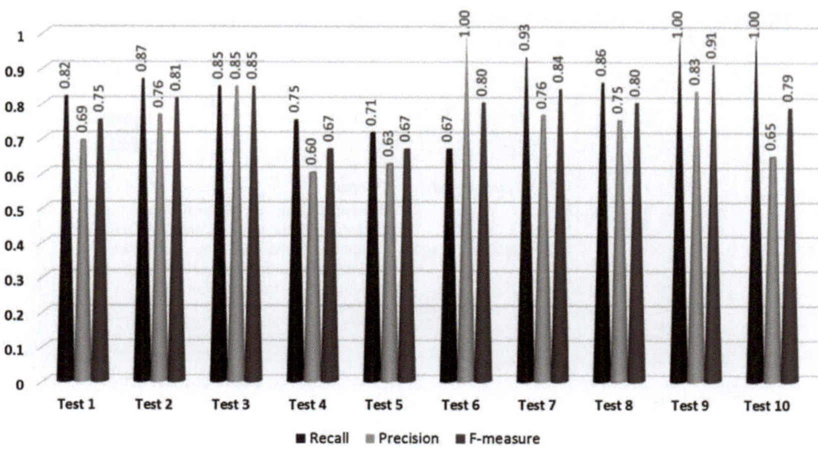

Fig. 2. Evaluation results of proposed approach

Therefore, we are convinced that the proposed approach is adequate to achieve its set objective of semi-automatic business categorization on SNSs.

A screenshot of the CoDiT system showing the official Facebook page of IBM company[9] is given in Fig. 3. As illustrated, the Facebook platform returns only one category for IBM, i.e. 'Company' (cf. category list in Fig. 2)[10] which does not sufficiently help to understand what the given company deals with.

The CoDiT system through the proposed approach has been able to determine several relevant categories for the company including the 'Company' (the general category), 'Computers', 'Consulting', 'Education', 'Research', 'Engineering', 'Technology', 'Telecommunications', 'Information technology', 'Design' (broad business domains), and 'Computer games', 'Computer hardware', and 'Computer software' (low-level categories) that substantially reveal the nature of the business and its offerings.

It is important to note here that while some of the given high-level categories such as 'Education' and 'Research' tend to be ambiguous and thereby need more drilling down to understand the area of education and research that the company operates in, the combination of such high-level categories with other high or low level categories implicitly declares the important relations such as 'Education' and 'Research' combined with 'Computers', 'Technology', and 'Engineering' indicates that the company would be dealing with the education and research in the fields of computers and information technology.

---

[9] https://www.facebook.com/IBM/.

[10] As retrieved on March 22, 2017.

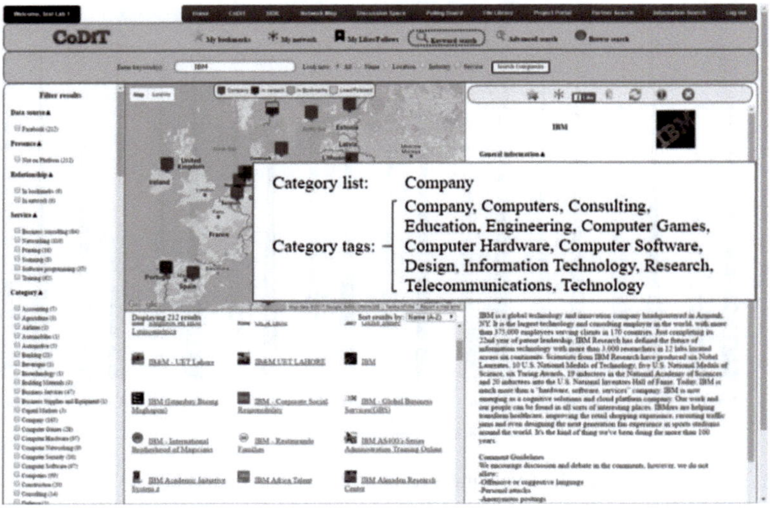

Fig. 3. Illustration of semantics-based business categorization approach

7 Conclusion

In this paper, we have addressed the issue of different business categorization schemes being varyingly used by the existing SNSs. In doing so, we have proposed a content-oriented approach for determining the relevant business categories on the basis of semantical and morphological analysis of the textual business information available in the business profile. The applicability and usability of the proposed approach is demonstrated within a web-based tool that supports the integrated business page search over multiple SNSs. The accuracy of the proposed approach depends on three factors: (1) the amount of information available in the business profile (business description), (2) the quality and depth of the corpus/thesaurus, and the morphological analyzer referenced to generate the synonyms and morphological forms respectively, and (3) the comprehensibility of the given business category list. However, given that these three components are appropriate, the approach is found to be adequate in attaining the task of semi-automatic characterization of businesses into the meaningful and appropriate categories.

References

1. Boyd, D.M., Ellison, N.B.: Social network sites: definition, history, and scholarship. J. Comput.-Mediated Commun. (2007). doi:10.1111/j.1083-6101.2007.00393.x
2. Lin, K.-Y., Lu, H.-P.: Why people use social networking sites: an empirical study integrating network externalities and motivation theory. Comput. Hum. Behav. **27**(3), 1152–1161 (2011)

3. Jefferson III, C.E., Traughber, S.: Social media in business. In: How Social Media Can Help Small Businesses and Non-Profit Organizations, pp. 2–3 (2012)
4. Kietzmann, J.H., Hermkens, K., McCarthy, I.P., Silvestre, B.S.: Social media? Get serious! Understanding the functional building blocks of social media. Bus. Horiz. **54**(3), 241–251 (2011)
5. Papacharissi, Z.: The virtual geographies of social networks: a comparative analysis of Facebook, LinkedIn and ASmallWorld. New Media Soc. **11**(1–2), 199–220 (2009)
6. Stelzner, M.A.: 2014 social media marketing industry report: how marketers are using social media to grow their businesses. In: Social Media Examiner (2014)
7. Memon, A.B., Meyer, K.: CoDiT: an integrated business partner discovery tool over SNSs. In: Working Conference on Virtual Enterprises, pp. 631–638 (2015)
8. Felt, A., Evans, D.: Privacy protection for social networking APIs. In: 2008 Web 2.0 Security and Privacy (W2SP 2008) (2008)
9. Simon, H.A.: The Sciences of the Artificial, vol. 136. MIT press, Cambridge (1996)
10. Hevner, A.R., March, S.T., Park, J., Ram, S.: Design science in information systems research. MIS Q. **28**(1), 75–105 (2004)
11. Peffers, K., Tuunanen, T., Rothenberger, M.A., Chatterjee, S.: A design science research methodology for information systems research. Journal Of Management Information Systems **24**(3), 45–77 (2007)
12. March, S.T., Smith, G.F.: Design and natural science research on information technology. Decis. Support Syst. **15**(4), 251–266 (1995)
13. Cole, R., Purao, S., Rossi, M., Sein, M.: Being proactive: where action research meets design research. In: ICIS 2005 Proceedings, 27 (2005)
14. Nunamaker, Jr., J.F., Chen, M.: Systems development in information systems research. In: Proceedings of the Twenty-Third Annual Hawaii International Conference System Sciences, pp. 631–640 (1990)
15. Takeda, H., Veerkamp, P., Yoshikawa, H.: Modeling design process. AI Mag. **11**(4), 37 (1990)
16. Feng, X., Shen, J., Fan, Y.: REST: an alternative to RPC for Web services architecture. In: First International Conference Future Information Networks, ICFIN 2009, pp. 7–10 (2009)
17. Biemann, C., Heyer, G., Quasthoff, U., Richter, M.: The Leipzig Corpora Collection-monolingual corpora of standard size. In: Proceedings of Corpus Linguistic (2007)
18. Richter, M., Quasthoff, U., Hallsteinsdóttir, E., Biemann, C.: Exploiting the Leipzig Corpora Collection. In: Proceedings of the IS-LTC (2006)
19. Huang, A.: Similarity measures for text document clustering. In: Proceedings of the Sixth New Zealand Computer Science Research Student Conference (NZCSRSC 2008), pp. 49–56 (2008)
20. Shrestha, P.: Corpus-based methods for short text similarity. In: Rencontre des Étudiants Chercheurs en Informatique pour le Traitement automatique des Langues, p. 297 (2011)

Holistic Design of Visual Collaboration Arenas and Intelligent Workspaces

Frank Lillehagen[1(✉)], Sobah Abbas Petersen[2], and Sven-Volker Rehm[3]

[1] Commitment AS, Lysaker, Norway
frank.lillehagen@commitment.no
[2] SINTEF Technology and Society, Trondheim, Norway
[3] WHU – Otto Beisheim School of Management, Vallendar, Germany

Abstract. Future industrial and societal projects must be designed for sustainable operations, evolutionary capabilities, and business operations. To exploit the potential of digitalization, we must design practical cases and roles, workspaces and collaboration spaces, creating evolutionary action- and work-sensitive contexts. Intelligent workspaces and operation models will complement, enhance, and replace natural language specifications, coded systems and information flows. Design of visual knowledge models, enabled by Active Knowledge Architectures, will revolutionize industrial computing and collaboration. The MADONE partners have performed industrial and public pilot projects verifying that sector adaptable platforms give actors agile approaches and evolving collaboration capabilities and services. Evolutionary workplaces and collaboration spaces resolve present challenges and open new opportunities, supporting flexibility, adaptability, reusability, traceability, predictability and sustainability. Holistic design of projects and operations is the industry case demonstrator described.

Keywords: Holistic design · Agile approaches · Intelligent workspaces · Visual collaboration arenas · Sustainable operations and Practice-driven innovation

1 Present Use of ICT

Most projects, system developers and consultants, architects and users, are still supported by domain-specific layered approaches and paper-based methods and disjoint work environments. Each layer is divided in discipline-dominated stages connected by gateways, and supported by linked application systems. Instant collaboration, dynamic viewing, data analyses, knowledge sharing and reuse, and competence transfer among stakeholders, users and suppliers is limited, if not altogether prohibited. Agile design approaches to visual enterprise arenas and workplace design, responding to growing variety, emergence and complexity of markets and companies are being researched [1], but holistic design of reusable knowledge-driven solutions are so far ignored. There are still political and commercial barriers preventing new styles of computing, transforming coded applications and workplaces to dynamic model-based, architecture-driven workplaces and visual work environments.

L.M. Camarinha-Matos et al. (Eds.): PRO-VE 2017, IFIP AICT 506, pp. 688–695, 2017.
DOI: 10.1007/978-3-319-65151-4_61

Most industries and public sectors are involved in innovation projects developing Cyber-Physical Systems (CPS) [2–4]. CPSs are a result of progress in sensor technology and digital technologies, but does not enable cyclic design. CPS presents a new level of prescribed intelligence that is characterized by interaction and collaboration of computing and physical processes, as well as structured human machine interaction.

Future computing will be composed of these components: hardware, software, smart digital devices, and Active Knowledge Models (AKMs). Categories of AKMs support cyclic design and execution of Visual Collaboration Arenas (VCAs), evolutionary platforms and intelligent workspaces, and will enable autonomous data, knowledge and work management. The Active Knowledge Modelling (AKM) technology [5] enables disruptive new approaches, so existing ICT business, research and education will be transformed. Collaboration across teams of users, designers, suppliers, and digital actors implies that they own and manage their workspace data and tasks, discipline parameters and design and engineering rules.

2 Design and Innovation of Visual Collaboration Arenas

Dynamic CPS design and operation will enable new applications in numerous public domains, like eHealth, where new solutions will enhance healthcare practices and services. Dynamic CPS design will also have beneficial impacts in industrial domains, such as Factories of the Future (FoF), where business models may be influenced by data from the sensing devices of a CPS. However, in most sectors there are life-cycle challenges and needs, such as innovating new approaches and practical methods for design and operation of new products and processes. This practice-driven innovation and learning and cyclic design and execution is not supported by CPS systems.

The discovery of human mental models [6] created in our brain when performing or observing practical work and events enable humans to capture practical work-sensitive knowledge and build new services [7]. AKM partners [8, 9] have invented an at-the-workplace modelling approach enabling workers to express their tacit knowledge and design mental models as digital models as work is being performed.

2.1 Implementing Visual Collaboration Arenas

VCAs are supported by Model-based, Architecture-driven (MBAD) project platforms and workplaces, and are built by these collaborating teams:

- A user-team composed of users, engineering and supplier experts, and use-case experts is responsible for customer solutions, capabilities and values.
- A knowledge modelling team composed of people with competence in holistic design methods and principles, and in building knowledge products, Active Knowledge Models (AKMs) and Active Knowledge Architectures (AKAs).
- An Evolutionary Project Platform (EPP) team with competence in using the core EPP &VCP tools, reusing knowledge models, and extending the contents, methods and capabilities, managed in the Project Knowledge Repository.

Reference project and sector-solution AKAs will be built to ease front-end loading, supporting cyclic design and execution, and kick-starting new projects cutting calendar times and costs by factors. Figure 1 illustrates the transformation of project design and execution enabled by VCAs. One key characteristic of the new agile approach is user-enabled visual modeling rather than prescribed coding to capture work-sensitive context. A second key characteristic is: supporting categories of users in capturing and sharing situations, decisions, dependencies, and local pragmatic knowledge spaces by modelling role-oriented workspaces. To implement these characteristics software will be applied as an enabler for workspace and knowledge modelling of AKA and MBAD workplaces, supporting enhanced communication, collaboration, configurations and competence transfer. The AKM approach [8, 9] and holistic design methods will have revolutionary impacts on business models, project methodologies, organizations, products and processes, knowledge management and reuse, and ICT development across industries and public domains.

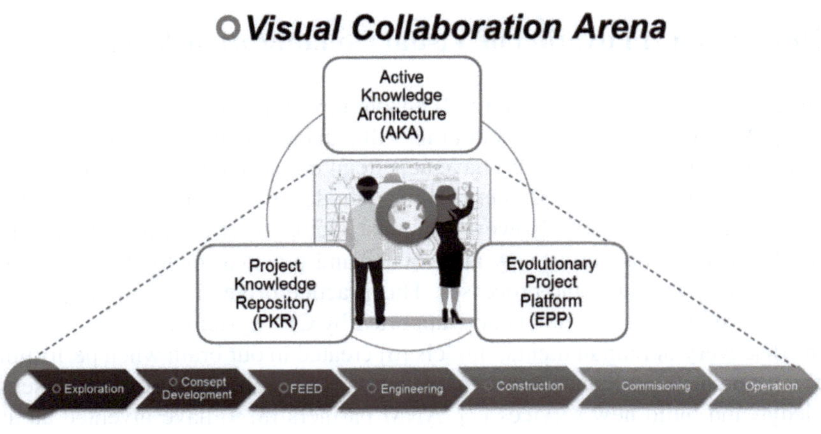

Fig. 1. New approaches and methods for project VCA design and operation.

2.2 The Industrial Pilot

Building on the insight from many Oil & Gas fields and exploration projects a holistic design approach [9] to field development and operations is conceived and tested. This pilot will combine the insights from the Woodside[1] project with state of the art knowledge capture and modelling, and create a practical demonstrator that validates holistic design methods and enhanced life-cycle collaboration and interaction.

The Woodside project (SPE MS176813) has documented that the Capex can be reduced by 10–35%, and the Opex by 30–80%, and reliability increased from 95 to 97+ % by adopting low-manned/unmanned remotely operated facilities [10]. The prerequisite for such success is that the operations philosophy and model is defined upfront in

[1] http://www.woodside.com.au/Pages/home.aspx

the concept phase, acknowledging that the operations model is a design driver, not as it is today, where the facility design drives the operations model. The operations model with facilities and resources and product design models support the stated mission, as illustrated in Fig. 2. The architecture of the pilot consists of role and task specific collaboration spaces that support the early phases (Concept & FEED) of a project that delivers an operations model and product design supporting the stated mission. The mission statement should be articulated on the form; a minimal manned, remotely operated installation that is profitable at a price point of $25/bbl.

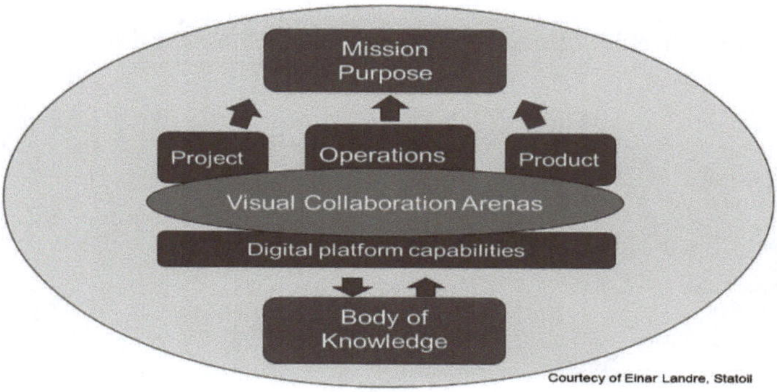

Fig. 2. Capabilities and knowledge models for designing Visual Collaboration Arenas.

Our approach is to combine the insights from the Woodside project with state of the art knowledge capture and modelling, and to create a technical demonstrator that validates new holistic design methods for projects, products and work environments.

3 Towards Holistic Project Design and Operations

The people responsible for designing projects and enterprises and operations must apply holistic thinking and adapt and implement the VCA concepts and AKM methods [9]. Holistic design of projects, products, organizations and processes implies modelling top-down to support resources and time, bottom-up to capture work-sensitive data and workspaces, and inside-out to balance discipline parameters across life-cycles and value-chains. Supporting holistic design requires fine-grained knowledge modelling of workspaces and collaboration spaces, and support for conceptual design based on active knowledge models of life-cycle operations and customer values.

Active knowledge models and architecture elements will be major assets in the growing Circular Knowledge Economy and the Digital Single Market [11, 12].

3.1 The Evolution of Design Methods

Design methods have been a major domain for research and development, since the early 1980's when Beitz and Roth extended product design to embrace manufacturing, and

Hubka introduced the principles of design embodiment to separate conceptual design properties and the balancing of discipline parameters and their tolerable values. Design embodiment implies that properties and parameters are modelled separately, and parameters are balanced across disciplines before they are embedded in objects.

The Holistic Design methods must be implemented, adapted and validated in industrial pilot projects. The core knowledge domains, the design meta-knowledge, as illustrated in Fig. 3 are composed of concepts, capabilities, properties, qualities, shapes and volumes, features, eco-norms and rules, and extensive life-cycle services.

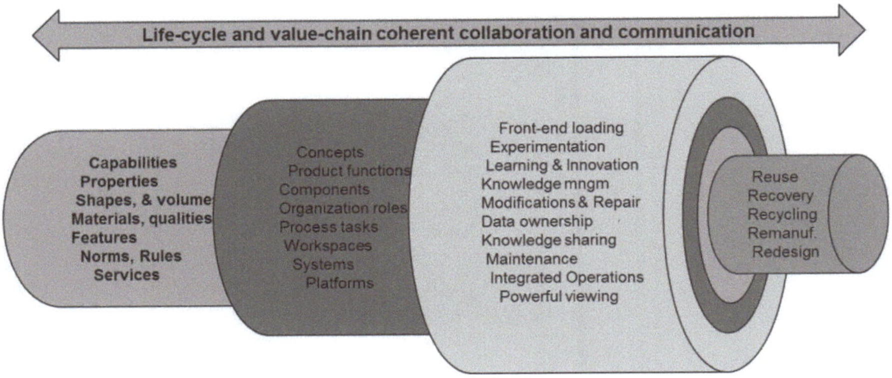

Fig. 3. Evolutionary VCA design of industrial meta-knowledge concepts.

4 Novel Paradigm-Shifting Concepts

There are several paradigm-shifting concepts supporting the design and operation of VCAs, designing life-cycle workspaces, agile workplace approaches, and emergent methods, platforms and solutions meeting growing market needs and opportunities. The most important concepts enabling emerging approaches and solutions supporting concurrent project design and sustainable operations are:

1. *Enterprise Knowledge Spaces - multi-dimensional knowledge spaces emergent models, collaboration, and data and knowledge management*
2. *Context-rich Workspaces – enable simultaneous workplace design and execution*
3. *Sector-specific Knowledge Architecture - integrating operations and new methods*
4. *Model-based Architecture-driven Collaboration (MBAD) - configuring agile solutions and enhancing collaboration*
5. *Contributions to Sustainability - Concurrent Modelling and Operation, enabling life-cycle design and execution*

The major concepts, their properties, enabling capabilities and business impacts are illustrated in Fig. 4, and will be explained in the following sub-sections.

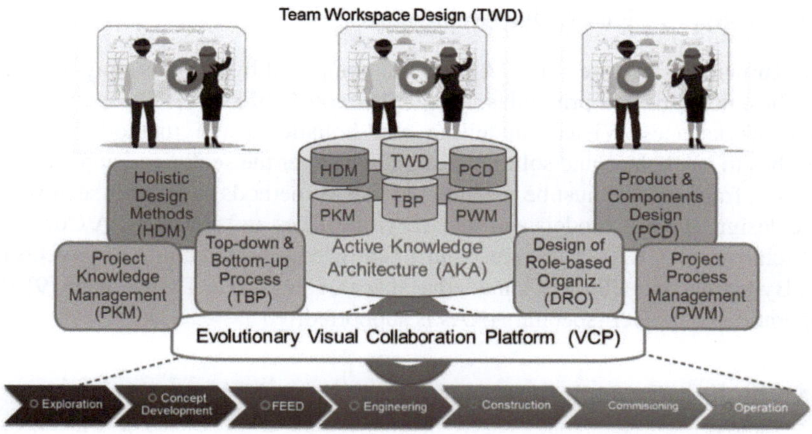

Fig. 4. Emergent networked enterprises – enabling life-cycle design and operation.

Multi-dimensional enterprise knowledge spaces, smart role-oriented organizations, workspace properties, AKA modelling, and the AKM methodologies and principles are explained in more detail in the entries of the AKM blog [1].

4.1 Enterprise Knowledge Spaces

Enterprise Knowledge is created in multiple dimensions by the people involved in the various enterprise activities and domains [7]. The nature of practical knowledge spaces and workspaces must be understood by applying visual design modeling to capture work-centric knowledge and context. Enterprise knowledge spaces span the individual workspaces, the organizational space of product design and development, the organizational network space of collaborating entities and further to the societal space where an organization and its work are affected by the environment they operate in and the social norms and legislation. Knowledge, data and experience sharing must be facilitated, and knowledge assets management and reuse will be decisive services for future competitiveness and progress.

4.2 Context-Rich Workspaces

Existing organizations, composed of hierarchies, static networks and collaborating teams require innovative design to fit the design, production and life-cycle support of projects, products and operations. The people assigned to roles must be supported by reusable MBAD agile workplaces, allowing them to perform at-the-workplace design, modelling and task execution, closing the gaps between project stages. Visual modelling of work-sensitive data and contexts enable capture of tacit knowledge in digital models, which could enhance their mental models for enhanced local work execution, coordination, collaboration and work management [8].

4.3 Sector-Specific Knowledge Architectures

Active Knowledge Architectures (AKAs) are composed by collaborating teams, agile approaches, novel design principles, and active models of knowledge spaces and role-oriented workspaces. Visual modelling and holistic design methods enable new approaches to workplace and solution design, whatever the sector and application. The present EA frameworks must be extended by AKM methods to support sector-specific holistic design of AKA models and MBAD workplaces and solutions. A Core Knowledge Architecture (CKA) can be reused in all knowledge architectures of projects in any sector. By graphic modelling of knowledge spaces, using the IRTV language [9], design and operation of project- specific AKAs is supported.

4.4 Model-Based, Architecture-Driven Collaboration

Collaborative open innovation and learning, and continuous design and operation of emergent networked solutions is enabled. Agility and emergence are achieved by building MBAD workplaces and collaboration spaces, providing capabilities for autonomous sharing of views and for extending and modifying AKMs and AKAs.

Design modelling of conceptual objects, capabilities, features and properties is supported, and discipline parameters, values and goals are balanced to support design embodiment and creation of design, configuration and collaboration rules. Decision-support, predictability, traceability and assessment of trends will provide users enhanced capabilities to deal with uncertainties and assess risks. Change management is minimized by product family variants and comparable alternatives.

4.5 Contributions to Sustainability

The model-based, architecture-driven approach is ideal for what is described as the reindustrialization of industry and enhanced international collaboration.

As illustrated in Fig. 5, common approaches for industrial and public enterprises can be composed by architecting teams applying fine-grained modelling methods. Adding

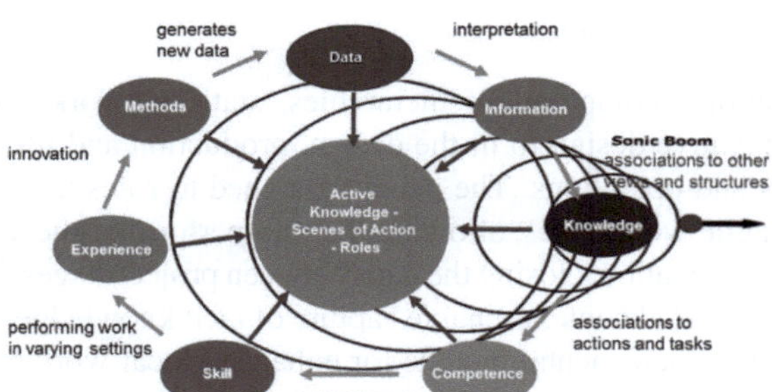

Fig. 5. Knowledge concepts, classes and categories will be built, managed and reused.

designer and user teams, modelling to cover structures and aspects of product, organization, process and system, enables and is enabled by the design of sector-specific knowledge models and architectures.

5 Conclusions

To meet the rapidly growing challenges and opportunities industry and public sector are facing [11, 12], there is an urgent need for new ways of building and applying computing power. The AKM technology enables the implementation of new concepts, capabilities and properties required to provide new, agile approaches, adaptive methods, and visual work environments. Future research, innovation and experimentation, must focus on developing and providing sector-specific and life-cycle agile approaches, holistic design methods, knowledge architectures and open modelling and computing platforms. Active knowledge models of approaches, methods, solutions and operations will be normalised and managed for reuse in private and public sector knowledge bases.

References

1. Jørgensen, H., Lillehagen, F.: content of the Active Knowledge Modelling blog. http://activeknowledgemodeling.com/
2. Lemke, M.: Cyber-physical systems and advanced computing opportunities in horizon 2020. In: Presentation at EU DG Connect- A3, Brussels, January 2013
3. Lee, E.: CPS foundations. In: Proceeding Design Automation Conference 2010, Anaheim, USA (2010)
4. Lee, I., Sokolsky, O., et al.: Challenges and research directions in medical cyber-physical systems. Proc. IEEE **100**(1), 75–90 (2012)
5. Lillehagen, F., Krogstie, J.: Active Knowledge Modeling of Enterprises. Springer, Heidelberg (2008). doi:10.1007/978-3-540-79416-5
6. Craik, K: Mental Models, Papers of Human Reasoning (1947/1948)
7. Chesbrough, H.: Open Services Innovation: Rethinking Your Business to Growth and Compete in a New Era. Jossey-Bass, San Francisco (2011)
8. Lillehagen, F., Krogstie, J., Petersen, S.: What Systems Engineering Need to Embrace, Paper in SE Newsletter. http://www.ppi-int.com/newsletter/syen-049.pdf
9. Lillehagen, F., Petersen, S.A., Krogstie, J.: Enabling holistic design, innovation and learning. In: The XXIII ISPIM Conference – Action for Innovation: Innovating from Experience, 17–20 Jun 2012
10. Edwards, A.R., Gordon,B. StepChange global: using unmanned principles and integrated operations to enable operational efficiency and reduce Capex and OPEX costs
11. Digital Single Market. https://ec.europa.eu/digital-single-market/en/digital-single-market
12. Circular Economy. http://www.eea.europa.eu/publications/circular-economy-in-europe

Designing an Open Architecture for the Creative Industry

Christian Zinke(✉), Michael Becker(✉), and Stephan Klingner(✉)

Institute for Applied Informatics at the University of Leipzig,
Hainstraße 11, Leipzig, Germany
{zinke,becker,klingner}@infai.org

Abstract. Companies in the Culture and Creative Industry are characterized by highly networked value chains. However, this value network lacks a profound support in terms of information technology and structure resulting in time-consuming and error-prone manual labor. To overcome these challenges, we conceptualize an application framework for creative industries. In particular a software architecture design and a data design will be proposed with the help of a design science research approach. The goal of the resulting application framework is to support the digital transformation of companies in the creative industry towards collaborative networks.

Keywords: Music business · Framework · Design science research · Collaborative networks

1 Introduction

The Culture and Creative Industry (CCI) is an emerging sector, with progressively increased significance. In 2014 the core sector of CCI had 4.4% of total GDP (558 billion Euro) and 3.8% of total EU workforce [1]. The current trend of digitalization leads to significant changes in the value chain of CCI, especially in music business [2–5]. For example, through digitization music production does no longer require a recording studio and new digital distribution channels like music and video streaming portals weaken the influence of major labels [3]. While these developments are headed by major companies, small enterprises lack accurate digital support within their value chain. This became a significant challenge for the domain as recent studies show [6]:

- The majority of companies in CCI are very small and small enterprises (99%).
- An average of 4.33 employee per enterprise renders an efficient division of work impossible.
- Cooperation and highly interactive networks are a substantial part of the value chain (93% of all enterprises).

Thus, the CCI in general and music business in particular, are already highly networked. According to Ewig's [7] collaboration business transformation pyramid the described small enterprises can be classified as a network on organizational structure level. This is challenged by a lack of information structure and technology, which includes the absence of unified and standardized exchange formats within the domain.

L.M. Camarinha-Matos et al. (Eds.): PRO-VE 2017, IFIP AICT 506, pp. 696–703, 2017.
DOI: 10.1007/978-3-319-65151-4_62

Due to the wide variety of data formats, manual consolidation of data sets is necessary, which is time-consuming and error-prone. Thus, SMEs in music business have a data-based information structure – which means that there is no cross-functional information flow [8]. In addition, conducted questionnaires and workshops show high usage of proprietary software (like Excel) as well as a lot of manual work, which can be categorized as a very low information technology maturity (see Fig. 1). Though the dimensions of Ewig's business collaboration pyramid have interaction effects with each other, the remainder of this paper focuses on information structure and information technology due to space limitations. We aim at conceptualizing an Information System (IS) and, thus, for our paper organizational questions are of minor importance. Analytically, small enterprises are on a preliminary stage to (goal-oriented) collaborative network organizations (CNOs) [9], lacking suitable information technology. Among others the forms of CNOs are virtual organizations or virtual enterprises [10].

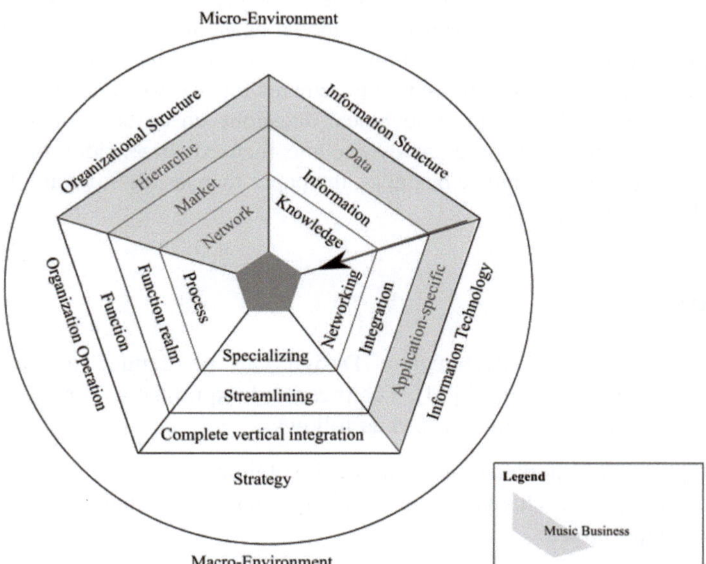

Fig. 1. Maturity of small enterprises within music business, according to Ewig [7]

The huge value network of the music industry and the resulting huge amount of requirements are challenging. Resulting mass-customization, from single worker (local workspace) via enterprise level (server) to collaborative network (cloud and web services), require a very flexible approach. However, the small stakeholders in music business lack the time, money and software solutions that fit their specific needs. Thus, open and scalable solutions are necessary to support the transformation process to CNOs. In summary, SME in music business need improved information structure and technology in order to evolve to a CNO (virtual network). Both will be addressed within this paper with the help of a design science research approach.

The leading research question is, how to design an IS architecture to support digital transformation of SME in music industry?

2 Methodology

The presented paper is conducted through an IS Design Science Research approach. The major task and result of design science research is to create an artefact, which is "by definition, a purposeful IT artifact created to address an important organizational problem" [11]. We will focus on the design of a solution for the given problem. The detailed requirements – briefly described in Chapt. 1 – are derived from workshops and expert interviews with stakeholders of the music industry as well as analysis of available documentations (e.g. from label management or DDEX). Following common design science research methodologies for IS, the next step from requirements is the design of a possible solution, which will be presented next [12]. As a research in process this work is limited to a conceptual model as an artefact and cannot provide a concrete implementation or an evaluation [12]. Further on, the proposed concept will be used to iterate and collect additional requirements for real world application in order develop requirements that supports technical decisions on costs, complexity, performance and applicability. In order to evolve the focused dimensions of information structure and technology in music business, the paper focuses on Software Architecture Design and Data Design [13].

3 Design

Amongst other, Software Architecture Design can be defined as "a high-level abstraction of software systems" [14]. The presented requirements for such a software system architecture can be summarized as follows:

- Scalable from local applications to network solutions
- Support the digital exchange within music business value chain
- Flexible enhancement

As shown in Fig. 2, the proposed architecture of the framework consists of a runtime environment providing horizontal services. On top of the general environment, the installation of various small applications (so-called apps) shall be possible in order to support the individual value chain for each stakeholder within the value network. Each app provides specific functionalities that are required by one or more stakeholders.

The app management layer is responsible for integrating apps into the runtime environment. The apps are managed by the framework through simple policies (e.g. naming conventions, meta-data for apps (Dublin Core[1]), data access rules, dependencies) [15]. The management layer ensures the unified and standardized structuring of apps.

[1] http://dublincore.org/.

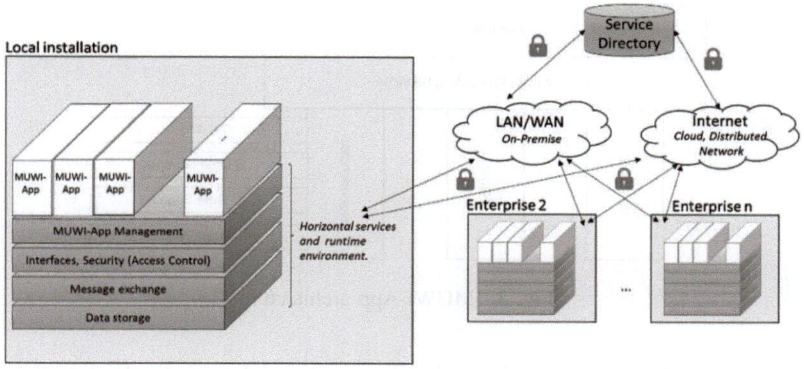

Fig. 2. Architecture to support small enterprises in music business

In order to enable data exchange between different software systems and the platform interfaces are needed. Interfaces to other software systems are the first step moving to the integration stage on information technology level of the business collaboration pyramid [7]. However, the apps should be integrated on data side through common data schemas and protected through access rules.

The message exchange layer enables the communication between different apps. Therefore, this layer may use the Music Business Ontology (MBO) [16] which specifies a unified message format. Based on this format, apps can access data provided by the data storage layer. The unified format allows for transformation of company-specific formats and, thus, reduces transaction costs.

Every company might maintain its own local installation of the framework. In addition to these local installations, a service directory containing apps has to be established. While an internal service directory only contains dedicated apps, an external directory which is available via internet connection, provides access to third party apps.

We will use the term framework, which consist of a set of elements and its relations, including economical, organizational and software-technical elements. An application framework is such a framework for other software artefacts (apps). An app is the smallest executable software artefact, which provides a specific functionality or service to the user. The proposed architecture of the app is described in Fig. 3. In particular, an app has two main components: the user interface and the internal data processing services. In order to ensure compatibility to the platform three information are mandatory: a name (conforming to naming conventions), meta-data (see Dublin Core) and the dependencies. The dependencies are important to ensure functionality of the apps. In order to do so, we suggest that the used interfaces (e.g. to ERP or CRM systems), Linked Data (LD) Data Schema, LD Data Sources (e.g. SPARQL endpoints) and the platform version need to be described.

Besides software architecture, data design is an important aspect in transformation of companies towards collaborative networks. As stated above, open and scalable solutions are required and, thus, a linked data approach is proposed. Linked data is an

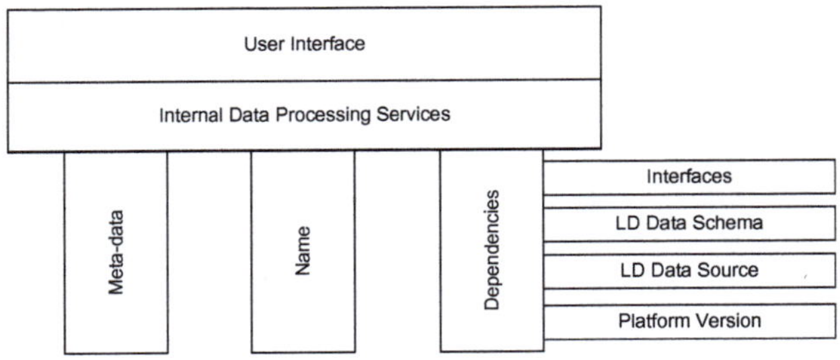

Fig. 3. MUWI-App architecture

approach applied for creating and distributing structured data on the Web with the help of RDF (Resource Description Framework) graphs. In order to make data accessible and enable automated processing, the Linked Data approach extents the vision of Semantic Web [17, 18]. Big players like BBC (British Broadcasting Corporation) already use this technology (with DBPedia[2] and MusicBrainz[3]) [19]. Linked data is suitable because heterogeneous data sources can be used across the value network, which will boost production efficiency of the small enterprises. However, Linked Data may lack in performance and practicability.

The proposed framework allows to create flexible apps for specific purposes, which **access** and enhance information and **knowledge** within the **network** (on server or via internet) easily due to the linked data approach. On information technology side, the approach goes beyond the integration level, because it is not about integration of existing tools, it will combine information from various sources and supports information flows all over the value network. Due to the linked data approach, the provided information are stored as graphs and new knowledge can be easily discovered and extracted [20]. Thus, the approach has the potential to boost the music business to a knowledge level of information structure and network level on information technology side.

4 Related Work

This work has a strong link to software ecosystem (SE) research, which understands SE as "a set of actors functioning as a unit and interacting with a shared market for software and services, together with the relationships among them. These relationships are frequently underpinned by a common technological platform or market and operate through the exchange of information, resources and artefacts." [21]. The MUWISTAR framework is a kind of a software ecosystem, and further a two-sided market solution, which addresses developers as well as customers [22]. Thus, the framework is a kind of a hub – an exchange platform [23], with many-to-many relations within the software supply chain [24]. While research on software ecosystem focuses on reports on

[2] http://wiki.dbpedia.org/.

[3] https://github.com/LinkedBrainz/MusicBrainz-R2RML.

procedures [25], the current work concentrates on software and data design. The framework allows for using apps as a kind of software component or plugin.

However, the research is also linked to software component research. There is a huge variety of components definitions and approaches, e.g. [26, 27]. By lack of space, we only introduce a small selection of software component literature. According to Heineman and Councill "[a] software component is a software element that conforms to a component model and can be independently deployed and composed without modification according to a composition standard." [28]. The definition is extended by two other definitions: the component model and the software component infrastructure [27, 28]. The component model specifies the composition and interaction [28] – also called bindings [29]. The infrastructure ensures the compliant performance of the components [28], also described as system platform [29], which is the presented application framework. Software components approaches are quite similar to plug-in architectures, with practical differences in simplicity of configuration and administration [27].

5 Conclusion and Further Work

The progress of digitalization led to various challenges in the music business. While in the past the focus was on the substitution of physical distribution of music with digital alternatives, with the ascension of streaming and downloads today's challenges lie in the collection, processing and analyzing of data. To master the data, adequate software support is required.

Consequently, the paper proposes a concept for a software architecture and data design as a solution for the current challenges for the music business. This solution aims at providing a powerful, extendable software support, suitable also for the various individual companies and small and medium enterprises (SMEs). However, also organizational questions are important and one of the dimensions of collaborative networks, which have been also addressed in further works.

Yet this architecture is still mainly in the conceptual phase, so that various proposed technical approaches might be subject to changes to better suit the needs of the music business domain. As the concepts represent the best option from a theoretical perspective, it might be possible that requirements occur during implementation and practical evaluation, leading to architectural or technical changes. For example domain- or technology-specific parameters can lead to the substitution of the semantic web approach with common data format approaches, since technical decisions are always a trade-off between costs, complexity, performance and applicability. The technically most advanced solution does not inevitably represent the best approach. Therefore, the priority during the implementation is to create an easy usable and affordable system suiting the needs for the multitude of small and medium enterprises in the music business. This might require a revision of the technical concepts outlined in the paper.

Currently we are working on a first implementation of the presented concept as an open source solution. After developing a first prototype a workshop based evaluation with domain experts will follow. In the long run, we aim to establish a framework community within CCI, aiming at developers as well as users. At this moment the work is still in process and there are no technical artifacts developed yet. Following Gregor and Hevner [30], the solution maturity of the presented case is low, while the domain maturity is high – thus our solution have research opportunities and knowledge contribution for the domain (improvement).

Acknowledgments. This work has been done within the frame of the joint research project "MUWISTAR" which was funded by the German Ministry of Education and Research (Grant Number: 01IS16018B) under the supervision of the PT-DLR. The authors thank for the funding.

References

1. Forum D'avignon: The economic contribution of the creative industries to EU GDP and employment (2014). http://www.forum-avignon.org/sites/default/files/editeur/2014-Oct-European-Creative-Industry-GDP-Jobs-full-Report-ENG.pdf
2. Bauckhage, T.: Das Ende vom Lied. Zum Einfluss der Digitalisierung auf die internationale Musikindustrie. Stuttgart, 113f (2002)
3. Kusek, D., Leonhard, G., Lindsay, S.G.: The Future of Music. Manifesto for the Digital Music Revolution. Berklee Press, Boston (2005)
4. Moreau, F.: The disruptive nature of digitization: the case of the recorded music industry. Int. J. Arts Manag. **15**(2), 18–31 (2013)
5. Bourreau, M., Moreau, F., Gensollen, M.: The digitization of the recorded music industry. Impact on Business Models and Scenarios of Evolution. SSRN J. (2008). doi:10.2139/ssrn.1092138
6. Bertschek, I., Ohnemus, J., Erdsiek, D., Kimpeler, S., Rammer, C., Shala, E.: Monitoringbericht 2016: Ausgewählte wirtschaftliche Eckdaten der Kultur-und Kreativwirtschaft. Langfassung. ZEW-Gutachten und Forschungsberichte (2017)
7. Ewig, M.: Der Transformationsprozess zum collaborative business. Eine strategische, organisatorische und informatorische Betrachtung. Schriften zur Wirtschaftsinformatik, Bd. 17. Lang, Frankfurt am Main, New York (2006)
8. Ehrenberg, D., Ewig, M.: Collaborative Business—eine Herausforderung für die Wirtschaftsinformatik. In: Fink, K., Ploder, C. (eds.) Wirtschaftsinformatik als Schlüssel zum Unternehmenserfolg, pp. 43–71. DUV, Wiesbaden (2006)
9. Camarinha-Matos, L.M., Afsarmanesh, H.: On reference models for collaborative networked organizations. Int. J. Prod. Res. (2008). doi:10.1080/00207540701737666
10. Camarinha-Matos, L.M., Afsarmanesh, H.: Collaborative networks. A new scientific discipline. J. Intell. Manuf. (2005). doi:10.1007/s10845-005-1656-3
11. Vaishnavi, V., Kuechler, W.: Design Research in Information Systems (2004)
12. Peffers, K., Tuunanen, T., Rothenberger, M.A., Chatterjee, S.: A design science research methodology for information systems research. J. Manag. Inf. Syst. **24**(3), 45–77 (2008)
13. Chatterjee, S., Hevner, A.: Design Research in Information Systems. Theory and Practice. Integrated Series in Information Systems, vol. 22, 1st edn. Springer, Berlin (2010). doi:10.1007/978-1-4419-5653-8
14. Solms, F.: Software Architecture Design (2014)
15. Weinreich, R., Sametinger, J.: Component models and component services: concepts and principles. Component-Based Software Engineering: Putting Pieces Together, pp. 22–64 (2001)

16. Schumacher, F., Gey, R., Klingner, S.: Semantics for the music industry. In: Sack, H., Filipowska, A., Lehmann, J., Hellmann, S. (eds.) the 10th International Conference, Leipzig, Germany, pp. 77–83. doi:10.1145/2660517.2660531
17. Berners-Lee, T.: Linked Data (2009). https://www.w3.org/DesignIssues/LinkedData.html. Accessed 27 Mar 2017
18. Feigenbaum, L., Herman, I., Hongsermeier, T., Neumann, E., Stephens, S.: The semantic web in Action. Sci Am. (2007). doi:10.1038/scientificamerican1207-90
19. Bizer, C., Heath, T., Berners-Lee, T.: Linked data-the story so far. Semantic services, interoperability and web applications: emerging concepts, pp. 205–227 (2009)
20. Bizer, C., Lehmann, J., Kobilarov, G., Auer, S., Becker, C., Cyganiak, R., Hellmann, S.: DBpedia - a crystallization point for the Web of Data. Web Semant. Sci. Serv. Agents on the World Wide Web (2009). doi:10.1016/j.websem.2009.07.002
21. Jansen, S., Brinkkemper, S., Finkelstein, A.: Business network management as a survival. Software ecosystems: analyzing and managing business networks in the software industry **29** (2013)
22. Roson, R., et al.: Two-sided markets: a tentative survey. Rev. Netw. Econ. **4**(2), 142–160 (2005)
23. Burkard, C., Widjaja, T., Buxmann, P.: Software ecosystems. Bus. Inf. Syst. Eng. (2012). doi:10.1007/s12599-011-0199-8
24. Ladid, L., Montes, A., Bruck, P.A., Ferri, F., Chbeir, R. (eds.): Proceedings of the Fifth International Conference on Management of Emergent Digital EcoSystems - MEDES 2013. The Fifth International Conference, Luxembourg, Luxembourg, 28 October 2013–31 October 2013. ACM Press, New York (2013)
25. Manikas, K.: Revisiting software ecosystems Research. A longitudinal literature study. Journal of Systems and Software (2016). doi:10.1016/j.jss.2016.02.003
26. Clemens, S., Dominik, G., Stephan, M.: Component Software: Beyond Object-oriented Programming. Addison-Wesley, Reading (1998)
27. Duvigneau, M.: Konzeptionelle Modellierung von Plugin-Systemen mit Petrinetzen, vol. 4. Logos Verlag Berlin GmbH, Berlin (2010)
28. Heineman, G.T., Councill, W.T.: Component-Based Software Engineering. Addison-wesley, Reading (2001)
29. Crnkovic, I., Sentilles, S., Vulgarakis, A., Chaudron, M.R.V.: A classification framework for software component models. IEEE Trans. Softw. Eng. (2011). doi:10.1109/TSE.2010.83
30. Gregor, S., Hevner, A.R.: Positioning and presenting design science research for maximum impact. MIS Q. **37**(2), 337–356 (2013)

Collaboration in Food and Agribusiness

The Role of ICTs in Supporting Collaborative Networks in the Agro-Food Sector: Two Case Studies from South West England

Marco Della Gala(✉) and Matthew Reed

Community and Countryside Research Institute, University of Gloucestershire, Gloucester, GL2 9HW, UK
{mdellagala,mreed}@glos.ac.uk

Abstract. Over recent years, in a wide range of countries, grassroots initiatives have emerged aimed at overcoming the limits of the mainstream agro-business system. These initiatives aim at improving farmers' access to local and regional markets and consumers' access to fresh local produce. Among these initiatives, Food Hubs have emerged as a promising way to improve local food supply systems. They represent collaborative networks of producers and consumers that aggregate, distribute, and market local food products. ICTs enable these collaborative networks by allowing information exchange among their actors and by providing collaborative tools that allow quick co-ordination between members of the network. The paper aims to analyse how the adoption of ICTs have fostered the development of new, initiatives oriented at establishing local food networks and to reconnect producers and consumers. The study will present results from the analysis of two food-hub initiatives based in South West England, which are adopting informative systems to support their activities and to implement novel business models: Stroudco Food Hub and Dean Forest Food Hub.

Keywords: Food hubs · Alternative food networks · Local food system

1 Introduction

Over the last three decades, in the academic and policy discourses a common concern has arisen about the sustainability of the agro-food system. The mainstream procurement system is vertically and horizontally integrated, global in scale, and aimed at maximizing efficiency and profit [1]. This model, based on economic efficiency and profit maximization, has resulted in negative environmental and social externalities [2, 3]. The increasing concentration of large corporations operating in the processing and retail sectors has led both to the crisis of trust in placeless and uniform products among consumers, and to power asymmetries along the food supply chain [2, 4]. The loss of bargaining power and constant cost-price pressure on commodity production has resulted in a decline in farm numbers, with consequences for rural areas [3]. In this context, driven by consumers' renewed interest in locally and sustainably produced foods, grassroots initiatives based on new forms of collaboration between

L.M. Camarinha-Matos et al. (Eds.): PRO-VE 2017, IFIP AICT 506, pp. 707–714, 2017.
DOI: 10.1007/978-3-319-65151-4_63

producers and consumers have emerged [5–8]. These initiatives include direct-to-consumer sales, pick your own, farmers' markets, box schemes, community-supported agriculture, collective buying groups, and community gardens. Typically grouped under the umbrella of 'alternative food networks' (AFNs) [9], they represent collaborative networks allowing for the development of new forms of relationship and governance, enabling a re-distribution of value to primary producers [3, 4].

Even if there is a common agreement that AFNs could offer the opportunity to revitalize local rural communities, they face many difficulties attempting to minimize the number of intermediaries in the food supply chain. The direct marketing activities in the AFNs are highly labour-intensive, profitable levels are low, due to a low volume of sales, high logistic and marketing costs [8]. Food Hubs (FHs) have been emerging as a way to face these challenges of coordination of marketing functions and efficient distribution management of local foods [1, 3, 8].

In this paper, we aim to explore the role of ICTs in fostering the development of FHs in the establishment of local food networks. In particular, the paper will addresses the following research questions (RQs):

- RQ1: Does the adoption of ICTs support the rise of new collaborative networks within the "alternative" food supply chains?
- RQ2: How do the adopted ICTs tools enable collaboration and coordination among all the networked actors in the identified case studies?

The paper is organized as follows: the Sect. 2 introduces the theoretical background about Food Hubs initiatives, while in the Sects. 3 and 4 the two case studies are presented and discussed. In the final section, we propose our conclusions.

2 Food Hubs (FHs): Theoretical Background

The concept of a Food Hub is a recent addition in the literature on AFNs. Scholars and public institutions have worked to elaborate a comprehensive definition of FH: Morely et al. [11], Horrel et al. [12], Horst et al. [13] and USDA [14] focused their attention on the functional aspects of co-ordination, looking at FHs as an intermediary between many local producers and suppliers and customers, including institutions, food service firms, retail outlets, and consumers. All these authors specified that the main functions characterizing FHs are information management, aggregation, distribution, and marketing of source-identified food products. Blay-Palmer et al. [15], in their definition of FHs, highlighted the sustainability aspect of FHs, while other authors try to balance the functional aspects with the civic and sustainable ones. In their study Fisher et al. [16] stated: "Food hubs are, or intend to be, financially viable businesses that demonstrate a significant commitment to place through aggregation and marketing of regional food." In the same vein, Franklin et al. [17] and Franklin and Morgan [18] pointed out that community food hubs provide to local producers and consumers the coordination of activities such as sourcing, supply, and/or marketing and distribution of products. According to these authors, the primary goals of FHs are environmental protection goals, and the economic viability of local farmers. With social motivations such as community cohesion, social gain, healthy eating, and local food access, as secondary goals. With a similar perspective, Berti and Mulligan [3], in their definition of FHs, highlighted both their role as intermediary organization, and capacity to operate as "activator" and "animator" of a strategic network involving all the actors in the short food supply chain. In such a network, producers preserve their identity, their organizational independence and their strategies, but, at the same time, all the actors collaborate to achieve mutual convenience. Together they co-produce shared economic and socio-environmental values to be distributed within the network and positively affect the entire local community.

Scholars proposed different perspective in FHs' definition, as well as noting the variety of organizational structures, target customers, ownership and control, function and operation [10, 11, 13, 14]. Despite this diversity it is possible to observe a common agreement about the potential of FHs to overcome the distributional limitations of small-scale AFNs and to help initiatives to 'scale-up' and deliver benefits for local communities [1–3, 8, 14, 16, 19].

The main services provided by the FH organization to coordinate the activities of its networked partners and manage the goods and information flows are:

- Logistics. Aggregation (on-farm pick up and on-FH drop off), product storage, re-packaging for distribution (customer location delivery and/or delivery management at the FH's drop off points) and relative information management with order consolidation for each producer and customer order management;
- Marketing. Recruitment of producers and consumers, internal communication management, product identity and branding activities, as well as sales management;
- Community engagement. Communication with farmers and consumers to identify needs for the following season, collaboratively planning cropping. Organising social events to allow meetings and engender trust between farmers and consumers. Creating and promoting educational programmes and training events.

One of the main role played by Food Hubs is building an effective information flow and transparency among the actors adhering to this form of AFN [14].

The advancement of the ICTs and the rapid growth of e-business have offered the space for new business models that, in line with FHs' objectives, allow for novel ways to create, co-produce and distribute value. The adoption of ICTs and its support to the supply chain management represent a great opportunity to assist the operations of Food Hubs [6]. FHs can take advantage of services and functionalities that allow them to manage inventory and online catalogues, allowing consumers to place online orders and carry out payments, supported by order processing and logistic activities. ICTs enable FHs to establish connections between buyers and sellers and to share data among all the parties in the network. As Barham et al. stated, "it is not coincidental that the emergence of the regional food hub concept is occurring at a time when technology is increasingly accessible and portable" [14].

The overall online FHs' value proposition relies in reducing search, transaction and coordination costs for buyers and sellers adopting an online food hub model that has been defined by Horst et al. [13] as an "internet-based online directory and marketplace that fosters efficient connections between local and regional food producers and consumers"

3 Two Case Studies from the South West England

The case studies were two FHs initiatives both located in Gloucestershire, a predominantly rural County in the South West England. The two FHs are respectively Stroudco CIC and Dean Forest Food Hub Ltd. On February 2017 by the means of semi-structured interviews to FHs key members; we collected data on the FHs' structure, their processes, the volume of their trading activities and on how the adoption of the ICTs affected the operations and coordination management activities in both the case studies. The interviews were oriented to investigate the main actors, and processes, as well as the impact of the ICTs in terms of enabling a better information flow management both for decision-making and for operational processes.

3.1 Stroudco

The Stroudco Food Hub is a member-owned Community Interest Company (CIC) jointly controlled by all its producers and consumers members. It started its trading activities in 2009 in Stroud by launching its online food hub system. The town of Stroud has a population of 13,260 inhabitants (2011 census) and displays socio-economic characteristics typical of English semi-rural communities. The area is well known for its long established local food movement which includes one of the most popular farmers' market in the UK, as well as a community-supported agriculture (CSA) project and a co-operative allotment project of national importance [17]. In this context, in 2008, two local food activists set up a community-led FH. The Stroudco's value proposition was to provide, locally produced food to low-income households living in a specific area of Stroud who were not able to afford the products sold in the Stroud's farmers market. At the same time, the business model was oriented to give to local producers (located within 15 miles of Stroud), who could not be engaged in the other AFNs in Stroud, to access a local market at higher than wholesale prices. The aims were to build connection between local consumers and producers, to develop a more sustainable local food culture and resilient community. Central to the Stroudco were the adoption of a web-based ordering system, to manage supply and demand of local food, on fixed order cycle, combined with the use of a school hall, located in a deprived area, as the drop off point for producers and pick up point for consumers.

The initiative received a grant of approximately £70,000 for the development of FH's web-based platform and for the set-up costs.

To guarantee the economic sustainability of the initiative, the FH has adopted a revenue model based on two sources of income: consumer households pay a membership fee of either £2 per month or £1 per order, plus £2 if they choose for the home delivery service, and producers pay 8% of gross sales made through Stroudco.

In their first year of trading 8 producers and 20 consumers were engaged in the FH as members to run monthly trading activities. After few years, the marketing activities were oriented to recruit new members from across Stroud to reach a critical mass of orders. Moreover, the range of available products was broadened with the inclusion of non-local foods provided by a wholefood wholesaler, with a mark-up at 28% above wholesale. Stroudco also employed a manager to carry on the day-to-day running of the hub with the support of some volunteer. Currently, the number of Stroudco member has reached almost 500 consumers and 60 producers, with the number of collected orders ranging from 20 to 50 per week.

Central to Stroudco is an internet-based administration system. Stroudco started its activities adopting a self-designed system, developed as an open source project, free and easy to copy. On May 2016, the FH switched to a new platform named Open Food Network (OFN) UK, a software platform supporting food hubs management and operations, provided by the global not-for-profit foundation Open Food Foundation and customized by some of the FH's members. The new platform is enabling the food hub to manage efficiently their main processes and operations. It offers functionalities to the FH's suppliers, who are trained by the FH's members involved in the platform customization in managing their own description and contacts, as well as their catalogue by controlling products descriptions, prices, and their stocks. Consumers can join Stroudco and, through an online shop front, get information about producer, products, the full price breakdown, as well as order and paying. The platform offers to the FH's staff tools to set the order cycles, to add mark-ups and shipping fees, orders consolidation and procurement as well as order fulfilment. The platform also provides tools for Customer Relationships Management and for reporting. The Stroudco allows the direct communication between consumers and producers through a blog. Furthermore, through the web portal and the newsletter, Stroudco advertises the social events organized to foster the relationships and connections among its members.

3.2 Dean Forest Food Hub

The Dean Forest Food Hub is a workers' co-operative and a social enterprise. It started its operations on July 2013 thanks to the initiative of two of the eight key members who currently manage and control the FH. The project started without any founding grant, but with the support of Stroudco that helped by providing advice on the FH model and the Stroudco software. The software was then set up and customized by one of the founders who has a background in software engineering.

The area of Forest of Dean surrounds the second largest Crown Forest in England with 110 Km^2 of mixed woodland. It has not traditionally been an agricultural area and, in contrast to Stroud it is not characterized by the presence of many AFNs schemes and people in the area found difficult to access to fresh local produce. Spreads around the forest are a large number of un-connected market gardens, orchards, cheese makers, and meat producers. The objective of the Dean Forest Food Hub is to provide everyone in the Forest of Dean to access affordable, quality local food that is fair for the producer. The FH's value proposition is to provide a web-based platform representing a single place to source food from over 20 local producers, whose sustainability is checked by the FH's staff, in an easy and convenient way. The FH provides a network of 11 accessible pick-up points located around the forest. At the same time, the FH provide to producers a platform to access the local market in an efficient way aggregating orders coming from several consumers on a weekly order cycle and providing a single drop-off point. The model adopted by the FH is a low margin model in which producers set the sale price. The FH works to link farmers with each other, with farm tours for exchanging ideas on best practice, as well as to connect consumers and producers with social events like the "Forest Food Hunt". The FH also uses a forum and social medias to foster interaction among people engaged in the initiative.

The revenue model is based on the income provided by the margin of 10% on the sale price for the local produce and a mark-up of 40% for non-local products. In addition, the home delivery service entails a £2.50 charge.

In July 2013, the Dean Forest Food Hub started its trading activities with just one producer and a few consumers ordering 3-4 boxes per week, with volunteers running it. Now the number of producers has grown to 20, with 600 registered consumers and 3 people have been employed. The FH is collecting an average of 50 orders per week for an average value of £4,400 per week and these numbers are growing every years especially after the Dean Forest Food Festival held every autumn.

At operational level, similarly to the Stroudco FH, the Dean Forest Food Hub is opening and closing at a fixed time each week. Producers register to the online platform and get a producer agreement electronic survey to fill in. Then, they decide whether they prefer to be trained to manage their own page where they can describe their production methods, list their produce for sale with stock levels and prices, or if they prefer, allow the FH's staff to do that for them. Consumers can buy from the list of produce available up to three days before the food drop, as well as directly contact producers to ask any questions. FH's staff then process consumers' orders collected and registered through the web system and each producer receives its own order. In this phase, FH's staff communicates with producers located close to one another and involved in the same order to facilitate a joint delivery to the FH's drop-off point. Producers have two days to deliver their products to the drop-off point provided by the producer who was the first to be engaged in the FH initiative. Then a team of roughly 30 volunteers and the FH's staff pack everything into the right boxes according to the picking lists generated by the software. When all the boxes are ready, the FH's staff, according to a shipment roster, distribute them to the network of pick-up points, or, if consumers opted for the service, they provide home delivery. All the sales data are stored and every season analysed by the FH's staff, identify any gaps in supply or demand, to carry out with produces a pre-season crop planning for following season.

4 Discussion

This study let us to positively confirm that ICTs represent a useful tool for supporting sustainability initiatives within local food supply chains supporting the rise of new business models such as the online FHs adopted by the initiatives we investigated (RQ1). The adoption of online FH models helped FHs to reduce their operational costs. We observed that the web platforms adopted by the two case studies, with different levels of sophistication, allowed the FH initiatives to be more efficient as well as automating and standardising processes, supporting volunteers whose help in carrying out FHs activities. The adoption of ICTs enabled the two FHs to face the challenges imposed by the complexity of activities typical of FHs and including the management of seasonality and perishability of products, the inconsistency and unpredictability of supply, working with multiple suppliers and having multiple incoming and outgoing logistics (RQ2). With the timely provision of salient information, as in the case of the Dean Forest Food Hub, networked actors are enabled to optimize their logistical activities. In terms of social benefits, ICT solutions help foster better relations between consumers and producers. By improving the flows of information, good practices are shared and the isolation of small business overcome. While forums and social media foster online communities linking consumers to one another and to producers.

5 Conclusions

From the case studies above, we make the following observations:

Firstly, this type of FH is often dependent on donations, grant funding and voluntary work, which limits the model's overall resilience. ICTs could play an important role in lowering costs and making it easier to establish a FH. Simultaneously, leveraging on their capacity to aggregate local productions, the FHs could differentiate their business model by wholesaling food to institutional buyers such as schools, in addition to retailing food to households. In this case, the adoption of an online auction tool allowing buyers to get information to attain the produce they desire could be beneficial.

Second, confirming Matson & Thayer's studies [7], FH seem to be a successful business model when it addresses the needs of local food deserts. In the Dean Forest Food Hub, consumers perceive the FH as the most convenient way to source local fresh food, in the absence of other AFNs, and the initiative has more opportunities. While the Stroudco FH showed some limits in the scaling up of the initiative that can be due to the presence of other popular AFNs in Stroud. The argument could be made that there is currently a degree of saturation in the alternative food market of the region and people prefer to be engaged in face-to-face interactions occurring in other forms of AFNs.

The study is limited by the lack of data on how consumers and producers perceive online FHs and a deeper analysis of what are the main factors limiting the scaling up of such initiatives. Confronting this question, observed by others in initiatives in UK, and in other countries, would help us to investigate if the online FH model is sustainable and if people could rely on it as the sole source of their food.

This paper is an exploratory study aimed to deepen the knowledge on FHs and the role ICTs play in fostering the rise of new forms of AFNs, we are conducting further research aimed at overcoming limits of the present work as well as to explore the potential of mobile applications in the context of local food. These technologies might offer the exchange of contextualized knowledge, which might overcome limits of the current model with sporadic direct meetings, and persuade more people in to choose the online FH, thus helping the initiatives to scale up.

Acknowledgments. A Marie Skłodowska-Curie IF of the EU's Horizon 2020 program, SOFIA (G.A. 702884), has supported this work. This paper only reflects the authors' views and funding agencies are not liable for any use that may be made of the information contained herein.

References

1. Cleveland, D., Müller, N., Tranovich, A., Hinson, K.: Local food hubs for alternative food systems: a case study from Santa Barbara County, California. J. Rural Stud. **35**, 26–36 (2014)
2. Jablonski, B., Schmit, T., Kay, D.: Assessing the economic impacts of food hubs on regional economies: a framework that includes opportunity cost. Agric. Res. Econ. Rev. **45**(01), 143–172 (2016)
3. Berti, G., Mulligan, C.: Competitiveness of small farms and innovative food supply chains: the role of food hubs in creating sustainable regional and local food systems. Sustainability **8**, 616 (2016)
4. Volpentesta, A., Ammirato, S., Della Gala, M.: Classifying short agrifood supply chains under a knowledge and social learning perspective. Rural Soc. **22**(3), 217–229 (2013)
5. Stroink, M., Nelson, C.: Complexity and food hubs: five case studies from Northern Ontario. Local Environ. **18**(5), 620–635 (2013)
6. Kurnia, S., Hill, S., Rahim, M., Larsen, K., Braun, P., Samson, D.: Open food network: the role of ICT to support regional food supply chains in Australia. In: 26th Australasian Conference on Information Systems, Adelaide, Australia (2015)
7. Matson, J., Thayer, J.: The role of food hubs in food supply chains. J. Agric. Food Syst. Commun. Devel. **3**(4), 43–47 (2016)
8. Krejci, C., Stone, R., Dorneich, M., Gilbert, S.: Analysis of food hub commerce and participation using agent-based modeling: integrating financial and social drivers. Hum. Factors **58**(1), 58–79 (2016)
9. Renting, H., Marsden, T., Banks, J.: Understanding alternative food network: exploring the role of short food supply chains in rural development. Environ. Plann. A **35**, 393–411 (2003)
10. Volpentesta, Antonio P., Ammirato, S.: A collaborative network model for agrifood transactions on regional base. In: Lytras, Miltiadis D., Ordonez de Pablos, P., Ziderman, A., Roulstone, A., Maurer, H., Imber, Jonathan B. (eds.) WSKS 2010. CCIS, vol. 112, pp. 319–325. Springer, Heidelberg (2010). doi:10.1007/978-3-642-16324-1_34
11. Morley, A., Morgan, S., Morgan, K.: Food Hubs: The 'Missing Middle' of the Local Food Infrastructure? Cardiff, Wales (2008)
12. Horrell, C., Jones, S., Natelson, S., Williams, K.: An Investigation into the Workings of Small Scale Food Hubs., London (2009)
13. Horst, M., Ringstrom, E., Tyman, S., Ward, M., Werner, V., Born, B.: Toward a more expansive understanding of food hubs. J. Agric. Food Syst. Commun. Dev. **2**(1), 209–225 (2011)
14. Barham, J., Tropp, D., Enterline, K., Farbman, J., Fisk, J., Kiraly, S.: Regional food hub resource guide (No. 145227), Washington, DC (2012)
15. Blay-Palmer, A., Landman, K., Knezevic, I., Hayhurst, R.: Constructing resilient, transformative communities through sustainable "food hubs". Local Environ. Int. J. Justice Sustain. **18**(5), 521–528 (2013)
16. Fischer, M., Pirog, R., Hamm, M.: Food hubs: definitions, expectations, and realities. J. Hunger Environ. Nutr. **10**(1), 92–99 (2015)
17. Franklin, A., Newton, J., McEntee, J.: Moving beyond the alternative: sustainable communities, rural resilience and the mainstreaming of local food. Local Environ. **16**(8), 771–788 (2011)
18. Franklin, A., Morgan, S.: Exploring the new rural-urban interface: Community food practice, land access and farmer entrepreneurialism. In: Sustainable Food Systems, pp. 166–185. Routledge, London (2014)
19. LeBlanc, J., Conner, D., McRae, G., Darby, H.: Building resilience in nonprofit food hubs. J. Agric. Food Syst. Commun. Dev. **4**(3), 1–15 (2014)

Conceptual Framework for Managing Uncertainty in a Collaborative Agri-Food Supply Chain Context

Ana Esteso, M.M.E. Alemany(✉), and Angel Ortiz

Research Centre on Production Management and Engineering (CIGIP), Universitat Politècnica de València, Camino de Vera S/N, 46002 València, Spain
aneslva@doctor.upv.es, {mareva, aortiz}@cigip.upv.es

Abstract. Agri-food supply chains are subjected to many sources of uncertainty. If these uncertainties are not managed properly, they can have a negative impact on the agri-food supply chain (AFSC) performance, its customers, and the environment. In this sense, collaboration is proposed as a possible solution to reduce it. For that, a conceptual framework (CF) for managing uncertainty in a collaborative context is proposed. In this context, this paper seeks to answer the following research questions: What are the existing uncertainty sources in the AFSCs? Can collaboration be used to reduce the uncertainty of AFSCs? Which elements can integrate a CF for managing uncertainty in a collaborative AFSC? The CF proposal is applied to the weather source of uncertainty in order to show its applicability.

Keywords: Agri-food supply chains · Collaboration · Uncertainty · Conceptual framework

1 Introduction

The term "agri-food supply chain" (AFSC) has been defined as a set of activities necessary to bring agricultural products "from the farm to the fork" [1–4]. Therefore, both vegetable and animal-based products are produced in and distributed by AFSCs [5].

AFSCs are subjected to many sources of uncertainty. If these sources of uncertainty are not managed properly, not only the AFSC performance may be negatively affected but also the customers service levels and the environment would be also affected. In this sense, collaboration is proposed as a possible solution to reduce this negative impact. For that, a conceptual framework (CF) for managing uncertainty in a collaborative context is proposed. In this context, this paper seeks to answer the research questions (RQ):

RQ1. What are the existing sources of uncertainty in the AFSCs?
RQ2. Can collaboration be used to reduce the uncertainty of AFSCs?
RQ3. Which elements can integrate a CF for managing uncertainty in a collaborative AFSC?

L.M. Camarinha-Matos et al. (Eds.): PRO-VE 2017, IFIP AICT 506, pp. 715–724, 2017.
DOI: 10.1007/978-3-319-65151-4_64

Since horticulture sector has received the least attention in the literature and the production processes of meat and horticulture sectors are extremely different, this paper focuses on the crop-based AFSCs.

Therefore, the main contributions of this paper are the identification of the existing sources of uncertainty in crop-based AFSC, and the proposal of a CF for reducing these uncertainties through the collaboration of the AFSC members. For that, literature search related to collaboration in AFSC is carried out within well-known databases, such as Springer, Elsevier, and many others. To the best of our knowledge there are few papers dealing the collaboration as a tool for reducing uncertainty in AFSCs and, some authors have stated that more research on supply chain collaboration is needed in order to cope uncertainty in the agricultural sector [2, 6].

The remainder of this paper is organized as follows. In Sect. 2, the existing sources of uncertainty in crop-based AFSC are detailed. A reflection of the impact of collaboration over these uncertainties is performed in Sect. 3. As a result, the CF for managing uncertainty in a collaborative AFSC context is proposed in Sect. 4. Finally, conclusions are exposed in the last section.

2 Crop-Based AFSC Sources of Uncertainty

Crop-based AFSCs are subjected to many sources of uncertainty which are mainly related to inherent characteristics of the agri-food sector. If these sources of uncertainty are not managed properly, they can have a negative impact on the AFSC performance, its customers, and the environment. However, if the level of uncertainty is reduced, the supply chain performance will be improved. Therefore, the aim of this section is to answer the Research Question: What are the existing sources of uncertainty in the AFSCs?

Supply chains uncertainty commonly refers to situations in which decision-makers have not enough information about objectives to make decisions; have a vague idea of the supply chain and/or its environment; are not able to predict the impact of decisions on supply chain's performance; or lacks effective control actions [7, 8].

According to [9], we are in the realm of decision making under uncertainty if it is ignored the probability of occurrence of the possible specific outcomes. In addition, when making a decision under uncertainty, the decision maker may or may not know the different outcomes that can occur [10].

This paper proposed a CF (Fig. 1) for the AFSC sources of uncertainty classification. This framework has been based on the CF in [11] where the SC uncertainties are divided into supply, demand, process and planning & control uncertainties. This classification has been extended by adding the sources of uncertainty related to products and to environment. For the purpose of this paper, although the sources of uncertainty are interrelated, we consider it more appropriate to group them into different categories to which they make reference. The categories proposed for the crop-based AFSC sources of uncertainty are product, process, market and, environment.

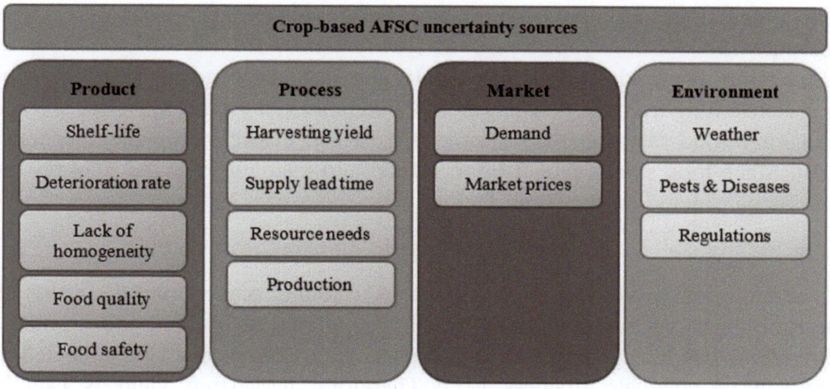

Fig. 1. Conceptual framework for the uncertainty sources of crop-based AFSCs

The identified sources of uncertainty related to crop-based AFSC products are:

- Uncertainty on shelf-life. The product shelf-life is the time during which the product losses its tacit initial characteristics becoming a non-value item for customers [12]. Then, the product shelf-life and physical state are not necessarily interrelated since many products deteriorate after the end of their shelf-life. Hence, product shelf-life may reflect its marketable life [13]. As the shelf-life of a product is the period of time during which quality losses do not exceed a tolerated level, the product's time and temperature history must be known; if not, the shelf-life is uncertain [14].
- Uncertainty on deterioration. Deterioration of products is the process where items decay, get damaged or spoiled, being impossible to use them for their original purpose [15]. It can be classified as age-dependent on-going deterioration and age-independent on-going deterioration [13]. Agri-food products are goods subject to age-dependent on-going deterioration. Most authors talk about constant or probabilistic deterioration rates, however, it can be considered as uncertain as the quantity and quality deterioration over time can be unknown.
- Uncertainty on lack of homogeneity of products. Agri-food sector is characterized by the lack of homogeneity of the product, so the products obtained after harvesting differ in some attributes (maturity, color, bacterial level, various size and weights of items…) that are relevant for customers because they require to be served with homogeneous units of the same product [16]. Correct handling of the lack of homogeneity in the product and its inherent uncertainty is important to reduce and avoid inefficiencies of the supply chain and improve customer service level [16].
- Uncertainty on food quality. Food quality is the combination of food features that establishes the customer satisfaction and compliance to legal standards [17]. It usually refers not only to the physical properties of food products, but also to the customer perception of it [18]. Product quality is characterized by properties such as texture, taste, flavor, smell, color, presence of pathogens, toxins or hormones… [17–19]. Some of these attributes can be easy to measure while others are subject to customer's perception, making its assessment very challenging (e.g., taste) [19].

Then, there is uncertainty in food quality as it is subjective so it cannot be certainly measured.

- Uncertainty on food safety. Food safety generally refers to the prevention of illnesses resulting from the consumption of contaminated food [18]. There is a need to guarantee food safety as the customer's trust and market acceptance depend on it [20]. Since food safety cannot be measured and guaranteed in the final product, it can be considered an uncertain factor.

The uncertainty sources related to crop-based AFSC processes are:

- Uncertainty on harvesting yield. The crops' ripening process and the capability of performing harvesting operations are highly influenced by land and weather conditions, so harvesting yield worsens if part of the crops cannot be collected at the moment of adequate ripeness [21]. Therefore, harvesting yield is usually an uncertain factor in terms of product quantity, quality and harvesting time. This is related to the uncertainty in supply of raw material as the SC stage after harvesting will not know the quantity, quality and time of the supply until it is received.
- Uncertainty on supply lead time. The lead time is the time taken from the beginning of a process to its end. AFSCs are characterized by their long supply lead times as many crops spend from six to nine months since their planting until their harvesting [1, 21]. Supply lead time can be considered an uncertain factor as the needed time for crops to grow is generally long, seasonal and, weather and yield dependent [22].
- Uncertainty on resource needs. Resources needed for harvesting, which can be established by the number, capacity and productivity of machines and laborers, are limited [21]. Given the uncertainty on the harvesting quantity, the resource needs cannot be known until the harvest is done.
- Uncertainty on production. Production depends on the raw materials received, as their quantity, quality and characteristics are not known a priori. This uncertainty provokes the need of having alternative recipes in order to produce the same final product [5, 11].

The uncertainty sources related to crop-based AFSC markets are:

- Uncertainty on demand. Demand of agri-food products is not only related to product and quantity, but also to the quality and safety requirements of the customer and factors such as remaining shelf-life of the product. Demand uncertainty reflects the uncertainty of customer demand for a product [23]. Natural causes as seasonality and weather as well as promotional activities can cause variability in customer demand, creating uncertainty [1].
- Demand can be dependent of the remaining shelf-life of products, inventory level, time, market trends or price; demand can follow a distribution function or it can be completely unknown [15].
- Uncertainty on market prices. Market prices are volatile and keep changing across the day [24]. The variability of prices in the different stages of supply chains are caused by dynamic factors such as the price of substitute products, inflation, production costs, import, export, customer demands, seasonality, product availability and the supply-demand balance [25].

The uncertainty sources related to crop-based AFSC environment are:

- Uncertainty on weather and land conditions. Weather conditions, such as temperature and precipitation, mainly affect the harvesting yield and activity. The harvesting process is complex as it dispose of limited resources and, it gets even more complex when considering the uncertainty related to weather conditions [21]. Weather and land conditions cannot be known with certainty.
- Uncertainty on pests and diseases. Agri-food products can be contaminated by pests and biotic hazards such as bacteria, viruses and other emerging pathogens [26]. Yield losses can be reduced by protecting the crops from various diseases with pesticides [27]. Pest and disease infestations are random factors that could be controlled by management [28].
- Uncertainty on regulations. The regulatory framework of the agri-food sector, comprised by public and private regulations dealing with food quality and safety, set the diverse requirements for tracking and tracing capabilities [20]. There is uncertainty on the appearance of new, more stringent, regulations.

It is worth mentioning that different relationships exist among the sources of uncertainty described. For instance, uncertainty on weather implicitly originates uncertainty in harvesting yields.

3 Impact of Collaboration on Crop-Based AFSC

Supply chains have been defined as goal-oriented networks in which their partners intensively collaborate with each other towards a common goal [29]. Then, the collaboration on supply chain means that two or more chain members actively and jointly work (spanning the organizations boundaries) for fulfilling and satisfying consumers' needs [2]. With collaboration, stakeholders are able to share their assets and capabilities so they can reduce the uncertainty, share the risk and cost, and serve customers at the right time, quantity, and quality without disregarding the interest of other stakeholders [30].

Collaboration is a powerful tool to improve the AFSCs performance. However, its implementation is complex as existing barriers potentially deteriorate collaboration among companies, e.g. the incompatibility of information exchange systems, the big quantity of enterprises making up a supply chain or the lack of trust between the parties. Despite this, collaboration is becoming more a necessity than an option [2].

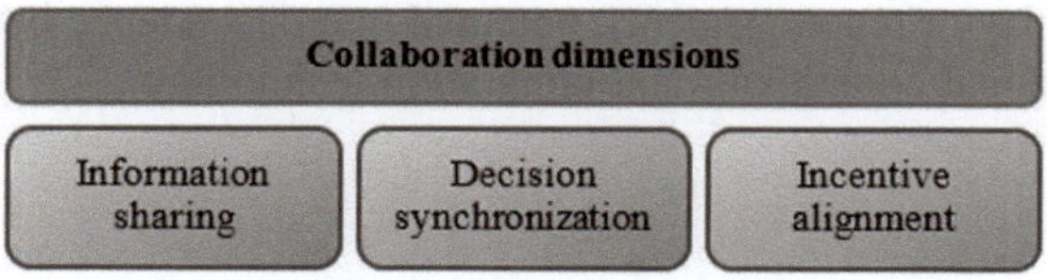

Fig. 2. Collaboration dimensions

The collaboration concept can be categorized into three interrelated dimensions (Fig. 2): information sharing, decision synchronization, and incentive alignment [31].

These three dimensions represent different levels of collaboration so that for changing from a level of collaboration to a superior one it is necessary to ensure the proper functioning of the previous collaborative levels. Different benefits and risks of collaboration can exist depending on the Supply Chain Activities [2]. According to these authors [30], the information sharing consists in capturing and disseminating timely information that is relevant for decision makers when planning and controlling supply chain operations; the decision synchronization consists in making planning and operational decisions jointly; and, the incentive alignment consists of the degree of sharing costs, risks and benefits between supply chain members.

Then, is it needed the collaboration to reduce the uncertainty on AFSCs? Supply chain collaboration can be necessary for various reasons. Collaboration is needed in AFSC for minimizing its costs, increasing the profits, ensuring the quality, and gaining customers trust [30]. Collaboration is also needed in the agri-food sector as AFSC are competing against other AFSC and single companies are not competing with each other anymore [32]. Another reason for collaborating in AFSC is given by the increased public pressure for transparency, traceability and "due diligence" throughout the AFSC due to the combination of social concern about food safety and the recent food crises [2]. These crises have emphasized the close interdependencies between AFSC actors and their need of cooperation in order to be a competitive AFSC and to ensure the meet of the customers' requirements related to food quality and safety [20].

However, an additional reason for applying collaboration in AFSC is the huge amount of sources of uncertainty that impact over its performance and which are mainly generated by the lack of information through the AFSC. Uncertainty can be reduced by supply chain collaboration [30, 32]. Sharing information reduces uncertainty as decision-makers dispose reliable data to conduct the decision making process (e.g. if the AFSC members share information about the traceability of the product, the food safety of the product would be guaranteed). Making joint decisions reduces uncertainty as decision-makers of two AFSC stages have all the information to make more appropriate decisions for both parts (e.g. farmers and producers decide jointly when to harvest, then the used capacities of both stakeholders can be optimized). The incentive alignment reduces uncertainty as the motivation to obtain maximum benefits make the stakeholders share high quality information (e.g. stakeholders could establish an equitable distribution of profits between them in order to reduce the share of profits).

Collaboration not only provide benefits, but also risks. The main risks in collaboration are [2]: the risk of failure (loss of the investment made, loss of time, and business plans delay or renouncement); potential interdependence between companies; increasing operational complexity and integration technology.

4 Conceptual Framework for Uncertainty Management Through Collaboration in AFSCs

In this section a conceptual framework (CF) to manage the inherent uncertainty sources of AFSCs through collaboration is proposed. Then, this CF tries to give and answer to the last research question: What elements can be considered for managing uncertainty by means collaboration in AFSC? The proposed elements for this CF are grouped into four blocks for AFSCs (Fig. 3): Sources of uncertainty, Management, Collaboration and Collaboration Impact. In the following, each element is described.

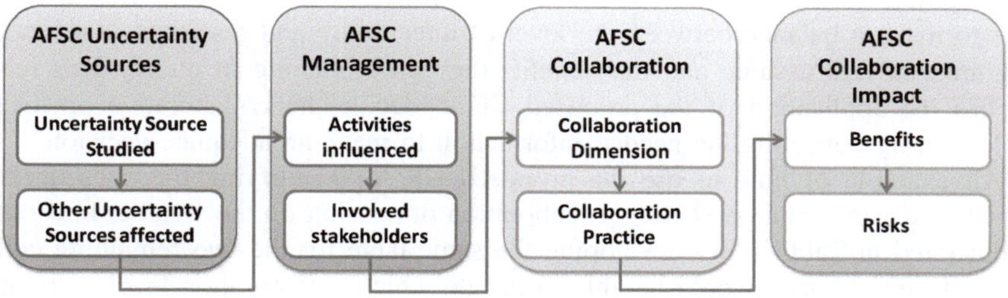

Fig. 3. Conceptual framework for managing uncertainty in a collaborative AFSC context

- AFSC Uncertainty Sources: in this block, the sources of uncertainty to be studied in the CF is indicated and the uncertainty sources affected by the studied one are identified.
  - Sources of uncertainty studied: the source of uncertainty to be managed is selected from the CF for the sources of uncertainty of crop-based AFSCs (Sect. 2).
  - Other Uncertainty Sources affected: Because different sources of uncertainty are not independent, the strongest relationship between the uncertainties studied and the other ones should be identified.
- AFSC Management: in this block, the activities and stakeholders influenced by the studied sources of uncertainty are identified.
  - Management activities influenced by the sources of uncertainty selected and the others affected by it should be determined.
  - Involved stakeholders related to the above activities should be determined with the aim of identifying the possible AFSC members for collaboration: farmers, processors, distributors, retailers and other stakeholders (NGO's, government…) [5].
- AFSC Collaboration: in this block, the collaboration dimensions to be employed to reduce the studied sources of uncertainty and their related practices are identified.
  - Collaboration dimension: the different collaboration dimensions (information sharing, decision synchronization, and incentive alignment) are detailed.
  - Collaboration practices: different collaboration practices can be adopted in order to establish the collaboration between stakeholders. Each collaboration practice will have a different impact on the AFSC.

- Impact on AFSC: the benefits and risks produced by the collaboration practice proposed are identified. For each collaboration practice could be made qualitatively and/or quantitatively:
  - Benefits of each collaboration practice should be detailed (assessed) on the AFSC characteristics and sources of uncertainty.
  - Risks for each collaboration practice should also be taken into account when analyzing the possible collaboration practice to be implemented.

When making the decision of which collaboration dimension to implement for reducing an uncertainty, the CF can be applied to collect information of the benefits, risks and other issues related to each collaboration practice. Although the highest collaboration level could offer more benefits in reducing uncertainty, decision-makers have to make a balance between the level of uncertainty and resources consumption they are ready to assume and the benefits they are obtaining in return. This reason justifies the application of the proposed CF to decide the collaborative practice to implement by collecting the needed information to make an adequate decision.

An example of how to use the proposed CF for identifying the consequences/ impact of the information sharing collaboration dimension on the weather uncertainty is illustrated in Table 1. By developing the same table for the two remaining collaboration levels the user would be able to decide which collaboration level is the most appropriate to his case. The objective of this example is not to show the whole decision process, but to illustrate the way to use the CF.

Table 1. Example for the conceptual framework completion.

CF Elements	Application
Uncertainty source studied	Weather
Other uncertainty sources affected	Harvesting yield, food quality and indirect effects related with changes in the distribution of pests and diseases
Activities influenced	Planning of harvesting operations (planting and harvesting scheduling, effective resource management among competing crops), Procurement
Involved stakeholders	Seed suppliers, Pesticides suppliers, Farmers and producers
Collaboration dimension	Information sharing
Collaboration practice	Sharing information among involved stakeholders on rainfall, water level in soil, use of pesticides and fertilizers and driving lanes of farm machines
Benefits	Predict the harvesting yield takes an input to multiple process, Optimize the use of pesticides, fertilizers and water
Risks	Technological risks for the necessity of sensors and properly information technologies

5 Conclusions

This paper has identified the existing sources of uncertainty in crop-based AFSC. A CF is proposed where these uncertainties are classified into product, process, market and environment characteristics. If these uncertainties are not managed properly, they can have a negative impact on the AFSC performance. As a solution, collaboration has been proposed as a possible solution to minimize this impact. To conclude, a CF to manage uncertainty in a collaborative AFSC context is designed. After completing this CF, it could be used by researchers and practitioners to determine the best way to reduce the studied uncertainty sources that affect their supply chains.

Acknowledgments. The first author acknowledges the partial support of the Program of Formation of University Professors of the Spanish Ministry of Education, Culture, and Sport (FPU15/03595). The other authors acknowledge the partial support of the Project 691249, RUC-APS: Enhancing and implementing Knowledge based ICT solutions within high Risk and Uncertain Conditions for Agriculture Production Systems, funded by the EU under its funding scheme H2020-MSCA-RISE-2015.

References

1. Taylor, D.H., Fearne, A.: Towards a framework for improvement in the management of demand in agri-food supply chains. Supply Chain Manag. Int. J. **11**, 379–384 (2006)
2. Matopoulos, A., Vlachopoulou, M., Manthou, V., Manos, B.: A conceptual framework for supply chain collaboration: empirical evidence from the agri-food industry. Supply Chain Manag. Int. J. **12**, 177–186 (2007)
3. Ahumada, O., Villalobos, J.R.: Application of planning models in the agri-food supply chain: a review. Eur. J. Oper. Res. **196**, 1–20 (2009)
4. Tsolakis, N.K., Keramydas, C.A., Toka, A.K., Aidonis, D.A., Iakovou, E.T.: Agrifood supply chain management: a comprehensive hierarchical decision-making framework and a critical taxonomy. Biosyst. Eng. **120**, 47–64 (2014)
5. van der Vorst, J.G., Da Silva, C.A., Trienekens, J.H.: Agro-industrial supply chain management: Concepts and applications. FAO (2007)
6. Borodin, V., Bourtembourg, J., Hnaien, F., Kabadie, N.: Handling uncertainty in agricultural supply chain management: a state of the art. Eur. J. Oper. Res. **254**, 348–359 (2016)
7. van der Vorst, J.G.A.J., Beulens, A.J.M.: Identifying sources of uncertainty to generate supply chain redesign strategies. Int. J. Phys. Distrib. Logist. Manag. **32**, 409–430 (2000)
8. Klosa, E.: A concept of models for supply chain speculative risk analysis and management. J. Econ. Manag. **12**, 45–59 (2013)
9. Samson, S., Reneke, J.A., Wiecek, M.M.: A review of different perspectices on uncertainty and risk and an alternative modeling paradigm. Reliab. Eng. Syst. Saf. **94**, 558–567 (2009)
10. Backus, G.B.C., Eidman, V.R., Dijkhuizen, A.A.: Farm decision making under risk and uncertainty. Neth. J. Agric. Sci. **45**, 307–328 (1997)
11. van der Vorst, J.G.: Effective food supply chains; Generating, modelling and evaluating supply chain scenarios. (2000)
12. Amorim, P., Günther, H.O., Almada-Lobo, B.: Multi-objective integrated production and distribution planning of perishable products. Int. J. Prod. Econ. **138**, 89–101 (2012)
13. Amorim, P., Meyr, H., Almeder, C., Almada-Lobo, B.: Managing perishability in production-distribution planning: a discussion and review. Flex. Serv. Manuf. **25**, 389–413 (2013)

14. Costa, C., Antonucci, F., Pallottino, F., Aguzzi, J., Sarria, D., Menesatti, P.: A review on agri-food supply chain traceability by means of RFID technology. Food Bioprocess Technol. **6**, 353–366 (2013)
15. Pahl, J., Voss, S.: Integrating deterioration and lifetime constraints in production and supply chain planning: a survey. Eur. J. Oper. Res. **238**, 654–674 (2014)
16. Grillo, H., Alemany, M.M.E., Ortiz, A.: A review of Mathematical models for supporting the order promising process under Lack of Homogeneity in product and other sources of uncertainty. Comput. Ind. Eng. **91**, 239–261 (2016)
17. Zwietering, M.H., van't Riet, K.: Modelling of the quality of food: optimization of a cooling chain. In: Management Studies and the Agri-business: Management of Agri-chains, Wageningen, The Netherlands, pp. 108–117 (1994)
18. Akkerman, R., Farahani, P., Grunow, M.: Quality, safety and sustainability in food distribution: a review of quantitative operations management approaches and challenges. Spectrum **32**, 863–904 (2010)
19. Apaiah, R.K., Hendrix, E.M.T., Meerdink, G., Linnemann, A.R.: Qualitative methodology for efficient food chain design. Trends Food Sci. Technol. **16**, 204–214 (2005)
20. Lehmann, R.J., Reiche, R., Schiefer, G.: Future internet and the agri-food sector: State-of-the-art in literature and research. Comput. Electron. Agric. **89**, 158–174 (2012)
21. Kusumastuti, R.D., van Donk, D.P., Teunter, R.: Crop-related harvesting and processing planning: a review. Int. J. Prod. Econ. **174**, 76–92 (2016)
22. Dreyer, H.C., Strandhagen, J.O., Hvolby, H.H., Romsdal, A., Alfnes, E.: Supply chain strategies for speciality foods: a Norwegian case study. Prod. Plan. Control **27**, 878–893 (2016)
23. Baghalian, A., Rezapour, S., Farahani, R.Z.: Robust supply chain network design with service level against disruptions and demand uncertainties: a real-life case. Eur. J. Oper. Res. **227**, 199–215 (2013)
24. Aggarwal, S., Srivastava, M.K.: Towards a grounded view of collaboration in Indian agri-food supply chains: a qualitative investigation. Br. Food J. **115**, 1085–1106 (2016)
25. Teimoury, E., Nedaei, H., Ansari, S., Sabbaghi, M.: A multi-objective analysis for import quota policy making in a perishable fruit and vegetable supply chain: a system dynamics approach. Comput. Electron. Agric. **93**, 37–45 (2013)
26. Opara, L.U.: Traceability in agriculture and food supply chain: a review of basic concepts, technological implications, and future prospects. J. Food Agric. Environ. **1**, 101–106 (2003)
27. Kruize, J.W., Wolfert, S., Goense, D., Scholten, H., Beulens, A., Veenstra, T.: Integrating ICT applications for farm business collaboration processes using FI Space. In: 2014 Annual SRII Global Conference, pp. 232–240. IEEE (2014)
28. Oriade, C.A., Dillon, C.R.: Developments in biophysical and bioeconomic simulation of agricultural systems: a review. Agric. Econ. **17**, 45–58 (1997)
29. Camarinha-Matos, L.M., Afsarmanesh, H.: Collaborative networks: value creation in a knowledge society. In: Wang, Kesheng, Kovacs, G.L., Wozny, Michael, Fang, Minglun (eds.) PROLAMAT 2006. IIFIP, vol. 207, pp. 26–40. Springer, Boston, MA (2006). doi:10.1007/0-387-34403-9_4
30. Prima Dania, W.A., Xing, K., Amer, Y.: Collaboration and sustainable agri-food supply chain: a literature review. MATEC Web Conf. **58** (2016)
31. Simatupang, T.M., Sridharan, R.: The collaborative index: a measure for supply chain collaboration. Int. J. Phys. Distrib. Logist. Manag. **35**, 44–62 (2005)
32. Fischer, C., Hartmann, M., Reynolds, N., Leat, P., Revoredo-Giha, C., Henchion, M., Albisu, L.M., Gracia, A.: Factors influencing contractual choice and sustainable relationships in European agri-food supply chains. Eur. Rev. Agric. Econ. **36**, 541–569 (2009)

Intelligent Food Information Provision to Consumers in an Internet of Food Era

Antonio Palmiro Volpentesta, Alberto Michele Felicetti(✉), and Salvatore Ammirato

Department of Mechanical, Energy and Management Engineering, University of Calabria, 87036 Arcavacata di Rende (CS), Italy
{antonio.volpentesta,alberto.felicetti, salvatore.ammirato}@unical.it

Abstract. Food information is a crucial tool for facilitating consumers in decision-making activities related to their consumption process. Recent advances in "Internet of food" technologies (such as food sensors, cloud computing, food data analysis, and mobile app technologies) makes possible to conceive new consumer information platforms. The rationale is to empower consumers by letting them get more relevant food information than they usually obtain through on-product labeling, mass media or other traditional channels. In this paper, we envisage a new generation of food information provision services, called intelligent food services (IFSs), which would be responsive to consumer's expectations and information needs. We outline IFS structure and main features as well as constitutive elements of user-IFS interaction context. Particularly, we focus on food-in-context awareness capability and we discuss its influence on consumer and IFS behaviors.

Keywords: Intelligent food services · Internet of food · Food-in-context awareness · Food information provision

1 Introduction

Food consumer behavior has changed substantially over the past decades. The contemporary food consumer, particularly the European consumer, has become more critical and outspoken, as he/she may be concerned with many heterogeneous attributes of food products. Along with, he/she demands and expects to get more relevant, accurate and reliable information necessary for his/her food decision making or learning.

These information needs may regard many heterogeneous elements pertaining to wellbeing, health, convenience, environmental, social, cultural, ethical and political concerns as consumers' choices are driven by many different motivations related to enjoyment (e.g. sensory quality, conviviality), health (e.g. diabetes, allergies, obesity), religion (e.g. halal, kosher), environment safeguarding or other special lifestyle (e.g. organic, vegetarian, no genetically modified foods). Recent research has shown that: (a) consumers who are environmental conscious and ethically concerned, give high value to food information relating to environmental and social issues [1]; (b) consumers who

L.M. Camarinha-Matos et al. (Eds.): PRO-VE 2017, IFIP AICT 506, pp. 725–736, 2017.
DOI: 10.1007/978-3-319-65151-4_65

want to make healthful food choices are more interested in information about food nutrition attributes, food origin and technological conditions under which the food has been produced and processed [2]; (c) as a reaction to frequent insertion of fraudulent, adulterated, misrepresented, and mislabeled food products into retail-to-consumer portion of food chains, many consumers strive for more and reliable information that guarantees the authenticity of their foods [3].

The challenge of food information management is to deliver the information that enables consumers to make appropriate choices according to their own individual objectives as they are involved in food consumption activities (planning, purchasing, preparation/cooking, eating and disposal/tidy-up). An effective and efficient food information service should deliver the right information to the right people, at the right time, and at the right place.

This challenge is particularly complex as it could require to meet a broad range of alternative information needs that are largely driven by the context in which food consumers make their decisions. This context may include many different entities (such as consumer, food, artifacts, and environment) and their attributes (such as identity, location, time, and activity currently involved in) depending on the situation they are relevant to.

Services that deliver massive and generic food information have a limited chance of success since they carry high search costs for the consumer and can hamper the ability to detect and correctly identify information that is needed in his/her decision or learning process [4, 5]. Employment of conventional channels (e.g., store shelf and package labels) allows neither to retrieve actionable information from sources that are appropriate for the current consumer's situation, nor, more in general, to provide personalized food information.

Today's consumers have access to a wealth of mobile app-based services that provide them with food information (food traceability, nutrition advices, recipes and purchasing support). However, the information provision of these services is neither contextualized nor consumer-centered. Other than the capacity to adapt to consumers' mobility, it does not seem much different from usual food information provision through conventional media or Web sites [6, 7].

A promising channel could be represented by a new generation of food information services which would empower consumers to have control over their own food as well as would be responsive to their contextualized expectations and information needs. These services could be based on the exploitation of recent advances of "Internet of food" technologies (such as food sensors, cloud computing, food data analysis, and mobile app technologies). The entry in the consumer market of some smart food applications and devices are clear signals in this direction: automated "food scanner" or "food sniffer" for the biomolecular food analysis, mobile apps that use camera photos for the quantification of food volume/weight/portion size or for the assessment of food quality, smart digital kitchen scale apps, intelligent package for food traceability or for improvement of food safety, and many others. Although these technology tools focus on specific functionalities and their data/information exchange with other systems is limited, they are at the cutting edge of current food information technology and give some clues about future food information services to consumers.

In this paper we envisage these new food information services that we call intelligent food services (IFSs), and we argue that they are characterized by having the following capacities:

- to be context aware;
- to transform data to knowledge/intelligence;
- to enable social connection/interaction;
- to run on cloud/app/sensor-based infrastructure.

Main research contributions of this paper can be summarized as follows:

- a functional framework for IFS and some real case examples and usage scenarios.
- an interaction context model, with a particular focus on food in-context awareness characteristic that distinguishes an IFS from other information services.

2 Towards Intelligent Food Information Services

"Internet of Food" is an offshoot of the Internet of things. It can be viewed as a network of smart food things, i.e., food-related objects and devices which are augmented with sensing, computing and communication capabilities in order to provide advanced services. Smart food things include sensor-equipped information artifacts (e.g., food labels with RFID or NFC tags), time-temperature indicators and other sensors on packages to detect spoiled foods, sensor devices that spots bacterial infection in food and water, kitchen devices that generate a record of compliance with food safety protocols, wearables to count bites and estimate calories, and so on.

In past years, research scientists have devoted considerable resources to the development of analytical tools for a quantitative and/or qualitative analysis of various food aspects, such as the identity of product and ingredients, region of origin and/or species, quality attributes and variety of ingredients. Until recently, their approaches had to be implemented in a laboratory with large and expensive equipment to get reliable data. New technological developments, especially in food sensor miniaturization, have made available hand-held and low-cost devices to capture food data or food-related entities data (e.g., data from label, package, container, environment), and to communicate them with a specialized smartphone/tablet app. Despite their miniaturization, these devices incorporate an analytical precision and resolution almost equivalent to bench-top instruments [8]. These advances are forging the convergence of consumer and enterprises technologies, and they are contributing to development of the "Internet of Food". Moreover, they make possible to conceive a new generation of food services that, throughout this paper, are referred to as intelligent food services (IFSs). These services are capable of carrying out intelligent functions (like sensing and monitoring, food data acquisition and analysis, food information searching and reasoning) to facilitate food decision-making.

The intelligence is essentially due to two main service characteristics:

- context aware. By leveraging on context-data acquisition and outcomes of a machine learning or a crowdsourcing process, IFSs are capable to identify and understand enough of a consumer's current situation in order to address his/her specific food information needs;

- knowledge leverage. By reasoning with identified current context items and available food knowledge resources (from simple food facts to food knowledge bases or food ontologies) IFSs are able to provide the user/consumer with personalized and context-sensitive food information.

Due to these characteristics, IFSs are most likely to be more effective than conventional food information services (product labeling, mass media or other traditional channels). For instance, they can help consumers with meal planning that is personalized according to their health condition and other factors such as food cost and affordability, and they can warn consumers about allergens or intolerance forms of food they are going to ingest, based on their known medical history.

On one hand, they empower consumers with information that was not previously accessible. Providing information on the safety and quality of foods and processes, as well as on issues around environmental, social, and ethical aspects, they let consumers have transparency on which trust can be built. In this sense IFSs could represent a means to create social food awareness. On the other hand, they reduce the consumer's cognitive load needed to interact within the context in which decisions are made.

Several real case examples (see next subsection) suggest a general framework describing IFS application systems. From the infrastructural point of view, IFSs could rely on cloud/app/sensor-based solutions. Service applications could run on a cloud computing infrastructure and be deployed via mobile device so they could interact with the user/consumer, food items and food-related entities through an app that has access to user's mobile device resources (e.g. built-in device sensors and local databases) or is

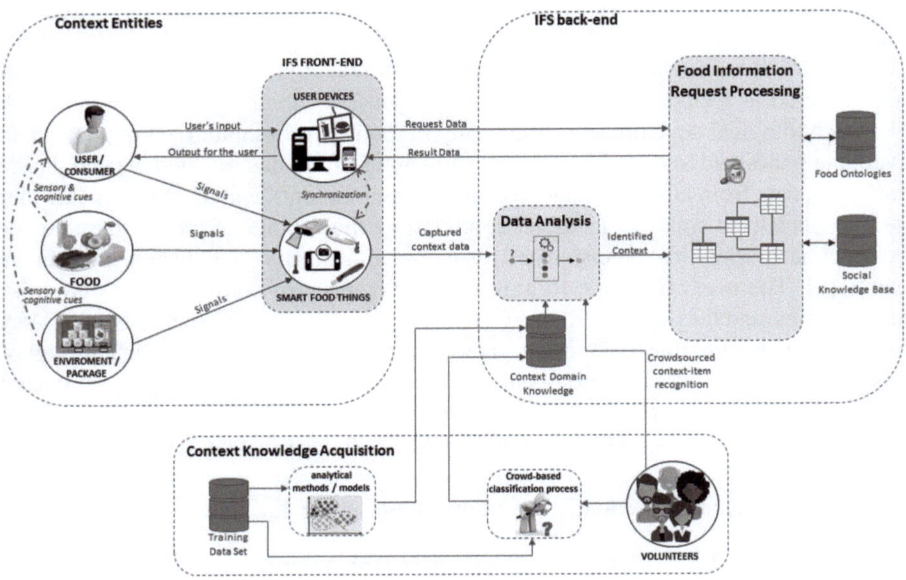

Fig. 1. Conceptual structure of an IFS application system.

connected to an external sensor device. Besides, they could interact with a sensor networked environment (e.g. a place where sensors are attached to food-related objects and connected to a wireless network) in order to detect food-related events. Having this in mind, we introduce a conceptual architecture for an IFS system, which is visualized in Fig. 1.

This structure can be considered as a kind of backbone for a new class of applications supporting intelligent food information provision. The IFS system front-end is the interface between the user/consumer and the IFS system back-end, and it is responsible for interactions with the external environment (user's request formulation, sensor data acquisition, and information presentation/visualization to the user); the IFS system back-end analyze context data versus domain-specific context knowledge (e.g., mining knowledge from lookup databases of previously identified food images, or of previously classified NIR spectra of food samples) to determine the current context configuration; successively, it exploits general food knowledge to adapt food information provision to the current user/consumer situation.

Domain-specific context knowledge can be acquired by using supervised learning from a training set of food samples data (e.g., previously classified NIR spectra of food samples) or by mining knowledge from a crowdsourced food properties database (e.g., a lookup database of previously identified food images).

2.1 Real Case Examples and Usage Scenarios

Over recent years, some pioneer companies have entered the food information market, exploiting benefits of IoF in order to provide consumers with food information. Such companies are bridging the gap between recent research advances in various scientific fields (such as spectroscopy [8, 9], machine vision [10, 11], hyperspectral imaging [12], odour analysis [13] and taste analysis [14]) and industry.

In what follows, we propose some usage scenarios, derived from real-world examples, to clarify how IFS are currently provided by these companies.

Usage scenario 1

A user is currently purchasing some meat in a store. He/she needs information about the freshness of that food. The user scans food with an odour-analysis based device (Smart Food Thing), able to acquire data about volatile organic compounds (VOCs) emitted by food [15]. The odour-analysis device is coupled to the user's smartphone via mobile app. Data are sent to a cloud-based engine able to perform a pattern recognition analysis to classify some food characteristics of that food item. Results of classification are processed by IFS back-end. The mobile app tells the user about the level of food freshness of the meat he/she analyzed.

FOODsniffer (http://www.myfoodsniffer.com/) and CDx inc. (www.cdxlife.com) are two examples of companies providing this kind of IFS.

Usage scenario 2

A user is going to eat a cooked meal in a restaurant. He/she needs information dealing with his/her diet. The user takes multiple pictures of food by means of his/her smartphone. That device acquires data about surface condition and volume of that food item. A data analysis unit, by mining knowledge from a food properties database, is able to recognize multiple food in user's plate and infer the mass of food products. IFS back-end processes food information exploiting a food knowledge database (e.g., nutritional facts tables). Moreover, data on user's food activities (e.g. historical data on previous food assumed the user during the day) and user profile (e.g. health related issues) are processed in order to provide the user with customized information. A mobile app informs the user with about the amount of calories and nutrition in his/her plate and the number of calories he/she can still consume in the rest of the day.

Calorie Mama (http://www.caloriemama.ai) and Lose it! (https://www.loseit.com) are two examples of companies providing this kind of IFS.

Usage scenario 3
A user is going to cook some food in his/her kitchen. He/she needs information about calories and nutritional facts of that food. The user takes a picture of food by means of his/her smartphone, acquiring data about surface condition of that food. Data analysis is based on a real-time crowdsourced process, as the picture is analysed by expert volunteers that manually recognize food items. Data about nutritional facts are processed by IFS back-end and information on calories and nutritional facts is provided through a mobile app.

An example of solution based on crowdsourced analysis process is represented by Rise (https://www.rise.us/).

3 The Interaction Context

Internet of Food (IoF) is an offshoot of the Internet of Everything. It can be viewed as a network of smart food things, i.e., food-related objects and devices which are augmented with sensing, computing and communication capabilities in order to provide advanced services. Smart food things include sensor-equipped information artifacts (e.g., food labels with RFID or NFC tags), time-temperature indicators and other sensors on packages to detect spoiled foods, sensor devices that spots bacterial infection in food and water, kitchen devices that generate a record of compliance with food safety protocols, wearables to count bites and estimate calories, and so on.

An interaction is generally understood as the effect two or more entities will have upon their counterparts as they perform actions on each other. The user-service interaction context is a set of entities with their relevant properties (called items) characterizing the situation the consumer is currently involved in, while he/she is interacting with the service [17].

In user-IFS interaction context modeling, four broad classes of context entities should be taken into account:

- **user:** a consumer who requires the information necessary for his/her food decision making or learning process as he/she is involved in food consumption activities in a real spatial environment; he/she interacts with an IFS through interface devices located in the environment;

- **food**: foodstuff that the consumer is interested in. Food related stimuli are perceived by the user and food characteristic data are acquired by the IFS during the interaction;
- **IFS interface devices**: they comprise devices that are used by the IFS system: (a) to take input from and deliver output to the user in the foreground of user's attention. These include food information artifacts (FIAs[1]), such as labels, tables, RFID chips, and NFC tags, that allow the user to get their contained information in the place where the artifacts are located; (b) to take input from the user in the background of user's attention, while he/she is involved in food consumption activities, such as many wearables for food intake monitoring [18]; (c) to take food and environment data with or without requiring user's action or attention. These include sensor equipped food packaging and containers, food appliances, as well as small tools designed for food-related functions (e.g. kitchen or cooking utensils);
- **environment**: physical and organizational environment where interactions take place (e.g. a home kitchen, a restaurant, a food shop, etc.). Environmental conditions have direct or indirect influence on consumer and service behaviour during the interaction. Physical properties, like light, humidity, temperature, localization, spatial layout of the environment, may change quality attributes of the food or consumers' perception of quality in food; organizational aspects, like rules, shop opening hours, working time, may drive the provision of information from the IFS.

According to many approaches for using and modelling context information, items of the above context entities fall into five categories [19]:

- **Identity**. A model of this item allow the service, or the user, to identify a context entity that is needed to know in the interaction with the counterpart. In particular, the user determines food identity by elaborating his/her food sensorial perceptions, like colour and appearance, taste, and odour, while the IFS system determines food identity by elaborating food data coming from instrumental measures of physical, chemical, biological, and microbiological food properties;
- **Time**. This item refers to temporal aspects of context entity properties. Item values may range from a current time representation to a complete time history of entity properties. When referred to food, values of this items allow to recognize or predict food quality over time. For instance, a time series of values of properties, like temperature, pH, or microbial growth, may help the user or the service to recognize when food is at its nutritional best and is safe to eat and when it should be disposed of to avoid ill health;
- **Location.** A model of this item may be quantitative or qualitative, and item values may represent current and previous positions of context entities in absolute or relative terms. When referred to food, location is a fundamental item of models for geographical traceability or geographic-based origin determination of food products.
- **Activity.** A model of this item describes fundamental changes of entity attributes that occur when a food activity is performed. In particular, changes of food characteristics, like temperature or size, may let the user or the service to determine the state progress

[1]. According to [20], a FIA is a physical entity expressly created to bear food information.

in a current consumer food activity (e.g. cooking); as a further example, chewing sounds may let a service to classify the food a consumer is eating.

- **Relations.** This item refers to relations a context entity has established with other context entities. A relation between two context entities expresses a semantic dependency that emerges from user-service interaction situations that these context entities are involved in. Relations between food and other entities are essentially relations of spatial proximity (e.g., relative distance and orientation). For instance, food data capture is strongly dependent on the relative distance and orientation of the food product and the sensor device.

4 Food-in-Context Awareness

Interaction context-awareness refers to the ability of the service (respectively, user) to acquire context item information and to use it in the interaction with the counterpart; context item information is acquired by capturing context data (respectively, sensory/ cognitive cues), analyzing them, and exploiting some context knowledge.

In an interaction session, context awareness has a significant influence on the behavior of the consumer, as service user, and on the behavior of the IFS, as food information provider. As matter of fact, context changes can trigger IFS/user actions on the counterpart, and context cues or data can support IFS/user to interpret actions performed by the counterpart. IFS and user mutually increase their context awareness, as they interact with each other. In particular, Fig. 2 shed light the role of context in an interaction between user and IFS, i.e. it further focuses on the Consumer-IFS interaction module reported in the functional architecture (see Fig. 1).

Food-in-context awareness is context awareness limited to food items, including relations with other context entities. In what follows we discuss more deeply user/ consumer and service food-in-context awareness and their roles in the interaction. Successively, we summarize main technical approaches that can be used to make an information service food-in-context aware, as they are aimed to automatically determine information on food characteristics and performances.

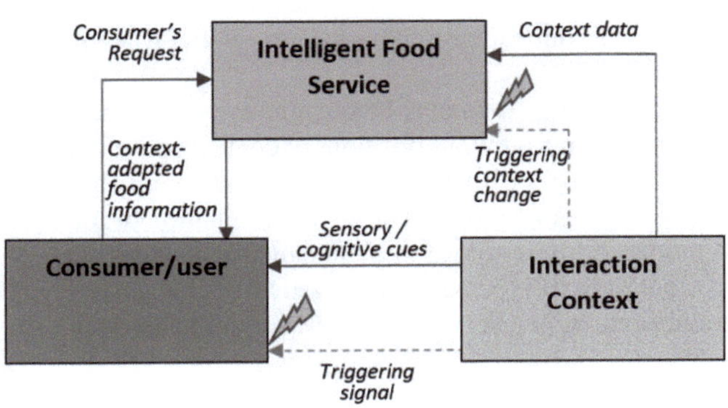

Fig. 2. Contextualized user IFS interaction.

User/consumer food-in-context awareness. It is the user's ability of knowing and experiencing contextual food items, i.e., sensory properties (such as appearance, taste, and odor) of food in the interaction context. Signals from contextual food can trigger a user's information need that in its turn can trigger a request to a food information service. For instance, the presence of a new food product can trigger the user need for nutrition or health information about that product (e.g. what vitamins have).

More important, in a contextualized interaction the user attempts to make sense of data and information delivered by the service provider, within his/her current situation and his/her own knowledge acquired from past experiences. Contextualization is absolutely essential both to let the consumer make appropriate choices in his/her food consumption activities in which he/she is currently engaged and to enable consumer's informal learning process that is crucial for his/her future related behavior.

User food-in-context awareness is at the core of user contextualization, since it provides the user with sensory and cognitive cues that allow him/her to refer delivered data and information to food items in the interaction context:

- value-laden information embedded within a food product can be effectively disclosed only by associating the perception of food-related stimuli (e.g. smell, flavor) with the logical information provided by the service;
- information content of labels/tags can be properly interpreted only by taking into account spatial relations between food products and these labels/tags. Think of a label on a food-shelf; we automatically refer the label information content to the closest food product on the food-shelf, and the label information content changes meaning as the label has moved to another place;
- food information provided by the service can be directly validated only by knowing specific physical conditions (e.g. light, humidity, temperature, localization, spatial layout, package integrity) or organizational features (e.g. operation rules, shop opening) of the environment surrounding food products the information content is referring to. For example, the "best before date" indicates the last date by which a product flavor and/or quality is best, but what is the value of this information if the product package has been opened?

Service food-in-context awareness. It is the ability of the service to capture and analyze food data versus domain-specific food knowledge in order to acquire information on food in current context. Food data coming from instrumental measures of physical, physico-chemical, and kinetic food properties are correlated with sensor properties such as color, appearance, taste, odor, and sound.

Service food-in-context awareness is at the core of context-adapted information provided by an IFS that creates value in letting consumers make better informed food choices, while they are involved in related food activities. Context-adapted information provision is characterized by the following dimensions:

- **context-triggered**. Changes of some food items can be detected and used by an IFS as a means to trigger context data acquisition that, in turn, can lead to timely information provision, i.e., information delivered when and where desired or needed by the consumer. For instance, an IFS may alert the user of a sensed condition within a refrigerator that food spoilage may occur.

- **context-situated.** In a current interaction session, an IFS information provision makes exophoric reference to context entities (e,g, food products or food-related objects) surrounding the user/consumer who, in his/her contextualization process, is required to resolve this exophoric reference as well as to assign meaning to spatial constructs. Service context awareness lets an IFS make easy and smooth the consumer's contextualization process by eliding spatially-retrievable information and inserting a minimal amount of unnatural clarification statements, in a food information provision. For instance, in a food supermarket, consumers could be guided towards what they're looking for, by using simple spatial deictic expressions in utterances such as "take a left" or "head towards the stairwell".
- **context-focused**. The IFS satisfies contextualized needs of information, i.e., consumer's needs of information that can be derived from the knowledge of current food items. This kind of adaptation couples contextualization and personalization, as addressing not just decontextualized consumer's needs, but what the consumer needs in the current context (e.g., in that place, at that time). It exploits an explicit context model that takes into account many context entities and it is broader than the only consumer model limited to personal characteristics such as preference, background, attitudes, and lifestyle. For instance, an IFS can suggest restaurants or food stores based on the user's preferences and current location and time.

5 Conclusions and Future Works

Internet of food based solutions are promising a huge impact on both food business and food consumers. In this paper, the envisaged intelligent food services constitute a part of the Internet of food vision that is grounded on recent researches and technology advances.

In this work, we proposed a functional framework such services. We provided also some usage scenarios to clarify how emerging companies in food information market exploiting benefits of IoF to provide context based information services. Moreover, we have introduced and discussed the concept of food-in-context awareness as a crucial ability for these services in order to provide consumer's situation adapted information.

In our opinion, this constitutes a contribution to realistically conceive innovative food information services that could let consumers be more food aware and could help them to make more informed decision when involved in food related activities.

The emergence of these services poses new challenges and problems but it also gives new business opportunities for tech startups in the Food Information Ecosystem. A critical point concerns with the consumer acceptance of these new technologies. Future research will be addressed to apply the Technology Acceptance Model (or its extensions) to evaluate the individuals' acceptance of this new generation of food information services.

In the paper we have presented some real-case applications, however a comprehensive study of companies operating in the food information market is missing. Further research will be devoted to conduct a survey aimed to understand technology foundation and business models of startup companies leveraging on IoF technologies, and to identify potential trails leading to the emergence of IoF based ecosystems.

References

1. Ghvanidze, S., Velikova, N., Dodd, T.H., Oldewage-Theron, W.: Consumers' environmental and ethical consciousness and the use of the related food products information: the role of perceived consumer effectiveness. Appetite **107**, 311–322 (2016)
2. Lando, A.M., Labiner-Wolfe, J.: Helping consumers make more healthful food choices: consumer views on modifying food labels and providing point-of-purchase nutrition information at quick-service restaurants. J. Nutr. Educ. Behav. **39**(3), 157–163 (2007)
3. Downey, G.: Advances in food authenticity testing. Woodhead Publishing series in food science, technology and nutrition (2016)
4. Verbeke, W.: Impact of communication on consumers' food choices. Proc. Nutr. Soc. **67**(3), 281–288 (2008)
5. Bialkova, S., Grunert, K.G., van Trijp, H.: Standing out in the crowd: the effect of information clutter on consumer attention for front-of-pack nutrition labels. Food Policy **41**, 65–74 (2013)
6. Volpentesta, A.P., Ammirato, S.; Evaluating web interfaces of B2C e-commerce systems for typical agrifood products. In: Pittaway, L., Koh, S.C.L. (eds.) The Adoption of Innovation and Technology by Small and Medium Sized Enterprises. (special issue). International Journal of Entrepreneurship and Innovation Management, vol. 7, No. 1, p. 74 (2007)
7. Volpentesta, A.P., Felicetti, A.M.: Analyzing App-Based services providing consumers with food information. In: Spender, J.C., Schiuma, G., Noennig, J.R. (eds.) Towards a New Architecture of Knowledge: Big Data, Culture and Creativity. ISSN 2280-787X. Proceedings of 11th edition of the International Forum on Knowledge Asset Dynamics Dresden – Germany 15–17 June 2016
8. Sorak, D., Herberholz, L., Iwascek, S., Altinpinar, S., Pfeifer, F., Siesler, H.W.: New developments and applications of handheld Raman, mid-infrared, and near-infrared spectrometers. Appl. Spectro. Rev. **47**(2), 83–115 (2012)
9. Cozzolino, D.: The role of vibrational spectroscopy as a tool to assess economically motivated fraud and counterfeit issues in agricultural products and foods. Anal. Meth. **7**(22), 9390–9400 (2015)
10. Casale, M., Simonetti, R.: Review: near infrared spectroscopy for analysing olive oils. J. Near Infrared Spectro. **22**(2), 59–80 (2014)
11. Steele, R.: An overview of the state of the art of automated capture of dietary intake information. Crit. Rev. Food Sci. Nutr. **55**(13), 1929–1938 (2015)
12. Kong, F., Tan, J.: DietCam: automatic dietary assessment with mobile camera phones. Pervasive Mob. Comput. **8**(1), 147–163 (2012)
13. Pu, Y.Y., Feng, Y.Z., Sun, D.W.: Recent progress of hyperspectral imaging on quality and safety inspection of fruits and vegetables: a review. Compr. Rev. Food Sci. Food Saf. **14**(2), 176–188 (2015)
14. Peris, M., Escuder-Gilabert, L.: A 21st century technique for food control: electronic noses. Anal. Chim. Acta **638**(1), 1–15 (2009)
15. Jha, S.N., Jaiswal, P., Grewal, M.K., Gupta, M., Bhardwaj, R.: Detection of adulterants and contaminants in liquid foods-a review. Crit. Rev. Food Sci. Nutr. **56**, 1662–1684 (2015)
16. Banerjee, R., Tudu, B., Bandyopadhyay, R., Bhattacharyya, N.: A review on combined odor and taste sensor systems. J. Food Eng. **190**, 10–21 (2016)

17. Volpentesta, A.P.: A framework for human interaction with mobiquitous services in a smart environment. Comput. Hum. Behav. **50**, 177–185 (2015)
18. Bi, Y., Lv, M., Song, C., Xu, W., Guan, N., Yi, W.: AutoDietary: AWearable acoustic sensor system for food intake recognition in daily life. IEEE Sens. J. **16**, 806–816 (2016)
19. Zimmermann, A., Lorenz, A., Oppermann, R.: An operational definition of context. In: Kokinov, B., Richardson, D.C., Roth-Berghofer, T.R., Vieu, L. (eds.) CONTEXT 2007. LNCS, vol. 4635, pp. 558–571. Springer, Heidelberg (2007). doi:10.1007/978-3-540-74255-5_42
20. Smith, B., Ceusters, W.: Aboutness: towards foundations for the Information Artifact Ontology. In: ICBO (2015)

Risk and Uncertainty in Agriculture

A Literature Review on Risk Sources and Resilience Factors in Agri-Food Supply Chains

Guoqing Zhao(✉), Shaofeng Liu, and Carmen Lopez

University of Plymouth, Plymouth, Devon PL4 8AA, UK
{guoqing.zhao, shaofeng.liu, carmen.lopez}@plymouth.ac.uk

Abstract. Risk and uncertainty are ubiquitous and varied in agri-food supply chains. As environment volatility increases, only having capabilities to manage agri-food supply chain risks may not be enough, resilience factors also need to be integrated into daily operations. This paper undertakes a systematic literature review on risks sources and resilience factors in agri-food supply chains. A five-stage systematic review methodology has been followed. The findings suggest that agri-food supply chains are highly vulnerable to various risks due to its unique characteristics of products. Main risk sources include antibiotics resistance, weather related risks and natural disasters, policy and institutional risks, and unethical issues. Five key resilience factors identified from the literature are traceability, knowledge management, collaboration, culture, and agility. The paper makes a contribution to the extant literature in the field of agri-food supply chain risk management and agri-food supply chain resilience.

Keywords: Supply chain risks · Supply chain resilience · Inter-organisational knowledge management · Agri-food supply chains

1 Introduction

In the past few decades, there has been an increasing recognition that the world's agri-food supply chains have been experiencing major challenges due to an increasing level of globalization and innovation [21]. The increasingly important role of global agri-food supply chains was associated with increasing level of interconnectedness among suppliers, manufacturers and distributors, which resulted in higher dependency among entities in the supply chain as well as a higher level of complexity in the supply chain [8]. These resulted in the fact that agri-food supply chain can be running efficiently and effectively in the stable business environment, but are highly vulnerable to risks and disruptions in unstable business environment [21].

Agri-food supply chains have faced much unique vulnerability resulted from various types of risks; tackling these vulnerabilities may cause the increase of supply chain complexity and result in more instability and unpredictability [3, 18, 52, 53]. As a result of the negative consequence of agri-food supply chain risks, researcher and academic have called for more research in this area, to design more efficient and resilient supply chains.

L.M. Camarinha-Matos et al. (Eds.): PRO-VE 2017, IFIP AICT 506, pp. 739–752, 2017.
DOI: 10.1007/978-3-319-65151-4_66

In order to address the risk and vulnerability issues, the concept of resilience has received great attention in recent years. Sullivan-Taylor and Branicki [44] argued that building resilience in agri-food supply chain is an emergency in the face of the climate change, soil degradation, pest outbreaks and population growth. Macfadyen et al. [24] suggested ten pieces of advice to improve agri-food supply chain resilience in their food supply system such as maintain soil resources, encourage sustainable practices in livestock management and protect water resources. Although the concept of supply chain resilience has been described by many researchers, there is no consensus on defining the construct. For some researchers, resilience is a capacity to withstand/adapt to disturbances, while others think resilience as a "dynamic capacity to continue to achieve goals despite disturbance and shocks" [24]. Therefore, the confusion around the concept is not surprising [27]. For now, we rely on the definition proposed by Tendall et al. [45], which defined food system resilience as "capacity over time of a food system and its units at multiple levels, to provide sufficient, appropriate and accessible food to all, in the face of various and even unforeseen disturbances".

In this study, in order to operate agri-food supply chain efficiently and effectively, we aim to address two key questions about agri-food supply chains: (1) What are the main risk sources in the agri-food supply chains? (2) What are the key resilience factors that can be designed in an agri-food supply chain? In order to answer the above questions, the remainder of this paper is organised as follows. In Sect. 2, we present a systematic literature review methodology. In Sect. 3, we present several figures and tables to demonstrate the characteristics of the publications. In Sect. 4, we provide a classification of risk sources in the agri-food supply chains. In Sect. 5, an overview of resilience factors in the agri-food supply chains will be discussed. In Sect. 6, the main connections between resilience factors and risk sources will be discussed. Finally, conclusions are discussed in Sect. 7.

2 Review Methodology

This paper is following the systematic literature review methodology proposed by Denyer and Tranfield [9]. A systematic literature review is an overview of primary studies that used in a clear and reproducible manner. This study follows the five phases systematic literature review proposed by Denyer and Tranfield [9]: (1) Define the research questions; (2) Location the studies; (3) Studies selection and evaluation; (4) Analysis and synthesis; and (5) Results presented. The method tries to assure that the process of the systematic literature review is transparent, reproducible and comprehensive.

2.1 Define Research Questions

The first phase in conducting a systematic literature review is to define research questions, which should clearly focus on risk sources and resilience factors in agri-food supply chains. The research questions were formulated based on the following process: (1) Brainstorming all the external and internal factors of an agri-food supply chain, and how the agri-food supply chain can be affected by the internal and external factors

(2) Developing relevance trees to show the internal and external factors that have a positive effect on building agri-food supply chain resilience, and the factors that may be risk source of agri-food supply chains (3) Examining what might be possible approaches or strategies that can be used to reduce supply chain risks and enhance resilience?

2.2 Locating Studies

This phase is to consider which database is the most suitable to answer the research questions. Web of Science is a database that includes the global major journals and conference proceedings especially in Social Sciences, Arts and Humanities. Therefore, the Web of Science is identified as the source to search for relevant publications. In order to search for relevant publications, three groups of keywords were identified: (1) Words related to risk: risky, riskily, riskiness. We decided to use the term risk* to cover all possibilities; (2) Words related to resilience: resiliency, resilient; (3) Words related to agri-food supply chain: agriculture supply chain or food supply chain.

The comprehensive search of the Web of Science was based on all possible combination of group 1 and group 3 as well as group 2 and group 3. Only journals papers (articles and reviews) and conference proceedings were searched, limited to the areas of "operations research management science", "agricultural" and "food science technology" et al. We wanted to find state-of-art discussion on risk sources and resilience factors in the agri-food supply chains, therefore, we only consider the journal papers and conference proceedings published from 2000 and 2016. We consider the year 2003 as a turning point for research in supply chain resilience. This view is based on the result of literature review on enterprise and supply chain resilience by Kamalahmadi and Mellat Parast [21]. Their discovery indicates that there has been a sudden increase in the number of articles (supply chain resilience) published in 2004. We assumed that the papers published in 2004 were prepared in 2002 or 2003 after the "9/11" attacks in America, which damaged many supply chains across the globe. The initial search presented a total of 499 items.

2.3 Study Selection and Evaluation

After the initial search, then the articles were judged by the relevance of the abstract and the paper. The following criteria for inclusion or exclusion articles were used in this phase (Table 1). After this phase, 58 papers were selected for detailed analysis (Fig. 1).

Table 1. Criteria for inclusion or exclusion papers

First criterion: focus of the abstract	Abstracts focusing on risk sources in agri-food supply chains or/and agri-food supply chain resilience have been included
Second criterion: focus of the papers	Papers focusing on risk sources in agri-food supply chain or/and agri-food supply chain resilience have been included

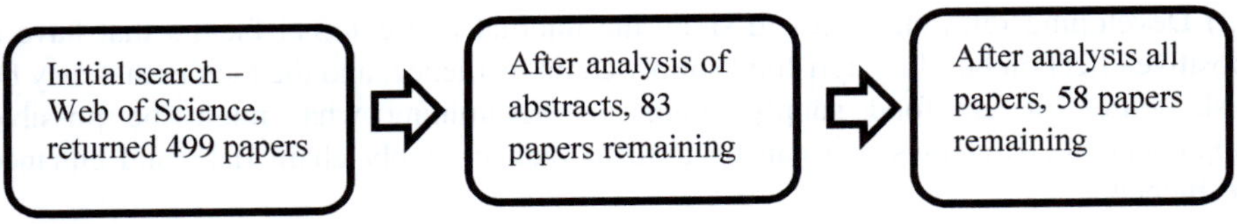

Fig. 1. Process of locating and selecting articles

2.4 Analysis and Synthesis

After selecting the most appropriate journal papers and conference proceedings for the purpose of this study, the papers were analysed and synthesised in two stages. The aim of the analysis is to examine and dissect different studies and identify the relationships between the elements [9]. Furthermore, synthesis is the integrating stage-to group the results of various studies "into a new or different arrangement and developing knowledge that is not apparent from reading the individual studies in isolation" [9]. The first stage is to concentrate on the categorisation of studies according to the criteria shown in Table 2. The second stage is to focus on how to identify and synthesize the main contributions of the identified publications to answer the research questions.

Table 2. Criteria for quantitative analysis of the papers [53]

Criterion	Type of analysis
Publication date	Verification of the timeliness of the theme
Publication source	Papers must be published in peer-reviewed journals and conference proceedings
Location	Analysis of the geographical dispersion of the papers based on the location of the authors
Methodology used	Analysis of the classification of articles and the approaches used in the studies

3 Characteristics of Publications

In this section, we present an overview of the main information of the 58 articles identified related to the risk sources and resilience factors in agri-food supply chains. The analysis of the publication date, publication source, methodology used and authors' affiliation are all aims at showing the context of the literature regarding the relationship between the themes of risk sources and resilience factors in agri-food supply chains. The identified publications will be analysed quantitatively.

3.1 Date of Publication

Figure 2 shows that a small fluctuation happened from 2000 to 2014, and then there has a big increase in publications of risk sources and resilience factors in agri-food supply chain from 2014 to 2016. The Fig. 2 also shows that there has been a small increase in

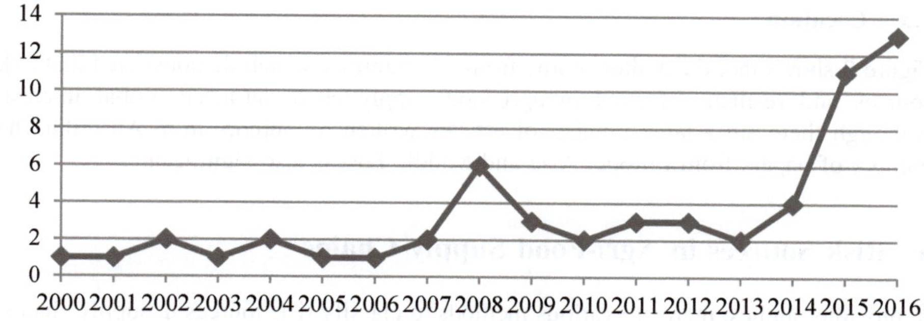

Fig. 2. Year-wise distribution of publications

publications in 2008. We assumed that the economic crisis between 2007 and 2009 encouraged researchers to do more on agri-food supply chain resilience. Most of publications were published between 2013 and 2016, which account for 52% of all identified publications. As a result, this study has been conducted in the early 2017, and we expect the number of publications in 2017 would surpass that in 2015 and 2016. The increase in publications indicates that researchers and practitioners have been more aware of the importance of risk sources and resilience factors in agri-food supply chains.

3.2 Publication Source and Methodology Used in the Papers

The papers have been published in 36 different journals mainly in *Supply Chain Management: An International Journal* (5), *British Food Journal* (3) and *European Journal of Operational Research* (3). As for the research methodology used in the papers, 19 papers used case study and 20 papers used empirical study. 12 of 58 papers used literature review as their research methodology, whereas only seven papers are conceptual study. It indicates that academic researchers and practitioners are less interested in conceptual studies in the area of risk sources and resilience factors in the agri-food supply chain.

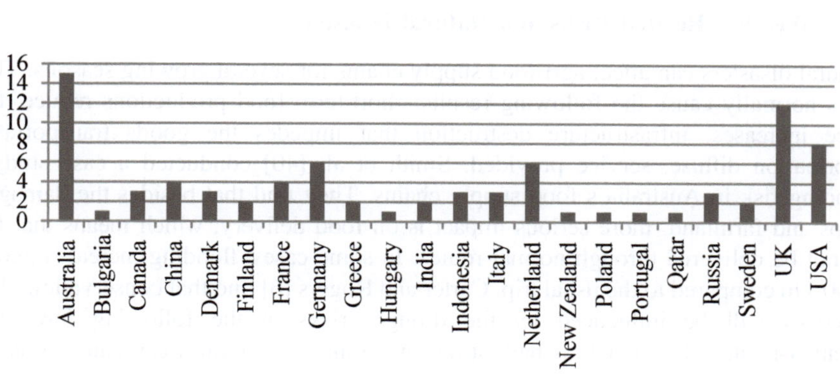

Fig. 3. Author's affiliation

3.3 Location

Figure 3 shows that the authors come from 22 countries, which demonstrated that risk sources and resilience factors in agri-food supply chain attracted global interest. Although there are a large number of articles written by authors from Australia, the number of papers from Europe, Asia and Middle East is also significant.

4 Risk Sources in Agri-Food Supply Chains

In previous studies, there are various methods to classify risk sources in supply chains. Based on the reviewed literature, risk sources can be divided into internal risk sources and external risk sources [50]. Within these two groups, it is not difficult to find that there are a number of common risk sources existing in almost any supply chains, as well as specific risk sources for agri-food supply chains [49]. These specific risk sources result from the specific attributes of agri-food supply chains, such as perishable characteristics of products and the rigid time constraints [47]. In the following, we will conduct a detailed analysis of specific risk sources existing in agri-food supply chains.

4.1 Antibiotic Resistance

Antibiotic resistance is emerging as a serious problem in food production sector, while clinical uses and misuses of antibiotics intensify the crisis [3]. Using antibiotics in food production not only broaden the role of agri-food supply chain just as a dispersal route for resistant bacteria and resistance genes, but also as an incentive for the sharing of resistance genes through horizontal gene transfer [20]. Resistant bacteria not only can cause contamination during the processing food products, but also can increase transmission route between humans [3]. The final result of the spread of resistant bacteria through food production is that human may be directly exposed to various bacteria from farmed animals [3]. International food standards highlight that it is necessary to consider the selecting and disseminating of foodborne resistance in food production risk analysis.

4.2 Weather-Related Risks and Natural Disasters

Natural disasters can affect agri-food supply chains for several growing seasons. These risks normally cause the following results: short-term food productions reduce, food price increases, infrastructure destruction that impedes the goods transportation, information diffuse, service provided. Smith et al. [40] conducted a case study of flooding risk in Australia's food supply chains. They find that besides the damage to crops and farmland, more serious impact is on food delivery, which means that food cannot be delivered through normal routes. In some cases, flooding increases another 1000 km compared to the usual trip. Carter and Rogers [6] find that conservation tillage practices will be influenced by the drought risks in the following few years. Weather-related risks (such as hail, strong wind and excess rain) can cause pests and diseases outbreaks subsequently. Smit et al. [39] proposed that the selection of appropriate corn seed was affected by the weather conditions in the last few years. Along with this route, Finger and Lehmann [15] find that farmers will increase investment in hail insurance after experiencing a hail event.

4.3 Policy and Institutional Risks

Policy and institutional risks have various impacts on agri-food supply chains. For example, these risks may alter the structure of the agri-food supply chains, may increase food product quality of agri-food supply chains, and may change the relationship among the agri-food supply chain members. Mittenzwei et al. [29] investigate the policy uncertainty in the agriculture sector in Norway. They find that 67% of farm in Norway are affected by market price support policy and subsidies from the government, which is a large proportion compared to other countries. The heavily relying on subsidies of farm income in Norway form a potential source of uncertainty as policies, in principle, may be changed frequently.

4.4 Unethical Issues in Agri-Food Supply Chains

Several authors have conducted research on unethical practices that can cause supply chain uncertainty. For example, Christopher and Peck [7] proposed that tangible supply chain cost increase will be caused by unethical business practice, such as monitoring business transactions and expenses on lobbying governments to update policies. Gonzalez [18] and Fraizer et al. [16] separately examined that unethical behaviour may help the firm to acquire profits but can cause expense on the whole supply chain. After collecting data from four focal manufacturers, four first-tier suppliers and four first-tier customers in Indonesian food industry, Simangunsong et al. [36] observed three unethical practices that can cause supply chain uncertainty in the food supply chain. First, collusion among suppliers of the same product, which involves the timing and pricing of supplies for the purchasing organisation. Second, organisations may seek chance to impact food policies so that the competitors may have to recall their products or packaging, whereas the organisation's own product or packing remains within regulations. Finally, anti-competition behaviour has been observed among large food retailers.

5 Resilience Factors in Agri-Food Supply Chains

This section will demonstrate the major enablers of supply chain resilience first (Table 3), and then summarise the major resilience factors exist in the agri-food supply chain according to our literature review.

5.1 Traceability

Traceability refers to the ability to trace and track food and food ingredients in agri-food supply chains or trace and track food in three stages: food production, processing and distribution [48]. Several authors indicate to adopt food traceability in agri-food supply chain have various advantages. First, food traceability has an

Table 3. Resilience factors in agri-food supply chain

Resilience enablers	Description	Supporting literatures
Agility	Agility is defined as "the ability of a supply chain to rapidly respond to change by adapting its initial stable configuration" [51]	[7, 14]
Collaboration among suppliers	Pettit et al. [30] define supply chain collaboration as "the ability to work effectively with other entities for mutual benefits"	[2, 21, 32]
Risk and revenue sharing	"Risk and revenue sharing is a kind of supply chain contract which makes it possible to share risks among supply chain partners" [43]	[12, 28, 43]
Trust	"Trust is generally seen as a precondition for risk sharing" [38]	[12, 13, 28]
Visibility	Francis [17] defined visibility as "the identity, location and status of entities transiting the supply chain, captured in timely messages about events, along with the planned and actual dates/times of these events"	[7, 38, 41]
Sustainability	"Sustainability is important for maintaining a value, awareness, society, and business reputation as well as enhancing a business environment and cooperation along a supply chain" [11]	[10, 28]
Adaptive capability	The adaptive capacity involved three phases, which are readiness, responsiveness and recovery [37]	[41]
Knowledge management and supply chain structure	"Knowledge and understanding of supply chain structures-both physical and informational-are important elements of supply chain resilience" [31]	[4, 7, 19]
Traceability	"Traceability is the ability to trace and track food, and food ingredients through the supply chain; thus, all stages of production, processing and distribution" [48]	[28, 46, 48]
Flexibility/Redundancy	Having multiple suppliers, multiple transportation channels, flexible supply base are examples can help to increase supply chain resilience [37]	[7, 21, 31, 37]
Supply chain risk management culture	"Culture of risk management should extend beyond the boundaries of corporate risk and business continuity management" [7]	[7, 50]

important role in recalling contaminated products and hindering counterfeited products from reaching the market [46]. Second, applied integrated traceability systems can improve recall efficiency, supply chain transparency, inventory and revenues; more importantly, it can help to increase customer trust on food safety [28]. Third, food traceability has a positive effect on monitoring food characteristics.

Supply chain visibility has some similar function with traceability such as monitor the supply chain in real time. Pettit et al. [30] defined visibility as "the knowledge of the status of operating assets and the environment". No matter which term is used, traceability or visibility, they both are all heavily rely on close collaboration between suppliers and customers, are all heavily rely on investment in information sharing [7, 42].

5.2 Inter-organisational Knowledge Management

Through systematic literature review, we find that knowledge management is an important construct in supply chain resilience due to frequent cited reference to knowledge management practices [4, 7]. After collecting data from nine VOAD lead member organisations, Scholten et al. [35] examined that horizontal and vertical collaboration, risk awareness, supply chain reengineering and knowledge management constitute the foundation of supply chain resilience. Esper et al. [10] suggest that creating customer value need supply chain members to integrate demand process and supply process through inter-organisational knowledge management. They also highlight that knowledge-sharing capabilities has a positive effect on supply chain cost reduction, and supply chain cost reduction influence supply chain resilience. Lingegard and Lindahl [23] did a survey from customer's side and supplier's side separately. They find that inter-organisational knowledge transfer not only can produce profits, but also play an important role in reducing environmental impact and increasing cost efficiency and quality. Except for these authors, other researchers also did a lot of research in inter-organisational knowledge management. For example, knowledge sharing has a positive effect on market orientation strategy, increase customer satisfaction and level of service between logistics service provider and customer [1, 33].

5.3 Supply Chain Collaboration

While agri-food supply chains are extended across the globe, it is obvious that agri-food supply chains become longer than before [21]. The unique characteristics of agri-food products require that the agri-food supply chain maintains the food quality across the whole process from initial production to end customers [29]. Therefore, a high level of collaboration among agri-food supply chain entities is necessary [12, 30]. Cao et al. [5] defines collaboration as "the collaborative activities of information sharing, goal congruence, joint decision making, resource sharing, incentive alignment, collaborative communication and joint knowledge creation among independent supply chain partners". Scholten and Schilder [34] proposed that supply chain collaboration reduces the impact of disruption through building the same goal and presenting clearly business needs. Through exploring Australian citrus supply chains, Ali and Shukran [2] find that long-term relationships between supply chain members could be better able to deal with divergent risks such as price fluctuation, opportunism, high operational costs, and behavioural uncertainties. Prima Dania et al. [32] conducted a literature review about collaboration and sustainability in agri-food supply chains. They find that vertical collaboration, horizontal collaboration and mixed vertical and horizontal collaboration have a positive effect on agri-food supply chain in term of mitigating environment impacts as well as to achieve socio-economic development. Leat and Revoredo-Giha [22] also find that vertical collaboration and horizontal collaboration in supply chain members can facilitate supply chain risk management after they have an in-depth investigation on ASDA Porklink supply chain in Scotland. After conducting 16 semi-structured interviews in food processing industry, Pettit et al. [30] concluded that information sharing, collaborative communication, mutually created knowledge and joint relationship efforts play important roles in increasing agri-food supply chain resilience. An empirical study conducted by Manos et al. [26] revealed that while collaboration in the daily operation is necessary for supply chain collaboration, the structure of the agri-food supply sector along with the attribute of products impinges the intensity of collaboration, to more operational and tactical level, as well as, to logistics-related activities. They also find that the intensity of collaboration can be seriously affected by trust. Finally, Soni et al. [42] use an interpretive structural modelling approach to analysis all major enablers of supply chain resilience. They find that supply chain collaboration is ranked second among fourteen enablers of supply chain resilience.

5.4 Supply Chain Risk Management Culture

In today's unstable business environment, it is very important to have a risk perception for an organisation. Christopher and Peck [7] highlighted that supply chain risk management culture is a critical element for organisation to develop a resilient organisation. Sheffi [37] pointed out that culture has an important impact for an organisation to survive from supply chain disruptions. Manning and Mei Soon [25] conducted a literature review on strategic resilience in the food supply chain, where they find that culture has a positive effect when organisations face food fraud issues. Vlajic et al. [49] refers that risk management culture is indispensable for an organisation. Smith [41] point out that risk management culture, agility, collaboration and visibility, all have a positive effect on supply chain resilience. Finally, Christopher et al. [8] argued that there are two most common approaches to global sourcing risk mitigation, one is risk management culture, and the other is global sourcing reengineering.

5.5 Agility

Agility is defined as "a strategic ability that assists organisational rapidly to sense and respond to internal and external uncertainties via effective integration of supply chain relationships" [14]. Soni et al. [42] think agility is the most important one among 14 enablers of supply chain resilience. Sullivan-Taylor and Branicki [44] use organisational theory to explore resilience factors in SMEs, where they find that agility was regarded as an important capability which has received great support among 11 SMEs decision makers.

6 Discussion

By being aware of resilience factors and risk sources identified in the literature, an agri-food supply chain entity can modify their organisational resilience factors easily according to generate balanced resilience (Fig. 4). In this context, risk sources will either be tackled completely or offset to a controllable level by an organisations capability to adapt. Furthermore, we can imagine that daily operations will be more efficient and effective as a result of the continuous process of tweaking resilience factors to meet unstable agri-food supply chains. On the other hand, unbalanced situation between resilience factors and risk sources which is easily to meet in day to day operations. For example, excessive resilience factors compared to risk sources can erode revenue. Likewise, if more profit is invested in building supply chain risk management culture, it is possible to return to a situation where traceability system becomes dated. This will result agri-food supply chain in a high risk state which will cause high consequences events occurring.

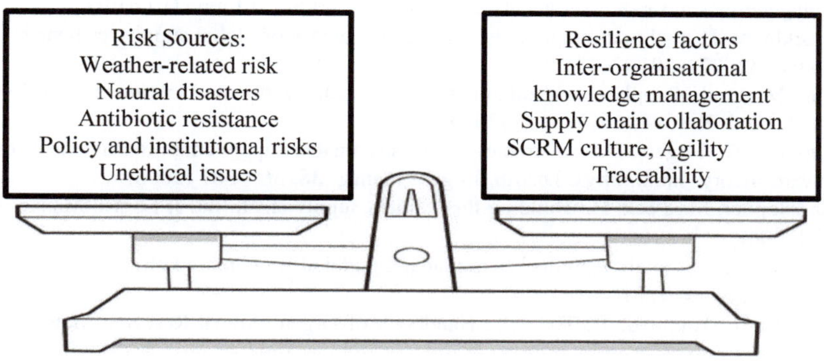

Fig. 4. The balance between resilience factors and risk sources

7 Conclusions

In this study, we conducted a systematic literature review to identify risk sources and resilience factors in agri-food supply chains. Through this process, we identified 58 publications, the majority of them are journal papers, a minority of them are conference proceedings. Main risk sources identified from the literature include unethical issues, antibiotic resistance, policy and institutional risks as well as weather related risks and natural disasters. At a supply chain level some of the risks are partially controllable, for example, unethical issues and institutional risks, but this also depends on the level of agri-food supply chain integration and collaboration. In addition, more empirical studies are needed to have a deep understanding of the damage of antibiotic resistance and unethical issues to agri-food supply chains. As for resilience factors in agri-food supply chain, literature has widely discussed are traceability, inter-organisational knowledge management, supply chain collaboration, supply chain risk management culture and agility. Although some of the resilience factors have been widely discussed in agri-food supply chains, the relationship between several key factors of agri-food supply chain resilience is not well understood. For example, the literature is not clear on whether there is a relationship between inter-organisational knowledge management and traceability. Also, there is little insight into the dynamics and development of traceability, and how traceability can enhance supply chain resilience in agri-food supply chains. Future work will investigate relationships between the risk sources and resilience factors, in order to develop a framework for agri-food supply chains.

References

1. Abid, M., Ali, B.: Antecedents and effectiveness of CKM: an empirical study. J. Basic Appl. Sci. Res. **4**, 104–117 (2014)
2. Ali, I., Shukran, K.: Management supply chain risks and vulnerabilities through collaboration: present and future scope. J. Dev. Areas **50**, 335–342 (2016)
3. Bengtsson-Palme, J.: Antibiotic resistance in the food supply chain: where can sequence and metagenomics aid risk assessment? Curr. Opin. Food Sci. **14**, 66–71 (2017)
4. Blackhurst, J., et al.: An empirically derived framework of global supply resiliency. J. Bus. Logist. **32**, 374–391 (2011)
5. Cao, M., et al.: Supply chain collaboration: conceptualization and instrument development. Int. J. Prod. Res. **48**, 6613–6635 (2010)
6. Carter, C.R., Rogers, D.S.: A framework of sustainable supply chain management: moving toward theory. Int. J. Phys. Distrib. Logist. Manag. **38**, 360–387 (2008)
7. Christopher, M., Peck, H.: Building the resilient supply chain. Int. J. Logist. Manag. **15**, 1–13 (2004)
8. Christopher, M., et al.: Approaches to managing global sourcing risk. Supply Chain Manag. Int. J. **16**, 67–81 (2011)
9. Denyer, D., Tranfield, T.: The Sage Handbook of Organisational Research Methods. Sage, London (2009)
10. Esper, T., et al.: Demand and supply integration: a conceptual framework of value creation through knowledge management. J. Academy Mark. Sci. **38**, 5–18 (2010)
11. Faisal, M.N.: Sustainable supply chains: a study of interaction among the enablers. Bus. Process. Manag. J. **16**, 508–529 (2010)
12. Faisal, M.N., et al.: Supply chain risk mitigation: modelling the enablers. Bus. Process. Manag. J. **12**, 535–552 (2006)
13. Faisal, M.N., et al.: Information risks management in supply chains: an assessment and mitigation framework. J. Enterp. Inf. Manag. **20**, 677–699 (2009)
14. Fayezi, S., et al.: Understanding and development of supply chain agility and flexibility: a structural literature review. Int. J. Manag. Rev., 1–30 (2016)
15. Finger, R., Lehmann, N.: The influence of direct payments on farmers, hail insurance decisions. Agri. Econ. **43**, 343–354 (2012)
16. Fraizer, G.I., et al.: Just-in-time exchange relationships in industrial markets. J. Marketing. **52**, 52–67 (1988)
17. Francis, V.: Supply chain visibility: lost in translation? Supply Chain Manag. Int. J. **13**, 180–184 (2008)
18. Gonzalez, C.: Climate change, food security, and agrobiodiversity: toward a just, resilient, and sustainable food system. Fordham Env. Law Rev. **22**, 11–19 (2011)

19. Hong, Y., Choi, T.Y.: Unveiling the structure of supply networks: Cases in Honda, Acura and Daimler Chrysler. J. Oper. Manag. **20**, 469–493 (2002)
20. Johnson, T.A., et al.: Clusters of antibiotic resistance genes enriched together stay together in swine agriculture. mBio **7**, e02214–e02215 (2016)
21. Kamalahmadi, M., Mellat Parast, M.: A review of the literature on the principles of enterprise and supply chain resilience: major findings and directions for future research. Int. J. Prod. Res. **171**, 116–133 (2016)
22. Leat, P., Revoredo-Giha, C.: Risk and resilience in agri-food supply chains: the case of the ASDA PorkLink supply chain in Scotland. Supply Chain Manag. Int. J. **18**, 219–231 (2013)
23. Lingegard, S., Lindahl, M.: Integrated product service offering for rail infrastructure – benefits and challenges regarding knowledge transfer and cultural change in a Swedish case. J. Cleaner. Prod. **98**, 166–174 (2015)
24. Macfadyen, S., et al.: The role of food retailers in improving resilience in global food supply. Global Food Security **7**, 1–8 (2015)
25. Manning, L., Mei Soon, J.: Building strategic resilience in the food supply chain. British Food J. **118**, 1477–1493 (2016)
26. Manos, B., et al.: A conceptual framework for supply chain collaboration: empirical evidence from the agri-food industry. Supply Chain Manag. Int. J. **12**, 177–186 (2007)
27. Melnyk, S.A., et al.: Understanding supply chain resilience. Supply Chain Manag. Rev. **18**, 34–41 (2014)
28. Meuwissen, M.P.M., et al.: Certification in meat supply chains. J. Agribus. **21**, 167–181 (2003)
29. Mittenzwei, K., et al.: Combined effects of climate change and policy uncertainty on the agricultural sector in Norway. Agri. Syst. **153**, 118–126 (2017)
30. Pettit, T.J., et al.: Ensuring supply chain resilience: development of a conceptual framework. J. Bus. Logist. **31**, 1–21 (2010)
31. Ponomarov, S.Y., Holcomb, M.C.: Understanding the concept of supply chain resilience. Int. J. Logist. Manag. **20**, 124–143 (2009)
32. Prima Dania, W.A. et al.: Collaboration and sustainable agri-food supply chain: a literature review. MATEC Web of Conferences. In: 3rd Bali International Seminar on Sciences & Technology. EDP Sciences, Les Ulis (2016)
33. Rollins, M., et al.: Inter-firm customer knowledge sharing in logistics services: an empirical study. Int. J. Phys. Distrib. Logist. Manag. **41**, 956–971 (2011)
34. Scholten, K., Schilder, S.: The role of collaboration in supply chain resilience. Supply Chain Manag. Int. J. **20**, 471–484 (2015)
35. Scholten, K., et al.: Mitigation process – antecedents for building supply chain resilience. Supply Chain Manag. Int. J. **19**, 211–228 (2014)
36. Simangunsong, E., et al.: Managing supply chain uncertain with emerging ethical issues. Int. J. Oper. Prod. Manag. **36**, 1272–1307 (2016)
37. Sheffi, Y.: Preparing for the big one. IEE Manuf. Eng. **84**, 12–15 (2005)
38. Sheffi, Y.: Supply chain management under the Threat of International Terrorism. Int. J. Logist. Manag. **12**, 1–11 (2001)
39. Smit, B., et al.: Corn hybrid selection and climatic variability: gambling with nature? Can. Geogr. **41**, 429–438 (1997)
40. Smith, K., et al.: The resilience of long and short food chains: a case study of flooding in Queensland. Aust. Agri. Hum. Values **33**, 45–60 (2016)
41. Smith, R.: Operational capabilities for the resilient supply chain. Supply Chain Pract. **6**, 24–35 (2004)
42. Soni, U., et al.: Measuring supply chain resilience using a deterministic modelling approach. Comput. Ind. Eng. **74**, 11–25 (2014)

43. Spekman, R.E., et al.: An empirical investigation into supply chain management: a perspective on partnerships. Supply Chain Manag. Int. J. **3**, 53–67 (1998)
44. Sullivan-Taylor, B., Branicki, B.: Creating resilient SMEs: why one size might not fit all. Int. J. Prod. Res. **49**, 5565–5579 (2011)
45. Tendall, D.M., et al.: Food system resilience: defining the concept. Glob. Food Secur. **6**, 17–23 (2015)
46. Thakur, M., Hurburgh, C.R.: Framework for implementing traceability in the bulk grain supply chain. J. Food Eng. **95**, 617–626 (2009)
47. van der Vorst, J.G.A.J., Beulens, A.J.M.: Identifying sources of uncertainty to generate supply chain redesign strategies. Int. J. Phys. Distrib. Logist. Manag. **32**, 409–430 (2002)
48. van Rijswijk, W., Frewer, L.J.: Consumer perceptions of food quality and safety and their relation to traceability. British Food J. **110**, 1034–1046 (2008)
49. Vlajic, J.V., et al.: A framework for designing robust food supply chain. Int. J. Prod. Econ. **137**, 176–189 (2012)
50. Waters, D.: Supply Chain Risk Management: Vulnerability and Resilience in Logistic. Kogan Page Limited, London (2007)
51. Wieland, A., Wallenburg, C.M.: The influence of relational competencies on supply chain resilience: a relational view. Int. J. Phys. Distrib. Logist. Manag. **43**, 300–320 (2013)
52. Xiaoping, W.: Food supply chain safety risk evaluation based on AHP fuzzy integrated evaluation method. Int. J. Secur. Appl. **10**, 233–244 (2016)
53. Zimmermann, R., et al.: The influence of supply chain on the innovation process: a systematic literature review. Supply Chain Manag. Int. J. **21**, 289–304 (2016)

The Semantic Web as a Platform Against Risk and Uncertainty in Agriculture

Wilmer Henry Illescas Espinoza[1], Alejandro Fernandez[2,3], and Diego Torres[2,3,4(✉)]

[1] Universidad Técnica de Machala, Machala, El Oro, Ecuador
willescas@utmachala.edu.ec
[2] LIFIA, Fac. Informática, UNLP, 1900 La Plata, Argentina
{Alejandro.fernandez,diego.torres}@lifia.info.unlp.edu.ar
[3] Comision de Investigaciones Científicas de Buenos Aires (CIC), Buenos Aires, Argentina
[4] Departamento de Ciencia y Tecnología, UNQ, Bernal, Argentina

Abstract. In this article, we discuss existing literature on DSS in agriculture, on DSS that use data available in the Semantic Web, and on Semantic Web initiatives focusing on agriculture information. Our goal is to assess the readiness of the Semantic Web as a platform to empower DSS that can keep risk and uncertainty in agriculture under control. Key agricultural activities targeted by DSS reported in literature are nutrient management, insect and pest management, land use and planning, environmental change and forecasting, and water and drought management. The most relevant use of Semantic Web in DSS, is in data analysis, as a means of making DSS more intelligent. There are initiatives to produce vocabularies and semantic repositories in the domain of agriculture. However, data and models are still isolated in specific domain repositories, and interoperability is still weak.

Keywords: Decision Support Systems · Semantic Web · Agriculture

1 Introduction

We make decisions many times a day. The strategy we use depends on the importance of the decision. Intuitively, the more important the decision, the harder we need to think about it. Complexity, impact, uncertainty and risk are aspects that define the importance of the decision. The impact of a decision can be expressed as a function of its consequences (economic, health of people and environment, etc.). When factors not under control of the decision maker can negatively impact the result of the decision we talk about risk. The higher the probability and/or impact of a risk, the more thought needs to be put into making a decision.

When we do not count with all the information we need, or when the information we have is not completely accurate, we make our decisions under uncertainty [1]. Although we can decide on a given course of action, sometimes we can still be uncertain about its result. Frequently, the results of our actions depend on the response of what

L.M. Camarinha-Matos et al. (Eds.): PRO-VE 2017, IFIP AICT 506, pp. 753–760, 2017.
DOI: 10.1007/978-3-319-65151-4_67

we act upon, or the actions taken by others. Uncertainty introduces risk, and consequently increases the complexity of our decisions.

Mathematics and information technologies offer a rich variety of tool to help practitioners make decisions. These tools, generally called Decision Support Systems (DSS), are available in multiple domains. Our interest centers in agriculture. Decisions regarding planning, soil management, crop health, crop varieties, and commercialization were once made on the basis of common practices. However, globalization and constant climate change have become a source of complexity, uncertainty and risk. Moreover, decisions in any of the components of the agriculture value chain have far reaching consequences for the economy of the organizations, the health of people, and the environment.

DSS vary in complexity, strategies to support decision makers, and applicability. There are tools that support multiple stakeholders making decision that satisfy, as good as possible, the stakeholder's multiple constraints and requirements. There are tools that apply mathematical models to select from multiple, competing alternatives. There are tools that attempt to mimic how experts make decisions. There are tools that help decisions makers find, filter and analyze information.

Every decision we make requires information. The more relevant and high quality information we count on, the better are our chances to make a good decision. DSS can obtain information from sources internal or external to the organization. We are particularly interested in DSS that exploit information available on the World Wide Web. The Web is a constantly growing source of information, created by collaborating individuals around the world. However, most of the information published on the Web is targeted to humans, making the task of automated extraction and processing difficult and sometimes impossible. Luckily, there is a layer on the Web that has been specially prepared for machines. It is called the Semantic Web.

In this article, we review and integrate existing literature on DSS in agriculture, DSS that use data available in the Semantic Web, and Semantic Web initiatives focusing on agriculture information. Our goal is to assess the readiness of the Semantic Web as a platform to empower DSS that can keep risk and uncertainty in agriculture under control.

The remainder of this article is organized as follows. Section 2 introduces key concepts of Decision Support Systems and Semantic Web. DSS in Agriculture and DSS and the Semantic Web are introduced in Sects. 3 and 4 respectively. Section 5 discusses the presence of Agriculture Data in the Semantic Web. Finally, conclusions and challenges are described in Sect. 6.

2 Background

Decision Support Systems (DSS) have evolved since the 1970s. They are generally defined as computer-supported systems that use data and models to help system managers to analyze semi structured problems [2]. A DSS is "a computer-based system that aids the decision-making process" [3], and "an interactive, flexible, and adaptable computer based information system, specially developed for supporting the solution of a non-structured management problem for improved decision making" [2]. DSS are the subject of specialized conferences and workshops such as those organized by the European Working Group on Decision Support Systems [4], and the theme of specialized journals such as Decision Support Systems and Electronic Commerce [5].

In terms of application domains, DSS can be classified as: Personal (PDSS), Collaborative or Group (GSS), Negotiation Support Systems (NSS, Intelligent Decision Support Systems (IDSS), Knowledge Management Support Systems (KMSS), Business intelligence (BI), Data Warehousing (DW), or Enterprise Reporting and Analysis System (EIS). From the perspective of the types of core artifacts used to support decision making, they can be arranged as: Model-Driven DSS, Communication Driven DSS, Data Driven DSS, Document Driven DSS, and Knowledge Driven DSS.

The Semantic Web is a portion of the Web where the information is described in a machine-understandable format. The term Semantic Web was introduced by Berners-Lee as an evolution of the Web 2.0 [6] as a set of technologies that provides a better knowledge representation with the use of ontologies, software agents, and logic rules. Information in the Semantic Web is mainly described as RDF resources and OWL is the language to describe ontologies. RDF allows users to describe meaning and OWL increase them with inference rules and a specific domain. Additionally, SPARQL is a query language for RDF, which applications can access to RDF stores similar to SQL in a traditional database [7]. The Semantic Web is defined as a layered architecture. Each layer is built in a particular technology.

3 DSS in Agriculture

Mir and colleagues [8] provide a comprehensive overview of the role of DSS in agriculture. According to the authors, the key agricultural activities targeted by DSS reported in literature are nutrient management, insect and pest management, land use and planning, environmental change and forecasting, and water and drought management.

DSS focusing on nutrition aim at optimizing the use of fertilizers (which heavily impact cost) given various environmental and crop conditions. Some reported systems consider in addition the reuse farm by-products such as manure. Most commonly found DSS in this area are mathematical models of crop growth such as CERES [9], and expert systems such as Farm-N [10]. There is an ongoing trend towards making nutrition DSS available over the Web.

A similar review and classification was conducted by Manos and colleagues [11] for publications in the period 1987-2001. The majority of the articles (59,2%) reported on advisory DSS that offered advice on strategic and tactical planning. In a smaller but still significant proportion, were articles reporting on control DSS (18.4%), and forecasting DSS (14.3%).

As early as 1993, [12] reported on the existence of 67 different expert systems dealing with plant protection. A key factor when dealing with insect and pest protection is to minimize the impact that chemicals have on the environment, while still being able to keep crops healthy. Disease expansion modelling and forecasting are commonly used decision support strategies in this area.

Land use and planning require dealing with complex trade-offs among the objectives of the various involved stakeholders (land-owners, farmers, governments, biodiversity protection organizations). Multi-objective models (especially goal programming) are frequently used mechanisms to implement DSS. In addition, planning support systems normally involve some form of geographic information systems functionality.

4 DSS and the Semantic Web

The most relevant use of Semantic Web in DSS context is the "use ontologies and rules as a means of making DSS more intelligent" in data analysis [13]. Much of the works could be viewed as continuation of the Expert Systems family of DSS, because they are using the SW standards such as RDF or OWL as an evolution of the use of raw data into knowledge representation [14–18]. The use of ontologies provides both a complete specialized domain knowledge model and a set of inference rules and querying to be applied in that model.

Semantic Web data can be used in different ways to power DSS; some approaches take advantages using RDF and OWL as formats to allow integration and systems communication [19–21]. Another improvement of the use of Semantic Web in DSS is the Ontology development, which is utilized on top of data to provide domain description and to integrate querying and reasoning [19, 20]. The reuse of ontologies or vocabularies is promoted by the Linked Open Data movement.

The main challenges in the use of Semantic Web in DSS are related to make easier and flexible the integration methods of data and systems. Another challenge is how to capture knowledge naturally generated in informal contexts, and then make a matching with ontologies that describe it. The challenge here is to make this usable by a machine. In this direction, the study of the co-evolution between the social and the semantic web remarks some achievements in this direction [22].

Mendoza and colleagues [23] studied collaborative decision making using the Semantic Web as a platform. They identified challenges in three areas: the selection of vocabularies, the selection of data sources, and the retrieval and fusion of data. These challenges, if not tackled translate to an additional effort in the integration process, the need to discard data, and potential inconsistencies and lack of data-quality in the final product.

5 Agricultural Data in the Semantic Web

Sanders and colleagues propose a model to study the next generation of agricultural systems data, models and knowledge [24]. The model is a pyramid with data at the bottom, information on top of it, then knowledge and finally wisdom. According to this model, Linked Data conforms the base of the pyramid, the semantic web is at the information level, semantic technologies conform the knowledge level, and at the top we find Decision Support Systems. Applications constitute a "knowledge chain" that transform data into information, then into knowledge and finally into wisdom.

At the data layer we find raw data descriptions, for example, the controlled vocabulary AGROVOC by the Food and Agriculture Organization (FAO) [25]. Government and research have been the traditional sources of raw data (e.g., weather, statistics). The ubiquity of sensors and the new role of users as content producers introduce new actors in model definitions [24] and data collection. Examples of this change are the use of citizen science activities to collect data [26] or to validate data directly in the field [27, 28].

When data is aggregated with formal descriptors we look at the information layer. There, we find semantic repositories. The FAO-VEST/AgroPortal map [29] that includes 299 RDF ontologies related to agriculture, crop and it lifecycle [30] ontologies belongs to the information layer. At this level we also find agriculture ontologies such as those described in [31, 32]. When elements in the information layer are linked among them, the knowledge layer is generated [33].

The transformation from data to knowledge requires the definition of models, for example, nutrition or climatological models which combine knowledge representations, a software infrastructure, and hardware infrastructure. There are groups dedicated to model this processes such as the AGMIP project [34, 35] related to agricultural simulation and climate impacts, or the Geoshare[1] group, which includes a broad range of agricultural data and analysis tools, among others.

DSS, Recommender Systems, Expert Systems and Advisory Systems are based on the relationships among different actors in the agriculture lifecycle, such as farmers and agricultural domain experts. These kinds of systems work at the knowledge and wisdom layers of the information chain. For their implementation, challenges still remain. Data and models are still isolated in silos, in specific domain repositories and the interoperability is still weak [24]; nevertheless, the use of ontologies could improve this by making possible the standardization of vocabulary, and data formats.

6 Conclusions: Opportunities and Challenges

The Semantic Web is a collaboratively constructed data repository. It depends on a sound theoretical model (ontologies and logic) and mature technology (the WWW). It shows characteristics of the collective intelligence [36] initiatives that made projects such as Wikipedia the center of today's information seeking.

As discussed in Sect. 5, the number of vocabularies and ontologies available for the domain of agriculture is growing. However, initiatives that use Semantic Web data to support decision making in agriculture are rare.

The Semantic Web, via initiatives like Linked Open Data, attempts to coordinate independent and previously disconnected efforts to standardize data representation formats, and vocabularies. Interoperability between applications depends on using compatible formats and unique identifiers to refer to the same entity. For example, to publish data that refers to the "Potato Beatle" (or Leptinotarsa decemlineata) its URI (http://aims.fao.org/aos/agrovoc/c_30034) should be used instead of any language

[1] https://mygeohub.org/groups/geoshare last accessed on May 2017.

specific string that would require human interpretation. Application developers need to learn these vocabularies and entity identifiers in order to create real Semantic Web aware systems.

The Semantic Web is an ecosystem that only flourishes when those that constitute it play according to its rules. Data generators (e.g., governmental agencies, research laboratories, technology providers) should participate in vocabulary standardization initiatives and publish data according to agreed vocabularies, aiming at the five stars of Linked Data[2]. Application developer need to learn and user existing vocabularies, consequently avoiding effort duplication. Whenever possible, application developers should contribute to making the Linked Data Cloud richer and up to date. Web site creators, even though their main primary audience consists of humans, should consider using approaches such as Microdata and RDFa, to make the data in their web-sites available to software agents.

Decision making requires timely, relevant, high-quality information. For certain topics such as classification of crop varieties and insect species there are mature, trustable sources (e.g., Universities). However, data related to more dynamic phenomena such as climate, and to recent development such as innovative products and methods, require that multiple perspectives are represented and made available. Paradigmatic cases can often be found around topics where competing and often contradicting opinions are seen. In such scenarios, it is important to develop trustable participative decision making systems that account for evidence and offer provenance traceability.

Acknowledgments. Authors of this publication acknowledge the contribution of the Project 691249, RUC-APS: Enhancing and implementing Knowledge based ICT solutions within high Risk and Uncertain Conditions for Agriculture Production Systems (www.ruc-aps.eu), funded by the European Union under their funding scheme H2020-MSCA-RISE-2015.

References

1. Kochenderfer, M.J., Reynolds, H.J.D.: Decision Making Under Uncertainty: Theory and Application. MIT Press, Cambridge (2015)
2. Power, D.J.: Decision Support Systems: Concepts and Resources for Managers. Greenwood Publishing Group, Westport (2002)
3. Turban, E.: Decision Support and Expert Systems: Management Support Systems. Prentice Hall PTR, Upper Saddle River, NJ, USA (1993)
4. Zaraté, P., Kersten, G.E., Hernández, J.E. (eds.): Group Decision and Negotiation. A Process-Oriented View, vol. 180. Springer International Publishing, Cham (2014)
5. Decision Support Systems. Elsevier. ISSN: 0167-9236
6. Berners-Lee, T., Hendler, J., Lassila, O.: The Semantic Web. Sci. Am. **284**, 34–43 (2001)
7. Hendler, J.: Web 3.0 Emerging. Computer (Long. Beach. Calif). 42 (2009)
8. Mir, S.A., Qasim, M., Arfat, Y., Mubarak, T., Bhat, Z.A., Bhat, J.A., Bangroo, S.A., Sofi, T.A.: Decision support systems in a global agricultural perspective - a comprehensive review. Int. J. Agric. Sci. **7**, 403–415 (2015)

[2] Linked Data - https://www.w3.org/DesignIssues/LinkedData.html. Last accessed on April 2017.

9. Ritchie, J.T.: Model for predicting evaporation from a row crop with incomplete cover. Water Resour. Res. **8**, 1204–1213 (1972)
10. Jorgensen, M.S., Detlefsen, N.K., Hutchings, N.J.: FarmN: A decision support tool for managing Nitrogen flow at the farm level. EFITA/WCCA. 25–28 (2005)
11. Manos, B., Ciani, A., Bournaris, T., Vassiliadou, I., Papathanasiou, J.: A taxonomy survey of decision support systems in agriculture. Agric. Econ. Rev. **5**(2), 191–203 (2004)
12. Edwards-Jones, G.: Knowledge-based systems for crop protection: theory and practice. Crop Prot. **12**, 565–578 (1993)
13. Blomqvist, E.: The use of Semantic Web technologies for decision support–a survey. Semant. Web. **5**, 177–201 (2014)
14. Bouamrane, M.-M., Rector, A., Hurrell, M.: A hybrid architecture for a preoperative decision support system using a rule engine and a reasoner on a clinical ontology. In: Polleres, A., Swift, T. (eds.) RR 2009. LNCS, vol. 5837, pp. 242–253. Springer, Heidelberg (2009). doi: 10.1007/978-3-642-05082-4_17
15. Bouamrane, M.-M., Rector, A., Hurrell, M.: Experience of using OWL ontologies for automated inference of routine pre-operative screening tests. In: Patel-Schneider, Peter F., Pan, Y., Hitzler, P., Mika, P., Zhang, L., Pan, Jeff Z., Horrocks, I., Glimm, B. (eds.) ISWC 2010. LNCS, vol. 6497, pp. 50–65. Springer, Heidelberg (2010). doi: 10.1007/978-3-642-17749-1_4
16. Buranarach, M., Supnithi, T., Chalortham, N., Khunthong, V., Varasai, P., Kawtrakul, A.: A semantic web framework to support knowledge management in chronic disease healthcare. In: Sartori, F., Sicilia, M.Á., Manouselis, N. (eds.) MTSR 2009. CCIS, vol. 46, pp. 164–170. Springer, Heidelberg (2009). doi:10.1007/978-3-642-04590-5_15
17. Tao, C., Solbrig, Harold R., Sharma, Deepak K., Wei, W.-Q., Savova, Guergana K., Chute, Christopher G.: Time-oriented question answering from clinical narratives using semantic-web techniques. In: Patel-Schneider, Peter F., Pan, Y., Hitzler, P., Mika, P., Zhang, L., Pan, Jeff Z., Horrocks, I., Glimm, B. (eds.) ISWC 2010. LNCS, vol. 6497, pp. 241–256. Springer, Heidelberg (2010). doi:10.1007/978-3-642-17749-1_16
18. González, A.R., Fernandez, J., Jimenez, E., Mencke, M., Radzimski, M., Gomez, J.M., Alor-Hernandez, G., Posada-Gomez, R.: MEDFINDER-Using semantic web, web 2.0 and geolocation methods to develop a decision support system to locate doctors. In: WEBIST, pp. 288–293 (2009)
19. Baker, C.J.O., Shaban-Nejad, A., Su, X., Haarslev, V., Butler, G.: Semantic web infrastructure for fungal enzyme biotechnologists. Web Semant. Sci. Serv. Agents World Wide Web. **4**, 168–180 (2006)
20. Bell, D., Nguyen, T.: Proximal business intelligence on the semantic web. In: Nelson, M.L., et al. (eds.) Sustainable e-Business Management. LNBIP, vol. 58, pp. 145–159. Springer, Heidelberg (2010)
21. Bouamrane, M.-M., Rector, A., Hurrell, M.: Semi-automatic generation of a patient preoperative knowledge-base from a legacy clinical database. Move Meaningful Internet Syst. OTM **2009**, 1224–1237 (2009)
22. Torres, D.: Co-Evolution between Social and Semantic Web (2014)
23. Mendoza, L., Zuccarelli, G., Díaz, A., Fernández, A.: The semantic web as a platform for collective intelligence. In: Baloian, N., Burstein, F., Ogata, H., Santoro, F., Zurita, G. (eds.) CRIWG 2014. LNCS, vol. 8658, pp. 255–262. Springer, Cham (2014). doi: 10.1007/978-3-319-10166-8_22
24. Jones, J.W., Antle, J.M., Basso, B., Boote, K.J., Conant, R.T., Foster, I., Godfray, H.C.J., Herrero, M., Howitt, R.E., Janssen, S.: Toward a new generation of agricultural system data, models, and knowledge products: State of agricultural systems science. Agric. Syst. (2016)

25. Caracciolo, C., Stellato, A., Morshed, A., Johannsen, G., Rajbhandari, S., Jaques, Y., Keizer, J.: The AGROVOC linked dataset. Semant. Web. **4**, 341–348 (2013)
26. Reges, H.W., Doesken, N., Turner, J., Newman, N., Bergantino, A., Schwalbe, Z.: COCORAHS: the evolution and accomplishments of a volunteer rain gauge network. Bull. Am. Meteorol. Soc. **97**, 1831–1846 (2016)
27. Chaudhary, S., Bhise, M., Banerjee, A., Goyal, A., Moradiya, C.: Agro advisory system for cotton crop (2015)
28. Walisadeera, A.I., Wikramanayake, G.N., Ginige, A.: Designing a farmer centred ontology for social life network. In: DATA, pp. 238–247 (2013)
29. Jonquet, C., Toulet, A., Arnaud, E., Aubin, S., Yeumo, E.D., Emonet, V., Pesce, V., Larmande, P.: AgroPortal: an open repository of ontologies and vocabularies for agriculture and nutrition data. In: GODAN Summit (2016)
30. Thunkijjanukij, A., Kawtrakul, A., Panichsakpatana, S., Veesommai, U.: Rice production knowledge management: criteria for ontology development. Thai J. Agric. Sci. **42**, 115–124 (2009)
31. Xie, N., Wang, W., Yang, Y.: Ontology-based agricultural knowledge acquisition and application. In: Li, D. (ed.) CCTA 2007. IFIP, vol. 258, pp. 349–357. Springer, Boston, MA (2008). doi:10.1007/978-0-387-77251-6_38
32. Pokharel, S., Sherif, M.A., Lehmann, J.: Ontology based data access and integration for improving the effectiveness of farming in nepal. In: Proceedings of the 2014 IEEE/WIC/ACM International Joint Conferences on Web Intelligence (WI) and Intelligent Agent Technologies (IAT), vol. 02, pp. 319–326. IEEE Computer Society (2014)
33. Kang, J.C., Gao, J.L.: Application of ontology technology in agricultural information retrieval. Adv. Mater. Res. **756–759**, 1249–1253 (2013)
34. McDermid, S., Gowtham, R., Bhuvaneswari, K., Vellingiri, G., Arunachalam, L.: The impacts of climate change on Tamil Nadu rainfed maize production: a multi-model approach to identify sensitivities and uncertainties. Curr. Sci. **110**, 1257 (2016)
35. Elliott, J., Kelly, D., Chryssanthacopoulos, J., Glotter, M., Jhunjhnuwala, K., Best, N., Wilde, M., Foster, I.: The parallel system for integrating impact models and sectors (pSIMS). Environ. Model Softw. **62**, 509–516 (2014)
36. Malone, T.W., Bernstein, M.S.: Handbook of Collective Intelligence. MIT Press, Cambridge (2015)

Challenges and Solutions for Enhancing Agriculture Value Chain Decision-Making. A Short Review

Jorge E. Hernandez[1(✉)], Janusz Kacprzyk[2], Hervé Panetto[3], Alejandro Fernandez[4], Shaofeng Liu[5], Angel Ortiz[6], and Marco De-Angelis[7]

[1] University of Liverpool Management School, Liverpool, UK
J.E.Hernandez@Liverpool.ac.uk
[2] IBSPAN, Systems Research Institute, Polish Academy of Sciences, Warsaw, Poland
[3] UL, Université de Lorraine, Nancy, France
[4] UNLP, Universidad Nacional de La Plata, La Plata, Argentina
[5] UoP, University of Plymouth, Plymouth, UK
[6] UPV, Universitat Politècnica de València, Valencia, Spain
[7] The Institute for Risk and Uncertainty, University of Liverpool, Liverpool, UK

Abstract. Increasingly challenging global and environmental requirements have resulted in agricultural systems coming under increasing pressure to enhance their resilience capabilities. This in special to respond to the abrupt changes in resource quality, quantity and availability, especially during unexpected environmental circumstances, such as uncertain weather, pests and diseases, volatile market conditions and commodity prices. Therefore, integrated solutions are necessary to support the knowledge-management, collaborative ICT solution, risk management and regulation management across agriculture stakeholders. Therefore, and based on the on-going work under the H2020 RUC-APS project research network, this book chapter is oriented to contribute to agriculture value chain decision-making field to cover the current need on gathering a common understanding and appreciation of new trends in agriculture value chain, in special the multi-disciplinary challenges. For this, a short a literature review is conducted to summarise the main findings on real application and current research trends. This within the objective to propose an integrated framework based on better use of communication ways, standardised structures, development of training and awareness, regulation based initiatives and vertical Integration.

Keywords: Agriculture value chain · Collaboration · ICT · Risk management · Case studies · Review

1 Introduction

In order to understand the agriculture concept from the operations and supply chain management perspective, the agribusiness terminology was established by [1] and can be understood as the sum of all operations involved in manufacture and distribution of

L.M. Camarinha-Matos et al. (Eds.): PRO-VE 2017, IFIP AICT 506, pp. 761–774, 2017.
DOI: 10.1007/978-3-319-65151-4_68

farm supplies, production operations on the farm, and the storage, processing, and distribution of farm commodities. But, considering the current decision-making challenges in agribusiness, specially regarded to promote costless coordination of production and distribution, finding solutions to fixed market imperfections and consequent price distortions and how to include private strategies in agriculture and related sectors [2], uncertainties in information across the agribusiness related stakeholders have oriented agribusiness analyst to get focuses primarily on the following main topics: agricultural environment and resources; risk and uncertainty; food and consumer economics; prices and incomes; market structures; trade and development; and technical change and human capital. These topics remains open in terms of required support and solutions, but more important, open to support research from theory and practice. In this context, uncertainties in information implies none-effective decision-making processes for farmers and to each related participant who belongs to the agriculture value chain.

In addition to this, and as established by [3], new kind of uncertainties coming from the climate global change issue is now another point of concern in agriculture and, even if it is a well-known issue, empirical research results has just been started to be released [4–8], but, even though, analysis on the main implications to agribusiness, decision-making, and collaborative networks in agriculture is still presented as a gap in the international literature. Thus, and as a source of uncertainty, climate change drives another type of uncertainties regarded to the lack of complete knowledge about the ecosystems reactions to climate change. This has important implications on how decision-making approaches are to be adapted to these new challenges. In fact, one of the main goals in agriculture and for the whole agri-food sector, is to find the right responses and strategies to the agribusiness challenges in a much faster way [9], but also dealing with the main uncertainties collaboratively. In addition to this, it is important to consider the role that farmers can play in overcoming these uncertainties if they are supported accordingly. This means providing them the right guidance, information, training and collaborative approach for developing solutions to their problems. But, due to the lack of information (specially regarded to the local regions cultures), this is certainly becoming a major task every day more. Thus, and considering current agribusiness based framework analysis done by [10, 11], practitioners and researcher are still looking at finding the efficient ways to answer questions like: how current growing in risk and uncertainty affects agribusiness stakeholders?; is the development and adoption of new technologies adding value to agribusiness related activities?, how can rapid market responsiveness be implemented so support changes in industry structure? and; are collaborative networks applicable in agribusiness domains to deal with interoperable aspects?.

Therefore, in the light of these current open challenges in agribusiness, the aim of this research is to provide an up-to-date contribution to field of Agriculture Value Chain decision-making, in special by updating and contrasting main challenges and requirements based on current literature and case studies. To accomplish this, the rationale is supported by considering following structure: (1) in the second section the research method is explained; next (2) the brief literature review on cases, knowledge management, collaborative ICT, risk management, regulations in agriculture value chain management is presented; after this (3) a brief analysis is presented in the section four within the purpose of addressing the main recommendations, from research, in order to support the main challenges and requirements from agriculture value chains, thus the RUC-APS framework is proposed and; finally (4) main conclusions and further research is presented.

2 Research Method

Considering the existing literature review in the field already performed by [3, 12–21], the method to support this review will consider sources from journals, books and reports in field of agriculture within a view of: value chain, ICT, risk, regulations and case studies. For this purpose, a qualitative analysis is to be performed to provide the current pictures on the already mentioned challenges. The main selected sources for this review are: http://scholar.google.com, http://www.scopus.com and http://www.sciencedirect.com.

Therefore, the main objective from this brief literature review is identify the main gaps and trend in the current research, understand the main agriculture value chain challenges and requirements, realise how theory and method is supported by empirical evidence and to understand how the main application are taking place in the field. The main findings from this research are presented in the following sections.

3 Short Literature Review on Challenges and Solutions for Enhancing Agriculture Value Chain Decision-Making

Regarding to the findings in agriculture needs from [30], it was shown that nearly a third of the global population relies on agriculture for a living, and the growth in this sector has been at least twice as effective at reducing poverty as growth in other sectors. But, progress on agriculture-based solutions can be frustratingly slow, therefore practitioners, researchers and academics are every day more involved in this field. In fact, challenges in agriculture might vary from biological science, going through health-care to social science and technologies. Which topics has been extensible reviewed [22–27]. But also, from the agribusiness decision-making point of view [28, 29], there is a high need for generating integrated and collaborative solutions, so that farmers can be embedded in the participative solutions generation process. Therefore, this review section is to be focused on decision-making process related to agriculture value chains.

In fact, a high variety of new digital applications, oriented to accelerate the improvement on productivity and growth in this sector [30], can be found, but not all of them are effective or resilient enough once agriculture value chains are facing unexpected events. As a tool, ICTs can provide the forum to access information and the necessary training to agriculture value chain stakeholders by enhancing their communication strategies, thus their decision-making process. ICTs will consist of electronic and digital based solutions for capturing, processing, sharing, storing and retrieving information, hence for broadcasting and using data and images through technology based mechanism [31]. In this context, the dilemma in most of the agriculture domains is regarded to decide and realise whether to move towards to a more traditional, organic farming or to a modern biotechnology-based agriculture [32], which necessarily implies the combined use of: Knowledge Management, ICT, Collaborative solutions, Decision Support Systems and regulation management. However, the scenario is even more complex, and a well and up-to-date understanding is required.

In fact, whether a wide variety of agricultural technologies and sustainability pathways are required to co-exist (worldwide at least), the current need from agriculture value chain stakeholders have moved from choosing between existing technologies to focus on the new technological developments through innovation [33]. But this has also led to the wide unused number of technologies as well the clueless from farmers about what the main criteria for selected the right solution might be. Therefore, by considering agriculture value chains market's needs, agri-food supply (farmers and manufacturers) and demand (supermarkets and other food retailers) established by [34], the following section presents the key findings in author contributions. This starts by considering we challenges addressed for veridical collaboration, information sharing and climate change within a view of agriculture value chain. From this perspective, and considering the current agribusiness value chain challenges, papers were reviewed and selected. Regarding to this, agribusiness decision-making related paper were selected on the key following domains: Collaborative ICT, Risk Management, Ontology driven, Technology transfer, Regulation analysis considering the following approaches: Supply chain management, Multi-stakeholder, Decision Support System, Real-life, Case study.

3.1 Case Studies Analysis in Agriculture Value Chains Decision-Making Challenges

There are many challenges involved in the agriculture value chains. These challenges can be seen from several angles and their implication can be grouped in three main themes, such as: vertical integration, information sharing and regarding the uncertainties due to the climate change. From this analysis is depicted that since the 80's there is a continuous interest for developing solutions to support these challenges. In overall, the analysis considers references that discusses the agriculture value challenges from a real-life case study point of view (see Table 1).

As depicted in Table 1, it can be found that vertical Integration and information sharing are two topics widely discusses, as well climate change. In addition, it is also possible to realise that authors also address ICT aspects to be considered once setting up potential solutions to food contamination problem, food security policies and postharvest practices, where the main objective in supporting these challenges is to ensure the food quality and safety.

In addition to this, one of the key identified challenges is regarded on how managing the knowledge across the agriculture value chain and their stakeholders. This since the level of tacit knowledge is very high, thus the main solution for these challenges will be around gathering the tacit knowledge to make it explicit. Therefore, the knowledge management might be contrasted across the agriculture value chain

Table 1. Case Studies based on main agriculture value chains decision-making challenges.

Author	Agriculture value chain decision-making challenges	Main aspect to support
[35]	India horticulture industry has ineffective information communication between producers and end-customers. The government introduced a physical wholesale market terminal to allow producer and end-customers to meet and share information	Vertical Integration
[36]	Both wholesalers and retailers need to know producers and production information.	Vertical Integration
[37]	Most farmers use wire phone or cellular phone to seek information. The Internet is not a popular method as lack of infrastructure, the cost of using the internet and the literacy rate of farmers.	Information Sharing
[38]	Farmers need a wide range of information to make a good decision. Information for farmers is very fragmented and unreliable. It is suggested to use a database that store information all together to facilitate farmers' decision making.	Information Sharing
[39]	The common way for India farmers to get reliable information is to go to external organisations. External organisations are usually far from farmers. Farmers need to drive there and it is very costly and time-consuming. The access to information is restricted or prohibited. Access to digital information is a bottleneck for HVC performance improvement in India.	Information Sharing
[40]	Choosing the right are for growing vegetable is a major issue. In special under climate change, hence it is suggested to use information communication between nation, regional and local-level management.	Climate change
[41]	Under a Value Chain Approach, environmental parameters, such as temperature, affects the product cycle time, in this case the example of grape was studied, where it was realised the agriculture value chain, due to high temperatures was required now to deal with 's faster ripening process time.	Climate change
[42]	Weather tracking database predicts the weather and makes planning arrangement, which successfully improves the effectiveness of producing quality grape.	Climate change
[43]	The quality of vegetable will be indirectly affected by climate change due to the change of pest species. A model shows the relationship between the temperature and the species of pests helps predict and control pest in agriculture.	Climate change

stakeholders, thus be used for developing more efficient solutions. For this purpose, the following section, by considering the knowledge management aspects, gather the number of authors contributing to the combined perspective of Knowledge Management, Collaborative ICT, Risk Management, Ontology driven, Technology transfer and Regulation analysis; versus Supply chain management, Multi-stakeholder, Decision Support System, Real-life and Case study.

3.2 Knowledge Management, Collaborative ICT, Technology Transfer and Risk Analysis Contributions to Agriculture Value Chain

From Table 1 analysis, it is depicted that the main challenges remain on how to determine the right selection and application of existing and emerging technologies, as well as on how to consider the adequate ongoing R&D for small farmers at small-scale food processing operations, therefore to move toward reducing the cost of food. But this also within an special focus of making a significant contribution to food production, environment and also to provide a good living for the operators/farmers [34]. From this, it also important to consider that due to the great advancement on ICTs, a high advancement in agriculture planning has ben also produced. One of the reasons for this is due to the fact that, ICT's can not only be cost-effectively and practically employed to facilitate information delivery, but also to support an effective knowledge sharing among farmers and stakeholders [44]. Hence, the success of agriculture value chain will necessarily depends largely on decisions by stakeholders on questions such as what to grow, where to sell, how to maintain the main sources, and how to manage common resources [45].

It is also acknowledged that stakeholders, involved in agricultural and rural development, are highly required to communicate, negotiate and to reach decisions that can achieve results. The main failures are commonly regarded to the extension on inability to deal with communication concerns. In fact, and based on [46], works at the farming/producer level are often ineffective in their communication with partners, which is due to the lack in training in methods of communication. They often have technical, but not communication orientation [47], which generated an unbalanced situation. Thus, and due to the variety of uncertainty sources in weather, soil, water and land conditions, diverse models, methods of analysis and solutions are needed on which the knowledge from farmers will be gathered and manged accordingly. This will activate the need of using different ways to support the variety of challenges in agriculture value chains, but in special to develop usable solutions to farmers [48]. Nevertheless, with the rapid development of information technology, the agriculture information dissemination models are constantly evolved and required of analysis for solutions [19]. Table 2 shows, therefore, the main findings for Supporting Agriculture Value Chain Decision-making considering a multidisciplinary approach.

Aligned with this, Table 2 shows where the key authors contribute to the main areas. Thus, it depicts the fact that, in general the agriculture value chain is widely known, and a variety of solutions and approaches are considered to overcome most of the challenges.

Nevertheless, not all the approaches are considered in the same way, and certainly they do not weight the same. This is the clear case of Collaborative ICT and Regulation analysis. In fact, where collaborative solutions are required at every level, there is an evidence that regulations advancement are not always aligned and up-to-date with these requirements. In addition to this, whether the application based research marks a high presence on authors contributions, it is also evidence the connection from theory and practice is low. This means that contributions on theory are still a pending matter once looking at real-life applications. Whether theory in operational research and ICT developments are high, these are good under a theoretical aspect, but lacks on

Table 2. Contribution analysis to Agriculture value chain decision-making.

Dimension/approach	Supply chain management	Multi-stakeholder	Decision Support System	Real-life Case study
Knowledge management	[30, 32, 49]	[47, 49, 50]	[47, 51, 52]	[12, 18, 30, 47, 49, 50]
Collaborative ICT	[19, 20, 53–55]	[14, 53, 56, 57]	[15, 20, 51, 53, 58–60]	[12, 21, 30, 53, 56–58, 61, 62]
Risk management	[17, 55]	[17, 63, 64],	[17, 65]	[17, 63–65]
Ontology driven	[48, 55, 66–69]	[63, 66, 68, 70]	[66, 68–72]	[48, 63, 67, 69, 71, 72]
Technology transfer	[30, 73]	[12, 73–75]	[12]	[64, 73, 75, 76],
Regulation analysis	[15, 33, 48]	[63, 77, 78]	[74, 78]	[63, 78]

applicability. Moreover, the development of decision support systems is also wide, and most of the researchers look at its applications, but just a few look at the value chain and/or multi-stakeholders approach. Which means the challenges on developing collaborative and participatory agriculture value chain decision support systems remains as an open topic. An interesting aspect was the evidenced on using/creating ontologies for supporting the ICT development of agriculture value chain solutions. Nevertheless, even if a variety of cases can be found in this topic, the use of ontologies still lacks on their real applicability, in especial to support the technology transfer aspects and interoperability across agribusiness technologies. In fact, decision support systems based training on agriculture value chain stakeholders is a key aspect, but has been vaguely covered by research authors and it is depicted as one of the less covered topics, thus a high level of opportunities for enhancing this topics as a research theme in agriculture value chain is depicted.

4 Analysis

From the short literature review, and aligned with the contribution from [79], it is realised that main barriers for adopting ICT solutions are: (1) the lack of physical and human resource infrastructure, (2) too much innovation blocks the use of older tested and in use technologies imposing an unacceptable cost, (3) ICT adoption based on working within communities takes longer in many cases because of the lack of understanding and awareness of the needs and challenges of small-scale farmers, (4) Ensuring leadership within the political and governmental environment, (5) Developing leadership and agents of change at all levels including communities, (6) Sharing ICT adoption funding including public/private partnership and (7) Sharing details of successful projects including business opportunities and their benefits.

Therefore, at the agriculture value chain level, the creation of efficient agricultural market, which delivers agricultural products, from the farmer to the consumer is a need. This implies that, behind every challenge and contributions, there is a need for efficiently make functioning agriculture value chains to commit with the markets, thus to make producers and consumers increase their benefits. But unfortunately, the supply chain management models are not as efficient as desired, and ICT integrations are still an open requirement to support the agribusiness based decision-making.

The challenges facing supply-chain management and agri-business can be seen from three main perspectives. In the first place, the lack of accessibility to regulated markets generates difficulties to establish standardised agriculture value chains solutions. In the second place, the lack of participatory developments, implies a lack on effective ICT developments for Agriculture value chain stakeholders, specially farmers. Finally, lack on standard regulations that understand the micro-levels of the value chain, implies inefficiencies across the value chain stakeholders.

In this context, from the reviewed papers, and by analysing and understating the main implications from coming from Tables 1 and 2, the following suggestions for supporting the current challenges and solution generations for enhancing the Agriculture Value Chain Decision-making are addressed:

- **Better use of communication ways:** Once the Agriculture value chain is formed, and in order meet their desired objectives efficiently, the information sharing is essential, thus collaborative ways must be set in place, specially to monitor and trace information between stakeholders.
- **Set standardised structures:** Through standardised structures it will possible to achieve more effectively the efficiency desired levels. In this context, standards might follow two approaches: (1) the first is regarded on how the agriculture products are produced, packaged, transported and delivered; (2) the second is regarded to ICT systems to be used across the value chain. Therefore, these standard approaches will enable stakeholders to efficiently manage their inefficiencies as well as to interoperate better with the high variety of systems available on these agriculture value chain environments.
- **Development of training and awareness:** Due to the current changes and evolution on market needs, hence into agriculture value chain structures, specialists, that will understand the high variety of value chain structures, is required. Hence, training, coaching, counselling and mentoring can be extended to all the parties in the supply chain. In this way, collaborative ICT solution might be better applied in several levels of the value chain.
- **Regulation based initiatives:** Agriculture regulations plays a leading role, in special with the new globalisation trends. International value chains are everyday more common; hence, robust and adaptable regulations are required to deal effectively with unexpected uncertainties from each region. The objective of this approach, is to generate consistent agriculture value chains across every level, thus to mutually reinforce them and commit with the common contradictory objectives from regions and stakeholders, therefore, standard protocols (ontologies) must be in place to support collaborative ICT, Risk management and regulation development.
- **Vertical Integration:** Considering the new trends on technologies as well as the dynamics of world economy, agribusiness stakeholders, in special farmers, are required to get collaborative involved, so that the continuous provision of safe and ample raw materials can be guaranteed amongst farmers, processors and traders. Therefore, the vertical integration will promote shorter value chains and an

increment on total returns shares. Therefore, to cope with the main uncertainties, farmers will get more incentives to achieve value chain requirements, such as certifications and global environmental requirements. Therefore, agriculture stake holder will be in a better position to use standardised technologies to share information and support collaborative decision-making processes.

4.1 The RUC-APS Framework Proposal

Therefore, to provide a crystallised view on how a potential solution might looks like, the Fig. 1 presents the RUC-APS framework. Through this, an advancement in agriculture based-decision making is provided. Thus, the agriculture value chain will be seen in terms of the integration of Global Agribusiness, Risk and Uncertainty, end-user driven solutions, inputs, products for exports, packaging & cold storage, processing and distributions. Therefore, the agriculture production systems, and its impact over the end users, will be mainly driven by participatory ICT developments.

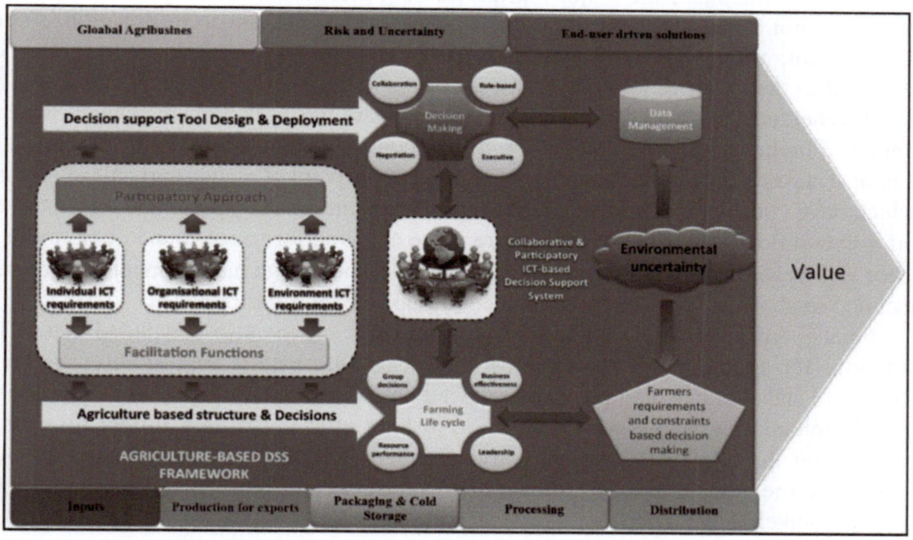

Fig. 1. The RUC-APS Framework. (sources: www.ruc-aps.eu)

As depicted in Fig. 1, the RUC-APS framework is oriented to contribute to the generation of horizontal and vertical collaboration strategy for supporting agriculture value chain in terms of: the organisations development for building mutual and beneficial value chain relationships in agriculture. For this the proposed RUC-APS framework propose enhancing the interactions between small and medium farmers with major value chain actors (often smallholders and businesses in the upstream chain segment) and larger, better-endowed businesses further downstream; and, to integrate this with policies that will support the environment on which value chain actors operate. Therefore, RUC-APS provide innovation for the development of agriculture production systems and their impact over the end-users by focusing on participatory ICT developments.

5 Conclusions

From this brief literature review, it can be realised that there is a clear evidence that current growing in risk and uncertainty are affecting affects agribusiness stakeholders' decision-making, especially in terms of dealing with the key commodities, such as price. Thus, if the supply chain management is improved in the agriculture sector, it will lead farmers to improve their business scenario. In fact, the key aspects addressed from authors were vertical integration, information sharing and climate changes, as main source of current challenges to be supported.

In this sense, it was noticed that one of the critical aspect to improve the agriculture supply chain management is the one regarded to adoption of new technologies, which necessarily implies that the information flow should be managed standardly. This will enhance the information sharing, thus will create value and will improve the performance, even more once information sharing will be established across regions and sectors, hence rapid responses to the market will be required. In fact, as depicted from the reviewed literature, the major reasons causing information sharing issues are that producers not always have access to the right ICT, hence access to information is not that straight, which implies a current need in implementing collaborative network structure to deal with ICT interoperable aspects.

Another aspect is that agriculture value chains are facing is climate change, which implies a higher need for collaboration to overcome the main uncertainties, in special amongst stakeholders from similar latitudes. From this point of view, nearly all solutions which have considered a knowledge management point of view, presented an effective information flow, thus a better agriculture value chain performance. In addition to this, there was a clear evidence that authors dealing with knowledge management were more inclined to share more information, hence to improve their performance.

Finally, from the authors contribution analysis, it can be also concluded that ICT solutions for agriculture problems aims to increase information accessibility, variety, sharing to stakeholders, and present a relevant contribution to farmers, thus presenting a high potential of increasing the decision-making efficiently. As a further research, considering the RUC-APS project activities, this short review will be extended by supporting the generation of a validated agriculture value chain conceptual model for the main stakeholders' decision-making and the main ICT application will be addressed for the seven countries on which the project is being applied (UK, Spain, Italy, France, Poland, Chile and Argentina). In addition, an extended version of this literature review will be produced by analysing more international case studies and adding quantitative analysis for this review, as well as by establishing the most up-to-date agriculture value chain road-map and covering the main interoperability due the main agriculture value chain integration requirements.

Acknowledgments. Authors of this publication acknowledge the contribution of the Project 691249, RUC-APS: Enhancing and implementing Knowledge based ICT solutions within high Risk and Uncertain Conditions for Agriculture Production Systems (www.ruc-aps.eu), funded by the European Union under their funding scheme H2020-MSCA-RISE-2015.

References

1. Davis, J., Goldberg, R.: A concept of agribusiness. Division of Research. Graduate School of Business Administration. Bost. Harvard Univ. (1957)
2. Zylbersztajn, D.: Agribusiness systems analysis: origin, evolution and research perspectives. Rev. Adm. (2016)
3. Yousefpour, R., Jacobsen, J., Thorsen, B., Meilby, H.: A review of decision-making approaches to handle uncertainty and risk in adaptive forest management under climate change. Ann. For. (2012)
4. Myers, S., Smith, M., Guth, S., Golden, C.: Climate change and global food systems: potential impacts on food security and undernutrition. Annu. Rev. (2017)
5. Thamo, T., Addai, D., Pannell, D., Robertson, M.: Climate change impacts and farm-level adaptation: economic analysis of a mixed cropping–livestock system. Agricultural (2017)
6. Altieri, M., Nicholls, C.: The adaptation and mitigation potential of traditional agriculture in a changing climate. Clim. Change (2017)
7. Alam, M., Siwar, C., Murad, M., Toriman, M.: Impacts of climate change on agriculture and food security issues in Malaysia: an empirical study on farm level assessment (2017)
8. Lobell, D., Asseng, S.: Comparing estimates of climate change impacts from process-based and statistical crop models. Environ. Res. Lett. (2017)
9. Yearbook, F.: World food and agriculture. Food Agric. Organ. United. (2013)
10. McKenzie, F., Williams, J.: Sustainable food production: constraints, challenges and choices by 2050. Food Secur. (2015)
11. Boehlje, M., Roucan-Kane, M., Bröring, S.: Future agribusiness challenges: Strategic uncertainty, innovation and structural change. Int. Food. (2011)
12. Suprem, A., Mahalik, N., Kim, K.: A review on application of technology systems, standards and interfaces for agriculture and food sector. Comput. Stand. Interfaces (2013)
13. Mahmood, H., Ahmad, M., Ahmad, T.: Potentials and prospects of precision agriculture in Pakistan-a review. Pakistan J. Agric. (2013)
14. Kruize, J.W., Robbemond, R.M., Scholten, H., Wolfert, J., Beulens, A.J.M.: Improving arable farm enterprise integration - Review of existing technologies and practices from a farmer's perspective. Comput. Electron. Agric. **96**, 75–89 (2013)
15. Martin, G., Martin-Clouaire, R., Duru, M.: Farming system design to feed the changing world. A review. Agron. Sustain. (2013)
16. Aqeel-Ur-Rehman, Abbasi, A.Z., Islam, N., Shaikh, Z.A.: A review of wireless sensors and networks' applications in agriculture (2014), http://www.sciencedirect.com/science/article/pii/S0920548911000353
17. Zougmoré, R., Partey, S.: Toward climate-smart agriculture in West Africa: a review of climate change impacts, adaptation strategies and policy developments for the livestock, fishery. Agric. (2016)
18. Dercon, S., Gollin, D.: Agriculture in african development: a review of theories and strategies. Annu. Rev. Resour. Econ. **44**, 1–41 (2014)
19. Zhang, Y., Wang, L., Duan, Y.: Agricultural information dissemination using ICTs: A review and analysis of information dissemination models in China. Inf. Process. Agric. **3**, 17–29 (2016)
20. Kaur, H., Goraya, S.: Role of cloud based technologies in agriculture process across countries: a review. Int. J. Comput. Sci. (2016)
21. Gangurde, P., Bhende, M.: A review on precision agriculture using wireless sensor networks. Int. J. Eng. Trends Technol. **23**, 426–431 (2015)

22. Mittler, R., Blumwald, E.: Genetic engineering for modern agriculture: challenges and perspectives. Annu. Rev. Plant Biol. (2010)
23. Opara, L.: Traceability in agriculture and food supply chain: a review of basic concepts, technological implications, and future prospects. J. Food Agric., Environ (2003)
24. Hillocks, R.: Farming with fewer pesticides: EU pesticide review and resulting challenges for UK agriculture. Crop Prot. (2012)
25. Shalaby, M., Al-Zahrani, K., Baig, M.: Threats and challenges to sustainable agriculture and rural development in Egypt: implications for agricultural extension. J. Anim. (2011)
26. Pant, L., Hambly-Odame, H.: Innovations systems in renewable natural resource management and sustainable agriculture: a literature review. African J. Sci. Technol. (2009)
27. Nagpure, A., Choudhary, B., Gupta, R.: Chitinases: in agriculture and human healthcare. Crit. Rev. (2014)
28. Iglesias, A., Quiroga, S., Moneo, M., Garrote, L.: From climate change impacts to the development of adaptation strategies: challenges for agriculture in Europe. Clim. Change. (2012)
29. Irvin, R., Stansbury, J.: Citizen participation in decision making: is it worth the effort? Public Adm. Rev. (2004)
30. Warshauer, W.: How Digital Is Solving Three Problems in Agriculture| TechnoServe - Business Solutions to Poverty, http://www.technoserve.org/blog/how-digital-is-solving-three-problems-in-agriculture
31. Zappacosta, M.: Information technologies for rural development: between promises and mirages. Info. **3**, 521–534 (2001)
32. de Wilt, J.G., Diederen, P.J.M., Butter, M., Tukker, A.: Innovation challenges for European agriculture. Foresight. **3**, 341–352 (2001)
33. Viaggi, D.: Research and innovation in agriculture: beyond productivity? Bio-Based Appl. Econ. (2015)
34. Lee, J., Gereffi, G., Beauvais, J.: Global value chains and agrifood standards: challenges and possibilities for smallholders in developing countries. Proc. Natl. Acad. Sci. U.S.A. **109**, 12326–12331 (2012)
35. Mittal, S.C.: Role of Information Technology in Agriculture and its Scope in India
36. Dolan, C., Humphrey, J.: Governance and trade in fresh vegetables: the impact of uk supermarkets on the african horticulture industry. J. Dev. Stud. **37**, 147–176 (2000)
37. Gummagolmath, K., Sharma, P.: User centric ICT model for supply chain of horticultural crops in india. Agric. Econ. Res. Rev. **26**, 91–100
38. Awuor, F., Kimeli, K., Rabah, K., Rambim, D.: ICT Solution Architecture for Agriculture. In: Conference Proceedings 978–1 (2013)
39. Rao, N.H.: A framework for implementing information and communication technologies in agricultural development in India
40. Challinor, A., Wheeler, T., Garforth, C., Craufurd, P., Kassam, A.: Assessing the vulnerability of food crop systems in Africa to climate change. Clim. Change **83**, 381–399 (2007)
41. Jones, G., Davis, R.: Climate influences on grapevine phenology, grape composition, and wine production and quality for Bordeaux, France. Am. J. Enol. (2000)
42. Webb, L., Whetton, P., Barlow, E.W.R.: Modelled impact of future climate change on phenology of wine grapes in Australia. Aust. J. Grape Wine Res. **13**, 165–175 (2007)
43. Thomson, L.J., Macfadyen, S., Hoffmann, A.A.: Predicting the effects of climate change on natural enemies of agricultural pests (2009)
44. Annor-Frempong, F., Kwarteng, J., Agunga, R., Zinnah, M.M.: Challenges and prospects of infusing information communication technologies (ICTs) in extension for agricultural and rural development in Ghana. J. Ext. Syst. **23**, 36–46 (2006)

45. Rivera, W., Alex, G.: Agriculture and Rural Development Discussion Paper 12 Extension Reform for Rural Development (2004)
46. Röling, N.G.: Extension science: information systems in agricultural development. Cambridge University Press (1988)
47. Vodt, K.W., Kuiper, D., Röling, N.: The edited proceedings of the European Seminar on Knowledge Management and Information Technology (1989)
48. ur Rehman, A.: Smart Agriculture: An Approach Towards Better Agriculture Management (2015)
49. McCullough, E., Matson, P.: Evolution of the knowledge system for agricultural development in the Yaqui Valley, Sonora, Mexico. Proc. Natl. (2016)
50. Zewge, A., Dittrich, Y.: Systematic mapping study of information communication technology research for agriculture (in case of developing Countries) (2015)
51. Rose, D., Sutherland, W., Parker, C., Lobley, M.: Decision support tools for agriculture: towards effective design and delivery. Agricultural (2016)
52. Barlett, P.: Agricultural decision making: Anthropological contributions to rural development (2016)
53. Jain, L., Kumar, H., Singla, R.: Localization of information dissemination in agriculture using mobile networks. Crit. Infrastruct. Proc. (2014)
54. Holzworth, D., Huth, N., Zurcher, E., Herrmann, N.: APSIM–evolution towards a new generation of agricultural systems simulation. Model. Softw. (2014)
55. Berger, T., Troost, C.: Agent-based Modelling of Climate Adaptation and Mitigation Options in Agriculture. J. Agric. Econ. (2013)
56. The Guardian: How ICT tools are improving efficiency of agricultural development| Global Development Professionals Network| The Guardian, https://www.theguardian.com/global-development-professionals-network/2013/jan/24/data-collection-evaluation-technology-agriculture
57. CARDI: Regional Synthesis of ICT Uptake and Usage in Agricultural Value Chains in the Caribbean (2015)
58. Lipper, L., Thornton, P., Campbell, B., Baedeker, T.: Climate-smart agriculture for food security. Nat. Clim. (2014)
59. Mbũgwa, G.W., Prager, S., Krall, J.: Utilization of spatial decision support systems decision-making in dryland agriculture: a Tifton burclover case study. Electron. Agric. (2015)
60. Kaloxylos, A., Groumas, A., Sarris, V., Katsikas, L.: A cloud-based Farm Management System: Architecture and implementation. Electron. Agric. (2014)
61. Patel, H., Patel, D.: Survey of Android Apps for Agriculture. Int. J. Inf. (2016)
62. Williams, T., Mul, M., Cofie, O., Kinyangi, J.: Climate Smart Agriculture in the African Context (2015)
63. Banson, K., Nguyen, N.: Using system archetypes to identify drivers and barriers for sustainable agriculture in Africa: a case study in Ghana. Syst. Res. (2016)
64. Rosenzweig, C., Elliott, J., Deryng, D.: Assessing agricultural risks of climate change in the 21st century in a global gridded crop model intercomparison. Proc. (2014)
65. Pham, H.: Design of environmental performance measurement systems for agriculture (2016)
66. Walisadeera, A., Wikramanayake, G.: An ontological approach to meet information needs of farmers in Sri Lanka. Comput. Sci. (2013)
67. O'Leary, D.: A multilingual knowledge management system: a case study of FAO and WAICENT. Decis. Support Syst. (2008)
68. Kawtrakul, A.: Ontology engineering and knowledge services for agriculture domain. J. Integr. Agric. (2012)

69. Xie, N., Wang, W.: Ontology and acquiring of agriculture knowledge. Agric. Netw. Inf. (2007)
70. Zheng, Y., He, Q., Ping, Q., Ze, L.: Construction of the ontology-based agricultural knowledge management system. J. Integr. Agric. (2012)
71. Song, G., Wang, M., Ying, X., Yang, R., Zhang, B.: Study on precision agriculture knowledge presentation with ontology. AASRI Procedia. (2012)
72. Alfred, R., Chin, K., Anthony, P., San, P., Im, T.: Ontology-based query expansion for supporting information retrieval in agriculture. 8th Int. (2014)
73. Ahuja, L.R., Ma, L., Howell, T.A.: Agricultural system models in field research and technology transfer (2002)
74. Ploss, S.: Conflict and decision-making in Soviet Russia: a case study of agricultural policy, 1953–1963. (2015)
75. Norris, W.C.: Responding to the technological challenges of small scale agriculture [Text of speech presented at the banquet of the Beltsville Agricultural Research Center Special Symposium Research for Small Farms, 17 November 1981]. Misc. Publ. - U.S. Dept Agric. (1982)
76. Reij, C., Waters-Bayer, A.: Farmer innovation in Africa: a source of inspiration for agricultural development (2014)
77. Norton, G., Alwang, J., Masters, W.: Economics of agricultural development: World food systems and resource use (2014)
78. Freeman, P., Freeland, R.: Politics & technology: US polices restricting unmanned aerial systems in agriculture. Food Policy (2014)
79. Mahant, M., Shukla, A., Dixit, S., Patel, D.: Uses of ICT in Agriculture. People (2012)

Author Index

MIX
Papier aus verantwortungsvollen Quellen
Paper from responsible sources
FSC® C105338

If you have any concerns about our products,
you can contact us on
ProductSafety@springernature.com

In case Publisher is established outside the EU,
the EU authorized representative is:
Springer Nature Customer Service Center GmbH
Europaplatz 3, 69115 Heidelberg, Germany

Printed by Libri Plureos GmbH
in Hamburg, Germany